THE ARCHITECTURE OF Frank Lloyd Wright

THE ARCHITECTURE OF

Frank Lloyd

Neil Levine

Wright

PRINCETON UNIVERSITY PRESS

Parts of this book previously appeared in somewhat
different form in the following publications: *AA Files:
Annals of the Architectural Association School of
Architecture* 3 (January 1983) and 11 (Spring 1986);
Art in America 71 (September 1983); *C. G. Jung and the
Humanities*, ed. Karin Barnaby and Pellegrino d'Acierno
(Princeton: Princeton University Press, 1990); *The Nature
of Frank Lloyd Wright*, ed. Carol R. Bolon, Robert S.
Nelson, and Linda Seidel (Chicago and London:
University of Chicago Press, 1988); *In Search of Modern
Architecture: A Tribute to Henry-Russell Hitchcock*,
ed. Helen Searing (New York, Cambridge, Mass., and
London: The Architectural History Foundation and
MIT Press, 1982); *The Wright State: Frank Lloyd Wright
in Wisconsin* (Milwaukee: Milwaukee Art Museum, 1992);
and *Wright Studies* 1 (1992)

Frontispiece. Taliesin (Wright House and Studio),
Hillside, Wis., begun 1911. Entrance court, looking toward
living wing (c. 1915)

Library of Congress Cataloging-in-Publication Data

Levine, Neil
The architecture of Frank Lloyd Wright / Neil Levine.
p.   cm.
Includes bibliographical references and index.
ISBN 0-691-03371-4 (cl : alk. paper)
1. Wright Frank Lloyd, 1867–1959—Criticism and
interpretation.   1. Wright Frank Lloyd, 1867–1959.
II. Title.
NA737.W7L46   1995   720'.92—dc20   95-32307   CIP

Publication of this book has been aided by a grant from
the Graham Foundation

This book has been composed in Bauer Bodoni and
Futura

Princeton University Press books are printed on acid-free
paper and meet the guidelines for permanence and
durability of the Committee on Production Guidelines for
Book Longevity of the Council on Library Resources

Printed in Hong Kong

10 9 8 7 6 5 4 3

Contents

To Gill, Vince, and my parents

Preface and Acknowledgments

Research projects that eventuate in books the length of this do not generally begin as a diversion. This one did. It had its origins in a detour to a Frank Lloyd Wright house on a field trip to visit recent museum architecture in Western Massachusetts for a course I was teaching with my colleague John Coolidge. As we were planning the day, he recalled that the Baird House in Amherst was quite nearby other things we were to see and suggested we include it on our itinerary. When I objected on grounds of relevance, he insisted, saying that it would be inexcusable to deny the students such an extraordinary opportunity. I assume he was also thinking of me, and for that I shall always be grateful to him. The night following the visit, I dreamt about the building, and then again the night after that. I could not get the image of it out of my mind.

A small grant from Harvard University allowed me and my wife, Gillian, to drive across the country in the Bicentennial summer of 1976 and visit over a hundred and fifty buildings. My initial idea was to do a short, interpretive study focusing on Wright's later work. The ultimate goal of that first trip, if I had to pin it down, was to see, and judge for myself, the Marin County Civic Center (the greatest surprise, however, turned out to be Hollyhock House). William Storrer's guide to Wright's buildings had just come out (1974) and was invaluable. Robert Twombly's biography had also recently appeared (1973), and John Sergeant's book on the Usonian houses (1976) made it seem as if a new era in Wright scholarship was opening.

But I had no intention of doing anything like either of them. The two models I had in mind for the book I was planning were Vincent Scully's intensely argued and eye-opening essay on Wright, published by Braziller in 1960, and Norris Kelly Smith's later elaboration of the "content" of Wright's architecture, published in 1966. I had known and been deeply impressed as an undergraduate by Scully's writing on Wright. As a graduate student of his at Yale, I came to appreciate more fully, through attendance of his lectures as well, the unique and profound understanding he offered of Wright's architecture and of its place in the history of modern culture. To Scully's ability to see, analyze, and describe architecture in its broadest possible frameworks—social, intellectual, topographical, and historical—this book owes its most significant debt.

Over the next few years the project began to grow in scope as I began teaching courses on Wright. Conversations with Arthur Drexler were always meaningful and encouraging. I shall never forget one of the first, in which he described to me the singular importance he attached to Wright's work and the need to reassess its role in the development of modern architecture. Holding his two hands, palms up, imitating a balance, or scales, he said: "If you put Wright on one side of the balance and Mies, Gropius, and Le Corbusier on the other, and even throw in Aalto for good measure, Wright will outweigh them all in significance." The thing that tipped the scales in my particular endeavor, however, was the increasing availability of published documentation of Wright's career and, ultimately, the accessibility of the archives of The Frank Lloyd Wright Foundation at Taliesin West. For this, we are all indebted to Bruce Pfeiffer, whose energy, wisdom, care, and professionalism have made the study of Wright a completely different sort of matter from what it was twenty years ago. A grant from the Graham Foundation for Advanced Studies in the Fine Arts allowed me to complete an initial investigation of materials in the Wright Archives in 1983. Several return trips to Taliesin West were always greeted with solicitude by Pfeiffer and his growing staff. Among these, I should particularly like to thank Oscar Muñoz, Indira Berndtson, Penny Fowler, and Margo Stipe. The notes to this book attest to the knowledge they willingly shared with me.

Many other individuals and institutions contributed to the thinking and the documentation involved in the final work. David Van Zanten and I have conversed about Wright and Chicago on countless occasions over the years, and I have always come away with some new thought or approach to an issue. Robin Middleton read parts of the manuscript in its initial stages, as well as the final product, and made numerous helpful suggestions. His invitations to lecture at the Architectural Association School of Architecture in London offered me an important public forum early on to test and develop my ideas. Other such occasions were provided by the Graham Foundation Seminars, the Sir Banister Fletcher Lectures at the Bartlett School of Architecture and Planning, University College, London, and the symposia on Wright and related subjects I was privileged to participate in at Harvard's Graduate School of Design, the University of Chicago, Columbia University, the University of Michigan, and the Museum of Modern Art in New York. Students in the courses I have given on Wright at Harvard have made many important contributions, and the reader will find their names recorded in the notes.

A generation of scholars working on Wright came into maturity during the past twenty years, and from them and their writing I have gained much. To Jack Quinan, Kathryn Smith, Donald Hoffmann, Jonathan Lipman, Anthony Alofsin, Robert Sweeney, Mary Jane Hamilton, and Narciso Menocal, I am enormously grateful. This book is the richer for their insights and help. Virginia Ernst Kazor, Curator of Hollyhock House, has been instrumental in my research on the building in her charge. Tom Beeby, Jeff Chusid, and Tom Heinz have each enlightened me in different ways through their understanding of Wright. I was fortunate to be able to interview Lloyd Wright before he died and to discuss his father with William Wesley Peters and Edgar Kaufmann Jr. on several occasions before they died. I also owe much to Richard Carney, Carter Manny, John Geiger, Edgar Tafel, Cornelia Brierly, John Rattenbury, and Arnold Roy, all of whom shared their personal knowledge of Wright and his architecture with me. In addition to instructing me in certain aspects of Japanese architecture and art, my colleague John Rosenfield provided information on the Rogers Lacy Hotel project as well as an introduction to Stanley Marcus, who shared with me his memories of the house project he commissioned from Wright. Rifat Chadirji and

Ellen Jawdat helped sort out the complexities of the Baghdad commissions. Gira and Gautam Sarabhai graciously informed me of Wright's project for their family's store in Ahmedabad. David Doyel, Breen Murray, Anthony Aveni, and Barbara Groneman all went out of their way to assist me in understanding the ancient petroglyph boulders at Taliesin West. Peter Goss facilitated access to the Taylor Woolley Archive at the University of Utah and offered valuable advice on interpretation. Others who have aided in significant ways include Nan Rosenthal, Alice Friedman, Jan Vleck, Meryle Secrest, Francesco Passanti, Mark Reinberger, John Vinci, Paul Turner, James Pouros, Joe Price, Phil Feddersen, Randolph Henning, and Jayne Kramer.

A number of people at research facilities with significant holdings of Wright material were exceedingly helpful. I cannot thank enough the following individuals and their staffs: Elaine Harrington and Meg Klinkow, Frank Lloyd Wright Home and Studio Foundation; Shonnie Finnegan, University Archives, State University of New York at Buffalo; Janet Parks, Angela Giral, and Adolf Placzek, Avery Architectural and Fine Arts Library, Columbia University; Nancy Young, Special Collections, University Libraries, University of Utah; Susan Buchel, Marcia Stout, and Blair Davenport, Scotty's Castle, Death Valley National Monument; and Enrique Vivoni, Archivo de Arquitectura y Construcción, Escuela de Arquitectura, Universidad de Puerto Rico. Ford Peatross kindly showed me the Wright drawings in the collection of the Library of Congress; Terry Marvel made the relevant material in the Milwaukee Art Museum available to me; Andrew Cooper, Miriam Gaber, Brent Sverdloff, and Gene Waddell processed my orders for photocopies of correspondence and manuscripts from the Getty Center for the History of Art and the Humanities; Jacqueline Cox and Michael Halls gave me access to the Ashbee journals in King's College Library, Cambridge. In addition, I should like to express my gratitude to Robert Holland, at Stronghold, Yoshihisa Aibe, Imperial Hotel, Tokyo, and Greg Novak, of the Arizona State Land Department, for their assistance.

A close reading of Wright's buildings was crucial to this project, and many individuals gave generously of their time in allowing me to intrude on their lives. Permission from Olgivanna Lloyd Wright to see the interior of Taliesin on my first trip there in 1976 had a powerful effect on how I would come to understand her husband's architecture. Subsequent visits to Taliesin and Taliesin West were obligingly arranged for by Bruce Pfeiffer, Richard Carney, and Charles Montooth. Kinshasha and Houston Conwill turned my first look at Hollyhock House into an extended "holiday adventure in Romanza," to use Wright's words, and Ginny Kazor made each return trip equally meaningful. Tom Schmidt and Lynda Waggoner did everything one could ask for to make Fallingwater a very special experience. Members of the staff, including Nancy Morrison, Dorothy Schrock, Joan Wilson, and Skip Robinson, were especially helpful and informative. Betty Leigh, John Michiels, and Frank Pond opened up Unity Temple for me on more than one occasion; and Donald Hallmark was equally gracious at the Dana House. Harold Price kindly arranged for a tour of the family office tower.

Among the many people who opened up their homes and shared with me their experiences of living in a Wright house, and often that of commissioning and building one, I should like to thank Mr. and Mrs. Albert Adelman, Eril Altay, Professor and Mrs. Theodore Baird, Ruth and Quintin Blair, Lewis Bradford, Mr. and Mrs. Erling Brauner, James Bridges and Jack Larsen, Gus Brown, Mr. and Mrs. Eric Brown, Jean Canavera, Mr. and Mrs. Robert Coleman, Nicole Daniels, William Dring, Barbara and Robert Elsner, Dr. and Mrs. Fineberg, Jorgen and Hannah Fogh, Betty and Louis Frank, Harriet and Samuel Freeman, Anthony and Mary Gholz, Harvey Glanzer, Elizabeth Halsted, Professor and Mrs. Albert Hastorf, Mr. and Mrs. Bruce Lloyd Haynes, Mr. and Mrs. Head, Jerome Jacobi, Ellen Johnson, Dr. and Mrs. Toufic Kalil, Lucile Kinter, Abe Kirshenbaum, Mr. and Mrs. Kenneth Laurent, Lillian and Curtis Meyer, Mr. and Mrs. William Miller, Maya Moran, Dr. and Mrs. Franklin Nelson, Arch Oboler, Mike Osheowitz, Mary and William

Palmer, Bette and Ted Pappas, Ruth and John Pew, Mr. and Mrs. Eric Pratt, Jack Prost, Mr. and Mrs. Milt Robinson, Mr. and Mrs. Donald Schaberg, Alice Shaddle, Dale Smirl, Sara and Melvyn Maxwell Smith, Mr. and Mrs. Walter Sobel, Donna Taylor, Mrs. Van Loben Sels, Mrs. William Walker, Mr. and Mrs. Carlton David Wall, Thomas Walsh Jr., Christine and David Weisblat, Gladys and David Wright, Mr. and Mrs. James Yoghourtjian, and Lucille and Isadore Zimmerman.

I am very grateful to the following, who provided photographs or helped in the search: James Ackerman; Pierre Adler, Anne Dixon, Matilda McQuaid, Christopher Mount, Peter Reed, and Terry Riley, Department of Architecture and Design, Museum of Modern Art, New York; Laurence Bain and Tessa Mahoney, Michael Wilford and Partners; Mary Berner, Corporate Public Information Worldwide, S. C. Johnson & Son; Melanie Birk, Public Relations, Frank Lloyd Wright Home and Studio Foundation; David Blanchette, Illinois Historic Preservation Agency; Mosette Broderick; Nicolette Bromberg and Andy Kraushaar, State Historical Society of Wisconsin; David Brown, Sydney Opera House Trust; Jack Brown and Mary Woolever, Art Institute of Chicago; Ann and Henry Carawan; Mikki Carpenter, Christine Schiller, and Laura Billingham, Department of Photographic Services and Permissions, Museum of Modern Art, New York; Maristella Casciato; Guy Chase, Richard W. Bock Sculpture Collection, Greenville College; Jocelyn Clapp, Bettmann Archive; Julia Converse, Architectural Archives, University of Pennsylvania; Carol Corey, Knoedler & Company; Harold Corsini; Dennis Crompton, Archigram Archives; Francesco Dal Co; Dandelet; Mary Daniels and Martha Mahard, Francis Loeb Library, Harvard University; Sam Dickerson, Black Star; Carina Duren, Museo Nacional de Antropología, Mexico; Kathleen Economou, Hedrich-Blessing; Scott Elliott; Minna Elsilä, Alvar Aalto Foundation; Evan Firestone and Susan Wells, University of Georgia; David Fishman, Robert A. M. Stern Architects; Eileen Flanagan, Chicago Historical Society; Aaron Green; Pedro Guerrero; Laura Harden, Sotheby's; John Harkness,

The Architects Collaborative: David Heald and Samar Qandil, Solomon R. Guggenheim Museum; James Helyar, Spencer Research Library, University of Kansas; Simon Herron; Lucien Hervé; Institute of Contemporary Art, Boston; Ward Jackson; William Jerousek, Oak Park Library; Hank Johnston; Jorge Juarez, Instituto Nacional de Antropología e Historia, Mexico; Isabella Ketchum; Anne Kreamer; Sarah Larsen and Clinton Piper, Fallingwater; Margaret Kimball and Linda Long, Special Collections, Stanford University Libraries; Jeff Levine, John Weber Gallery; Letje Lips, Netherlands Architecture Institute; Joan Lukach; Nancy Lyon, Manuscripts and Archives, Yale University Library; Alex MacLean; Yoshihiro Maeda, Imperial Hotel, Tokyo; Darwin Matthews; Dorothy McLaughlin; Mercedes Matter; Luigi Mumford, Art Institute of Chicago; Keisuke Naito, Kikutake Architect & Associates; Graham Nickson; Kevin Nute; David Phillips; Lisa Licitra Ponti; Sergio Pozzati, Fototeca ASAC, Biennale di Venezia; Eric Rayman; Cervin Robinson; Laura Rosenstock, Department of Painting and Sculpture, Museum of Modern Art, New York; Drew Ross and Peter Schmid, University Libraries, University of Utah; Ben Schnall; Barbara Shapiro Comte; Dorothy Shields, Art and Architecture Library, University of Michigan; Erica Stoller and Sheila Masselli, Esto Photographics; William Straus; Anna Tonicello, Archivioprojetti Angelo Masieri, Istituto Universitario di Architettura di Venezia; Evelyne Tréhin, Fondation Le Corbusier; Robert Venturi and Link Tran, Venturi, Scott Brown and Associates; Skot Weidemann; and Liz Weisberg, Artists Rights Society. For their outstanding photography, I am indebted to John Cook, Linda McCausland, Peter Cirincione and Joe Nucci at Pro B & W Photo Lab, Bruce White, and Bob Zinck and Steve Sylvester at Widener Photographic Services, Harvard University.

The support of my own institution in the protracted process of completing the manuscript is greatly appreciated. Harvard University was extremely generous in its provision of paid and unpaid leaves. My colleagues in the Fine Arts Department were incredibly helpful and supportive, especially during the six years when I was Chair and concurrently trying to finish a major part of the research and writing. To Deanna Dalrymple, the Department Administrator, I owe a special thanks. She has stood behind me from the beginning and always found a way to make sure that things got done—and with marvelous equanimity. I am also very grateful to Chris Hummel, Jeannie Davis, Gary Ralph, Reid Ackley, and Michael Nolen for their sometimes heroic efforts in deciphering my handwriting to produce a speedily typed text. Both Victoria Newhouse and Bill Rawn read the final manuscript and made useful suggestions. Kathryn Taylor had the generous and brilliant thought of putting me in touch with Elizabeth Powers, who has been an extraordinary editor to work with—enthusiastic, insightful, tough at times, sensitively pressuring, and always understanding in both intellectual and personal terms. Gretchen Oberfranc

did a remarkable job editing the text, not only bringing clarity to it when that was lacking but also making important and substantive corrections. Phil Unetic produced what I thought was nearly impossible: a design that in no way imitates or trivializes Wright yet says something appropriate and unique to a book about his work.

Finally, I want to thank Gillian Levine, who undertook that first Wright "grand tour" with me in 1976 and has remained my constant interlocutor on the subject. Bringing to bear on our discussions her own expertise in contemporary art, she has consistently made me rethink my positions and helped me see things in a new perspective. She has been a powerful aide and a patient companion. My debt to her is incalculable.

Cambridge, Mass., 1995

1. Frank Lloyd Wright
in his office, Taliesin West,
Scottsdale, Ariz. (1947).

Introduction

There was a time when no discussion of modern architecture could take place without including Frank Lloyd Wright. The open plan, fragmented volumes, dynamic space, natural materials, and integral structure of his buildings helped establish the basic terms of the discourse. But now his work is studied only cursorily, if at all, in architecture schools, and it is even more unusual to see references to Wright in serious journals of theory and criticism. A few years ago, when I mentioned to the British architect James Stirling that I was doing a book on Wright, he looked at me quizzically and said: "Do we need *another* one?" When I asked what he meant, he replied: "We already have *one*. Isn't that enough?" He was no doubt referring to Henry-Russell Hitchcock's *In the Nature of Materials* (1942), a book that neither Wright nor Hitchcock was ever satisfied with but that, for better or worse, has remained until only very recently Wright's one-volume *oeuvre complète*.[1]

There is a great paradox here, for despite all assumptions about Wright's irrelevance, he remains the most popular and most celebrated architect of this century. In a poll conducted by the editors of *Architectural Record* in 1981, to cite just one example, architecture students voted Wright their "favorite" architect and Fallingwater their "favorite" building by runaway margins, while practitioners voted Wright their "favorite" architect by a margin of two to one.[2] The usual explanation is that Wright's influence has been so broad and so pervasive that it is below the normal threshold of recognition and almost second nature by now. It is an issue not of a particular style or manner of building, as in the case of Mies, Le Corbusier, or Kahn, but of an attitude, a principle, a general approach to the making of an environment.

Wright himself believed this to be true of his work, and was never averse to acknowledging it. When Thomas

Creighton, editor of *Progressive Architecture* in the 1950s, asked him to "assess his influence and contribution," Wright replied:

I appreciate your thought for me. But, dear man, comparisons are odious.

What would you think of getting together composers influenced by Beethoven?

He is dead.

I am alive and laughing.

As a matter of fact, Thomas, whom would you leave out![3]

By the 1950s, when Wright was in his eighties, his preference for "honest arrogance" over what he called "hypocritical humility" had reached legendary proportions. A story in *Look* magazine in 1957, two years before he died, reported that he "agreed on the witness stand that he was the world's greatest living architect." When his wife protested, saying, "Frank, you should be more modest," Wright replied: "You forget, Olgivanna, I was under oath."[4]

When one considers the issue in purely personal terms, it is perhaps no wonder that a backlash occurred. Many younger architects, critics, and historians in the 1950s and 1960s came to regard Wright as a somewhat annoying—yet vaguely threatening—superannuated folk hero, living out a mythic existence in a world of his own devising in rural Wisconsin and Arizona, totally divorced from the political, social, economic, philosophic, and artistic problems of the real world.[5] In his flowing cape and porkpie hat, he appeared terribly corny; and the kitschy quality attributed to his buildings and projects of the later years made them seem beyond the pale. Who should care, anyway, about someone who disdained all schools and professional organizations and took every opportunity to say so?

The only way to deal with him was to play his own game—and ignore him. Philip Johnson said it best. In front of a student audience at Harvard's Graduate School of Design in 1954 he called Wright "the greatest architect of the nineteenth century."[6] That cut to the quick and was, as

Johnson later admitted, "the worst thing I ever said about Mr. Wright." Johnson, like so many others who were trying to establish a personal stake in modern architecture, was "annoyed" by Wright's arrogance and "contempt" for others. "Was he born full-blown from the head of Zeus that he could be the only architect that ever lived or ever will?" Johnson asked rhetorically. A profound "dislike" conspired with a grudging sense of "admiration" to place Wright and his work at a safe remove.[7]

Johnson spoke for most of his contemporaries when he characterized Wright as the "greatest architect of the nineteenth century." That explained, in one neat phrase, Wright's romanticism, his pantheistic Naturalism ("with a capital N"), his lingering traditionalism, his idealism, and his attachment to the values of rural America. In the 1940s and 1950s, while Gropius was putting into practice a curriculum for the education of the modern "teamwork" designer, while Mies was providing the elements for a standardized, corporate architecture, and while Le Corbusier was beginning to build in raw concrete the brutal forms of a new, collective urban vision, Wright seemed to be living out the dream of the "rugged individualist" at his country retreats in southern Wisconsin and the Arizona desert, with only occasional forays to New York City to wag his cane at the workmen on the Guggenheim Museum site who were erecting the monumental ziggurat he thought of as his "Archeseum."

For the past twenty years and more, this love-hate relationship with Wright has persisted. But modern architecture has changed. Gone is that unquestioning moral belief in the historical validity of the machine aesthetic that at first deified and then dismissed Wright. A broader understanding of what constitutes the modern experience in architecture is being elaborated, and with that effort has come the demand for a more comprehensive and balanced account of its historical development. And so the answer to the question of whether we need "another" book about Wright is surely yes. "The oeuvre of Wright bulks too large," wrote Hitchcock while preparing *In the Nature of Materials*, "to be merely taken for granted. Either finally to accept it wholly; or, if necessary and partially, to reject it, we must learn in the fullest historical and critical way what it is."[8] Notwithstanding Hitchcock's own analysis, as well as the important studies by Bruno Zevi (1947), Grant Manson (1958), Vincent Scully (1960), Norris Kelly Smith (1966), and Robert Twombly (1973/79), there still seems to be ample need for the kind of serious investigation Hitchcock called for.[9] The numerous publications on various aspects of Wright's life and work that have appeared during the time the present volume has been in preparation, along with the major Wright exhibition at New York's Museum of Modern Art in the spring of 1994, are ample testimony of this.[10]

■ ■ ■

One of the challenges that makes the study of Wright so fascinating and yet so problematic is the sheer span of time involved. His career started well before the turn of the century and ended in 1959, just prior to the election of John F. Kennedy. Added to this is Wright's enormous productivity, far greater than that of any other avant-garde architect of this century. He built more than four hundred buildings and designed at least twice as many more. He was also a prolific writer, producing nearly twenty books and contributing countless articles to publications ranging from professional journals like *Architectural Record* to newspapers and popular magazines like *Esquire*.[11]

Wright's career encompasses the entire development of modern architecture, from its beginnings in the 1880s in the steel-frame, tall office buildings of Chicago to its institutionalization on an international scale in the post–World War II era. Born in 1867, Wright was of the same generation as the traditionalists Henry Bacon (b. 1866), Edwin Lutyens (b. 1869), and John Russell Pope (b. 1874) and as the early modernists Peter Behrens (b. 1868), Irving Gill (b. 1870), Adolph Loos (b. 1870), Joseph Hoffmann (b. 1870), and Auguste Perret (b. 1874). He was, however, the only one of the latter group to remain on equal footing with the next

generation of modernists and would take his place with Gropius, Mies, and Le Corbusier in the immediate postwar period as one of the "form givers" of modern architecture. In this regard, one should remember that Wright was almost an exact contemporary of three of the key figures in the development of modern painting: Matisse (b. 1869), Kandinsky (b. 1866), and Mondrian (b. 1872).

If the length of Wright's career and the extent of his output appear to make the historian's task of categorizing and thematizing especially difficult, the teleological vision of modern architectural history has tended to ease that task enormously by presenting a limited picture of Wright's contribution and achievement. Following the conventional account of modern architecture dating from the late 1920s and early 1930s, most studies have taken the so-called Prairie Style that Wright developed during the years he practiced in Oak Park (1889–1909) as their central focus and defining term. Wright's realization of the Prairie House became the object toward which all his earlier work appeared to lead and the *locus classicus* from which almost all his later work was seen to diverge. Its historical significance was directly related to the development of the International Style in Europe in the late teens and twenties.

Known in part through the German publications of Ernst Wasmuth in 1910–11, the buildings of Wright's early years were considered to have exerted a powerful influence on younger Europeans, whose steel, concrete, and glass structures of the twenties showed the way in which Wright's fragmentation and decomposition of traditional form could be used to create a machinelike, abstract architecture of lines and planes in space.[12] But once Wright's Prairie Style was defined as the catalytic agent in this development, Wright himself was relegated to the role of forerunner. His Prairie Style buildings were treated as the mature statement of his art, and little serious attention was paid to the post-1909 work, which was generally felt to have represented a regression. Wright was, to all intents and purposes, stereotyped as a domestic architect—and a regionalist at that—who had somehow emerged from the provincial confines of

Midwest America with all the built-in virtues and vices of the archetypal Noble Savage.

In the later 1930s, however, after Wright's own architecture showed signs of having been reinvigorated by the lessons of European modernism, critics turned their attention to him once more. But then, because of the extraordinary richness and diversity of imagery of such buildings as Fallingwater, Taliesin West, and the Guggenheim Museum, as compared to the relative uniformity of their European counterparts, this later work was seen as the personal, romantic, and idiosyncratic production of someone who followed only the whims of his individual genius. Where the earlier work displayed a consistent pattern of planning and a rational use of materials that rigorously conformed to clearly established types, the later work seemed to disregard any discernible formula in the search for novelty and variety of expression. No longer the Noble Savage, Wright was now the parvenu Populist, even further removed from the cultivated world of mainstream academic modernism than he had been in his youth.[13] The production of Wright's maturity and later years thus diminished, when it did not actually contradict, the "advances" made by the earlier work. In this way, a wedge was driven not only between Wright and his younger contemporaries but between Wright and his younger self.

■ ■ ■

This book had its genesis in Wright's later work and its impetus in the deconstruction of the myth of Wright as the American Noble Savage gone astray. Growing up in New York, I knew the Guggenheim Museum first, and then Beth Sholom Synagogue. Marin County Civic Center was built while I was taking my first college courses in modern architecture. When I later became intrigued with Wright's architecture, these were the buildings that struck me as revealing new ways of looking at Wright and seeing him as an integral part of the development of modern architecture. Fortunately, this was also the moment when the elitism and "good taste" of modern art was being called into question by an interest in popular culture that soon manifested itself in Pop Art, so there was little anxiety about preserving modern design from the "nefarious" and "vulgar" influence of kitsch that Wright's later work was felt so manifestly to exhibit. Since that time, numerous studies of individual Wright buildings, or groups of buildings, by scholars as well as former clients have helped to document the terrain of these later years.[14] Even more important has been the extraordinary contribution of Bruce Brooks Pfeiffer, the Director of Archives of the Frank Lloyd Wright Foundation, whose twelve-volume collected works of Wright and multiple editions of correspondence have provided the fundamental basis for a reassessment of the architect's career as a whole.[15]

A distinct advantage to the retrospective approach is that it helps avoid the temptations and pitfalls of a proleptic history. I have no interest whatsoever in proving that Wright was the first to do one thing or another, or that in doing so he inevitably led to such and such a development of which he might be considered the "forerunner." Instead, I approach Wright's career and work as a continuous field, embedded in a larger cultural and historical context, but with its own special dynamic. What interests me is the fundamental historical problem of determining when a major change or shift in focus takes place in an artist's work and what effects it has. This, rather than any preconceived model of formal development, has determined my approach.

The major shift in focus in Wright's career occurred in the year 1909–10, when he left Oak Park for Europe with the wife of a former client, never to return to his family or practice in that Chicago suburb. His first stop was Berlin, to initiate and oversee the publication of his work by Wasmuth, but he spent most of the year in Italy. The German editions ultimately helped to make him a figure of international renown, but the time spent abroad had an even more decisive effect in reorienting his work toward issues very different from those that had occupied him in his suburban practice.

The immediate outcome was the construction of Taliesin, a combined house and studio on an estate in southern Wisconsin that would remain his primary dwelling and office for the rest of his life. As a manifesto of what he believed architecture should be, Taliesin became Wright's public persona and principal form of advertisement.

After 1910, Wright can no longer be considered simply an American architect, nor can his ambitions be narrowly defined as domestic. Though he continued primarily to build houses, and stressed as never before their local and regional characteristics, the larger issues of history, representation, symbolism, context, and meaning that his later work engages raise questions of an entirely different order. Wright's Prairie Style buildings of the Oak Park years may be characterized as a search for types—images of home, work, or worship—in their distillation of nineteenth-century traditions. His work after 1910 reveals a quest for a more profound synthesis of architecture and nature that involves a radical reinterpretation of the classical theory of art as the "imitation" of nature. In rejecting the nineteenth-century opposition of form and function, wherein the sign of progress became the dissolution of historical and natural references following the model of engineering, Wright set himself apart from the younger European modernists who maintained that only the pure, geometric shapes of a "machine aesthetic" were the architect's proper response to the demands of the Industrial Revolution. Wright's work, by contrast, reveals the degree to which the dialectic of abstraction and representation, so fundamental to the development of modern painting and sculpture, also informed the architectural discourse of this century.

■ ■ ■

Nature was Wright's constant preoccupation, and the way he abstracted and represented it in his architecture will be the underlying theme of this book. The first two chapters, dealing with the period from 1889 to 1909, provide a background for the more mature work. Because of the relatively

uniform and progressive character of these early designs, a series of examples will be used as illustrations. In the succeeding chapters, where buildings or projects take on more individuated and highly charged symbolic meanings, I will generally focus on one or two examples from each decade or phase to characterize the evolution of Wright's thought. These are the ones to which he devoted his most intense efforts and in which he was able to exercise the greatest freedom in developing the program. Each will be treated monographically and subjected to close reading and analysis.

After the review of the Oak Park period, Chapter III will deal with Wright's trip to Europe and the house he designed for himself in Fiesole. The fourth chapter will be devoted to Taliesin. Built in 1911 upon Wright's return from Italy, it was designed to look like a natural ledge or rock outcrop, a "brow," as Wright later said, for the hill on which it was sited.[16] The relation with the landscape was no longer abstract, as in the Prairie Style houses, where a congruence was achieved through the means of allusion or analogy. The relation between Taliesin and its landscape setting is immediate, and the boundary between the two often indistinguishable. Wright generated the shapes of Taliesin by direct reference to natural ones, drawing the surrounding landscape into an illusion of heightened reality through a process of representation that was to inform, in one way or another, all his later work.

Wright had done nothing like Taliesin before, nor would he do anything quite like it for another twenty-five years, until he built Fallingwater in 1935–37. This is the drama of Wright's mid-career crisis. To understand it, one must refer to events in his personal life. Wright built Taliesin as a token of love, a place to cohabit with Mamah Borthwick (Cheney), the woman with whom he had eloped to Europe.[17] The house was designed to embody, in its embrace of the hill, the two lovers' natural, if not conventional, union. But less than three years after it was finished, disaster struck. While Wright was in Chicago supervising another job, one of the household staff set fire to Taliesin and hacked to death anyone who tried to escape. Among the seven people murdered were Borthwick and her two children.

The experience for Wright was traumatic. He did not return to Oak Park, but removed himself even farther from Chicago in the second half of the decade. First he went to Tokyo to supervise construction of the Imperial Hotel, and then to Southern California to design a house and art center for Aline Barnsdall in Hollywood, called Hollyhock House. Romantic, perhaps even escapist, these buildings, which are the subject of Chapter V, show the effect of the Taliesin tragedy in their repression of any unmediated reference to natural forms and their sublimation of the relation between building and nature through the explicit means of symbolization. Nature was interpreted as a constant source of disaster, whether by earthquake, fire, or flood, and it was architecture's role to overcome and subdue these violent forces.

This confrontational attitude only gradually began to give way during the mid- and late twenties to a feeling of resignation and acceptance of nature as an independent force. The ground for this change was the desert environment of the Southwest. Chapters VI and VII focus on the project for the A. M. Johnson Desert Compound and Shrine in Death Valley and the plan for the San Marcos-in-the-Desert Hotel in the Phoenix South Mountains.

The challenge of the desert was quickly joined by another, more directly professional one that would serve, over the next two decades at least, to keep the aging Wright (he was sixty-one in 1928) fully involved in the debate over the direction modern architecture should take. For the first time in his life, Wright was faced with the competition of a younger generation of modernists, more radical than he in their opposition to tradition. He found a second wind in counteracting the International Style's abstraction and machine aesthetic with a renewal of the naturalism and representational directness of Taliesin. Out of this came Fallingwater and Taliesin West, the two buildings of the thirties that form the subjects of Chapters VIII and IX. Enriched with a new psychological complexity and sense of the limits

of human intervention in the workings of nature, they introduce a temporal dimension to his architecture that established a framework for a reengagement with history.

In his major projects of the 1940s and 1950s, especially the Guggenheim Museum, the Plan for Greater Baghdad, and the Marin County Civic Center (the subjects of the final two chapters), Wright sought to reaffirm the representational power of monumental public architecture in the face of growing corporate anonymity. Transforming easily recognizable historical models into extended institutional metaphors at the scale of the city or region, he brought into focus, in what are still extremely controversial designs, the issue of the accommodation of modern architecture to the urban and suburban contexts. As the imagery of these buildings became more and more geared to their function as public signs, the architecture Wright produced in his last years revived the dismissive criticism of the twenties and thirties, but in even more exacerbated form. The word "fantasy" became the typical epithet. In the Conclusion I will take that criticism into account by offering a new interpretation of Wright's contribution to modern architecture on the model of his own engagement with the language of the fairy tale.

■ ■ ■

Any study of a single artist runs considerable risks, overemphasis on biography and reinscription of the myth of individual genius being the most obvious ones. But the "death of the author," as Roland Barthes maintained, entails the "birth of the reader."[18] Reading necessitates a text, and the text of Wright's architecture is in large part written in autobiographical terms. Most modern artists have helped to create their own myths, Le Corbusier's *Oeuvre complète* being a prime example. But few, if any, modern architects have implicated their private lives in such accounts to the degree that Wright did.[19] Indeed, only Picasso and Hemingway, in this century, offer comparable examples of artists whose work is so intimately and explicitly a matter of autobiographical expression. Who knows what Le Corbusier's wife's name was or whether Gropius had any children? What difference does it make where Aalto's grandparents lived or what type of car Mies drove? Wright made all such aspects of his private life a matter of public record, through his buildings and his writings, and the analysis of his work must therefore take this into account.

Which brings me to my final caveat. The modernist injunction against biography goes hand in hand with an ambivalence about accepting the artist's own explanation of his or her work. The "intentional fallacy" is grounded in the formalist definition of modern art, which maintains that the work must "speak for itself" through the clarification of its own special means of expression. No other medium can do or say the same thing. From the very earliest evidence we have, Wright was profoundly impressed by this concept. He referred throughout his life to the chapter "Ceci tuera cela" ("This Will Kill That") in Victor Hugo's novel *Notre-Dame de Paris*, where it is stated that the invention of movable type and the printed word had "dethroned" architecture and removed its power of expression.[20] Wright always argued that he would be the Dante of the twentieth century who would return architecture to its place of prominence in the hierarchy of the arts and restore its capacity to move souls and influence minds.

Ironically, he often resorted to words to do that. Sometimes it would simply be the name of a building, like Taliesin, Romeo and Juliet, or Fallingwater. At other times, it might be a full-fledged text describing the building, like a chapter in his *Autobiography*.[21] Still other times, it might be marginal notes on a drawing: in the case of the Guggenheim Museum, the legend "Ziggurat" is coincidentally spelled backwards as "Taruggitz" (fig. 291); in the project for a Steel Cathedral of 1926, the words "Spider's Web," "Fish Net," "Passion Vine and Flower," "Fringe," "Pendent," "Stalactite," and "Stalagmite" are listed as the architecture's verbal equivalents in conjunction with the elevation of the structure. Wright's verbal explanations of his intentions in building will thus be considered part of the text, like the glosses in the margins of a pre-Gutenberg manuscript. For Wright's thinking of architecture in relation to words and to the representational function of language provides, in my view, the most immediate access to understanding the very special effect of his buildings as well as their broader social meaning.

I

Beginnings of the Prairie House

*A*ny study of Frank Lloyd Wright must start in Oak Park, that prim and proper suburb to the west of Chicago where, at the age of twenty-two, Wright built a house for himself and his family in 1889 and where he lived and practiced until 1909. Supported by an upper-middle-class community of progressive, right-thinking, churchgoing Midwesterners, Wright developed in his Oak Park Studio the revolutionary form of the Prairie House that would bring him national and international recognition by the time he was forty and ultimately affect every aspect of twentieth-century architecture.

Oak Park today looks a little less affluent than in the days when it was known as "Saint's Rest." Though only a fifteen-minute commute by rail to Chicago's Loop, it retains the small-town flavor that allows it still to boast that it is the largest village in the world. It therefore came as something of a shock to see in the center of the main shopping street, when it was bricked over in the 1970s to create a pedestrian mall, a double fountain with portrait reliefs dedicated to the town's two most famous citizens: Frank Lloyd Wright and Ernest Hemingway. Although the mall has since been undone and the fountain removed, seeing Wright and Hemingway in this unexpected way, growing up side by side in suburbia, gave pause for reflection on what different meanings Oak Park had for each.

Hemingway, a generation younger than Wright, was born in Oak Park in 1899, grew up there, and completed his education there. But he left as soon as he could, and never returned. He went to Europe and became a member of the international literary scene. Though his prose style remained as Midwestern as Wright's architectural style in its stripped-down matter-of-factness, Hemingway's writing was always cosmopolitan.

Wright, by contrast, chose to live in Oak Park. When he left, after more than twenty years, it was not to live in Europe, or New York, or even Chicago, but to go even further into the hinterland, to the farm in Wisconsin where his mother was brought up and where he spent his summers as a boy. In contrast to Hemingway, who would spend most of his life moving between France, Italy, Spain, Cuba, Key West, and Idaho, Wright established roots and believed in the need for them to nurture one's art. By comparison with the international style of Hemingway, Wright's style was self-consciously insular, not to say provincial, and Oak Park played a formative role in his development.

A solid base in the community is, of course, necessary for an architect to build and maintain a practice. This naturally ties the architect, more than the writer, to a place. But there was also a generational difference between Wright and Hemingway regarding the significance of what I have called the "provincial." The avant-garde art movements of the turn of the century flourished as never before, and indeed never since, on the periphery rather than in the center. Glasgow, Barcelona, Turin, Vienna, Darmstadt, Brussels, and even Nancy replaced Paris, London, Rome, New York, and Berlin as centers of artistic progress in the 1890s, in the wake of the longstanding critique of the metropolitan academies by critics as different in their positions as Hugo, Ruskin, Viollet-le-Duc, and Morris.

Chicago, with its extended ring of suburbs on the prairie, was part of this diffusion. Compared to the "decadent," European-oriented East centered on New York, Chicago had come to represent by the early 1890s the hope for a new American culture. Hamlin Garland, one of the early leaders of the literary movement that came to be known as the Chicago Renaissance, and a transplanted Easterner himself, believed that "provincialism" should be seen in a positive rather than a negative light. In 1892 he argued that "provincialism" was just another word for "decentralization" and that "we have had too little of it." A regionalism grounded in the new social and economic conditions of the Midwest, he maintained, would usher in an era of "the indigenous and the democratic" in art.[1]

In 1890 Chicago was chosen to host the World's Columbian Exposition, the international event that was to celebrate, under the pretext of the four-hundredth anniversary of the "discovery" of America, the emergence of the United States as an international power. It also marked a decentering of American industrial power and culture that would bring into open conflict the academic ideals of the Eastern professional establishment and the more "provincial," progressive, and self-consciously modern attitudes of the Chicago architects who were to become known collectively as the Prairie School.[2] The original creative impulse for that development came from Louis Sullivan. But what began in the commercial heart of downtown Chicago soon found, through the leadership of Wright, its main inspiration, much of its clientele, and its fullest expression in the down-to-earth, open-minded world of suburban Oak Park.

■ ■ ■

Frank Lloyd Wright was a Midwesterner by birth. He was born in 1867 in the small, agricultural market town of Richland Center, Wisconsin, about twenty-five miles northwest of Spring Green and Helena Valley, where his mother's family lived and where he himself would eventually make his home.[3] His father, William Cary Wright, a sometime lawyer, music teacher, and itinerant preacher, left New England in 1859 for southwestern Wisconsin, where he met Anna Lloyd Jones, whom he married in 1866. Wright's mother was born in Wales to a family of strong Unitarian faith. Brought to the United States as a small child, she grew up with her nine brothers and sisters on the farms her parents established in Wisconsin, first in Rock River Valley, then in Spring Green, and finally in Helena Valley, just across the Wisconsin River from Spring Green.[4] After moving to McGregor, Iowa, in 1869 and then to Pawtucket, Rhode Island, in 1871, the young Wright and his family lived in Weymouth, Massachusetts, for about four years before returning to Wisconsin.[5]

Back in Wisconsin, the family settled in Madison, where Wright began high school. He never received a diploma, however, for he dropped out in the spring of 1885, around the time his parents divorced and his father left home. To help support his mother who, Wright claimed, always intended her son to be "an Architect," Wright took a job in the office of Allan D. Conover (*A* I, 8). He worked there for nearly a year before enrolling in 1886 for two semesters, under Conover's tutelage, as a special student in the University of Wisconsin. About the only stable element in Wright's years of growing up was the family's farmland in Helena Valley. Beginning in 1878, he returned there each summer to work for his uncles. The attachment he developed to that landscape and its agrarian mode of existence remained with him for the rest of his life. In Wright's later construction of his artistic autobiography, this original experience of nature took on emblematic meaning.[6]

In the beginning of 1887, at the age of nineteen and a half, Wright left Madison for Chicago to look for a job as an architect. For someone with virtually no training or experience, Wright could hardly have picked a better place or a better time. After the Great Fire of 1871, which nearly leveled the city, and the economic depression of 1873, which retarded construction until the end of the decade, Chicago was in the midst of an unprecedented building boom. Young firms, such as Burnham and Root, Adler and Sullivan, and Holabird and Roche, following the lead of William Le Baron Jenney, were developing the potentialities of fireproof, steel-frame skyscraper construction to create those pragmatic commercial structures that were coming to characterize the Chicago School of architecture.[7]

Wright got a job almost immediately, though not with one of the firms involved in the reconstruction of the Loop. He was hired by Joseph Lyman Silsbee, whose practice was mainly domestic, although he had designed a church for Wright's uncle Jenkin Lloyd Jones in Chicago (1885) as well as the Lloyd Jones family chapel in Helena Valley, on which Wright had worked in the summer of 1886 (fig. 75).[8] Silsbee, who had come to Chicago from Syracuse at the beginning of the eighties, introduced Wright to the Shingle Style mixture of Queen Anne and Colonial elements that formed the basis of his picturesque approach to design. Although Wright probably used family connections to get the position with Silsbee, he soon proved himself capable enough to secure a job as a draftsman in one of Chicago's leading firms. Within about a year from the time he joined Silsbee, Wright was hired by Adler and Sullivan to work on the monumental Auditorium Building, on which construction had begun in the summer of 1887 (fig. 384).[9] Wright's facility in drawing stood him well, and by the middle of 1890 he was promoted to the position of head draftsman in what was fast becoming one of the outstanding architectural offices in America.

The nearly six years that Wright worked for Adler and Sullivan marked the apogee of the firm's success and creativity. Sullivan was producing such designs as the Wainwright Building (1890–91), the Getty Tomb (1890), Fraternity Temple (1891), the Schiller Building (1891–92), the Wainwright Tomb (1892), and the Transportation Building for the World's Columbian Exposition (1890–93). Wright worked on a number of these—as "a good pencil in the Master's hand" (*A* I, 102)—but he was soon given primary responsibility for the few domestic commissions the firm still accepted. In this capacity, he designed the Charnley House, prominently located on Astor Street on Chicago's fashionable Near North Side (fig. 3), as well as a house for Sullivan's brother Albert on Chicago's South Side (both 1891–92). In these, Wright applied the "considerable light on practical needs of the American dwelling" he felt he had gained working in Silsbee's office (*A* I, 106), to which he added a formal, geometric precision and schematic regular-

3. Adler and Sullivan (Wright, principal designer): Charnley House, Chicago, 1891–92 (c. 1893).

4. Adler and Sullivan: Wainwright Tomb, Bellefontaine Cemetery, St. Louis, 1892.

ity reminiscent of Sullivan's quasi-classical, typological distillations of the programs of the modern tall office building and tomb (figs. 4, 5).

For about a year after leaving Madison, Wright lived alone in Chicago. Eventually, his mother and younger sister Maginel joined him, and they all moved to Oak Park. After living for a time in the house of a friend, the Reverend Augusta Chapin, then pastor to the Unitarian congregation in Oak Park, Wright and his mother bought a parcel of land in 1889 on the corner of Forest and Chicago Avenues. The property contained a small house on the Chicago Avenue

side of the lot and a barn near the corner. Wright had met Catherine Lee Tobin a little while before and intended to marry her and build a home on the site of the barn, adjacent to the existing house his mother and sister would continue to occupy. Sullivan agreed, as part of his contract, to advance Wright enough money to help pay for construction. Wright was married in June 1889 and moved into the small, gabled, Shingle Style house with Catherine by the end of the following winter (fig. 9). Three of their six children were born within the next four years.

To support his growing family as well as his own somewhat reckless spending habits ("So long as we had the luxuries the necessities could pretty well take care of themselves," he always liked to say [A I, 115]), Wright began taking on work outside the Adler and Sullivan office, in violation of the terms of his contract. Between 1890 and 1893 he designed at least six "bootlegged houses," as he later called them. They exhibited a great variety of approaches, from the Shingle Style Emmond House in La Grange, Illinois (1892), and the gambrel-roofed Dutch Colonial version for the Warren McArthurs in Chicago (1892), to the explicitly classical, eighteenth-century design of the Blossom House (1892) and the overtly Sullivanesque Harlan House (1891–92), both also in Chicago (figs. 6, 7). When Sullivan found out about these moonlighting activities in 1893, so the story goes, he refused to sign over the deed for Wright's Oak Park house that had already been paid off, and Wright quit.[10] Wright then set out on his own and soon established a reputation as a leading young designer in the field of domestic architecture.

■ ■ ■

The Chicago of 1893, when Wright opened his own office, was very different from the burgeoning city he had moved to in 1887. First of all, the entire country was in a recession that would last for several years. But other, more profound changes had occurred between 1887 and 1893. In that short time, not only had the form of the steel-frame building become an established type, characteristic of Chicago, but a

5. Adler and Sullivan: Wainwright Building, St. Louis, 1890–91.

6. Blossom House, Chicago, 1892 (c. late 1930s).

7. Harlan House, Chicago, 1891–92 (before July 1897; demolished).

the Plan of Chicago, which would be published at the end of the following decade (1909); and such recently completed classical structures as the Public Library (1890) and the Art Institute (1892), both by the Boston firm of Shepley, Rutan, and Coolidge, the successors to Richardson, testified to the type of grandiloquent design that would be demanded of architects under this new system.

Clearly, the kind of domestic planning Wright had learned from Silsbee would mean as little in this context as the rigorous approach to functional analysis or the poetic elaboration of an original type of ornament he had learned from Sullivan. Indeed, Sullivan's own career was on the wane. His firm was seriously hurt by the recession of 1893 and, even more, by an unwillingness, or inability, to come to terms with the new classicism and professionalism now instituted as the norm by such large, seemingly anonymous offices as D. H. Burnham and Company and McKim, Mead and White. Sullivan's uncompromising individualism and abstract lucubrations on the relation between form and function isolated him in the defensive posture of provincial critic. Sullivan lambasted the academic influence of the "eastern establishment," eventually describing the Fair as a "lewd exhibit of drooling imbecility and political debauchery," indicating a state of "dementia" in the American mind that would set back the course of architecture "for half a century . . . if not longer."[12]

Wright therefore found himself in a curious and difficult position in 1893. All his experience was in suburban domestic architecture or commercial design, whereas the new impetus was toward monumental urban architecture of just the classical sort detested by his "lieber meister" Sullivan. Wright felt the change in the air and submitted a grandiose classical composition in a competition for the Milwaukee Public Library and Museum in 1893 (fig. 8). His project, with its symmetrical disposition of pedimented pavilions linked by open colonnades and crowned by a central dome, though ultimately derived from Perrault's west facade of the Louvre, clearly made reference to the monumental classical structures around the Fair's Court of Honor.[13] And although it did not even receive an honorable mention,

new urban vision of classical order had emerged out of the World's Columbian Exposition to regularize and control the helter-skelter growth of the city. Planned by Daniel Burnham, John Root, Charles McKim, and Frederick Law Olmsted beginning in late 1890, the fair opened in Jackson Park on the shores of Lake Michigan to enthusiastic notices in the spring of 1893.[11] Against the backdrop of the urban "jungle" that Chicago had become, with its stockyards and factories, slum housing, and unplanned commercial development, the "White City" presented an ideal for monumental civic improvement that would soon capture the popular imagination and become known as the City Beautiful Movement. As early as 1895, Daniel Burnham began working on

8. Milwaukee Public Library and Museum project, 1893. Perspective.

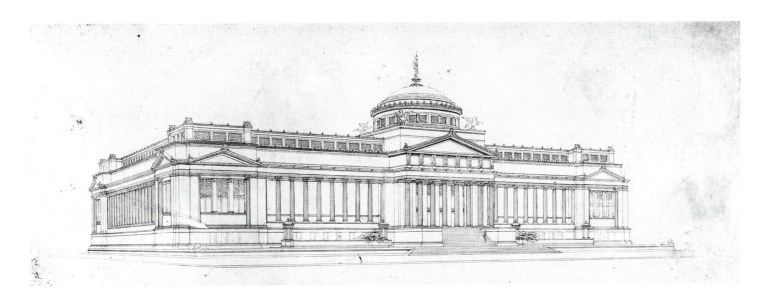

Wright exhibited the project in 1894 as his first contribution to the annual Chicago Architectural Club exhibition. Recognition from none other than Daniel Burnham came soon thereafter and led to the most serious decision Wright had yet to make about the direction his career would take.

Burnham was about to lose his chief designer, Charles Atwood, who had been responsible for much of the Fair's actual appearance.[14] Impressed, no doubt, by the evidence of promise shown in Wright's Milwaukee competition project, Burnham apparently was also struck by the urbanity and dignity of Wright's first independent commission, the Winslow House (fig. 2), built in 1893–94 in River Forest, Illinois, just opposite the home of Burnham's friend Edward Waller. According to Wright, Burnham called the design "a gentleman's house from grade to coping" (*A* I, 123). He quickly sought to hire Wright, though not without attaching certain important strings. Meeting with Wright in Waller's house, Burnham promised to make him a designer in his firm on the condition that he first enrich his background in classical architecture. According to Wright, Burnham offered to send him "to Paris, four years of the Beaux Arts. Then Rome—two years. Expenses all paid." As he later recalled, in one of the most memorable narratives of his *Autobiography*, Wright "sat, embarrassed, not knowing what to say." For a moment, the direction of his career hung in the balance. But the force of Sullivan's example was too strong.

Wright replied: "It's too late now, I'm afraid. I am spoiled already. I've been too close to Mr. Sullivan. He has helped spoil the Beaux Arts for me, or spoiled me for the Beaux Arts, I guess I mean." Wright admitted that, "without a good education in the Classics," one could hardly "hope to . . . succeed." Yet he stood his ground, saying, "I just can't see it as a living. Somehow—it scares me" (*A* I, 123–24). He thus refused Burnham's offer, choosing to go it alone, as Sullivan had. He defined his goal of creating an indigenous architecture in radically personal and provincial terms, totally independent of the academic traditions and institutions of the East Coast and Europe. "I can't run away," he finally told Burnham, "from what I see as mine—I mean what I see as ours—in our country, to what can't belong to me, no I mean *us*, just because it means success" (*A* I, 125).[15]

Wright's decision to follow Sullivan's path, rather than the more conventional road to success promised by Burnham, did not necessarily imply that he would find it impossible to get work, but it did mean that he would be relatively isolated from the mainstream of corporate and civic commissions and would have to accept a somewhat limited sphere of action. This was to be essentially suburban, domestic work. Wright initially accepted that situation with zeal. He would be, he said, a missionary "in the cause of architecture," carrying Sullivan's message into the uncharted territory of residential design. "Adler and Sullivan had little time to design residences," Wright explained, "so largely, it remained for me to carry into the field of domestic architecture the battle they had begun in commercial building."[16]

By his own reckoning, then, Wright's early work during the Oak Park years must be viewed as a conscious effort to apply to the problem of the house Sullivan's approach to the design of the tall office building. It was a method based on principle rather than precedent, as he would always say. What Wright admired in Sullivan was not only his refusal to follow history blindly but also his belief in the individual artist as the "germ" of poetic expression. Rational analysis replaced mere adaptation or appropriation, while the abstract deduction of form from function gave rise to a type-solution that followed a kind of natural law. The resulting forms expressed, metaphorically, the emotional meaning attached to their functions. Form thus became "organic" and could be understood as the necessary outgrowth of indigenous conditions.[17]

The Wainwright Building, in particular, demonstrated to Wright the power of the individual to recast and re-create in his own terms, meaning those of his society, the classical language of architecture. "Do you realize," Wright asked in summing up Sullivan's legacy, "that here, in his [Sullivan's] own way, is no body of culture evolving through centuries of time but a scheme and 'style' of plastic expression which an individual, working away in the poetry-crushing environment of a more cruel materialism than any seen since the days of the brutal Romans, had made out of himself? Here was a sentient individual who evoked the goddess whole civilizations strove in vain for centuries to win, and wooed her with this charming interior smile—all on his own in one lifetime all too brief." Sullivan's "language of self-expression," according to Wright, was "as complete in itself" as that "of any of the great styles which time took so many ages to perfect."[18]

Wright's goal in carrying Sullivan's message into the field of domestic architecture was similarly to establish a *type* reflecting modern, and local, conditions of program, construction, and site. By the rigorous analysis of the relation of form to function, Wright believed he could (1) modernize the traditional house in both plan and construction, (2) give it coherent symbolic expression through the formulation of a type, and (3) adjust its general form to the specific character of the regional topography to make the type appropriate as a house on the prairie. The first phases of this effort followed Sullivan's example closely.

Wright's Own Oak Park House

The house Wright built for himself and Catherine in 1889–90 set the stage for the development that would reach its logical conclusion in the totally original Prairie House of the following two decades.[19] Though small—really no more than a cottage—and traditional in materials and massing, it epitomized Wright's idea of what a house should be. It was therefore already more a projection of an image than merely a dwelling (fig. 9). It was, in fact, so highly formalized an image, of such apparently recondite and idiosyncratic derivation, at least for Oak Park, that Wright's neighbors, according to him, did not quite know what to make of "the funny little house" and used to ask "if it were Seaside or Colonial."[20]

The two-storied house turns its flank to busy Chicago Avenue and faces west onto Forest Avenue. Both the ground floor, articulated by projecting bays, and the upper floor, composed of an enormous gable, are sheathed in wood shingles. The plan of the ground floor is quite free, with the stair hall, living room, and dining room opening into one another in a pinwheeling fashion around the central fireplace, which bears a moral scripture on its mantel (fig. 10):

Truth is Life.

Good Friend, Around These
Hearth Stones Speak No Evil
Word of Any Creature . . .

Wright House, Oak Park, Ill., 1889–90.

9. Exterior (before 1895).

10. Living room (restored).

11. Bruce Price: Chandler House, Tuxedo Park, N.Y., 1885–86.

The round-arched brick mass of the fireplace, set deep within an inglenook, forms an inner sanctum. Removed from the main flow of space, it becomes almost purely symbolic in function, providing a constant reminder and stable image of the mutual affection that ideally guides the family life revolving around it.

The exterior of the house is equally symbolic in intention. The expression is reduced to the triangular shape of a gable set like a classical pediment above a supporting base of bay windows. The composition is symmetrical and stable, belying the pinwheeling effect of the interior space, which is echoed only faintly in the curved projections of the brick terrace. Although one of the two bays of the ground floor serves as the entrance, and the other as a living room window, they are equal in size and shape and together support the overhanging gable. This motif, which dominates the facade, contains a central Palladian window lighting Wright's original second-floor studio.[21]

The geometric regularity of the design goes well beyond the picturesqueness of Silsbee's rather unsophisticated Shingle Style. It points to the much more recent development toward classical discipline and order that could be seen on the East Coast in the revival of the vernacular Colonial tradition in the domestic work of architects like Bruce Price and McKim, Mead and White. Though barely twenty-

two years old, and with no formal education to speak of, Wright was clearly *au courant*, and intelligent enough to realize what was most significant at the time. As Vincent Scully has convincingly shown, he very likely saw examples of such work in publications like George William Sheldon's *Artistic Country Seats* (1886–87) and adapted their part-Colonial, part-Seaside imagery to the landlocked community of Oak Park.[22]

The design of his Oak Park house already tells us much about Wright's architectural motivations. The exaggeration of the two main elements—the gable on the outside and the arched fireplace on the inside—proclaims his intention that the house be read as the projection of an image of shelter, while the conventional shapes these symbols of hearth and home take reveal the representational impetus of his thought. Clearly, Wright was not being "original" by inventing these forms, as his dependence on Price's Chandler House in Tuxedo Park, New York (1885–86), shows (fig. 11). But the issue is more than one of mere copying and has to do with the way in which Wright considered the traditional forms of architecture to be figures in a language of representation.

At the very beginning of his career, then, in a work of great personal significance, Wright came to grips with what had surely become by the end of the nineteenth century the most critical issue in architecture: the relationship between form, or style, and meaning. And he interpreted the issue in the complex terms of a theory of mimesis ultimately based on the model of nature. "Primarily, Nature furnished the materials for architectural motifs out of which the architectural forms as we know them to-day have been developed," Wright explained a few years later, "and, although our practice for centuries has been for the most part to turn from her, seeking inspiration in books and adhering slavishly to dead formulae, her wealth of suggestion is inexhaustible." Acknowledging that he understood "with what suspicion the man is regarded who refers matters of fine art back to Nature," Wright maintained that his work was "dedicated to a cause conservative" and was thereby "a declaration of love for the spirit of that law and order, and a reverential recognition of the elements that made its ancient letter in its time vital and beautiful."[23]

Although considered one of the "arts of imitation" in classical theory, architecture has generally been distinguished from painting and sculpture by virtue of its less literal, less direct, more mediated relationship to the natural world, it being maintained that architecture follows nature in its principles rather than in its forms. Indeed, in our post-Cubist, post-Bauhaus age, we all too readily assume that architecture is a completely abstract, nonrepresentational art that makes no direct reference to nature. Yet we can hardly deny that the conventional shapes of traditional architecture stand in virtually the same relation to nature as the shapes of a human figure in a painting do to the world of reality. Both depend on the mediation of historical models in the process of representation that Ernst Gombrich has called the "making and matching" of art imitating art. Ironically, the Neoclassical theorist Antoine-Chrysostôme Quatremère de Quincy had already used that argument to explain architecture's place among the "arts of imitation." The architect, he observed, does not proceed "like the painter copying a model [in nature], but like the student who embraces the manner of his master to reproduce not what he sees but how he sees it done."[24]

Phrasing the issue in the language of his day, Wright called architecture "the most complete of conventionalizations," in fact, "the highest, most subjective, conventionalization of nature known to man."[25] The Froebel kindergarten method, emphasizing the underlying geometric order of nature, functioned as a kind of surrogate academic training for him. It provided a similar basis for understanding the theory of mimesis as a process of *abstraction from* the specific to the general, which is to say from the natural to the conventional. For this reason, Wright would maintain that not only were the principles of symmetry and proportion derived from nature but that the forms of the arch, the gable, and the column were "conventionalizations" of natural ones.[26] Indeed, only through acculturation do such

forms become so removed from their natural source as to appear "abstract." Abstraction would generally retain for Wright an epiphenomenal status, being the consequence of the simplifying, clarifying, and epitomizing process of representation rather than the independent agent of a purely geometric construct, as it later would become in the theories of Neoplasticism and Non-objectivity.[27]

What Wright meant by conventionalization is therefore only different in degree, rather than kind, from what occurs when a painter or sculptor fashions what might be called a "likeness" of nature. "As Nature is never right for a picture," Wright noted, "so she is never right for the architect—that is, not ready-made."[28] In effect, the conventions learned from previous works of art provide the models or schemata for the "making and matching" of artistic production. The conventions can, as Plato and Aristotle originally pointed out, operate both on the level of subject matter—as in the adherence to a type or genre—and on the level of form—as in the representation of specific elements or attributes.[29] In this way, a church could be likened to a religious painting, an important public building to a history painting, a palace to a state portrait, and a small country house to a landscape painting. And the elements of representation in a building, such as an arch, a gable, or a column, would be analogous to a face, a hat, or a tree in a painting.

Like most progressive thinkers of the time, Wright was wary of the overly literal and "realistic" reading to which the theory of imitation had been subjected by the middle of the nineteenth century, and for that reason he stressed, following the dictates of John Ruskin and Owen Jones, the processes of "conventionalization" and "interpretation" over mere "imitation." The "naturalistic" and "photographically" realistic "imitation" of nature shows little but "manual dexterity and a mechanic's eye," he noted in 1900, whereas the "conventionalization of natural things, revealing the inner poetry of their Nature," elicits a sense of "the Ideal."[30] The classical concept of the imitation of nature was an idealist construct, and with the demise of classical

idealism in the nineteenth century went the full meaning of the term "imitation." For Wright, to "conventionalize" and to "idealize" were one and the same thing.[31] This categorical interposition of the conventional in the theorizing of the relation between architecture and nature allows us to trace the source of Wright's thinking to the most advanced philosophical discussions of architectural representation at the very beginning of the modern age.

It was, significantly enough, during the Age of Enlightenment that the classical theory of imitation was applied to architecture in such a rational way as to affirm its representational basis while at the same time declaring its conventional status. Beginning with Vitruvius, architectural treatises had always referred to the primitive hut as the first stage in the development of architecture and had often derived certain decorative features, such as the Corinthian capital, from a specific model in nature. But in his *Essay on Architecture*, first published in 1753, the French theorist Marc-Antoine Laugier went one step further: he used the example of the primitive hut to testify to architecture's natural origins (fig. 12). Assuming its creators still to be living in a state of nature, Laugier's text explained how the primitive hut was not merely the first example of built form—an aboriginal shelter—but how the hut had to be seen as the natural prototype for the conventional forms of classical architecture.

Imagining four trees joined at the tops of their trunks by horizontal branches and supporting others set at angles, Laugier pictured in the celebrated frontispiece of the second edition of his book (1755) what he considered to be the most rational, and therefore natural, form of construction. He explained how the Greeks and their followers first understood this and so took the hut as the natural model for their temples. They transformed the various parts of the hut into stone, turning the tree trunks into columns, the horizontal branches into entablatures, and the angled branches into pediments.[32] Thus the classical temple imitated in permanent materials the forms of nature and therefore could be considered the representation of the natural prototype of the hut. Once made permanent in stone, the conventional forms of the temple became the ideal nature for later architects to refer to and to represent, just as the marble figures of Phidias or Praxiteles formed the images of ideal nature for the classical painter and sculptor.

Similarly, following the same mimetic theory of transformation from prehistorical natural prototype into ideal historical archetype, all other architectural forms—from the arch and the dome to the pyramid and the hearth—could be understood as figures in the representational language of architecture. But Laugier's construct remained the essential one, for it explained more than just the natural origin of individual elements. In his image of the hut, the four trees acting as uprights are still rooted in the ground, and the leaves prefiguring roof tiles literally grow on branches silhouetted like acroteria against the sky. Laugier's hut thus affirmed one of the ultimate aims of architectural representation, which is the establishment of a continuity between figure and ground, the building being the figure and its natural setting, the ground. This illusion of continuity between building and site can be considered the architectural equivalent of the illusion of three-dimensional objects in space in the two-dimensional medium of painting.

By the end of the eighteenth century, Laugier's theory was elaborated and historicized in the widely read writings of the academician Quatremère de Quincy. Though never denying the representational significance of the model of the primitive hut, Quatremère clarified its quasi-natural status at the same time as he allowed it a more or less purely conventional, "fictional" existence.[33] This opening of a wedge in the idealist equation of nature and history might lead, on the one hand, to the full-blown architectural naturalism of an Etienne-Louis Boullée (fig. 233) or a Ruskin, though more often it would result in the study of history in its own right. As architects and writers increasingly stressed the role of history in the process of reification of nature, the historical styles of eclecticism, at least in the popular mind and in much of the United States, fundamentally replaced nature as the model for imitation. Eventually, the vernacular followed the academic, and the forms of the clapboard Greek Revival town hall as well as the Shingle Style house came to be charged with an equal degree of representational meaning.

Wright's architecture at the end of the nineteenth century emerged from a resolution of the tension between the vernacular and the academic without compromising the representational basis of either. While his classical project for the Milwaukee Public Library and Museum showed the more conventional and academic use of historical precedent, his own house in Oak Park indicated how he could exaggerate the representational element of the vernacular gabled roof to express in a much less academic form the image of shelter. Where the one made use of the monumental forms suitable for a public edifice, the other revealed Wright's ability to vary the mode of representation to express the more rustic and mundane.

Although Wright would very shortly, and very emphatically, reject the strict classical conventions as "dead formulae," he never denied the broader implications of the theory of mimesis itself.[34] Both the Milwaukee Public Library and Museum and his own Oak Park house are representational buildings of a very conventional sort, using traditional forms and materials to symbolize function through association. The more important question for Wright was how to get beyond the formulaic and back to "the spirit of that law and order . . . [and] the elements that made its ancient letter in its time vital and beautiful." The answer lay in Sullivan's example of schematic abstraction based on typological analysis. In the highly stylized expression of the Winslow House, Wright clarified and simplified the shape of each figurative element, separating one from the other by a change in material or a starkly drawn outline to produce the desired effect of "an expression pure and simple, even classic in atmosphere."[35] The horizontal stratification of those elements served to intensify the naturalistic meaning of Laugier's model by underscoring the intimate relation of building to ground and sky.

Winslow House

In the context of the evolution of late nineteenth-century American domestic architecture, Wright's Oak Park house was just a few steps behind the latest developments on the East Coast. In this respect, it was similar to Sullivan's own buildings of the late eighties, such as the Auditorium (1886–89) and the Walker Warehouse (1888–89) on which Wright had worked. Where Sullivan based his designs on the archetypal clarity and monumentality of the late, urban Richardson Romanesque, in particular the Marshall Field Wholesale Store in Chicago (1885–87), Wright sought his models in the suburban version of the late Shingle Style. But when one thinks of the Marshall Field Store and the nearly contemporary Allegheny County Courthouse (1883–88), or of Price's Chandler House and McKim, Mead and White's Low House in Bristol, Rhode Island (1886–87), the question almost immediately arises: How far could the vernacular be pushed in the direction of classical order and monumental-

13. McKim, Mead and White: Taylor House, Newport, R.I., 1885–86.

ity without having to adopt the actual conventions of the classical style?[36]

The issue facing architects like Sullivan and Wright at the end of the eighties was therefore whether to allow the implicit classicism to surface in a pronounced use of historical precedent, as McKim, Mead and White did in their Boston Public Library (1887–92), or to press for more and more abstract patterns of the "law and order" Wright spoke of through an emphasis on program and construction. Sullivan followed the latter course and produced his first *typical* design in the Wainwright Building of 1890–91 (fig 5). In the field of domestic architecture, the problem was the same. Even before they designed the Low House, McKim, Mead and White had turned toward the explicit use of classical precedent in their Taylor House of 1885–86 (fig. 13).

After finishing his own house, so similar to the Low House, Wright had to decide which way to proceed. In some of the "bootlegged houses," like the Blossom House (fig. 6), he adopted the straight classical conventions of the Taylor House.[37] In the McArthur House, next door, he remained a bit looser in his historical references. In the Harlan House, however, he followed the Sullivanesque style he used in domestic work for his employers (figs. 3, 7). And it was that abstract, synthetic approach that Wright relied on in the Winslow House, his first independent commission, in order to turn the conventional representation of shelter illustrated by his own Oak Park house into the more essential and stylized concept of the Prairie House.

The Winslow House set the standard for the Prairie House (fig. 2). Although scholars usually regard the Willits House in Highland Park, Illinois, of almost ten years later, as the first "true" Prairie House, Wright called the Winslow House "the first 'prairie house'" and always considered it the original expression of the type. It provided the example for the six "propositions" he formulated in 1894 as the basis for the Prairie House.[38]

William Herman Winslow was only thirty-six (ten years older than Wright) when he commissioned the house in 1893, the year of the World's Columbian Exposition. A leading manufacturer of ornamental iron and bronze, he had met Wright in his business dealings with the firm of Adler and Sullivan. As Leonard Eaton has shown in his pioneering study of Wright's clients, Winslow set the pattern for the typical Wright client of the Oak Park years.[39] A businessman, a Republican, and a member of the upper middle class, he was also nonconformist in religious matters (he belonged to the Society for Ethical Culture) and a very strong family man. The close-knit Winslow family, which included three children, found recreation in music; Winslow himself enjoyed woodworking, printing, photography, and the challenge of mechanical invention.

Winslow purchased the lot for the house from Edward Waller, who owned a large tract of land at the extreme western edge of River Forest, in a bend of the Des Plaines River. The town, just to the west of Oak Park, was somewhat more exclusive than its neighbor. The setting of the Waller estate was bucolic and wooded (fig. 14). Winslow's property, located on the east side of Auvergne Place, diagonally opposite Waller's own house, formed a broad expanse of prairie raised above the river and looking gently down to it toward the west (fig. 15).

Wright sited the house well back from the street, up on the rise, and set it off from the street by a formal stone terrace with a reflecting pool in the middle. A central entrance, surrounded by a decorated stone frame recalling that of the Wainwright Tomb, projects out from the main wall plane to highlight the symmetrical composition of the facade (fig. 2).

Winslow House, River Forest, Ill., 1893–94.

14. Exterior (1905).

15. View from rear, looking southwest (1905).

16. Plan, ground floor (redrawn c. 1940).

The pale smooth surface of the frame contrasts with the tawny-colored Roman brick of the ground floor, as well as with the (now) darker and more textured plaster frieze of the second floor. The frieze is thrown into shadow by the deep overhang of the hip roof, which is pinned low in its center, directly behind the entrance, by the broad mass of the stone-capped chimney. The house, which was originally to have had an octagonal pavilion extending into the rear garden on the right, balancing the porte-cochere on the left, gives the appearance from the front of a self-contained, freestanding classical block.

The plan of the Winslow House was laid out on equally classical and formal principles (fig. 16). It is governed by the axial placement of the broad fireplace in the exact center of the rectangular block. The fireplace occupies the entire rear wall of the entrance hall, which is flanked on the left by a library and on the right by the living room. Standing directly opposite the entrance, it becomes the internal focus of the design and acts as a pivot for the spatial composition. The fireplace divides the front half of the house from the rear and determines a counterclockwise path that moves through the enfilade of rooms along the front, around the living room on the side, and into the rear dining room that projects from the central core into the garden. Cut out of the block in the corner between the living room and the dining room is an open porch; directly across from this is the kitchen and pantry area that fills out the corner adjacent to the porte-cochere. The garden facade re-

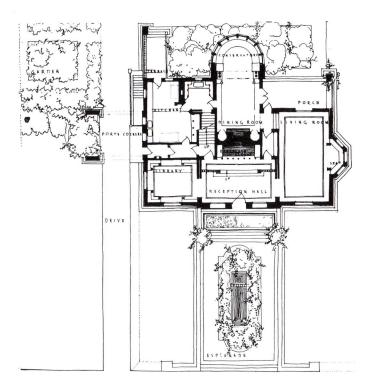

flects the disjointed, partially eroded nature of the plan at the rear (fig. 17). Unlike the extremely planar composition of the front, it presents an informal grouping of separate volumes that project and recede in depth: on the left, the void of the porch; in the center, the curved bay of the dining room; on the right, the octagonal stair tower cutting through the roof above the pantry.

The contrast between the symmetrical, strictly formal street facade and the informal, picturesquely composed garden facade emphasizes the degree to which Wright meant

17. Winslow House. Garden facade.

the public face of the house to be read as a symbolic representation of domestic order.[40] Each individual part of the composition is outlined and related to the others in precisely modulated divisions (fig. 2). The house rests on a projecting stone water table, which Wright compared to the stylobate of a Greek temple. He noted that the "low platform under the building" was designed to create the impression that the house begins "*on* the ground, not *in* it" and thus lies "comfortably and naturally flat with the ground."[41]

Above the line of the water table, all the divisions of the facade are arranged in strongly demarcated horizontal bands echoing the flat, level expanse of the prairie. The ground floor, containing the more public spaces of the library, reception hall, and living room, is faced with brick that is relieved only in the center by the slightly projected stone frame of the entrance. The brick facing continues

above the floor level of the second-story bedrooms to reach the height of the windowsills. There, a change in material, color, and texture occurs. A band of patterned plaster runs around the top of the wall, just under the "sheltering overhangs" of the eaves, to group all the smaller bedroom windows into a continuous "simple frieze."[42] The shadow line thus created allows the gently sloping hip roof to appear to float and provide, as Wright would say, a sense of "broad shelter in the open, related to vista." The "quiet sky line" that he believed "natural" to the "quiet level" of the prairie is broken only by "one massive chimney" in the center, which projects an image of domestic warmth as it anchors the building firmly to the site.[43]

The division of the Winslow House into a series of horizontal layers marked by changes in material and expressing differences in function was a direct translation into domestic terms of Sullivan's design of the tall office building (figs. 2, 5).[44] The high ground floor of public or communal rooms, faced in Roman brick, corresponds to Sullivan's unification of the first and second stories of the Wainwright Building to provide space for functions of a public nature, such as the main lobby, stores, and banks. Sullivan faced the two lower stories with sandstone ashlar and gave them a broader scale than the ones above in order to form a solid base for the upper grid of offices. The plaster frieze of the Winslow House, integrating the bedroom windows into a single decorative pattern of light and shade, corresponds to the "honey-comb" of "typical offices" that Sullivan treated as an overall pattern of interwoven lines of vertical brick piers and horizontal terra-cotta spandrels. Finally, the prominent hip roof of Wright's house corresponds to the attic and projecting cornice of Sullivan's design, capping the structure, as Sullivan said, in a way "specific and conclusive as it is in its very nature."[45]

The force of Sullivan's example for Wright was that it presented not merely a solution to a particular problem but the "birth" of "a true normal type." According to Sullivan, the Wainwright Building revealed "the pervading law of all things organic, and inorganic, . . . that the life is recognizable in its expression, that form ever follows function." Its power as an image derived from an expression of emotional meaning that led both Sullivan and Wright to compare it to an organic "entity." Sullivan believed that the architect had to ask "what is the chief characteristic" of any building type, then "heed the imperative voice of emotion," and finally embody that emotional character in a form of architectural equivalency that could stand as a metaphor of function.[46] In ways that directly parallel Symbolist practices in contemporaneous European art, the emphasis is taken off the associational references of conventional forms and replaced by a more synthetic expression of programmatic meaning.[47]

In the Wainwright Building, the emotional sense of loftiness and power of commercial enterprise that Sullivan considered "characteristic" of the tall building is not expressed by the representation of a classical temple or Gothic tower, as it would have been in the ordinary skyscraper of the period. Rather, it is projected through the vertical lines of the structure itself, which are stylized, powerfully emphasized, and florescently climaxed in the cornice. Similarly, in the Winslow House, the elements of a house are analyzed into their constituent parts: entrance, ground-floor reception rooms, upper-floor bedrooms, roof, and chimney. These are then synthesized into an image of domesticity that is not merely represented by any one or other conventional form, such as a gable or pediment, but is expressed in the emotional terms of horizontal lines that echo the earth and carry the sense of human warmth, comfort, and security—the opposite of Sullivan's aspiring and dominating image of commercial power, yet achieved by the same means of programmatic abstraction in terms of type.

The emotional attributes of a suburban house are almost diametrically opposed to those of the urban high-rise, and Wright understood this difference completely. A house had to signify comfort, a sense of belonging, a feeling of privacy—in a word, the idea of shelter. "The horizontal line," Wright wrote, "is the line of domesticity."[48] On the flat prairie of the Midwest, breadth would be a sign of shelter, as height was a sign of power and success in the city. Wright assumed "that *shelter* should be the essential look of any dwelling," for that idea was "probably rooted deep in racial instinct." The low horizontal lines that "identify themselves with the ground" and "make the building belong to the ground," he believed, offer a sense of "comfort" and "repose" that satisfies the human need for a feeling of belonging.[49]

In the Winslow House, for the first time in his work, "the *sense of shelter* in the look of the building," which Wright felt to be the primary characteristic of the Prairie House, infused every aspect of the design with an expressive meaning that was more than skin deep.[50] While the calm horizontal lines and deep overhanging planes make the house seem at one with the site, the massive central chimney literally pins the structure to the earth and establishes an emotional core for the *"sense of shelter"* in the almost "instinctual" relation between hearth and home. Seen directly

18. Winslow House. Entrance hall.

upon entering the house, the fireplace fills the entire field of vision, like a stage set, to act as a synecdoche for the house (fig. 18). Raised three steps above floor level, on a podium separated from the main flow of space by low balustrades, the fireplace is set well behind an arcaded screen. Cushioned benches at both ends of this recess might lead one to think of it as an inglenook, but Wright took the symbolism far beyond the generalized medievalism of the Shingle Style. Norris Kelly Smith has interpreted the arcade as a rood screen, thus giving the alcove the religious character of a chancel.[51] Perhaps even more to the point, and in keeping with the classical bearing of the house, the arcade can be

read as an internalized loggia, just barely masked by the framing frontispiece of the entrance and acting, like its Renaissance prototype, as a public space of familial representation.[52]

The central fireplace reminds us to some degree of Wright's own house, but there the more conventional inglenook is an isolated, off-center element. Like the roof gable of the facade, it functions as a traditional symbol of domesticity. In the Winslow House, the fireplace is so broad in treatment and so open to view that it appears to be the very backbone of the house, as the roof above is its shelter. "The big fireplace in the house below became now a place for a

19. William C. Gannet[t], *The House Beautiful*, 1896–98?. Layout and graphic design by Wright; typography and printing by William Herman Winslow.

r^al fire," Wright later wrote, and "the *integral* fireplace became an important part of the building itself" (*A* I, 138–39). In the Winslow House, the formal equation of hearth and home became a fundamental element of the Prairie House type, transmitting the emotional content of the type through the very core of the building. "It comforted me to see the fire burning deep in the solid masonry of the house," Wright added, and this was "a feeling that came to stay" (*A* II, 141).

Functioning as a synecdoche, the fireplace in the Winslow House expands and personalizes the domestic imagery of the exterior to permeate the entire house with a rarefied, almost ethereal atmosphere of what in the 1890s had come to be thought of as the charm of the "aesthetic." Distinctions between the religious and the secular, the public and the private are sublated. At the center of its own world, in the bucolic environment of the suburb, the house becomes a sanctified, exalted place of bliss. No phrase describes this better than "The House Beautiful," the title of a sermon by the Unitarian minister William C. Gannett, which Wright and Winslow thought so appropriate to their common endeavor that they published it jointly just a few years after the house was finished. Wright did the layout and graphic design, and Winslow the typography and printing in the basement of his new house (fig. 19).[53]

The Gannett text opens with a line from Paul—"A building of God, a house not made with hands"—that is elaborated to become the closing sentence of the first chapter: "The house in which we live is a building of God, a house not made with hands." The main body of the text describes how all the aspects of a house, from its physical structure to its furnishings, are nothing as compared with its inner soul. This is "The Dear Togetherness," the title of the last chapter, that makes a house a home:

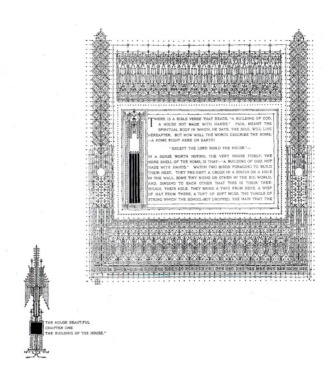

And still one thing remains to furnish the house beautiful,—the most important thing of all, without which guests and books and flowers and pictures and harmonies of color only emphasize the fact that the house is not a home. I mean the warm light in the rooms that comes from kind eyes, from quick unconscious smiles, from gentleness in tones, from little unpremeditated caresses of manner, from habits of fore-thoughtfulness for one another,—all that happy illumination which, on the inside of a house, corresponds to morning sunlight outside falling on quiet dewy fields. It is an atmosphere really generated of many self-controls, of much forbearance, of training in self-sacrifice; but by the time it reaches instinctive expression these stern generators of it are hidden in the radiance resulting. It is like a constant love-song without words, whose meaning is, "We are glad that we are alive together." It is . . . cheer; it is peace; it is trust; it is delight; it is all these for, and all these in, each other. . . . The variant dispositions in the members of the home, the elements of personality to be "allowed for," add stimulus and exhilaration to this atmosphere. Shared memories make part of it, shared hopes and fears, shared sorrows; shared self-denials make a very dear part of it.

Thus is it at its happy best; but even when the home-love is not at its best, when moods at times prevail, and cold looks make a distance in the eyes, and someone grows recluse and selfish to the rest, even then the average and wont of love may keep the home not wholly undeserving of its coronation name, "a building of God, a house not made with hands." Certainly love is the force by which, and home the place in which, God chiefly fashions souls to their fine issues.

The "home-nest," as Gannett called it, is

A world of care without;
A world of strife shut out;
A world of love shut in![54]

This is a blissful "togetherness," where "you and I should have made a happy world, if we were the only two in it."[55] It becomes translated into reality as the totally privatized, atomized world of the suburban family, who find refuge from the city in the country, separated from others like themselves in their oasis of individualism.

The Winslow House expresses all of these beliefs, including their less placid, more complicated underpinnings.[56] The formal street facade is both inviting and aloof (fig. 2). It marks the thin line between "a world of strife shut out" and "a world of love shut in." The entrance, with eyes open and alight like a face, is contained and surrounded in a frame that, by its references to Middle Eastern models, seems to function equally as a veil, protecting the occupants from the too inquisitive looks of outsiders and masking the inner world of family life.[57] The curiously high center of gravity of the facade, with its extraordinarily broad proportions and hooded lid, reinforces this mixed message of private security and public distance.

The fireplace is also a double-acting element. It echoes and reinforces the formal expression of shelter carried by the street facade while projecting onto the enclosed family rooms across the rear garden a vision of the more complex interactions of individual members within the family group (fig. 16). What appears at first to be a static, symmetrical, classical plan is turned into an asymmetrical, freewheeling pattern of movement by the presence of the fireplace; and that freedom is progressive, so that by the time one reaches the rear part of the house, the sense of axiality and symmetry is almost completely eroded. Opposite the entrance, facing the public reception area, the fireplace provides the general image of family "togetherness." On its other side, however, the different rooms break out into conflicting configurations, as might the individual family members in the daily patterns of their lives.

As the emotional core of the house, the fireplace holds in balance the worlds of the private and the public, the individual and the group, the formal and the informal, that the two different facades of the exterior of the house discretely express. Gannett's text of *The House Beautiful* stressed the need for "many self-controls," "much forbearance," and "training in self-sacrifice" in order for the various individuals who compose a family to arrive at the blissful state of "togetherness." What he referred to as "that unselfing of each one for the other's sake" could not, and in fact does not, occur on a constant daily basis—and that is what the Winslow House ultimately expresses.[58] There is the ideal, and there is the reality, the one predictable and orderly, the other accidental and serendipitous.

If the design of the public facade of the Winslow House established the Prairie House type categorically and unconditionally, it also implied through its implacable formality and irreducible frontality that such a suburban house had to respond to many different and often conflicting conditions. The house had to address the street as part of a larger community. It had to be generous and open in its self-presentation to the street, for the Midwestern suburban community was by its very nature a coming together of neighborly and generally like-minded individuals. But one of the main purposes in leaving the city was to gain a certain amount of space and privacy for the family, so the house had to clarify the line between the communal space of the neighborhood and the private space of the house. And finally, to enable that ideal of family life to flourish, the various individual members of the group had to be able to exercise a certain degree of freedom on a fairly constant basis so as not to feel that the "dear togetherness" was too overbearing or constraining.

The Winslow House projected a handsome, "dignified" face toward the street, radiating from within, as Gannett might say, "the warm light in the rooms that comes from kind eyes." The low horizontal lines and flat planes seem to want to extend beyond themselves to connect to the neighbors' lawns (fig. 2). The family is thus defined as a self-contained group; the relationship with the larger collectivity is only implied. The private nature of their world is reinforced by the overriding image of shelter, carried by the roof and its central chimney/fireplace motif. The conflict between the desire for individual space and privacy and the concern for group togetherness and community action is brought into the open at the rear of the house, where everything appears accidental and haphazard rather than typical and designed.[59] There, the extreme fragmentation and atomization of the modern suburban dweller's way of life is given full expression, and the result is disjunction and discontinuity. There is no transition ground between the two sides of the house, only a breakdown in the principle of organization that reveals itself in the progressive erosion of the surface. There seems to be no continuity, therefore, between the activity of the family as a group and the activities of its individual members; just as there seems to be no easy line of connection between the desire for privacy of the individual family and the concern for community otherwise expressed.

Some might object to thinking of such an exquisite and sophisticated building as Wright's Winslow House in such problematic terms. Given that Wright was only twenty-six when he designed it, one might argue that its discontinuities are less a matter of conscious design than of inexperience.[60] Wherever the truth lies, it is clear from the direction of Wright's work that the Winslow House established the house-type and clarified the issues he would attempt to integrate more fully over the next fifteen years of practice.

How could one weave together the various private interests of individuals with those of the family group while at the same time linking all of these larger individual entities to the more amorphous one of the suburb itself? What could be the basis for a new form of collectivity responding to the dispersed conditions of such a fragmented world? The answer Wright would eventually propose lay outside the Sullivanesque framework of the Winslow House—in a radical reification of space as the essential medium of architectural design. But the Winslow House always remained, in its uncanny reserve, the fundamental diagram of social and artistic forms activating that new space.

20. Unity Temple, Oak Park, 1905–08. Interior.

20. Unity Temple, Oak Park, 1905–08. Interior.

II

Abstraction and Analysis in the Architecture of the Oak Park Years

As an epigraph for *The House Beautiful*, *Wright chose Alfred, Lord Tennyson's poem "Flower in the Crannied Wall," which he incorporated within a highly elaborate border. Originally published with The Holy Grail in 1869, it is one of Tennyson's best-known, later "speculative" poems. Addressing the question of the relation between microcosm and macrocosm, spirit and matter, appearance and reality, the short poem describes the removal of a natural object from its place of growth and suggests that the very process of abstraction may stand as a metaphor for the artistic act:*

Flower in the crannied wall,
I pluck you out of the crannies;—
Hold you here, root and all, in my hand,
Little flower—but if I could understand
What you are, root and all, and all in all,
I should know what God and man is.[1]

The theme of this poem would haunt Wright throughout the early years of his practice and serve as a leitmotif of his architecture at least until the building of Taliesin. "A rhythmic changing play of ordered space and image seeking trace" is the way Wright described the effect of the "interlinear web" of his graphic designs for Tennyson's and Gan-

21. Wright House. Playroom addition, 1895–98. Interior, looking east.

nett's texts (fig. 19).[2] Translating words into people and graphic design into built form, that description might easily serve for the architecture of the Oak Park years as well.

■ ■ ■

Wright's work between 1893 and 1909 can be conveniently divided into two phases, to each of which he consciously provided a *terminus ad quem* by means of a retrospective publication. The first phase concludes in 1900 with

his friend Robert Spencer's lengthy and copiously illustrated article "The Work of Frank Lloyd Wright" in Boston's *Architectural Review*. The second phase ends in 1909 with Wright's preparations for the publication in Berlin of the Wasmuth monograph, *Ausgeführte Bauten und Entwürfe von Frank Lloyd Wright* (1910[–11]).[3]

During the entire period, Wright maintained an office in downtown Chicago, essentially for business meetings, but the real work of designing from the late 1890s on took place in Oak Park. Following the pattern of the English Arts and

Crafts Movement, Wright hoped to integrate work and family life under one roof in an environment close to nature and free from the stresses of city life. To adapt the small house he had built in 1889–90 to his growing family and practice, he added two separate wings between 1895 and 1898. These reveal, in their different ways, his growing interest in the dynamics of spatial composition, the controlling force of geometry, and the literary and symbolic attributes of form. Free to write his own program, and cognizant of the public statement the work would make, Wright explored a number of new ideas that would reappear intermittently and in different combinations over the years to come.[4] Outside the normal pattern of his commissioned work, the renovations point to the more experimental side of Wright's thought and therefore make a good place to begin.

In the first campaign of renovation, an addition to the southeast created space for a new kitchen and maid's room on the ground floor. This allowed Wright to make the former kitchen into a dining room, thus liberating the original dining area for a study.[5] More significant from an architectural point of view is the children's playroom occupying the entire second floor of the new wing. It is one of Wright's first dramatic interior spaces (fig. 21). A fifteen-foot-high barrel vault, delineated by ribs and lit by a skylight, turns the multi-use space into a noble basilica. In the semicircular lunette above the fireplace at the far end, a mural depicts a scene from the tale of the "Fisherman and the Jinni" in the *Thousand and One Nights*.[6] Wright intended "a lesson to be drawn from the subject-matter by the children" (*A* I, 110). At the opposite end of the space, on the railing of the gallery used for theatrical productions, a plaster cast of the *Winged Victory of Samothrace* stands directly over the vaulted entrance. Its shape echoes the hovering form of the Jinni and complements its Middle Eastern heritage with one of the most celebrated monuments of the Hellenistic world (fig. 22).[7]

23. Wright House. Studio addition, 1898. Perspective and plan.

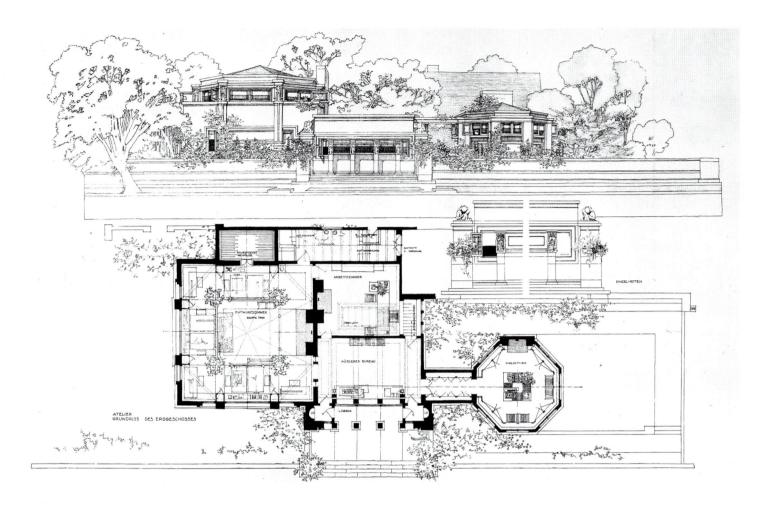

The second campaign of renovation was even more ambitious. Following the birth of his fourth child in 1895, Wright turned his original second-floor studio (over the living room) into a dormitory for the children. To replace it, he created a multiroom complex on the north side of the house, containing a reception hall, a library/conference room, a drafting room, a vault, and a private office for himself (fig. 23). This was one of Wright's first attempts to connect a series of distinct and highly articulated spaces along a continuous axis. A low, heavily lidded rectangular loggia serves as the entrance and as the link between a small, octagonal library and the larger octagon of the drafting room rising from a square base. All the rooms are skylit. The hermetic atmosphere and mysterious sense of light bring to mind the progression of space around a medieval cloister or the chancel of a cathedral, just as the octagonal shape of

both the library and the upper level of the drafting room recall medieval baptisteries and chapterhouses.[8] The geometric clarity of the rendition, however, tends to limit the representational impact and cause one to read the overall form as a concatenation of large-scale building blocks. The polyphonic composition of disjunct volumes marks a decisive break with the synthetist approach of Sullivan.

In his free and inventive attitude to tradition, Wright, at least at this stage in his career, was not alone. As H. Allen Brooks has amply demonstrated, he was in fact a fully integrated member of the younger profession.[9] While envisaging a special role for his Oak Park Studio as a place for avant-garde experimentation, Wright had much to gain from close contact with his peers.[10] During the 1890s, he first shared office space in Chicago with a former colleague from Silsbee's office, Cecil Corwin, before joining Dwight

24. Bagley House, Hinsdale, Ill., 1894 (c. late 1930s).

Perkins, Myron Hunt, and Robert Spencer in a loft in Steinway Hall. These architects formed the nucleus of the group that would later be known as the Prairie School. Along with Richard Schmidt, Hugh Garden, Arthur Heim, George Dean, and others, the young Wright took part in meetings, social gatherings, and exhibitions in which the major issues of the day were debated and discussed.

Following the World's Columbian Exposition, Chicagoans felt their horizons widen and believed themselves to be assuming a new leadership role in architectural matters. As newcomers to the profession, the members of the Steinway Hall group were concerned with making an architecture that was in tune with the times yet characterized by a regional sensitivity. Sullivan was the *éminence grise*, the spiritual leader for whom a number of the group had in fact worked. But other ideas were also beginning to take hold. An important offshoot of the Arts and Crafts Movement was developing in Chicago, and in 1897 it found a home in Jane Addams's Hull House. Wright, Perkins, Hunt, and Spencer were all charter members of the Chicago Arts and Crafts Society, which set out to reform the Victorian house on the modern lines Wright had already laid out in the Winslow House and the publication of *The House Beautiful*.[11] Wright would continue to be involved both directly and indirectly with this aestheticizing reform movement, eventually trying to redirect its energies from Ruskin's and Morris's ideal of handicraft toward acceptance and incorporation of the machine as a way of achieving more modern results. Wright's lecture at Hull House in 1901 on "The Art and Craft of the Machine" represented his most forceful statement of that position.

Along with the other young architects in Chicago, Wright was introduced to international developments in the Arts and Crafts Movement. Through the English *Studio* magazine, in particular, he would have seen the work of M. H. Baillie Scott, Charles Robert Ashbee, C.F.A. Voysey, and Charles Rennie Mackintosh. It was also at this time, and in such publications, that he probably became aware of the more radical investigation of geometric abstraction and stylized decoration that was evolving among the group that would be known as the Viennese Secessionists. Indeed, Wright's studio addition to his Oak Park house parallels, when it does not actually predate, the work of Joseph Maria Olbrich, Josef Hoffmann, and others.[12] As another significant aspect of these Arts and Crafts ideals, Wright came into contact with the art of the Middle East and Asia. The importance of Islamic art, which he had known through his reading of Owen Jones, had already been reinforced by Louis Sullivan's interest. The very different lessons of "simplicity" and "elimination of the insignificant" that Wright felt he learned from Japanese art also began to affect his work at this time.[13]

Wright's work between 1894 and 1900 follows no single, straightforward course, as it fundamentally would in the following decade. It took him a certain amount of time to try out different approaches and, especially, to see how the Sullivan model could be expanded and reworked to suit his own purposes. The work of these years shows an openness to new and progressive influences, despite the strong will to create something personal and integral. At the same time, a significant undercurrent of traditionalism continues to mark it in a pronounced way. The gambrel-roofed, Ionic-porticoed Bagley House (1894) in Hinsdale, Illinois (fig. 24), is even more explicitly Dutch Colonial than the McArthur

25. Wolf Lake Amusement Park project, Chicago, 1895. Perspective and plan.

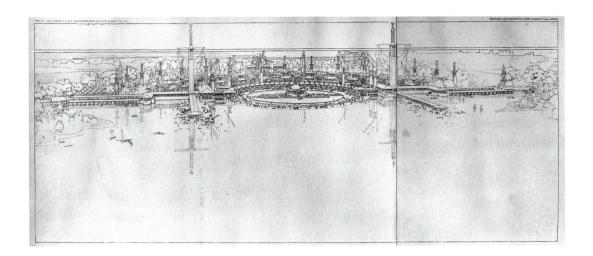

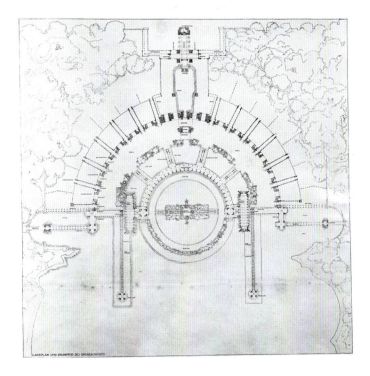

of his thinking still derived from Sullivan. The chief effect of Sullivan's example initially was to lead Wright to develop his own synthesis of the classical style out of the Winslow House. In the wake of the Chicago Fair of 1893, Wright gave up the strict classicism of the Milwaukee Library and Museum to produce an abstracted, "secessionist" version of the White City's Court of Honor for Edward Waller's proposed Wolf Lake Amusement Park in 1895 (fig. 25). Here, the axial Beaux-Arts plan and exedra of festive structures are rendered in the Sullivan manner of stripped-down geometric shapes, ornamented in flat floral patterns.[14] The low-income housing schemes of the same year for Waller and for the Terre Haute Trust Company, in Chicago, as well as the projects for the Luxfer Prism Office Building (1895) and the All Souls Building (Abraham Lincoln Center) for his uncle Jenkin Lloyd Jones, designed in association with Dwight Perkins in 1897, all show Sullivan's diagrammatic approach to design applied to different building types.

The most consistent line of development in Wright's work during these years was in the private, suburban house, where the model remained the Winslow House. Step by step, from the project for the McAfee House (1894) for the north Chicago suburb of Kenilworth, through the Heller House (1897) and the Husser House (1899), both in Chicago, Wright worked his way toward integrating the disjunctive aspects of the Prairie House prototype into a new

House of two years before. The Gothic Roloson townhouses in Chicago (also 1894) and the Tudor Moore House in Oak Park (1895) are just two further examples of Wright's willingness to preserve intact certain aspects of the historical language of architectural representation while analyzing how they could be simplified, rationalized, and thereby "modernized."

These various strains in Wright's work tended to remain fairly discrete, and at times even superficial; the core

26. McAfee House project, Kenilworth, Ill., 1894. Plan.

27. Heller House, Chicago, 1897.

28. Husser House, Chicago, 1899 (before March 1908; demolished).

form of open spatial composition directly related to the experiments made in his Oak Park Studio addition.[15]

In the McAfee House project, Wright reduced the traditional, almost Palladian mass plan to a single room in depth (fig. 26). By equating the axis of movement with the definition of space, he gave the interior a dynamic sense of direction and outward flow. Designed for the shore of Lake Michigan, the McAfee House points in the direction of the view. Diagonal shifts in axis, recalling the Shingle Style "butterfly plan," create angled projections from the wall plane.[16] These interpenetrating diagonals, crossing at the rear fireplace, run counter to the underlying rectilinear pattern to expand the space outward in a broad fanning motion.

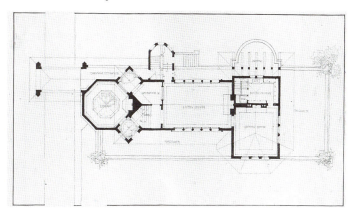

In the Heller House, located at the edge of Chicago's Hyde Park section, Wright again used the Winslow House's horizontal layering, Roman brick, rhythmically grouped windows, decorative plaster frieze, and low sheltering roof. But in response to the narrow city lot, he notched the exterior corners, treating them as reentrant angles (fig. 27). The interior space of the living and dining rooms expands into a Greek cross that projects into tall bay windows forming balconies, like protective parapets, under the second-floor eaves.

Finally, in the Husser House, which also looked out over Lake Michigan, though broadside, Wright compressed the cross-shaped space into separate wings, reaching out in a pinwheel pattern and terminating in open octagonal bays or porches, snugly sheltered under exaggeratedly deep eaves (fig. 28). With the basement here treated as a raised ground floor, the center of gravity became even higher than in the Winslow House. The brooding image of protectiveness that resulted seemed to be designed to counteract the generous exposure of interior space.

The Husser House calls to mind the rear of the Winslow House, with its bristling projections, deeply cut hollow voids, and lack of the "sweet reasonableness of form and outline naturally dignified" that Wright achieved in the symmetry and "repose" of the more representational parts

of the Winslow House. It was Wright's last explicitly Sullivanesque design. During 1900 and 1901, in a series of projects culminating in the Willits House, he found a way of resolving the conflicting demands of freedom and order by reversing the very terms of the argument so as to redefine the problem from the inside out.[17]

In the Winslow House, Wright started with the image of a self-contained block, which was then opened up on the

29. Bradley House, Kankakee, Ill., 1900.

rear, in ways that would not be very noticeable, to give the interior of the house a measure of the spacious breadth he perceived in the expanse of the prairie. "To bring the outside world into the house, and let the inside of the house go outside" was the way he later described this first intimation of how the Prairie House should be integrated with its site (*A* I, 139). Here, the structural and decorative bases of Sullivan's work were of little help. Clearly, this is the fundamental reason why the Winslow House and those that immediately followed it remained so tentative and, indeed, disjunctive.

In looking back on this moment in his career, Wright stressed the limitations of Sullivan's teaching in helping him formulate the idea of shelter as a spatial experience. He described Sullivan's approach as two-dimensional: although "the Wainwright [Building] went very far," it "was still a mere facade." Sullivan's buildings lacked that "still-mysterious third dimension." Only in his ornament did Sullivan achieve "an integral sense of the whole." For his part, Wright "wanted to see . . . a building continuously plastic from inside to outside." "I longed to see the thing go through and 'button at the back,' become genuinely unitarian," he said. "Or to come through from within and button at the front would do as well, if that was any easier."[18]

The "genuinely unitarian" solution Wright sought thus involved a radical reworking of the Prairie House type in terms of its spatial structure. With this emphasis on the third dimension—or sense of depth—a new simplicity and geometric clarity entered his work. The infusion of those elements also brought an increasing, and somewhat antagonistic emphasis on abstraction, to which Wright's designs of the first decade of the century owe so much of their unusual power. The simplicity and geometric clarity appear first in two houses built in 1900 in Kankakee, Illinois, the one for the family of B. Harley Bradley (fig. 29) and the other for that of his brother-in-law, Warren Hickox. Eschewing the heavy masonry of the earlier Sullivanesque houses, Wright chose a system of partially exposed, wood-stud construction sheathed in stucco. This lighter method of building resulted in a more open composition of solids and voids—structural members interwoven with thin flat planes—that probably owed something both to the Arts and Crafts Movement and to Japanese esthetics.

Reworking these two designs for publication in the *Ladies' Home Journal* in 1901, Wright produced even more extended, open, and spatially dynamic plans for what he called "A Home in a Prairie Town" and "A Small House, with 'Lots of Room in It.'"[19] As part of this presentation of his ideas to the general public, Wright also showed how a neighborhood might be formed out of such independent yet spatially interactive units (fig. 30). The "Quadruple Block Plan" grouped four houses, each one pinwheeling around a central fireplace core, in clusters interlaced by paths and lines that visually linked them yet kept each house at an appropriate distance from the others.[20]

Willits House

The house Wright built for the Willits family in Highland Park in 1902–1903 gave full expression to these various ideas and codified both the elements and the imagery of the mature Prairie House. Ward Winfield Willits was, like Winslow, an independent businessman involved in manufacturing. Born of a pioneering family in western Illinois in 1859, he had not yet turned twenty when he went to work for a

30. "Quadruple Block Plan" project, 1900. Perspective and plan.

company that made railroad equipment. By 1891, he was vice-president of the Adams and Westlake railway supply manufacturing company, and he became its president in 1904, the year after his new house was completed. Willits bought the property in the northern suburb of Chicago in the early part of 1902, and Wright's working drawings were done by the beginning of the summer.[21]

For the flat, expansive lot on Highland Park's fashionable Sheridan Road, Wright began with the asymmetrical, pinwheeling plan of the smaller, second *Ladies' Home Journal* project, but regularized it to give it the formality, axiality, and order of the Winslow House (fig. 31). Set well back from the street, the house extends out in all four directions on a cross-axial plan that is anchored in the center by a fireplace (fig. 32). This essential element of representation and family unity becomes the source of the spatial energies of the house, while at the same time it focuses all movement on the center. As each wing of the ground floor of the two-story structure—entrance and reception area on the right, living room in the center, dining room on the left, and kitchen/servants' area at the rear—projects directly from the core, the circulation pattern is forced into the reentrant angles or deflected to the edges. The frontality of the Winslow House thus becomes a purely formal gesture to the street, an ideal counterpoint to the reality of family life within.

To construct this image of suburban domestic life, Wright followed the example of the Kankakee and *Ladies' Home Journal* houses. He jettisoned the Winslow House's thick Sullivanesque surface of Roman brick and stone belt courses in favor of a lighter screen of plaster trimmed with wood stripping. In place of the shadow-giving decorative frieze, he inserted a continuous band of casement windows beneath the eaves. These windows stop just short of the corners to leave a void that would deny the sense of solid containment and allow the overhanging hip roof to appear to float free. The lower, even broader horizontal roof extends from the open porch of the dining room on the left to the porte-cochere adjoining the entrance hall on the right, reinforcing the sense of dynamic space. As the lower roofline slices through the central living room bay, it indicates the penetration of one volume through another in a sequence of overlapping planes. The low base of the porch/porte-cochere, stretched laterally between "out-reaching" piers topped by flat urns, continues around the front of the house to form the girding parapet of the open terrace that extends the living room bay toward the street in a gesture of formal openness and receptivity.

In the Willits House, Wright translated the Prairie House type into three dimensions to achieve the ordered expression of spatial freedom and openness he had sought since the Winslow House. While preserving the horizontal stratifications of the Winslow House in the thin wood stripping and window bands, he gave the functional differentiation a spatial definition. Instead of merely being described on the two-dimensional surface of the wall, the horizontal layering is projected in depth through the successive planes of parapets, window bays, wall screens, piers, and rooflines. Where in the Winslow House the formal elements of protective shelter, such as the solid stone frame of the door and the capping hip roof, are agents of closure and containment, in

Willits House, Highland Park, Ill., 1902–03.

31. Exterior (before March 1908).

32. Plan, ground floor (redrawn c. 1940).

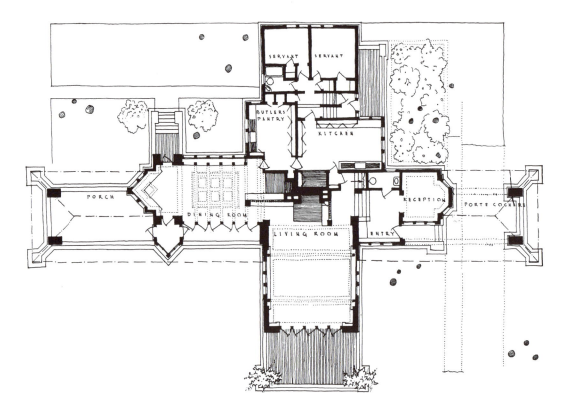

the Willits House those same elements have become the low parapets, freestanding piers, screen walls, and free-floating rooflines marking the interpenetration of interior and exterior space.

Although the facade presented to the street is as symmetrical as that of the Winslow House, one does not enter the Willits House through a central door. The path from the street is off-center, running alongside the driveway to join the house at the corner of the porte-cochere. The entrance is reduced to a slot of space, perpendicular to the drive, created by a break and dislocation in the wall plane under the eaves of the lower roof (fig. 33). One slides between two layers of space in the angle between the wings, thus allowing the projecting central pavilion to preserve its ideal, formal integrity. Movement within the house is determined by another sequence of screens, angling off the central fireplace and directing the view outward along the continuous lines of wood-strip moldings and under the protective overhang of the eaves.

The interior spaces overlap one another along the pinwheeling pattern of the projecting fireplace screens. This interpenetration of volumes is translated into a direct interaction between inside and outside, as the spaces of the rooms to either side of the living room are allowed to seep into partially enclosed porches under the continuous lower roof. Instead of being mere appendages, as in earlier Shingle Style dwellings, these porches are half-inside, half-outside interstitial spaces. Where the prow-shaped end of the dining room projects through the porch into the garden, one has the impression that the interior space of the house has literally been pulled out from the core, like a plastic, fluid medium, merging laterally with the exterior in an ever-expanding plane.

Conceived as a series of layers permeating and permeated by space, the Willits House becomes an enveloping presence in its suburban context. The sheltered interior extends its domain into the communal space of the neighborhood, forming a kind of aura or protective envelope of

shared space around the privacy of the home. The house is the center of a field of energy that is the activated space of family life. Revolving around an internal core, the disparate and highly individuated parts coalesce into the conception of community planning that Wright visualized in the Quadruple Block Plan. The individual unit—whether the family as a whole or its separate members—becomes the multifocal key to a new collective order wherein space functions as the dissolver of distinctions and the connector of disparities. The private subsumes the public as the individual subsumes the group in an expression of integral order in which the abstract gridded lines of the house seem totally congruent with the abstracted landscape of the typically man-made, suburban plat of the Midwest.

Dana House and the *Flower in the Crannied Wall*

The fragmentation and decomposition of the Willits House brought the imagery of the Prairie House to a point of high tension between the poles of abstraction and representation, or convention and nature, as Wright defined those terms. As he became aware of the problems of interpretation posed by this highly analytical approach to design, the relation between abstraction and representation emerged as a major preoccupation in his writing and work. "It is fair to explain

34. Dana House, Springfield, Ill., 1902–04. Exterior (c. early 1950s).

the point," he wrote in 1910, "which seems to be missed in studies of the work, that in the conception of these structures they are regarded as severe conventions whose chief office is a background or frame for the life within them and about them."[22] Two years before, he had remarked that the "broad simple surfaces and highly conventionalized forms" of his architecture were the "inevitable" result of his intention to make the houses a "framework for the human life within their walls and a foil for the nature efflorescence without." He explained that the imagery of the Prairie House was "conventionalized to the point where it is quiet and stays as a sure foil for the nature forms from which it is derived and with which it must intimately associate."[23]

One way in which Wright attempted to deal with the issue so as to reduce the effects of abstraction was to use nature itself as an extension of the architectural forms.

Planters, window boxes, and urns were designed to make "natural foliage and flowers" an integral part of the house. "This efflorescence" of the building's piers and parapets, Wright believed, made the Prairie House seem "to blossom with the season."[24] Another device, more explicitly calling attention to the natural origin of the architectural forms, was to choose a particular plant as the overall "grammar" of a building. Abstracted into a geometric figure, the natural form would provide the basis for the plan as well as the elevations, and perhaps appear more overtly in the decorative designs of the leaded glass windows, lampshades, and rug patterns.[25] By this means, an "organic" unity of design would be implanted in the whole as a subliminal natural pattern.

One of the most fully realized examples of such grammatical underpinning is the house designed for the wealthy

35. Dana House. Entrance (before March 1908).

mining heiress and social activist Susan Lawrence Dana, built in Springfield, Illinois, at just about the same time as the Willits House, though finished a year later (1904).[26] For this extremely large project, with a budget that allowed for an unusually elaborate decorative program including free-standing sculpture, Wright chose the indigenous sumac plant as the leitmotif. A frieze of stylized sumac grows under the shadow of the eaves and into the beveled, green, copper-sheathed gable of the roof (fig. 34). The leaded-glass archivolt within the entrance forms an abstracted, semicircular wreath over the door (fig. 35).[27] Inside the stairhall, which is suffused with natural light from above and resonates with

the trickle of water into a pool diagonally opposite the fireplace, the hanging lamps and carpet patterns continue the sumac theme (fig. 36). Yet, despite its recurrence, the form of the plant remains so conventionalized that it is never reduced to a literal representation. Similarly, the traditional parts of the house, such as the arched door, the gable, and the frieze, are so fragmented and decomposed that the overall image of shelter seems to dissolve and give way, as in the Willits House, to a gridlike plaiting of vertical and horizontal piers and planes.

There is no doubt that Wright was keenly aware of the resulting tension in the design. For the very spot that would

Dana House.

36. Entrance hall.

37. *Flower in the Crannied Wall,* by Wright and Richard Bock (before March 1908).

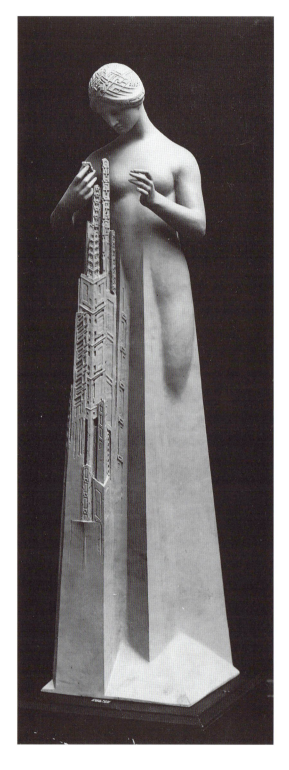

be seen immediately upon entering the house, where the world of nature outside is transformed into the man-made world of architecture inside, he designed a piece of sculpture that embodies, in its binary form, the dialectical forces of abstraction and representation. Entitled *Flower in the Crannied Wall* after the poem by Tennyson, the sculpture was executed and cast in terra-cotta by Richard Bock.[28] The poem itself is inscribed on the rear of the base, reiterating what it means for an artist to *abstract* nature so as to *re-present* it.[29]

Wright's image of the *Flower in the Crannied Wall* is a female muse of architecture, like the one pointing to the primitive hut in Laugier's frontispiece, but here contemplating a tower of Froebel-like blocks (fig. 37). Placed directly on axis, the buff-colored female figure appears through the arch of the entrance, in the dimness of the vestibule, like a nymph chanced upon in a glade (fig. 35). With the light behind her coming through a skylight, as well as from a trough below, she slowly emerges as if through a mist. Her thin, vertical figure, like a chink of light, throws the arch into relief, making it seem truly cavernous. The entrance becomes the cranny in the wall in which the flower of the figure takes root.

The *Flower in the Crannied Wall* depicts a young maiden building an abstract, crystalline tower out of interlocking, geometric blocks. At first the meaning seems obvious: the maiden is the muse of architecture, and the tower, her creation, is a pure abstraction. But the image is more complex. The small decorative block in the figure's hand is surely the flower plucked "out of the crannies" in the wall. Understanding the part should reveal the meaning of the whole. Stylized and conventionalized to fit into the overall design of the tower, it is like one of the geometricized sumac leaves that serve as the building blocks of the house itself. Neither natural form nor abstract pattern predominates.

Even though the completely abstract design of the tower is contrasted with the quite sensuous representation of the woman, both tower and woman emerge from the same rudimentary block of brute matter or stone and thus derive from the same natural basis. As a result, we read the image of architecture not simply as a pure abstraction but rather in the dialectical terms of nature and geometry brought together to produce a composition of conventionalized, or stylized, forms grounded in the world of representation and taking its order from that creative impulse. The sculpture thus embodies Wright's awareness of the distinction between the abstract and the natural, as well as his belief that abstraction and representation must be held in balance, for the conventionalized forms of architecture can emerge only out of the process, and through the medium, of representation.[30]

Geometry, as Wright later claimed he learned from his Froebel training, allows the architect "to seize upon essentials" and thereby condense into an expressive image "that inner harmony which penetrates the outward form or letter, and is its determining character." This *typical* form, Wright noted, is "what Plato called . . . the 'eternal idea of the thing.'"[31] The danger for the artist is to lose sight of the source. The *Flower in the Crannied Wall* can therefore also be read as a portent or, at the very least, an indication of the hermetic self-centeredness that can result from an unmitigated obsession with abstract geometry.[32]

Larkin Building and Unity Temple

To maintain a balance between the extremes of abstraction and representation remained Wright's ideal for the rest of the decade. That goal, however, became increasingly difficult to achieve. Having developed the Prairie House to a point of near systematization, Wright had only to elaborate or refine the type, a process that in itself led to greater and greater simplification and standardization of elements. But the drive toward abstraction had a more deliberate, even willful, side, as can be seen in the two major nondomestic buildings Wright designed during the period. The Larkin

38. Larkin Building, Buffalo, N.Y., 1902–06 (c. 1906; demolished).
Exterior, from southeast.

by Wright as an industrial artifact "built to house the commercial engine of the Larkin Company" (fig 38).[34]

Surfaced in brick trimmed with stone, the five-story steel and concrete structure was almost entirely self-contained and closed off from the outside. The exterior was treated as "a simple cliff of brick hermetically sealed," according to Wright (A I, 151), to keep out the noise and noxious fumes of the surrounding factory environment. The building was planned around a skylit atrium court (fig. 39). The floors thus formed galleries ringing the central open space and rising up through the full height of the building. Continuous vertical piers were plaited with inset spandrels, as Sullivan had done for the main "beehive" of offices of the Wainwright Building and of the later Guaranty Building, which he built on the same model in Buffalo (1894–95). The resultant grid in the Larkin Building created a web of space that interiorized Sullivan's concept and made it over in spatial terms. Wright related the gathering of coworkers to a "family gathering" and asserted that "the top-lighted interior created the effect of a great official family at work in day-lit, clean airy quarters."[35] The image of space itself, as an abstract construct, thus replaced the hearth or fireplace of the home as the communal focus of the office building.

With that central focus as the core of his design, Wright analyzed the various functions of the building into distinct operational units that would surround, support, and, in his words, "articulate" the main idea of the "Larkin family" headquarters (A I, 151–52).[36] File cabinets were lifted off the floor and integrated within the spandrels between the piers of the atrium court or those of the exterior wall. Likewise, stairways were removed from the central space, to allow for freedom of movement through and around it, and were placed in large hollow piers set "free of the central block" at the four exterior corners (A I, 151; fig. 40). Heating and ventilating ducts were also relegated to the outer shell. Placed just behind the stair towers, they were separately articulated in flat, hollow shafts that rose above the cornice of the main building. To one of the long

Building of 1902–1906 and Unity Temple of 1905–1908 were commissions of a size and scale large enough to allow the development of complex spatial ideas. Unburdened by the conventions and personal sentiments attached to the individual, private house, Wright could give free rein to a more abstract notion of form. Both the Larkin Building and Unity Temple would grow out of the same concern for programmatic analysis in terms of type that the Winslow House originally owed to Louis Sullivan, but neither of them would depart as much as the succeeding Prairie Houses did from Sullivan's structural language of form.

The commission for a new administration building for the burgeoning mail-order business of the Buffalo-based Larkin Soap Manufacturing Company came into Wright's office in late 1902 as a result of the impression Wright's domestic work had made on the vice-president of the company, Darwin D. Martin, while visiting his brother William in Oak Park.[33] The site for the building was the industrial area on the south side of Buffalo, near the harbor. Locked between the tracks of the New York Central Railroad and the existing warehouse and factory buildings of the Larkin Company, the new administration building was conceived

Larkin Building.

39. Interior (before March 1908).

40. Plan, ground floor.

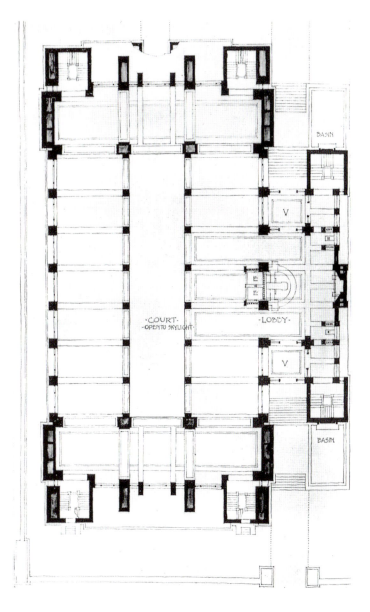

sides of the structure, an annex containing lounges, restrooms, the reception area, and other ancillary facilities was created by pulling out from the main body of the building a separate unit composed of two, shorter hollow square piers. The gap between became the main entrance to the atrium court. By means of this disjunction, Wright was able both to preserve the self-contained integrity of the central

space and to produce the dramatic effect of seeming to arrive within the very heart of that space almost at the moment of entering the building.

The result of this type of Sullivanesque programmatic analysis was an exterior expression of an almost purely geometric form. Each rectangular element sings out as a discrete unit within a reticulated composition of forceful presence and scale. Aside from the two piers in antis on the narrow front and rear facades, topped by Richard Bock sculptures of figures supporting globes symbolizing the Larkin Company's international aspirations, none of the elements could be read as anything more than a functional device. And thus their abstract geometry predominates. Wright described the design as an "utterance of a plain, utilitarian type," maintaining that the program itself called for "less architecture in quotation marks and more engineering."[37] In response to criticism from the older architect Russell Sturgis, Wright wrote:

> *Concerning the aesthetics of the bare, square forms . . . he [Wright] prefers to think in terms of clean, pure, unadulterated forms. A clean cut, square post could not be improved . . . by chamfering the edges. There is a certain aesthetic joy in letting the thing alone which has for centuries been tortured, distorted, and dickered with in the name of Art. . . . I confess to a love for a clean arris; the cube I find comforting, the sphere inspiring. In the opposition of the circle and the square I find motives for architectural themes with all the sentiment of Shakespeare's "Romeo and Juliet": combining these with the octagon I find sufficient materials for symphonic development. I can marry these forms in various ways without adulterating them, but I love them pure, strong, and undefiled.*[38]

The "pure," declarative geometry of the Larkin Building expresses the mechanical workings of the structure in a metaphorical way that allows one to speak of a "machine esthetic." Unburdened by traditional references or associations, these straightforward geometric units permitted Wright to expose and describe, with a directness and bluntness appropriate to the "character and brutal power" of the program and site (*A* II, 151), the various mechanisms that ensured the proper functioning and spatial integrity of the structure's symbolic interior core. In that sense the Larkin Building is, in effect, a negative cast, the exoskeleton of an idea. Wright called it an "affirmative negation," his "first

protestant" building. He intended its extremely reductive form to be a "genuine and constructive affirmation of the new Order of this Machine Age"—a "genuine expression of power directly applied to purpose, in the same sense that the ocean liner, the plane or the car is so."[39]

■ ■ ■

In the design for Unity Temple, undertaken during the construction of the Larkin Building, Wright gave a more positive cast to the enclosure of space, while at the same time relating the geometric forms of the building to certain traditional ideas of places of worship and to the spiritual meaning of space as a place of communion and interaction. Unity Temple is the name by which Wright liked to refer to the church for the Unitarian congregation of Oak Park that he was commissioned to design in the fall of 1905, following the fire that destroyed an earlier structure on a different site.[40] Wright was a member of the congregation and had a number of friends on its building committee. Moreover, his uncle Jenkin Lloyd Jones was the most celebrated Unitarian minister in the Chicago area. Whatever questions might have arisen over his radical artistic position, it was known that Wright had worked on earlier buildings for the Unitarians when he was a draftsman in the Silsbee office.[41]

The newly acquired site for the church was a prominent corner on Lake Street, the major east-west thoroughfare of Oak Park. For mainly economic reasons, Wright decided to build the church of monolithic reinforced concrete. The form work required lent itself to the repetitive, geometric character of the shapes used to create the building's image (fig. 41).[42] Following the example of the Larkin Building, Wright closed the structure off from the noisy Lake Street side and located the entrance at the rear, between the church proper and a lower building, called Unity House, which was designed to serve the social and educational functions of the congregation (fig. 42).

The bipartite arrangement of the Unity Temple complex therefore developed directly from the Larkin scheme.

The main differences were in the relative size and hierarchical distinction of the two parts. In the Larkin Building, the narrow, single-bay annex was articulated as a kind of file drawer pulled out of the side of the main rectangular block. Unity House, on the other hand, is wider than the church proper and about half as deep. It acts as a frame and a podium for the main auditorium, cupping it from behind and throwing it into relief.

The plan of Unity Temple, like that of the Oak Park Studio, is a perfect square, in contrast to the double-square rectangle of the Larkin Building.[43] The centrality of the geometry was further emphasized by the four hollow inset corner piers, which define a stubby Greek cross and contain the heating and ventilating ducts. Behind them, in the reentrant angles of the cross, four larger hollow piers enclose stairs leading to two tiers of balconies (fig. 20). The central space, which is nearly a cube, is entirely covered by a grid of amber-tinted skylights. The arms of the cross terminate in clerestories that ring the room with a continuous band of natural light.

Unlike the Larkin Building, where the complex volumes of the exterior essentially mask the singular interior space, the geometric forms of the exterior of Unity Temple, blocky and abstract as they are, reproduce a direct impression of the space inside, like a *repoussé*. In describing the building many years later, Wright maintained that his primary motive was "to keep a noble room for worship in mind, and let that sense of the great room shape the whole edifice. Let the room inside be the architecture outside," so that *"it may be seen as the soul of the design"* (*A* II, 154, 158)

The four arms of the Greek cross project from the main cube of space. The upper rows of piers in front of the bands of clerestory windows are topped by flat, cantilevered slab roofs that direct the interior space outward. The wall plane behind the conventionalized ivy capitals of the piers reads like a membrane. In the reentrant angles, the hollow stairway piers are set free of the mass but kept below the height of the projecting rooflines—indeed, to the same height as

the sill of the clerestories—so as to read in spatial rather than structural terms.

Cubical, stark, and abstract as it is, the exterior of Unity Temple is much less brutal and mechanistic than the Larkin Building. Wright laid special emphasis on the programmatic issue of character and expression. But he did not want a typical-looking church. "Why [have] the steeple of the little white church?" he asked. "Why *point* to heaven?" The fundamental liberalism and enlightenment rationalism of the Unitarian religion called for something humanistic and abstract: "a temple," Wright thought, "as a meeting place" (*A* II, 153–54). He therefore rejected the "nave and transept of the cathedral type" in favor of an "auditorium" that would be "a frank revival of the old temple form," that is to say, of the Early Christian and Byzantine periods. Such a solution would permit "the speaker [to be] placed well out into the auditorium, his audience gathered about him in the fashion of a friendly gathering."[44] Mysterious and aloof, perhaps even somewhat masonic in character, the exterior of Unity Temple would withdraw from the outside world to an inner harmony and peace.[45] The spiritual meaning of the building would be revealed on the exterior as a direct outgrowth of the space of that secularized "meeting place."

Wright designed Unity Temple to lead the worshiper slowly yet inexorably from the busy, mundane life outside into the calm, boundless space of a "thought-built" world within (*A* I, 158). Paths partially sheltered by the overhanging slab roofs of the barely projecting arms of the cross lead down both sides of the cubical block of the church to stairways contained within the arms of Unity House. Highly abstracted, cruciform-shaped urns terminate the parapets and establish the "grammar" of the composition. The raised podium, or terrace, turns inward to face a loggia linking Unity Temple and Unity House. The transverse foyer, at the same level as the latter, but halfway between that of the basement and main floor of the church, is extremely low and relatively dim (fig. 43). The open view into Unity House focuses on the fireplace of the rear wall. The view to the church proper, in the direction of the street, is blocked by a flat, framed panel

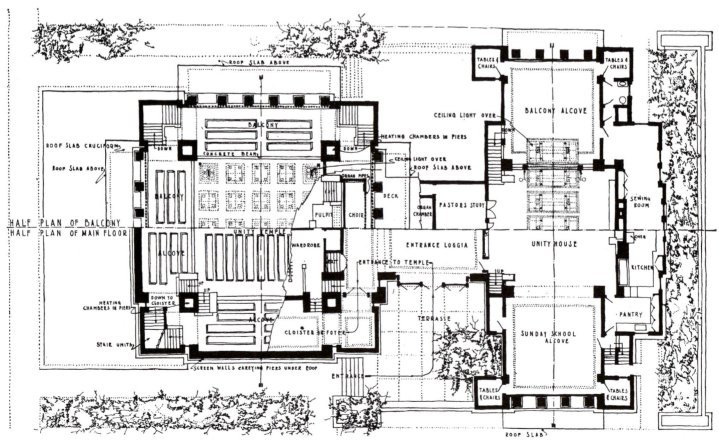

Unity Temple, Oak Park, 1905–08.

On opposite page:
41. Exterior (c. 1910).   42. Plan (redrawn c. 1940).

Below:
43. Longitudinal section.

that extends beyond the corners of the foyer and leads the eye around to the concealed, peripheral entrances to the "temple" (fig. 42).

The low, even more dimly lit doorways of the church are reached by turning ninety degrees one way and then another through the square anterooms contained within the hollow corner piers. Ahead are dark, tunnel-like passages approximately four feet below the level of the auditorium (fig. 44). Wright called these subterranean passages "cloisters" in recognition of their dual function as circumambient space and surrounding enclosure. A narrow slot of light along the top of the inside wall exposes the floor of the church, and in the gap between that wall and the corner piers, stairways lead up to the raised interior space.

The view up the stairs is directed toward the skylights, which flood the space with an amber glow (figs. 45, 20). From the top of the stairs, the light spreads beyond the edges of the room through the surrounding band of clerestory windows. The floor, open to the cloisters below, seems to swell up within the space into an elevated platform, free of material constraints. The passage from darkness to light is thus perceived as a movement from one plane of experience to another—from confinement to openness, from obscurity to clarity of thought and action.

Around three sides of the room, balconies are suspended within the alcoves created by the corner piers. The ones on the lower level are raised like bridges, while the upper tiers are articulated with strips of wood molding and

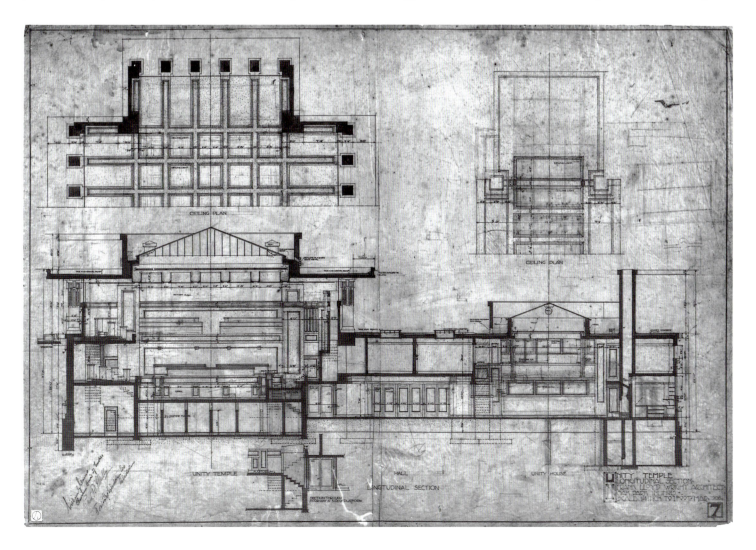

Unity Temple.

44. "Cloister" beneath auditorium floor.

45. Auditorium, corner and ceiling.

46. Auditorium, looking toward pulpit with side doors open.

inset colored squares to look as if they are floating in front of the clerestory windows. On the fourth side is a diaphanous screen of crisscrossing lines and interweaving planes that compose the podium, choir, and organ loft. The pulpit, as Wright intended, is placed well into the room so as to welcome and draw the congregation around it.

Perhaps the most telling aspect of the interior space of Unity Temple is the way in which Wright choreographed the means for departure. Instead of the usual practice of turning one's back to the pulpit to exit toward the street, one passes to either side of it and down a few stairs to the level of the cloisters, where sections of the panel that originally blocked the view from the entrance unexpectedly open into the space of the foyer (fig. 46). There is therefore no retracing of steps, but simply a resumption of interrupted movement. The movement is perceived as a continuous loop, and the overall pattern of circulation within the church becomes a kind of dance directed by light. In that dance, the space of the building becomes the spiritual ground of the architecture; and the figure of movement expresses the unitarian idea in terms of the three-dimensional experience of space.

When Wright later came to describe the interior of Unity Temple in his *Autobiography*, he explained some of its imagery in naturalistic terms. He stated that he wanted the skylights to create an effect of "light [that] would, rain or shine, have the warmth of sunlight." Giving a literal reading to the feeling that the auditorium floor rises like a

plateau above the surrounding valley of cloisters through the billowing, cloudlike formations of the suspended balconies, Wright maintained that his intention was "to get a sense of a happy cloudless day into the room" (*A* II, 158).[46] While such representational imagery may indeed help describe the experience of Unity Temple on a metaphorical level, it is the abstractness of the spatial conception of the building that actually dominates our understanding and seems to have directed Wright's contemporaneous accounts of it as a reconstitution of the "old temple form" into a "thought-built," modern "meeting place."

The square plan defined by inset corner piers represents a highly conventionalized image of the Greek-cross type that ultimately refers to Early Renaissance and Byzantine examples.[47] The characteristic dome, which would have been lit from above by an oculus, is abstracted by Wright into the cubic block that rises out of the projecting drum of colonnaded clerestory windows on the model of the Oak Park Studio. The interior of Unity Temple is even more perspicuously realized as a purely spatial composition of interweaving lines and overlapping planes (fig. 20). A grid defined by the square pattern of skylights, and made manifest in the clerestory windows and corner piers, establishes the abstract framework. The wood stripping on the cream-

colored plaster helps to dematerialize all the surfaces and thus override any structural reference or reading. The key is the treatment of the corner piers.

In a preliminary sketch, the corner piers terminate in powerful capitals, rigidly coursed in deep horizontal bands and topped by a wide echinus, like those in the Larkin Building (fig. 47). In the final version, Wright eliminated any reference to traditional tectonic imagery by suppressing the relation between load and support. The pier is articulated by a paneled frame that *bends* around the corner so as to deny a structural significance to that stiffening edge and to turn the form into a weightless plane (fig. 45). At the juncture with the ceiling, the moldings on the vestigial echinus block likewise spread apart before meeting at the corner to connect the vertical element of the pier with the overhead plane of the skylights. From within the well of the corner skylight, thin vertical members drop down into the space of the room to support lights, which in the earlier scheme were attached to the face of the upper balconies. In this way, the spatial grid itself is made palpable by the lines of force moving through it.

Nothing appears solid in Unity Temple. The eye is never arrested by a structural joint or connection. The plastic lines that articulate the space dominate and cause the overlapping planes to appear to float above and behind one another in a general expansion outward of space from within. The effect of looking through great depths of receding space is like an implosion of traditional architectural form, as if the facade of the building has been wrapped around the center to create a world where space and depth, rather than mass and volume, reign supreme.

In this new spatial construct of Unity Temple, foreground and background interrelate and become one. Space bends around corners. Verticals and horizontals intertwine. Distinctions between container and contained disappear. Solid and void elide in an overall continuity of space. Distinctions between decoration and construction, between ornament and building, are treated essentially as a matter of scale. The cross-shaped urns of the entrance prefigure the space of the interior. The abstract, fluid medium of space becomes the solution within which all contradictions and conflicts are resolved. This is the integral thinking Wright called "genuinely unitarian."

The design of the space of Unity Temple substantiates the effect of abstraction as an expression of unitarianism. The movement from the outside into an interior of freedom and openness is felt as a progression toward reason and light. The power of reason, not mystical faith, is responsible for this sense of serenity and peace. Space, as a logical construct, becomes the highest expression of the unitarian oneness of mind and body, of love and thought, of faith and reason. In the reciprocity between interior and exterior, between detail and whole, between mass and void, evidence of conflict and contradiction disappears in the fluid space that increasingly took over as the abstract ground of Wright's architecture by the middle of the first decade of the twentieth century.

Cheney House

The Larkin Building and Unity Temple remain almost isolated examples of significant nondomestic work during this period. In response to their public and institutional charac-

ter, Wright developed the abstract aspects of his geometric approach, with a relative lack of concern for the dissolution of traditional values that implied. Indeed, in the exceedingly demonstrative utilitarian character of the former, and the intensely sublimated spirituality of the latter, the non-referential, highly conventionalized geometric forms offered appropriate typological expression. Domestic architecture, however, continued to be more problematic and conflicted. The tension between the natural and the machine-made, the individual and the general, the representational and the abstract was by definition imposed by the program and had to be accounted for in the elaboration of any typical solution.[48]

Between 1903, when the Larkin Building was begun, and 1909, when he closed his Oak Park office, Wright built more than forty-five houses and designed at least twenty-five others that never reached the point of construction. Of these, the Cheney House in Oak Park (1903–1904) and the Robie House in Chicago (1908–1910) may be considered among the most typical. In the Cheney House, as in the contemporaneous Martin House in Buffalo, Wright brought the building lower to the ground by adopting a much broader system of proportions. With this development came a return to the heavier forms of masonry construction. Perhaps for this reason the Cheney House illustrates more clearly than any other building of the period how completely Wright had reworked the Winslow House paradigm in three-dimensional, spatial terms to give it the freedom and openness it originally lacked, but without compromising the effect of containment and privacy that ensured its protective character of shelter.

Edwin H. Cheney manufactured engineering equipment. His wife, Mamah (pronounced Máy-mah) Borthwick, had grown up in Oak Park and was one of the best-educated women among Wright's clients of the period, having earned a Bachelor's and a Master's degree in literature from the University of Michigan. She worked as a librarian for a number of years before returning to Oak Park to settle into married life. The Cheneys purchased a lot just around the corner from Wright's own house, and both Edwin and

Cheney House, Oak Park, 1903–04.

48. Aerial Perspective.　　　　　　　　　　　　　**49.** Plan (redrawn c. 1940).

Mamah were close friends of the Wrights. Whether or not Mamah was responsible for the decision to hire Wright, it was probably not long after the house was built that she and Wright fell in love, an event that would culminate in their elopement to Europe five years later.

Although expansive in relation to its site, the Cheney House is quite small compared to the Willits, Dana, and Winslow houses. Wright treated it as a one-story bungalow set, like a small temple or pavilion, above a raised basement, disguised along the front by a terraced embankment (fig. 48). The lower level was reserved for the servant's quarters, heating, storage, and a separate apartment (in place of the garage originally indicated on the plans).[49] The main floor of the house is divided lengthwise in half by the line of the broad fireplace, which backs onto a corridor linking the four bedrooms and bathroom (fig. 49).

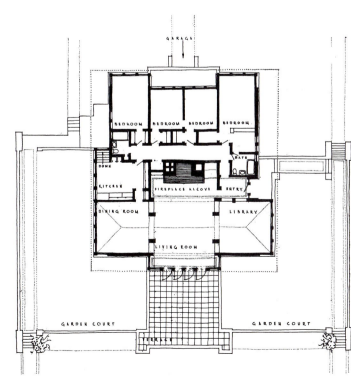

50. Cheney House. Interior, living room looking toward library.

The front half of the house is treated as a single space, symmetrically subdivided by screens into a living room in the center and dining room and library at either end. The reticulated wood and plaster structure of these freestanding partitions is integral with the visual framing of the walls, onto which the wood stripping of the hipped ceiling is brought down to allow the ceiling to appear to expand beyond the confines of the structure (fig. 50). The main volume of the space is defined by the continuous, tentlike ceiling. The central section of the living room broadens out into another volume crossing it at right angles. Kept to the height of the freestanding screens, its decklike ceilings reinforce the intimate, human scale. On one side, this lower space burrows deep into the core of the house to incorporate the fireplace alcove; on the other, it extends toward the street and into the light to open, opposite the fireplace, into a continuous screen of French doors leading to a terrace surrounded by a low brick wall.

Wright evolved the Cheney House as an abstracted, dissected, almost transparent version of the Winslow House.[50] The stone frame of the central entrance of the earlier design is pulled out from the block to form the front wall of the terrace (figs. 2, 48); the planes of Roman brick to either side of the Winslow doorway become the walls of the garden courts; the plaster frieze under the eaves is fragmented into bands of windows alternating with recessed brick panels; and the heavy hip roof of the Winslow House is reduced to a thin canopy suspended from the thick mast of the chimney projecting through it. What was once a solid wall combining the functions of support, enclosure, and penetration in the Winslow House has been separated into three different elements (and planes) discretely performing the three different functions, while the earlier, homogeneous system of support has been clarified into a composite structure of piers and planes riven by space.[51]

The stylized elements of the Winslow House are thus abstracted and subjected to further analysis. The house has been exploded, as it were, into its constituent parts to allow each of the conventional elements—roof, wall plane, corner pier, chimney, window band—to stand on its own without any direct connection to the traditional core or mass of the building still evident in the Winslow House. As the door

51. Cheney House. Exterior.

frame of the Winslow House is pulled out to become the garden parapet wall of the Cheney House, and the roof plane of the Winslow House is made to float above the continuous window band of the Cheney House, the geometric shape and order of the elements come to dominate their representational character and thus force a much more complex reading than before. It is not that the traditional representational character of those elements is entirely forsaken; it is just that their degree of stylization has been stretched beyond the norm.

In its simple, primal form, the Cheney House epitomizes the fully developed Prairie House type. Inside, it is low, dark, snug, and cozy at the same time that it is spacious, light, airy, and open. Outside, it is a mysterious combination of belvedere and bunker, a balance of opposites impossible to define in any more singular way. The garden and terrace walls that permit the interior space to expand out to their edges also rise just high enough under the eaves to allow only a slit of shadow to be seen from the street (fig. 51). This give-and-take between the private house and its setting is reinforced by the site planning. The garden

courts and terrace form a buffer between house and street. The low garden and terrace walls that parallel the street, and the symmetrical walks penetrating them at their extremities, form an imaginary block within which the house appears as a microcosm of the suburb of Oak Park. The platted grid of the neighborhood is echoed in the orthogonal network extending the house out to the street, thus making the individual house concentric with the larger order of the man-made environment.

In its relation to its site, the Cheney House is typical of the mature Prairie House and therefore allows us to reflect on Wright's conception of the meaning of the Prairie House in terms of nature and the landscape. The chief characteristic of the prairie, according to Wright, was "its quiet level." Thus one "should recognize and accentuate this natural beauty" by modifying the traditional form of the house to emphasize "gently sloping roofs, low proportions, quiet sky lines, suppressed heavy set chimneys and sheltering overhangs, low terraces and out-reaching walls sequestering private gardens."[52] These would be the conventions for establishing a formal congruency.

But because nature in the suburb was itself an abstraction—a matter of real estate—the image of prairie-ness, or level-ness, was almost purely conventional and easily reduced to a generalization. What existed more particularly as a precondition for building was the regular, repetitive, orthogonal plat of the Midwestern grid.[53] And this, in its schematic abstraction, seems to have provided the specific ground for Wright's forms. Congruency with the grid allowed the house to allude, by way of analogy rather than homology, to the landscape type. The actual forms of the house did not imitate those of nature directly, nor did they grow out of or depend upon the natural conditions of the prairie. This is no doubt what Wright meant when he said that "in the conception of these structures they are regarded as severe conventions whose chief office is [as] a background or frame for the life within them and about them" and "as a distinct chord or contrast, in their severely conventionalized nature, to the profusion of trees and foliage with which their sites abound."[54]

With this in mind, it is hardly surprising to find that the typical Prairie House, though abstractly in harmony with its environment, is in actuality relatively isolated from it. It is a discrete incident in a landscape that it is meant to recall only in a very generalized way. In the Winslow House, that isolation is stated by the facade, but the rear garden actually connects the house to the surrounding landscape in a direct and traditionally American way. A typical Shingle Style house might have a formal entrance on the street, yet open onto a rear garden in a casual, pragmatic manner. But as Wright worked through the Winslow House model to get it to "come through and button up at the front," something curious happened. The private part of the house was brought into the public domain, and contact with the landscape was established through a formal garden or series of terraces in the front. This solution visually resolved the tension (in the Winslow House) between front and rear, or formality and freedom, but it isolated the house from its surroundings more than ever before. It reduced the relation with nature to an abstract idea.

The rear of the Cheney House gives onto an alley and was originally meant for a garage. Similarly, the rear of the Willits House is given over to service facilities, and the relation to the "backyard" is left unarticulated. With the "front yard" idealized as a formal expression of shelter, the house becomes a self-centered, symbolic object deriving its only direct connection with the ground from its fireplace core. In that regard, the so-called Prairie House becomes as hermetic and self-generating a form as the crystalline geometric tower in the *Flower in the Crannied Wall*.

It can be argued that this aspect of Wright's work is more a matter of circumstance than intention, that, given the opportunity to work with more interesting and "natural" sites, Wright would have found ways to adapt his buildings to the landscape in a more supple manner. Both the Coonley House in Riverside, Illinois (1906–1909), and the contemporaneous project for the McCormick Estate on the shore of Lake Michigan at Lake Forest present casual, loosely jointed plans with two-sided buildings zoned into wings more or less following the lay of the land (figs. 52, 63). But the effect of the Coonley House is still of a highly formalized and generalized relation to the site, in which Wright distorted the principles of the Prairie House about as much as possible without losing a sense of cohesion and integrity.

The Hardy House (1905), which steps down the steep bank of Lake Michigan at Racine, Wisconsin, is a further example of the Prairie House somewhat modified to conform to the exigencies of the landscape (fig. 137). Yet another is the Glasner House in Glencoe, Illinois (1905), where the house is built at the edge of a ravine yet remains fundamentally aloof from it, establishing a purely visual—that is to say, abstract—contact (fig. 53).[55] But Wright's usual approach, no matter how dramatic or irregular the landscape setting, remained the highly formalized, rigorously geometric one typified by the Cheney House. This can perhaps be seen most pointedly in the project of 1909 for the University Heights (Como Orchards) Summer Colony in Montana's Bitter Root Valley (fig. 54), where, almost without any

52 (*above left*). Coonley House, Riverside, Ill., 1906–09. Site plan (before March 1908).

53 (*above right*). Glasner House, Glencoe, Ill., 1905. Perspective and plan.

54 (*below*). University Heights (Como Orchards) Summer Colony, Bitter Root Valley (near Darby), Mont., 1909. Perspective.

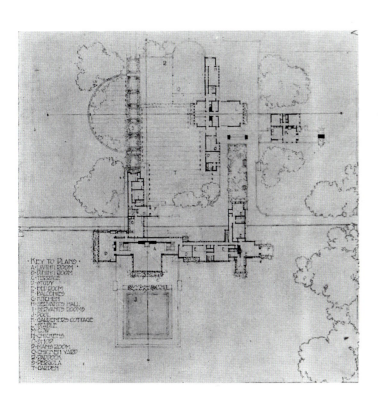

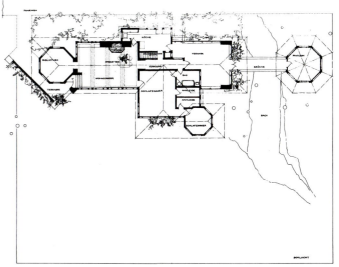

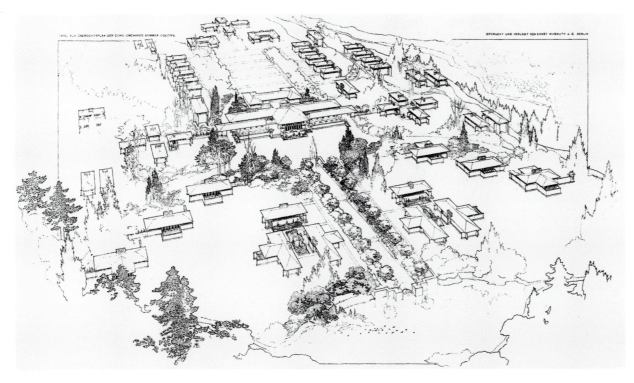

55. Robie House, Chicago, 1908–10. Exterior (late 1950s).

regard for specific topographical or regional factors, the various isolated and self-centered Prairie Houses, some based directly on the Cheney House, are laid out symmetrically to form a group plan recalling in many respects Louis XIV's palatial retreat at Marly.

Robie House

The house that can be considered the final outcome of the process of abstraction and analysis begun in the Winslow House—and the one usually thought of as the ultimate ex-

pression of the Prairie House type—is the residence Wright built in 1908–10 for the family of the bicycle and automobile parts manufacturer Frederick C. Robie.[56] By Wright's own reckoning, it is the most elaborate, extreme, and conclusive expression of the type in terms of formal "articulation," as he called it, and imagery (fig. 55).[57] The long, narrow structure occupies a corner site next to the University of Chicago campus, facing south toward the former Midway Plaisance of the 1893 Fair, a block away.

Robie had studied mechanical engineering at Purdue University before entering his father's business in 1899. He and his wife, Lora, bought the corner lot on Woodlawn Ave-

56. Robie House. Plans, ground floor and second floor (redrawn c. 1940).

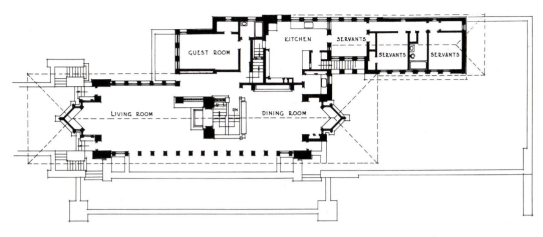

UPPER FLOOR

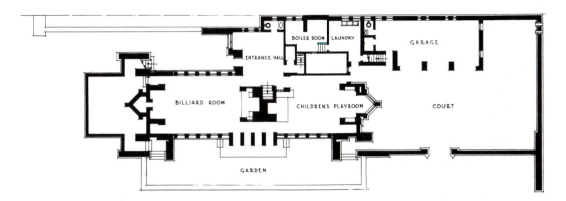

LOWER FLOOR

nue and Fifty-eighth Street, near her alma mater, in the spring of 1908. Although Wright would describe the house he began designing that summer as a "city dwelling,"[58] Hyde Park was a low-density area of mainly single-family houses that might be characterized more aptly as a "street-car suburb."

The three-story brick and stone house is low to the ground, yet deeply undercut with great shadowed voids that make it appear buoyant and spacious. The abstraction of parts into type-elements and the extremely broad scale of their elaboration make the house at first difficult to read as anything more specific and definitive than an image of shelter-as-such, what Wright liked to think of as an "umbrageous architecture."[59] All is seemingly reduced to roofs suspended above volumes screened and faced by protective

planes. No entrance is visible, no ground floor as such, nor anything much more than a single, major floor with a minor addition above it. Wright described the Robie House as a "single room type" dwelling and did everything to stress that abstract spatial conceit.[60]

The "single room" forms virtually the entire main floor of the house (fig. 56). It stretches out to contain a continuous living and dining room, partially divided by a central fireplace, and rests on the base of a ground floor, which is treated as a raised basement. A billiard room and a children's playroom lie along the front of that floor, with the entrance hall at the rear. The interior of the main floor opens onto the street in a balcony that runs along its entire southern exposure; at the corner, it becomes an open brick porch (fig. 60). These "out-reaching" spaces are girded by

57. Robie House. Living room, looking toward fireplace (1910).

staggered brick parapets and bridges floating just below the overhanging, cantilevered roofs. A wing comprising a guest room, kitchen, and servants' rooms slips behind, and is nearly hidden by, the formal living/dining space that is projected out to the street as if it were "the house." An abbreviated third floor of bedrooms is tucked around the mass of the central chimney to create an aerie or "belvedere," as Wright called it, out of what might otherwise be thought of as an attic.

The plan of the Robie House is simplified, clarified, and reduced nearly to the point of pure abstraction. A central fireplace/stairway forms the core and focus of a space that is continuous around it (fig. 57). In terms of its disposition of functional areas and exaggeration of the formal living/dining space, the Robie House carries the Prairie House type to an extreme that represents an almost mannered solution.[61] The separate pinwheeling volumes of the Willits House are condensed into one and stretched to the limits from the core. Each aspect of the earlier Prairie House that

was intended to increase the sense of interior openness is further fragmented and articulated to enhance that effect.

Where the fireplace in the earlier dwellings forms a solid wall from floor to ceiling, in the Robie House it is sunk into the floor to give a sense of vertical continuity, and opened at the top to allow the space to flow through from one area to the other. Where one of the wings of the Willits House was given a prow-like termination to direct the view out, both ends of the Robie House culminate in such diagonally set bays, which are further articulated by a double set of staggered, inset piers (fig. 58). These define slots of space to either side of the prow, increasing the illusion of depth and uncontained space. At the same time, on the exterior, the long, horizontal bands of bridges, balconies, and parapets, which weave in and around the recessed flat piers in response to the outward pressure of space, provide a heightened sense of privacy that is further dramatized by the hovering roof plane extending well beyond the edges of the enclosed space.

The Robie House stakes itself out on, and screens itself off from, the street, while at the same time it offers an illusion of total freedom of movement and infinite expanse of space within. This balance of opposites is only the most prominent of the many dualities the house expresses. Approaching from the south, the passerby sees the nearly symmetrical composition of the main facade on Fifty-eighth Street, with the balcony of the main floor projecting above a low, walled terrace (fig. 55). Aside from the gate in the solid wall that originally led to the garage and service court, the house is entirely self-contained and offers no apparent means of access. As in the Willits and Cheney houses, Wright masked the main entrance in order to preserve the formal design of the street facade. But here, instead of simply placing the entrance to one side of the main facade, he removed it to the rear (fig. 56). The effect is to affirm the reflexive nature of the house as an independent object with its own internal sense of logic.

A path leads halfway down the length of the house, behind the projecting prow and porch on Woodlawn Avenue, to a low, fairly insignificant doorway opening into a small, dimly lit reception area that feels almost underground. A narrow stairway cuts through an arch in the solid mass of the chimney to reach the upper floor. The intimate scale and prominence of stair and chimney subliminally call to mind the disposition of seventeenth-century Colonial houses, a reference that throws into even sharper relief the modern, machinelike quality of the detailing both inside and out.[62]

The narrow stairs lead from one world to another. At the top of the short but steep climb the well opens into the suffused light of the main floor, where low, perforated screens just barely define the multidirectional space (fig. 59). As one looks from the dining to the living area, it would seem that nothing exists as solid enclosure; no two surfaces appear to remain on the same plane. As each plane folds

Robie House.

59. Dining room, looking toward living room (1910).

60. Exterior, pier and porch at end of living room.

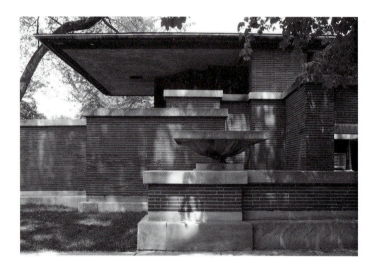

The surrounding "wall," which is composed almost entirely of leaded-glass floor-to-ceiling doors and waist-high windows, sits within a reticulated frame of square-cut vertical and horizontal members. This framed window-wall is separated from the ceiling by a plaster band and gives the impression of a screen of light, a "fence" providing privacy around the idealized, domestic world of the Robies. At another scale, the dining room table and chairs define a room within a room.

The only element in the main space of the house that seems solid and anchored to the earth is the enormous, H-shaped central fireplace. Sunk into the floor and cut out at the top, it appears to rise uninterrupted from the ground through the ceiling and roof (fig. 57). It provides the element of rootedness and permanency that allows for the openness and indeterminacy of the rest. As an isolated, autonomous source of strength and focus, it brings to the representational imagery of the Prairie House a compelling, and nearly overwhelming, aspect of abstraction.

The Robie House is an expression of the tensions that characterize the modern house in its suburban setting. A refuge from the hustle and bustle of the city, it is open to the beneficent effects of nature, yet sternly independent and protective of its inhabitants' privacy. Emerging from the distinctions between city and country, work and leisure, men and women, family and community that the suburb gave rise to, its fragmented appearance responds to the conflicting pulls of these opposing forces. The integrated central heating and electric lighting that allowed Wright to create the perfectly controlled environment for family gathering around the fireplace or dining table are precisely what give this machine-age structure its ability to recall with such atavistic force the images of a Colonial past. But while the chimney mass in the center (with the stairway tucked behind it) and the "beamed" ceilings of the two "rooms" on either side substantiate the underlying domestic imagery of a tradition deeply rooted in the past, the streamlined, smooth planes of the exterior swiftly and almost violently interrupt that reading with a counterimage of the twentieth century (fig. 60). To contemporaries, in fact, the building

into the next, or recedes behind a projecting pier, one gets the impression of a continuously expanding composition of geometrically defined space.

The ceiling is articulated by wide cross-strips of oak, like the beams of a Colonial parlor (fig. 58). But here they are flat and purely decorative, and the ceiling is stepped up in the center. The strips themselves do not rest on the outside walls, as if they were members of support, but rather reverse back on themselves to form rectangular, floating panels. The electric light fixtures projecting toward the center from the lower deck of the folded plane reinforce the image of a canopy held in place by tension.

looked more like an ocean liner than a house—a "ship of the prairie," as it was soon called, or a "Dampfer House," as Wright himself described it in his *Autobiography*.[63]

To account for such fluctuating, oscillating imagery, the development of the Prairie House from the Winslow House to the Robie House must be understood in terms of a radical restructuring of the language of architectural representation akin to the invention of Cubism in painting by Picasso and Braque at the same moment in France.[64] Within the traditional framework of the house-type, Wright dissected and pulled apart the planes, fracturing the image and opening it up to a freedom of space and ambiguity of relationships that was quintessentially modern. Having condensed the representation of shelter into the highly conventionalized Symbolist language of the Winslow House, Wright then began to deconstruct the stylized imagery by subjecting each element to analysis. The result is precisely comparable to the Analytic Cubism of Picasso and Braque that culminated in their work of about 1908–10.

In Wright's Robie House, as in Picasso's contemporary portraits, the conventional image of house (or person) is broken down into a series of intersecting, overlapping, and nearly autonomous planes (figs. 60, 61). Where a molding would traditionally define the shape of a window or the boundary between wall and ceiling, just as the contour of a cheek or the brim of a hat might distinguish those forms from the background against which they are seen, planes now overlap in shallow depth to create ambiguous geometric shapes in constantly shifting patterns.[65] The elision of windows and walls creates "window-walls," while the incorporation of porches within the spatial framework of the house denies normal distinctions between figure and ground, turning the house inside out. Although the presence of such indices of representation as roof, chimney, balcony, and urn (or, in a Cubist painting, forehead, eyes, nose, and mouth) continues to allow conventional readings, the constantly shifting relations of the parts sets up a tension between the poles of abstraction and representation that is more extreme than any previous art had produced. The image, while rooted in the real world, seems to exist in an autonomous space of its own, not quite an illusion but not quite a denial of it either.

The reification of space as the destabilizing ground for representation gave the fully matured Prairie House its extraordinary sense of vitality. The Robie and Cheney houses conjoin the organic vitality and freedom of nature with the rational control and order of the machine to create an image that expresses, in its tense balance of opposites, the interrelationship of the private and the public, the individual and the group, the family and the community in a form at once historically evocative and radically modern. The illusory world of spatial continuity that Wright created in these houses in Chicago and its surrounding suburbs offered their inhabitants a vision of plenitude and control, as the house took on the aspect of an abstraction that subsumed the prairie unto itself.

62. Wright House project, Fiesole, Italy, 1910. Aerial perspective and plan.

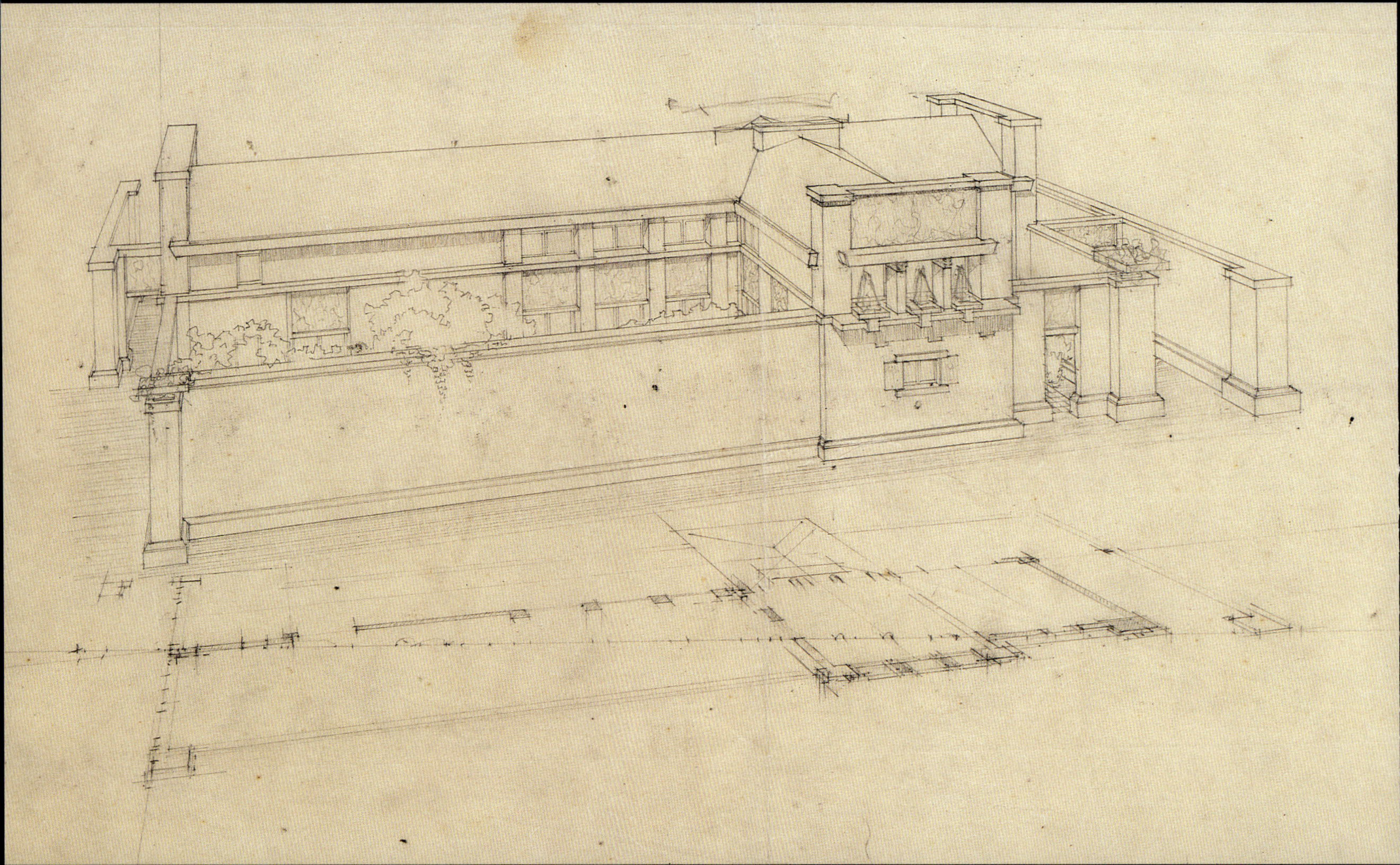

Voluntary Exile
in Fiesole

In the early fall of 1909, less than a year after Unity Temple opened for its first service, and even before the Robie House was completed, Wright closed his Oak Park office and eloped to Europe with Mamah Cheney. Although he returned to the United States a year later, he would never reestablish his suburban Chicago practice or rejoin his wife, Catherine, and their six children. Wright described the "rebellion" against his past life as a "struggle for inner freedom" and characterized the "spiritual adventure" of the year abroad as a period of "voluntary exile" (A I, 167, 169).[1]

What was Wright trying to get away from, and why did he feel it necessary to make such a break? These questions, which are fundamental to an understanding of his work, involve a complex interaction of professional, personal, and artistic factors. In recalling that moment twenty years later, Wright stated that "everything, personal or otherwise, bore down heavily on me. Domesticity most of all." "Weary, I was losing grip on my work and even interest in it," he explained. "The effort . . . now seemed to leave me up against a dead wall. I could see no way out. Because I did not know what I wanted, I wanted to go away." He characterized the situation in Oak Park as a "closed road" and gave the trip

63. McCormick House project, Lake Forest, Ill., 1907–08. Perspective.

to Europe an even more categorical meaning by equating it with his earlier move from Madison to Chicago (*A* I, 166, 165, 167).

No period in Wright's career seems less understood than this one. Yet, as brief as it is, none is greater in its ramifications. Few historians have devoted much time to it.[2] Although the documentation is exceedingly spotty and, on the whole, unhelpful, I believe it is essential to focus special attention on this year. If the answers are not easy to come by, at least the questions can be raised.

■ ■ ■

Among the various personal, professional, and artistic factors involved in Wright's decision, the most immediate, though not necessarily the most critical, was his growing disenchantment with the life he and his wife had settled into. Between 1900 and 1908, as his career progressed, Wright grew further and further apart from Catherine. Family commitments, which took time and energy away from work, made the situation worse and the breakup of the

marriage inevitable. By 1909, the family had grown to six children. At the same time, Wright's studio and office, located in the same house, had become one of the busiest in the area. "The establishments began to compete," he wrote, and "the architect absorbed the father in me" (*A* I, 111). As Wright spent more and more time on his work, Catherine spent more and more time with the children. "I found my life in my work," he told a reporter for the *Chicago Tribune* in 1911, while "Mrs. Wright had found her life in her children." "Mrs. Wright had little time to be interested in my work and I had little time to be interested in hers. . . . And so we grew apart."[3]

The disjunction between life and work, which Wright would always consider "inorganic," was made all the more perspicuous by the illicit love affair he had been carrying on for some time with his former client Mamah Cheney. Wright believed her to be more in sympathy with his efforts, and he was attracted to her intellectual and spiritual qualities, which he found lacking in his wife.[4] And Cheney no doubt felt Wright's artistic career to be closer to her interests than her husband's business activities.[5] After a number of years of seeing each other, in a not so clandestine fashion it appears, they decided to marry. Wright asked Catherine for a divorce in 1908. She supposedly agreed on the condition that he and Cheney spend a year without seeing each other as a test of their love. When that love proved lasting, but Catherine reneged on her agreement, Wright decided he and Cheney had no other option but to elope.[6]

It is hard to draw the line, however, between personal and professional problems. In Wright's case in particular, the desire to force a complete unity of life and art resulted in a constant assimilation of personal issues to professional and artistic ones.[7] Indeed, there is ample evidence to suggest that, by 1908, Wright felt his work was getting nowhere and, like his married life, was settling into a formula. Commissions for houses were still coming into the office, but few presented any real challenge. Missing entirely were the kinds of major jobs that he might have expected as a result of the Larkin Building and Unity Temple.[8] Looking back over the previous fifteen years of independent practice, during which time he had built approximately seventy-five buildings, he could see very little of major significance. Houses comprised most of the work, and most of these were in Oak Park or in one of the nearby suburbs. Beyond that, there was only the summer colony planned for University of Chicago professors in Montana; a rural school for his aunts on the family farmland in Wisconsin (Hillside Home School); a tiny bank, much reduced in size from the original design, built in 1905 in Dwight, Illinois, a small crossroads town about thirty miles west of Kankakee; and, most recently (1909), a combination small bank/hotel for the medium-sized town of Mason City, Iowa.[9]

Wright's production was therefore quite inconsequential when considered in relation to the incredible boom in monumental civic building in the United States, and particularly the Midwest, that took place after the recession following the Columbian Exposition of 1893. The prolific output of such firms as McKim, Mead and White, Daniel H. Burnham, Cass Gilbert, Carrère and Hastings, Cram, Goodhue and Ferguson, not to mention Charles Platt, Ernest

Flagg, and even the younger John Russell Pope, must have been a bitter pill to swallow for an architect who considered himself, rightly or wrongly, the most creative of his time. For this very reason, one should not underestimate, as some historians have, Wright's failure in 1907–1908 to secure the commission for the estate of the wealthy Chicago industrialist Harold F. McCormick (fig. 63). There can be little doubt that when Platt, the Beaux-Arts-trained author of *Italian Gardens* (1894) and designer of estates in the classical manner, received the commission instead and produced his scheme for the Villa Turicum (fig. 64), Wright began to see the writing on the wall.[10] (A possible commission for the Henry Ford estate hit a snag soon thereafter.[11]) The analogy with Sullivan's decline from national prominence could hardly have gone unnoticed. It was, in fact, in the late summer of 1908, around the time he heard about the loss of the McCormick commission, that Wright asked his wife for a divorce.

The financial panic in the fall of 1907 produced only a short-term decline in building opportunities. Yet Wright felt the effects very keenly. In December of that year, while negotiations were proceeding with the McCormicks, he remarked to Darwin Martin that "work seems at a standstill entirely." He expected that "a hold-fast and hangtight period ahead" might last "for two years," but added: "I am ill prepared for it and what the outcome will be I cannot say." About a year later, in December 1908, he wrote to Martin confirming his dire prediction: "My affairs are not in good order. This year has been a great disappointment so far as opportunity to work is concerned."[12] Whatever appearance of equanimity Wright was able to preserve in that letter was completely dispelled in his personal contacts with colleagues. C. R. Ashbee, the English Arts and Crafts architect who found Wright "full of fire and belief" when they first met in Chicago in 1900, reported on his second visit in December 1908 that Wright had grown "bitter" and had "drawn in upon himself."[13] Ashbee related this situation to Sullivan's plight.

Perhaps the clearest indication of Wright's inability to break out of a certain stereotype and make significant headway in the professional world can be seen in the generally negative critical response his work received. One of the very few positive notes was struck by the portfolio of Wright's architecture published by Herbert Croly in the *Architectural Record* in March 1908, accompanied by Wright's essay "In the Cause of Architecture."[14] Yet, just one month after this lavish spread, the *Record* published a damning critique of the Larkin Building, almost as if to set the record straight. (Unity Temple, it should be noted, received no serious critical attention in the national press.)

In his article of April 1908, the aged, but still highly respected Gothic Revivalist Russell Sturgis could find nothing whatsoever to praise in the Larkin Building, declaring that no one who knows anything about the history of architecture "will fail to pronounce this monument . . . an extremely ugly building. It is, in fact," he went on, "a monster of awkwardness" (fig. 38). By trying to show "what else might have been done, had the architect felt that he could not bear to turn out a building so ungainly, so awkward in grouping, so clumsy in its parts and in its main mass," Sturgis in effect declared Wright to be totally egotistical and unconcerned with other people's feelings and opinions. He condemned Wright's solution as "wholly repellant [*sic*] as a work of human artisanship which might have been a work of art and is not."[15]

Wright was taken aback by the vehemence of this critique. In a response, which he probably intended for the *Record* but which got no further than a small Larkin Company brochure put out the following year, he stated that the building was designed "for the man . . . of the future . . . and not for the man who, startled, clutches his lifeless traditions closer to his would-be-conservative breast and shrieks, 'It is ugly!'" Wright tried to counter Sturgis directly by saying that, although "it may be ugly," the Larkin Building "is a bold buccaneer, swaggering somewhat doubtless, yet acknowledging a native god in a native land with an ideal seemingly lost to modern life—conscious of the fact that because beauty is in itself the highest and finest kind of morality so in its essence must it be true."[16]

Wright believed, as he often stated, that he was preeminently responsible for the development of a "native" American architecture, which he liked to call the "New School of the Middle West."[17] Many of his colleagues, however, were reluctant to grant him even this distinction. In the same month that Sturgis's diatribe appeared, in one of the first articles to treat the subject of the new regionalism, Wright's fellow Chicagoan Thomas Tallmadge stressed Louis Sullivan's primary role in the endeavor and simply lumped Wright, along with George Maher, Dwight Perkins, Howard Shaw, Max Dunning, and Wright's own assistant Walter Burley Griffin, among "that little band of enthusiasts" who had "furthered the movement."[18]

Whenever Wright's work was treated in a more positive vein, it was almost always qualified as something curious or eccentric and thus not to be taken too seriously or deemed of permanent value. Even those who were close to Wright and considered him a friend wrote of his work in this way. Typical was the poet Harriet Monroe. In her review of Wright's contribution to the Chicago Architectural Club's annual exhibition at the Art Institute in 1907, she started by noting that "Mr. Wright has cut loose from the schools and elaborated his own system of design," with the result that "his work is thus a most interesting experiment." When called upon to assess "the measure of his success," however, Monroe had to answer that "his limitations are obvious enough." She characterized "the more ambitious buildings"—meaning Unity Temple and the Larkin Building—as "fantastic blockhouses, . . . without grace or ease or monumental beauty." When it comes to public architecture, she explained, "Mr. Wright's system of design seems inadequate to the strain imposed upon it." She allowed that "his dwellings, on the contrary show its charm" and "express our hospitable suburban American life, a life of indoors and outdoors, as spontaneously as certain Italian villas express the more pompous and splendid life of those old gorgeous centuries." But in the face of such competition, Monroe ultimately found Wright's work, no matter how "graceful" or "charming," "so unusual" that it must be said to be "at times even bizarre."[19]

Again, Wright felt the need to respond. But this time he was more disheartened than angry and could only wistfully remind his friend Monroe that even "in conservative England as in France" his designs had been "accorded the rare virtue of originality without eccentricity."[20]

The charges of youthful experimentation and eccentricity were not easily dismissed in the conservative architectural climate prior to World War I. And they stuck to Wright for many years to come. In his review of the Wasmuth portfolio in 1912, the progressive critic Montgomery Schuyler maintained that "the stark unmodelled" character of Wright's buildings "give [them] an air of something

rude, incomplete, unfinished," so that "the buildings seem 'blocked out,' and awaiting completion rather than completed."[21] Even Wright's friend and esteemed colleague C. R. Ashbee, in the introduction Wright asked him to contribute to the smaller volume of work published by Wasmuth in 1911, ended his appraisal by noting that there was something lacking in Wright's buildings. "I would like to touch [them] with the enchanted wand," he wrote, "to clothe them with a more living and tender detail." But "I do not know how, and the time is not yet—nor would I like to see Wright do it himself, because I do not believe he could."[22] One wonders who, other than Louis Sullivan, might have written a more unqualified appraisal.[23]

■ ■ ■

The questions surrounding Wright's work on a professional level can hardly be dissociated from the issues that work posed in a more purely artistic sense. Wright later remarked that during the years he might have needed it most—in the period up to 1909, when he was absorbed in the development of the Prairie House—he lacked any meaningful critical discourse with peers and colleagues.[24] This could help to explain the rather dry and repetitive manner his work began to assume from at least 1907 on. House after house repeats the same basic plan-types. Whether brick or wood and stucco, the elevations seem to grow out of a single mold. Elaboration and refinement of a formula were, in fact, endemic to the very program of typological design Wright inherited from Sullivan (which may have had a similarly debilitating effect on him).

The Robie House, for all its power of expression, has a tightness and predictability that were not apparent in the earlier Cheney and Martin houses, when Wright was still experimenting and searching for new forms and ideas. The power seems to be an affect, rather than an effect, of the work. The result is a kind of mannerism that Wright realized was particularly detrimental to an artist at the beginning of his career. "The manner of any work (and all work of any quality has its manner)," Wright explained just a few years later, "may be for the time being a strength; but finally it is a weakness."[25] His own designs of the two or three years before leaving Oak Park surely made him terribly aware of this. Houses like the ones for the Steffenses in Chicago and the Ingallses in River Forest, both of 1909, were labored and vapid in expression; the City National Bank and adjoining hotel in Mason City, Iowa (1909–11), was thin and uninspired, a mechanical reduction of the Unity Temple *parti* to a level that could hardly be compared in conception, imagination, or resolution to Sullivan's coeval bank at Owatonna.

Yet the problems Wright faced went beyond the lack of challenging commissions, cool critical reception, and formulaic production. There was something fundamentally intractable and hermetic about his very system of design, which, perhaps in retrospect only, could be appreciated for the tension of opposing forces it set into motion. The ultimate irreconcilability of these forces may well have made Wright realize that he was playing a game in which "articulation" was the only evidence of progress or change. The "freedom" he sought depended on the acceptance of certain conventions or rules—like the grid of the suburban street pattern—which permitted only a circumscribed number of moves. The evolution of the Prairie House was a kind of academic exercise, a search for the ever-new and more elegant solution to a prescribed problem. Although it may seem like heresy to compare his early work to a school exercise, it could be argued that this is exactly what Wright was alluding to when he likened leaving Oak Park to the earlier departure from his high school environment in Madison.

Not surprisingly, some critics and historians have maintained that the conflicts Wright felt in his private life were simply manifestations of the more profound conflicts in his work. Norris Kelly Smith has forcefully argued that the contradictory pulls toward expression of the individual, on the one hand, and the family group, on the other, may explain the tension between freedom and order that characterizes Wright's domestic work. According to this analysis,

the conflict between personal identity and institutional being—the private and public realms—posed by the Prairie House was irresolvable in the suburban context. Seeing the impossibility of his work altering the conventional framework of suburban life, and likening this situation to the frustrations of his own married life, Wright felt the only way out was to disengage himself entirely from the situation.[26]

Notwithstanding the appeal of this argument, especially its deconstruction of the myth of Wright as the "persecuted genius" in favor of John Berger's idea of a "failure of success," it reduces the problems of the Prairie House to a programmatic definition.[27] The most powerful and radical aspect of Wright's early work was the independence he gave to certain formal elements of design, to the extent that they began to read as abstract units. The resulting emphasis on space, however, added a level of complexity that Wright did not seem capable of fully understanding or articulating at the time. The opposition between abstraction and the conventions of representation reached a level of intensity about the time Wright began designing Unity Temple. It, like the Larkin Building, gave him the rare opportunity to design a large public space. In equating the spiritual meaning of the building with its expression of space, Wright disengaged the characteristic elements of church design from almost all traditional representational meaning. He later wrote that he "let the room inside be the architecture outside" so that "*it may be seen as the soul of the design*." But that description was written almost a quarter of a century later. In 1908, Wright had nothing to say about "space," nor did he even use the word.

Wright's lack of a full awareness of what he was doing—the discovery of space that he later felt to be his major contribution to the creation of modern architecture—reveals the degree to which he must have sensed he was working in the dark and needed a certain distance or perspective. What Wright had evolved in the form of a spatial architecture contradicted the premise of typological abstraction derived from Sullivan. In the establishment of a type and its refinement over time, one is concerned with the building as an object, a thing, an "entity" unto itself. The self-centered, reflexive nature of the Willits House attests to this primary purpose; the elaborate articulation of its type in the Robie House reveals how much the rest of the process is merely a matter of working things out. The same could be said for the evolution from the Larkin Building to Unity Temple, but there the conflicting role of space becomes painfully evident; and the typological distinctions themselves begin to blur as office building and church are both defined by the common "domestic" reference to a space, or place, of "family gathering."

Wright's discovery of space as the basic element of architectural design points away from the object, not toward it. The fulfillment of this idea implies a relation of the building to the outside world and its extension into the landscape, which the inward-looking concern for type denies. The pinwheeling plan of the Willits House illustrates the delicate balance of centrifugal and centripetal forces that reached a point of extreme tension in the Robie House. Only a complete break with those conventions typical of the suburban world in which Wright was working could allow him to extend the openness of plan and interaction between interior and exterior that he achieved in the design of individual buildings to the larger question of the relation of building to landscape. But for that to happen, "nature" would have to be set in opposition to "culture" as the fundamental basis for design.

■ ■ ■

From the point of view of Wright's own sense of his work, then, we can perhaps now better understand what he meant when he said: "Because I did not know what I wanted, I wanted to go away." But we should be wary of drawing too simple a conclusion, considering only lack and leaving desire out of the equation. Wright *was* unfulfilled in his marriage. He *was* in love with another woman and frustrated in his inability to make a new life with her. He *was* disturbed by the reception of his work and bitter over the incapacity

of critics to see its value. And he *was* at an impasse in his thinking about design. But he had also arrived at a point when he needed time and distance to evaluate what he had accomplished and where it might lead, which points to the more positive aspects of his decision to dissolve his fifteen-year-old practice.

Wright needed to expand his horizons. The "spiritual adventure" he spoke of was as much professional as it was personal. The only time he had ever been out of the country—indeed, out of the Midwest—was a short trip to Japan he and his wife took with the Willitses in the winter of 1905. The importance Wright gave in his *Autobiography* to the story of Burnham's offer to send him to Europe at the beginning of his career and the somewhat wistful account of his refusal clearly indicate that an extended "study tour," and not just a family vacation, was always in the back of his mind. When invited in 1901 to visit Ashbee in England, Wright answered that, although it was "one of the most real of many known temptations," he felt it necessary to refuse on the grounds of "poverty."[28] Ashbee extended that invitation again in 1908, with the promise of a trip through Sicily, the rest of Italy, and Germany, as well as England. "Believe me, it is worth doing and doing now!" He added, "and also I think you need it."[29] Wright obviously agreed, for he immediately wrote back: "No temptation to 'desert' was ever so difficult to resist as this one." For various reasons, however, he would have to "postpone the visit" but would "join [Ashbee] in England within a year."[30]

In some ways Europe was just a symbol; in others it represented a very real challenge. Italy, of course, was at the crux of the matter. Since the middle of the eighteenth century at least, the Grand Tour had been a kind of passport to the highest levels of professional achievement, whether in England, France, Germany, or, more recently, the United States. The very person to whom Wright lost the McCormick job had made his reputation by a careful study of Italian Renaissance villas and gardens. Wright himself used the Ecole des Beaux-Arts as a yardstick to measure his compositional skills.[31] Wright knew he would probably never be able to become a nationally, not to speak of internationally, recognized architect without having had the experience of seeing Italy firsthand. It was as much a matter of learning as it was of testing himself against the past. And the time had never been more ripe, for unlike the typical traveling student, Wright had by then developed an architectural personality and way of thinking that could only be enriched, and not circumscribed, by the experience. Perhaps that is what Wright meant us to understand when he later wrote that he "had resisted up to this time" taking such a trip, "only dreaming of Europe" (*A* I, 165).

Berlin, Florence, and Fiesole

A series of events that came to a head in 1909 resulted in Wright's final decision to leave. During the previous year the Berlin publishing house of Ernst Wasmuth had contacted him with a proposal to publish a monograph of his work in its ongoing series on contemporary architecture, Sonderheft der Architektur des XX. Jahrhunderts. This volume would include plans and photographs and appear in a relatively small format (*Frank Lloyd Wright: Ausgeführte Bauten*, 1911). Wright apparently persuaded Wasmuth to publish in addition a much larger and more lavish portfolio of engravings (the Wasmuth portfolio, or *Ausgeführte Bauten und Entwürfe von Frank Lloyd Wright*, 1910[–11]).[32] To oversee production, Wright felt he would eventually have to go to Europe.

When Ashbee visited Oak Park in December 1908 and invited Wright to join him the following spring in Italy, Wright mentioned the "German business" but said he would have to "postpone the visit" for anywhere up to a year. He explained that he had received some work "quite unexpectedly" (the bank and hotel project in Mason City, as well as the Lexington Terrace Apartments). He thought he should "make hay while the sun shines, particularly as this year has been a lean one."[33] In effect, he was bound to wait until he could obtain a divorce at the end of the "year of probation" his wife had stipulated (*A* I, 167). The work done in the meantime, he thought, would bring in enough money to support his family while he was abroad.

In late June 1909, Mamah Cheney took her two children for a summer vacation with a friend in Boulder, Colorado. She told her husband that she was leaving for good and would never return to live with him. When Wright found out in September that Catherine still refused to grant a divorce, he decided there was nothing to do but "take the situation in hand and on my own" (*A* I, 166). (Work on the Wasmuth portfolio provided a good moral rationalization for the trip.) After contacting Cheney, he left for New York. She followed soon after, arranging for her husband to pick up their children in Colorado.[34] Wright and Cheney sailed for Europe in early October, to settle first in Berlin. After about a month, their illicit relationship was uncovered by a reporter for the *Chicago Tribune* and blasted across the front page of that newspaper on 7 November. Wright was publicly denounced for having "abandoned" his wife in "an affinity tangle of character unparalleled even in the checkered history of soul mating." As the publicity continued over the next few days, with Wright described as the "erring husband" and Cheney as a "vampire" and his "soulmate" in their "spiritual hegira," the pair let it be known, or at least it was reported, that they were leaving Berlin for Japan.[35] This may have been simply a ruse, for they remained in Berlin a month or so longer.

At the time Wright arrived, Berlin was at the very center of modern architecture in Europe. Having just completed his most powerful and radical work for the AEG, Peter Behrens was attracting into his office such younger architects as Gropius, Mies, and Le Corbusier, all of whom worked for him during 1909–10.[36] Yet, although Wright felt that the recent developments in Germany and Austria were more in tune with his way of thinking than those anywhere else in the world, he decided to go to Italy to prepare the drawings for the monograph.

After a trip to Paris in January with Cheney, who then went off to Sweden and Leipzig for work of her own, Wright first rented a villa in Florence, on the south bank of the Arno just below the Piazzale Michelangelo, across from the church of Santa Croce. There, he and a former draftsman from his Oak Park studio, Taylor Woolley, were later joined by his oldest son, Lloyd. By the end of March, Wright moved to Fiesole, perhaps in anticipation of Cheney's arrival. Once the drawings for the portfolio were finished, sometime in the spring of 1910, Woolley and Lloyd Wright left for a trip through Italy and France, at the end of which Wright met up with his son to visit Paris, Versailles, and the château country. In the meantime, Wright went to Leipzig to rejoin Cheney and bring her back to the quaint hill town of Fiesole, overlooking Florence.[37]

Before the outbreak of World War I, Florence had not yet relinquished to Paris the role of expatriate artistic community, and the city was still "the paradise of exiles and the retreat of Pariahs" described by Shelley almost a century before.[38] At the time Wright and Cheney were in Fiesole, their neighbors included the English writer and esthetician Violet Paget (who wrote under the pseudonym Vernon Lee), just below in San Domenico; Bernard Berenson and Mary Costelloe, at the Villa I Tatti in Settignano; their librarian and secretary, the English architectural critic Geoffrey Scott and his close friend, the landscape architect Cecil Pinsent; the German sculptor Adolf Hildebrand, in Bellosguardo; and the Chicago sculptor Larkin Mead, the French composer Claude Debussy, and the German collector of modern art Helene Kröller-Müller, in Florence.[39] Whether the couple from Oak Park was also thinking of such earlier liaisons as Elizabeth Barrett and Robert Browning, Sophia Peabody and Nathaniel Hawthorne, or even the Berensons, Wright was aware of the romantic implications of their choice of domicile. "How many souls seeking release from real or fancied domestic woes have sheltered in Fiesole!" he asked. "In ancient Fiesole, far above the romantic city of Cities, I, too, sought shelter there in companionship with

her who, by force of rebellion as by way of Love, was then implicated with me" (*A* II, 168).[40]

By the first decade of the twentieth century, Florence and its surrounding countryside had also become the main center for the recently revived study of the Italian Renaissance garden. Here, just a little more than a decade before, Charles Platt had gathered much of the material for his seminal book *Italian Gardens*, as well as the ideas for his design of the McCormick House. Between 1894, when Platt's book was published, and the end of the first decade of the twentieth century, the subject of Italian villas and their gardens had become extremely popular. Notable works were produced by Charles Latham and H. Inigo Triggs, among others.[41] But Edith Wharton's *Italian Villas and Their Gardens* (1904) stands out for its sensitive text as well as for its striking illustrations by Maxfield Parrish. The book was, as Wharton herself noted, based on ideas she had gleaned from reading and talking with Violet Paget. Following many of Paget's thoughts, Wharton maintained that there was still "much to be learned" from the "old garden-magic" of Italy, where the "transition from the fixed and formal lines of art to the shifting and irregular lines of nature" was so "subtle" and so gradual that house and landscape always "formed a part of the same composition."[42]

The house Wright and Cheney occupied, the Villino Belvedere, is a small, unpretentious stuccoed structure set into the hillside and stepped down in section, like most of its neighbors, to follow the contours of the steeply sloping site (figs. 65, 66). On one side, it opens onto a terraced walled garden that was originally connected to the larger Villa Belvedere to the east. The ground slopes so precipitously from the entrance facade on the upper Via Montececeri (the continuation of the Via Giuseppe Verdi) that the main floor of the house is located one story below, at the level of the garden, but still far enough above the lower Via della Doccia that both floors have unimpeded views of Florence.[43] The earth-toned stucco walls of the house, continuing into those of the garden and then bleeding into the walls of the adjoin-

Villino Belvedere, Fiesole.

65. Facade, via della Doccia (1910).   66. From above, looking southwest (1910).   67. Garden (1910).

ing houses, form an uninterrupted band that seems from a distance to be just a ridge in the natural terracing of the hillside.

In a letter to Ashbee, Wright described the house as a "little eyrie on the brow of the mountain above Fiesole—overlooking the pink and white Florence, spreading in the valley of the Arno below—the whole fertile bosom of the earth seemingly lying in the drifting mists or shining clear and marvelous in this Italian sunshine—opalescent—irridescent [*sic*]."[44] Among the photographs of the house, mostly taken by Woolley, are views of "the high-walled garden that lay alongside the cottage in the Florentine sun or arbored under climbing masses of yellow roses" that Wright described in his *Autobiography*. One can even see in one of them "the white cloth on the small stone table near the little fountain, beneath the clusters of yellow roses, set for two" (fig. 67) that he later so tenderly recalled (*A* I, 168).

Wright and Cheney do not appear to have taken much part in the social life of the Anglo-Florentine community.

They kept to themselves, as if on an extended honeymoon, "closing the medieval door" of their home "on the world outside" (*A* I, 168). Wright began the introductory text for the Wasmuth portfolio and collaborated with Cheney on translations of the Swedish feminist Ellen Key's books on free love and marriage as well as of Goethe's nature poetry.[45] In his *Autobiography*, Wright describes "long walks along the waysides of the hills above," past the *pietra serena* quarries on Monte Ceceri and through the pine woods to Vallombrosa, stopping at a "cloistered little mountain-inn," then "back again, hand in hand, miles through the sun and dust of the ancient winding road, an old Italian road, along the stream. How old! And how thoroughly a road" (*A* I, 168).

It was not just the landscape that interested them. Wright saw everywhere the pervasive and "harmonious" interaction between man and nature, as evidenced by the artistic remains of a culture with roots deep in Antiquity and the Middle Ages. He described how he and Cheney "poked

68. Wright House project. Ground-floor plan and elevation.

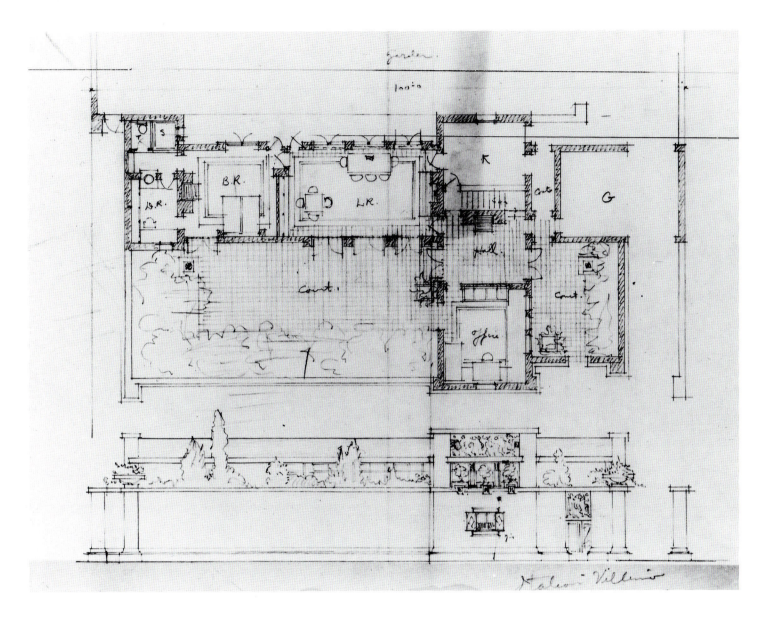

into the unassuming corners where this wondrous brood of Florentines—painter sculptors, sculptor painters and painter sculptor architects worked."[46] The two of them went from museum to museum and building to building, "saturated with plastic beauty, beauty in buildings, beauty in sculpture, beauty in paintings until no 'chiesa,' however rare, and no further beckoning work of human hands could draw or waylay us any more" (*A* I, 168). Yet, despite this exhausting summary, we do not know in any detail what the two of them visited. Wright kept no journal and wrote few letters.[47]

Wright was so impressed with what he and Cheney saw and did in Italy that he referred to the time spent there as "a dream in realization," and he even appears to have contemplated what it might be like to live and work in Fiesole on a more permanent basis (*A* I, 168). That would be the only reasonable explanation for the design of a combined house and studio made sometime during the summer of 1910 (figs. 62, 68).[48] It is long, tall, and narrow. Except for the entry just to the right of a projecting frontispiece, it presents a solid wall to the street, as do most of the other villas in Fiesole. The T-shaped plan allows for a group of

69. Michelozzo di Bartolomeo: Villa Medici, Fiesole, c. 1455.

small, walled gardens and service courts to be sequestered within its angles. Most uncharacteristically for Wright, the low tiled roofs do not end in gables but are masked by parapeted pavilions that rise above the roofline and terminate in flat cornices.[49] The one serving as a frontispiece on the entrance side contains a large classical relief above a triple opening with topiary work, the whole central composition being defined by projecting antae or piers. Classical reliefs also appear above the entrance and in the transom panels over the ground-floor windows looking onto the walled garden.

Although the intended site for the house is not known, it seems to be a flat terrace or a sliver of land, not unlike the property just to the west of Michelozzo's mid-fifteenth-century Villa Medici (fig. 69). The American philosopher Charles A. Strong bought this narrow ledge overhanging San Domenico a year or so later, and in 1912–14 Cecil Pinsent and Geoffrey Scott designed a villa for him about the same

size and shape as Wright's.[50] It is indeed intriguing to think that this plot, immediately adjacent to what is usually considered to be the first Italian villa and garden of the type refined in the sixteenth century by Raphael and Vignola, might have been the site Wright had in mind for himself.

Although in no way as explicitly Italianate, or classical, as the Pinsent-Scott design, Wright's building would have been even more at home in its environment than Strong's Villa Le Balze. To achieve this effect, Wright turned toward the most urban and public forms of expression he had developed during the previous decade, eschewing the typical "sheltered" look of his Prairie House and recalling rather the quasi-classical, monumental Unity Temple and Larkin Building. The prominent placement of sculptured relief panels, set discreetly within frames rather than continuously as a frieze, goes back even further in his work to the project for a Village Bank of 1901 or the Roloson townhouses in Chicago of seven years before that. At the same time, the treatment recalls such Florentine models as the Palazzo Pandolfini, originally designed as a villa by Raphael in the early sixteenth century.[51]

Wright's house project for Fiesole begins to reveal how significant the Italian experience was to be for him and why he chose to live in a place where, to most progressive thinkers of the time, architecture would seem to have come to a stop with the Renaissance. Rather than staying in Berlin—that hotbed of developing modernism, where the role of the machine in generating form and meaning was just coming into its own—Wright saw in the villas and gardens of the hill towns surrounding Florence something more meaningful for the development of his own work. There, architecture and nature were brought together in a remarkable union that satisfied his need to experience—at its source—a world in which the mimetic theory of art could be understood all over again.

The Fiesole project formalized the Prairie House type, not in terms of greater abstraction but in terms of classical ordonnance and site planning. The gridded facades, filled with panels of relief sculpture, rise above the low rooflines and mark the boundaries of secret gardens enclosed, like those of the surrounding Italian villas, by high, blank walls. There is little of the typical Prairie House's sense of extension into the landscape by means of overhanging eaves and open porches, and yet a much more real interaction with the hillside site takes place through the characteristic use of walled gardens to produce an effect similar to the terracing of the Villa Medici.

■ ■ ■

The study of Italian architecture led Wright to review his own work, to reorder its basic elements so as to reinforce his growing concern for integrating building and setting in a more direct and positive way than he had been able to accomplish before. In the introduction to the Wasmuth portfolio, Wright described some of his perceptions and thoughts. He began by referring to the "splendid" architects

Brunelleschi, Bramante, Sansovino, and Michelangelo that he had had the "privilege of studying." But like the good former reader of Ruskin and Viollet-le-Duc that he was, he condemned the "fake ideals of the Renaissance" as a matter of course.[52] Yet he found an "ineffable charm" in Italian architecture that had nothing to do with "the rarefied air of scholasticism or pedantic fine art." "It lies close to the earth. Like a handful of the moist, sweet earth itself, it is so simple that . . . it would seem unrelated to great purposes. It is so close that almost universally it is overlooked." It was less the "'good school' performances" of Renaissance architects that inspired him, he noted, than "those indigenous structures" like his own rented house, "the more humble buildings everywhere which are to architecture what folklore is to literature." "Though often slight, their virtue is intimately interrelated with environment and with the habits of the people," and "of this, there is greater proof in Italy than elsewhere."[53]

In Italy, Wright discovered, as had so many architects before him, that the classical was less style or a set of rules than an underlying system of order that gave to all structures, whether pretentious or not, a common language of form appropriate to the natural setting:

Buildings, pictures and sculpture seem to be born, like the flowers by the roadside, to sing themselves into being. . . .

No really Italian building seems ill at ease in Italy. All are happily content with what ornament and color they carry, as naturally as the rocks and trees and garden slopes which are one with them.[54]

In making the distinction between "high" and "low" versions of a common architectural culture, and in stating a clear preference for the values expressed by the more "humble," "folk" variant, Wright defined the essential lines of a modern interpretation of Mediterranean classicism that would become prevalent later in the century.[55] With the Renaissance as a foil, he articulated the concept of a "native" architecture, as distinguished from a "national" one. To the "highly selfconscious academic" architecture that derived from the Renaissance masters and soon spread all across Europe—becoming "German or Italian, French, Dutch, English or Spanish in nature, as the case may be"—Wright contrasted an "indigenous" architecture, "close to the earth" and "one with" the "rocks and trees and garden slopes," a vernacular tradition that gave birth to "buildings that grew as folk-lore and folk-songs grew." "Another and truer Renaissance" based on these "humble buildings" meant "a return to simple conventions in harmony with nature."[56]

From his European experience Wright believed he learned how architecture might overcome the limits of history and style to establish a more intimate bond with culture through the land. Behind the forms of the Renaissance he saw the more basic ones of a vernacular or primitive tradition in which a "simplified" set of conventions preserves and expresses fundamental values of the indigenous culture. The persistent analogy with folklore and folk music implied that there is a universal language of form that can be varied to meet the needs of the most diverse and individual situations. These two poles—the universal and the individual—provided a much broader framework for thinking about architecture than had Wright's earlier concentration on types, with the categorical oppositions of family and community, public and private, order and freedom, and abstraction and representation.

Not long after returning to the United States, Wright assessed his trip in a letter to Darwin Martin:

I am better qualified by my experience in every way to do stronger work than before. What I have seen and felt in the old world (and I have seen it pretty thoroughly) has mellowed many harsh crudities and rubbed off many corners. I think I am a stronger man and a better architect. But that remains to be proven.[57]

Wright's trip to Europe raised the stakes of his enterprise considerably and shifted it to a new ground. He now aligned himself with the folk-hero poet whose special persona gives voice to universal cultural meanings and values. But to assume that role in the modern world demanded a powerful defense mechanism, and this is something Wright may even have deliberately calculated in "deserting" his family and running off with the wife of a neighbor and former client. If he had been frustrated by the lack of important commissions before, and embittered by insensitive criticism, the "voluntary exile" and self-destructive assumption of the role of pariah would ensure even greater isolation from the world of institutional authority on which architecture ultimately depends. "It may be that this thing [the trip to Europe] will result in taking my work away from me," Wright self-righteously explained to a reporter for the *Chicago Tribune* upon his return:

If I were a writer or a musician or an actor or a painter my work would still be mine, but with an architect it is another matter. An architect comes into as intimate contact with his client as does a physician. . . .

There will be people who will be unwilling to have me in that intimate relation. I shall have buildings to design, of course. But I shall not have as many as I would have if this thing had not happened. I shall not have as many as I would have if I had been content to live dishonestly.[58]

Wright's trip thus gave a truly ironic modern twist to the traditional Grand Tour. Where that had invariably served to guarantee an architect's social and artistic acceptability, Wright's year abroad made it literally impossible for him to return to his Oak Park practice. Using whatever means of publicity and self-advertisement that were at his disposal, he became, at once, an architect of international renown. No longer willing to be looked upon as a regional designer (though, granted, one of exceedingly refined taste), demonstrating to perfection the domestic virtues of the Arts and Crafts Movement, Wright would succeed where Sullivan had failed. His work would no longer be constrained or defeated by the social or political system because it would be produced deliberately outside that system. "I am cast by nature for the part of the iconoclast," Wright wrote to Ashbee from Fiesole in 1910. "I must strike—tear down before I can build—my very act of building destroys an order."[59]

Undercutting society's power to deny him success, Wright placed himself outside the establishment. He declared himself an artist—in the strictest sense of the word—upon whom only history might pass judgment. Like a painter or poet, Wright felt he could proceed on instinct alone, without immediately concerning himself with func-tion, social purpose, or modern technology. His work would emerge directly out of the contact with nature that he now saw as the sole and eternal source of art. His buildings would have to be accepted, first and foremost, as expressions of the relation between man and nature. They would be the de-institutionalized and privatized expressions of a personal worldview grounded in the universe he would create for himself in the house and studio he began building in Wisconsin hardly more than six months after returning from Fiesole.

The Story
of Taliesin

I was a hero in trouble:
I was a great current on the slopes:
I was a boat in the destructive spread of the flood:
I was a captive on the cross:
I went afar, and I was chief:
I was a leader, with abundance, who saw beyond the present....
Of those that be beneathe sky, when all the truth is bare,
none lives entirely to the mind of such as know him there.[1]

So ends the "Book of Taliesin," a collection of epic poems, religious songs, elegies, and prophecies attributed to the Welsh bard who began his career as a court poet in the sixth century and eventually became the mythological poet-prophet of medieval Wales for whom Wright named the house he built for himself and Mamah Borthwick (Cheney) less than a year after returning from Europe (fig. 70).[2] The house, which began as a lyrical and romantic interpretation of nature, ended, like its namesake, on a more elegiac note. The intimate relation with the landscape setting was entirely new in Wright's work, while the choice of a legendary figure of medieval Europe to symbolize its meaning was an indication of Wright's desire to expand the provincial confines of his earlier work.[3]

Unlike the medieval Taliesin, however, who performed an integral role in his society's political and cultural life and whose poetry was an instrument in his patron's struggles for power, Wright, in building Taliesin, removed himself even further from the center of political and cultural authority than he had done by his "voluntary exile" in Fiesole. Ironically, then, the adoption of Taliesin as his alter ego threw into sharpest relief Wright's alienation from society and served to emphasize the role of "iconoclast" that he took to be the fate of the modern artist-architect. As the self-contained world of the Prairie House was left behind, a disengagement of such proportions occurred that nature now replaced culture as the direct source for Wright's architectural ideas. The cultural gap was filled by the narrative of myth.

Taliesin was a direct outcome and logical extension of Wright's year in Europe. It was intended to be a "transference" from Fiesole to Wisconsin of the new life he and Borthwick had begun in Italy. It was designed as a "refuge" and "retreat" for "the woman, the work, and himself." It would be their home as well as the office-studio from which he would launch his new practice, and eventually the school where he would propagate his ideas.[4]

Taliesin was therefore never just a house—not merely a building, that is. It signifies a domain, a country estate, reestablishing the proprietary hold Wright's Welsh forefathers had on the land they settled in south-central Wisconsin in the previous century. Taliesin collapses past and present history into a complex representation of place. At once house, farm, studio, workshop, school, and family seat, it is a complete expression of Wright's integration of architecture and nature. But even more than that, Taliesin was intended from its outset to tell a story with a specifically autobiographical meaning, forming an image of Wright's personal life woven into the fabric of his family's land.[5]

Site and Design

When Wright returned to Oak Park in early October 1910, it was only for a short time; Cheney was to remain in Berlin until the following summer, when her husband finally agreed to grant her a divorce. Wright's most immediate problem was where to live. Catherine still refused to divorce him. For the time being, Wright chose to remain at the Oak Park house, but in totally separate quarters. Clearly, this arrangement could not last, so one of the first things Wright did was to draw up plans for the subdivision of the house and studio into an apartment for his wife and children and another one to provide them with rental income.[6] He must also have been thinking about what to do with his elderly mother, who still lived in the house next door and whose life was deeply bound up with his.

Oak Park proved to be extremely uncomfortable socially for Wright, as one might have expected.[7] Professionally, things were no better. When Wright left the year before, he had turned over his office to the architect Hermann von Holst and had entrusted certain ongoing projects (such as Mason City) to assistants who had been with him for a number of years, assuming that the income from this arrangement would support his family in his absence. Although he may have overestimated, he came to believe that work to be completed on his account or "held over" until his return had been "unscrupulously taken from him" by his former employees.[8] This was undoubtedly one of the factors that persuaded him to move his practice elsewhere. "I will not try any of the old guard again," he wrote to Taylor Woolley. "All the architects about here are inimical—nothing to expect of them or of those whom I once regarded as my own architectural family."[9]

We have no evidence of what Wright did at the time, if anything, to find a new place to settle. We do not even know for sure when, or whether, Cheney planned to rejoin him. In any event, after completing the introductory text for the

Wasmuth portfolio in November and December, and upon learning of certain problems with the publication, Wright decided to return to Berlin. He remained in Europe from late January through March 1911, during which time he and Cheney surely discussed future plans. We know nothing of what transpired, except that Wright once again came home alone.[10]

Within a month of this second return, events began to move rapidly, though not necessarily straightforwardly, toward the purchase of property in the Helena Valley community of Hillside, Wisconsin, where the Lloyd Jones family farmlands were located. On 3 April, Wright reported to Darwin Martin on the "successful" results of his negotiations over a new contract with Wasmuth before asking if he could use some of the money he owed Martin "to help [his] mother out of a tight real estate situation." A week later, he informed Martin that the deal had gone through: "I helped mother buy a small farm up country on which she had a contract for purchase and had paid $500.00, hoping to sell her Oak Park property to redeem the contract." Wright added that he "went up with her [to Wisconsin] to close it and see about building a small house for her."[11]

The first plans for Taliesin were drawn up in April 1911, and work was under way by May. Cheney returned to America sometime in June to take her children to Canada for their summer vacation. Following divorce proceedings in early August, she reverted to her maiden name and took up residence at Taliesin in the fall. Wright did not move there permanently until all work on the house was nearly completed, a few days before Christmas 1911. When reports first surfaced in the Chicago newspapers about this latest turn of events, Catherine Wright vehemently denied any suggestion that her husband and Borthwick could be living there together, claiming that Wright "built that house as a house for his mother."[12] Had she been fooled, or was there some truth in what she said?

The April 1911 plans for Taliesin are indeed titled "Cottage for Mrs. Anna Lloyd Wright" (fig. 71). They show

an L-shaped structure composed of a living wing joined to a "working room," or studio, by a generous open loggia and terrace. The living wing, which was eventually built almost exactly as it appears in this plan, contains an enormous living room connected to a master bedroom by a second outdoor terrace, as well as a smaller bedroom, servant's room, bathroom, and large kitchen. The "working room," with a fireplace equal in size to that of the living room as well as its own enclosed porch, was to be approximately thirty-four feet long by seventeen feet wide.

By June 1911, when Cheney returned from Berlin, these plans had been revised and expanded to become simply a "Cottage and Stable," with Anna Lloyd Wright's name eliminated from the legend. The only change in the living wing was the addition of a small sitting room at the far end of the suite of rooms (figs. 72, 73). The other changes were: (1) an addition to the "working room" amounting to an increase in size of about 50 percent; (2) a new and fairly extensive farmyard and stable area; and (3) a continuous driveway forming an entrance court that shows the beginnings of a hilltop garden in the center of the complex.

In his public remarks at the time, Wright never mentioned his mother in relation to Taliesin, maintaining that it was his idea to settle in Wisconsin and build on his family's land.[13] Only much later did he reveal that his mother had purchased the property for him. "Foreseeing the plight I would be in" upon returning from Europe, Wright stated in the second edition of his *Autobiography* (1943, p. 167), she "bought the low hill on which Taliesin now stands" and "offered it to me as a refuge."[14] This admission probably reflects the truth, but the actual story is more complicated.

To begin with, Wright himself put up some, if not most, of the money for the land. Although Anna Lloyd Wright clearly figured in the original scheme for Taliesin, it seems doubtful that the house was ever intended exclusively for her. More than likely, before he could be sure that Mamah Cheney would actually return, Wright thought of sharing the Wisconsin house with his mother, if not as a

Taliesin.

71. First project ("Cottage for Mrs. Anna Lloyd Wright"), April 1911. Plan.

72. Final project, June 1911. Plan (redrawn c. 1940).

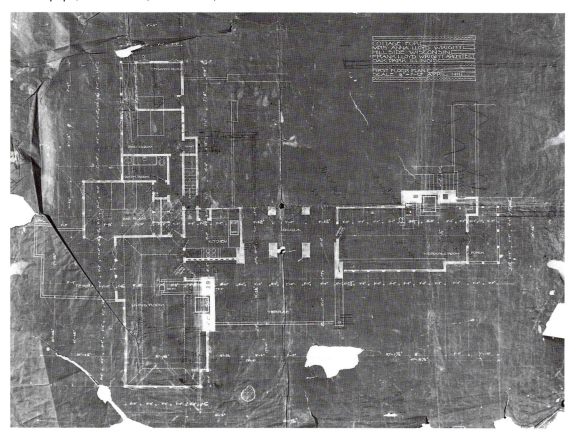

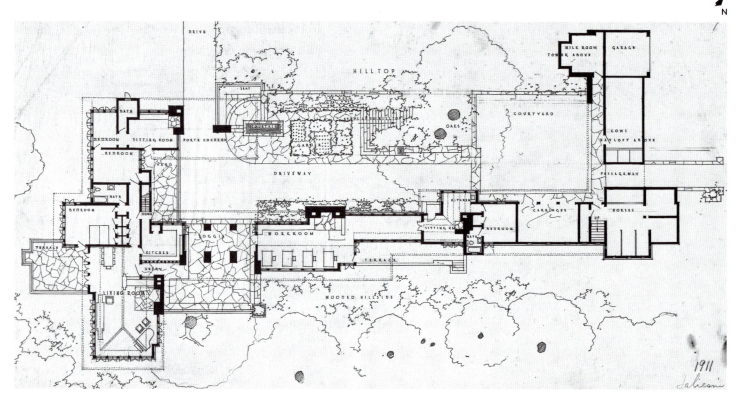

73. Taliesin. Final project, June 1911. Elevations and section.

full-time residence then at least as a weekend or vacation "retreat."[15] It was important, however, that the property not be in his name, because Catherine could then have a legal right to it. Publicly, at least, his wife was willing to be part of the ruse.[16]

A number of details about the project make it almost certain that the original plan was as much for Wright as for his mother. Although it is true that Wright's mother probably felt somewhat uneasy about living in Oak Park next door to her son's spurned wife and that much of her family, including her sisters Ellen and Jane, her brother Enos, and her daughter and son-in-law Jane and Andrew Porter, were living in Hillside, it is also fair to say that no site in all of Helena Valley could have been less appropriate for a sixty-nine-year-old woman than the hill on which Taliesin is located.[17] (It is therefore hardly surprising that, after she "gave" Taliesin to Wright in June 1911, she went to live down by the main road near the Hillside Home School, close to her sisters' and daughter's houses.) Furthermore, it is very difficult to conceive of a single, elderly woman occupying such grandiose quarters as the original plan called for—again re-

membering that, when it became his own house, Wright made no significant changes to the living wing. And finally, how else can one explain the existence of a "working room" thirty-four feet long by seventeen feet wide, at the entrance to the property (just the location of Wright's office/studio later at Taliesin West) if it was not for the architect's own use?

But the most compelling reason for believing that Wright designed the house for himself, and that the registration of the deed of sale as well as the building plans in the name of his mother were essentially for legal reasons, is the particular choice of site. When Wright finally revealed his mother's role in the affair, he specified that she "had bought the low hill" that "was one of my favorite places . . . as a boy" (*A* II, 167). Wright's sister Maginel later confirmed that "Mother knew the hill that was Frank's favorite . . . and had made a present of it to Frank."[18]

In his *Autobiography*, Wright explained that he loved the hill for its liberating sense of space and vista, which he compared to the experience of looking down to earth from an airplane: "When you are on its crown you are out in mid-

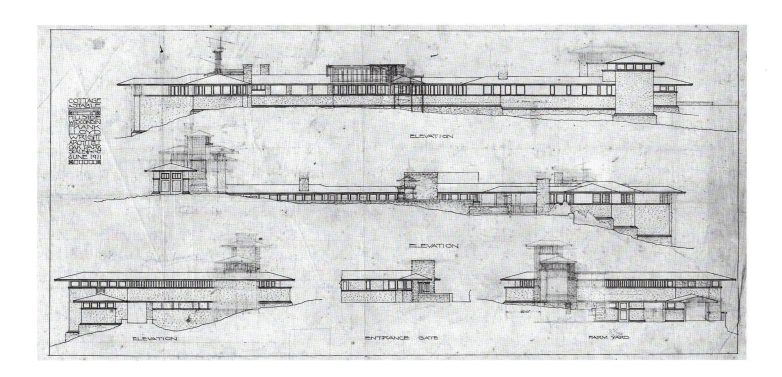

74. Spring Green and Helena Valley, Wis.

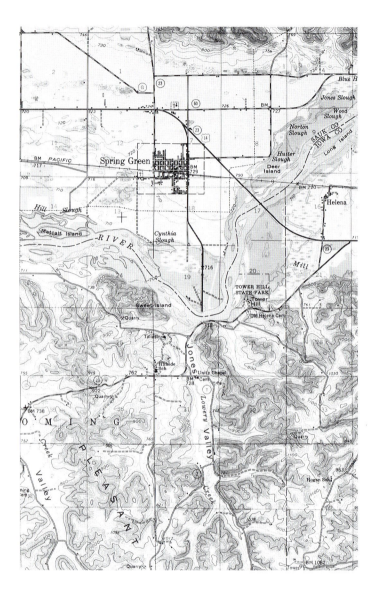

air as though swinging in a plane, as the Valley and two others drop away leaving the tree-tops all about you" (*A* I, 170). The sense of immersion in the landscape was matched by a feeling of strategic control over the valley. Commanding the view from the bend in the river up the valley to its wooded slopes in the distance, the hill had come to represent for Wright a place where one could feel the presence of nature's regenerating force. It was there, he remembered, that "pasque flowers grew . . . in March sun while snow still streaked the hillsides" (*A* I, 170). Before Taliesin was even a house, then, it was a hill. Whether or not his mother was also to have lived there, the design of the house was predi-

cated on the existence of the hill and the meanings Wright associated with it. Of these, surely the most decisive was that it ultimately would provide a home for Mamah Borthwick, "she for whom Taliesin had first taken form" (*A* I, 189).

■ ■ ■

The Helena Valley community of Hillside, Wisconsin, where Wright's grandparents settled in the early 1860s, is about forty miles west of Madison.[19] It is separated from the town of Spring Green, about two miles to the north, by the Wisconsin River, which flows from east to west at this point (fig. 74). The rich farmland of the valley supported not only the farmstead of Richard Lloyd Jones but also those of four of his sons, Wright's uncles Enos, Thomas, John, and James. It also provided a desirable rural environment for the progressive Hillside Home School established by Wright's aunts Ellen and Jane in the 1880s.[20] Although Wright's parents never actually lived there, Wright himself spent summers working on his uncle James's farm in the late 1870s and early 1880s. And it was in this agrarian, familial environment that Wright got his earliest experience in building and saw the first design of his own realized.

In the summer of 1886, while still living in Madison, Wright worked on the Lloyd Jones family chapel, called Unity Chapel, for the site where the family had traditionally held "Grove meetings . . . after each harvest" in an expression of "unity and thanksgiving."[21] The small, Richardsonian, Shingle Style building, designed by Silsbee, is located next to the family cemetery at the southeastern corner of the valley, near James Lloyd Jones's farm (fig. 75). The following year, Wright's aunts asked their nephew to design a school building in place of the original homestead (which was moved to a new site). Wright's first built work, the original Shingle Style Hillside Home School, was set near the base of the hill on the west side of the valley (fig. 76).

Less than ten years later, in 1896–97, Wright designed a windmill for the top of that hill. He once again used cedar

75. Joseph Lyman Silsbee: Unity (Lloyd Jones) Chapel, Hillside, 1885–86.

76. Hillside Home School: original building (right middleground) 1887; addition (center) 1901–03; and Romeo and Juliet Tower (on hill in distance) 1896–97.
View from other side of main road (now State Highway 23), looking north (before March 1908).

77. Romeo and Juliet Tower. Plan.

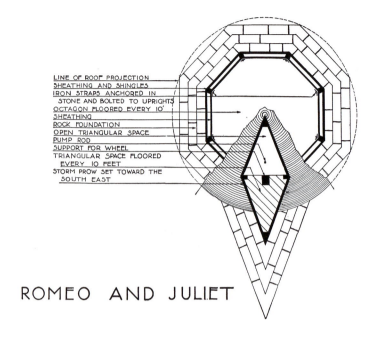

LINE OF ROOF PROJECTION
SHEATHING AND SHINGLES
IRON STRAPS ANCHORED IN
STONE AND BOLTED TO UPRIGHTS
OCTAGON FLOORED EVERY 10'
SHEATHING
ROCK FOUNDATION
OPEN TRIANGULAR SPACE
PUMP ROD
SUPPORT FOR WHEEL
TRIANGULAR SPACE FLOORED
EVERY 10 FEET
STORM PROW SET TOWARD THE
SOUTH EAST

ROMEO AND JULIET

shingles as the cladding material, but he gave the tower a bold geometric form as a structural solution to the expression of the tower's role as a landmark (fig. 77).[22] The pump rod and support for the wheel are carried up within an acutely angled lozenge shape pointed southeast to deflect blasts of wind like a "storm prow" (*A* I, 131). This angular element is inserted halfway into a larger octagonal volume that contains and supports it throughout nearly its full height. Wright called the composition Romeo and Juliet, likening its conjugate geometry to an amorous union. In a letter to his aunts he explained what must have seemed a somewhat mystifying symbolism:

Of course you had a hard time with Romeo and Juliet. But you know how troublesome they were centuries ago. Each is indispensable to the other . . . neither could stand without the other. Romeo, as you will see, will do all the work and Juliet cuddle alongside to support and exalt him. Romeo takes the side of the blast and Juliet will entertain the school children. Let's let it go at that. (A I, 132)

The emphatic geometry of the Romeo and Juliet Tower was contemporaneous with the studio and playroom additions to Wright's Oak Park house. It also shared their liter-

ary and symbolic allusiveness. Wright chose the story of the building of the tower as one of the opening episodes of his *Autobiography*. Turning it into a kind of fairy tale—the first draft begins, "Once upon a time were two matriarchal maiden sisters in a Southwestern-Wisconsin Valley, known far and wide as the Lloyd-Jones sisters"[23]—he used the Shakespearean romance as a story within the story, on the model of the narrative technique of the *Thousand and One Nights*. The particular reference to gender distinction and gender conjunction in the tower's form predates its occurrence in the sculpture of the *Flower in the Crannied Wall* and thus already discloses something of the extremely personal meaning Wright always attributed to the landscape of Helena Valley.[24]

Wright visited the valley often during the years he lived in Oak Park, and he built two more structures there between 1900 and 1909. In response to increased enrollments and programs at the Hillside Home School, he added a new complex of buildings in 1901–1903, just below the original structure (see fig. 76). Built of rock-faced ashlar sandstone on a steeply sloping site, this grouping provided pavilion-like spaces for a gymnasium, an assembly hall, a drawing studio, and a laboratory, all connected by galleries of classrooms and corridors bridging service drives.[25] The pavilion containing the assembly hall, based on the Oak Park Studio, was designed as a two-story space, with a square balcony rotated forty-five degrees within the orthogonal arrangement of piers supporting the roof (figs. 78, 79). The resultant spatial dynamism is expressed on the exterior in tall window bays projecting through recessed corner piers under a floating hip roof, a solution that became the model for Unity Temple. But unlike the abstract treatment of that interior space, the detailing of the Hillside assembly hall was deliberately given a "Welsh feel," because the room was intended to serve, in part, as a memorial to the sisters' immigrant parents, Richard and Mary Lloyd Jones, and as an expression of the continuity of their teaching and example in the philosophy of the school.[26]

The final building Wright designed in the area before 1911 was a small, compact, fairly conservative, shingled

Prairie House for his sister Jane Porter and her husband, Andrew (1907), at the time the latter became business manager of the Hillside Home School. The house was called by the Welsh name Tanyderi, meaning "under the oaks." Unlike Taliesin, Tanyderi was tucked out of sight of the valley and set like a discrete, prismatic cube in distinct contrast to the foliage surrounding it.

By the time he began designing Taliesin, Wright thus knew the "valley of the god-almighty Joneses" intimately. One of a series of fertile valleys lying between soft, rolling hills leading down to the Wisconsin River, Helena Valley is defined on the east by the nearly solid wall of the three "guardian hills" of the family clan, named by them Bryn Mawr, Bryn Canol, and Bryn Bach (fig. 74).[27] These come right to the river's edge. On the west, the floor of the valley rises more gradually and more irregularly to Pleasant Ridge. At its southerly point, the valley splits in two, with a low ridge coming between. Here, two spring-fed streams join to run north into the bend in the river. The path of the western branch (which the main road, now a state highway, follows) skirts a group of hills along the eastern slopes of Pleasant Ridge.

Farthest to the southwest is the hill topped by the Romeo and Juliet Tower, below which sits the Hillside Home School, marking the site of the original Lloyd Jones homestead. Next is the conical Midway Hill, rising abruptly from the cornfields and pasture lands around it. And finally, directly north of it, is the hill on which Taliesin was built, angling its way out to the southeast to form a kind of promontory at the point where the valley opens out and the river takes a deep bend to the south below Spring Green. As the most northerly of these hills, it has a view down the entire length of the valley and up the river as well. From its slopes, Wright noted, "you could look out upon the great sandy and treeless plain that had once been the bed of the mighty Wisconsin of ancient times" (*A* I, 3).

The way in which Wright sited Taliesin provides the key to understanding its meaning and underlies all other aspects of it. To take advantage of the panoramic vista without compromising the integrity of the hill by building on top

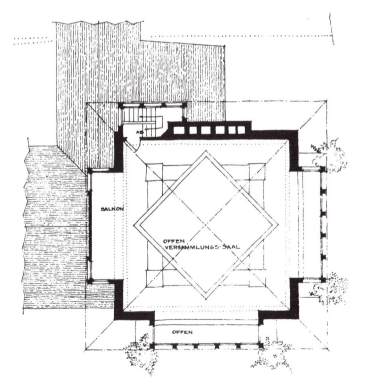

of it, Wright wrapped the wings of the house around its two prominent sides, but well below its crown (figs. 70, 72). The house became, as Wright later wrote, "the 'brow' of the hill," and thus the very image of Taliesin, which means "shining brow" or "radiant brow" in Welsh (*A* I, 171).[28] Following the contours of the hill, one wing parallels the bend of the river while the other points upstream to the northeast.

In the original plan of April 1911, the living section on the southeast flank of the hill was connected to the studio by an open loggia and terrace (fig. 71). The house, which backs up against the slope of the hill, was entered from the rear through the courtyard formed by the angle of the two wings. The approach to the rectangular court was originally to have been from the northwest, down a flight of steps behind the chimney of the studio (the access drive perpendicular to the studio would apparently have come from the south over the hill). The house was sited about fifty degrees east of south, so that as you passed through the court, between the hill crown on the right and the studio on the left, and then turned into the loggia, you would have had a view of the lower end of the valley as it opens into the Wisconsin River, framed by the double set of stone piers of the loggia.

In this first project, the living wing is composed of a large living room forming a kind of head at the river end, with terraces on either side for shoulders, a kitchen and master bedroom as its trunk, and a tail of smaller bedrooms, with a bathroom running alongside the walled kitchen court. The casual and linear arrangement of rooms off a long central corridor, though it has some antecedents in Wright's work, is fundamentally new and looks forward to the telescoping, polliwog plans of his later Usonian houses, just as the angled relation of studio to living wing predicts their frequent L-shaped configuration (fig. 203). The way the kitchen and master bedroom overlap the central rectangular space and butt up against the corridor recalls the Glasner House, in which Wright also had to deal with a sloping hillside site (fig. 53). There, too, a large fireplace was set on the long side of the living room, which, like the living room in Taliesin, doubles as a dining area. The projecting terraces of Taliesin, however, relate the house to the site in

a much more intimate way; even had the bridge and tea house for the Glasners been built, a highly formal distinction would have been maintained between house and hill.

The key to the site planning of Taliesin, however, lies not so much in the extensions or projections over the hillside and into space but rather in the connection established by the courtyard to the hill behind. In effect, Wright turned the Prairie House paradigm inside out. "There is no backyard," he later wrote. "Taliesin is all front yard" (*A* II, 425). Or rather, one might say, as the "backyard" courtyard became the front yard, it extended its domain through the house to encompass the panorama that frames its rooftops (fig. 80). The bird's-eye perspective in which Wright made this most evident also clearly illustrates the relation between the courtyard plan of Taliesin and the earlier courtyard plans for the Coonley and McCormick houses (figs. 52, 63). In those, Wright "zoned" the house into a series of wings set around a courtyard that functions as the main entryway. In the first plan of Taliesin, this scheme was only partially adumbrated; but in the revised and expanded project of two months later, Wright completed the other half of the three-sided courtyard to embrace the hill from behind.

In the June 1911 plan, Wright more than doubled the total length of the studio wing to provide not only more work space but also an apartment for an assistant, as well as a wagon shed and stable under the same roof (fig. 72). These units were staggered along a narrow drive that replaced the former rectangular court. The main approach was removed to the upper end of the living wing to cut between the hill and the walls of the house (fig. 81). The entrance drive, narrowed considerably by the addition of a sitting room on the inner side of the former servant's room, now lined up with the opening of the loggia. A porte-cochere, balanced on a broad stone pier similar to those of the loggia, was attached to the chimney mass of the sitting room. The view from the main entrance was thus channeled toward the opening to the river, as the relation between hill and valley was reinforced by the rise of the hill crown on the left.[29]

The hill became a constant presence in the experience of the house. Upon reaching the loggia, you turned to the

PRELIMINARY STUDY OF
TALIESIN SPRING GREEN
WISCONSIN

Taliesin.

80 (*above*). Aerial perspective, looking east (c. 1912).

81 (*right*). Main entrance (before October 1915).

Taliesin.

On opposite page: 82. Court, looking northwest from porte-cochere to stable (c. 1912).   83. Hill and belvedere, looking west (c. 1915).

left into what Wright described as "a sort of drive along the hillside flanked by low buildings on one side and flower gardens against the stone walls that retained the hill crown on the other" (*A* I, 173; fig. 82). At the end of the studio/apartment section of this wing, the drive widened into a farmyard, opposite the wagon shed, before passing under a bridge connecting the horse stalls to the rest of the stable wing extending up the slope of the hill and terminating in a garage backing onto the milk room and ice house set into the hill. Above the milk room, Wright built a tower (penciled in on the June drawings), which provides a point of orientation and a belvedere (fig. 83). The tower indicates the deepest penetration of the house into the hill and can thus be read as an eccentric vertical axis staking the building to the site. From it the house unwinds in a spiraling, clockwise direction around the hill and out to the entrance (fig. 80).[30] Instead of revolving around an internal element, such as the fireplace core of the typical Prairie House, Taliesin takes its direction from an external, natural feature of the landscape.

As noted before, the design of June 1911, which was followed with only minor variations, differed from the original scheme in three significant respects. First, the buildings now formed an enclosed, loosely U-shaped courtyard embracing the hill. Second, along the edge of the driveway forming the court, Wright created a garden to define a more gradual transition from house to hill, as well as to help connect the house itself with the larger treatment of the landscape implicit in the third new development: Taliesin was no longer just a house and studio but was a full-fledged country estate, not unlike the typical European or Colonial American ones of the preindustrial period. The land, which had been his family's means of sustenance, would once again be farmed, while its income-earning potential would be extended by the inclusion of the permanent headquarters of Wright's architectural practice and, eventually, school (figs. 84, 85).

In other words, by the time Cheney came back from Europe to join him, Wright had concluded that "Taliesin should be a garden and a farm behind a workshop and

a home." "The place was to be self-sustaining, if not self-sufficient and with its domain of two hundred acres, [it would provide] shelter, food, clothes and even entertainment within itself." It would have "its own light-plant, fuel-yard, transportation and water system." As the "architect's workshop," it would be "a dwelling as well for young workers who came to assist" and "a farm cottage for the farm help." All the land just beyond the enclosed hill garden was planned for crops or grazing. There were to be apple and plum orchards farther up the hill to the west; vineyards "on the south slope of the hill" down from the tower, with orchards for smaller fruit bushes beyond; a vegetable garden below the kitchen and living wing to the east; pasture lands lower down the slopes for cows and sheep to graze; and finally, a pond to the northeast for geese and ducks. Wright envisaged the estate as a single totality: "I saw it all, and planted it all and laid the foundation of the herd, flocks, stable and fowls as I laid the foundation of the house." "Taliesin was to be a complete living unit," encompassing everything "from pig to proprietor" (*A* I, 172–73).

■ ■ ■

The concept of a country estate on the European model was the subject of much interest in American architectural circles during the first decade of this century. In his review of Barr Ferree's *American Estates and Gardens* (1904) in the

84. *Taliesin. Estate plan (c. 1912).*

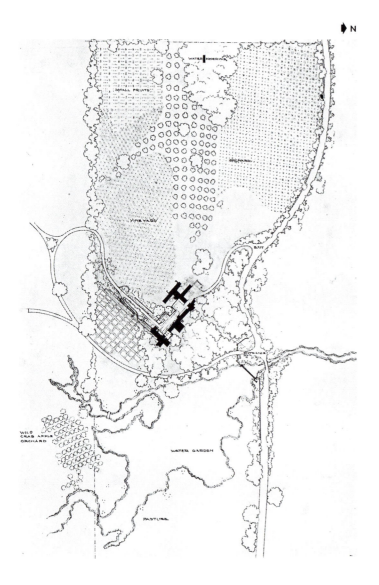

♦ N

July 1905 issue of *Architectural Record*, Herbert Croly noted that the American estate was "the creation of the past ten years," obviously referring to Richard Morris Hunt's Biltmore (1895). He added that "the majority of them are probably not more than five or six years old." By *estate*, Croly specifically meant a permanent dwelling in the country, like those of the landed aristocracy of Britain, France, and Italy, where the "proprietor . . . generally derives an income from his estate, and is attached to it by all sorts of family and personal ties, and whose house has settled down into an architectural efflorescence of a neatly parted and combed landscape."[31]

Croly contrasted this tradition with the typical American "country houses erected for habitation during a few months in the summer and generally surrounded by a comparatively small amount of land," or those used for weekends, where the "relation to the country remains essentially casual and artificial." Whereas Americans consider the city house their primary place of residence, "the owners of the big English [or continental European] estates live in the country, and sojourn for some months of each year in the town." As a result, "country life" for them is not "a vacation" but rather "a patient, leisurely, submissive, and even contemplative habit of mind." Croly believed that the social barriers preventing the "European 'bourgeois'" from entertaining the thought of living a "genuine country life" did not exist in America, and that it was simply a matter for Americans, whether millionaires or otherwise, to learn how "literally and metaphorically to cultivate their gardens."[32]

The major architectural difference between the country house and the country estate lay in the relation between house and landscape. Typically, Croly wrote, "it is the house which the American considers first, last and always—no matter whether the house be a villa or a palace in a park." "The grounds are generally slurred," he added, and "the garden and the other landscape accessories are inadequate to the scale of the house." In planning an estate, by contrast, the land comes first. "When a residence is erected on an estate of five hundred acres, the house should become merely an incident in the lay-out of the whole estate," with its design "adjusted to the lay-out of the land." The transition from one scale to the other was to be effected by the "flower-garden" in the "immediate vicinity of the house," so that house and garden form a single totality as the central focus of a larger pattern of development. In Croly's view, "Italian villas and their gardens," along with "English country mansions," provided the most suitable models. The Italian villas are to be preferred, not only because they give the impression "that the architecture belongs to the landscape," but also because "their propriety as country houses is fundamentally a matter of intelligent design."[33]

Wright's conception of Taliesin as a country estate closely paralleled Croly's definition and would have been unthinkable without his own recent European experience.[34]

85. Taliesin. Distant view from Midway Hill, looking north (c. 1915).

He intended Taliesin to be a continuation of the new life he had begun with Cheney in Italy, and the revised and expanded project of June 1911 coincided with her return. Prior to that, Wright may well have considered Taliesin only a weekend or vacation "retreat" from city life. This seems to be the most logical explanation for the project he prepared for a house and studio for himself on Goethe Street in Chicago (fig. 86) at about the same time he undertook the first design for Taliesin. Located on the Near North Side, close to the lake and within walking distance of the Loop, the site was just four blocks north of the house at 25 Cedar Street that he had rented for himself and his mother.[35]

Wedged between other houses on a narrow city lot, the four-story townhouse was to have had a duplex apartment above the ground-floor office and second-floor studio/drafting room. A double-height living room topped by a skylight and surrounded by a music balcony over the rear dining room would have been the central feature. The facade derives directly from the design for Fiesole less than a year before. Projecting terminal piers contain a tripartite composition defined by narrower piers in antis, with sculptural relief panels filling the spandrels between the two upper levels of windows. For this urban setting, Wright obviously felt that the quasi-classical, formal treatment of his Italian project was most appropriate.

When the decision was made to concentrate all resources on Taliesin as the permanent place of residence and simply retain rented quarters as a pied-à-terre in town,

86. Wright Townhouse project, Chicago, 1911. Perspective.

On opposite page:

87. Taliesin. Hill garden with *Flower in Crannied Wall* (c. 1912).

Wright did not reject his recent Italian experience as irrelevant but rather turned to different aspects of it. Along with the notion of a full-fledged country estate on the European model, he looked to the Italian Renaissance villa and garden for ideas about site planning and landscaping, if not actual details of house design. Wright said that the terrain of southern Wisconsin reminded him of the "'pastoral' beauty" and "'human' . . . scale and feeling" of the Italian

landscape, and he claimed that it was "more like Tuscany, perhaps, than any other land."[36] The hillside siting of Taliesin followed the characteristic manner of Florentine and Roman villas. Indeed, the basic concept of Taliesin recalls the Villino Belvedere, which Wright had described to Ashbee as a "little eyrie on the brow of the mountain."

When Taliesin was expanded into an estate, Wright turned his attention to the question of landscaping. The increased length of the studio wing, combined with the added stable wing, created an enclosed courtyard. This became the nucleus of an overall design in which Wright adapted the various components of the typical Italian garden to relate house to landscape in a hierarchically ordered pattern. "The house, the flower-garden, the grove, the fountains, and the water system" were, according to Charles Platt, the "main features of the [Italian] villa" to be manipulated to create the impression of a gradual transition from the rational order of built form to the free and natural beauty of the surrounding landscape.[37] At Taliesin, Wright designed the enclosed hill garden as a "formal garden" and called it a "flower-garden," on the model of the Italian *giardino segreto* (fig. 84). On the southern slope of the hill, following the entrance drive past the gate of the courtyard, he created a "terraced garden" mirroring the vegetable garden on the other side of the drive. This characteristically Italian feature formed the transition to what Wright called the "wild garden," like the Italian ilex grove, surrounding the house and acting as a buffer between it and the working farmlands beyond.

The connection between the orchards and the cattle pasture in the valley was made by manipulating the element of water. Wright dammed the stream at the base of the hill to make a "water garden," as he called it. This "raised the water in the valley to within sight from Taliesin" and at the same time created a pond for ducks and geese (*A* I, 173). The dam made a waterfall with enough force to activate a hydraulic ram that lifted the water to a stone reservoir built on the hill just above the house. From there, the water could be channeled into a series of pools and fountains in

the formal hill garden before it irrigated the vegetable gardens farther down the slopes.

The formal garden in the center of the composition continued the line of the terraced garden flanking the drive. Modeled on a *giardino segreto*, it was designed as a suite of small, boxed-in flower gardens set against the stone parapet acting as a retaining wall for the hill crown. About two-thirds of the way down the drive toward the rear stable court, where the hill begins to rise, Wright inset a flight of steps leading to a clump of oak trees and, at the beginning of this stairway, placed a cast of the *Flower in the Crannied Wall* (figs. 87, 82). In the plan of June 1911, there is an exedra

adjoining the pier of the porte-cochere, delineating the turn in the drive (fig. 72). Realizing the greater significance of the shape as a symbolic rather than functionally expressive form, Wright transposed it to the top of the steps to create a semicircular stone seat enclosing the grove of oak trees. For the center of this exedra, he designed a semicircular pool with a fountain directly on axis with the line of the retaining wall of the hill crown. This line marked the division between the untouched world of nature and the ordered world of man.

At the lower end of the garden, next to the porte-cochere, Wright built a right-angled stone seat, enclosing

88. Taliesin. Entrance to living quarters (c. 1912).

two sides of a square and framing a narrow, rectangular stone basin containing a pool and another fountain. The water flowing through the flower beds would be collected here before it was channeled to the lower vegetable garden. On the way, it would pass through another rectangular basin, this one under the loggia, tucked between two piers next to the door of the living quarters (fig. 88). The path of entrance into Taliesin was thus marked, on the left, at the porte-cochere and, on the right, at the loggia, by water. The water coming down the hillside would appear to be making its way to the river, which could be seen through the opening of the loggia. House and landscape would thus seem to form one continuous world. With the fountains flowing and the sound of water playing on the surface of the pools, with the rich color and perfumed air of the tightly packed flower beds, the sensuous and "secret" hilltop garden, hidden behind the porte-cochere, in the center of the court, defined the constant source of nature's vitality out of which the rest of the house and grounds could be seen to have grown.

The hillside siting, the terracing, the enclosed flower garden, the belvedere-like tower, the stone seats and exedra, the sculptured term, and especially the fountains, pools, and controlled use of water—all are reminiscent of such Italian examples as the Villa Medici in Fiesole, the Villa d'Este in Tivoli, the Villa Lante at Bagnaia, and, per-

haps most of all, the Aldobrandini and Torlonia villas at Frascati.[38] But the Italian villa and garden also had a less obvious effect on the planning of Taliesin. In response to the Renaissance designs he saw in Italy, Wright began to free himself from dependence on the underlying classical patterns of symmetry and "simple axial law and order" that had been so basic to his earlier work. In an important sense, then, Italy also taught Wright what not to do, or at least what he no longer had to do to achieve a sense of classical unity and order.

Taliesin has none of the formality of the Prairie House type. This is evident both in the plan and in the use of materials. Even in the most casual and open plans of Wright's earlier work, such as those for the Coonley and McCormick houses, where separate wings interlock in a loose and somewhat disjointed manner, there is a classical ponderation and reciprocity of parts that results in a disguised, though no less instrumental, symmetry (fig. 52). This is even more apparent at the level of the part, or zone, than the whole. In the Coonley House, the living/dining wing and the stable wing are both formal, symmetrical, T-shaped configurations, while the bedroom wing is a Willits-type pinwheel plan. In the McCormick House (fig. 63), the absolutely symmetrical, U-shaped living/dining wing is mirrored at a reduced scale by the bedroom court, much as the larger church and smaller parish house components of Unity Temple are related to one another. The materials in Wright's Prairie Houses further emphasize the abstract formality of the design. In the Coonley House, for instance, the off-white plaster surfaces are regularized and contained by their wood stripping, while the colorful frieze of geometric abstraction is used to articulate linkages and to set off such projecting, centralized pieces as the living room pavilion. Whether it be the brick of the Robie and Cheney houses or the lapped wood and plaster of the Glasner House, the materials almost always play a recessive, generalizing role.

In Taliesin, materials and plan emphasize the building's informality, its irregularity, and its intimate relation to the natural surroundings. Piers, chimneys, parapets, and lower walls are all built of limestone quarried just a mile away; intervening wall surfaces are roughly stuccoed with plaster made of the yellowish sand from the banks of the Wisconsin River; and the complex, multilevel roof is covered with cedar shingles left to weather.[39] Taliesin looks "homemade," as Wright said, "made out of the rocks and trees of the region" so as to be "part of the hill on which it stands."[40] The stonework, in particular, looks "raw." It is quarry-faced and set in a pattern of randomly projecting blocks, producing a knobby, textured surface. By comparison with his earlier work, the materials have an undisguised naturalness. The rock-faced ashlar in the Hillside Home School of ten years before was laid evenly to produce a smooth, continuous surface (fig. 78). Each block was squared to make tight, definitive joints, and the chisel-drafted margins of the corner stones cause the entire surface to seem "laid on," producing an optical effect of solidity. Taliesin, by contrast, feels as solid as the earth. Nothing about it appears artificial.

The natural roughness and irregularity of Taliesin are not confined to its physical structure but can be felt in the unusual freedom and casualness of the plan. It was in fact "in the *constitution* of the whole, in the way the walls rose from the plan and the spaces were roofed over" that Wright said he found "the chief interest of the whole house" (*A* I, 175). There is no obvious order of a formal or abstract sort in the overall grouping of the parts, nor is there any symmetry in the individual parts themselves.[41] Each wing is loosely organized in itself and joined to the next in a meandering pattern that appears to unwind slowly around the hill. There is none of that rigid orthogonal plaiting and interweaving of rectilinear elements that characterized even the most open of Wright's Prairie Houses and gave them an internal, self-contained sense of order. At Taliesin, the order is more subtle. It is contingent and circumstantial, deriving from Wright's intention to follow the natural contours of the site. When he decided categorically that "it was unthinkable that any house should be put *on* that beloved hill" but had to "be *of* the hill belonging to it . . . [like the] trees and the

ledges of rock" (*A* I, 171), he rejected any conventional method of axial composition based on the flat, abstract grid. He turned to diagonal axes, believing these could more closely approximate nature's path of least resistance and thus accommodate the building to its site.

Wright had experimented with organizing rooms along an implied diagonal axis in just a few projects of the previous decade.[42] Of these, only the Glasner House was built. With a site similar to Taliesin's in terms of slope, the Glasner House played off a diagonal geometry against the controlling orthogonal axis (fig. 53). An eccentrically located fireplace in the living room is on a forty-five-degree line of sight from the corner entrance, and the same angle determines the disposition of the bedrooms and octagonal sewing room that step out over the ravine. A longitudinal axis defined by the two larger octagons of the library and projected tea house stabilizes the plan in a rectilinear fashion, however, making the diagonal seem somewhat out of place.

At Taliesin, the only significant right angle is the one the drive takes rounding the porte-cochere. But even there, the recess of the kitchen court and the jog in the axis from the porte-cochere to the loggia throw the grid out of kilter and force a diagonal reading. Almost all the rooms are connected to each other, and entered, at their corners (fig. 72). The lines of sight thus carry diagonally across from room to room to emphasize the sense of space. But above all, Wright used the diagonal axis to extend the views beyond the confines of the house, to relate interior to exterior in a totally unexpected and unmediated way.

If, wherever one turns, a vista cuts across architectural boundaries and makes inside and outside seem like a single, continually expanding space, that sense of oneness with the land is most fully expressed in the commanding diagonal view from the living room over the valley and river below. The rectangular living room, which is entered from the corner of the courtyard, occupies the angle between the loggia and the dining terrace. Its diagonal axis is the resultant of their perpendicular spatial directions.[43] From inside the

89. Taliesin. Living room, looking southeast (late 1930s).

cavernous loggia, there is a preliminary view of the valley and river, just over the parapet of the terrace (fig. 88). Before coming out into the open, however, you turn ninety degrees to the right. Through the Dutch door of the corner entrance of the living room, there is another vista, this time across the room and over the dining terrace. The view is up the valley toward the family chapel.

You still have no idea of the expanse of the living room, for the large fireplace and bookshelf seat block the view, forming an inglenook in the path of entry (fig. 72). In

forcing you to cross the room before being able to look down its length, this corner element powerfully defines the implied diagonal axis of the space; at the same time, the inset, notched corner and diagonally placed piano at the far end of the fireplace wall reinforce the spatial twist. Once you come around the bookshelf and are opposite the fireplace, the view opens into an arc of 270 degrees. It cuts across the room and over the hills in a single, effortless, arching movement that seems to follow the curve of the earth, as the stone fireplace to the rear, diagonally opposite the corner window, anchors the vista in the hill behind (fig. 89). The cater-cornered placement of these two points of reference helps give the impression of shearing along the diagonal; and, with the planes of the hip ceiling spreading above and the floor sliding out toward the light, you have the boundless sense of being outside, in the center of things, in a space turned inside out.[44] It is almost as if Wright had been able to re-create indoors that boyhood experience on the hill of feeling "out in mid-air as though swinging in a plane."

The diagonal shear of the living room traces the axis from the hill to the bend in the river (fig. 80). The rough stone fireplace mass replaces the hill crown as the center of an arch sweeping across the landscape. Taliesin is thus not to be looked at as much as it is to be looked from. It is more akin to a natural outlook than a house. And this feature, more than anything else, differentiates Taliesin from the Prairie House. In those quintessentially suburban structures, Wright concentrated on the self-contained form of the house to create "a sense of 'shelter' in the look of the building." The Prairie Houses are all distinctly imageable. A single view can and does contain the meaning of the Robie House or the Willits House or the Coonley House, and Wright felt it was possible to record this message in the perspectives he drew of these buildings. There is no perspective of Taliesin other than the one drawn from above and behind it, looking through it, so to speak, over the valley.[45] There are no photographs of the building from the "outside"— that is, from the valley—that are either intelligible or truly memorable. The views of the "inside"—the court—are in essence views of, or from, the hill. What we remember about Taliesin is the way it embraces the hill to afford views of the larger world of which it is a part (fig. 70).[46]

Taliesin is an incident in the landscape, and thus its system of order is not independent of nature. In no previous building had Wright so utterly disconnected one section from another as he did at Taliesin by inserting the open loggia between the living and studio wings. The hill literally passes through the house. The house does not just cling to it, but appears from the entrance gate to be a part of the hill of

which the drive is simply an open cut. Taliesin only seems asymmetrical and discontinuous when it is considered out of context, for it is the hill that completes the house and makes the marriage of architecture and nature an affair of mutual interdependence. The typical Prairie House always asserts its own limits and edges so as to condense the image of the landscape in itself. In Taliesin, the line between building and landscape was deliberately blurred so that it would not be "easy to tell where pavements and walls left off and ground began" (*A* I, 173).

Wright pictured Taliesin as "a home where icicles by invitation might beautify the eaves" and "prismatic crystals in pendants sometimes six feet long, glittered between the landscape and the eyes inside." The connections were to be more than just visual and involve all the senses. "In spring," he noted, "the perfume of the blossoms came full through the windows, the birds singing then, the while." And because almost all the ceilings were simply the exposed undersides of the roofs, the bird songs would be accompanied by "the sweeping, soft air of the rain" heard as a "music on the roofs." Finally, when weather permitted, Taliesin would "open to the breezes of summer and become like an open camp," reducing even further the barriers between inside and outside (*A* I, 176).

The stone floors and piers continued uninterrupted from the courtyard into the house and studio, relieved in the same manner and color as outside by sand plaster and wood trim. The twists and jogs of the plan turned the space into a latticework of light and shadow. Overhead, the effect of dappled light coming through clerestories set between the angles of the roofs reinforced the sensation of walking along a country path or stopping to rest in the shade of some trees. Wright intended Taliesin to be "a natural house, not natural as caves and log-cabins were natural but native in spirit and making." "I wished to be part of my beloved Wisconsin," he wrote, "and not put my small part of it out of countenance" (*A* I, 171). The name of the Welsh poet Taliesin, as already noted, means "radiant" or "shining brow," literally referring to his forehead. In designing Taliesin as an outlook and conceiving the house as the "brow," or forehead, of the hill "rising unbroken above to [its] crown" (*A* I, 173), Wright made nature both the subject and object of its architecture. With Taliesin, nature as an expression of the self became the content, not just the context, of his work.

The Figure of Taliesin

The experience of nature in Taliesin is complex. One is not merely afforded views of the world beyond; one's gaze is always directed back to the center, the internal focus of the hill crown (fig. 87). There, at the edge of the steps leading up to the grove of oak trees encircled by the stone seat, stands the *Flower in the Crannied Wall*. In its twofold aspect, the statue induces us to reflect upon the dyadic character of the relation between building and landscape. The female figure's gaze is absorptive and engrosses ours (fig. 37).[47] In this transference of insight, we become increasingly aware of the representational dimensions of the site.

The name Wright chose for the house signals that he meant it to have a more than literal connection to the landscape and to figure, or represent, something special about the site and his relation to it.[48] Taliesin has both a literal and a figurative meaning, which in itself immediately suggests that the building can be read on more than one level. As Wright explained in his *Autobiography*, "literally the Welsh word means 'shining brow'" and therefore describes the external appearance of the house on its hill. But he was just as quick to point out that "many legends cling to the name in Wales" (*A* I, 170). Indeed, there is good evidence that he was not even thinking of the English meaning of the Welsh word when he first named the house but was only referring to the poetic figure of Taliesin.[49]

As the name of the chief bard and archetypal poet-prophet of Wales, Taliesin signified the inspired nature of the poet through the radiance of his "shining brow." "There was the legend of Taliesin, the primeval artist with the shining brow!" Wright later wrote, so "why not a 'shining brow' for the hill?" Wright obviously relished the *double entendre*, with its conflation of nature and myth, figure and landscape, and building and personage. "Taliesin was an ancient bard, in Wales, who sang the glories of Fine Art," Wright began his first article about the building, "but he is now a house in Wisconsin."[50] The references to nature in the house were thus filtered through the figure and legend of Taliesin.

In fact, there were two Taliesins: the historical figure who lived in the latter part of the sixth century, and the folk hero mythicized out of him.[51] The historical Taliesin began his bardic career in the service of Cynan Garwyn, Lord of Powys. Early on, he left his homeland to become the court poet of Urien Rheged and his son Elphin. It was in the kingdom of Rheged, singing the praises of his adopted masters, that he achieved his greatest renown. Taliesin's songs and poems are preserved in the "Book of Taliesin," a thirteenth-century manuscript that was first published by W. F. Skene in 1868 and then in a facsimile edition by J. Gwenogvryn Evans in 1910, the year of Wright's trip to Europe, followed by an English translation five years later.[52] Interspersed with the elegies, eulogies, and prophecies considered to be authentic records of the historical Taliesin are other poems describing his magical transformations from one natural shape to another. In "The Festival," Taliesin declares to his competitors and audience:

I have been a blue salmon,
I have been a dog, a stag, a roebuck on the mountain,
A stock, a spade, an axe in the hand,
A stallion, a bull, a buck,
A grain which grew on the hill,
I was reaped and placed in an oven,
I fell to the ground when I was being roasted
And a hen swallowed me.
For nine nights I was in her crop.
I have been dead, I have been alive,
I am Taliesin.[53]

In the celebrated song of "The Battle of the Trees," Taliesin attributes his divinatory and shape-shifting powers to his primordial, supernatural origin:

Not from a mother and father was I made;
As for creation, I was created from the nine forms of
  elements:
From the fruit of fruits, from the fruit of God at the
  beginning;
From primroses and flowers of the hill, from the blooms of
  woods and trees;
From the essence of soils was I made,
From the bloom of nettles, from water of the ninth
  wave.[54]

The legendary Taliesin, the primeval poet who could tap the very source of divine wisdom and knowledge through his art, became the hero of the Hanes Taliesin, the folktale or fairy tale of Taliesin, which dates back at least to the late Middle Ages. It was translated by Lady Charlotte Guest in her publication of *The Mabinogion* (1838–49) and further popularized by the one-volume edition of that highly acclaimed work that appeared in 1877 (when Wright was ten years old). Guest's translation formed the basis for the well-known versions in Bulfinch's *Mythology* (*The Age of Chivalry*, 1858) and Sidney Lanier's *Knightly Legends of Wales; or, The Boy's Mabinogion* (1881). Intended for children (and it would have been as a child that Wright first heard the tale), the story recounts how Taliesin was reborn as an artist through the inspiration of nature and explains his various metamorphoses as the means he used to flee his homeland in order to practice his art.[55]

The story is set in the time of King Arthur. A witch called Ceridwen, who is both the Goddess of Nature (the "White Goddess" in Robert Graves's phrase) and the Poetic Muse, has a son named Afagddu, who is the ugliest young man alive.[56] To provide him with the gifts of beauty and knowledge, she prepares a brew of herbs and plants and orders a blind man named Morda and a youth named Gwion

Bach to watch over the Cauldron of Inspiration and Knowledge and keep it boiling for a year and a day (fig. 90). But while she was away "culling plants and making incantations," three drops containing "the grace of Inspiration" splashed onto Gwion Bach's fingers. He put them into his mouth, "and when he swallowed them he became the greatest sage on earth, knowing everything, past, present and future."[57]

Immediately realizing that when Ceridwen returned she would pursue him with vengeance, Gwion Bach fled for his life. Fully aware of her cunning, he transformed himself into a hare. But she became a greyhound and chased him to the river. He jumped in and swam away in the form of a fish; Ceridwen continued the chase as an otter. He took to the air as a bird; she pursued in the form of a hawk. Just when she was about to swoop down upon him, "he espied a heap of winnowed wheat on the floor of a barn . . . and turned himself into one of the grains." She then metamorphosed into a black hen and swallowed him, keeping him in her womb for nine months.

When the hen/Ceridwen finally delivered him and saw how beautiful he was, she could not bear the thought of killing him. So she placed him in a coracle, or skin bag, and threw it into the sea. After some time (forty years according to certain versions), the bag made its way along the coast into the fishing weir of the lord Gwdyddno Garanhir, whose son Elphin had been granted the catch of salmon as a gift from his father. When Prince Elphin saw only the bag and no fish, he was greatly dismayed—until his servant opened the bag and revealed the brilliant forehead of a boy. "Behold a radiant brow!" cried the servant. Elphin declared: "Taliesin be he called."[58]

Taliesin soon proved himself more valuable than any catch of fish. He became Elphin's bard, bringing great power and riches to his master. Through his poetic, magical, and divinatory powers, he established himself as the chief bard of the kingdom of Gwynned. When the king asked Taliesin where he came from, the bard responded:

I was revealed in the land of the Trinity;
And I was moved through the entire universe;
And I shall remain till doomsday, upon the face of the
*   earth.*
And no one knows what my flesh is—whether meat or fish.

And I was nearly nine months in the womb of the witch
*   Ceridwen;*
I was formerly Gwion Bach, but now I am Taliesin.[59]

Taliesin's identity ultimately remains a mystery, for it is bound up in the riddles that form the basis of his art. In describing the wind, he told his audience:

It is in the field, it is in the wood,
Without hand, and without foot,
Without signs of old age,
Though it be co-aeval
With the five ages or periods;

.   .   .   .

It is also so wide;
As the surface of the earth;
And it was not born,
Nor was it seen.[60]

In his various manifestations, Taliesin is himself a riddle. The legendary Taliesin thus poses the riddle of art. Nature is the source of inspiration and knowledge, symbolized by the vessel, or cauldron, from which Taliesin's shape-shifting powers derived. Although art is an illusion, a mysterious form of creation, it gains its power over the mind from the imitation of nature. Just as Taliesin transformed himself from a hare to a fish to a grain of wheat, the artist creates his images by means of representation. Taliesin warned the other bards contesting his place that it was not enough to know the technique of rhyming. The true artist must "know" more, for he re-creates the world in images by giving them a name; and to do that the artist had to know "the name of the firmament, / And the name of the element, / And the name of the language, / And the name of your district."[61]

Wright's choice of the name "Taliesin" for his house suggests his understanding of the meaning of the legend as a metaphor for the riddle of art and nature. Wright had come to believe, as he wrote in his Wasmuth introduction less than a year before, that there is a profound connection between architecture and folklore. Buildings that "fitted into the environment . . . with native feeling" were "buildings that grew as folk-lore and folk-song grew." Folktales revealed the "source of inspiration."[62] The tale of Taliesin told of the regenerative power of nature—how the artist might be given such new life by it as to become a new person with a new name (Taliesin instead of Gwion Bach). It then described, through the image of exile, how the work of art, as an imitation of nature, may become indistinguishable from the artist himself, so that the act of representation is perceived as the creative act.

The legend of Taliesin expressed Wright's vision of the rebirth of his own art and life in exile through renewed contact with nature, and it allowed him to suggest the breadth of that vision and to represent it in mythical terms. Taliesin personified Wright's quest for an expression of the elemental basis of architecture and became Wright's alter ego. Wright "dedicated" his house to the bard, as he said, so that "Taliesin might come alive again." Wright thereby added his own transformation to the riddle of Taliesin: "Taliesin was an ancient bard, in Wales. . . . But he is now a house in Wisconsin"; "Taliesin was a story and therefore had to run the gauntlet"; "But Taliesin lived where I stood. So I believed"; "Taliesin, voluntary exile, in his shining brow declares. . . ."[63]

Taliesin as the First "Natural House"

Wright was always as adamant about preserving the integrity of architecture and its independence from the other arts as he was about following the example of nature. Although he considered music "a sympathetic friend . . . from which he need not fear to draw," literature and painting were evil influences. Wright believed from his earliest reading of Victor Hugo that modern architecture was "cursed by literature."[64] This feeling of combativeness toward the other "arts of imitation" eventuated in his later defense of "organic" architecture over the two-dimensional "picturizing" of the International Style. The theory of mimesis, which was first set forth in Plato's *Republic* in reference to poetry, was most easily transferred by analogy to painting and sculpture. To name his own house and place of business after the literary figure of a poet was thus to underscore his awareness of the indebtedness of his architecture not to literature as such but to the theory of representation that ultimately derived from it.

In the context of Wright's career, Taliesin must be understood as a reaction to the problems posed by the increased role of abstraction in his architecture of the previous decade. Taliesin is an investigation of the ways in which architecture could substantiate a more direct form of representation. As a work of such an experimental—one might almost say hypothetical—order, it should be read as a meditation on nature represented in the terms of architecture. It was and would remain—with constant addition, elaboration, redesign, and alteration—the only real sketchbook Wright ever kept, an ever-changing record of his architectural response to nature and the surrounding landscape.[65]

Although his work between about 1905 and 1909 seemed to lead toward an art of pure abstraction, Wright, like Picasso at about the same time, refused to accept certain formal consequences of Analytic Cubism. Both artists rejected abstraction as such in favor of a renewed emphasis on the role of representation. Two very revealing pieces of evidence support this interpretation of Wright's development and point to close links with Picasso's move toward Synthetic Cubism.

In 1912, shortly after Taliesin was designed and while the final details of planning and construction were being overseen by him, Wright wrote a short book. Ostensibly devoted to Japanese pictorial art, but in effect a theoretical essay on the role of representation in the plastic arts, *The Japanese Print: An Interpretation* remains Wright's most cogent discussion of the mimetic theory of art.[66] Basing his interpretation on Plato's conception of "the 'eternal idea of the thing,'" Wright sought the meaning of all art in the conventionalization of nature through the judicious and sensitive use of geometry. Geometry, he noted, allowed the artist "to seize upon essentials" and give to the image of a natural form "that inner harmony which penetrates the outward form or letter, and is its determining character." To imitate nature by "right aesthetic conventionalization," Wright concluded, was the highest aspiration of art. Through the process of expressing the ideal nature of a thing—the oakness of an oak tree, or the acanthusness of an acanthus leaf—the artist reveals the essential "life-principle" of his culture.[67]

The other indication of Wright's intense concern about revising and redefining his earlier thoughts on the concept of "conventionalization" can be seen in his reuse of the *Flower in the Crannied Wall* to define the pivotal spot of his hillside dwelling. Instead of appearing, as in the Dana House, framed by an arch on the central axis of the skylit entrance hall, the figure at Taliesin is placed out in the open, at the edge of the drive, up against the hill slope (figs. 35, 87). Like a classical term at the base of the steps leading to a sacred grove of oak trees on the hill, combining references to both the Mediterranean and the Druidic worlds, the statue occupied the very center of the courtyard, halfway down the drive.[68] Facing the porte-cochere, it appeared to the visitor as the first sign of inhabitation of the site (fig. 82; this photograph was used by Wright as the frontispiece for the initial publication of Taliesin, in *Architectural Record* in January 1913[69]). Transplanted, as it were, "root and all" from a sheltered domestic environment, the image embodying Wright's conception of architecture as an ideal balance of abstraction and representation was released from its preexisting framework of conventional typological references to take its place directly in apposition to nature.

In Taliesin, the sculptured figure appears to grow out of the hillside. It no longer points to a distinction between geometry and nature, or abstraction and representation, as it did in the Dana House, but rather signifies a continuity or identity of the two. Rising from a low stone wall along the edge of the hill garden, the *Flower in the Crannied Wall* occupied the point where nature and architecture come together—the juncture of the natural and the man-made—with the hillside "rising unbroken above to crown the exuberance of life" and the house growing like a ledge beneath it (*A* I, 173). The two aspects of the sculpture, its naturalistic figure and its abstract tower, now find their direct referents in the juxtaposition of landscape and building.

In its reincarnation in Taliesin, the *Flower in the Crannied Wall* takes on a more definite figurative meaning as it literally embodies the spirit of the place. The generalized personification of Tennyson's poem becomes, as Thomas Beeby has convincingly shown, the goddess of nature Ceridwen.[70] As the poetic muse of the legend, she made the bard Taliesin from the youth Gwion Bach. She oversaw his various transformations until finally reconceiving him with the mark of a "shining brow." At the edge of the hillside embraced by the buildings of Taliesin, the *Flower in the Crannied Wall*, as the goddess of nature Ceridwen, mediates between the worlds of nature and man and represents, both literally and figuratively, the direct transformation of the one into the other.

Wright described Taliesin as the first "natural house," thereby distinguishing it categorically from the Prairie

House (*A* I, 171). In its architecture, he believed, he had achieved an equivalence for nature. Although the actual forms of the hip roofs, freestanding piers, and paneled planes remind us to some degree of his earlier work, Wright transfigured the conventional models by reworking the forms so as to represent directly, through the abstract means of wood, stone, and plaster, the very appearance of nature. As he explained,

Taliesin was to be a combination of stone and wood as they met in the aspect of the hills around about. The lines of the hills were the lines of the roofs. The slopes of the hills their slopes, the plastered surfaces of the light wood-walls, set back into shade beneath broad eaves, were like the flat stretches of sand in the river below and the same in color, for that is where the material that covered them came from.

The finished wood outside was the color of gray tree-trunks, in violet light.

The shingles of the roof surfaces were left to weather, silver-gray like the tree branches spreading below them. (*A* I, 174)[71]

Wright wanted the house literally to look like part of the hillside, to "belong to that hill, as trees and the rock ledges did" (*A* I, 171). Unlike the Prairie House, which was to serve as a "foil" for the surrounding landscape, Taliesin was to be an extrusion of its site. The relation with nature was no longer one of analogy, mediated by historically determined conventions of type, but one of homology, articulated by continuities of structure and surface.

The horizontal lines and low-slung forms of the Prairie House paralleled the lines and forms of the prairie, but the representational elements of the house type predominated. The image was bounded by the conventions of base, pier, and roof. The result was always a house *on* the prairie or, more precisely, "in a prairie town." In the Prairie House, the word "prairie" qualified the word "house." The house never lost its identity as a figure abstracted from its ground. In Taliesin, Wright worked to the opposite end. The house was to be "part" of the "countenance" of the landscape first, and

a house second. It was to be seen not as something added to the landscape but as an integral part of it. Nature—the hill—came first, and was modified to become a house.

A major difference from the Prairie House involved a change in the scale of representation. This was achieved through a completely new relation between material and image, which parallels Picasso's development of Synthetic Cubism in painting. What had been limited to the scale of the part in the more literally naturalistic aspects of the Prairie House was now expanded to the shape of the whole. What had more often than not been a matter of decoration now became an issue of construction.[72] In order to ensure an illusion of continuity between figure and ground, Wright made the skin of the house, so to speak, look like the skin of the surrounding landscape (fig. 81). He said that he "scanned the hills of the region where the rock came cropping out in strata to suggest buildings" and took the appearance of these "outcropping ledges in the facades of the hills" as the model for the stonework of the house. He specifically directed the masons to imitate the "pattern" of the rough ledges exposed in the quarry on the hill just to the northwest (*A* I, 173).[73] Banding the face of the hill in a series of horizontal layers, Taliesin thus formed the image of a natural outcrop (fig. 91).

The illusion of continuity with nature is only an illusion, however, and this must be kept in mind when as-

92. Antoni Gaudí: Parc Güell, Barcelona, 1900–14. Entrance pavilion.

93. H. H. Richardson: Ames Gate Lodge, North Easton, Mass., 1880–81.

Hoenderloo (1914–20), for instance, Taliesin is neither cute nor *gemütlich*; nor does it rely on sentimental attachment to a local vernacular or "national" style. Compared to the literalness of organic expression in Gaudì's Parc Güell (1900–14; fig. 92), where one expects to be attacked by gnomes or fairies at any moment, Taliesin is totally inert and abstract.

Perhaps the most telling comparison is with Richardson's Ames Gate Lodge at North Easton, Massachusetts (1880–81; fig. 93). There, Richardson mounded up small boulders and rocks to create a great rubble construction that gives the appearance of the abode of a strange, antediluvian creature. The texture, which overrides and contradicts the tectonic structure of the building, produces a decorative surface that looks almost as if it had been piled up by the monster that presumably still creeps around within. The Ames Gate Lodge is primitivistic in a Mannerist sense, going back at least to Giulio Romano, and stays safely within the confines of a rustic mode.

The naturalism and primitivism of Taliesin are of another order, and a completely modern one at that. The relation between figure and ground that previously had been transmitted through conventional forms and signs is now conveyed directly through the abstract shapes of the materials themselves. This abstraction has to do with a progressive distinction between form and content, a disengagement of

sessing both the significance and the modernity of Taliesin. Taliesin does not actually look like a rock outcrop, nor did Wright ever intend such a narrowly realistic reading. Although one can trace the romantic naturalism of Wright's thought back to Ruskin, there is absolutely nothing descriptive or illustrative about the physical fabric of the building. There are no naturalistic details, carefully wrought to bring out their individual color and charm. Quite the contrary: Taliesin is stony hard. Nor does Wright's naturalism seem to have anything in common with late nineteenth-century tendencies toward primitivism, as expressed in the work of H. H. Richardson, Antoni Gaudì, Bernard Maybeck, and H. P. Berlage. Unlike Maybeck's multimedia houses in the Bay Area, or Berlage's St. Hubertus Hunting Lodge at the shapes taken by the materials from their traditional representational contexts. In the examples of Gaudí, Berlage, and Maybeck, or even Wright's earlier work, the materials compose or form the particular elements of the design; and no matter how much they are highlighted or emphasized, they always remain neutral or transparent as regards content. Their job is to support and give a figure to the image.[74]

In Taliesin, by contrast, the piers and parapets of stone, the planes of plaster, and the lines of shingled roof are experienced primarily as disembodied material presences, shapes disengaged from any figurative role (fig. 81). They are, in that regard, much like the shapes Picasso was using in his contemporaneous collages and Synthetic Cubist paintings, shapes completely abstract in outline yet often either cut out of real materials like wallpaper or oilcloth, or painted to imitate their textures and designs in the most literal way (fig. 94). As these discrete shapes are synthesized into the image of a person or thing on the plane of the supporting canvas, Picasso's revolutionary method of collage, especially as translated into Synthetic Cubism, proposed the possibility for representation outside the limits of traditional illusionism. Similarly, in Taliesin, the stone laid up in strata on the pattern of the surrounding outcrops, by virtue of its own material reality as shape, forces us to read the building, as a whole, as a natural extension of the hillside. Paradoxically, the denial of the traditional transparency of the material (or object), characteristic of Renaissance and post-Renaissance art, makes the representation contiguous with its physical ground and therefore convincingly readable as a single Gestalt.

Wright wanted to extend the representational possibilities of architecture beyond the bounds of the object in order to make its presence felt in the world. In expanding the role of representation from an almost exclusive attention to the part to a focus on the whole, and in switching the emphasis from the figure itself to the relation of figure to ground, Wright made Taliesin a function of its natural context. From this perspective, building for Wright would thenceforth be a means for modifying nature and no longer an

object qualified by it. Although Wright's conception of a "natural" architecture turned on a belief in the mythic significance of the natural forms of the landscape that seemed to run counter to the evolving structure of modern thought, it was his work at Taliesin that most emphatically established the idea that the creation of a sense of place would be a fundamental criterion of authenticity and meaning in twentieth-century architecture.

Taliesin as Self-Representation

Wright's assertion of nature as the only model for Taliesin expressed, as boldly as any reference to the machine or technology, the modern myth of making architecture outside of history. Wright believed his work could "safely abandon forms . . . held through habit or tradition" because "it

[went] to the roots."[75] This meant, of course, that the synthesis of the past took place in the activity of the self. As romantic as Wright was, he was also enough of a realist to understand that the meaning of his work derived from a purely personal interpretation of nature. In the secularized and industrialized world of the twentieth century, the credibility or authenticity of such a vision could be realized only in autobiographical terms. The sense of place that gives Taliesin its aura of enchantment depends on a reverence for the landscape that was inextricably linked to its identification with Wright's own being.

"Taliesin lived where I stood. So I believed," wrote Wright. As the *Flower in the Crannied Wall* would immediately suggest to the visitor on entering its precinct, Taliesin was charged with an anthropomorphic significance that substantiates the meaning of its representational character. As much as it was intended to be a natural part of the landscape—"a 'shining brow' for the hill"—Taliesin was conceived as an embodiment of "the primeval artist with the shining brow," the legendary poet who had "come alive again."[76] When the building was completed, Wright said that "its countenance beamed, wore a happy smile of well-being and welcome for all" (*A* I, 176). Describing the building as a person in disguise, Wright noted how "the living things of Art and Beauty belonging to the place—become like Taliesin's own flesh."[77] And when reporters came to sniff out stories about the "immoral" ménage of Wright and his "soulmate," he noted how "Taliesin raged, wanted to talk back—and smiled. . . . It made its way through storm and stress, threats and slanderous curiosity to its happiness for more than three years and smiled—always" (*A* I, 177).

Taliesin was, in effect, Wright's alter ego. His friend Richard Bock called it a "self-portrait."[78] It was the persona Wright fashioned for himself to perpetuate the "unconventional life" of self-imposed exile. But that was only half the story. Much of Wright's inspiration for this career change came from Mamah Borthwick, and Taliesin was built to celebrate their unconventional union. If Taliesin was Wright's

alter ego, the hill it was designed to consort with was its female companion. As much as he identified himself with the house, Wright identified Borthwick with the hill, the two so closely knit that "hill and house could live together each the happier for the other" (*A* I, 170, 171). Newspaper stories based on interviews with Wright referred to Borthwick as "Mamah of the Hills."[79] "Her Life," Wright said, was "built into the house" (*A* I, 168).

During the year they spent abroad, Wright and Borthwick had become deeply interested in the "free love" philosophy of the Swedish feminist Ellen Key, who maintained that relations between the sexes should not be bound by rules of convention and that marriage should be solely a matter of natural affinity. Wright's vision of Taliesin was of such a marriage, a union between male and female partners consecrated not by legal convention but rather by the "higher" law of nature. He described Taliesin as "a house that hill might marry and live happily with ever after," deliberately phrasing the remark in the idiom of the fairy tale to which the house was "dedicated" (*A* I, 171).

The architectural reference to an amorous union with very clearly implied sexual overtones immediately recalls the earlier Romeo and Juliet Tower (fig. 77). In that structure, which can be seen from Taliesin as a landmark in the valley, the sharp-edged, diamond-shaped upright penetrates and is engulfed by the swelling octagonal volume that supports it. "For the life of this harmoniously contrasting pair," as Wright put it, "Romeo . . . will do all the work and Juliet cuddle alongside to support and exalt him." In Taliesin, Wright inverted the relation between male and female to make the hill more than just a passive support.[80] Soft and rounded, it rises up through the hard, angular forms of the embracing house to stand out as a kind of *mons Veneris*, revealing the dependence of Taliesin's work on nature and Wright's future "realization" of that on collaboration with his "faithful comrade" Borthwick. (*A* I, 168). House and hill were to complement each another, together creating a much larger whole. In this sense, then, the statue of the *Flower in the Crannied Wall*, itself a product of the intersection of female and male elements, represents the tutelary deity of the site as it indicates the very spot where hill and house come together (fig. 70).

Taliesin was to be more than just a symbol of union. It was built around the ideal of a collaborative life that Wright and Borthwick had already embarked on while living in Fiesole. With Borthwick's background in literature and skill at languages, they together translated Goethe. "A Hymn to Nature," one of the results of this collaboration, was featured in the first volume of the *Little Review*, published by their friend Margaret Anderson in early 1915. They also worked on translations of Key's writings, jointly publishing her *Love and Ethics* in 1912. A translation of *The Morality of Woman and Other Essays* appeared under Borthwick's name alone in 1911, followed by *The Woman Movement* and *The Torpedo under the Ark: "Ibsen and Women"* (both in 1912) and an article on "Romain Rolland" in the *Little Review* in 1915.[81] Furthermore, as Wright's son John recalled, collaboration at Taliesin was a two-way street. When Wright was away on a job, Borthwick "took charge of the drafting room during his absence."[82]

■ ■ ■

The establishment of Taliesin and the rejuvenation of Wright's career coincided with the full flowering of the Chicago Renaissance. This burst of intellectual excitement in literature, the theater, and the other arts centered around Floyd Dell, who became editor of the *Friday Literary Review* in 1911; Maurice Browne and Ellen Van Volkenburg, who started the Chicago Little Theater in 1912; Harriet Monroe, whose *Poetry* magazine was founded the same year; Francis Fisher Browne, who published *The Dial*; Ralph Fletcher Seymour, the publisher; and Margaret Anderson, whose *Little Review* first appeared in 1915. Theodore Dreiser returned to Chicago at this time to do research for his novel *The Titan* (1912); Carl Sandburg and Sherwood

Anderson began their literary careers; and the Armory show, originally seen in New York, exposed the Midwest to the most recent advances in European painting and sculpture (1913).

Wright and Borthwick were friendly with many of the leading figures in the Chicago Renaissance. They contributed both money and articles to Anderson's *Little Review*, and Ralph Fletcher Seymour published their translations of Key's work.[83] As Chicago emerged from its regional and provincial status to become a national and even international center for the arts and literature, Wright and his architecture seemed poised to ride the crest of the wave. Moreover, the Prairie School was receiving serious attention from large-scale developers, commercial interests, and government clients.

Although Wright continued to receive more commissions for private houses than other types of work, the balance now began to shift perceptibly. In 1911, he designed and began construction of a large pavilion for Banff National Park in Canada, as well as an important hotel in Lake Geneva, Wisconsin. He also designed a hotel for downtown Madison and a Catholic church for suburban Zion, Illinois, before beginning the project for his first real skyscraper, the twenty-two-story San Francisco Call Building, commissioned by the Spreckels real estate interests around 1913 for a prominent site downtown. In the same year came the two most important jobs of this period: Midway Gardens, built on Chicago's South Side in 1913–14; and, following a trip to Japan with Borthwick in early 1913, the commission to build Tokyo's Imperial Hotel (fig. 98). At the same time, Wright embarked on projects for a Carnegie library in Ontario (1913), a bank in Spring Green (1914), and the United States Embassy in Tokyo (1914).

Even before the commissions for Tokyo and Midway Gardens came in, Wright felt confident enough to plan for the expansion of the office and drafting room section of Taliesin. A large, two-story addition was designed to project beyond the workroom on the northeast (see figs. 80, 84).[84]

He also included a dormitory wing to provide lodging and dining space for an increased number of draftsmen. This section, not actually built until the 1920s, was to be perpendicular to the stable wing, just beyond the tower and milk room.

All of the large-scale public buildings produced in the early years of Taliesin were very different from Taliesin itself. The Imperial Hotel, Midway Gardens, the Carnegie library, and the Tokyo embassy were in fact the most formal and symmetrical designs Wright had done since the early Beaux-Arts scheme for the Milwaukee Library and Museum of twenty years before. It was as if these projects of an urban and public character naturally elicited a reaction against the freedom allowed for in what was ultimately a rural and very private retreat. Where the loose, open, and casual treatment of Taliesin was expressed through a use of natural materials imitating the appearance of stone, wood, and plaster in their raw state, the formal public buildings were overloaded with highly wrought schemes of decorative sculpture, indicating the representational character of the structures through the most elaborate form of architectural "cookery" Wright had yet indulged in.

The houses designed during this period, however, began to reflect more directly Wright's thinking about Taliesin. In the Angster House in Lake Bluff, Illinois (1911), and the second Little House, called "Northome," in Wayzata, Minnesota (1912–14), Wright adopted the casual planning of Taliesin, with its implicit diagonal geometry, to open up the interiors and give them a sense of direct contact with the outdoors. And in the unbuilt projects for the Cuttens in Downer's Grove, Illinois, and for Wright's lawyer Sherman Booth in Glencoe, Illinois (both undertaken in 1911), Wright divided the house, as in Taliesin, into discrete wings to allow the landscape to penetrate the building and make the building seem part of its natural surroundings (fig. 95). For the Booth House, which was sited on the edge of a ravine and designed at approximately the same time as Taliesin, Wright used bridges and causeways to connect the far-flung pavilions and interleave them with the various levels of the site in a way that almost predicts the organic quality of Fallingwater.[85]

Almost, that is, because the Booth House, like the others of this period, retains much of the formality of the Prairie House type as well as the abstract use of materials. In fact, most of the houses of these years are not so different from those that came before Taliesin. Obviously, a certain "enlightened" life-style, as well as a natural context to fit, were prerequisites for a real Taliesin. But the issue goes deeper. Taliesin was, for Wright, a very personal and radical experiment that could be applied only gradually to his work for others, a purpose he gave to the architect's own house that, from Schindler, Neutra, Gropius, and Johnson to Venturi, Moore, and Gehry, has become the norm for the modern architect in the United States.

It is therefore not surprising that the influence of Taliesin on Wright's other work should have been so slow to appear. What is surprising, however, is that the impact took nearly a quarter of a century to manifest itself fully, as it finally did in Fallingwater. This is especially curious because the Cutten and Booth houses, to take just two examples, already seemed to be heading in that direction. But something happened within less than three years of the completion of Taliesin that decisively changed the course of Wright's career. And that change was so sweeping, so profound, and so ineluctable that, from 1914 until well into the twenties, the rigid formality and symmetry of the public buildings such as Midway Gardens and the Imperial Hotel more or less dominated everything he did, domestic or otherwise.[86]

■ ■ ■

During the period following the construction of Taliesin, Wright rented an office in Chicago (first in the Fine Arts Building and then in Orchestra Hall) where he handled ordinary business matters. While supervising the building of

95. Booth House project, Glencoe, Ill., 1911–12. First scheme, 1911. Perspective.

Midway Gardens during the spring and summer of 1914, he generally spent a number of nights in Chicago at the apartment he kept on Cedar Street, leaving Borthwick, her children (when they were visiting her), and his draftsmen and other employees alone at Taliesin. Among the latter were Julian and Gertrude Carleton, Barbadian immigrants whom Wright had hired three months before to do the cooking, serving, and general housework. The husband, who was by all reports a morose and unstable paranoid, apparently believed he was being "jumped on" and hounded either by his employers or by one of the other employees.[87]

On 15 August 1914, while Wright was in Chicago, Julian Carleton took it into his head to exact revenge as he was serving the midday meal. Borthwick and her two young children, John and Martha, were sitting on the screened terrace off the living room overlooking the lake. Two draftsmen, Herbert Fritz and Emil Brodelle, Wright's carpenter

William Weston, his son Ernest, whom Wright had taken on as an apprentice, the Taliesin foreman Thomas Brunker, and the gardener David Lindbloom were gathered in the separate men's dining room located at the opposite end of the house, just behind the porte-cochere. After making sure that everyone was seated, Carleton locked the doors, poured gasoline around, and set the house ablaze. He then picked up a hatchet and ran to the screened terrace. Apparently aiming first for Borthwick, he "cleft the woman's skull with a clean blow"[88] before striking and killing her two children. After that he ran toward the locked men's dining room, set it alight, and hacked at the six others as they tried to escape.

In the end, the toll was seven dead, two wounded, and the entire living wing of Taliesin gutted by fire. Carleton himself was found later that evening, hiding in the basement furnace, where he had swallowed some muriatic acid that killed him before he could be brought to trial. Although rumors quickly spread that he was acting out of moral revulsion at Wright's sinful "lovenest," as local preachers and newspapers constantly referred to Taliesin, it was generally considered that he was simply insane.[89]

Wright was informed of the fire (though not of the murders) by telephone while at the Midway Gardens site. His son John, who was working with him, remembered how "suddenly all was quiet in the room, . . . then a groan. . . . He [Wright] clung to the table for support, his face ashen."[90] They took the train back to Spring Green, accompanied by Edwin Cheney, and only then learned of the murder of Borthwick and the others. Arriving in the evening to find "that devastating scene of horror," Wright was stunned beyond comprehension by the vision of the "charred and terrible ruin" and "its mortal sacrifice" (A I, 190, 192). He walked around in near shock. All that he then lived for, as he later wrote, had been swept away "in terror and in flames." "Tragedy suddenly destroyed that life forever," he said, "and left a black hole, the smoking crater of a volcano upon the hill where once Taliesin stood." The painful image of death and destruction remained in his mind as "a black gaping wound . . . where once Taliesin shone."[91]

In preparing to bury Borthwick the following day, Wright cut down the remains of the hill garden and filled the simple pine casket with "the flowers that had grown and bloomed for her" (A I, 189). Toward the end of the day, he, along with his son John and two nephews, transported the body to the graveyard next to the family chapel. More of the flowers were heaped upon the casket so that the whole looked like "a mass of flowers" when it was lowered into the grave. Wright remained alone to fill the hole as night fell. As he was waiting, he said he "felt, dimly, the far-off shadows of the ages, struggling to escape from subconsciousness and utter themselves . . . then—darkness" (A I, 189–90).

No marker or monument of any sort was placed over the grave, for Wright believed Borthwick's absence, like her former presence, was "forever" connected to the hill Taliesin had embraced: the "black hole in the hillside" was enough to reveal that "Mamah was gone" (A I, 191). In a eulogy he published a few days later in the local newspaper, Wright made it clear that only a "Taliesin the II" raised "from the ashes of Taliesin the first" would be a fitting remembrance, and he declared his intention to rebuild the house "for the spirit of the mortal that lived in it and loved it—and will live in it still."[92] To fix that continuity in space and time, Wright noted that he made one significant change from the original plan in the rebuilding that was completed in the following years: "Where scenes of horror had identified the structure with ugly memories," now "an open stone-floored loggia looked up the Valley to the Lloyd-Jones Chapel" (A I, 192). The loggia, which lies on the axis of the statue of the *Flower in the Crannied Wall*, opened up the view to allow the tutelary deity of the site to look directly down to the cemetery and thereby renew contact with the spirit of place that had given "Taliesin the first" its purpose in life (figs. 70, 75).[93]

That sentimental, symbolic gesture simply emphasizes the extent to which Wright translated personal devastation into architectural terms. The event was, in every sense of the word, traumatic. Wright later reported that he initially broke out in boils, had "continuous nausea," and lost a great deal of weight. He then began to think he was going blind. He had to get eyeglasses for the first time in his life and believed that he "might not be able to see at all." Once he realized he was not actually losing his eyesight, he understood that the problem was psychological: he claimed he "could see forward but . . . could not see backward." "All I had to show for the struggle for freedom of the past five years that had swept most of my former life away," he said, "had now been swept away." More than ever, he now identified himself with the void Taliesin had come to represent: "The gaping black hole left by fire in the beautiful hillside was no less empty, charred and ugly in my own life" (A I, 190–92).

In his *Autobiography*, Wright gave a gripping and revealing account of his state of mind in the days immediately following the event.

Those nights in the little back room were black, filled with strange unreasoning terrors. No moon seemed to shine. No stars in the sky. No frog-song from the pond below. Strange, unnatural silence, the smoke still rising from certain portions of the ruin.

Unable to sleep, I would get up, numb, take a cold bath to bring myself alive, go out alone on the hills in the night, not knowing where. But I would come safely back again with only a sense of black night and strange fear.

Then,

After the first anguish of loss, a kind of black despair seemed to paralyze my imagination in her direction and numbed my sensibilities. The blow was too severe. (A I, 190)

Finally,

as I looked back I saw the black hole in the hillside, the black night overall. And sinister shadows. Days strangely without light would follow the black nights. Totally— Mamah was gone. (A I, 191)

Dramatic and sensational as Wright's account may read, it clearly must be considered more seriously than most historians and critics have done. With the understanding that we are dealing as much with an event as with someone's interpretation of it, we may begin to explain some of the reasons for Wright's strange and apparently erratic development over the next two decades. For the lasting effect of the murder of Borthwick and the others was to turn Wright away from Taliesin and the poetic synthesis of architecture and nature he had tentatively achieved in it. He compared the event to a nightmare:

The fact remains—until many years after, to turn my thoughts backward to what had transpired in the life we lived together at Taliesin was like trying to see into a dark room in which terror lurked, strange shadows—moved— and I would do well to turn away. (A I, 191)

For most of the next two decades Wright did turn away from Taliesin, both figuratively and literally. Until the final years of the twenties, he did not even live there on anything like a continual basis. But the creation of Taliesin had irrevocably changed his idea of architecture, and everything he did after the fire was determined in one way or another by it. Taliesin removed Wright's architecture from any narrowly functionalist concern for typological expression. In opening up the hermetically sealed environment of the earlier Prairie Style buildings, Taliesin showed the way in which their spatial implications could be fulfilled in a larger and more profound synthesis of architecture and nature. In the directness of its representation of natural forms through the use of "raw" materials, Taliesin rejected the imperatives of a machine esthetic to concentrate more intensely and more immediately on the integration of man with his natural surroundings. And in establishing architecture as the authentic ground for this reintegration of man and nature, Taliesin revealed the extent to which myth, history, and symbol would ultimately have to be redefined in modern terms as part of a uniquely personal process of the creation, or rather, re-creation of a sense of place.

In time, Wright rebuilt Taliesin much as it was. (He even rebuilt it a second time after another, less tragic fire, in 1925.) And eventually its principles, and even its forms, would be applied to buildings as diverse as Fallingwater (fig. 196) and the Marin County Civic Center (fig. 396). Its siting in relation to the landscape, its direct reference to natural forms, its spatial continuity, its enchanted setting, its symbolic use of water and natural features of the landscape—all these became basic characteristics of Wright's later work.

But perhaps even more significant is the fact that Taliesin remained throughout Wright's life a personal story—a poetic narrative—as much as a house. He made many changes to Taliesin over the years, some functional, some merely cosmetic. But he always left the hill crown intact, or "undisturbed," as he more gently put it. He always thought of it as the center of the house, the object and the subject of

96. Taliesin. View from hill to living wing, with Ming Tub installed in mid-1950s.

its embrace, and he continually meditated on its mythological dimension. In time, he removed the statue of the *Flower in the Crannied Wall* from its prominent location at the base of the steps of the hill and placed it underground, at the entrance to the root cellar. The displacement of the tutelary deity, perhaps occasioned by its all too personal associations, left an ellipsis in the story Taliesin told. To fill that narrative void, Wright eventually placed an enormous ceramic pot on top of the hill, as if to signify the return of all things to their source (fig. 96).[94] Like the Cauldron of Inspiration and Knowledge in the tale of Taliesin, it serves as a metaphor for the origin of the poetic imagination. As a sym-

bol of nature's fertility and regenerating force, it remains a constant reminder of the legendary figure of the "shining brow" of Taliesin to which it gave birth in the first place—*in illo tempore*.

Few artists have suffered the kind of personal loss Wright did, nor have any perhaps equaled him in fulfilling the modern project of making the artist's persona and individual experience the very ground of authenticity. Tragedy authenticated the fictive history of the place and gave it a real history of its own. The final events in the story of Taliesin in turn historicized nature, providing a new temporal and psychological dimension to Wright's architecture. The affective and complex meanings of his later work are bound up in this. The story of Taliesin, as related in Wright's *Autobiography* and as dramatized by the site, provided the place of origin. A visit to Taliesin became a prerequisite to commissioning a design from Wright. Taliesin was a sign of Wright's creativity and a test of the client's commitment.[95] It stood for Wright and revealed what the client might expect. House and person, architect and legendary poet-hero, Taliesin described the ground where Wright's created self-image intersected the historical realities of his life to support and continually reconfigure, throughout that life at least, the sense of myth he believed could be restored to modern architecture.

97. Hollyhock (Barnsdall) House, Los Angeles, Calif., 1916?/18–21. West facade.

Building against Nature on the Pacific Rim

Wright's architecture in the years immediately following the murders and fire at Taliesin is arguably the most problematic of his career. Too often simply dismissed as an expression of withdrawal from a hostile world—a world in the throes of war—the work forces us, by its highly charged symbolism and overdetermined atavism, to appreciate the impact of biographical factors in the genesis of Wright's forms and ultimately to realize how fully he could make the subject of his own life the object of his art.

Two major projects of the period were always linked in Wright's mind with the holocaust at Taliesin. The building of the Imperial Hotel in Tokyo and the commission for the cultural center and Hollyhock House for Aline Barnsdall in Los Angeles came right after the fire and gave Wright the opportunity to distance himself, both literally and figuratively, from that traumatic event for nearly a decade (figs. 97, 102). Wright spoke of these two projects as a "relief," a

"refuge," and a "rescue" from Taliesin. (*A* I, 194–95). In them he sought to work through the meaning of the tragedy and to counteract its effects through a transference of the idea of a "natural architecture" onto the more remote plane of public, monumental expression.

The Imperial Hotel and Hollyhock House share a similar approach to planning and decoration. Both are grand, scenic compositions in the classical manner, treated with decorative exuberance and emblematic purpose. Both are extremely ambivalent in their respect for the machine and strangely defensive in their relation to their settings. Wright used the same terms to describe both of them, terms he had never used before. He hoped to create in these buildings a world of "romance," "poetry," "magic," and "mystery." They were to be "symphonic" and "epic" in scope and "romantic" in their expression of a sublimated "ideal" (*A* I, 212, 224–26, 229, 233).

More important, Wright approached the design of the two buildings in a way almost opposite to that of Taliesin. No longer conceiving an architecture at one with a benevolent landscape, he imagined the process of building as a confrontation with the violent and irrational forces of nature embodied in the unstable, seismic conditions of the Pacific Rim. "Building against doomsday," as he later put it, he returned, almost with a vengeance, to historical forms and conventional patterns, even recalling, as in Hollyhock House, the pyramidal, hieratic shapes of Precolumbian temples and sanctuaries.[1] Regressive and defensive by comparison with Taliesin, these buildings were designed against the background of Fujiyama, the volcanic "sacred mountain" that came to symbolize for Wright nature's inexorable force.

Imperial Hotel

The Imperial Hotel was different from Hollyhock House in one very important respect. Whereas the house for Aline Barnsdall and the cultural center to surround it were commissioned and designed after the fire, the Imperial Hotel had already been in the works.[2] Its relation to the fire is therefore more ambiguous and conflicted.

As Japan advanced in its program of modernization and Westernization under the Meiji dynasty, the idea of replacing the outmoded nineteenth-century hotel that served a central role in that process began to be discussed seriously in official circles in 1910. In the following year, Wright's friend Frederick W. Gookin, a Chicago banker and collector of Japanese prints who was in contact with Aisaku Hayashi, the new managing director of the hotel, recommended Wright for the job. Although it is now known that Hayashi had requested preliminary designs from the American-trained Japanese architect Kikutaro Shimoda, hotel authorities seem to have been less than enthusiastic about the design Shimoda proposed in early 1912.[3] By this time, Wright had begun corresponding with them. Following a six-month delay occasioned by the death of Emperor Meiji on 30 July, Wright went to Tokyo to meet Hayashi and discuss the matter further.

Wright spent the early part of 1913 in Tokyo with Borthwick. During this time he studied the site, acquainted himself with local building materials, and reviewed the program. He received provisional approval to proceed with the project and began the sketches that would eventually be developed into the preliminary plans drawn up at Taliesin upon his return and shown at the annual Chicago Architectural Club Exhibition in April 1914 (fig. 98). This, of course, was prior to the fire.[4] In the meantime, however, no doubt owing partly to the outbreak of world war and partly to political unrest following the death of the emperor, all proceedings relative to the hotel were put on hold.

It was only after the fire at Taliesin, and following the enthronement of the new emperor Taisho in November 1915, that Hayashi was directed to visit the United States to study modern American hotels more closely and to review Wright's plans. He spent part of February 1916 with Wright in Wisconsin, at which time he authorized him to develop and complete the plans.[5] By the end of the year the commission was official, and Wright left Taliesin to spend the winter of 1917 in Tokyo. This time he went with his new paramour, Miriam Noel, as well as his son John.[6] His objective was to gather the information necessary to turn the preliminary plans into a final project that could be translated into working drawings during the ensuing year. One problem, above all, obsessed him. Because the downtown site was a drained marsh in a highly earthquake-prone area, Wright paid particular attention to the structural issues involved in designing a building to withstand seismic tremors. The question of foundations became uppermost in his mind.[7]

The final stage of plans and working drawings was begun under Wright's direction back at Taliesin. It occupied him and his staff, including the Japanese architect Arato Endo, well into 1918. Construction was scheduled to begin in the fall (although it did not actually start until August 1919), and Wright left for Tokyo with Noel at the end of October 1918. Except for very brief yearly visits to the United States, he would remain in Japan for most of the next four years (for thirty-five out of forty-five months, to be exact). Living at the site, in the annex of the hotel he redesigned after a fire destroyed the original one in late 1919, Wright completed the final plans and supervised the construction. The north wing and part of the central section were opened to the public in July 1922, just before Wright's departure; the remaining south wing was opened the following November.[8]

Design and construction of the Imperial Hotel was a long and complicated affair. From beginning to end, it took nearly a decade. Originally conceived prior to the Taliesin fire, the hotel was almost completely replanned after that event. Although the basic idea of the composition developed in 1913–14 remained, Wright claimed that once he was in Japan "most of th[ose] plans . . . were thrown away." "Captured by Romance living in the life of a unique people, hoping to leave them my sense of themselves," he said that between 1917 and 1922 "a world in itself began to take shape in that transition building, created spontaneously" (*A* I, 224, 225). Having begun as a highly abstract and rational organization of architectural elements resulting in large part from functional considerations, the form of the hotel soon evoked a more profound sense of history and place.[9] It became a building that Wright believed would be a "not unworthy associate of the noble native buildings in view across the palace-moat, one that would stand there no less richly imaginative than their own buildings wherein the Old was in the New as the New was in the Old" (*A* I, 224–25). The

hotel was now, in his words, an "elemental romance" of architectural discourse "addressed to the Japanese people as an epic of their race."[10]

Wright's aggrandizement of the hotel into an "epic poem" of "the Japanese people" was a logical, if not wholly predictable, response to the nature of the commission. The Imperial Hotel was more than just a hotel. It was a government building of the highest representational order, one intended literally to *represent* Japan, in Japan, to the foreign visitor. The hotel was a joint venture of the Imperial Household and leading industrialists of the country. The first, European-style Imperial Hotel was built between 1888 and 1890—from plans originally submitted by the Berlin firm of Ende and Böckmann, as redesigned by Yuzuru Watanabe—to accommodate foreign guests as well as to provide a place for public receptions, various forms of entertainment, and private meetings involving state officials, local businessmen, and visitors. The centrally located downtown site, in the Hibiya government district, opposite Hibiya Park, looked diagonally across the moat to the grounds of the Imperial Palace. Wright's brief was to replace the older hotel, on the adjoining lot, with more modern and up-to-date accommodations to receive foreigners and to act as "a clearing house for Japan's social obligations to 'the foreigner.'"[11]

Wright immediately saw the hierarchical distinction between the two parts of the program and realized he was dealing not with "a hotel at all in the accepted sense of that term" but rather with "the social center of the life of the Japanese Capital."[12] The *parti* he adopted for his 1913–14 plan reflects the distinction between functional "hotel" and representational "social center," combining the two in a Beaux-Arts composition of a palatial type akin to the ancient Buddhist temple complexes and monasteries of Nara in its formal order and containment.[13] From the very beginning, Wright rendered the functional with a curious mixture of rational efficiency and ceremonial display—the old and the new, the modern and the traditional.

The oblong four-acre site faced Hibiya Park to the west and was hemmed in by dense downtown development

98. Imperial Hotel, Tokyo, 1913–23 (demolished). Preliminary perspective (1913–14).

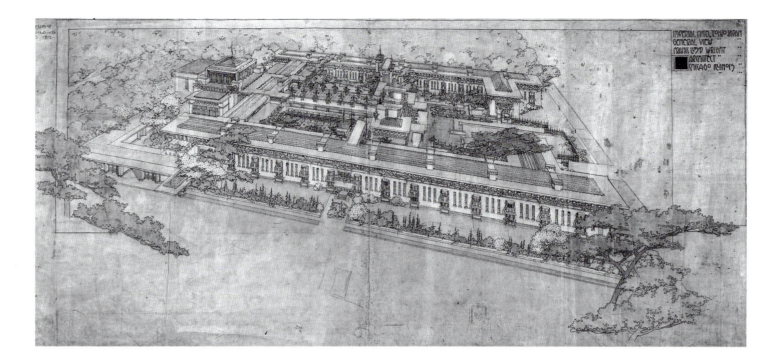

on the other three sides. Wright filled it with an open, H-shaped, courtyard plan (fig. 99). Two low, three-story wings containing the 285 guest rooms ran the five hundred foot length of the site along the two side streets, forming a barrier protecting the series of interior courtyards that gave access to and isolated the spine of public spaces. This central, processional sequence led from a low porte-cochere, entered at the rear of a forecourt defined by a large reflecting pool, through the main lobby and public dining room into a grouping of more monumental reception rooms that ultimately rose to a height of seven stories. The central section was connected to the outside wings by a double system of cross-axial circulation. At the lower end, open arcades and bridges connected the lobby to the guest bedrooms. At the upper end, a three hundred-foot-long, twenty-foot-wide promenade, or galleria, formed a link between the two wings while also serving as an entrance hall for the ground-floor cabaret-restaurant, the second-floor one thousand-seat theater, and the top-floor banquet hall, which occupied the crowning structure terminating the main axis and dominating the wings and courtyards below.

Although Wright believed that the design, "as a sys-

tem of gardens and sunken gardens and terraced gardens . . . and roofs that are gardens," was fundamentally Japanese in conception, the hierarchical distinction between the private "hotel" part and the public "social center" was drawn in a traditional Beaux-Arts manner. The lower, and much simpler, outside wings framed the composition and set off the taller, more elaborate central section, which Wright referred to as forming "a great building in itself."[14] In the final plans, this representational center, surrounded by terraced gardens, was given the shape of a Latin-cross church (fig. 100). In this way, Wright's plan for the Imperial Hotel recalled such well-known examples of Beaux-Arts planning as Julien Guadet's *grand prix* project of 1864 for a Hospice in the Alps (fig. 101). Indeed, just as Guadet gave his scheme a "character" suitable to a monastic establishment by treating it in a cisalpine Romanesque style, Wright gave a certain Oriental local color to his preliminary design by flaring the eaves of the roofs at the edges and mounting them in stages to create an overall pagoda-like effect.

More important than any superficial *japonismes* it might display, the rendering exhibited in Chicago in 1914 illustrates a competing and perhaps even more powerful

99. Imperial Hotel. Preliminary plan, ground floor (1913–14).

100. Imperial Hotel. Final plan, upper level, banquet hall.

101. Julien Guadet: Hospice in the Alps project, Ecole des Beaux-Arts, Grand Prix, 1864. Perspective.

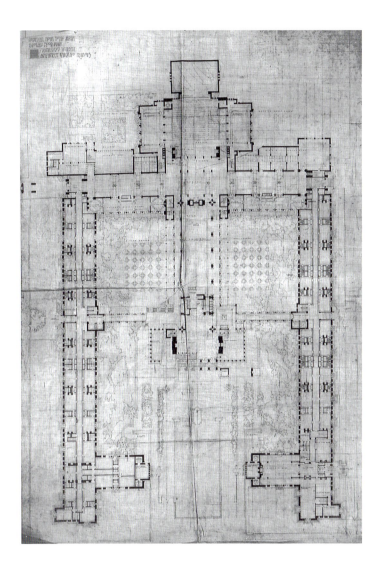

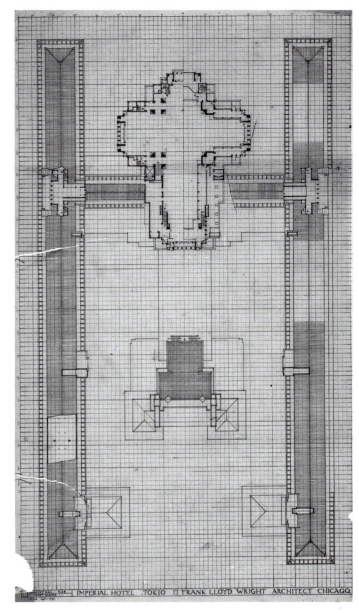

modern imagery underlying the design and controlling the plan. Instead of taking the perspective from the front of the building, as he usually did—and as he would later do for the final project of 1919—Wright drew the original design for the Imperial Hotel from the side.[15] This view not only downplays the classical nature of the plan but also forces one to see the building as a swift, efficiently designed, forward-moving object rather than as a static, symmetrical pattern.

Wright compared the Imperial Hotel to a modern "ocean liner" and indicated that this was his original concept for the building.[16] Although he believed that traditional Japanese wood construction had set an example for modern architecture in its precocious development of "modern standardizing," the "elimination . . . of the insignificant," and the "conservation of space and honest clean use of materials," Wright felt all that had been lost in Japan's recent history of industrialization and Westernization (*A* I, 196, 224). Furthermore, the hotel had to be built of masonry for fireproofing, and the Japanese had not yet, according to Wright, been able to translate into masonry the protomodern characteristics of the "ancient Japanese dwelling." Wright wanted the Imperial Hotel to set an example for the Japanese, in "masonry building," of the "conservation of space, energy and time by concentration and the invention of practical ways."[17] The modern ship illustrated how to do that:

The Imperial [Hotel] is the first great protest against the Gargantuan waste adopted by Japan from the old German precedents when there were no better ones. Since then the world has moved with incredible rapidity. Conservation of space by concentrated conveniences has gone far. The ship began it, the Pullman car took it up, the Ocean Liner went further and now the modern Hotel, on costly ground, is at work upon it.[18]

Wright's purpose was directed as much by moral concerns as it was by architectural ones. He believed that the efficient organization of space characteristic of the modern ocean liner should be adopted "for the sake of a better order." His minimal-sized, low-ceilinged guestrooms, in contrast to the grand public spaces, were offered as a "protest" against the Victorian, or rather Bismarckian, idea of a hotel, which he described as a collection of oversized and overstuffed rooms "in which to spread around a freight car load of baggage," where there was "an enormous upholstered platform, seven feet square, three feet above the floor—to sleep on," and where there was "boy San just outside the door day and night" in order to help "stall and feed and groom and bed that captious animal" known as "the average guest."[19]

This association between the Imperial Hotel and an ocean liner is quite different from Wright's earlier defense of the stripped-down, abstract quality of the Larkin Building as having "the same claim to consideration as a 'work of art' as an ocean liner, a locomotive or a battleship."[20] That claim issued from an esthetic point of view, not unlike Le Corbusier's "eyes which do not see" in his *Vers une architecture* of fifteen years later. On the contrary, the image of the Imperial Hotel as an ocean liner, rather than as a work of art, foreshadows the later functionalist criteria of Ernst May, Gropius, and others for the *existenzminimum* of a rationalized housing scheme based on the well-equipped ship's cabin—what Le Corbusier and Mies would refer to as a "floating apartment house."[21] Wright's conception of the Imperial Hotel grew out of the concern for creating an idea of community, "a world complete within itself."[22]

Wright's unusually small, efficiently designed guest rooms were arranged like cabins in a regular grid around the perimeter of the "floating hotel." The central well was given over to communal spaces running from the "bridge house" of the lobby across the "poop deck" over the dining room to the "raised quarter deck" of the cabaret, theater, and banquet hall. Wright thought that "in the New Imperial the quality of beauty and integrity of the whole is established by making each unit (albeit a smaller unit) an integral part of a great and harmonious whole." "That broader relationship," he went on to say, "affords a richer experience, a fuller life for each individual than could possibly be, where more license in more space would turn that individual loose at the expense of the whole." The "concentration of space" in the ocean liner, which Wright experienced firsthand each time he went back and forth to Tokyo, helped establish "the degree to which the human animal will submit to the larger and the finer interest."[23]

At the earliest stages of the project, then, the model of the ocean liner inflected the relatively traditional conception of the plan in the direction of functional astringency—without, however, any loss of the ceremonial qualities appropriate to a place of dining and entertaining under the

102. Imperial Hotel. Final perspective (1919–20).

Imperial aegis. The original design, with its thin, soaring roofs and elegant central pavilions, projects a lighthearted, joyful, even gay quality, much like the contemporaneous Midway Gardens. But that image changed by the time the building was built, to become a dour and ominously solemn mass of brick and lava stone.

If at the start Wright compared the hotel to a passenger ship, he soon began referring to it as a "battleship." As he studied the foundations in relation to the problem of earthquakes, he came to realize that "the ground in a serious quake . . . undulates like waves at sea." It was then, he said, that "the idea of building a super-dreadnought, flexible as a ship is flexible, floating it on the mud as a battleship floats on salt-water, gradually unfolded itself to me."[24] The shift from a luxurious and pleasurable ocean liner to a

dreadnought, the most up-to-date battleship in the world at the time, illustrates the change in conception after the fire at Taliesin.

As a battleship, the hotel took on the confrontational stance Wright projected in the powerful, nearly head-on perspective showing the final, more massive and ponderous design of 1919–20 (fig. 102).[25] The little pagoda-like roofs were eliminated; the batter of the lower walls was increased; and the banquet hall was raised to form a great central pyramidal mass gradually descending over the lower buildings on all sides. Reinforcing the confrontational nature of the structure were two pairs of sculptured warriors designed to stand in the forecourt, flanking the pool and porte-cochere (fig. 103). The conjunction of the square-jawed *Vikings* and slant-eyed *Samurai* may have been

103. Imperial Hotel. Entrance, with pool and Viking sculpture (before April 1923).

intended to symbolize the willingness of Japan to join forces with the Allies in World War I. Yet their placement at the entrance, directly opposite one another, presented an oddly bellicose introduction to the "social center" where East was to greet West and where both were to communicate on a new common ground.[26]

The militaristic imagery and confrontational nature of the final design arose from several not unrelated factors. To some extent, conflict was built into the project from the outset. Wright had a vision, perhaps somewhat patronizing at the beginning, of his architecture operating in the middle ground between "old" and "new," East and West. "The New Imperial Hotel is not an American building in Tokio any more than was inevitable in the circumstances." "It is not a Japanese building" either, he said, "nor [was it] intended to be an Oriental building." It was to be "a building that respects Oriental tradition, at the same time that it keeps its own individuality as a sympathetic friend on Japanese soil." His "mission," as he put it, was "to assist Japan to her own architectural feet, to help find an equivalent for her ancient supremacy in Art."[27] This meant showing the

Japanese how to reinterpret their own traditions, in masonry construction, to satisfy modern needs, "in short, . . . to help Japan make the transition from wood to masonry and from her knees to her feet without too great loss of her own great accomplishments in civilization" (A I, 225).[28]

Wright soon realized, however, that he had grievously misjudged the situation. The modern industrial methods of construction, and organization of labor that underlay his design had almost nothing to do with Japanese traditions and methods of handicraft production. Once having understood this, Wright said he "tried faithfully—sometimes frantically and often profanely—to teach them how to build it, half-way between our way and their way." But finally, "instead of wasting them by vainly trying to make them come our way—we went with them their way. I modified many original intentions to make the most of what, I now saw was naturally theirs." Only then did "the countenance of the building . . . emerge from the seemingly hopeless confusion" (A I, 217).[29]

The complex profiles and decorative elaboration, especially along the rooflines and in the ceiling supports, would provide a masonry analogue for traditional timber framing and bracketing. But beyond the matter of detailing, Wright needed a single, overriding motif to resolve the conflicts in his original design. This appeared totally unpredictably following the coincidental disaster at Taliesin and the outbreak of World War I in August 1914. It was so all-encompassing that Wright even seems to have been able to convince himself that the building owed its very being to the change.[30] Whereas he almost invariably gave the earliest date of a meeting with a client as the date of a building's conception, and sometimes even predated that, in the case of the Imperial Hotel he postdated the preliminary project. In his Autobiography, Wright described the initial meeting with the Japanese representatives of the emperor as having taken place three years after the fact. He claimed they "had gone around the world to find an architect," and when "they came to the reconstructed Taliesin, Taliesin II," in

1916, they "fell in love with the place" (*A* I, 193). Indeed, they were so "impressed" by it that they decided to offer him the commission for the hotel. It was almost as if, by an act of will similar to the reconstruction of Taliesin itself, Wright believed he could deny any evolution in the design of the hotel so as to give the impression that it grew "spontaneously" out of a coherent impulse traceable to his defiant resolve after the fire and murders to get "up in arms" and fight against "the brutalizing Taliesin had received" (*A* I, 193). To illustrate the meaning of the building as an expression of this resolve, Wright described it as "a form seen to be bracing itself against storm and expected temblor."[31]

Wright later characterized the entire Japanese experience as a protracted campaign of "building against doomsday." He never tired of affirming that every design decision following resumption of work on the project after the disastrous events at Taliesin was aimed at dealing with that "terrible natural enemy to all building whatsoever—the temblor!" (*A* I, 214). The floating foundations, the system of cantilevered construction, the pools of water, the splayed base giving the building its low center of gravity, the jointed monolithic walls of double-shell construction, and the lightweight lava-stone trim and copper roof—all these features, by his account, were developed in an effort to combat the devastating effects of earthquakes and the raging fires that follow.[32]

The changes Wright made after 1914 were not just a matter of technological adjustment. The more he studied the situation of building in Tokyo, the more he thought about the broader historical and geographical implications of ancient "Yedo." Searching for a way to understand and thereby express the natural history of the site, he came to see the problem in mythological terms, centered on the archetypal image of the "sacred mountain" Fujiyama (fig. 104). Rising out of the Pacific Ocean, "venerable, white hooded, inviolate against a golden sky," the volcanic mountain seemed to Wright to embody the very force of the temblor and thus become emblematic of the place (*A* I, 216, 201):

From infancy, as a sort of subjective contemplation, the minds and hearts of the Japanese are fixed upon the great calm mountain God of their nation—the sacred Fujiyama brooding in majesty and eternal calm over all. They deeply worship as the mountain continually changes moods, combining with sun and moon, clouds and mist in a vast expression of elemental beauty the like of which in dignity and repose exists nowhere else on earth.

It is not too much to say that the "sacred mountain" is the God of old Japan: Japan the Modern Ancient.

And yet the dreaded force that made the great mountain continually takes its toll of life from this devoted people, as the enormous weight of the deep sea beside their tenuous island, the deepest sea in the world, strains the earth-crust opening fissures in the bottom of the great valley in which it rests and the sea rushes down to internal fires to become gas and steam expanding or exploding internally causing earth convulsions that betray the life on the green surface.

Great wave movements go shuddering through the body of their land spasmodically changing all overnight in immense areas. Whole villages disappear. New islands appear as others are lost and all on them. Shores are reversed as mountains are laid low and valleys lifted up. And always flames! The terror of it all faces conflagration at the end. (*A* I, 213)

More powerful an image of the land than any stylistic reference to Japanese architecture might have been, Mount Fuji became Wright's totalizing motif. As he developed the design of the building between 1917 and 1919, the form of the hotel, though hardly Japanese in any of its details, came to represent that land as a poetic response to the power of its "calm mountain God."[33] The building lost any resemblance to the lighthearted and fanciful Midway Gardens. Gone were the thin, stepped pagoda roofs and festive poles and banners perforating the floating planes of terraces and roof gardens. Instead, there was a new bulk and weight. The central mass of the banquet hall and theater was heightened

104. Katsushika Hokusai: *Tagonoura Bay, at Ejiri, on the Tokaido Road*, in *Thirty-six Views of Mount Fuji*, early 1830s.

105. Imperial Hotel. View from Hibiya Park (before April 1923).

and given a ponderous hip roof that spread out over the side pavilions as it descended. The whole complex was compacted into a powerful pyramidal shape echoing the natural form of Fujiyama and thus aggressively substantiating the architecture's historical and territorial imperative (fig. 105).

The volcanic imagery of the Imperial Hotel affected the design through and through, and even became part of the building's promotional literature (fig. 106). It was integral to Wright's structural calculations and played an important part in the choice of materials. The stone used for all exterior and interior finishes was a spotted, greenish, solidified lava called Oya. It was cheap, relatively soft, easy to

work, and considered a rather "plebeian" material by the Japanese. Wright apparently discovered it only after construction was well under way and could therefore make use of it only in restricted, decorative ways. Had he been aware of it earlier, he claimed, he would have made the entire building out of lava: his "chief regret" was "that the Imperial Hotel is not all Oya stone."[34] As the stone came from the lava deposits in "a flood . . . moving down to the site in Tokyo, in a stream that kept pouring into the building for four years," the hotel looked to Wright like a volcanic cone in the making, "a self-formed building, deposited in strata, gradually rising uniformly over the whole area." Had it been completely covered in lava, the building, he believed, would have formed a truly "sculptural whole" and crystallized, in effect, the eruptive force of Fujiyama in an ever-present image of "impending disaster" comparable to that of its mythic, natural model.[35]

Despite all the compromises and changes that occurred in the design and building of the Imperial Hotel, Wright always considered it one of his most significant works, if not the most significant one. Historians, on the other hand, viewing it mainly in terms of his stylistic development, have usually dismissed it as turgid and retardataire.[36] Wright considered it important for three reasons. First, it was a major public building, international in scale, a commission that ranked with the jobs a Burnham, a McKim, or later a Hood, a Gropius, or an S.O.M. might get.[37] Second, it was an engineering achievement, proving he could handle such jobs. (In fact, the hotel withstood a minor tremor in April 1922, even before it was finished; and on 1 September 1923, it survived the catastrophic Great Kanto earthquake, the most destructive ever recorded in Japan, with more than 100,000 people killed, nearly double that injured or missing, and three-quarters of the housing stock of Tokyo destroyed.) But beyond that was what the building meant to Wright in personal terms. It proved to him that he could successfully confront the irrational force of nature and develop the architectural means to sublimate its destructive power.

An earthquake represented for Wright the "most terrible natural enemy to all building whatsoever." Though "unconquerable, for it is mightier than any force at man's command," one nevertheless could "fight" and "outwit it."[38] The experience in Japan, as he described it almost ten years later in his *Autobiography*, remained permanently etched in his mind:

The terror of the temblor never left me while I planned the building nor while, for more than four years, I worked upon it. Nor is anyone allowed to forget it—sometimes awakened at night by strange sensations as at sea, strange unearthly

THE JEWEL
OF THE
ORIENT.

K. OKURA JR., PRESIDENT
T. INUMARU, MANAGER

IMPERIAL HOTEL

1925

and yet rumbling earth-noises. Sudden shocks, subsidence—and swinging. Again shock after shock and upheaval, jolting back, and swinging. A sense of the bottom falling from beneath the building, terror of the coming moments as cracking plaster and groaning timbers indicate the whole structure may come crashing and tumbling down. There may be more awful threat to human happiness than earthquake—I do not know what it can be. (*A* I, 214)

As World War I proceeded to wreak destruction throughout Europe, and as Japan entered the fight on the side of the Allies to protect its own sphere of influence, the Imperial Hotel rose up between the confronting warriors representing the West and the East like the indomitable Fujiyama.[39] Although it is clear that Wright meant the building to mark its time in history through its warlike imagery, it is even more important in the long run to realize the extent to which Wright assimilated that conflict to his own personal tragedy. "To produce the image of what one fears in order to protect oneself from what one fears," wrote Rosalind Krauss in relation to European Surrealism, "is the strategic achievement of anxiety, which arms the subject in advance against the onslaught of trauma, the blow that takes one by surprise."[40]

Mount Fuji displaced the hill crown of Taliesin in Wright's mind, as its volcanic effects did that of the fire. Wright interpreted the construction of the Imperial Hotel as evidence of his own ability to survive catastrophe. The experience for him recalled the mythical phoenix rising from the ashes. He later referred to such resilience on his part as "snatching victory from the jaws of defeat" (*A* II, 446). Wright directly equated the devastating force of earthquakes with the conflagration and deaths at Taliesin. "In spite of all my reasoning power and returning balance I was continually expecting some terrible blow to strike," he remembered of his life after the fire. "The sense of impending disaster would hang over me, waking or dreaming. This fitted in well enough with the sense of earthquake, from the actuality of which I should have to defend the new building

[of the Imperial Hotel]" (*A* I, 194). And when he had to choose a metaphor to describe what Taliesin looked like after the fire, we should recall that he identified the site with his image of Japan, seeing in place of his home in Wisconsin "the smoking crater of a volcano upon the hill where once Taliesin stood."

Hollyhock House

If the process of building the Imperial Hotel in the face of "impending disaster" took on a mythical meaning for Wright, Hollyhock House first fully embodied the effects of that experience in architectural form. Hollyhock House and its accompanying cultural center were designed to be built on the same "red line of seismic convulsion" as the Imperial Hotel, though on the other "rim of the Pacific basin."[41] Because almost all the actual planning for the complex took place while Wright was working on the hotel in Tokyo, it represents his first unqualified response to the elemental forces of nature encountered in the Pacific. Unlike the hotel, whose standard Prairie Style forms were given a certain local inflection reshaped to suggest a more inclusive natural image, Hollyhock House was created out of an entirely different set of historical conventions—those of Precolumbian America—which Wright believed might represent his ideas more emphatically.

Few modern houses in the twentieth century have been designed with such monumental purpose as Hollyhock House (figs. 97, 107). Fewer still have been invested with the degree of symbolic expression normally reserved for buildings of a more public nature. Soon after Wright had begun working on a project for a small theater for the wealthy oil heiress Aline Barnsdall, sometime in 1915 or early 1916, she urged him to stretch his imagination to the limit. "You will put your freest dreams into it, won't you!" she wrote. "For I believe so firmly in your genius that I want to make it the keynote of my work."[42] Wright saw a major opportunity when it eventually came to designing an entire cultural cen-

107. Hollyhock (Barnsdall) House, Los Angeles, 1916?/18–21. Patio-court (c. 1923).

ter around a house for his enthusiastic client. "Why not make the architecture stand up and show itself . . . as Romance?" he asked. "The architect's plans joyfully traveled the upward road of poetic form and delighted Miss Barnsdall. I could scarcely have keyed the 'romanza' too high for her . . . had I made it a symphony." He later realized, however, that there were those who would feel "that the architect had indulged himself . . . regardless of the task with the machine he had set himself" (*A* I, 226, 229, 233).[43]

Hollyhock House was built in the Hollywood section of Los Angeles at the first peak of excitement over that city's role in the fast-growing motionpicture industry. The house, which was to be the nucleus of a cultural center devoted mainly to the dramatic arts, is located on Olive Hill at the

108. Hollyhock House and Olive Hill Cultural Center. Final scheme, 1920. Perspective looking south from Hollywood Boulevard, showing artists' studios and cinema (foreground), Residence A and Barnsdall House (top middle) (1921).

109. D. W. Griffith: *Intolerance,* 1916. Great Gate of Bel.

edge of the Los Angeles basin, just before the Hollywood foothills begin to rise. With the city below to the southeast, the San Gabriel Mountains in the background to the north, the San Bernardino Mountains in the far distance to the east, and the Pacific Ocean sweeping across the horizon from west to south, the house is perched on the acropolis of Olive Hill like an ancient palace or citadel, isolated from the real world by a surrounding moat of boulevards and streets (fig. 108). Wright called it Aline Barnsdall's "little queen-dom" and said it was conceived as "a holiday adventure in Romanza" (*A* I, 233, 228).

■ ■ ■

"You'll want when you see it to call it Egyptian," wrote a reporter just after the house was completed, until "you real-ize that in the Nile country, in all the stretches of the north African plains, there is no building that could truly be called Parent of this one." Then, "the 'Aztec!' you exclaim; and you are closer to the truth, when your eyes equate it with the charm of the courts and the patios and the bowers, and the gardens and the siesta spots and the flat roof lines. But you are still wrong." Rather, he concluded, you should "think of a good size pueblo on one of New Mexico's mesas or low clean bluffs seen in some parts of the foothills of the Sierras. Refine the outline[s] somewhat, without losing their strength, tint it as near as an approach as possible to the silver green slopes of these same foothills and bower it with verdure and you will approach the conception of the exte-rior of Miss Barnsdall's home."[44]

Hollywood had already become the land of make-believe in that "desert of shallow effects" Wright called Los Angeles (*A* I, 235). Soon after Colonel William Selig sent some of his staff there in 1907 to shoot *The Count of Monte Cristo,* the movie industry began establishing permanent studios to take advantage of the perpetual sunshine and ex-traordinary natural scenery. Movie lots began springing up all over Los Angeles, but especially in Hollywood, with sets resembling the rock-cut temples of Abu Simbel for Cecil B. DeMille's *Ten Commandments* (1923) or a Middle Eastern bazaar for Douglas Fairbanks's *Thief of Baghdad* (1925). The first and greatest of these spectacular outdoor dream worlds was D. W. Griffith's Babylonian palace for *Intoler-ance,* built in 1916 on Sunset Boulevard, just a block or so to the east of Olive Hill, and left standing for a number of years afterward as a kind of memorial to that epic (fig. 109). As the palaces in which the movies were shown, along with those in which the stars lived, were becoming as exotic as

110. Hollyhock House. Aerial view of Olive Hill (c. 1924).

the sets themselves, a context was established that Wright could hardly ignore, especially when Nebuchadnezzar was the next-door neighbor.

Located just below the crown of Olive Hill and enclosing a central courtyard, Hollyhock House steps down to the south in a series of platforms and terraces that terminate in a low semicircular bastion, making the southern flank of the building seem impregnable from Sunset Boulevard (fig. 110). The private entrance on the north, from

Hollywood Boulevard, is protected by a deep forecourt that reaches out to the driveway and is bordered by animal pens on one side and a forty-foot-long porte-cochere on the other (fig. 111). For most of its length, this covered passage has openings at eye level, recalling to the newspaper reporter "apertures in great moat walls," and providing intermittent glimpses of the Pacific Ocean that establish from the outset the thematic link between mountain and sea.[45] Near the end, the passage narrows into a corbelled tunnel that finally

111. Hollyhock House. Entrance.

pushes through a pair of swinging, solid concrete doors, like a ceremonial causeway opening into the shaft of a man-made mountain.[46]

Inside, the verdant, sun-drenched courtyard offers a sanctuary of peace and serenity (fig. 107). Like a crater open to the sky, it is surrounded by shaded loggias and pergolas that were cooled by a stream of water fed by a fountain and pool.[47] Outside, the monolithic appearance of the smooth, lightly tinted walls, roofs, and parapets—layered and canted as they rise, and almost completely unpunctured by windows or doors—makes the house seem to be part of the hill, at once reinforcing the temple-like character of the precinct and calling to mind the ancient monuments of Mesoamerica and the Middle East (fig. 97).[48] But finally, the

luxuriousness of the setting, the sleek beauty of the forms, and the sense of enchantment within provide a visual experience that, more than any other serious work of architecture, speaks of the world of romance represented by Hollywood in the late teens and twenties.

■ ■ ■

In late 1914 or early 1915, "shortly after the tragedy at Taliesin," as Wright later recalled, he met Aline Barnsdall in Chicago, where she was involved in the Little Theater movement (*A* I, 225). The granddaughter of William Barnsdall, who drilled the world's second producing oil well in Titusville, Pennsylvania, and opened the first refinery in America in 1860, Barnsdall (born 1882) was educated in Europe, where she studied theater and acting with Eleonora Duse. Upon returning to the United States at the outbreak of war, she became a codirector of the Players Producing Company in Chicago's Fine Arts Building before lending her support to Maurice Browne and Ellen Van Volkenburg's Chicago Little Theatre, located in that same building where Wright's office had previously been. One of her ideas was to finance the construction of a completely new theater for the company. She chose Wright for this job, and in 1915–16 he produced a preliminary scheme envisioning a circular space containing the stage and auditorium capped by an octagonal canopy roof—a sort of permanent circus or odeum, with shades of Pompeii (fig. 112).[49]

Following a trip to California in the summer of 1915, Barnsdall had a change of mind and decided that the future of experimental theater lay out west. She moved to California in early 1916, and over the next three and a half years she and Wright discussed the theater as well as the design for a house to be built in conjunction with it. She rented an existing facility in Los Angeles for the 1916–17 season, with Norman Bel Geddes as her stage designer and Richard Ordynski as director. But the venture was unsuccessful, and she closed the company at the end of the season.[50]

In the meantime, planning for new construction proceeded in fits and starts. At first, the theater took precedence. Hearing from Barnsdall in July 1916 that she was "looking for land," Wright probably did some more preliminary studies for the theater, and perhaps even some sketches for the house, before returning to Tokyo in the winter of 1916–17. Although it is unclear when the Olive Hill site first came up, it seems that it was fairly early on in the process.[51] But when Barnsdall's father died in February 1917, after having apparently visited the site with her and given his consent to its purchase, everything was put on hold until the estate could be settled. Barnsdall described the "theatre site" to Wright at this time as "the *real* inspiration" and expressed the hope that he "could see it in relation to the new building in L.A."[52]

Early in the summer of 1918, Barnsdall assured Wright that construction would begin "in the fall," despite the fact that she seems to have been considering other sites for her operation.[53] But only in the following year did things become more settled as the purchase of the Olive Hill site neared agreement. In early April, Wright's assistant Rudolph Schindler asked Barnsdall for the "sketches" that she had in her possession as well as a "regular survey of the lot," so that the office could "go ahead with the execution of [final] plan[s] and building."[54] Barnsdall closed on the property in late June, and, after a visit to Los Angeles in September to sign the contract, Wright prepared the final plans for the house, which were mainly completed between January and March 1920.

Originally part of the Los Feliz Rancho, Olive Hill comprised a thirty-six-acre block bordered by Sunset Boulevard on the south, Hollywood Boulevard on the north, Vermont Avenue on the east, and Edgemont Street on the west. The hill took its name from the olive trees planted on its slopes in the 1890s. The hollyhocks growing wild there provided the decorative theme for the house and gave Barnsdall the idea of naming her house after "her favorite flower" (*A*, I, 226).

Rising to a height of nearly 490 feet above sea level, and at least 100 feet above the surrounding streets, the site

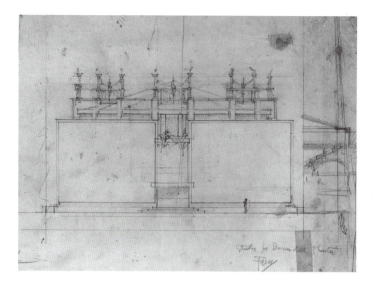

was a prominent landmark. Located at the northeastern corner of Hollywood, where the tracks of the Pacific Electric streetcars coming from downtown Los Angeles turned west from Vermont Avenue into Hollywood Boulevard, Olive Hill, along with Mount Hollywood to the north, formed a kind of natural gateway to Hollywood.[55] For many years Angelenos had come to the "Mount of Olives" to celebrate Easter sunrise services, a purpose Barnsdall recognized in declaring to the press, upon announcing her plans for building, that she would "keep [the] gardens always open to the public . . . who wish to come here to view sunsets, dawn on the mountains, and other spectacles of nature visible in few other places in the heart of the city."[56]

As Wright began to develop the plans for what Barnsdall ultimately intended to be a complete art center, including theaters for both drama and movies, residences for artists and production staff, income-producing shops, a rooftop restaurant above the theater, and public gardens—all surrounding her own hilltop residence—the nature of the hill site and its setting in the surrounding landscape seemed to demand a monumental solution. He turned the site into an outdoor sanctuary for the arts. Like a temple—or "a miniature palace of some ancient civilization," as Bel Geddes described an early version of the design—the house was to command the hill, with the buildings for cultural activities set around its base (figs. 113, 114). In the initial master

113. Hollyhock House and Olive Hill Cultural Center. Final site plan (1920).

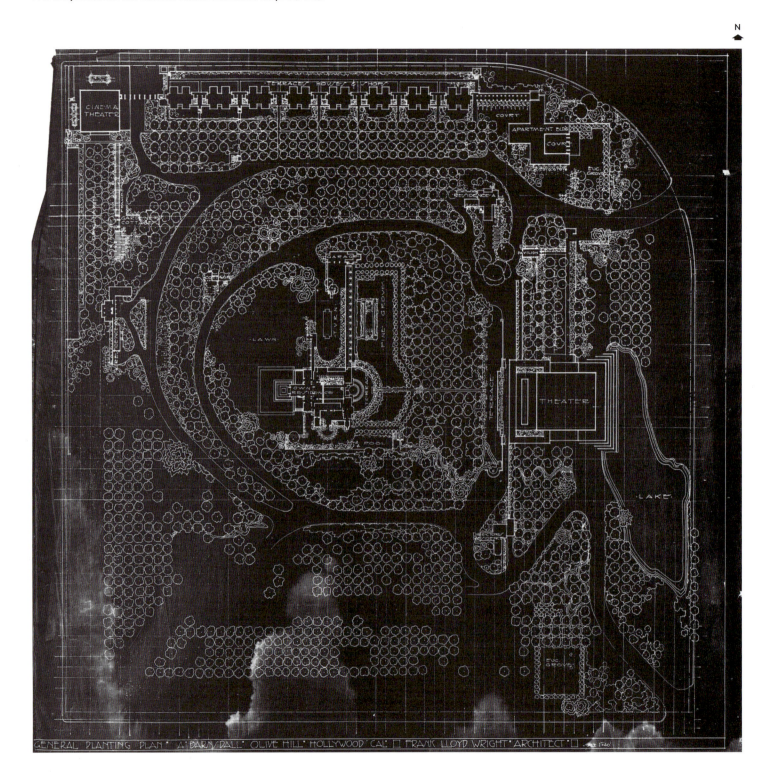

Hollyhock House and Olive Hill Cultural Center.

114. Sketch of theater and Olive Hill looking west from Vermont Avenue (1919).   115. Theater project, final design, 1920. Model, Vermont Avenue facade.

plan of 1919, only two other structures in addition to the house and theater were demanded: a house for the theater director and a dwelling for the actors (both located along the eastern edge of the site). But by the following year, the program was expanded to include a larger apartment house at the corner of Vermont and Hollywood, a row of combined shops and artists' residences along Hollywood, a cinema at the corner of Hollywood and Edgemont, as well as several subsidiary dwellings for the various people who would run the art center and manage the estate Wright referred to as Barnsdall's "little principality" (*A* I, 233).[57]

If the house formed the nucleus of the design, the theater provided the public facade (figs. 114, 115). It was to be linked to the house by an axial path leading up the hillside, and the prominent and oversized moldings framing its cubic mass were to characterize it as a symbolic portal. As all the buildings took on a solid, monumental appearance of weight and authority, the theater design of 1915–16 lost its festive, Pompeian character. The basic *parti* of the circle in a square was retained, but it was rendered in more Greek, or at least Hellenistic, terms under an exterior casing of massive Precolumbian-inspired forms. With a clerestory rising

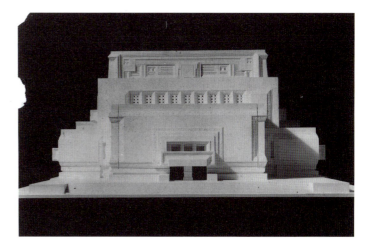

above a ceiling in the form of a laylight, covering both auditorium and stage, the theater was conceived as an indoor-outdoor space (fig. 116). According to Bel Geddes, Wright kept referring to the model of "the classic Greek theater" and said his project was based on "the classic Greek stages [which] were without equipment for lighting and scenery."[58] In this, Wright seems to have been completely in tune with developments in Los Angeles. Already in 1916, one of the natural amphitheaters in the Hollywood Hills had been used for an open-air production of *Julius Caesar*. This

Hollyhock House and Olive Hill Cultural Center. Theater project.

116. Interior perspective (c. 1919).

117. Final design, 1920. Model, interior.

led to the creation of the Hollywood Bowl in 1919–22 and of the Greek Theater in Griffith Park, just north of Olive Hill (proposed in 1919 and built a decade later).[59]

In Wright's theater, the bowl of seats would have made a continuous circle with the rear wall of the stage, designed as a cyclorama; and, with low freestanding piers separating the two areas rather than a proscenium arch, the space would have formed a single arena under the continuous ceiling (fig. 117). In the final design of 1920, a series of outdoor terraces would have led to a rooftop restaurant over the backstage area, looking up to Hollyhock House, while a lake in front of the theater, at ground level, would have formed a reflecting pool toward the street.

Despite the importance of the theater to the project, Hollyhock House was built first.[60] Site preparation began in the fall of 1919, and foundations were ready to go in by the

early spring of 1920. Because Wright was in Japan much of the time, his son Lloyd, who had gone out to California in 1910 to work with Irving Gill, shared responsibility for supervision with Rudolph Schindler, the Viennese-born architect who had joined Wright at Taliesin in 1918.[61]

Little, if anything, went according to schedule. Although it is unclear whether Wright had intended the building to be constructed of reinforced concrete, a more conventional system of hollow terra-cotta tile and wood framing, covered with stucco, was used to convey the impression of solid masonry forms. Work halted not long after it had begun, when problems with the contractor arose in the fall of 1920. Disagreements between Wright and Barnsdall, mostly over the theater, resulted in even more serious delays and setbacks. Throughout the whole affair, Barnsdall would maintain that "the Theatre is the 'Problem.'"[62] It was partly a question of funds and partly a matter of design. In any event, even before the house was finished in late 1921, the scope of the project was greatly curtailed, and only two of the subsidiary buildings were completed (Residences A and B). In recompense, Hollyhock House came to bear the full expressive charge of the general scheme, metaphorically and perhaps even literally taking over some of its dramatic functions. But it was always in Wright's mind much more than just a house, for "Miss Barnsdall wanted no ordinary home." Although she was, according to him, "as near American as any Indian," she was about "as domestic as a shooting star" (*A* I, 226, 229).

■ ■ ■

Hollyhock House was one of the very few opportunities Wright had in domestic design to develop a program of such scope. Earlier there had been the Coonley estate and the McCormick project. The other major undertaking of a similar nature was, of course, Taliesin. After Hollyhock came Fallingwater and Wright's desert compound of Taliesin West. But Hollyhock House is different from all of these. It has the formality of the early Prairie Style, but none of its domesticity. It is more explicitly regional and more specifically oriented to the natural forms of the landscape, yet is nowhere nearly as naturalistic and integral to its site as the two Taliesins or Fallingwater. Like the Imperial Hotel, Hollyhock House is a "transitional" building; but unlike its immediate predecessor, it represents a single point of view and is prophetic in that regard. Its subject matter is nature—or, more precisely, the forces of nature—and the relation between building and landscape is expressed in a symbolic language that predicts the major themes of Wright's later work.

Southern California was a totally new experience for Wright. Its natural beauty made it seem to him "a land of romance." But he also felt, just as profoundly, that its natural beauty had not yet been recognized in any "type" of building "characteristic" of the region, and that most of its architecture was a misguided effort to escape from the realities of the landscape and to deny its potentially devastating effects.[63] With the Barnsdall commission, Wright was, for the first time in his life, forced to confront the issue of American regionalism as an outsider. In the Imperial Hotel, he had deliberately chosen to make a compromise with his Prairie Style to avoid anything that might look too "Oriental." The architecture's relation to nature was ultimately an abstraction, for the downtown urban setting of the building had no immediate connection with the actual landscape.

In the case of Hollyhock House, Wright was presented first and foremost with a landscape situation. Early on in the process, Barnsdall had told him that the hill would be "the *real* inspiration," and throughout their later discussions both of them described the project as "working out this hill."[64] Wright instinctively associated the situation with Taliesin, as can be seen in a notation on a series of sketches for the overall treatment of the site (fig. 118). But the scrubby hills and powerful mountain ranges of Southern California presented an austere environment quite alien to the lush, rolling countryside of south-central Wisconsin, which, Wright noted, "picks you up in its arms and so gently, almost lovingly, cradles you."[65] Never before had

Wright faced a landscape of such elemental power and dramatic presence. "Hollyhock House was to be a natural house in the changed circumstances," he later wrote. It was to be "native to the region of California" and thus embody and dramatize the characteristic features of the region for "a client who loved them and the theater."[66]

Wright was hardly alone in this search for regional expression. Across America, the adoption of explicitly regional styles was already beginning to alter the course of modern architecture. Nowhere was this more apparent than in California, where the progressive work of Greene and Greene, Irving Gill, and Bernard Maybeck had come almost completely to a halt by 1916. Instead, the Spanish Colonial style of the early missions had been accepted as the most logical expression of local conditions, especially after the 1915 Panama-California Exposition in San Diego. While Wright despised such "sentimental bosh," he agreed that the style of the mission buildings "just happened to be more in keeping with California."[67] In searching for an "imaginative California 'Form,'" something "romantic" and "beautiful

119. Hollyhock House. Plan (redrawn c. 1940).

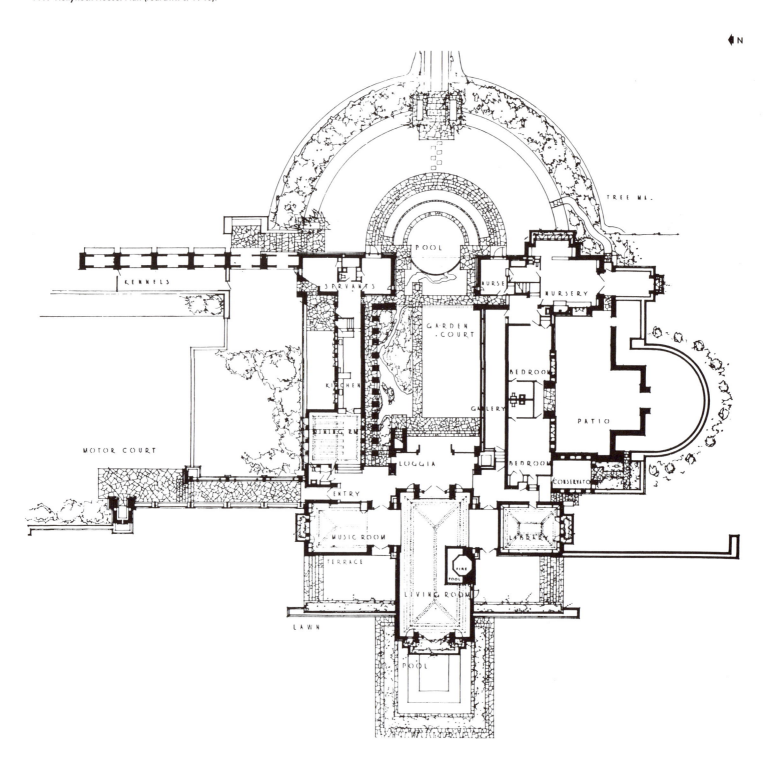

in California in the way that California herself is beautiful," he felt inspiration could be found in "cool *patios*" enclosed by "plain, white-plastered walls," creating a "refreshing foil for exotic foliage" in "oases kept green by great mountain reservoirs." But Wright also believed his program called for something more monumental and "not so domestic as the popular neo-Spanish of the region" (*A* I, 234, 227, 240, 232). By reference to the native forms of Precolumbian Mexico and the American Southwest, he sought to achieve a more "elemental" expression of the powerful forces of nature that define the landscape of Southern California.

For the plan of Hollyhock House, Wright returned to the "zoned plan" he had developed for the main house of the Coonley estate and later used in modified form at Taliesin (fig. 119). As adapted to the Olive Hill site, it became the most classically balanced and self-contained composition he ever produced for a house. In the Coonley House, the major functions (living, dining, kitchen and servants' quarters, bedrooms, guest rooms) were placed in separate wings (fig. 52). These were raised above the driveway to form a *piano nobile* and were linked in a broad, open U to take advantage of the view to the Des Plaines River. At Taliesin, the different wings were set along the contours of the hill, just below the crown, and were only loosely connected to one another (fig. 72). By contrast, the four main wings of Hollyhock House enclose a patio court in the local Spanish Colonial tradition. The axiality and symmetry of the design give it a specifically classical formality relating it to Midway Gardens and the Imperial Hotel; yet the plan of Hollyhock House is more domestic in type.[68] In its complex play of longitudinal and transverse axes terminating in divergent circular shapes, it recalls certain eighteenth-century French *hôtel* plans, exemplified by the Hôtel de Salm in Paris (fig. 120). (An exact replica of this was built in San Francisco in 1915 as the French pavilion for the Panama-Pacific Exposition and then rebuilt in 1919–24, on a site in Lincoln Park overlooking the Pacific Ocean, as the permanent home of the California Palace of the Legion of Honor.)

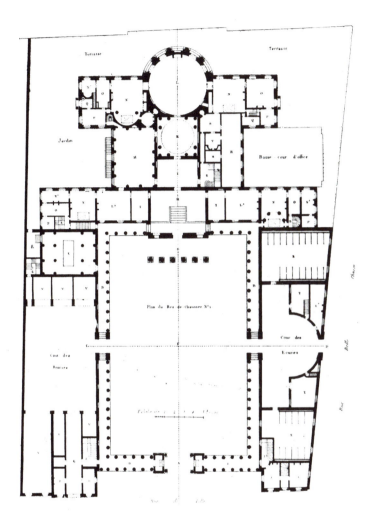

Hollyhock House is organized around two major axes: the central one runs east-west through the patio, or garden court; the other extends north-south through the entrance, or motor court. Each terminates in a semicircle, as in the Hôtel de Salm. A central opening into the patio on the east forms a monumental "courtyard entrance" along what would have been an almost ritually formal path through the woods from the theater below (see fig. 113).[69] But the main entrance to the house, from the motor court, is shifted off axis. It slides into the northwest corner, thus producing one of the many distortions that give the plan the pinwheeling effect characteristic of Wright's work in general. The long sides of the patio are bounded by the dining/kitchen/servants' wing on the north and the guest-bedroom wing on

121. Hollyhock House. Preliminary perspective, looking east.

122. Hollyhock House. Patio-court, looking east.

123. Theater, Priene, c. 300 B.C. Reconstruction by Armin von Gerkan, 1921.

the south. The former closes the house off from the motor court, and the latter opens onto a walled garden, which in turn is ringed by the semicircular retaining wall.

The central east-west axis parallels the mountains to the north and connects the reflecting pools at each end of the house. To the east, the axis passes under the family bedroom wing, which forms a bridge over a circular pool marking the upper end of the patio. A stand of pine trees, backed by a taller one of eucalyptus, was to have formed a silvery green screen between the pale stucco walls of the house and the distant, sandy-colored mountain slopes (fig. 121).[70] To the west, the axis passes through the loggia and then the living room, which faces the Pacific Ocean. A square reflecting pool in front of the living room balances the circular one to the east.

Unlike almost all Wright's earlier houses, Hollyhock House is a closed composition turning inward on itself. Despite its elevated site, the views are limited and highly controlled. All the spaces, however, open generously into the central patio, making the house seem "half house and half garden"—which is, Wright told Barnsdall, what "a California house should be" (fig. 107).[71] The patio was originally designed to be part formal and manicured, part informal and wild, again reminiscent of such eighteenth-century prototypes as the romantic *jardin anglais* set within the classical framework of Ledoux's Hôtel de Thélusson. At Hollyhock House, a stream meandering through lush foliage and connecting the reflecting pools was originally separated from the rest of the garden by a stone path.

The secluded oasis thus became an idealized landscape suggesting, in its forms, an open-air theater. Although it is not known whether dramatic productions were ever intended to be staged there, the bedroom bridge could have functioned as a proscenium arch, separating the raised stage beyond the circular pool from the orchestra occupying the manicured garden, while the flat roofs of the surrounding wings could become balconies for overflow crowds (fig. 122).[72] More in keeping with the antique source of Wright's design for the actual theater, however, the whole arrange-

ment could be seen in reverse. Then the stepped semicircular *cavea* around the pool would define the perimeter of the auditorium. The action would take place, as in a Greek theater of the Hellenistic period, on top of the flat roof of the loggia, functioning as a true proscenium, in front of the episcenium formed by the canted roof of the living room (figs. 107, 123).

However this central arena was used, its design was clearly more than a literal response to the program. The stylized, freestanding hollyhocks sprouting from the corner stairway are inset with mask-like faces (fig. 124). Recalling Mexican Gulf Coast agricultural deities guarding a sacred precinct, they recur in pairs to define a processional way up

124. Hollyhock House. Stairway to roof.

125. Chicomecoatl (agricultural deity), Veracruz, Mexico, Postclassic.

to the multilevel roof garden (figs. 125, 126). The entire sequence takes on an extraordinarily ceremonial air. The roof terraces, like temple platforms, are linked to one another by stairways and bridges and seem to have been designed for some symbolic purpose beyond the viewing of contemporary drama and dance.

The movement follows a spiraling, counterclockwise path, fully encircling the open court and making one realize that this is not just a roof garden. Rather, it is a "roof observatory," as a contemporary newspaper report aptly called it, "to view sunsets, dawn on the mountains, and other spectacles of nature."[73] As at an ancient Amerindian observa-

tory, such as the Caracol at Chichén Itzá, or the Palace complex at Palenque (fig. 127), one mounts from one platform to the next, to yet a higher one, until the panorama of Los Angeles unfolds below and one has the impression of being suspended between the mountains and the sea under "the serene canopy of California blue" (*A* I, 228).

The exterior of Hollyhock House reflects the surrounding mountain shapes, which Wright described as "curious tan-gold foothills ris[ing] from tattooed sand-stretches" (*A* I, 239). Hollyhock House is the one building Wright placed *on* the hill (or nearly so) and for which he made the profile of the roof the most conspicuous feature of the design. After first trying a conventional hip and then a tall, tepee-like shape, he chose a truncated talus, which is banded by a ridge, or frieze, of conventionalized hollyhocks to "adorn the hill crown" (*A* I, 231; fig. 128). Instead of relating house to ground through the extended horizontal line of the eaves, the truncated shape floating above the line

126. Hollyhock House. Roof terraces and patio-court, looking west.

127. Palace, Palenque, Chiapas, Mexico, eighth century.

of hollyhocks relates the building to the sky and allows for the effects of aerial perspective in a landscape where, as Wright noted, "foreground spreads to distances so vast" that "human scale is utterly lost as all features recede, turn blue, recede and become bluer still to merge their blue mountain shapes, snow capped, with the azure of the skies" (*A* I, 239). It was "in the *silhouette* of the Olive Hill house" that Wright meant to express "a sense of the breadth and romance of the region."[74]

As observers pointed out from the moment Hollyhock House was finished, its imagery derives from the two historical models Wright felt were most appropriate to the region. The stepped and layered horizontal masses recall the "mesa

128. Hollyhock House. West elevation.

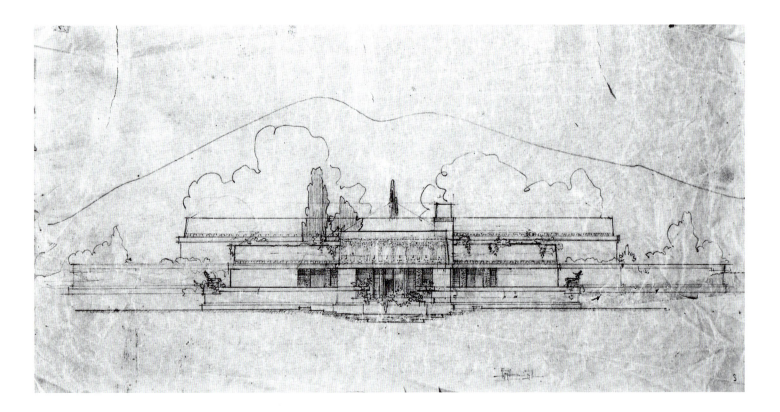

silhouette," as Wright's son Lloyd put it, "characterized and developed by Pueblo Indians" in their terraced adobe constructions.[75] More significant and more obvious, perhaps, are the shapes of Precolumbian Mexican architecture. The profile of the high canted attic, and the squat proportions resulting from the mid-height placement of the continuous decorative frieze, immediately bring to mind the temples of Palenque, Uxmal, and Chichén Itzá (fig. 127), just as the banded, enframing moldings of the theater project recall the more compressed and earth-bound forms of Mitla and Monte Albán.[76]

■ ■ ■

While the blatant use of Precolumbian forms may be quite unnerving to those who simply want to see Wright as a progenitor of modernism, it should be noted that Hollyhock House was not his first design to incorporate archaic Amerindian motifs. Both the A. D. German Warehouse, in Richland Center, Wisconsin (1916–21; fig. 129), and the Bogk

House in Milwaukee (1916–17), were built before it.[77] All three examples thus come almost immediately after the fire at Taliesin. Although this return to a deeply rooted American tradition may have had a particular regional justification in Southern California, it clearly reflects Wright's larger purpose, after the events of August 1914, to redefine the relationship of his architecture to the natural landscape. Prefiguring D. H. Lawrence's appeal to the artists and writers of the United States to "Listen to Your Own" and "take up life where the Red Indian, the Aztec, the Maya, the Incas left off," so as to "pick up the life-thread" of "the great dusky continent" of America, Wright likewise saw in the architectural culture "which Cortes and Columbus murdered" a "spirit of place" that could be made to represent his own revision of nature.[78]

Precolumbian architecture represented for Wright, as he later wrote, a repository of "might," of "strength," of "gigantic power" and "force." In his view it was neither "sensuous" nor "humanistic," but aggressive, defiant, and warlike. "The Mayan grew by war," Wright wrote. "He was a

great ritualist. He was a Godmaker through force. Flesh lives in his architecture only as a gigantic power." As an "architecture beyond conceivable human need," it was "truly monumental." As a "greater elemental architecture than anything remaining on record anywhere else," it offered the archetypal image of permanence "made one with the . . . land."[79]

Even though Hollyhock House was built of stuccoed hollow tile and wood, Wright retained the solid, layered, and earthy forms of the indigenous architecture of precolonial times for their powerful expression of nature. He felt in the "primitive character" of Maya architecture "the purest kinship to elemental nature" and used "the extended plateaux [the Maya] terraces made and . . . the mighty scale of [their] horizontal stone constructions" as the natural expression of the "vast perspectives" afforded by the "arid, sunlit strand" of California.[80] In Hollyhock House, Precolumbian architecture provided more than just an expression of monumentality, as it had done in the German Warehouse and the Bogk House. In Los Angeles, it became a model and an equivalent for the shapes of the landscape itself.

Wright described the forms of "primitive American architecture" as "abstractions" of natural forms, and their ritual purpose as "cosmic as sun, moon, and stars!" They were "earth-architectures: gigantic masses of masonry raised up on great stone-paved terrain, all planned as one mountain, one vast plateau lying there or made into the great mountain ranges themselves." As Maya "buildings grew to be man-mountains," they were "made one with the surrounding features of mountainous land"; and because "all were built as and for grandiloquent religious rituals to stand forever in the eye of the sun as the earthly embodiment of the mystery of human majesty," Wright claimed that "man was made into, built into, living harmony with the surrounding mountains" and consequently recognized himself in his architectural forms "as a mighty son of Earth!"[81]

The compacted, stratified, sloping planes of the four wings of Hollyhock House create a man-made crown for Olive Hill, while the patio court in its center forms a crater of space where the images of mountain and water are brought together to create a microcosm of Los Angeles itself. Like the valley of Los Angeles, the court is surrounded by mountains protecting it from the desert and "kept green" by water from "great mountain reservoirs" channeled through to the Pacific Basin. The stream of water in the patio court was to be fed by an underground source pumped to the surface in the circular pool under the bridge, located at the highest point of the site. From the circular pool, the water would have flowed into the open to irrigate and refresh, then passed underground again before reappearing in the square reflecting pool just beyond the living room (figs. 107, 119).[82] But unlike its exclusively outdoor use in the court at Taliesin, the water emerges inside Hollyhock House in the trough around the hearth of the fireplace, which is set under a skylight (fig. 130).[83] Thus at the very core of the house, the homestead so to speak, the four natural elements of earth, air, fire, and water are combined in a mythical union ultimately defining the meaning of the house as a form of control of the landscape.

The main iconographical weight of Wright's houses was almost always carried by the fireplace, which he liked to see "burning deep in the masonry of the house" and expressed on the exterior by "a broad generous" chimney. Hollyhock House is no exception. Even though its chimney is inconspicuous, the fireplace is the most iconographically charged of any Wright produced after the one for the Winslow House of a quarter century before. Its placement and design are unique. The living room is a self-contained volume, a perfectly symmetrical double-square covered by a tent-like hip ceiling.[84] The fireplace is set in the middle of the long side, diagonally opposite the entrance, at the juncture of the central axis and the secondary, north-south cross-axis linking the library and music room. It is constructed of blocks of decorative, cast concrete and projects a third of the way into the room. Set between the opening to the library and a floor-to-ceiling door leading to an outdoor terrace, and framed by two diagonally placed couches, it appears almost to be freestanding.

The location of the fireplace in the center of the long side of the room gives it a special significance. Wright almost invariably set the fireplace on the short side, thinking of it as the backbone or core of a space emanating from it. In the typical Prairie House, such as the Willits or Robie House, one enters the living room around the fireplace and senses it in the background as a three-dimensional, sculptural presence (figs. 56, 59).[85] In Hollyhock House, it is both a focal point and a pictorial element designed to be read narratively (we should remember Wright's description of the house as a "romance") and to provide a visual link between the secluded oasis of the patio and the view beyond the Hollywood Hills to the Pacific Ocean.

Dramatically lit by the skylight, the large sculptured mantel projects well out into space. It presents an asymmetrical, abstract, geometric composition that is totally different from the typically decorative and symmetrical designs of Wright's earlier work, such as the pattern of hanging wisteria in the Martin House in Buffalo or the frieze of ferns and birch trees on each side of the brick mantel in the living room of the Coonley House. The asymmetry of the Hollyhock composition derives from the narrative and figurative content of its imagery (fig. 131).[86] The scene reads from left to right, or east to west, following the direction of the sun through the southern sky and the geometric progres-

sion from one reflecting pool to the other. Against the background of a large circular shape on the left is superimposed a fretted, vertical element recalling the anthropomorphized hollyhocks outside. Both of these forms are then reproduced at two smaller scales, as if mirrored on the surface of water. The resulting dynamic shape opens into an inset panel on the lower right that contains a series of horizontal stripes that are first deflected down and then out into diamond shapes, expanding like water seeping into the ground.

The composition then turns counterclockwise into another inset panel, this one containing a grid of vertical striations that continue across the top, like a sky in the background. The whole design is locked in place and held in suspension by the notched square shapes on the left and right, which overlap the two deeply cut vertical channels. The channel on the left is taller than the one on the right. Its chamfered outside edge causes an illusion of perspectival diminution that reinforces the reading from left to right.

The geometric forms seem part mechanical, part organic, and the rhythmic action described by the big ratchet wheel on the left immediately recalls the mechanomorphic imagery of Picabia's and Duchamp's contemporaneous paintings and assemblages, especially the latter's *Bride Stripped Bare by Her Bachelors, Even (The Large Glass)* (1915–23).[87] The figurative content of Wright's design becomes all the more obvious when the mantel is seen obliquely, as is normal on entering the room. Then the tall, conventionalized hollyhock takes on the stature of a figure in three-quarter profile, and the whole scene is thrown into deep perspective. One has the impression of looking over a vast landscape from a high seat or throne. Indeed, this reading coincides with Lloyd Wright's explanation of the scene as depicting Barnsdall, as an Indian princess, surveying the desert from her throne.[88]

Poised in mid-air and hovering gravely between hearth and skylight, the mantel presents an image of man and nature in a turbulent world of cyclical change. The circular forms on the left describe a rhythmic and recurrent action moving through the composition to the right, always

130. Hollyhock House. Living room (restored).

131. Hollyhock House. Fireplace mantel.

to turn back on itself. The constant stream of water around the hearth underscores the ebb and flow of existence, while the skylight literally enforces the natural cycle of night and day. To the destructive and transformative power of fire is added the healing and regenerative force of water. Again, one is reminded of the alternating energies of Duchamp's *Large Glass*; but perhaps even more apropos is the synthesis of cosmic forces represented in Navajo sandpaintings, which Wright no doubt knew by that time. In these, the image of equilibrium is usually contained by the elongated form of a rainbow guardian surrounding the field on three sides (fig. 132). Especially in the Whirling Logs type, the characteristic placement of the head of the female deity in the upper left-hand corner opposite her inverted skirt in the upper right reminds us of the two notched squares Wright used to contain his design.

Nor was the purpose of such ceremonial paintings so far removed from Wright's. They were drawn on the ground in the middle of the hogan beneath the smoke hole, under the direction of the singer, or medicine man, and the person to be brought back into equilibrium with the world was placed within the painting.[89] Wright described Barnsdall's purpose in commissioning the house as an attempt to give

stability and focus to her life. She was "a restless spirit—disinclined to stay long at any time in any one place," he noted. At first he could not understand "what she wanted a beautiful home for—anyhow or anywhere," until he "came to see that *that* was just *why* she wanted one" (*A* I, 228).

The mantel is one part of the larger composition of the fireplace. It is set midway between the octagonal hearth and the skylight. The two couches placed diagonally in front of it parallel the hearth and thus set the fireplace apart from the rest of the space (fig. 130).[90] Appearing to rise freestanding out of the earth and into the sky, with water around its base and light and air on all sides, the fireplace becomes an *axis mundi*, or cosmic pillar, bringing to mind Brancusi's contemporaneous columnar sculptures, such as the *King of Kings* (1920) or the first *Endless Column* (1918). Again, like Duchamp's *Large Glass*, Wright's fireplace connects a lower, earth-bound, watery world to a higher, more ethereal, light-filled plane.[91]

The shape of the hearth is a median term between the circular and square reflecting pools. It is set within a rectangular basin mirroring the skylight and lined in gold tile. At night, the stream of water reflects both the starry sky and the flickering flames of the fire. During the day, it catches the glint of the sun's rays filtering down from above.[92] The central feature of Hollyhock House is at once a fireplace, a waterplace, and a lightplace. Fire and water emerge from the cracks and crevices of the earthy stone floor under the blistering sun of "the serene canopy of California blue" to condense in one complex form Wright's perception of the violent forces of nature:

Stone is the basic material of our planet. It is continually changed by cosmic forces, themselves a form of change. Contrasted with these great mineral masses of earth structure—this titanic wreckage—are placid depths and planes of mutable water or the vast depth-plane of the immutable sky hung with evanescent clouds. And this creeping ground-cover of vegetable life, more inexorable than death, is rising from it all, over all, against all, texturing with pattern, infinite in resource, and inexhaustible in variety of effect. This is the earthly abode of the buildings man has built to work, dwell, worship, dance and breed in.[93]

Hollyhock House gave form to Wright's vision of the landscape and history of Southern California. A sham construction in itself, it is fittingly all about image—and image-making. Through its theatrical adaptation of historical forms, it represents an idealization of the powerful forces of nature in an elemental expression of Southern California. To appreciate its uniqueness and significance in this regard, one has only to contrast it with the casual Japanese-inspired bungalows of the Greene brothers, the simplicity of Irving Gill's stripped-down Mission Style, and the more explicit revivalism of Goodhue's Spanish Colonial. Those earlier attempts to fit in with the region were, Wright believed, either "sentimental," "antiseptic," or just "fashionable," designed to appeal to the Californian "née Iowan, Wisconsoniano, Ohioan" (*A* I, 227, 240). His vision of Los Angeles, the "poetic thing this land was before this homely mid-west invasion" (*A* II, 239), derived from a cataclysmic interpretation of a landscape described by Southern California's poet lau-

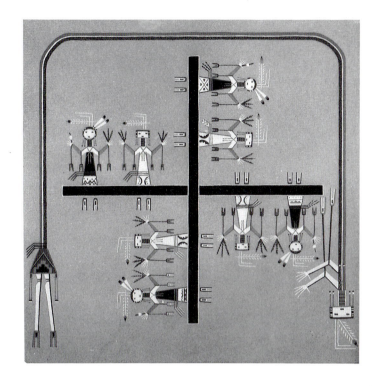

reate John Steven McGroarty in 1921 as "a city where it seemed that neither God nor man intended a city should be." It was a "place in the sun," as Frank Fenton later wrote, that "rested on a crust of earth at the edge of a sea that ended a world."[94]

Water, of course, was one major problem for Los Angeles. "Water is all that enables them to have their being there," wrote Wright. "Water comes, but comes as deluge once a year to surprise the roofs, sweep the sands into ripples and roll the boulders along in the gashes combed by sudden streams in the sands of the desert—then—all dry as before" (*A* I, 249, 239). But if the flow of water could be controlled, earthquakes could not. An abiding fear of earthquakes reaches back in Los Angeles history to the account by Father Crespi in 1769 of the first Spanish settlement, when the missionaries were welcomed by three severe quakes the night they arrived in the valley.[95]

In 1923, while living in Residence B on Olive Hill following his return from Tokyo, Wright wrote a brochure about building in Los Angeles, ominously entitled *Experi-*

menting with Human Lives. In it he described the drama of the Southern California landscape in terms of its violent history:

This great basin of the Pacific is overloaded,—overloaded with gigantic waters. Occasionally, as faults and fissures occur in its floor owing to the strains of this overload, water rushes down with enormous pressure to internal fires—creating steam and gasses of incalculable power, seeking escape through other internal crevices leading to the upper air and convulse and alter the conformation of the earth-crust in doing so. If this, as a theory of seismic convulsion is too simple to be scientific, . . . the fact remains that the red line of seismic convulsion clings to the rim of the basin.[96]

Wright noted that "Los Angeles, San Francisco, Tokio [are] all on the rim of this great basin." His mythic interpretation of California, however, did not grow out of a memory of the San Francisco earthquake of 1906 but rather from the experience of "building against doomsday" in Tokyo. Wright specifically remarked that Hollyhock House was built on the same "red line of seismic convulsion" as the Imperial Hotel. According to Bel Geddes, he told Barnsdall that, as he "walked over [Olive] hill," he began thinking about the design in "the same way [as] on the Tokyo hotel" where "earthquakes had to be provided for."[97]

Wright maintained that "the terror of the temblor" never left him during the period he was traveling back and forth between the West Coast and Japan. The fixation on "the sacred Fujiyama brooding in majesty and eternal calm over all" that he ascribed to the Japanese became his own. Nowhere is this more evident than in the preliminary sketches and studies for Hollyhock House. In almost all of them, a conical, Fuji-like mountain rises behind the building to the west, where in reality no such hill can be seen.[98] In the sequence of elevation studies, the rounded hill that bounds the composition in its horizontal extent and caps the mounting, truncated forms with its pyramidal mass is cleft in the middle (fig. 128). This cut occurs directly over a verti-

cal jet of water from the circular pool at the top of the open patio court. In the perspectival studies, invariably drawn from the southwest, the ascending and descending lines of the conical mountain describe a catenary curve that draws the man-made forms of the house into a symbiotic relationship with the site (fig. 121).

In a preliminary draft of the chapter on Hollyhock House for the *Autobiography*, Wright remarked (in what for him was a highly unusual psychological allusion) how the "sub-conscious" came into play in this design:

The great architect, Richardson . . . once said "the first principle of Architecture is to get the job."

A thoughtless remark.

Only an inferior architect, such as Mr. Richardson was not, ever gets a job. The job invariably gets him—and how!

This "job" got me entirely. . . . The sub-conscious is a mill effectively and brilliantly at work "creating" what the conscious mind can only sift, compare and arrange and ruin. . . . And it started to grind on Hollyhock House, to render "Romanza."[99]

Hollyhock House became the antitype of Taliesin in terms of both its natural imagery and its historic form. The building of the Imperial Hotel brought Wright into direct contact with the possibility of natural disaster on a scale that made the conflagration at Taliesin pale by comparison. Wright saw in this confrontation a way of distancing himself from his past. The archetypal shape of the volcanic Fujiyama replaced "the smoking crater" of the hill at Taliesin with a potent image of symbolic substitution. The association of that natural image in Hollyhock House with the prehistoric forms of Amerindian architecture provided an appropriate way of contextualizing, and thereby objectifying, the meaning of his personal experience.

Under the shelter of the mountains and looking out to the sea, Hollyhock House gave mythopoeic expression to the California landscape. In the cool living room, with its waterplace, lightplace, and fireplace beside the sun-baked patio, it gave vent to the destructive force of fire and guided its transformative power through the regenerative flow of water, underscoring the cyclical pattern of death and rebirth as the very ground of its design. While its central court, open to the sky and rimmed by terraced platforms encircling the stream-fed garden, formed an image of the earth subdued and quieted by man, the rarefied atmosphere was rendered even more dreamlike and ideal by the allusions to a distant historical past.

■ ■ ■

Barnsdall probably never really thought of Hollyhock House as her "home." Wright made it quite clear, both in what he designed and in what he wrote, that his intention was never simply to provide a functional solution to a domestic problem. Monumentality was uppermost in both their minds. It is therefore not surprising that Barnsdall hardly ever lived in Hollyhock House and that she offered it to the City of Los Angeles, within two years of its completion, as the nucleus of a municipal art center. Following much debate, and after the California Art Club agreed to act as an intermediary, the city accepted the gift in early 1927, at which time the land and its buildings became known as Thomas Barnsdall Park, in memory of her father.

Many reasons have been put forth to explain this peremptory disposal: high taxes, exorbitant maintenance costs, problematic living conditions, lack of need for a permanent residence of such size, philanthropy, the demise of the theater component, even real estate profiteering. Interestingly, Wright stressed the social question. A friend of Emma Goldman, Barnsdall was well known as a promoter of left-wing causes. Wright acknowledged the enormous disparity between Barnsdall's ideological position and the house she had been given to live in: "They said in Hollywood, Aline Barnsdall was a Bolshevik. . . . They rather sneered . . . at one whose ideas were 'proletariat' and hard, while living soft herself like a princess in aristocratic seclusion" (*A* I, 233). But such an apparent mismatch cannot

fully explain Barnsdall's action, for she commissioned Wright to design another house (in Beverly Hills) at about the same time she offered Hollyhock House to the city.[100] Which leads one to suspect, as most observers have, that her fundamental reason for giving away Hollyhock House was the very one for which she initially commissioned Wright to design it: that it should become a public arena in which Los Angeles might find forms of artistic expression appropriate to its new "place in the sun."

For many years, however—indeed, until quite recently—Hollyhock House seemed hardly to fulfill its idealistic social mission. Abandoned and unused during the years of high modernism, it fell into a premature state of ruin. Whether or not it qualifies as the first modern ruin, this condition of dysfunction made its expression of the "spirit of place" even more poignant.[101] One is forcefully reminded of Louis Kahn's conception of how meaning in architecture emerges out of the transcendence of mere building or function:

When a building is being built, there is an impatience to bring it into being. Not a blade of grass can grow near this activity. Look at the building after it is built. Each part that was built with so much anxiety and joy and willingness to proceed tries to say when you're using the building, "Let me tell you about how I was made." Nobody is listening because the building is now satisfying need. The desire in its making is not evident. As time passes, when it is a ruin, the spirit of its making comes back. It welcomes the foliage that entwines and conceals. Everyone who passes can hear the story it wants to tell about its making. It is no longer in servitude; the spirit is back.[102]

Hollyhock House will always be like a stage set for a play that could never be acted out, nor ever had to be, in reality. For the building itself was conceived as a work of pure representation, its fictional story line being understood in its mute, historic forms.

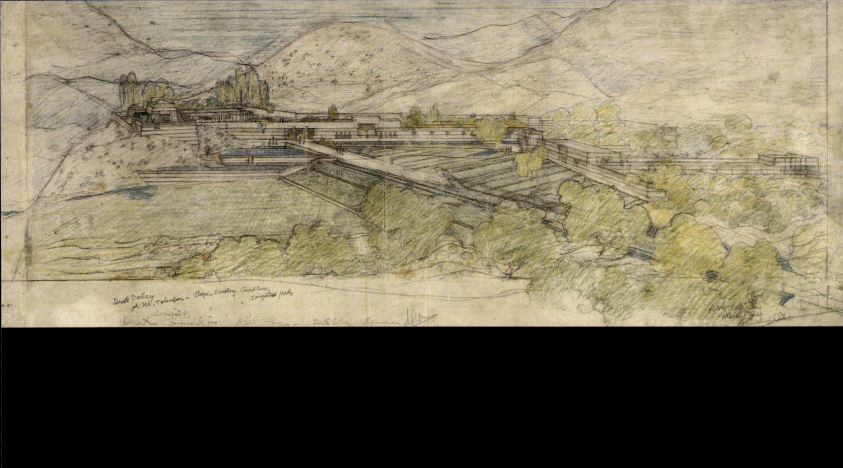

VI

From Los Angeles to Lake Tahoe and Death Valley

T*he 1920s was a critical decade in the history of modern architecture. In the turbulent atmosphere of postwar Europe, the "machine aesthetic" of Gropius, Mies, Le Corbusier, Oud, and others vied with the more conservative Expressionists and the more radical functionalists and Soviet "formalists" for dominance over the fairly moribund academic establishment. By 1925, the "esprit nouveau" of a Machine Age architecture, as Le Corbusier called it, had given rise to what would eventually be recognized as the International Style.*

Fully aware of these developments, Wright wrote in 1928 one of the first reviews of the English translation of Le Corbusier's *Towards a New Architecture* (1927).[1]

In the United States, the same period witnessed the remarkable development of the modern skyscraper, beginning with the Chicago Tribune Competition of 1922–23, and culminating in the pre-Depression designs for the Chrysler Building (1927–29), Empire State Building (1929–31), and PSFS Building (1929–32). The American city, with its stepped-back slabs towering sixty to one hundred stories above the canyon-like grid of streets, offered the vision of a "magic mountain" to some, the prophetic outlines of a "Metropolis of Tomorrow" to others.[2] At the same time, the other half of this modern metropolitan equation, the suburb, grew at an unprecedented scale, with places like Shaker Heights, Mariemont, River Oaks, and Beverly Hills being just a few prime examples.

In all of these developments, however, Wright played almost no part. In Europe, his work began to be seen as irrelevant and out-of-date; and in America, he was now even more of an outsider than before. Despite, or perhaps just because of that, the twenties proved to be one of the most innovative decades of his career. Though marked by very little actual building, this was the period during which Wright consolidated the ideas he had developed in the Imperial Hotel and Hollyhock House and worked them into a less extravagant, less personal, more generic form of expression particularly appropriate to the landscape and culture of the Southwest.[3] Designing mainly for the hills, mountains, and deserts of California in the first half of the twenties (the subject of this chapter) and then moving for a time to Arizona at the end of the decade (the subject of the next chapter), Wright now came into direct contact with Native American civilization. Bringing to that experience a renewed and highly self-conscious determination to be "modern," he concentrated on evolving a rigorous, logical, and industrialized system of construction and planning that would give an "integral" sense of "reality" to his formal vision of the region (*A* I, 235). The three major components of this singular combination of modernism and primitivism were the textile-block method of reinforced-concrete construction, the grid system of diagonal planning, and a new spatial conception based on the model of the vessel or pot.

■ ■ ■

Wright left Japan for good in late July 1922. Although he first returned to his home base at Taliesin, his plans soon took him back to Los Angeles, where he opened an office in the early winter of 1923.[4] He had high hopes for himself following the Tokyo venture. From this important international commission he expected to gain the kind of fame and recognition he thought would attract the wider, corporate clientele that now dominated American building. Profusely illustrated articles in *Architectural Record* and *Western Architect* (the former with a text by Louis Sullivan) gave ample publicity to the work and stressed the large scale of the operation, the organization of a complex office and work force, and, in particular, the advances in structural engineering developed to carry the project to a successful conclusion. Wright clearly wanted to appear as an architect of the most professional sort, capable of handling major corporate jobs, and not just custom-designed houses for the upper middle class.

It was no doubt partly to establish such a new professional identity that Wright decided to move his architectural practice from the Midwest to California. Opportunities not open to him in the well-established Eastern and Midwestern cities might be available to him there.[5] Furthermore, he had closed most of the doors on himself in Chicago by his activities during the previous decade. Even before the fire at Taliesin, he had dissociated himself from the efforts of his former assistants and colleagues in Chicago, castigating their work in the May 1914 issue of *Architectural Record* as "half-baked, imitative designs—fictitious semblances—pretentiously put forward in the name of a movement or a cause."[6] Moreover, by 1922 "very few of the old acquaintances and friends" remained in Chicago, as he wrote to Darwin Martin, and he felt completely "cut off" from professional life there.[7] In any event, by the end of the teens the progressive cultural scene in Chicago had nearly totally dissipated. The leaders of the Chicago Renaissance in literature, the theater, and the arts had gone elsewhere—to New York or, like Barnsdall, to California—while the architects of the Prairie School who remained in the Midwest either became as conservative and eclectic as the rest of the country or, like their one-time mentor Louis Sullivan, received fewer and fewer commissions.[8]

If the desire to reestablish his professional identity was one reason for Wright to move to California, another even stronger one was his determination to regain his position at the forefront of contemporary architecture. A good indication of the thoughts going through his mind upon his return from Japan can be gleaned from a letter written to the Dutch architect H. P. Berlage in November 1922, following a critique by Berlage of the "romanticist" strain of his work. Berlage no longer saw in Wright the basis for a "collective" renewal of "principle" growing out of the "rationalism of the machine," but only a "personal originality" that had failed to "answer to this [machine] ideal formulated so precisely by himself" in his earlier writing and buildings. Describing the difficulty of his position, Wright agreed that his recent work might appear to have lost contact with the main thrust of modern developments. He fixed the blame on the professional isolation that had been forced upon him:

Yes—you are right!—I have been romancing—engaged upon a great Oriental symphony—where my own people should have kept me at home busy with their own characteristic industrial problems—work which I would really prefer to do and to have done.

But, dear Dr. Berlage—I am branded as an "Artist" architect and so under suspicion by my countrymen.[9]

Wright realized, as he had in 1909, that to change direction he had to uproot himself. Following in the footsteps of his former associate in Sullivan's office Irving Gill, his own assistant Rudolf Schindler, and his eldest son, Lloyd, he moved to Southern California with the idea that it offered the last opportunity in America for the growth of an indigenous modern architecture. On that final frontier were fewer stifling traditions; and whatever traditions there were, such as the Spanish Colonial, easily lent themselves to interpretation in modern terms. Wright saw the move as an opportunity for a rational reinterpretation of the forms he had developed in his most recent work in accord with the advanced structural principles that had guided his earlier thinking.

By the time he moved to Los Angeles, Wright had certainly become aware of recent developments in European architecture through his working relationships with Anto-

nin Raymond on the Imperial Hotel and Schindler on Hollyhock House. During this period as well, he would attract from Europe such younger architects as Richard Neutra and Werner Moser to work for him. Erich Mendelsohn and H. Th. Wijdeveld, the editor of the influential Dutch journal *Wendingen*, also became close acquaintances.[10] Although the extent to which his thinking was affected by such contacts is unclear, it is apparent that Wright felt the need to reassert his own commitment to the ideals of modernism at the very same time those ideals were undergoing radical revision in Europe.

In many ways, Wright found himself in a position not so different from the one the leaders of European modernism encountered after the war. As recent scholarship has shown, the work of Picasso, Braque, and Matisse, for instance, was diverted from its radical prewar involvement with modern formal issues of abstraction and ambiguity toward a conservative and decorative neoclassicism bent on reestablishing the narrative basis for a national style concurrent with the political "retour à l'ordre."[11] In the field of architecture, Expressionism after the war followed a similar course. And although the later reaction of Le Corbusier and the architects of the Bauhaus in favor of a geometric purism has commonly been viewed as a complete turnabout, it has been convincingly shown that the adoption of rational techniques of standardization and prefabrication were part and parcel of the postwar effort to deny to architecture any frivolous "art for art's sake" pretention so as to renew its cultural role in the serious matter of national reconstruction.[12]

Wright defined his purpose after returning from Japan as a conscious act of renewal. Referring to the elaborate designs for the Imperial Hotel and Hollyhock House as an extended "holiday" that diverted him from "getting buildings built by machine and true to modern mechanical processes," he soon acknowledged that, even before Hollyhock House was completed, he had serious misgivings about the direction his work had taken: "Conscience troubled me a little—that 'voice within' said, 'What about the machine crying for recognition as the normal tool of your age?'" He concluded that although he "had, not yet, descended to make believe," he had come dangerously close to conforming with his own derisive image of California building as a "shallow sea of cheap expedients" in a "desert of shallow effects" (*A* I, 224–25, 229, 235, 252).

■ ■ ■

Wright's immediate response to the situation he faced in California took a characteristically modern turn. He began thinking in terms of materials and sought a "mechanical" means of construction that would be appropriate to local conditions. "The gnawing of the old hunger for reality," as he put it, would be satisfied only when "some system of building construction [was found] as a basis for architecture" (*A* I, 235). The desiderata were numerous and complex. First of all, the system had to be economical. Not only did the materials have to be "cheap," but "skilled labor" had to be reduced to the barest minimum, if not eliminated entirely. Standardization and mechanization were essential, but large-scale factory production of prefabricated parts was out of the question. "Manhandled units weighing 40 to 50 pounds," in conjunction with a simple method of assembly based on rational organization of preexisting components, provided a solution (*A* I, 235).

But that was not all Wright demanded. He wanted a building system that would be appropriate on every level to the culture and topography of Southern California. It had to be responsive to the seismic conditions of the region. It had to make use of local materials so as to take on the coloration and texture of the area. It had to resonate, somehow, with the traditional materials and methods of construction of a region whose history included both Spanish and ancient and modern Amerindian cultures. The system therefore had to retain, or at least suggest, a sense of "true mass" while offering the possibility of a "rich encrustation" of integral decoration. It had to look "permanent," yet have the integrity of a "system" (*A* I, 236, 235).

The result was Wright's "textile-block" method of construction, which dominated his design thinking from 1923 until the end of the decade and reappeared sporadically throughout the remainder of his career.[13] The basic element of the system, as it was finally worked out after a number of experiments, was a sixteen-inch-square tile of cast concrete, a little less than four inches thick at its borders but hollowed out on the rear (fig. 134). Semicircular grooves along all four edges were left to contain steel reinforcing rods. First, the vertical rods were set up, sixteen inches on center, and a row of blocks was slid between them. After each course of blocks was in place, a horizontal rod was laid in the exposed upper groove and tied to the vertical rods to create a tensile structural grid. Grout was then poured into the joints around the rods as additional blocks were added, creating a continuous, reinforced-concrete fabric that could act both in compression and tension and could therefore be used for floors, walls, and ceilings. The walls were intended to be double in thickness, leaving a hollow space for insulation.

The flat blocks were cast at the site, with sand and crushed stone from the immediate vicinity used in the aggregate, whenever feasible, to impart to the concrete the color of the surrounding soil. The effects of mass would echo the solid masonry structures of the Spaniards and Native Americans, while the tile-like shape of the block was similar to that of the traditional adobe brick. Because the process of casting allowed for any amount of integral decoration, and because the method of aligning block with block allowed for continuous, repetitive patterning over the entire surface of the wall, the textile-block system afforded a rational, standardized, and modern means for reinterpreting the traditional ornamental textures and patterns of earlier regional architectures, both European and Amerindian.

The resonances with local traditions and cultures went deeper than mere appearance, however, and struck a chord that ultimately touched on the very definition of architectural space. Wright's description of the method of construc-

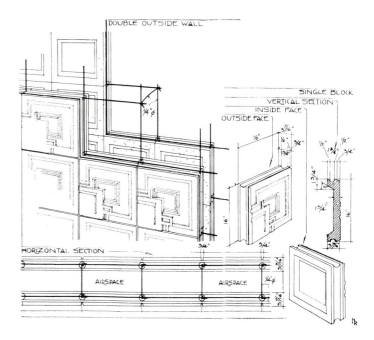

134. Textile-block building system. Section of Ennis House wall, based on original drawing by Richard Neutra (1924–25).

tion as "textile-block" carried a whole series of allusions within it.[14] References to weaving and pottery making, both traditional forms of Native American craft, became associated in his mind with the molding of shelter and the creation of space. Wright pictured himself as a "weaver" and described what he was doing as making "a 'weaving' in building." With "steel for warp and masonry units for 'woof,'" he would fabricate with purely modern materials and specifications "a free masonry fabric" that could be compared in the richness of its textures and the variety of its patterns with the woven baskets and rugs of the indigenous cultures of the region (*A* I, 245, 235; fig. 178).

Wright also saw the intimate connection between weaving and architecture that had long been suggested by historians and theorists, from Gottfried Semper on, as a major link in the evolution of built form.[15] And thus the image of weaving soon suggested another, more solid one to Wright, one closer to the ceramic craft that historically succeeded basket-making traditions. "Then I saw the 'shell,'" he wrote. "Hollow wall-shells for living in! The 'shell,' as human habitation." Continuously formed into a container-like shape from a single plastic material, the "shell" had volume and thus made manifest "the sense of interior space coming through." Wright described how, with all openings woven as integral features of the shell, "the rich encrustation of the shells visible as mass" could then be displayed as "the true mass of the architecture" (*A* I, 235–36).

The textile-block system brought the "romance" of Wright's vision of California under the control of materials to counterbalance the regional imagery by the requisites of modern industrial techniques. In his book *Wie Baut Amerika?* (1927), Richard Neutra, who worked with Wright on several projects using the textile-block method, concluded a survey of modern American building techniques with a description of Wright's work in California. In addition to stressing the modernity of the technique, he compared the results, both formally and spatially, with the Native American pueblos of the Southwest.[16] In this way,

Neutra hinted at what were in fact the larger—one might even say megastructural—implications of the textile-block system at the level of urban and regional planning.

With the unit-based nature of the system as the underlying factor throughout, Wright developed the spatial implications of the textile-block in two parallel ways. First, the hollow, shell-like structure came to be thought of in volumetric terms and was thus shaped in cubical or cylindrical forms. When combined with one another on the mountainous terrain of the region, these forms could jog in plane or overlap in section to create a stepped profile, like the pueblos referred to by Neutra. This adaptation to the landscape logically suggested to Wright a method of planning with diagonal axes and spaces that almost completely replaced his previous orthogonal geometry, which had grown out of the urban and suburban grid. Diagonal planning gave Wright's architecture a new freedom and openness that aligned his work of the twenties with some of the more radical designs of the younger Europeans. Thus, like the unit system of the textile-block structural method out of which it grew, diagonal planning combined a renewed sense of modernity with a resonance of the region's past.

Textile-Block Buildings

Wright built four concrete-block houses in the Los Angeles area between 1923 and 1925. He also began construction of a combined school and playhouse building for Aline Barnsdall on her property at Olive Hill, but this was left incomplete. (It was later turned into a terraced park.) Although he produced a number of other important projects, Wright never established the kind of reputation he had enjoyed in Oak Park. This meant, on the other hand, that he never had the occasion, or the need, to repeat himself. There is little formulaic about the California work.

Like Barnsdall herself, who continued to be a patron as well as a major contact, many of Wright's clients had some connection with Chicago and the Midwest. The first of the four houses was in fact for a former client, Alice Millard, whose wood-and-stucco Prairie Style house in Highland Park, Illinois, was built in 1906. Widowed and living in Pasadena, she ran a rare-book and antique business. The house Wright designed for her in early 1923 was to combine living and work. After preparing at least one preliminary plan for the lot his client originally purchased, he apparently persuaded her to buy a less expensive, though more "interesting," nearby ravine site. This gave him the opportunity to deal with what he considered a characteristically Californian terrain in a characteristically Californian way.[17]

The house was to be small and inexpensive, as well as very personal. Wright named it La Miniatura, surely a reference to its diminutive size, and perhaps even to that of its owner, but also meaning in Spanish a "miniature" or manuscript illumination, the kind of precious object its rooms were to display in an atmosphere quintessentially regional. Inspired by the need for economy, Wright made this his first experiment with the unit system of concrete-block construction (figs. 135, 136). In this initial use, however, there were not as yet any vertical or horizontal steel reinforcing rods. The blocks were "knit" together by inter-locking flanges along their edges and laid on conventional mortar beds.

The cubical, three-story house is set at the rear of the lot, against the wall of the ravine, and is entered from behind, at the second-floor level. A romantically bridged loggia, connecting the house to the garage, leads into a two-story living room that occupies the entire front half of the structure and overlooks the ravine. Its perforated facade forms a dappled sunscreen above spindling, textured piers that give onto a projecting balcony. One level below is the dining room, with a terrace leading to a narrow, wedge-shaped reflecting pool eked out of the bottom of the ravine. Above the main two-story space is a roof garden. At the rear, behind a transverse fireplace/stairway core, are stacked the service areas, bathrooms, and bedrooms.

The basic three-story scheme of the Millard House was not entirely new in Wright's work. He had used it nearly twenty years before in the Hardy House in Racine, Wisconsin (1905), a small Prairie Style dwelling designed to step down its precipitous lakeside site (fig. 137). Lower and more horizontal in expression than La Miniatura, its bedrooms were placed to either side of the transverse fireplace/stairway core, under a characteristically spreading hip roof. Also much more formal than its later California counterpart, the Hardy House has a symmetry as absolute as any of Wright's public buildings of the Oak Park period, with its two doorways on the street balancing one another on either side of an entry hall.

The most significant differences between the earlier and later houses are the materials and the overall shapes they help create. In contrast to the open, broadly sheltered, pavilion-like Hardy House, built of wood lath and plaster trimmed with oak stripping, the concrete-block Millard House is much more closed and contained within its tight, cubical massing. The flat roof, in particular, gives it a volumetric clarity and sense of modernity similar to the contemporaneous projects by Le Corbusier for his Citrohan House (1922), a resemblance not overlooked by critics at the time.[18] But whereas the open-air roof garden would become

135. Millard House, Pasadena, Calif., 1923–24. Garden facade (c. 1926–27).

On opposite page:

136. Millard House. Longitudinal section and structural details.

137. Hardy House, Racine, Wis., 1905. Perspective from lake.

one of Le Corbusier's "five points of a new architecture" and a leitmotif of the International Style in general, Wright's precocious use of it here clearly derives from the more ceremonial version of it in Hollyhock House.

La Miniatura was, in effect, Wright's first revision of Hollyhock House "in terms of modern industry and American life" (*A* I, 241). The unit system of the concrete-block structure governed the design in plan, elevation, and section to ensure a thoroughgoing structural integrity. Functions of support, screening, and enclosure were differentiated by the types of block used. These varied from a totally flat, undecorated version used for solid interior walls, to a cross-shaped pattern, either embossed or actually perforated, used for exterior screening walls, to a type with a square boss on its face and a U-shaped channel on its side, joined back to back with a mate to form the vertical piers of repetitive, embedded rectangles. These structurally distinct, decorative components give the flat, stuccoed masses of the earlier Hollyhock House a physically active presence, while their geometric incisions multiply the effects of light and shadow. The variegated, interlocking shapes provide a textural distinction that Wright believed would complement the forms of the tall eucalyptus trees enframing the house. His colored renderings illustrate how intimately he thought the structure would relate to its luxuriant setting (fig. 138). Textured like the trees, La Miniatura rises from the ravine floor through the forest cover of foliage into a diaphanous, ornamental crown that brings to mind the Temple of the Sun at Palenque, not as a prototype or model, as in Hollyhock House, but as a resonant after-image.

■ ■ ■

This first concrete-block house thus came very close to Wright's ideal of "a distinctly genuine expression of California" that would be, at the same time, an "indigenous" modern architecture (*A* I, 241). It also came very close to the ideal of the "natural house" that Taliesin had promised, a dwelling "native to the region" and growing out of it as "the trees

and rock ledges did." But the Millard House was still essentially a static spatial composition of closed volumes organized almost exclusively on orthogonal lines. In this regard, it was not much different from Hollyhock House or, indeed, the Hardy House, and certainly much less supplely integrated into the actual topography of its landscape setting than Taliesin. The flexibility and reflexivity that were inherent in the fully evolved textile-block system of construction, and so appropriate to the earthquake-prone terrain of Southern California, would be developed by Wright in his next few buildings and projects as a new approach to planning based on the diagonal axis.[19] This determinate diagonality, whether explicitly expressed in non-orthogonal geometries or merely implicit in the oblique definition of space as in Taliesin, would not remain confined to an expression in plan but would determine the section and elevation of buildings as well.

Wright most probably began discussions with Alice Millard about her prospective house in early February 1923, soon after arriving in Los Angeles. Plans were approved by mid-March, and construction started in the spring. At about the same time, he began preparing designs for what would have been his most significant Los Angeles venture, the so-called Doheny Ranch Project (figs. 139, 140). Involving him throughout the spring, summer, and early fall of 1923, the project issued directly from the thinking that went into La Miniatura and produced a large repertory of designs that Wright would adapt for other clients.

Mystery surrounds this project. There is, in fact, no direct evidence linking Wright with Edward Laurence Doheny, the conservative oil magnate and business tycoon, who was one of the wealthiest and most powerful people in Los Angeles until his implication in the Teapot Dome Scandal in 1924. Robert Sweeney has suggested that the project may have been a purely speculative joint venture on the part of Wright and John B. Van Winkle, a Los Angeles real estate promoter. Whatever the case may be, the site was specific and Wright worked from a plot plan of the Doheny Ranch Tract dated February 1923.[20]

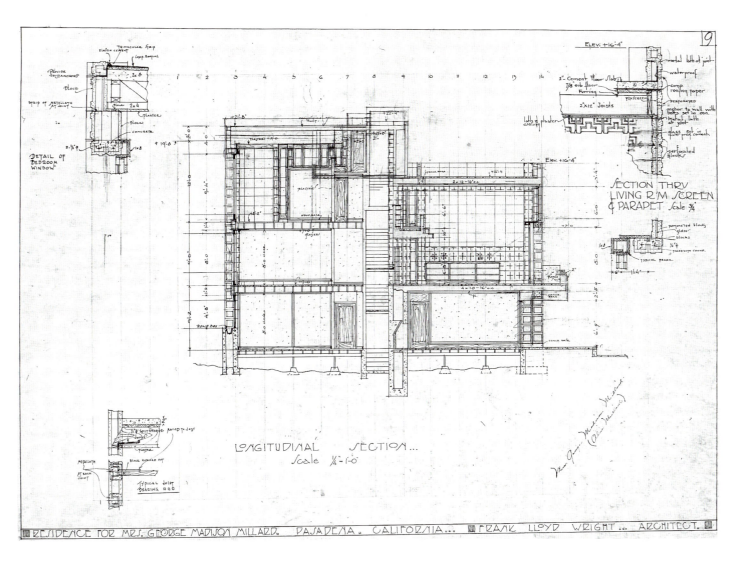

Elev. +16'-4"

SECTION THRU
LIVING R'M SCREEN
& PARAPET Scale ¾"

DETAIL OF
BEDROOM
WINDOW

LONGITUDINAL   SECTION...
Scale ¼"= 1'-0"

RESIDENCE FOR MRS. GEORGE MADISON MILLARD. PASADENA. CALIFORNIA... FRANK LLOYD WRIGHT ... ARCHITECT.

TAFEL. XV. PERSPEKTIVE VOM HARDY-HAUS. RACINE WISCONSIN   GEDRUCKT UND VERLEGT VON ERNST WASMUTH A.-G. BERLIN

138. Millard House. Perspective, from garden.

Doheny Ranch project, Los Angeles, 1923.

139 and 140.　Perspective.

141. Doheny Ranch project, House C. Perspective and plan.

142. Hokusai: *Reflection on the Water at Misaka, Kai Province*, in *Thirty-six Views of Mount Fuji*.

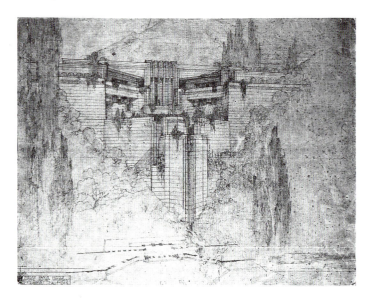

Extending north from Sunset Boulevard to the east of Coldwater Canyon, the four-hundred-plus-acre site along the northeastern edge of Beverly Hills jutted like a finger into the Santa Monica foothills. In the shallow canyon bordered on three sides by rugged, steeply sloping hills that offer dramatic views over the city toward the Pacific Ocean, Wright projected more than twenty-five individual houses to be built of textile-block construction and to form terraced and hanging gardens along the hillsides. The stepped and layered forms recall Hollyhock House in their dependence on Precolumbian and Pueblo examples. At the same time,

the basic concept of treating the houses, along with the access roads, as part of the hills, so as to leave the "contours of the hills undisturbed" (as later noted by Wright on fig. 140), clearly took its cue from Taliesin. Some of the houses become arched bridges over ravines; others stretch out in long horizontal platforms; still others emerge like natural promontories from an existing chasm. Almost all the houses were designed to be continuous with the roadway going beneath, through, or above them and were conceived in section as a series of diagonally stepped-back, superimposed ledges. Those that were to be descended into from a rooftop garage remind one of the ancient cliff dwellings at Mesa Verde or Canyon de Chelly; those with gardens and pools on their roofs, and that were to be entered from garages located underneath the main living floor, predict Le Corbusier's later scheme for the Villa Savoye (1928–30).[21]

As for the interior spaces, Wright obviously felt that a non-orthogonal geometry was more accommodating to such a terrain. One of the most spectacular houses, referred to as House C in the drawings, spans a waterfall (fig. 141). Probably to be located at the head of the canyon to the north, it develops around an open court defined by the splayed, angled walls of the natural cleft. The chamfered square court was rotated forty-five degrees and set like a cut diamond in the hillside. The diagonals define the major axes: the transverse axis forms terraces along the contours of the hill; the longitudinal one reaches out from the fireplace, set in a pool deep in the cave-like living room, to a projecting hexagonal terrace. Its wedge shape reflects the conical hill behind, like Hokusai's mirror image of Fuji reflected on the water at Misaka (fig. 142). Below, the angled planes split to permit the mountain stream running under the court to cascade down the ravine.

The diagonal axis of House C allowed Wright to externalize the conjunction of architecture and nature, symbolically contained within the closed shapes of Hollyhock House, and thus directly implicate the building in its natural setting. The vertical lines of the piers of the recessed cen-

143. Little Dipper School and Community Playhouse, Olive Hill, Los Angeles, 1923. Perspective, from west.

tral living room, coming down to a point at the base of the hexagonal balcony, literally read like water falling over a path of boulders. Looking like an image of the waterfall coursing through it, the house is an obvious predecessor of Fallingwater (fig. 196).

■ ■ ■

Whereas Fallingwater may have been an indirect outcome of the Doheny Ranch Project, there were several more immediate results. One of the designs was reused for the Ennis House, built on Los Feliz Heights in North Hollywood in 1924–25. And the final two textile-block buildings in Los Angeles that we shall look at, the Little Dipper and the Freeman House, are both reflections of its approach to site planning.[22] While the Millard House was in its earliest phases of construction and the Doheny drawings were being worked on, Wright began the building that would prove to be the most radical departure in planning of the entire group. The progressive school and community playhouse designed for Barnsdall's estate on Olive Hill in the summer of 1923, and called the Little Dipper because of its shape, was only partially built (in November 1923) before being turned into a wading pool and park by Schindler and Neutra in 1925. According to Kathryn Smith, it was commissioned by Barnsdall in anticipation of her decision to give the buildings on Olive Hill to the City of Los Angeles as a cultural center.[23]

The Little Dipper was sited to the west of Hollyhock House, halfway down the slope to Studio Residence B, on the house's main east-west axis (fig. 143; the site is just off the photograph, to the left, in fig. 110). In the final version of the design, the combined schoolroom and playhouse build-

144. Little Dipper. Plan.

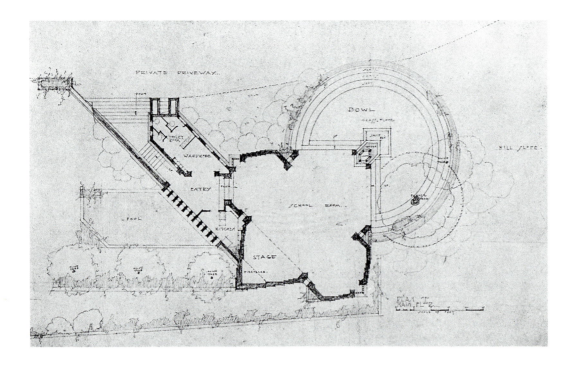

ing was reached from the upper drive by a bridge. A raised stage occupied the corner of the enclosed space, opposite a "bowl" of outdoor seats (fig. 144). Performances could thus be viewed from inside or out, depending on the weather.[24] A viewing terrace and pergola balanced the complex to the north and stepped down the steeply sloping site in a series of terraces and retaining walls. All walls were to be of textile block. The building itself, which formed a distended square in plan defined by the intersection of two elongated hexagons (ultimately deriving from the assembly hall of the Hillside Home School), was to be encased in nearly freestanding, angled "shells," producing a stellate, bastion-like profile. The flaring copper roof over the central clerestory acted as a canopy for the roof garden enclosed by the angled parapet walls.

The design was based on the rotation of a square, resulting in an overall forty-five-degree geometry. The steep slope of the site clearly inspired this solution. By setting the building at an angle to the main east-west axis of the estate, Wright was able to tuck it tightly into the hillside. The contour lines establish points of reference to which the diagonal

geometry bends and inflects. Entered from the upper drive that encircles Olive Hill, the building angles out from the hill like a spur. The diagonal path from the roof terrace leads down an enclosed bridge, lit from the side by vertical slits of glass set into the concrete piers. Movement down the slope follows a seemingly natural course, gently deflected by three forty-five-degree bends. Two offset, elongated hexagons define the overall length of the building and determine the first two angled shifts. At the crossing of the two major hexagons, within the deformed square of the schoolroom, the axis again shifts forty-five degrees to angle out through the corner, split by the diagonally placed piers. The longitudinal axis of the structure, under the clerestoried central section, ends in vertical slots of perforated concrete block. The main transverse axis reaches back to the fireplace to direct the view through the hexagonal pool and sandbox in the corner into a broad arc that expands over the bowl of seats defining the eastern and southern horizon.

Like the symbolic hearth of Hollyhock House, the diagonal axis of the Little Dipper conjoins images of earth, air, fire, and water. But instead of being abstracted from nature, the elements are, as in the Doheny House C, literally connected in space by the axis. The diagonal thus effects the union of natural elements at the scale of the landscape itself. This metaphysical dimension amply suggests the role the diagonal would play in returning Wright's architecture to a spatially freer and more naturalistic form of expression.

■ ■ ■

Around the time construction was halted on the Little Dipper, or very soon thereafter, Wright began the designs for the textile-block house in which he would show how a less eccentric, less explicit form of diagonality could achieve similar results in terms of dynamic spatial experience and flexible site planning. The house for Harriet and Samuel Freeman was a direct outcome of the Little Dipper in more than one way. It was commissioned in late 1923 and built over the next two years for the sister and brother-in-law of Leah Press Lovell, the progressive schoolteacher Barnsdall had asked to advise Wright on what might be needed for her school and playhouse. In the process, she also acted as the contact between Wright and the Freemans.[25]

The site of the Freeman House is similar to that of the Little Dipper in strictly topographical terms (fig. 145). The steep slope at the base of the Hollywood Hills, facing due south toward the intersection of Hollywood Boulevard and Highland Avenue, is reached from an upper drive. Following the example of Taliesin, Wright folded the house back on itself ninety degrees at the bend in the drive. An entrance loggia is located at the corner between a garage (where his own studio at Taliesin is) and the house itself (where the living wing at Taliesin is). The house angles down the hillside, like the Little Dipper, but more in the shape of a square ladle. The flat roofs become extended terraces as the building steps down the slope, with the upper one serving as a roof garden. The wall along the drive steps back in a series of jogs to conform to the changes in level. In an early design for this rear elevation, Wright had thought to echo the

downward slope by canting the concrete-block walls inward, following the example of the upper part of Holly-hock House. In the end, however, he decided to give all the outer profiles of the house, in both elevation and plan, the square shape of the sixteen-by-sixteen-inch concrete block and to reserve any expression of diagonality for the ornamental pattern within that block and, by extension, the spatial pattern within the essentially square plan of the house.

Like the Little Dipper, the Freeman House is entered from above and behind. A long, narrow passage leads from the corner loggia to the living room (fig. 146). As in the Little Dipper, this entry passage is aligned with the rear wall of the main space to become the back of a fireplace. But whereas the entry into the Little Dipper was deflected forty-five degrees along the side of one hexagon, and the fireplace was set on the diagonal in the corner of another, the entry into the living room of the Freeman House is through a corner, and the fireplace is located in the middle of one side of an absolutely square room.

Piers on either side of the fireplace support two deep ceiling beams that extend across the space to a bank of windows looking south over the city (fig. 147). The piers opposite the fireplace are matched by others along the side walls, inset equidistantly from the corners. The corners are left completely open. The horizontal sheets of plate glass are butted directly, with no vertical mullion, in one of Wright's first uses of a true corner window.[26] The view from the entry through the far corner is unimpeded and has an immediate impact. The diagonals of the square define a space that appears to extend well beyond the perimeters of the geometric figure; and the room takes on the virtual shape of the Little Dipper schoolroom, with the open corners offering a panoramic vision akin to that building's bowl of seats. As if to acknowledge this relationship and its new spatial implications, Wright placed a circular pot in the corner, just in front of the window, which appears in the photograph of the view from the house before it was refurnished by Schindler (fig. 148).[27] The curve of the jar, swelling out under the arch of its

Freeman House, Los Angeles, 1924–25.

145. Aerial perspective, from entrance side on north.

146. Plan, ground floor.

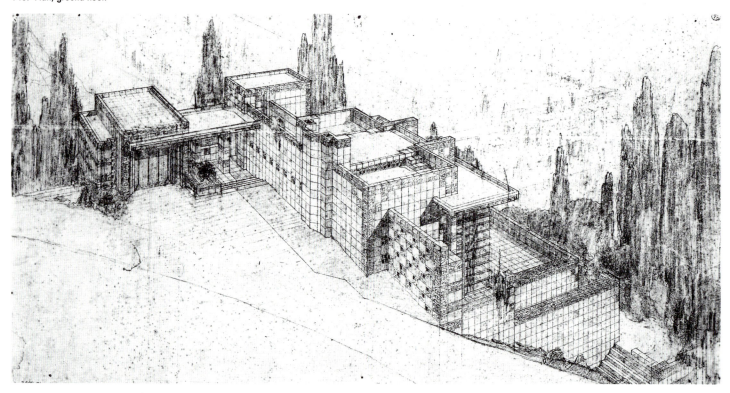

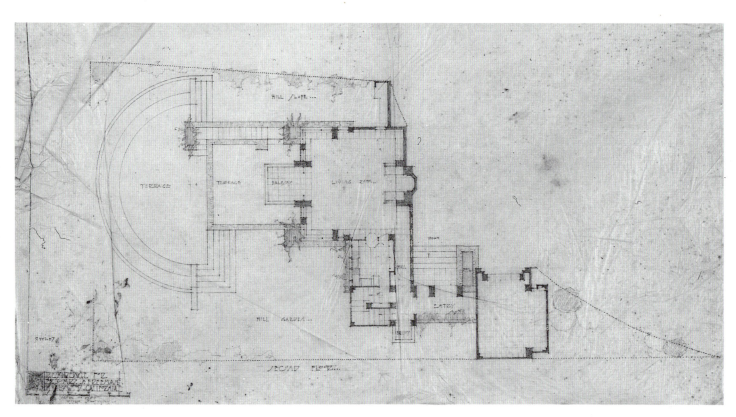

Freeman House. Living room

147 (*above*). Looking diagonally across to southwest
(c. 1928).

148 (*right*). Corner window (c. 1924–25).

149. Cooper House project, La Grange, Ill., 1890. Plan of house and elevation of barn.

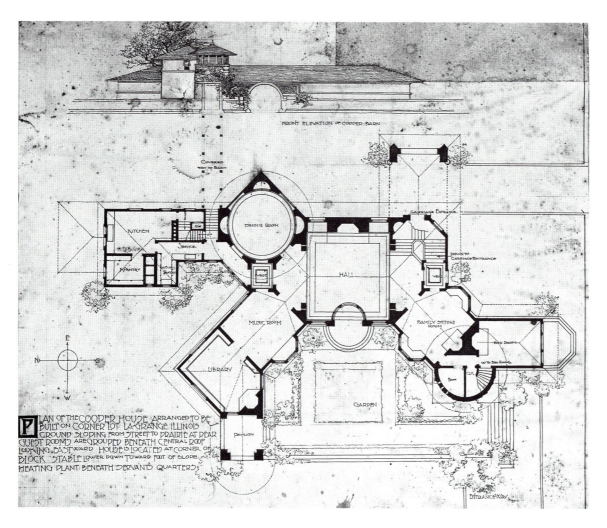

handle, becomes a metaphor for the sense of expanding space contained under the overarching beams of the living room ceiling and formalized in the exedra of the lower garden retaining wall.

■ ■ ■

Wright's development of diagonal planning in the early 1920s was not totally without precedent in his earlier work, nor was it without parallels in contemporaneous artistic movements in Europe. Indeed, the diagonal axis has played an important role in planning throughout history—here one immediately thinks of the Acropolis in Athens, Hadrian's Villa, and the radiating avenues of Baroque cities and gardens—but its deliberate use in the design of buildings themselves is a relatively modern development. To the classically trained architect, the diagonal implied irregularity and irrationality. Its appearance in the rib vaults, canted piers, and flying buttresses of medieval cathedrals was one of the traditional criticisms of Gothic architecture. The recourse to diagonal shifts in axis as a way of accommodating the desire for a more picturesque aspect and casual feeling, particularly in domestic architecture, thus came to the fore only in the later nineteenth century, on the heels of the Gothic Revival.

Wright was influenced by this development and employed diagonal shifts in axis from the very beginning of his career as a way of opening up the plan and giving direction to the interior space, as in his "butterfly plan" for the Cooper House in La Grange, Illinois, of 1890 (fig. 149).[28]

Such dispersive tendencies were soon overcome, however, by the move to more compact and classical solutions, as in the Winslow House, where the grid of the suburban site makes itself felt as the underlying principle of order. In the mature Prairie House, the desire for a sense of free-flowing space led Wright to open up the corner and deny its role of containing and bounding interior space, although any explicit use of diagonals was restricted to the rotation of small square bays to form terminating projections of the orthogonal axes themselves (fig. 56).[29]

Aside from a few instances like the Glasner House, it is quite apparent that in the earlier stages of his career Wright considered the diagonal axis unconventional and too radical for the average client. He generally restricted it to buildings for himself or members of his family, where he could experiment, as in the main assembly hall of the Hillside Home School (fig. 79). It was only in Taliesin that Wright freed the interior almost completely from the regulating lines of an orthogonal grid. In sympathetic response to the angled slope of the site, an assertive diagonal axis defines the main space of the living room to provide an unbounded sense of immediacy with the landscape outside (figs. 72, 89). The great chimney mass in the one corner and the window diagonally opposite it become like two ends of a bow strung in tension by the implied diagonal axis. The eye traverses the space in a flash and perceives in an instant the sense of oneness with the landscape. The diagonal axis cuts across boundaries and makes connections immediate, while the arching line of the bow-like ceiling ties the interior panorama to the curve of the distant horizon.

An integral part of the "natural architecture" of Taliesin, the diagonal axis appeared only tentatively in a few domestic commissions between 1911 and 1914, and then was almost completely repressed for a good eight or nine years. When Wright returned to it in the early 1920s, he did so at the very moment he sensed the need to renew the modernist focus of his work, and for this reason it is interesting to note the parallels with advanced European thinking of the time. The diagonal had been proposed in the late teens by Rus-

sian Constructivist artists such as Malevich and Tatlin as the very index of modernity (fig. 294). Its vital, dynamic line was likewise emphasized by Kandinsky in his writings and teaching at the Bauhaus in the early twenties.[30] But it is in Holland, the country where Wright's architecture was most esteemed and where, since the early teens, his work had been most influential, that the parallels are the clearest.

The spatial experience of virtual, or implied, diagonality in the Freeman House immediately recalls Piet Mondrian's contemporary Diamond paintings, just as the explicit diagonality of the Little Dipper reminds one of Theo Van Doesburg's diagonal "counter-compositions" of 1924–25 (figs. 150, 151). Mondrian adopted the diamond format as early as 1918–19 for a series of grid paintings continuing through 1921, followed by another group of four works (1925–26) in which the square central space projects a sense of dynamic continuity, but without forsaking the orthogonal structure of vertical and horizontal lines. Van Doesburg, the spokesman for the De Stijl group, made diagonality the *sine qua non* of what he described as a new Elementarism, attributing to its dynamic form a spiritual "space-time" dimension he believed would help break down the traditional barriers between art and life.[31]

In avant-garde European circles, diagonality became a polemical, and at times explosive, issue.[32] In its very form anticlassical and antiacademic, it was adopted more often than not for theoretical reasons. Wright's return to the diagonal axis in the early 1920s, by contrast, had a much more broadly defined purpose, driven by spatial and structural as well as contextual and psychological factors. The diagonal had always been for him, even in its restricted use in the Prairie House, a very practical means for cutting across the boundary between indoors and outdoors. It therefore had an empirically understood spatial dimension that marked its use as a sign of modernity. The freedom and flexibility it afforded in relating building to natural environment, which he had exploited so fully in Taliesin, was called forth once again by the mountainous terrain of Southern California. The textile-block method of construction, developed in re-

150. Piet Mondrian: *Painting, I*, 1926.

151. Theo Van Doesburg: *Counter-Composition V*, 1924.

152. Imperial Hotel. Design for floor plate (c. 1920).

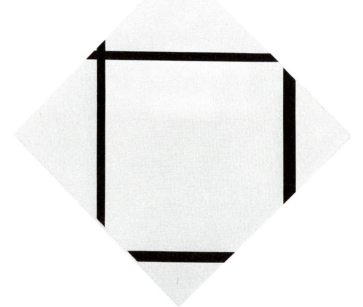

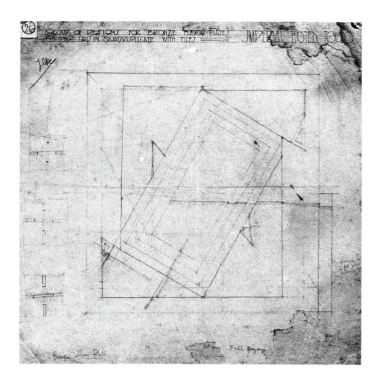

sponse to local conditions, further suggested the return to the diagonal. Given the modular system of a square grid directly expressed in the lines of the adjoining blocks of the floor, the almost automatic response was to draw the diagonal from corner to corner to define the greatest internal dimension.

At the level of content, the purpose of the textile-block system as in part a counteraction to seismic disturbances also played an important role. Wright viewed the diagonal as an image of unrestrained force, erupting out of the confines of the orthogonal grid. Its architectural expression might therefore be seen as an acceptance and reflection of nature's own force. In this regard, it is fascinating to note how Wright allowed the repressed diagonal to surface in the decoration of a number of his buildings between 1914 and 1922, and most particularly the Imperial Hotel.[33] In the square bronze floor tiles of the reception areas, for instance, and the carved facing blocks of lava, he used a complex diagonal geometry to animate, break up, and give illusionistic depth to the surface (fig. 152). In some cases, a layered pattern results from multiple rotations; in others, an angular insertion cuts into the block to deny its foursquare integrity; and in still others, the constantly overlapping and shifting planes of the carved lava seem to express the turbulent tilting and folding action of earthquakes. Indeed, Wright's description of the way he intended to combat the force of earthquakes in the hotel is much more suggestive of these decorative designs than of the plan or engineering of the building itself.[34]

Wright always later referred to the diagonal axis as the "reflex." The "reflex," he believed, allowed for "a perfect flexibility," a sense of being "at ease." In its automatic—one might say unconscious—aspect, it implied a lack of resistance, a relaxation of the will that "yields to circumstances, to pressure" and produces "a plastic form."[35] In its expression of plasticity, the "reflex" diagonal subsumed in one general form the modern notions of freedom of space, dynamic movement, and intimacy with nature. In the final two projects we shall now turn to, the Lake Tahoe Summer Resort and the Johnson Death Valley Compound, Wright developed these ideas to produce buildings that expand the plastic role of the diagonal from plan to section and from the single building to the grouping of buildings. At the same time, he reached back into the history of each site to secure for the buildings' forms a temporal, and not just spatial, continuity with the landscape.

Lake Tahoe Resort

Lake Tahoe and Death Valley are two of the most remarkable natural environments in California. Both are located along the eastern fault line of the Sierra Nevada mountain chain, at the edge of the Great Basin extending across Nevada and Utah. One is an alpine lake, the other a desert sink. As opposite in geological and environmental terms as they might be, they nevertheless share many features. Both exhibit the effects of the great volcanic forces and glacial activity that determined the physiography of the region. Both were inhabited by significant groups of Native Ameri-

cans. And both were becoming prominent in the late teens and twenties in the growing tourist business that was turning California's eastern mountains and deserts into real stage sets to match, and sometimes even to supplant, those of its movie industry. Wright's designs for the two sites grew out of these conditions and reflect in their unique forms his different reactions to those environments.

Despite the large scale of both projects and the enormous amount of creative effort that Wright put into them, little is known about the actual circumstances of either. What is almost certain, however, is that the one for Lake Tahoe came first, beginning around June 1923.[36] Like the Doheny project, which it directly followed, the Tahoe Resort may well have been a real estate promotion scheme that never got beyond the preliminary design stage. The site, nearly 240 acres at the southern tip of the lake, known as Emerald Bay, was owned by the Armstrong family of Oakland, California. Whether it was their idea to commission Wright or one that was proposed to them by others, they appear to have taken advantage of the publicity from the event to raise the value of their property, which they sold for a significant profit less than five years later.[37]

On the California-Nevada border, about 175 miles northeast of San Francisco, Lake Tahoe is, as Mark Twain described it, "a noble sheet of blue water lifted six thousand three hundred feet above the level of the sea, and walled in by a rim of snow-clad mountain peaks that towered aloft full three thousand feet higher still!" Originating with powerful volcanic forces followed by continuous glacial action, it reaches depths of 1,645 feet below its surface elevation of 6,229 feet. Its name comes from the Washoe word for "Big Water," or "Water in a High Place." In his promotional book of 1915 marking the completion of the Rim of the Lake road and the development of the local tourist industry on a new scale, George Wharton James called Tahoe the "Lake of the Sky."[38]

The area owned by the Armstrongs was, as James noted, "the choicest portion of Lake Tahoe."[39] Named for the brilliant color of its crystal-clear water, Emerald Bay is

153. Lake Tahoe, Calif./Nev. Emerald Bay.

154. Lake Tahoe Resort project, 1923–24. Photomontage of Emerald Bay, showing Inn buildings on Fannette Island, pontoon bridge with attached boats, and cabins along shore.

Lake Tahoe Resort project.

155. Fir Tree Cabin. Perspective and plan.

156. Big Tree (Wigwam) Cabin. Plan and elevation.

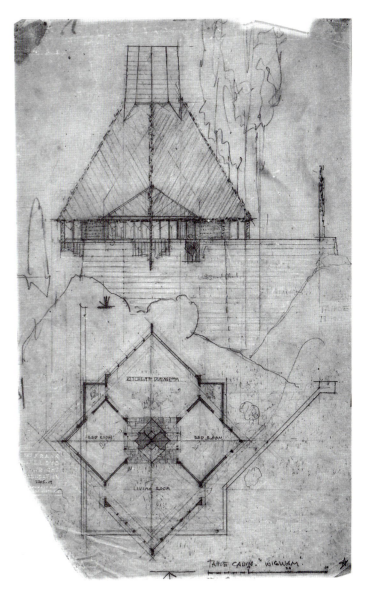

closed in by steep, dark, pine-covered walls of glacial mo-
raines, rising up to snow-capped mountain peaks, and
edged with nearly white, superfine sandy shores (fig. 153).
Near the center of this almost perfect oval hollow is a small,
tree-covered granite island, the only one in Lake Tahoe.
Wright made Fannette Island the focus of the plan, locating
the quadrangle of the Emerald Inn on its western edge and
connecting it to the shore by a pontoon bridge. Houseboats
would be moored to this floating structure, while cabins on
the shore stepped up the precipitous slopes between the
dense fir trees. Wright used the modernist technique of
photomontage, apparently the only time he ever did, to emphasize the subtle, nearly imperceptible nature of this intervention in the landscape (fig. 154).[40]

Although the overall plan of the resort defined by the
inn, the docks, and the bridge was laid out on strictly orthogonal lines, almost all of the individual cabin and house-
boat designs exhibit extremely varied diagonal planning
techniques. In some of the shore cabins, for example, such
as the one called the Fir Tree Type, Wright expanded the
open-angled plan of the Doheny House C to allow the bed-

room wings that project from the central octagon of the living room/kitchen area to enclose a terrace broadened out to
120 degrees (fig. 155). In others, where there was not enough
level land, he went even further in developing some of the
spatial implications of rotation. The Big Tree (Wigwam)
Type Cabin, for instance, is composed of a square rotated
forty-five degrees within another, like the assembly hall at
the Hillside Home School (figs. 156, 79). But here the rotated
square is made the larger of the two and thus projects
through the outer casing of the terrace to emphasize in a
much more dynamic way the full extent of the diagonal. An
abstracted "totem pole" at the outer end of the angled ter-

Lake Tahoe Resort project.

157 (*left*). Family Barge. Sketch elevations and plans.

158 (*right*). Barge for Two. Plan (redrawn c. 1940).

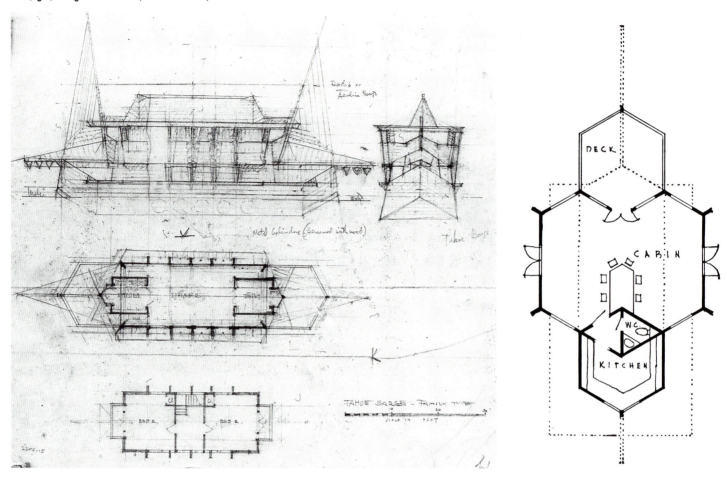

race wall stakes the composition to the ground as it opens out along its rotational path above the slope.

A few of the houseboats, such as the Catamaran, were based on the idea of a raft and given a rectangular shape. Almost all the others, however, evolved from the diagonal geometry suggested by the boat's prow. For the largest one, the Family Barge, with prows at both ends, Wright returned to the plan of the Robie House, eliminating everything but its main volume and thereby exaggerating its boat-like character (fig. 157). He also expanded the angle of the prow from forty-five to sixty degrees. In the smaller Barge for Two, he took advantage of this change to make a rippling, complex shape of three interlocking hexagons, with the long central axis from the open foredeck to the enclosed kitchen in the aft extending from point to point (figs. 158, 159).

In the designs for the Tahoe Summer Resort, the diag-onal geometry is not limited to the plans but is reflected in the sections and elevations as well. The materials and shapes were chosen for their direct relationships to local conditions. The shore cabins were to be constructed of poly-chrome-stained boards above white, textile-block bases and terraces made with the beach sand and thus blending in color and texture with the shoreline. The steep, pyramidal forms of the lapped wood roofs, edged with verdigris copper hips and ridges, would have echoed the shape and color of the surrounding conifers; at the same time, their tall central chimney masts and color decoration referred to the tepees of the local Washoe people, who until recently had set up their camps at Lake Tahoe for similar seasonal purposes.[41]

The diagonal geometry enabled Wright to represent architecturally both the permanent natural features of al-pine conditions and the more transient character of a partic-

159. Lake Tahoe Resort project, Barge for Two. Perspective.

ularly indigenous and expressive type of nomadic shelter. The undercutting of a sense of permanence with an implication of impermanence struck a particularly modern note. The reference to nomadic forms of shelter, along with the incorporation of boats as an essential feature of the design, reinforced this association with contemporary concerns.[42] But unlike the abstract geometric shapes that the younger Europeans were giving to their habitable volumes, Wright deliberately chose to make his Tahoe cabins and boats carry an imprint of the region's cultural and natural history. The specific choice of model allowed him to subvert the typical conception of the rustic mountain camp and replace its easily assimilable frontier image (traceable back to the Adirondacks) with a more remote, atavistic type. Any false

sense of permanence and control was denied by the fundamental transience of a type that made evidence of human construction seem, in Wright's drawings, to be totally dependent on the accidents of nature and, in the photomontage, to be almost inconsequential in view of the immense body of water lifted up by the surrounding, towering mountains.

Death Valley

Wright's work in California culminated in the project for Death Valley, begun a little over half a year after the one for Lake Tahoe. Though one of the least well known and least

160. Death Valley, Calif. View north, toward Grapevine Canyon.

documented of all his works, it is certainly one of the most consequential.[43] It marked his first contact with the desert, the environment that would serve as the basic ground for his later work, much as the prairie had done prior to 1910. So taken was Wright with the area that he ended up designing a winter dwelling for himself nearby.

The site was extraordinary for both its natural and its human history, so much so that it had already acquired a mythic place in the American mind.[44] Lying below sea level, like a deep trough between the surrounding mountain peaks of the Panamint and Amargosa ranges, the dry, ancient lake basin of Death Valley is situated at the upper edge of the Mojave Desert, on the California-Nevada bor-

der, about two hundred miles southeast of Lake Tahoe (fig. 160). Though the same in shape and orientation, it is in every respect the inverse of that sparkling alpine environment. It is almost as if, like a vision nearly completely evaporated and eroded, Death Valley is Lake Tahoe at a much later stage in the earth's history. And where the name Tahoe derives from Native American lore and connotes a sense of a spiritual, life-giving, natural force, Death Valley received its sinister name from those forty-niners who survived the disastrous attempt to drive a short-cut through it in their quest for gold.

Programmatically, the two projects were also nearly inversions of each other. The one was a summer resort for lakeside vacationers planning stays of limited duration in a festive setting suitable for families and different-sized groups; the other was a solitary, permanent winter retreat in an eerie, remote canyon high above the desert floor for a millionaire Chicago insurance man, his wife, and a reclusive friend. Where for the Tahoe project Wright designed a series of wonderfully varied, small-scale objects of an impermanent, seasonal nature to convey a camp-like atmosphere, in the project for Death Valley he proposed the exact opposite. It was to be more an earthwork than a building (fig. 133). And the application of the diagonal axis to the overall scheme allowed Wright to endow the continuous, low-lying forms of the connected structures with a sense of the ever-changing, imperceptibly shifting quality of the desert landscape itself. Wright always referred to the project as the A. M. Johnson Desert Compound and Shrine. When his design was rejected in favor of the Spanish Colonial hacienda that was actually built, the owner called it Death Valley Ranch (fig. 169). But that name has not stuck either. Rather, tourists from around the world have come to know the buildings in Grapevine Canyon as Scotty's Castle.

Wright's client, Albert Mussey Johnson, was president of the Chicago-based National Life Insurance Company of the United States of America, for whose headquarters in Chicago Wright would design a spectacular skyscraper using the cantilevered construction of the Imperial Hotel, with a curtain wall set back in stages and clad in iridescent sheets of copper and glass.[45] A straitlaced religious fundamentalist and supporter of the evangelist Paul Rader, Johnson was trained at Cornell as a mining engineer. But after suffering a broken back in a train wreck while on a trip to inspect some Colorado mining properties, he had to give up that career. He then moved to Chicago, where he acquired a major interest in the National Life Insurance Company in 1902 and became its president four years later. Always attracted by the romance of the Far West, as well as the bracing effect it had on his health, Johnson early on began grubstaking the notorious prospector Walter Scott.[46]

Death Valley Scotty first went out to Death Valley in 1884 to work for a survey party running the state boundary line between California and Nevada. He also worked for the Harmony Borax Works on their 20-Mule Team wagons and then as a cowboy before signing on as a performer in the Buffalo Bill Wild West Show. After leaving the troupe in 1902, he got the idea that all he had to do to get rich was to claim to have discovered a gold mine in Death Valley. Gullible Eastern businessmen would flock to grubstake him. One taker was Julian Gerard of the Knickerbocker Trust Company of New York, but the longest lasting was Albert Johnson. Gerard, when he suspected Scotty's secret mine was merely a hoax, pulled out of the three-way partnership, but Johnson, even when he realized there was no gold mine, continued to support Scotty as a companion and friend. It was to be a lifelong friendship that centered on their love of the desert landscape of Death Valley, a landscape Scotty knew better than anyone else. "I don't know of any other man in the world that I would rather go on a camping trip with than Scott," Johnson wrote to his wife, Bessie, in 1906, following one of his first, abortive attempts to get Scotty to show him the mine.[47] Soon thereafter, Johnson began spending his winter vacations in Death Valley on more extended camping trips with Scotty; and by 1915, he started purchasing land in the northern reaches of the Grapevine Mountains, in the area known as Grapevine Canyon.

Death Valley had been the home of a fairly vigorous borax mining industry since the 1880s, centered around Ryan, farther south in the Black Mountains. Following the gold mining boom of the first decade of the twentieth century, during which Scotty made his name, so to speak, the activity in precious metals and in borax began to diminish. At the same time, the frontier myth of Death Valley began to be popularized, attracting the more adventuresome type of tourist to the area. In the late teens and early twenties, Western writers like Dane Coolidge and Zane Grey featured it in their stories.[48] Erich von Stroheim filmed the horrifying

161. Death Valley, northern area.

concluding scenes of *Greed*, based on Frank Norris's novel *McTeague* (1899), on location in Death Valley in the summer of 1923; and in the following winter Hollywood's first all-color film, Zane Grey's *Wanderer of the Wasteland*, was shot there. The first automobile road was begun in the fall of 1925, and by the following spring a hotel opened at Stovepipe Wells. The final step in this changeover from frontier economy to tourist attraction took place in 1927, when Borax Consolidated closed its mines and opened instead the elegant Furnace Creek Inn, designed by the Los Angeles architect Albert C. Martin.

On their first camping trips, Johnson and Scotty set up light wood-and-canvas tents on what was the former Stain-

inger Ranch, where the German immigrant Jacob Staininger had established a grape, fig, and vegetable farm in the 1880s that gave Grapevine Canyon its name. The site on a wide bend in the upper reaches of the canyon, at a comfortable altitude of three thousand feet, was fed by a number of underground springs and was accessible by road (fig. 161).[49] Earlier, the largest Shoshone village in the area had been located there, home of the *pakwinavi*, or regional chief. It would prove to be a perfect spot for establishing a more permanent camp. By 1921, partly at the behest of his wife, Johnson decided to do just that. Construction began the following year on a frame-and-stucco two-story house, garage, and cook house, under the supervision of F. W. Kropf.

162. F. W. Kropf: Johnson Ranch, Death Valley, 1922–24 (c. 1924).

Other smaller structures were added over the next two years, so that by 1924 the ranch, where Scotty could stay throughout the year, had scattered about the site a chicken house, a dog house, a crafts or foreman's house, and a separate toilet cellar. The buildings were simple, unadorned boxes, about as bleak and uninspired as could be (fig. 162).[50]

At some point, Johnson began thinking of enlarging the group and giving it a more substantial and elaborate architectural treatment. For this he first turned to Wright, whom he would also commission to design his company's headquarters in Chicago. The latter project was undertaken in the summer of 1924, although it may have been discussed earlier.[51] It is almost certain, however, that work on the desert home preceded the office building, because we know that Wright visited Johnson's newly erected lodgings in Death Valley perhaps as early as December 1923 but no later than, and in all likelihood at, the beginning of March 1924. "We took a trip into Death Valley together," Wright later recalled, "where he [Johnson] and Death Valley Scotty had made a place in which to live. He drove his own car, a Dodge, I rode beside him and Nature staged a show for us all the way" (*A* I, 253).[52]

Wright pictured Johnson as someone "extraordinarily intelligent," "intensely interested in ideas," and very possessive of them. "Now, Mr. Wright, remember!" Johnson reportedly said in discussing the National Life Insurance Company Building, "I want a Virgin. I want a Virgin" (*A* I, 253, 252).[53] But if Johnson was "a strange mixture of the fanatic, the mystic, Shylock, the humanist," it was the usurer's stinginess that came to the fore in the case of his winter retreat (*A* I, 253). Wright, it appears, was expected to incorporate the existing structures in his overall scheme. This was a very unusual constraint for him to accept, but jobs were rare at the time, and the site and program presented a unique challenge.

Wright probably began designing soon after receiving a letter from Johnson, dated 16 March 1924, supplying the levels of existing structures on the site (fig. 163). It was prob-

ably also at this time that he received the large color photograph over which he sketched his earliest ideas (fig. 164). The design went through at least two preliminary stages before being worked up into presentation drawings in the late fall and early winter of 1924–25.[54] The overall concept of the site plan never varied; the only changes would be in the main house and chapel complex.

Wright's impulse was to unify the disparate structures in a single megastructure articulated in relation to the landscape as a whole and fully open to it rather than closed in on itself (fig. 133). The existing buildings were joined together and extended by intersecting horizontal bands of textile-block construction forming causeways, covered loggias, and walled precincts, as well as enclosed living and working spaces. The original rectangular house in the center of the composition, directly facing the access road to the southeast, was turned into a guest house. It was connected to the toilet cellar and cook house behind, as well as to the garage and chicken house to the right and in front, to form a service court or "compound," as Wright called it, using a term of Southeast Asian derivation he undoubtedly picked up in Japan.[55]

The low wall enclosing the compound joins building to building to form a dynamic, De Stijl–like composition (fig. 165). A stream issuing from the springs higher up the hill flows through the service court, which is bridged over in

163. Johnson Desert Compound project, Death Valley, 1923?/24–25. Preliminary site plan.

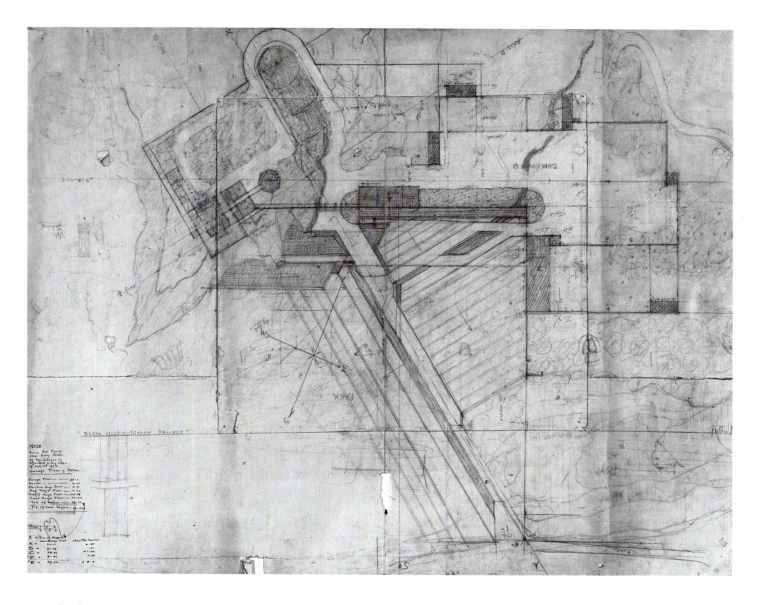

part. In the main, L-shaped forecourt, bounded by the garage on the right and the guest house to the rear, the water is collected in a long, trough-like basin. As it overflows the edge, it is channeled into a series of pools that take on the angled contours of the sloping land, which in turn is terraced and divided into strips for cultivation. The driveway cutting across this court at an angle of thirty degrees forms a raised causeway, acting as a dam or sluice gate to control the water irrigating the terraced gardens.

The main entrance to the complex is located at the end of this drive, just to the left of the guest house, in front of which is a pool in the shape of an equilateral triangle. Be-

yond a columned portico, the inner court leads back on the right, at an angle of 60 degrees, to the service court and across a stream of water on the left, at a less acute, 120-degree angle, to the entirely new construction of the Johnson House and Chapel. The octagonal mass and spire of the chapel direct the view to a circular fountain that terminates the diagonal axis of the drive on the slopes of Windy Point Hill.[56] Pumped from the triangular pool below, water cascades down the sand garden forming a base for the terrace of the main house and chapel. This L-shaped building is angled thirty degrees southeast of the line established by the long wall of the entrance portico and guest house to align

Johnson Desert Compound project.

164. Preliminary sketch over photograph (by Charles W. Beam) of site.

165. Final site plan.

N

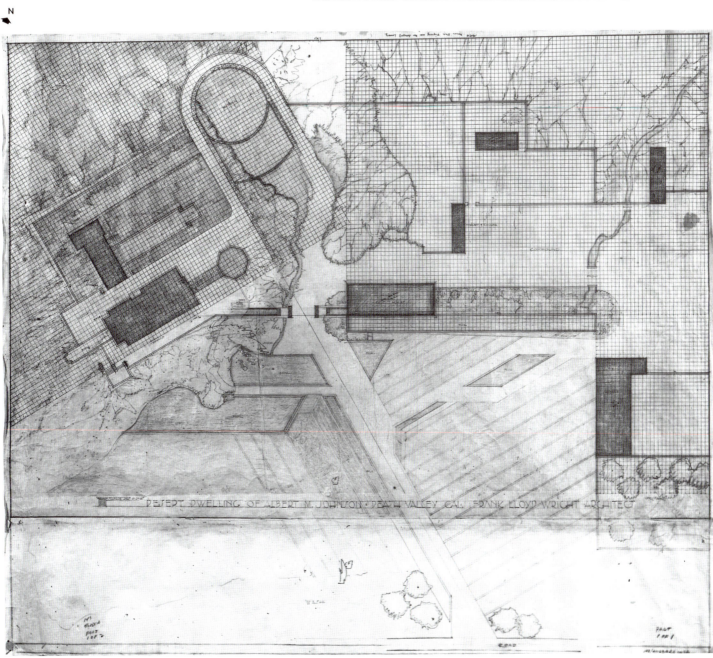

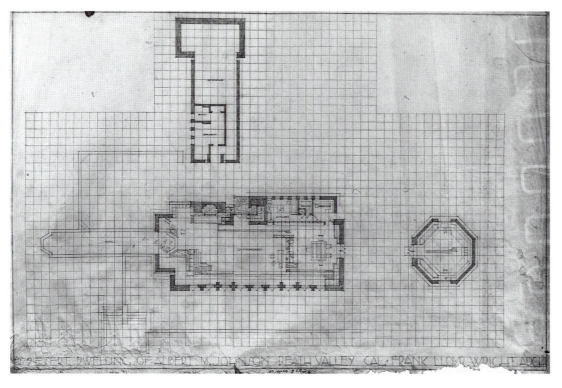

Johnson Desert Compound project.

166. Plan of house and chapel, second floor.

167. South elevation of house and chapel.

168. Sections through living room and bedroom wing of house.

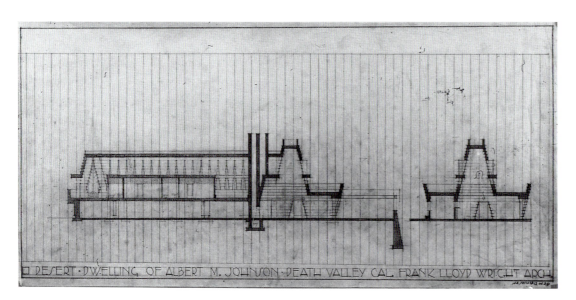

with the spur of land pointing down the canyon to the valley (fig. 133).

The new L-shaped building, which received the most attention as the plans were developed into presentation drawings, is composed of three parts. These are separated into discrete units on the ground level, but are linked by bridges on the second floor (fig. 166). The first unit is the chapel, or shrine, at the northeast end, which the Johnsons no doubt intended to use in their effort to convert the native population to Christianity. Its octagonal form echoes the dome-shaped *kahni* the Shoshone traditionally built for use in the winter.[57] The entrance to the chapel is under the bridge, directly opposite the door into the dining area of the house. The main body of the house, which is slightly bigger than the original one (the guest house in the new configuration), comprises a combined dining and living room whose entire southeast wall is lined with floor-to-ceiling doors opening onto a terrace leading down to plunge pools (fig. 167). The cross-section of this room is a two-stepped pyramid, making the tall central area a double-height volume and the outer two bands low, single-story spaces covered by outdoor platform terraces (fig. 168).[58] The two-story volume is contained within walls battering in at a fifteen-degree angle to form a long, Maya-style corbel vault over the entire length. The bedroom wing, located above a partial ground floor devoted to storage and servants' quarters, is perpendicular to the living room and faces southwest, opening onto terraces and balconies with views down the canyon.[59]

The final plans for the project were drawn on gridded or lined paper, following the four-foot unit system Wright had employed in the Imperial Hotel and adapted for his textile-block system of construction. The thirty/sixty-degree geometry, which was used to a much different effect in the Tahoe project, here resulted in a radical degree of asymmetry for Wright.[60] The layered composition of long horizontals, with their battered profiles and canted roofs, derives from his attempt, first in Hollyhock House and then in the Doheny project, to find in the architecture of the Maya and American Pueblos an appropriately "earthbound" form for the mountainous region of the Southwest. In the Johnson Desert Compound, following Lake Tahoe, Wright inflected those forms toward the shapes produced by the nomadic tribes of the Great Basin, thereby giving them the jagged, almost savage look he associated with the "strange firm forms" of the desert (*A* II, 453).[61]

The repeated geometric motifs, forming bands of stepped and herringbone designs, may have been inspired by the patterns of local Shoshone, or Panamint, baskets, which Bessie Johnson collected, but the overall effect of the project seemed too rude and uncivilized to the Johnsons (compare fig. 178). According to Hank Johnston, Death Valley Scotty's biographer, Albert Johnson rejected Wright's project, despite its "indigenous purity," as being too much "in keeping with one's idea of an adobe Indian village—not a real hacienda, which we wanted."[62] Wright, on the other hand, implied that Johnson never really had it in him to go through with the project. "He was intensely interested in ideas," Wright wrote, "though not himself the kind of man inclined to build much. He seemed rather of the type, called conservative, who, tempted, will sneak up behind an idea, pinch it behind and invariably turn and run" (*A* I, 252).[63]

In late 1925 Johnson turned to a former Stanford classmate of his wife, an engineer named Matt Roy Thompson, for a much more ordinary and domestic-looking Spanish Colonial design. Thompson, who supervised Johnson's building operation from 1926 to 1931, was soon joined by the Chicago designer C. Alexander MacNeilledge, hired to direct the overall planning, and then, in 1928, by the architect Martin de Dubovay. Thompson's original scheme for enlarging the existing house was to duplicate it with a second building to the rear, leaving a courtyard in between. Arcaded porticoes were added to unify the whole. With the help of MacNeilledge and Dubovay, the decorative treatment became much richer, with tile roofs and medieval towers creating a picturesque skyline (fig. 169).

The placement of a Chimes Tower at the spot where Wright's chapel was to have been, and the plan for a foun-

169. C. Alexander MacNeilledge (with Matt Roy Thompson and Martin de Dubovay): Death Valley (Johnson) Ranch , late 1920s. Aerial perspective, from south.

170. Thompson, MacNeilledge, and de Dubovay: Scotty's Castle (Johnson Ranch), 1926–31. Aerial view, looking south.

tain court between it and the house, made use of some of Wright's ideas. But the kidney-shaped pool directly in front of the house, defining the circular drive leading to the central portico, was a purely conventional, textbook solution, which, like everything else, gives Scotty's Castle the appearance of a self-contained, proto-Disney world of fantasy completely at odds with the surrounding landscape and cultural milieu (fig. 170). It is in contrast to this that Wright's conception of the building as an earthwork becomes all the more vivid. Inspired by the desert, which he had come to know for the first time, as well as by the Native American cultures that had preceded him at the site, Wright allowed the angled slopes of the surrounding hills to inform the geometry of the plan so as to link building and landscape in a

more dynamic way than he had ever achieved before, while at the same time he gave the building a form and texture that resonated with indigenous traditions.

■ ■ ■

Grapevine Canyon is an isolated spot on the extreme northeastern rim of Death Valley, more than 130 miles from the southern entrance through Saratoga Spring and almost 60 miles north of Furnace Creek. The road running north passes over sand dunes and salt flats after dipping to 282 feet below sea level, the lowest point in the Western Hemisphere (fig. 161). It is bounded by steep mountain ranges on both sides, rising to over 11,000 feet in the Panamints on the west and to nearly 9,000 in the Amargosa on the east. The sloping alluvial fans angling down from the hills and canyons constantly remind one of the powerful seismic and volcanic action that created this enormous, sun-bleached fault basin and gave birth to the local Native American myth of its origin. To put a halt to tribal bickering and warfare, the gods, it is said,

blew off the tops of the mountains and poured molten rock upon the warriors. The warring tribes fled blindly. The earth turned to jelly beneath them. It trembled and shook and ran in ripples under their flying feet. Great rents appeared in the earth and cut off all escape. The gods split a mountain chain open and poured an ocean of water through the gap. What is now Death Valley became an inland sea.

By this time the gods were interested in their work. They loaded the waters of the inland sea with salt and then dried the waters up. They tossed the mountains around in liquid form and solidified them with vertical rivers dropped from the sky. When the cooling waters washed away a mountain range another was thrust up to take its place. The new range was twisted, split, and stood on end. At length, the gods thought that the Indians had been punished enough. Besides, the gods were getting tired. So they stopped the tor-

171. Ubehebe Crater, Death Valley.

172. Death Valley. Road up Grapevine Canyon, with Chimes Tower and Johnson Ranch in distance.

rential rains, took all the moisture from the air and left Death Valley to slip and settle into its present form.[64]

The volcanic Ubehebe Crater, its name thought by some to mean "Big Basket in the Rock," is located at the north end of the valley (fig. 171).[65] Owned by Johnson as part of Lower Grapevine Ranch, it forms a natural signpost where the side road leading up into Grapevine Canyon branches off to the northeast (fig. 161). Leaving the valley behind, with the peak of Tin Mountain rising to a height of nearly 10,000 feet across to the southwest, the canyon first narrows and then opens out as the road takes a sharp bend due east before beginning its final climb through the Grapevine Mountains, the northernmost group in the Amargosa Range (fig. 172). Johnson and Kropf located the original two-story frame-and-stucco house of 1922 parallel to this road but set back on a rocky ledge, just above the bed of the stream that flows from the spring about a mile farther up the hill (fig. 162). With the garage in front of it and the cook house behind it to the east, the main axis of the house was centered on the lower wall of the canyon closing the view to the south, making the house appear, as Scotty's Castle still does today, as if it were designed without any regard for the lay of the land (fig. 170).

Instead of merely embellishing what already existed, Wright reoriented the entire composition through the use of the "reflex" diagonal. He deemphasized the importance of the existing buildings in the more confined upper end of the site in order to direct the view across the valley to the southwest. This was done by (1) adding the entirely new house and chapel at the western edge; (2) pivoting that unit to follow the spur of land angling down the valley; and (3) focusing attention on the shifting sightline by the diagonal causeway connecting the access road to the main entrance across the bed of the canyon.

For anyone driving up the canyon from the valley, the spire of the chapel would have acted as a landmark, in the way the Chimes Tower still does, to indicate the approach to the site at the bend in the road. But rather than allowing you

to enter the compound from below, at the bend, as one still does today, Wright's plan would have made you continue to climb the road beyond the house before forcing you to turn around on yourself 120 degrees (fig. 165). The real drama of the landscape would then have unfolded as you followed the causeway angled toward the rounded hill of Windy Point, lying just behind the entrance court of the house (fig. 133). When you passed along this embankment, the vista to the southwest, focusing on Tin Mountain, would have opened up to your left, and the panorama of Death Valley in the

173. Johnson Ranch. View west across front garden toward Tin Mountain.

distance would have been defined by the span of the causeway (fig. 173). Like the leading edge of this sweeping arm, the house at the end would have jutted through the wall of the portico at an angle of 150 degrees to project the axis of the canyon across space through the seventy-foot-long pool of water sticking out from it like a finger.

The diagonal axis of the Death Valley project functions on a metaphorical level as well as a formal one and points to a new stage in Wright's conception of architecture in its representation of nature. The extraordinary horizontal extension of the main facade of the complex establishes a man-made horizon line against which the seismic folding, faulting, and tilting that originally created the landscape can be felt in the disruptive asymmetries and angularities of the layout (figs. 133, 165). In breaching the self-contained form of Hollyhock House and allowing its mesa-like elements to look as if they had been deposited and shifted with the gradual movement of the earth's crust, Wright represented the activity of a constructive rather than destructive nature.

The extruded, fluid forms of the Johnson Compound appear to have been shaped and laid low over time by the process of continuous erosion that made the "striated and stratified masses" of what Wright later called the "noble architecture" of the "great nature masonry" of the desert (A I, 304). Indeed, the triangular bed of irrigated land, kept in check by the pivoting causeway, holds in suspension the image of an alluvial fan in the making. The angle of the dam, as it responds to the insistent pressure of earth and water against its upper edge, reveals a new symbiotic relationship between architecture and nature. The resolution of the conflict between force and resistance occurs along the elastic and responsive line of the diagonal that Wright likened to a natural "reflex" and believed to be particularly appropriate to the desert.[66]

As mentioned earlier, Wright described the "reflex"

diagonal as "the natural easy attitude" for organizing buildings in relation to one another and to the landscape. Unlike the domineering rigidity of "the major axis and the minor axis of classic architecture," the diagonal "yields to circumstances, to pressure."[67] By identifying the diagonal with a motor reflex, Wright emphasized the involuntary aspect that made it seem so natural a response to the intractability of the desert. The diagonal causeway in the Death Valley project is the first example in his work of such a bending to the dictates of nature. The dam does not rigidly hold back the silted mass indicated in the foreground of the perspective, but yields to the pressure (fig. 133). In that give-and-take with the landscape, nature appears not as a hostile force to be contained and controlled but as a self-governing process, partially, and perhaps only temporarily, channeled to human purposes.[68] Nature becomes an active figure in the representational process of architecture.

The attitude toward nature expressed in the Death Valley project cannot be divorced from Wright's choice of style or from the mythological construct that Death Valley itself had come to represent. Death Valley was, and still is in many ways, the last frontier. It is the Achilles' heel of the American myth. Romantic figures like Death Valley Scotty survived there as they could nowhere else. With the coming of the automobile and mass communication, however, what could never be conquered by brute force was taken over by what Guy Debord has called the "society of the spectacle."[69] Myth and reality nearly completely overlapped. The radio program "Death Valley Days" began in 1930, just three years after the borax mining stopped. And only four years before that, Erich von Stroheim powerfully exploited Death Valley's "hellishness" in the final scene of *Greed*, shot the summer before Wright's visit to Johnson's ranch. Escaping to the desert in hope of salvation after murdering his wife, McTeague eventually lies broiling in the sun, without water and without any means of transportation, handcuffed to the friend he has beaten to a pulp.

Wright avoided all the easy, obvious characterizations of the place for which the archetypal huckster Scotty or the evangelical missionary Johnson might have provided the perfect pretext. Instead of turning to an imposed tradition of colonial domination (the Spanish Mission style), as Johnson's next team of designers almost immediately did, Wright identified the site with the culture that had survived there over millennia and had only recently been displaced by incursions of the White Man. In returning this human element to the figure of the landscape, Wright denaturalized Death Valley as a universal sign of inferno and offered a design for collaborating with, rather than dominating, both the landscape and its Native American cultural traditions.

Wright's Own Desert Dwelling

The degree of Wright's engagement with the problems posed by building in Death Valley is evidenced by his project for a Desert Dwelling for himself, apparently done in conjunction with the commission from Johnson. Almost nothing is known of this project, except the two autograph drawings by Wright: a plan, and a side elevation and partial section (figs. 174, 175).[70] Perhaps designed for a site in Grapevine Springs at the base of Grapevine Canyon, diagonally across the road from Ubehebe Crater (fig. 171), the building seems to emerge from its desert setting as a direct response to that dormant volcanic cone and the various issues it raised in personal and formal terms.[71] Condensing images of natural crater and man-made vessel into a singularly original form of sheltering container, Wright's Desert Dwelling integrates structure and shape by means of a newly articulated spatial model.

The compact two-story house is clearly as symbolic and as imagistic in intention as was Wright's original Oak Park house and studio. Set on a ledge and approached through an angled forecourt forming a "desert compound," the house is composed of two parts: an octagonal concrete-block shell, about sixteen feet high, surrounding a central open "patio" about forty-two feet in diameter; and a split-

On opposite page: *Wright Desert Dwelling project, Death Valley?, 1924–25.*
174. Elevation and partial section.   175. Plan.

level, right-angled block, or tower, tucked behind that, containing the various rooms and services.[72]

The walls of the octagon are corbeled out and split into laminae, like the petals of a desert flower, to hold in tension an overhead awning. The awning was to have had a central oculus, directly over the circular pool in the desert floor that establishes a vertical axis from earth and water to light and sky around which the house revolves. Defining that axis, on the far wall of the court directly opposite the entrance, is a monumental fireplace and chimney. Rising through the full height of the court like a backbone or spine, it divides the split-level living quarters from the representational vessel of space in front. To one side of the hearth, a stairway leads down to the lower servant's room, kitchen, and dining room; to the other, stairs lead up to the bedrooms, study, and roof garden. Closets and bathrooms are located in the central service core behind the chimney, while balconies overlooking the patio court angle out from its flanks.

At first glance, the house has the appearance of a barbican, obviously defensive in nature. But that image soon dissolves into something halfway between a natural crater and a man-made cistern or vessel protected from, yet receptive to, the elements. The defensive, inward-looking *parti* of a courtyard dwelling immediately reminds us of Hollyhock House, where the patio court similarly was open to the sky and contained a body of water (fig. 107). But the forms of Hollyhock House, as well as its materials of construction, were quite different. The sham wood-and-stucco walls and canted roofs recall the shapes of Maya temples in an unusually direct, historicizing way. In the project for the Desert Dwelling, the plastic treatment of the forms seems to result from the special characteristics of the textile-block method of construction and its associations both with basketry and with pottery making. No direct reference is made to any particular historical type of architecture: the building appears to grow out of the ground in an entirely unexpected, yet natural way.

The historical references are of a more general sort, archetypal and embedded one within another. On the most obvious level, the compact central-plan building, open to

the sky, can be likened to the indigenous Shoshone *kahni*, a low, domed structure with a fire hole in the middle of its partially excavated floor. Within the broader context of Amerindian culture, this dwelling-type clearly relates to the sacred form of the kiva. In Wright's work, with its deep roots in the Western tradition, the octagonal plan can be traced back to the medieval sources of the library and studio of his Oak Park house and other Shingle Style buildings (figs. 23, 24). But where its earlier uses may simply have been as a Richardsonian device, its reappearance in the chapel of the Johnson house project clearly points to the relation of that centralized plan-type to the Early Christian martyrium and to the symbolism of death and resurrection through immersion associated with it in the later medieval baptistry, where the building becomes a symbolic vessel for the activity it is meant to contain.[73]

What underlies the form, both in Wright's understanding of its historical significance and in his delicate rendition of it for the desert setting of Death Valley, is, indeed, the image of a vessel or container. In the legend of Taliesin, the Cauldron of Inspiration and Knowledge was literally a source of regeneration. Wright undoubtedly had that connection in mind when, during the years he was in East Asia, he purchased a group of Chinese Tea Jars, which he then incorporated in the reconstruction of Taliesin (fig. 176). He placed them on the ledges and parapets of the house as if to signify the new meaning he was trying to impart to those walls that had been transformed by the fire into the "smoking crater of a volcano." They were, in Wright's words, part of "the story within the story: ancient comment on the New" (*A* I, 177).

By the mid-1920s, the idea of the fired vessel or pot had become for Wright a highly charged image of regeneration; and its shape, totally continuous and protective yet wholly responsive to its contents, presented a new model for representation.[74] Unlike the classical archetype of the hut, the vessel or pot was plastic rather than clastic, spatial rather than structural. Unlike other archetypal models, such as the cave or the tent, the pot provided a continuous image of inside and outside at once, while remaining stable and

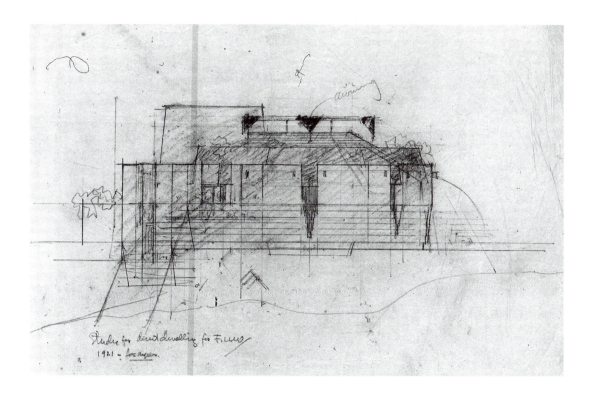

Study for desert dwelling for F. LL Wright
1921 - Los Angeles.

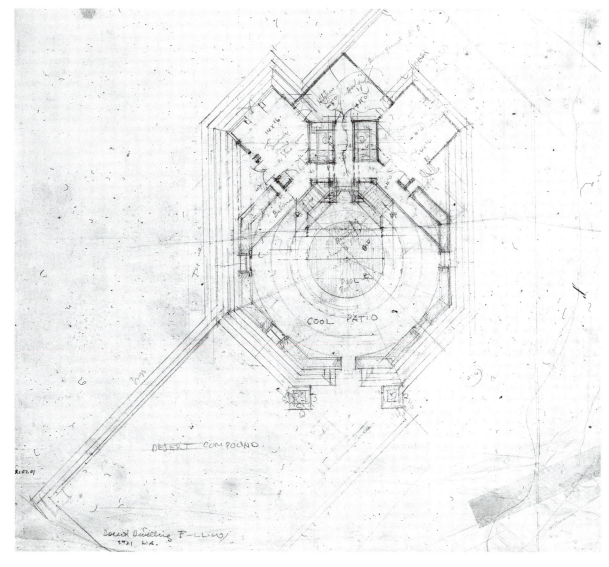

COOL PATIO

DESERT COMPOUND

Desert Dwelling F-LL Wright
1921 L.A.

176. Taliesin. Pool in court with Ming Tea Jar (1936).

177. Prehistoric Native American pithouse. Reconstruction.

178. Panamint Basket, Great Basin, Calif, early 1900s.

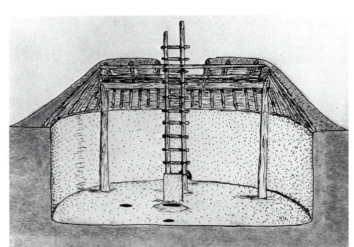

woven by the Shoshone, and collected by Bessie Johnson, which were thought to have preceded the more permanent fired-clay vessels of the later Pueblo cultures (compare fig. 178). These echoed the decorative patterns of the forms of his desert dwelling and the textile-block method of constructing it; but even beyond that, they would have called to mind the sequence of transformations from one material to another that might lead from the impermanent to the permanent—from portable container to built form.[78]

In his only essay treating the history of architectural development, a part of which was published in the following decade, Wright described how man, who "probably first lived in stone caves, when he did not live in trees," soon learned a new method for shaping the structures around him subsequent to his change from basket making to the production of pottery:

permanent in shape.[75] By its very nature, the earthenware vessel or pot was *of* the earth, a realization in three-dimensional form of the holes in the ground that may have served as the basis for the pithouses of prehistoric Native Americans and, according to Wright, as the actual prototype for the kiva, the earliest sacred architectural form of the early inhabitants of the Southwest (fig. 177).[76]

If the first pots Wright prized came from Asia, it was his experience of the Southwest and its Native American cultures that gave him a historical rationale for such a model that can surely stand up to Laugier's defense of the hut.[77] In Death Valley, Wright would have seen baskets

While still dwelling in caves . . . man perhaps learned to make utensils out of wet clay. He burned them hard for use. These utensils he seems to have made with a higher faculty. His instinct became an aesthetic sense of environment. It taught him something of form. He learned from the animals, the serpents, the plants that he knew. Except for this faculty he was no more than any other animal.

Still clinging to the cliffs, he made whole caves out of wet clay and let the sun bake the cave hard. He made them just as he had made the vessels that he had previously put into the fire to bake and had used in the cave in the rocks. And so, once upon a time, man moved into his first earth-built house, of earth.

This large clay cave or pot of the cliff-dwellers, with a lid on it, was among the first man-made houses. The lid was troublesome to him then and has always been so to subsequent builders.[79]

If the kivas in cliff dwellings like those in Mesa Verde represented the original form of the storage pot or cistern and thereby derived their sacred meaning from that primary transformation, as suggested by Alfred Kidder in his classic *Introduction to the Study of Southwestern Archaeology* (1924), the even earlier version of the woven basket carried the image of the protective vessel of space back to a prelithic, truly hut-like condition, providing a mythic dimension to Wright's theory to match Laugier's own. Ignoring the fact that the cliff dwellings he had in mind were constructed of coursed stone rather than of molded clay, Wright was able to imagine a perfectly consistent historical evolution of form. And this revelation of a different, more plastic model of representation provided him with a new basis for design.

The model of the vessel or pot, first represented in the Desert Dwellings, gave Wright the means for articulating a conception of architecture as space. From the mid-1920s on, and only from that time on, he began speaking of his buildings as vessels of space and of his architecture as an "architecture of the *within*."[80] Only a short time before, he said, he read Okakura's *Book of Tea* and discovered in its pages Lao-tse's description of "the reality of the building" as "the space within," from which he extrapolated back to reinterpret such earlier buildings as Unity Temple.[81] Iconicizing, as it were, the fluid medium of architecture, the fired-clay vessel came to embody, in its very being, the symbolic idea of regeneration Wright was always to ascribe to the creation

and modeling of space. Releasing him from almost all ties to traditional structural conventions, this archetypal form also slowly eased the way back to the direct representation of natural appearances that had characterized Taliesin.

As one might expect, Wright's Desert Dwelling gave the thoughts expressed in the project for A. M. Johnson a more speculative and more personal cast. It provides a *terminus ad quem* to the sequence of designs leading from the Imperial Hotel through Hollyhock House and the Doheny House C. It isolates the specific form of the volcanic crater, condenses the building's imagery into it, and substantiates the building's meaning through it. Image, structure, and space fully coincide as the woven textile-block shell recreates the volume of the nearby "Big Basket in the Rock." Filled with water, the dormant, quiescent crater transforms the death-dealing volcano into a life-giving vessel. The regenerative impulse is articulated by the collocation of the four elements of earth, air, fire, and water along the main vertical axis of the house.

Redefining the meaning of shelter as a sense of well-being within, the house shifts the emphasis from a distanced and vicarious visual control of the landscape, dependent on an outward-directed "view," to a more receptive and fully integrated conception of the fundamental interiority of spatial experience.[82] The oculi above *and* below, revealing depths of blue sky over one's head and of water beneath one's feet, circumscribed by laminae of cement and sand tinted lavender by the desert sun, become the vanishing points of a circumambient space that draws in the abstract Renaissance construct of the horizon line to implicate the upright human body in its surround. The distinction between a "public" space of interaction and a "private" space of looking on dissolves. As Wright's Oak Park House and Fiesole project were, respectively, preparations for the Prairie House and Taliesin, the Desert Dwelling served throughout the remainder of Wright's career as the model for an evolving phenomenological definition of architecture as "man in possession of his earth."[83]

VII

Writing *An Autobiography,* Reading the Arizona Desert

Neither his international venture in Japan nor his relocation to Southern California opened up the new opportunities that Wright anticipated. Rather, the contrary turned out to be true. After leaving Los Angeles definitively in the early spring of 1924, Wright built only three buildings during the rest of the decade: a summer house for the most loyal of his early clients, the Martins of Buffalo (1926–28); a house for Richard Lloyd Jones, a cousin in Tulsa, Oklahoma (1928–31); and a temporary camp for himself in the Arizona desert, called Ocatilla (1929).

The first of these, which Martin wanted "as cheaply done as possible," engaged Wright in only a half-hearted way. The second, after much compromise and a good deal of misunderstanding, turned out to be an aesthetic dead-end. The third, however, was linked to one of Wright's most important projects, the San Marcos-in-the-Desert Hotel in the Phoenix South Mountains, and served as his introduction to the area where he would remake his life in the 1930s.[1]

The second half of the twenties was not only the most fallow period of Wright's career; it was also the most frustrating and disruptive from a personal point of view. These two facts are inextricably linked. Indeed, one could argue that the most important work Wright produced during the later twenties was not a building at all but the story of his life. He began writing his *Autobiography* in 1926, in the midst of his greatest personal turmoil.[2] Much of the book was written in 1928–29, while he was preparing the project for the Arizona desert. Wright's account of his personal difficulties and of the Arizona experience that followed define the turning point in the three-act drama of *An Autobiography*, published in 1932.

Excerpts from *An Autobiography*

In its original form, Wright's *Autobiography* was divided into three books, each of which is composed of numerous short chapters or sections.[3] Book One bears the twofold title "Family Fellowship." It begins with a "Prelude" describing a nine-year-old Wright walking in the snow with his uncle John Lloyd Jones on his farm in Hillside, Wisconsin, before proceeding to an account of the family settlement of Helena Valley in the mid-nineteenth century. Following Wright's youth and apprenticeship in Adler and Sullivan's office, Book One ends with Wright's first marriage, the building of his Oak Park home, the raising of his family, and the opening of his office in 1893.

Book Two, entitled "Work," returns to the Lloyd Jones farm for an introductory description of "The Field" in mid-summer.[4] After a discussion of the Winslow commission and the meeting with Burnham at which Wright rejected the offer of training at the Ecole des Beaux-Arts, there follows a history of Wright's work and thought as it developed from the mid-1890s through the mid-1920s. The elopement to Fiesole, the construction of Taliesin, and the fire and murders of the summer of 1914 occupy center stage and set in motion the events that culminate in Wright's personal, professional, legal, and financial setbacks of 1925–28. After a long, detailed account of these events, Book Two ends with the section "Autumn," a conflicted scene of sadness and

thanksgiving set in the family chapel in Helena Valley where Wright had his first experience building.

Book Three, entitled "Freedom," marks a new beginning. It opens with the work in Arizona before going on to discuss projects such as the St. Mark's-in-the-Bouwerie Tower (1928–30) in the context of his developing philosophy of architecture and urbanism for the American utopia he now referred to, cryptogrammically, as Usonia (*A* I, 299ff.).[5] This final book is very much a work in progress.

Sullivan's *Autobiography of an Idea* (1924), published the year he died and the first copy of which, Wright reported, Sullivan presented to him, was obviously a precedent (*A* I, 264). But Wright's act of writing (and dictating) was not a postscript to a career of building, nor was it intended to be. It was cathartic, but also much more than that. From a historical point of view, it was constitutive and programmatic. If Taliesin was the "charm" that works "on everybody that comes within its atmosphere," as Wright wrote to Darwin Martin in 1929, the *Autobiography* was the lure that would bring people into its aura.[6] Understanding the role of the press as few twentieth-century architects have, Wright created in the story of his life an explanation of his art and a scenario to engage the imagination of prospective clients. Where other architects wrote polemical tracts for an audience of peers, Wright embedded his architectural theory in a narrative that appealed to a wide readership.[7] Few of those who were attracted to his work after 1932 had not read the *Autobiography* first. What they wanted and expected from his architecture was something closely related to his life. *An Autobiography* thus functioned as a pretext rather than a postscript.

The life that Wright presented was a heroic story of overcoming all odds, of winning out in the face of extreme adversity. It was a very special case of the modern myth of the artist as persecuted genius. The persona Wright had begun to fashion in his "voluntary exile" in Fiesole was substantiated by the events that followed closely on his return to America and the construction of Taliesin. The dramatic conclusion to Book Two of the *Autobiography*, and the happy outcome projected in Book Three, turn on these events. It is therefore important to look at them in greater detail.

■ ■ ■

The turmoil in Wright's life began not long after the Taliesin holocaust, when he responded to one of the supposedly numerous women who had sent him notes of condolence and sympathy with an invitation to meet him in his Chicago office, thus initiating a most ill-starred affair.[8] Maud Miriam Noel was a wealthy widow, two years younger than Wright, who had been living in Paris until the outbreak of the war. Pursuing a career in sculpture, she apparently moved about in literary and artistic circles, claiming as friends Elie Nadelman, Ossip Zadkine, and Leon Trotsky. Her cosmopolitan air immediately impressed Wright, who found her "brilliantly intellectual" and "sophisticated." Her dress was "in the mode"; she wore a monocle "with which she played as she talked"; she smoked cigarettes; and "her latest study" was "psychology." Wright found her "wonderful, not only as a literary woman but as an artist."[9] She was "stunned" by "the touch of genius" in his work and found his art "stupendous." "In his dark eyes," she wrote, she "could see the deep soul of the artist." There was also his "gift of picturesque words," the "passion" of his thought, the "admiring" acquaintances, the "exquisite" taste of his personal lifestyle.[10] But perhaps most of all, each saw in the other a companion in misery.

When Noel told him how she had been the victim of "a luckless love affair," Wright said he felt that "life had crashed for her with much the same sorrow as mine" (*A* I, 200). From the letters that have been preserved, it would seem that they were both desperate for love. Even before their first meeting, Noel wrote that "if my friendship can serve you in any way, it is yours . . . as the stars, and the trees and the blue hills are yours!" To which Wright re-

sponded: "I hunger for the living touch of someone. . . . Yes—at times almost *anyone* or *anything*. A hunger that makes merely *living* itself a tragedy." Events moved with incredible rapidity. Accepting an invitation to spend Christmas Eve at Wright's house on Cedar Street, Noel addressed him the next morning as "Lord of my Waking Dreams!" saying, "I have called thee friend who art my master! Let me crown your head with a wreath of violets and bind your hair with fillets of gold, like Alcibiades at the feast of Agathon. You have touched me with the edge of the far outspreading wing of your love and I kiss your feet with my trembling lips—I am your prisoner."[11]

Within an extremely short time, however, this high-strung emotionalism, in which Noel compared her love to "a conversion, an apotheosis," was joined by expressions of guilt, self-recrimination, suspicion, and jealousy. She warned Wright: "I will come into your life for a little while and then I will lose you because you will never understand, and then, like Hagar, I will go forth to hunger and thirst in the wilderness, alone with my Ishmael, the poor frail child the world calls love."[12] In his weakened and vulnerable state, Wright at first overlooked certain traces of serious psychological imbalance and drug addiction that Noel maintained were merely the effect of her own recent "grief." Wright wanted to believe that her "enlightened comradeship" would bring "help, light to see by."[13]

Noel went to live with Wright at Taliesin in the spring of 1915. But within less than a year their relationship began to deteriorate. Wright said it was like "the leading of the blind by the blind" (*A* I, 201). She accused him of unbridled egotism, hypocritical sentimentality regarding Mamah Borthwick, and infidelity. His motives in relation to herself were completely selfish and materialistic, she claimed; but even that might not have been so bad were it not for the fact that he refused to give anything of himself in return. He was, she added, incapable of love, out of fear of being "possessed." In one of her letters to Wright, stolen by a vengeful housekeeper and leaked to the press, Noel described him as "a small, narrow mind that could suppose somebody was endeavoring to possess him because that one loved him and depended on his loyalty and affection." It ended with this revealing image: "I suppose this morning you are walking to and fro (rapt in admiration of yourself and your house), uttering high sounding phrases on freedom, denouncing your marriage, morality, family, to the admiration of yourself and your housekeeper."[14]

Wright, for his part, characterized Noel as a neurasthenic, "psychopathic" woman whose "unnatural expression, mental and emotional, spoiled life entirely for days at a time" and ultimately caused such "disintegration from within" that all "life seemed paralyzed by subtle poison" (*A* I, 295, 203, 257).[15] In a letter to his son John, Wright denied Noel's allegation of selfishness and materialism, claiming that "a relation that was a disinterested one for me seems to have been a calculated one for her." "She has made my life a living hell off and on during the months I have known her," he added, blaming her for exploiting his state of emotional vulnerability: "I must take the consequences of not caring much what became of me at a time when I was all ready to die for the sake of dying. She caught me in that mood and has taken advantage of it ever since."[16]

For reasons that are not easy to understand, Wright and Noel stayed together, more or less, for seven or eight years, continuing their stormy affair in Tokyo during the construction of the Imperial Hotel. Noel's "emotional nature grew more and more morbid," according to Wright, and "domestic drama increased at the expense of good sense and domestic peace."[17] Yet, when they returned to America at the end of 1922 and Wright finally received a divorce from Catherine, the two of them were married. The secret midnight ceremony in November 1923 symbolically took place in the middle of the bridge over the Wisconsin River just below Taliesin. Wright thought that this expression of devotion on his part would make matters better. But "instead of improving with marriage, as I had hoped, our relationship became worse" and "resulted in ruin for both."[18]

Wright was shuttling back and forth between Los Angeles and Taliesin during this final phase of their relationship, and the strain was obviously too much. In April 1924, less than half a year after their marriage, Noel left Wright to live in Los Angeles, where she claimed she was going to start a movie career. That was hardly the end of her, though. When Wright began divorce proceedings little more than a year later and Noel discovered that his purpose was to marry another woman he had met in the meantime, she became so vindictive and vengeful that Wright's life was thrown into utter chaos.

The woman Wright had met and fallen in love with in late 1924, and who was eventually to restore a certain equanimity and order to his life as his third and last wife, was Olgivanna Lazovich Hinzenberg (née Olga Ivanovna Lazovich), a handsome twenty-six-year-old Montenegrin of noble birth and mystical inclinations.[19] The daughter of a supreme court justice and granddaughter of a general, she was educated in czarist Russia. After leaving her Russian architect husband, Vlademar Hinzenberg, at the end of the war, she went to Paris and joined Georgi Gurdjieff's Institute for the Harmonious Development of Man, spending four years as a student and instructor at the movement's headquarters in Fontainebleau. She had come to Chicago to discuss business matters with her husband, who was there at the time. After going to live with Wright at Taliesin in early 1925, she was divorced from Hinzenberg in April of that year.[20]

On the surface, then, things seemed to be looking up for Wright in the winter and spring of 1924–25. The four textile-block houses in Los Angeles had been completed or were close to being finished. The Nathan Moore House in Oak Park was being remodeled, and work was going ahead on the drawings for the Johnson complex in Death Valley, the Chicago skyscraper for the National Life Insurance Company, the Nakoma Country Club in Madison, and the Automobile Objective and Planetarium for Gordon Strong in western Maryland (fig. 292).[21] To help with this work,

Wright took on a number of new draftsmen, including the Swiss architect Karl Moser's son Werner and the young Austrian Richard Neutra, who had just left Erich Mendelsohn's office in Berlin. (Neutra worked at Taliesin from November 1924 to February 1925 and functioned as translator when Mendelsohn came to visit Wright that winter.)

European architects had taken a renewed interest in Wright's activities, and by late 1924 two major publications of his recent work were being planned. The first, edited by the Dutch architect H. Th. Wijdeveld, initially appeared in serial form in early 1925 in the Amsterdam School's magazine *Wendingen*, before being published later that year in book form as *The Life-Work of the American Architect Frank Lloyd Wright*. The second, edited by the German architect Heinrich de Fries and featuring Wright's buildings in Los Angeles and Lake Tahoe, was published in Berlin in 1926. Although neither publication had the novelty of the original Wasmuth portfolio, both kept Wright's name in the limelight of international avante-garde developments.[22]

Yet these events were only the calm before a storm that put Wright totally out of commission for almost three years. On a windy evening in April 1925, a second fire broke out at Taliesin, this time due to faulty wiring. Although no one was hurt, the physical damage was much greater than before. The cost of rebuilding the house and studio placed Wright in enormous debt. But the fire proved to be just the initial setback. The most devastating blows came from the denouement of Wright's affair with Noel, a melodrama that left him homeless and unequipped for work for a significant period of time.[23]

Once Lazovich received a divorce from Hinzenberg, Wright filed for a divorce himself, charging Noel with desertion (July 1925). At first, the proceedings seemed to go smoothly. But when Noel found out about Wright's relationship with Lazovich, and shortly thereafter about the child that had been born to them out of wedlock (December 1925), she flew into a rage and began doing everything she could to destroy their relationship and make life impossible

for them at Taliesin. First, she tried to have Lazovich deported as an alien; then, she publicly announced she would sue Wright for divorce on the grounds of physical cruelty; and finally, she laid siege to Taliesin, taking out a warrant for Wright's arrest and attempting to occupy the house as her rightful due (June 1926).

In order to cover his debts, now amounting to over $43,000, due in great part to legal costs, Wright was forced to mortgage Taliesin completely. By September 1926 the Bank of Wisconsin was about to foreclose on the mortgage and take over Taliesin, eventually forcing Wright to auction off his collection of Japanese prints. But in the meantime, things had gotten even worse on the legal front. Noel shared the same lawyer with Hinzenberg, and Lazovich's former husband was now induced to join the battle against Wright, since his own child, Svetlana, was involved.

When Noel sued Lazovich at the end of August for alienation of affection in the amount of $100,000, Wright went into hiding with Lazovich and the two children. They secretly rented a lakeshore cottage in Minnesota, where they lived for almost two months. Once their absence was made known, Hinzenberg sued Wright for alienation of affection and obtained a writ of habeus corpus to secure custody of his daughter. Warrants were issued for the arrest of the couple on the charge of adultery; and, since they had crossed a state border, Mann Act charges were also brought. When their whereabouts were discovered in late October, Wright and Lazovich were arrested as fugitives from justice and for violation of the Mann Act. They spent at least one, and perhaps two, nights in the Hennepin County Jail before being released on bail. The Mann Act charges were eventually dropped, and Hinzenberg withdrew his suit after coming to an agreement with Lazovich about custody of Svetlana.

Wright, however, was enjoined from returning to Taliesin by the Bank of Wisconsin until his debt was paid off. He and Lazovich spent the winter and early spring traveling between California, New York, and Washington, D.C. In April 1927, while they were in New York fighting deportation proceedings that had been brought against Lazovich and her children, the bank sold off Taliesin's livestock. But the new lawyer Wright hired, Philip La Follette, the future governor of Wisconsin, was able to work out a deal with the bank in May that gave Wright a year to pay off his debt and allowed him to return to work at Taliesin. The only catch was that he could not live there illegally with Lazovich, that is to say, without being married.

Wright was finally granted an interlocutory divorce from Noel in late August 1927, which meant that he would have to wait a year before remarrying. The fairly large cash settlement and alimony were paid, in part, by the recently formed corporation Frank Lloyd Wright, Inc., which came about through the efforts of Philip La Follette and the help and support of friends and former clients, including Darwin Martin, Queene Ferry Coonley, Alfred MacArthur's brother Charles, and Alexander Woollcott. Just when things were looking up, toward the end of 1927, the Bank of Wisconsin discovered that Wright had been living at Taliesin with Lazovich and denied him any further access to his house or studio, claiming that "the premises were being used for immoral purposes" and "the mortgage was outraged" (*A* I, 292).

Coincidentally, Wright received a request from Albert Chase McArthur, a former apprentice and the son of an early client, to advise him on the textile-block system McArthur was contemplating using for the Arizona Biltmore Hotel, a luxury property in Phoenix he was designing for his brothers Charles and Warren Jr. This soon turned into a contract to consult on the spot, in Phoenix.[24] With no other work in sight and nowhere else to go, Wright and Lazovich spent the first part of 1928 in Arizona, before repairing to La Jolla, California, for the summer. However elated Wright might have felt as a result of the commission he received while in Phoenix to design the equally luxurious desert resort for the San Marcos Hotel in nearby Chandler, the final, and nearly ruinous events in the Noel-Taliesin saga were still to be played out.

The due date on Wright's debt to the Bank of Wis-

consin passed without his being able to pay, and the bank took over title to Taliesin with the intention of auctioning everything. A chattel mortgage sale was announced for late May 1928 (although it apparently never took place), at which Wright's farm equipment and all personal belongings were to be placed on the block. With no other bidders, the bank bought the property back with the understanding that Frank Lloyd Wright, Inc. would come up with enough money to take it off their hands, which the corporation did by the end of September. In the meantime, Wright and Lazovich, who were still being pursued with an insane jealousy by Noel, were finally married on 25 August 1928 in Rancho Santa Fe, outside La Jolla. After a honeymoon in Phoenix, where Wright presented the preliminary project for the San Marcos-in-the-Desert Hotel to the client, Dr. Alexander J. Chandler, the Wrights were finally able to return to Taliesin in October. Miriam Noel Wright died a little over a year later.

Wright's description of his travails and final success struck a particularly resonant chord in the American popular mind, especially in the early years of the Depression. Wright was not just your average modern artist misunderstood by society. He was someone who had fought the "*system,*" as he said, and who was willing to take on all the worst elements of capitalist society without compromising his principles (*A* I, 282). He "stood firm," he wrote in the concluding section of Book Two of the *Autobiography,*

while newspaper-men, editors, reporters, camera-men, publishers, lawyers, petty officials, federal, state, county, local officials, lawyers in Washington, lawyers in Minneapolis, lawyers in Chicago, lawyers in Milwaukee, lawyers in Madison, lawyers in Baraboo, and in Dodgeville and Spring Green,[25] newspaper-men everywhere, judges, commissioners, prosecuting attorneys, process servers, sheriffs, jailors, justices of the peace, federal immigration officers, police officers, Washington officials, senators and congressmen, governors—has "authority" anything else?—did their worst. And that is, their best. (A I, 273)

Wright described himself as having descended to "the bottom of the vulgar pit" and come out a better artist for it (*A* I, 273). Such resiliency was less the sign of the martyr than the stamp of the survivor. Indeed, Wright's critique of the "*system*" reads like a typical list of the enemies of the American "rugged individualist." The desert of the Southwest was therefore the perfect place for the story to conclude. In the designs for Arizona done in 1928–29, Wright gave full scope to the themes developed in the Death Valley project; and the symbiotic relation between architecture and nature first mooted in Taliesin came closer to becoming normative in his work.

Phoenix and Chandler

Located at the divide of the Salt and Gila Rivers in south-central Arizona, Phoenix was first laid out in 1870. Until about 1400, the area had been home to the Hohokam, who had developed a sophisticated canal system to irrigate the arid desert land at approximately the same time the Anasazi were building their cliff dwellings farther to the north. In 1865 the United States Army established a camp in the vicinity to protect miners and ranchers who feared hostility from those tribes that had succeeded the Hohokam in the Salt River Valley. The town of Phoenix grew up to service Camp McDowell and its dependents. Among its original founders was the former Confederate soldier, Union Army scout, prospector, rancher, and alcoholic, Jack Swilling, who rediscovered the Hohokam irrigation system and promoted its revival as the basis for a viable regional economy. The mythic name Phoenix was given to the town in recognition of its rebirth from the ruins of a distant past.[26]

Between 1912, when Arizona was admitted to statehood, and 1929, Phoenix grew into a significant agricultural and resort community. Much of the impetus came from the construction of the Roosevelt Dam (1906–11), the nation's first major reclamation project. Health seekers, who had started coming to Phoenix for its warm, dry climate as early as the 1880s, were soon displaced by more well-heeled winter vacationers and tourists from the East and Midwest, a trend promoted in large part by local boosters and businessmen. A mainline railroad connection through Phoenix arrived in 1926, and scheduled airline service started the following year. Two downtown hotels, the San Carlos and the Westward Ho, opened in 1928 to compete with the earlier Hotel Adams. The final stage in the evolution from frontier mining and ranching town, to health spa, to vacation resort for the wealthy was reached in February 1929 with the opening of the Arizona Biltmore Hotel. Reporting in the *American Mercury* a few months later, the local writer Goldie Weisberg commented on the changes: "Today Phoenix no longer thinks of itself as first of all a health-seeker's paradise. There is no rule against regaining one's health here, but it is not in the best of taste to discuss it. Phoenix is going metropolitan. It is turning smart."[27]

The Arizona Biltmore Hotel was planned for a two-hundred-acre site six miles northeast of the city, between Squaw Peak and Camelback Mountain (fig. 180).[28] With its elaborate sports facilities and extensive gardens, its individual bungalows spread out beyond the main hotel building on manicured grounds, and its price tag of $2 million, the Arizona Biltmore was intended by the McArthur brothers to upstage other out-of-the-way resort hotels, such as the nearby Ingleside Inn (1908), the San Marcos Hotel in Chandler (1912–13), and the Jokake Inn in Scottsdale (1924), and to give new meaning to the concept of the luxury resort in Arizona.

Wanting to develop a suitable and striking image for the complex, which had already been through a preliminary design stage, Albert McArthur contacted Wright about using the textile-block system of construction. This was in early January 1928, at the moment Wright was being forced by the bank to desist from living with Lazovich and their children at Taliesin. Wright not only offered advice but suggested that his own services might be used in helping the McArthurs adapt the block system to their needs.[29] He was invited to Phoenix with his family and left Taliesin on

13 January. On 25 January 1928 Wright signed a contract with the McArthur brothers "for three months for his services in establishing suitable technique for use of the Textile and Blockslab Construction, invented and owned by him, in the plans for the Biltmore Hotel, of which Albert Chase McArthur is architect."[30]

Construction of the hotel was originally planned to start in the late spring. Delays set the timetable back until the summer, and the three-month clause in Wright's contract was extended. Work was completed early the following year, and the hotel opened in late February 1929. Wright's role in its design has never been fully revealed. He maintained, both publicly and privately, that he was essentially a technical consultant. Although certain features of the interior might lead one to see some greater impact of his thinking, the overall plan and details of construction suggest fairly strongly that his role was essentially just as he described it.[31] The real importance of the Arizona Biltmore, as far as Wright's career is concerned, is that it brought him to Phoenix and set the stage for his meeting with Alexander Chandler, the owner of the San Marcos Hotel, who was to commission Wright to design a totally new facility that would rival the Arizona Biltmore by the natural beauty of its setting and the elegance of its accommodations.

Dr. Alexander John Chandler was one of those rare clients for whom Wright had only unqualified admiration and praise. "He is an ideal client, a gentleman," Wright wrote his son John soon after their first meeting. Chandler's ideas apparently fully coincided with Wright's. His "dream," Wright said, was to build "an undefiled 'desert resort' for wintering millionaires," the "preservation of Arizona desert beauty" being his highest priority.[32] The only problem was that he was perhaps too much of a dreamer, a trait that would only endear him even more to Wright. Chandler never had enough money of his own to finance the undertaking, nor was he ever able to convince enough lenders of the efficacy of his idea for an "undefiled 'desert resort'" designed by Frank Lloyd Wright, despite Wright's constant assertions that a modern, rather than a traditional Spanish

building, would give "the distinction and celebration" that would act "like a magnet" and prove to be an economic advantage "looking toward the future."[33]

Chandler was eight years older than Wright and had lived in the Phoenix area since moving there in 1887, the same year Wright left Madison for Chicago. He was one of the area's most powerful and respected citizens, a leading figure in the development of irrigation for large-scale agricultural production (mainly cotton and alfalfa) and the founder of the town where he lived and which he named after himself.[34] The son of a minister, Chandler was born in Canada and studied veterinary surgery in Montreal, where he earned his degree in 1882. After five years of practice in Detroit, where he became acquainted with Queene Ferry Coonley's father, Dexter Ferry, who would eventually help finance some of his agricultural operations in Arizona, Chandler, like Albert Johnson, felt the lure of the West (and of the money to be made there) and applied for the job of territorial veterinary surgeon of Arizona.

He worked with the stock-raising interests of the cattle industry until 1891, when he resigned his position to begin an entrepreneurial career of irrigation and land reclamation projects. By the end of the first decade of the new century, he had accumulated approximately 18,000 acres of farmland in the Salt River Valley, known as the Chandler Ranch, and operated the largest privately owned canal system south of the Salt River, the Consolidated Canal Company. As a consequence of the federal Salt River Project, begun in 1903, Chandler eventually sold his canal system to the United States government. When the Roosevelt Dam was completed in 1911 and a new federal law limited holdings of land served by it to 160 acres, Chandler began subdividing his ranch. He founded the town of Chandler in 1912 to help attract settlers and to provide them with a community center, based on the model of the City Beautiful, that would be "the Pasadena of Arizona."[35]

The town of Chandler is situated on a relatively flat mesa about twenty-three miles southeast of Phoenix, halfway between the Salt and Gila Rivers (fig. 180). It was laid

180. Phoenix and surrounding area. A = Arizona Biltmore Hotel; B = Chandler; C = Ocatilla site; D = San Marcos-in-the-Desert Hotel site; E = Keith property ("cove"); F = Taliesin West.

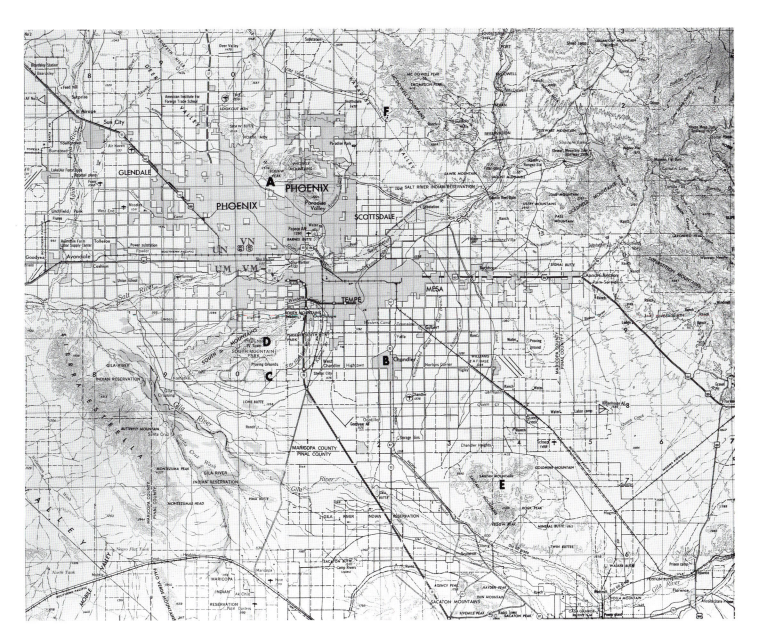

out on a standard grid, with a plaza planned as a park in the center, to be surrounded by arcaded buildings in the Spanish Colonial tradition of Mexico and the American Southwest.[36] The first public building begun was, significantly, the San Marcos Hotel (1912–13). From the very beginning, Chandler believed that winter tourism for wealthy Easterners would become a major industry of the region. He called in Arthur Benton and later Myron Hunt, the Los Angeles architects responsible for California's epoch-making Spanish Mission Style hotel, the Glenwood Mission Inn in River-

side (begun 1902), to create one of Arizona's first luxury winter resorts. Named after Fray Marcos de Niza, the first missionary to enter Arizona (1539), it remained for the next fifteen years or so, as George Wharton James wrote, "the one unique hotel of the State—the caravanserai on the whilom-desert that is to Arizona what Frank Miller's Glenwood Mission Inn is to California; a gathering place for men and women of refinement, used to luxury, yet appreciative of those larger and finer things that deserts, not cities, afford."[37] Though offering its guests the proximity of the desert, with barbecues, camping, and riding excursions available to those who desired to rough it, the hotel, which is connected to a golf course by a manicured lawn once filled with elegant bungalows, is in fact in the center of the town and was designed to provide a very sheltered and urbane environment for its well-heeled guests.

By the mid-1920s, however, the habits of the wealthy were changing enough to convince Chandler that a more secluded resort in the desert could be a real success. With the serious downturn in the cotton industry resulting from the postwar glut on the market, Chandler also realized that he would have to invest more heavily in the tourism industry if he was to compete with the other new resorts, including the Jokake Inn and the Arizona Biltmore. Between 1924 and 1926 he bought about eighteen hundred acres of land ten miles to the west of Chandler, on the southern slopes of the Phoenix South Mountains (then called the Salt River Mountains), where he built a permanent stable and Desert Lodge (including a fifteen-foot-high communal barbecue) as an extended facility for his guests. At the same time, he persuaded his friend William Sproule, president of the Southern Pacific Railroad, to route the new mainline to Phoenix through Chandler on its way from New Mexico to California. In October 1926, Chandler became a regular stop, and the railroad began advertising the service on a nationwide basis.

By the end of 1927, Chandler had all he needed to begin a new campaign of building—all, that is, except an architect. When Wright showed up in Phoenix that winter to work for the McArthurs in the demeaning, "behind the scenes" capacity of technical advisor, Chandler saw the solution to his problem. "Learning I was in the neighborhood," Wright recounted, "he came to see me and invited my little family and myself to come and see him at his pleasant 'San Marcos'" (*A* I, 301). This first meeting took place in March 1928.[38] Wright spent two days in Chandler discussing the building and visiting the site. He was bowled over by the "weird, colorful, wind-swept, wide-sweeping terrain." "There could be nothing more inspiring on earth than that

spot in the pure desert of Arizona," he wrote. Such an "ideal site unspoiled" was "the rarest and most fortunate occurrence in any architect's life" (*A* I, 304, 302). Indeed, he was so eager for the job that he agreed to produce "as many beautiful drawings to illustrate the project as would enable [Chandler] to finance the project," and eventually even offered his services to help in fund-raising.[39]

Wright began working out ideas for the building in the first weeks of April, and by the end of the month he wrote to Chandler that "all [is] ready now to make drawings. The scheme has taken shape definitely."[40] Some drawings were done by the end of May, but the bulk of the preliminary sketches were completed during the summer months, which Wright and Lazovich, with their children, spent in La Jolla prior to their marriage. During their honeymoon in Phoenix in early September, Wright showed Chandler the designs, and a contract for final plans and specifications, to be completed by 1 January 1929, was signed on 25 September. Some of this work was done when Wright returned to Taliesin. But much remained to be completed and, in Wright's view, could be completed only at the site itself.[41] (The working drawings, in fact, were not sent out for final estimates until the following May.)

Wright spoke to Chandler in the spring of 1928 of "camping down near the building site" in order to do some "actual building experiment" with the concrete-block technique. It was written into the contract that Wright would "personally be present at all times during the construction work," and Chandler noted to Wright that "this will require that you live here, but I believe this is in accordance with your wishes."[42] He expected to be able to get his financing together so that construction could begin in the coming winter season. Wright planned to arrive, with a full staff of draftsmen, around the middle of January. When Chandler was unable to assure housing for the group at a reasonable cost, Wright apparently decided to go anyway and build a camp near the site, assuming Chandler would supply the land.[43] Following a telegram from Chandler urging him to come as soon as possible, Wright set out for Arizona on

Ocatilla (Wright Camp) site, Phoenix South (formerly Salt River) Mountains, Phoenix, Ariz.

181. View north.　　182. View south.

15 January 1929 with his entire family, a nursemaid for the two small children, and six draftsmen, a carpenter/handyman, and their relatives or friends—a total of fifteen people in all—to spend the next four months camping in the desert and working on the final plans for the San Marcos-in-the-Desert Hotel.[44]

Ocatilla

Wright's mobile office staff and family arrived in Chandler toward the end of January. Having decided to combine living and working quarters in a single camp, Wright chose a spot near the building site so that the temporary structures could be used to oversee construction the following season. The camp was built on land provided by Chandler and was finished within several weeks. It was named Ocatilla, after the spindly, thorny, scarlet-flowered candlewood, known also as vine-cactus, that dotted the area.[45]

The camp was located to the south of the elevated hotel site, on a rocky mound at the base of the South Mountains, where a valley leading up to the future hotel opened out to the desert (figs. 180, 181).[46] It was a ten-mile drive on an absolutely straight road leading west out of Chandler. After the first seven miles through irrigated fields of alfalfa and grain, the South Mountains begin to rise on the right into a dark, furrowed, and serrated wall running at a thirty-degree angle from northeast to southwest. Beyond, and just behind them, the grander Sierra Estrella cut across in a southeasterly direction, following the Gila River and dropping down to the desert in the south to provide a vista over the Salt River Valley that swings around to the southeast toward the Santan and Sacaton ranges. Highlighted against the shadowy ridge of the South Mountains and running in a north-south direction almost perpendicular to the road out of Chandler was the barrow-like, "spreading, rocky mound" on which Wright decided to build (*A* I, 302). Nearly three hundred feet long and about one-third as wide, it rose at a fairly steep angle to a height of almost twenty-five feet,

just enough to provide the kind of commanding panorama one experiences at Taliesin. Wright said it gave the feeling of a "room sixty miles wide, as long and tall as the universe" (*A* I, 308; fig. 182).

The camp was planned as a "compound" composed of separate cabins connected by a continuous, low wall (fig. 183). The floors of the cabins were wood, as were the board-and-batten sides; the roofs were canvas stretched over wood frames, tilted at a thirty/sixty-degree angle (fig. 184).[47] Triangular canvas flaps were mounted on rubber hinges at the ends of the roofs for ventilation. The lower section of the board-and-batten walls formed part of the continuous enclosure that zigzagged from cabin to cabin, following the

183. Ocatilla, 1929 (demolished). Plan.

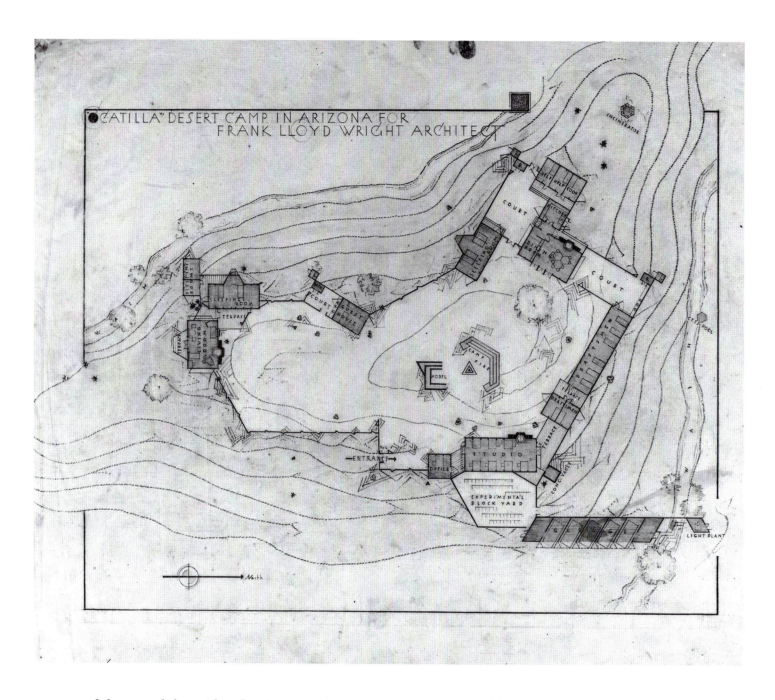

contours of the mound that widened as it rose at its upper end to angle off in a northwesterly direction.

The entrance to the camp on the east slope ran parallel to the north-south axis of that side of the mound and led directly to Wright's office and the drafting room behind it. Beyond that, at a 120-degree angle, were the draftsmen's sleeping quarters, connected by an enclosed court at the upper end of the hill to the dining room, kitchen, and ser-

vice quarters. Closing this corner of the site, where the mound widens to its greatest extent, was the cabin for Will Weston and his wife, the only other married couple among the group. The enclosing wall, now following the narrowing neck of the mound, angled in at 210 degrees to the guest cabin and its enclosed court, which made a final zigzag before joining Wright's own quarters at the southwest corner of the compound. These included a sleeping cabin for him-

Ocatilla.

184. Exterior, from southeast (1929).

185. Preliminary sketches.

186. Central court with campfire and concrete blocks for San Marcos-in-the-Desert Hotel (1929).

self and Olgivanna, a smaller one for the two children, and a separate living room with an angled terrace looking directly south toward the conical Lone Butte, three miles away, and Pima Butte beyond it in the distance, two strange and solitary dark presences on the horizon (fig. 182).

The cabins were built out from the sides of the hill on a raised structure of two-by-fours, with the floor level well below that of the hilltop (fig. 185). The hill therefore retained its original shape and profile, as at Taliesin, rising up to a central spine that was high enough to block views from one cabin to another and, in Wright's words, "to give *a measure* of privacy to all" (*A* I, 305). At the highest point of the hill, toward the north, there was a campfire. A twenty-five-foot-wide bank of seats enclosed in its angle the equilateral triangle of the pit that directed the view over the tops of the cabins and across the southern horizon. The prow of this seat pointed sixty degrees west of north in the direction of the gorge leading into the South Mountains and up to the site of the future San Marcos-in-the-Desert Hotel. The facing tier of seats became the backdrop for a full-scale plaster model of a section of the textile-blocks for the hotel that Wright made while living at Ocatilla (fig. 186).

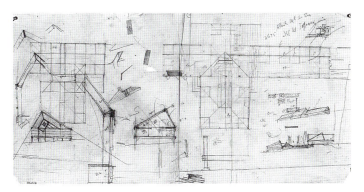

187. Ocatilla. Interior, Wright living quarters (1929).

Wright characterized the "ephemeral" quality of Ocatilla as "a preliminary study" for San Marcos, in which the pattern of desert forms might be outlined and considered in greater detail before being fixed in more "permanent" materials (*A* I, 306, 305). Ocatilla was, in effect, a piece of the desert marked off to be experienced and represented as architecture. "The Arizona desert itself was architectural inspiration and actually the architect's workshop," Wright said. The design of Ocatilla can therefore best be understood as a kind of *plein-air* sketch of the desert, using its forms, shapes, and colors as models for adapting human life to the special conditions of desert living. The compound was to be, in Wright's words, "as appropriately 'nature' in Arizona as Arizona cacti, rocks and reptiles themselves" (*A* I, 309, 305).

Forms devised to respond to the particular problems of function attain, in Ocatilla, the immediacy of imagery often associated with a sketch, along with the mobile, shifting character resulting from the subtle changes in atmosphere. The enclosing, ground-hugging walls of board-and-batten were designed to keep vermin, snakes, and the like out of the camp. The horizontal lines of the battens echoed "the striated and stratified masses" of the desert terrain, while the angular, zigzagging plan reinforced the impression of buildings snaking their way along the ground. The color of the paint was a "dry rose to match the light on the desert floor" (*A* I, 304–5).

The luminous canvas roofs were intended to "afford generous diffusion of light within" and, as in Wright's earlier project for a Desert Dwelling, to trap the warmth of the winter sun (fig. 187).[48] The profile of the roof combined references to work and to context. "The factory roof section," Wright noted in a letter to Darwin Martin, "is an ideal cross-section for school purposes as well as for working purposes" from the point of view of light reflection and light diffusion.[49] In the context of the Arizona desert, the sloped canvas tent tops seen in juxtaposition to one another were meant to be read in relation to the lines of the "uptilting planes" of the surrounding mountains. (*A* I, 304). Noting that the "cross-section of the talus at the base of the mountains is the hypotenuse of a 30–60 degree triangle," Wright adopted for the section of the roof "the one-two [thirty/sixty-degree] triangles seen made by the mountain ranges around about the site."[50] Color was called upon to expand the reference from topography to the flora suggested by the camp's name. The little triangles within the gable ends were painted the red of the candlewood flower to "make the cabins bloom with these scarlet one-two triangles like the one-two triangles of the ocatilla bloom itself" (*A* I, 305).

As a sketch, Ocatilla conjures up multiple and overlapping images. Its wriggling, serpentine wall, camouflaged to match the color of the ground, makes it seem like one of the pale-colored sidewinders it was designed to keep out. The angles of the canvas roofs, reminiscent as they are of the factory and the workplace, reflect the shapes of the mountains in the background, while the spots of color in their gables call to mind the red blossom of the spindly cactus for which the camp was named. Wright regarded the imagery of the camp in even more fluid terms, in relation to its "transitory" character (*A* I, 305). He compared the white canvas roofs to "the dazzling white of Arizona clouds." The flaps that opened to allow breezes to flow through reminded Wright at times of "wings" and at other times of "sails." As the cabins were being finished, he thought they would look "like a group of gigantic butterflies," but then added: "when these white canvas wings, like sails, are spread, the buildings . . . will look like 'desert ships'" and "the group . . . like some kind of desert fleet."[51]

Wright meant Ocatilla to capture the essence of impermanence and represent it architecturally in organic terms. The mere fact of making a tent was not enough. Wright chose his words in describing the imagery of Ocatilla as precisely as he chose its architectural forms. He wrote that "'Ocatilla' is Ephemera. To last a few years,—to drop a seed or two."[52] The linguistic reference, like the architectural ones, was specific and organic rather than general and abstract. Ephemera are minuscule mayflies that can spend anywhere from six months to three years as larva before metamorphosing into slender, delicate flies, with membranous wings, that live for just a few hours, at most a day. Reproducing by dropping their eggs into water, they are particularly subject to wind. Wright analogized the struggle of their life cycle to the transient existence of his camp. Owing to the heat and rattlesnakes, it had to be abandoned before the end of May. "Although ephemera," Wright wrote, "our 'desert ships' are strong enough to meet the 'desert devils' as they come whirling across, miniature cyclones, slender, whirling columns of dust passing along the ground rising high in the air, one or two to be seen somewhere all the time. . . . The ephemera will all shudder when a 'devil' comes along to grasp and shake them, but they will not give way." "To last a few years,—to drop a seed or two," Ocatilla represented "ephemera as preliminary study" (*A* I, 307, 306).[53]

■ ■ ■

The imagery of Ocatilla reflected the fragility and mortality of life in the desert. In this, as in many other ways, it owed much to Wright's experience in Death Valley. On a superficial level, however, there is one major difference, and that is the lack of any explicit reference in Ocatilla to Amerindian forms, Southwestern or Mesoamerican. In a sense, Ocatilla is both more abstract and more directly representational than the Death Valley work—somewhat more like Taliesin,

one could say. But the references to Native American civilization are there, and they must be recognized to understand the full meaning of the design and its implications as a "preliminary study" for the more "finished" San Marcos-in-the-Desert.

With its arid, bleached court rising through luminous wings of brilliantly white canvas, Ocatilla offered itself up to the sun, that all-powerful agent of life and death in the desert that Wright assumed to have been the spirit worshiped by the prehistoric inhabitants of the area. The basis for this belief were the Hohokam petroglyph boulders he discovered nearby.

Across the mesa from the camp are great low-lying mounds of black, burnt rock covered with picture writing scratched on the surface by the Indians who came there at sunrise to worship the sun, the greatest evidence of the Great Spirit they knew.

The desert is prostrate to the sun.

All life here is sun-life: and dies a sun-death. Evidence is everywhere. (*A* I, 304–5)[54]

It is not known whether Wright was aware that archaeological and anthropological investigations were just beginning in the area of the Salt River Valley.[55] Nor is it known whether he and Olgivanna were in touch with any of the artists and writers in the Taos community who were so interested in seeking a rapport with Native American culture. Wright's interest in Amerindian civilizations, from the mid-teens on, certainly paralleled D. H. Lawrence's. His references to "sun-life" and "sun-death" immediately recall Lawrence's discourses on the animism of Native American thought and its expression of an "elemental life of the cosmos" that he believed underlay the American "spirit of place."[56]

Whatever the case, Wright certainly embraced a more thoroughgoing "primitivism" than at any previous time in his life. "Soon we become sun-worshippers ourselves," he wrote of his stay in the Phoenix South Mountains. "As the great morning breaks far off over the blue mountain ranges we stamp the board floors, rush out to catch the first warming rays, and see 'Ocatilla' with its saguaro sentinels bathed in golden light." Ocatilla, he said, was designed to offer "a free sun-life of the wide spaces" with only "mild shelter, but no defenses" (*A* I, 308, 310, 307). Each container-like cabin was treated as an individual vessel of space. This allowed the sun to penetrate fully from above and to give to each part of the compound, as to the whole, a sense of being contained within the circle of the sun's powerful rays.

Wright observed how vegetation, like all animal and human life in the desert, seeks to arm itself against the very power to which it owes its existence, but also how the relentless energy of the sun finally dominates and subdues all: "There seems to be no mortal escape, even in death, from this earth-principle—or is it sun-principle—of growth. This creative creature of the sun." He concluded that the "extraordinary style and character here in the desert" was "born of the desperate nature of the struggle in the sun to survive the sun" (*A* I, 307).

As a temporary settlement, Ocatilla might reflect such primitivizing thought without necessarily embodying it in its forms. But the question Wright posed to himself while living there and working on the design of the San Marcos-in-the-Desert Hotel was how to make an image of permanence in a landscape "scarred by conquest," where nothing man-made could long survive (*A* I, 307). The answer lay in a naturalism revitalized and reinforced by its association with primitivism. In the first draft of his description of Arizona for the *Autobiography*, written in 1929, Wright recounted what had been going through his mind:

Great buildings would be man's natural contribution to this land he invades and would subdue as his home. . . .

Great buildings would be as easy for him here as the primitive cliff-dweller's house was to the primitive cliff-dweller himself if the educated man could only forget and rediscover himself, —allow the child in him to live. . . .

If the archetypes of Architecture were all lost and man

stood here, his experience with the architecture of the ages deep in him only as instinct, conscious of his present power gained by the machine, —to begin to build, —what would he do?

I have often wondered as I've studied these great significant lines, the dramatic silhouettes of the dark masses so grandly cut out against the crystal sky, at the same time delighted by the consciousness of wealth in vivid-bloom under foot. . . . The varied cacti-lives meantime rise stark and strange against the colorful strata of the endless walls and massive roofs of this Arizona-world.

Man has yet built very little that would do here at all. . . .[57]

As we dare enter into this great domain what should we do to . . . prove some spiritual constructive kinship. . . ? Perhaps we already are too sophisticated to enter into the great-spirit animate here.

Do we know enough, yet, to make room for it to enter us in order that we might do so?[58]

San Marcos-in-the-Desert would be to Ocatilla not simply as Death Valley was to Tahoe or the Anasazi cliff dwellings in Canyon de Chelly are to the Navajo hogans erected beneath them. That equation is an opposition of the permanent and the impermanent, the monumental and the quotidian. Wright was seeking a dialectical relation between the two, where permanence and impermanence would be functions of each other. The unique temporal framework of desert conditions, already sensed by him in Death Valley, prompted Wright in the San Marcos project to delineate a space for the representation of change.

San Marcos-in-the-Desert Hotel

The San Marcos-in-the-Desert Hotel was to be located about a mile north of Ocatilla, on the southern slopes of the Phoenix South Mountains (figs. 180, 181). But to say a mile hardly describes the psychological distance that separated

188. San Marcos-in-the-Desert Hotel project, 1928–29. Panoramic photo of view from site, looking south (1928).

the two sites. "For the jaded millionaires who still loved beauty and sought solitude in beautiful surroundings," Chandler wanted to remove the hotel as much as possible from any connection with the flat, cultivated lands of the Salt-Gila basin (*A* I, 308). The hotel was therefore sited well beyond the first range of foothills, across a hidden valley. To get there meant a fairly arduous trek through the rugged terrain of washes and arroyos cutting through the outlying foothills. Heading north, you left the vast Salt River Valley behind. The track skirted a series of rocky mounds before coming to the wash, or ravine, that curved around and finally led into the gorge that cut through the elevated site Chandler himself apparently chose. As you rose to the level at which the hotel was to be, the landscape dramatically opened up to the south and east (fig. 188). But the lower range of hills in the near foreground provided a sense of containment that made the location as much a natural solarium as an amphitheater.[59]

The 110-room hotel was planned on a diagonal thirty/sixty-degree geometry to conform with the rugged desert landscape (fig. 179). The hotel stepped up the hillside so that the building, including the foundations, could be constructed without altering the existing contours and surfaces, aside from "a single cut in the ledge and consequent filling below the cut."[60] The wash leading to the gorge was to be used as the entrance road (fig. 189). It was to be unpaved;

passage would be ensured in all seasons by channeling any flow of water around it and underneath the building through a series of pools to the side.

The road runs under the building, which bridges the wash to create a covered court. Above the entrance, on the bridge over the wash, are the monumental public spaces of the hotel, announced from the distance by the tall water tower. A double-height lobby and mezzanine lounge occupy the first and second levels; a skylit dining room, or arbor, as Wright referred to it, is located on the top level. From this central volume, basically a rhomboid in plan, one range of rooms stretches out to the east and another to the west, along the contours of the mountain slopes. The one on the east takes a straight path from the lobby at an angle of 120 degrees; the other first shoots out to the southwest along the ridge of the wash to round a spur before cutting back at a right angle to follow a line approximately 30 degrees north of west. A shorter, prow-like wing coming straight out of the southwest corner of the central volume and containing studio apartments is tucked behind this second wing.[61]

Each of the main lateral wings was designed in section to form three levels of terraces receding in depth as they rise (fig. 190). There is a corridor at each level along the rear, or inside, forming a horizontal circulation spine. The section was worked out so that the roof of the room on the lower terrace becomes the floor of the balcony above it, and thus

San Marcos-in-the-Desert Hotel project.

189. Perspective of entrance.

190. Section through guest room wing (redrawn c. 1940).

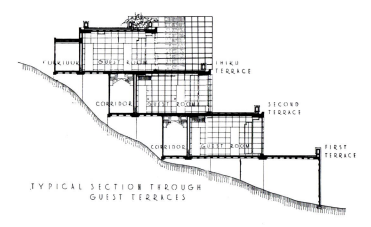

TYPICAL SECTION THROUGH
GUEST TERRACES

each guest room faces south and opens onto an unroofed balcony almost the same size as the room.[62] To ensure privacy in a lateral direction, the individual guest balconies were separated from one another either by vertical fins or by intervening balconies planted to become hanging gardens and alternately containing pools of water. An upper roof garden connected the public spaces in the center to the individual guest cottages and villas (see figs. 193, 194) that were to be built at the extremities of the two lateral wings as well as farther up the slopes of the mountainside. The exposure of every part of the building to the sun, along with the resulting panoramic vista, was the prime motive in Wright's

planning. "The far-flung, long-drawn-out levels of the terraces afford each room, each bathroom, each closet, each corridor, sunlight," he said. "Every portion of the building . . . is free to the sun and also to magnificent views." (*A* I, 309; *A* II, 314).

San Marcos-in-the-Desert was to be constructed of textile block, and the project represents the culmination of Wright's efforts in the twenties to perfect this modern system of streamlined, standardized production. In the specifications for the hotel, he noted that "the ferro-block system to be used is designed to produce a one-process, monomaterial building out of the materials of the site itself so far as and wherever possible." "The aim in this effort," he continued, "is to bring to the building field the same advantage of manufacture and standardization that characterize [*sic*] all other American industry with natural increase of economy and greater structural integrity."[63]

By the time these specifications were written in late November 1929, Chandler was having considerable trouble raising the $750,000 that was calculated as the price for the building.[64] The stock market crash in October rendered Chandler's chances slimmer and slimmer. No doubt,

191. Le Corbusier: Durand Housing Development project, Oued Ouchaïah, Greater Algiers, 1932–34. Perspective.

Wright hoped to impress Chandler with the efficiency and cost-saving features of his system ("All the dovetailing of various trades having been abolished"), but there was more to it than that. By the end of the 1920s, Wright had come to align his stance on many issues, both in practice and in theory, with recent developments in European modernism. The description of his machinist ethic for the San Marcos-in-the-Desert Hotel was matched by an esthetic that paralleled in numerous ways avant-garde practices in Europe.

More than any building Wright had designed since the Larkin Building, San Marcos-in-the-Desert was an instrument for performing a specific function. It was a machine for taking advantage of a specific climate, at a specific time of the year, for a specific clientele. The plan diagrams the relations between individual and group activity along functional lines of circulation and use in which movement is essentially lateral and nondirectional.[65] The section can be read almost as a scientific solution to the problem of bringing light, air, and greenery into the individuated cells of the building's occupants. It is fascinating in this regard to note how closely Wright's design mirrors a contemporaneous one by Marcel Breuer for a hospital in Elberfeld (1928) and another by Le Corbusier for a housing complex overlooking the sea on the outskirts of Algiers (1932–34; fig. 191). The stepped profile, with circulation along the rear and views

along the front, has in fact become the paradigm for the modern vacation resort, in which the spectacle of nature is the objective and the privacy of experience the vehicle.[66]

The "modernism" of San Marcos-in-the-Desert is felt in the outward form of the building as much as in its structure and plan. Historians and critics had already begun to note a correlation between some of Wright's concrete-block houses in Los Angeles, such as the Millard House, and the work of Le Corbusier and Oud. The San Marcos-in-the-Desert project went much further in the direction of simplification and broadening of forms, disengagement from ornamental patterning, and rejection of any vestigial, historical references.[67] Key to this was Wright's revision of the decorative character of the concrete block itself.

In its earliest stages of development, the textile-block system maintained important references to handcrafted artifacts such as baskets and rugs. The interwoven vertical and horizontal lines of steel reinforcing rods established, like the warp and woof of a fabric, a grid that controlled the overall design. The decorative geometric pattern of each block was contained within the square, emphasizing its shape; and the larger image of the building was perceived as a multiplication of individual units, with each one retaining its separate, ornamental identity (fig. 134). In the project for San Marcos, Wright made the vertical pattern continuous

across the horizontal joints (figs. 189, 192). For the first time, the separate blocks were designed to be read as part of a larger, abstract pattern conceived at the scale of the building itself. This pattern was essentially a kind of vertical fluting or pleating that would have produced a general effect of light and shade without depending upon or delineating any internal decorative order.

Abstract as it might appear, the overall pattern was still a pattern, not simply a flat, rendered surface. For his model, Wright turned from weaving directly to the example of nature. He found the structural analogue for what he now preferred to call the "block-shell system" in the saguaro cactus. "The sahuaro," he remarked, "is a perfect example of 'reinforced' construction. With its interior vertical rods it holds upright the great columnar mass for six centuries or more," and around these rods grows "the flesh of the sahuaro" (*A* I, 304). As can be seen in the model erected in the court of Ocatilla, the blocks were designed to make a continuous pattern of vertical pleats, like the fluted surface

of the saguaro, while every so often these ridges were notched to approximate the stippled arris of the flute itself. This creates a pattern of light and shade that is "gros-grained like the sahuaro" and produces the effect of "the dotted line" Wright believed to be the "outline in all desert creation."[68] The rippling, pleated surface would have created a vertical counterpoint to the "long-drawn-out levels of the terraces" and given the building a thick-skinned shell like the one the saguaro grows as its defense against the desiccation of the sun.

Curiously, the drive to simplify form and broaden its scale did not lead Wright away from the model of nature and toward a purist geometry of non-objectivity; instead, it had the opposite effect.[69] In the San Marcos project Wright came closer to the direct representation of nature than in anything he had done since Taliesin. He was very conscious of this and declared that the design of the hotel "was to embody all that was worthwhile that I had learned about a natural architecture" (*A* I, 302). Aside from a very general, indeed subliminal, relation to the terracing of prehistoric Amerindian cliff dwellings or Great Houses, like the one at Chaco Canyon, San Marcos-in-the-Desert appears to bear no significant historical imprint at all. Where the difference between the impermanent character of the Lake Tahoe project and the permanence of the Johnson Death Valley Compound was expressed in a historical distinction between Plains Indian and Pueblo/Precolumbian forms, the difference between the ephemeral in Ocatilla and the monumental in San Marcos was represented by different natural models.

Wright said that he "used the surrounding giant growth, Sahuaro, as motive for the building": the hotel "was to grow up out of the desert as the Sahuaro grew."[70] The contrast between the two types of cactus, the saguaro and the ocotillo, stood for the difference between the "preliminary study" of the camp and the final design of the hotel. Both types of cactus exist in the same environment and thrive under similar conditions, but where the ocotillo is a slender, formless shrub—more a bush than a tree—with spiny stalks that sway and flutter in the wind, the saguaro, like a sentinel, is a monumental arborescent figure in the landscape. Solid and fluted like a Doric column, it is usually equipped with one or more limbs that extend parallel to its stately trunk as if to declaim its great age in pantomimic gesture. In contrast to the relatively short-lived ocotillo, the saguaro impressed Wright with its perdurability. He referred to "the great sahuaro, standing there erect, six centuries old" as "the king of the cacti" and considered it a permanent fixture and symbol of the Arizona desert. As "an abstraction of cactus life in masonry shells made more cactus than any cactus," the hotel, in Wright's view, thus took on the cast of "a human habitation to live in as long as the mountain lasts" (*A* I, 305–6, 309).

■ ■ ■

In contrast to Taliesin, but analogous with Ocatilla, San Marcos-in-the-Desert represents not a single image but rather a compound one. In fact, a simple glance at the project would probably not call to mind the figure of a cactus as quickly as it would the ledges of an eroded hillside. The terracing of the wings along the contours of the mountain slopes gives the impression of a series of natural ledges cut into the mountainside (fig. 179). In an article in the April 1928 issue of *Architectural Record*, written just when he began working on the San Marcos project, Wright hinted at the importance such an image would have: "The rock-ledges of a stone-quarry are a story and a longing to me [read: Taliesin]. There is suggestion in the strata and character in the formations. I like to sit and feel it, as it is. Often I have thought, were great monumental buildings ever given to me to build, I would go to the Grand Canyon of Arizona to ponder them."[71] He ended by reminding the architect, in a kind of self-explanatory way, that

As he takes the trail across the great Western Deserts—he may see his buildings—rising in simplicity and majesty from their floors of gleaming sand. . . .

For in the stony bone-work of the Earth, the principles that shaped stone as it lies or as it rises and remains to be sculptured by winds and tide—there sleep forms and styles enough for all the ages for all of Man.[72]

A few months later, in a subsequent article on concrete, Wright noted how the textile blocks of his San Marcos design could be seen as arresting the erosion of the mountainside and recomposing the stone in its original place:

I am writing this on the Phoenix plain of Arizona. The ruddy granite mountain-heaps, grown "old," are decomposing and sliding down layer upon layer to further compose the soil of the plain. Granite in various stages of decay, sand, silt and gravel make the floor of the world here.

Buildings could grow right up out of the "ground" were this "soil," before it is too far "rotted," cemented in proper proportions and beaten into flasks or boxes—a few steel strands dropped in for reinforcement.

Concrete, Wright went on to say, is a kind of "artificial stone," a modern expedient that differs from its natural correlate mainly by virtue of its "binding" medium, cement. This makes concrete a "compound," or "conglomerate," that suggests a different kind of expression from stone. Concrete, being more "plastic" as a material, wants to be stamped, cast, or impressed with a pattern that will "flow" across its surface and carry in its impress the sign of organic life, with "such effects . . . as may be seen in stone when fossil remains of foliage or other organic forms . . . are found in it."[73]

The "artificial stone" of the concrete blocks of San Marcos-in-the-Desert thus inherently called for a superimposed, organic imagery to provide it with the compound meaning "natural" to it. Wright contended that an architecture "indigenous" to the Arizona desert would be "patterned after . . . the Sahuaro, cholla or staghorn but stratified in masses noble and quiet like the great nature masonry rising from the mesa floors." The architect's job was "to

193. San Marcos-in-the-Desert Hotel project, Young House. Perspective.

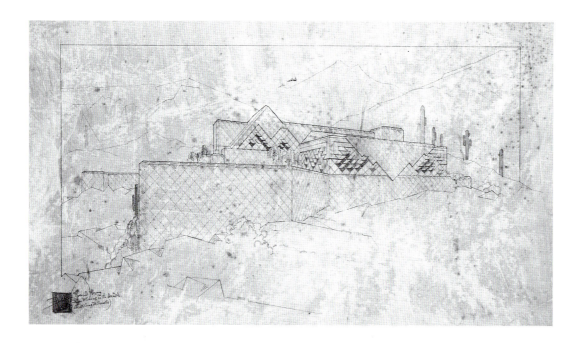

harmonize his building masses with topography and his building-walls with the nature-creation they consort with."[74] In San Marcos-in-the-Desert, the vertical lines of the saguaro imbue the horizontally layered "masonry shell" with the vitality of organic growth that Wright called "plasticity."

Wright suggestively described the overall design of the hotel as "an abstraction of mountain region and cactus life" (*A* II, 314). The two layers of imagery oscillate, somewhat like those vertically ridged plastic pictures that reveal one scene when viewed from one angle and a quite different one from the other. Sometimes it is the image of the mountain that is emphasized; at other times it is the cactus. As the concrete-block surface of the building breaks in and out at a thirty- or sixty-degree angle, one sees echoed in its forms the crystalline shapes of the rocky landscape, which are picked up and made even more prominent in the peaked roofs of the dining "arbor" and one of the outlying cottages (fig. 193). In another, the continuous vertical pleating rising straight out of the ground, and set in sharp contrast to the streaked and patchy mountainside, reflects the forms of the saguaros drawn like sentinels against the lines of the terraces (fig. 194).

The most conspicuous transformation of the image of

"mountain region" into "cactus life" occurs, appropriately, in the center of the composition, above the wash that serves as the entrance road, and in line with the sheets of water that cascade down the angle between the lobby and the east wing of guest rooms. The large-scale vertical pleats of the piers of the two-story lobby and dining room are carried through the roofline into a water tower sheathed in concrete block and verdigris copper (fig. 189). In compliance with Chandler's wish to complete the desert theme of his hotel by having open-air organ concerts, where the sound would echo across space from mountain to mountain, Wright placed organ pipes in the upper part of the tower and took advantage of the similarity in shape between them and the stalks of the saguaro to create the impression that the water tower "rises like a giant sahuaro from the gorge."[75]

Because it was "intended to give 'voice' to the whole," as Wright said, "this tower as a natural expression of the sahuaro-motive that also qualifies the other building forms" naturally became "the only efflorescence anywhere."[76] By locating the entrance and public spaces of the hotel over the wash and designing the water tower above it on the model of a giant saguaro, Wright made the unique and powerful drama of desert life the focus of the design. The lateral wings extending from the tower thus no longer read simply

194. San Marcos-in-the Desert Hotel project, Cudney House (Sahuaro). Perspective.

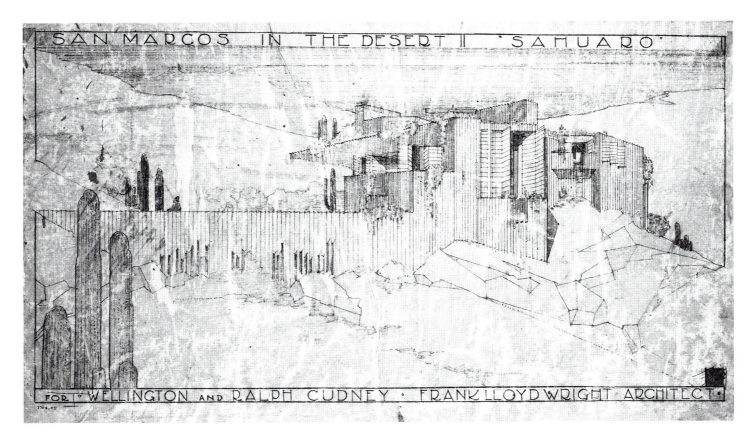

as eroded, rocky ledges. They visibly become the wide-spreading roots of the cactus, which reach out over great distances to the shallow pools that line the receding terraces (fig. 179).

The combined "abstraction of mountain region and cactus life" gives the project for San Marcos-in-the-Desert a deep-seated tension that sets up new relations between figure and ground. In Taliesin, the figure of the outcrop functioning as a "brow for the hill" was singular and static (fig. 91). There was an untroubled, unself-conscious seamlessness of figure and ground. In Hollyhock House, Wright pictured the building in relation to a mountain backdrop that was purely imaginary (fig. 128). Figure and ground were distinguished from each other as history and nature. The projection of the one onto the other made a metaphor out of the building. In the Death Valley project, Wright retained the historically circumscribed forms of Hollyhock House but dislocated them and shifted them about in response to the pressure of the forces of erosion (fig. 133). The link between historical form and natural image, however,

was mechanical. The lines of the building trace the effects of a process without being fundamentally transformed by them. Figure becomes ground by substitution.

In the project for San Marcos-in-the-Desert, figure and ground—cactus and mountainside—interpenetrate and substantiate one another in a dynamic way. The lines of the building's surfaces describe an image of change and growth out of and over against the forces of decomposition.[77] One is hard pressed to keep the building from receding into the landscape. An elevation sketch, in particular, shows the hotel as a locus of natural forces coming into focus at the center but dissolving into the landscape at the edges (fig. 195). The building becomes a parturition of nature, condensing in its figural status the multiple indications of the ever-present ground.

Wright described the Arizona desert as a "titanic, ancient battle field" in which one could see the drama of life and death acted out as if in slow motion (*A* I, 307). Everywhere were signs of violence, armed struggle, defiance, and capitulation. The power of the sun and the force of ero-

195. San Marcos-in-the-Desert Hotel project. Sketch elevation.

sion were the two major protagonists. The project for San Marcos-in-the-Desert reenacts that drama as architectural representation. Its text, like the libretto for an opera, is provided by the description in Wright's *Autobiography* of the tenacity of desert growth in the face of unyielding geological force:

Everywhere around us see this stern, armed, creeping cover of "growth!" Ocatilla, greasebush, palosverdes, mesquite, bignana, cholla, suhuaro [sic]. *Eternal mysterious purpose desperately determined, continually seeking conquest, in due course, of this titanic, ancient battle field. To what end?*

And this inexorable grasp of vegetation on the earth itself is more terrifying to me here as a principle at work . . . than are all the others put together.

There seems to be no mortal escape, even in death, from this earth-principle—or is it sun-principle—of growth. This creative creature of the sun.

Death being necessary to this creative creature's increase, death was invented.

Is this extraordinary style and character here in the desert of extremity born of the desperate nature of the struggle in the sun to survive the sun? Every line and the very substance of the great sweeping masses of rock and mesa speak of terrific violence. All are scarred by conquest, marred by defeat of warring forces.

Yet, subsidence, as we may see now in the stream lines of these endless ranges of mountains coming down gently to the mesa, has in this geological period found comparative repose. To these vast, quiet, ponderable masses so made by Fire and laid by Water, both architects, now comes the sculptor—Wind. Wind ceaselessly eroding, endlessly working to quiet and harmonize all traces of violence until a glorious unison is bathed in light that is eternity. (A I, 307–8)[78]

Wright's text reinforces our first impression of the San Marcos project: the geological ultimately overrides the vegetal. But the text also makes it clear that the former must be seen in terms of the latter if the image is not to be lifeless. The process of erosion becomes the formative agent—a curious idea from the point of view of architecture.[79] Architecture, by definition, is a matter of building, of constructing, not of dissolving and wearing away. The architect is supposed to be someone who takes a positive hand in this matter. Wright, however, likens his role as form-giver to that of midwife, an agent overseeing and assisting in the natural processes of geological formation.[80]

The self-effacing tone of this characterization of the architect should not be taken as a prescient expression of the postmodern concept of the "death of the author." Rather, it affirms in the fullest the image of the modern architect as inspired genius, the persona Wright originally affected through his engagement with the figure of Taliesin and now returned to in all senses of the word. The resurgent unity and organicism in the work in Arizona in the late twenties was accompanied by a renewed and intensified ego-involvement. The radical identification of architecture with nature went hand in hand with a quasi-mystical divinization of man's creativity. While camping at Ocatilla in the spring of 1929, Wright wrote: "A true announcement of the law of creation, if a man were found worthy to declare it, would carry Art up into the Kingdom of Nature and destroy its separate and contrasted existence."[81] "We are at the fountain-head of all forms whatsoever," he had written a little more than a year earlier:

The integrity of it all as an expression *is now a matter of the creative-artist's Imagination* at work.

Where is he? And if he *is, may he be trusted with such power? Yes, if he has the Gift. If he is "God" in the sense that "man-light" lives in him in his work.*[82]

Never before had Wright's ideal of a representational architecture been expressed in such extramundane terms. One is reminded of the ancient story of Zeuxis, whose pictorial depiction of grapes was supposedly so lifelike that it fooled the birds who tried to eat them. One is also reminded of the story of Daedalus, the designer of the spiral labyrinth at the Palace of Knossus, in which he and his son Icarus were imprisoned. When they attempted to escape by fashioning wings for themselves in imitation of birds, and Icarus flew too close to the sun, the wax melted and he plummeted to his death in the sea. The regenerated and dynamic naturalism of the San Marcos project, however, speaks not at all of virtuosity or hubris. Quite the contrary. The meaning of the classical myths is subverted by a profound and subtle fatalism, manifested architecturally in the seemingly effortless, extrusive character of the design, to which Wright gave verbal expression in the closing remarks ("Postlude") of the final book of *An Autobiography*, which opened with the trip to Arizona. "The order of change" that "I have sought

as a natural order," he wrote, is a function of "growth," and the inevitability of "death [merely] a crisis of growth" (*A* I, 371).[83]

■ ■ ■

The fate of San Marcos-in-the-Desert was tied up with economic and social issues well beyond Wright's control. When he and his group left Ocatilla toward the end of May 1929, as the heat became unbearable and rattlesnakes, scorpions, "and various other damage dealing insects [started] appearing," they fully expected to return the following autumn.[84] The working drawings for the resort were sent out for bids by the end of the first week of May, and a number of responses were received before they broke camp. During the summer of 1929, however, signs of the difficulties that lay ahead began to appear. Chandler was finding it impossible to line up backers for the project, and Wright's unconventional system of construction was no help. On 24 October 1929, otherwise known as Black Thursday, Wright wrote a concerned note to Chandler from Taliesin: "There seems to be a 'big silence' out in the West," he began. "Many rumors regarding the San Marcos-in-the-Desert, many questions too from various directions."[85]

The stock market crash eventually put an end to Chandler's fund-raising efforts, as well as the ones Wright took up on his behalf. Wright produced the final estimate of $743,969.71 for the hotel on 20 November. A few days later Chandler made a deal with the owners of the Ritz-Carlton Hotel in New York, offering them operating control in the hope that this would ease the way to financing the project. Wright made additional drawings in January and February 1930 to bolster Chandler's efforts, but by the spring of that year, it appears, both he and Chandler had given up any hope that the hotel would be built. Fallingwater, a vertical slice of San Marcos, and Taliesin West, a conflation of the impermanency of Ocatilla and the durability of the hotel, are lasting reminders of what the building might have been.[86]

196. Fallingwater
(Kaufmann House),
Mill Run, Pa.,
1934–37.
View from south,
below second falls

The Temporal Dimension of Fallingwater

VIII

T here is a story, said to be apocryphal, that when Philip Johnson and Henry-Russell Hitchcock were planning, for New York's fledgling Museum of Modern Art, the exhibition of contemporary architecture that was to canonize the International Style and the discussion turned to the question of which Americans to include, Johnson dismissed Hitchcock's suggestion of Wright, claiming he was dead. Whatever phrase was actually used, Wright's passing from the picture by the late twenties was a common refrain.

He himself was quoted in *Architectural Record* in 1929 as saying: "I have been reading my obituaries to a considerable extent over the past year or two, and think, with Mark Twain, the reports of my death greatly exaggerated."[1]

By 1938, things had changed dramatically. Wright's name was on the tip of everyone's tongue. In January of that year *Time* magazine featured him in a cover story; an entire issue of *Architectural Forum* was devoted to his work; and

the Museum of Modern Art gave him its first major one-building exhibition by a living architect.[2] The building that was the subject of the exhibition, and that was featured as the background for Wright's portrait on *Time*'s cover, was Fallingwater, the weekend house designed for the wealthy Pittsburgh department-store owner Edgar Kaufmann in 1934–35 and built during the next two years (fig. 196). As the iconic work of Wright's rise to the status of culture hero, as well as of his return to the forefront of modern architecture, Fallingwater must be viewed as Wright's most significant building of the mid-1930s. Yet, although Fallingwater can now be seen as a logical outgrowth of Wright's work of the teens and twenties—from Taliesin to San Marcos-in-the-Desert—that was not always the case, especially when his architecture of those years was so little known or appreciated. But other factors also led critics and historians to see a definitive break in Wright's career at this point and to talk of a "revival," or "renaissance." However exaggerated that may be, there is little doubt the house would look exactly as it does were it not for certain events that took place during the four years just preceding it, and so it is to an overview of these that we turn first.[3]

■ ■ ■

Following the stock market crash and during the early years of the Depression, Wright spent most of his time writing, lecturing, and generally preparing for better economic times. This is when he completed *An Autobiography* and published *Modern Architecture* (1931), the Kahn Lectures he gave at Princeton University in May 1930. He also published the *Two Lectures on Architecture* (1931) given at the Art Institute of Chicago in October 1930 on the occasion of the exhibition of his work that had started at the Architectural League of New York and then traveled to Amsterdam, Berlin, Frankfurt, Stuttgart, Antwerp, and Brussels before returning to the United States at the end of 1931. He completed *The Disappearing City* in 1932, the first important exposition of the ideas to be embodied in his later project for Broadacre City, and prepared for publication a "complete works" of his buildings and writings (1929–31), as well as a book based on the *Architectural Record* articles of 1927–28, to be entitled "Creative Matter in the Nature of Materials" (1932).[4] Between 1930 and 1935, he also published more than thirty articles in professional and popular journals.

Wright's marriage to Olgivanna Lazovich and their return to Taliesin had an important stabilizing influence at this critical juncture. With her background in the mystical and organic philosophy of Georgi Gurdjieff and her experience as a student and instructor at the Institute for the Harmonious Development of Man, she collaborated with Wright in creating the Taliesin Fellowship (opened October 1932) as a place for young men and women to live and work in an environment where architecture and life would be fully integrated with nature.[5] Learning would come from doing, which meant that Wright would be assured of a steady supply of help in the way of food production and building construction and maintenance, not to speak of mere baby-sitting. Even more to the point, the apprentices, as the Taliesin Fellows were called, would form a solid core of trained craftsmen ready to assume supervisory roles in building once the Depression was over.

The idea for the Fellowship went back to the fall of 1928, when Wright proposed to establish the Hillside Home School of Allied Arts. Its purpose was "to harmonize the spirit of art and the spirit of the machine" in an "uncompromisingly modern" environment that would be, at the same time, a "farm school" where "the students themselves . . . [would] get their own living as far as possible from the ground itself." Combining training in the so-called fine arts and the industrial arts under the general framework of architecture, students would design and produce objects for use, ranging from glassware to textiles to building plans, that not only would be marketable but would also serve as examples for "all the design-forms of American industrial production now characterizing our homes and our lives."[6] The program was closely related to that of Eliel Saarinen's Cranbook Academy of Art at Bloomfield Hills, Michigan, designed by the Finnish immigrant architect in 1924–25 and officially opened in 1932, as well as to that of its more celebrated predecessor, the Bauhaus, formed by Walter Gropius out of a union of the schools of Fine Arts and Arts and Crafts in Weimar in 1919 and then relocated in 1925–26 to new Gropius-designed headquarters in Dessau.[7]

This reaction to, and competition with, contemporary European architecture and education was not an isolated event. Between 1928, when he reviewed Le Corbusier's seminal *Towards a New Architecture* and first took a public stand on developments in Europe, and 1932, when he was included in the Museum of Modern Art's International Style exhibition as a foil to the more radical "machine esthetic" of Le Corbusier, Mies, Gropius, and Oud, Wright engaged in an often heated debate with his younger colleagues that continually forced him to define himself and that ultimately galvanized him into action.[8] It was also the first time that Wright's own work was subject to wide critical attention, which did not always prove to be a happy experience for him. The polemical, professedly avant-garde movement championed in the United States by Hitchcock and Johnson and in Europe by Sigfried Giedion, among others, presented a challenge to Wright's authority and historical significance such as he had never faced before.[9]

From the time he joined Sullivan's office until well into the 1920s, Wright never thought of himself as anything other than the most advanced and accomplished modern architect in the world. Now, all of a sudden, it was becoming clear that he had been overtaken by a younger generation of European modernists. The pure white forms and gleaming metal columns and strip windows of their buildings made his work seem not merely dated and old-fashioned but even *traditional*, thereby throwing into doubt its very relation to modernity. So powerfully did this realization impress itself on Wright that, from this moment until the end of his life, he never stopped railing against the "sterile" and formalistic "picture-buildings" of "gas pipe, thin slabs and naked steel work" designed by "sophisticated, ingenious, cleverly curious" European modernists that "smell of the dissecting room" and would have us all "embalmed alive."[10]

Wright castigated the International Style as merely a narrow tributary stemming from his own work, simplifying it, and reducing it to a repeatable aesthetic formula. Playing into the widespread isolationist mood of America, he called the European modernists "predatory 'internationalists'" and cautioned most vociferously against listening to their American "propagandists" (meaning Hitchcock and John-

son), who were "ready to hinder and betray native progress." He compared the International Style to the Beaux-Arts classicism of the turn of the century and referred to Sullivan's dire prediction of the effects of the Columbian Exposition of 1893 in warning of the powerful hold the new style could have on the country "for another thirty years" if it was not combated and kept in check.[11]

Just as Wright was stimulated by the wave of academic classicism following the 1893 fair to formulate and develop his Prairie Style, he at first welcomed the challenge of a new "enemy" from abroad for similar reasons. "I believe Le Corbusier and the group around him are extremely useful," he wrote in 1931, "extremely valuable, especially, as an enemy."[12] Wright was always quick on the counterattack. When Hitchcock declared in the catalogue of the International Style show that "the day of the lone pioneer is past" and "throughout the world there are others beside Wright to lead the way toward the future," Wright characterized "this alleged invention [as] an attempt to strip hide and horns from the living breathing organism that is modern architecture of the past twenty-five years." He retorted: "It is the thing said that is more important, now, than the manner of saying it. Our pioneer days are not over."[13] Two years before that, after Hitchcock had written him off as an architect more in tune with the tradition of nineteenth-century "eclecticism" than with the values of contemporary modernism, Wright revealed the full extent of his passion—and will—to vindicate himself: "I warn Henry-Russell Hitchcock right here and now that, having a good start, not only do I fully intend to be the greatest architect who has yet lived, but the greatest who will ever live. Yes, I intend to be the greatest architect of all time. And I do hereunto affix 'the red square' and sign my name to this warning."[14]

The challenge represented by the International Style was not only personal. It was a challenge of a philosophical nature, pitting one conception of architecture against another. Wright felt that the purely geometric "'surface and mass' abstractions" of the new architecture, "stripped clean of all considerations but Function and Utility" in response

197. Taliesin Fellowship Buildings (renovation and enlargement of Hillside Home School), Hillside, begun 1932–33. Aerial perspective.

to a misplaced form of "machine worship," necessarily removed architecture from the realm of symbolic form, causing it to deny and "to force issue upon Nature."[15] To the geometric abstraction of International Style modernism, Wright offered a highly figurative naturalism (figs. 179, 191); to the Europeans' mechanistic functionalism, he countered with a romantic expressionism; to their rigorous Taylorization and standardization, he proposed instead a material- and site-specific ad-hocism; and to their collectivist vision of a regularized urban order, he opposed a pragmatic individualism based on typically American patterns of land use and development (figs. 198, 199).[16]

The prospect of an International Style forced Wright to examine his own position and to articulate his approach to design in a way that clearly distinguished him from those he perceived to be his enemies. The result was a concentration and intensification of those characteristics of his work that were peculiarly his own, which in the end meant the thoroughgoing naturalism of Taliesin.

■ ■ ■

The renovation and enlargement of Taliesin was, in fact, one of the most important projects Wright undertook after the San Marcos resort fell through and before Fallingwater was begun. In preparation for the first group of Fellows, arriving in the fall of 1932, Wright planned an extensive network of buildings to create a kind of campus out of the original Hillside Home School (fig. 197).[17] The major new element was a large, central drafting room abutting the original physics laboratory and drawing studio. Begun in 1933, though not finished until several years later, this clerestoried space has a factory-shed roof supported by a dense wood-truss ceiling that Wright likened to an "abstract forest."[18] In a preliminary stage of the design, the main units were aligned orthogonally and related, as in Hollyhock House, by cross-axes terminating in large exedrae, but in the final project, a wing containing machine-craft shops and apprentices' rooms angled off the far end of the drafting room to align with paths leading up the hillside toward Midway Hill and Wright's house.

The purpose of the building campaign, like that of the Fellowship itself, was to restore Taliesin and the Hillside Home School to their original educational, domestic, and professional functions. Wright was particularly concerned that the new buildings be as much in keeping with the older ones as the expanded Fellowship program was with the original uses of the site. "As fate would have it," he noted, "I had recourse only to the materials . . . in which the early buildings were originally built." "That they [the additions] are not 'modern' as use of steel, concrete, and glass would have made them" was therefore "beside the mark."[19] In certain other projects, however, where the situation warranted it, Wright did use such materials precisely for their "modern" effect. The projects of 1931–32 for the Capital Journal Newspaper Plant in Salem, Oregon, and the House on the Mesa for Denver, Colorado, offered streamlined silhouettes that were clearly meant by Wright to prove that he could compete with the younger Europeans on their own terms.[20]

Some of that same competitiveness lay behind the project for Broadacre City, the model of which was produced in 1934–35 as a kind of private WPA program to provide work for the Taliesin Fellows during the Depression

198. Broadacre City project, 1929–35. Model.

199. Le Corbusier: Contemporary City for 3 Million Inhabitants project, 1922. Perspective.

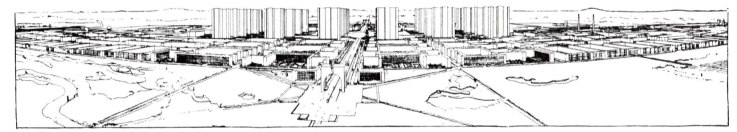

(fig. 198). Conceived in the late 1920s, following Le Corbusier's revolutionary proposals for a "contemporary city" planned around the imagery of modern technology, Broadacre City offered an agrarian alternative (fig. 199). In direct opposition to Le Corbusier, Wright called his guiding principle "Ruralism as distinguished from '*Urbanisme*'" (*A* I, 321).[21] His decentralized, land-based scheme would guarantee each citizen a minimum of one acre to live on and to farm in an effort to reintegrate life in the United States on the model of Taliesin.[22] Modern in its acceptance of the automobile as the generator of a boundless sub-urban development that would be "nowhere unless everywhere," and utopian in its elimination of real estate speculation and rent in favor of a cooperative system based on social credit, Broadacre City combined a number of earlier, unbuilt projects, such as the San Marcos Water Gardens, Doheny House C, the Gordon Strong Automobile Objective, the Tahoe Fir

Tree Cabin, and the St. Mark's-in-the-Bouwerie Tower, in a loosely organized framework that reflects, in its schematic and overly fragmented form, the unreality of the studio, or classroom, out of which its design emerged.[23]

Because of his deep belief that a building must respond directly to its site and to the materials used in its construction, Wright needed a real client and a real program to fulfill his artistic ideals. One even wonders whether Wright would have undertaken a project such as Broadacre City had he had more work at the time. It did, however, serve its purpose in a number of ways. It provided work and design experience for the new apprentices while initiating them into Wright's principles and procedures of design. When it was exhibited in the spring of 1935 in New York, and later in Pittsburgh and Washington, D.C., it was accompanied by major press coverage that provided a significant source of advertising for Wright and the Fellowship. It also proved, in

Willey House, Minneapolis, Minn., 1932–34. First scheme, 1932.

200. Perspective.

201. Preliminary plan, upper floor.

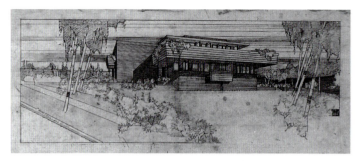

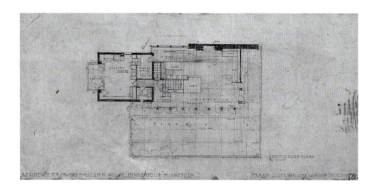

the process, that he was no less capable than the younger Europeans of considering architecture's larger social role and its relation to the development of modern life. Perhaps most important, though, it furnished Wright and the new Fellowship with a permanent, experimental terrain on which could be modeled every conceivable type of building that might be needed once the construction industry got back on its feet.

The fundamental unit of Broadacre City was the single-family house. It ranged in size and type from the "minimal," one-car, do-it-yourself prefab to a five-car dwelling of "machine-age luxury" based on the Denver House on the Mesa. In between was an enormous variety of possibilities, each of which in turn could be adapted to a particular region of the country, the climate, and its actual site. That kind of experimentation, adaptation, and diversification became the single most characteristic aspect of Wright's later work—almost his signature, if that is not a contradiction in terms. Certain basic principles of site planning, construction, and interior organization underpinned the varied results, much as they had, in different ways of

course, the Prairie House. Wright called the basic, least elaborate ones Usonian, and eventually considered them all, following the precedent of Taliesin, examples of the "Natural House."[24]

■ ■ ■

The predecessor of the Usonian House, and the prototype for many of its characteristic features, was designed in late 1933–early 1934 and built for Nancy and Malcolm Willey in 1934 in a suburb of Minneapolis.[25] It was a scaled-down version of a slightly earlier scheme for the same site, done in 1932, which the academic couple had to forgo for financial reasons. That project became the basis of Fallingwater. The first scheme called for a two-storied, flat-roofed, brick-and-wood structure that dramatically cantilevered from a wall built against the north lot line (figs. 200, 201). The combined living and dining room of the upper floor was planned along the lines of implied diagonal axes, like the main room of Taliesin.[26] Floor-to-ceiling glass doors opened onto a roof deck that projected the view over the Mississippi Valley below. The upturned, efflorescent shape gave the impression of a flower growing from a vine on the wall.

Wright called the second, reduced scheme for the Willey House "The Garden Wall." It is a single-story structure that occupies an ell in the angle of the wall (fig. 202). Like the later Usonian Houses that derive from it, it is a light, wood-and-brick structure that sits on a relatively thin concrete "mat" serving as the foundation. A dining nook connected to a laboratory-like kitchen features as part of the living room (fig. 203). The bedrooms form a tail, "sequestering," as Wright said, a private garden within the ell.[27] The house literally depends upon the garden wall as it forms a kind of lean-to recalling the primordial "northern house" Viollet-le-Duc illustrated in his *Habitations of Man in All Ages* (fig. 204).[28] The simplified, though no less potent, diagonality of the final plan, bodied forth in the expansive, pivoting action of the terrace, underscores the sense of movement down the hillside from the upper wall. With the

Willey House. Second scheme, 1933–34.

202. Aerial perspective.

203. Plan.

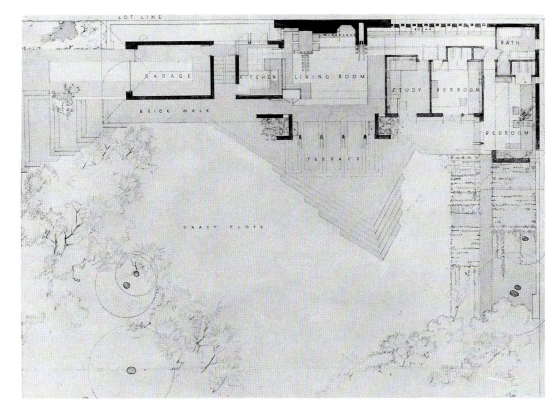

ground thus figured in it, the lean-to shelter becomes an aspect of a much larger whole.

In the design of the Willey House, Wright responded keenly and accurately not only to the site but also to the new economic and social realities of the 1930s. He completely revised his earlier conception of the ideal domestic environment to meet the changed conditions of a more simplified and casual life-style. The Usonian House that evolved out of the Willey House was "streamlined" in plan to accommodate new patterns of family life and entertainment.[29] The combination of simple, modern shapes with warm, natural materials proved to be particularly appealing to a middle-class market as a subtle compromise with the more astringent forms of the International Style. The original scheme for the Willey House would provide the basis for such later examples as the Sturges House (1939–40), the Lewis House

204. Viollet-le-Duc: House of the Arya, in *The Habitations of Man in All Ages* (1875).

(1939–42), and the Affleck House (1941), as well as the Suntop Homes (1938–39); it would in turn help prepare the way for the postwar development of the Bay Region Style in America as well as the different versions of Scandinavian Modern in Europe.[30]

If the Willey House was the prototype for the Usonian House, the Willeys were the prototypical clients. Born into a family that owned a string of small-town newspapers and educated at Clark and Columbia universities, Malcolm Willey joined the Department of Sociology at the University of Minnesota in 1927, where he later became Dean and Vice-President for Academic Administration. His specialty was the sociology of the communications industry, in particular, the effect of newspapers and radio on contemporary society. As clients, he and his wife, Nancy, were the first of a series of forward-looking, middle-class academics and journalists that would include the Jacobses, the Lewises, the Popes, the Hannas, the Lusks, the Bairds, the Rosenbaums, and Alma Goetsch and Katherine Winkler. They constituted a very

different and more varied type from the upper middle-class and wealthy group of businessmen and women who generally hired Wright in the years prior to the crash.[31]

For the more elaborate version of the "Natural House" that would cost more than the $5,000–10,000 the average Usonian did prior to World War II, as well as for the more grandiose public buildings for which Wright began to receive commissions, the clients were again much more varied than those of the earlier years. One group totally new for Wright was the wealthy Jewish merchant, often of German extraction. Two such men were responsible for major house commissions that came into Wright's office at almost exactly the same time, in November–December 1934, just as the Willey House was being finished. The first was Stanley Marcus, of the Neiman-Marcus Department Store in Dallas; the second was Edgar Kaufmann, of Kaufmann's Department Store in Pittsburgh. Both were alumni of Ivy League universities, the former of Harvard and the latter of Yale, and both went to Wright because they wanted something of special artistic merit. (The other famous German Jew to commission a building from Wright was Solomon R. Guggenheim, but that project was still a few years down the line.)

The project for the Marcus House in Dallas, developed concurrently with the one for Kaufmann, expanded the second scheme for the Willey House on a much more lavish scale (figs. 247, 248). Although it was never built, it served as the basis for the plan of Taliesin West and will be discussed in more detail in the following chapter. The Kaufmann House, which grew out of the first scheme for the Willeys, is the focus for the remainder of this chapter.

Fallingwater, Edgar Kaufmann, and Bear Run

Fallingwater is the name Wright gave to the "forest lodge" he designed for Edgar Kaufmann, his wife Liliane, and their son Edgar Jr. as a year-round weekend retreat in the Allegheny Mountains south of Pittsburgh, near the West Virginia line (fig. 196).[32] The Kaufmanns, who had been going to the area for a number of years, generally referred to the house by its most prominent natural feature, Bear Run. But, as Wright's name for it suggests, the building represents much more than a physical attribute of its site: it embodies an image of nature in flux. Designed "to the music of the stream," as Wright told his client, for "one who liked to listen to the waterfall," Fallingwater materializes the temporal dimension of architecture.[33] In so doing, it offers an expression of antithesis and mutability that can be considered definitive of modern architecture.

Though essentially known by most people through the dramatic view of it from below, Fallingwater exists as a complex of changing aspects of which that view is only one (figs. 206, 217, 227). It is rough stone and smooth concrete, crevice and plane, vertical pier and horizontal parapet, projecting volume and deep void, cave-like interior and open-air terrace, rock, tree, leaf, fire, and water, all woven into a hallucinatory, magical image by daring engineering and delicate site planning. "Fallingwater is a realized dream," wrote the architect Paul Rudolph. "It touches something deep within us about which, finally, none of us can speak."[34] Rudolph's reference to a dream may therefore be more apt and more helpful than one might at first have thought. The dream, in twentieth-century art, has served as a paradigm for the concept of duration, a temporal state existing within, yet unmeasured by, real time. It has also been

used to describe the mutability of images when they occur outside of conscious thought. With this in mind, perhaps we can begin to explain how Fallingwater works on us, if not all that it may mean.[36]

■ ■ ■

When Edgar J. Kaufmann asked Wright to design the family's mountain retreat toward the very end of 1934, there began a relationship between architect and client based on the kind of mutual trust, admiration, and respect that existed between Wright and few other clients. From then until his death in 1955, Kaufmann commissioned six or more additional projects from Wright, and often helped when most needed to support the activities of the Taliesin Fellowship.[37] Kaufmann, who was forty-nine years old when he first met Wright in 1934 (and thus nearly twenty years his junior), was the owner and president of Pittsburgh's largest department store. Kaufmann's was a family business, founded in 1871 by Edgar's immigrant father and three uncles; he took over in 1913 and controlled the operation until it was sold to the May Company in 1946. In 1909, Kaufmann married his first cousin Lillian Sarah Kaufmann (she changed her name to the more elegant Liliane in the 1920s), who became celebrated as a hostess in local circles. She took a keen interest in the running of the store but never, it would appear, became involved in her husband's passion for architecture.[38]

Active in local politics and community affairs, Edgar Kaufmann was admired for his business acumen as well as for his personal vitality, magnetism, and urbanity, although to some his brilliance appeared unconventional and even eccentric. Distinguishing himself from those Pittsburgh moguls and scions, from Frick and Mellon to Heinz and G. David Thompson, who made the collecting of painting and sculpture a *sine qua non* of financial success, Kaufmann apparently wanted to be known for his interest in architecture. To a reporter preparing an article on the department store for *Fortune* magazine in 1944, Kaufmann

Wright brought to Fallingwater an extreme degree of personal involvement and subjectivity. "You got your money's worth out of an architect if ever a man did," he told his client. "All we need is one more commission into which I put as much of myself as I did into this one to go out of the picture here [at Taliesin]." Wright spoke of Fallingwater as his own child. "We 'nursed it' to a conclusion," he wrote to Kaufmann, later confiding to him in a most extraordinary statement: "I would deny you nothing I had to give, short of suicide."[35]

declared that he liked "above all else to build houses." That may have been an unusually modest claim, for Kaufmann was not only one of the founding members of the Allegheny Conference on Community Development (1944), which oversaw the resurgence of downtown Pittsburgh in the late 1940s and 1950s, but he also provided the seed money for the construction of Pittsburgh's Civic Auditorium in the new Lower Hill (completed 1962).[39]

Kaufmann's earliest efforts at building do not reveal a special talent for seeking out architects with particularly advanced ideas. Rather, they exhibit the outward signs of someone who very much wanted to "assimilate" and be accepted in the most fashionable social circles.[40] The family house in the wealthy northern Pittsburgh suburb of Fox Chapel was designed by the Beaux-Arts trained architect Benno Janssen, of the firm of Janssen and Cocken. Built in 1924–25 and called La Tourelle, it is a picturesque brick-and-stone Norman farmhouse, in the manner of Mellor, Meigs, and Howe, and typical of Philadelphia's Main Line. The same firm was called upon to remodel the department store in 1927–30 and give its ground floor a "modern" face-lift. In the following year (1931), Kaufmann had an addition in the "rustic-rocky" mode made to the family's weekend house at their mountain property in the Alleghenies. (The original house was a simple "Readi-cut" summer cabin, built from a kit in 1921, and did not even involve the services of an architect.)

What apparently changed Kaufmann's mind about architecture and influenced him to turn to Wright were the artistic ideas of his son.[41] Edgar Kaufmann Jr., who was to become director of the Department of Architecture and Design at the Museum of Modern Art in New York and eventually a professor of architectural history at Columbia University, had gone to Europe in the later twenties to study painting and graphic art. When he returned to the United States in 1934, he read Wright's *Autobiography* and was so impressed with it that he soon joined the Taliesin Fellowship in October as one of its early members, even though he had no intention of becoming an architect. Kaufmann Sr., who

had begun corresponding with Wright about ideas for civic improvements for Pittsburgh in the late summer, visited his son at Taliesin with his wife in November 1934. The following month he invited Wright to Pittsburgh to discuss the idea of building a planetarium, based on the Gordon Strong project of 1924–25, and to advise on a public works program for the city. It was during this trip, in mid- to late December 1934, that Kaufmann asked Wright to design a new office for himself in the department store (completed 1936–37) as well as a new weekend house to replace the simple cabin near Bear Run.[42]

By 1934 Kaufmann owned approximately sixteen hundred acres of unspoiled, rugged, upland forest on the Allegheny Plateau, about a two-hour drive or train ride south of Pittsburgh. Situated along the Youghiogheny River between the towns of Ohiopyle and Mill Run, in an area of otherwise disused coal mines and poor farms, the densely wooded property, covered mainly with oak trees and rhododendron, lies within the folds of the Ohiopyle Valley between Laurel Hill and Chestnut Ridge (fig. 205). The name Ohiopyle, as Donald Hoffmann notes in his excellent history of Fallingwater, is of Native American derivation. It means "a white-water place" and perfectly describes the most characteristic and important natural feature of this uplifted and deeply eroded landscape.[43] Kaufmann's property follows the winding and precipitous course of a mountain stream, called Bear Run, which begins on Laurel Hill and works its way down through the sandstone cliffs of an old glacial ravine, falling nearly fifteen hundred feet in four miles to empty into the Youghiogheny. About half a mile before it reaches the river, it takes a sharp dogleg north; and as it straightens out again, it drops in a series of dramatic falls over large boulders strewn in its bed.

The area within this crook of Bear Run, which is mainly on the flatter south bank, was first developed as a camp in 1890 by a group of Masons from Pittsburgh. After that venture failed, another Masonic group took it over in 1909, calling it the "Syria Country Club." This lasted until 1916, when the land was leased by Kaufmann's Department

205. Bear Run and Youghiogheny River. A = Fallingwater (and guest house); B = entrance to property; C = access drive; D = site of original cabin.

Store as a "Summer Club" for its women employees, providing them with a variety of sports and social activities in a healthy, relaxed, "back-to-nature mode of living," as it was described in a camp brochure of 1926.[44] Its paternalist character was made even more evident when the Kaufmann family built their own cabin not far from the other club buildings in 1921. Although an employees' organization was finally able to purchase the sixteen hundred acres outright in 1926, helped by a mortgage from Edgar Kaufmann, the summer camp fell into disuse during the Depression. In 1933 Kaufmann took over title to the property and began planning for its improvement.

After implementing careful conservation measures in 1932 and 1933 to preserve the beauty of the forest and its abundance of wildlife and fish, Kaufmann focused his attention on turning the family's modest summer cabin into something more permanent and worthy of its site. This would necessitate a complete rebuilding. The only question was where. The cabin was originally located farther upstream than the club buildings, on higher ground, but in a less open and less interesting area, quite distant from the stream (see fig. 205). In 1930 the dirt road alongside it was paved and turned into a state highway, making traffic a major problem. A new site had to be chosen.

The choice of site seems to have been the main purpose of Wright's first visit to the Ohiopyle Valley. He was taken there by Edgar Kaufmann shortly before Christmas 1934.[45] When he saw the area of the falls farther down the glen, where Kaufmann told him the family and their friends liked to swim and picnic, Wright was apparently immediately struck with its possibilities. As Kaufmann considered the more practical problems of building in such an exiguous spot, hemmed in by a steep, rocky cliff on one side and with a precipitous drop on the other, Wright reportedly insisted: "You love this waterfall, don't you? Then why build your house miles away, so you will have to walk to it? Why not live intimately with it, where you can see and hear it and feel it with you all of the time?" Whether or not this quotation is verbatim, it is part of the myth that has grown up

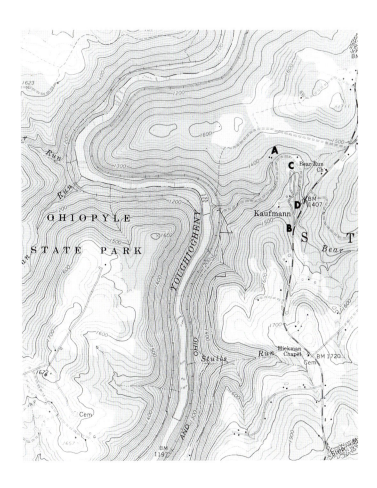

around this building. What we do know for sure is that Wright wrote to Kaufmann on 26 December 1934, upon returning to Taliesin: "The visit to the waterfall in the woods stays with me and a domicile has taken vague shape in my mind to the music of the stream. When contours come you will see it."[46]

Convinced that the house should be built somewhere around the falls, Kaufmann had a topographical map of the area drawn up and sent to Wright in early March 1935 (fig. 208). Before it arrived, however, the Kaufmanns had another meeting with Wright when they went out to Arizona in mid-February to visit their son at Chandler, where he was working with the Fellowship on the Broadacre City model.[47] Wright visited the Bear Run site again in the spring or early summer of 1935, clearly anxious about the very complex problems involved with situating a house over a mountain stream and falls. Following that second visit, Kaufmann wrote to Wright advising him that the house should cost no more than $20,000–30,000.[48]

Another part of the myth surrounding Fallingwater, and perhaps the most interesting, is that for almost precisely nine months Wright did not touch pencil to paper but just let the design germinate in his head. On 22 September 1935 Kaufmann, who was on a business trip to Milwaukee, called Wright to say that he would like to stop off at Taliesin to see the preliminary studies for the house. According to Edgar Tafel, one of Wright's apprentices, that was the signal for "Mr. Wright . . . to start drawing." "The design just poured out of him." Plans, sections, and elevations were all done within a few hours, Tafel reports, and the house received the name Fallingwater just before noon, when Kaufmann arrived. Whether it is true that no sketches preceded the ones shown to Kaufmann, it is entirely accurate to say, as Tafel and others have, that from this initial drafting of the project, "the basic design never changed."[49]

A set of plans was completed and sent to Kaufmann on 15 October. Wright's involvement in the project was such that he made a third visit to the site a few days later (19 October 1935). The first set of working drawings was produced in January 1936, although quarrying of stone had begun the month before. After a series of engineering reports in March and April, requested independently by Kaufmann to allay his fears about the feasibility of the design, construction went ahead early in the spring of 1936. Wright visited the site in mid-April and again in early June, during which time he continued to make minor adjustments and refinements in the design.[50] The first-floor slab was poured in mid-August, and the second floor by mid-September. After a slight delay due to concerns over cracks that appeared in the concrete, followed by tests by outside engineers, work proceeded throughout the winter and spring of 1937 on exterior and interior finishes. The house was completed in the fall of 1937, at a cost of approximately $80,000, a little over a year and a half after it was begun. A separate guest house, including a four-car garage and servants' quarters, that was intended from the outset to be added on

the rear, higher up the side of the glen, was designed in 1938 and finished in the following year. The final bill came to approximately $145,000, a little more than half of what the Kaufmanns paid for their Norman farmhouse in town, though quite a bit more than they had originally intended to spend on a weekend house in the country.[51]

Materials, Siting, Design

Fallingwater combines the seemingly accidental naturalness of Taliesin with the geometric order and structural logic of Wright's work of the mid- to late 1920s. A binary opposition of stone and concrete expresses this conjunction on a basic, material level. The stone, quarried less than five hundred feet from the actual site, was reserved for all vertical, load-bearing piers and walls; reinforced concrete was used to create the stack of horizontal balconies, or trays, cantilevered from the rock ledge over the bed of the stream (figs. 206, 207).[52] The trays, bounded by curved parapets, weave through the vertical stone structure to provide the living spaces for the house. These are continuous inside and out. Where one tray overlaps another, doors and windows of plate glass in steel sash are inserted to mark the distinction between interior room and outdoor terrace. The lowest tray forms the main floor of the house and contains a single space combining the functions of living, dining, reception, and library. The middle tray, with its main terrace forming the roof of the living room, contains the two master bedrooms plus a small guest room, each with its adjacent terrace. The top tray, roofing over the second-floor bedrooms and forming an aerie within the overarching branches of the tall oak trees, became the domain of Edgar Jr.[53]

The idea of combining stone and concrete was a consequence of the decision about the precise placement of the house: the structural interaction between the two different materials was determined with respect to the scanty footing offered by the site. Wright's prime objective was to make the relation between house and waterfall as intimate as

Fallingwater (Kaufmann House), Mill Run, Pa., 1934–37.

206. Entrance side from east.

207. Section (north-south) through living room.

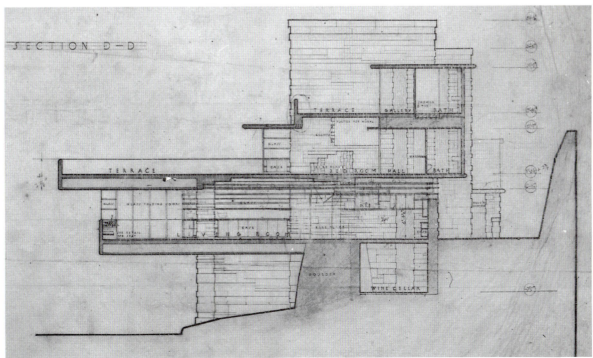

208. Fallingwater. Topographical map of site (March 1935).

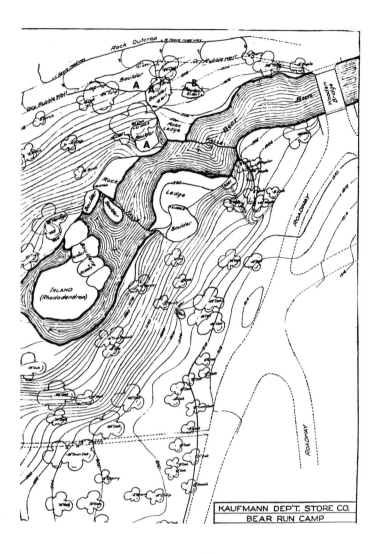

KAUFMANN DEP'T. STORE CO.
BEAR RUN CAMP

possible. To that end, he placed the house over the water-fall, on the steep, boulder-strewn north bank of the stream, rather than facing it from the wider and flatter south bank. Edgar Kaufmann was apparently taken by complete surprise. When he initially showed Wright the area, he reportedly took him down the old stone steps on the south bank of the stream to the "flat expanse of rock at the base of the falls" where the family "liked to bask between forays into the ever-icy water," and from which point one would have a splendid view of "the torrent pouring over the fractured ledge."[54] The assumption was that Wright would place the house somewhere down there, looking up at the falls. When Kaufmann realized how different Wright's intentions were, he raised certain objections from the point of view of engineering, to which Wright, we are told, retorted: "Nature

cantilevered those boulders out over the fall. . . . I can cantilever the house over the boulders."[55]

As can be seen from the topographical map Wright had to work with, the site on the north bank of Bear Run forms a narrow shelf making an almost perfect thirty/sixty-degree triangle between the steep rock outcrop (along the northern edge) and the first falls (to the left, or southwest, of the wooden bridge; fig. 208). The shelf spreads out to the west and south from the point where a wooden bridge crossed the stream. The base of the triangle follows the southwesterly flow of the stream, while the hypotenuse, running due west, lines up with the edge of a dirt road (indicated on the map by the dry rubble wall) that ran along the face of the cliff from the bridge to a cottage farther up the hill. The western boundary of this triangle is defined by a group of three large boulders (A on the map) that follow the line of the ledge that determines the fall. Another, more isolated boulder stands a little to the east of them (B on the map).

The foundations were to fit within the triangular shelf defined by the stream, the road, and the three westernmost boulders (fig. 209). The bridge was rebuilt in stone and concrete and the road between the house and the cliff was preserved. A staggered stone wall following the edge of the drive creates an almost solid backbone on the north, to which the horizontal trays of reinforced concrete were attached and from which they were cantilevered into space (fig. 206). An enormous, three-story chimney mass, set at an angle to this rear wall, was built up from the isolated, easternmost boulder to become the fulcrum of the design and anchor the whole structure in space.

The nearly fifteen-foot cantilever of the living room floor is partly supported by three "bolsters," as Wright called them, that angle up from the rock ledge (fig. 215). The even greater cantilever of the second-floor terrace is partly supported by the two free-standing piers in the living room; the weight of the enclosed section of the second floor, along with that of the entire upper story (all of which is contained within the angle of the chimney mass and the north wall of the house), serves to counterbalance the effect of the canti-

Fallingwater.

209. Preliminary plan, foundations.

210. Preliminary plan, ground floor.

N

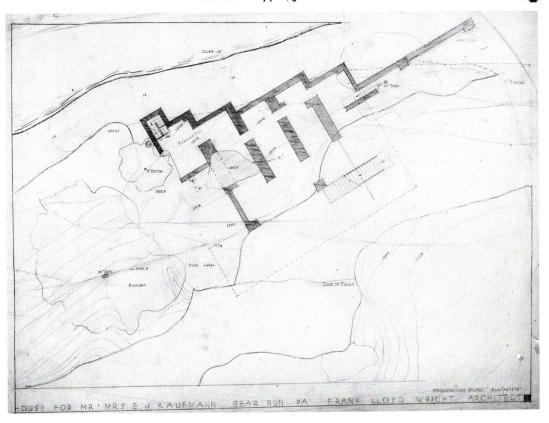

HOUSE FOR MR + MRS E J KAUFMANN BEAR RUN PA FRANK LLOYD WRIGHT ARCHITECT

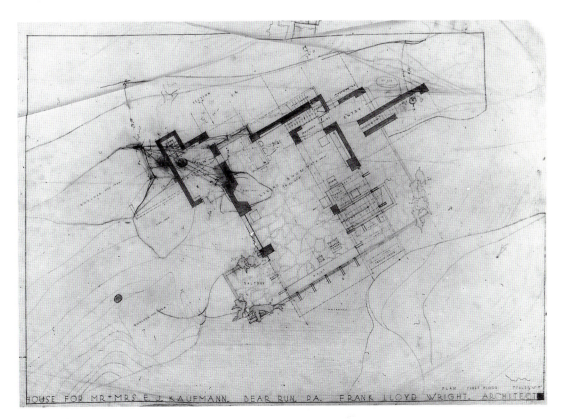

HOUSE FOR MR + MRS E J KAUFMANN BEAR RUN PA FRANK LLOYD WRIGHT ARCHITECT

211. Fallingwater. Plan, ground floor.

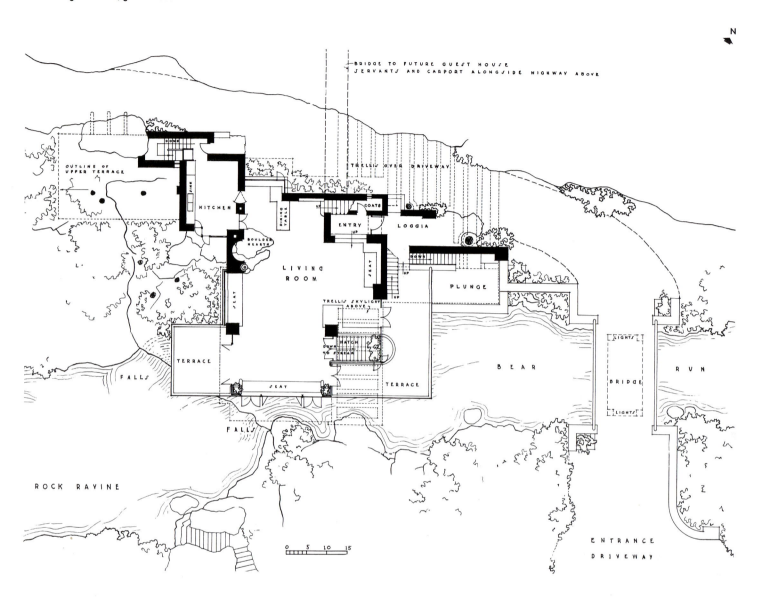

lever (fig. 207). Visually, the composition is stabilized by the trellis of reinforced-concrete beams that continues the slab of the second-floor tray through the rear wall of the house and ties the floating layers of living space into the face of the cliff (fig. 206). As a result, the tunnel-like driveway beneath becomes a fully integrated part of the design.[56]

Wright chose to make the plan of Fallingwater orthogonal in contrast to the triangular shelf on which it is superposed. The interaction of the two geometries is reflected in the general pivoting of the plan and in the resulting diagonal axes that govern its spatial form. The east-west path of the existing road served as the datum line. Although most reproductions illustrate the plan squared to the page,

Wright's earliest drawings show that it was consistently placed at an angle to the sheet (figs. 209, 210). Working with the inherent geometry of the rock shelf, Wright established the outlines of the house, as Donald Hoffmann has convincingly shown, by using a thirty/sixty-degree triangle.[57] With its hypotenuse set to the edge of the drive, against the dry rubble wall indicated on the topographical map, and with the thirty-degree angle toward the bridge, Wright drew along the short arm of the triangle (the one lining up with the three boulders and facing southwest) the structural supports in stone, beginning with the most important one forming the chimney. By sliding the triangle to the right, he established the other supports parallel to it on an approxi-

212. Fallingwater. Living room, looking south.

mately twelve-foot module. The leading edge of the trays cantilevered from them, paralleling the course of the stream, was drawn along the side opposite the sixty-degree angle, thus giving the house the southeast orientation Wright generally preferred. In keeping with the orthogonal grammar of the plan, Wright then established the rear wall of the house, on the north, by a staggered line of wall sections implicitly describing, by their zigzag movement, the diagonal of the hypotenuse.

Seen in this way, the plan reveals its dynamic, reactive character. It appears to have pivoted southeast, from the point where the road nears the bridge, as a result of pressure from the land mass behind, only to be stopped in its track by the projecting boulders. The effect is a concentration of the final scheme for the Willey House. There, the front terrace pivots thirty degrees into space to suggest an underlying relation to the slope of the land. Wright described Fallingwater as "an extension of the cliff beside a mountain stream."[58] The entire house, not just a part of it, swings with the glen to align with the stream, thus incorporating within its space the sense of direction and motion of the body of water beneath it.

The spatial definition of the interior of Fallingwater likewise depends on lines generated by implied diagonal axes. The main floor, entered at ground level, is devoted almost exclusively to a multipurpose family living room, approximately forty-eight feet deep by thirty-eight feet wide (fig. 211). The flexible, open plan is loosely organized around a central atrium-like space, illuminated from above by a large, nearly square, recessed ceiling panel, which is supported at its four corners by stone piers (the fourth being the right pier of the fireplace; fig. 212). The various functions are zoned into pockets of space that pinwheel around this open core, sometimes overlapping and sometimes projecting from it. Just to the left of the entrance is a seat with a built-in phonograph next to it. Beyond that is the skylit area of the study, or library. Projecting between the two piers at the far side of the room is a family sitting area that opens to the left and to the right onto outdoor terraces overlooking the stream. And just to the left of the fireplace is another built-in seat, under the window, forming a more cozy sitting area next to the fire. To the right of the fireplace and set back into the rear stone wall of the house is the dining area (fig. 213). On one side it opens to the kitchen, and on the other to the stairway leading to the upper-floor bedrooms.

The materials used inside are the same as those outside, an identity that is reinforced in two key places by the actual intrusion of an element from outside. The walls and piers are stone; the ceiling, forming the underside of the upper slab, is plastered and painted the same color as the parapets. The floor is covered in flagstones, similar in color and texture to the stones in the bed of the stream. They are waxed, except for a single boulder that projects above floor level to become the hearth of the fireplace. The surface we see is actually the upper part of the isolated, easternmost boulder used in the foundations of the house (see fig. 210). As it emerges in its raw, natural state as the base of the living room fireplace, its role in anchoring the composition is transformed from a literal to a figurative one (fig. 213).[59]

This emphasis coincides, from all we can tell, with the particular significance Wright attached to the boulder.

Based on his visits to the site with the client, he understood that this was the rock on which Kaufmann liked to sit. While working on the plans, Wright apparently would think out loud: "The rock on which E. J. sits will be the hearth, coming right out of the floor, the fire burning just behind it."[60] For Wright, at least, this boulder, as the seat of the house, served to identify subject and object—site and building—through the continuous involvement of its occupant. Bear Run would thus not remain externalized as an object but would be internalized as the very subject of the house.

The fireplace, the most powerful element in the room, is located in the far corner of the central space and calls attention to itself. Its stone hollow forms a blunt, cavernous half-cylinder. In the lefthand pier is a hemispherical depression in which there is a large, spherical red kettle that can swing into the fire for boiling water or mulling wine. Diagonally opposite the fireplace, behind the pier of the library, is a second element that works with the fireplace to determine the spatial shape and meaning of the room by relating it directly to the natural world outside (figs. 211, 214). This is the glass hatch under the skylight that opens through the floor and connects to a suspended stairway leading directly down to the stream (fig. 215). Wright had thought that he could "deepen the stream for a swimming pool" at this point. When that proved impossible, and a plunge pool was created nearer to the road and bridge, he insisted on retaining the hatch and stairs, admitting the originally intended use was perhaps only a pretext: "We got down into the glen to associate directly with the stream and planned the house for that association. Hence the steps from living room to stream." He told Kaufmann he thought "this feature necessary from every standpoint."[61]

Fireplace and hatch each reveals, within the space of the living room, the direct association of the house with its site, the one by its protruding "boulder hearth," the other by its stairs to the stream. Taken together, as they are meant to be, they describe a diagonal line across the room that traces the underlying geometric relation between building and site. Though different in material and function, the fire-

Fallingwater.

213. Fallingwater. Living room, looking toward fireplace.

214. Living room, hatch.

215. Steps from hatch and "bolsters" supporting living room floor.

place and hatch are both semicircular. They are the only non-rectilinear shapes in the plan of the house.[62] This was clearly a very conscious decision on Wright's part. In the earliest plans, dating back to the fall of 1935, the rear wall of the fireplace formed three sides of an octagon, and the outside wall of the hatch was square (fig. 210). Over the course of the next several months, Wright changed the shape of the wall of the hatch to a half-circle in response to the curved profile adopted for the top of the terrace parapets. At the same time, he gave the fireplace a thirty/sixty-degree triangular plan. This picked up the angle of the boulder of the hearth and pointed in the direction of the hatch. To reinforce the link between the two corners of the room containing the main symbolic elements relating to the stream, Wright finally made the fireplace the same semicircular shape as the hatch, at about the same time the plunge pool was being designed and the hatch was being justified on essentially symbolic grounds.[63]

The curved outside wall of the hatch echoes the hollow cavity of the fireplace in space. The line of reflection inscribes a thirty/sixty-degree diagonal across the central square of the living room. This parallels the angle of the falls, as well as the line of the rear cliff and road. The diagonal connection between hearth and hatch thus describes the dynamic spatial shear of the room while at the same time internalizing the datum line from which the house was pivoted over the ledge and stream (figs. 208, 209). The responding diagonal cross-axis, which leads from the entrance to the southwest corner of the room opening onto a cantilevered terrace, thus naturally follows the path of the stream below defined by the projecting ledge.

The enclosed areas of the second and third floors of bedrooms conform fairly exactly to the shape of the triangular rock ledge between the road and the stream and thus serve to counterbalance the deep cantilevers.[64] The two

216. *Fallingwater. View from high point of south bank of Bear Run.*

upper floors are stepped back as they rise, creating the impression, as in the San Marcos-in-the-Desert project, that they form part of the natural terracing of the hillside (fig. 216). When the guest house was completed, this illusion was made even more convincing (fig. 217). But there remains a fundamental difference between the San Marcos project and Fallingwater on this score, which has to do with the effect of materials.

In the San Marcos resort, a single material was to have been used throughout the entire structure. The concrete

block employing crushed stone from the site would have preserved for the building a consistently eroded appearance, despite the imprint of vegetal imagery based on the vertical ridges of the saguaro cactus. In Fallingwater, stone and reinforced concrete were not only differentiated according to structural capacity and use, but everything was done to sustain and highlight that difference in a visual sense. The hard gray sandstone was laid in flat, uneven courses, rough edges out, as if to emphasize the aspect of compression. The concrete, by contrast, was painted to take

217. Fallingwater. South facade, with guest house above.

any sense of weight off it so that its role in tension would be felt.

The treatment of materials in Fallingwater also had significant representational motivations. The stone masonry was based on the model of Taliesin, while the painting of the wide bands of reinforced concrete, which in the elevations and sections of the building might seem to bear a close relationship to the International Style, had a more complex origin and purpose. Suffice it to say for the moment that Wright did not originally intend to paint the concrete but to give it an expressive texture and natural coloration by coat-

ing it with gold leaf. When this proved too expensive and too difficult to persuade the client to accept, Wright thought of an aluminum leaf. When that idea was rejected, he experimented with a paint containing mica flakes, which came in both a "glittery type or [a] very soft flock effect," believing that such a coruscated finish would be "more sympathetic with the stone surface" and make the concrete trays "'glisten' down among the masses of green leaves." For reasons of ease and efficiency of application, it was eventually decided to settle for a flat cement paint of a "warm, light ochre, almost pale apricot in color," which preserved the autumnal

Ludwig Mies van der Rohe: Tugendhat House, Brno, Czechoslovakia, 1928–30.

218. Garden facade.   219. Plan, lower floor.

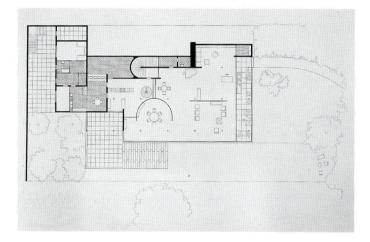

cast of the gold leaf if not its rich glow. The same color was to be maintained on all roof surfaces as well. Wright specified that they were "to blend in with the parapets and . . . have a thin coat . . . of light colored (cream colored to light gold) gravel spread over [the] final coat of asphalt."[65]

Fallingwater was to be seen from above as well as from below. It was meant to recede into and emerge from the landscape. Its exterior surfaces were to reflect the environment just as its interior was to reveal actual traces of it. From the simple conclusion that this is a building fully integrated with its setting, the geometry of its plan and the composition of its forms and surfaces lead us to ask: What more did Wright mean when he said Fallingwater was designed "to the music of the stream"? To begin to answer

that, we must look more closely at Fallingwater's language of expression, which, of necessity, brings up the question of precedents.

Terms of Expression

When the Department of Architecture and Design of the Museum of Modern Art gave its one-building exhibition to Fallingwater in early 1938, and thus its modernist imprimatur, it called attention to the appearance in the work of features that had been particularly associated with the International Style. Where earlier projects by Wright like the House on the Mesa or the Salem Newspaper Plant had a certain streamlined look, Fallingwater seemed to many observers to have fully integrated not just the forms but also the principles and structural methods established in the architecture of the European avant-garde.[66]

The most obvious similarity between Fallingwater and some of the earlier houses by Le Corbusier or Mies lies in the use of undecorated, horizontal elements of flat, painted concrete to define an abstract De Stijl–like pattern of sliding, floating, and overlapping planes in space (figs. 218, 219). The transparency and autonomy of the open, volumetric composition relies heavily on a dynamic asymmetry and looseness in planning that Wright appears to have evolved in relation to his younger contemporaries. The bold scale of the unrelieved surfaces was new, as was the sense of almost complete dematerialization aided by the use of paint, flat roofs, and the continuous bands of steel-sash windows. The appearance of hovering above the ground, or rather of being suspended in space, almost as if on *pilotis*, gives Fallingwater, despite its intimate connection to the site, a pneumatic quality quite at odds with the earlier sense in Wright's work of rootedness to the earth.

The open plan of Fallingwater went even further in the direction of the characteristic International Style "free plan" than the first scheme for the Willey House. The staggered, continually shifting planes of the rear stone wall cre-

ate a rhythmic composition that reminds one specifically of Van Doesburg and Mies (fig. 211). As in so many of the latter's designs of the twenties and early thirties, the dynamic, open relationships formed by parallel and perpendicular wall planes describe a space that is coextensive with the larger field of the building's site. The freestanding piers in Fallingwater's living room punctuate the interior space like Mies's cruciform-shaped columns or the concrete posts in Le Corbusier's Dom-ino grid. The contrapuntal use of the semicircular fireplace and hatch to create incidents of a special nature within the field also finds a parallel, if not its source, in Mies's and Le Corbusier's house plans of the previous decade.[67]

All of which is not to say that Wright simply adopted a new manner of design. Rather, he incorporated aspects of the International Style into his work to help free it of certain traditional attitudes toward decoration, massing, and formal planning and thus open it up to new possibilities of expression. In effect, Wright turned it to his own purposes. Where the white planes of stucco in the work of Mies, Le Corbusier, or Neutra read as absolutely flat and stretched tightly around clear, cubic volumes of space, in Fallingwater the concrete parapets are thick and curved and organic by comparison.[68] Instead of clarifying the pure, optical shapes of geometry, the compacted layers of trays reveal a three-dimensional depth. What in elevation appears to be a flat De Stijl–like pattern in reality becomes a plastic interaction of sculptural elements that push and pull in relation to the dark depths of the hillside perceived through the alternating window bands. The sensation is one of substance rather than abstract shape, of something physical and almost palpable rather than ideal and "non-objective."

In this regard, it should also be noted how distinctly Wright treated materials and how differently he conceived of structure. In contrast to the abstract, diagrammatic grid of Le Corbusier's Dom-ino system of reinforced-concrete construction or Mies's or Neutra's parallel solutions for steel framing, the structural system Wright adopted for Fallingwater made reference to natural forms and was intended to

have a representational effect. Instead of appearing neutral and passive, like Le Corbusier's *pilotis* at the Villa Savoye or Mies's chrome-sheathed columns in the Barcelona Pavilion, the concrete "bolsters" supporting the projecting tray of the living room and the brackets attaching the west terrace to the topmost boulder are tense, active, figurative expressions of the natural forces at work in the structure (fig. 220).

Wright often compared the plastic continuity in reinforced-concrete cantilevered construction to the structure of a tree: "Steel in tension enables the support to slide into the supported, or the supported to grow into the support as a tree-branch into its tree-trunk" (*A* I, 355).[69] Just as often, he would use a muscular, tactile analogy, comparing the way a cantilever works to the way "a waiter's tray rests on his upturned fingers" (*A* I, 147). In Fallingwater, both references come into play. Viewing the house from the side makes clear how the tree analogy works, the rear stone wall of the structure rising vertically as the trunk and the trays cantilevered from it like branches (fig. 206). Actual trees were in fact allowed to grow through the concrete trellis, or entrance "arbor," as Wright sometimes called it, as well as through the spreading terraces at either end of the house. The ridges of their bark were echoed in the striated surface of the stone wall (fig. 230). Whereas the "bolsters" under the main tray are noticeably like "upturned fingers," the western terrace that projects from the bedrooms grabs onto its

221. Le Corbusier: De Mandrot House, Le Pradet, France, 1930–31.

222. Fallingwater. Cliff face on north side of Bear Run.

natural support by three finger-like grips that were meant to look as if they were "clutching big boulders."[70]

Any comparison between Fallingwater and Le Corbusier in terms of the use of materials might at first seem gratuitous, until one takes into account the fact that Wright's combination of natural stone and painted concrete, though inimical to the machine aesthetic of the twenties, had achieved a high degree of visibility in Le Corbusier's work of the early thirties. In the De Mandrot House at Le Pradet (1930–31) and the later Villa le Sextant at La Palmyre–les Mathes (1935), Le Corbusier combined roughly laid local stone with smooth plaster (fig. 221); and he used rubble stone in contrast to concrete for the lower curved wall of the Swiss Dormitory at the Cité Universitaire in Paris (1930–32). In the two earlier buildings, which were illustrated in the International Style show catalogue, the boulder-like stones are laid in a random manner, much as they would be in traditional peasant rubble construction. The effect is of a surface pattern, like a mosaic or a terrazzo floor.

In Fallingwater, the manner of laying the stone was entirely different, and the effect is of a natural rather than a man-made order. Only roughly squared, their thickness resulting from the height of the rifts or strata of the nearby quarry, the stones were laid in horizontal courses, with the flatter ones projecting to form long, irregular ledges. The result was less an expression of surface pattern than of a compacted, stratified mass. "The stone," Wright said, "was intended to blend with that of the glen," referring to the eroded rock ledges exposed in the cliffs along the banks of the stream (fig. 222).[71] The purpose was, in effect, to maintain their appearance, just as the stone in Taliesin was laid to preserve the "raw" look of an outcrop.

■ ■ ■

Fallingwater represents a new stage in Wright's work insofar as the idea of a "natural architecture" was revived and reinstated in a fresh way. The line reaching back to Taliesin depends, in the final analysis, on the work of the twenties.

Taliesin.

223. Bridge and dam at lower entrance.

224. Bedroom terrace.

The diagonal planning and stepped section responding to the sheer, sloping site derives from the textile-block buildings and projects for California and Arizona. A number of these, beginning with the Doheny House C and including the Death Valley and San Marcos designs, were planned to be built over a gorge or ravine, with water channeled under and through the building. In these same projects, Wright turned the flat roofs into open terraces and observation decks in order to take advantage of dramatic views, an idea that went back to Hollyhock House, where one also finds, for the first time, the symbolic conjunction of fire and water as a key element of the plan.

Of crucial importance in the phenomenological definition of Fallingwater's interior space is its continuation and development of the model of the vessel, or clay pot, that came to the fore in the work in Death Valley. Fallingwater was conceived as a stack of superposed trays, shaped like broad, shallow basins. Each is folded along its base for rigidity and turns up in a continuous plane to form the lip or parapet that contains the fluid space within. Through the use of poured-in-place concrete, Wright was able to overcome the compartmented, basket-like forms of the earlier textile-block buildings and achieve an uninterrupted molded surface. In fact, the cantilevered slabs were not intended to support the parapets in a traditional "post and beam" way. According to Wright, they were originally supposed to "carry the floors" so that "the two [might] work together as one," as the sides and the base of a molded pot flow into one another without "separations and separate joints." Although he found this impossible to realize in actual constructed fact, the trays, with their upturned, rounded edges, read as much like the overflowing pools of a cascading fountain as they do a spreading canopy of receptacles for the organization of living space in direct relation to the natural environment (figs. 216, 196).[72]

The essential term in Fallingwater's expressive language is, however, Taliesin. Fallingwater is the only building, so far as I know, that Wright ever directly compared to his own house. "The same thought applied to Taliesin that

applied later to Bear Run," he said.[73] In Taliesin, one can find all the basic elements that were eventually recombined in Fallingwater. There are the falls created by the dam, to make the lake below the house, and the bridge that serves as the threshold (fig. 223); there are the terraces and the balconies that reach out over the void to link interior and exterior (fig. 224); there is the combination of rough stone and smooth plaster in the hill-hugging forms (fig. 81); and, above all, there is the incorporation of a key feature of the landscape, in one case the hill, in the other the stream and falls (fig. 70). Significantly enough, these very aspects of Taliesin were being reworked and redesigned in the years just before and during the conception of Fallingwater, so that one can even speak of a dialogue or discourse between the two houses, with Taliesin providing the opening phrases and basic terms, and Fallingwater a response and conclusion.[74]

The most obvious and, from Wright's point of view, most profound similarity between Fallingwater and Taliesin lay in the use of materials and the way they relate to the site. Both houses were built of locally quarried stone intended to suggest the appearance of an outcrop or cliff face. In both, the rugose texture of the stone was accentuated by a contrasting, smoother surface of plaster or cement. While the natural references in the two situations differed in relation to the differing contexts, what is important to consider here is the identity and significance of the natural referent. Wright did not believe materials were inert, meaningless substances to be exploited and manipulated for purely formal or functional purposes. In 1928 he devoted six of the nine articles written for the *Architectural Record* to "The Meaning of Materials," describing them as "gifts of Nature" through which "the story and the song of *man* will be *wrought*": "Each material has its own message and, to the creative artist, its own song. Listening, he may learn to make two sing together."[75]

Between 1914 and 1934, Wright almost never specified stone for construction. One important exception was the summer house for the Martins on Lake Erie, near Buffalo (1927–28).[76] Darwin Martin was one of Wright's closest friends. He helped pay for the Wasmuth publications and continued to help support Wright throughout the teens and twenties. Wright remembered him especially as the person on whom he could count during the time he was trying to return to Taliesin and regain it as his place of work. In Wright's mind, stone was intimately connected with Taliesin and the countryside around Spring Green.

He began the article on stone in 1928 with a description of "the country between Madison and Janesville, Wisconsin," lying in "the old bed of an ancient glacier-drift." Noting the "vast, busy gravel-pits [that] abound there, exposing heaps of yellow aggregate . . . sleeping beneath the green fields," he remarked: "I never pass without emo-

tion."[77] Wright's feeling for stone was one and the same as his feeling for Taliesin; and when Wright spoke of stone, he meant Taliesin. For many years following the murders and fire at Taliesin, Wright substituted the artificial, "cooked" material of concrete block for its natural analogue. But just as he never stopped thinking about Taliesin, so he never stopped thinking about stone and its source in the image of the quarry that lay behind Taliesin. In the article of 1928, he confessed: "The rock ledges of a stone-quarry are a story and a longing to me."[78]

In Fallingwater, Wright responded to that "longing." But the "story" had become much more complicated since his relatively simple and straightforward use of stone in Taliesin, most noticeably as a result of the experience of building in Japan, California, and Arizona, where less gentle landscapes, with very different histories, gave stone a further meaning. In the interim, Wright had come to see "stone [as] the basic material of our planet," revealing the "cosmic law" of change. In the first of his articles of 1928 on "The Meaning of Materials," the one devoted to stone, he exclaimed that the architect could "read the grammar of the Earth in a particle of stone! Stone is the frame on which his Earth is modelled, and wherever it crops out—there the architect may sit and learn." He continued to reflect on the significance of stone as a sign of transformation throughout the time he was designing Fallingwater. "Disintegrated by temperatures, ground down by glaciers, eroded by wind and sea, sculptured by timeless forces qualifying each other," stone, he wrote in 1937, "is continually changed by cosmic forces themselves a form of change."[79]

Modeled on Taliesin and recapturing its fundamental sense of oneness with the land, Fallingwater is different from its predecessor precisely in its involvement with change—and thus with the action of time. Where Taliesin was designed to be a representation of the static appearance of nature—an outcrop as the "brow" of the hill it embraces—Fallingwater was quite literally made to be an intervention in the dynamic flux of natural processes and thus to represent such changes as occur over time. One of the

225. Fallingwater. Perspective, from southwest.

things that allowed Wright to achieve this quality of apparent movement, as well as the ambiguity of imagery that went with it, was the International Style.

As already suggested in the compound imagery of Ocatilla and San Marcos-in-the-Desert, Wright took advantage of the simplified, large-scale, geometrically distinct shapes typical of the International Style to enforce the one-to-one relation between architectural form and natural object in Taliesin. But he also exploited the very abstractness of these shapes to imply multiple references to constantly shifting and overlapping images so that the temporal dimension of Fallingwater would take into account not just the movement of water but all the other elements of the environment that are affected by it. Fallingwater is ultimately about the cumulative effect of stone, water, trees, leaves, mist, clouds, and sky as they interact over time. It was conceived, as Wright said, as an integral part of "living down in a glen in a deep forest."[80]

Fallingwater in Experience

The most dramatic, memorable, and well-known image of Fallingwater is the view from the southwest, just below the first falls, where the house seems to rise from the stream and float effortlessly over it. It is the view Wright chose for the perspective he drew for Kaufmann as most fully representing the total effect of the house in its site, as well as the one most often reproduced in photographs (fig. 225).[81] But, as a conclusive image, it can be very deceptive, because the view it represents does not actually reveal itself until after one has seen the house, experienced its interior space, and left. Like an inverted, Baroque *vol d'oiseau*, the perspective is ideal and recapitulative, collapsing the disparate perceptions of experience into one. To understand the house, then, we should not start with it, but end with it, building toward it step by step.

226. Fallingwater. Access road, from northeast.

Fallingwater is normally approached from the east by a curving gravel drive that comes off the state highway south of Mill Run and follows the bend the stream takes to the north (fig. 205). The drive passes from a heavily forested area into a more open one as it begins to descend to join the south bank of the stream (fig. 226). The descent, though gradual, is perceptible and becomes very much an aspect of the approach. The first view of Fallingwater is from slightly above, off to one's right, down in the glen. It is seen through a veil of trees, as if rising up the far bank of the stream (fig. 227). Unlike Taliesin, where one's first glimpse of the house, from the base of the hill, was of strong, deeply undercut horizontal ledges beetling protectively above, at Fallingwater the image one retains is of something more fragile and evanescent, like bands of smoke or mist gently ascending and about to dissipate or evaporate. The nearer one approaches, the more solid the forms become. The voids between them begin to read as dark, hollow recesses in the rock, paralleling the stratified layers of the eroded cliff on the far bank of the stream, which comes into full view just before the drive finally descends to stream level to cross a bridge (fig. 228).

At the bridge, the entrance drive meets another dirt road coming up the south bank of the stream from the railroad line that lies along the ridge, about a half a mile to the southwest (where Bear Run empties into the Youghiogheny River; fig. 205). Any guests arriving at this now-defunct private station would have ascended a steep grade set back from the stream. They would have had no view of the house until they almost passed it to join the main drive at the

bridge. Fleeting glimpses head-on through the trees might well have seemed more like flashes of light than anything substantial and real.

From the bridge, Fallingwater takes on a more active appearance and begins to look like the "extension of the cliff beside a mountain stream" that Wright intended. Its stone base and walls become visible as part of the rocky ledge from which they emerge. The reinforced-concrete balconies and slabs extend into space like projecting ledges, overlapping one another above the water. One hears the sound of the falls but cannot see them. One senses a drop-off beyond the house, but only the height of the trees and the depth of the sky suggest that. Stopping at this point on the bridge, suspended above the rushing stream, at almost the same level as the main floor of the house, one sees Fallingwater for the first time close up, as it expands gravity-free to inscribe its own world of space in what seems to be its own time zone.

The approach by bridge romantically distances the house both in place and in time, following the precedent of Taliesin. At Fallingwater, however, the bridge is much closer to the house, actually an integral part of it, and immediately establishes certain basic themes of the house. The abutments of the bridge, which are constructed of the same thin ledges of quarried stone as the house, blend into the natural stone walls of the stream. Joining the lower walls of the house on the downstream side, they form a seamless transition between architecture and nature. The concrete span of the bridge, on the other hand, is like the cantilevered trays of the house. Its softly rounded parapets effect a fluid connection between the stone piers of the banks, suggesting an allusion to moving water. This dual reference was pointed out by Lewis Mumford shortly after the house was completed: "The stones represent, as it were, the earth theme; the concrete slabs are the water theme."[82]

The imagery becomes more complex as one crosses the bridge. The drive bends around the rear of the house and cuts between it and the cliff (fig. 229). The horizontal lines of the stone walls of the house, which are extended left and right into space by the concrete beams and slabs, echo the strata of stone ledges in the walls of the glen, while the rip-

Fallingwater.

227 (*above*). Distant view from access road, looking southwest.

228 (*right*). View from bridge (1937).

Fallingwater.

229. Entrance drive, under trellis.

230. Trellis at entrance with tree growing through it.

On opposite page:

231. Fallingwater. Living room, diagonal view across from entrance.

only—like the obdurate outcrop it represents. In Fallingwater, the references multiply and overlap. From the far end of the bridge, the tall, thin, willowy-looking wall stubs merge with the forest of surrounding trees (fig. 206). The beams that tie the house into the cliff become an arbor-like trellis. This overhead canopy of branches shades the path, giving a dappled light. Wright reinforced the analogy by allowing two tulip poplars to grow through the trellis, bending the concrete beam around them (fig. 230).[83] Their trunks shared the rugose texture and dark color of the wall and thus appeared to be one in nature with it.

The small pentagonal lights along the edge of the trellis were meant to represent pendent leaves. The relation of upstanding vertical trunk to hanging, outstretched branch would have been even more richly developed by the paint Wright had intended to use on the concrete. The burnished light ochre color was chosen to match "the sere leaves of the rhododendron," the main foliage (along with oak) that characterizes the site. The coruscated surface would have allowed the concrete, in Wright's words, to "'glisten' down among the masses of green leaves" with a "stone-like" cast.[84]

The forms of Fallingwater act as double- and even triple-functioning elements, relating to a stone/water, tree/leaf, and cloud/mist imagery. The boundaries between these various sets of references are fluid, and for this reason one's perception of Fallingwater is constantly shifting. Under the shade of the entrance arbor, the stone/water imagery reasserts itself. Water can be seen seeping naturally out of the cliff face on the right. It also streams out from a spout in the pier next to the entrance into a small basin that functioned as a footbath.[85] As you pass between the stone walls of the loggia into the deep recess of the entry area, you hear the water and feel its moisture. The transition from outside to inside is so orchestrated as to seem like a gradual change in atmosphere and light rather than a change of place.

pling effect of the cliff is picked up by the staggered vertical slots in the rear wall of the house. Connected to the cliff by the transverse trellis beams, the wall of the house and that of the cliff together give the impression of a notch or natural pass.

Again, one is reminded of the original entrance to Taliesin (fig. 81); but that impression only serves to emphasize how much more fluid and multivalent the imagery of Fallingwater is. The stone in Taliesin reads as stone—

The gray-blue flagstone paving of the bridge and loggia continues right into the house as the surface of the living

room floor. The floor is raised three steps above the loggia and vestibule so that you feel, even when inside, that you are still climbing up the slope of the ledge from the lowest point at the bridge. The only surface difference between inside and outside is that the flagstones inside are waxed and polished to give them a shiny, reflective appearance. This causes the eye to skim the surface quickly, following the line of the diagonal axis across the room toward the light at the far side, which comes through the band of windows and doors that open onto terraces projecting over the ravine (fig. 231). The raised floor and centrally recessed ceiling give a lift to that diagonal, recalling the arching vista in the living room at Taliesin. But where that room roots you solidly to the earth, the shiny surface of the flagstone floor in Fallingwater has a slippery look and feel that suggest the instability of moving water underfoot.

The reference to the stream below the living room floor is not merely metaphorical. As noted earlier, one of the actual boulders of the rock ledge projects through the surface as the hearth of the fireplace (fig. 213); and at the opposite corner of the room, a glass-enclosed hatch opens to reveal a view of the stream as well as a stairway leading down to it (fig. 214). The specific references to stone and water intersect in a chiasmic relationship. Water, or at least some form of liquid, was an integral part of the fireplace. Suspended within the stone cavity, the spherical kettle was intended to bring its liquid contents into direct contact with the fire. "The warming kettle will fit into the wall," Wright reportedly told his apprentices while designing the apparatus: "It will swing into the fire, boiling the water. Steam will permeate the atmosphere. You'll hear the hiss."[86]

The combined visual, tactile, aural, and olfactory sensation of water in contact with stone is inversely restated in the juxtaposed hatch. Located under a skylit trellis of concrete beams, the twelve-foot-long opening brings directly into the room the view, sound, smell, and moisture of the water rushing over the stone bed of the stream. The reflective surface of the shallow stream appears to be continuous in color and texture and substance with the waxed flagstone floor. The cool, damp air coming off it is funneled through the hatch, while the steady burble resonates in the curved chamber of the concrete parapet.[87]

The stream is brought into direct apposition with the living room floor along a line that parallels the actual ledge of the falls (see figs. 208, 210). The polished flagstones reconstitute the rocky bed of the stream. Their uneven surface reflects the light filtering through the trees in a constantly changing pattern. The irregular outline of their raised joints recreates the swirling movement of the stream as it rounds the bend before meeting the ledge. Walking across the imaginary line between the projection of the stone through the hearth and the opening of the floor at the hatch, one is made aware of the changes in level that determine the direction and flow of the water and is thus subliminally induced to project one's thoughts beyond the space of the room. As the floor continues through the plate-glass doors onto the terrace, the dark flagstone surface turns up into a rounded concrete parapet. In its light, airborne mass, this shape echoes the color and texture and trajectory of the cascade of white foam that spills over the rock ledge just below it (fig. 232). One can only imagine that the pressure of water welling up in the terrace is released in the overflow of the cantilever.

The sensation of movement in Fallingwater is matched by an equally powerful one of suspension. What makes this most apparent on the inside of the living room, not to speak of the upper bedroom floors, is the canopy of trees that becomes, by extension, the exterior walls and roof of the house (figs. 212, 214). The tree/leaf imagery first stated at the entrance returns to help situate the interior in its larger context. Once again, the freestanding stone piers silhouetted against the windows and glass doors on the far side of the room merge into the background of tree trunks, while the horizontal trellises that branch off them, with their leaf-like pentagonal lights, shade the terraces that seem to hang in the trees. Seeming is replaced by being on the westernmost terrace, where three oak trees were planned to grow through the floor to provide a natural canopy of foliage (they did not survive), and on the upper bedroom terraces, where the existing forest cover performs that function.

In the living room, the continuous glass enclosure of the southern half of the space, beginning at the corner of the library and going all around to the seating area next to the fireplace, offers a panorama of foliage and sky that puts one in mind of looking out from a perch in a tree. The height of the floor above the stream and the steep rise of the opposite bank give one the sensation of being *in* the trees, looking out from them as from a tree house.[88] The continuation of the arbor-like trellis of the east terrace in the skylight over the library and hatch links the tree/leaf imagery to the stone/water imagery at the point where the house is most fully understood as being suspended between earth and sky.

The vertical axis—of tree, of hatch, of fireplace—is the experiential axis of Fallingwater. Paradoxical as it may seem, it is precisely the sensation of suspension that grounds the perception of Fallingwater in bodily experience. The importance of the fireplace and hatch in expressing Fallingwater's relation to the site makes clear how much the experience of that association depends upon the reaction of all the senses, and not just that of sight alone. The response to Fallingwater is multisensory and kinesthetic.[89] The sound and feel of water permeate everything and are everywhere, but its presence is especially felt underfoot. The connection to the stream is not a disembodied, optical one. It is felt through the whole body, through all the senses. The awareness of the swiftly moving water in the boulder-strewn stream comes "from the ground up," as Wright would insist, as does the sensation of suspension over the ledge of the falls. The waxed floor of the living room imparts a sense of fluid motion to the body and suggests the suspended animation of the drop of the waterfall from one level to the next. The rise of the boulder at the fireplace and the fall of the water under the hatch situate the occupant of Fallingwater in that time between.

The experience of Fallingwater is not complete, however, insofar as it ever can be, until you are able to look back on it as a passage of time. Although the association with water is the key to almost every aspect of the house, one of the most remarkable facts about Fallingwater is that the water is hardly visible until you leave. The stream is seen only briefly as you pass over the bridge, and then not again until it appears, though just barely, through the hatch in the floor. From the outdoor terraces, you become aware of the precipitous drop-off as the deep, narrow gorge falls away directly beneath you; but your awareness of the water depends more on hearing than seeing.

The view of the water cascading down the glen is reserved for the final moment in the perception of the place as a whole, when you leave the house proper, cross back over the bridge, descend the path on the opposite bank to the flat rock below the first falls, and look up from the point where Wright's perspective was drawn (fig. 225).[90] What is then seen is something already known, but not yet visualized as such. Everything comes together, as it were, around the falls, to amplify them as the underlying factor in the design. Yet even here, the process of visualizing is undercut by the insistent appeal to the other senses—of touch, of smell, and especially of hearing. The noise of the falls can be deafening, but even when the water is low it is an insistent distraction.

The sound of this final view helps preserve in one's memory, almost like a mnemonic device, the multivalence of Fallingwater's imagery. Vision has been privileged in

Western thought and art for its power to order the chaos of experience into controllable, knowable entities. When we say "I see," we mean "I understand." The thought or image has been clarified in the mind by being distinguished and differentiated from others so that no confusion may arise. Hearing is a different story. When we say "I hear you," that means "I am registering the words you speak, but I neither fully comprehend nor entirely agree. I'll have to think it over." Even when we finally see Fallingwater in relation to the waterfall, or perhaps *only* when we see the two together in the inverse relation to each other that the name of the house implies, do we fully register the degree to which the architecture blurs all boundaries and works to erase all distinctions.

Fallingwater in Time

The fluctuating, multivalent imagery of Fallingwater relates to the compound references of Ocatilla and San Marcos-in-the-Desert. But whereas those presented essentially either/or situations, Fallingwater is both/and.[91] The shifting and overlapping images involve general conditions of physical and atmospheric change over time, and our sensory response to them is called upon to focus and adjust the image to the actual experience of the place.

Combining our first impressions with our last, and trying to synchronize them with the passage of time in the house, we almost surely will find that our reading hovers between alternatives. In reference to the most salient feature of the site, and the one for which the house is named, we ask if it is really "falling water," as certain impressions would support. Or is it "water in suspension," like the dew on leaves? Or is it perhaps even "rising water," like mist in the air?[92] The actual experience of Fallingwater supports all these readings, while Wright's perspective rendering offers a suggestion of how they may be linked within the larger cyclical order of natural change that the house represents.

First, the house depends on the stream. It extends from the cliff like the boulders and ledges of rock it resembles and over which the white water flows. While the deeply raked and randomly laid stone literally reproduces the eroded appearance of the cliff face, the two terraces cantilevered over the falls, being broader in scale and flatter in treatment than the stone walls, echo the large boulders in the streambed. But that is only an initial impression. Their rounded, fluid contours and light, insubstantial surface relate more to water than to stone. The different directions in which these two airborne masses point correspond almost exactly to the relative disposition of the two lower falls (fig. 196). Appearing to spill out from the stone masses on either side of them like the actual falls between the banks of the stream, the two cantilevered trays effect changes in level in the house that echo those in the stream, so that the house becomes a natural step in the descent of Bear Run to the river.[93]

As the water rushes down the glen and under the bridge, it gathers force, creating mist and foam. Where it passes beneath the living room floor, the cantilevered terraces seem to hover weightlessly above the stream, suspended, as it were, in the air. Rising through the dense cover of trees, the billowing forms turn into cloud-like shapes that seem to condense, into bands, the mist and spray coming off the falls. Soft, ethereal, intangible, almost vaporous in substance, the terraces open into trellises and filter through the trees to join with the clouds and sky, thus completing a cycle of transformation of nature that is activated by the replenishing, vitalizing element of water (fig. 225).

The image of a cascade bringing water down from the hills to nourish the ground is reflected back on itself in the moisture rising into the air eventually to return as rain. The image of a tree growing from the ground into the sky effects the vital connection. The natural cycle of growth, decay, and regeneration, which is ultimately what Fallingwater is about, would have been richly amplified by the illusion of dying leaves that Wright had hoped to project by coating the parapets in a burnished gold leaf. Although the "glisten" of water on leaf was lessened by the resort to a flat paint, the pale-apricot color was still, as Wright said, "in [the] key of the sere leaves of the rhododendron."[94] Rhododendron are evergreen, so it is obvious that Wright had wanted to express not merely a seasonal change but a more absolute sense of death and rebirth. In fact, just a few years prior to the Kaufmann commission, he referred to the legendary story of the oracle of Zeus at Dodona to describe the meaning of "falling leaves" in terms of a modern narrative of regeneration:

The Greeks supposed trees the earliest dwellings of the Gods. Zeus spoke his truest oracles through the rustling of the leaves. And although, in the combined voice of all the poets, the falling leaf has been metaphor of everything that dies, the Forest corrects our faith for we know now that the race of leaves grow off and do not fall off, and, owing to natural science, their "speech" is more a marvel of sensibility today—than in the twilight of the "Gods."

In a finer poetic sense, too, the leaves fall to a new glory.[95]

Wright meant Fallingwater to represent nature in process—to suggest the phenomenon of change over time. The sound of Fallingwater and the references to hearing and listening that abound in Wright's descriptions of the building are not coincidental. Sound and hearing are functions of time and necessarily introduce that element into the visual field, as pure opticality does not. The sound of Fallingwater fills the space of the glen and surrounds us like nature. The movement of the stream continues throughout the year; the seasonal variations in intensity of the white water are registered and reverberated by the house. The question one constantly asks is not *where* this or that begins or ends, but *when*. And the answer is never.

The temporal dimension of Fallingwater must have strongly impressed one of its first visitors, John McAndrew, then curator of Architecture and Industrial Art at the Museum of Modern Art.[96] The catalogue he produced for the exhibition of the building in early 1938 was based on a sequence of views located in time and space by the sign of a moving eye on a small plan repeated beneath each photograph. These culminate in a double photographic image showing the house from the exact same spot in the daytime and at night. The point was to show that the experience is ultimately of *duration*, to use Bergson's popular term, rather than mere *time*. It is, in other words, of a phenomenal rather than a literal order of being.[97]

■ ■ ■

Wright was not alone among modern architects in his desire to endow buildings with a temporal dimension. Le Corbusier, among others, tried to free architecture from the static appearance of classical monumentality and to open it to phenomenological experience. By analogizing architecture to boats, cars, or planes in his designs of the twenties and thirties, he posited the building as a type of conveyance from which the occupant/passenger might observe the world in passing, like the stop-time images of a silent movie. (In the postwar period, as in the design for the reconstruction of St. Dié, he literalized the connection between movement and time by giving the scale of the plan in hours and minutes.) This essentially kinetic and sequential understanding of the issue was summarized and widely popularized in Sigfried Giedion's *Space, Time, and Architecture* (1941), based on the Norton Lectures given at Harvard University in 1939–40 following his first visit to the United States.[98]

How much Giedion's conception of a "space-time" architecture actually owed to this first encounter with Wright's work in person is difficult to discern. Significantly, Fallingwater is absent from Giedion's book. Giedion, like Gropius and Le Corbusier, defined the temporality of architecture in the literal terms of the observer's movement and chose to reproduce Muybridge-like photographs of sequential images, time exposures, and even Cubist-inspired col-

Etienne-Louis Boullée: Newton Cenotaph project, 1784.

233. Section, daytime.

234. Section, night.

lages to make his point.[99] Wright, by contrast, attempted in Fallingwater, where the sound is at least as important as the view, to do something quite different: to suggest by the static forms of a building the sense of duration one might experience in an instant of time.

Such an ambition has traditionally been the prerogative of poets, musicians, and painters, something Wright himself was well aware of. A figurative artist like Poussin might depict the change of seasons in the sequential imagery of multiple canvases (for example, *The Four Seasons*, 1660–64) by relying on the beholder's habitual willingness to accept the narrative continuity of virtual time, just as the non-objective painter Rudolf Bauer pushed the analogy with music to its limits in composing a four-part work (*Tetraptychon*, 1926–30) as a "symphony in four movements" (fig. 308). But architects have usually felt constrained by the physicality of their medium to assume temporality to be a function of real movement and linear time. A "visionary" architect like Boullée, in his project for a Cenotaph for Isaac Newton (1784), thought it possible to suggest the evolution from night to day within the same virtual space only by using the techniques of pictorial or theatrical representation (figs. 233, 234). His contemporary Ledoux, likewise, used pictorial means to suggest the durational aspects of certain of his designs for the Ideal City of Chaux (1780–1802; fig. 235).[100]

The desire to involve time in the perception of actual buildings, however, at least in the modern age, has usually relied on the appeal to history, where a reuse of earlier forms might bring to mind a train of associations. In the eighteenth-century English Garden, this could result in the creation of an Elysian Fields or a Vale of Arcady in which one might, as in a painting by Claude or a poem by James Thomson, feel transported into a world distant in time. Recreated ruins were especially efficacious, as they carried on their surface the very imprint of nature's relentless activity (fig. 236). The ruin thus became the most characteristic image of the temporal dimension in post-Renaissance architecture.

Fallingwater is different though, and remains almost unique even in Wright's work. It relies on the purely architectural forms of its natural imagery to enforce a temporal reading without recourse either to historical allusion or to pictorial or other means of expression.[101] Nor is Fallingwater merely a representation of natural activity. Rather, it is an elaboration and a compounding of preexisting conditions into the realm of phenomena. One is therefore reminded of a long tradition of architecture using nature in movement, as in the gardens of Renaissance and Baroque Italy and France, to give buildings a more direct connection with the changing natural world they in fact replace. Water, in the form of pools and, especially, fountains, played a sig-

235. Claude-Nicolas Ledoux: House of Surveyors of Loue River, Ideal City of Chaux, c. 1790s.

236. William Chambers: Ruined Arch (with Temple of Victory in distance), Kew Gardens, Richmond, England, 1759–60.

nificant role in making the observer believe he or she was witnessing an event with a temporal dimension. As with all such illusions, however, when the play is over, the action stops, leaving us merely with a sense of what was and what might be once again. The fountains at Versailles, for instance, were turned on only for certain occasions and then only for a certain amount of time. In those moments, one might imagine an eternity, but eventually it all ends and real time supersedes. What is so extraordinary about Fallingwater is that it never stops. When one leaves, one expects it to be turned off—but it can never be (fig. 196). Reality and illusion coincide.

Fallingwater is continuous—with the falls that preceded it, and with the entire natural system that grows and develops around them. In a sense, Fallingwater can be said to historicize the landscape and thus give to nature a history and a meaning beyond the present. Permanence, that quality which had for so long seemed at odds with modernism, was reintroduced but transformed into an aspect of impermanence. It is surely for such reasons that Rudolph described the weekend house for the Kaufmanns as a "realized dream." Always all things at once, it remains as magical, as hallucinatory, and as ethereal as a cascade of white water or an early morning mist (fig. 227).

The Traces of Prehistory at Taliesin West

If Fallingwater both appeals to an extremely broad audience and is one of the few among Wright's later buildings to attract serious consideration in the academy, the same can hardly be said for Taliesin West, the winter home and headquarters for the Taliesin Fellowship that Wright began building in the desert outside Phoenix a few months after Fallingwater was finished.[1] In many ways the two are antithetical. One is all about water and vegetation, and is set deep within the folds of a glen. The other spreads out low to the ground, under the sun, on the slopes of an arid desert mountainside (figs. 196, 259).

One is rectilinear, smooth, and made of such sleek modern materials as reinforced concrete and plate glass set in steel sash. The other is angular, rough, and composed of primitive-looking rubble walls topped with canvas set in crude wood frames. One is engaging, almost mesmerizing, like the waterfall it incorporates. The other is offputting, even forbidding, like the desert it holds at bay (figs. 217, 237).

Taliesin West is strange and enigmatic, not just from the point of view of modern architecture, but from nearly any point of view. Philip Johnson once described how, to the uninitiated, the complex appears to be "a meaningless group of buildings."[2] For such reasons, no doubt, historians and critics of modern architecture, following their greater interest in social housing, urban planning, and buildings for industry, have tended to marginalize it and to concentrate on Wright's Usonian houses and Johnson Wax Company headquarters (1936–39) when discussing Wright's work of the later 1930s. Not only do those buildings conform more closely to the social and esthetic criteria established by modernism; they also fit, at least superficially, much more comfortably into its developmental pattern. But from any point of view seeking to comprehend Wright's work as a whole and its complex relation to modern art as a whole, Taliesin West is the critical building of the later 1930s and the link between Fallingwater and the Guggenheim Museum (1943–59).

At a deeper level than style or appearance, Taliesin West and Fallingwater have much in common. Both deal with the issue of permanence versus impermanence that came to the fore in Wright's work in the twenties. Both are reactions to the abstraction Wright perceived to be at the basis of the International Style. Both use the contrast of materials as a ground for expression. And both make an engagement with the dimension of time a determinant factor of form. Even the conspicuous differences in outward expression may be taken as evidence of Wright's conscious effort, in the later 1930s, to find the particular and appropriate image for each program and each site or region of the country.[3]

Where Fallingwater and Taliesin West truly diverge, ironically, is in their relation to Taliesin. Fallingwater returned to it to reconstitute its meaning as another form of experience. Taliesin West, by contrast, emptied it of a certain meaning in creating its double. Before Taliesin West, there was only Taliesin. After Taliesin West, everyone, including Wright, began referring to Taliesin as Taliesin North or Taliesin East. Taliesin, which had always represented a singular identity of person and place was now qualified by another. And as Taliesin, in time, became the other, Taliesin West assumed the role of defining Wright's architecture and persona to the outside world. In Wright's architecture, diversity and complementarity replaced unity and singularity. Once the provincial Midwesterner, involved in internecine struggles over leadership of a regional school or private battles with the law over affairs of the heart, he was now viewed by the world as the intrepid "frontiersman," the protean, modern Noble Savage who received outsiders at "the fountainhead" of his desert camp like a tribal chief, leading his loyal followers into a world of replenished vigor and hope, safe from contact with the discontents of civilization.[4]

When one went out to Taliesin West in the 1940s or 1950s to commission a building from Wright or to study his architecture and perhaps meet the man, the experience, most writers noted, was "extraordinary" and "magical." Something well beyond the mere integration of building and landscape struck them. Hitchcock spoke of the "almost prehistoric grandeur of this camp." Philip Johnson dwelled on its "hieratic aspects."[5] Everyone was impressed with the ritualistic sense of space and time that seemed to relate to a profound and distant mythic past. Wright, who was normally averse to admitting any influence, especially any reference to history, found himself responding to a visitor:

You are perfectly right in feeling the primitive in Taliesin West. In the ancient days of the race men were close to nature as a child to its mother. . . .

Sophistication came with Science and what we call education to wean or warp them away from the simplicity of that childhood. . . .

Well, Fowler [McCormick]—Taliesin West is modeled with that higher understanding—deeper than the simplicity of the barbarian, not copying his forms but drinking understanding from the springs from which he drank unconsciously. . . .

Modern art feels the need of the inner strength that comes from this eternal inspiration.[6]

In Taliesin West, Wright built upon his earlier interest in the architecture of the indigenous Precolumbian inhabitants of the American Southwest but clarified its formal expression as an extension of the temporal dimension of

Fallingwater. The natural environment of the desert was inextricably linked with its cultural history, so that geological time could be reinvested with the meanings of historical time and history revalorized through such an identification with nature.

The Search for a Site

According to Olgivanna Wright, the decision to winter in Arizona on a regular basis went back to the initial trip to Phoenix in 1928.[7] Wright was getting on in years and the question of health was an important factor. But it was only after the stock market crash and with the establishment of the Taliesin Fellowship that any steps were taken in this direction. According to Wright's secretary, Eugene Masselink, the idea of moving everyone from Wisconsin to Arizona in the winter, as a kind of "working vacation," was proposed in the late fall or winter of 1933–34 for the following year.[8] By then, economic and pedagogic concerns had made the move even more appealing. During the cold winter months Taliesin, in conjunction with the expanded Hillside Home School, cost enormous sums to heat and maintain; the weather, moreover, made it quite difficult to carry on the kinds of outdoor work activities that the program of the Fellowship contemplated.

In the early fall of 1934, Wright contacted Alexander Chandler to ask if the Fellowship might use one of his facilities as temporary quarters while he looked for a site on which to "begin to build a camp this winter that we can go into regularly every winter from now on." When Chandler delayed responding, Wright threatened to "take to the desert and move from place to place—nomads, as the spirit moves."[9] Chandler then offered the use of La Hacienda, a subsidiary inn he owned and operated. A group of about twenty-five strong left Wisconsin toward the end of January 1935.

The major work that winter season was the construction of the model of Broadacre City, which was to begin its

exhibition schedule in New York later that spring before going on to Pittsburgh, where the arrangements were being made by Edgar Kaufmann. Wright did preliminary studies for a new, reduced version of the San Marcos-in-the-Desert Hotel for Chandler (called the Little San Marcos), no doubt a payment in kind for his client's hospitality. He also began looking for land, but that was to prove to be a much more protracted affair than anticipated.

The search for a suitable site eventually occupied Wright for a period of nearly three years. At first, he looked toward the Santan Mountains, lying about seventeen miles southeast of Chandler, just south of the citrus farming community of Chandler Heights, in the direction of the Casa Grande ruins along the Gila River (fig. 180). He was shown a 640-acre tract in the "cove" on the north side of the mountains, looking over the citrus groves past Mesa and toward the McDowell Mountains that closed the vista to the north. The land in this still quite remote and undeveloped part of the region was owned by a local farmer and small landholder, Dewey Keith, with whom Wright carried on a cat-and-mouse game of haggling over price and other details beginning when Wright got back to Taliesin in mid-April 1935. Soon the mayor of Chandler, J. Lee Loveless, entered the picture as an intermediary, offering to put Wright in touch with other possibilities in the vicinity of Keith's property if a deal with the latter should fall through.[10]

Nothing materialized by the end of 1935, so Wright asked Chandler if the Fellowship could return in January 1936 to spend another winter at La Hacienda, hoping this time "to begin building a camp" and that he, Chandler, "might lead us in the right direction and help us secure the necessary ground." Wright added that last year they had "looked about above Chandler Heights among the homesteaders there but I am not sure we don't want to go in the other direction toward the Salt Range again," referring to the area where Chandler still owned land and where Ocatilla had been built.[11]

The Fellowship spent the first three months of 1936 in Chandler, at the La Hacienda Inn. Although Chandler himself was in deep financial trouble and apparently could not help, Wright was able to work out what he thought was a satisfactory arrangement with Loveless to purchase a half-section of federally owned land just south of Goldmine Mountain on the east edge of the Santan range, looking toward the Superstition and Dripping Spring Mountains (fig. 180[E]). Having put down money by the end of March, Olgivanna was confident enough to write to the Hannas, for whom Wright was designing a house in Palo Alto (built 1937), that "we are coming back [to Arizona] in December, since we bought lots of desert and mountains about 17 miles from here!" After the Fellowship returned to Wisconsin in mid-April, the purchase was announced in the local newspaper.[12]

But complications soon arose, as they so often did when it came to money and Wright. First of all, Chandler was refused an important loan, which not only scotched the Little San Marcos project but also threw his entire hotel operation into question. This led Wright to wonder whether it was still worth thinking about building near Chandler. Learning from Loveless that the government land he thought he bought was actually only for lease and that, by law, he also had to buy Keith's property in order to be able to purchase a key piece of federal land he needed to put together a viable parcel, Wright balked and accused Loveless of deceiving him.[13] Wright may have had a problem with cash flow, for he wrote to Keith independently to tell him that "if we could get slow enough and begin within our means we might work out a deal with you," in response to which Keith offered a smaller parcel of 120 acres at a much reduced price. Wright then wrote to Loveless, apologizing for his accusations and telling him that he was "minded to take Keith on."[14] The moment was past, however, confidence had been shaken, and Keith sold off all his land to none other than Alexander Chandler, who had been informed that Wright had "failed to take it." In fact, Wright had admitted to Chandler only weeks before that the deal involving Loveless looked "so complex" that he hadn't "much interest in it."[15]

Another important reason for Wright's hesitation to close any deal involving land in the Santan range was the opposition of his wife and others to locating in such a remote spot. "To most of the camp (Mrs. Wright included), San Tan seems like too much pioneering," Wright told Chandler in September 1937. "They prefer to go nearer to Phoenix."[16] In fact, Wright may have already had something in mind by the time he wrote this. Having come down with a severe case of pneumonia in December 1936 that knocked him out for more than two months, he had decided, given the amount of work then in the office, to cancel the Fellowship's winter trip to Arizona. When he recovered, the family took a trip to Palo Alto in mid-March so that Wright could oversee the initial stage of construction of the Hanna House. To facilitate his recuperation, the family decided to return to Taliesin by way of Arizona. Bruce Pfeiffer has suggested that it was during this short sojourn, in the early spring of 1937, that Wright first heard of the land he eventually bought northeast of Phoenix, above Paradise Valley, on the southern slopes of the McDowell Mountains.[17]

Whatever the case, Wright said nothing about this possibility to Chandler when he wrote in September to tell him of his plans to look in the Phoenix area and to ask if the Fellowship could again make use of the La Hacienda Inn (which Chandler no longer controlled). In fact, in November of that year, Olgivanna told friends that the Fellowship was "planning for a trip to Arizona in January" but would "not build the camp." They would go with "sleeping bags and small tents" and remain "ever-moving in caravan for 3 months." Wright reiterated this intention to Chandler in early December, saying that "we've decided to spend the money on camping equipment and go directly into the desert where we will build. We don't know just where that will be yet. I am coming West to reconnoiter pretty soon now."[18]

Once in Phoenix, Wright and his wife were able to firm up a part-purchase, part-lease agreement by the end of December. Records show that this deal involved, at the beginning at least, probably no more than half a section (320 acres) of land in Paradise Valley (then unincorporated, now part of Scottsdale), which Wright liked to refer to as Maricopa Mesa (within a few years Wright's holdings increased to nearly 800 acres). Stephen D. Pool, who worked in the State Land Office and whom Wright may have initially contacted earlier that spring, sold Wright 160 acres of his own property and arranged for the lease of a contiguous 160-acre parcel (figs. 238, 180[F]).[19] The land was unimproved and had no history of water, which no doubt affected the price. Wright wired the Fellowship, and by 31 December 1937 they were making plans to travel south "in several days."[20]

■ ■ ■

Wright later described the three-year search for a site that ended up, fittingly enough, in Paradise Valley as a kind of pilgrimage to the Promised Land, compressing the events into a mythical *wanderjahr*: "Every Sunday, for a season, we swept here and there on picnics. With sleeping bags we went to and fro like the possessed from one famous place to another. Finally I learned of a site twenty-six miles from Phoenix, across the desert of the vast Paradise Valley. On up to a great mesa in the mountains. On the mesa just below McDowell Peak we stopped, turned, and looked around. The top of the world!" (*A* II, 452). The panorama of the desert across the southern horizon suggested to the seventy-year-old Wright a collapse of history into the timelessness of a present that could be registered but never truly known. The design of the camp would have to reflect that perception:

Just imagine what it would be like on top of the world looking over the universe at sunrise or at sunset with clear sky in between. Light and air bathing all the worlds of creation in all the color there ever was—all the shapes and outlines ever devised—neither let nor hindrance to imagination— nothing to imagine—all beyond the reach of the finite mind. Well, that was our place on the mesa and our buildings had to fit in. It was a new world to us and cleared the slate of the

pastoral loveliness of our place in Southern Wisconsin. Instead came an esthetic, even ascetic, idealization of space, of breadth and height and of strange firm forms, a sweep that was a spiritual cathartic for Time if indeed Time continued to exist in such circumstances. (*A* II, 453)

The land lies at the foot of the McDowell Mountains at an elevation of nearly sixteen hundred feet (fig. 239). The mountains, trending northwest, rise to a height of over four thousand feet. Wright's property is located at the base of a spur that projects to the southwest, forming a double-humped mound identified on the earliest published plan as Maricopa Hill (fig. 238[B]).[21] At an elevation of over nineteen hundred feet, this protruding ridge creates a deep, cove-like gully that swings around to the north and throws into powerful relief the two highest points in the McDowell range, the pyramidal mass of Thompson Peak in the foreground and the broad, horned McDowell Peak behind it and slightly to the west. To the east and south of Maricopa Hill, the McDowell Mountains level out toward the Verde River Valley (about twenty miles east) into a vast tableland, from the floor of which rise, mysteriously unannounced, a group of strange, conical, volcanic buttes that give the landscape an unearthly air (fig. 240). The two most prominent are Black Mountain closer to the north (with the elevation marker Verde; fig. 238[D]) and Sawik Mountain farther to the south. Lower, craggy hills, the nearest one known as Little Black Mountain (fig. 238[E]), appear in between as if satellites of the former. Behind them in the distance, though now sometimes barely visible due to pollution, are Granite Reef and the Superstition Mountains.[22]

Beyond the sloping crater top of Sawik Mountain, the broad basin of the Salt River Valley dips down to the Santan and Sacaton Mountains, which loom up on the distant horizon along the edge of the Gila River (fig. 241). Directly south, there is an unobstructed view over Tempe and Chandler extending fifty miles or more to the Sonoran Desert, until the southern tip of the Sierra Estrella, behind the South Mountains, slides across the western horizon. In the

238. Paradise Valley and McDowell Mountains. A = original turnoff from Shea Boulevard and beginning of access road;
B = Maricopa Hill; C = petroglyph remains; D = Black Mountain; E = Little Black Mountain.

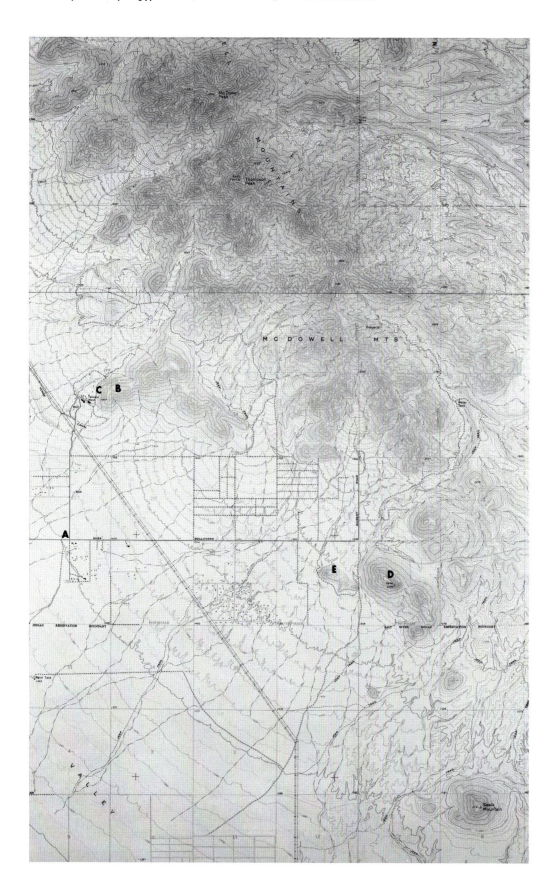

239. Taliesin West. Aerial view, from southwest (November 1949).

Taliesin West.

240. View southeast along base of McDowell Mountains to Verde River valley.   **241. View southwest to Salt-Gila River Valley.**

foreground, about seven miles to the southwest, the long, serrated ridge of the north-trending Phoenix Mountains begins with the characteristic humped mass of Camelback, followed by the reclining shape of Mummy Mountain, and then Squaw Peak, before dying out toward the northwest in the upper ranching lands where Paradise and Deer Valleys come together (fig. 242). Barely visible at the time would have been the suburban fringes of Phoenix and the small town of Scottsdale. Although its population was not much more than one thousand, the latter was already becoming known as a center for the arts and luxury resort inns.[23]

Paradise Valley was, and still is, less isolated than the Santan Mountains, but the Maricopa Mesa site is grander and has a much more commanding position than the possibilities Wright was offered farther south. The latter were hemmed in and had little elevation. The site at the base of the McDowell Mountains has an expansive outlook over the entire Salt-Gila River Valley, as well as a commanding amphitheatric backdrop that gives it the magical quality of a mythical "high place." Indeed, the site was previously inhabited, or at least used, by the Hohokam for just this reason, and evidence of their occupation made it clear that the site had a special meaning for them.[24]

The location was, it would appear, one of those numerous ceremonial, hunting and gathering, or boundary hill sites, possibly for seasonal use, strung in a circle around the central cultivated valley, in communication with similar

ones to the north and south of Phoenix.[25] On the ground, Wright found an unusual amount of rubble-like stone, pieces of volcanic rock varying in color from burnt umber to steel blue and purple. Farther uphill were some extraordinary conformations of even larger boulders, one of which, just below the southern ridge of Maricopa Hill, includes an enormous flat stone, taller than a man, propped up against the sky and facing west (fig. 282). On the slopes beneath this and a bit more to the north, there was a sizable group of boulders incised with ancient petroglyphs (fig. 243). Significant finds of potsherds, grinding stones, and even grinding pits with corn still in them were made by Wright and his apprentices in the area.[26]

Wright's interest in the indigenous cultures of the Southwest began as far back as Hollyhock House. It became less explicitly a matter of style and more importantly an issue of content during the time he was in Arizona in the late twenties. This shift dovetailed with the considerable changes in attitude toward Native Americans that were to occur in the socio-political as well as the cultural-anthropological arenas in the 1930s. In 1933, following Franklin Roosevelt's election, a Senate commission was established to recommend steps to overhaul the much criticized Indian Service. John Collier was appointed Commissioner of Indian Affairs, and in June 1934 the Wheeler-Howard (Indian Reorganization) Act was signed into law, repealing the allotment acts, reasserting tribal rights of ownership, easing

Taliesin West.

242. View west to Phoenix Mountains.

243. Hohokam petroglyph boulder at base of Maricopa Hill, now above pool in main terrace prow (1938 or early 1939)).

the way for credit and agricultural development, and generally supporting the values of native culture over the previous policy of forced assimilation.

By 1939, the results of this new attitude were celebrated in the popular *Indians of the Americas* by Edwin R. Embree, director of the Rockefeller Foundation. Like Collier's own book of the same title, which appeared nearly a decade later, Embree told the story of Native American culture as a continuous narrative, beginning with the ancient "classic" civilizations of the Maya, Inca, and Aztec and culminating in those of North America. The reader gained a profound respect for the Native American populations of the Southwest, which might otherwise have been dismissed as a provincial backwater.[27]

The effects of these changes were particularly felt in the region in which Wright chose to settle. Precisely during the years when he was looking for land, Harold Gladwin and his Gila Pueblo group were undertaking the first major archaeological investigations in the Salt-Gila Valley. The dig at Snaketown, just southwest of Chandler, began in 1934–35, and the discovery of the ball court there would provide one of the strongest arguments for a direct link between local Hohokam culture and the "higher" civilizations of Mesoamerica.[28] The second phase of this dig lasted from 1937 to 1942, and it is known that members of the Taliesin Fellowship visited the excavations while in the process of constructing Taliesin West.[29]

Struck as he was with the "magnificence" of the natural features of the site, and awed by their "mystic" overtones, Wright took into equal account the topographical and the ethnographical aspects of the landscape as determining factors in the design of Taliesin West (*A* II, 453). To "fit in" with the surroundings, he made reference to certain natural objects and phenomena, as he had done in Fallingwater; but to register the effects of cultural continuity over time, Wright literally appropriated extant traces of the prehistoric past to align his buildings with the cosmic purposes those traces suggested. Taliesin West must therefore be read, in terms of its site, more as an excavation of it than as an intervention in it.

Planning as Orientation

Taliesin West was planned *in situ*. Within the first month or so (January–February 1938), temporary wood-and-canvas shelters for drafting, cooking, and eating were set up in the wash to the west and slightly south of the spot chosen for the permanent structure. The apprentices camped out in sleeping bags and tents. The Wrights stayed at the nearby Jokake Inn until a group of "sleeping boxes," simple cubicles of wood covered with canvas, were built for them on the far side of the intended construction site, close to Maricopa Hill. These were eventually connected by a concrete floor and

244. Taliesin West. Preliminary plan.

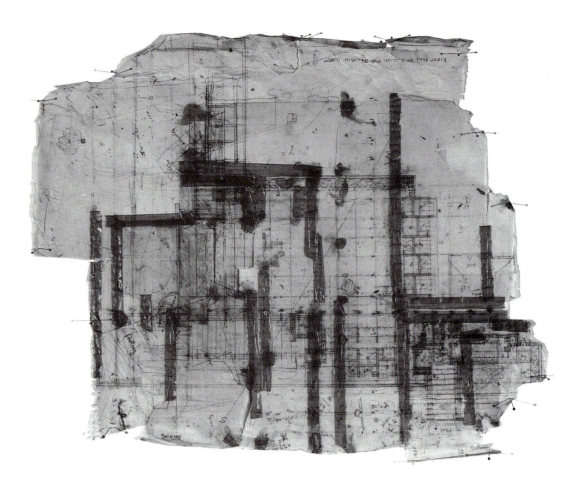

enclosing walls of wood siding to form an atrium-like structure Wright called Sun Trap, which served as a semipermanent residence for the family until the living quarters of Taliesin West were completed a year or so later.[30]

Designing and drafting took place outdoors, and for this reason, as Bruce Pfeiffer points out, a brown butcher paper was used to cut down on glare.[31] The preliminary studies for Taliesin West tell a fascinating, and quite unexpected, story. If the conventional wisdom says that Wright did not do sketches until the design was fully formed in his mind, Taliesin West turns out to be a major exception, because there are at least two preliminary stages of the plan preserved that do not correspond with any known elevation or section or, indeed, with the final project. That such drawings exist for a design for Wright's own use and for a project where he was living at the site is perhaps even more interesting. The preliminary studies for Taliesin West give the lie to

the myth that Wright's buildings (such as Fallingwater) were born fully conceived, as if "the thing had simply shaken itself out of my sleeve" (*A* I, 179). Rather, these early plans reveal a persistent study and analysis of the actual conditions of the site.

The location selected for the permanent structure was in the southwest quadrant of the quarter-section Wright purchased outright. It forms a headland just below the sixteen-hundred-foot contour line where the slope begins to level out a bit more gradually (fig. 238). Washes along the northwest and southeast give a shape and directionality to the land mass. Wright's first ideas for the camp, as he liked to call the place, are recorded in a sketch plan that has only recently come to light (fig. 244).[32] It shows an orthogonal grouping of buildings loosely organized around a rear open court. A long drafting room on the front is joined by an open walkway to an L-shaped structure intended as Wright's liv-

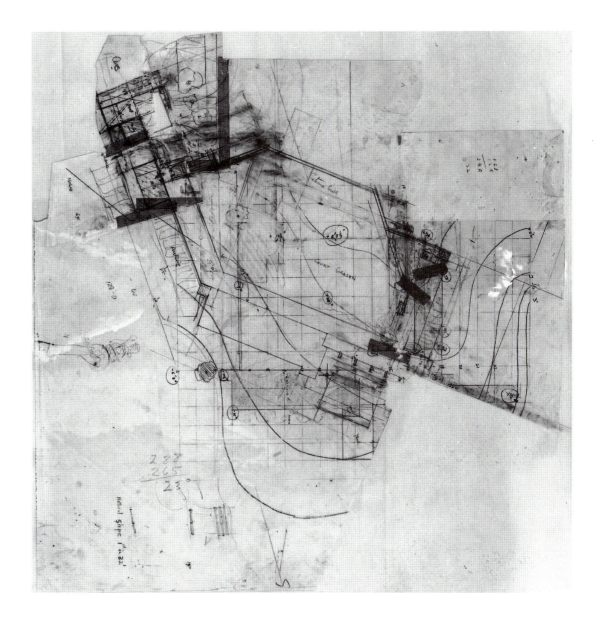

ing quarters. A pergola behind those two elements connects them to the open quadrangle, defined on the right by a wing running perpendicular to it and on the left by a terrace wall that ends at the upper left-hand corner of the plan in a structure containing Wright's office and areas for workshops and help. The access road is indicated as coming in from the lower left and terminating in a parking area (with shops) at the southwest corner of the compound. Aside from the absolute orthogonality of the plan, the other most notable feature is its orientation. Compass points indicate that the lateral, or longitudinal, axis (which for simplicity's sake

I shall generally refer to as the east-west axis, in contradistinction to the transverse, or north-south, axis) defined by the pergola is rotated approximately thirty degrees east-southeast as Fallingwater was, so that the drafting room and living quarters face the morning sun.[33]

A second stage in the planning process reveals a distinct uneasiness with the sense of closure resulting from a purely rectilinear solution, along with a series of moves questioning the basic orientation of the main buildings (fig. 245). Over an indication of the contour lines, the drafting room was first drawn almost due south, at plus-or-minus

246. Taliesin West. Plan (redrawn c. 1940).

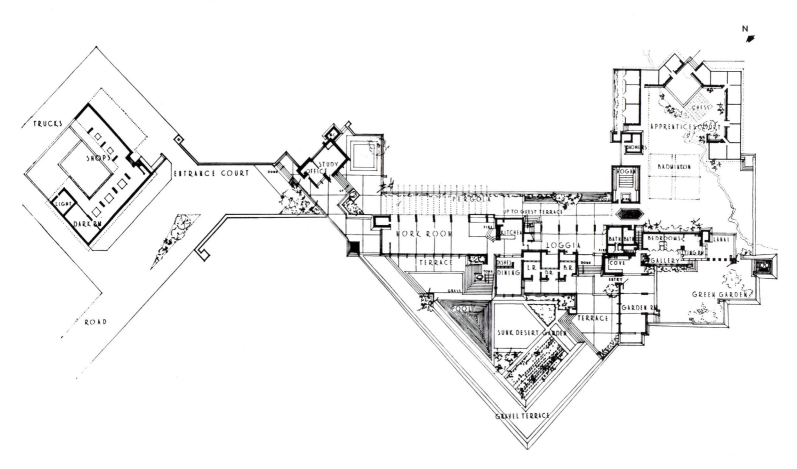

five degrees east-southeast. The compass point was then shifted, and the entire plan was rotated over the original to bring the drafting room into an orientation approximately thirty-five degrees west-southwest. The rear "court garden" became a skewed hexagon, and the terrace wall, parking area, and office and workshops faced due west at an angle of approximately 120 degrees to the pergola and rear wall of the drafting room. The plan was literally cranked open by the application of a hexagonal geometry similar to the one Wright was experimenting with in the Hanna House; but the openness was essentially internal—a response to configurations of topography—and did not take into account more broadly defined aspects of the site.

The final plan retained the basic west-southwest orientation of the second stage but replaced its "soft" hexagonal geometry with a "harder" forty-five/ninety-degree one based on the rotation of a square dynamically articulated as the pivoting of a prow (fig. 246). The module is a sixteen-foot square etched in the concrete platform connecting the various structures. The five basic units seen in both previous plans, now somewhat differently disposed, are: workshops, Wright's office, drafting room, Wright family living quarters, apprentice court. A pergola remains the lateral spine; and an open loggia, around which are grouped the kitchen and dining room (along with some senior Fellows' bedrooms) forms the link between the drafting room and the L-shaped Wright house.[34]

At the entrance on the west, joining the carpark, is a squarish workshop building rotated forty-five degrees and thus establishing the geometrical order of the camp. A court leads to Wright's office (and study), set on the same forty-five-degree grid. The angled prow at the beginning of the pergola opposite the office marks the pivotal point, or hinge, in the shift of the grid. All the units along the lateral spine—the drafting room, kitchen/dining/loggia link, Wright living quarters, and apprentice court with its connecting cinema—conform to the orthogonal grid. All, that is, except for the small, rotated-square opening at the top of the apprentice court which, along with the workshop building, was added by Wright in the final stages of the plan.[35] This ro-

Marcus House project, Dallas, Tex., 1934–36.
247. Plan.   248. Model.

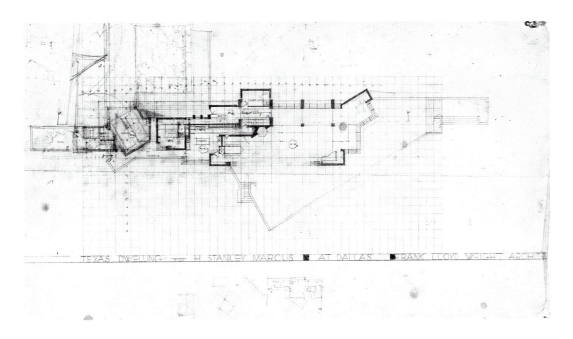

TEXAS DWELLING FOR H. STANLEY MARCUS AT DALLAS FRANK LLOYD WRIGHT ARCHIT

tated square, approximately the same size as the main part of Wright's office, reverberates the diagonal impulse of the grid shift at the upper extremity of the plan in concert with the larger workshop building at the other end, which in turn provides a counterbalance to the powerful projection of the angled prow in front of the drafting room.[36] The triangular prow, the most significant addition to the third and final stage of the plan, provides a terrace overlooking the desert and unifying the main communal spaces of drafting room, dining room, loggia, and Garden Room (the space in the Wright house set aside for social functions involving the Fellowship).

The diagonality of the plan of Taliesin West can be traced back to the project for the Johnson Compound in Death Valley, Wright's first experience in dealing with the desert (fig. 165). Wright usually referred to the projects for Ocatilla and San Marcos-in-the-Desert as the sources (*A* II, 315, 453; figs. 183, 179). More immediate ones would be the plan of the Willey House (1933–34) and the project for the Marcus House (1934–36), both of which employed a rotated, projecting, prow-like terrace to mediate between building and landscape and both of which would have been very much in Wright's mind while he was looking for a site (figs. 203, 247).[37]

The plan of the Dallas house for Stanley Marcus, who had become the leading force in his family's Neiman-Marcus Department Store by the mid-1930s, was a conscious elaboration and expansion of the second scheme for the Willey House.[38] Including the walled terraces, the house would have been over 230 feet long and about 70 feet deep, just a little smaller than the drafting room/living quarters section of Taliesin West (fig. 248). The original site was a sloping terrain that dropped fairly rapidly to the east. Wright set the house into the slope, parallel to the access road, orienting all the rooms to the southeast. The two-story service and bedroom wing at one end burrows into the hill slope, while the large living/dining room occupies the entire east half of the ground floor. The extensive openings of its front wall, composed of sliding glass doors that can be entirely pushed aside to make the space of the room continuous with that of the terrace, provide views to the south and east.

Wright's earliest sketches show that the terrace was pivoted from the upper corner of the living room much as if the large rectangle of that space had simply been cranked thirty degrees southeast, the rotation of the garage to the left echoing the movement. As in the Willey House, the projecting terrace would have made the living room floor appear to be continuous with the ground while directing the view, through its pivoting action, across the sloping terrain. The terrace itself forms a thirty/sixty-degree triangle that overshoots the far end of the room, its leading edge paralleling the contour lines and thus locking the house into the site. Carrying out the theme of a pavilion open to the landscape, Wright designed the roof to look like an awning, with a superstructure composed of forty-four-foot-long steel trusses angled at fifteen degrees like booms, along which would have rolled removable shutters, or "aeroshades," and from the tips of which would have hung insect screens to protect the inhabitants when the floor-to-ceiling glass doors of the living room were open.[39]

Despite the very obvious relation between the Marcus House and Taliesin West, especially when one considers the tent-like superstructure that both share with Ocatilla, it is interesting that Wright did not immediately start the process of planning his desert camp with it in mind.[40] The first sketch, as mentioned, was entirely orthogonal. On one level, this can be interpreted as illustrating Wright's penchant for beginning each project afresh, although that assumption is too often belied by reality. Another interpretation might be that the introduction of the diagonal was always a "reflex action" for Wright, in other words, a reaction to an orthogonal premise in response to particular conditions and contingencies. That conclusion might be closer to the truth, at least at this stage in his career. But what is probably the "real reason," as Mies would say, rather than just a "good reason," is that Wright started from a unique set of considerations in planning Taliesin West—considerations so different from those posed by the Willey site, the Marcus site, or even the Death Valley site that the precedent offered by those diagonal plans may not at first have been apparent to him at all.[41]

The diagonality of the earlier buildings resulted essentially from considerations of what I should like to call *siting*. By this I mean relating the building to the topographical and geological conditions of the land. Death Valley, Ocatilla, San Marcos-in-the-Desert, and the Willey and Marcus houses were all designed to be site-conforming. Angles of rotation or displacement were meant either to follow the contours of the land or to act as a mediating device. There is some of that in Taliesin West. The diagonal projections resulting from the rotation of squares reflect the pattern of washes and give the platform on which the various structures sit the general shape and sense of direction of the land mass beneath, although it is quite clear that Wright had to do a good deal of digging and filling to produce this impression. But the plan of Taliesin West was not an issue of *siting*. Rather, it was a matter of *orienting*. And by this I mean the coordination of visual axes with distant landmarks and associated directional points.

The shifted grids of Taliesin West relate more importantly to lines of sight than they do to contours of land. The fundamental move in planning Taliesin West was the deviation from a basic east-southeast orientation to a west-south-westerly one. This opened up all sorts of possibilities, some perhaps totally serendipitous, that the original orientation, typical of Wright's reliance on passive solar energy, had precluded. Instead, the plan was keyed off the distant mountains, which Wright clearly understood to have had special meaning for the ancient inhabitants of the area.

In the first sketch, the lateral axis of the camp would have terminated in the side of Maricopa Hill (fig. 244). By angling the plan off its southern tip, Wright allowed the main axis to slip by the hill and point directly toward the volcanic buttes of Black Mountain and Little Black Mountain (fig. 238[D,E]). In doing that, he inevitably, and indeed almost inescapably, aligned the transverse, north-south axis with Thompson Peak, the pyramidal mass in the center of the McDowell chain.[42] The crossing of the axes occurs precisely at the point where the major change in direction of movement takes place, at the end of the loggia that leads to the prow. This crucial spot, as we shall see, was to be marked with numerous devices to cue the visitor as to its importance, the most significant of which may well have been a rooftop observatory intended to be built above the windowless cinema Wright liked to think of as a kiva, the ceremonial center of Pueblo religion.[43]

The rotational shift of forty-five degrees that takes place on the prow redirects the view toward the saddle of Maricopa Hill and thus realigns the central open space of Taliesin West with the area where the major Hohokam artifacts and petroglyphs were found. This axis extends in the opposite direction toward Shaw Butte and the Phoenix North Mountains, while the main lateral axis points toward the Hieroglyphic Mountains in the distance. Although the topographical alignments delineated by the plan were surely not meant to be as exacting as they might have been in "primitive" times, a fact borne out by the way in which Wright typically skewed the axes ever so slightly to articulate actual paths of movement, they were, at least in Wright's mind, partially based on the extant prehistoric

signs. Indeed, while working on the design he is reported to have said to his apprentices: "When the Indians come back 2000 years from now to claim their land, they will note we had respect for their orientation."[44]

Construction as Consolidation

If the plan of Taliesin West was generated by ideas quite different from those that underlay what might otherwise seem to be obvious precedents in Wright's work, the same is only partially true for the design of its physical fabric. The desert camp is a low-lying, basically one-story megastructure composed of distinct and quasi-independent units linked by a platform, terraces, walkways, and bridges, much like the Johnson Death Valley Compound. (The second-story guest terrace, or deck, over the loggia and dining room, was an early addition to the original structure.) The units themselves were built of stone and concrete and covered with canvas roofs to have the nomadic, tent-like character of Ocatilla and yet the permanence associated with masonry construction. As in Ocatilla, the angle of the tent top was meant to echo the surrounding mountain slopes. But a reflection of the natural surroundings was only part of what Wright hoped to achieve in the appearance of Taliesin West and was more a means than an end in itself.

The "desert rubble stone," as Wright called it, forming the walls, piers, and parapets, resulted from an agglomerative process in which "raw" material lying around the site was simply consolidated into a "cooked" product. The small and quite plentiful boulders and fractured rocks were placed flat side out in wood forms. With smaller stones slipped between them to fill the gaps, a lean mixture of concrete was poured in from behind to bind the mass together, allowing the multicolored rocks to appear as if suspended in a "mosaic" of what Le Corbusier would later term *béton brut* (fig. 249). The mottled surface reproduced with intensity the complex visual effect of the desert mountains that Wright described as "tattooed" and "spotted like the

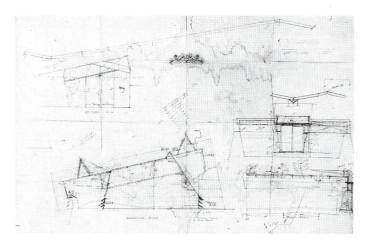

Given this underlying imagery of a container for liquid, an appropriately natural pattern was found to activate its surface. The walls were generally grooved at varying heights to break up the sense of mass and give a "flowing" effect. The model was quite literally the eroded streamlines typical of canyon walls in the area.[46]

The sense of time and age implicit in the consolidated and eroded appearance of the "desert rubble stone" walls was highlighted by the much more transient character of their covering. All the main structures were covered by canvas panels stretched within an exposed framework of dark-brown stained, rough-sawn redwood trusses. The fin-like rectangular frames are angled at a fifteen-degree slope and attached like C-clamps to the supporting base of masonry (fig. 250). Some of the overhead canvas panels could slide back and forth to let in more light and air, while those along the side and ends were designed to flap up and down or in and out, often in combination with painted wood panels.[47] At the ends, long notched poles, sometimes painted in multicolored patterns, were used to hold the flaps in position, much as the Plains Indians did to secure the door flaps or draft holes of their tepees.[48] Exoskeletal, angular, spotted with color, and bristling with projections, the roofs that emerged from the lower stone walls seemed armed for defense, like the scaly carapace of a local horned lizard or Gila monster peering out from the rocks on the ground.[49]

The combination of stone base and wood-and-canvas roof was subject to differing interpretations, depending on the function and placement of the particular space to be contained. Unlike the cabins at Ocatilla, there was no single type-solution. The two most characteristic and unusual types are what might be called the pavilion and the cavern, corresponding very roughly to the conventional archetypes of tent and cave.[50] The pavilion type, which was essentially a canopied shelter made by placing a series of wood-and-canvas frames over widely spaced masonry supports, was adopted for the two largest communal rooms. The drafting room is six and a half modules, or a little over one hundred feet long, each bay as defined by the roof trusses being half

leopard's skin" while at the same time "often patterned like hieroglyphics."[45] The design of the walls thus suggested a cultural reading as well as a purely topographical one.

The masonry walls, ranging anywhere from two to over ten feet tall, were generally battered inward at an angle of fifteen degrees, matching the angle of the roofs and translating into the third dimension the diagonal "reflexes" of the plan. Some, like those of Wright's office, have a double batter, with the upper part canted out fifteen degrees like the flanged neck of a beaker. Others, like the massive construction behind the kitchen, continue straight up from the lower batter, following a characteristic Toltec-Maya profile. Still others are canted out first and then batter in to reproduce quite explicitly the shape of a wide-bellied basket or jar.

Taliesin West.

251. Drafting room, interior (1947).

252. Garden room, interior (1947).

253. Wright office, interior.

a module wide (fig. 246). Closed in at the west by the solid structure of the vault and at the east by the fireplace and kitchen wall, it was originally totally unenclosed on the side toward the pergola and generously open to the terrace, called Indian Rock Terrace, overlooking the pool and the prow (fig. 251). The Garden Room in the Wright house is approximately three and a half modules, or fifty-six feet long. With its rear to Sunset Terrace, it opens onto the enclosed garden on the east and was intended, as noted before, to function as the main space for social occasions of the Fellowship (fig. 252). Partly because of the slant of the roof, but mostly because of the open bay structure and canvas (now plastic) covering, these rooms seem as much outdoor as indoor spaces, providing shelter without a sense of enclosure. The natural light is a constantly shifting, constantly varying presence.

The cavern type, as I have called it, was meant to provide a more definite feeling of enclosure and focus. Aside from the so-called Cove, which was designed as an intimate and private space at one end of the Garden Room, the two most telling examples of this second type are Wright's office and the cinema-theater, which was sometimes called a kiva and sometimes a hogan.[51] The Native American reference is not inconsequential. The cinema-theater is a small, rectangular, solid masonry structure with openings only for air vents. Being in it feels like being underground. Wright's of-

fice is literally partially underground, although its roof was more typically wood and canvas (figs. 253, 249, 1). Set into the hillside on a diagonal, its rear clerestory openings reveal the ground outside to be at nearly eye level. The mysteriously cool atmosphere smells of the earth and puts one in mind of the prehistoric pithouses of the region, where, in a similar fashion, the ground was partially excavated and then bermed to provide a supporting ledge for the superstructure of wood. As the first structure a visitor might enter, the office immediately suggests the relationship Wright wanted to establish in Taliesin West between natural and cultural representations. All superficial resemblances to local topography, flora, or fauna are filtered through the archetypal transformation from cave to cistern to pithouse that the prehistoric inhabitants of the area had earlier effected.[52]

■ ■ ■

Although an accurate account of the construction history of Taliesin West, including later changes and additions, must await further documentation, some indications can be given here. Work began in the late winter of 1938 in the area of the drafting room. According to William Wesley Peters, Wright's chief draftsman, the first two elements of "desert rubble stone" masonry to be built were the vault and the kitchen/serving tower at the two extremities.[53] By May 1940, when the camp was first published in *Arizona Highways*, the drafting room, the kitchen and dining area, the loggia and upper guest deck, Wright's office, and a good part of the Wright living quarters and apprentice court were finished. By the early part of the following season, Wright was able to say that "Taliesin West is now quite complete. The small cinema comes into action as we go to press. Some of the boys are hammering away at the final furnishing in the rooms. . . . The pools are filled. . . . We have hot water, and life is already taking on a more civilized character."[54] By the end of the spring of 1941, the fourth year of building, the initial campaign of construction can be said to have come to an end.

Interestingly, it is only at about that time that the name Taliesin West was finally chosen.[55] "As a name for our far-western desert camp," Wright wrote in the second edition of his *Autobiography* (1943), "we arrived at it after many more romantic names were set up and knocked down. The circumstances were so picturesque that names ran wild—so we settled sensibly to the one we already had" (*A* II, 452). Names meant a lot to Wright, so we should not simply leave it at that. Names like Hollyhock, Fallingwater, and perhaps Taliesin came even before the buildings were begun. We know of some in the case of Taliesin West that were tried and vetoed. "Desert Camp" was one, and "Tali-

esin in the Desert" another; still a third was "Rockledge." The most curious, however, was "Aladdin."[56]

Wright often referred to the figure of Aladdin in the tales of the *Thousand and One Nights* as "a symbol for creative desire and imagination" (*A* I, 178), just as he had very early in his career chosen another theme from these Arab folktales and fairy tales for the mural decoration of his children's playhouse.[57] Aladdin was the son of a poor tailor in China, who died when Aladdin was ten, leaving the young boy to care for his mother. Meeting a sorcerer from Morocco, he came into possession of the charms of the magic ring and lamp that allowed him to call into being anything he desired. To marry the sultan's daughter and provide her with a place to live, he conjured up a palace that "only magic could have brought into being," one "beyond the power of mortal kings" and for which "no masons are to be found who can produce such work."[58] The palace was miraculously transported from China to the North African desert.

In many ways Aladdin was a figure like Taliesin, a poor boy from nowhere who got lucky and who was able to stretch his imagination beyond the capacity of normal human beings. Wright obviously felt a kinship to both folkloric figures, just as he saw the Welshness of the one and the desert romance of the other as appropriate to his two houses. But whereas Taliesin (in Wisconsin) was essentially a personal affair, the program for the Arizona winter headquarters had grown into a communal, if not totally public, undertaking. Surely this is one reason why the name Aladdin did not seem very "sensible."

But why did it take so long to decide on the name the Fellowship "already had," and what did it convey in its qualified form? Most, if not all, of the names Wright devised for buildings derived from their representational character vis-à-vis nature. But unlike Fallingwater or Ocatilla, or later Wingspread or Eaglefeather, for instance, Taliesin West is not primarily a representation of nature.[59] It is about the desert in Arizona, to be sure, but it never condenses into an image of the landscape, be it a simple one like Taliesin or a more complex one like Ocatilla. The cultural context out-

254. Taliesin West. Terrace prow, with drafting room to left, dining room straight ahead, and Sawik Mountain in distance (1939 or early 1940).

weighs and overrides the natural one. For this reason, it would seem, Wright ultimately chose a name that linked him and the Fellowship to the place, and did so by providing essentially locational and orientational information. Taliesin West is Taliesin moved west—and facing west, as all indications at the site proved its former inhabitants did.

Orientation and direction based on earlier remains were not only key to the planning of Taliesin West; they were essential to its physical fabric and expression. Not all the rocks and boulders retrieved from the site were incorporated into the masonry substructure of the buildings and parapet walls. Certain special ones, those incised with ancient petroglyphs or distinguished by size or shape, were reused in isolation in conspicuous locations, consciously re-

ferring to their former disposition and in full recognition of their original power to articulate human movement and action.[60] The two most prominent are the one at the beginning of the pergola, just opposite Wright's office (fig. 237), and the one on the main terrace prow, above the pool, in front of the drafting room (fig. 254).

These two were set in place in the earliest stages of construction, even before the buildings around them were finished. They were removed from where they were found at the base of Maricopa Hill (see fig. 243), but were carefully repositioned in accordance with their original orientation (compass readings were taken before removal).[61] Although such an act of decontextualization would not be condoned today, the intention was clearly restorative rather than destructive and was more analogous to the work of Viollet-le-Duc or Sir Arthur Evans than it was to that of Lord Elgin. Marking the focal points of a ceremonial spatial pattern and orienting the visitor, as well as the seasonal occupant, to the lines of sight established by the plan, the petroglyph boulders become crucial elements in articulating the building's meaning.

Over the years Wright made a number of changes to Taliesin West to accommodate the growth of the Fellowship from approximately thirty to more than sixty members. In 1951–52, a cabaret-theater was added behind his office, and the kiva was turned into a library; shortly thereafter, the dining room was moved into part of the loggia, which was glassed in; and in 1957, a large music pavilion was built behind the cabaret-theater. But none of these changes was as important as the continual addition of new stone markers, modifications in the disposition of existing ones, or adjustments to the path of movement itself. The petroglyph boulders and other stone markers used to program one's experience of Taliesin West make it evident that the building fits into a larger time frame than might have been expected. They give a temporal dimension to the experience that makes the building seem to share a history with that of its site. Nature, as an object of representation, is viewed as inseparable from its historical manifestations.

Space as Processional

In the late 1960s it became fashionable to talk about "the processional element in architecture" and even "to process" (pro-cess') rather than simply "to walk through" a building. Philip Johnson is probably as responsible as anyone for this emphasis; and it was his recent experience of "the hieratic aspects of architecture" in Taliesin West, "the processional aspects," as he went on to describe them in a lecture in 1957, that may well have been the source of this discovery, or rather rediscovery, of a type of movement more charac-

teristic of ancient temple or palace complexes than of modern schools of architecture.[62] The processional movement in Taliesin West, however, was linked directly to its unique educational program. It was enacted in real time and space in the spiral pattern determined by the rotated square of the plan and was represented in symbolic form in the Fellowship logo adopted at the time Taliesin West was under construction (fig. 264).[63]

If the experience of Fallingwater can be likened to listening, Taliesin West is a journey. It is like going to one of those large, remote, multibuilding complexes, such as Mycenae, Hadrian's Villa, Machu Picchu, or Teotihuacan, where the individual unit may not count as much as the whole, and the whole, that is to say, the grouping of buildings, must be perceived as part of an even larger whole, meaning the landscape. Changes in level, angles of view, sightings of natural landmarks, a multiplicity of guideposts—all these factors become part of a journey that starts well before you arrive at the site and ends at a clearly defined goal, where the purpose of the journey is disclosed.

The trip to Taliesin West usually begins in Phoenix, which in 1940 was still more a large town than a city. (Its population increased sevenfold during the following two decades, from 65,000 to approximately 440,000 by 1960.[64]) Heading east and north through Scottsdale (whose population increased even more staggeringly, from a mere 1,000 in 1940, to 10,000 in 1960, to well over 100,000 by 1990), you then take Shea Boulevard, which runs east across the floor of Paradise Valley toward the McDowell Mountains (fig. 180). In 1938 the road had not yet been paved, and during the early years of its use by the Fellowship it was often flooded and impassable. Nowadays, the trip is much less treacherous, unless you do not know where to turn off. (The first Fellowship sign, with its spiral pointing north, is almost totally invisible amid the developments that have recently engulfed even this part of the valley and fundamentally changed the way the site is approached today.)

Shea Boulevard ascends ever so gradually. The high

Taliesin West.

255. Distant view from beginning of access road.

256. Access road, just beyond Verde Canal.

Taliesin West.

255. Distant view from beginning of access road.

256. Access road, just beyond Verde Canal.

ridge of the McDowell Mountains rises up from the group of conical hills in the distance and then folds back across the northern horizon in ponderous masses, angling up and away to the northwest. Against this powerful backdrop of mountains, the valley to the right drops in expansive stages of irrigated fields down through the Salt-Gila River basin. The turnoff to Taliesin West came just before Shea Boulevard draws even with the projecting spur of Maricopa Hill (fig. 238[A]). When you turned left and headed north, you would begin to feel the excitement of the place as you started climbing toward the mountains. Over the next mile and three-quarters, the access road rises two hundred feet to the base of Maricopa Hill.

Until recently, there was no development along this road, and it ran dead ahead for a mile, dipping slightly and then rising. Before the dip, one could just spot in the distance something unusual on the high shelf of land against the mountainside (fig. 255), though what it might be was impossible to tell at first. There was the shimmering image of a broken horizontal line, flickers of white, brown, red, and beige against the receding, greenish-blue mass. Perhaps it was just an escarpment or gash in the land, perhaps just a mirage. But the hard edge of the white line could soon be read as a plane dug into the shelf and forming some sort of habitation.

Once the road dipped, you lost sight of this high place. Soon after you reemerged, the road passed through the gates of Wright's property, which in time were marked by low, inconspicuous blocks of "desert rubble stone" and a tall, saguaro-like stanchion growing out of an open red square containing a double-square spiral, with a single-square spiral behind it pointing north.[65] The road then climbed more rapidly, bending to the left and right. Giant, gesturing saguaros acted like sentinels to mark its path. One had the distinct impression that at least some of them were transplanted expressly for that purpose.[66] Glimpses of the camp came and went between the twists in the road and the bushes of palo verde, cholla, and mesquite. It was hard to distinguish building from landscape, because the color and texture of the walls are virtually the same as the sandy, rock-strewn ground.

As the road twisted and turned, the mountains came in and out of view, and you realized that you were not heading directly into them but skirting their flank. The encampment appeared off to the right. As you got closer, the distinct shapes of Maricopa Hill, Thompson Peak, and McDowell Peak imprinted themselves on your mind, while the perimeter of the lower valley was clearly defined by the Santan Mountains to the southeast and the Phoenix Mountains to the west (fig. 256). The road then swept around to the west before finally heading northeast to point you in the direction of the double-humped shape of Maricopa Hill, on the ridge

Taliesin West.

257. Maricopa Hill, from access road.

258. Eagle Stone, at beginning of dual carriageway laid out in 1959.

of which you might see, if you looked very closely, a precariously balanced, light-colored stone object, appearing as a kind of subliminal sign (fig. 257).

After completing the wide turn, the road bent sharply left about five hundred feet before the entrance court, at which point the retaining wall of the prow, with the main buildings tucked in behind it, then as now, comes clearly into view. They sit directly beneath McDowell and Thompson Peaks as you face northeast (fig. 258). A divided driveway runs straight along the west wall of the terrace prow. Its beginning is marked by a tall menhir, or standing stone, raised on a low parapet and aligning directly with the north-south axis of the camp that passes through the loggia in the direction of Thompson Peak. Swelling out from its

narrow foot into a broad chest, the stone is like a great bird that has just descended from the mountains and alighted. Called the Eagle Stone, it reminds one of Brancusi's contemporaneous *Birds*. With its reference to a prehistoric, Neolithic culture, it instantly situates Taliesin West in relation to a mythic, though no less real, past.

From this point to the entrance court is a short, straight drive. But that is not the way one would have approached the camp throughout most of Wright's lifetime. This final leg of the entrance road was laid out in 1959, and the introductory menhir should therefore be read more as a footnote than a foreword. Originally, the main access road branched off quite a bit farther to the south, before the final bend it now takes (fig. 238). Just on the other side of the Old Verde Canal, it swept around to the west, following the canal and the wash, before turning into the entrance court. Along its sweeping arc, you would have had a continually changing panorama of the camp against the mountain backdrop (fig. 259). First, the low-lying buildings would have appeared framed by the broad, cleft McDowell Peak; then, further around, the point of the prow would have locked directly on the axis of Thompson Peak; and finally, as you approached from the west, the buildings would have appeared to be nestling under Maricopa Hill (see fig. 239).

To frame that final image, which is so reminiscent of the way the Bronze Age citadel of Mycenae appears to sit in the lap of Mounts Marta and Lara, Wright built a low stone tablet inscribed with the name "Taliesin West" and opposite it, on the upper side of the court, a Light Tower (1947; fig. 260).[67] This highly visible structure is composed of a tall, thick plane supported at a fifteen-degree angle by a wedge-shaped buttress. From it projects the symbolic spiral of the Fellowship, with an arrow pointing toward the entrance at the base of the hill. The axis from the entrance court to Maricopa Hill was reinforced in the 1950s by the placement of a small menhir and petroglyph boulder halfway between the tablet and the tower, in line with the saddle of Maricopa Hill. (When looked at in three-quarter profile, as one would in moving around it, the stele also becomes the

Taliesin West

259. View from southwest along original access road (1939 or early 1940).

260. Main entrance court, looking east to Maricopa Hill.

first in a series of stones and other objects marking the lateral, east-west axis.)

The Light Tower also functions as a gate. It would seem from extant visual evidence, including drawings, photographs, and film, that a second access road entered the camp from the rear, giving the final leg of this first part of the journey an even more ritualistic aspect (fig. 261).[68] Although probably not made until the first campaign of building was over, the road is clearly visible in an early sketch by Wright, framing the complex as a diamond (fig. 262). (Only traces of it still remain.) It forked right after the canal, running almost due east toward the saddle of Maricopa Hill. Following the path of the wash, it paralleled the southeast wall of the prow, affording views of the strange group of hills in the distance to the southeast (fig. 289). It then took a ninety-degree turn toward McDowell Peak after passing

around the walled garden of the Wright living quarters. Heading northwest, it cut between Sun Trap and the apprentice court before making another ninety-degree turn directly behind the camp, under Thompson Peak (figs. 261, 263). From this vantage point, the buildings would almost

Taliesin West.

261. Aerial view, looking southwest (c. 1946–47).

262. Preliminary perspective.

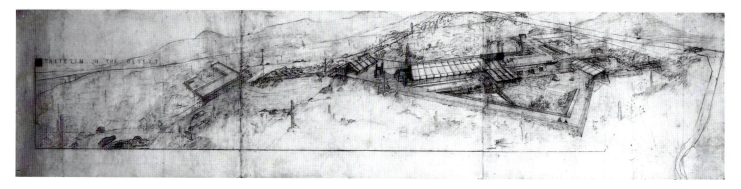

Taliesin West.

263. Sequence of stills from Gerald Loeb film recording arrival by car (April 1945).

264. Entrance, with dual Fellowship signs (1940).

265. Hohokam petroglyph boulder at entrance.

Distant view,
from southwest

Wright living quarters,
from south

Wright living quarters,
from southeast

Rear of drafting room,
from northeast

Wright office,
from northeast

have disappeared beneath the cut in the hillside created by the pergola. Descending in a southwesterly direction toward Wright's office, the visitor would finally be deposited in the entrance court, where he or she would again be brought face to face with the double-humped form of Maricopa Hill, within whose protective hollow the camp is understood to be contained (fig. 260).[69]

Both the main clockwise approach from the west and the counterclockwise path from the east circumambulating the buildings define the initial segment of a spiral pattern of

movement that Wright mapped out for the visitor, as it were, at the flight of steps leading down into the camp. To either side of this narrow slot of space were vertical posts with the double-square Fellowship spiral pointing inward (fig. 264). Sometime in the 1940s, these were removed. What remains, instead, is less demonstrative though more indicative of the iconographical meaning of the symbol. A low, oblong petroglyph boulder was placed on the ground to the right of the steps (fig. 265). Clearly visible among the other humanoid and animal signs is a Hohokam double-square

Taliesin West.

266. View from entrance, with Wright office on left.

267. Entrance area, with steps in front of Wright office and Maricopa Hill in background.

268. Petroglyph boulder at beginning (west end) of pergola.

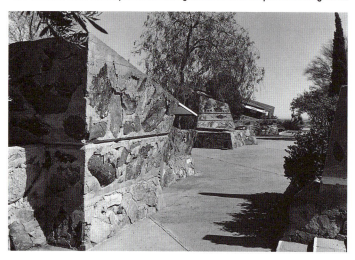

spiral whose interlocking forms add a historical resonance to Wright's logo and embed the program of Taliesin West in the cultural continuum of the site.[70]

The petroglyph boulder with the double-square spiral also serves to underscore the major, forty-five-degree rotation in axis that takes place just inside the compound (see fig. 246). It picks up the angle of the stela placed midway between the Light Tower and the signature tablet to fix it firmly in line with the lateral axis of the pergola, defined, at the near end, by the large petroglyph boulder referred to before (fig. 237) and, in the distance, by the volcanic mountains to the southeast.

The entrance to Taliesin West is like a defile (fig. 266). You go down three steps, turn right almost immediately at the side of Wright's office, pass between the eroded-looking walls, and come out to a wide flight of steps (fig. 267). These ascend in the direction of Maricopa Hill, between the partially buried structure of Wright's office and the projecting prow of the pergola-passageway. The line of sight follows the diagonal of a rotated square (the center of which was subsequently filled by a circular fountain) over the top of a large standing stone, later placed on the wall of the rear garden court.

Wright's office logically serves as a transitional space. Its kiva-like interior has an initiatory effect (fig. 253). When you reemerge from it into the harsh sunlight of the desert, you realize you have completed the first stage of the journey and are ready for the final one. The grid shift occurs as you mount the steps toward the petroglyph boulder, which clearly defines the axial rotation of the camp by the directionality of its placement and imagery (figs. 237, 268). The large boulder is one of the pair Wright set up during the initial stages of construction, this one being composed of two blocks cemented together. Inscribed by the prehistoric Hohokam with signs that may possibly relate to hunting imagery, it is extremely striking because of its division and patination.[71] Taking into account, we are told, their original

Taliesin West. East end of pergola.

269. With wooden bridge (early 1940).

270. With stone bridge, water tower, and Madonna Stone being set in hexagonal pool (early 1949).

orientation, Wright joined the two blocks so that the signs on the flat side face the entrance, and the line of the seam, as well as the angle of the images, points in the direction of the southeasterly path of movement along the rear circulation spine of the camp.

The petroglyph boulder defines the main lateral axis of Taliesin West, which follows the contours of the mountain slope as it cuts between a retaining wall and the rear of the drafting room. The figures and arrows pecked into its surface direct you up the flight of steps and around the stone to the right. Until certain changes were made after Wright's death that blocked the end of this axis in order to enlarge Olgivanna Wright's living quarters, the boulder pointed toward the conical mountains in the distance.[72] This view was framed, almost perfectly, by the tunnel-like passage of the pergola (fig. 237). Megalith and mountain, in apposition to one another, described a line of orientation that linked building to landscape across space and through time. Appearing in perspective as an integral part of Taliesin West, the Fuji-like shape of the volcanic butte was immediately perceived as a raison d'être of the design.[73]

The importance Wright attached to this sighting is attested to by the sequence of changes he made along the axis to frame the mountain and magnify its significance. At first only a wooden bridge, spanning an elongated, hexagonal reflecting pool, connected the rear of the Wright living quarters to the cinema-kiva (figs. 269, 246).[74] In the mid-1940s the front half of the pool was skewed to give it a more dynamic shape, and perhaps to take into account the slightly off-axis view of Black Mountain, just beyond and to the north of Little Black Mountain. At the same time (probably by 1946), a small petroglyph boulder with figural markings on its rounded top surface was placed in the narrowed angle of the near corner of the pool, its oblong shape following that of the pool.

Around 1947, plans were drawn up to rebuild the earlier wooden bridge in stone.[75] This bridge was set to the east of the original one and was supported by two inclined piers

echoing the shape of the distant buttes (fig. 270). A tall water tower was constructed at the junction of the bridge and the Wright house. It was initially flat-topped, but buttressed on its outer side at an angle parallel to the inner face of the bridge piers. Finally, a tall menhir, sometimes called the Madonna Stone, was set in the pool just in front of the

271. Taliesin West. East end of pergola, showing water tower with flat cantilevered roof and Madonna Stone moved to far side of bridge (1956).

272. Taliesin West. East end of pergola, with stone pediment on bridge and angled water tower roof (February 1957).

273. Lion Gate, Mycenae, thirteenth century, B.C.

opening of the bridge, creating a vertical line through it and transcribing the east-west axis onto the side of the distant mountain.

Even more pronounced changes were made in the mid-fifties. The roof of the water tower was projected over the bridge; the pool was extended beyond the piers; and the tall menhir was removed to the far side of the bridge. The standing stone now functioned more as a negative than a positive shape, appearing as a slit or crack in the angled opening (fig. 271). By 1956–57, the changes that ultimately made the far end of the lateral axis of Taliesin West into a symbolic representation of the distant mountain were realized. The most important of these was the erection of a rude, freestanding pediment on the bridge, directly over the pool (fig. 272). Continuing the lines of the inclined piers, it transformed the void below into a positive, triangular shape, as if to bring the mountain into the camp itself. The lower part of the pediment was split and opened in a slot; the peak was unified by a ceramic Ching dynasty relief panel depicting a group of figures taking part in a theatrical representation in an outdoor architectural setting. Wright modified the roof-

274. Taliesin West. Plan (1959).

line of the canopy projecting from the water tower to reflect the angled planes of the pediment and its internal scene. And so as not to divert attention from this complex symbolic form, he removed the menhir to a position marking the corresponding north-south axis.[76]

The shape and placement of the pediment, with its sculptured relief panel, leave little doubt that Wright had in mind such images of ancient architecture as the Lion Gate at Mycenae, which Vincent Scully, in his contemporaneous book on Greek architecture, *The Earth, the Temple, and the Gods*, was interpreting in similar and not entirely unrelated terms (fig. 273).[77] By the end of his life, Wright's desire to link Taliesin West with the significative forms of the landscape in as physical a way as possible led him well beyond the bounds of local cultural traditions to a more inclusive historical position.[78] Indeed, menhirs, or standing stones, are more Celtic than Amerindian. Wright's ultimate, unrealized plan for articulating the axis from the entrance of the pergola to the mountains in the southeast was based on

the prehistoric alignments at Carnac in Brittany. In a project that he seems to have developed over a period of time, Wright planned a row of eight standing stones to march across the valley toward Black Mountain, beginning just beyond the bridge and terminating in a semicircular pool on the far side of the wash that determined the path of the counterclockwise access road (fig. 274).[79]

No matter how much the link between building and distant mountains was elaborated and reinforced during the two decades Wright occupied Taliesin West, it had from the very beginning a ritualistic sense of necessity that must be understood in terms of the overall circulation pattern of the site. Whether one approached the camp by circling around from the west or by taking the more circuitous, counterclockwise road from the east, the path described an inwardly spiraling movement. The petroglyph boulder at the pivot of the plan (the one across from Wright's office) signaled the continuing course of that path through the building, while at the same time indicating its redirection outward (see fig. 246). The internal circumvolution takes the visitor down the pergola, onto the terrace prow, around its perimeter, and to the petroglyph boulder in the angle between the drafting room and the original dining room, so we shall follow this route to complete the procession.

The tunnel-like appearance of the east-west axis of the camp gives it a compelling directionality (fig. 237). The tilted petroglyph boulder at the entrance, the angled mass of the stone vault at the near end of the drafting room, and the projecting prow of the passageway platform define a channel that is covered through nearly half its length by a low redwood trellis. The pergola is similar to the "arbor" drive at Fallingwater. Cut into the hillside, it accommodates the nearly five-foot drop to the level of the drafting room floor and provides a continuous shaded access to that space along its flank.

As you walk through the pergola, you can see the top of the hill slope on the left at almost head height, with the result that the "desert rubble stone" retaining wall literally reads as a section of the mountainside. The framed view of the mountain at the end is dramatically enhanced by the play of light and shade, which begins with the rhythmic pattern of the trellis but develops into more powerfully contrasted areas. The pergola stops where the rear wall of the kitchen batters out. Originally, as you emerged into the glare of the sun, the passageway was almost immediately constricted by an eighty-foot-long pool along the base of the retaining wall. Right after that, the axis jogs half a module to the right to line up with the center of the pool under the bridge (and, before it was removed, the pediment above it).

It is at this point that the corresponding north-south axis begins to make its presence felt. The front wall of the long, narrow pool was broken, about a third of the way down its length, by a spur of "raw" desert projecting through the retaining wall into the concrete walkway (figs. 246, 269). Like the boulder-hearth of Fallingwater and the hill crown of Taliesin, this intrusion of nature serves to recenter and reorient the composition. As you looked beyond the lump of earth and stone to locate its source, you

saw the massive form of Thompson Peak in the near distance. Its apparent continuation in the projecting spur would have had the physical and psychological effect of making you veer to the right, where the deep, dimly lit space of the loggia carries the eye out to the light of the terrace prow (fig. 275).

The loggia functioned as a vestibule for the Fellowship dining room (before part of it actually became the dining room itself) as well as the entrance portico to the Wright living quarters. It is the turning point in the building, where the north-south axis crosses and takes over from the east-west one.[80] The view south through the loggia passes directly over the twin peaks of Papago Park to the ridge of the Phoenix South Mountains. To the north, the loggia perfectly frames the pyramidal mass of Thompson Peak (fig. 276). Its battered and canted profiles appear to have been expressly designed to contain the mountain's bulk in their grip. The proximity of Thompson Peak may well account for the fact that Wright did very little else to reinforce this axis as compared to the east-west one. Only very late in his life did he cut a stairway through the retaining wall, directly opposite the loggia opening, to the side of which he placed the menhir that had earlier marked the end of the east-west axis. And as part of the larger plan to extend that axis across the desert floor by an alignment of eight standing stones, an avenue of fourteen menhirs was projected to march up the slope toward Thompson Peak (see fig. 274).

The passage through the loggia along the north-south axis gives you, really for the first time since arriving at Taliesin West, a view of the vast expanse of the desert below. Your natural impulse is to descend the two broad flights of steps to the gravel path that runs around the edge of the prow. The view across the southern and western horizons slowly unfolds to reveal the sweep from the Santan Mountains in the southeast to the Phoenix Mountains and the Hieroglyphic Mountains in the northwest. Your eye follows the spiraling movement of the path, which becomes a raised embankment that lifts you high off the desert floor. As you walk down the length of one side of the prow, your path

Taliesin West.

275 (*right*). View through loggia to terrace prow and desert (1940).

276 (*below*). View through loggia to Thompson Peak (late 1940s).

277. Taliesin West. West edge of terrace prow, with original dining room, guest deck, and drafting room in foreground, Wright office in background to left, and McDowell Mountains in the distance.

parallels, in reverse, the access road that forked off to the east. At the tip you are forced to turn north. Looking toward Wright's office, where you first came in, you now see the entire stretch of buildings contained under the ridge of the McDowell Mountains (fig. 277). An angled belfry over the stairs leading to the guest terrace points to Thompson Peak and aligns the prow with it.

The triangular shape of the terrace appears like a reflection of the mountain on the desert floor. Within the "desert garden" planted as an oasis in the center of the terrace is a pool that actually reflects the mountains (fig. 278). More important, it also reflects another large petroglyph boulder that sits on a pyramidal base high above the pool and whose shape is nearly congruent with that of Thompson Peak. The relation between architecture and landscape is again af-

firmed, as it was at the entrance to the camp, by an apposition of boulder and mountain. And because you are heading back toward the entrance, you instinctively connect this one with the other one in your mind.

The new boulder, however, appears to be round and has no visible markings on its face. To reach it, you have to follow the length of the pool to the end of what Wright called Indian Rock Terrace. It is only from there, when the boulder is seen silhouetted against the side wall of the dining room and in relation to Sawik Mountain, that the cryptic markings on its faceted surface become visible (fig. 254). Unlike the one at the entrance, this boulder makes you walk around it to appreciate its full locational significance.

From the end of Indian Rock Terrace, which runs across the front of the drafting room, you can just begin to

Taliesin West.

278 (*above*). Hohokam petroglyph boulder and pool in front of drafting room, with Thompson Peak directly behind (early 1940).

Below: Petroglyph boulder above pool.

279 (*left*). From base of steps.   280 (*right*). Rear face.

281. Taliesin West. Petroglyph boulder above pool with Maricopa Hill directly to east.

Taliesin West.

282. Propped stone on Maricopa Hill, from rear looking west.

283. View west to Phoenix Mountains, from petroglyph boulder above pool.

make out the concentric circles and squiggly lines that define the reptile, water, but predominantly solar imagery incised on the north-facing and upward-slanting facets of the prehistoric stone (fig. 279). The boulder sits on a battered rectangular base, which projects from the corner of a stepped platform that rises abruptly from the end of the path like a metaphorical mountain top. As you mount the twelve steps behind the boulder in the direction of the corner entrance to the drafting room, the three facets covered with petroglyphs gradually reveal themselves. Your own movement around the boulder causes the descending arc of sun symbols (concentric circles) on the top and rear faces to appear to move across the sky, from east to west, in the opposite direction from you (fig. 280), and thus to connect the Hohokam relic with the site on Maricopa Hill where it was originally located and in relation to which it is oriented. In fact, the axis of the boulder above the pool, which is defined by the top ridge of its faceted surface, aligns with the saddle of Maricopa Hill and thus completes the cycle of coordinates plotted by the processional space of Taliesin West in returning to the forty-five-degree diagonal axis delineated by the entrance court and Wright's office (figs. 281, 246).

The boulder nestles in the angle of the drafting room and former dining room as in the protective hollow of a hill. It points directly up the side of Maricopa Hill toward the

light-colored stone object we subliminally registered earlier on. This is an enormous stone propped up on the ridge of the hill, just to the south of the saddle (fig. 282). Whether its positioning resulted from natural or human means is hard to tell. Its manifestly supernatural appearance may well have played a part in the earlier Hohokam occupation of the site; it surely reinforced Wright's sense of the significance the site had for its previous occupants.[81]

Facing west and reflecting the setting sun, the propped stone makes manifest, at the end of the procession through Taliesin West, the most immediate and direct connection the camp has to its natural and historical surroundings. Taking its orientation from the propped stone, as if to realign the camp with the powerful natural forces it reveals, the petroglyph boulder above the pool lines up with the corner of the stepped base to carry the eye across the pool, the terrace, and the plain of Paradise Valley, to the ridge of the Phoenix Mountains where the equinoctial sun sets (fig. 283).

The vertical axis of the petroglyph boulder, whose prehistoric signs link water and earth to sun and sky, becomes "the still point of the turning world," to use T. S. Eliot's contemporaneous poetic image.[82] In its function of centering perception, it literally turns you around the steps behind it to face the desert. At that moment of disclosure, you sense

284. Taliesin West. Petroglyph boulder above pool, from drafting room.

in the twist of your own body the final turn in the spiral path you have taken, beginning with the turnoff from Shea Boulevard you can now see in the near distance. Seeing where you came from while being where you were heading has an effect of déjà vu. The experience of discovery becomes one of rediscovery, of a site already inhabited and described: "Finally I learned of a site . . . across the desert of the vast Paradise Valley. On up to a great mesa in the mountains. On the mesa just below McDowell Peak we stopped, turned, and looked around. The top of the world!" (*A* II, 452).

The processional movement through Taliesin West becomes, in part, a ritual formalization of the first sighting of the place and thus a continual re-experiencing of the finding of the Promised Land. The desert is not only made available to the visitor in this way, but is foregrounded in the view from the drafting room as the everyday focus in the life of a Taliesin Fellow (fig. 284).

The "Terror of History" and the Ruin

Wright's engagement with the prehistoric art and symbolic systems of the Hohokam can be more fully understood when seen in terms of the development of modernism during and after World War II. Interest in myth, ritual, sign, and sym-

bol had come to dominate avant-garde artistic thought and practice in the wake of Surrealism, and contact with the cosmic forces revealed through the efforts of so-called primitive artists was felt to be the only way by which modern artists might revitalize an arid, abstract formalism so as to confront what Mircea Eliade called the "terror of history."[83] One has only to think of Jackson Pollock, Barnett Newman, Adolph Gottlieb, Max Ernst, or Matta to be reminded of some of the painters associated with the phenomenon. Among architects, Wright was exceptional in sensing the issue and in formulating a response so early. His appropriation and consolidation of the actual traces of prehistory at Taliesin West bore little relation to the image-making of his projects of the twenties, as the interest now shifted from mere formal representation to the reconstitution of experience and function.

It was this idea of recapturing some of the "inner strength" and "simplicity" he attributed to "the primitive" who lived "close to nature" that most clearly aligns Wright's intentions in Taliesin West with the younger group of artists known as the Abstract Expressionists. Referring to themselves in the early 1940s as the Myth Makers, Gottlieb, Pollock, Newman, and Mark Rothko turned to the hieratic form of "primitive" art, and in particular Native American art, out of the belief that its "timeless" symbols expressing the "powerful forces . . . of the natural world" would enable them to restore a mythic dimension to the language of modern art (figs. 285, 286).[84] Books like Robert Goldwater's *Primitivism in Modern Art* (1938) and exhibitions at the Museum of Modern Art, such as "Prehistoric Rock Pictures in Europe and Africa" (1937) and "Indian Art of the United States" (1941), provided an important intellectual underpinning.[85]

The primitivism of the 1930s and 1940s can be related to instances in the earlier part of the century, and even in the latter part of the nineteenth century, but certain aspects are particularly characteristic of its later manifestation. Among these are the focus on the hieratic and the ritualistic,

285. Adolph Gottlieb: *Pictograph*, 1946.

286. Jackson Pollock: *Wounded Animal*, 1943.

with a consequent deemphasis of the naturalistic and the representational. The purpose was less to imitate the appearance of nature than to reveal its fundamental and tragic "verities."[86] This could be accomplished only by the use of signs or symbols, rather than more traditional means of representation. Their greater degree of conventionalization and concreteness, it was felt, allowed such signs to evoke, like hieroglyphs, a range of feelings and relationships unavailable to the more descriptive representational image. Gottlieb's Pictographs and Pollock's Totem paintings, like Wright's Taliesin West, function as signs to orient or direct the viewer to the "universal" aspects of their subject matter. And because of their "universal" meaning and "timeless" validity (read: abstractness), such "primitive" signs could be used almost ready-made—not represented, as it were, but simply appropriated as a preexisting symbolic system.[87] The operative model for reading such a work, involving the complex layering of "primitive" means and modern intentions, became the map.

As Leo Steinberg first pointed out in reference to painting, the process of decoding such a work of art positions the viewer/participant in a new relation to the object. The object no longer functions as a surrogate image but becomes a plane of reference parallel to the actual ground along which we move.[88] The virtual condition of the "flatbed picture plane," as Steinberg called it, was literalized in the environmentally scaled, site-specific sculpture of the 1960s and 1970s known as Earthworks, where prehistoric or "primitive" models such as labyrinths, solar calendars, mounds, and ceremonial pathways map a surface of lines and spatial markers that are decoded in relation to an external set of referents (fig. 287).[89]

Taliesin West should be seen, both historically and theoretically, as a bridge between the pictorial conception of art as a map and its extension in three-dimensional space in the sculpture of Earthworks. Its orientational plan makes the low, spread-out compound appear more like lines of direction than a place of habitation, calling to mind such celebrated prehistoric examples as the Nazca lines on the desert

287. Robert Smithson, *Spiral Jetty*, Great Salt Lake, Utah, 1969–70.

288. Nazca Lines, Southern Peru, c. 500.

pampas of southern Peru (fig. 288).[90] And much like those cryptic markers, Taliesin West is read as a palimpsest, where different stages in the occupation of the site have helped define the overall pattern of land use (fig. 289). The complex of buildings overlooking Paradise Valley thus becomes a nexus of indications, like the Nazca lines, pointing to distant landmarks while providing, in the framework they form, a center for certain ritual activities and ceremonial movements.

The processional type of movement in Taliesin West and its spiral configuration derive from the "primitivism" of its conception and operate on the model of mapping. A path of movement laid out to ensure a sense of formality and predestination represented a radical reversal of the conventional modernist idea of the "free plan," and it was no doubt for this reason that Philip Johnson saw the "hieratic aspect" of Taliesin West as so unique. The so-called free plan had its experiential counterpart in Le Corbusier's notion of the "architectural promenade."[91] A promenade is disinterested movement; it is the movement of the *flâneur*, the movement of filling in, or taking up, time. The idea of the promenade is based on freedom of choice, an absence of hierarchies, the equality of all approaches. The idea of processional movement implies direction, distinction, and prescription, along with a certain type of group coordination. It is communal

rather than individual, always a kind of pilgrimage rather than merely a *sortie*.[92]

The sign of the spiral, which appears in Taliesin West both as a Hohokam petroglyph and as the Fellowship logo, maps the spatial movement onto a mythic plane that transforms the procession into an archetypal journey through the desert in quest of spiritual regeneration. To the Hopi of the Southwest, the spiral represents the path one must take on the "Road of Life" in order to return to the center, symbolizing the "Sun Father, giver of life." Often depicted as a double spiral, the image could represent the "four directional migrations" the different clans had to undertake "before they all arrived at their common, permanent home."[93] To the Pueblo people, the spiral is often associated with the replenishing element of water, as it is in Taliesin West. In many archaic cultures, like Bronze Age Crete or Pharaonic Egypt, the labyrinth or spiral carried similar evolutionary and salvational meanings.[94] Unlike the straight line, which implies progress with no looking back, or a meandering path of personal choice and reconsideration, the spiral defines a directed movement that is circumspect at the same time. One proceeds ahead, but at each turn with a view to the past.[95] In Taliesin West, the metaphorical journey through the desert goes back and forth on itself, passing one sign after another until the high point of land is

289. Taliesin West. Aerial view, looking southeast (November 1949).

reached, where there is water and where, as Wright said, "it would be like on top of the world looking over the universe. . . . Light and air bathing all worlds of creation in all the color there ever was" (*A* II, 453).

■ ■ ■

Where Wright's Taliesin West can be said to differ from almost all related expressions of myth and ritual is in the application of the concept of metaphor. In Taliesin West, the reconstitution of a mythical past was not meant to remain a purely vicarious or virtual experience. It was, in fact, lived through, on a cyclical basis, by the Taliesin Fellowship. Every year, the Fellowship made its "hegira," "pilgrimage," or "trek," as it was variously called, to Arizona in December, around Christmas, to return to Wisconsin after Easter.[96] The dates coincide with the solar calendar. Arrival was around the winter solstice, and departure around the vernal equinox. In Wisconsin, from April through November, the Fellowship could perform all the tasks of the agricultural cycle, harvesting their produce before returning to the regenerative atmosphere of the desert. Wright described the experience of Taliesin West as "clear[ing] the slate of the pastoral loveliness" of Taliesin in Spring Green and, by contrast, providing an "ascetic" world "of strange firm forms, a sweep that was a spiritual cathartic for Time if indeed Time continued to exist in such circumstances" (*A* II, 453). The cyclical pattern of occupation of Taliesin West realized in actual practice the myth of "the eternal return" that Mircea Eliade described as the fundamental "'primitive' ontological conception" of "the abolition of profane time and the individual's projection into mythical time."[97]

In his brilliant analysis of the problem of modern historicism in relation to the "terror of history" that formed the final section of his book *Cosmos and History: The Myth of the Eternal Return*, begun in 1945 and published in 1949, Eliade distinguished the archaic and traditional views of a timeless and mythic past, based on an identification of history with nature, from the modernist belief in the tem-

poral actuality of an ever-changing historical present that defines itself by its dissociation from the periodic and cyclical existence of nature. Observing, however, in the aftermath of two world wars, the "despair" and bankruptcy of such a modernist position that ultimately denies any meaning to history, Eliade pointed to "the reappearance of cyclical theories in contemporary thought" as a sign of the effort to reorient man's understanding of himself in relation to the past and, by extension, to nature. Citing T. S. Eliot and James Joyce in particular, he noted how this new attitude proposed, "rather than a resistance to history, a revolt against historical *time*, an attempt to restore this historical time, freighted as it is with human experience, to a place in the time that is cosmic, cyclical, and infinite." Indeed, in the *Four Quartets*, published in 1943, Eliot spoke of the need "to apprehend / The point of intersections of the timeless / With time," for "Only through time time is conquered."[98]

The destruction wrought by World War II was to have a particularly profound effect on architectural thought, the significance of which Wright seems to have sensed from the very beginning. Against the background of the unprecedented devastation of European and Japanese cities, epitomized for most by the bombings of Hiroshima and Dresden, the goal of reconstruction took the form of a new concern for permanence. Architects sought what Giedion and others called a "new monumentality," a sense of permanence at odds with the earlier modernist belief in functional adaptability and immediacy.[99] This "new monumentality" was a search for the "timeless," that which transcends mere temporality and appears to have a life *over* time, not simply *in* time.

A sense of the timeless could, however, be achieved in many different ways. Mies, in his designs for the school of architecture at the Illinois Institute of Technology in Chicago (begun 1939–42), which were almost exactly contemporaneous with the building of Wright's own school at Taliesin West, reduced the rich formal vocabulary of classicism to its bare, syntactical bones. The buildings expressed a truly "time-less" world of abstract, absolute value through

290. Mies: Illinois Institute of Technology, Chicago, begun 1939–42. Crown Hall, preliminary scheme (early 1950s). Perspective.

a kind of ur-classicism (fig. 290). They would exist outside time, offering an image of timelessness through absence. By contrast, Wright's Taliesin West, which set the stage for much of the "primitivizing" work of Le Corbusier and others after the war, expressed the condition of timelessness through presence. The sense of myth, ritual, and history provided the framework—and justification, as Eliade pointed out—for this expansion of the momentary and the immediate, the here and now, into the recurrent and the repetitive, the forever. The timelessness of the forever, that which always existed and will always exist, naturally devolves from a pattern of echo and reverberation, which led Wright, like so many romantics before him (and so many modern architects after him), to the image of the ruin, but also to a view of history that made no distinctions among nature, prehistory, and history, properly speaking.

The ruin, from the late eighteenth century on, has stood for the idea of reversion, along with the possibility of regeneration.[100] As an image of the interaction of nature and culture suspended in time, it was an obvious metaphor for the expression in building of the timelessness embodied in mythic thought. Everything about Taliesin West suggests that Wright conceived of it as a ruin. The construction technique of the "desert rubble stone" walls produces an effect of consolidation that reminds one of "restored" portions of masonry at archaeological sites. The luminous framed superstructure protecting the masonry from the elements further adds to that effect. The ancient petroglyph boulders and standing stones isolated in significant locations or aligned with distant landmarks allude to the existence of a former, now vanished civilization.[101]

None of this went unnoticed by the early visitors who were guided around the site by either Wright or his apprentices. The tour must have included some reference to this prehistoric horizon, for many of the visitors came back describing the camp as a recycled, reconstructed ruin. Elizabeth Gordon, the editor of *House Beautiful* and a friend of the Wrights, wondered why "the massive walls look as if they had been cast in place 100,000 years ago." She then remarked that "when the first enclosing walls were completed, the effect must have been that of a magnificent ruin, and even now that the house is complete and lived in, there is a feeling of something almost prehistoric in the masonry that surrounds it."[102] Wright loved to quote his wife, who said that Taliesin West "looked like something we had been excavating, not building" (*A* II, 454).[103] He himself described the desert camp as looking "as though it had stood there for centuries" (*A* II, 454).[104]

As an idea, the ruin offers the basis for starting again, for refashioning the world on the model of the past. In this way, it embodies the principles of "archetype" and "repetition" that Eliade singled out as essential to the cyclical character of mythic thought.[105] But as a praxis, the ruin can be understood in a number of ways. Ordinarily, it implies some form of distinction, if not necessarily opposition, between "nature" and "culture." The ruin makes manifest the transition from the one state to the other (fig. 236). Most romantic descriptions of ruins stressed the melancholic aspect of nature's victory over culture, of time overcoming human history. By contrast, most contemporary thought seems to find in the ruin an almost purely cultural construct, historical in significance and divorced from its alliance with nature.[106] Wright, however, understood the ruin, and especially the prehistoric ruin, in a more plastic way, as existing midway between the dominions of nature and culture. In Taliesin West, it is hard to tell where nature leaves off and history begins, or vice versa (figs. 265, 267). Were the masses of rubble-like stone and boulders found at the site previously incorporated in earlier constructions? Or were they simply deposited there by geological activity? This fluid conception of the ruin exposed the very continuity of natural and human history that Wright shared with certain prominent prehistorians of the time, including V. Gordon Childe.[107]

Wright's most extended comments on the architecture of ruins appeared in 1937 in *Architecture and Modern Life*, the book he coauthored with Baker Brownell. Wright's thesis was that the boundary between nature and architecture, and thus nature and history, was fluid and that both shared a common and continuous history. "The land is the simplest form of architecture," Wright began, and thus building is "simply a higher type and expression of nature by way of human nature."[108] Natural history may precede architec-

tural history in time, but eventually both come to share the same space in consciousness. The ruin offers a bridge from the one to the other, a bridge, it should be noted, that leads both ways.

"Let us now go nearer to the grand wreckage left by this tremendous energy poured forth by man in quest of his ideal, these various ruined cities and buildings built by the various races to survive the race," Wright wrote. "These buildings . . . wrested by his tireless energy from the earth and erected in the eye of the sun" are "now fallen or falling back again upon the earth to become again earth." The architecture of ruins, in its quasi-natural, quasi-cultural state, he suggested, reveals the mythic origins of architecture, not as an archetypal form (à la Laugier) but as a condition of time and place:

Today we look back upon the endless succession of ruins that are no more than geological deposits washed into shore formation by the sea, landscape formed by the cosmic elements. . . . The buildings are now dead to uses of present-day activity. They were sculptured by the spirit of architecture in passing, as inert shapes of the shore were sculptured by cosmic forces. Any building is a by-product of eternal living force, a spiritual force taking forms in time and place appropriate to man.

. . . It begins always at the beginning.[109]

The traces of prehistory at Taliesin West are meant to effect a continuity between nature and culture and to return the present inhabitants, periodically, to their "beginning." History, no longer merely a sequence of discrete, momentary occurrences, is reidentified with the timeless periodicity of nature's cycles. In the life of the Taliesin Fellowship, that act served as the basis for a re-ritualization of art, something that has become a continuing and recurring theme in modern art. Whether or not such Earthworks as Robert Smithson's *Spiral Jetty*, Richard Long's *Walking a Line in Peru*, Robert Morris's *Observatory*, or indeed, Wright's Taliesin West could, can, or ever will function as their prehistoric models might have is, in a way, beside the point. By their mere existence they bear silent witness to what T. S. Eliot described as the inescapable significance of the mythic experience in modern times:

> *A people without history*
> *Is not redeemed from time, for history*
>   *is a pattern*
> *Of timeless moments.*[110]

If the "authenticity" of Taliesin West is in this way beside the point, its modernity is very much to the point. Unlike the site in the Santan Mountains that Wright rejected, the one in the McDowell Mountains was never out of sight of civilization. Much of Taliesin West's poignancy, and to many its deeply tragic air, comes from the contrast its "ruinousness" offers to the suburban sprawl of Scottsdale at its edge. The closer civilization comes—and it is extremely close by now—the more Taliesin West seems to have to say. It would appear that Wright knew full well that all modern attempts to re-create the mythic are purely personal and bound in time. The profound irony of Taliesin West lies in the realization it forces upon us that, compared to the ruin (Wright said "degeneracy") of modern civilization for which it might be taken as an antidote, its own architecture of ruins can all too easily be read, in empirical terms, as an effect of "development," rather than in the metaphoric terms in which it was composed.

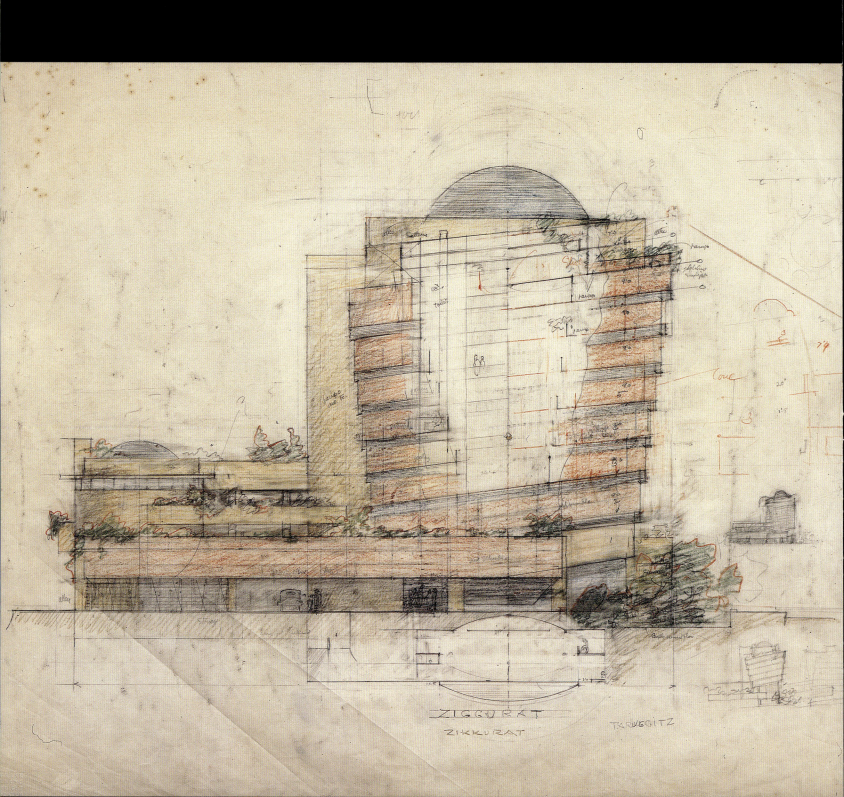

The Guggenheim Museum's Logic of Inversion

In the early summer of 1943, Hilla Rebay, curator of New York's Museum of Non-objective Painting and of its parent organization, the Solomon R. Guggenheim Foundation, wrote to ask Wright if he would come to New York to discuss the possibility of designing a building to house their important collection of contemporary paintings. "I feel that each of these great masterpieces should be organized into space and only you so it seems to me would test the possibilities to do so," Rebay began.

In Berlin I once saw your exhibition which Mendelsohn arranged, I believe. . . . His functionalism does not agree with non-objectivity. . . . I do not think these paintings are easel paintings. They are order creating order and are sensitive (and corrective even) to space. As you feel the ground, the sky and the "in-between" you will perhaps feel them too; and find the way. I need a fighter, a lover of space, an orig-

inator, a tester and a wise man. Your three books which I am reading now gave me the feeling that no one else would do. . . . I want a temple of spirit, a monument![1]

Not realizing Rebay was a woman, and apparently unimpressed by the name Guggenheim, Wright responded that he had been unable to stop off in New York on a recent

East Coast trip because he had to get back to Taliesin to attend a birthday party. (He did not say it was his own.) He then added, somewhat curtly, that he did not "know of any definite Eastern commitment at the moment" and suggested that Rebay and his "wife" might "run down" to Taliesin "for a week end."[2]

The casualness, not to say naiveté, of Wright's response did not seem to disturb Rebay unduly. She wrote back in a businesslike manner: "As much as I would love to see Taliesin and be with you, it would take too long to arrange. Mr. Guggenheim is 82 years old and we have no time to lose. . . . Please come to New York." She noted she was not a man and gently reminded Wright that Solomon R. Guggenheim "is a great man, full of vision, courage and understanding."[3] She did not feel it necessary to say that he was one of the richest men in the world and had endowed one of the most significant private foundations devoted to the encouragement of modern art. Wright got the message after this second letter and was in New York in a few days.

What might appear on the surface to be simply a misunderstanding actually has a great deal to tell us about the way in which Wright's later career was to unfold. Wright prided himself on his artistic integrity. The refusal to compromise his principles, as he saw them, had led to greater and greater isolation from the profession and the world at large. He would never compete with other architects for a job, nor would he openly solicit one. He liked to say: "I don't go to clients. They come to me."[4] And he meant that literally. They came to his home, which was also his office. This took care of two problems at once. Clients could see, before any actual designs were produced, an example of what they might be getting; in the process, they would be entering into any future agreement on Wright's own terms.[5]

This attitude was not as imperious or as arrogant as one might think. In fact, it was probably quite the reverse. If Wright's self-imposed isolation reveals a certain defensiveness (read: provincialism), then the self-exposure by means of Taliesin precluded, up front, any later misunder-

standing on the part of the client of what he or she could expect. Wright would rarely, if ever, have to deal with criticism or disappointment from a client after the fact, leaks and cost overruns notwithstanding.[6]

The rebuff to his invitation to "run down" to Taliesin "for a week end," followed by his immediate agreement to meet Rebay and Guggenheim in New York on their turf, signaled the beginning of the expansion of Wright's practice in the later years to encompass a much more widely distributed, more complex, and more varied range of projects and buildings. These would include university structures, churches, theaters, government buildings, high rises, and civic centers throughout the United States, Europe, and the Middle East. The Taliesin Fellowship continued to produce houses for a mainly middle-class clientele, but Wright himself focused most of his energies on the public buildings. In Wright's mind, as in world opinion, the Guggenheim Museum was without any question the most important of them.[7]

Owing in part to the prominence of its location in New York City and in part to its status as a leading cultural institution devoted exclusively to the exhibition of avant-garde art, the Guggenheim Museum came to be seen as the summation of Wright's architectural thought and thus, to all intents and purposes, the building by which his ultimate significance for modern architecture would generally be judged (fig. 347). The conflicts and ambiguities in that judgment not only reflect the complex character of Wright's response to the program but also expose, sometimes quite painfully, the many difficulties modern architecture *and* art have faced once they left the isolated arena of the avant-garde to become the accepted cultural expression of the establishment in the post–World War II era.

Hard as it may be to realize today, there was but one strictly modern building of prominence in New York City when the Guggenheim Museum was commissioned: the Museum of Modern Art built by Philip Goodwin and Edward Durell Stone in 1938–39 (fig. 334). The situation was hardly different elsewhere. Until the late 1940s, modern architecture was essentially an experimental, exurban, and elitist proposition. After the war, it became the norm. Architects, who had previously seen their careers more in terms of the modern painter or sculptor than in those of the traditional businessman-architect, now faced not just the problem of large-scale production but also the task of providing new and valid forms of cultural expression and symbolism within the language of modern architecture.[8]

Wright had already begun to outline certain approaches to this "search for a new monumentality" in Taliesin West. The use of masonry, a strong processional concept of space based on the spiral, and a reliance on archaic historical references would all come to play an important role in the design for the Guggenheim Museum. To translate that remote and private world into the public sphere, Wright turned to the unifying form of the circular plan and the universalizing shape of the dome. Historically, they had always been the type of monumental and sacred space.[9] The combination of the spiral and the circle, which gave the Guggenheim's design the characteristically modern dynamism and utopian bearing called for by the museum's program, would, at the same time, throw into relief the functional problems of adapting a visionary scheme to an institution—the museum—that was ultimately unwilling or, more accurately, unable to dispose of many of its traditional attitudes and to resolve the inherent conflict between its philosophical mission and more up-to-date commercial methods and practices.

In the Guggenheim Museum, Wright revived the classical idea of the "great room," but gave it an entirely new twist[10]—what I call its "logic of inversion." The thought behind the design can be traced back to a series of projects for public buildings involving the use of the circle, the dome, and the spiral during the previous several years. To understand more fully the uniqueness of the Guggenheim solution, we should first take a brief look at some of those earlier efforts.

Circular Plans and Domed Spaces

Like many architects, Wright ascribed a symbolic meaning to geometry. As early as 1912, in his essay on *The Japanese Print*, he noted how there resided in each basic geometric shape "a certain psychic quality which we may call the 'spell-power' of the form, and with which the artist freely plays, as . . . the musician at his keyboard with his notes." These "geometric forms," he explained, "have come to symbolize for us and potently to suggest certain human ideas, moods and sentiments—as for instance: the circle, infinity; the triangle, structural unity; . . . the spiral, organic progress; the square, integrity." Over the years, Wright elaborated and expanded those references. The triangle, by its association with hands clasped in prayer, stood for "aspiration," while the circle, by its reference to the sun, the moon, and the other planetary spheres, took on a cosmic meaning of "universality."[11] Though diverging in nuance and detail, Wright's symbolic reading of geometry generally coincided with the ideas of contemporary artists like Kandinsky, Gleizes, and Tatlin, the first two of whom were to be so richly represented in the Guggenheim collection.[12]

For an architect, of course, geometry implies a three-dimensional development, and here is where Wright's interest in the circle can be seen to have dovetailed so perfectly with the search for a plasticity of expression that led him to the archetype of the vessel as the basis for modeling architectural space. The circular form created a seamless, all-embracing shape, the ultimate image of oneness and fullness. It should therefore come as no surprise that Wright's first building based on the geometry of the circle was designed in 1924–25, at precisely the moment he was developing the octagonal, central-plan Desert Dwelling for himself. The design for an Automobile Objective and Planetarium for the Chicago real-estate entrepreneur Gordon Strong came as close to a visionary project as Wright would ever produce (fig. 292).[13]

Gordon Strong Automobile Objective and Planetarium project, Sugarloaf Mountain, near Dickerson, Md., 1924–25.

292. Aerial perspective.   293. Elevation and section.

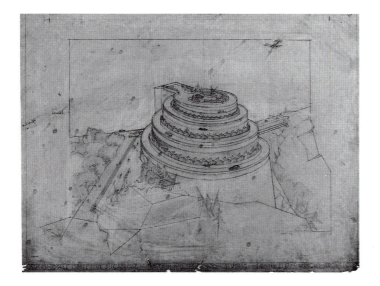

Strong owned Sugarloaf Mountain in the wilderness area of western Maryland, then about a two-hour drive from Washington, D.C., which he hoped to transform into a destination for the weekend automobile outings that were just becoming popular with the growth of highways in the mid-1920s. With little specific direction from the client (except the demand to accommodate a sizable number of people and cars), Wright conceived the idea of making a planetarium the central feature of a building that would otherwise be almost entirely composed of a double helix of ramps for the ascent and descent of cars (fig. 293). The planetarium,

which replaced Wright's first idea for a theater, undoubtedly seemed a more appropriate use for the spiral form of the "fabulous Tower of Babylon" on which he consciously based the design.[14] (The Mesopotamian ziggurat was traditionally considered the first example of a monumental building devoted to the purpose of astronomical observation.) The planetarium was to be composed of a hemispherical dome, 150 feet in diameter, around the perimeter of which would be space allocated for aquariums and natural history exhibits. The dome, however, would not be visible from the exterior, for it was completely encircled by a double-deck system of ramps designed to afford the visitor a continuously changing panorama of the "landscape revolving about them."[15] At the top, a figure-eight loop formed a bridge over a roof-garden restaurant.

The circle and the spiral were thus initially associated in Wright's mind with the creation of a public space for leisure activity and cultural events, a social and intellectual gathering place, in other words. As a response to the automobile, the spiral added a special note of modernity to what Wright otherwise described to his client as "a noble 'archaic' sculptured summit for [the] mountain."[16] This explicit historicizing clearly distinguishes Wright's design from the slightly earlier *Monument for the Third International*, proposed by Vladimir Tatlin in 1919–20 to house offices, meeting rooms, and other related functions of the International in a series of geometric solids rotating differentially within an Eiffel Tower–like steel spiral (fig. 294). The "archaic" aspect of Wright's image was picked up by Le Corbusier in his project of 1928–29 for a Musée Mondial, or Museum of World Culture, to be built on the outskirts of Geneva as part of a utopian project for a Mundaneum in conjunction with the League of Nations (fig. 336).[17]

Although Wright produced no new circular design for at least another ten years, he incorporated the project for an Automobile Objective in the various studies for Broadacre City, retaining the association of ziggurat and community gathering place with mountaintop setting. In both the original presentation of the idea in *The Disappearing City* (1932)

294. Vladimir Tatlin: *Model for Monument for the Third International,* 1919–20.

and the large model executed in 1934–35, the design plays a significant part in Wright's overall scheme for a decentralized city.[18] Located in the corner that is the highest point of the four-square-mile area shown in the model, the Automobile Objective would become the pivot of four such sections rotating around its central axis. Indeed, Wright planned these spiraling structures to be dotted around the countryside, beckoning from their hilltop locations and providing a focus for their regional communities as the cultural centers of the new, automobile-oriented utopian society of Usonia. Designed to contain planetariums, auditoriums, museums, restaurants, meeting rooms, and the like, such megastructures would remain one of the essential elements of Wright's later proposals for the reconstruction of the city, as in the Pittsburgh Point Park Civic Center scheme of 1947 and the Plan for Greater Baghdad of ten years later (figs. 367, 410).[19]

When Wright returned to investigating the various possibilities of the circle, he made the obvious connection between its geometry and the element of water. The relation between streamlining and the use of curves first appeared in the Salem Capital Journal newspaper plant project (1931–32), which otherwise remained essentially an orthogonal scheme. The Johnson Wax Company headquarters, designed in mid-1936 and completed in 1939, grew out of this project and developed the fluid effects of streamlining through a more integral use of circular forms (figs. 295, 296).[20] The smooth brick, the shiny tubes of Pyrex glass, and the sleek metal fittings are all layered in long horizontal bands. The main, double-height "workroom" ringed with galleries is totally closed off from the outside environment by a nearly solid brick wall. The corners of the wall are curved, while the top opens in a continuous "rift" of glass tubing that forms a lip of light between the wall and the skylit ceiling. The ceiling appears to float and dematerialize in the cool, diffused light filtering through the circular, lily-pad capitals of the tapering "dendriform" columns that articulate the orthogonal spatial grid of the room in a gently swaying movement. The illusion, like that of an Egyptian hypostyle hall, is of an aqueous, underwater environment.

The smooth, fluid space was meant to create a modern sense of business efficiency while at the same time providing the employees with a soothing, reposeful atmosphere in which to work.[21]

It was only in the upper part of the administrative section of the building, however, that the circular forms of the plan were truly developed in a three-dimensional way, and this section was designed last.[22] The penthouse, as it is called, is composed of two wings of offices shaped into semicircular-ended oblongs. These swing out at forty-five-degree angles from a similarly shaped connecting court in a way that uncannily resembles some of Piranesi's fanciful reconstructions of Roman ruins, especially his vision of the Nymphaeum of Nero (figs. 297, 298).[23] The points of rotation are marked by cylindrical stair and elevator towers that

Johnson Wax Administration Building, Racine, Wis., 1936–39.

295 (*left*). Interior (c. 1939).

296 (*below*). Exterior, after addition of Research Tower (far left) and advertising department (behind glass bridge over entrance court), 1943–50 (1950).

297. Johnson Wax Administration Building. Plan, penthouse level.

298. Giovanni Battista Piranesi: *Plan of the Nymphaeum of Nero,* in *Le Antichità Romane,* vol. 1, 1756.

299. Jester House project, Palos Verdes, Calif, 1938. Model.

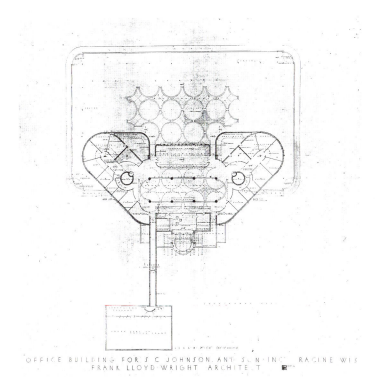

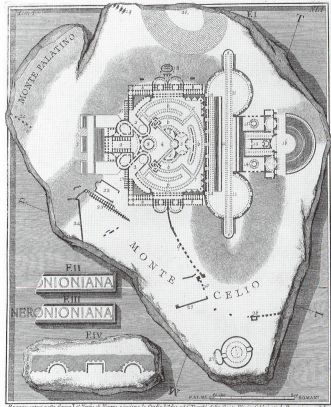

project through the roof to serve as heating and ventilating flues. Beneath the penthouse, at the mezzanine level, is a semicircular auditorium. Also at this level, a narrow bridge connects the main building to a squash court on the far side of the carport. This is covered by a continuous barrel vault, semicircular in section and composed entirely of light-filled Pyrex tubes attached to arched steel frames.

Seeing these circular forms emerge during the later stages of construction of Johnson Wax must have particularly struck Wright, for in 1938 he began to use the circle and the dome in a much more comprehensive and unqualified way.[24] Three projects from that year—two of them, significantly, for important cultural or civic purposes— illustrate this point. All three were designed for sites with direct access to water. The single house among the group, the project for Ralph Jester, was for a bluff overlooking the Pacific Ocean at Palos Verdes, California. Quasi-independent cylindrical elements made of curved plywood sheets define the interior spaces, while the sweeping arc of a circular pool provides the unifying element in the form of an overflowing basin of water (fig. 299).[25]

EXTENSION AND TERMINAL OF MONONA AVENUE
SEVEN ACRES OF MADE OVER EXISTING RAILROAD TRACKS,   FOR PARKING.
LAKE WATER THROWN UP INTO MONUMENTAL FOUNTAINS.   MONONA AVE.   "THE CITY GOES TO THE LAKE"   SEVEN MONTHS WATERDOMES, FIVE MONTHS EVERGREENS, INSTEAD
CIVIC AUDITORIUM SEATING 10,000, FRONTING OLIN TERRACE.
COUNTY JAIL AND OFFICES,   CITY HALL,   UNION RAILROAD DEPOT.   COST $17,500,000,   RAISED BY ___? (SEE KAUFMANN A LA PITTSBURGH.)

On opposite page:

300. Monona Terrace (Olin Terraces) Civic Center project, Madison, begun 1938. First scheme. Aerial perspective, looking southeast (redrawn 1953).

301. Aerial view of Madison, looking southeast over Lake Monona with State Capitol in foreground.

302. Monona Terrace Civic Center project. First scheme. Longitudinal section (1938).

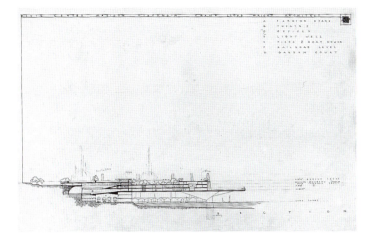

Of the two nondomestic commissions, the one that most closely relates to the Johnson Wax building—indeed, literally grows out of it—is the project for a lakeshore civic center for Madison, Wisconsin, originally called Olin Terraces but soon known as Monona Terrace. It was designed in the late summer and fall of 1938 at the request of a group of citizens who were hoping to avoid a more mundane city-county office building by presenting an alternative solution.[26] Instead of a single building to house the combined government offices, Wright proposed a landscape-like megastructure (fig. 300). Taking its cue from John Nolen's earlier City Beautiful plan for Madison, Wright's scheme projected into one of the two lakes bordering the downtown area in order "to recover the waterfront for urban use" and make the lake part of "the life of the entire city."[27]

The site was the end of Monona Avenue, three blocks southeast of George Post's grandiloquent State Capitol (1906–17) and directly on axis with its nearly three-hundred-foot-high granite dome (fig. 301). Wright proposed to terrace over the existing railroad tracks along the lakeshore, creating a new underground terminal within a multilevel civic center complex (fig. 302). In the shape of a monumental hemicycle, it was supported, like a pier, by reinforced-concrete pylons that carried the weight of the structure onto pilings driven into the lakebed. Cantilevered out from these, just above water level, was a semicircular car deck joining a lakefront drive.

The upper level of the terrace, given over to pedestrian promenades and automobile parking, was cut away to disclose sunken gardens between three large glass domes forming the basis of cascading fountains.[28] The cylindrical structures beneath them contained the municipal and county offices (to the left and right) and the civic auditorium (in the center). The enveloping domes described a right-angle triangle on the plan of the penthouse section of the Johnson Wax building. The Piranesian reference of that plan, which is made even more explicit here, informs the spatial experience of the complex as a whole. Circulation starts at the top and descends into the half-revealed lower depths along

deep flights of steps, long tunneled driveways, and multiple sequences of ramps. Below the four levels devoted to the auditorium and the city and county offices and courts are still others where the railroad station and the city and county jails share the watery environment with a boat basin for summertime leisure activities (fig. 303).

Deliberately intended as a "completion of capitol-park and the capitol building," Wright's Monona Terrace project echoed the classical forms of the City Beautiful scheme while at the same time subverting their meaning (fig. 301).[29] The central dome of the civic auditorium aligns with Post's, while the two smaller ones, over the city and county structures, point due west and south, following the orientation of the wings of the Capitol, which Post had rotated forty-five degrees off the city grid in relation to the cardinal points. Instead of a single, hegemonic dome symbolizing government authority, Wright made three—and the largest of them was for a place of social gathering and cultural activity rather than for a specifically government use.[30]

Even more significant were the differences in form and material. Wright's domes are pure hemispheres and rise directly from ground level (indeed, the "buildings" they cover are subterranean), unlike Post's stilted, Baroque, Michelangelesque structure that towers above the city.[31] Moreover, Wright's were to be of transparent glass rather than stone, literally revealing the normally secret workings of government agencies. The effect of dematerialization would have

Monona Terrace Civic Center project.

303. First scheme. Perspective, from lake (redrawn 1953).

304. Second scheme, 1954–55. Plan, upper level.

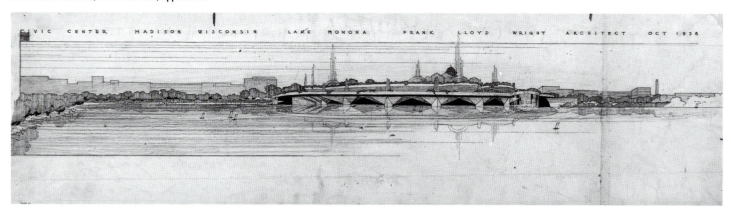

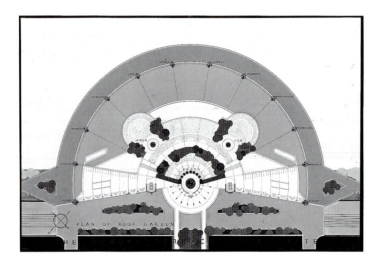

been even further enhanced by the constant stream of water cascading down the sides of the domes and creating rainbow-like effects of light.

The cultural focus of the project and its large ambitions at redeveloping and reconstructing an entire segment of the city went far beyond the intentions of Madison politicians. But the project did not die. It was revived by Wright in 1941 and then again in 1952–56, at which time the government office buildings were eliminated and the plan was devoted entirely to cultural activities. Theaters, art galleries, exhibition halls, a gymnasium, and meeting rooms replaced the city and county functions, while the upper esplanade level was turned into a roof garden symbolizing the scope of the project in cosmic terms.[32] The three water domes were dedicated to the Earth, the Moon, and the Sun (fig. 304). The Earth, the largest one, is in the center, directly in line with the Capitol dome. The smaller domes of the Moon and

Sun are on the radii, pointing due west and south. The hemicycle is divided into eighteen-degree segments. Around the perimeter are twelve smaller fountains dedicated to the signs of the zodiac, first described by the early astronomers of Mesopotamia in their effort to chart the divisions of time in terms of the movements of the planetary spheres.

The final version of Monona Terrace would thus have offered the citizens of Madison a civic center in the shape of a large-scale planisphere, translating the forms of the State Capitol into natural materials and signs and relating the daily activities of the city to a more universal frame of reference. The radiating lines would have described a path across the horizon, following the far shore of the lake, and thus making this extension of the city appear concentric with the larger order of nature.

■ ■ ■

The third project of 1938, and the only one actually built (at least in part), was Florida Southern College, a co-educational Methodist school situated on a small lake in the citrus-growing area of central Florida.[33] Wright's task was to design a major addition to a campus that was begun in the mid-twenties as a Neo-Georgian complex loosely organized on the lines of Jefferson's University of Virginia. Here again, Wright followed classical precedent while molding it to his own purposes. He adopted the two essential ideas of Jefferson's prototypical Southern campus plan: the central motif of the dome and the connective tissue of covered porticos.

305. Florida Southern College, Lakeland, Fla., begun 1938. Aerial perspective.

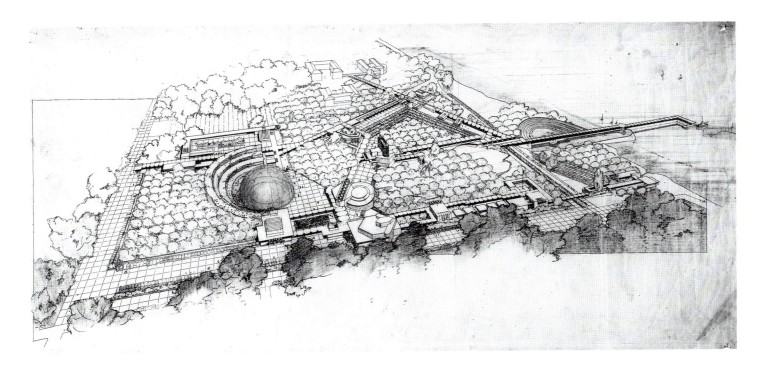

The dome, however, was brought down to ground level and turned into water; and instead of laying out the porticos on a hierarchical, orthogonal grid, Wright allowed the "esplanades," as he called them, to zigzag among the low orange trees in a loose "reflex" pattern that preserved the inherent quality of the site as a grove leading down to the lake (fig. 305).[34]

The plan, which Vincent Scully has convincingly suggested owes much to Hadrian's Villa, uses circular and semicircular classical motifs to define the major axes as well as to provide a symbolic system of signs.[35] At the upper end of the site, near the entrance, a triangular plaza is anchored at its corners by the Administration Building, the circular Roux Library, and the classroom (seminar) buildings. Dominating this plaza, and the entire campus falling away from it, was to be an eighty-foot-high water dome framed by a landscaped exedra. The dome, like those for Madison, would have been created by closely spaced jets around the rim of a circular basin.[36]

This mutable, light-filled hemisphere replaced the static image of Jefferson's focal Pantheon-library with a fluid one that directly related the educational program to the specific character of the site. Rising higher than the circular library diagonally opposite it, the dome of water symbolizes the nourishing power of nature and physical activity in the process of education. Its outflow irrigates the citrus grove from which the school buildings grow, running under the various buildings, and reappearing here and there, before being channeled into a lakeside swimming pool shaped like Hadrian's Canopus and serving as the backdrop for a semicircular, outdoor Greek theater.

The Florida Southern work became a kind of laboratory for Wright's experimentation with circular planning. The original Greek Theater went through at least two revisions, finally ending up as a semicircular bowl tangent to a completely circular swimming pool created by damming the lake.[37] The final plans for the main library were worked out in 1941–42, at which time Wright designed an Industrial Arts Building with a central rotunda to serve as a lecture hall. Related to these, Wright also produced two independent house designs in this period based on the geometry of the circle. In the canal-side weekend cottage in Fort Lauderdale for Ludd Spivey (1939), the president of Florida Southern, a completely circular, inverted cone, with an overhanging balcony overlooking the water, serves as the main social space; and in the adobe Burlingham House for El Paso,

306. Florida Southern College, Music Building project, 1942–43. Sketch plan and section.

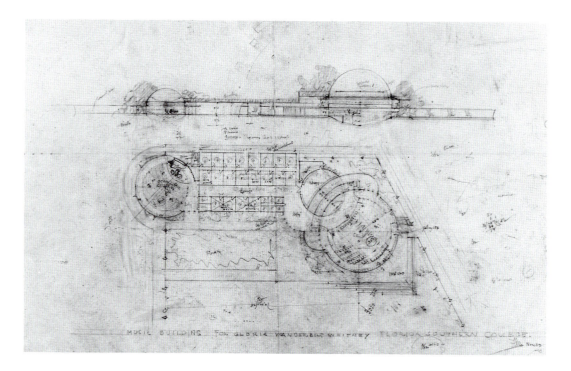

Texas, a patio court is created by shifting, intersecting arcs (1940–42; fig. 356).[38]

Although aspects of both house designs would feed into the planning of the Guggenheim Museum, one final project for Florida Southern seems more relevant, especially from a programmatic point of view. This was the Music Building that Wright was asked to design in 1942 for the site along the street to the right of the campus entrance, where the 1938 master plan had called for a "model theater." Spivey hoped to interest Mrs. Cornelius Vanderbilt Whitney in it as an alumnus of the college.[39] The finished designs from late 1943 show two circular auditoriums, one to seat five hundred people and the other for smaller chamber concerts, linked by a lower skylit wing containing classrooms (fig. 306).

Before anything further was done to implement this scheme, however, it seems to have been incorporated in a larger project proposed as a memorial to Gertrude Vanderbilt Whitney (Mrs. Harry Payne Whitney), the founder of the Whitney Museum in New York, who died in 1942. Emphasizing her interest in modern American art, the memorial was enlarged to include an art museum and studio facil-

ities, for which Wright provided plans in the early months of 1944. Ironically, the memorial music and art building was put on the back burner at the very moment Wright began to sketch out his ideas for the museum in New York that was intended, in part, to rival the Whitney and would be Wright's first public building based on the geometry of the circle and with a domed space as the central element of its design.

Guggenheim's Foundation and Rebay's Program of Non-objectivity

If the commission to design the Guggenheim Museum is arguably the most important of Wright's career, it was certainly the most time-consuming. The project involved Wright in varying degrees of intensity for nearly sixteen years, eventually leading him in 1954 to rent, on a permanent basis and in the city he had so often reviled, a suite in the Plaza Hotel, which he redecorated and named Taliesin the Third. Plans for the museum were begun in late 1943, reviewed by the client in 1944, and formally approved in

1945. Economic conditions in the immediate postwar period caused Guggenheim to delay. When he died in 1949, the project was called into question. After much debate, changes in personnel, and revisions to the design, construction finally began in 1956 and took a little more than two years to complete.[40] Wright supervised a good deal of it personally until his death in April 1959, six months before the museum was finished. When it opened in October it provoked probably more public discussion and critical attention than any previous modern building. Much of that revolved around the question of function, and so it is imperative for us to reconstruct what Wright was called upon to produce and how his ideas related to those of his original client.

Solomon R. Guggenheim belonged to one of the richest and most influential families in America, whose fortune had come from the mining of copper, tin, gold, diamonds, and rubber in the United States, Canada, South America, and Africa. The business was started by his father, Meyer Guggenheim, a Jew who had emigrated to the United States from Switzerland with his father, a tailor by trade, in 1847 at the age of nineteen.[41] Born in 1861, Solomon was the fourth oldest of the eight sons who inherited the company known as M. Guggenheim's Sons (incorporated 1882), out of which was later formed the partnership of Guggenheim Brothers (1916). Considered the most social, outgoing, and dandyish of the partners, Solomon became their major public relations figure. An inveterate hunter, he established shooting lodges in Scotland, Idaho, and eventually Yemassee, South Carolina, near Charleston, where he and his wife, Irene, a Rothschild, also had a winter home on the Battery.[42] Solomon owned an estate on Long Island, Trillora Court, an Italian villa originally known as Villa Carola when it was built for his brother Isaac in 1918–19 by H. Van Buren Magonigle. He also had a summer house called The Towers on the New Jersey shore, at the "Jewish Newport" resort of Elberon, as well as an apartment-sized suite in the Plaza Hotel, where he lived when in New York City and where he kept the major part of his ever-growing art collection.

Under the guidance of his wife, Solomon Guggenheim at first collected Old Master paintings, along with German and Italian primitives, exhibiting a taste in art as traditional in its orientation as was his taste in architecture and his lifestyle in general. But all that changed abruptly in the later 1920s, when, in his mid-sixties, he met a young, German-born artist, the Baroness Hilla Rebay von Ehrenwiesen (1890–1967). As Joan Lukach has shown, she would channel his interests in art toward a single, overwhelming passion: the abstract painting based on pure geometry that had been developed in Europe around 1910 by Wassily Kandinsky and others.[43]

Hilla Rebay was born in Strasbourg into the family of a Bavarian career officer. She studied art in Cologne and Paris after falling under the influence of Rudolf Steiner's mystical, religio-philosophical school of theosophy. After exhibiting in the Munich Spring Secession in 1913 and the Paris Salon des Indépendents, she moved to Berlin, where she spent the war years in direct contact with the fast-developing avant-garde art scene there. She became a close friend of Hans Arp and joined Der Sturm in 1917, where her paintings were shown alongside those of Kandinsky, Klee, Léger, Marc, Gleizes, and Ernst. It was also there that she met and became infatuated with Rudolf Bauer (1899–1953), the egomaniacal abstract painter who believed not only that he and Kandinsky were the two greatest living artists but also that they had transcended and superseded all previous art through their discovery of the cosmic "realm of the spirit" in the pure abstraction that Bauer and Rebay would christen "non-objectivity" (figs. 308, 309).[44] Bauer founded his own art movement, later a gallery (called Das Geistreich), and exercised a powerful, controlling influence over Rebay for nearly the remainder of his life, despite the tension and destructiveness of their personal relationship.

Partly to get away from Bauer and partly to prove herself, Rebay went to New York in 1927, as so many other Europeans were doing, in search of the modern "metropolis of tomorrow." Through art-world connections, she quickly moved into the upper-class circles that included the Whitneys, the de Peysters, the Burdon-Mullers, the Speyers, and the Guggenheims. To support herself while waiting for more long-term results from the exhibitions of her work that she was able to arrange, Rebay took on portrait commissions. Through the New York banker James Speyer, whose family was from Pittsburgh and was related to the Kaufmanns, she met Irene Guggenheim, who purchased some of her work and befriended the young artist, taking Rebay under her wing and arranging portrait commissions for her. One of those was of her husband, who sat for his portrait in 1928.

In her zeal to convince others of the supreme value and achievement of non-objective painting, Rebay became "a magnificently human projectile," as Wright later noted.[45] Her effect on Solomon Guggenheim was almost immediate. He later likened it to a religious conversion. Out of his new-found belief that "non-objectivity . . . eventually will have the greatest effect on leading the brotherhood of mankind to a more rhythmic creative life and so to peace," Guggenheim, under the direction of Rebay, began collecting contemporary abstract art with a dedication, as well as the wherewithal, few others of his generation possessed.[46]

In the summer of 1929, Rebay escorted the Guggenheims on their first European buying trip. They visited Kandinsky's studio in Paris and purchased his *Composition 8*, a major painting of 1923. By the end of the trip, Solomon Guggenheim had decided "to invest in a non-objective collection and leave it to the Metropolitan Museum," Rebay told Bauer, and had placed an account "at [her] disposal" for the purchase of works of art. By 1930, Guggenheim began thinking about building his own museum, which Rebay started referring to as a "Temple of Non-objectivity."[47] Rebay soon acquired paintings by Mondrian, Gleizes, Léger, Moholy-Nagy, and Delaunay, while continuing to increase the holdings of Bauer and Kandinsky. After a second trip to Europe in the summer of 1930, when they went to the Bauhaus to visit Kandinsky, Solomon Guggenheim redecorated his Plaza Hotel suite in a modern style and installed three rooms with paintings from the burgeoning collection.

Although the Depression put a temporary halt to Guggenheim's buying, the collection had grown to such an extent by 1933 that a Guggenheim Museum was apparently suggested as part of the cultural mall for Rockefeller Center that would also include the Museum of Modern Art and a new Metropolitan Opera House.[48] Rebay consulted the Viennese architect Frederick Kiesler, who was living in New York, about the project. Although discussions lasted until 1936, nothing came of the proposal. The desire on the part of both Guggenheim and Rebay to make the collection public and thereby gain a wider audience for abstract painting led them, beginning in 1936, to organize a series of traveling exhibitions. The final one opened in New York in January 1939 to coincide with the World's Fair. Called the "Art of Tomorrow," it inaugurated the new temporary Museum of Non-objective Painting, located on East Fifty-fourth Street, around the corner from the just completed Museum of Modern Art.[49]

The former townhouse was remodeled under the supervision of William Muschenheim, following Rebay's ideas. The galleries were done in soft, restful tones of white and gray, creating an atmosphere at once subdued and luxurious (fig. 307). The floors were laid with thick gray carpeting, and much of the wall surface was covered in pleated gray velour. The paintings, set in enormous silver frames "like precious stones," and hung against the velour background at nearly floor level, were to be viewed, under indirect lighting, from soft, velvet-covered seats while music of Bach and Chopin was piped into the room.[50] The museum remained at this location for ten years, during which time its reputation as a highly focused, rather eccentric, and quite personal institution developed in obvious comparison to its near neighbor, the more broad-based and market-oriented Museum of Modern Art.

Even before the temporary Museum of Non-objective Painting opened, Guggenheim set in motion plans for building a permanent home for his collection, which numbered over eight hundred works by 1939. In 1937 he established the Solomon R. Guggenheim Foundation to ensure the "promo-

307. William Muschenheim (with Hilla Rebay): Temporary Museum of Non-objective Painting, New York, 1939 (exhibition view, *In Memory of Wassily Kandinsky,* 1945).

tion and encouragement of art and education in art and the enlightenment of the public."[51] One of the foundation's principal objectives was the creation of a permanent museum to carry out the program of education. Rebay was initially named curator of the foundation, and then director. Shortly before the opening of the temporary museum, her duties were spelled out by Guggenheim to include everything from "the selection of pictures for exhibition [and] their arrangement and hanging," to "advice as to acquisition of new pictures," to "the consideration . . . of all scholarship and educational work, any and all lectures, talks or other statements as to the nature and meaning of the art, including the compilation of the catalogues." Guggenheim thus entrusted to Rebay complete direction of the foundation in matters of art, and it was she who determined its policies.[52]

Rebay expressed her ideas about art and defined the program of the Guggenheim Foundation in the essays she wrote for the catalogues accompanying the exhibitions held between 1936 and 1939. The source of Rebay's thinking lay in Kandinsky's writings, especially his *Concerning the Spiritual in Art* (1912) and *Point and Line to Plane* (1926), the latter co-translated by Rebay for an American audience in 1927.[53] Added to her characteristically modernist amalgam of spiritualism, German idealism, and Hegelian historicism was a good dose of Nietzschean and Crocean aesthetics and Bergsonian Creative Intuition. A dualistic opposition of matter and spirit underscored a linear theory of history that envisioned the final state of artistic progress, indicating the triumph of intuition over intellect, in the spiritual efflorescence of the type of abstract art she called non-objective.[54]

Rebay described the history of modern art as a progressive realization of the irrelevance of natural objects as models for pictorial representation, likening this to the shift from a pre-Copernican to a post-Copernican world: "The object is just as far from being the center of art as the earth is from being the focal point of the universe."[55] A series of experiments beginning in the nineteenth century led inexorably to this discovery. According to Rebay, "in an impres-

sionistic picture the painter reproduces a sensation or image he has received from nature" rather than making "a faithful copy of nature"; in the "expressionistic picture," the "painter uses even more artistic choice in emphasizing or exaggerating certain lines which strongly express what he considers worthwhile"; the "cubistic picture uses the object still more freely, . . . creating inventive form combinations in which nature is still needed for inspiration"; penultimately, "the abstract picture abstracts the object to its last constructive part," though it still "includes suggestion and reminiscence of an object to satisfy those who look for one"; finally, "the Non-objective picture stands by itself as an entirely free creation, conceived out of the intuitive enjoyment of space," with no reference whatsoever to the "objective" forms of nature.[56]

Abstraction was, in Rebay's way of thinking, simply a highly conventionalized mode of representation, a definition that Wright himself would have accepted. Non-objectivity, on the other hand, was an art of pure "space, form and line" directed toward the creation of "rhythmic balance" and "order." It was "the artistic realization of the present intense dynamic impetus of our time" and represented the culmination of all progress "from the materialistic to the spiritual."[57] In the search for "constant change in

308. Rudolf Bauer: *Tetraptychon: Symphony in Four Movements (Scherzo; Allegro; Andante; Allegretto)*, 1926–30.
309. Wassily Kandinsky: *Dominant Curve*, 1936.

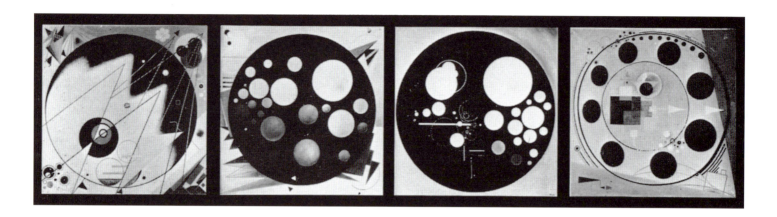

movement and form," the non-objective painter uses the "absolute forms" of geometry in the same way the composer uses musical notes (fig. 308). "The three basic forms of absolute beauty" were, according to Rebay, the circle, the square, and the triangle. It was with "these basic forms, like the keyboard of a piano," that the painter develops "themes."[58]

Although Rebay refused to admit that any of these "absolute" shapes of geometry might "stand as a symbol for some material object, or subjective thought," she ascribed a formal significance to each of them:

The circle is a self-centered continuity in itself, isolated and floating in its own concentration. . . . The square, compared to the circle, is a more powerful form of relationship

in space. The triangle directs its points from an indifferent base, but it is the only basic form submittable to variation of its dimensions without losing its identity as an absolute form.[59]

Rebay generally felt it necessary to resort to nature for "proof," however. The absoluteness and perfection of geometric shapes were demonstrated by their reflection in natural forms—the circle, for instance, being "realized in the appearance of the sun and moon." The pure shapes of geometry, she explained, point "beyond earthly reminiscence" to a world of space that may not be the material one of nature but is "definitely cosmic" (fig. 309). Because of its spatial rather than temporal character, non-objectivity transcends the "time-bound" world of music to engage the spectator in "the timeless quietness of a painting." In this way, non-objectivity prepares us "to receive the relaxing influence of nature's peace."[60]

Though programmatically antisymbolic and antireferential, non-objective paintings clearly had, for Rebay, a source in nature: "The cosmic order of creation [is] made visible in them." Non-objective paintings, she maintained, "are alive with spiritual rhythm and organic with the cosmic order which rules the universe," the "cosmic rule of sun, stars and earth." Like religious icons, they reveal a higher form of reality, which Rebay compared to the ideal world of pure, eternal forms described by "the great Lao Tze" and

Plato. "Being worlds of their own," works of non-objective art are "like the sun, the moon, the rain or the growth of a flower," she wrote. "The finality of these organic creations" puts them beyond words to describe. They are "prophets of spiritual life" heralding "the religion of the future." The experience of such paintings is epiphanic: "The startling advent of the first experience in feeling beauty in a non-objective picture seems to take a veil off eye, mind and soul, thus opening new vistas of joy beyond all former experience."[61]

The key factor in this interpretation of artistic experience as the "religious spirit of intuitive creation" was the substitution of passive reception for active engagement. The exercise of "intellectual willpower," in Rebay's view, was "inferior to intuitive response" on the part of both the artist and the spectator. "The intellectually conscious approach prevents spontaneous joy and a sensitive reaction to the wealth of creation." Intuition is a matter of feeling rather than understanding, and the act of submission "beyond all will or wishes" allows one to become "receptive to the influence and visual expression of cosmic power." "We are merely tunnels through which the spiritual wave must pass," Rebay declared. "All we can do is to refine and perfect this wave and keep the body receptive and sensitive." To be capable of moving the spectator, the work of art had to be "organic" in the sense of being "a flawless continuation of intuition from beginning to end."[62]

The communication through intuition gave non-objective art a value of a very practical sort, as well as an ethical purpose that lay well beyond that possessed by all previous, "materialistic" forms of art. On the more mundane level, non-objective painting acted as a physical and mental release of tension. "The contemplation of a Non-objective picture offers a complete rest to the mind," Rebay wrote. "It relaxes the fatigued intellect and elevates" the beholder "into the cosmic beyond where there is no meaning, no intellect, no explanation but something infinitely greater—the wealth of spiritual intelligence and beauty." The only way to describe this experience, however, was again in terms of natural images. Non-objective paintings, according to Rebay, "help one to forget earth and its troubles as most people do when they are looking up into the vastness of the starlit sky. One does not ask there, either, for meanings, symbols, titles, sense or intellectual explanation. One looks up and feels a vast beauty, and when the eye returns to the ground, its troubles seem to be much smaller."[63]

In this experience of "relaxation," "connecting the on-looker with the beyond of earth," was revealed the spiritual purpose of non-objective art. Rebay profoundly believed that the submission of the self to the power of non-objectivity would usher in "the bright millennium of cooperation and spirituality." "Where religions failed to stop murder and brutality," the "intuitive power" of non-objectivity "will spread and succeed . . . in creating understanding and consideration of others." "The pictures of non-objectivity," she wrote, "are the key to a world of unmaterialistic elevation. Educating humanity to respect and appreciate spiritual worth will unite nations more firmly than any league of nations." Only non-objectivity had this potential, for, unlike all previous art, its language was universal. Whereas earlier representational paintings, "using the individual language of a nation as a medium, are necessarily limited, intuitive creations are understandable to all nations alike through the universal language of art." "Educating everyone to intuitive reaction," Rebay admitted, "may seem to be Utopia," but "Utopias come true."[64]

Rebay's rhetoric was as messianic as her message was religious. She believed that the "spiritually gifted collector" Guggenheim had, with "intuitive foresight," "recognized the spirit of a new epoch leading into the future and proclaiming the unmaterialistic, non-objective age after centuries of materialistic confusion."[65] Rebay insisted that art had the power to transform human life. It was only a matter of faith. That "advance guard of elite" who had already received the message were duty-bound to prepare others for its "joyous influence" and "healing embrace." The ultimate goal had to be "the religious welfare of mankind."[66] This is how she conceived of the mission of a museum to house the non-objective paintings in Guggenheim's possession and what its architecture would have to represent despite the very material constraints of that medium:

The rare art collection of the Foundation creates a center of spiritual power. With it, a precious, priceless, non-commercial, and distinctive nucleus of influential masterpieces is starting the new art center of the world. It is to be a quiet, peaceful, elevating sanctuary for those who need a cultural life, and those who, by its influence, will become leaders of the future.[67]

Wright's Original Design of 1943–44

In many ways, Wright was both the least likely and the most likely choice to turn this vision of a "peaceful, elevating sanctuary" into the reality of a building when, in the early part of 1943, Guggenheim gave Rebay the go-ahead to begin planning for a permanent museum. Wright had never hidden his feelings about painting in general and modern art in particular. By almost any critical standard, he could be called a philistine, a member of those very masses Rebay wished to educate. Furthermore, the art Rebay championed was both abstract and European, just the kind of "sterile" foreign importation Wright had so vociferously opposed in the campaign against the International Style he continued to wage throughout the 1940s and 1950s.[68]

Yet, despite these obvious differences, Wright had much in common with Rebay and the art she championed. In his own decorative designs for the Coonleys, Midway Gardens, and the Imperial Hotel, for instance, he had pioneered a "non-objective" type of imagery that closely paralleled its pictorial development in Europe after 1910. Wright was of the same generation as Kandinsky and Mondrian, being a year younger than the former and four years older than the latter. And like them, though to a much more expressive and explicit degree, he derived his sense of geomet-

ric form from nature, finally evolving, as both of them did, a spiritual interpretation of the character of organic design and a cosmic vision of its implications.

More important in this context, however, is the degree to which Wright's "organic philosophy" could be read between the lines of Rebay's own exegesis of Kandinsky's art and thought. Indeed, only very shortly after meeting him, Rebay acknowledged to Wright how she felt that "in many ways [we] are so much alike in our reactions to earth, nature, and creation itself." Wright was precisely the type of misunderstood "genius" Rebay admired most.[69] Who else, indeed, was there by 1943 to rival Wright on that score? Certainly not Le Corbusier yet, nor Mies, nor Gropius, not to speak of Mendelsohn, Oud, or Kiesler. It was, in fact, in 1943, at the height of World War II, that Ayn Rand featured Wright as the embattled, egocentric, visionary hero of *The Fountainhead*, the quintessentially American rugged individualist. And although it is not clear how important it was for Guggenheim that the architect hired during this time of international crisis be an American, it is certain that Wright was the only American Rebay felt was worth considering.

The choice of Wright as architect for the Guggenheim Museum was by all accounts Rebay's own rather than Guggenheim's, although it is clear she did not arrive at the idea immediately or without help from others. Guggenheim apparently put all his trust in her on this matter, just as he did on all curatorial matters.[70] In the late spring of 1943, Rebay began canvassing her friends as to who they considered "a remarkable architect," stating that she herself was "often astonished how banal they all are." In response, her close friend Làszlò Moholy-Nagy, who had emigrated to Chicago, where he established the New Bauhaus in 1937, listed almost everyone but Wright and Mies. He mentioned Le Corbusier, Gropius, Neutra, Breuer, Aalto, and even George Keck, Paul Nelson, Werner Moser, Mart Stam, William Lescaze, a William Humbly, plus himself! Rebay had other intentions. She thanked Moholy for his advice, saying, "I think that Le Corbusier, Gropius and Neutra, whose development I well know, would never do for the work I have in mind." She intimated that she was looking for something more grand and monumental than technological and functional, something more in line with the "temple" or "sanctuary" she had earlier spoken of.[71]

Wright had recently been very much in the news, with a retrospective exhibition of his work at the Museum of Modern Art through the fall and winter of 1940–41, followed by the publication of Frederick Gutheim's collection of Wright's writings (1941), Hitchcock's *In the Nature of Materials* (1942), and the second edition of *An Autobiography* (1943), the "three books" Rebay was most likely referring to in her initial letter to Wright of June 1943. Rebay's connections, however, were primarily European, and it was probably not she who first thought of asking Wright. But when Wright's name was brought up by Irene Guggenheim, it apparently took little time for Rebay to be convinced of his appropriateness for the job. Less than a month after the search had begun, she wrote to Wright, saying, "functionalism does not agree with non-objectivity. . . . I want a temple of spirit, a monument! And your help to make it possible. . . . May this wish be blessed."[72]

Once the question was settled of where the first meeting would take place, Wright went to New York in mid-June to meet Rebay and Guggenheim. Although Guggenheim reportedly thought that some of Wright's recent buildings were "crazy," he apparently stressed to Wright that he wanted a museum unlike any other that existed, that only a totally radical solution would be appropriate to the type of paintings to be exhibited.[73] Wright must have assured him there would be no problem on this score, for the preliminary meeting was a success. On 29 June a contract was drawn up for a building to cost no more than $1 million, including the site. Since there was no site yet, the contract stipulated that if none was found "by July 1, 1944, this agreement shall be canceled."[74] Finding a place to build thus became the first priority. Wright offered to help, as that was clearly in his interest.

Wright returned to New York in early July and was escorted around the city by Robert Moses, New York's Parks Commissioner (who also happened to be distantly related to Wright by marriage). They looked at sites on Park Avenue, one next to the Museum of Modern Art, and another outside the city, in a park Moses had just created in the Spuyten Duyvil section of Riverdale, near the Henry Hudson Parkway.[75] The "hilltop" site overlooking the Hudson River was Wright's favorite. In reporting to Guggenheim on his findings, he denigrated the in-town sites as "the NOW. . . . not the future." Rather than "tie us down to the conventional idea of the Art Museum on hard pavements," the park site, Wright emphasized, would allow them to "build a new type of Treasury for works of art, one that would be a haven of refuge for city dwellers" and "the natural object of organized pilgrimage." He predicted that the new park "within a decade will be to Greater New York what Central Park is now to little old New York."[76]

Any idea of building outside the city, however, was soon scotched, for Rebay and Guggenheim wanted an easily accessible, highly visible presence in the cultural center of the city. In the meantime, Moses suggested another possibility, which Wright felt was the best of the "mid-traffic" sites considered so far. It was the southeast corner of Madison Avenue and Thirty-seventh Street, next to the Morgan Library, occupied by a nineteenth-century brownstone mansion that was formerly the residence of J. P. Morgan Jr.[77] While Guggenheim and Rebay investigated the idea of doing something in relation to Columbia University, the Morgan site remained the most promising possibility, at least in Wright's mind, until the decision was made in mid-March 1944 to purchase a property on the corner of Fifth Avenue and Eighty-ninth Street, a few blocks north of the Metropolitan Museum and directly opposite Central Park. Wright quite liked the chosen location and told Rebay that such "frontage on Central Park will be [the] preferred place for dignified or important buildings" within ten years, even though it "seems far away now."[78]

The program discussed at the first New York meeting was summarized by Guggenheim in the contract drawn up in late June 1943. The museum was to include "a suitable exhibition gallery, a small auditorium, offices and penthouse accommodation for rest and recreation, small study rooms for classwork and several larger studios for guest artists . . . all according to the requirements of Curator, Hilla Rebay."[79] To this were soon added a film center, a restaurant, and a small experimental theater for sound and projection.

Rebay set the tone and established the character of the museum. In the initial letters to Wright even before he came to New York, she described the collection as containing the "greatest masterpieces of art in existence." But because they are not "easel paintings" in the traditional sense of the word, meaning they do not create an illusion of perspectival three-dimensional space, she noted that they would have to "be organized into space." "As you feel the ground, the sky and the 'in-between' you will perhaps feel them too," she hoped, "and find the way." "I know what is needed," she added. "Nothing that is heavy, but organic, refined, sensitive to space most of all."[80] The space should help create an "order" appropriate to the paintings that would allow them to be received in the "spirit" they were created.

Rebay had been dreaming about her "temple of spirit" for more than ten years and had discussed it with Rudolf Bauer, among others, on numerous occasions.[81] As she first imagined it in 1930, she told Bauer: "I believe that a museum should be built in a fabulous style, with a room for resting, a large room, where pictures can be well cared for, so as always to rotate, only a few to be hung." This main space was preceded by an antechamber with "blue ceiling lights, like Napoleon's Tomb in Paris; a room for composure, warmth, and rest, where one can get away from the noise of the streets before entering the temple of art." The visionary "Temple of Non-objectivity and devotion," as she called it ("'Temple' is better than 'Church'"), would exude a sense of permanence and "reach a standard to enable it to endure well past the year 2000." "Yes, one could build something fabulous, it must become the standard for greatness for all nations, truly the Temple of Peace in the universe."[82]

When the possibility of building within the context of Rockefeller Center came up in the mid-1930s, Rebay refined her ideas and made them more precise by contrasting the Guggenheim Museum with its projected neighbor, the Museum of Modern Art. Hers, she said, "will be much grander, more exalted, nobler and more important than their museum which will have many floors with offices and constantly changing exhibitions and activities." Again, she referred to the proposed Guggenheim Museum as an "edifice, or temple," in order to communicate the proper sense of monumental, nonfunctional imagery it had to embody.[83]

Rebay discussed the idea with Bauer over the next few years, and he agreed with her dislike for "constantly changing exhibitions" and stressed that the building should be large enough so that the pictures would not have to be rotated. "The collection must not change," he stated, "it must be a permanent one." He allowed that a single, separate room could be set aside to "show new works not belonging to the collection." Bauer compared the museum, as a type, to the church and said it should be built in a "timeless" style, developing "from this exterior, a crescendo towards the interior."[84] According to Richard Hennessey, both Bauer and Rebay seem to have arrived at the notion that ramps should replace stairs in order to create a more organic, more contemplative environment, and that the paintings themselves should not be framed but set directly into niche-like cavities in the walls.[85] "Long before I knew you," Rebay later wrote to Wright, "my coming museum was to go up as a spiral and have no stairs, nor was an entrance to be seen."[86]

There is no way of knowing whether this last statement is entirely accurate. In 1937 Rebay proposed a pavilion around a circular courtyard to exhibit the Guggenheim Collection at the 1939 New York World's Fair, but it was only one-story high (fig. 310). Each pie-shaped gallery projected from a ring surrounding the enclosed garden, like the spokes of a wheel.[87] The interiors that she created for the temporary Museum of Non-objective Painting in 1939, on the other hand, give evidence of what she considered to be the most crucial aspects of displaying works of art. She believed that the design had to create a total environment or ambience conducive to an "intuitive" response. It should be a soft, rarefied, and relaxing atmosphere, hushed and somewhat mysterious, like that of a church (fig. 307). Background music and dim lighting were key elements in ensuring that the passive, contemplative spectator, overcome by waves of spiritual energy, would be wafted to higher levels of being.

Rebay naturally took Wright to see the Museum of Non-objective Painting when he came to New York in June 1943. Afterward, she sent him a note to remind him that she wanted nothing that smacked of natural, "earthly" imagery. Although impressed with the Johnson Wax building, she told him to "forget the 'forest,' the trees, as we want no abstraction of any existing growth." She elaborated on her concept of a sanctuary for the spirit, imploring Wright to embody its "cosmic breath" in his design:

With infinity and sacred depth create the dome of spirit: expression of the cosmic breath itself—bring light to light! . . . Let us not compare, not outshine, not contrast anything— let us be reverent to the spirit in everything created. . . . In dignity, quiet and out of love for the magic spell of spiritual order and infinite grace, let us create a shrine to forget our personal illusions to be healingly embraced with perfected harmony by the order of spiritual reality.[88]

Although Rebay was the intellectual force behind the program and was mainly responsible for articulating it, Solomon Guggenheim clearly had veto power, and thus his interests and ideas were naturally taken into account by any architect as savvy as Wright. He respected Guggenheim for his forward-looking attitude toward art. Early in their discussions, Wright described the project to him as "a true memorial . . . to your vision as a pioneer," "your memorial building."[89] The Guggenheim Museum was, in effect, to be a memorial to its founder and a permanent home for his collection.

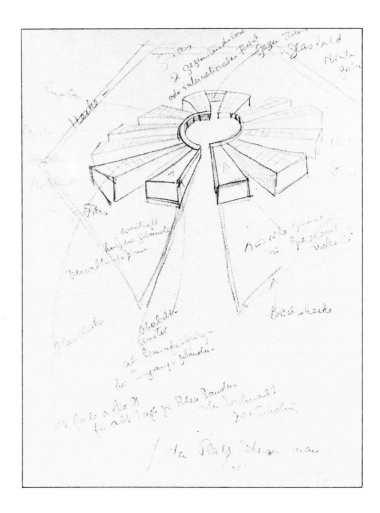

Guggenheim agreed with Rebay that an appreciation of the "permanent, silent and powerful influence" of non-objective art would lead people "to higher realities of aesthetics, . . . beyond materialistic needs," and that this "is the only solid way to peace" and "the brotherhood of mankind."[90] But on a more prosaic and personal level, Guggenheim saw art as a special form of relaxation. "All day as a businessman I look at graphs and figures," he told Daniel Catton Rich in 1932. "It's good to come home at night and look at these paintings. They rest my eyes." And to Rebay he wrote in 1944: "What relaxation you have given me in the way of Non-objective Art, which has proven such a diversion for me from my many business matters."[91] To preserve in a public building this type of intimate experience, Wright said, Guggenheim insisted the museum be like one's own home or, indeed, the artist's studio. "Mr. Guggenheim wanted his people to see a picture much as the artist himself saw it in changing light and whoever owned it might see it." "He wanted," Wright explained, "a home for these paintings"; they "were not only to be seen but *enjoyed*."[92]

From all that we can tell, however, Guggenheim agreed with Rebay that the "home" the museum was to provide for the foundation's collection was in no way to be thought of as either a small-scale, unimposing, domestic environment or a flexible, utilitarian space for changing exhibitions and a constantly growing collection. Nor was it to be analogous to, say, the Frick Museum. Wright often stated that, at the outset of their discussions, Guggenheim insisted he did not want "just another museum." He wanted Wright to create an environment specifically adapted to the revolutionary forms of the paintings in the collection, which would serve to encourage changes in the way people thought about and looked at paintings.[93]

One idea, above all, seems to have been beyond dispute: the Guggenheim Museum was to house, in a permanent fashion, a collection of paintings that would be considered more or less complete when Solomon Guggenheim died, and absolutely so when Rebay did. Guggenheim envisaged the projected building, in 1944, as "enclosing all of our present paintings, and probably some additional ones which we will have acquired in the meantime." In the adjunct to his will, written five years later, he told the trustees of the foundation that it was his "wish that during the lifetime of Miss Rebay the Foundation accept no gifts and make no purchases of paintings without her approval, and that after her death the Foundation make no addition to its collection of paintings, unless they come from Mr. Bauer."[94]

The program for the Guggenheim Museum was, in many ways, as open-ended as the one for Aline Barnsdall's cultural center on Olive Hill. Like the earlier project, it included living quarters for staff along with facilities for the presentation of works of art. Moreover, it would initially be designed without a definite site—something Wright rarely did—as a way of "showing the possibilities of building . . . the ideal building."[95] As a "memorial building," the museum would have to be *representational* in the traditional

sense of the word, which is to say, impressive, perhaps even theatrical. It was to be elitist, didactic. It was to create an atmosphere that would sweep people off their feet and elevate them into the spiritual realm of non-objectivity. It was to do that through the ordering power of space. It was in no way to be a "functionalist" solution to the problem. It was to be a temple, a monument, a "dome of spirit," a modern-day church. It would be the *gesamtkunstwerk* of the twentieth century, with the "greatest architect" alive, according to Rebay, providing a "suitable" atmosphere for the viewing of paintings by the two greatest painters in history, Kandinsky and Bauer.[96] It would be a permanent "home" to the achievements of non-objectivity. The Guggenheim Museum, as Wright was told of it in 1943, was to be a sacred building in a secular society, an expression of the utopian ideals that modern art instilled in those who believed it to be the twentieth-century counterpart of religion.

■ ■ ■

Wright did not immediately turn to the Gordon Strong project as a point of departure, even though the hilltop site he originally preferred in Riverdale could have been likened to Sugarloaf Mountain. Robert Moses remembered from their reconnaissance trip that Wright began by thinking of a composition of "low horizontal buildings." This is substantiated by Wright's report to Guggenheim, in which he said that the Riverdale site would give them "the chance to create a truly creative group of buildings . . . , embracing gardens and attractive courts."[97] No drawings exist from this very preliminary stage, and it is doubtful any were made. But we know that Wright continued to think in terms of a low, spreading building even after the decision to remain within the city. He kept up a fairly regular correspondence with Rebay in which he outlined his developing thoughts. Toward the end of the summer of 1943, she cautioned that "this crawling in wide extensions" lacked a certain spiritual expression and advised Wright to think more loftily: "I feel that what we are doing, and what I want to see expressed, is completely a new task, which will inspire you to a sensitiveness, that will not only spread horizontally, but also vertically, up to the infinite infinity of space." She wanted the building to combine the "two poles" into "the one rhythm," to "embrace the sky as much as the earth."[98]

During the fall of that year, Wright worried about the "unwillingness of the Guggenheim people to close a deal promptly" and kept pushing for the site next to the Morgan Library. In his mind, he actually began to think of the deal as done and probably began drawings at that time.[99] In early October he told Herbert Johnson, who had just commissioned the Research Tower for the Racine headquarters, that he was "using the technique" of Pyrex glass tubing developed in the earlier Johnson Wax building "to build a great million dollar building on Madison Avenue next [to] the Morgan Library . . . to house the Guggenheim Collection."[100] If indeed Wright had actually reached the point of deciding on the materials he would use, he certainly did not tell Rebay or Guggenheim that he had gotten so far ahead of the game. On the contrary, he wrote to Rebay in mid-December, saying how desperate was his "hope [that] we can get a plot" soon, since "I am so full of ideas for our museum that I am likely to blow up or commit suicide unless I can let them out on paper. That building ought to show how to show a painting." Two weeks later, he sent Rebay a telegram: "BELIEVE THAT BY CHANGING OUR IDEA OF A BUILDING FROM HORIZONTAL TO PERPENDICULAR WE CAN GO WHERE WE PLEASE. WOULD LIKE TO PRESENT THE IMPLICATIONS OF THIS CHANGE TO MR. GUGGENHEIM FOR SANCTION."[101]

Wright followed this up with a letter to Guggenheim in which he concluded that "it now seems probable that our desire for a horizontal building is incompatible with real estate values in that part of New York where you would be pleased to have the museum built." To inspire Guggenheim to action, he noted: "I can see a tall building of a new type perfectly appropriate to our purpose having monumental dignity and great beauty, requiring about half the ground area we have been looking for." He asked if he might come to New York to settle, at least provisionally, on some location ("to take an option on the plot for, say, sixty days") so that he could "prepare tentative sketches showing the possi-

bilities of building . . . the ideal building." Guggenheim, however, firmly believed that once the war was over prices would come down and told Wright "this is not the time to act."[102]

Fearful that the project might get bogged down, Rebay pushed Wright to go ahead with the plans in the hope they might entice Guggenheim into building. The idea was to take the location next to the Morgan Library as an imaginary site, something Wright had no doubt already done. In early January 1944, he sent a telegram to Rebay to assure her that his revised idea for a "PERPENDICULAR" building should in no way make her think of "OFFICE ARCHITECTURE." Rather, he had in mind a "NOBLE BUILDING MORE APPROPRIATE TO TIME SPACE AND PURPOSE. SPACIOUS HORIZONTALLY GOING UPWARD ON WINGS."[103] By 20 January, the design had begun to take shape along the lines of the Gordon Strong project.

Realizing how thoroughly unexpected such a building might appear, Wright felt compelled to warn Rebay (and thus Guggenheim) that they "may be shocked by what is in my mind when it gets on paper." "The whole thing will either throw you off your guard entirely or be just about what you have been dreaming about!" "Anything more modern, less stuffy and conventional, you have never seen," he added. "Nor anything so ideal for your purpose." By way of explanation, Wright began by saying that, for non-objective paintings to be fully appreciated, they "must be related to environment in due proportion." He criticized the conditions in the existing temporary galleries, remarking that the excessive height of the ceilings tended to "dwarf" the "significance and scale" of the paintings and that the textured coverings of the walls were distracting. "A museum should have above all a clear atmosphere of light and sympathetic surface," he said. He particularly opposed the heavy gilt frames, claiming that frames were not necessary at all: "Frames were always an expedient that segregated and masked the paintings off from [the] environment to its own loss of relationship and proportion, etc., etc."[104]

Wright maintained that his design would emphasize the totality of the aesthetic experience by making painting and architecture work together to form a unified environment with an all-pervasive atmosphere of receptivity. The building would be "one extended expansive well proportioned floor space from bottom to top." The ease of it would be like "a wheel chair going around and up and down, *throughout*."[105] There would be "no stops anywhere"; the only visible interruptions would be "such screened divisions of the space gloriously lit within from above as would deal appropriately with every group of paintings or individual paintings as you might want them classified." There would be "day-light throughout," making "the atmosphere of the whole . . . luminous from bright to dark."[106] A "superb entrance" would lead into "a top-lighted court" where there would be "galleries running around the sides," with "a great calm and breadth pervading the whole place." The plan would be "adaptable to the [typical] New York plot depth of 100 feet or less and more or less length. . . . A corner, however, is necessary."[107]

Despite the rather lengthy description of the project, Wright did not actually provide Rebay with a visual image. A week later he did so, although in a rather offhand way. In a chatty letter otherwise devoted to the doings of his daughter Iovanna, who had been seeing Rebay in New York, Wright remarked that "the antique Ziggurat has great possibilities for our building. You will see. We can use it either top side down or down side top." After informing her of his work for the Whitneys at Florida Southern, he ended by saying that he hoped to see Rebay "before long," at which time "we'll have some fun with the modern version of the Ziggurat."[108]

■ ■ ■

The first presentation of the preliminary plans most probably took place in late February or March 1944.[109] It is unclear whether Rebay was accompanied by Guggenheim at this meeting. It is also unclear how "shocked" she (they) was (were). What we do know is that, following it, attention turned to more specific issues of interior arrangement and refinements to the program. These revisions were further complicated by the announcement in late March that a site on upper Fifth Avenue, at the southeast corner of Eighty-ninth Street, had been purchased.[110] Wright, of course, was greatly "relieved" by that turn of events, even though it would necessitate redrawing all the plans. He told Rebay that he thought "the idea suits the [new] plot we have even better than the imaginary one." In terms of overall area, the two plots were "nearly *almost exactly the same*." The major differences were that the Fifth Avenue site was shorter though deeper and had its corner exposure on the left side rather than the right.[111]

With the site finally settled, Rebay and Wright turned to specifics. They decided that a restaurant should be included, that there should be space for a film center, and that there should be provision for a separate "grand gallery" in which to exhibit the major paintings of the collection. Rebay described this last feature, in almost funereal terms, as an "impressive quite high roofed hall, a sanctum and as quiet as possible, carpets and softness to rest the greatest of all paintings permanently." Wright thought this "Holy of Holies" should be on the *piano nobile*, or "main floor, not on the ground floor." Rebay also requested a completely separate area, or wing, in which to install the representational paintings Guggenheim had collected as historical "precursors" to non-objectivity.[112]

Very little had been said so far about how the paintings would actually be installed in a building composed of a single continuous ramp. Rebay showed some signs of worry over the need to exert oneself by constantly climbing. "Never speak of 'a climb' in the new building," Wright responded. "You only take an easy walk slightly—very slightly—uphill." He added, no doubt thinking of Rebay's concern for Guggenheim, that "the whole building will be a paradise for elderly or tired people to see beautiful things."[113] Rebay was already receiving dire warnings from friends like Moholy-Nagy and Bauer, who had no particular fondness for Wright, that the building would never work as a museum. Discussions on that score became heated only after the revised preliminary plans were approved, although

Solomon R. Guggenheim Museum, New York, 1943–59. Scheme C, 1943–44.

311. Perspective.   312. Plan.

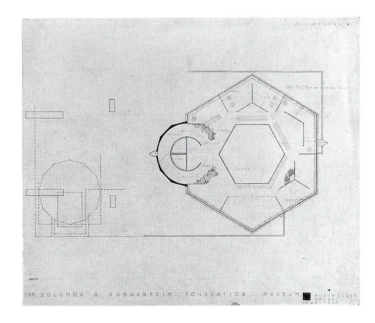

it may well have been a growing "'nervous' state of apprehension" on the part of both Rebay and Guggenheim that led to a full-scale review of the plans in July 1944.[114]

Between the fall of 1943 and early spring of 1944, Wright worked up four different versions of the preliminary design, which he called schemes A–D. This, for him, was a highly unusual procedure and can probably be explained by the original indecision over a site, coupled with the extraordinary importance of the job. After learning of the purchase of the Fifth Avenue property, Wright revised the scheme he thought best to conform with the actual site.[115] In July, he took the plans to New Hampshire, where Guggenheim was vacationing, to go over them with him and Rebay. On 27 July, Guggenheim approved the design and authorized Wright "to proceed to make detailed plans" as well as a model.[116]

Schemes A, B, C, and D were all based on the same *parti*; only their geometries and brightly colored marble exteriors differed. One was hexagonal, the other three variations on a circle. The colors ranged from red, to white, to orange, to a combination of white marble and verdigris copper. The key element was an approximately eight-story "tower" occupying the right half of the site (figs. 311, 315). This more or less freestanding unit contained the galleries around an open, skylit atrium, or "crystal court," as Wright called it.[117] In the basement was an auditorium, and around the top ring of galleries were artists' studios. A taller and much thinner vertical circulation core intersected one side of the main tower and joined it to a lower, four-story wing hooking around the left side of the site. This section provided space for storage, classrooms, and Rebay's apartment. A domed "ocular chamber" for experimental sound and light projections occupied the front corner. This wing was raised on piers to allow for off-street parking. It was connected to the circulation core and gallery tower by a series of terraces and bridges serving as roof gardens. The ground floor of the museum proper was entirely open to the street, making the tower seem to float above it.

The project based on the hexagon (scheme C) was the only one of the four to have level gallery floors rather than a continuous inclined ramp (figs. 311, 312). A subsidiary ramp, however, spiraled around the outside of the vertical circulation core (containing two quarter-circle elevators) to connect one level of galleries to the next. The walls of the galleries tilted out at an angle and were washed with natural light from a band of skylights made of Pyrex glass tubing. Their exterior surface was covered in verdigris copper sheets, while the solid bands above and below were revetted

Guggenheim Museum.
313. Scheme B, 1943–44. Perspective.
314. Scheme A, 1943–44. Perspective.

perspective shows a pool and fountain in the center, dramatically spotlit by the telescopic "crystal court."

The key to the final two schemes (A and D) was the inversion of the pyramidal ziggurat and the crowning of its atrium court with a tubular glass dome. The differences between the two final schemes were more a matter of development and refinement than of basic premise. In fact, only one of the two (A) was worked out, and it was this one that formed the basis for Wright's presentation to Guggenheim and Rebay in New Hampshire.[118] A colored, cutaway elevation/section shows how the interior space opened up as it rose under the shallow glass dome (fig. 291). The drawing is labeled "Ziggurat," under which is written the German spelling of the word, "Zikkurat," as if to emphasize the archaeological reference of the form. Even more significant, however, is the word "Taruggitz," written just to the right of the other two.[119] The spelling of ziggurat backward functions as a verbal analogue for the process of inversion by which Wright arrived at the "top side down" form of this scheme. It not only reveals his self-consciousness in appropriating the ancient, historical model of the ziggurat, but also suggests the intention that it be read *in opposition to the past*.[120]

Scheme A was broader and squatter in proportion than scheme D. Its middle rings were differentiated from the lower and upper ones by being tilted out at an angle to create the impression of an organically expanding volume (figs. 314, 315). The plan was generated from the intersection of a smaller circle with a larger one, the composition of the two looking like the abstracted section of a human eye (fig. 316). The broad arc of the public entrance occupied the quadrant between the cylindrical circulation core, near the center of the plot, and the pier at the edge of the sidewalk that supported the bridge-like terrace of the canopy. To the left was the protected off-street delivery and parking area, with direct access to offices and storage areas above. To the right, the nearly quarter-circle wall of plate-glass doors revealed the expanse of the circular "crystal court," lit from above by the approximately eight-story-high glass dome.

in white marble. An extruded, hexagonal roof-comb of glass tubing linked the circulation core to the open court of the gallery tower by an inverted light trough.

That same skylight arrangement appeared in scheme B, but there it connected a cylindrical, brick circulation tower to a red marble ziggurat based on the Gordon Strong Tower of Babel (fig. 313). In this version, the galleries followed an inclined ramp winding around in a counterclockwise fashion and narrowing as it rose through approximately six turns. The outside walls were perpendicular and the distance between them, from one revolution to the next, provided space for the continuous band of skylights. The

Above:
315. Guggenheim Museum. Scheme A. Section.

Below: Guggenheim Museum. Schemes A/D.

316 (*left*). Plan, ground floor.

317 (*right*). Plan, main floor (second level).

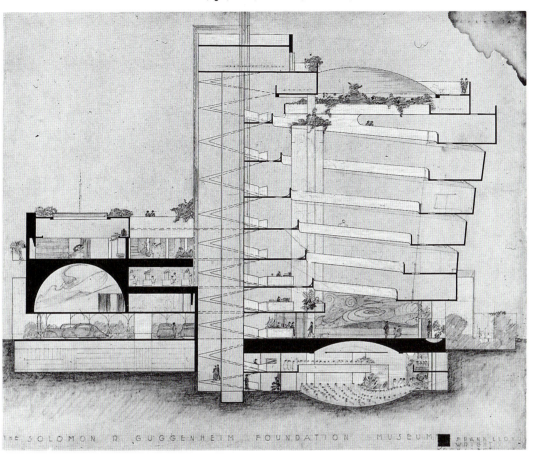

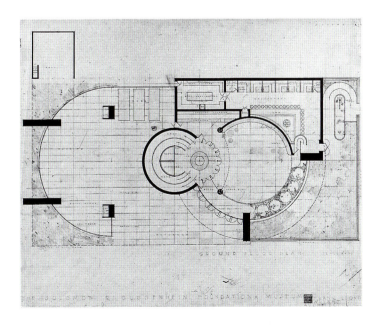

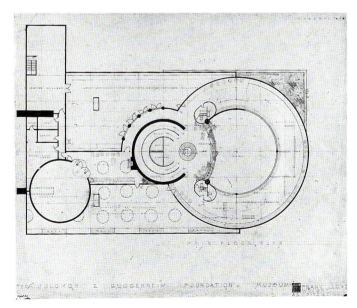

Behind a curved mural above a continuous bench-seat, the dramatic and monumental public space led to a restaurant. A continuation of the plate-glass wall in the other quadrant facing the street allowed light to flood in at ground level. It provided a view of the outdoors to relieve "museum fatigue" and a point of orientation in an otherwise hermetically sealed, climate-controlled, self-enclosed space.[121]

The actual entrance to the galleries was through a semicircle of glass doors that led to a circular reception desk under the bow-shaped balcony of the second, or main, floor. The semicylindrical elevator core, surrounded by a double-helix system of ramps, gave access to the basement auditorium and to the main information and sales desk on the second floor (fig. 317). Immediately behind the vertical circulation core, on this floor, was a corridor leading to a large storage area that could also be used for "intimate galleries" (presumably the ones for the "historical precursors") as well as to the domed "ocular chamber" for experimental films. Tucked behind them was a "sales gallery." (The upper floors of this wing were set aside for additional storage, classrooms, administrative offices, and a penthouse apartment for Rebay.)

The main ramp of the galleries began at the second-floor sales desk and wound its way up counterclockwise, without interruption, through six turns (fig. 315). A "rift" of tubular glass beneath each successive overhang washed the tilted plane of the curved outside wall in a continuous stream of natural light, while a band of glass set into the floor of the ramp near the interior parapet allowed the light from the dome to penetrate from one floor level to the next. The galleries, which expanded outward as they rose, remained the same in width until the top level, although they gradually increased in height. At the top, the ramp wound around a ring of artists' studios, encircling the base of the glass dome, before emerging onto a roof terrace. Movement up or down the spiral structure could be accomplished rapidly by means of the elevator, or a little more slowly by taking the concentric ramps surrounding it, or even more

slowly, but more profitably and enjoyably, by following the main ramp of galleries along which the spiritually elevating non-objective masterpieces were to be installed as independent "features" of the overall spatial experience.[122]

■ ■ ■

Above and beyond the hypothetical nature of the site, many important aspects of the museum's design were not fully worked out in schemes A–D. Neither the materials nor the methods of construction were explicitly indicated, nor was the system for hanging and installing the paintings, although Wright had begun to develop ideas on this matter (fig. 318). The schematic nature of the design even extended to the system of circulation, which did not clearly show any definite sense of direction or climax, despite the basic linearity of the spiral form.[123] When Wright was forced to adapt scheme A to the actual Fifth Avenue site, in all likelihood for the presentation in July 1944, he began to pin down many of these issues, and the final working drawings of a little over a year later reflect the changes. But the main point of discussion between Rebay and Wright following Guggenheim's approval of the revised preliminary plans centered on their adaptability to the specific needs of exhibiting and viewing works of art.

Wright's scheme for an inverted ziggurat with a single uninterrupted gallery unfolding along a continuously inclined ramp was so seemingly relentless in its logic and so self-contained in its form that Rebay, though deeming it "wonderful in itself" and enthusiastic about its cosmic "embrace" of sky and earth, was concerned about whether the building would not dominate and overpower the paintings. "While I have no doubt that your building will be a great monument to yourself," she wrote to Wright in January 1945, "I cannot visualize how much (or how little) it will do for the paintings. . . . We need a monument to painting also which is our main interest." Rebay was apparently egged on by her friends, who warned her of Wright's intransigence

and dislike for modern art and suggested that she get a second opinion on the design of the building's interior from another architect, such as Mies.[124]

Rebay never pursued this option, but she did push Wright to be more specific about "how a painting should be built in—how light it will be," about "how definitions can be given to different sections before entering them without wall inscriptions," and about how she could "close some of the galleries against noise   against each other—[to] create intimacy and peace."[125]

Wright tried to assure Rebay that "the great ramp" could be cut "into separate rooms or alcoves or sub galleries lengthwise or crosswise" and that, by its very nature, it "yields infinite possibilities of division—privacy—or whatever have you, when and wherever you want it." But he constantly returned to the overall conception as the essential issue, claiming that "the building itself . . . creates an atmosphere congenial to the type of painting you are representing," in contrast to "the orthodox environment" in which "modern painting of the non-objective type has been out of place." By its acknowledgement and transformation of the "*principles* represented by those works" into an environment "integral" with them, the building would allow the paintings to appear "more brilliantly effective" than ever before.[126]

Rebay wanted to be convinced, so she asked Wright to construct a test wall in early 1945. He had already produced some sketches showing alternative systems of movable partitions, screens forming alcoves, different-shaped compartments, and even "loose-leaf" hinged panels, all related to seating arrangements similar to those in the temporary museum (figs. 318, 307). Wright felt that a test wall would not be as informative as the large plexiglass model he was building, and he urged Rebay to wait until that was finished.[127] He maintained that no tests or partial mock-ups would really tell her anything, for they could never reproduce the actual conditions of natural light and three-dimensional space of the *entire* building in which the paintings would

eventually be seen and on which their perception, in the fullest sense of the word, would depend.

Wright tried to explain that a painting is not an isolated phenomenon or aesthetic object independent of outside influences and forces, existing in a neutral (read: "orthodox") environment. Its spiritual significance could be appreciated only when it "appears integral with the environment," and the environment could be judged, like the painting, only in its actual presence. The situation might be likened to a problem in acoustics. Regardless of countless theoretical calculations and small-scale models, the sound of the music ultimately depends on the total spatial and structural organism of the hall as finally realized in actual materials and dimensions.[128]

"The Modern Gallery" of 1945

Wright called the final project for the Guggenheim Museum "The Modern Gallery." The plans and model were completed during the summer of 1945, and their announcement was treated as a major public event. An initial presentation took place at a luncheon held for the press at the Plaza Hotel on 9 July 1945.[129] Between then and 20 September, when the model was exhibited at a second press conference (fig. 319), Wright completed a revised set of plans, dated 7 September 1945, and signed and approved by Guggenheim. *Time*, *Life*, *The Museum News*, *Architectural Forum*, *The Magazine of Art*, and *Mouseion* devoted articles to the new building.[130]

Following the first revision of the previous July, the final plans were adapted to the site on the corner of Fifth Avenue and East Eighty-ninth Street, comprising a little over half the block facing Central Park. From a purely physical point of view, there were two main differences between this site and the imaginary Morgan Library one: first, it was more square in shape, being shorter and deeper (145 by 25 feet); second, it was west-facing, with its corner on the north, rather than north-facing, with its corner on the west. To accommodate the difference in orientation, Wright flipped the plan over, placing the spiral "tower" element at the corner to the left (north), and the subsidiary office/apartment/ocular chamber wing against the lot line of the existing townhouse on the right (south) (fig. 324).

To compensate for the reduced length of the plot, Wright took advantage of the greater depth to rotate the cylinder of the vertical circulation core thirty degrees off the line it had occupied in scheme A parallel to the street. The elevator core was brought closer to the center of the main circle of the museum, making it a more integral part of the overall spatial flow and creating a dynamic interaction between the different-sized circles of the main gallery, the ocular chamber, the circulation core, and its two attendant service nodules.[131] An open court was introduced between the circulation tower and the adjacent wing, bringing light into the offices and rooms around it and exposing the circular shaft of the tower in its full, 125-foot height.[132]

Describing the building as a "steel basket shot with concrete," Wright told the reporters at the first press conference that it would be as "plastic [as] the form of a rising spiral" and "virtually indestructible by natural forces."[133] The prestressed reinforced-concrete structure, using expanded steel mesh, was to be surfaced with concrete shot from a gun under high pressure. The vertical circulation core, with its two continuous pipe shafts for heating and ventilating ducts, created a backbone for the rest of the structure (figs. 320, 325). The floors of the ramp were stiffened by their upturned parapets and were designed to be supported mainly by the splayed bands of enclosing wall. (In the early stages, thin, cigar-shaped columns, like struts, helped to brace the floors near their inner edge.) The system was a realization of Wright's idea for the trays of Falling-water, where he wanted to make the parapets and floors totally integral by supporting the latter from the former. In the proposed solution for the Guggenheim, "the construction of the great ramp," Wright said, "like that of a sea-shell, is clear of interior supports of any kind, the fibrous floors being carried throughout from the outer walls."[134]

Instead of being revetted with thin slabs of marble, the exterior surfaces of gunnite were to be coated with a sand-blasted and polished marble aggregate, so as to give the appearance of being "a monolith without joints."[135] Almost all the sources of light, as well as the cylindrical elevator shaft, were to be of Pyrex glass tubing, a material Wright had been experimenting with for use as a walling element and as a means of domical construction in the design of the Research Tower and advertising offices of the Johnson Wax Company (1943–50; fig. 321). The question of color, however, was left somewhat vague, because Rebay and Wright could not seem to come to an agreement. Wright favored red for the exterior, with a tone like "rose with white veins," and, at least initially, a very light "warm-grey" for the interior. Rebay thought red too "materialistic."[136] Wright did, however, specify red marble slabs, cut in squares, to cover the entire ground floor, both inside and out.

The glass tubing was used structurally in situations that called for it to be laid horizontally and vertically as well as circularly. In the preliminary scheme A, the twin quarter-circle elevators occupied the rear half of the circular shaft that was, in turn, encased in a solid wall surrounded by a double ramp. The circulation tower thus became a fairly dark and tight space (fig. 316). The ramp was now reduced

319. Wright with model of "The Modern Gallery" (September 1945).

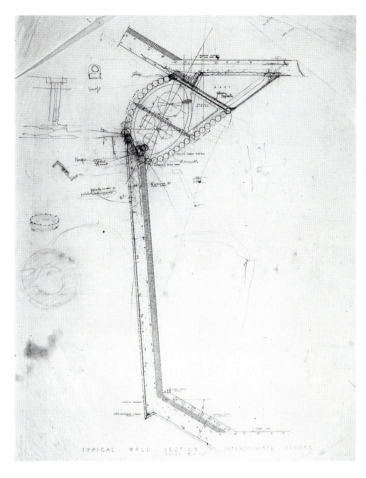

On opposite page:
320. Guggenheim Museum. "The Modern Gallery," 1945. Model, interior.

Above, left:
321. Johnson Wax Administration Building. Advertising department, reception area, 1943–50.

Above, right:
322. Guggenheim Museum. "The Modern Gallery." Section through exterior wall.

Left:
323. Guggenheim Museum. "The Modern Gallery." Glass tubing details.

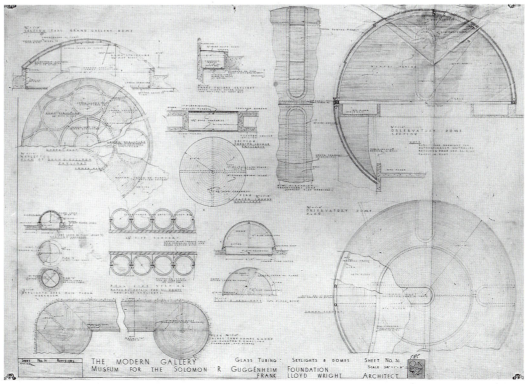

to a single depth by making it double-tiered, leaving an open lightwell between it and the elevator shaft. The latter was redesigned as a clear semicircular tube of Pyrex glass, creating a freestanding, translucent column in space extending from the ground level up to the glass dome that capped it (fig. 320). (At one stage in the design, Wright rotated the semicircular shaft 180 degrees to project its convex face into the space of the ramp.) The skylights, or "rifts," running along the outer edge of the galleries of the main ramp were composed of a double layer of horizontal glass tubes attached to metal frames and welded to steel struts that also served to brace the concrete structure (fig. 322). Within the hollow, at the base of the trough, were lighting fixtures to supplement the daylight; along the top, a plate mirror was to reflect the light onto the outwardly tilted wall surface.

Both the main atrium court and the circulation tower were covered with domes of glass tubing laid in diminishing concentric circles (fig. 319). The glass tubes, jointed with mastic, were also employed in the numerous smaller bubble skylights throughout the building (fig. 323). The twenty-five-foot-diameter revolving dome over the circulation tower was hemispherical, whereas the nearly sixty-foot-diameter one over the main court was segmental in shape. The latter was also double in thickness to allow the trapped space to be heated or cooled. The stainless steel tubes keeping the two layers apart were arranged in a pattern of circles diminishing in size toward a compression ring at the top, a design similar to the dome planned for the reception area of the advertising offices of the Johnson Wax Company headquarters (fig. 321). Because of the double layer of tubing, the oculus would have been "translucent rather than transparent"; and in the diffused, opalescent light, the descending circles of reflective stainless steel would have looked like droplets of water in suspension.[137] Much more than merely a neutral covering now, the dome reverberated in space the underlying geometry of the building and provided an appropriately dematerialized conclusion.

Aside from the flipping of the plan and the new diago-

nal orientation of the circulation tower, the basic organization and interrelation of functions remained the same as in scheme A. Everything, however, was made more fluid, more dynamic, and more dramatic. Wright took advantage of the added depth of the lot to make the vehicular entrance a through-drive curving around the circulation tower and exiting onto Eighty-ninth Street. The red marble paving beginning at the sidewalk and continuing through to the rear made the ground floor, inside and out, seem like a permanent "red carpet" laid out on Fifth Avenue to welcome the visitor to the inner sanctuary of the foundation.

The central court was meant to be a spacious, light-filled reception area, full of activity and giving both visual and physical access to the various functions contained within the museum (figs. 324, 320). It opened onto a terrace with a tea garden, a half-flight below, that was reached by a ramp continuing on to a café-restaurant. Beyond a circular information desk, embraced by a bow-shaped glass wall echoing the balcony above, was the lower lobby of the circulation tower. In the center of this circular space was the glass-enclosed tube of the elevator shaft and, around that, separated by a lightwell, was the two-tiered "fast ramp" giving access to the first level of galleries, where the "great ramp" began, as well as to the four-hundred-seat auditorium/cinema/theater in the basement.[138]

The upper lobby, on the *piano nobile*, was defined by a large, lens-shaped planter overlooking the circular reception space and sunken tea garden (figs. 325, 320). From one end of this seed-like shape, a ramp led down past a screen wall perforated with circular openings to the double-height Grand Gallery, located above the restaurant and surrounded on the inside by a continuous balcony. This was the "inner sanctum," or "Holy of Holies," in which Rebay intended to exhibit the most monumental and most important paintings of the collection. At the other end of the planter, beyond one of the service shaft nodules, was the foyer leading to the wing containing the "ocular chamber," which Wright had redesigned in accordance with the recommendations of the German avant-garde filmmaker

Guggenheim Museum. "The Modern Gallery."

324. Plan, ground floor.

325. Plan, main floor (second level).

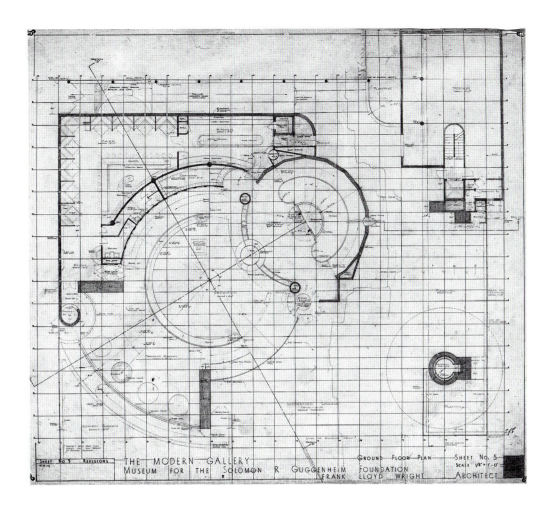

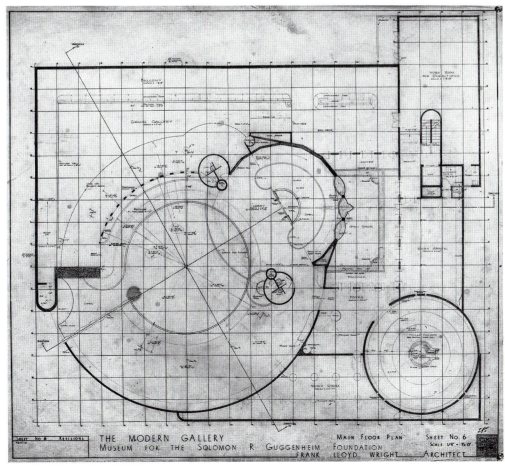

Oskar Fischinger, acting as Rebay's advisor on this and other related matters. Fischinger told them that the small experimental theater should be "half-spherical, like a big planetarium." With the projection and sound equipment located in the center and the audience sitting around its side, "the spheric projection surface would produce," he said, "a cosmic feeling of endless space without perspective."[139] Wright sank the sound and projection equipment in a pit one floor below the hemispherical dome and placed reclining chairs in a circle around it.

The second-floor lobby was also where the main ramp of galleries began, or, rather, ended its spiral movement through six complete revolutions starting at the top level of artists' studios. The parapet along the interior edge was given a gently curved, upturned lip. The "rift" of glass tubing along the top edge of the exterior wall created a continuous band of natural light. The walls themselves were tilted back at a slight angle, and a three-foot-deep base projected out from them at an angle reflecting that of the skylit "rift."[140] Floors, walls, and ceilings thus merged into one another with no abrupt transitions.

Wright's intention was "to provide [a] perfect plasticity of presentation."[141] The paintings were to sit directly on the angled base of the wall, which would be washed with natural light from above. Aside from acting as a support for the paintings, this plane would reflect light onto the ceiling at the same time that it would keep visitors from approaching the works of art too closely. By "plasticity of presentation" Wright meant that everything necessary for the installation and protection of the paintings would be taken care of by the architecture itself. Consequently, there would be "no hanging of the pictures." In contrast to Rebay's temporary museum, where the paintings were similarly placed near floor level, all frames and glass would be eliminated. Nothing but space was to come between the beholder and the individual work of art.[142]

As Wright developed the idea that the building itself would amount to a "frame," the actual movement of the visitor through its space began to demand greater definition

than originally indicated in the preliminary scheme A.[143] The key element, of course, was the spiral ramp surrounding the atrium court. Although the court always provided a sense of centrality and orientation, its power to act in a concerted fashion with the ramp depended on a number of factors, perhaps the most significant being directionality. In the earlier studies, it appears that Wright assumed the visitor would walk up the ramp. But as the design was refined and elaborated, and once the elevators were enclosed in the freestanding translucent cage of glass tubing and surrounded by a "fast ramp," he seems to have realized that the real significance of the museum's spatial experience depended on the same inversion of normal habits of perception as did the initial idea of turning the ziggurat upside down. Everything in the final design of "The Modern Gallery" thus pointed upward, to a spiritual height where the body is released to find its way back down to earth along the liberating path of non-objectivity.

The various changes Wright made in the design of the interior all emphasized what he described as the "skyward" expansion of its central space toward the "flood of sunlight, illuminating the grand ramp."[144] The semicircular tube of the elevator shaft materialized the vertical *axis mundi* defined by the oculus of the dome and thus signaled to the visitor that the tour of the collection must start at the top. The visitor would either take the elevator directly up or use the "fast ramp," perhaps stopping first on the main floor to prepare for the experience by seeing the "masterpieces" in the Grand Gallery.[145] To ascend slowly through the glass tube in the plunger-type hydraulic elevators specified by Wright would have been like levitating in a weightless, gravity-free environment, the kind of feeling one now can get, for no apparent spiritual purpose, in any of John Portman's Hyatt-Regency hotels (fig. 320).

In the 1945 project for the Guggenheim, the skyward idea was directly linked to Rebay's spiritual program, where art was an "unearthly," disembodied experience of the "cosmic breath." To underscore that, Wright planned the elevators actually to rise above the top level of galleries to a glass-domed, nearly hemispherical space serving as "an observatory where an adequate astronomical telescope will be installed for general study of the cosmic-order."[146] The dome over this sky-room was to revolve, thus preparing visitors for the spiraling course of their descent down the main ramp. That began, one level below the central dome, where a lens-shaped planter, similar to the one on the *piano nobile*, projected into space to mark the beginning of the spiral with the organic image of a seedpod.

Movement down the spiral was counterclockwise and was intended by Wright to feel effortless, as if one were being carried along on the crest of "a curving wave that never breaks." The elevator, Wright would say, did "the lifting, the visitor the drifting."[147] At the bottom of the well, which narrowed as it reached the lower lens-shaped planter suspended above the ground floor, the direction of movement was reversed. Visitors descended either into the Grand Gallery or wound around the elevator cage in a final, small eddy that took them out of the flow of the stream and deposited them in the main pool of space of the central court. There one could rest, meet friends, socialize, purchase catalogues, go to the restaurant, have tea or coffee, and eventually either return to the galleries to continue the visit or leave the museum in a suitably relaxed and uplifted state.

■ ■ ■

The project for "The Modern Gallery" that emerged by 1945 posited a conception of the museum-going experience and an interpretation of museum architecture that would remain constant despite the changes the design underwent before being built nearly eleven years later. Many different considerations were bound up in the spiral form adopted. Thinking of museum architecture in general, Wright wanted natural light. He believed, as most traditional architects did—and as architects since Kahn do again—that paintings should be seen in the changing conditions of natural light. This would not only enhance their qualities as works of art but would also provide a less harsh and less relentless environment in which to view them. The question of "museum fatigue" was uppermost in his mind. The slow downward "drift" along the ramp was one answer; another was the orientational device of the central court.

From the point of view of the client's particular needs, and here I am thinking of both Guggenheim and Rebay, Wright envisioned the building, again in quite traditional terms, as a memorial, a temple, a spiritual sanctuary. But he also believed that any effect of "grandomania" must be avoided: thus the domestic scale of the galleries (generally a little over nine feet high and less than twenty-five feet deep) and the constant focus on the social gathering place at ground level.[148] Neither Wright nor his client thought of the museum as a place merely for the specialist or art lover. Rather, it had a missionary, proselytizing role, which meant it should define "a new, more liberal idea of the nature of a public museum" and provide "a more broad and enjoyable" museum-going experience than was usually the case with museums devoted to more historical collections.[149] For Rebay, as for Guggenheim, art's utopian social values were primary.

This brings us to the most unusual and most challenging aspects of the design, those generated by considerations of the special character of the paintings to be shown. Wright felt that the radical nature of non-objective art demanded an equally radical architectural solution, one that freed the paintings from the traditional form of display in a frame on an upright wall. The elimination of frames and glass, the relatively casual placement of the paintings on the baseband against the sloping wall, and the downward angle at which they were to be seen all conspired, in Wright's view, to make the looking experience a more immediate, a more felt, and a more integral one. The curve of the wall behind the paintings was meant to "liberate" them in space, so that each individual work could be appreciated in a uniquely compelling way.[150] (Wright liked to compare this solution to a sparkling "jewel" or precious "signet" as it is "set" in a ring, instead of a lifeless, flat picture "hung" on the wall.) "The substitution of an *atmosphere* for a form," as he put it, offered "a new unity between beholder, painting and architecture."[151] This naturally gave the building *as a museum* a very complex, even radical significance. But before we turn to that, we should look briefly at how the building came to be what we can see and more or less experience today.

From "Modern Gallery" to Guggenheim Museum

It is often said that architecture gains in clarity and intensity of expression from the constraints imposed by the client and the program during the later phases of design development. If this is true, and there is good reason to believe it is, the transformation of "The Modern Gallery" into the Guggenheim Museum would be the exception that proves the rule. Where construction at Hollyhock House was aborted when desire and funds for the cultural center disappeared, "The Modern Gallery" became a shell in which to accommodate the demands of a new client, a new director, a new program, and an inflated economy, not to mention a set of restrictive building codes.

Between September 1945 and August 1956, when ground was broken, the project went through numerous reviews and revisions. Wright compromised on many points simply to get the building built. He reduced the height considerably; eliminated such expensive luxuries as the marble facing and ground-floor paving; gave up the tubular glass for the elevator and the dome, substituting more prosaic and structurally simpler solutions for both; added interior supports that interrupted the continuity of the ramp; and sacrificed the rooftop observatory, roof garden, ring of artists' studios, and the "ocular chamber." Most important, perhaps, the provisions he had made for the installation and lighting of the works of art were completely disregarded when they were not actually undone. All that really remained was the underlying order of the vessel-like container and the logic of inversion on which its spatial concept of an "easy downward drift" depended.[152] Still, that is enough for us to feel many of the effects Wright intended

and to sense what he meant to convey about the museum-going experience when he turned the Tower of Babel upside down.

■ ■ ■

War shortages and the sharply rising cost of materials presented the first serious obstacles to the immediate and full realization of the 1945 project. Guggenheim was reluctant to move quickly, believing that prices would come down in the not too distant future.[153] The estimate on the 1945 project was $1 million, already a third over what Guggenheim had agreed to for the building alone in the original contract two years earlier. By June 1946, Wright's revised estimate came to $1.5 million. To cut costs, he investigated alternative methods of construction, such as welded steel, and proposed reducing the height of the museum by one level. By the end of that year, a new contract was signed for a building to cost $1.5 million.[154]

Further costs were incurred by the foundation's purchase of additional properties on Fifth Avenue and Eighty-eighth Street that eventually allowed the museum to occupy the entire blockfront. At about the time "The Modern Gallery" plans were first shown in New York, discussions began on a parcel adding thirty feet of frontage on Fifth Avenue as well as an outlet on Eighty-eighth Street. This property was acquired in 1946, and Wright redrew the plans the following year to incorporate the added space. He also proposed an annex to house the temporary museum on the Eighty-eighth Street section, with the intention that this two-story structure eventually become part of the permanent museum. To save money, Guggenheim and Rebay decided to remodel the recently acquired townhouse on Fifth Avenue to serve as the temporary home for the collection.[155]

By 1948, the estimated cost of Wright's design had risen to $3 million, a figure that Guggenheim could in no way accept. Wanting desperately to see the museum built and realizing that Guggenheim, now eighty-six years old, was in failing health, Wright proposed a scheme for cost-cutting that drastically reduced the size of the building (by about 380,000 cubic feet). He then suggested that the foundation "sell the 5th Avenue property for a good price—say a million or more—and apply to the city for a good site in some of the parks or on some boulevard, free."[156] But Guggenheim was not interested in either idea and seemed content to wait. Furthermore, with the expense of remodeling the new temporary quarters at 1071 Fifth Avenue and reinstalling the entire collection, even Rebay now cooled on the idea of immediate construction of Wright's design. She realized that once her "Maecenas" died, the trustees of the foundation would no doubt weigh her operating budget against all future construction costs. And in fact, that is exactly what Guggenheim himself set out in his will.

Solomon Guggenheim died in November 1949 after a protracted bout with cancer. He had come to fear, after all the waiting, that the whole affair might fizzle due to the recent inflation. Wright had promised him that he could bring the building in for a maximum of $2 million, and that is the amount Guggenheim earmarked for it in his will.[157] But nothing in the will specifically stated that Wright was to be the architect. When rumors reached him at Taliesin that the trustees were being warned about his cavalier attitude toward budgets and were showing some "reluctance . . . to go into action on the building," Wright wrote to the head of the board, playing on his emotions and appealing to his sense of loyalty. "The fact is Mr. Guggenheim employed me and trusted me," Wright said. "Were it not for my promise to Mr. Guggenheim several weeks before he died that I would be building this building for him . . . for two million dollars—I would be quite content to withdraw and leave the matter to the trustees." "But," Wright sanctimoniously added, "I do have a conscience in this matter, whether they have any or not. . . . Mr. Guggenheim wanted me to assure him that the building would be built substantially as he saw it (making the changes I suggested)—and I gave him my promise." Wright stressed that the museum was to be a "memorial to Solomon R. Guggenheim" and that "no carping, doubting building-committee is going to hamper the ef-

fort." "Unless released by an authority now above and beyond his will," Wright warned, "I am ready to keep my promise" to accomplish this "herculean task requiring all the encouragement and support Mr. Guggenheim himself would have given to me had he lived to do so."[158]

The will remained in probate for over a year. During that time, it became quite clear that the building would go ahead, and that Wright would be its architect, but that Hilla Rebay would no longer be its guiding force, a fact that would have an untold effect on the final outcome of the building. In early April 1951 the foundation purchased the final corner property on Fifth Avenue and Eighty-eighth Street, giving it the entire blockfront opposite Central Park.[159] Within a week of the announcement in the press, a devastating critique of Rebay's policies appeared in an article in the Sunday *New York Times*, written by the art critic Aline Louchheim (later Saarinen).

Louchheim took Rebay to task for the "mystic double-talk" of her writings, as well as her "doctrinaire attitude" and "exclusive addiction to non-objective art," which Louchheim described as "at best but a small current in the stream of modern art." She publicly condemned the foundation's "evasiveness" and "stalling" in regard to the issue of building the museum as stipulated in its donor's will. Questioning whether the foundation, as presently constituted, was in fact living up to its responsibility regarding its "educational and artistic purposes," Louchheim suggested that "perhaps the Foundation would better serve the public interest if it would place the new Wright building and the Guggenheim collections and monies under the jurisdiction of one (or perhaps jointly of two) of the existing museums of modern art," meaning the Museum of Modern Art and the Whitney.[160]

Between April 1951 and the following March, when she formally submitted her resignation as curator and director of the foundation, Rebay gradually receded from the picture and Wright began to deal directly with a new, more business-like administration headed by Harry Guggenheim, Solomon's nephew. Wright would now be kept to the bud-

Guggenheim Museum. Revised "Modern Gallery," 1951–54.

326. Perspective (1951).

327. Section.

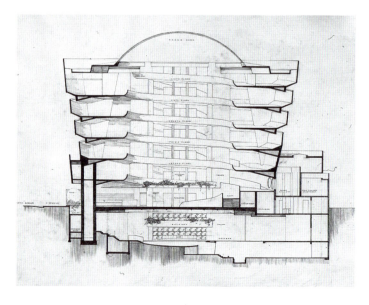

get, and there would be little talk of "domes of spirit" or "cosmic breath." Wright's immediate task was to adapt the existing plans to the $2 million budget, while at the same time expanding them to fill the enlarged site.

Work on the new plans proceeded throughout the second half of 1951. They were approved by the foundation's board of trustees in early February 1952 and, with minor revisions, submitted to the New York City Building Commission for a permit in late March.[161] The most obvious change in response to the new site conditions was the reversal of the two main elements of the composition so that they once again occupied the positions they had in the preliminary schemes of 1944 (fig. 326). The full exposure of the main spiral to the south substantially increased the amount of natural light in the galleries while at the same time making the inverted ziggurat the most visible element when approached from lower Fifth Avenue.

328. Guggenheim Museum. Revised "Modern Gallery." Plan, ground floor (1952).

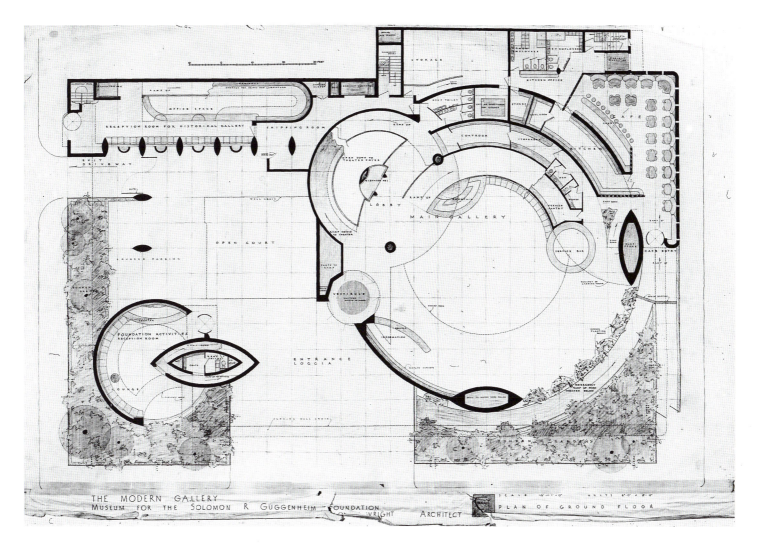

To a certain extent, Wright followed the simplified plans he had developed for Solomon Guggenheim in 1948. The tower was reduced in height by a story but given a broader, more saucer-like section (fig. 327). The tubular glass dome remained more or less the same in diameter, however, since the open well of the atrium court, instead of widening as it rose, now retained a constant diameter throughout. By contrast, the gallery ramp narrowed at every turn as it descended to ground level, ever so slightly increasing the feeling of momentum.

One fundamental change was that the main ramp now continued right down to the level of the court, instead of terminating at the upper lobby of the *piano nobile*, which was eliminated as a cost-cutting measure. Wright took advantage of this to give a sense of climax to the spiraling path. At ground level, it swung back on itself in a swirling reverse curve to empty out, as it were, into a lens- or pod-shaped fountain and pool in front of the elevator (fig. 328). By contrast, the elevator was deemphasized as an architectural feature. With its Pyrex glass tubing replaced by a solid concrete wall, it was no longer exposed; and with the "cosmic" observatory eliminated, it rose only as far as the top level of the main ramp.

Cost was also a determining factor in the other major change in the main gallery, a change that in this case affected the structural system. When the original idea of using prestressed concrete proved too expensive and a welded steel option was found not to work, Wright turned to a more conventional system of concrete reinforced with steel rods. To transfer the load of the cantilevered ramps to the outside walls, as well as to stiffen them, Wright introduced a series of vertical fins or "webs," as he called them, running from the second floor to the base of the dome. Set at intervals of thirty degrees, the webs widened as they rose and thus created separate alcoves, or "chambers," for organizing exhibitions into smaller, more coherent groupings (see fig. 340).[162] They also provided a rhythmic pulse that gave the building a more organic expression. Wright now talked less of the museum's inspiration in the Mesopotamian ziggurat and more of its snail-like nature, likening the structure to a "chambered nautilus" in whose "harmonious fluid quiet" the paintings were nestled. In keeping with this imagery, the exterior of the building was designed to be a "glistening" white marble aggregate, left matte with polished highlights.[163]

Although the administrative wing was separated from the main gallery by a somewhat larger court than before, it was brought into a much closer visual relationship by its circular design (fig. 326). The program for this element had, in fact, greatly changed. It was now called the Monitor, as if to suggest a nautical image for its function of oversight. Rebay's ocular chamber and duplex penthouse apartment were eliminated, and the structure was now entirely devoted to administration and business. The plan consisted of a small, circular ring surrounding a top-lit inner court that was intersected on its south side by a relatively large, lens-shaped stack containing an access ramp wrapping around the services (fig. 328). A reception area and lounge occupied the ground level, just to the left of the main entrance loggia; above that were two stories of offices, connected to the museum by the bridge-terrace over the entrance; and on the top level was a circular roof garden, surrounding the projecting stack of the Monitor, which lit the central court and gave the small building its name.

Behind the Monitor, and connected to it by the offices along Eighty-ninth Street, was a fifteen-story building, the top thirteen floors of which were to be built at a later date as income-producing studios and apartments, setting an example to be followed by the Museum of Modern Art in the early 1980s and by the Guggenheim itself at the end of the decade. The first and second floors of this tower slab were to be built immediately to house the "historical gallery" for the representational "precursors" of non-objective painting. In the basement would be carpentry shops and storage.

The recessive, unrelieved square grid of the tower-block acted as a foil to the plastic, streamlined shapes of the "memorial gallery," as Wright now called the museum in the inscription over the Fifth Avenue entrance. The continuous parapet ran the entire length of the block, defining the building's relation to the street in a quite formal manner, almost like the stylobate of a temple. Wright used all the available area under the parapet and around its sides for sunken gardens, to set the "memorial gallery" off from the rest of its environment and to call attention to its very special nature as a sanctuary for the contemplation of art. He insisted that the museum should be perceived "as a temple of adult education and not as a profit-seeking business-venture." "The nature of the building design," he wrote in his accompanying description of the project, "is such as to seem more like a temple in a park on the Avenue than like a mundane business or residential structure."[164]

Aware of Rebay's decreasing influence in the project, but unwilling to give up completely the idealistic, "doctrinaire" position she maintained against the business-like, "carnival-atmosphere" of many other museums, Wright held to the idea of the museum as a temple, but gave it a less "cosmic," more "unitarian" tone than before. In describing to his new clients the various amenities of the plan, he stressed the museum's socially redeeming values. "There are many innovations in the building all on the side of convenient exposition and enjoyable social experience," he told them, "accommodation for the pictures, comfort for the visitors come to view them, their refreshment and social intercourse meantime encouraged, should they wish to have them."[165]

As the imagery of the 1951 design subtly shifted emphasis from the cosmic/historical to the fluid/natural, the revolving, glass-domed, roof observatory of "The Modern

Gallery" was replaced by a new symbolic device. A semi-abstract piece of open metal sculpture was placed above the lens-shaped stack of the Monitor (fig. 326). The panel was composed of tiers of smaller fin-shaped elements joined to little open circles. Deriving from the intersection of two circles, the biconvex shape had become the characteristic element in the plan of the Guggenheim. It was repeated, at various scales, in the vertical ducts of the main gallery, in the ground-floor information desk, and, most significantly, in the fountain and pool at the base of the reversed curve of the main ramp (fig. 328).

Representing the lentil seed from which its name derived, the shape could be read either as an image of germination or as a sign of vision, taking the lens shape at its secondary level of meaning. Wright seized upon this ambiguity of readings to make "the oval seed-pod containing globular units," as he put it, the "symbolic figure" of the building. At the base of the ramp that now directly connected the dome to the ground, the "synthetic" form of the seedpod gave the spiral a symbolic origin and termination in nature, thus joining vision to growth—seeing to becoming—in its reflexive shape.[166]

■ ■ ■

When the plans were filed with the Building Commission, thirty-two violations were found, and a building permit was denied. That number was subsequently reduced to eleven by the Board of Standards and Appeals and the permit was finally issued in March 1956. The most important violations, from the point of view of design, had to do with the dome, the circulation tower, and the structure of the ramp.[167] The commission considered that the dome's extremely thin double layer of glass tubing did not meet the necessary fire-resistance rating and would thus have to be changed to another material. The openness of the circulation tower likewise contravened the fire laws. Not only did the lightwell have to be closed in, but additional fire stairs had to be added, which would further change the pattern of circula-

tion in the building. Finally, the prohibition against expanded steel mesh for reinforcing resulted in the change in profile of the internal parapet of the main ramp from a gently upturned lip to an angled, hard-edged plane.

Hearings over the permit dragged on throughout the next few years, during which time Wright continued to make changes necessitated by economic factors as well. For reasons both of cost and occupancy ratios, the tower apartment building was eliminated. So too was the connecting wing of offices and educational facilities linking it and its now defunct "historical gallery" to the small Monitor, which survived as the only remnant of the original administrative quarters. To compensate as best he could for this major loss of space, Wright enclosed the circular roof garden of the Monitor to make a director's office and trustees' lounge. A rectangular balcony was cantilevered from it to tie in with the long horizontal band of the museum's first-floor parapet. Needless to say, the relief sculpture of seedpods containing globular units was sacrificed.

To comply with code requirements, Wright eliminated the lightwell in the circulation tower and replaced the generous open semicircle of the fast ramp with a much tighter, triangular tower containing a normal stairway (fig. 329). The elevator shaft was isolated and enclosed by a solid wall. To accommodate an additional enclosed fire stair (plus a freight elevator), the space between one of the circular service nodules and the outer wall of the ramp was filled in. This destroyed the symmetry of their relation to the circulation tower and the smooth flow of space along that section of the ramp. To create a passageway, the ramp was bowed out into the space of the open court in a countercurve. In some ways compensating for the lost vertical emphasis of the elevator shaft, this bulge acted as a strong spatial beat in concert with the constant pulse of the webs.

The need to redesign the dome using a structural material other than Pyrex tubing forced Wright to deal with a problem that he had not really faced when he first added the interior webs to the spiral structure. With its graduated pattern of open circles, the original dome had a bubble-like

329. Guggenheim Museum. Final plan, first level (second floor) (1958).

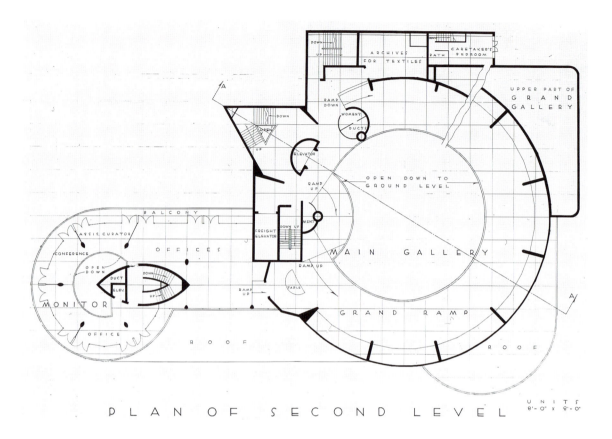

PLAN OF SECOND LEVEL

effect that was completely unrelated to the structural diagram of forces traditionally associated with ribbing or coffering. Its dematerialized appearance, like water suspended in the sky, was consistent with the original design of the ramp as a "coiled spring."[168] The vertical lines of the webs added a very different element that suggested a more traditional relation between structural support and dome.

At least three different schemes for the dome were developed. One, which may date from as early as the summer of 1953, was essentially a translation of the original design into different materials. The graduated stainless steel circles became concrete rings holding glass bubbles. Above an air space was an overall skylight.[169] Between the fall of 1954 and early 1956, Wright experimented with a more structurally rational solution emphasizing the segmentation of the space by the webs (fig. 330). Diagonal struts supporting individually curved compartments of frosted wire-glass created a shallow, Byzantine-type pumpkin dome, with space for murals indicated in the lower segments. A plenum chamber filled the center, and a lapped-glass outer skylight covered the whole.[170]

The most classical solution, and the one that provided the structural basis for what was finally built, was developed by Wright in 1956, coinciding with a trip to Rome that summer. The webs were again carried up into the dome by diagonal struts, which were joined in pairs by hairpin bends near the oculus (figs. 331, 332). This concrete framework of ribs supported an outer shell of lapped glass, as well as a coffered dome of sandblasted glass that was hung from it on the inside. The reticulated grid of the inner dome recalled quite explicitly the dome of the Pantheon, with which Wright is known to have compared his design for the Guggenheim at the time.[171] Cost was again a major factor, so that by December 1956 the suspended shell was eliminated; and when it came time actually to construct the dome, the framework of paired hairpin struts containing translucent glass was built without the coffering that was designed to offer an illusion of a metastructural sort (fig. 333).

The double-shell dome, with its inner one of a distinctly smaller diameter, came as a logical conclusion to the studies made to adapt the structure of the ramp to economic and code requirements. Following the introduction of the vertical webs that increased in depth as they rose, Wright gave up the expanded mesh reinforcing that had originally generated the curved section of the interior parapet. The more simply constructed angled parapet that hung off the inner edge of the ramp paralleled the angle of the webs. In part to emphasize the inclining lines and in part to cut costs in formwork, Wright increased the depth of the ramp as it rose to maintain a constant cantilever beyond the edge of the webs. In contrast to the 1945 project, where the atrium court expanded upward and outward to a saucer dome that capped it at its widest point, the central space now diminished in diameter as it rose to form an ever-narrowing cone. The interior thus redressed the inverted spiral of the exterior in spatial terms, making a fully three-dimensional double helix. The Pantheon-like inner shell of sandblasted glass coffering would have given shape to that space and delineated the full effect of the building's underlying logic of inversion.[172]

■ ■ ■

The confrontation with building codes and budgets resulted in considerable changes in design, but these were as nothing compared to the results of changes in policy of the Guggenheim Museum after Harry Guggenheim's ascendancy to power, Rebay's forced resignation, and the appointment of James Johnson Sweeney as the new director. The purpose and program of the museum, as Wright and Rebay originally understood them, were so radically and irrevocably redefined that very little about the building still made sense. Save for starting all over from the beginning, which nobody wanted to do, the only possible outcome could be a profound and lasting dislocation of the shell of the building from its functional significance.

On the heels of Louchheim's devastating critique and Rebay's subsequent resignation in March 1952, Harry Gug-

genheim made it known that "a more flexible artistic formula than the present one" would be sought by the museum. With the appointment of Sweeney later that year, this new "flexible" program began to take shape.[173] Its implications were basically twofold: first, the museum would no longer be devoted exclusively to the non-objective form of abstract painting that Rebay had championed; and second, the collection would no longer be a permanent "memorial" to Solomon Guggenheim and considered complete when Rebay died. Following from these decisions, the museum would no longer limit itself to exhibiting only the two-dimensional art of painting, nor would the building be exempt from having to provide space for temporary exhibitions as well as all the administrative and curatorial needs attendant on a constantly growing collection and schedule of changing exhibitions.[174] The Guggenheim Museum was, in effect, to rival the Museum of Modern Art as an institution of experimentation and taste-making across the whole range of modern art, a program hardly inimical to Sweeney who had previously been the director of MOMA's Department of Painting and Sculpture.

Where Wright and Rebay seemed to get along in a very special sort of way, realizing each other's idiosyncrasies but usually agreeing on fundamentals, Wright and Sweeney saw eye to eye on almost nothing. Wright considered him one of "the common or garden variety of 'museum men,'" a "professional showman" with no sense of purpose or integrity. Wright came to view the entire affair after Sweeney's appointment in October 1952 as "A DUEL BETWEEN UNCLE SOL'S MAN, MYSELF, AND HARRY'S MAN, SWEENEY," in which "UNCLE SOL'S MAN HAS NOT MUCH CHANCE BECAUSE UNCLE SOL IS DEAD."[175]

To satisfy the requirements of a full exhibition schedule as well as an ever-expanding collection, Sweeney made his demands for space known in the middle of 1954 and asked Wright to figure out how they could be accommodated. Wright responded by reminding him that, because of budgetary as well as zoning restrictions, "we cannot build Solomon R. Guggenheim's Memorial and at the same time build whole big buildings for carpentry, photography, storage, conservation, etc., etc." In any event, Wright thought

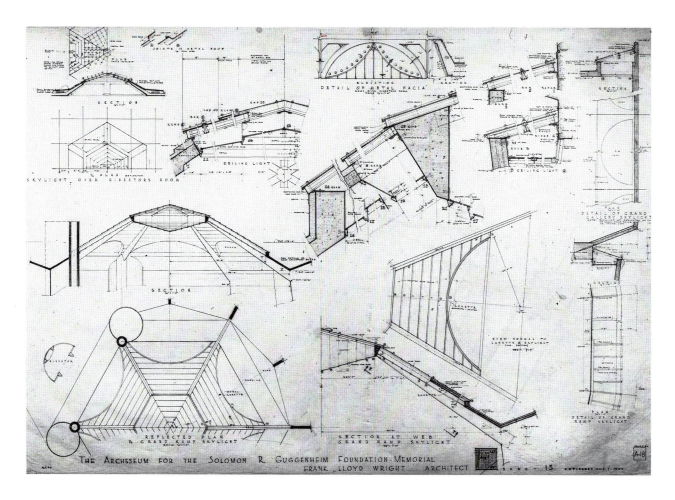

THE ARCHESEUM FOR THE SOLOMON R. GUGGENHEIM FOUNDATION-MEMORIAL
FRANK LLOYD WRIGHT ARCHITECT   SHEET 13

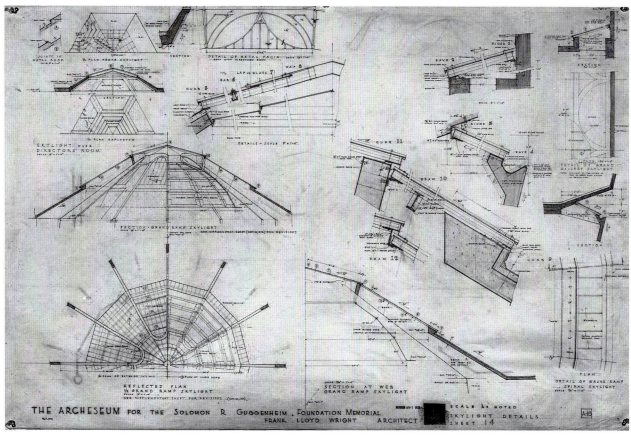

THE ARCHESEUM FOR THE SOLOMON R. GUGGENHEIM FOUNDATION MEMORIAL
FRANK LLOYD WRIGHT ARCHITECT   SKYLIGHT DETAILS   SHEET 14

On opposite page: Guggenheim Museum. "The Archeseum," 1954–56.

330. Plan, section, and details of dome (August 1955–April 1956).

331. Plan, section, and details of dome (August–September 1956).

Below: Guggenheim Museum.

332. "The Archeseum." Section (August–September 1956).

333. Final section (1958).

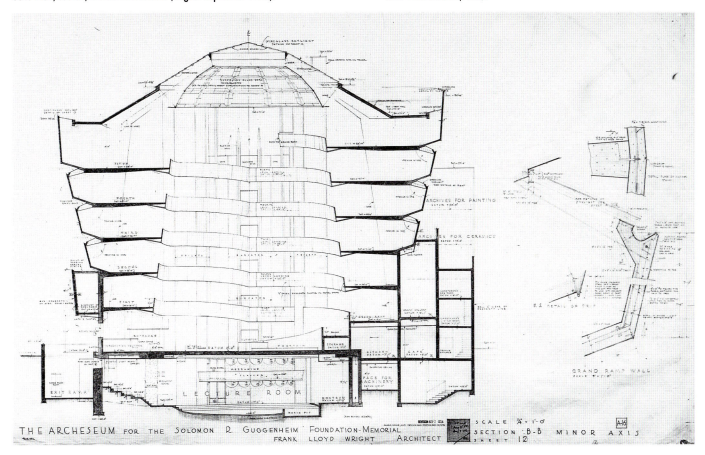

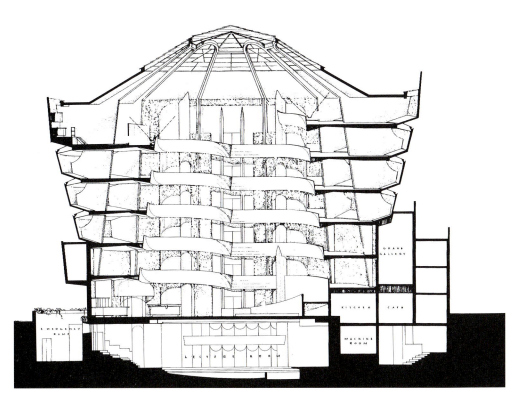

these demands totally out of line with what had earlier been decided: "Your experts want about the entire area of the Guggenheim lot or about 23,000 sq. ft., excluding any building for exhibition purposes whatever and allowing only a reasonable amount for the corridors, circulation, etc. . . . Something, James, is radically wrong." A choice had to be made between the "noble Memorial" Solomon Guggenheim desired and the "group of sizable factories" Wright felt Sweeney was now requesting.[176]

Squabbles over space allocation continued into the period of construction. Wright took a strong position on the matter, maintaining that a museum should not be run as "a big business," and especially the Guggenheim, given its founder's original vision. "The very heart of his memorial," Wright believed, would "go out when the museum as a business came in." "What the museum as a business of trading, collecting, circulating, exchange and purchase, shipping in and shipping out requires is an office building," he stressed over and over again, "and Mr. Guggenheim left no money to build one." Wright allowed that such a structure could be "added to the present memorial without harm," as he had earlier proposed in the apartment tower, but unless an effort was made to adhere to the original purpose of "The Modern Gallery" as "a unique quiet retreat" in which "to see a painting in an atmosphere suited to inspire the beholder," the building and its program would be fundamentally compromised.[177]

The disagreements over general matters of policy could never, in effect, be settled to the benefit of the building's original conception as a "memorial gallery," and Wright realized that.[178] The really acerbic arguments between him and Sweeney thus developed around the more specific issues of installation techniques and interior disposition. Coming from the modernist tradition of the "clean, well-lighted place," with its anonymous surfaces, flexible partitions, and artificial lighting, Sweeney disagreed with just about everything Wright proposed. On the matter of color, Sweeney wanted to paint the entire interior white. Wright, whose final choice was a soft ivory tone, countered

that Sweeney's "whitewash" would be antagonistic to subtle variations in color and value in the paintings and make the museum look like "the toilets of the Racquet Club."[179] Sweeney also wanted the "rift" of natural lighting to be blacked out and a trough with fluorescent lights to be hung from the ceiling in front of the paintings. Wright tried to convince Sweeney, and Guggenheim, that such a method of artificial lighting was too harsh and smacked of the way dealers spotlighted their wares for sale. But his criticisms fell on deaf ears.

Sweeney could and did what he threatened. The "virginal whiteness" of the interior, as one disturbed observer at the opening exhibition said, resembled a kind of "three-dimensional Suprematism" totally at odds with Wright's soft, relaxing atmosphere.[180] But the one thing Sweeney could not really undo, no matter how hard he tried, was the actual physical structure of the ramp, with its tilted outside walls and angled base-band. He tried to have all the webs built out to within six feet of the parapet in order to create a series of distinctly separate compartments, but that was not countenanced by the trustees.

The critical problem, as Sweeney saw it, was the angle at which the paintings were intended to be seen and the distance by which the base-band separated them from the viewer. This, of course, was the heart of Wright's conception and was literally built into the building. In early 1958 Wright prepared a number of drawings to show how the art should be installed according to his specifications, and he produced a booklet with explanatory text (fig. 344).[181] Sweeney brought the issue to a head in July 1958 by threatening to resign. A compromise was worked out by Harry Guggenheim and the trustees: Sweeney and Wright would each design an installation, and the results be compared.

Wright suggested that the test "be done before any public opening. Say not earlier than May first [1959]."[182] He died a month before that. Sweeney's proposal, which was totally inimical to Wright's design, carried the day. To compensate for the angle of the wall and its distance from the viewer, the paintings were mounted on "tripods" sticking out from the wall three feet or more (fig. 340). Thus suspended in space, the paintings were effectively disjoined from the architectural "frame" Wright conceived for them. Although Sweeney left the Guggenheim a year after it opened, his "solution" set a pattern of alienation of art from the architecture of the museum that has held sway in varying degrees of intensity ever since.

■ ■ ■

The building permit for the Guggenheim was issued in late March 1956. Demolition and site work began in May and construction started that spring. The contract was let for $2.5 million, and the final cost was approximately $1 million over that.[183] Among the last cost-saving measures, aside from the radical simplification of the dome, was the substitution of a slick plastic paint in a somewhat dead, cream-colored tone for the honed and polished marble-aggregate surface of the exterior. The building took a little over two years to finish and was completed in October 1959.[184] There was a four-block line of nearly three thousand people waiting to get in on a Wednesday afternoon at 2:00. On the following Sunday, more than ten thousand people queued up to visit what was by all accounts the most extraordinary and most controversial example of modern architecture yet built in a major city and for a public use.

The Optimistic Ziggurat

The critical controversy surrounding the Guggenheim Museum began soon after ground was broken. In a letter of protest apparently inspired by Sweeney and made available to the *New York Times* in December 1956, twenty-one New York artists asked the museum's board of trustees "to reconsider the plans for the building," which they deemed "not suitable for a sympathetic display of painting and sculpture." "The basic concept of curvilinear slope for presentation of painting and sculpture," they said, "indicates a

callous disregard for the fundamental rectilinear frame of reference necessary for the adequate visual contemplation of works of art."[185] Among those who signed the letter were Willem De Kooning, Adolph Gottlieb, Philip Guston, Franz Kline, Seymour Lipton, and Robert Motherwell. Among those missing were Hans Hofmann, Jasper Johns, Barnett Newman, Robert Rauschenberg, Ad Reinhardt, and Mark Rothko, not to speak of those artists more closely associated with the movement of Geometric Abstraction.

Wright responded by telegram, denying the very assumption on which the criticism was based. "THERE IS NO 'RECTILINEAR FRAME OF REFERENCE' WHATEVER FOR THE EXHIBITION OF A PAINTING," he declared, and any such assumption is merely "THE INCUBUS OF HABIT." In an interview with Aline Saarinen (formerly Louchheim) published in the *Times* nine months later, he argued that the real issue always was and always would be a matter of innovation versus habit. What he was trying to do, he said, was to design "a museum specifically for the advanced type of paintings [Solomon Guggenheim] collected" and "to create an atmosphere suitable to the paintings."[186]

Wright argued that modern abstract art (of the non-objective sort or not) had engendered a new kind of pictorial space that had nothing to do with traditional perspectival illusionism based on the relationship of vertical and horizontal lines. Removed from that tectonic ground, modern paintings should no longer be seen within the traditional framework of orthogonal space. Wright further believed that his design indicated the direction future art would take. "Once he stops having to think in terms of rectangles, the painter will be free to paint on any shape he chooses—even to curve his canvas if he wants," he told Saarinen.[187] And indeed, the shaped canvas, "specific objects," Earthworks, conceptual and installation art were all just around the corner and would soon be seen to their greatest advantage in exhibitions at the Guggenheim during the sixties, seventies, and eighties—but that was still a number of years off. The critical debate about Wright's design was limited to conventional notions of painting and sculpture understood within the context of conventional ideas of how a museum should operate.[188]

Although the public reception of the Guggenheim Museum was immediately and overwhelmingly positive, the reaction of critics and professionals was quite mixed. There were those who appreciated the daring spatial and sculptural form of the building to such an extent that any of its contextual or programmatic shortcomings were irrelevant; but many others could in no way accept what they perceived to be Wright's overriding disregard for everything but his own "organic" idea of what the building should be. Henry-Russell Hitchcock hailed the museum as Wright's "swan-song," comparing it in significance to Beethoven's late quartets. Peter Blake, editor of *Architectural Forum*, claimed it had to be judged more as a "monument" than a "museum." As a work of "pure art," it belonged among the greatest works in the history of Western architecture, in the company of those by "architects like Phidias, Brunelleschi, Michelangelo, and Wren."[189]

For the social critic Lewis Mumford, that was not enough. The Guggenheim might be compared in its monumentality to the Pantheon and Hagia Sophia, but ultimately it is such an "all-or-nothing building," full of "hollow rhetoric" expressing "an ego far deeper than the pool in which Narcissus too long gazed," that the building's real purpose and meaning might truly be served only by turning it into a museum of Wright's own architecture. Philip Johnson, who was fast becoming the leading museum designer of the period, interpreted the apparent perversity of Wright's conception as the key to what made the building "magnificent," indeed, "incomparable." He called it "Wright's greatest building," "one of the greatest rooms of the 20th century," albeit an "art defying architecture!"[190]

Most art critics and museum professionals took a harsher line, seeing Wright's creation as an attack on painting and sculpture. It was "a cultural horror, a new disaster inflicted upon art," exclaimed Hilton Kramer, "an architecture totally irrelevant to its purposes, an architecture which succeeds in having only one 'organic' function: to call attention to itself." Some critics, like Tom Hess, editor of *Art News*, were willing to admit that "it takes Wright's kind of egomania to smash the pattern"; as a result of the Guggenheim, "perhaps the idea of a museum will now be thought about again, and as a new concept." But almost all agreed fundamentally with John Canaday of the *New York Times*, who characterized the building as "a design of shaped space sufficient unto itself" in which "a war between architecture and painting" was forever to be waged. "If he [Wright] had deliberately designed an interior to annihilate painting as an expressive art, and to reduce it to an architectural accessory," Canaday wrote, "he could not have done much better."[191]

Ironically, though perhaps understandably, one of the few critics to put a finger on one of the most original and successful aspects of Wright's design was Sweeney, the very person who had done as much as anyone to counter Wright's ideas and alter the original design and programmatic intent of the building. Writing just a few months after the opening, he pointed to the "'great-room' character" of Wright's design as "the most individual and gratifying feature of this building as an art museum." "Its effect on the public is immediately noticeable," he said:

There is a sociability in participation evident on all sides among the spectators. The play of light and color from one side of the building to the other and the mobile rhythms of the ramp parapets awaken a liveliness in the visitor. At the same time the theme of ample spacing, set by the wide open core under its lofty dome, gives the interior a tone of serenity in which even the constant movement of a thousand visitors is effectively absorbed.

Sweeney concluded that "it is in this social aspect that Frank Lloyd Wright's building has struck its most original museum note."[192]

Most critics and commentators, whether positive or

334. Philip L. Goodwin and Edward Durrell Stone: Museum of Modern Art, New York, 1938–39.

negative, tended to judge the building in typically modernist terms. If it was successful, it was so for purely formal reasons—as a space, as a shape, as a sequence of movements. If it failed, it did so for functional reasons—the difficulty of installation, the awkward system of lighting, the inadequacy of storage, office space, and other facilities. Aside from such comments as Sweeney's relating to its "social" significance, little was said about the building's highly configured symbolic and representational character. References to the Pantheon, to Michelangelo, to the idea of a "great room" carried some implications of the traditional bearing of the design; acknowledgment of its "organic" appearance and shell-like character reminded the reader that Wright was not merely interested in abstract form as such.

The building clearly posed a difficult question of interpretation and has continued to remain highly problematic. Much of the difficulty has to do with the type of building it is. With its monumental dome and processionally organized space, the Guggenheim shares certain important features with the classical museum of the past; yet it looks nothing like, say, John Russell Pope's nearly contemporaneous National Gallery of Art in Washington, D.C. (1937–41). The Guggenheim is archetypally modern in its dynamic spatial form, yet something about it resists interpretation in strictly modern terms.[193] But beyond these considerations, there is one other important factor to remember: the Guggenheim Museum has never been seen as it was planned to be. Not only have judgments been based on distorted evidence but, by 1959, when the building was completed, few people recalled the design of "The Modern Gallery" of 1945.

■ ■ ■

Form and function are intimately, indeed indissolubly, interconnected in the Guggenheim Museum, and any interpretation of its meaning must begin with an understanding of the original intent of its program and client. Hilla Rebay did not want a typically "functional" modern building, and

that is precisely why she chose Wright. She wanted a "temple," a "sanctuary for art," a "dome of spirit," as she phrased it. Whatever this might look like or mean, it certainly was diametrically opposed to the principles on which most advanced modern designs for museums were then being based, and it is with that in mind that one must assess Wright's work.[194]

The Museum of Modern Art in New York (1938–39) had established the image of a modern museum just four years before Guggenheim commissioned Wright (fig. 334). Gone were the portico and the dome, as well as any reference to the symmetry, monumentality, or formal procession of the classical temples of the past. Instead there was a free-flowing, flexible, loft-like space wrapped in a nonrepresentational casing of office- or factory-like character. Artificial lighting and easily movable partition walls created the desired interior space of a "museum without walls."[195] Everything could be shifted to accommodate whatever "new directions" contemporary art might take.

In 1943, in *Architectural Forum*, Mies van der Rohe published a project for a Museum for a Small City that gave an ideal form to this program for a modern museum.[196] In this daringly minimal design, there are literally no walls as such. A slab roof, raised on widely spaced point-supports,

335. Mies: Museum for a Small City project (for *Architectural Forum*), 1941–43. Interior perspective.

336. Le Corbusier: Museum of World Culture (Musée Mondial), Mundaneum project, Geneva, Switzerland, 1928–29. Plan, section, and elevations.

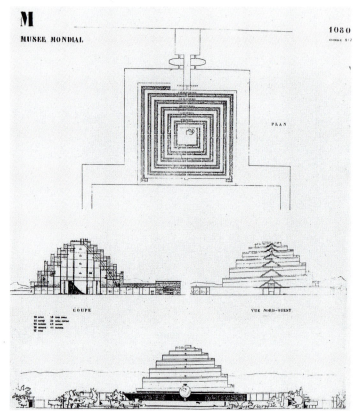

covers the glass-enclosed space (fig. 335). Asymmetrically placed panels, set in dynamic groupings, serve as vertical supports for the exhibition of paintings, which, as a result, look as if they are floating free in space. Pieces of sculpture are likewise isolated on their bases to form collage-like compositions in conjunction with the freestanding panels. Flexibility, light, space, and immediacy are the keynotes of this image of a sublimated functionalism.

In his continuing series of designs for museums, beginning in 1928–29 and culminating in the construction of the Museum of Western Art in Tokyo (1956–59), Le Corbusier combined the modern idea of flexible space with concerns for circulation and expansion that approach somewhat more closely Wright's ideas. The Musée Mondial, already referred to, was designed for the utopian Mundaneum project of 1928–29. Following the model of Wright's Gordon Strong Automobile Objective and Planetarium, it was a multistory ziggurat, here square in plan and pedestrian in scale (fig. 336). The museum was intended to be universal in scope and to exhibit, in an interdisciplinary fashion, the entire history of civilization from "prehistoric times" to the present. Le Corbusier adopted the spiral form of the ancient ziggurat as an "organic" expression of the "uninterrupted succession" in the "chain of knowledge upon which human works unfold across the centuries." Beginning at the top,

the visitor would experience the "widening links" and "accumulating" information of history as the galleries descended to the ground level.[197]

The explicitly representational character of this early design was almost immediately rejected by Le Corbusier and his critics as regressively monumental and eclectic, although he would retain the abstract spiral form for almost all his later museum designs. Collapsed into a single level of galleries raised on *pilotis*, and thus purged of its former associations, the square-spiral plan became Le Corbusier's museum-type. First proposed in 1930–31 as a Museum of Contemporary Art for a site outside Paris, it was fully elaborated into the Museum for Unlimited Growth for Philippeville, Algeria (1939), before being built in Ahmedabad in 1952–54 and then in Tokyo (followed by Chandigarh) during the years the Guggenheim was going up (fig. 337). The main purpose of the design was to offer flexibility in the present and provide for expansion in the future. From the beginning, Le Corbusier explained, his intention was to es-

337. Le Corbusier: Museum for Unlimited Growth project, Philippeville, Algeria, 1939. Model.

tablish a type-solution that would be "expandable at will." The key factors were "standardization," "modularity," and "regularity."[198]

The square-spiral form was ideal for these purposes. It permitted "unlimited growth" by an accretive process that always maintained the basic form of the original nucleus, an ordered process Le Corbusier liked to illustrate by abstracting the image of a snail shell into the mathematical formula of a logarithmic spiral. Starting from the central core and working its way out, the interior gallery space could be manipulated by partitions to flow in any direction, just as new "modular" units could be added without disturbing the general appearance or functioning of the whole. But to generate a workable formula for a completely flexible museum from the essentially unilinear and inward-turning shape of the spiral, Le Corbusier was forced to renounce the inher-

ently processional and directional aspects of its circulation pattern as well as the historical and natural allusions of its symbolic imagery.[199]

■ ■ ■

In contrast to the museums of Le Corbusier and Mies, which developed from generically modernist conceptions of space and use, Wright's design for the Guggenheim Museum grew out of a very specific set of aesthetic, institutional, and symbolic concerns that subsumed and redefined all spatial and functional considerations. In response to his client's wishes, Wright rejected the notions of flexibility and open-endedness in favor of a monumentality and sense of permanence suitable to a "memorial" collection. In answer to Rebay's desire for a didactic display of modern art's evolution toward its spiritual end, Wright chose the directional and progressive form of the spiral to create a processional space oriented around a focal, rotunda-like core. And to express in the physical shape of the building both the "cosmic" aspirations of non-objective art as well as the "spiritual realm" to which Rebay believed a "feeling" for such art would lead, Wright chose to emphasize rather than deny the historical and natural allusions of the ziggurat form.

Wright interpreted the mission to create a "congenial" atmosphere for the works of art as a process of representation in itself. He intended the forms and spaces of the museum to be homologous with those of the paintings to be displayed within it. An early sketch, for instance, shows a non-objective tondo installed on the ramp (fig. 338). Paintings and building were to be concentric with one another and conform to the same principles of design.[200] The complex circular geometry of the building directly related to the cosmic, space-time imagery of Kandinsky and Bauer (figs. 308, 309).[201]

Rebay and Wright talked at length about the symbolism of geometry. Rebay claimed she always had a spiral in mind as the form for her "dome of spirit": it combined the vertical and the horizontal into "the one rhythm," a unified

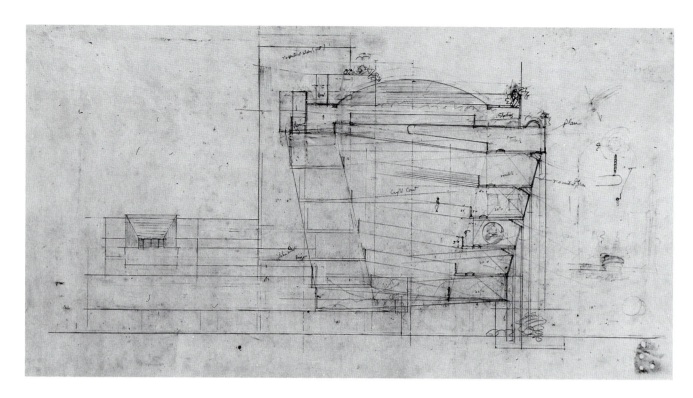

impulse that would "elevate" one "up to the infinite infinity of space" and would "embrace the sky as much as the earth." Wright agreed that the circle embodied a sense of infinity and of universality; its three-dimensional extension in the spiral expanded that meaning to encompass a dynamic sense of growth and development. In Rebay's view, this "organic" form was the very sign of the artistic "masterpiece"—"a flawless continuation of intuition from beginning to end."[202]

The spiral also contained the possibility for expressing two extremely important aspects of Rebay's program, namely, the idea of artistic progress and the sense of communal absorption in that process. The development of modern art to its ultimate stage of non-objectivity was, in her view, linear and progressive. Each new stage represented an advance on the past in a continuous development from materiality to spirituality. To appreciate this, one had to witness the evolutionary cycle unfold.[203] A spiral organization of circulation permitted the development of modern art to be experienced as a self-referential, teleological fact.

As in Tatlin's *Monument for the Third International* (fig. 294), the spiral functioned not only as a sign of modernity; it was also an image of communal activity in which striving, aspiration, and progress toward a socially desirable and useful goal predominated. In following its predetermined course, individuals would be caught up in a force much larger and more powerful than themselves. Both Rebay and Guggenheim felt that the spiritual emanation of non-objective paintings represented such a force and that the proper "sanctuary" for their display should also be a center for significant social activity. Wright's original project, with its restaurant, tea garden, artists' studios, roof garden, and film center, responded to that ideal. The glass-enclosed elevator leading up to the astronomical observatory provided a dramatic staging point for the communal event while at the same time giving it an otherworldly focus.

The mythico-historical source for this symbolism of the spiral, to which both Wright and Tatlin referred, was the Tower of Babel (fig. 339). In it were embodied human aspiration, infinite progress, and communal activity. Based on ancient descriptions enlivened by numerous pictorial representations from the Middle Ages through the Renaissance, the biblical Tower of Babel had come to stand in the popular mind for the ancient Mesopotamian ziggurat. Circular rather than square in plan, it represented the sacred mountain, or "high place," even more faithfully than its historical counterparts did.[204] The historical ziggurat was a temple tower in the form of a mountain linking earth and sky. It was a source of fertility, the mountain from which water flowed. It was the sanctuary of God, the place of epiphany where He appears to man. It was the throne to which God descends from heaven to earth. It was also traditionally considered to be the first example of an astronomical observatory.[205]

The biblical account of the Tower of Babel created a more tragic and human image. After the Flood, the survivors traveled as a group from Mount Ararat to the plain of Shinar (Genesis 11:1–9). As a new home for themselves, they planned to build a city with an enormous tower marking the center. When God saw that this tower was to reach to heaven, he punished Noah's progeny for their hubris by destroying the commonality of their language (hence Babel = babble). Unable to communicate with one another, the various groups, each now speaking its own language, went their separate ways, and the tower was left forever incomplete.

In his discourse on the relation between architecture and the printed word in *Notre-Dame de Paris,* a book that was so important for Wright throughout his career, Victor Hugo capitalized on the incompleteness, indeed, incompletability of the Tower of Babel to make it the symbol of "the grandeur of the edifice which printing has erected" in its assumption of architecture's role as society's main tool of communication. The linguistic "construction which grows and mounts in spirals without end," in "a confusion of tongues, ceaseless activity, indefatigable labour, fierce rivalry between all of mankind," and which includes novels, poems, plays, encyclopedias, and newspapers was, Hugo wrote, "the human race's second Tower of Babel."[206]

Beyond the purely formal characteristics that can be associated with it as an ascending spiral, the Tower of Babel thus describes the conflict of universality versus particularity of expression and of cohesion versus dispersion of social forces in terms of the different effects of architecture and language. Little of that broader context of meaning can be discerned in the earlier Gordon Strong project (fig. 292). There, the gathering of people in their cars is rather unceremoniously followed by a general dispersion. As in the constantly narrowing ascent of the Tower of Babel, where there is no human end in sight, the cars proceed in a line upward only to return back on themselves. In a very real sense, perhaps, Wright understood that frustration and lack of fulfillment were the perfect expression of an automobile outing.

The program of a museum, and especially one devoted to the exhibition of contemporary art, gave reason for a more complex interpretation of the mythico-historic model. In an interview in *Time* magazine published shortly after the plans for "The Modern Gallery" were made public, Wright explicitly referred to the social and cultural dimensions of the project. "Democracy demands this type of building," he said. "The thing you can't get any more in church you ought to get here: the health, vitality and beauty of the human imagination."[207]

Wright performed two related operations on the Tower of Babel that irrevocably altered its meaning. First, he turned it inside out, hollowing out the core and rotating the spiral around the central space. That space appeared in the early elevation/section as an inner luminescence or glow (fig. 291). Clearly a response to the urban setting, this internalization nevertheless produced a basis for reflexivity and self-realization in the path of movement that was missing in the purely centrifugal pattern prescribed by the ancient prototype. Second, and much more deliberate in its revisionism, was the inversion of the source. This characteristically modernist strategy of defamiliarization, or estrangement, was laid bare by the linguistic device of spelling the word "Ziggurat" backward ("Taruggitz"), thus indicating how the design should be read.

To read the ziggurat from the top down rather than from the bottom up, in other words, to view the spiral's completion in its end rather than its beginning, entirely reoriented the building in social as well as phenomenological terms. The inverted pattern of circulation redefined the relation between means and end exemplified in the mythico-historic source. The Tower of Babel recedes in stages as it spirals upward, but it can never reach the ultimate goal. The human means at its disposal can only point ineffectually to the unattainable infinite "beyond." The other-directed process is one of ill-conceived expectations constantly frustrated.

By inversion, the circulation pattern in Wright's design implies completion and self-fulfillment along with the prospect of continuous renewal (figs. 338, 320). To start by going straight to the top and then working one's way down grounds the experience in the immediacy of the present. Movement from the unknown to the known becomes a voyage of discovery that always returns to a point where the knowledge and experience gained can be utilized again and shared with others. Implied in a return to where one started is the possibility of beginning again; and implied in the dynamically expanding shape of the spiral is the idea that no repetition of the experience will ever be the same.[208]

When Wright was asked in 1945 by the *Time* reporter how he had arrived at the unfamiliar form of the building, he replied that the "basic idea" came from the ancient Middle Eastern ziggurat. But it was only when "he turned it upside down" that it could work. He explained that, because of its "pyramidal" shape, "the ziggurat is pessimistic." While pointing upward, it dies out in the ground. Inverted, however, it can be made into a container of "pure optimism"—an "optimistic ziggurat."[209]

Wright's deconstruction of the Tower of Babel reveals the conflicts in the model at the same time that it offers a resolution of them. In this regard, it must be seen as a utopian project, in both the social and the artistic senses of the word.[210] The inward-turning spiral follows from Taliesin West but reconfigures the "myth of the eternal return" as a path to social reconstruction through the experience of art. In the Tower of Babel, the centrifugal pressures of the uphill struggle, resulting in lack of cooperation and communication manifested themselves in the disintegrative effects of language (fig. 339). Artistic and architectural unity decreased in inverse proportion to the increase in linguistic disunity.

The gentle "stroll down" the self-renewing loop of the Guggenheim spiral gathers its participants into a continuous flow that converges on the social space at the center (fig. 342).[211] The integration of art and architecture by means of a "perfect plasticity of presentation" was thought by Wright and Rebay to reflect the integrative effect of modern, nonobjective art. Such art, in Rebay's view, spoke a "universal language" that had the power to usher in "the bright millennium of cooperation and spirituality" even "more firmly than any league of nations." One should remember that the United Nations headquarters was in fact built while "The Modern Gallery" was on hold (1947–50) and that many observers at the time had the vision, as Lewis Mumford expressed it, of an architecture that might suggest "the dawning concept of world government or make visible the love and cooperation that are needed for its success."[212] Harrison and Abramovitz's United Nations clearly relied more on simultaneous translation than on architectural symbolism to break down the barriers of political and cultural difference. Wright's design for the Guggenheim, for better or worse, can almost surely be said to have initiated the popular postwar idea that the art museum would be the ideal instrument for bringing together people of differing classes, races, and political persuasions.

■ ■ ■

The utopian idea of the integrative effect of art, as understood by Wright and Rebay, was given metaphorical expression in the actual space and rhythm of the building. Rebay believed that, to receive the enlightening effects of art, one had to submit "beyond all will or wishes" to its "influence."

The descending spiral provided a path of least resistance, as it were, which Wright emphasized in describing it as a "drifting" motion. After taking the elevator to the top, the visitor "drifts down" the curving ramp, carried along by its slow, regular, pulsating movement (fig. 340). No level horizon line is visible across the open well—only the rising and falling shapes of the parapets, curling like undulating water (fig. 341).

The buoying effect of the building's interior space is not adventitious but was a direct consequence of Wright's intention to create an illusion of a fluid "environment."[213] The concentric circles of tubular glass forming the dome of the earlier project of 1945 would have given the impression of a rippling surface of water spreading over the central space (cf. fig. 321). The curving, upturned parapets would have carried the illusion down to the base of the court, to the place where Wright eventually designed the lens-shaped pool and fountain to indicate where the flow of the ramp begins and ends (fig. 342). The implosive pressure of the ramp on the inner space is eased by the two outlets, one above and the other below (fig. 343).

The space of suspension between the dome and the pool is like few others and has its mythical parallel in a world not too far removed from that described in the biblical account of the Tower of Babel. Traditionally, the dome in architecture has been seen as modeled on the "dome of heaven."[214] Whether interpreted in Christian or secular terms, the image is a static one. Wright's watery dome, by contrast, issues from the description in Genesis 1:6–7 of the creation of the firmament before it is actually named and given the form of Heaven (Genesis 1:8). The firmament is created "in the midst of the waters" to "divide the waters from the waters" (that is, "the waters which were under the firmament from the waters which were above the firmament"). Recalling the landscape of the Tower of Babel after the waters of the Flood receded, Wright's suggestion of a world just preceding the particularization of Heaven (and Earth) offers a vision of infinite potential as a fluid, polymorphous environment.

Wright likened the state of pure potentiality of the Guggenheim space to the suspended animation of a "quiet unbroken wave." "The impression made upon one" by the interior space of the building, he wrote, is "similar to that made by a still wave, never breaking, never offering resistance or finality to vision. It is this extraordinary quality of the complete repose known only in movement that characterizes this building." More than any other, it was this image he tended to repeat to critics and reporters. "You will *feel* the building . . . as a curving wave that never breaks," he assured Aline Saarinen. "You will feel its quiet and its consistency."[215]

The creation of a feeling of suspension in space and time was Wright's answer to the question of what environment would be most conducive to preparing the museum-goer for the "relaxing influence" and "healing embrace" of non-objective art. But it was more than that too, for Wright conceived of this mode of reception as the basic precondition for entering the world of artistic illusion as such. Works of art image landscapes, environments, spaces, and things in a framework separate from reality. As an extension and container of those fictive worlds, the interior of the Guggenheim Museum was designed to mirror their irreality. The space of perception was defined as a potentiality of contem-

342. Guggenheim Museum. Interior, view down to pool and fountain at base of ramp.

343. Guggenheim Museum. Interior, dome.

344. Guggenheim Museum. Installation proposal, "The Masterpiece" (April 1958).

THE MASTERPIECE

plation removed from the mundane limits of time and space. The museum collapses seeing into being by assuming the "willing suspension of disbelief," normally associated with the act of looking at pictures, into its own physical form.[216]

Wright thought of the museum as an extruded artist's easel and often justified the angle of the outer walls against which the paintings were to lean by comparing it to the angle of the easel in an artist's studio.[217] The "new unity between beholder, painting and architecture" that Wright hoped to achieve represented a short-circuiting of the role of the traditional museum and a powerful critique of its usual mode of operation. Solomon Guggenheim's paintings were not to be regarded as a "collection" of rare objects removed from their original contexts and offered up to the connoisseur for analysis and delectation. The nearly ground-level placement of the pictures brought them into a more intimate relation with the viewer. Their tilt was supposed by Wright to make viewing more easy and "natural."[218]

The lack of frames and glass removed another layer of mediation. The distancing base-band, however, kept the "overcurious observer" from "inspecting" the works too closely. There would be no aggressing on pictures in Wright's museum: each would be "master of its own allotted space" (fig. 344).[219] In the "laid back" environment of the fluid ramp, as Wright pictured it, a child might be seen playing with a yo-yo—a perfect metaphor for the spatial continuity of the building—while her parents and others are "taking in" the message of a "masterpiece." The Guggenheim may well have been the first museum designed at least as much, if not more, for the Sunday outing as for the specialist's research trip.

At the core of Wright's conception, however, there is more than one paradox. The free-form architecture eschewing a "rectilinear frame of reference" was interpreted by many artists and most critics as warring with painting and condemning it to subservience. Wright, by contrast, maintained that "in any right-angled room the oblong or square flat plane of a picture automatically becomes subservient to the . . . architecture." He was not alone in maintaining that pictures hung flat on walls in rectangular frames are easily reduced to the status of a postage stamp. He believed that his system of placing the paintings against a tilted, outward curving wall would "liberate" them from the control of an external "background" and give them the breathing space they need to be seen as individual objects in their own right.[220]

A further extension of this paradox involves the relation between art and the environment. The disjunction between painting and architecture lay at the basis of most criticism of the building. Wright did not deny the point completely, for a certain "detachment" was necessary in his view to achieve the "liberation" of painting from its subservient, two-dimensional existence as merely an aspect of or "hole in the wall." Wright argued that "a picture (like sculpture and like a building) [is] a *circumstance* in nature, sharing light and dark, warm and cold, changing with every subtle change."[221] Perhaps not so ironically, then, it was this perception of the total environment in which art is seen that led Wright to create a system of exhibition that emphasized, as never before in a museum, the dependence of art on its context.

The Guggenheim Museum calls into question almost all previous assumptions about how art should be seen. It offers no firm ground, no consistent horizon line, no tectonic structure in which paintings, not to speak of sculpture, can

345. Donald Judd: *Untitled,* Guggenheim International Exhibition, 1971.

346. Frank Stella: *Darabjerd I,* 1967.

be conventionally displayed. The transparency of the relation of the upright human figure to the parallel picture plane is intruded upon by the destabilizing effect of the building on the body. The involvement of the body in the act of looking brings to the space of art the body's own space. Real time and real space work their way into the situation to extend and ultimately to break down the traditional boundaries and limits of art.[222]

The Guggenheim Museum predicted in many ways the changes that occurred in art in the years immediately after it was finished. Begun as a building exclusively to show painting of a very specialized type, it ultimately came to exhibit forms of art that were neither painting nor sculpture of the traditional sort. Sometimes it has been difficult to say whether it has simply adapted well to these new forms of expression or whether it has actually played some role in their creation. One of Donald Judd's first "contextual" works, for instance, was a site-specific piece for a Guggenheim International exhibition (1971; fig. 345). Its overall circular shape was clearly given by the geometry of the building, while the relation between the heights of the inner and outer cylinders was determined by the slope of the building's ramp in relation to an abstract horizon line. Artists as diverse as Mario Merz, Robert Morris, Carl André, Dan Flavin, and Jenny Holzer have all been challenged by the building to produce new work. If the move to the shaped canvas by so many artists in the 1960s seemed in some sense justified by the space of the recently opened Guggenheim, certain large-scale Earthworks like Smithson's *Spiral Jetty* (1969–70) are difficult to imagine without taking Wright's structure into account (figs. 346, 287).[223]

■ ■ ■

It is ironic, given the environmental and contextual implications of the Guggenheim Museum, that its relation to its own urban context is so problematic. The denial of the "rectilinear frame of reference" that opened the museum to new ways of dealing with the relation of art to the social sphere resulted in an intervention in the urban fabric that disrupted the orthogonal grid of the city and set the building in obvious opposition to that conventional social network. But to conclude from this that Wright was also "waging war" on the city would be as reductive as saying that the building was designed to "tyrannize" the art exhibited in it. The logic of inversion that governed the design was one of defamiliarization and destabilization intended to produce, in a quintessentially modern way, the outlines of a utopia.

From its origins, the concept of utopia has been fundamentally a literary one, in which an imaginary place of harmony and fulfillment is projected in opposition to the disorder and frustrations of everyday existence. Although it is usually traced back to Thomas More's early sixteenth-century description of an ideal commonwealth located on an island, one might well think of the city on the plain of Shinar planned by Noah's progeny as the originary case.[224] Indeed, the focal tower of that design, denoting a community center, would become a characteristic feature of modern utopian city design.

The Tower of Babel, and the city surrounding it, suffered the consequence of all utopias: private interests overwhelmed the public good. Its dystopic end became the perfect symbol for the nineteenth-century romantic realism of Victor Hugo. For him, utopia could not be *built*, only *written*. In the chapter "This Will Kill That" in his novel *Notre-Dame de Paris*, he described how literature had taken over the functions of social expression and representation from architecture following Gutenberg's invention of movable type at the end of the fifteenth century. More's *Utopia* appeared shortly thereafter. The "prodigious edifice" of Hugo's own "second Tower of Babel" remained "perpetually unfinished," a by-product of "the printing press, that giant machine, tirelessly pumping the whole intellectual sap of society [and] constantly spewing out fresh materials for its erection."[225]

Wright always considered Hugo's discussion of the battle between the book and the building essential to an understanding of architecture. In *A Testament*, published in 1957 as the Guggenheim was going up, Wright called "This Will Kill That" "the most illuminating essay on architecture yet written," adding that Hugo's "study of the tragic decline of the great mother-art [has] never left my mind." Even though Hugo maintained that there was no way in which architecture might ever again become the force for social change it once had been, Wright read Hugo more optimistically. He claimed that Hugo "went on to prophesy: the great mother-art, architecture, so long formalized, pictorialized by way of man's intellect could and would come spiritually alive again. . . . The soul of man would by then . . . be awakened by his own critical necessity."[226]

The Guggenheim Museum was not designed merely to liberate art. It had the much larger social purpose, as Wright said, of providing a modern substitute for religion.

As such, the building represents Wright's ultimate response to Hugo and to the challenge of language. His clients' utopian belief in non-objectivity as a "universal language" provided the opportunity and the rationale, and World War II the immediate context. Community and understanding were to replace disintegration and disagreement. The architectural solution was a deliberate reversal of a linguistic sign: Ziggurat became Taruggitz (just as Wright's model literary utopia, Samuel Butler's *Erewhon*, got its name by the reversal of the spelling of "nowhere," the literal meaning of the neologism "utopia" invented by More).[227] Building utopia would be made possible by rewriting history, not as it was but as it should be. The inversion of the Tower of Babel recovered the original impetus of utopia while redirecting it toward a more realistic and human end. The "downward drift" of the descending spiral would always bring the visitor back to the communal space of the central court, where the integrative nature of the art would be experienced as a function of architecture (fig. 342).[228]

In a way then, the Guggenheim Museum is twice removed from its gridlocked site on upper Fifth Avenue: once as a critique, and again as an alternative space (fig. 347). It operates in the spatio-temporal realm where utopia has always existed—"nowhere unless everywhere," as Wright liked to say—the realm of the imaginary and the fantastic.[229] The recovery of a representational role for architecture, in opposition to language, entailed the reinstitution of a language of representation peculiar to architecture's own special history as an instrument of the imagination. The metaphor of the endless wave translated the bodiless experience of daydreaming and sleepwalking, so characteristic of utopian literature, into a manifest space of potentiality.

For better or for worse—and Wright himself, as we shall see, would sense the problematic nature of the case—the Guggenheim Museum was never designed to have more than an abstract relationship with the city block on which it sits. The utopian program and its formal exegesis precluded all extrinsic concerns. The imaginary site at the beginning of the process subsumed the real one in the end.

347. Guggenheim Museum. Aerial view, from Central Park.

Signs of Identity in an Increasingly One-Dimensional World

In the discussion of Wright's later work, and here I am referring specifically to the decade 1949–1959, one quite small building has loomed especially large: the Morris Shop built in downtown San Francisco in 1949 (fig. 351).[1] The ostensible reason is the spiral form it shares with the Guggenheim Museum. Completed ten years before its progenitor, the Morris Shop was regarded as a preview of things to come. Interestingly, it predicted not so much what the Guggenheim would be like but what it would not be like, from an urban perspective, that is (fig. 350).

Its importance lay in its exterior address rather than its interior space—in its facade as an indicator of a new urban intention. This externalization of architectural effect as a sign of identity between building and context was to define Wright's later work in ways that are still difficult to assess fully. This final chapter will offer some suggestions.

One of the reasons for the difficulty of Wright's work in the fifties is its sheer quantity; another is its variety; still another, and undoubtedly the most important, is its apparent eccentricity in comparison with the rest of contemporary production. The latter aspect might seem most surprising, because it was during this period that Wright came closer to the center of mainstream modern architecture than ever before—perhaps too close for his own comfort, not to speak of that of his professional colleagues. An assertion of individuality became an efficacious means for maintaining the distance everybody seemed to desire.[2]

In the two years 1949–1950, Wright received more than sixty commissions. In 1949, he was awarded the Gold Medal of the American Institute of Architects, the most conspicuous sign of professional recognition. The same year also saw the appearance of the Hollywood version of Ayn Rand's *The Fountainhead*, starring Gary Cooper as Howard Roark, a.k.a. Frank Lloyd Wright, the bête noire of the architectural establishment. From 1949 until his death at the age of ninety-one ten years later, Wright was constantly in the news. He appeared on radio and television talk shows and in popular magazines such as *Time, Life, Holiday, Look, Esquire*, and the *Saturday Evening Post*, as well as on the lecture circuit in major universities around the country and in important gatherings around the world.[3] Wright became, in effect, the first superstar architect of the twentieth century. It was a role he relished, but one that also deflected criticism from the work and to the person. Some observers even read the shape of Wright's porkpie hat into his buildings.

Wright's popularity was in part the result of the general postwar acceptance of modern architecture. He rode the crest of that wave with skill and flamboyance. Modern architects throughout the world were now being called on to design everything from corporate headquarters to foreign embassies, from public high schools to public libraries. Modern architecture, in the post–World War II era, became the architecture of the establishment. As such, it became the new academy. The corporate style of the Miesian glass box, which seemed so perfectly to express the late capitalist society that called it into being, proliferated.

Reaction among architects to the "anonymity" of such "packaging," which "obliterates the past" and produces what Norman Mailer called the "empty landscapes of psychosis," came in many forms.[4] Almost all took some leaf out of the book of Expressionism. There was the Engineer's

Aesthetic, which favored complex, sometimes historicizing, often naturalistic effects of shell concrete construction. There was what the Museum of Modern Art dubbed the new architecture of "imagery," buildings that evoked "natural or man-made objects." This, of course, came very close to, and sometimes even overlapped with, Wright's "organic architecture." And, finally, there were the beginnings of Brutalism, Le Corbusier's highly expressionistic contribution to the postwar ethos, along with its overt antitype, the decorative formalism and historicism of such architects as Edward Durrell Stone, Minoru Yamasaki, and at times, Philip Johnson.[5]

Wright's architecture shared much with all these attempts to give meaning, individuality, and expression to the built environment. Appropriately chosen examples of Wright's work would not look out of place in an exhibition showcasing any of the above tendencies. But what is more interesting is what would remain eccentric and unassimilable. Wright had always resented the International Style. His work consistently resisted strict modernist classification. Before the war, such disagreement could be read as one of means rather than ends. With the onset of the fifties, however, the equation changed radically. While the other leaders of modern architecture all seemed to proceed on the basis of an unquestioning faith in the virtues of modernism, Wright began to challenge some of its basic premises in his final years. His attitude can best be described as conflicted.[6]

In 1948, in the introduction to the January issue of *Architectural Forum* devoted to his work of the preceding decade, Wright sounded a very disquieting note. "Contemporary art," he said, "cannot be ignored in any vital scheme of life. The Art of today is the art that really belongs to us: it is our own reflection. In our self-centered century what inspiration do *we* offer? The Past may well look with pity at the spiritual poverty of our civilization, the future will laugh at the barrenness of our Art."[7]

It should be noted that Wright said "we," not "it," when referring to contemporary art. The more Wright felt he shared in the collective responsibility for the effects of modern architecture on the environment, the more he began to distance himself from modern architecture's categorical self-referentiality, especially vis-à-vis the past. On a trip to Baghdad in 1957 to discuss the commission for an opera house, he remarked to a group of Iraqi architects that, although he realized he had been brought there "to help modernize" the city, they should understand that modern is "becoming a bad word" in architecture. In reviewing the edited transcript of the talk, he added that it posed "a hazard at best" to the environment.[8] In this situation as elsewhere during the fifties, Wright advised caution. On more than one occasion, he remarked that the architect "should rescue, not destroy"; he should show that he is "not destructive, but constructive" in dealing with "his inheritance from the past . . . to which he [usually] pays scant respect." The architect should think "not only to develop but to preserve" that which is "characteristic" of a place.[9]

One can find echoes of such sentiments earlier in Wright's career, in the late teens and twenties, for instance, in his consideration of local traditions and history in the design of the Imperial Hotel.[10] But the trajectory of Wright's thought in the fifties can more effectively be seen in relation to his immediate past. History as a matter of recuperation and reintegration began to redirect Wright's thinking in the later 1930s, when the temporal dimension of architecture became of fundamental importance to him. The intersection of nature and culture in Taliesin West introduced a register of effects that eventually allowed Wright to deal with the man-made and natural environments on relatively equal terms. The distinction of modernism versus traditionalism that was operative in the Imperial Hotel no longer obtained. Any site, any environment offered some visual evidence of preoccupation on the scale from nature to culture, and this had to be respected if the building was to become a meaningful part of the life around it.

The Italian architect Giovanni Michelucci described this characteristic feature of Wright's work in the early fifties as a "spontaneous mimeticism" ("spontanea mimesi"), an unconscious and undifferentiated drive to imitate na-

ture, whether in its raw "genuine" state or after it had been "collectively elaborated through history" onto the plane of culture. Michelucci characterized Wright's approach as that of a realist. "The context in which any building of his is to be inserted," he wrote, "is considered simply in terms of its actual reality as a physical fact."[11]

Realism is hardly the term that one would ordinarily apply to Wright's work of the fifties. Fantasy has been the more usual one. But perhaps there is a deeper connection between the two than one might initially suppose, and it is this I intend to explore. To see how Wright dealt with the problem of contextualization at the different extremes posed by the modern city and suburb, we will look first at two urban sites where infill was the issue. We will then look at an "edge-city" condition and a suburban site where historical and regional identity had to be extended and implanted in the natural environment.

Morris Shop

Wright's first contact with Lillian and Vere Morris, the owners of an elegant shop in San Francisco that sold contemporary furnishings and gifts for the home, came in 1944. About three and a half years before they commissioned him to redesign their store, the Morrises asked Wright to draw up plans for a house for an ocean-front property they had just bought in the fashionable section of Seacliff, at the northwestern edge of San Francisco.[12] Situated between Lincoln Park and the Presidio at China Point, the steep cliff offered dramatic views of the Marin Headlands and the Golden Gate.

Wright proposed a cliff-hugging structure of reinforced concrete that jutted out over the headland like a pier and telescoped down the face of the rock over a hundred feet to the edge of the water (fig. 349). The four floor levels suspended within the inverted cone were connected by ramps around an open circular well that extended down to the base. An opening at the bottom allowed the cool moist

349. Morris House project, San Francisco, Calif., 1944–46. Perspective from below.

350. Morris Shop, San Francisco, 1948–49. Exterior.

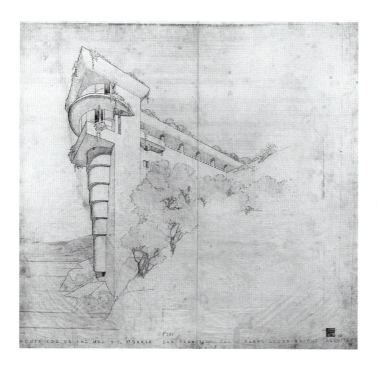

air of the water and the sound of the crashing waves to enter the hollow structure, which thus functioned as a combined draft/resonating chamber. While the streamlined exterior of the house gave the impression of a surface eroded by the action of wind and tide, its chalky, annular shape would have looked like a large sea snail, or conch, attached to the cliff face. Inside, the sound of the sea would have reverberated as if the house were a shell held to one's ear.[13]

It is important to stress the comprehensive and synesthetic naturalism of the house in order to appreciate fully the contrast with the design of the couple's downtown store as a response to a completely different, urban context (fig. 350). After the project for their Seacliff house was put on the back burner sometime in 1946 or 1947, the Morrises asked Wright to do a complete remodeling of their shop on Maiden Lane. The drawings were done in 1948, and construction was completed the following year.[14]

Maiden Lane is a short, two-block street—really more like a mews than a street—that begins in the middle of one end of Union Square, directly opposite the Saint Francis Hotel. Union Square has always been the center of the upscale shopping and hotel district of San Francisco; it was the first city park in the United States to receive an underground parking garage (1942). The lane itself is typically heterogeneous, containing a number of relatively tall buildings interspersed with two- and three-story shops. The Morris Shop specialized in modern glassware, silver, china, and linens, with separate departments for books and fine prints.

Wright adapted the circular plan of "The Modern Gallery" scheme of the Guggenheim Museum (1945) to the tight, party-wall situation, retaining more or less the plane of the original facade, but eliminating its plate glass "show windows" and opening up the existing two-story space within (fig. 351).[15] A ramp joins the two store levels in a continuous display of merchandise laid out on counters, in cases, and on shelves following the curving plan. The double skylight is masked by a suspended panel of convex and concave plexiglass bubbles that covers the entire central well. Hanging planters, a hemispherical aquarium, and

351. Morris Shop. Interior (1949).

several circular cutouts in the ramp wall for the display of objects and artwork help give the interior a dreamlike character that removes it entirely from the pedestrian world outside the door.

The "door," in fact, is a kind of airlock. A barrel-vaulted tunnel, half glass and half brick, half inside and half outside, creates a transitional, depressurized zone between the street and the shop (fig. 352). The glass half relates to the open interior, while the brick continues the closed surface of the facade. The facade is an almost completely flat brick plane on which is superimposed a slightly smaller rectangle, one brick thicker, and into which has been cut the single, asymmetrically placed arch of the entrance (fig. 353). The brick is a thin, tawny, Roman type. The relief panel is edged top and bottom with stone, and on the left with an open weave, allowing it to be read as a large, hinged plane. At night it is underscored by a row of small square lights set in plexiglass blocks behind square spiral grilles. The half-stilted semicircular arch is given exaggerated importance by four radiating bands of brick voussoirs.

From the outside, the contents of the interior are a total mystery. The store name was only barely visible on the

352. Morris Shop. Interior, entrance (1949).

etched block of stone in the entrance arch. Wright had apparently not wanted even that much visibility, for the presentation drawings simply show the name etched into the glass door at the end of the vaulted tunnel (fig. 353). Such a deliberate masking and concealment of internal structure, space, and function flew in the face of modern design, most particularly of the modern commercial store and shop front, in fact, just the kind Wright was replacing. Wright's perversity was not the result of ignorance. The plate-glass display window of the modern department store had been one of the most characteristic features of early modern architecture at the end of the nineteenth century. Sullivan's buildings, among others, had made the Chicago in which Wright first practiced one of the leading centers for this display technique. Indeed, Wright himself had produced a characteristically modern design for the Bramson Dress Shop, in Oak Park, in 1937 (fig. 354).

If the small specialty shop drew the attention of modern architects in the late twenties and thirties, in the postwar period it really took off as a field for modern design that quickly changed the face of the American city. Numerous books on the subject, with contributions by such well-known figures as George Nelson, Morris Ketchum, and Victor Gruen, appeared soon after the war. They all stressed that the design of a shop front had to accomplish four objectives: it had to attract the attention of the passerby; it had to "identify" the store by name and by the character of the goods it sold; it had to display the goods in a dramatic way that would "create the urge to buy"; and it had to provide an attractive entrance that would entice the customer to come in.[16] The large glass display window was taken for granted. The recent evolution of the "open front," by which the rear wall of the display window, or show window, was replaced with glass so as to allow one to see directly into the store, was felt to be a logical consequence of modernist principles of functional expression and transparency. And the development of the "exterior lobby," in which a part of the street was appropriated for the store's display, made the boundary between inside and outside so amorphous that the customer was actually drawn into the store without knowing it (fig. 355).

The "open front" store became a paradigmatic expression of modern architecture. Transparent, functionally expressive, clearly designed from the inside out, it was a perfect instance of the self-referential, modernist object-building. Wright's critique of the type in the Morris Shop can thus be taken as a partial critique of modern architecture. Indeed, when seen in the light of his earlier design for the Bramson Shop, the Morris Shop represents a rejection of certain formal principles that Wright himself had followed. But it is important to stress that the effects in this case are not merely formal.

Transparency involves an often unstated psychological dimension of vision. The hypostatization of the view in modern architecture reinforces the putative sense of mastery in the subject of the gaze and turns its object into a

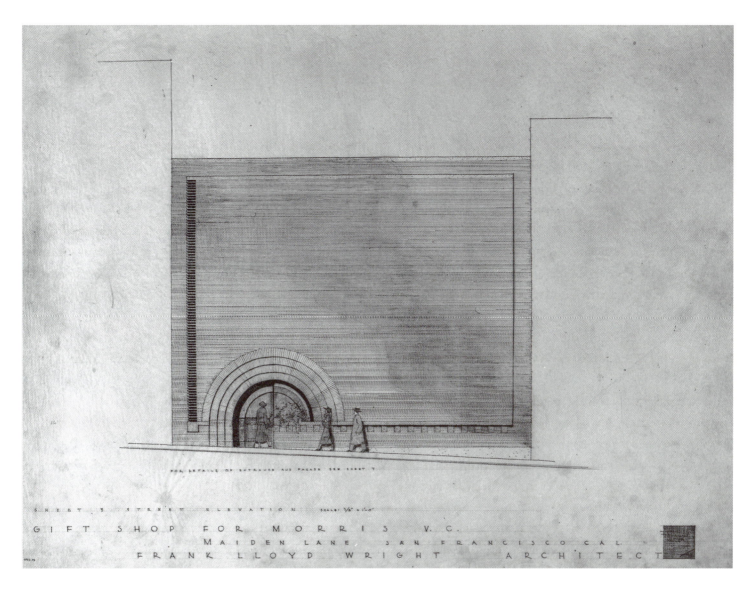

GIFT SHOP FOR MORRIS V.C.
MAIDEN LANE SAN FRANCISCO CAL.
FRANK LLOYD WRIGHT ARCHITECT

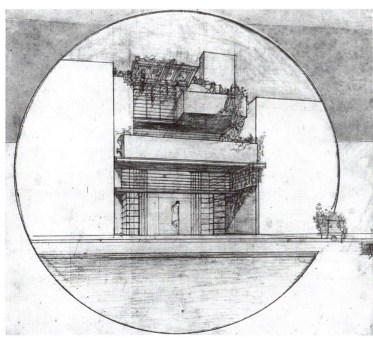

354 (*left*). Bramson Dress Shop project, Oak Park, 1937. Perspective.

355 (*right*). Ketchum, Giná & Sharp: Catty Patty Shoe Store project, for Kawneer Company, mid-1940s. Perspective.

commodity fetish. The display window was typically thought of as a "theater set," and the psychology of "window shopping," a vicarious experience.[17] Desire for the fetishized object was increased by the physical alienation of subject from object. In the Morris Shop, by contrast, the objects on display are seen only when they can actually be held in one's hand. The optic and haptic are never disjoined.

This is not to say that the Morris Shop is anticommercial. It is just that the fantasy world of consumerism is *contained*. Which brings us to the social dimension of Wright's critique. When Vere Morris saw the design and worried about the lack of visibility, Wright responded: "We are not going to dump your beautiful merchandise on the street but create an arch-tunnel of glass, into which the passers-by may look and be enticed. As they penetrate further into the entrance, seeing the shop inside with its spiral ramp and tables set with fine china and crystal, they will suddenly push open the door, and you've got them!"[18] Wright made the unstated voyeurism of the "open front" display window explicit, but immediately discharged it through action. In the "open front" store, the "window shopper" is literally exposed, as her or his fantasies and desires are materialized in full view of other passersby. In the Morris Shop, a boundary is maintained between container and contained, which preserves for the individual a sense of dignity and self-possession. The distinction between the public and the private that is integral to the urban order of the street is represented by the blank facade with its discreet, arched entrance (fig. 353).

■ ■ ■

The facade of the Morris Shop is clearly the most radical aspect of the design. As a wall bearing nothing and concealing everything, it is strictly representational. Though the logical choice for an opening in a brick wall, the arch strikes a particularly nonmodern note.[19] The very concept of *facade*, moreover, was contradictory to the idea of modernism. Following the belief that the exterior of a building should express the interior, the facade had become, by the end of the nineteenth century, simply a facing or extrusion of internal conditions of structure and space. The perception of a building became a matter of probing rather than scanning. The more one focused on the relation between inside and outside, the more the building was viewed as independent and isolated from its actual context. Wright's Bramson Dress Shop, like his Guggenheim Museum, is a perfect case in point. The circular frame of the perspective literally declares the building's "self-centered" isolation (fig. 354). One looks at it as if through the magnifying glass of modernist analysis.

The facade of the Morris Shop proposes a different sort of reading, one more like scanning. Instead of looking in and out, as it were, one reads from left to right.[20] The brick wall lines up flush with the adjoining facades to create a continuous ground that preserves the line of the street. Despite the relative inarticulateness and distinctly different scale of the barely relieved brick surface vis-à-vis its neighbors, the facade of the Morris Store describes an urban intention. The entrance arch, which at the time was felt to be the most unusual and even questionable aspect of the design, grounds the experience in a historical frame of reference.[21]

Early on, the arch was banished from the vocabulary of modern architecture. It spoke of the weight of tradition, of masonry structure, of hierarchy and symmetry, of enclosure and formal order. It also spoke, most eloquently, of connectedness and contextualism through its logical repetition in the arcade.[22] The arch and the arcade have traditionally been associated in urban terms with the making of a street and the announcement of the point of entry into a space beyond.

Wright often used arches in his Prairie Houses and public buildings of the Oak Park period but gave up the practice, to all intents and purposes, soon after establishing himself at Taliesin.[23] It returned in the early 1940s in the project for the adobe Burlingham House in El Paso (fig. 356). Significantly, it was in response to the regional context

356. Burlingham House project, El Paso, Tex., 1940–42. Preliminary sketch.

357. Le Corbusier: Maisons Jaoul, Neuilly-sur-Seine, France, 1954–56.

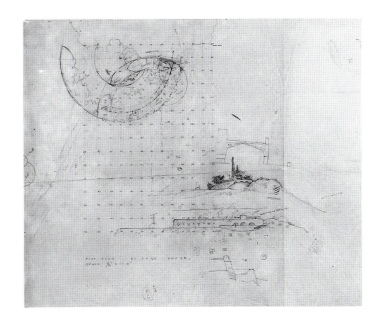

that Wright revived this seemingly regressive form. He considered it in representational terms. This is in marked contrast to Le Corbusier, for instance, who also began using arches and segmental Catalan vaults in a fairly concerted way from the late 1940s on, but who always rationalized their use in strictly structural terms.[24] His project for the Roq and Rob Housing Development (1949) and his Maisons Jaoul in the Paris suburb of Neuilly (1954–56) are well-known examples (fig. 357). The sheltering vault of the interior space is carried through to the exterior surface, where it is expressed as an extruded section. The representational character of the arch is denied along with any historical reference, as the arch itself is literally viewed askance.

The entrance arch of the Morris Shop cannot be related to a local vernacular as can the arches in the Burlingham House. Its position within the larger framework of the facade that the building presents to the street points to a more general reassessment of the relationship of modern architecture to the American urban environment. Its historical and contextual implications can probably best be understood diachronically rather than synchronically. The arch in the long, side street facade of Richardson's Glessner House in Chicago (1885–87) immediately comes to mind. Moreover, as Bruce Pfeiffer has noted, Wright was working on the text of his book about Louis Sullivan, *Genius and the Mobocracy*, at the time he was designing the store (it was published in 1949). Following in certain ways Richardson's example, Sullivan's small downtown banks, such as the ones at Owatonna, Minnesota (1906–1908), Sidney, Ohio (1917–18), and Columbus, Wisconsin (1919), established a significant precedent within the tradition of modern American architecture for the adoption of such a representational device as the arch for contextual ends.[25]

The Morris Shop thus became the link between late Sullivan and the revival of the wall and the arch in the work of Louis Kahn and Robert Venturi (fig. 403).[26] Although the strongly stated urban character of the store ultimately relies on typically modernist resources of material expressiveness and abstract formal composition, which give it a scale and a character somewhat at odds with its older neighbors, its critique of the self-referentiality of modernism at the level of program opened a way for further exploration of the issue of contextualism. The Morris Shop would not be typical of all Wright's later designs for cities,[27] but its critical thinking would undergird his most successful buildings of the fifties and provide a basis for more and more resonant historical referencing.

Masieri Memorial in Venice

The project that most clearly reveals Wright's increased involvement with history and local culture at the beginning of the fifties is the Masieri Memorial in Venice (fig. 362). It is significant that the commission came about as a result of his first trip to Italy since 1909–10. The occasion was the opening in Florence in May 1951 of an exhibition of his work, "Sixty Years of Living Architecture," and the award of an honorary degree by the Institute of Architecture of the University of Venice.

If Holland was the European country where Wright found his most appreciative audience during the teens and twenties, Italy took over that role in the post–World War II era. With architects and critics like Bruno Zevi, Giuseppe Samonà, Carlo Ludovico Ragghianti, and Carlo Scarpa devoted to him, Wright established a following analogous to the earlier *Wendingen* group. Key events in this development were the founding of the Association for Organic Architecture (A.P.A.O.) under the leadership of Zevi in 1945, Zevi's books on Wright and Organic Architecture (1945–47), the publication of the journal *Metron*, and the appointment of Samonà as director of the architecture school of Venice, also in 1945. The decision by Ragghianti's Studio Italiano di Storia dell'Arte to mount a major exhibition of Wright's work in Florence in 1951, at their headquarters in the Palazzo Strozzi, was a logical outcome.[28]

"Sixty Years of Living Architecture" was what later would be called a blockbuster exhibition. It comprised some eight hundred drawings and more than twenty models, including the very large one of Broadacre City. The émigré Philadelphia architect Oskar Stonorov, who had coedited the first volume of Le Corbusier's *Oeuvre complète* (1929) and had worked in partnership with Louis Kahn from 1942 to 1949, organized the exhibition. In recognition of the financial support given by Gimbel's Department Store of Philadelphia (through its owner, Arthur C. Kaufmann, a cousin of Edgar), the show opened in that city in January 1951 and remained on view through the following month. It traveled to the Palazzo Strozzi in May, and Wright flew to Italy to be present at the opening.[29] Aside from the normal professional accolades and events, Wright was presented with a distinguished medal by the Italian Foreign Minister Count Sforza in a ceremony at the Palazzo Vecchio. He then traveled to Venice, where, in addition to an honorary degree from the university, he received the Star of Solidarity from the city in a ceremony held in the Doge's Palace. (After Florence, the exhibition traveled to Zurich, Paris, Munich, Rotterdam, Mexico City, and New York, making its last stop in Los Angeles in 1954.[30])

During the time he was in Venice in June, Wright met the young architect Angelo Masieri. From a well-to-do family in nearby Udine, Masieri had graduated from the University Institute of Architecture of Venice in 1945 and had begun an informal partnership with his former teacher Scarpa the following year. His work between 1947 and 1951 was deeply indebted to Wright, whom Masieri apparently "loved and worshipped."[31] While he was a student, his father bought him a small house in Venice on the Rio Nuovo, where it joins the Grand Canal. It was a nondescript, three-story vernacular structure (fig. 358). Masieri and his wife, Savina, conceived the idea of asking Wright to rebuild it and apparently broached the subject to him on the occasion of his June visit. According to Elio Zorzi, Wright was intrigued with the possibility, and before he returned to the United States, he had a look at the site. The program called for three separate apartments, one per floor. One was to be for Angelo and Savina Masieri, a second was presumably for

the parents, and a third was to be a guest apartment that reportedly would be made available to Wright whenever he visited Venice.[32]

Nothing much happened for about a year. The following summer, the younger Masieris traveled to America to see Wright's buildings and to discuss the commission further. They went to Taliesin, although they never actually saw Wright.[33] On their way back from Fallingwater, they had a terrible automobile accident on the Pennsylvania Turnpike, in which Angelo Masieri and a young American architect friend who was driving were killed and Savina badly injured. This was on 28 June 1952. After several months of recuperation, Savina Masieri returned to Venice and decided, with the help of Angelo's parents, to go ahead with the project, but now as a memorial to her husband.

The Masieris consulted Samonà, as well as Scarpa and Zevi. By the end of the year, they had come up with two alternatives for a foundation that would be a living memorial. Both involved the school of architecture. One idea was to build a small apartment house, the rental income of which would be used for scholarship aid for students and for general program development; the other, more distinctive, was for a hostel that would provide lodging and a place to study for sixteen to twenty students, as well as a center for exhibitions, lectures, and other "collective activities." The choice was to be left to Wright.[34]

In December 1952, Savina Masieri wrote to Wright laying out the "two suggestions for [him] to consider," and noting that the idea for the hostel "appeals more strongly to us, owing to its higher moral meaning and adequacy," but most of all imploring him to carry on with the project despite the "changed circumstances." Wright responded on 30 December, saying that he was "willing" to proceed and that he thought "the dormitory for students would be best."[35] Working with drawings of the existing building and photographs of the site along with indications of allowable building heights and volumes within the zoning restrictions, supplied by Masieri under separate cover, Wright produced a design in less than a month. (One sketch is drawn directly

over the elevation sent by Masieri [fig. 363]; the finished perspective is dated 20 January 1953 [fig. 362].[36]) Wright had a formidable visual memory. His visit of eighteen months before must have remained extremely clear in his mind, for when Masieri saw the design, she said it looked as if it had been done "by heart." She was delighted by how "it fit perfectly into the plan of Venice."[37]

The site was uppermost in Wright's mind. Contextual issues dominated all others. The accommodations were in fact quite simple: the building would contain a library *cum* general meeting room, a kitchen and communal dining area, sixteen bedrooms, plus a rooftop apartment. No expression of "memorial" as such was intended, nor did Wright propose any. The site, on the other hand, presented an extraordinary challenge, with cultural and political im-

359. Masieri House. Distant view, from the Accademia.

360. Masieri Memorial project, 1951/52–55. Site plan. A = Masieri Memorial; B = Palazzo Balbi; C = Ca'Foscari (University).

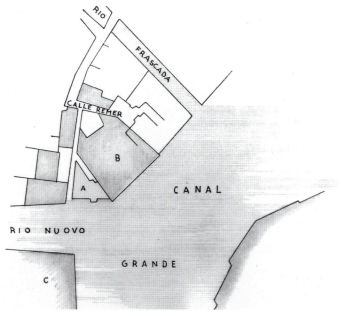

plications that ultimately defeated the idea of any modern intervention by a foreigner, no matter how sensitive the solution.[38] (The Masieri Foundation eventually chose to gut and remodel the interior of the house, leaving the exterior virtually untouched, a job undertaken by Scarpa in 1968.)

The Masieri House faces the Grand Canal, the most important artery of Venice and one of the most treasured urban environments in the Western world (figs. 359, 360). Though minuscule in terms of square footage, its location was one of the most prominent on the canal. Called the *volta de Canal*, it is the spot where the Rio Nuovo (Foscari) leading to and from the railroad station joins the Grand Canal to form its busiest intersection. It is at this point that the annual regatta terminates and where the ornamental pavilion

Masieri Memorial project. First scheme, 1953.

361. Plans, ground floor and mezzanine.

362. Perspective.

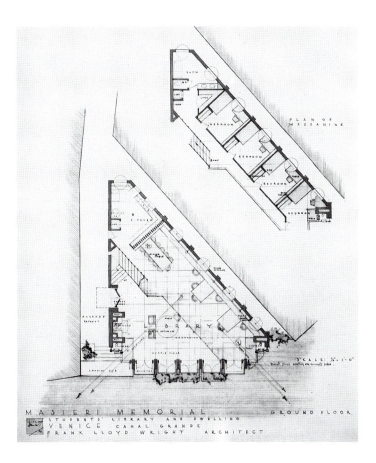

called the *macchina* is set up for the distribution of flags and prizes.

The *volta de Canal* can be seen from the Accademia, where it terminates the perspective framed, in the near distance, by the mid-eighteenth-century Palazzo Grassi on the right and by Baldassare Longhena's distinguished late seventeenth-century Palazzo Rezzonico on the left. The Masieri house forms a vanishing point in the far distance, between the imposing marble facade of the late Renaissance Palazzo Balbi (at the time, the headquarters of S.A.D.E., the electric power company of the Venice region; now the seat of the regional government) next to it on the right, designed by Alessandro Vittoria in 1582–90, and the richly encrusted, late Gothic Ca' Foscari, the home of the University of Venice (restored by Scarpa in 1955–56), diagonally across the Rio Nuovo, on the left. Of special significance in the distant view of the *volta* is that the apse of the Church of the Frari can be seen rising above the diminutive Masieri house (the

tower looms above the Palazzo Balbi). One of the conditions imposed on Wright was that this perspective had to be maintained.

The actual site is in fact very much like a vanishing point (fig. 360). It is a small, triangular, wedge-shaped plot locked in between the abutting Palazzo Balbi and a companion-like vernacular structure, from which it is separated by a narrow alley and landing stage. Wright's plan regularized these conditions (fig. 361). Following the zoning guidelines conveyed to him by the client, Wright made the memorial a right-angle triangle, with its hypotenuse paralleling the side wall of the Palazzo Balbi. A new alley, isolating it from that building, allowed light to be brought into the stack of bedrooms located along the rear spine.

The triangular shape was used to give a sense of spaciousness inside, as well as distant views outside along the diagonals defined by the open corners, a fact Wright duly noted on the plans. The building contained five levels, in-

363. Masieri Memorial project. Preliminary sketch of facade drawn over plans supplied by Masieri.

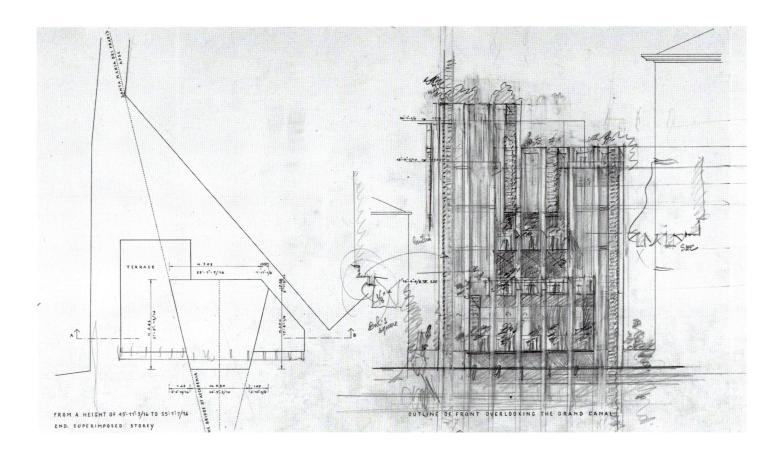

cluding (in the initial scheme) a mezzanine over the rear of the ground floor, plus a roof garden with a belvedere. The library occupied the front two-thirds of the main ground-floor space, with the dining area and kitchen beneath the mezzanine. Each of the other floors had space for four bedrooms.

It is not easy to read the disposition of the interior from the exterior, and in fact there is no straightforward correspondence between the two (fig. 362). The facade preserves a visual life of its own, pulsating on the surface in vertical lines and horizontal beats.[39] It was divided into five bays by clearly articulated vertical fins. This linear concrete structure was to have been faced with thin marble slabs—white with dark pink veins. The balconies, projecting through this mesh in groups of threes and fives, would have been faced with the same Pavanozzo marble. The potentially static, centralizing A:B:B:B:A rhythm they establish in the hori-

zontal dimension, slightly offset by the asymmetrical tower and extra balcony in the middle right register, would have been dynamically undercut by the high center of gravity created by the tall glass void of the double-height main-floor library.[40]

Beyond the recessed end bays, the two open corners were treated like vertical lanterns, composed of alternating sections of clear and blue-tinted Murano glass containing neon light tubes. The building's luminous edges would have made it appear to glow, while blending into the surrounding atmosphere. That sense of dematerialization so characteristic of Venetian architecture also governed the design in the vertical dimension. The flowering roof terrace and projecting belvedere were based on the typical *altana* and *liagò* of Venice that give its roofscape such a picturesque air. Wright's very first sketches have the belvedere on the left side of the roof, showing that he began by following almost exactly what existed (figs. 363, 358). Rendered in the more solid materials of concrete and marble, however, the belvedere in that position would have attracted too much attention to itself (and perhaps even blocked the view of the Frari apse). Shifted to the right, next to the taller Palazzo Balbi, it effected a smooth transition from one roofline to the other, acting almost like a volute.

The watery ground of Venetian architecture was also brought into play, both as a transparent and as a reflective plane. The perspectives of the Masieri Memorial show the vertical piers of the facade as if reflected in the water, like those of the celebrated Ca' d'Oro, which Wright's design resembles in more ways than just this (fig. 364). But the vertical continuity below water level was to be more than an illusion. Noting how "Venice does not float upon the water like a gondola, but rests upon the silt at the bottom of the sea," Wright designed the piers to "rise like reeds from the water" above concrete piles that "should be seen below the surface," reflection and reality thus becoming one.[41]

The outward-directed, contextual nature of the Masieri facade was remarked upon by the most perceptive critics of the time. The Italian art historian Sergio Bettini noted in 1954 that "Wright has set up a closer figurative relationship between the facade and the color surfaces of the Canal, than between the facade and the Memorial itself," meaning its interior spaces. This testified, in Bettini's view, to Wright's "full comprehension of Venice," where "the facades of . . . buildings failed to draw any sustenance, as it were, from their inner selves" and where the "spatial forms [of the city] are defined by the facades of the buildings that are bound together in a *continuum* of color."[42]

Bettini ascribed Wright's ability to respond so sensitively to Venice's architecture to an affinity in terms of style. "The anticlassical character of the city is in keeping with Wright's tastes," he said. Giovanni Michelucci, as already noted, attributed the connaturalness to more involuntary causes: Wright, the Noble Savage, reacted to the Venetian scene with a purely "spontaneous mimeticism."[43] There is

some truth in both statements, but there is also a great degree of reductiveness, not to speak of condescension, especially in the latter. Wright was deeply impressed by the historical significance of the site, and his response was a very conscious act of architectural accommodation.[44]

The composition of balconies projecting in rhythmically ordered groupings echoed the traditional facade patterns of Venetian palaces (fig. 362). The floor lines were carefully adjusted to mediate between the string-courses of the neighboring Palazzo Balbi and the window heights of the smaller structure on the left. The interplay of single- and double-height stories likewise reflected Renaissance conventions of ordonnance. The reticulated, open-work design of the facade struck an abstract balance between the filigree late Gothic of the Ca' Foscari and the more solid, compact, classical facade of the Palazzo Balbi. One can see how Wright worried about that balance being tipped too much one way or the other. He continually worked over the composition. At one stage of the design, he pulled the balconies back somewhat and made the horizontal lintels flush with the outer face of the vertical piers, even adding one along the top to cap the facade and thereby reinforce the more classical aspects of the Palazzo Balbi (fig. 365). Neither classical nor Gothic in any of its details—and here the exclusion of the arch is worth noting—the Masieri Memorial combines, in a fundamental way, the formal qualities of both

On opposite page:

365. Masieri Memorial. Revised design, 1954. Perspective.

periods, just as it manifests their shared compositional patterns.[45]

Wright forthrightly declared his contextual intentions in all his statements about the building, whether privately to his client or publicly. On his initial submission of the design, he told Masieri that he "wanted, by way of modern techniques, to make the old Venice Tradition live anew." He believed his design to be "entirely sympathetic to the culture with which [he was] asked to cooperate" and fully "in the Spirit of Venice." When he first exhibited the project at the National Institute of Arts and Letters in New York in May 1953, he explained that "the architect intended to lovingly cherish the ancient Venetian tradition by the finest resources of modern architecture," proving, in his view, that modernity did not have to be a "destructive cliché."[46]

Once the design became public and controversy began to grow, Wright defended the project on the grounds of historical sympathy and concordance with the site in a way, and with a sense of humility, he rarely, if ever, had shown before. To those who opposed the project, Wright countered: "All the work I do takes account of the culture of the place I do it in, and the nature of that place. . . . My concept of a structure in Venice reflects Venice—her age, her style, her nature. True modern architecture, like classical architecture, has no age. It is a continuation of all the architecture that has gone before, not a break with it." In opposition to his brand of "true modern architecture," Wright set the "so-called international school of architecture which makes a distinct break with the past, disregarding the contribution the past has made."[47]

The controversy over the Masieri Memorial sparked one of the first important public debates around the issue of modern architecture and historic preservation. It is ironic that a project so specifically designed to fit into its historic context should have caused such a stir, but Venice was a very special situation and Wright the most outspoken and notorious modern architect alive. Very little of the debate actually focused on the inherent qualities of the design, and much of it took place before people had even seen the project.

■ ■ ■

Building in cities is a matter of politics, and that was the art Wright probably excelled in least. In fact, an impolitic act on Wright's part set the opposition in motion. While the Masieri family was quietly preparing the groundwork for municipal approval of the project, and before any public announcement of it had been made, Wright allowed the design to be included in an exhibition of his work in New York, the May 1953 show at the National Institute of Arts and Letters. A review in the *New York Times* by Louchheim featured the Venice project prominently.[48] The Italian press soon picked up the story, and, with local pride hurt as a result of having been kept in the dark, the battle was on. Needless to say, the growing sense of American high-handedness and imperialism after the war played into this. By mid-December 1953, Masieri wrote to Wright that "the whole European press is interested in it." "Venetian people have an almost morbid susceptibility for what regards their own town," she noted.[49] To which she might have added that many cultured and powerful foreigners regarded themselves as Venetians when it came to preserving the heritage of that city.

The "polemic," as the Italians referred to it, carried on from the early summer of 1953 into the early part of 1955. Articles pro and con appeared in daily newspapers and weeklies in every major Italian city. The London *Times* and the *New York Times* also became involved. The professional journals, especially in Italy, devoted generous amounts of space to the issue.[50] In general, those against the project opposed it on preservationist grounds. They did not want any building destroyed, since every building, no matter how "insignificant," was part of the "texture" of the city. Underlying this reaction was the belief that any modern building would be an intrusion of a totally hostile character. The Milanese architectural critic and preservationist Antonio

MASIERI MEMORIAL CANAL GRANDE VENICE
STUDENTS' LIBRARY AND DWELLING
FRANK LLOYD WRIGHT ARCHIT

Cederna, for instance, stated that even if Wright were "ten thousand times greater than Michelangelo, he must not build on the Grand Canal. . . . Today, not even the Eternal Father can build there anymore."[51]

Defenders of the Wright project were generally of three sorts. Ardent "organicists" of the Zevi-led A.P.A.O. felt that nothing could be more important for Venice than to have an example of Wright's work in its midst. Others, like Michelucci, distanced themselves from Wright on ideological grounds, yet believed this particular project had great contextual merit. Still others, perhaps the large majority of modernists, defended Wright's building mainly on the basis of freedom of expression. Whatever the actual merits of the design, they maintained it should be built as an "expression of the voice of our own age."[52] The controversy offered a welcome opportunity to defend modernism against a withering traditionalism.

Interestingly, some among that largest group of "supporters," wittingly or not, probably prejudiced the case by using the occasion to take a swipe at Wright. The English critic J. M. Richards, for instance, in a widely publicized piece, called the Masieri Memorial "an arty little building" that was "so old-fashioned in style that it might have been pulled out of a drawer of Mr. Wright's unexecuted designs of around 1920." "We can reasonably regret that what had begun to look like a test case should end without the test in fact being made," Richards opined. Resorting to a modernist (via futurism) rhetoric of aggressive antihistoricism, foreshadowing Brutalism, Richards belittled Wright's accommodating gesture as "a tame . . . pussy-cat with a ribbon around its neck, more ready to purr than to pounce." Revealing, quite simply, fundamental "misconceptions about modern architecture on the part of Frank Lloyd Wright," the project, and the debate it engendered, left in Richards's mind "the main question unanswered: when we of the mid-twentieth century build in a historic setting, have we the *courage* to speak with our own voice and the skill to do so with *positive effect*?"[53]

With friends like that, Wright certainly did not need

any enemies. Americans with Italian connections, like the aging connoisseur Bernard Berenson and the convalescent Ernest Hemingway, were engaged by the press to join in the attack. Berenson characterized the memorial as "a model for a table ornament in a banqueting hall"; Hemingway more ruthlessly declared that everyone would be placated if "as soon as it is finished it is burned." Perhaps most significant was the reaction of certain wealthy "art lovers." Marie Truxtun Beale, an American socialite who had helped raise funds to restore the Basilica of St. Mark's, called the project "a piece of inexcusable vandalism" and reportedly threatened the mayor of Venice: "Defend your city. If you allow this, I will regret ever having done anything for you."[54]

Beale's comments, as well as Berenson's, Hemingway's, and Richards's, immediately preceded the meeting of the Municipal Building Commission that was to decide on the legality of the design. After two heated sessions devoted to the subject (16 and 21 April 1954), the commission put off any decision by maintaining that the agreement of the abutters first had to be secured, since the project violated minimum perimeter requirements. Although the electric power company that then owned the Palazzo Balbi agreed to waive its rights, public opinion moved in the direction of the preservationists. After two hearings by the Municipal Council, the project was turned down in November 1955 on the advice of Venice's Artistic and Technical Commission.[55]

■ ■ ■

The Masieri Memorial preoccupied Wright for at least three years, from December 1952 at the latest until mid-November 1955. Unlike its predecessor, the Morris Shop, it never received anywhere near the same critical acclaim. Perhaps this was due to its increased deference toward its cultural context, meaning essentially its historical frame of reference. Although Wright deliberately refrained from employing the arch as an element of design in a city largely characterized by it, he used the arch as a framing device—a proscenium—to place his project in perspective, while gain-ing for it a purely representational meaning (fig. 365). In the rendering of the Masieri Memorial, the silhouetted arch highlights the new within the context of the old, assuring the past a renewed place of representation in the present.

As Bruce Pfeiffer has documented, the project for the Masieri Memorial remained particularly significant for Wright. He kept the "drawing at his table, or nearby, for quite a long period of time" and "went back and worked on it each day." On the perspectival rendering, "he applied colors, and then took a single-edge razor blade and diffused them. Into the colors from color pencils he would blend graphite from an HB pencil, again and again working with his razor blade and eraser until he achieved the patina desired."[56] The effect of historical patination slowly works in the drawing to dissolve the screen distancing past from present—the arcade within which we stand from the representation in "modern dress" on the stage-set of Venice.

Plan for Greater Baghdad

The Grand Canal in Venice was a very different kind of site from downtown San Francisco. It is the paradigmatic place of spectacle, lacking all those modern realities like automobiles and industry that would undercut the illusions of the stage. Where Wright eschewed any reference to the theatrical aspects of display-window techniques in the Morris Shop and internalized the drama of shopping as a lived, kinesthetic experience, he played into the historic image of Venice in the Masieri project to revive the metaphor of the theater as a way of conceptualizing and representing the architectural re-creation of a historically defined cityscape (fig. 365). But although it is the role of the proscenium arch to bracket any anachronism that might result from a modern intervention in the urban setting framed by it, Wright adopted the twentieth-century theatrical convention of "modern dress" as a way of making the reinterpretation of the historical text relevant and meaningful in contemporary terms. Yet the more he thought about the issue, the more he

seems to have concluded that such a solution was a compromise and that the convention of "modern dress" could never offer more than an indeterminate sign of identity between building and place.

If any design of Wright's can be taken to illustrate how he thought modern architecture could effectively be staged in what can only be described as updated "period dress," it is the project he did for an opera house and cultural center for the outskirts of Baghdad in 1957–58 (fig. 375).[57] Authorized just slightly before the Marin County Civic Center, it represents, along with that building, Wright's most important government commission. It was also his most significant confrontation with a non-Western culture since the Imperial Hotel.[58] Europeans and Americans had changed some since that time in their attitudes toward Orientalism, colonialism, and the so-called Third World in general, though nowhere nearly as much as they would during the period following the Baghdad commission, which itself fell victim to the Arab nationalist and socialist revolution that ended the Hashimite dynasty in Iraq. Wright was only one of a number of important Western architects, including Le Corbusier, Aalto, and Gropius, brought in by the pre-Qasim government to help "modernize" Baghdad and provide the Iraqi capital with buildings epitomizing the latest advances in Western technology and design. Wright's response, much more than any of the others, articulates in figurative terms the problems of cultural identity and self-determination at a moment of impending change.

■ ■ ■

Iraq is the Arab name for Mesopotamia, the ancient site of the Sumerian, Assyrian, and Babylonian civilizations that was conquered by the Arabs in the seventh century and made the center of the Abbasid Caliphate by al-Mansur in the following one. The modern nation-state of Iraq, with its capital in Baghdad, was created as a British mandate in 1920 after the breakup of the Ottoman Empire, which had ruled the Fertile Crescent of the Tigris and Euphrates

Valley since the sixteenth century. A limited constitutional monarchy, modeled on that of Britain, was established, and Faysal, one of the two sons of Husayn, who had led the Arab Revolt in 1916, was chosen in 1921 to take over the throne.[59] In 1932, a year before King Faysal I died, Iraq was admitted to the League of Nations as an independent state.

Independence, of course, is a term open to interpretation. Iraq remained a client-state of Britain throughout the duration of the Hashimite dynasty. Faysal I was succeeded by his son Ghazi in 1933. When the latter died in a car accident six years later, his son was only four years old. Until Faysal II came of age in 1953, Iraq was ruled by his uncle, Abd al-Illah, as regent. Under the system in place until mid-1958, when a revolution led by the military toppled the regime, the monarch was answerable not only to the British but also to a highly unstable, constantly fluctuating coalition of wealthy landowners and tribal chiefs, Western-educated elite professionals, and powerful army officers.

Oil was the key to material progress and development in Iraq in the period after World War II. The British-controlled Iraq Petroleum Company was created in 1925, but Iraq lagged behind other countries in the region in the exploitation of its fields. In 1950, as production increased, Iraq renegotiated its agreement with the company to increase its profits substantially. Following the nationalization of the oil industry in Iran that year and the fifty-fifty split in profits with Aramco negotiated by Saudia Arabia, the Iraq Petroleum Company agreed in 1952 to give Iraq a similar fifty-fifty deal.

Iraq's revenues increased dramatically, almost quadrupling from $32 million in 1951 to $112 million in 1952. (They reached $237 million by 1958.) To manage these enormous sums, the government created a semiautonomous Development Board in 1950, which was receiving 70 percent of the annual oil revenues by 1952. Its object, according to the enabling legislation, was to present "a general economic and financial plan for the development of the resources of Iraq and the raising of the standard of living of her people." "This plan," the legislation continued, "shall define a gen-

eral program of the projects to be undertaken by the Board and shall include in its scope but not be limited to projects in water conserving, flood control, irrigation, drainage, industry and mining as well as projects for the improvement of communications by river, land and air."[60] Nothing was said about public buildings at this stage.

The Development Board's first six-year plan (for 1951–1956) emphasized what economists call "social overhead capital." The bulk of the funds was spent on infrastructure: major flood control, irrigation, and water storage projects to harness the country's agricultural potential. (The Tharthar Dam had the added purpose of protecting Baghdad from the annual flooding of the Tigris.) Transportation and communication, industry, and construction were given much lower priority. In response to political pressure against this long-term, trickle-down approach, which was felt by many to help only the rich, the Development Board modified its philosophy in its next effective six-year plan (1955–1960), which was budgeted at $1.4 billion. Investment in transportation and public building now amounted to a little under half the budget, with that portion being divided nearly equally between the two sectors.[61]

To maintain its authority and to counter the constant threat of insurrection, the government was looking for "widespread and visible benefits quickly."[62] Urban areas, particularly Baghdad, where dissension was most likely to develop, were targeted for housing, health, education, and welfare projects, as well as for civic and cultural buildings. Money was specifically appropriated for new museums of antiquities and of modern art, a new parliament building, a royal palace, an opera house, a stadium, and a new campus to house the recently created Baghdad University (1956). Beginning in 1956, a Development Week was celebrated each spring, at which time new projects were announced and those just completed were dedicated with great fanfare by the king.

At first there seemed to be no general policy or direction in the building program. Some commissions, like those for the Iraq Museum (museum of antiquities), the National

366. Minoprio & Spencely and P. W. Macfarlane: Master Plan for Baghdad, Iraq, 1956 (with overlay sketches by Wright, 1957).

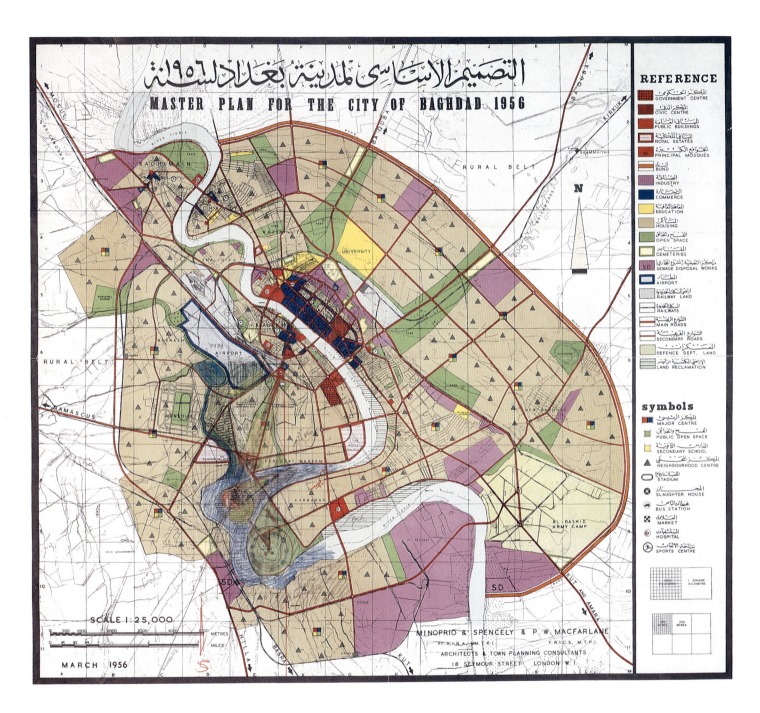

Parliament, and the Royal Palace, went to rather undistinguished architects, the first to the German Werner March, the latter two to the English firm of J. Brian Cooper.[63] In 1954 a competition was held for the National Bank of Iraq and, although Alvar Aalto and Gio Ponti were both invited to Baghdad, the Swiss architect William Dunkel was chosen. In 1955 Constantinos Doxiadis prepared a low-income

housing and community development program that would see partial implementation over the next four years; and Le Corbusier was initially contacted about the design of an Olympic stadium and sports complex.[64]

In December 1954, however, Minoprio & Spencely and P. W. Macfarlane, London planners active in the Middle East and South Asia, were called in to draw up a master plan for Baghdad that would eventually provide a focus to the program. Produced by the spring of 1956, the plan set forth an overall scheme for new street construction and public and private building, suggesting appropriate sites for a government center (west bank), a civic center (east bank), the university (south edge of town), and open green space (fig. 366). Following that, a series of discussions led to the gradual selection of a "panel of architects of world fame," as one report put it, to design key buildings.[65] The first of these commissions were decided upon in late 1956, and Wright's name was on the list. He was notified of the request for the design for "the Opera for the City of Baghdad" in mid-January and accepted almost immediately (24 January 1957). He was apparently invited to visit Baghdad during the second annual Development Week, in late March, to discuss the matter and see the site, but had to postpone the trip until May.[66]

In addition to Wright, the group of Western architects who were asked to participate in this high-profile enterprise would include Aalto, Le Corbusier, Walter Gropius and The Architects Collaborative, Oscar Niemeyer, and Ponti. Aalto was asked to do a museum for modern art, Le Corbusier a stadium and sports complex, Gropius and TAC the university, and Ponti a building to house the offices of the Development Board and the Ministry of Development. We know for sure that all but Gropius were contacted around the same time as Wright. Niemeyer was the only one to refuse, his reasons being political.[67]

Wright visited Baghdad during the last week of May, apparently the first of the group to do so. Aalto arrived in July, Ponti in August, and Le Corbusier in early November. Le Corbusier's visit overlapped with that of Gropius, who by that time had been given the commission to design the new Baghdad University, a project that Wright had already incorporated in his general plan.[68]

There was apparently a good deal of fluidity in discussions with the government, involving changes in site, expansion of the program, and even additional commissions. Wright played this game to the hilt, perhaps going too far

for his own good. The original invitation was for an opera house on a relatively small two-acre plot in downtown Baghdad.[69] This was part of the civic center that the 1956 master plan proposed for the densely built Rusafah section of the city and that would have entailed significant demolition of the historic core. Flying in over the city, Wright espied what he thought was a much more effective site: an island, locally known as Pig Island, at the southwest edge of the city, in the bend in the river between the Karradah peninsula (reserved in the master plan for use either as a park or as the site of the new university) and the Karradat-Maryam riverfront, where the new royal palace and foreign embassies were being built.[70]

The island would have been unthinkable as a building site until then; even the 1956 master plan fundamentally disregarded it as anything other than a place for a bridge crossing. Only with the flood-control measures just completed in that year, which finally alleviated one of Baghdad's most serious problems, could the river be looked to for a positive contribution to the urban landscape. The land in question did not fall under municipal jurisdiction but belonged to the royal household. Wright had to make a special request to the king, who turned over the island to him after Wright explained how it could be used to advantage. (Wright spoke of "the great historical river [being] celebrated" in his project.)[71] With this greatly enlarged and relatively isolated site, Wright was able to put forward the vision of a complete cultural and educational complex, providing the city with a new focus and scale, yet deeply rooted in Baghdad's historical beginnings (figs. 375, 376).

By the time he left for the United States, Wright apparently had (or at least believed he had) an agreement for a $45 million cultural center to include the opera house (which would double as a civic auditorium), a gallery of contemporary art, and an archaeological museum, all on the island in the Tigris, plus a separate commission for a central post office and telecommunications center in downtown Baghdad. There was also an understanding that he would include a proposal for the new university on the contiguous peninsula.[72] In developing the general scheme, Wright eventually added a botanical garden on the right (west) bank to complement the university.

The plans were done fairly rapidly. Most are dated June and July 1957, as is the report that accompanied the preliminary studies submitted to King Faysal and Crown Prince Abd al-Illah. After being reviewed in Baghdad, they were exhibited at the Iraqi Consulate in New York in early May 1958.[73] But clouds had already begun to appear on the horizon. An article in Boston's *Christian Science Monitor*, featuring a separate spread on Gropius's university, placed Wright's project in some doubt, claiming that his "whole Arabian Nights spectacular may be delayed pending the completion of hydrological studies of the flow of the Tigris" and that it "may not come to fruition" at all.[74]

It was not a scientific investigation of the site, however, that finally did in Wright's project. Faysal II and Abd al-Illah were assassinated in a coup d'état on 14 July 1958 that brought the revolutionary government of the military leader Abd al-Karim Qasim to power. Following a year of considerable turmoil and realignment of government agencies, during which little or no public building took place—and during which Wright himself died—the Hashimite program was reviewed. Although most of the earlier projects, except Wright's, were kept on the books, none but the Gropius university, the Ponti government offices, and, much later, a piece of the Corbusier scheme were implemented.[75]

■ ■ ■

Wright's designs for Baghdad differed from those of the other foreign architects at the levels of form, intention, and reference. While the differences may well reflect the political and ideological shift that took place in Iraq in 1958, to understand what that might mean in the broader context of East-West, First World–Third World cultural politics is another matter. Let us start by reconstructing how Wright approached the problem.

On his visit to Iraq in May 1957, Wright gave a talk to the Society of Engineers of Baghdad, describing his first impressions and outlining his general views. The talk was probably not at all what they wanted to hear, being more a critique of Westernization and modernization than a tribute to the power of those ideas to reform society. Contrasting, in a somewhat stereotypical manner, the "materialism" and "commercialism" of the West with the "spiritual integrity" of the East, Wright made no secret of where his sympathies lay.[76] He referred to the "old historical city" of Baghdad, going back to the reign of Harun ar-Rashid and the *Thousand and One Nights*; he spoke of the "Sumerian priority in the arts," of the "vigor" and "strength" of that era; he praised the "genius" of the culture "that produced the dome" and "the marvellous intricacy and beauty" of the faience decorative "flesh" of Islamic architecture. Reminding his listeners that this "great period in the life of the world . . . is still your period, I mean . . . your inheritance," Wright warned them not to "'sell out'" for the "wrong kind of success." He implored them to "reject the commercialization" of Western models so as to regain "contact with what is sound, what is deep in the spirit and what genuinely [is] yours."[77]

Wright's main point was that there is a *genius loci* and that it must be acknowledged and engaged for architecture to make a vital contribution to society. "Every nation has a genius of its own," he said. "Now in the push of modernism, . . . that ancient strength should not be weakened and lost. That background of your own culture should now be developed so genuinely, so broadly, and so individually . . . that no architect should come here and put a [Western] cliché to work." His role was not to bring to an "underdeveloped" nation the fruits of the technology of a more "advanced" one. He spoke of coming to learn and to help rather than to teach: "An architect must come to you to see the beauty of the life that was originally yours—understand the character and nature that made it beautiful and try by every means in his power to keep it alive by [the use of] modern science." The architect, especially the foreigner, should not come to the job with any preconceived notion of the value of "mod-

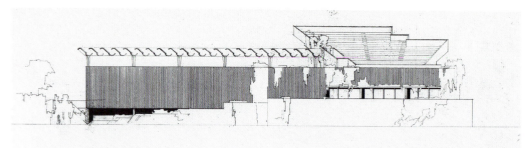

BAGHDAD / FINE ARTS BUILDING
ELEVATION SOUTHWEST   1:200

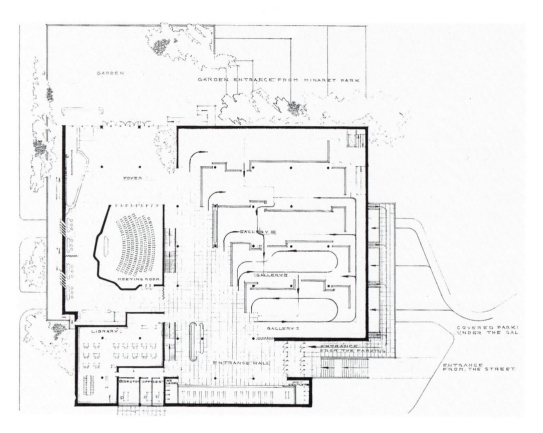

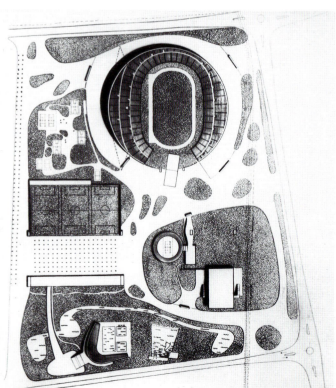

Top and center:
Alvar Aalto: National Art Gallery project, Baghdad, 1957–58.

367. Southwest elevation.

368. Plan, first floor.

Bottom:

369. Le Corbusier: Stadium and Sports Complex, Baghdad, 1955/57–80. General plan.

370. Walter Gropius and The Architects Collaborative: Baghdad University, begun 1957. Revised scheme, 1959–60. Aerial perspective, looking north.

ernization" but should look at the situation as a way "not only to develop but to preserve" what is "characteristic" of the place and its rich and long history. Wright ended the talk, no doubt unwisely in the light of future events, by recalling to his audience the value of living under a monarchy with deep roots in the past: "Kingdom has come to a point [in the world] where it is extremely decorative and valuable and interesting to the people." As subjects of a "democratic," constitutional monarchy, those present should consider themselves "all his Majesty the Baghdad citizen."[78]

The plans produced at Taliesin over the next few months mirrored these cultural and historical considerations. The process resulted in a design unique in Wright's *oeuvre* and worlds apart from those of the other Western architects. Rather than simply adapting modern architecture to local or regional conditions, Wright sought to remake what he referred to as the "historic nature" of Baghdad in contemporary terms.[79] By contrast, the other invited Westerners proposed buildings that were in essence the same as they might have designed for their home countries, which in fact many originally were. Despite its blue-tile surface and rooftop sculpture garden, Aalto's project for a National Art Gallery is almost identical to ones he produced for museums in Estonia and Scandinavia (figs. 367, 368). Le

Corbusier's Sports Stadium complex was directly based, as he himself remarked, on an earlier design of 1936–37 for the suburbs of Paris (fig. 369). Gropius's project for Baghdad University was designed around principles of American campus planning and administrative organization that TAC (The Architects Collaborative) had become experts in over the years (fig. 370).[80] (A few marginal nods were given to indigenous culture, as in the domed mosque, which, in its final form, was an Orientalizing pastiche of Saarinen's Kresge Chapel at MIT isolated in its own separate precinct on the northern edge of the site.)

The justification for such "regional adaptation" of International Style modernism lay in function. According to the theory of functionalism, with its basis in technological determinism and instrumental rationality, the solution to a design problem of a typological order had universal applicability. Particular local conditions having to do with climate or availability of materials or skilled labor, for instance, were only secondary factors that might inflect the design to give it an "authentic" regional flavor.[81] The significance of the measurable factor of climate, which was probably the most important distinguishing condition referred to by architects working in the Middle East at the time, was singled out by Gropius, Aalto, and Ponti as fundamental to their design decisions. Aside from the need for "the greatest possible flexibility of the organizational system," Gropius spoke of the "major problem" being "to counteract the excessive heat from May to September, often considerably higher than our blood temperature." "That hot wind," he told the reporter for the *Christian Science Monitor*, "is our main problem." The regional character of the design would thus be ensured, in his view, by the use of reflective white paint, glazed tiles, "plentiful waters," and roof overhangs, louvers, and grilles providing "shadow effects from the strong sunlight" (fig. 371).[82]

Gio Ponti was even more categorical in drawing the distinction between the inauthenticity of historical reference and the authenticity of climatological accommodation. The "initial conception" of his Development Board and Ministry of Development Building derived from the "climatic conditions of Baghdad" and from "that climatic local reality only," he stated, even though the building looks to all intents and purposes like his Pirelli Building in Milan raised on *pilotis* and surrounded at ground level by a portico (fig. 372). The standard International Style devices, in his view, perfectly adapted the building to its site. "The architecture," he asserted, "does not indulge in particular local [stylistic] motifs that, when interpreted by foreigners, even with the best intentions, are invalid, apart from being simple-minded and fatuous." Ponti rationalized this dismissal of historical context by pointing out that, at least from his Western perspective, there was only the climate to consider. The ravages of time and the constant flooding of the Tigris had effaced all historical examples "to which the architect could have referred." Any "genuine preexisting stylistic context," he concluded, "was destroyed by history."[83]

Wright never referred to the problem of the climate in describing how he developed his design (he no doubt took the issue for granted, based on his experience of living in Arizona); he was much more concerned with the "traffic problem" and the detrimental effect the automobile was having on the historical fabric of the city.[84] Nor did he define historical context as literally as Ponti did (*pace* Michelucci). For Wright, history entailed the cultural memory as much, if not more, than it did the physical remains of brick and mortar. History existed in a temporal, not merely a spatial, dimension. History is read, not seen. It is defined by writing. To speak of the culture where writing made its initial appearance as bearing no present trace of history was in his view impossible, the very evidence of the materialistic mode of thinking he had warned the Iraqis against.

The historical legacy of Baghdad is, in fact, more a literary image than a physical reality. It has mainly come down through books. The site where the Tigris and Euphrates rivers converge was chosen by al-Mansur, the second Abbasid Caliph, as the ideal location for the administrative center of his regime. The city was created virtually ex nihilo between 762 and 766. According to literary sources, it was laid out as an enormous circle and built of mud brick, with four gates oriented to the cardinal points in the image of the cosmos (figs. 373, 374). Al-Mansur called his Round City "the City of Peace" in reference to paradise.[85] Concentric walls defined the living quarters within the rim of a wheel at whose center stood the royal palace and mosque.

Baghdad reached its cultural zenith, it is commonly thought, during the reign of Harun ar-Rashid (786–809). The tales of the *Thousand and One Nights* are one of the lasting reminders of that period. Already by that time, much building had taken place outside the Round City; and by the middle of the tenth century, the government officially shifted its headquarters to the left (east) bank. What remained of al-Mansur's original city was soon destroyed by floods. The rest of the city was sacked by the Mongols in 1258, and by Timur the Lame in 1393 and 1401. Whatever was left was further confused in the minds of many Westerners, until well into the twentieth century, with the biblical narrative of ancient Babylon.[86]

Wright did not take any of this "history" lightly. This is not to say that he studied it in depth or had a firm scholarly grasp of its details, but only that it meant something to him.[87] In the letter to the Development Board accompany-

371. Gropius and TAC: Baghdad University. Revised scheme. Perspective, with faculty tower and administration building straight ahead and theater and art gallery on right.

372. Gio Ponti: Development Board and Ministry of Development Building, Baghdad, 1957–62. Model, looking east toward Tigris River.

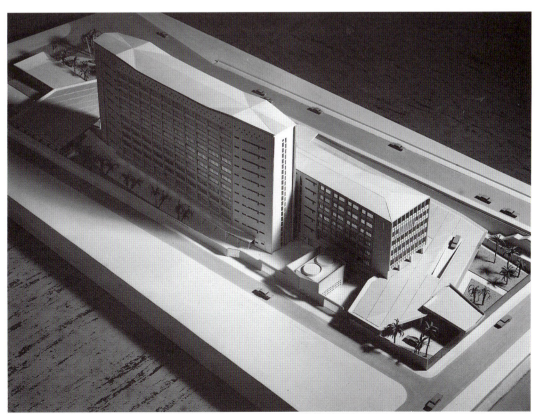

373. Baghdad. City plan showing medieval and modern structures.

374. Baghdad. Round City of al-Mansur, 762–66. Plan. Reconstruction by Jacob Lassner.

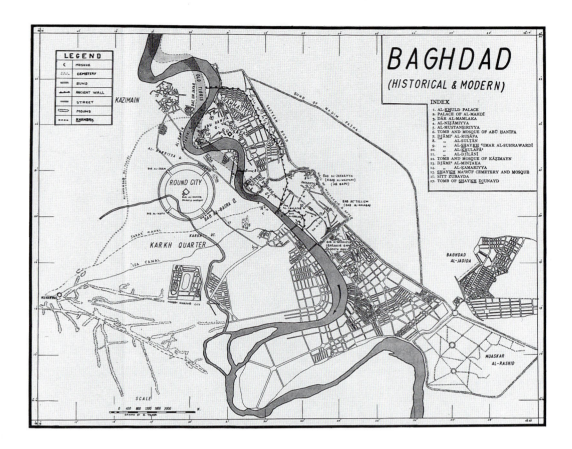

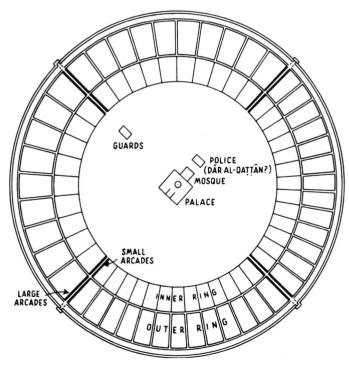

ing his plans, he described the project as "glorify[ing] IRAQ—its people and history." He listed the main historical agents informing his conception as "the great circular city of Harun al Rashid—the romance of the Thousand and One Nights—the story of Adam and Eve in the Garden of Eden."[88] In the text explaining the general idea of the project as well as its individual parts, he specified the particular ways in which the historical imagery determined the design.

The circular plan of "the original city of Baghdad" gave his design its geometric basis. The graded, natural earth mounds forming the "substructure" of the main buildings "revived" the characteristic "use of the ground that produced the architecture of [Mesopotamia]." The exterior spirals for roads and parking followed the same pattern as "the ancient ziggurat." All reinforced-concrete superstructures were revetted with "fired and glazed ceramics" meant to help "revive [traditional] crafts of the kiln," thus adding a social dimension to the historical reference. Finally, all decoration was to be "significant of Arabic history."[89]

"The general design," Wright explained, "is an attempt to see beyond the materialistic Western structures called 'modern' now barging in from the West upon the East, typical of Capitalism." The style was neither "modern" in that sense, nor a straightforward "copy" of the past. It was something in between, consciously meant to "demonstrate that if we are able to understand and interpret our ancestors, there is no need to copy them."[90]

■ ■ ■

Wright's Plan for Greater Baghdad, which is how he entitled the overall scheme, is an essay in archeourbanism—retrospective, imaginative, and reconstitutive all at once. It replicates, with almost perfect symmetry, the original plan of al-Mansur's Round City in another time and another place (figs. 376, 374). The circular university, along with its satellite island in the Tigris, becomes a new urban node at the edge of the existing city, a nucleus for future development on the model of its original counterpart on the opposite bank of the river. Like the City of Peace, it too describes an ideal landscape of paradisiacal significance.[91]

Almost due south of the center of Baghdad and south-southeast of the site of al-Mansur's construction, Wright's university and cultural center triangulates the topography of greater Baghdad to take into account the major pre- and postwar movement of population and administration into the Karradat and Maryam quarters on the right bank of the Tigris and into the Alwiyah and Karradah sections on the left bank. A large avenue indicated on the 1956 master plan connects the university campus to Sadun Street, the major modern thoroughfare connecting the southeastern section of the city to Rusafah (fig. 366). Joined by bridges to both banks of the river, the island cultural center is directly linked to the heart of downtown Baghdad by a new, tree-lined boulevard (named after King Faysal) that leads to the main railroad station at the edge of the bustling commercial quarter known as Karkh, just opposite Rusafah (figs. 375, 376).[92]

As already noted, Wright was particularly concerned about the "traffic problem" in modern Baghdad, and the impact of this consideration for movement of people and vehicles reminds us of certain City Beautiful schemes of the earlier part of the century (which, in their later Baghdad incarnation of the 1930s–1940s, Wright was in fact simply extending). I am not thinking here of the Chicago or San Francisco model of the downtown, government, civic center–type redevelopment, but rather of the Buffalo or Pittsburgh type of cultural and university complex in a park-like setting on the outskirts of the city. The Oakland section of Pittsburgh, a city Wright knew well and for which he designed a downtown redevelopment project (Pittsburgh Point Park Civic Center) that predicts certain formal aspects of the Baghdad project (fig. 409), functions as the university–cultural center of the city, and is connected to the railroad station and the commercial core by boulevards forming a larger triangle (fig. 377).[93]

One of the key features of the earlier Pittsburgh City Beautiful plan was the Cathedral of Learning, a forty-two-story tower/skyscraper containing the entire University of Pittsburgh in a single proto-megastructure (1925–37). This was matched in Wright's Baghdad scheme by a true megastructure of a diametrically opposed character. The broad, low, circular earthwork that constitutes the infrastructure and perimeter wall of the university campus is a three-level spiral road reflecting, in its shape, al-Mansur's original plan for Baghdad and, in its form, according to Wright, the ancient ziggurats of Mesopotamia (fig. 378).[94] The curvilinear path serves for access, vehicular communication from one part of the campus to another, and for parking.

The various departments, or faculties, are plugged into this "curriculum," as Wright called the vehicular network, by clipping onto its internal circumference. New ones

375. Plan for Greater Baghdad project, 1957–58. Aerial perspective, looking southwest, with Opera House on far end of island and University on Karradah peninsula in bend of Tigris River on left.

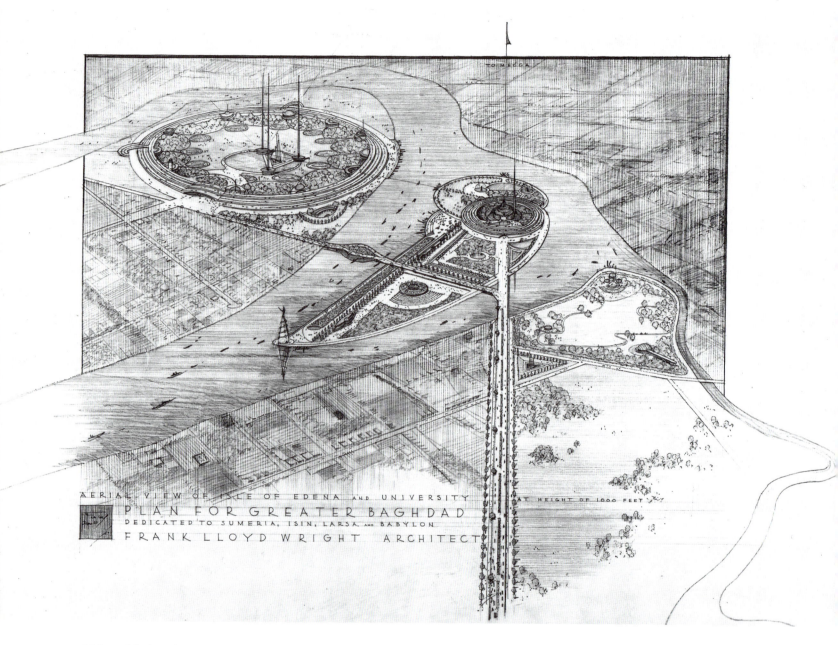

AERIAL VIEW OF ISLE OF EDENA AND UNIVERSITY AT HEIGHT OF 1000 FEET
PLAN FOR GREATER BAGHDAD
DEDICATED TO SUMERIA, ISIN, LARSA, AND BABYLON
FRANK LLOYD WRIGHT ARCHITECT

could be added or functions interchanged whenever necessary, although the location on the axis to Mecca was reserved for the faculty of religion and, as originally designed, culminated in a pointed, horseshoe-shaped dome similar to Baghdad's Kadhimain Mosque.[95] The central space of the campus, which is left free of traffic to become a park for pedestrians, contains a pool with fountains that is surrounded by radio and television broadcasting studios, symbolized by their tall antenna towers. (Iraq was the first Middle Eastern country to have a television station.) The significance of removing the library from the center to the periphery and of replacing it with elements of the "culture industry" will be discussed later.[96]

The plan for Baghdad University does not simply resemble al-Mansur's Round City in its superficial form but is a reinterpretation of that design at the more fundamental level of structure and meaning. In the original plan of Baghdad, the interstitial space of the concentric walls was used to

376. Plan for Greater Baghdad project. General plan.

377. Pittsburgh. Aerial view from the Golden Triangle (downtown) to Oakland, with the Cathedral of Learning (University of Pittsburgh), Carnegie Institutes, and Carnegie-Mellon University in distance.

378. Plan for Greater Baghdad project, Baghdad University. Perspective, with mosque on far side (later obliterated).

provide living quarters for the royal city's inhabitants. These were arranged in sectors according to tribal groupings and separated by intermediate streets (fig. 374). Located around the inner circumference of the thickened wall, comparable to Wright's vehicular levels, were accommodations for the different government offices and members of the royal household. This inner ring, added after the initial stage of construction, can thus be likened to Wright's additive and interchangeable faculty buildings lining the inner edge of the transportation loop. Finally, the royal palace and the mosque, with its dome defining the open center of the Round City, were translated into the towered broadcasting stations of the university, where communication and dissemination of information, rather than entrenched power and tradition, are given preeminence.

The central focus, coherence, and singularity of the City of Peace are thus transformed at the core to create an image of modern Baghdad that refers to the past while being

grounded in the present. The conflict between the traditional religious focus of Arab education and the secular humanism guiding the new university toward a more "modern" approach to scholarship was only one aspect of contemporary cultural policy highlighted by Wright's design. Another had to do with a more explicitly political discourse. Iraq, like Egypt, was caught between two historical cultures, the one ancient and pre-Islamic, the other medieval and Islamic. A modern regime had somehow to balance these two legacies. Wright's conflation of al-Mansur's Islamic capital for the Abbasid Caliphate with the Babylonian and Sumerian ziggurat was fortuitous in allowing him to express the idea of a modern Islamic culture supported and served by a unique, originary civilization.[97]

■ ■ ■

The plan for the Opera House and its island site condensed and elaborated the ideas introduced in the University (fig. 376). The name Wright gave to the polliwog-shaped island provides the first clue. It was changed from Pig Island to Edena in reference to the marshland south of Baghdad where the biblical Garden of Eden is believed by many to have been located.[98] Eden thus joined Babylon and Baghdad in Wright's scheme to encompass the three historic horizons of Iraqi culture. As the representation of the legendary site of the beginning of the world, Eden almost had to be an island—autonomous, embryonic, omphalic.

The Isle of Edena was shaped, graded, and consolidated by Wright into its streamlined, germinal form. At the end of the tail on the upstream side, facing the old city, is a statue of Harun ar-Rashid. Made of gilded sheet metal over a steel frame, it was to rise to a height of three hundred feet above a spiral base representing a procession of camels (fig. 375). The design was clearly based on the minaret of the Great Mosque at Samarra (847–61), the town, about sixty miles north, that was built in the ninth century to replace Baghdad for a brief interregnum as the capital of the Abbasid Caliphate (fig. 379). This highly unusual form of the

minaret has most often been connected with the earlier Mesopotamian ziggurat, serving as the model for most popular images of the Tower of Babel.[99] For Wright, it became a perfect vehicle for stating, at the tip of the composition of the Isle of Edena, the theme of cultural continuity developed throughout the design.

The avenue leading from the statue of Harun ar-Rashid to the Opera House at the head of the island is treated as a cultural mall. On the near side of the cross-axis is a lens-shaped museum for contemporary art, in which a central gallery is surrounded by lower, smaller-scaled ones on the model of John Soane's Dulwich Gallery. Beyond that is a long clerestoried building with a high battered base, devoted to the exhibition of ancient Mesopotamian sculpture. In between these two structures, filling out the protuberance of the island, are lines of domed kiosks forming a shopping bazaar and a casino (*kazinu*) for eating, drinking, and general socializing, like those on the banks of the Tigris off Abu Nawas Street. These latter elements were intended to bring to the island some of the aspects of daily life in contemporary Baghdad and to provide a certain commercial vitality to the scheme.[100]

The focus of Edena is the building for the opera that generated the entire project (figs. 380, 381). The Iraqi Symphony Orchestra was created in 1941, and Western classical music had become a significant interest of middle- and upper-class residents of Baghdad by the mid-fifties. (The socialist government that came to power in the revolution of

Plan for Greater Baghdad project, Opera House.

380. Aerial perspective with Garden of Eden behind.

381. Plan, entrance level.

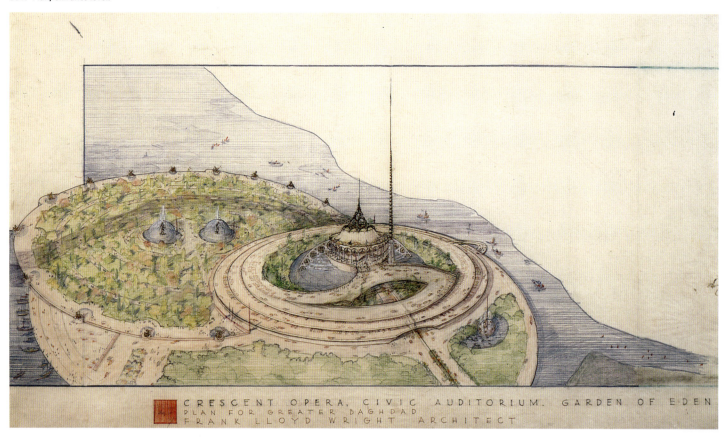

CRESCENT OPERA, CIVIC AUDITORIUM. GARDEN OF EDEN
PLAN FOR GREATER BAGHDAD
FRANK LLOYD WRIGHT ARCHITECT

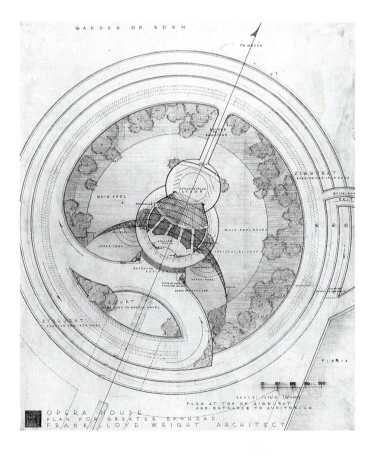

OPERA HOUSE
PLAN FOR GREATER BAGHDAD
FRANK LLOYD WRIGHT ARCHITECT

1958 retained the Opera House in its first development plan and even announced an international competition in 1962 to choose a new architect.)[101] Wright, however, seems to have sensed a certain anomaly in the situation and proposed a flexible hall that could be expanded from approximately 1,600 seats to anywhere from 5,000 to 7,500, to serve as a civic auditorium for conventions, public celebrations, and larger political gatherings.[102] This redefinition added a certain national dimension to the program, while the idea of a multi-use auditorium led Wright to look carefully again at Adler and Sullivan's Auditorium (fig. 382).

The Baghdad Opera House is one of the most elaborate buildings Wright designed and demands a close reading of its various elements before one can attempt a general assessment. "King Faisal Avenue," which runs southwest from the main railroad station, forms the axial approach to the building. (It actually continues under the building as a tun-

382. Adler and Sullivan: Auditorium, Chicago, 1886–89. Interior (c.1890).

nel opening onto a vista across the Tigris in the direction of Mecca.) The Opera House as such is a circular structure surrounded by an alabaster colonnade and topped by an openwork, gilded metal crown containing a statue of Aladdin. The tent-like pavilion rises out of a circular pool. It is stabilized on either side by flying buttresses that take the form of incurving half-arches. The pool is surrounded by a garden, which in turn is surrounded by three spiraling roadways raised on banked earth.

The ground-level tunnel under the main structure leads to a planetarium, on the domed ceiling of which floats the floor of the theater (fig. 383). The surrounding ziggurat takes cars through three revolutions, where there is parking for almost two thousand automobiles, before depositing attendees at the front entrance. This is marked by a tall, tapered antenna symbolizing the "Sword of Mohammed." Entrance to the nearly circular, bowl-shaped auditorium is through an ethereal arcade illusionistically representing tied-back curtains.[103]

The interior space is shaped by interlocking spherical surfaces (fig. 384). The *cavea*, or auditorium, forms a shell angling down toward the stage.[104] The proscenium arch, by reflection, starts a rippling action in the opposite direction that spreads over the seats in an expanding series of curves. The model for this was the Chicago Auditorium (fig. 382). The earlier ceiling design, derived from acoustic calculations, appeared to represent the movement of sound waves in space. Wright emphasized the representational aspects of its translation in Baghdad both in instrumental and in anthropomorphic terms. He said it was "like a great horn," "carrying sound as would the hand cupped above the mouth."[105] The outermost arch served as a track for sliding screens to close off the rear part of the theater when not needed, a provision for flexibility also indebted to the Auditorium.

But there is one significant way in which the ceiling of the Baghdad Opera House is different from that of the Auditorium, and this is what carries the full impact of the building's representational charge. In Baghdad, the largest arch, the one farthest removed from the proscenium, continues beyond the outer walls of the building into the surrounding pool. One immediately thinks of Le Corbusier's project for the Palace of the Soviets in Moscow (1931; fig. 385), especially in light of Gropius's pastiche of it for his arcaded, multi-use, civic auditorium for Tallahassee, Florida, designed in 1956 and published in *Architectural Forum* early in the following year.[106] But Le Corbusier's giant parabolic arch was the actual structure from which the roof of the hall was hung and was never meant to be seen from inside. In the Baghdad project, the arch reads as an integral feature of both the interior and the exterior space of the building (figs. 380, 383).

In part, the so-called "crescent arch" of the Baghdad Opera House was intended by Wright to carry the image of sound into the environment, across the actual threshold of hearing, as a "poetic extension of the acoustic principle involved."[107] This highly imagistic interpretation of the program of an opera house brings to mind Jørn Utzon's prizewinning entry in the Sydney Opera House competition of 1955–57 (fig. 386). Its exposed, interlocking concrete shells look as if they were designed to project and resonate sound across Sydney harbor. Their color and shape convinced the jury (which included Eero Saarinen) of the building's appropriateness to "the total landscape of the harbour,"

Plan for Greater Baghdad project, Opera House.

383. Lateral section. 384. Longitudinal section.

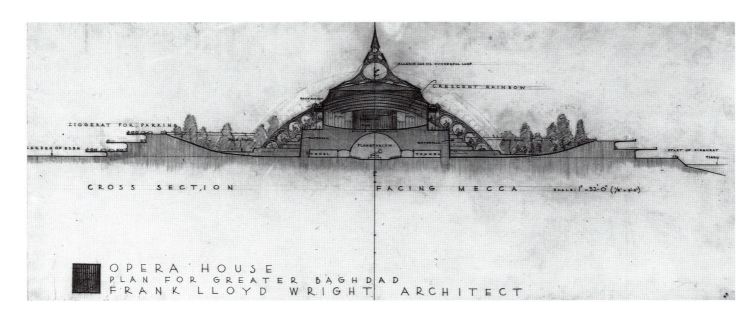

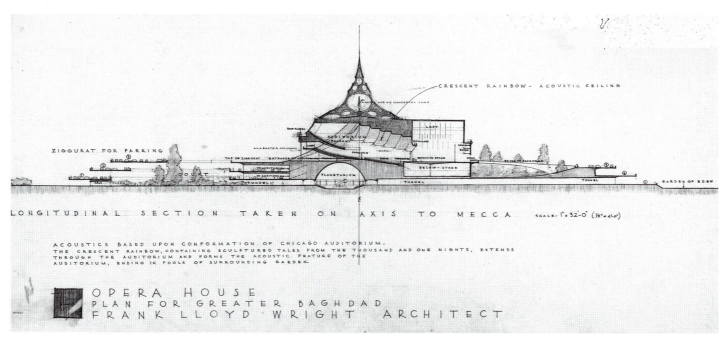

385. Le Corbusier: Palace of the Soviets project, Moscow, 1931.

386. Jørn Utzon: Opera House, Sydney, 1955–73. Model (1955–56).

because the "white sail-like forms of the shell vaults relate as naturally to the harbour as the sails of its yachts."[108]

There is good reason to believe that Wright knew the Sydney design. The competition results were published in the months between the commission from the Development Board and his visit to Baghdad.[109] Though comparable in certain respects to Utzon's solution, Wright's is much more *operatic*, by which I mean that his does not simply take music and the natural environment into account but includes all the narrative and historical components that are part of the *gesamtkunstwerk* that opera uniquely represents. The key to this conception is the "crescent arch," which functions as a synecdoche for the design as a whole.

In referring to the arch as a "poetic extension of the acoustic principle involved," Wright meant the phrase to be taken literally as well as figuratively. At the simplest level, the arch is the efflorescence of the proscenium and stage on the exterior. But it is not just that. Its traceried design contains a group of roundels depicting "sculptured scenes" from the *Thousand and One Nights*. These celebrated tales, which date back at least to the ninth century, were a national folk literature that had particular relevance for Baghdad, since many of the stories were set in the court of Harun ar-Rashid. Wright had always been drawn to them as a source of imaginative and didactic force (fig. 21). In the project for the Baghdad Opera House they became, by virtue of their universal appeal, an ideal frame for his larger narrative.[110]

The tales of the *Thousand and One Nights* are recounted by Shahrazad to the King Shahrayar in an attempt to ward off her own death at his hands. Having been the victim of adultery, Shahrayar swore to sleep with a different woman each night before killing her. To save the young women of her land and to cure the king of his misogyny, Shahrazad volunteered to become one of his victims but was able to stave off the devastating consequences by telling him stories each night that had to be continued the following night. So enraptured was Shahrayar with her storytelling

that he let these trysts go on long enough—a "thousand and one nights"—to fall in love with her and marry her.

The *Thousand and One Nights* symbolizes the power of art and illusion over even life and death. Of particular significance in the context of an opera house for Baghdad, it inscribes the world of fantasy in the lunar path of the night. Wright's "crescent arch" frames this nighttime activity. Time is suspended within the space of the arch in synchrony with the virtuality of theatrical time. The crescent, as a symbol of the Islamic world, serves to contain that experience in the particular narrative context to which it is addressed.[111] The figure of Aladdin, standing in Wright's mind for the "human imagination," occupies the apex of the arch under the pinnacle of the crown, orchestrating the events by rubbing his "wonderful lamp" (fig. 384).[112]

The fantasmatic character of the *Thousand and One Nights* was to suffuse the "crescent arch" so completely that it would be magically transformed—before our very eyes, one is tempted to say—into an illusion of paradise. The Islamic symbol representing the waxing moon would metamorphose, Wright noted on the drawings, into a "crescent rainbow" as an effect of the fountains cascading beneath the arch. Against the background of the southern sky, the rays of the sun would refract and reflect in the drops of water spraying over the gilt bronze curve of the traceried arch (figs. 380, 383). And through this rainbow would appear, over the annular wall of the ziggurat, a landscape representing the Garden of Eden. Lushly planted along the Tigris, like the idealized landscape in the Bible, it contained statues of Adam and Eve under small water domes. The image of paradise represented in abstract geometric terms in al-Mansur's original circular City of Peace was thus reconfigured, on the model of Genesis 2:6, through "a mist from the earth" that "watered the whole face of the ground."[113]

■ ■ ■

Wright's project for the Baghdad Opera House is a proscenium that transforms the architecture of the university and cultural center into a performance art of synesthetic character and operatic scope. Sound becomes water; water, light; and light, story and image. Framed by the "crescent rainbow," the Isle of Edena, the Tigris River, and the city of Baghdad create a real-life setting for a play about themselves. The extravagant illusionism leads one into a realm of fantasy that is in many ways more "literary" than strictly "architectural." The Opera House is like an image from the *Thousand and One Nights*.

The "architecture of fantasy," as Ulrich Conrads and Hans Sperlich called it in their book by the same name (1960), was an important part of the architectural climate of the 1950s. One has only to think of the interest in Gaudí (fig. 91); Art Nouveau; the French "visionary" architects Ledoux (fig. 235), Boullée (fig. 233), and Lequeu; Simon Rodia; and Expressionism in general.[114] Some of this interest was di-

rected toward social utopianism, some toward structural pyrotechnics, and some toward organic or figurative ends. Much of the specifically expressionistic side owed a good deal to earlier experiments in "national romanticism." Wright's Plan for Greater Baghdad, while certainly a part of this development, is highly unusual in its ascription to architecture of the role of reconstructing urban history.

If the idea of historical reconstruction is one that is fundamentally contrary to the principles of modernism, then the adoption by architecture of a literary program to accomplish that end only increases the contrariety. For this reason, no doubt, most architects, critics, and historians would shudder even to consider Wright's Baghdad project in the same breath as, say, al-Mansur's Round City or the Kadhimain Mosque, and would probably more readily compare it to John Nash's Royal Pavilion at Brighton (1815–23). The Brighton Pavilion, with its "Kubla Khan"–like allusions to "sunny pleasure-domes" in Xanadu and "gardens bright with sinuous rills," instantiates the relation between Orientalism and fantasy that has come to be accepted in modern Western thought as virtually one of synonymy. Its Orientalism, which amounts to a pastiche of motifs from a wide range of sources, clearly reflects the colonialist and imperialist impulses that Edward Said has so powerfully described as informing the attitude.[115] The Royal Pavilion is a *souvenir* as well as a trophy, a bijou brought back from the East. The deliberate act of decontextualization functions as a sign of power.

But Wright's Baghdad project, by contrast, is about contextualization, and the questions it poses regarding power relations are therefore quite different. Which brings us back to the origin of the commission and the general political and economic framework in which it took place—meaning "development." As neocolonialist promotion of development replaced colonialist control of raw materials in the 1950s, the architectural stage shifted from the home country to the alien one, and the architect was faced with a choice of accommodation or imposition. More colloquially, one could say that the choice was between a local-aid, bootstrap operation and a massive dose of technological assistance and hardware.

The reading I have presented of Wright's scheme places it squarely in the camp of the former—a quite unpopular one in the 1950s—and assigns most of the Baghdad projects by the other Western architects to the camp of the latter. Wright saw his role as that of a revitalizing agent, using modern methodologies to give new meaning and value to historically determined local conditions.[116] His project took the cultural history of the area as its ground, building upon that social construction of reality a new focus for developing Baghdad. Gropius, Ponti, and Aalto, on the other hand, essentially limited their accommodating gestures to climatological considerations, thereby reducing the city's significance to a matter of natural history. In contrast to Wright's Garden of Eden for the Opera House, where nature itself is historicized into a cultural artifact, Gropius's campus assumes the ahistorical and timeless conditions of a specific type of natural environment as the virginal ground for a regional adaptation of novel, Western forms. As in traditional colonial architectures in the Middle East and elsewhere, the alien land is thought of simply as a natural resource to be exploited and developed, having no cultural means for representing itself and thus totally dependent on those imposed from outside.

One could endlessly debate which position is more patronizing: exporting and acclimatizing, or trying to work within (and perhaps even to help revive) another nation's traditions.[117] There is no doubt, however, that the latter is more difficult, if not impossible, and more subject to "fantasy." But unlike the purely imaginary world of Nash's Brighton Pavilion or, for that matter, Disneyland (opened 1955), the "fantasy" of Wright's Baghdad project is much more akin to what Tzvetan Todorov has described as the "ambiguity of vision" of the "fantastic," the "hesitation" between the assurances of the "real" and the disequilibrium of the "imaginary." Operating within the "duration

of the uncertainty," the "concept of the fantastic is therefore to be defined in relation to those of the real and the imaginary."[118]

Wright's Plan for Greater Baghdad stretches the limits of verisimilitude, constantly changing temporal focal length. It offers an imaginary journey through a reconstructed past on very nearly the site where that past once may have existed. History is thus realized as a complex pattern of archeological representations.[119] The multiple historical images and layers in this vision of the "fantastic" cohere to form a well-orchestrated event celebrating the Hashimite monarchy. That accomplishment was probably a major reason the project was rejected by the new military regime (another being the successor regime's stated desire for explicitly "modern" representations of its industrial base). In reconstituting the history of the site through his own form of archeourbanism, Wright constructed a history for Faysal II that would celebrate him as a cultural leader in the eyes of his people.[120]

The circular precinct of the university reestablished the determining context of the situation as the original foundation of Baghdad by the Abbasid Caliph al-Mansur, from whom Faysal could trace a direct line of descent (figs. 375, 374).[121] The "rainbow crescent" arch of the Opera House, with its images of the *Thousand and One Nights*, joined with the statue of Harun ar-Rashid to elaborate the cultural flowering of Baghdad under the Caliphate in its pre-Ottoman, pre-Western state of independence (fig. 380). The Garden of Eden, along with the foundational ziggurats, revealed the ancient and even originary basis of Iraqi civilization, into which the minaret-like "Sword of Mohammed" infused new blood.

The two art museums, but especially the Opera House, gave evidence of the continuing beneficence to be derived from a constitutional monarchy that traced its roots back to such an august past. Looking like a princely palace of medieval Islamic times, surrounded by pools, fountains, and gardens and topped by an openwork metal dome representing nothing so much as a crown, the Opera House clearly defined the royal presence as the centering factor in Iraq's "development."[122] Not only was it Faysal who gave the island to Wright—and thus to his city and nation—but it was the very successes of the first stage of the Development Board program under his reign, concentrating in particular on flood-control measures, that allowed the scheme to become a possibility.

One could take a cynical attitude and say that such an "architecture of fantasy" was particularly suitable for the situation, since the monarchy Wright represented was in fact more a fabrication of the West than an indigenous product of Iraq's history. But that would miss the real point of Wright's design, which is not the legitimation of the Hashimite dynasty but rather the democratization of its cultural institutions and their increased accessibility to the Iraqi people. "You are all his Majesty the Baghdad citizen," Wright told the professional audience of architects and engineers in Baghdad in the spring of 1957, "just as we [in the United States] have his Majesty the American citizen." Hokey as that might sound, the utopianism expressed itself in architectural terms quite similar to those used by Fourier. Where Fourier modeled his phalanstery on the image of Versailles so as to give each inhabitant a taste of what previously only Louis XIV and his court had enjoyed, Wright opened the royal pavilion in the park to a never-ending stream of automobiles and placed the crown of the building under the aegis of Aladdin, the poor tailor's son, the archetypal child of the streets who "made it" by chance.[123]

The Plan for Greater Baghdad takes architecture into the problematic realm of wish-fulfillment, where desire rather than need, as Kahn would say, is entertained. But it always retains an element of reality, for it lays bare the mechanisms by which the illusions are brought into play. This is the significance of the representation of the "Sword of Mohammed" as a television antenna and of the assignment of the normally central role of the library in a university campus to radio and television broadcasting studios (figs. 375, 376). The prominence of these elements of the

"culture industry," as it were, helps to blur the line between desire and need, but without erasing it.

The Baghdad project is composed of mediated images—ones supplied by books, legends, and traditions of storytelling. Consistent with its contemporaneous appearance in the early stages of Pop Art, the mediated image provided a basis for social and political comment through a form of representation in quotation marks. Sensing the inadequacy of modern architecture to deal with the historical traditions and context of Iraq, while at the same time realizing the ineffectualness of trying to rebuild that past in its own terms, Wright used the mediated image as a way of describing an urban vision for Baghdad. Unlike the Western "hardware" proposed by the other architects invited, Wright offered an architectural equivalent of "software" that no machinery yet in place could process. It is perhaps not surprising that California's Marin County, so close to the center of the American defense industry and its high-tech subsidiaries, would be the place where Wright's final ideas about architecture and context were realized.

Marin County Civic Center and Fairgrounds

Wright received the commission for a combined civic center and fairgrounds for Marin County, just across the Golden Gate from San Francisco, a few weeks after returning from his visit to Baghdad in May 1957. The designs were done in tandem and have a number of features in common, the most important, from our standpoint, being the inclusion of the automobile as a key element in the planning and the signal form of representation evolved for a characteristic suburban site (figs. 348, 390).[124]

The suburban landscape of the United States began to be defined in an architectural sense in the 1950s in ways that had only been theorized or tentatively suggested before. With the postwar baby boom, the growth of the automobile industry, and the passage of the Interstate and Defense Highways Act (1956), regional shopping centers, regional high schools, suburban corporate headquarters and industrial parks, grouped service and tourist facilities, and eventually regional civic and cultural centers demanded architectural solutions. From the point of view of expression, the most salient new conditions were the scale and speed of the highway and the consequent anonymity and centerlessness of the average site. The dislocation and decentering, along with the corollary disintegration of the edges of the city, seemed drastically to reduce the traditional division between nature and culture. It became an almost indefinable blur between "real estate" and "the media."[125] Wright's posthumously built design for Marin County is one of the earliest and still quite rare examples of a serious architect's attempt to come to terms with this issue.

■ ◻ ■

Marin County came into its own after the completion of the Golden Gate Bridge in 1937 and the postwar economic boom and population expansion. Including within its boundaries the cities and towns of Sausalito, Mill Valley, Tiburon, Corte Madera, the county seat of San Rafael, San Anselmo, and Novato, it was one of the richest and fastest-growing areas in post–World War II America. Between 1940 and 1960 its population tripled, and by 1969 it had become the fifth richest county in the United States.[126] Occupying the peninsula north of San Francisco at the base of the historic wine-growing Sonoma and Napa Valleys, and endowed with oceanfront beaches, rugged mountains, picturesque fishing villages, and lush lowlands, Marin County offered the perfect environment for the fulfillment of the American Dream. Here, the suburbanized "rugged individualist" could live less than twenty miles from the center of San Francisco in an Arcadian landscape not too unlike that predicted in Wright's Broadacre City and exuberantly imaged in the expanded Living City of 1958 (fig. 387).

The idea of grouping all the county offices and agencies, law courts and jail, and library within a complex containing a civic auditorium, public recreation facilities, and

county fairgrounds grew out of the same trend toward stronger regional planning and government that was earlier reflected in Broadacre City. By the 1950s, the needs of Marin County had outstripped the available facilities in downtown San Rafael, just as the old-fashioned "cracker-barrel politics" answering to special local interests no longer seemed applicable to the growing desire for a systematic public administration based on broader county concerns. Between 1952 and 1956 two proposals emerged from the deliberations of the five-member Board of Supervisors that oversaw the running of county affairs: one would establish an independent county administrator; the other would create a government center to consolidate all county offices under this new centralized form of administration. Although curtailed in its powers, the post of county administrator was approved in 1956 at the same time that the Board of Supervisors agreed to go ahead with the purchase of a site for a civic center.

Spurred by the leadership of Vera Schultz, its first woman member (elected 1952), the Board of Supervisors appointed a site committee in 1953 to look into the question of relocation. Three sites along Highway 101, the county's main north-south artery, were considered. Because of lingering opposition on the part of certain conservative politicians who did not want to leave downtown San Rafael, the purchase agreement for a 140-acre site in Santa Venetia, just north of the San Rafael city limits (annexed 1969), was not concluded until April 1956. In the meantime, a search committee began looking for an architect. Toward the end of the interview process, Wright's name came up, although he would not consent to be interviewed. When he was assured that the formal process had been concluded (without positive result), he agreed to meet the members of the committee while he was in the Bay Area to deliver the Bernard Maybeck Lectures at the University of California, at Berkeley, in late April 1957. This was about a month before the trip to Baghdad.[127]

Published accounts offer differing versions of exactly how negotiations developed. What is clear, however, is that Wright returned to the San Francisco area at the end of July to sign the contract, and it was on this second trip that he was shown the site for the first time.[128] After several months devoted to space analysis and programming, in which the San Francisco office of Wright's former apprentice Aaron Green played a large role, sketch plans were more or less completed by the end of December. The preliminary plans for the Civic Center, including a master plan for the entire site, were presented to the board on 25 March 1958 and formally approved one month later. A model, along with detailed drawings of all the buildings for the fairgrounds and ancillary service facilities, was produced by early autumn (fig. 391).[129] Only the working drawings remained to be finished when Wright died in April 1959. Construction on the first phase of the $8 million undertaking began in February 1960. The Administration Building was completed two and a half years later (fig. 393). The second phase, including the Hall of Justice, was begun in May 1966 and completed in January 1970 (fig. 394). Other parts of the master plan have been realized since then, though not always in accord with Wright's designs.[130]

■ ■ ■

By incorporating the county fairgrounds in the project, the Board of Supervisors was able to make use of the parimutuel funds available from the state for county fairs and thus reduce the overall cost for the complex. But fair-

grounds required a large, open, and easily accessible site. The 140-acre parcel of former farmland is east of the six-lane highway, just beyond the gap between Puerto Suello Hill and San Rafael Hill, where the Coastal Range of mountains, culminating in Mount Tamalpais to the south, comes down to Gallinas Valley and levels out into San Pablo Bay (fig. 388). The hilly, southern part of the site, which was reserved for the Civic Center proper, is elevated quite a bit above the northern section of low, flat marshland allocated to the fairgrounds. Fed by an underground stream, the marsh was to be drained at the state's expense to create a lagoon linked to the bay by the South Fork of Gallinas Creek, which was to be dredged and widened to form a navigable waterway for recreational use.

Ringed by softly rolling hills of a tawny, almost golden color on nearly three of its sides, the site could easily have reminded Wright of the Roman *campagna*. The Coastal Range rising up to the west and the marshes draining into the inland sea of the bay give it a distinctly Mediterranean character. Indeed, the wineries established by Italian, French, and German immigrants in the mid- to late nineteenth century in the Napa and Sonoma Valleys to the north, like the ones for the Christian Brothers, Beringer, and Charles Krug, attest to this cultural-geographical link by the styles of their architecture. The six-lane strip of highway, however, introduces a different note, one that irrevocably alters the way in which the landscape, and everything placed in it, is viewed. In fact, just a mile to the north of the Civic Center site, plans were already under way for the Northgate Shopping Center, a sixty-store complex connected to an industrial park the same size as the Civic Center/Fairgrounds site.

Wright was particularly attentive to two aspects of the problem: the representational demands of the program; and the character of the site. In a talk to the citizens of Marin County at a gathering in the high school auditorium at the time he came to sign the contract, Wright made it clear that uppermost in his mind was "what we do to represent Marin County in these buildings." That representation, in his view, had to be integrally connected with an expression of

388. Marin County Civic Center and Fairgrounds, San Rafael, Calif., 1957–70. Aerial view looking west, with Gallinas Creek in foreground and Mount Tamalpais in distance.

the natural setting, "something commensurate with the beauty of the County," since living in such a "beautiful environment" was what brought people to Marin County in the first place. "The good building," Wright told the audience, "is not one that hurts the landscape but is one that makes the landscape more beautiful than it was before that building was built. Now in Marin County you have one of the most beautiful landscapes I have seen. . . . I am here to help make the buildings of this county characteristic of the beauty of the county."[131]

Wright's resort to the words "beauty" and "beautiful" must be read in relation to the problem (one that would con-

tinue to plague modern architects) of combining the desire for monumental expression with the alien, highway setting of suburbia. The residents of Marin County envisaged the project as creating "a whole aura for our life in the County" that would be "the focus for our political and cultural life . . . for many many years to come." Wright saw the means for accomplishing this in the "new opportunity" and "great chance for free, open spacing [and] ground room" afforded by the site.[132]

The planning director of the Marin County Planning Commission, Mary Summers, who also chaired the architect selection committee, took the by then conventional position that "a group of buildings [arranged] like a campus" would be the ideal solution. Indeed, this is how the neighboring Northgate Shopping Center and almost all such suburban complexes were invariably planned.[133] Wright's immediate reaction to the problem, which he outlined on his July visit to the site and which remained consistent throughout the design process, went contrary to this received opinion. To give the project a definite and "particular character," he said, one had to abandon the campus concept of a "group of buildings." "To be something all-together," and in saying this he was including the landscape, "you can't just build one building here and another building there, and another one over there without reference to a great coherent scheme for the whole." He told the audience that what they could expect from him was a "scheme coordinate," implying a megastructural concept based on the classical principles of concatenation and regularity.[134]

■ ■ ■

Three knolls define the southwestern quadrant of the site, the highest one (a little over 150 feet) being in the corner nearest the highway interchange (fig. 389). A fourth, smaller hillock, in conjunction with two of the others, makes an almost straight line parallel to the highway at an angle of 140 degrees to the line joining the highest one. As can be seen from a very early sketch on the topographical plan provided him, Wright's impulse was to link the hilltops; and this idea became the basic *parti* of the design. But instead of following the contours of the hills as he had, for instance, at Taliesin or San Marcos-in-the-Desert, Wright boldly projected the main government building as a bridge joining one hill to the next (fig. 390). Each of the three intervening depressions or valleys was in turn articulated as a spanning element. These open spans serve as access roads for traffic proceeding from the entrance along North Pedro Road to the parking areas between the hills and the highway. The recreational and service structures related to the fairgrounds were placed either in the valley, around the lake

created from the marshland, or along the linear highway spine, where they could act as a buffer against traffic noise (fig. 391). The fundamental concept of the civic center as a bridging of nature ultimately determined every aspect of the building's use and meaning.[135]

The Civic Center proper is over a quarter mile long. It is composed of two arcaded wings of unequal length joined by a domed rotunda. The wings are each four stories high and form gallerias around skylit courts, originally planned to be open to the sky. The ground level is composed of wide sweeping arches of reinforced concrete that span the roads running through them and support the upper three stories (fig. 392). The exterior glass walls of the office floors are surrounded by five-foot-deep balconies, which are protected by a suspended, sunshading screen of metal-lath and cement-plaster arches (on the second and third floors) and oculi (on the fourth).[136] The openings diminish in size as they rise to the overhanging vaulted roof, a thin concrete shell sprayed with an aqua-blue plastic membrane that is trimmed with a gold, anodized aluminum cornice of pendant balls in semicircular frames representing drops of water. Originally, the roof was also to have been a burnished gold, to match the color of the hills and blend with the building's beige stucco surface.[137]

The first phase of construction involved the shorter wing of the Administration Building at the southwest corner of the site (fig. 393). It houses all the major departments of the county in flexibly designed space, as well as the public meeting rooms and library in the more formal, central rotunda. This wing emerges from the side of the hill and runs in a northeasterly direction. After spanning the entrance road, it dissolves into the domed library that crowns the next hill. A hilltop garden, serving as an outdoor terrace for the cafeteria, forms a prow overlooking the lagoon and fairgrounds. The Hall of Justice wing, which was built in the second phase of construction, begins at the rotunda, with its top floor level with the garden terrace.[138] It cranks around the rotunda forty degrees to parallel the highway and send its four-tier bridge of arcades over a small intermediary

389. Marin County Civic Center and Fairgrounds. Topographical map, with Wright sketches.

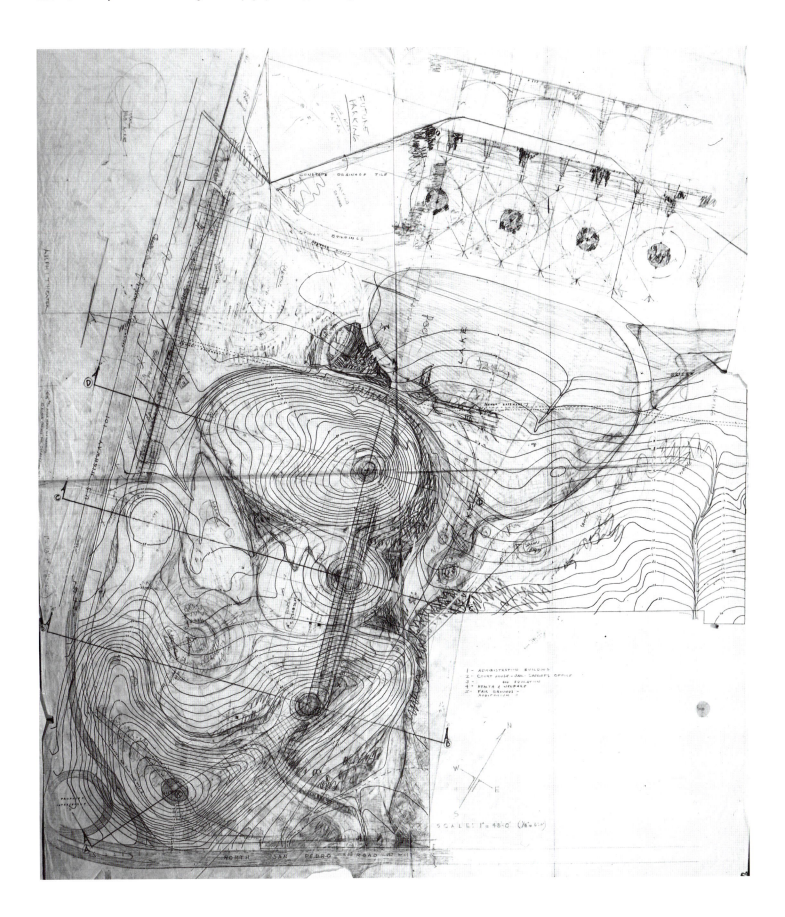

Marin County Civic Center and Fairgrounds.

390. Aerial perspective, looking west.

391. Model, from above.

MARIN   COUNTY   GOVERNMENT   CENTER
FRANK   LLOYD   WRIGHT   ARCHITECT

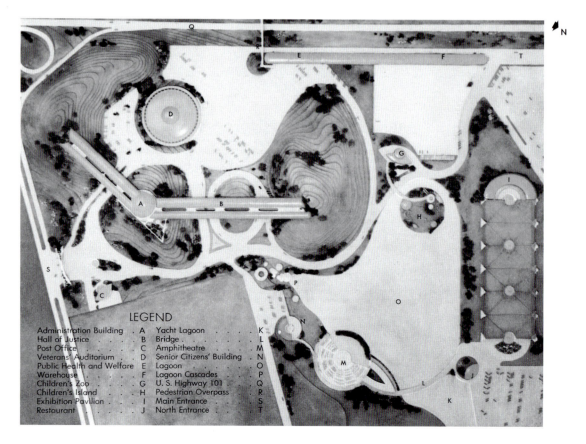

LEGEND

Administration Building	A	Yacht Lagoon	K
Hall of Justice	B	Bridge	L
Post Office	C	Amphitheatre	M
Veterans' Auditorium	D	Senior Citizens' Building	N
Public Health and Welfare	E	Lagoon	O
Warehouse	F	Lagoon Cascades	P
Children's Zoo	G	U. S. Highway 101	Q
Children's Island	H	Pedestrian Overpass	R
Exhibition Pavilion	I	Main Entrance	S
Restaurant	J	North Entrance	T

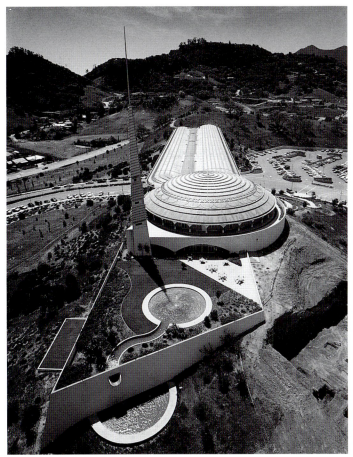

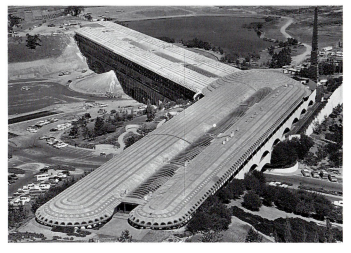

Marin County Civic Center

392 (*above*). Exterior.

393 (*below, left*). Administration Building, library rotunda, and garden (built 1960–63).

394 (*below, right*). Hall of Justice, under construction (built 1966–70).

395. Marin County Civic Center. Entrance and interior galleria of Administration Building (c. 1963).

hillock before sinking into the steep southern slopes of the most northerly hill (fig. 394). The two wings of the megastructure thus form a wide-angled V that comes to a point at the domed rotunda. This vertical axis is marked by a gold anodized aluminum television tower that rises over two hundred feet into the air.

Although the building can be said to have a center, it has no ends. It begins and ends in the hills in a way that allows the mind to imagine it as a fragment of a much larger whole. The entrances to the building are not at its beginning, middle, or end, but somewhere in between. The escalators and elevators within the abutments of the drive-through arches take you up through the hollow between the two ranges of offices or courtrooms (fig. 395). The dual-causeway traffic pattern of the gallerias interiorizes the bridge-like imagery and defines a smooth flow of movement around the periphery and toward the center, where the

domed rotunda joins the two wings. The space of these wings flows out around the base of the rotunda into the hilltop garden terrace adjoining the cafeteria. This externally oriented communal social space is treated as the symbolic center of the building. The dome is reflected in a circular fountain that overflows into a curvilinear conduit, channeling the water through the retaining wall of the prow into a semicircular catchment at its base (fig. 393). The water re-emerges beyond the road as a cascading stream feeding the man-made lake (fig. 396).[139]

The water flowing from the hilltop terrace forms the physical and symbolic link between the Civic Center and the various cultural and recreational facilities of the fairgrounds (figs. 390, 391). The view through the arch proposed for the main entrance to the complex along North Pedro Road would have defined the axis that runs from the hills to the lagoon. Along the north shore of the lagoon was to have been the main exhibition pavilion, a large, open-air, canopied structure built of concrete pylons, steel cables, and sheets of suspended plastic fabric (fig. 397).[140] To one side of it was an outdoor restaurant and to the other a children's zoo connected by a curving bridge to a children's island at the west end of the lake. Closer to the roadway leading to the Hall of Justice was a circular amphitheater and swimming pool, based on the Greek design for Florida Southern College; between that and the cascade was a smaller circular building for senior citizens.

A causeway bridge from the amphitheater to the exhibition pavilion separated the lake from a saltwater boat basin at the head of the creek joining San Pablo Bay. Between the fairgrounds and the highway was a long, narrow building serving the Public Health and Welfare departments as well as the Department of Public Works. A biconvex-shaped post office, originally planned to be placed at the base of the hill between the Hall of Justice and the highway, was built on the east side of the complex, near the main entrance. The Veteran's Memorial Auditorium, which was initially designed as a domed rotunda within the open V of the Civic Center, was later built, according to a some-

396. Marin County Civic Center. View from lake.

397. Marin County Civic Center and Fairgrounds, Exhibition Pavilion project. Perspective from edge of lagoon.

what different plan, on the site reserved for the enclosed area of the exhibition pavilion, on the far shore opposite the island intended for the children's playground.[141]

■ ■ ■

The related images of bridge and water, combined with that of mountain, underlie the design of the Marin County Civic Center and, in so doing, echo the most characteristic features of the environment. Whether one approaches the complex from the south across the Golden Gate Bridge, from the east across the Richmond–San Rafael Bridge, or from the north around the top of San Pablo Bay, one is constantly made aware of these elements in the landscape, though in

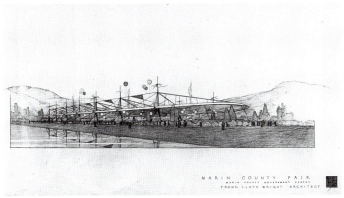

398. Pont du Gard, near Nîmes, France, late first century, B.C.

399. D. H. Burnham and Co. (Charles L. Morgan designer): Skyscraper Bridge project, Chicago, c. 1927–28. Aerial perspective from Lake Michigan.

no way is one fully prepared for their particular crystallization in Wright's design. From Highway 101, the building establishes a scale appropriate to the environment (fig. 348). The rhythm of the arcades picks up the movement of the road. The structure spanning the low-lying hills looks like an overpass. In its flatness and boldness, it reads at great speed. The pinkish-beige color of the cut-out shapes of the arcades causes them to sing out against the blue vaults and dome of the roofs. The gold tower of the television antenna signals from a distance the building's government function

of public works, which the arcades flatten into the shape of a roadside sign.

The relaxed pace of movement within the complex contrasts with the speed of the highway. The winding roads slow vehicles to a typical suburban "school zone" speed at which the characteristic features of the place become uniquely intense.[142] When seen closer up in this way, the Marin County Civic Center becomes more complex in meaning and its imagery denser. As a bridge, it symbolizes the concatenating function of regional government, where the needs of many different cities and towns are coordinated by a single, central, policymaking organization. In a metaphoric sense, the form allows for an experience of the openness of government: unlike an ordinary building, a bridge can never really be closed (fig. 395). One can actually go through the Civic Center at all times of the day or night, even up to the observation deck under the western portico of the dome.

To describe the Marin County Civic Center as a bridge, however, is somewhat misleading. Wright no doubt had the Golden Gate in mind, but in no way does his building refer either to its modern engineering or to the structure of a typical truss or suspension bridge. The Marin County Civic Center is less about spanning space than it is about conveying ideas, more about processing information than about moving things or people. For this reason, Wright gave the building the form of an aqueduct rather than a bridge— in fact, the most famous aqueduct in history.[143] The Roman Pont du Gard, near Nîmes, is the very image of a far-reaching regional scheme of public works, a sign of the positive effects of large-scale planning and centralized administration (fig. 398), and it conveys that meaning through its integration of man-made form and natural landscape.

Though the choice of an ancient Roman aqueduct as the model for a modern government center may at first appear gratuitous, the aqueduct as a type—and especially its updated form, the viaduct—has played a significant role in the history of megastructures. In the late 1920s, Charles Morgan (who shortly thereafter formed a limited partner-

400. Le Corbusier: City planning study, Rio de Janeiro, 1929–30. Aerial perspective.

401. Carioca Aqueduct (Los Arcos), Rio de Janeiro, eighteenth century. Postcard sent by Wright to Darwin Martin, 1931.

ship with Wright) published a Skyscraper Bridge for the lakefront of Chicago, in which the piers of the viaduct, ascending more than twenty-five stories in height, contain offices beneath the roof-level highway (fig. 399). Raymond Hood proposed a variant solution, also in 1928, for retrofitting the bridges across the Hudson and East Rivers in New York City.[144] The best-known examples of the adaptation are Le Corbusier's urban renewal projects of 1929–34 for Rio de Janeiro, São Paulo, Montevideo, and Algiers (fig. 400). Although none of these is detailed with arches in a historicizing way, it is quite likely that they were directly inspired by the eighteenth-century Carioca Aqueduct (called los Arcos) in Rio, which Le Corbusier would have seen on his trip there in December 1929. By then, the aqueduct had been converted into a viaduct for use by the Santa Thereza Tramway Company. When Wright visited Rio two years later to serve as a juror in the Columbus Memorial Lighthouse Competition, he was undoubtedly impressed with the way that structure sits in the Rio landscape, for he sent a postcard of it to Darwin Martin (fig. 401).[145]

When Wright returned to the Brazilian example in the Marin County Civic Center, he took the viaduct back to its original form as an aqueduct for specific representational purposes. The water that flows from the prow into the lagoon looks as if it has been drawn out of the surrounding hills by the building and conducted through the site to convey a message of collective enterprise at the scale of the region (fig. 388). The Pont du Gard offered a ready-made, highly legible, and very accessible model of the integration of building, landscape, and program of public works. The deliberate and unequivocal reference to it in the Marin County Civic Center sets Wright's last major building apart from those of most of his contemporaries. But it is not simply a matter of historicism.

There was a general "return of historicism," as Nikolaus Pevsner ruefully noted in 1961, that began in the late 1940s and to which even Le Corbusier's Brutalist buildings, such as the High Court of Justice at Chandigarh (1951–56) or the Maisons Jaoul, can be related (fig. 357). The revival of

interest in the dome and the arch, noted earlier, played an important part here. In Le Corbusier's work, however, the historical references, which are extremely generalized and abstracted, tend to be treated in such a way as to cause their conventional meanings to be denied or, at the very least, subverted.[146] Eero Saarinen, Philip Johnson, Oscar Niemeyer, and even Walter Gropius, among countless others, employed traditional motifs and, especially, screening arcades for what were usually purely decorative, or at most vaguely figurative, purposes (fig. 372). Rarely was a specific historical prototype like the Pont du Gard consciously adopted *in toto* for the symbolic and contextual possibilities it represented.[147]

To many, Wright's procedure in the design of the Marin County Civic Center appeared, and still appears, inconsistent with the ideals of modern architecture exemplified in his own earlier work.[148] Although this judgment entails a very selective sampling that leaves out, or at best marginalizes, say, Hollyhock House, the Death Valley project, and probably even the Imperial Hotel, it is quite true that the Marin County design differs markedly from the approach to the integration of building and context illustrated

402. Hubert Robert: *View of the Pont du Gard, 1786.*

by Taliesin and Fallingwater (though not the Winslow House or the Guggenheim Museum). It also differs considerably from the projects for Venice and Baghdad, which brings the discussion closer to home.

In most of the work by Wright we have surveyed, the question of representation has been paramount. Often, as in Taliesin and Fallingwater, the parameters of the program were such as to restrict the language to what one might characterize as the lower orders of *genre* or *landscape*, that is to say, the domestic and the natural.[149] The Venice and Baghdad projects raised the level of representational rhetoric by virtue either of the historical context or of that combined with a monumental program. The Marin County Civic Center and Fairgrounds presented a curious case, one in which the choice of site seemed completely at odds with, even recalcitrant to, the mode of representation called for.

Wright felt it necessary in the Marin County project to create a historical context in order to fulfill the demands of the program.[150] The building meant to serve as a center for the governmental and cultural facilities of the region was "nowhere." (The scenario was akin to a science-fiction story

or, indeed, a utopian novel like *Erewhon*.) What existed was a highway and a landscape, the latter on the verge of becoming "real estate." Wright told the citizens of Marin County that it was this fragile, amorphous thing called their "landscape" that was their sign of identity and their reason for being where they were. The Civic Center thus had to do much more than just "fit in" to the landscape or "preserve" a part of it. It had to *frame* and *represent* the landscape to make "the landscape more beautiful than it was before that building was built." In other words, it had to reconstitute the natural context as a historical phenomenon.

The Marin County Civic Center represents a rare form of architecture: an architecture of pure representation. Maybe it is for this reason that it reminds us even more of Hubert Robert's painting of the *Pond du Gard* than of the Pont du Gard itself (fig. 402). Supremely functional though it is, and delighted in by its users as so few modern buildings of its sort are, the Marin County Civic Center is almost more like an eighteenth-century garden fabric than anything else. In the strictest sense of the classical meaning of representation, it is an idealization of nature, an "improvement" on its existing state and an "elevation" of its mundane, everyday condition to a higher level of significance and value. It is a kind of "instant" culture or history, comparable in that sense to Le Corbusier's Chandigarh or Louis Kahn's Dhaka (fig. 403).

But Wright's Marin County Civic Center is different from Chandigarh and Dhaka in a very important sense, which speaks directly to its contextual significance. The government centers by Le Corbusier and Kahn establish their credibility to a large extent by the material, tectonic stress of their forms. This was a time-honored way of making the new monumental. There has always been a moral argument for construction in the durable, physical evidence of it. Wright's response to building along a highway in suburbia reflects a different set of presuppositions about architectural representation in the contemporary world that paradoxically relies much less on historical precedent.

Construction becomes simply a support for the appearance of the building as a sign (fig. 348). Following the line of reasoning set forth by Hugo in his discussion of the erosion of architecture's physical embodiment of meaning in traditional tectonic terms and its irrelevance in the face of the insubstantial, yet more effective means of mass communication such as the printed word, Wright reinterpreted the modernist concepts of dematerialization and transparency on the signifying level of form. With the reduction of the building's fabric to a gossamer, almost volatile surface that makes its appeal primarily to the mind's eye, the surrounding landscape reconfigured by it so dominates the architectural scene that it ultimately is responsible for valorizing the building's message.

The environmental feedback of the building increases the more it is seen in perspective. From above, on the ridge of Puerto Suello Hill, the entire landscape is defined by its radius vectors. The Coastal Range on the west is literally drawn into the lagoon that leads the eye out to the bay (figs. 388, 390). To the south, the city of San Francisco appears beneath the Twin Peaks, directly beyond the hills and inlets of southern Marin. Reminded thus of Daniel Burnham's City Beautiful plan for San Francisco (1905), one begins to see Wright's project as a regional extension and radical reinterpretation of the concept of "civic center" in a suburban form of *civitas*.[151]

Although the suburb has been with us for quite a long time now, we still do not seem able to think of it in the same way as the city. There are departments of urban studies and urban planning in universities around the world, but few, if any, of suburban design. Wright's design for Marin County made a significant effort to describe how the context of the suburb might be defined. In that process, architecture is called upon to do both less and more than before. The Marin County Civic Center offers an instructive comment on the change in the relative value of building as opposed to landscape—or historical convention as opposed to nature—that we have traced throughout the course of his career.

In the early Beaux-Arts Wolf Lake Amusement Park or Milwaukee Public Library and Museum of the 1890s, as in Burnham's City Beautiful projects, building and convention dominated landscape and nature (fig. 25). The garden formed the entourage of the city. Nature functioned as a retainer. With the Prairie Style, that order began to be inverted (fig. 63). History and convention receded into the background, so that nature and the landscape could predominate. Marin County represents a final stage in this evolution. Foregrounding the historical sign of nature's transformation into culture as a purely representational device, Wright's final building creates a sense of place that seems particularly appropriate for a world in which the "terror of history" has made even the reality of nature seem surreal.

New York:
the shadow of the
box for which —

we start from " Oca-
tilla " the ephemera
in the background.

Conclusion: Wright and His/story

By now, I hope, the reader has formed a picture of Wright's architecture and career that is more comprehensive and more complex than those previously available. I have tried to avoid certain stereotypes inherited from the past that have served mainly to marginalize him. In this more inclusive view, Wright is not merely a domestic architect, nor is his historical significance only that of a precursor or progenitor of modern architecture. Though usually site-specific and extremely sensitive to context, the work is not thereby simply a manifestation of national culture. Wright is as far from being the American Noble Savage as he is unlike the vulgar populist pandering to the debased tastes of the middle class. As the most prolific and engaging modern architect of his generation, he can hardly any longer be seriously identified with Howard Roark, the embittered, antisocial egomaniac of *The Fountainhead*.[1]

Still, you might say, we are left with other stereotypes that have been reinscribed and even reinforced in this book: Wright the individualist, Wright the romantic, Wright the naturalist, even Wright the ornamentalist and historicist. But where those characterizations have most often been used either to qualify the modernity of Wright's work or to dismiss it entirely from the canon of the "modern movement," here they have been presented as positive contributions to the work's peculiarly contemporary meaning. Instead of relegating Wright to another century (as Philip Johnson tried to do), we have good reason to regard him as the Other of this century—not the antimodern traditionalist, it should be noted, but the modernist's double and complement (fig. 404). Most religions have exploited the anxieties instilled in their adherents by the designation of an antitype, and Wright played the role of devil's advocate more fervently than any follower of the International Style could ever have dreamed possible.

■ ■ ■

Wright was positioned as an outsider from the very beginning of his career. After working with Sullivan and rejecting Burnham's offer of schooling at the Ecole des Beaux-Arts, plus a job in one of the largest architecture firms of the period, Wright made his name in the relatively isolated field of suburban housing, as a bohemian "artist-architect." The trip to Europe, followed by the self-imposed exile in Wisconsin, established a pattern of brief contact/prolonged disengagement vis-à-vis the centers of professional, academic, and artistic power that soon translated itself into a lasting critical distance. After the radical statement of the Oak Park work illustrated in the Wasmuth publications, which Mies was later to describe as having "invigorated a whole generation of young Europeans," Wright's retreat to Taliesin signified to most contemporary critics a regression from the theoretical implications of the earlier work to an outdated naturalism that effectively transformed him from the eccentric American "secessionist" he had been in the eyes of the traditionalists into the antitype of the modernist.[2]

The critical reception of Wright from the early twenties on reflected the need of the "modern movement" to establish its autonomy and originality. Where the Dutch architect Oud could claim in 1918 that Wright had "created a new 'plastic' architecture," akin to futurist experiments in painting, that "opens up entirely new aesthetic possibilities for architecture" in its emphasis on the "primary means" of the medium, only seven years later he would completely reverse himself, saying that the International Style (he called it "cubism in architecture") "arose in complete independence of Wright" and that "in reality the two were wholly different, nay rather opposed to one another." Berlage, we remember, had already raised the specter of the "jealous eye" of Eurocentrism (1921), just as he preceded Oud in his dismissal of Wright's continuing relevance to European

concerns. The opposition of Wright's "romanticism" to the International Style's "classicism," of his individualism to their collectivism, of the "sensuous abundance" of his figurative forms to their "puritanic asceticism" aiming at "the humble level of an abstraction," made the temptations of Wright's example to Oud "more harmful, indeed, than the impediments which an academic architecture puts in the way of a rising functional art of building."[3]

Just as Viollet-le-Duc needed the academic counterpoint of the Beaux-Arts, so too did the International Style need Wright. When the exhibition of "Modern Architecture since 1922" was held at the Museum of Modern Art in 1932 to show how "a single new style had come into existence" based on "a general discipline of structure and of design in the terms of the day," Wright was included even though his work had no logical place in it. According to the exhibition's organizers, there was a "definite breach between Wright and the younger architects who created the contemporary style after the War," and thus "an essential and insuperable difference" existed between their architecture and his. The museum's director, Alfred Barr, admitted in the foreword to the catalogue that, "as the embodiment of the romantic principle of individualism," Wright's work was to be viewed as a foil and "a challenge to the classical austerity of the style of his best younger contemporaries." He was the "exception," Barr noted, "the exception that illustrates the rule," as Philip Johnson often reiterated. Wright's romanticism validated the International Style's claim to the authority of a new classicism.[4]

Hitchcock's essay on Wright for the catalogue, however, went further than merely setting him up as a foil. It constructed an artistic biography around the myth of the Noble Savage that portrayed Wright as a kind of backwoods child of nature: "The influences which surrounded his [Wright's] youth in the [eighteen] seventies and eighties in the isolation of Madison, Wisconsin, were far different in every way from even the provincial calm of Purmerend [Oud's birthplace] or La Chaux-de-Fond [sic; Le Corbusier's birthplace]." Contrasting what one is supposed to assume was the unusual cultural richness of these two European towns with the intellectual barrenness ("isolation") of the capital of Wisconsin, Hitchcock went on to say: "Behind Wright was only Sullivan. In his early years architecture had no existence until he created it. Behind the young Europeans were Berlage, Wagner, Behrens, Perret, Hoffmann, Van de Velde, Loos, and above all Wright himself. If his buildings were not at hand, there was nevertheless the monograph of his work which few then knew in America. Instead of the feeble dome of the Madison Capitol there was Hagia Sophia itself at the end of a journey briefer than Wright's from Weymouth. And not only Hagia Sophia but all the varied wealth of the past down through the architecture of Schinkel, Labrouste, and Cuijpers in the previous century." As a fitting cautionary note to this fable, Hitchcock declared: "But now conditions are changed. No young architect anywhere grows up in quite the isolation of Wright's youth. . . . The day of the lone pioneer is past."

Natty Bumpo, Daniel Boone, and Davy Crockett had in fact supplanted the Native American as the Noble Savage by the end of the nineteenth century. As the updated and ethnically corrected image of the unspoiled, untutored indigenous American, Wright the "frontiersman" comes almost completely out of the woods. He knew no architecture, saw no architecture, and, unlike the younger Europeans, apparently was not even able to read about it. They might thumb through his Wasmuth portfolio, but he (despite all evidence to the contrary) could not and did not consult anything but "the book of Man and of Nature," as Hitchcock coyly phrased this preliterate backwoodsman's simple intellectual diet. Wright, Hitchcock concluded, could blaze new trails because "there was much he never had to unlearn."[5]

What began, no doubt in good faith, as a rather naive way of accounting for an unexpected historical phenomenon became over the following decades a now condescending, now mean-spirited way of discounting Wright. Like the belated writer of a chain letter whose origins are hardly any longer recognizable, Manfredo Tafuri in the mid-1970s

could characterize Wright as a "Big Child" who had "a memory . . . deprived of history" and whose timeless, natural "realm," like that of the Noble Savage, "was [simply] the flux of existing"—"a realm of the aspiration to childhood," Tafuri was quick to point out, that was "typical of the American public."[6]

There is a tendency to marginalize the Other in evolutionary as well as constitutional and psychological terms, and the characterization of Wright as the "lone pioneer"/Noble Savage did just that. Writing in the pages of the Paris avant-garde art magazine *Cahiers d'art* in 1932, the young Swiss critic Sigfried Giedion stated that the "organic" approach to design "symbolized" by Wright and the "mathematic and formalist tendency" represented by Le Corbusier were not simply two different options available to the contemporary architect but rather two "different stages of a single line of development." "From the point of view of history," therefore, it was only the work of the "young Wright . . . from about 1893 to 1910" that was significant. The "naturalistic form" of his later work signified "a sort of renunciation of the notion of architecture," "a flight into solitude," a regression to "the distant romantic memories of his youth." And any architecture "infested by psychology, working upon the feelings and deriving its effects from associations of ideas provoked by the objects represented," was, in Giedion's view, in direct opposition to the characteristically "abstract mode of expression of the twentieth century," which "simply aims to serve a function" by the adaptation of those "elements peculiar to its own medium."[7]

Despite an abiding admiration for some of Wright's later work, as well as a growing realization of the value of "the organic perception of the world" in solving many of the problems European architects faced in the later 1930s, Giedion only touched upon Taliesin and Johnson Wax in his Norton Lectures at Harvard in 1938–39, which were published as *Space, Time and Architecture* in 1941. Although he continued to add recent buildings by architects like Le Corbusier, Gropius, Mies, and Aalto to later editions of the book, he never saw the need to do so in the case of Wright.

As representative of the timeless "urge toward the organic," Wright's architecture was less important for its actual historical development than "as an index" of an attitude toward design. "To imitate or even to follow him" was therefore never the issue.[8]

Throughout the 1930s, European critics tended to accept Wright's marginality and to follow closely Oud's interpretation of the independence of European developments. P. Morton Shand, the English translator of Gropius's *The New Architecture and the Bauhaus* (1935), criticized Wright's "reactionary stylistic mannerisms" after 1910, stating that "Wright's positive achievements . . . are in every case coincident with his earlier career [1893–1909]" and that "the decorative-structural bias he gave to European functionalism just as it was emerging from theoretical abstractions into rational forms" both "debauched" and "corrupted its primitive purity." In dismissing Wright's literary style along with his architecture, Shand revealed an outspoken ethnocentrism and increasing anti-Americanism: "The trouble with him [Wright], *as with so many Americans*, is an inability to achieve coherently sustained expression in a now half-forgotten language."[9] Following on this, Nikolaus Pevsner decried the influence of "Wright's *seconda maniera*" on the "Dutch and German phantasts" of the Expressionist school, noting that, fortunately, "Wright's influence on early Gropius [was] a transitory one." He was also content to report that when Le Corbusier was asked to contribute an article to the 1925 *Wendingen* publication in which Oud's critique appeared, Le Corbusier supposedly claimed to be ignorant of Wright's work, replying to the editor: "I do not know this architect."[10]

Disinformation generally gave way to other forms of dissociation in the discourse of the postwar era. Some followers of the twenties' line, especially the English, retained the animus, and often even the turns of phrase, expressed by Shand and Pevsner. Colin Rowe, for instance, cautioned against focusing too much attention on Wright's work on the grounds that it "debauched American taste." Reyner Banham devoted less than four pages of his *Theory and Design in the First Machine Age* (1962) to a discussion of

Wright, and those pages, it should be added, essentially reviewed what certain Europeans (particularly Oud) had said about him. Unconcerned with the truth or full context of Le Corbusier's remark, Banham repeated the alleged response reported by Pevsner, as "verified" by André Lurçat and with the cachet—and added authority—of being in French: "Connais pas cet architecte" (a curiously incomplete sentence in its lack of a proper subject). Anecdotal evidence seemed to suffice. Later, Banham quoted a remark by Leonard Eaton that "summed up" to Banham "the difference between the first and last Mr. Wright," irregardless, once again, of the facts: "Before 1910 it took intelligence to employ Wright, but after 1935 it took only money."[11] The devil could appear in many forms, but to the "puritanic ascetic" it was always a temptress prostitute. Thus despite their many differences, the fear of *nouveau riche* vulgarity rejoined Banham to Rowe in a campaign to rout out kitsch that would find even more dedicated spokesmen in Tafuri and others in the 1970s and 1980s.[12]

In postwar Italy and, especially, the United States, where Wright's work was followed most closely, the oppositional nature of his position took on its most psychologically and politically interesting form. We must remember, of course, that the period from the 1940s through the end of the 1950s, when Wright received his greatest public exposure and acclaim, also witnessed the worldwide growth of American political, military, economic, and cultural hegemony, along with the emergence of the Ugly American. In Italy, where International Style modernism had seriously compromised its reputation in the eyes of many by its association with the Fascist government of Mussolini, Wright was championed, for a time at least, as the anticollectivist architect of "organic" principles and "democratic" design. Bruno Zevi, who had studied under Gropius at Harvard, spearheaded the movement.[13] In the United States, by contrast, where European modernists such as Gropius, Mies, Breuer, Moholy-Nagy, Albers, and Hilbersheimer had established themselves by the mid-1940s as the new academy, Wright's position was interpreted somewhat differently. There was no denying the enormous creativity and vitality he still showed in his late seventies and eighties, but an important cautionary note had to be sounded.

The critical approach that would dominate thinking about Wright for almost the next quarter century crystallized soon after the January 1948 issue of *Architectural Forum* illustrating the entire range of his recent work—from the projects for the Guggenheim Museum, the Morris House, the Rogers Lacy Hotel, and the First Unitarian Church outside Madison, to the completed work at Taliesin West, the Johnson Wax headquarters, and the Florida Southern campus, not to speak of the numerous Usonian houses both planned and built. Just a month later, in a symposium held at the Museum of Modern Art on the subject of "What Is Happening to Modern Architecture?" Hitchcock declared: "It is hard, unless we turn to that extraordinary man, Frank Lloyd Wright, to find much wealth or variety or range of expression in modern architecture at the present time." "Frankly, I do not see anybody in the world who has his capacity for variety of expression," he added. "A range of expression sufficient for several centuries seems to be concentrated in that man's last few years' projects, as shown in the January number of the *Forum*."[14]

But Hitchcock did not stop there. With Breuer, Gropius, Johnson, Edgar Kaufmann Jr., Eero Saarinen, and Vincent Scully all present on the panel, he pronounced the key qualification in the critical reception of Wright:

Now, with Mr. Wright there is a danger, for he is obviously the Michelangelo of the twentieth century. Michelangelo was not good for his contemporaries, and, least of all, for his students. . . .

We [therefore] cannot learn from Mr. Wright, but he can indicate to us . . . that he is less of an enemy of the International Style than he claims to be, and that there are many possibilities of expression within the frame of reference of modern architecture.

By virtue of the analogy to Michelangelo, Wright's antitypal status was given a historical legitimacy. Wright's "genius" was not denied; it was simply displaced, analeptically as

well as proleptically. "Michelangelo," Hitchcock noted, "was a master who looked forward, not to what was going to happen in ten years, but to what was going to happen in fifty years."[15]

At precisely the same time this historical equivalency was being proposed for Wright, Colin Rowe was establishing the identity between Le Corbusier and Michelangelo's younger academic counterpart, Palladio. Wright-as-Michelangelo removed the chronological-developmental issue that plagued Giedion and Oud, so that with Le Corbusier-as-Palladio the question of opposition could be understood purely and simply in terms of style and pedagogy. "Is not the contrast between Le Corbusier's *prisme pur* and Wright's luxuriant forms but another manifestation of the Classic-Romantic dichotomy?" Philip Johnson asked somewhat disingenuously in 1949. The answer, of course, was both yes and no. The terms were not equal when reproduction was at stake. Johnson repeated the view that "Frank Lloyd Wright is our Michelangelo," and by that he meant that Wright was outside the canon, an "enigma," a historical anomaly, an evolutionary sport, someone who could get away with breaking the rules but whose "grand distortions" would inspire only Mannerism in his followers and the taste for kitsch.[16]

Established opinion now maintained that the problem with Wright was that he was unteachable and inimitable. The idiosyncratic, often seemingly extravagant nature of his work could even prove subversive in an era when the principles of European modernism were being instituted in American schools of architecture.[17] The situation was described by Scully just two years after Wright's death:

The excellent students who flocked to Gropius and his associates at Harvard and elsewhere during the forties were indoctrinated with a deep suspicion of Wright's motives and a kind of sociological contempt for his buildings. Soon the younger architects were themselves acting as critics in most of the better architecture schools throughout the country, and today they have become the deans of many of them. For this reason, no serious attempt to teach and develop the principles of Wright's design has been consistently sustained in America, outside of Wright's own inbred Taliesins.[18]

Wright, for his part, fulfilled the role of anti-academic perfectly, and even added a strong antiprofession stand (architecture as a profession being another inheritance of the Palladian era). "You learn nothing about architecture really worth knowing in school," Wright told the San Rafael High School audience in 1957. "When you go to be educated," he warned his own Fellowship, "you go up against a pile of rubbish, and you paw around in that scrap heap . . . and come out with nothing." The "educated man," he added, is "a menace to society." International Style modernism was merely a contemporary "formula" replacing the earlier classical ones contained in books like Palladio's. "Only academics and governments could ever look upon such narrow abstraction with tolerance." The profession, in Wright's view, simply reproduced the formulas learned in school.[19]

Not surprisingly, Wright made few friends in the academic and professional worlds, not to speak of government circles. Those most eager to forgive the barbs of his criticism maintained at best a love-hate relationship. Indeed, literary historians as well as anthropologists have noted that the so-called civilized person's relationship with the Noble Savage often follows the same dynamic as the one of love-hate. Respect for the Savage's natural (read: noble) innocence is countered by disgust for his appalling, all too often savage, behavior. At the root of the phenomenon was the murder of Captain Cook by the very "noble savages" he discovered and praised. An arrogant and unsubmissive example of the type (today we might call him "uppity"), Wright thus presented the greatest cause for anxiety—and repression.

In this context, let us simply recall some remarks of Philip Johnson in a talk to a professional society of architects in Seattle in 1957:

Mr. Wright has been annoying me for some time. (I didn't say that he wasn't a great architect.) He says that my

house, . . . the Glass House . . . [is] a box. He once said (he's much cleverer, of course, than all the rest of us so you can't say these things as well as he does) that my house is a monkey cage for a monkey. . . .

He can have his opinions. . . .

[But] I find very annoying . . . his contempt . . . for all architecture that preceded him. Was he born full-blown from the head of Zeus that he could be the only architect that ever lived or ever will? . . .

Then almost worse is the contempt for the people who are going to come after him—and this is where it hurts us most, we slightly younger, older architects. He is determined that there shall not be any architect after him.

After going on to criticize Wright for everything from the inappropriate choice of materials, to a lack of concern for clients' privacy, to a "very careless" attitude toward construction, Johnson prefaced his concluding discussion of Taliesin West, which he described as "brilliant," "magnificent," "exciting," "the essence of architecture," by speaking of Wright as "a man that never gave up; the great American that perhaps we can admire at the same time we dislike him as much as I do."[20]

■ ■ ■

To understand more fully the problematic nature of Wright's relationship with modern architecture, one must turn from words to practice. Here the conflict between emotional engagement and critical distance reveals itself more directly in the form of repression. There has been, to use Harold Bloom's phrase, a profound "anxiety of influence" operating throughout the world of modern architecture in relation to Wright.[21] It goes back at least to the 1920s, when Oud argued for the independent and parallel evolution of "cubism in architecture" in Europe against his own earlier position that Wright's fragmentation of volumes and hypostatization of space in the Prairie House had formed the basis for subsequent developments. But it was in the 1940s

405. James Stirling: Florey Building, Queen's College, Cambridge, England, 1966–71.

406. First Unitarian Church, Shorewood Hills, Wis., 1946–52. Perspective.

and 1950s, when Wright's work was actually more visible and more closely studied, that it became almost a commonplace to say that his impact on modern architecture had become either so negligible or of such a generalized nature as to be impossible to define and thus irrelevant to discuss. And so it is to the postwar era that I shall confine this very brief overview.

The fact is, Wright's influence on modern architecture since 1945 has been as determinate as it is extensive. Quite simply, it is rarely if ever acknowledged. It extends from the use of materials and techniques of planning to the level of symbolic representation and the reconceptualization of the relation between building and environment; it includes not only the work of acknowledged followers like Carlo Scarpa, Harwell Hamilton Harris, and Bruce Goff, but also that of Mies, Aalto, Kahn, Le Corbusier, Stirling, Johnson, Rudolph, and Venturi, to name just some of the most prominent figures. Wright's invention of "desert rubble stone" as an analogue for traditional masonry in Taliesin West and his related treatment of brick and glass in the Johnson Wax buildings set a precedent for the Brutalist revival of monumental masonry in Le Corbusier's *béton brut* and Stirling's red-brick university buildings of the 1960s (figs. 249, 296, 357, 405). The Brutalist aesthetic, as Banham described it, was as much about the symbolic and the imagistic as it was about materiality and monumentality. Here again, Wright's emphatically representational designs of the forties, such as the Guggenheim Museum, the Morris House, or the First Unitarian Church of Shorewood Hills, Wisconsin (1946–52; fig. 406), all published in the 1948 *Forum*, set the stage for the organic expressionism of Le Corbusier's Chapel at Ronchamp (1950–55) and Saarinen's TWA Terminal at JFK (then Idlewild) Airport (1958–62).[22]

The pronounced articulation of structural and volumetric elements in the designs of Kahn and Rudolph from the late fifties, like the Richards Medical Laboratories at the University of Pennsylvania by the former or the Art and Architecture Building at Yale by the latter, have often been related to early Wright (for example, the Larkin Building).

407. Kahn: Adath Jeshurun Synagogue and School Building project, Philadelphia, 1954–55. Plan.

408. Huntington Hartford Hotel and Sports Club project, Los Angeles, 1946–48. Clubhouse plan, entrance level.

409. Carlo Scarpa: Luciano Veritti House, Udine, Italy, 1955–61. Plan.

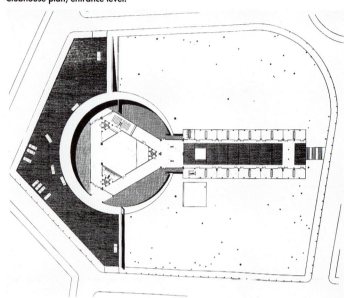

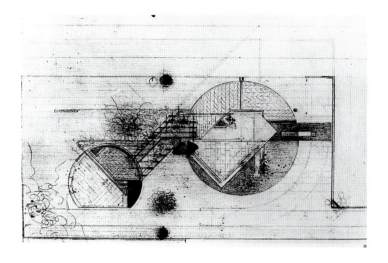

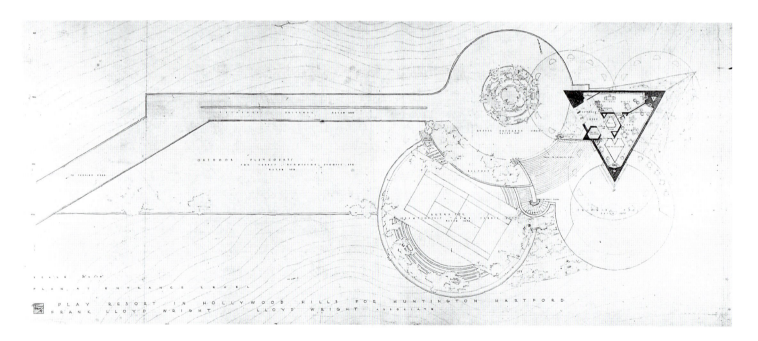

The overriding geometric order and clarity of Kahn's seminal work of the period, however, is even more closely indebted to Wright's contemporaneous plans based on circles and equilateral triangles, such as the Huntington Hartford Resort (figs. 407, 408). This geometry, along with the increasing interest in historicism evidenced by Wright at this time, shows up clearly in some of Philip Johnson's circular plans as well as in Carlo Scarpa's houses, tombs, and mu-

seums (fig. 409).[23] (Scarpa's color-pencil drawing technique is a direct inheritance from Wright.)

Wright's large redevelopment schemes of the late thirties and forties, like the combined ziggurat/parking garage/civic center for Pittsburgh Point Park (1947), predicted the scale and even many of the actual forms of Kahn's proposals for Philadelphia of the mid-fifties to early sixties (figs. 410, 411). One can also trace many of the ideas about

410. Pittsburgh Point Park Civic Center project, Pittsburgh, 1947–48. First scheme, 1947. Aerial perspective.

411. Kahn: Civic Center (Market Street East) project, Philadelphia, 1956–57. Aerial perspective.

412. Kiyonori Kikutake: Marine City project, 1962. Model.

413. Ron Herron and Brian Harvey (Archigram): Walking City: New York project, 1963–64. Photomontage.

414. Robert Venturi (Venturi and Rauch): Thousand Oaks Civic Center project, Thousand Oaks, Calif., 1969. Plan.

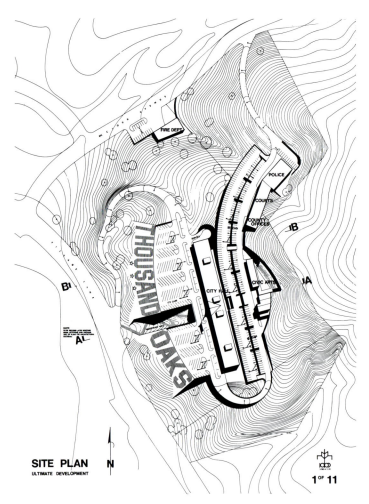

415. Philip Johnson: Own House, New Canaan, Conn., begun 1947–49.

metamorphosis, flexibility, and mutability of the mega-structural proposals of the Japanese Metabolists and the London-based Archigramists of the early sixties to Wright's forward-looking designs of the previous two decades, his characteristic clip-on tree-like structure for the tall building being perhaps the most telltale sign. (figs. 412, 296). Even the fantasmatic, futuristic, and "ludic" qualities stressed by Banham in his analysis of the movement find their most obvious precedent in Wright's imagery (figs. 413, 387).[24] Reduced to the level of a Hyatt-Regency Hotel lobby or a shopping mall, Wright's Guggenheim Museum atrium-court and Marin County Civic Center galleria have become ubiquitous (figs. 320, 395).

Wright's greatest impact in the postwar years was surely in the design of the suburban house and the integration of building and landscape, features of his work so seemingly organic that they would be naturalized in contemporaries' minds and therefore the origin in Wright generally overlooked. This extends all the way from Harwell Hamilton Harris and the Bay Region Style of the forties, to Aalto in Finland, to Venturi's work of the late fifties on. In Venturi's case, it is not merely the design of the house that reflects issues first adumbrated by Wright but also the architecture of the highway and suburban landscape, as in the Thousand Oaks Civic Center project of 1969, where the representational and planning strategies of Wright's Marin County Civic Center are redeployed (figs. 414, 391).[25]

But once again, Wright's influence in this area is not always as obvious as one might assume, a most interesting case in point being Philip Johnson's New Canaan estate, where lake, hill, and man-made structures are woven together in a way inconceivable without the model of Taliesin (figs. 415, 90). Given what we know of the personal relationship between Johnson and Wright, and the amount of contact between the two of them during the 1940s and 1950s when the Glass House and its environs were being developed, it is not at all surprising that Johnson should have modeled his house in certain significant ways on Wright's. It is also not surprising that Johnson should have chosen utterly to disregard the influence of Taliesin in the article he wrote for London's *Architectural Review* (1950) cataloguing the sources of his design (including Le Corbusier, Mies, Van Doesburg, Choisy, Schinkel, Ledoux, Malevich, and an anonymous ruin).[26]

John Andrews: George Gund Hall, Graduate School of Design, Harvard University, Cambridge, Mass., 1968–72.

416. Entrance side.   417. Garden side.

It is, however, quite surprising to discover how much the building designed in the late 1960s by John Andrews to house Harvard's Graduate School of Design owes to Taliesin West (fig. 416). This, naturally, is not disclosed on its public face, but only behind the scenes (fig. 417). The sections of the two buildings are almost identical: a covered loggia or pergola acts as a linear circulation spine on the one side; and a sloping shed-roof with light-diffusing panels covers the drafting room on the other (see fig. 277). It is true that the programs for the two structures were the same, namely, an architecture school. But it is hard to believe that the architect handpicked for the job by Harvard's chairman, José Luis Sert, would have deliberately turned to a Wrightian model for the institution that stood most for the

things Wright so vehemently opposed. There would seem to be only two possible explanations: either Andrews was unconscious of the source; or he felt he had disguised it enough so that it would not be noticed. Whichever the case may be, the result is evidence of a repressed relation in which Wright's influence appears only in subliminal form.

Such repression seems to be characteristic of Wright's reception and the usual way his influence has made itself felt.[27] It not only explains why Wright's architecture has never furnished a *style*, as has Mies's, Le Corbusier's, Kahn's, or even Gehry's; it also begins to explain more adequately how the love-hate relationship with Wright has played itself out in and through the academy. It is extraordinary how often one hears how an early exposure to Wright was the reason for someone deciding to become an architect, this being followed by a "learning" process (read: unlearning) in which Wright is replaced by those more in touch with the "real" world.

Here is Charles Moore's account:

When I was deciding that I wanted to be an architect, almost the only great buildings that I had ever seen were Frank Lloyd Wright's. He was the first architect I ever had heard of. . . . Buildings of his . . . were the first that ever moved me, and remain among the very few that have ever moved me deeply. His Autobiography *was the first architectural book I ever read.*

But Moore was quick to add: "His work is special to a place and a time that are both just out of reach. . . . Wright was not, like Le Corbusier, a 20th-Century man."

Moore pictured Wright as a kind of natural instrument of magic powers, a redoubtable fairy-tale figure of another age and place. He compared him to a

great tree you might find in an Indian fable, a tree of unsurpassed grandeur and breathtaking beauty, suitable for meditating under, hidden in a Himalayan fastness at the end of a perilous journey to which only the strong should aspire. The tree's greatness lies in its remoteness: It is and must be unique, magic, and those who seek to smuggle back shoots from it expose us all to Doom.[28]

■ ■ ■

Wright's architecture is embedded in narrative. Most ready access to it is the story of his life. Wright never chose, as did Le Corbusier, to present his work autonomously—as a matter of information—and anonymously—as the third-person editor of an *oeuvre complète*. Rather, he presented it in the guise of a fairy tale whose heroes were Taliesin and Aladdin.[29] "The fairy tale, which to this day is the first tutor of children because it was once the first tutor of mankind, secretly lives on in the story," wrote Walter Benjamin in 1936. "The liberating magic which the fairy tale has at its disposal does not bring nature into play in a mythical way, but points to its complicity with liberated man. A mature man feels this complicity only occasionally, that is, when he is happy; but the child first meets it in fairy tales, and it makes him happy." Benjamin asserted that "the first true storyteller is, and will continue to be, the teller of fairy tales." "His gift," he concluded, "is the ability to relate his life; his distinction to be able to tell his entire life." What differentiates him from others, we should add, is that he retains the capacity to relate to a world of fantasy that helps structure the child's personality but that is normally repressed before the onset of adulthood.[30]

Wright's interest in preschool education as a process of socialization through storytelling can already be seen in the playroom he designed for his children in the Oak Park house (fig. 21). Froebel blocks were only one part of a larger program for stimulating the child's mind and imagination. The beneficial and even more pervasive effects Wright attributed to fairy tales and folktales are illustrated by the prominence of the mural from the *Thousand and One Nights*.[31] Throughout Wright's *Autobiography* and later career, the narrative structure of the fairy tale played an essential role. One of Wright's last, uncompleted projects was to write a history of architecture for children in the *Wonderful World of . . .* series published in England in the 1950s. This reminds us of Viollet-le-Duc, who spent the last years of his life writing children's books (for the same house that published Jules Verne), out of the belief that only a preemptive strike could neutralize the repressive effects of formal, academic training in architecture.[32]

One of those Viollet caught in his narrative web was Wright.[33] Wright's own educational program for the Taliesin Fellowship grew out of the Gothic Revival precept that thinking should be a part of doing. In contrast to university schools, where professional education in architecture had lodged since the founding of the Ecole des Beaux-Arts, the Fellowship was antitheoretical and antiformulaic. Wright's role as "Master of Taliesin" reflected the fundamental differences between his approach to the teaching and practice of architecture and the "experimental research" in design carried out under the Bauhaus and Corbusian curriculums. The modern architect, in their view, could be analogized to the scientist, technologist, or engineer. He was a problem-solver, "proceeding in the manner of the investigator in his laboratory."[34] "When a problem is properly stated," Le Corbusier liked to say, "it inevitably finds its solution." No endorsement of his Modulor was more prized than the one from Einstein (it "makes the bad difficult and the good easy"), which Le Corbusier quoted time and again as ultimate authority.[35] The "five points of a new architecture" were like the five orders in Palladio's handbook, an abstract, demonstrable schema based on experience and fact.

In opposition to the idea of the professional architect as problem-solver, Wright offered the storyteller's magic of the fairy-tale hero. Taliesin and Aladdin had much in common. Both were naïfs, children from simple, humble backgrounds who received their special gifts by chance. The gift was the power to transform the mundane world of reality into the imaginary realm of artistic representation.[36] Taliesin and Aladdin describe figures of artistic practice operating in a world with no fixed rules, where the ground of representation is constantly shifting. The terms are personal and changeable at will. The condition is in fact a very modern one.

Taliesin and Aladdin are thus very different from Michelangelo. They react to their surroundings with a childlike sense of immediacy, without the inherited conventions of an ideal style. They retell the "initiatory ordeal," as Mircea Eliade has put it, of "passing . . . from ignorance and immaturity to the spiritual age of the adult" without forgoing the originary "complicity" with nature. They present a model of the artist as medium rather than inventor, magician rather than researcher.[37] Instead of producing an object through calculation, they call forth images as if by midwifery.

Wright always liked to say about a design he was particularly proud of that "the thing had simply shaken itself out of my sleeve" (*A* I, 179). That explained the lack of preliminary sketches and supported the myth of spontaneous generation. But how do you teach magic without reducing the process to a bag of tricks? This is what other architects asked themselves.[38] The theory of functionalism as the master code of modern architecture provided a rationale for the inventive response to new problems, new needs, new materials. "Form ever follows function," Louis Sullivan first wrote: where functions change, new forms need to be conceived. Le Corbusier's *Towards a New Architecture* and Gropius's *New Architecture and the Bauhaus* were both elaborations of this principle. Wright's dictum that "form and function are one" confused the issue.[39] Where functionalism had denied precedence to any conventional referent in its materialist definition of formal invention, Wright's organic conflation of form and function retrieved the natural referent as a basis for a renewed form of architectural representation.

P. Morton Shand quoted Oud's comment that "the process by which Wright's work came into being remains a perfect mystery to me" in order to deny Wright's relevance to the modern movement. But he tendentiously eliminated Oud's prefatory remarks: "Whereas it is a peculiarity of our

day [1925], that even the work of the cleverest nearly always betrays how it grew to be such as it is, with Wright everything is, without being at all perceptible [that it took] any mental exertions to produce. Where others are admired for the talent with which we see them master their material, I revere Wright because the process . . . remains . . . a perfect mystery."[40]

As should be clear from my descriptions of Wright's buildings, I do not believe that their gestational process is unrecoverable or that the data Wright relied on in developing his response to a site or a program cannot be recuperated and the design process reconstructed. The "mystery" of Wright's magic becomes opaque only when one looks at the problem through a screen of functionalist preconceptions. Wright's representational approach to architecture, which can be traced back to the origins of classical theory, short-circuits modern logic, causing one either not to register the obvious connections and references (Fallingwater as falling water) or not to acknowledge the illusions intended (Hollyhock House as Fujiyama; Baghdad Opera House as "crescent rainbow"). Refusing to accept, on the other hand, the classical distinction between nature and culture that always placed a strict barrier of idealism between natural history and human history, Wright worked his transformations along a sliding scale of references, favoring now one end and now the other, to give the beholder the impression that the building had simply been *teased* out of its environment.

The continuum of the environment that was Wright's constant preoccupation, from the early Prairie House and Taliesin through Fallingwater and the Marin County Civic Center, involved an engagement with time and history that fundamentally set his work off from mainstream modernism. To be modern meant to be of one's ("our") own time. Authenticity was guaranteed by the "espirit nouveau." The "spirit of the times," or *zeitgeist*, called for new solutions to new problems, which would result in a "new world of space." Wright opposed an *authenticity of place* to this *au-*

thenticity of time (and space). The diachronic "once upon a time" of the folktale and fairy tale was used by Wright to clear a way for the setting he proposed to provide.[41] Authenticity for Wright meant a rootedness to place that could occur only through the narrative framework of time. To create such a sense of place, temporal boundaries had to be transgressed: the history of a place transcends the individual and the momentary. The authenticity of place, by its incorporation of multiple temporal as well as topographical horizons, not only calls into question the modern ideal of functional originality, but also undermines, for the very same reasons, the modernist belief in transparency.

The narrative mode has often been seen as antithetical to modernism, which is supposed to be open-ended, free, aleatoric. Narrative is described as coercive, moralizing, manipulative, totalizing.[42] Indeed, both Taliesin and Taliesin West were prescriptive communal organizations, in which the hearing and retelling of the narratives of the sites were part of the initiation rite of the Fellowship and a fundamental activity throughout its existence. (A visit to the buildings today still entails a listening experience, as one of the members of the Fellowship "guides" the visitor through its story.[43]) But might we not also understand the narrative mode in a subversive sense, as providing an outlet for that which can never be contained within the pure (purist) definition of modernism?

The narrative and the scientific can be defined as two modes of legitimating knowledge. The scientific is denotative, axiomatic, and open to the assertion of truth; the narrative is connotative, reiterative, and achieves legitimacy through belief. This opposition well describes certain essential differences between Wright's *Autobiography* and Le Corbusier's *Oeuvre complète*. The latter's scientific tone and abstract formulas, like the "five points," seem at first more liberating and conducive to originality and inventiveness than Wright's narrative structure, which appears to demand nothing less than a conversion. But the narrative mode of the storyteller's art ultimately engages the listener in a dialogue that allows new shades of meaning to emerge from the fact of interaction.[44]

When one considers the history of modern architecture in its broadest perspective, which is to say, from the eighteenth century to the present, the relation between narrative and scientific discourse becomes a dialectical one. What on the surface may appear coercive and retrogressive often turns out to be subversive and progressive. The narrative impulse underlying the English landscape garden called into question the rational order of French academic classicism and gave us the picturesque. The narrative intervention of the story of the building of the primitive hut in the otherwise fairly conventional expository text of Laugier's *Essai sur l'architecture* helped to discredit the mythology of the orders. And the narrative histories and tales that Viollet-le-Duc and Ruskin, among others, related about the origins and development of Gothic architecture undercut the classical abstractions of academic theory. In fact, the fairy tale as such, which has been described by both Eliade and Benjamin as a desacralized, humanized form of myth, was first made the object of collection and publication by Charles Perrault at precisely the same moment (the end of the seventeenth century) that he and his architect brother Claude were laying a rational foundation for the adaptation of classical theory to the increasing scientific pressures of a modern world through their writings on art and architecture.[45]

■ ■ ■

Wright's critique of the materialism and scientism of modern architecture and society produced an important legacy that will take many generations to digest fully. Over and against the instrumentalization of built form, he proposed a vision of architecture as human shelter that maintained an integral relation to the site at the same time as it expressed institutional values in a symbolic language comprehensible to a broad segment of the population. The expressive range of that deliberately non-elitist language was supported by a system of representation that was as traditional in intention as it was modern in inflection. Memory and history were increasingly called upon to solidify the relation between public and private, city and country, urban and suburban experience that Wright continually stressed as essential to ensure a humane living and working environment.

The representation of a kind of unity and continuity that few in the twentieth century still believed to be possible was Wright's ultimate aim and what led him to choose the particular means of expression he did. While writers from Ernst Bloch and Walter Benjamin to Mircea Eliade and Bruno Bettelheim have stressed how folktales and fairy tales permit access to a world of desire and imagination that ultimately allows the child, when grown up, to cope successfully with the "terror of history," the great Russian Formalist Vladimir Propp exploited the archetypal character of the genre to formulate the first structural analysis of narrative.[46] Wright, too, used the form as a means to a larger end. His architecture does not take us back to childhood, as some might claim; but it does intentionally preserve those characteristics of wonder, and immediacy, and credulity, and complicity that we associate with the world of childhood

and that modern artists from Picasso, Klee, Miro, and Ernst to Calder, Pollock, Dubuffet, and Oldenburg have sought as a source of "primitive" inspiration.[47] Wright hoped to "allow the child in him to live." That happened enough for us to be able to experience many buildings of his, no matter how many times we visit them, as if always for the first time and, at that time, as if never for the last time.

The imagery of nature, as the complement of culture, was Wright's model for such illusions of continuity. The "mystery" of his "creations" mirrors the fundamental mystery of the universe. There is a profound romanticism in that unwillingness either to rationalize nature as "sun, space, and greenery" and exploit it as "real estate," or to adopt the heroic, machine-age counterposition of alienation.[48] Wright's rejection of the instrumentalization of nature in favor of its representation carries a deep moral and ethical charge that is hardly spent yet. One can only assume that as the technological dream of early modernism is counterbalanced by the growing importance of ecological, environmental, and contextual concerns, Wright's position in the history of twentieth-century architecture will be revised as his/story is retold.

Notes

Abbreviations
(For additional information on the sources listed below, see Bibliographical Note.)

AJ   *Architects' Journal*
AF   *Architectural Forum*
ARec   *Architectural Record*
ARev   *Architectural Review*
CT   *Chicago Tribune*
ENR   *Engineering News-Record*
FLW   Frank Lloyd Wright
FLWN   *Frank Lloyd Wright Newsletter*
JRIBA   *Journal of the Royal Institute of British Architects*
JSAH   *Journal of the Society of Architectural Historians*
NYT   *New York Times*
PSR   *Prairie School Review*
PA   *Progressive Architecture*
WA   *Western Architect*

A   Frank Lloyd Wright, *An Autobiography*. London, New York, and Toronto: Longmans, Green, 1932. See Introduction, note 21, below.

Alofsin, *Lost Years*   Anthony Alofsin, *Frank Lloyd Wright: The Lost Years, 1910–1922. A Study of Influence*. Chicago and London: University of Chicago Press, 1993.

Brownell and FLW   Baker Brownell and Frank Lloyd Wright. *Architecture and Modern Life*. New York and London: Harper & Brothers, 1937.

Gill, *Many Masks*   Brendan Gill. *Many Masks: A Life of Frank Lloyd Wright*. New York: G. P. Putnam's Sons, 1987.

Gutheim, *FLW on Arch.*   Frederick Gutheim, ed., *Frank Lloyd Wright on Architecture: Selected Writings, 1894–1940*. New York: Duell, Sloan and Pearce, 1941.

Hitchcock, *Materials*   Henry-Russell Hitchcock. *In the Nature of Materials: The Buildings of Frank Lloyd Wright, 1887–1941*. New York: Duell, Sloan and Pearce, 1942.

LApprentices   Bruce Brooks Pfeiffer, ed., *Frank Lloyd Wright: Letters to Apprentices*. Fresno: Press at California State University, 1982.

LArchitects   Bruce Brooks Pfeiffer, ed., *Frank Lloyd Wright: Letters to Architects*. Fresno: Press at California State University, 1984.

LClients   Bruce Brooks Pfeiffer, ed., *Frank Lloyd Wright: Letters to Clients*. Fresno: Press at California State University, 1986.

FLWM   Bruce Brooks Pfeiffer and Yukio Futagawa, eds. *Frank Lloyd Wright*. 12 vols. Tokyo: A.D.A. EDITA, 1984–88. Vols. 1–8, *Monograph*.

FLWPS   Bruce Brooks Pfeiffer and Yukio Futagawa, eds. *Frank Lloyd Wright*. 12 vols. Tokyo: A.D.A. EDITA, 1984–88. Vols. 9–11, *Preliminary Studies*.

FLWR   Bruce Brooks Pfeiffer and Yukio Futagawa, eds. *Frank Lloyd Wright*. 12 vols. Tokyo: A.D.A. EDITA, 1984–88. Vol. 12, *In His Renderings*.

Scully, *Wright*   Vincent Scully Jr. *Frank Lloyd Wright*. Masters of World Architecture Series. New York: George Braziller, 1960.

Secrest, *Wright*   Meryle Secrest. *Frank Lloyd Wright*. New York: Alfred A. Knopf, 1992.

Smith, *Wright*   Norris Kelly Smith. *Frank Lloyd Wright: A Study in Architectural Content*. Orig. pub. 1966. Rev. ed. Watkins Glen, N.Y.: American Life Foundation & Study Institute, 1979.

Sweeney, *Wright in Hollywood*   Robert L. Sweeney. *Wright in Hollywood: Visions of a New Architecture*. New York, Cambridge, Mass., and London: Architectural History Foundation, MIT Press, 1994.

Twombly, *Wright*   Robert C. Twombly. *Frank Lloyd Wright: His Life and His Architecture*. New York: John Wiley & Sons, Wiley-Interscience Publication, 1979.

Princeton Lects.   Frank Lloyd Wright. *Modern Architecture, Being the Kahn Lectures for 1930*. Princeton: Princeton University Press, 1931.

London Lects.   Frank Lloyd Wright. *An Organic Architecture: The Architecture of Democracy*, Sir George Watson Lectures of the Sulgrave Manor Board for 1939. London: Lund Humphries, 1939.

Wasmuth I   Frank Lloyd Wright. *Ausgefürhte Bauten und Entwürfe von Frank Lloyd Wright*. Berlin: Ernst Wasmuth, 1910[–11].

Wasmuth II   Frank Lloyd Wright. *Frank Lloyd Wright: Ausgefürhte Bauten*. Berlin: Ernst Wasmuth, 1911.

Wendingen 1925   H[endrikus] Th[eodorus] Wijdeveld, ed., *The Life-Work of the American Architect Frank Lloyd Wright*. Santpoort, Holland: C. A. Mees, 1925.

Ashbee Journals   Ashbee Papers, Journal, Modern Archive Center, King's College Library, Cambridge, England.

FLWF   Frank Lloyd Wright Archives, Frank Lloyd Wright Foundation, Taliesin West, Scottsdale, Ariz.

J. L. Wright Papers   John Lloyd Wright Collection, Drawings and Archives, Avery Architectural and Fine Arts Library, Columbia University, New York, N. Y.

Klumb Archive   Henry Klumb Archive, Archivo de Arquitectura y Construccíon, Escuela de Arquitectura, Universidad de Puerto Rico, San Juan.

Woolley Archive   Taylor Woolley Archive, MS 452, Manuscripts Division, Special Collections, University of Utah Libraries, Salt Lake City.

Wright-Martin Papers   Frank Lloyd Wright–Darwin D. Martin Papers, MS 22.8, University Archives, State University of New York, Buffalo.

Wright-Polivka Papers   Jaroslav Joseph Polivka. Papers Concerning Frank Lloyd Wright, 1945–1959, MS 48, University Archives, State University of New York, Buffalo.

Introduction

1. Hitchcock, *Materials* was published soon after Wright's retrospective at the Museum of Modern Art in 1940–41, in lieu of a catalogue. It remained the basic record of Wright's work until the mid-1980s, when the twelve-volume compendium by Bruce Brooks Pfeiffer and Yukio Futagawa began to appear (see note 15 below).

2. Walter F. Wagner Jr., "Profile of the 1981 Graduates: Conservative, On-Track, Main-Line Modernists," *ARec* 169 (January 1981): 89.

3. Quoted in "FLW: His Future Influence," *PA* 49 (September 1968): 143.

4. Quoted in "A Visit with Frank Lloyd Wright," *Look* 21 (17 September 1957): 31.

5. A succinct account of this attitude is given by Vincent Scully in "The Heritage of Wright," *Zodiac* 8 (1961): 8–13.

6. Philip Johnson, "The Seven Crutches of Modern Architecture," orig. pub. *Perspecta* 3 (1955), repr. in Johnson, *Writings* (New York: Oxford University Press, 1979), 140.

7. Philip Johnson, "100 Years, Frank Lloyd Wright and Us," orig. pub. *Pacific Architect and Builder* (March 1957), repr. in Johnson, *Writings*, 194.

8. Henry-Russell Hitchcock, "Frank Lloyd Wright at the Museum of Modern Art," *Art Bulletin* 23 (March 1941): 76.

9. Bruno Zevi, *Frank Lloyd Wright* (Milan: Il Balcone, 1947); Grant Carpenter Manson, *Frank Lloyd Wright to 1910: The First Golden Age* (New York: Reinhold, 1958); Scully, *Wright*; Smith, *Wright*; and Twombly, *Wright*. Manson's pioneering study was originally a doctoral dissertation in the Department of Fine Arts, Harvard University, in 1940, and Hitchcock consulted the manuscript in the preparation of *Materials*. To the list of general studies of Wright mentioned in the text should be added: Zevi, *Frank Lloyd Wright* (1979; rpt. Zurich and Munich: Verlag für Architektur Artemis Zürich, Les Editions d'Architecture, 1981); Otto Antonia Graf, *Die Kunst des Quadrats: Zum Werk von Frank Lloyd Wright*, 2 vols. (Vienna, Cologne, and Graz: Hermann Böhlaus Nachf., 1983); Daniel Treiber, *Frank Lloyd Wright* (Paris: Fernand Hazan,

1986); Grant Hildebrand, *The Wright Space: Pattern and Meaning in Frank Lloyd Wright's Houses* (Seattle: University of Washington Press, 1991); and Donald W. Hoppen, *The Seven Ages of Frank Lloyd Wright: A New Appraisal* (Santa Barbara: Capra Press, 1993).

10. In addition to the books and articles of the 1980s and 1990s that will be referred to in relevant notes, a number of important newsletters and journals specifically devoted to Wright have appeared. These include: *Wright Angles: Newsletter of the Frank Lloyd Wright Home and Studio* (begun 1976); *The Frank Lloyd Wright Newsletter* (1978–82); *Frank Lloyd Wright Quarterly* (begun 1990); *Journal of the Taliesin Fellows* (begun 1990); and *Wright Studies* (begun 1992). The Wright exhibition at MOMA was accompanied by the catalogue *Frank Lloyd Wright: Architect*, ed., Terence Riley, with Peter Reed (New York: Museum of Modern Art, 1994).

11. The most complete guide to Wright's buildings is William Allin Storrer, *The Frank Lloyd Wright Companion* (Chicago: University of Chicago Press, 1993). The best bibliography, though now somewhat out of date, is Robert L. Sweeney, *Frank Lloyd Wright: An Annotated Bibliography*, Art and Architecture Bibliographies, no. 5 (Los Angeles: Hennessey & Ingalls, 1978). Two early, synoptic collections of Wright's writings are: Gutheim, *FLW on Arch.*; and Edgar Kaufmann and Ben Raeburn, eds., *Frank Lloyd Wright: Writings and Buildings* (Cleveland and New York: Meridian Books, World Publishing, 1960). A five-volume collection of writings, edited by Bruce Brooks Pfeiffer, began appearing in 1992: Bruce Brooks Pfeiffer, ed., *Frank Lloyd Wright: Collected Writings* (New York: Rizzoli, Frank Lloyd Wright Foundation, 1992–1995), vol. 1, *1894–1930* (1992); vol. 2, *1930–1932* (1992); vol. 3, *1931–1939* (1993); vol. 4, *1939–1949* (1994); vol. 5, *1949–1959* (1995). Unfortunately, these came out too late to be of general use in this book.

12. Wasmuth I and Wasmuth II. Both works have been republished a number of times. For a more precise dating of the original publications and a critical appraisal of their impact in Europe, see Alofsin, *Lost Years*, 72, 78.

13. For a brief summary of this position, see Kenneth Frampton, *Modern Architecture: A Critical History* (New York and Toronto: Oxford University Press, 1980), 186–91. Wright's critical reception will be treated more fully in the Conclusion.

14. Among these are: John Sergeant, *Frank Lloyd Wright's Usonian Houses: The Case for Organic Architecture* (New York: Whitney Library of Design, Watson-Guptill, 1976); Donald Hoffmann, *Frank Lloyd Wright's Fallingwater: The House and Its History* (1978; 2d ed. rev., New York: Dover, 1993); Herbert Jacobs and Katherine Jacobs, *Building with Frank Lloyd Wright: An Illustrated Memoir* (San Francisco: Chronicle Books, Prism Edition, 1978); Paul R. and Jean S. Hanna, *Frank Lloyd Wright's Hanna House: The Clients' Report* (Cambridge, Mass., and New York: Architectural History Foundation, MIT Press, 1981); Hoffmann, *Frank Lloyd Wright's Robie House: The Illustrated Story of an Architectural Masterpiece* (New York: Dover, 1984); Joseph Connors, *The Robie House of Frank Lloyd Wright* (Chicago and London: University of Chicago Press, 1984); Margaret Helen Scott, *Frank Lloyd Wright's Warehouse in Richland Center, Wisconsin* (Richland Center: Richland County Publishers, 1984); Edgar Kaufmann Jr., *Fallingwater: A Frank Lloyd Wright Country House* (New York: Abbeville Press, 1986); Jonathan Lipman, *Frank Lloyd Wright and the Johnson Wax Buildings* (New York: Rizzoli, 1986); John Gurda, *New World Odyssey: Annunciation Greek Orthodox Church and Frank Lloyd Wright* (Milwaukee: Milwaukee Hellenic Community, 1986); Aaron G. Green and Donald P. DeNevi, *An Architecture for Democracy: Frank Lloyd Wright—The Marin County Civic Center* (San Francisco: Grendon, 1990); Susan J. Bandes, ed., *Affordable Dreams: The Goetsch-Winckler House and Frank Lloyd Wright*, special issue of *Kresge Art Museum Bulletin* 6 (East Lansing: Michigan State University, 1991); Hoffmann, *Frank Lloyd Wright's Hollyhock House* (New York: Dover, 1992); Kathryn Smith, *Frank Lloyd Wright, Hollyhock House and Olive Hill: Buildings and Projects for Aline Barnsdall* (New York: Rizzoli, 1992); James Steele, *Barnsdall House: Frank Lloyd Wright*, Architecture in Detail (London: Phaidon, 1992); Alvin Rosenbaum, *Usonia: Frank Lloyd Wright's Design for America* (Washington, D.C.: Preservation Press, National Trust for Historic Preservation, 1993); *The Solomon R. Guggenheim Museum* (New York: Guggenheim Museum, 1994); and Sweeney, *Wright in Hollywood*. To these monographs should be added the eight-volume series of *Frank Lloyd Wright: Selected Houses*

(Tokyo: A.D.A. EDITA, 1989–91), edited by Bruce Brooks Pfeiffer and Yukio Futagawa.

15. Bruce Brooks Pfeiffer and Yukio Futagawa, eds., *Frank Lloyd Wright*, 12 vols. (Tokyo: A.D.A. EDITA, 1984–88): vols. 1–8, *Monograph*; vols. 9–11, *Preliminary Studies*; vol. 12, *In His Renderings. LApprentices; LArchitects; LClients*; Pfeiffer, ed., *Frank Lloyd Wright: The Guggenheim Correspondence* (Fresno, Calif., and Carbondale and Edwardsville, Ill.: Press at California State University and Southern Illinois University Press, 1986); and Pfeiffer, ed., *Frank Lloyd Wright: The Crowning Decade* (Fresno: Press at California State University, 1989). To this primary documentation should be added the following important publications: Patrick J. Meehan, ed., *The Master Architect: Conversations with Frank Lloyd Wright* (New York: Wiley-Interscience Publications, John Wiley, 1984); Meehan, ed., *Truth Against the World: Frank Lloyd Wright Speaks for an Organic Architecture* (New York: Wiley-Interscience Publications, John Wiley, 1987); Meehan, ed., *Frank Lloyd Wright Remembered* (Washington, D.C.: Preservation Press, National Trust for Historic Preservation, 1991); Randolph C. Henning, ed., *"At Taliesin": Newspaper Columns by Frank Lloyd Wright and the Taliesin Fellowship, 1934–1937* (Carbondale and Edwardsville, Ill.: Southern Illinois University Press, 1992); Edgar Tafel, ed., *About Wright: An Album of Recollections by Those Who Knew Frank Lloyd Wright* (New York: John Wiley, 1993); and Pedro E. Guerrero, *Picturing Wright: An Album from Frank Lloyd Wright's Photographer* (San Francisco: Pomegranate Artbooks, 1994). Meehan also published the very useful *Frank Lloyd Wright: A Research Guide to Archival Sources* (New York and London: Garland, 1983). Wright's correspondence has been made more accessible through the publication of Anthony Alofsin, ed., *Frank Lloyd Wright: An Index to the Taliesin Correspondence*, 5 vols. (New York and London: Garland, 1988).

Partly as a result of the increased availability of such research materials, studies of Wright have become more numerous in recent years. Among those that appeared too late for me to make significant use of (or of which I became aware too late) are: Jean Castex, *Frank Lloyd Wright: Le printemps de la Prairie House* (Liège: Pierre Madarga, 1985); Donald Leslie Johnson, *Frank Lloyd Wright versus America: The 1930s* (Cambridge, Mass., and London: MIT Press, 1990); James F. O'Gorman, *Three American Architects: Richardson, Sullivan, and Wright, 1865–1915* (Chicago: University of Chicago Press, 1991); Robert McCarter, ed., *Frank Lloyd Wright: A Primer on Architectural Principles* (New York: Princeton Architectural Press, 1991); and Kevin Nute, *Frank Lloyd Wright and Japan: The Role of Traditional Japanese Art and Architecture in the Work of Frank Lloyd Wright* (New York: Van Nostrand Reinhold, 1993).

16. FLW, *An Autobiography* (London, New York, and Toronto: Longmans, Green, 1932), 170 and passim. In Welsh, the word *Taliesin* means "shining" or "radiant brow." The larger context of its meaning for Wright will be fully discussed in Chapter IV.

17. Borthwick was Mamah Cheney's maiden name, to which she reverted upon her divorce from Edwin Cheney in August 1911.

The Cheneys had two children, both of whom were visiting their mother at the time. A third child, whom they raised following the death of Mamah's sister, had remained in Oak Park. I would like to thank Mrs. Richard B. Hart and Dale Smirl for this information.

18. Roland Barthes, "The Death of the Author" (1968), repr. in Barthes, *Image-Music-Text*, ed. and trans. Stephen Heath (New York: Hill and Wang, 1977), 142–48. For a semiological interpretation of Wright, see Daniel Treiber, "Frank Lloyd Wright," *CREE* 3 (August–September 1974): 104–14.

19. No other twentieth-century architect has inspired anywhere near the kind of biographical interest that Wright has. Some of the books are pure gossip, others for children, still others quite scholarly. Among them are: John Lloyd Wright, *My Father Who Is on Earth* (New York: G. P. Putnam's Sons, 1946); Aylesa Forsee, *Frank Lloyd Wright: Rebel in Concrete* (Philadelphia: Macrae Smith, 1959); Finis Farr, *Frank Lloyd Wright: A Biography* (New York: Charles Scribner's Sons, 1961); Doris Ransohoff, *Living Architecture: Frank Lloyd Wright* (Chicago: Britannica Books, 1962); Herbert Jacobs, *Frank Lloyd Wright: America's Greatest Architect* (New York: Harcourt, Brace and World, 1965); Olgivanna Lloyd Wright, *Frank Lloyd Wright: His Life, His Work, His Words* (New York: Horizon Press, 1966); Corinne J. Naden, *Frank*

Lloyd Wright: The Rebel Architect (New York: Franklin Watts, 1968); Kenneth G. Richards, *People of Destiny: Frank Lloyd Wright* (Chicago: Childrens Press, 1968); Paul Salsini, *Frank Lloyd Wright: The Architectural Genius of the Twentieth Century*, ed. D. Steve Rahmas (Charlotteville, N.Y.: SamHar Press, 1971); Charlotte Willard, *Frank Lloyd Wright: American Architect* (New York: Macmillan, 1972); Twombly, *Wright*; Gill, *Many Masks*; Wendy B. Murphy, *Frank Lloyd Wright*, Genius Series (Silver Burdett Press, 1990); Yona Zeldis McDonough, *Frank Lloyd Wright*, Chelsea House Library for Biography (New York and Philadelphia: Chelsea House, 1992); Secrest, *Wright*; and Alexander O. Boulton, *Frank Lloyd Wright, Architect: An Illustrated Biography* (New York: Rizzoli, Frank Lloyd Wright Foundation, 1993). This list, of course, does not include Ayn Rand's *The Fountainhead*, a *roman à clef* published in 1943 and released as a movie in 1949 starring Gary Cooper as Howard Roark, a.k.a. Frank Lloyd Wright. Nor does it include the more recent fictionalization of Wright's life up to 1914 in the novel by Meyer Levin, *The Architect* (New York: Simon and Schuster, 1981). The tragedy at Taliesin in 1914 served as the subject for Daren Hagen's opera *Shining Brow*, which premiered at the Madison (Wisconsin) Opera in April 1993.

20. For representative examples, see FLW, "The Art and Craft of the Machine," orig. pub. Catalogue of the *Fourteenth Annual Exhibition of the Chicago Architectural Club* (1901), repr. in Kaufmann and Raeburn, *Frank Lloyd Wright: Writings and Buildings*, 55–73; and FLW, *A Testament* (New York: Horizon Press, 1957), 18–19. For a fuller treatment of Hugo's essay and its relation to modern architecture, see my "The Book and the Building: Hugo's Theory of Architecture and Labrouste's Bibliothèque Ste. Geneviève," in *The Beaux-Arts and Nineteenth-Century French Architecture*, ed. Robin Middleton (London: Thames and Hudson, 1982), 138–73. For later discussions of the subject, see Narciso Menocal, "Frank Lloyd Wright as the Anti-Victor Hugo," in *American Public Architecture: European Roots and Native Expressions*, ed. Craig Zabel and Susan Scott Munshower, Papers in Art History from the Pennsylvania State University, vol. 5 (University Park: Pennsylvania State University Press, 1989), 139–50; and Sidney K. Robinson, "Frank Lloyd Wright and Victor Hugo," in *Modern Architecture in America: Visions and Revisions*, ed. Richard Guy Wilson and Robinson (Ames: Iowa State University Press, 1991), 106–11.

For an early, and concise, statement of the necessity for each artistic "medium" to be "true to conditions of its existence," see FLW, "A Philosophy of Fine Art" [1900], in Pfeiffer, *Collected Writings*, 1:42–43.

21. Wright's *An Autobiography* remains the fullest account of his thinking about architecture. It was begun in 1926 and first published in 1932. A revised and expanded version appeared in 1943 (New York: Duell, Sloan and Pearce). A third, revised and expanded version appeared posthumously in 1977 (New York: Horizon Press). They will henceforth be referred to as *A* I, II, and III.

Chapter I
Beginnings of the Prairie House

1. Hamlin Garland, *Crumbling Idols: Twelve Essays on Art Dealing Chiefly with Literature, Painting and the Drama* (1894; ed. Jane Johnson, Cambridge, Mass.: Harvard University Press, Belknap Press, 1960), 7, 9–10. The essay "Provincialism," which forms the first chapter of *Crumbling Idols*, was originally published as part of "The West in Literature," *Arena* 6 (November 1892): 669–76. On the Chicago Renaissance, see especially Bernard Duffey, *The Chicago Renaissance in American Letters: A Critical History* ([East Lansing]: Michigan State College Press, 1954); Hugh Dalziel Duncan, *The Rise of Chicago as a Literary Center from 1885 to 1920: A Sociological Essay in American Culture* (Totowa, N.J.: Bedminster Press, 1964); and Dale Kramer, *Chicago Renaissance: The Literary Life in the Midwest, 1900–1930* (New York: Appleton-Century, 1966).

2. The basic work on the Prairie School is H. Allen Brooks, *The Prairie School: Frank Lloyd Wright and His Midwest Contemporaries* (New York: W. W. Norton, 1972).

3. For the most recent, and accurate, biographies of Wright, see

Twombly, *Wright*; Gill, *Many Masks*; and Secrest, *Wright*. The birth date of 1869, which Wright always gave, was accepted until Thomas S. Hines Jr. published the correct date in "Frank Lloyd Wright—The Madison Years: Records versus Recollections," *Wisconsin Magazine of History* 50 (Winter 1967): 109–19.

4. On the history of the Lloyd Jones family in Wisconsin, see Maginel Wright Barney, *The Valley of the God-Almighty Joneses: Reminiscences of Frank Lloyd Wright's Sister* (1965; rpt. Spring Green, Wis.: Unity Chapel Publications, 1986); Thomas Graham, ed., *Trilogy: Through Their Eyes* (Spring Green: Unity Chapel Publications, 1986); *A Lloyd Jones Retrospective* (Spring Green: Unity Chapel Publications, 1986); and Franklin Porter and Mary Porter, eds., *Heritage: The Lloyd Jones Family* (Spring Green: Unity Chapel Publications, 1986). For a broader treatment of the Welsh immigration, see Phillips G. Davies, *The Welsh in Wisconsin* (Madison: State Historical Society of Wisconsin, 1982). For the less well-known subject of Wright's paternal ancestors, see Donald Leslie Johnson, "Notes on Frank Lloyd Wright's Paternal Family," *FLWN* 3, no. 2 (1980): 5–7.

5. It was apparently while living in Weymouth that Wright's mother, who took a particularly active role in her only son's education, became interested in the Froebel kindergarten method. She purchased a set of the geometric blocks and colored paper "gifts" for him to play with. This experience of combining and recombining abstract forms to create highly integrated structures analogous in their patterns to those in nature, Wright always maintained, had a profound impact on his later thinking. For Wright's account, see *A* I, 11. The subject of Froebel's influence on Wright has inspired a large debate. See Grant C. Manson, "Wright in the Nursery: The Influence of Froebel Education on the Work of Frank Lloyd Wright," *ARev* 113 (June 1953): 349–51; Stuart Wilson, "The 'Gifts' of Froebel," *JSAH* 26 (December 1967): 238–41; Richard C. MacCormac, "Froebel's Kindergarten Gifts and the Early Work of Frank Lloyd Wright," orig. pub. *Environment and Planning B* 1 (1974), rev. and repr. in Robert McCarter, ed., *Frank Lloyd Wright: A Primer on Architectural Principles* (New York: Princeton Architectural Press, 1991), 99–123; Edgar Kaufmann Jr., "'*Form* Became *Feeling*': A New View of Froebel and Wright," orig. pub. *JSAH* 40 (May 1981), repr. in Kaufmann, *9 Commentaries on Wright* (New York, Cambridge, Mass., and London: Architectural History Foundation, MIT Press, 1989), 1–6; Kaufmann, "Frank Lloyd Wright's Mementos of Childhood," orig. pub. *JSAH* 41 (October 1982), repr. in Kaufmann, *9 Commentaries*, 19–35; and Jeanne S. Rubin, "The Froebel-Wright Kindergarten Connections: A New Perspective," *JSAH* 48 (March 1989): 24–37.

6. *An Autobiography* begins on a winter morning in Helena Valley with the young Wright walking in the snow with his Uncle John (p. 1). Twenty-two of the first twenty-eight pages of the *Autobiography* are devoted to Wright's early experiences on, or recollections of, the family's Wisconsin farmland.

7. The classic study of the so-called Chicago School is Carl W. Condit, *The Chicago School of Architecture: A History of Commercial and Public Building in the Chicago Area, 1875–1925* (Chicago and London: University of Chicago Press, 1964).

8. For Silsbee, see Susan Karr Sorell, "Silsbee: The Evolution of a Personal Architectural Style," and "A Catalog of Work by J. L. Silsbee," *PSR* 7 (1970): 5–13, 17–21. On Silsbee's work for Jenkin Lloyd Jones and the Lloyd Jones family, see Joseph Siry, "The Abraham Lincoln Center in Chicago," *JSAH* 50 (September 1991): 235–65. Elizabeth Wright Ingraham, "The Chapel in the Valley," orig. pub. *FLWN* 3, no. 2 (1980), repr. in Porter and Porter, *Heritage: The Lloyd Jones Family*, 3–15.

9. There has been some debate as to when Wright joined Sullivan's office. In his study of Sullivan, Robert Twombly maintains that it was "probably early in 1888" (Twombly, *Louis Sullivan: His Life and Work* [New York: Viking, 1986], 173). It should be noted that Wright worked for Silsbee at two separate times; in between, he did a short stint in the office of William W. Clay.

10. For a slightly different account, see Twombly, *Sullivan*, 233–38.

11. On the World's Columbian Exposition, see David F. Burg, *Chicago's White City of 1893* (Lexington: University Press of Kentucky, 1976) and Reid Badger, *The Great American Fair: The World's Columbian Exposition & American Culture* (Chicago: Nelson Hall, 1979).

12. Louis H. Sullivan, *The Autobiography of an Idea* (1924; rpt. New York: Dover, 1956), 322, 325.

13. An early treatment of this important project is in Henry-Russell Hitchcock, "Frank Lloyd Wright and the 'Academic Tradition' of the Early Eighteen-Nineties," *Journal of the Warburg and Courtauld Institutes* 7 (January–June 1944): 46–63. It is not easy to understand how Wright became so proficient in classical design without the normal training in that discipline. Did he get it from Sullivan? That is probably a large part of the answer. His Wolf Lake Amusement Park project of 1895 (see Chapter II) certainly supports this contention. In any event, it is intriguing to recall the almost Freudian slip H. P. Berlage made in an article of 1912 on "Neuere amerikanische Architektur" when discussing Wright's educational background: "Frank Lloyd Wright is a student of Sullivan's and is an architect of very special importance. I do not know whether Sullivan studied in Paris, but Wright is a student of the Ecole des Beaux-Arts" ("The New American Architecture [1912]: Travel Impressions of H. P. Berlage, Architect in Amsterdam," orig. pub. *Schweizerische Bauzeitung* [14, 21, and 28 September 1912], trans. Lily Boecher in Don Gifford, ed., *The Literature of Architecture: The Evolution of Architectural Theory and Practice in Nineteenth-Century America* [New York: E. P. Dutton, 1966], 611). It may be that Berlage misunderstood the "young colleague of [his] who worked in Sullivan's office" and who showed him around the Chicago area on his trip in 1911 (p. 615). Or perhaps he just could not believe that any young American could have arrived at the level of compositional and stylistic sophistication Wright did without such formal training as that offered at the Ecole. There is a contemporary English translation of the Berlage article (perhaps supplied by Wright and, if so, perhaps done by Mamah Borthwick) dated 30 March 1912, in Box 3-15, Wright-Martin Papers. A more extensive discussion of Berlage's trip appeared in his *Amerikaansche Reisherinneringen* (Rotterdam: W. L. and J. Brusse, 1913).For a recent study of Wright and the "academic tradition," see Patrick Pinnell, "Academic Tradition and the Individual Talent: Similarity and Difference in the Formation of Frank Lloyd Wright," in McCarter, *Wright*, 18–58.

14. Atwood had been hired to replace John Root, who died in February 1891. But his serious emotional and health problems, involving drug addiction, rendered him almost useless to Burnham by early 1894. Although Atwood died in 1895, it is clear that Burnham was aware much sooner that he would have to find a replacement for him. This was suggested in an unpublished paper on Atwood by Ann Lorenz Van Zanten.

15. Wright's account of his decision to reject the academic road of easy success and go it alone is foreshadowed in Viollet-le-Duc's pseudo-autobiography, *Histoire d'un dessinateur: Comment on apprend à dessiner* (Paris: Bibliothèque d'Education et de Récréation, J. Hetzel, 1879).

16. FLW, "In the Cause of Architecture," *ARec* 23 (March 1908): 156. Robert Spencer, a friend and colleague of Wright, originally made this point in print in the first lengthy critical article about Wright's work: "Mr. Wright has been doing for the typical residence and apartment house what Sullivan has done for the theatre and office building" (Robert C. Spencer Jr., "The Work of Frank Lloyd Wright," *ARev* [Boston] 7 [June 1900]: 66).

17. For the fullest expression of Wright's understanding of Sullivan's lesson, see FLW, *Genius and the Mobocracy* (New York: Duell, Sloan and Pearce, 1949).

18. Ibid., 80, 56.

19. The most recent publication on the house is Ann Abernathy, with John G. Thorpe, eds., *The Oak Park Home and Studio of Frank Lloyd Wright* (Oak Park, Ill.: Frank Lloyd Wright Home and Studio Foundation, 1988). An early discussion is "Successful Houses, III," *House Beautiful* 1 (15 February 1897): 64–69.

20. FLW, *Genius and the Mobocracy*, 42. Until more work is done on the Shingle Style in Chicago, it is difficult to know how much Wright was exaggerating the unusualness of his design. Silsbee certainly did things like it, though never as singular in expression. George Maher, who was in Silsbee's office at the same time Wright was, also apparently produced similar designs, though probably on the heels of Wright's.

21. As his family grew in size, Wright built a separate studio on the Chicago Avenue side of the house (1898), at which time the second-story room under the gable was partitioned into dormitory-like bedrooms for boys (on the Chicago Avenue side) and girls (on the other).

22. Vincent J. Scully Jr., *The Shingle Style and the Stick Style: Architec-*

tural Theory from Downing to the Origins of Wright (1955; rev. ed., New Haven, Conn., and London: Yale University Press, 1971), 159. Cf. George William Sheldon, *Artistic Country-Seats: Types of Recent American Villa and Cottage Architecture, with Instances of Country Club-Houses*, 2 vols. in 5 pts. (New York: D. Appleton, 1886–87). Although Sheldon did not illustrate Price's Chandler House (fig. 11), he did illustrate Price's Kent House, also in Tuxedo Park and of the same date (1886) and style. The Chandler House was first published in the journal *Building* 5 (18 September 1886). Sheldon also included McKim, Mead and White's Taylor House in Newport (fig. 13).

23. FLW, "In the Cause" (1908): 155.

24. Ernst H. Gombrich, *Art and Illusion: A Study in the Psychology of Pictorial Representation*, A. W. Mellon Lectures in the Fine Arts (1956), Bollingen Series 35, no. 5, 2d ed. rev. (Princeton: Princeton University Press,1961); and Antoine-Chrysostôme Quatremère de Quincy, *De l'architecture égyptienne, considérée dans son origine, ses principes et son goût, et comparée sous les mêmes rapports à l'architecture grecque* (Paris: Barrois l'aîné et Fils, 1803), 42. For a clear exposition of the *natura naturata/natura naturans* debate in the theory of architectural imitation, see in addition to the *Architecture égyptienne*, Quatremère's articles on "Architecture" and "Cabane" in *Architecture*, 3 vols., in *Encyclopédie méthodique* (Paris: Panckoucke, 1788; H. Agasse, 1798–1825), 1:109–27, 382–86.

25. FLW, "In the Cause" (1908), 162; and FLW, "A Philosophy of Fine Art" [1900], in Bruce Brooks Pfeiffer, ed., *Frank Lloyd Wright: Collected Writings*, vol. 1, *1894–1930* (New York: Rizzoli, Frank Lloyd Wright Foundation, 1992), 43. The latter essay, apparently prepared for delivery to the Architectural League of the Art Institute of Chicago in 1900, formed the basis for Wright's most explicit discussion of the theory of mimesis in relation to the concept of conventionalization in his later *The Japanese Print: An Interpretation* (1912; rpt. New York: Horizon Press, 1967). Although the theory underwrote his architecture throughout his career, the role of tradition or history as the informative agent of convention significantly changed for him, as we shall see, after 1910.

26. FLW, "In the Cause" (1908): 153, 161. See also Brownell and FLW, esp. 44–49, 273ff.

27. For a further discussion of this, see Chapter X.

28. FLW, "In the Cause" (1908): 155. For another view of Wright's use of nature, see Donald Hoffmann, *Frank Lloyd Wright: Architecture and Nature* (New York: Dover, 1986).

29. Wright specifically referred to Plato in *Japanese Print*, esp. 16–18. The two essential ancient texts are Plato's *Republic*, Book X; and Aristotle's *Poetics*.

30. FLW, "Philosophy of Fine Art," 42–43. See also Henry Blackman Sell, "Interpretation, Not Imitation: Work of F. L. Wright," *International Studio* 55 (May 1915): lxxix–lxxxiii. In a short piece about the Badlands in 1935, Wright continued to assert that "Nature needs from man not imitation but interpretation. It is quite another thing, as you may learn" (in Gutheim, *FLW on Arch.*, 196). For Ruskin's condemnation of "direct imitation" and his espousal of the "noble abstraction" of "conventionalism," see esp. *The Stones of Venice* (1851–53), 1: chap. 20, par. 25; 2: chap. 6, par. 43; and 3: chap. 4, pars. 19–26; and *Lectures on Architecture and Painting* (1854), addenda to lectures 1 and 2. For Owen Jones's view, see *The Grammar of Ornament* (1856), passim. In contradistinction to the idealist definition of "imitation," conventionalization involved a close relationship between image and medium, taking into account the nature of the materials used, the shape of the support, and the physical conditions of production (cf. FLW, "Philosophy of Fine Art," 42). In contrast to the restricted range of prototypes available to classical "imitation," conventionalization allowed for a more inclusive body of historical and natural models, the very term implying the creation of a new set of standards.

31. FLW, "Philosophy of Fine Art," 42–43.

32. [Marc-Antoine] Laugier, *Essai sur l'architecture*, 2d ed. (1755; rpt. Farnborough, Hertfordshire: Gregg Press, 1966), esp. 8–12. Wright was conversant with this argument and reiterated it in Princeton Lects., 57–59 ("The Passing of the Cornice"); and *A* I, 360. For a recent translation of Laugier's text, see Laugier, *An Essay on Architecture*, trans. Wolfgang Herrmann and Anni Herrmann, Documents and Sources in Architecture, 1 (Los Angeles: Hennessey & Ingalls, 1977).

33. In his *Architecture égyptienne*, Quatremère refers to the hut as a "fiction agréable" and as a "fiction habituelle" (pp. 242–43), definitions he repeats in the article on "Architecture" in the *Encyclopédie* (p. 115).

34. His strongest statement of the theory, as noted above, is in his 1912 publication of *The Japanese Print*.

35. FLW, "In the Cause" (1908): 160.

36. James O'Gorman's *Three American Architects: Richardson, Sullivan, and Wright, 1865–1915* (Chicago: University of Chicago Press, 1991) unfortunately came out too late to be of use to me. Wright's own interpretation of the Richardson-Sullivan legacy is most fully explored in his *Genius and the Mobocracy* (1949). It should be noted that the Richardson-Sullivan-Wright trinity, to which Wright was consciously associating himself at this point, was a construct of the historiography of modern American architecture adumbrated by Lewis Mumford in the 1920s. Following its promotion of European modernism in the International Style show of 1932, the Museum of Modern Art gave its support to this construction of an autonomous American tradition: first by mounting an exhibition of Richardson's work in 1935, accompanied by the publication of Henry-Russell Hitchcock's *The Architecture of H. H. Richardson and His Times* (1936); then by helping fund Hugh Morrison's *Louis Sullivan: Prophet of Modern Architecture* (1935); and finally by devoting an exhibition to the work of Wright in 1940–41, followed by the publication of Hitchcock, *Materials* a year later.

37. The Taylor House was first published in Sheldon's *Artistic Country-Seats* in 1886–87.

38. FLW, "Recollections: United States, 1893–1920," *AJ* 84 (16 July 1936): 78 and (30 July 1936): 142; FLW, "In the Cause" (1908): 156–57.

39. Leonard K. Eaton, *Two Chicago Architects and Their Clients: Frank Lloyd Wright and Howard Van Doren Shaw* (Cambridge, Mass.: MIT Press, 1969), 67–74; and Eaton, "W. H. Winslow and the Winslow House," *PSR* 1 (1964): 12–14 (the entire issue is devoted to the Winslow House).

40. This point forms a significant part of Norris Kelly Smith's influential discussion of the social content of the Winslow House in Smith, *Wright*, 83–87.

41. FLW, "In the Cause" (1908): 159; *A* I, 139; FLW, "Recollections," 77; and *A* II, 139.

42. FLW, "In the Cause" (1908): 157, 160.

43. Ibid., 157; FLW, "Recollections," 77; and Wasmuth I, caption pl. 1.

44. Sullivan's explanation of the rational design of the tall office building is contained in "The Tall Office Building Artistically Considered," orig. pub. *Lippincott's* 57 (1896), repr. in Louis H. Sullivan, *Kindergarten Chats and Other Writings*, Documents of Modern Art, 4 (New York: George Wittenborn, 1947), 202–13. Wright's account of the impact the Wainwright Building made on him when he was in Sullivan's office is in *Genius and the Mobocracy*:

[W]hen he brought the drawing board with the motive for the Wainwright outlined in profile and elevation upon it and threw the board down on my table I was perfectly aware of what had happened.

This was a great Louis H. Sullivan moment. The tall building was born tall. . . . [H]ere was the "skyscraper": a new thing beneath the sun, entity imperfect, but with virtue, individuality, beauty all its own. Until Louis Sullivan showed the way, high buildings lacked unity. . . . [His was] the master mind that first perceived the high building as a harmonious unit—its height triumphant. (P. 79)

[G]iven a novel problem of that moment . . . his fine mind instantly saw its chief characteristic. Aware of its nature he got its real sense. It was tall! . . . Look back and see the interminable vistas of interior structure ignored and falsified in exteriors without any sense of the nature of the problem as you see a type in the Wainwright. (Pp. 59–60)

45. Sullivan, *Kindergarten Chats*, 203, 208, 206.

46. Ibid., 203, 208, 206; and FLW, *Genius and the Mobocracy*, 79.

47. The years 1886–91 represent the high point of Symbolism in poetry and the plastic arts. Wright's emphasis on the roofline, or general silhouette of the building, as indicating characterological meaning ("In the Cause" [1908]: 159) may be directly related to synthetist techniques of expression. In this re-

gard, Narciso Menocal has relevant things to say about Sullivan in his *Architecture as Nature: The Transcendentalist Idea of Louis Sullivan* (Madison: University of Wisconsin Press, 1981), 128.

48. Wasmuth I, par. 20. Later in life, Wright changed the phrase, calling the "horizontal line . . . the true earth-line of human life, indicative of freedom" (*A* II, 349).

49. FLW, "Recollections," 77; and *A* I, 140, 145.

50. *A* II, 142. There is a minor orthographic difference in the first edition, where the phrase reads: "the sense of 'shelter' in the look of the building" (p. 139).

51. Smith, *Wright*, 85.

52. I am grateful to Timothy Love, a former student at Harvard's Graduate School of Design, who pointed this out in one of the Wright seminars he took with me.

53. William C. Gannet[t], *The House Beautiful*, In a Setting Designed by Frank Lloyd Wright and Printed by Hand at the Auvergne Press in River Forest by William Herman Winslow and Frank Lloyd Wright during the Winter Months of the Year Eighteen Hundred Ninety Six and Seven (River Forest, Ill.: Auvergne Press, 1896–97?). Although the title-page gives the date of publication as 1896–97, Mary Jane Hamilton has recently shown that the book was not finished until 1898 (Mary Jane Hamilton, *Frank Lloyd Wright and the Book Arts* [Madison: Friends of the University of Wisconsin–Madison Libraries, 1993], 58–64). See also Patrick J. Meehan, *Frank Lloyd Wright: A Research Guide to Archival Sources* (New York and London: Garland, 1983), 199. Gannett was a friend of Wright's uncle, Jenkin Lloyd Jones. The sermon in question was delivered in Jones's All Souls' Church in Chicago, on which Wright had worked when he was in Silsbee's office. It had previously been published in Boston in 1895, as well as in a Hungarian translation in Kolozsvar (now Cluj), Romania, in 1896. On Wright's own life-style as a reflection of Gannett's ideas, see Meg Klinkow, "Wright Family Life in the House Beautiful," *Wright Angles: Newsletter of the Frank Lloyd Wright Home and Studio Foundation* 17 (Summer 1991): [3–6].

54. Gannet[t], *House Beautiful*, [3], [6], [33–35], [38–39].

55. Ibid., [41–42]. The phrases are quotations from "The Story of William and Lucy Smith."

56. Norris Kelly Smith has much to say on the long-range effects of these attitudes on Wright's later work and private life in Smith, *Wright*, 97ff.

57. David Gebhard related the facade of the Winslow House to the Turkish Pavilion at the World's Columbian Exposition in "A Note on the Chicago Fair of 1893 and Frank Lloyd Wright," *JSAH* 18 (May 1959): 63–65. The latter structure was an adaptation of the pavilion-like early eighteenth-century Fountain of Ahmed III located in front of the Imperial Gate of the Topkapi Palace in Istanbul.

58. Gannet[t], *House Beautiful*, [38].

59. This was first pointed out in 1900 by Robert Spencer: "The street facade . . . is simple with a breadth of treatment that carries the exquisite refinement of its detail with perfect dignity. Within the grounds to the rear we are afforded a more intimate knowledge of the conditions of life within and the scheme becomes less reticent and is more picturesque without sacrificing the quiet formality of the whole" (Spencer, "Wright," 65).

60. That is precisely Brendan Gill's argument. He contends that the complexities of the rear simply show that "Wright had plainly lost control of the design" and "was unable to make an appropriate exterior accommodation" (Gill, *Many Masks*, 110). Few critics, however, have accepted this position. Spencer's early comments would seem to reflect quite accurately Wright's intentions and the artistic fulfillment of them.

Chapter II
Abstraction and Analysis in the Oak Park Years

1. Tennyson, *The Holy Grail, and Other Poems* (Boston: Fields, Osgood, 1870), 165. The poem is quoted here the way Wright reproduced it in William C. Gannet[t], *The House Beautiful*, In a Setting Designed by Frank Lloyd Wright and Printed . . . by William Herman Winslow and Frank Lloyd

Wright. . . . (River Forest, Ill.: Auvergue Press, 1896–97?). Later editions of Tennyson's work show minor variations in orthography and punctuation.

2. Wright, in Gannet[t], *House Beautiful*, [1] (verso of title page).

3. For complete references, see Chapter I, note 16, and Introduction, note 12. This practice of summing up his achievements continued throughout Wright's career: the Wijdeveld *Wendingen* and de Fries publications of 1925 and 1926, respectively, closed the Taliesin-California period (see Chapter VI); the *AF* issues of January 1938 and January 1948 served similar functions in his later years (see Chapters VIII–X). It should also be noted here that Wright's article "In the Cause of Architecture" in the March 1908 issue of *ARec* was accompanied by a fairly complete retrospective selection of photographs of his work.

4. Another important design of this sort, to be discussed in Chapter IV, is the Romeo and Juliet tower that Wright built for his aunts, Ellen and Jane Lloyd Jones, at their Hillside Home School property in Helena Valley, Wisconsin, in 1896–97.

5. The most reliable account of the changes Wright made to the Oak Park house is Ann Abernathy, with John G. Thorpe, eds., *The Oak Park Home and Studio of Frank Lloyd Wright* (Oak Park, Ill.: Frank Lloyd Wright Home and Studio Foundation, 1988), 3–7. For a contemporary appraisal, see Alfred H. Granger, "An Architect's Studio," *House Beautiful* 7 (December 1899): 36–45.

6. Designed by Wright, the mural was painted by Orlando Giannini, according to Abernathy, *Oak Park Home and Studio*, 26. In *FLWM*, vol. 1, Pfeiffer attributes the mural to Charles Corwin, the brother of Wright's friend Cecil Corwin (p. 22).

7. The *Winged Victory of Samothrace* had only recently been discovered and placed at the head of the main stairway of the Louvre. I owe these observations to Linda Phipps, a Fine Arts graduate student at Harvard who took my seminar on Taliesin in the fall of 1987–88 and wrote her Qualifying Paper on Wright's use of plaster casts during the Oak Park years.

8. The intermediary for this medievalism would have been H. H. Richardson, especially his domestic and small library plans, like the ones for Woburn (1877–78) and North Easton (1880), both in Massachusetts, and Billings, Vermont (1885–86). Evidence of Wright's dependence on Richardson's plans of this type may also be seen in his project for the Baldwin House in Oak Park (1895). For a more general treatment of this relationship, see James F. O'Gorman, "Henry Hobson Richardson and Frank Lloyd Wright," *Art Quarterly* 32 (Autumn 1969): 292–315.

9. H. Allen Brooks, *The Prairie School: Frank Lloyd Wright and His Midwest Contemporaries* (New York: W. W. Norton, 1972), esp. 3–87. See also Mark L. Peisch, *The Chicago School of Architecture: Early Followers of Sullivan and Wright*, Columbia University Studies in Art History and Archaeology, 5 (New York: Random House, 1964); and Brooks, *Frank Lloyd Wright and the Prairie School* (New York: George Braziller, Cooper-Hewitt Museum, 1984).

10. For Wright's own comments on the experimental character of his studio, see FLW, "In the Cause of Architecture," *ARec* 23 (March (1908): 163–65.

11. See Robert Judson Clark, ed., *The Arts and Crafts Movement in America, 1876–1916* (Princeton: Princeton University Press, 1972); Brooks, *Prairie School*, 16–20; Wendy Kaplan, ed., *"The Art that is Life": The Arts & Crafts Movement in America, 1875–1920* (Boston: Museum of Fine Arts, Little, Brown, 1987); and Richard Guy Wilson, "Chicago and the International Arts and Crafts Movements: Progressive and Conservative Tendencies," in *Chicago Architecture, 1872–1922: Birth of a Metropolis* (Munich: Prestel-Verlag, Art Institute of Chicago, 1987), 208–27. On the social and economic aspects of these changes, and Wright's response to them, see David P. Handlin, *The American Home: Architecture and Society, 1815–1915* (Boston and Toronto: Little, Brown, 1979), esp. 232–329; and Gwendolyn Wright, *Moralism and the Model Home: Domestic Architecture and Cultural Conflict in Chicago, 1873–1913* (Chicago and London: University of Chicago Press, 1980), 105ff.

12. There has been a long tradition of placing great stress on the putative influence of Viennese Secessionism on Wright's work, with Unity Temple (1905–1908; fig. 41) or the Hillside Home School Assembly Building (1901–1903; fig. 78) usually singled out as being indebted to Olbrich's Secession Gallery

(1898–99). Aside from the fact that the latter design should probably be read in much more traditional, classical terms than is normally the case, it is quite clear that Wright's Oak Park Studio served as the basis for his own later designs and predicts in every important way the geometric abstraction of the Olbrich building. When one considers the work of Wagner or Hoffmann, not to speak of Loos, Mackintosh, or Behrens, it is hard to find anything that can be even remotely considered proto-Wrightian before 1898. More recently, Anthony Alofsin has tried to make the case that the German and Viennese influence on Wright became most pronounced only after Wright's trip to Europe in 1909–10. See Alofsin, *Lost Years*, esp. 16–19, 79ff.

13. FLW, *The Japanese Print: An Interpretation* (1912; rpt. New York: Horizon Press, 1967), 19. See also *A* I, 195–204. For explicit *japonismes* at this time, one could point to aspects of the Bradley and Hickox houses in Kankakee, Ill. (1900); the Foster House, Chicago (1900); and the Davenport House, River Forest, Ill. (1901). For a more expansive reading of the Japanese influence on Wright, see Kevin Nute, *Frank Lloyd Wright and Japan: The Role of Traditional Japanese Art and Architecture in the Work of Frank Lloyd Wright* (New York: Van Nostrand Reinhold, 1993). See also Julia Meech-Pekarik, "Frank Lloyd Wright and Japanese Prints," *Metropolitan Museum of Art Bulletin* (Fall 1982): 48–56; and Meech-Pekarik, "Frank Lloyd Wright's Other Passion," in Carol R. Bolon, Robert S. Nelson, and Linda Seidel, eds., *The Nature of Frank Lloyd Wright* (Chicago and London: University of Chicago Press, 1988), 125–53.

Wright acknowledged the impact Jones's *Grammar of Ornament* (1856) had on him in *A* I, 74.

14. Although all the drawings for this project, and especially the finished renderings, were probably not in Wright's hand, it is important to note the high degree of finish in the elegant Beaux-Arts use of India ink and wash in the rendered plan of the project.

15. The development outlined here is directly based on the work of Hitchcock and Scully.

16. The earliest example of Wright's use of the "butterfly plan" is his precocious design for the Cooper House (1890) for La Grange, Ill., which he claimed was a development of the project he showed to Louis Sullivan in 1887 when applying for a job. For its importance in relation to Wright's later work, see my "Frank Lloyd Wright's Diagonal Planning," in Helen Searing, ed., *In Search of Modern Architecture: A Tribute to Henry-Russell Hitchcock* (New York, Cambridge, Mass., and London: Architectural History Foundation, MIT Press, 1982), 138ff.

17. The opposition of "freedom" and "order" is Wright's, as are the terms, although at the time he usually preferred to use the word "individuality," in the sense of individuation of parts, for "freedom." He often coupled "order" with "law," as in "law and order." See FLW, "In the Cause" (1908): 155, 160–65; Wasmuth I, pars. 2, 7, 19; and *A* I, 139–45. Cf. Vincent J. Scully Jr., *The Shingle Style and the Stick Style: Architectural Theory from Downing to the Origins of Wright* (1955; rev. ed., New Haven, Conn., and London: Yale University Press, 1971), 155–64.

18. FLW, *Genius and the Mobocracy* (New York: Duell, Sloan and Pearce, 1949), 59–60.

19. FLW, "A Home in a Prairie Town," *Ladies' Home Journal* 18 (February 1901): 17; and FLW, "A Small House with 'Lots of Room in It,'" *Ladies' Home Journal* 18 (July 1901): 15.

20. The plans were commissioned by Edward Bok, president of the Curtis Publishing Company. The "Quadruple Block Plan" appeared in the February 1901 *Ladies' Home Journal*. Wright reworked it as the basis for a twenty-four-unit development for Charles E. Roberts, for Oak Park, in 1900–1903.

21. The contract drawings are dated June 1902. The fullest account of the client and the history of the building is in Mark David Linch, "Ward Winfield Willits: A Client of Frank Lloyd Wright," *FLWN* 2, no. 2 (1979): 12–17; and Linch, "The Ward Willits House by Frank Lloyd Wright," *FLWN* 2, no. 3 (1979): 1–5. Cf. also Linch, "Design Origins of the Ward Willits House," *FLWN* 3, no. 1 (1980): 7–11. In the winter of 1905, Wright and his wife took a two-month vacation in Japan with Ward and Cecilia Willits. After this, the two families seem to have drifted apart, the extended trip together perhaps being a cause. In concert with the social ambitions of his wife, Ward Willits became

active in local political affairs, eventually being elected to the governing Board of Commissioners of the town of Highland Park in 1914.

22. Wasmuth I, par. 17.

23. FLW, "In the Cause" (1908): 163, 162, 161.

24. Ibid., 161. The historical figure who comes most immediately to mind in his use of existing nature as a supplement to architectural form is Etienne-Louis Boullée. In a rewriting of the traditional *paragone*, he maintained that what gives the architect his special advantage and makes him the most versatile manipulator of the language of representation is his ability literally "to bring nature into play" ("mettre la nature en oeuvre"). See Boullée, "Architecture: Essai sur l'art," in Helen Rosenau, *Boullée & Visionary Architecture, including Boullée's "Architecture, Essay on Art"* (London and New York: Academy Editions, Harmony Books, 1976), 140.

25. Wright explains this method in "In the Cause" (1908): 159–61. For a later gloss on the subject, see his *The Natural House* (New York: Horizon Press, 1954), 181–83.

26. Commissioned in 1902, the final plans of the house are dated 18 January 1903. Unlike most of Wright's houses of the period, this one involved a partial "remodelling" of an existing structure. In order to please the client's mother, who died one year after the house was finished (Dana's husband had died in 1901), Wright preserved the library of the original house as a sitting room directly behind the reception hall, in the angle formed by the dining room. The barrel-vaulted dining room and gallery/library wing, the latter built concurrently with the rest of the house, reveal the importance of Wright's 1895–98 additions to the Oak Park House and Studio as a source for the spatial geometries of the work after 1900. For more complete information on the client and the house, see James R. Allen et al., *Dana-Thomas House, Springfield, Illinois: Frank Lloyd Wright, Architect* (Springfield: Dana-Thomas House Foundation, 1989); and Allen, John Patterson, and Richard Taylor, "Frank Lloyd Wright and Springfield's Lawrence School," *Historic Illinois* 4 (April 1982): 2–3, 12–13. I would like to thank Donald Hoffmann, who is presently working on a monograph of the house, for providing me with the last reference.

27. Although Wright referred only to the sumac plant in his early discussions of the house ("In the Cause" [1908]: 161), he later noted on a drawing of the entrance arch the phrase "butterfly wreath," leading Bruce Pfeiffer to prefer an insectile source for the transom motif. See Bruce Brooks Pfeiffer and Yukio Futagawa, *Frank Lloyd Wright: Selected Houses*, vol. 1, *Frank Lloyd Wright . . . Frederick C. Bogk* (Tokyo: A.D.A. EDITA, 1991), 16.

28. For this commission in particular, as well as the Wright-Bock collaboration in general, see Donald P. Hallmark, "Richard W. Bock, Sculptor. Part II: The Mature Collaborations," *PSR* 8 (1971): 5–29; and Richard W. Bock, *Memoirs of an American Artist*, ed. Dorathi Bock Pierre (Los Angeles: C. C. Publishing Co., 1989), esp. 44–99.

Wright originally assigned the sculptural figure to the Belgian-born Chicago sculptor Albert L. van den Berghen. Although Wright had employed Bock a number of times before (for the frieze of the Heller House; the statue of John Lloyd Wright as *Goldenrod* in the Oak Park House; and the sculpture for the Oak Park Studio addition), Bock was busy on other projects and was unavailable at the time. Van den Berghen produced a *maquette* that shows an upright Grecian figure (somewhat in the style of St. Gaudens's *Statue of the Republic* for the 1893 Chicago Exposition) standing in front of a naturalistically rendered vase. Her arms are outstretched, holding flowers or leaves, as if she were arranging the vase. (A photograph is preserved in the Archives of the Frank Lloyd Wright Home and Studio. I am grateful to Meg Klinkow for providing me with a photocopy and description of it.) Wright was not happy with the result and convinced Bock to take over. According to him, "Frank's idea for the figure was well conceived but far from solved" (Bock, *Memoirs*, 81). Bock then went on to do the relief for the fountain in the entrance hall, called *The Moon Children*, based on a design by Marion Mahony. Bock later worked on the sculpture for the Larkin Building and Midway Gardens.

29. The importance of this sculpture for Wright is partially indicated by the fact that he reproduced it three times: as the concluding image of the retrospective album of his work in the article "In the Cause of Architecture" (1908): 221; as one of the key illustrations for Ashbee's introduction to Wasmuth II

(p. 5); and, in a second cast, as the central focus of his design for Taliesin in 1911 (see Chapter IV).

30. A different interpretation of the sculpture is given by Narciso Menocal in "Taliesin, the Gilmore House, and *The Flower in the Crannied Wall*," *Wright Studies* 1 (1992): 66–82. An important aspect of the sculpture, to be considered in the context of Taliesin (Chapter IV), is its gendered form. There is a binary opposition of male and female elements, with the figure clearly representing the female as the generative force (Mother Nature?) and the male tower its artistic product. Corroboration of this particular division of gendered characteristics can be found in Wright's design for the entrance stairway to the Dana gallery/library. As reproduced in Wasmuth I (pl. 31 [d]), it shows the crystalline tower of the *Flower in the Crannied Wall* as the newel. In construction, however, the tower was replaced by a male figure, a plaster cast of Michelangelo's *David* ("In the Cause" [1908]: 174). The sculptural concept of a figure emerging from the block of stone, yet not fully revealed, obviously derives from Rodin's contemporaneous reworking of Michelangelo's "unfinished" works.

31. FLW, *Japanese Print*, 18.

32. For a more reflexive and more universalizing reading of Wright's use of geometry in these years, see Otto Antonia Graf, *Die Kunst des Quadrats: Zum Werk von Frank Lloyd Wright*, 2 vols. (Vienna, Cologne, and Graz: Hermann, Böhlaus Nachf., 1983).

33. William E. Martin was, in fact, about to commission a house from Wright, to be built in Oak Park in 1903. The definitive work on the Larkin Building is Jack Quinan, *Frank Lloyd Wright's Larkin Building: Myth and Fact* (Cambridge, Mass., and London: Architectural History Foundation, MIT Press, 1987). For Wright's own account, see *A* I, 151–52 ("The Protestant"); "The New Larkin Administration Building," orig. pub. *The Larkin Idea* 6 (November 1906), repr. in *PSR* 7 (1970): 15–19, and in Quinan, *Larkin Building*, 140–44; FLW, "Reply to Mr. Sturgis's Criticism," orig. pub. *In the Cause of Architecture* (Buffalo: Larkin Company, April 1909), repr. in Quinan, *Larkin Building*, 165–68; and "In the Cause" (1908): 166–67. For the first important European review of both the Larkin Building and Unity Temple, see H. P. Berlage, "The New American Architecture (1912): Travel Impressions of H. P. Berlage, Architect in Amsterdam," in Don Gifford, ed., *The Literature of Architecture: The Evolution of Architectural Theory and Practice in Nineteenth-Century America* (New York: E. P. Dutton, 1966): 614–15.

34. FLW, "In the Cause" (1908): 166.

35. FLW, "New Larkin Administration Building," in Quinan, *Larkin Building*, 140; and *A* I, 152. The background for the spatial idea is the arcade, or galleria, of the nineteenth century. For the Chicago transformation of this idea in terms of the office building block, see Meredith L. Clausen, "Frank Lloyd Wright, Vertical Space, and the Chicago School's Quest for Light," *JSAH* 44 (March 1985): 66–74.

36. For an excellent discussion of the operational factors involved, see Quinan, *Larkin Building*, 44–84. Reyner Banham presents an important analysis of the structural and functional aspects of the design in *The Architecture of the Well-Tempered Environment* (London: Architectural Press, 1969), 86–92. See also Banham, "Note: The Services of the Larkin 'A' Building," *JSAH* 37 (October 1978): 195–97.

37. FLW, "In the Cause" (1908): 159; FLW, "Reply to Mr. Sturgis," in Quinan, *Larkin Building*, 166.

38. Ibid., 167.

39. FLW, "Recollections: United States, 1893–1920," *AJ* 84 (30 July 1936): 142; and *A* II, 150–51.

40. No book yet exists on Unity Temple; in fact, very little of substance has been written on the building. Joseph Siry briefly discusses the commission in terms of Wright's relations with the Unitarian community in "The Abraham Lincoln Center in Chicago," *JSAH* 50 (September 1991). A senior honors thesis at Harvard University by David Shklar, "Frank Lloyd Wright's Design of Unity Church" (1980), provided me with many important insights and much new information.

Wright's own accounts of the building are contained in "In the Cause" (1908): 212, and *A* I, 152–64. Wright also had a hand (and a voice) in the brochure produced by the pastor of the congregation during the construction of the building: Rodney F. Johonnot, *The New Edifice of Unity Church, Oak*

Park, Illinois. Frank Lloyd Wright, Architect (1906; rpt. Oak Park: The Unitarian Universalist Church, 1961).

41. Cf. Siry, "Abraham Lincoln Center," 235–65.

42. Early drawings of the building suggest that Wright originally conceived of the structure in brick. This would be logical, following the precedent of the Larkin Building.

43. It should be noted that between the Oak Park Studio and Unity Temple stands the design of the assembly hall at the Hillside Home School (1901–1903; figs. 78, 79). There is a clear progression from the octagon within a square of the first building, to a square rotated forty-five degrees within a square at Hillside, to the final square within a square of Unity Temple. For a further discussion of the Hillside building, see my "Wright's Diagonal Planning," 249–50.

44. FLW, "In the Cause" (1908): 212. On the question of historical references, it is interesting to recall Wright's comments on the building committee's reaction to his design: "At this moment the creative architect is distinctly at disadvantage as compared with his obsequious brother of the 'styles.' His brother can show his pattern-book of 'styles,' speak glibly of St. Mark's at Venice or Capella Palatine, impress the no less craven clients by brave show of erudite authorities—abash them. But the architect with the ideal of an organic architecture at stake can only talk of principle and sense" (*A* I, 162). Kevin Nute, *Wright and Japan*, 167, offers the intriguing thought that Wright's insistence on the word *temple* may refer to Japanese religious architecture. Following the suggestion of Masami Tanigawa, he points to the relation of the Unity Temple plan to the *gongen-zukuri* type of the seventeenth-century Tōshōgū and Daiyūin shrines at Nikkō, which Wright apparently visited on his 1905 trip to Japan (pp. 148–49, 167–70). But whether Wright was able to abstract the plan diagram from the overly elaborate, almost baroque, profusion of decorative ornament is another matter.

45. In his discussion of the building in 1912, Berlage compared its form and scale to "an Egyptian temple" ("New American Architecture," 614).

46. It should also be noted that Wright used the analogy of a holy man climbing a mountain, and then returning to the valley, to impart to the building committee a sense of the character of his design (*A* II, 153).

47. Johonnot's description of the building in his 1906 brochure stresses these traditional sources of the design. In explaining the appellation "temple" instead of "church," Johonnot noted: "This usage . . . keeps us in line with the Biblical use of the terms; for in it the word 'temple' is always used to designate a house of worship, while the word 'church' always refers to the body of worshippers. . . . The term is further made specially fitting here because the building has the feeling and to some extent the form of an ancient temple." He elaborated: "The religious feeling . . . has been reached in this structure not by the adoption of . . . the Gothic style of the Middle Ages, but by a frank return to the simpler and more ancient forms of religious architecture" (*New Edifice*, [2], [13]). For a possible connection of nomenclature and plan to Japanese architecture, see note 44 above.

48. For a somewhat different, more sociological interpretation of the tension in the work of the Oak Park years, see Smith, *Wright*, 71–114.

49. The apartment was set aside for a relative of the Cheneys. An independent garage was built between the house and the alley. The plans of the house including the garage were drawn up in mid-December 1903 and revised between 18 January and 3 March 1904. But see note 50 below.

50. An earlier scheme for the house, dating perhaps from October–November 1903, follows a more monumental, fully expressed two-story *parti* that is much less dependent on the Winslow House.

51. In the contemporaneous two-story Martin House in Buffalo, the abstraction and dissection of the structure resulted in the division of the corner piers into differentially-sized buttresses set at right angles to one another, which became Wright's characteristic solution to the problem of the exterior corner. The corners of the Willits House, and especially the Dana House, show this idea at an earlier stage of development. In the Dana House, for example, the projecting corner piers are kept distinct from and lower than the three uprights that rise into the windows of the second story. Those represent, however, only two terms of the Martin equation. In the Martin House, the tall piers supporting the roof are distinguished from thinner ones in-antis, as well as from outer ones set like buttresses at ninety-degree angles to them.

52. FLW, "In the Cause" (1908): 157.

53. Wright seems to have been well aware of this irony. He wrote: "A building should appear to grow easily from its site and be shaped to harmonize with its surroundings if Nature is manifest there, and if not try to make it as quiet, substantial and organic as She would have were the opportunity hers.*" The footnote reads: "In this I had in mind the barren town lots devoid of trees or natural incident, town houses and board walks only in evidence" ("In the Cause" [1908]: 157). This conception of imitating a Nature that might only appear to the artist as an ideal construct is entirely in line with Neoclassical thought.

54. Wasmuth I, par. 17.

55. It is important to note that both of these 1905 designs were produced soon after Wright's return from his first trip to Japan.

56. For a discussion of the client and the building history, see Leonard K. Eaton, *Two Chicago Architects and Their Clients: Frank Lloyd Wright and Howard Van Doren Shaw* (Cambridge, Mass.: MIT Press, 1969), 126–33 (which includes a reprint of an interview with Robie and his son, "Mr. Robie Knew What He Wanted," *AF* 109 [October 1958]: 126–27, 206, 210); Donald Hoffmann, *Frank Lloyd Wright's Robie House: The Illustrated Story of an Architectural Masterpiece* (New York: Dover, 1984); and Joseph Connors, *The Robie House of Frank Lloyd Wright* (Chicago and London: University of Chicago Press, 1984). See also Irma Strauss, "An Interview with Lorraine Robie O'Connor," *FLWN* 3, no. 4 (1980): 1–3.

57. Wasmuth I, caption pl. 37. The Coonley House, however, was the house Wright considered to be his best of the period (*A* I, 164).

58. Wasmuth I, caption pl. 37.

59. Ibid., par. 18.

60. Ibid., caption pl. 37.

61. In describing the genesis of the design, Wright noted that he started with the Tomek House, "a characteristic 'prairie house'," which he "later elaborated into the plan of the Robie House" (ibid., caption pl. 35). Connors, in his study of the Robie House, stresses the antecedence of the Tomek House in order to develop a design sequence in the face of a lack of other preliminary sketches and studies.

62. I owe the observation about Colonial references to Vincent Scully.

63. *A* I, 251; and Hoffmann, *Robie House*, passim.

64. For a more extended treatment of this congruence, see my "Abstraction and Representation in Modern Architecture: The International Style and Frank Lloyd Wright," *AA Files: Annals of the Architectural Association School of Architecture* 11 (Spring 1986): 3–21. Analogies of this sort can be tricky, yet also extremely revealing. They are often used to serve polemical purposes. Since the later 1930s, Le Corbusier's architecture of the twenties has usually been offered as the architectural analogue of Cubist painting. See, e.g., John Summerson, *Heavenly Mansions and Other Essays on Architecture* (1949; rpt. New York: W. W. Norton, 1963), 177–94 ("Architecture, Painting and Le Corbusier"); and Colin Rowe and Robert Slutzky, "Transparency: Literal and Phenomenal," orig. pub. *Perspecta* 8 (1963), repr. in Rowe, *The Mathematics of the Ideal Villa and Other Essays* (Cambridge, Mass., and London: MIT Press, 1976), 159–83. In fact, Le Corbusier's Purism came into being a good fifteen years after Cubism, and Le Corbusier himself saw it as a reaction against, and a successor to, that earlier movement. Interestingly enough, J.J.P. Oud's critique of Wright in Wendingen 1925, 85–89, was based on the argument that Wright had refused to carry through the ideas of Cubism to their logical (that is, abstract) conclusion—the same critique Le Corbusier and Amédée Ozenfant made of Picasso and Braque in their *Après le cubisme* (Paris: Editions des Commentaires, 1918). Scully compared Wright's Robie House to Cézanne as well as to Braque and Picasso (Scully, *Wright*, 21).

65. Wright later commented that Sullivan's ornament led toward the kind of "flattening" out of space that became characteristic of Cubism: "Into the living intricacy of his loving modulations of surface, 'background'—the curse of all stupid ornament—ceased to exist. None might see where terracotta left off and ornamentation came to life." Wright continued: "Background disappeared but surface was preserved. There was no sense of background, as such, anywhere. All was of the surface, out of the material" ("In the Cause of Architecture, V: The Meaning of Materials—The Kiln," *ARec* 63 [June 1928]: 556, 560).

Chapter III
Voluntary Exile in Fiesole

1. The phrase "spiritual adventure" is in FLW to D. D. Martin, 16 November 1909, Box 3-3, Wright-Martin Papers.

2. Ostensibly, Manson, Smith, and Twombly each devotes a chapter to the subject (entitled, respectively, "Flight," "Crisis," and "Affinity Triangle"), but none actually deals with the year spent in Europe. Edgar Kaufmann Jr., "Crisis and Creativity: Frank Lloyd Wright, 1904–1914," orig. pub. *JSAH* 25 (December 1966), repr. with changes in Kaufmann, *9 Commentaries on Frank Lloyd Wright* (New York, Cambridge, Mass., and London: Architectural History Foundation, MIT Press, 1989), 87–102, offers important insights. Alofsin, *Lost Years*, which was published while this book was in press, finally provides a more complete historical account and analysis (esp. pp. 29–100). A key problem, however, remains the lack of documentation about the time Wright spent in Italy. In addition, no correspondence between Wright and Cheney has yet surfaced.

3. "Spend Christmas Making 'Defense' of 'Spirit Hegira,'" *CT*, 26 December 1911, 1.

4. Wright liked to refer to Cheney as a "faithful comrade" (*A* I, 168).

5. Cf. Robert L. Sweeney, *Frank Lloyd Wright: An Annotated Bibliography*, Art and Architecture Bibliographies, no. 5 (Los Angeles: Hennessey & Ingalls, 1978), xxv; and Gill, *Many Masks*, 199ff. I owe much of my knowledge of the relationship between Wright and Cheney, and its effect on Wright's work, to Anne Nissen, who wrote a paper on the subject in the Taliesin seminar she took with me at Harvard in the fall of 1987–88.

6. "Wright Reveals Romance Secret," *CT*, 31 December 1911, 4; and *A* I, 166. For a somewhat different account, see Gill, *Many Masks*, 203–4.

7. Wright's correspondence with Darwin Martin provides interesting evidence of this assimilative process. In a letter probably written in November 1910, Wright said: "I have had a vision of life which has come to me with my work—I wanted to live, as I would work, with *organic integrity*—a whole man—a *unit*." Speaking of himself in the third person, he went on to explain what had gone wrong: "He was blind. He turned to dreams that he could make come true and for twenty years 'stood pat.' Stood, however, with revolutionary ideas, a growing contempt for conventions which his work revealed to his sight as shams and expedients—a resentful rage at heart at the unreasoning institution of marriage" (Box 3-5, Wright-Martin Papers).

8. Already by 1902, Wright was apparently feeling the curse of being labeled a domestic architect. William E. Martin reported to his brother Darwin that Wright "says it is strange that he is only known as a residence architect—when his best and largest experience [in Sullivan's office] was in large buildings" (William E. Martin to Darwin D. Martin, 2 November 1902, Box 1-12, Wright-Martin Papers).

9. On the Montana work, see Delton Ludwig, "Frank Lloyd Wright in the Bitter Root Valley of Montana," *FLWN* 5, no. 2 (1982): 6–16; and Donald Leslie Johnson, "Frank Lloyd Wright's Architectural Projects in the Bitterroot Valley, 1909–1910," *Montana: The Magazine of Western History* (Summer 1987): 12–25. On the bank buildings, see Craig Zabel, "The Prairie Banks of Frank Lloyd Wright," *FLWN* 5, no. 1 (1982): 3–13.

10. McCormick, who would remain a friend and supporter of Wright throughout his life, was married to Edith Rockefeller, the daughter of John D. Rockefeller. It was apparently she who disliked the Wright design and preferred Platt. The loss of the McCormick commission was usually seen as a major blow to Wright's career until Norris Kelly Smith downplayed the issue in order to make the case that Wright did not leave his practice because he was failing to get jobs. On the contrary, his commissions were increasing, and, according to Smith, "by 1909 many of the ideas he had advanced . . . had been accepted throughout the country." Wright's "failure," in Smith's view, was not that of unpopularity but rather a "failure of success," meaning that the architecture by which Wright had intended to revolutionize society had simply been appropriated and co-opted by that society (Smith, *Wright*, 109–14). That position was largely adopted by Twombly in his biography of Wright.

Soon after it was finished, Platt's Villa Turicum was given lavish coverage in the architectural press ("The Renaissance Villa of Italy Developed into a Complete Residential Type for Use in America: The House of Harold F. McCormick, Esq., at Lake Forest, Ill. Charles A. Platt, Architect," *ARec* 31 [March 1912]: 200–25). On Platt, see Keith N. Morgan, *Charles A. Platt: The Artist as Architect*, American Monograph Series (New York, Cambridge, Mass., and London: Architectural History Foundation, MIT Press, 1985).

11. Gill relates the story of the interview with Henry Ford in *Many Masks*, 203. The Ford commission eventually went to the firm of von Holst and Fyfe, Hermann von Holst being the architect to whom Wright turned over his office when he left Oak Park in October 1909. Marion Mahony, who had been one of Wright's draftspersons, did the design for von Holst in 1912. The house was begun in 1913 but finished by another firm. See David Van Zanten, "The Early Work of Marion Mahony Griffin," *PSR* 3, no. 2 (1966): 5–24.

12. FLW to Martin, 19 December 1907, Box 3-1; and FLW to Martin, 2 December 1908, Box 3-2, Wright-Martin Papers.

13. Ashbee Journals, 21 December 1908 (Chicago).

14. FLW, "In the Cause of Architecture," *ARec* 23 (March 1908): 155–221. It should be pointed out that under Croly's progressive direction the *Record* had published, although anonymously, a laudatory article on Wright about two and a half years previously: "Work of Frank Lloyd Wright—Its Influence," *ARec* 18 (July 1905): 60–65.

Again, particularly since Smith's book of the mid-1960s, the fashion is to see Wright as a "failed success" rather than as a "persecuted genius." Yet I see no evidence for denying the fact that, at least until the 1920s in America and perhaps 1912 in Europe, Wright was either little known or considered to be an "eccentric."

15. Russell Sturgis, "The Larkin Building in Buffalo," *ARec* 23 (April 1908): 312, 317–18.

16. FLW, "Reply to Mr. Sturgis's Criticism," orig. pub. *In the Cause of Architecture* (Buffalo: Larkin Company, 1909), repr. in Jack Quinan, *Frank Lloyd Wright's Larkin Building: Myth and Fact* (Cambridge, Mass., and London: Architectural History Foundation, MIT Press, 1987), 168.

17. FLW, "In the Cause" (1908): 156.

18. Thomas E. Tallmadge, "The 'Chicago School,'" *ARev* (Boston) 15 (April 1908): 73.

19. Harriet Monroe, "In the Galleries," orig. pub. *Chicago Examiner*, 13 April 1907, repr. in H. Allen Brooks, ed., *Writings on Wright: Selected Comment on Frank Lloyd Wright* (Cambridge, Mass., and London: MIT Press, 1981), 112.

20. FLW to Monroe, c. 18 April 1907, quoted in Twombly, *Wright*, 124–25. To whom in England or France Wright may have been referring is open to question. No one comes to mind. It is particularly poignant, in this regard, to note what Ashbee wrote in the privacy of his journal on his second trip to the United States in 1908–1909. In the entry of 21 December 1908, written in the playroom of Wright's Oak Park house, he expatiated on the "bizarreness" of Wright's architecture (Ashbee Journals, October–December 1908); and in an entry of January 1909, written in Pasadena, he compared the work of Charles Greene with that of Wright: "There is in his [Greene's] work more tenderness, more subtlety, more self-effacement than in Wright's work, and it is more refined and has more repose. Perhaps it is looser in strength, perhaps it is California that speaks rather than Illinois, anyway, the work—it is, so far as the interiors go, more sympathetic to me" (Ashbee Journals, 1909).

21. Montgomery Schuyler, "An Architectural Pioneer: Review of the Portfolios Containing the Works of Frank Lloyd Wright," orig. pub. *ARec* 31 (April 1912), repr. in Schuyler, *American Architecture and Other Writings*, ed. William H. Jordy and Ralph Coe, 2 vols. (Cambridge, Mass.: Harvard University Press, Belknap Press, 1961), 2:640.

22. C. R. Ashbee, "Frank Lloyd Wright: A Study and an Appreciation," orig. pub. (in German) Wasmuth II, repr. (in English) in *Frank Lloyd Wright: The Early Work* (New York: Bramhall House, 1968), 8.

23. It was precisely Sullivan to whom Wright turned in the early 1920s when he wanted someone to review the Imperial Hotel, the building he later thought would establish his reputation around the world (see Chapter V).

24. See especially FLW, "In the Cause of Architecture: Second Paper," *ARec* 35 (May 1914): 405–13.

25. Ibid., 408.

26. Smith, *Wright*, esp. 71–114. For Wright's own analysis of the situation

in these terms, see the letter to Darwin Martin of November 1910 quoted in note 7 above.

27. Smith, *Wright*, 109ff. The reference is to John Berger, *The Success and Failure of Picasso* (Baltimore: Penguin, 1965). See note 14 above.

28. Quoted in Alan Crawford, "Ten Letters from Frank Lloyd Wright to Charles Robert Ashbee," *Architectural History: Journal of the Society of Architectural Historians of Great Britain* 13 (1970): 65.

29. Ashbee to FLW, 25 December 1908, Ashbee Journals, October–December 1908. Ashbee planned the trip so that Wright would arrive, probably in Naples, in mid-March; travel through Sicily, mainland Italy, and Germany; then stay with him in England in April; and return to his family in Oak Park by May. Ashbee was to act as a kind of cicerone-chaperon, making sure that Wright returned safely to his family in Oak Park: "You want a holiday! I wonder if you know how good your home really is. Leave it for a while and come back and see!" (ibid.). It is probable that Ashbee knew nothing of the Cheney affair at this time. It is also clear that Wright had no intention of going to Europe without his lover and did all he could to hide this fact, as diplomatically as possible, from Ashbee.

30. FLW to Ashbee, 3 February 1909, Ashbee Journals, 1909 (in Crawford, "Ten Letters," the date is given as 3 January 1909).

31. In 1908, for example, he described his work in the following way: "In laying out the ground plans for even the more insignificant of these buildings a simple axial law and order and the ordered spacing upon a system of certain structural units definitely established for each structure in accord with its scheme of practical construction and aesthetic proportion, is practiced as an expedient to simplify the technical difficulties of execution, and, although the symmetry may not be obvious always the balance is usually maintained. The plans are as a rule much more articulate than is the school product of the Beaux-Arts" (FLW, "In the Cause" [1908]: 160).

32. Many of the mysteries surrounding this venture have finally been clarified in Alofsin, *Lost Years*, esp. 11–12, 54–55, 72–78. Wright stated in his *Autobiography* that the invitation from Wasmuth came as a result of the impression his work had made on Kuno Francke, a professor of Germanic Studies at Harvard University, when the latter visited Wright in Oak Park probably in early February 1908. There is, however, no direct evidence for this story. Alofsin suggests that the Berlin architect Bruno Möhring may have been the go-between (p. 12). We know that Wasmuth was in touch with Wright at least by December 1908, because Wright mentioned the publication to Ashbee at that time (Crawford, "Ten Letters," 66).

The smaller, and less expensive, of the two publications came out under two titles. The German edition, which appeared as volume 8 in the series Sonderheft der Architektur des XX. Jahrhunderts, was entitled *Frank Lloyd Wright: Ausgeführte Bauten*. The American edition was entitled *Frank Lloyd Wright: Chicago*. Both were published in 1911. The larger, and much more lavish Wasmuth portfolio was published mainly at Wright's own expense and was, in fact, largely subsidized by three former clients, Charles E. Roberts, Francis W. Little, and Darwin D. Martin, all of whom Wright thanked at the end of his introductory text. Although bearing the date of publication of 1910, it apparently only came out the following year, in fact after the smaller volume.

Wright described the relationship between the two publications in a letter to Ashbee: "In addition to [the large portfolio]—or rather before I undertook it—they had written to me—in America—for material for a Sonderheft to appear in a regular series now in publication. This material to consist wholly of photographs of actual work and plans. . . . This work was their enterprise—but I had counted on the two appearing together. The monograph giving the office-ideal,—the architect's rendering of his vision—his scheme graphically proposed in his own manner—the Sonderheft, the photographs, of the results in brick and mortar" (FLW to Ashbee, 24 July 1910, Ashbee Journals, 1910).

33. FLW to Ashbee, 3 February 1909.

34. Gill offers another interpretation of the suddenness with which everything happened. He notes that Cheney had gone to Colorado to visit a friend who was pregnant. The shock of the friend's death in childbirth, in October, precipitated Cheney's departure and "perhaps" even an "ultimatum" to Wright to accompany her to Europe (Gill, *Many Masks*, 203–4). The story of the elopement was reported in the *CT*, 9 November 1909, p. 7 ("Cheney Cham-

pion of Run-away Wife"). Edwin Cheney's testimony during the divorce proceedings of 3 August 1911 leads one to suspect that Mamah Cheney's actions were premeditated. The direct examination by Mr. Fassett went as follows:

Q. After your marriage you [Edwin Cheney] and the defendant [Mamah Borthwick Cheney] lived together as husband and wife for how long?
A. Until June 28th, 1909.
Q. What happened on that date affecting yourself and the defendant, Mamah Borthwick Cheney?
A. Mrs. Cheney left me, stating that she was not going to return.
Q. She stated to you that she was not going to return?
A. Yes, two or three days prior to that she so stated.

(Appendix B, 3 August 1911, State of Illinois, County of Cook)

I would like to thank Anne Nissen for supplying me with the copy of the Cheney divorce proceedings.

35. "Leave Families; Elope to Europe," *Chicago Sunday Tribune*, 7 November 1909, p. 1; "Stoutly Defends Erring Husband," *CT*, 8 November 1909, p. 7; and "Cheney Champion of Runaway Wife."

36. Although Gropius, Mies, and Le Corbusier all worked for Behrens in 1909–10, only Gropius was apparently in Berlin when Wright was there. See Alofsin, *Lost Years*, 33; and Franz Schulze, *Mies van der Rohe: A Critical Biography* (Chicago and London: University of Chicago Press, 1985), 38–41.

37. Our knowledge of these events is still quite hazy. Lloyd Wright's reminiscences are quoted in Sweeney, *Wright: Bibliography*, xxi–xxii. See also David Gebhard and Harriette Von Breton, *Lloyd Wright, Architect: 20th Century Architecture in an Organic Exhibition*, Art Galleries, University of California, Santa Barbara, 23 November–22 December 1971 (Santa Barbara: Regents, University of California, 1971), 17–18; and Kaufmann, *9 Commentaries*, 96–98. For the most recent account, see Alofsin, *Lost Years*, 40–48. Gebhard and Von Breton place the trip to Paris in May, implying that the work on the drawings was done by early April and that Lloyd Wright and Woolley had left Fiesole by then. Alofsin maintains that the work was not completed until June, and that Wright's trip to Paris to meet his son did not occur until "midsummer." He then goes on to say that "in the late spring or early summer" Wright "went to Leipzig and returned with Mamah Cheney" to Fiesole, which would coincide with the moment that Woolley and Lloyd Wright began their tour of Italy and France. A letter from Wright to Ashbee of 31 March 1910 establishes that Wright was in Fiesole by that date (Ashbee Journals). One of the reasons offered in the press for Cheney's remaining apart while Lloyd Wright was working with his father was the moral one.

For a discussion of the preparation of the drawings for publication, mainly from a connoisseurial point of view, see H. Allen Brooks, "Frank Lloyd Wright and the Wasmuth Drawings," *Art Bulletin* 48 (June 1966): 193–202.

38. Letter from Percy Bysshe Shelley to Thomas Medwin, 17 January 1820, quoted in Giuliana Artom-Treves, *The Golden Ring: The Anglo Florentines, 1847–1862*, trans. Sylvia Sprigge (London, New York, and Toronto: Longmans, Green, 1956), 18.

39. See Clara Louise Dentler, *Famous Foreigners in Florence, 1400–1900* (Florence: Bemporad Marzocco, 1964); and Van Wyck Brooks, *The Dream of Arcadia: American Writers and Artists in Italy, 1760–1915* (New York: E. P. Dutton, 1958). It should also be noted that Harriet Monroe spent the months of May through December 1910 in Europe and that Maurice Browne, who would found the Chicago Little Theatre in 1912, met his actress-wife, Ellen Van Volkenburg, in Florence in 1910. Browne and Van Volkenburg's company later performed in the Fine Arts Building, at which time one of their supporters, Aline Barnsdall, first came into contact with Wright (see Chapter V). See Maurice Browne, *Too Late to Lament: An Autobiography* (London: Victor Gollancz, 1955).

40. The section of the *Autobiography* devoted to Fiesole is entitled "In Exile" (*A* I, 168).

41. See Charles A. Platt, *Italian Gardens* (orig. pub. *Harper's* 87 [July and August 1893]; New York: Harper & Brothers, 1894); Charles Latham, *The Gardens of Italy*, 2 vols. (London: Country Life, George Newnes, 1905); H. Inigo Triggs, *The Art of Garden Design in Italy* (London, New York, and Bombay: Longmans, Green, 1906); George Sitwell, *An Essay on the Making of*

Gardens, Being a Study of Old Italian Gardens, of the Nature of Beauty, and the Principles Involved in Garden Design (London: John Murray, 1909); and Julia Cartwright, *Italian Gardens of the Renaissance and Other Studies* (London: Smith, Elder, 1914).

42. Edith Wharton, *Italian Villas and Their Gardens* (1904; New York: Century, 1905), 12, 3, 7. Wharton dedicated the book to Paget and used her phrase "Italian Garden-Magic" as the title for the introduction (pp. 5–13). Wharton, who met Paget when she lived in Fiesole, at the Villa La Doccia, in 1903, admonished architects to "try to extract from them [Italian gardens] principles which may be applied at home. He [the architect] should observe, for instance, that the old Italian garden was meant to be lived in" (p. 11). The architect should therefore be wary of imitation: "Certain effects . . . are no doubt unattainable; but there is, none the less, much to be learned from the old Italian gardens, and the first lesson is that, if they are to be a real inspiration, they must be copied, not in the letter but in the spirit" (p. 12).

43. There is some confusion about the street address of the house. In the *Autobiography* (I, 168), Wright said it was on the Via Verdi. The Villino Belvedere, however, is located in the angle where the Via Giuseppe Verdi forks into the Via Montececeri and the Via della Doccia. At the time Wright lived there the northern fork did not change its name. The first publication of the house was "Wright's Fiesole Studio," *FLWN* 5, no. 1 (1982): 18, with photographs from the Woolley Archive, supplied by Peter L. Goss. See now also Giampaolo Fici and Filippo Fici, *Frank Lloyd Wright: Fiesole, 1910* (Florence: Minello Sani, 1992). The latter notes that the house was built around 1850 and that it was owned by Elisa Illingworth, an English woman who owned and lived in the neighboring Villa Belvedere, just to the east.

44. FLW to Ashbee, 8 July 1910, Ashbee Journals, 1910 (in Crawford, "Ten Letters," 67). For the relation of this description to the design of Taliesin, see Chapter IV.

45. Wright's Wasmuth text is dated 15 May 1910 in the German translation and June 1910 in the original English. In fact, Wright did not complete it until he returned to the United States. It held up publication and was only sent off to Wasmuth by the first week of December 1910.

Wright informed his friend William Norman Guthrie of the translations and asked for his advice in finding an American publisher. Guthrie responded that "radical literature does not sell in America" but suggested an agent in New York (Guthrie to FLW, 16 [?] May 1910, FLWF). These collaborative translations will be referred to in Chapter IV.

46. FLW to Ashbee, 8 July 1910.

47. Other than those taken in and around Florence, the photographs by Taylor Woolley offer views of Rome, Tivoli, Frascati, and Venice (Woolley Archive). Wright later referred to a visit to Palermo and Monreale in "In the Cause of Architecture, V: The Meaning of Materials—The Kiln," *ARec* 63 (June 1928): 560 (but see note 52 below). Aside from the stay in Paris, the trip with Lloyd to visit the châteaux of the Ile de France and Loire Valley, and two trips to England, we only know for sure that he visited Berlin, Darmstadt, Leipzig, Vienna, the Rhine Valley, and Oberammergau.

48. There are seven known drawings for this project. A perspective, which Wright gave to Henry-Russell Hitchcock in 1941, is now in the Avery Library, Columbia University. It is inscribed: "The Florentine Study for house for the Architect at Fiesole: 1910   To Russell Hitchcock at Taliesin 1941 FLLW." A similar perspective, with a more authentically Italian background (#1005.001, FLWF), has two inscriptions: along the top, "Studio for the architect—Florentine Study—Florence 1910"; on the lower left, "Villa Florence Italy—Via Verdi—Madame Illingworth—1910—Feb." Another less finished perspective has a plan drawn on the same sheet (#1005.003); and there are two aerial studies, one with a schematic plan (#1005.002 [fig. 62]) and one without (#1005.004, FLWF). Photographs of two sheets of studies are in the Woolley Archive. The more finished one contains a plan of the ground floor and an elevation of the entrance side (MS 452, #17). It is inscribed, on the verso, "Italian Villino," and, on the recto, "Florence. Mar 1910" (fig. 68). The other is a plan of the upper floor, with a partially finished elevation in a more preliminary stage of development (MS 452, #16). There is a low hip roof visible above the projecting pavilion and a sketch for a round arch for the garage entrance. The plans in the Woolley Archive indicate that the house would have had a master bedroom on the ground floor and a maximum of five bedrooms on the

upper story. Whether this was to accommodate draftsmen or visiting children is hard to tell. An office on the ground floor faces north, and a large space above it, running clear back to the fireplace mass of the hall, may have been planned as the studio (it also faces north).

Both finished perspectives show the villa reversed, as is the inscription on the drawing of the ground-floor plan in the Woolley Archive. The name Illingworth on one of the perspectives is that of Wright's landlady.

49. Note should be made, however, of the visible hip roof in the preliminary study in the Woolley Archive (MS 452, #16).

50. Erika Neubauer, "The Garden Architecture of Cecil Pinsent, 1884–1964," *Journal of Garden History* 3 (January–March 1983): 35–48. The Villa Le Balze, as it is known, is now the Charles A. Strong Center of Georgetown University. Fici and Fici, *Wright*, 18ff., try to reconstruct the Wright project on the Villino Belvedere site, but it would have been much too cramped. If demolition were an option, Wright might have been contemplating the contiguous Villa Belevedere site, which would explain why its owner's name and address are on one of the perspectives.

51. Wright adapted the Fiesole project in 1956 for the Sottil House in Cuernavaca, Mexico—significantly, another Latin environment. I am grateful to Oscar Muñoz and Bruce Pfeiffer for pointing out this later project to me.

52. Wasmuth I, pars. 1, 5. Wright's mention of the work of Bramante and Sansovino in such a conspicuous position could lead one to infer that he visited Venice and Rome, and perhaps even Milan.

53. Wasmuth I, par. 1.

54. Ibid.

55. One can trace its evolution through the post–World War II interest of Le Corbusier and Brutalism in the Mediterranean vernacular (Greek islands, San Gimignano, and so on) right up through the work of Aldo Rossi and others. For a different interpretation of the "lessons" Wright learned in Italy, and especially Austria and Germany, in 1909–10, see Alofsin, *Lost Years*.

56. Wasmuth I, pars. 1, 3, 4.

57. FLW to Martin [12 October 1910; letter incorrectly dated "postmarked Oct. 12, 1930"], Box 5-32, Wright-Martin Papers.

58. "Spend Christmas Making 'Defense' of 'Spirit Hegira,'" p. 2. Wright concluded that "it will be a waste of something socially precious if this thing robs me of my work," and that "it will be a misfortune if the world decides not to receive what I have to give." The "arrogance" that has generally been ascribed to Wright may well date from this moment and be related to the issue of self-destructiveness.

59. FLW to Ashbee, 8 July 1910.

Chapter IV
The Story of Taliesin

1. *Poems from the Book of Taliesin*, ed. and trans. J. Gwenogvryn Evans (Tremvan, Llanbedrog, N. Wales: privately printed, 1915), 197–98. See note 52 below.

2. As noted above, Mamah Cheney reverted to her maiden name Borthwick after her divorce in August 1911. Awkward as it may be, I shall refer to her as Cheney up to that time, and Borthwick thereafter.

3. Aside from the collection of essays in "Taliesin: 1911–1914," *Wright Studies* 1 (1992), ed. Narciso Menocal (Carbondale and Edwardsville: Southern Illinois University Press, 1992) and the photographic monograph by Bruce Brooks Pfeiffer and Yukio Futagawa, *Frank Lloyd Wright: Selected Houses*, vol. 2, *Taliesin* (Tokyo: A.D.A. EDITA, 1990), there is no book-length study of Taliesin yet. Wright's description of it is contained in *A* I, 170–93 and 258–60. This was based on his previously published article "Taliesin: The Chronicle of a House with a Heart," *Liberty: A Weekly for Everybody* 6 (23 March 1929): 21–22, 24, 26–29. The two earliest publications are: "The Studio-Home of Frank Lloyd Wright," *ARec* 33 (January 1913): 45–54; and C. R. Ashbee, "Taliesin, the Home of Frank Lloyd Wright, and a Study of the Owner," *WA* 19 (February 1913): 16–19.

A significant recent essay on the building, and the one that inspired my own approach, is Thomas Beeby, "The Song of Taliesin," *Modulus: The Uni-*

versity of Virginia School of Architecture Review (1980–81): 2–11. For other insights and approaches, one should consult: Robert C. Twombly, "Frank Lloyd Wright in Spring Green, 1911–1932," *Wisconsin Magazine of History* 51 (Spring 1968): 200–17; Sidney K. Robinson, *Life Imitates Architecture: Taliesin and Alden Dow's Studio* (Ann Arbor: Architectural Research Laboratory, University of Michigan, 1980); and Walter L. Creese, *The Crowning of the American Landscape: Eight Great Spaces and Their Buildings* (Princeton: Princeton University Press, 1985), 241–78. Also worth consulting are: Wendingen 1925, 38–51; "Frank Lloyd Wright," *AF* 68 (January 1938): 2–23; George Nelson, "Wright's Houses," *Fortune* 34 (August 1946): 116–25; and Joan W. Saltzman, "Taliesin through the Years," *Wisconsin Architect* 40 (October 1969): 14–18.

An earlier version of this chapter appeared in my "The Story of Taliesin: Wright's First Natural House," *Wright Studies* 1 (1992): 2–27. An abbreviated, and somewhat different, version appeared in my "Under the Aegis of Taliesin," in Jonathan Lipman and Neil Levine, *The Wright State: Frank Lloyd Wright in Wisconsin* (Milwaukee: Milwaukee Art Museum, 1992), 32–43.

4. *A* I, 167; and "Wright Reveals Romance Secret," *CT*, 31 December 1911, p. 4. Although there is no direct evidence that Wright may have been thinking of a school as part of the original conception of Taliesin (1911–14), a letter from his mother, written in 1919, mentions that "you [Wright] talk of an architectural school of thirty young men" (Anna Lloyd Wright to FLW [1919], FLWF).

5. It is perhaps worth noting here that Taliesin, *not* Taliesin North or Taliesin East, was the name Wright gave to the house and the one he generally used. The addition of North or East came only in the 1940s, after Taliesin West was built. I shall also deliberately avoid the pedantic distinctions of a Taliesin I, II, and III established in Hitchcock, *Materials* in order to account for the rebuildings after the fires of 1914 and 1925. Building and rebuilding went on constantly and continuously from 1911 to 1959; but the core always remained the plan of the house, studio, and farm buildings begun in 1911. Wright's own references to a Taliesin the first, second, or third have more to do with his personification of the place, and thus a sense of linear succession, than with fundamental differences or changes in nature or character.

6. See D. D. Martin to FLW, 28 October 1910; and FLW to Martin, 30 October 1910, Box 3-4, Wright-Martin Papers. Work probably did not begin until the following summer.

7. Wright remarked that when former friends "learned he had not come [home] as a repentant sinner to rejoin the family" but instead to establish a new domestic and work environment that involved Mamah Cheney, he was shunned and treated like a "pariah" ("Wright Reveals Romance Secret"; and W. E. Martin to D. D. Martin, 10 October 1910, Box 3-4, Wright-Martin Papers).

8. "Wright Reveals Romance Secret." It could be conjectured that, had the arrangement worked out financially more as he had expected, Wright might have stayed longer in Europe, which would help explain the house project for Fiesole. The story of Wright's handing over his office is still not very clear. Before turning to the relatively little known German-born von Holst, he apparently approached Marion Mahony, Barry Byrne, and Purcell and Elmslie, all of whom refused. Cf. H. Allen Brooks, *The Prairie School: Frank Lloyd Wright and His Midwest Contemporaries* (New York: W. W. Norton, 1972), 148ff.; Gill, *Many Masks*, 208; and now Alofsin, *Lost Years*, 27–28, 67–70, 311–12. The largest group of works Wright may have considered "stolen" from him were the Rock Glen and Rock Crest houses in the Mason City subdivision that Mahony and Griffin undertook following Wright's bank/hotel job. Wright may well have assumed the whole subdivision should have been his, since he had made the initial contact with its developer, James Blythe.

9. FLW to Woolley, 22 April [1911], MS 452, Box 1-1, Woolley Archive.

10. As noted above, no correspondence between Wright and Cheney has so far surfaced.

11. FLW to Martin, 3 April and 12 April 1911, Box 3-9, Wright-Martin Papers. Owing to the economic crisis of the 1880s and subsequent overinvestment in land and equipment, the Lloyd Jones family had lost much of its holdings in the Helena Valley area by the first decade of the twentieth century. Wright thus had to buy back the land from others. The land for Taliesin was purchased from Joseph and Justina Rieder on 10 April 1911 (Anthony Alofsin, "Taliesin I: A Catalogue of Drawings and Photographs," *Wright Studies* 1 [1992]: 98–99). For the family history, see Chapter I, note 4 above.

12. "Architect Wright in New Romance with 'Mrs. Cheney,'" *Chicago Sunday Tribune*, 24 December 1911, p. 4. For a good summary of these events, see Twombly, "Wright in Spring Green."

13. The only references I have seen are in the two letters to Darwin Martin cited above (note 11). These probably should not be taken at face value, however. Martin was always criticizing Wright for his profligacy in money matters. Given his displeasure with Wright's intention to put money into the subdivision of the Oak Park house (for rental purposes), Wright could hardly have expected Martin to look favorably upon a request for money to help pay for a "farm" in the middle of Wisconsin. From a business standpoint (and that is generally the way Martin looked at any issue), this would have appeared to be sheer lunacy. It is also important to note that in the voluminous correspondence that has been preserved between Anna Lloyd Wright and her son there is not a single mention of the putative turnover of property.

14. Henry-Russell Hitchcock, who was working closely with Wright at the time the second edition of the *Autobiography* was being prepared, noted that Taliesin "was begun for his [Wright's] mother upon his return from Europe. But before it was completed he had decided to live there himself" (Hitchcock, *Materials*, 64.) This curious account, probably somewhat garbled, makes Wright's action seem duplicitous. Bruce Brooks Pfeiffer, in the text on Taliesin in *FLWM*, vol. 3, 138–39, is faithful to the 1943 *Autobiography*, maintaining that Taliesin was originally designed as "a summer house for his mother" but that "during the construction of the cottage, his mother urged him to take over the building and live there himself."

15. It would seem most likely that the bedroom at the southeast end of the living wing, with its connected servant's room, was for Wright's mother. When the plan was expanded in June 1911, that area was turned into a quasi-independent apartment, with its own kitchen, sitting room, and bathroom (cf. figs. 71, 72). Writing to Janet Ashbee in 1913, Catherine Wright noted that Anna Lloyd Wright was spending the "summer in her apartments in the house he [Wright] built at Hillside" (Catherine Lloyd Wright to Janet E. Ashbee, 28 July 1913, Ashbee Journals, 1913). Another factor to consider here is the 1911 project for a townhouse and studio that Wright designed for himself in Chicago, to be discussed below.

16. Other factors may well have played a part in Wright's thinking. Given his financial dependence on Darwin Martin, and the latter's moral indignation at his leaving Catherine, Wright did everything possible to conceal his affair with Cheney from Martin. In addition, Wright may have been concerned for his aunts Ellen and Jane, whose Hillside Home School was in terrible financial straits and could be badly hurt by any publicity resulting from his return to live nearby.

The title to Taliesin appears to have remained in Anna Lloyd Wright's name at least into the decade of the 1920s (Alfred MacArthur to D. D. Martin, 25 October 1920, Box 4-11, Wright-Martin Papers). Wright was divorced from Catherine in November 1922, and his mother died early the following year.

17. Living at Taliesin would have been particularly difficult during the strenuous winter months, a fact that induced Wright himself, in his late sixties, to build a winter headquarters in Arizona. Wright's mother did spend some summers at Taliesin (cf. note 15 above), as well as some months when Wright and his second wife, Miriam Noel, were in Tokyo for the construction of the Imperial Hotel.

18. Maginel Wright Barney, *The Valley of the God-Almighty Joneses: Reminiscences of Frank Lloyd Wright's Sister* (1965; rpt. Spring Green, Wis.: Unity Chapel Publications, 1986), 141.

19. The names by which the valley and the community are known can vary by author and over time. Indicated as Jones Valley on recent U.S. Geological Survey maps (fig. 74), and sometimes referred to as Wyoming Valley (despite the fact that the latter is the next one to the west), it was most commonly called Helena Valley by Lloyd Jones family members and their friends. The name Hillside was likewise the one most commonly used by the family to refer to the conglomeration of their houses and farms at the north end of the valley, around the family chapel and the Hillside Home School.

20. See especially, Barney, *The Valley*; and Franklin Porter and Mary Porter, eds., *Heritage: The Lloyd Jones Family* (Spring Green, Wis.: Unity Chapel Publications, 1986). On the Hillside Home School and the important

role it played in the development of progressive education in America, see Mary Ellen Chase, *A Goodly Fellowship* (New York: Macmillan, 1939).

21. Elizabeth Wright Ingraham, "The Chapel in the Valley," orig. pub. *FLWN* 3, no. 2 (1980), repr. in Porter and Porter, *Heritage*, 12. In his review of the building shortly after it was dedicated, William Gannett noted that "a boy architect belonging to the family looked after [the] interior [decoration]" (W. C. Gannett, "Christening a Country Church" [1886], repr. in *A Lloyd Jones Retrospective* [Spring Green, Wis.: Unity Chapel Publications, 1986], 14).

22. The shingles were replaced with lapped siding in 1939.

23. FLW, "Romeo and Juliet," p. 1, MS 2401.031 A, FLWF. In a letter to Darwin Martin of 27 March 1928, Wright noted that the manuscript of "Romeo and Juliet" was finished (Box 5-2, Wright-Martin Papers). In the tale of the building of the tower, Wright becomes the Aladdin-like child who somehow succeeds, despite enormous odds and without full rational explanation: "The Aunts made much of this boy although he was inclined to be a dreamer and wayward—or radical, they never knew just which" ("Romeo and Juliet," 1).

24. Conscious of the regressive attitude expressed in his earlier explanation of the tower's symbolism, Wright intended to end this section of the *Autobiography* in the following way:

> *I wonder if I shall live to see it [the tower] as I have already lived to see the very symbolism of Romeo and Juliet grow old-fashioned.*
>
> *Juliet, to be up to date, should have a wheel of her own. Yes—and a hill of her own, too.* ("Romeo and Juliet," 9)

This reflection was cut from the final draft.

25. I am grateful to John Geiger, a former Taliesin Fellow, for pointing out to me that the material is sandstone, rather than limestone. He remarked that Wright probably chose sandstone because of the ease in cutting and dressing it. He also noted that the stone came from the quarry located just to the southwest of the school (personal communication, 1 March and 21 April 1992).

26. Jane Lloyd Jones, "Jenny's Story: 'In Memoriam'" (1916–17), quoted in Thomas Graham, ed., *Trilogy: Through Their Eyes* (Spring Green, Wis.: Unity Chapel Publications, 1986), 39. Examples of "Welsh" detailing are the "druid" materials of oak and stone and the fire fenders "formed of the conventionalized Welsh hat" (ibid.). Indications of the memorial nature of the structure are the inscriptions from Gray's "Elegy" (a favorite poem of Mary Lloyd Jones) over the fireplace and from the fortieth chapter of Isaiah (a favorite of Richard Lloyd Jones) on the balcony.

27. Barney, *The Valley*, 56.

28. In the folkloric literature of Taliesin, the name of the poet is rendered both ways, although "radiant" tended to be the preferred one in the nineteenth century. This name and its meanings will be discussed more fully below.

It was in reference to the design of Taliesin that Wright first said: "No house should ever be *on* any hill or *on* anything. It should be *of* the hill" (*A* I, 171). It is interesting to note that Wright had previously used the distinction *on/of* in relation to decoration being "*of* the surface, never *on* it" ("In the Cause of Architecture," *ARec* 23 [March 1908]: 161).

29. In the later 1920s, after the second fire (1925), Wright changed the entrance, removing it from the southwest end of the living wing to the northwest corner of the stable and service wing. The description here follows the original pattern. For a record of what existed by early 1913, see "Studio-Home of Wright"; and Ashbee, "Taliesin." One of the most accurate and sensitive descriptions of the house is in Robinson, *Life Imitates Architecture*, 9–19.

30. I am indebted to David Van Zanten for making this observation on a trip we took together to the site. Considering Wright's interest in things Japanese, one could relate this technique of planning to his observation that "the Japanese approach to any matter is a spiral. Their instinct for attack in any direction is oblique and volute" (*A* I, 217).

31. Herbert Croly, "The American Country Estate," *ARec* 18 (July 1905): 1, 2. This is the same issue in which the laudatory review of Wright's work appeared (Chapter III, note 14), which would lead one to assume that Wright was aware of Croly's study.

32. Ibid., 1, 2, 4.

33. Ibid., 2–3.

34. Another factor that may have played a part in Wright's decision to move his entire operation to the countryside was his visit to Ashbee's home and workshop in the Cotswolds on his way back from Italy in September 1910. Ashbee had moved his Guild of Handicraft from the East End of London to Chipping Campden in 1902. For a description of that Arts and Crafts community, see Alan Crawford, *C. R. Ashbee: Architect, Designer, and Romantic Socialist* (New Haven and London: Yale University Press, 1985), 100–162. Any parallel would only be ideological, and not architectural, since Ashbee's headquarters did not involve estate-building as much as retrofitting and recycling an old village.

35. Though generally dated 1911, neither the exact date of the project nor the specific lot has yet been determined. A date prior to April 1911 is highly unlikely, given the fact that Wright was abroad from mid-January to the end of March. Of the two known perspectives, one shows a nineteen-foot-wide corner lot, perhaps bordering an alley (#1113.004, FLWF); the other indicates existing houses on both sides (#1113.001, FLWF).

36. FLW, "Why I Love Wisconsin," in Guthiem, *FLW on Arch.*, 158.

37. Charles A. Platt, *Italian Gardens* (1893; New York: Harper & Brothers, 1894), 19.

38. To the list of similarities should also be added the entrance "loggia" and the curious, very classical cyma reversa molding Wright used along the base of all the plaster exterior walls at the junction with the lower courses of stone.

39. Again, I am grateful to John Geiger for pointing out the use of limestone in Taliesin as opposed to the sandstone of the earlier Hillside Home School.

40. FLW, "Taliesin III," 8 June 1926, MS XXI/4, J. L. Wright Collection.

41. In his analysis of Wright's plan, done while taking my Taliesin seminar, Timothy Love made certain important discoveries concerning the planning of Taliesin. The most significant of these, from my point of view, is that the "eccentric," asymmetrical plan can be read as an eroded remain of an earlier symmetrical design that had been rotated and flipped over to align with existing topographical features, notably the oak trees on the hill crown as well as those lower down the hill, where the loggia and entrance terrace are.

42. See my "Frank Lloyd Wright's Diagonal Planning," in Helen Searing, ed., *In Search of Modern Architecture: A Tribute to Henry-Russell Hitchcock* (New York, Cambridge, Mass., and London: Architectural History Foundation, MIT Press, 1982), 249–52.

43. The actual alignment of the diagonal is nowhere as abstract as I have made it sound. The diagonal follows the "natural" axis that runs from the two oak trees within the exedra of the hill crown to the single large oak framed by the entrance loggia and terrace (see note 41 above).

44. These effects were continually reinforced by Wright in his various alterations to and enlargements of the living room over the years. Unfortunately, there are no photographs of the living room prior to the fire of 1914 that illustrate the view I have described.

45. This perspective (fig. 80), of which there are several versions, was prepared in late 1912 or 1913, at the time Wright was first contemplating a major enlargement of the studio and stable wing area to accommodate more draftsmen. Emil Brodelle, one of the draftsmen killed in the 1914 fire, worked on it. The design reflected in it appears in the plan published in Ashbee's article on Taliesin in the February 1913 issue of *WA*.

46. Walter Creese noted that "the architecture was something to see the landscape *through*." For this and other extremely perceptive remarks, see his *Crowning of the American Landscape*, 253–63.

47. The concept of the absorptive gaze comes from Michael Fried, *Absorption and Theatricality: Painting and Beholder in the Age of Diderot* (Berkeley, Los Angeles, and London: University of California Press, 1980).

48. Thomas Beeby first suggested the importance of Wright's Welsh background in the naming of the house (note 3 above). Many of my ideas stem directly from his. They have been enriched and expanded by Scott Gartner's "The Shining Brow: Frank Lloyd Wright and the Welsh Bardic Tradition," *Wright Studies* 1 (1992): 28–43.

49. The section on Taliesin in the *Autobiography* was written in 1927. On

23 July 1926, Darwin Martin sent Wright a copy of Arthur Granville Bradley's guide to Wales, *Highways and Byways in North Wales* (1898; 1st pocket ed., London: Macmillan, 1923), and marked the pages where the author recounted the folktale of Taliesin in discussing the village of that name (pp. 421–23). In a letter to Martin a few days later, Wright added a postscript:

N. B. The little book on Wales thoughtfully annotated by yourself just came in. I am glad to have it from your hand and I only now learn just what the word "Taliesin" means. It is worth knowing. Thank you very much, F. L. W. (FLW to Martin, 31 July 1926, Box 4-26, Wright-Martin Papers; emphasis added)

If Wright was telling the truth—and there is no reason to doubt he was—then Beeby's argument about the importance of the poetic figure of Taliesin takes on even more weight. In fact, the conventional interpretation of the house as a concretization of the English translation of the Welsh word becomes secondary. One is left with the alternative of seeing Wright's choice of name as extraordinarily fortuitous or uncannily clairvoyant, or perhaps a combination of the two. Cf. Grace Steth, "Wright's Taliesin Linked to Legendary Welsh Poet," *Capital Times* (Madison), 25 July 1951.

As for the specific translation of the name Taliesin, it should be noted that Bradley, like Guest, Peacock, and Bulfinch before him, translated it as "radiant brow." Of all the popular sources, apparently only Sidney Lanier offered the alternative of "shining brow" (see note 55 below). Wright used both translations in the article for *Liberty* magazine of 1929 ("Taliesin: Chronicle of a House," 21, 22); but from the time the *Autobiography* was published (1932), he generally favored "shining brow." Perhaps it sounded more modern to him than "radiant brow."

50. FLW, "Taliesin: Chronicle of a House," 22, 21.

51. On the elusive figure of Taliesin, see: D. W. Nash, *Taliesin; or, the Bards and Druids of Britain: A Translation of the Remains of the Earliest Welsh Bards and an Examination of the Bardic Mysteries* (London: John Russell Smith, 1858); John Morris-Jones, "Taliesin," *Y Cymmrodor: The Magazine of the Honourable Society of Cymmrodorion* 28 (1918); Ifor Williams, *Lectures on Early Welsh Poetry* (Dublin: Dublin Institute for Advanced Studies, 1944), 49–76; A.O.H. Jarman, "Taliesin," in Jarman and Gwilyn Rees Hughes, eds., *A Guide to Welsh Literature* (Swansea: Christopher Davis, 1976), 51–67; and Emyr Humphreys, *The Taliesin Tradition: A Quest for Welsh Identity* (London: Black Raven Press, 1983). An important contemporaneous source on the general subject of Welsh mythology is W[alter] Y[eeling] Evans-Wentz, *The Fairy-Faith in Celtic Countries* (London and New York: H. Frowde, Oxford University Press, 1911).

52. William F. Skene, ed., *The Four Ancient Books of Wales*, 2 vols. (Edinburgh: Edmonston and Douglas, 1868): the translations into English are in volume 1, the originals in volume 2; *Facsimile and Text of the Book of Taliesin*, ed. J. Gwenogvryn Evans (Llanbedrog, N. Wales: privately printed, 1910). Although the 1915 translation by Evans (see note 1 above) is now considered to be unreliable, it is relevant because of its contemporaneity. The best recent edition of the poems in English is *The Poems of Taliesin*, ed. Ifor Williams and trans. J. E. Caerwyn Williams (Dublin: Dublin Institute for Advanced Studies, 1968).

53. Ibid., xvi.

54. *The Mabinogi and Other Medieval Welsh Tales*, trans. and with an introduction by Patrick K. Ford (Berkeley, Los Angeles, and London: University of California Press, 1977), 185–86. This is the poem called "Cad Goddeu" in Welsh.

55. Lady Charlotte Guest [Schreiber], *The Mabinogion, from the Llyfr Coch o Hergest, and Other Ancient Welsh Manuscripts*, 3 vols. (London: Longman, Brown, Green, and Longmans, 1838–49). The one-volume 1877 edition (lacking the texts in the original Welsh) was published in London by B. Quaritch. An Everyman's Library edition was published by J. M. Dent in London and E. P. Dutton in New York in 1906. It should be noted that the Hanes Taliesin was not originally part of the *Mabinogion*, and was only appended to it by Guest and others.

Guest's translation of the Hanes Taliesin was preceded by the one attributed to William Owen (Pughe) and published in two parts as "The Mabinogi

of Taliesin," pt. 1, *The Cambrian Quarterly Magazine and Celtic Repertory* 5 (1 April 1833): 198–214; and pt. 2, *The Cambrian and Caledonian Quarterly Magazine* 5 (1 July 1833): 366–82. Just a few years earlier, Thomas Love Peacock had adapted the tale in his popular novel *The Misfortunes of Elphin* (1829). I am indebted to Scott Gartner for this information.

Gartner has comprehensively documented the involvement of the Lloyd Jones family in traditional Welsh folklore and persuasively shown how Wright would have been introduced to such stories as the tale of Taliesin ("The Shining Brow"). In her history of the family, Wright's sister Maginel referred to the importance of folktales and folklore (*The Valley*, esp. 51, 73). Bruce Brooks Pfeiffer, in *FLWM*, vol. 8, x, says that Wright "came upon The Mabinogion" during his 1956 trip to Wales. Wright himself referred to *The Mabinogion* only once in print. In 1957 he wrote: "Comes to mind a triad from the old Welsh *Mabinogion* defining genius: A man who sees nature. Has a heart for nature. The courage to follow nature" (*FLW, A Testament* [New York: Horizon Press, 1957], 81). Gartner has traced this triad back through Lanier's introduction to his *Knightly Legends of Wales; or, The Boy's Mabinogion* (1881; New York: Charles Scribner's Sons, 1884), xii, to the list of "Poetic Triads" published in 1792 by Edward Williams (Iolo Morganwg), the founder of Neo-Druidic "Bardism" and the most important progenitor of the Welsh Revival in the late eighteenth and early nineteenth centuries ("Some Account of Llywarç Hen, with a sketch of British Druidism," in William Owen, *The Heroic Elegies and Other Pieces of Llywarç Hen, Prince of the Cambrian Britons* [London: J. Owens and E. Williams, 1792]).

The reference to Iolo Morganwg, a kind of Horace Walpole cum Batty Langley of folklore, brings up the important point that Welsh folklore, language, and traditions, like most medieval culture, had essentially died out by the middle of the eighteenth century and thus had to be revived and, in many cases, reinvented. On this phenomenon, see Prys Morgan, "From a Death to a View: The Hunt for the Welsh Past in the Romantic Period," in Eric Hobsbawm and Terence Ranger, eds., *The Invention of Tradition*, Past and Present Publications (1983; rpt. Cambridge: Cambridge University Press, 1985), 43–100. For its effect in the region where Wright's grandparents settled, see Phillips G. Davies, *The Welsh in Wisconsin* (Madison: State Historical Society of Wisconsin, 1982), esp. 13ff. Alfred, Lord Tennyson, through his recounting of the legends of King Arthur in his *Idylls of the Kings* (1859–85), was perhaps the most significant figure in the general revival of medieval Celtic folklore, and we know that Wright was fond of his poetry from an early age.

Yet, it is important to note that Wright mentioned no specifically Welsh sources of Taliesin in the *Autobiography* or in the earlier article published in *Liberty*. Instead, he referred to the little-known play by the turn-of-the-century "genteel" New England poet Richard Hovey, whose "charming masque 'Taliesin,' had made me acquainted with *his* image of the historic bard" (*A I*, 170; italics added). Clearly, Wright was indicating not how he had learned of the Taliesin legend but only that Hovey's adaptation of it meant something special to him at the time. We know that in February 1908 Wright either purchased or was given *Taliesin: A Masque*, along with the three companion volumes that make up Hovey's incomplete *Launcelot and Guenevere: A Poem in Dramas* (New York: Duffield & Co., 1907). See Margaret Klinkow, *The Wright Family Library* (Oak Park, Ill.: Frank Lloyd Wright Home and Studio Foundation Research Center, 1994), 7. Originally published between 1891 and 1899 (*Taliesin* is the final volume of the series), the plays were almost immediately read as offering an alternative to the moralizing of Tennyson's version of the Arthurian legend. Taking as a main theme the illicit love between Guenevere and Launcelot, Hovey refused to criticize the pair as adulterers but rather proposed the modern idea that one might have to break the law in order to fulfill oneself as an individual. Guenevere became, in effect, an image of the "new woman" and Taliesin, the liberated poet, is "the modern creative man who dares to accept evil and passion and paradox as materials of emerging good" (Allan Houston Macdonald, *Richard Hovey: Man & Craftsman* [Durham, N.C.: Duke University Press, 1957], 93 and passim). It is interesting that Wright acquired the set of four volumes at the height of his own affair with Mamah Cheney. Finally, it should be noted that in the *Autobiography* the reference to the Hovey play occurs not within the "Taliesin" section but just prior to it, as the conclusion to the section entitled "Following Voluntary Exile at Fiesole: Sociological Consequences." There, Wright declared his belief in the sovereignty of the individual in matters of love and in the supremacy of love over the legal and social convention of marriage (*A* I, 169–70). The reference to Hovey thus signaled a fundamental aspect of Taliesin, the building, as an act of self-representation.

Hovey was best known at the time for his sensitive translations of Maurice Maeterlinck's Symbolist plays. Wright may well have come into contact with these through Sullivan, who owned a copy of Hovey's translation of *The Plays of Maurice Maeterlinck* (Chicago: Stone and Kimball, 1895). See Narciso G. Menocal, *Architecture as Nature: The Transcendentalist Idea of Louis Sullivan* (Madison: University of Wisconsin Press, 1981), 128. For more on the Wright-Hovey connection, see Anthony Alofsin, "Taliesin: 'To Fashion Worlds in Little,'" *Wright Studies* 1 (1992): 44–48. For a discussion of Hovey that places him within the context of an antimodernist stream of American artistic thought, see T. J. Jackson Lears, *No Place of Grace: Antimodernism and the Transformation of American Culture, 1880–1920* (New York: Pantheon, 1981), 98–138.

56. Robert Graves, *The White Goddess: A Historical Grammar of Poetic Myth* (New York: Creative Age Press, 1948).

57. Guest, *The Mabinogion* (1838–49; 2d ed. 1877, rpt. Chicago: Academy Press, 1978), 472.

58. Ibid., 473–74. It is interesting that Guest footnoted the phrase "radiant brow" to indicate that it was a translation of the word *Taliesin*, despite the fact that Elphin's response immediately succeeded the servant's declaration (p. 473). As noted above (note 49), Guest consistently translated Taliesin as "radiant brow," as did Bulfinch, A. G. Bradley, and Peacock; among the sources Wright may have known, only Lanier alternated between "shining brow" and "radiant brow," using the former translation in his introduction and reserving the latter for the text of the story.

59. *The Mabinogi*, trans. Ford, 172–73.

60. Guest, *The Mabinogion*, 485–86.

61. *The Mabinogi*, trans. Ford, 175.

62. Wasmuth I, par. 4.

63. FLW, "Taliesin: Chronicle of a House," 22, 21, 26, 28, 29. The very fact that myths and legends such as that of Taliesin were no longer "living" but had to be revived and reinvented, as Prys Morgan has shown (note 55 above), makes Wright's appropriation of it that much more problematic and modern.

64. FLW, "In the Cause" (1908): 162.

65. There are no preserved sketchbooks of Wright. As we know, he admonished young architects not to sketch out their ideas but to "conceive the building in the imagination, not on paper but in the mind, thoroughly—before touching paper" (FLW, "In the Cause of Architecture, I: The Logic of the Plan," *ARec* 63 [January 1928]: 49). Instead of sketching buildings, sites, or people while traveling, Wright apparently preferred to rely on the power of his visual memory. I should like to thank Bruce Pfeiffer for elaborating on this.

66. See Chapter I, note 25. It should be recalled that the germ of the argument in *The Japanese Print* had been formulated as early as 1900 in the lecture Wright prepared on "A Philosophy of Fine Art" (in Bruce Brooks Pfeiffer, ed., *Frank Lloyd Wright: Collected Writings*, vol. 1, *1894–1930* [New York: Rizzoli, Frank Lloyd Wright Foundation, 1992], 39–44). Wright referred to the conventionalizing of the Japanese print in his introduction to the Wasmuth portfolio (Wasmuth I, par. 4). Cf. Twombly, *Wright*, 148–51. For a contemporary critique, see Henry Blackman Sell, "The Artist as Master," review of *The Japanese Print: An Interpretation*, by Frank Lloyd Wright, *Little Review* 1 (January 1915): 17–19.

67. FLW, *The Japanese Print: An Interpretation* (1912; rpt. New York: Horizon Press, 1967), 18, 65–67.

68. The statue no longer remains in that place. It was probably removed sometime in the later 1920s, after the second fire (1925). Photographs exist showing it at the lower gate to the house, next to the dam and waterfall. It was later moved to the entrance of the root cellar. Narciso Menocal has suggested that beyond the classical and Celtic references there is an analogy with the image of the Virgin in the medieval *hortus conclusus* ("Taliesin, the Gilmore House, and the *Flower in the Crannied Wall*," *Wright Studies* 1 [1992]: 66–97).

69. "Studio-Home of Wright," 45. Taylor Woolley, who visited Taliesin

during construction, was apparently struck by the prominence of the figure and took a number of photographs of it, one of which is identical to the frontispiece for the *ARec* article (Clifford Evans Scrapbooks, MS 466, Woolley Archive).

70. Beeby, "Song of Taliesin," esp. 6–9.

71. The curious punctuation in the third sentence of the first paragraph may have occurred during revisions. In the original manuscript there were dashes between the second and third sentences, as well as between the first clause of the third sentence and the rest of that sentence (FLW, "Taliesin," p. 4, MS 1201.028 A, FLWF).

72. For a related discussion, see Thomas Beeby, "The Grammar of Ornament/Ornament as Grammar," *VIA* 3 (1977): 10–29.

73. According to a reporter who was shown the house by Wright soon after it was finished, the stone was "laid in close imitation of the cliff" where the stone was quarried ("Spend Christmas Making 'Defense' of 'Spirit Hegira,'" 2). Fig. 74 shows the quarry along the road west from Taliesin.

74. In the case of Richardson's Ames Gate Lodge, the material surface distorts the figure of a house and thus works by the Mannerist technique of contradicting normal expectations through the element of surprise.

75. Brownell and FLW, 15.

76. FLW, "Taliesin: Chronicle of a House," 22, 29. In fact, Wright described the stonemasons imitating the rock outcrops as "sculptors fashioning a statue" (*A* I, 174).

77. FLW, "Taliesin: Chronicle of a House," 28.

78. Richard W. Bock, *Memoirs of an American Artist*, ed. Dorothi Bock Pierre (Los Angeles: C. C. Publishing Co., 1989), 138.

79. "Wright Buries Mamah of Hills in Night Grave," *CT*, 17 August 1914, pp. 1, 7.

80. It should be recalled that Wright had thought of "updating" the symbolic interpretation of the Romeo and Juliet Tower he had sent his aunts in 1896–97 by adding a reference to the more active role of the modern woman (see note 24 above).

81. "A Hymn to Nature," *Little Review* 1 (February 1915): 30–32. A note preceding the poem explains: "This fragment, a 'Hymn to Nature,' unknown to us in the published works of Goethe, was found in a little bookshop in Berlin, and translated into English by a strong man and a strong woman whose lives and whose creations have served the ideals of all humanity in a way that will gain deeper and deeper appreciation" (p. 30). *Love and Ethics, The Morality of Woman*, and *The Torpedo under the Ark* were all published in Chicago by Ralph Fletcher Seymour. *The Woman Movement*, with an introduction by Havelock Ellis, was published in New York and London by G. P. Putnam's Sons.

82. John Lloyd Wright, *My Father Who Is on Earth* (New York: G. P. Putnam's Sons, 1946), 80.

83. See note 81 above; and Ralph Fletcher Seymour, *Some Went This Way: A Forty Year Pilgrimage Among Artists, Bookmen and Printers* (Chicago: R. F. Seymour, 1945).

84. This had to have been designed before February 1913, because it figures in the plans published by Ashbee in his article on Taliesin in the February 1913 issue of *WA*.

85. The commission for the Booth House came in early January 1911. The plans for the first scheme are dated April 1911 and thus are contemporaneous with the first project for Taliesin. Wright took the plot plan of the Booth site with him on his trip to Germany in January 1911, but it is doubtful that he got anywhere with the design until he returned. See Wright to Martin, 21 January 191[1], Box 3-4, Wright-Martin Papers (the letter was mistakenly dated 1910 by Wright). Both the Cutten project and the one for Booth carried over into 1912.

86. One can, of course, always find exceptions to prove the rule. In this case they would include the Allen House in Wichita, Kansas (1916–18) and the Yamamura House at Ashiya (near Kobe) in Japan (planned c. 1918; begun 1924).

87. "Wright Buries Mamah of Hills," 7. Secrest, *Wright*, 217, notes that Emil Brodelle, a draftsman, had apparently made racist remarks to Julian Carleton a few days before. For a possible connection to Borthwick, see note 89

below. The Carletons had been recommended to Wright by John Vogelsang, the restaurateur-manager of Midway Gardens.

88. "Awful Crime in Wisconsin: Mrs. Cheney and Five Others Slain in Frank Lloyd Wright Bungalow," *CT*, 16 August 1914, p. 1. As noted above (Introduction, note 17), the child of Borthwick's deceased sister, whom the Cheneys had raised as one of their own, had remained in Oak Park that day. Some early press reports mistakenly announced that three children had been killed.

Both Twombly, *Wright*, 167, and Gill, *Many Masks*, 229, give the date of the event as 14 August. The story in the *NYT* confirms the 15 August date: "Wild Negro Chef Kills 6, Wounds 4," *NYT*, 16 August 1914, p. 12.

89. The initial story in the *CT* of 16 August 1914 contained an interesting piece of information that was never really followed up by investigative reporters. After noting that Borthwick "had called them [the Carletons] ideal servants," the report went on to say that during the week preceding the event "something caused Mamah Borthwick to dislike [Julian] Carleton" and that "one of the survivors of the tragedy said whatever happened had led Mamah Borthwick to tell the negro and his wife their time would be up on Saturday night" (p. 1). In all the reports, stress was laid on the fact that Carleton was "negro." An editorial in the *CT* of 18 August 1914 pronounced the general judgment. Entitled "The Lunatic at Large," it referred to "the abnormal character of the negro Carleton" and "his attacks of 'temper,'" and described him as a "sporadic degenerate" who should have been locked up well before the event took place (p. 6). The element of racism clearly played a part. Cf. Twombly, "Wright in Spring Green," 200–210.

90. J. L. Wright, *My Father*, 81.

91. FLW, "Taliesin: Chronicle of a House," 26; FLW, "Taliesin III"; and FLW, "Taliesin: Chronicle of a House," 26.

92. *A I*, 192; and Twombly, *Wright*, 169. Wright included in his obituary quotations from Goethe's "A Hymn to Nature," the poem he and Borthwick had translated together.

93. It is difficult to reconstruct the scene of the murders exactly, but it would seem that Wright took certain liberties so as to be able to align the statue more precisely with the distant cemetery and family chapel. The loggia replaced the guest bedroom, next to the master bedroom, an unlikely spot for Borthwick and her children to have been at the time they were murdered. According to newspaper reports, they were on the terrace outside the dining area of the living room.

94. This was done sometime in the mid- to late 1950s. On the removal of the statue, see note 68 above.

95. It was also, needless to say, a prime advertisement: "Taliesin works like a charm on everybody that comes within its atmosphere," Wright wrote to Darwin Martin (7 September 1929, Box 5-25, Wright-Martin Papers).

Chapter V
Building against Nature on the Pacific Rim

1. "Building against Doomsday" is the title Wright gave to the section on the Imperial Hotel in the 1943 edition of the *Autobiography*; it was originally called "Why the Great Earthquake Did Not Destroy the Imperial Hotel."

The critique of the Imperial Hotel and Hollyhock House as tangential to Wright's career and irrelevant to the history of modern architecture goes back to the writings of architects and critics of the 1920s, including Giedion, Oud, and Hitchcock. In his seminal book *Modern Architecture: Romanticism and Reintegration* (1929; rpt. New York: Hacker Art Books, 1970), Henry-Russell Hitchcock, for instance, described the two buildings in the following way:

The Imperial Hotel . . . done in 1916 [sic] has been Wright's largest commission. Yet the design, despite its admirable plan, is redundant, overburdened with unskilfully exotic ornament, and except where the quality of the materials is well brought out, vastly ineffective. The interiors on which Wright expended apparently a considerable effort are incomparably worse than those however Louis XVI of any coëval Ritz.

. . . The Barnsdall [Hollyhock] house of 1917 [sic] is also one of his least successful buildings. The poured concrete [sic] smoothly surfaced enhances the

monstrous weight of the design. The ornament of unparalleled inappropriateness, suggesting whittling rather than moulding, has only the virtue of being well placed and of lightening somewhat an almost pyramidal gloom. . . . In his return to the experiment of 1904 in Unity Temple with monolithic construction [sic] the wealth of his clients [sic] permitted in this case full play to his intemperance in ornament. . . . Thus in his positive 'modernism' he produced a major work in many ways less satisfactory than the houses of the better Néo-Spanish architects of California such as Myron Hunt or George Washington Smith, [who were] at least negatively restrained in their nominal borrowing from the past. (Pp. 115–16)

In all fairness, it should be pointed out that Hitchcock liked the "elaborate plan" and siting of Hollyhock House, just as he appreciated the "admirable plan" of the Imperial Hotel.

As late as 1966, Norris Kelly Smith made no mention of the Imperial Hotel in his book on Wright and gave only the most slighting reference to Hollyhock House and the work that followed it in the Los Angeles area: "Wright had revealed in his design for the Barnsdall house a taste for impenetrable massiveness and austerity that is quite foreign to his earlier work. We can understand all this in terms of the personal anxieties of the architect, but it is hard to find here an affirmation concerning *res publica* or the image of the family that can be compared to what we see in both earlier and later buildings. He was working in a world to which he felt he did not belong, a world where he had no roots and no place, and where his chief need was not to define the nature of his participation but simply to be sheltered and made secure" (Smith, *Wright*, 125–26). While the fundamental perception of Smith's remarks may be true, a more meaningful interpretation of Wright's work in these years could be given by using the analysis in a constructive rather than a dismissive way.

Even the most recent monograph on Hollyhock House, by a scholar who has devoted a good part of her life to the subject, offers a less than positive view of Wright's achievement. Kathryn Smith concludes her study by saying that "although Hollyhock House is not one of Wright's best buildings, it is certainly his most interesting. Many factors contributed to its flaws. . . . While ignoring both structure and material, Wright sought new expression to give form to meaning. And while the various architectural elements of the building . . . do not come together to create an artistic synthesis, each reveals Wright in his struggle to break away from the Prairie House grammar and take a new direction. . . . Even the awkwardness of his choice of the literal imagery of the pre-Columbian temple shows Wright grasping for the essential, searching for beginnings" (*Frank Lloyd Wright, Hollyhock House and Olive Hill: Buildings and Projects for Aline Barnsdall* [New York: Rizzoli International, 1992], 202).

Underlying the difficulty and uncertainty in dealing with Hollyhock House has always been modern architecture's ambivalence about historical reference, just as the uncertainty about the Imperial Hotel can be traced to its symmetrical, monumental classical-type plan.

2. For the most recent and most accurate account of the years in question, see the important article by Kathryn Smith, "Frank Lloyd Wright and the Imperial Hotel: A Postscript," *Art Bulletin* 67 (June 1985): 296–310. This supersedes Robert Kostka, "Frank Lloyd Wright in Japan," *PSR* 3, no. 3 (1966): 5–23.

Wright wrote about the Imperial Hotel in a number of places. Most important are, in chronological order: FLW, "In the Cause of Architecture: The New Imperial Hotel, Tokio," *WA* 32 (April 1923): 39–46; FLW, "In the Cause of Architecture: In the Wake of the Quake; Concerning the Imperial Hotel, Tokio," pt. 1, *WA* 32 (November 1923): 129–32, and pt. 2, *WA* 33 (February 1924): 17–20; [FLW], "Facts Regarding the Imperial Hotel," in Wendingen 1925, 134–39; FLW, "Why the Japanese Earthquake Did Not Destroy the Hotel Imperial," *Liberty* 4 (3 December 1927): 61–66; FLW, "Why the Great Earthquake Did Not Destroy the Imperial Hotel," *Creative Art* 10 (April 1932): 269–77; and *A I*, 193–225.

The secondary literature on the building includes: Louis Christian Mullgardt, "A Building That Is Wrong," *Architect and Engineer* 71 (November 1922): 81–89; Louis H. Sullivan, "Concerning the Imperial Hotel, Tokyo, Japan," *ARec* 53 (April 1923): 335–52 (repr. in Wendingen 1925, 101–23); "The Effect of the Earthquake in Japan upon Construction," *WA* 32 (October 1923):

117–18; Sullivan, "Reflections on the Tokyo Disaster," *ARec* 55 (February 1924): 113–18 (repr. in Wendingen 1925, 124–33); Julius Floto, "Imperial Hotel, Tokyo, Japan," *ARec* 55 (February 1924): 119–23; Cary James, *The Imperial Hotel: Frank Lloyd Wright and the Architecture of Unity* (Rutland, Vt., and Tokyo: Charles E. Tuttle, 1968); Yoshio Watanabe, Tachu Naito, Shindo Akashi, and Gakuji Yamamoto, *Imperial Hotel, 1921–67* (Tokyo: Kajima Institute Publishing Company, 1968); Shinjiro Kirishiki, "The Story of the Imperial Hotel, Tokyo," *Japan Architect* 138 (January–February 1968): 132–38; Hessell Tiltman, *The Imperial Hotel Story* (Tokyo: Imperial Hotel, 1970); Nobumichi [Shindo] Akashi, *Kyu Teikoku Hoteru no Jisshoteki Kenkyu [Frank Lloyd Wright in Imperial Hotel]* (Tokyo: Tokodo Shoten, 1972); Antonin Raymond, *An Autobiography* (Rutland, Vt., and Tokyo: Charles E. Tuttle, 1973), 46–77; Robert King Reitherman, "The Seismic Legend of the Imperial Hotel: How Did It Really Fare in the Tokyo Earthquake of 1923?" *American Institute of Architects Journal* 69 (June 1980): 42–46, 70; and David B. Stewart, *The Making of a Modern Japanese Architecture: 1868 to the Present* (Tokyo and New York: Kodansha International, 1987), esp. 13–89. Appearing after my text was fundamentally written were: *The Imperial: The First 100 Years* (Tokyo: Imperial Hotel, 1990); Nan and Ivan Lyons, *Imperial Taste: A Century of Elegance at Tokyo's Imperial Hotel* (Tokyo and New York: Kodansha International, 1990); and Masami Tanigawa, "Wright's Achievement in Japan," in *Frank Lloyd Wright: Retrospective* (Tokyo: Mainichi Newspapers, 1991), 58–67. The hotel's one-hundredth anniversary publication, in particular, has a rich documentation of the pre-Wright and Wright buildings. I am grateful to Jayne Kramer for bringing it to my attention.

3. My chronology is indebted to the researches of Kathryn Smith (see note 2), supplemented by references to the commission in the Wright-Martin Papers and, wherever appropriate and feasible, by the hotel's own publication, *The Imperial: The First 100 Years*. According to the account in that publication, Shimoda went to the United States in the late 1880s or early 1890s after finishing the course in architecture at Tokyo's Industrial College in 1883. He worked for A. Page Brown in New York before joining Daniel Burnham's firm in Chicago. He received his Illinois license and opened his own office in Chicago before the end of the decade. In 1898, he returned to Tokyo and practiced there until 1909, when he went to Shanghai. It was while he was in Shanghai that Hayashi commissioned the Imperial Hotel design. Shimoda brought the plans with him to Tokyo in March 1912 (*The Imperial*, 94). The death of Emperor Meiji in July 1912 brought negotiations with Shimoda to a standstill and eventually gave Wright the opening he needed. In 1928, Shimoda published a book recalling the affair (*Shiso to Kenchiku*). His plans have apparently been lost.

What makes the involvement of Shimoda even more fascinating is that an architect by the same name worked as a draftsman for Wright around 1894 or 1895. In his *Autobiography*, Wright talks of having fired "Shimoda, a Japanese draftsman" for "speaking obliquely of a [certain] lady" and, when he refused to take no for an answer, having given him a kick that "landed him well down the half flight of the main public stair" of the Schiller Building. Wright noted that Shimoda then reported the incident to his uncle Jenkin Lloyd Jones, following which Wright kicked him "more thoroughly next time he came." Wright said "this finally settled it and Shimoda disappeared from the American scene, not very much worse for wear." Wright ended his account with the statement: "No, Shimoda was not a good Japanese" (*A* I, 121–22). Although it is not clear that the two Shimodas are one and the same, Wright's vituperation would lead one to believe they were.

Hayashi became manager and managing director of the Imperial Hotel in 1909, following a fairly long stint as the manager of the New York branch of Yamanaka Shokai, a company specializing in art and antiques. He had studied at the University of Wisconsin and was a close friend of the Japanologist Ernest Fenollosa. Shimoda claimed that Hayashi already knew Wright through his dealings in Japanese art, although it is not clear how well or by exactly when (*The Imperial*, 95).

4. Indeed, Emil Brodelle, one of the victims of the Taliesin fire, worked on the exhibited perspective.

5. The meeting of the board of directors took place on 30 November 1915. According to all evidence, it appears that Hayashi's decision to employ Wright was already a *fait accompli* and that the trip was merely a formality to "confirm" the commission (*The Imperial*, 95–96). Hayashi and Wright signed a Contract Memorandum on 17 March 1916 in Chicago for the design and supervision of the hotel.

6. Wright's relationship with Noel will be discussed in Chapter VII.

7. Wright hired the structural engineer Paul Mueller, with whom he had worked in the Adler-Sullivan office, to consult on this matter and eventually to go to Tokyo with him and work on the design.

8. A seven-story annex was built in 1954, and a ten-story addition in 1958. The hotel was demolished in 1967–68. The entrance pavilion and lobby were re-erected at the outdoor museum at Meiji Mura in 1970–85.

9. Cf. Sullivan, "Reflections."

10. *A* I, 212; and FLW, "In the Wake," 1: 129.

11. FLW, "New Imperial Hotel," 40. It was apparently Hayashi who saw the need to develop the "social" functions of the hotel. The site next to the original Imperial Hotel was occupied by the residence of the minister of Home Affairs. It was razed in 1918–19 to make way for Wright's building. The original Imperial Hotel was destroyed in a fire in April 1922. On the development of the Hibiya district in the immediately preceding period, see Stewart, *Modern Japanese Architecture*, 38–48.

12. FLW, "New Imperial Hotel, " 39, 42.

13. The laterality of the typical early Buddhist monastic plan is much more in evidence in the simpler, more open, and less articulated plans of Midway Gardens and the Tokyo embassy project. Cf. Kevin Nute, *Frank Lloyd Wright and Japan: The Role of Traditional Japanese Art and Architecture in the Work of Frank Lloyd Wright* (New York: Van Nostrand Reinhold, 1993), 146–49. For an ancient Japanese religious prototype for the Imperial Hotel, one would have to turn to the seventh-century Kawara-dera, or the eighth-century Daianji and Tōdaiji, both at Heijo. In the secular sphere, one could point to the Chōdoin, in the Imperial Palace at Kyoto, as well as the Kōkyo, or imperial residential quarter, adjacent to the palace precinct. How well Wright would have known any such plans remains a question. I am grateful to my colleagues John Rosenfield and Cherie Wendelken for sharing their insights on Japanese architecture with me.

14. FLW, "New Imperial Hotel," 42. It has been mooted that the Beaux-Arts composition of Wright's plan grew out of an earlier project for the building, presumably Shimoda's. Intriguing as this suggestion is, there is no way yet of verifying or denying it. There is evident in Meiji architecture from the turn of the century a movement away from the English Victorian and Prussian Neo-Renaissance toward an international-style Beaux-Arts classicism. This is particularly true of the work of Kingo Tatsuno and Tokuma Katayama.

15. This approach should be contrasted to the contemporaneous perspective of Midway Gardens (seen from the front) and compared with the earlier perspectives of the McAfee and Robie houses, for example.

16. FLW, "New Imperial Hotel," 42; and [FLW], "Facts," 139.

17. *A* I, 195–200, 224–25; and FLW, "New Imperial Hotel," 44–45, 39.

18. [FLW], "Facts," 139.

19. FLW, "New Imperial Hotel," 41.

20. FLW, "In the Cause of Architecture," *ARec* 23 (March 1908): 167.

21. Le Corbusier, *Towards a New Architecture* (1923; trans. Frederick Etchells, 1927, rpt. New York: Holt, Rinehart and Winston, 1976), 82–97 (the chapter was based on his article "Des Yeux qui ne voient pas . . .: Les paquebots," orig. pub. *Esprit Nouveau* 8 [1921]: 845–55). Mies called the German ship *Imperator* a "floating apartment building" in "Solved Tasks: A Challenge for Our Building Industry," lecture given in December 1923 and published in *Die Bauwelt* 14 (1923): 719 (Fritz Neumeyer, *The Artless Word: Mies Van der Rohe on the Building Art* [1986; trans. Mark Jarzombek, Cambridge, Mass., and London: MIT Press, 1991], 245). Le Corbusier made the reference in *The Radiant City: Elements of a Doctrine of Urbanism to be Used as the Basis of Our Machine-Age Civilization* (1935; trans. Pamela Knight, Eleanor Levieux, and Derek Coltman, New York: Orion Press, 1967), 118.

22. Brownell and FLW, 154; and FLW, "New Imperial Hotel," 42.

23. FLW, "New Imperial Hotel," 42.

24. FLW, "In the Wake," 1: 130, 129.

25. Antonin Raymond worked on at least one version of this perspective. It became a sore point in his relationship with Wright and ultimately a cause for the end of his work on the hotel. Raymond claimed that he was "bored"

with having to render the "elaborate detailing" and "extraordinary amount of ornamentation covering the building." "The exterior perspective of the Imperial Hotel, which I had to do to the minutest detail, was one of the main causes of my revolt" (Raymond, *Autobiography*, 71). A letter from Wright to Raymond, preserved in the Wright Archives, tells a different story. Wright fired him on 8 February 1921 with the following remarks:

The rendering was brought to me yesterday. I am disgusted. I find it hopeless.

After waiting something over one month more for something to make good your facile promises—I find this,—a greasy photographic print with about ten hours work upon it intended to resemble nothing so much as a dung hill in a mud puddle. (FLWF)

For an indication of what this version may look like, see Raymond, *Autobiography*, 72.

26. So far as I know, the only place where Wright described the attributes of the two warrior figures was in his article, "The New Imperial Hotel," in the April 1923 issue of *WA*, and there only in the captions. The Viking figure is described as "typifying the Occident" (p. 39), and the Samurai "the Orient" (p. 41).

27. FLW, "New Imperial Hotel," 44.

28. It goes without saying that this final statement should be taken both figuratively and literally: one of the reasons for constructing a Western-style hotel was to create an environment where Europeans and Americans could meet Japanese around tables with chairs.

29. In the early 1950s, Wright further elaborated on the compromises he made between modernism and tradition, and gave a less instrumental, more self-consciously cultural meaning to his actions: "I have sometimes been asked why I did not make the opus more 'modern.' The answer is that there was a tradition there worthy of respect and I felt it my duty as well as my privilege to make the building belong to them so far as I might" (*Sixty Years of Living Architecture: The Work of Frank Lloyd Wright* [New York: Solomon R. Guggenheim Museum, 1953], [7]). Resonances of this contextualist strain of thought in Wright's late work will be discussed in Chapter XI.

30. Wright did, however, make an important point of referring to the Imperial Hotel as a "transition building" (*A* I, 225), meaning not only that it was intended to effect a transition in the way of building and of life for the Japanese but also that it carried within its design the effects of a major transition in his own life and way of thinking about architecture. It was through the subject of "transition" that he introduced the discussion of Hollyhock House (ibid.).

31. Brownell and FLW, 133.

32. See especially *A* I, 213–16; and FLW, "In the Wake," pts. 1 and 2. An early description and set of specifications confirm that Wright had originally intended the roof to be "tiled with a specially designed clay tile, dipped in a copper greenslip" and the "trimming members" of the exterior brick walls to be of concrete "cast in wooden molds on the ground and set in place as stone or tile would." "The plans," he noted, "are designed for a structure of secure masonry supports set upon a concrete foundation. The foundation rests with ample area upon the gravel bed underlying the surface of the lot about six feet" (FLW, "The Imperial Hotel, Tokio, Japan. Frank Lloyd Wright—Architect. To be erected for the Imperial Hotel Company, Limited, Tokio, Japan," n.d., pp. 7, 4, MS 2401. 535 A, FLWF).

Stewart, *Modern Japanese Architecture*, 33, 43, points out that the system of reinforced brick construction used by Wright had been popular in Japan since the end of the nineteenth century, and that the "floating foundations" Wright claimed to have invented were introduced by the firm of Ende and Böckmann by 1895.

33. In a way, the Imperial Hotel was still fundamentally a Prairie Style building in its general form and details. This is especially evident in the pre-fire design. In submitting the building to such a totalizing natural motif as the shape of a mountain, Wright was following the line set forth in Taliesin but developing it in a more circumscribed way. The contradictions in scale between the overall shape and individual details proved difficult to manage in

many ways. The problem would remain with him throughout the work of the late teens and twenties and not really be resolved until the end of that decade (see Chapters VI and VII).

34. FLW, "In the Wake," 1: 130. Toward the end of his life, Hayashi reportedly told Kazu Shimizu that Wright first saw the Oya tuff used on a building in Tokyo while walking with him on Aoyama Avenue. Wright then went to the area where the stone was quarried and had the hotel buy three acres of mountain land in the village of Shiroyama, in Tochigi Prefecture (*The Imperial*, 98–99).

35. FLW, "Why the Earthquake Did Not Destroy the Hotel," 63; FLW, "In the Wake," 1: 130; and *A* I, 194.

36. An exception is Otto Graf, who devoted nearly half of the second volume of his study of Wright to an elaborate analysis of the geometry of the Imperial Hotel and its significance for Wright's entire *oeuvre* (*Die Kunst des Quadrats: Zum Werk von Frank Lloyd Wright*, 2 vols. [Vienna, Cologne, and Graz: Hermann Böhlaus Nachf., 1983] 2: 307ff). More recently, see Alofsin, *Lost Years*, 201–20.

37. In the concluding section of the two-part article "In the Wake of the Quake," published in *WA* in February 1924, Wright wrote: "To attack the popular giant [commercial architecture] openly is to go like David—sling and stone in hand. The stone in my sling is the Imperial Hotel. I, too, know my aim" (p. 20).

38. FLW, "Why the Earthquake Did Not Destroy the Hotel," 62–63.

39. The war broke out in Europe in the first few days of August 1914. President Woodrow Wilson declared American neutrality on 4 August. Japan entered the fray on 15 August, the same day as the Taliesin fire and murders, when it sent an ultimatum to Germany demanding the withdrawal of German warships from Chinese and Japanese waters within a month. It also demanded the surrender of Kiaochow to Japan by that same time. Japan acted in accord with the Anglo-Japanese Agreement of Alliance which had been renewed in 1911.

40. Rosalind Krauss and Jane Livingston, *L'Amour fou: Photography & Surrealism* (Washington, D.C., and New York: Corcoran Gallery of Art, Abbeville Press, 1985), 86 ("Corpus Delicti").

41. FLW, *Experimenting with Human Lives* (Chicago and Hollywood: Ralph Fletcher Seymour, Fine Art Society, Olive Hill, 1923), 1. The copy of this pamphlet I consulted has only the Fine Art Society, Olive Hill imprint. The information regarding Seymour comes from Robert L. Sweeney, *Frank Lloyd Wright: An Annotated Bibliography*, Art and Architecture Bibliographies, no. 5 (Los Angeles: Hennessey & Ingalls, 1978), 29.

There are now three books on Hollyhock House: Donald Hoffmann, *Frank Lloyd Wright's Hollyhock House* (New York: Dover, 1992); Kathryn Smith, *Frank Lloyd Wright, Hollyhock House and Olive Hill: Buildings and Projects for Aline Barnsdall* (New York: Rizzoli International, 1992); and James Steele, *Barnsdall House: Frank Lloyd Wright*, Architecture in Detail (London: Phaidon, 1992). The Smith book incorporates and supersedes her earlier "Frank Lloyd Wright, Hollyhock House, and Olive Hill, 1919–1924," *JSAH* 38 (March 1979): 15–33, to which my understanding of the commission was heavily indebted. See also: Francis William Vreeland, "A New Art Centre for the Pacific Coast," *Arts and Decoration* 28 (November 1927): 64–65; Norman Bel Geddes, *Miracle in the Evening: An Autobiography*, ed. William Kelley (Garden City, N.Y.: Doubleday, 1960), 146ff.; Harwell Hamilton Harris, *Architecture as an Art* (Clinton, Ia.: Fingernail Moon Press, 1969); Henry Sutherland, "Strange Saga of Barnsdall Park," *Los Angeles Times*, 15 March 1970, sec. C, pp. 1–3; Art Ronnie, "Hollyhock—The Wright House," *Westways* 66 (November 1974): 18–22, 86; K. Smith, "Aline Barnsdall, Hollyhock House—Los Angeles," *FLWN* 1 (January–February 1978): 9–10; Charles Lockwood, "The Wright House for the Wrong Woman," *Antiques World* (November 1980): 68–73; Esther McCoy, *Vienna to Los Angeles: Two Journeys* (Santa Monica: Arts and Architecture Press, 1979), esp. 79–83; Alice T. Friedman, "A House Is Not a Home: Hollyhock House as 'Art-Theater Garden,'" *JSAH* 51 (September 1992): 239–60; and Norman M. and Dorothy K. Karasick, *The Oilman's Daughter: A Biography of Aline Barnsdall* (Encino, Calif.: Carleston Publishing, 1993). I would like to thank Virginia Ernst Kazor for providing me with a copy of this biography. For early publications of drawings and photographs, see Wendingen 1925, 131–63; and H[einrich] de Fries, ed., *Frank Lloyd Wright: Aus dem Lebenswerke eines Architekten* (Berlin: Ernst Pollak, 1926). Wright's description of the commission is in *A* I, 225–34.

An earlier version of this section of the book appeared in my "Landscape into Architecture: Frank Lloyd Wright's Hollyhock House and the Romance of Southern California," *Art in America* 71 (September 1983): 150–65; and *AA Files: Annals of the Architectural Association School of Architecture* 3 (January 1983): 22–41.

42. Barnsdall to FLW, 27 July 1916, FLWF. The actual date of the commission has never been firmly established. Wright said he met Barnsdall "shortly after the tragedy at Taliesin while I was still in Chicago at the Cedar Street house. Henry Sell brought her to see me, in connection with a project for a theatre in which she was interested in Los Angeles" (*A* I, 225). A letter from Wright to Barnsdall, postdated "circa: 1915," talks of the theater project and even mentions a "Chicago scheme" (MS 1502.025, FLWF). The first dated letter is the one quoted here, written from Mill Valley, California, in which Barnsdall urges Wright to "work on the theatre plans and get them finished as soon as possible."

43. It should be noted that Wright alternatively used both the Spanish ("romanza") and English ("romance") spellings in his description of Hollyhock House. Although he particularly referred to the musical meaning of the term as a "free form" composition (*A* I, 227), he clearly was also alluding to the narrative conventions of the medieval adventure or love story as appropriate to the Spanish Colonial traditions of the region. For more on the self-criticism implied in the final phrase, see Chapter VI.

44. "New Home for Aline Barnsdall Crowning Olive Hill," *Hollywood Citizen News*, 2 September 1921. The author noted, however, that Wright described the style of the house as "simply Californian." I am grateful to Virginia Kazor for bringing this article to my attention. On the exterior color of the house, see note 70 below.

45. "Will Spend 1 Million Dollars on Olive Hill Improvement; Barnsdall Home Nearing Completion at an Expenditure of $150,000," *Hollywood Citizen News*, 8 July 1921. Again, I am grateful to Virginia Kazor for making this article available to me.

46. According to Charles Lockwood, Barnsdall later maintained that, because of the weight of the concrete doors, she needed "three men and two boys to help me get in and out of my house" ("Wright House," 71).

47. Although the pool still exists, the fountain and the stream have long since disappeared.

48. In early 1920, while the house was under construction, Barnsdall told Wright that she was planning, in the spring, to visit "Sicily, Greece, and Egypt—the two great architectures of the past," adding that "I am just ready for them" (Barnsdall to FLW, 29 January 1920, FLWF).

49. There is still some confusion about the date of the design illustrated in fig. 112 and whether it was for Chicago or for California (see note 42 above). For biographical and historical information about Barnsdall, see Hoffmann, *Wright's Hollyhock House*, 1–14; and Smith, *Wright, Hollyhock House and Olive Hill*, 15–23.

50. Constance D'Arcy Mackay, *The Little Theatre in the United States* (New York: Henry Holt, 1917), 156–58; and Sheldon Cheney, *The Art Theatre* (New York: Alfred A. Knopf, 1917), 197–98. Among the numerous luminaries of the movie world who attended the opening night of Barnsdall's Little Theatre of Los Angeles on 31 October 1916 were: Charlie Chaplin, D. W. Griffith, Cecil B. DeMille, Erich von Stroheim, Douglas Fairbanks, Francis X. Bushman, Theda Bara, Jesse Lasky, Samuel Goldfish (later Goldwyn), Thomas Ince, and Harold Lloyd (Bel Geddes, *Miracle*, 167). Between 1915 and 1922 or so there was a growing together of the so-called legitimate theater and the movies, which seemed to promise a fusion of the two fields. Aline Barnsdall was not the only one to think of establishing a little theater in Los Angeles: in 1917 the Pasadena Community Playhouse Group was founded by Gilmore Brown; and in 1918 Christine Wetherill Stevenson, a patroness of the Little Theater movement in Philadelphia, began her connection with Krotona by sponsoring thirty-five outdoor performances of "The Light of Asia."

51. Barnsdall to FLW, 27 July 1916. Barnsdall went on to say that she wanted "to get the land within the next two months" and "build [the] theatre

within the next six months." She was "only waiting for [her] father's very definate [*sic*] consent."

As evidence for the existence of drawings for the house prior to Wright's 1916–17 trip to Japan, both Hoffmann, *Wright's Hollyhock House*, 9, and Smith, *Wright, Hollyhock House and Olive Hill*, 39, refer to the recollections of Norman Bel Geddes and Antonin Raymond. In his autobiography published in 1960, Bel Geddes recalled a visit with Barnsdall to Wright's office in Chicago sometime in the summer of 1916, where they were shown drawings of the theater as well as the house. Of the house, Bel Geddes had this so say:

Its exterior was very original, although it looked more like a miniature palace of some ancient civilization than a contemporary private home. Aline was very interested in the location of the building on her property, and pointed out that the steep hill which dominated would affect all building plans. Wright agreed with this. "You are right this time, Aline. To plan a building you must start with the land. I have walked over your hill. The plan will fit it. I began the same way on the Tokyo hotel, only in this instance earthquakes had to be provided for." (Miracle, 156–57)

Raymond, who went to work for Wright at Taliesin in the late spring or summer of 1916, noted that, aside from "some early sketches made of the Barnsda[ll] House in Hollywood," there was "hardly any work in the office" (Raymond, *Autobiography*, 53).

Where Hoffmann allows that Wright might indulge in "sketching a project long before any site was secured" in order to "hold a client's interest" (p. 9), he never asserts that Wright designed the house without the Olive Hill site in mind. He simply wonders "how much of the house" Wright might have imagined before Barnsdall "bought the site" (p. 15). By contrast, Smith makes a point of maintaining that "when Wright made the drawings [of the house], Barnsdall had not chosen Los Angeles as the location" (p. 43) and that he therefore proceeded "with no site or definite location in mind" (p. 25). Although Smith uses Bel Geddes as a significant part of her argument for a 1916 date for the preliminary sketches of the house, she ignores his recollection of Wright's discussion of the site with Barnsdall. She does, however, refer to a 1958 letter from Wright to his son Lloyd noting that "Barnsdall had acquired Olive Hill on his advice" (p. 50). She suggests that this is possibly related to a request from Barnsdall of Wright, in early October 1918, to meet with her lawyer, if she was unable to be in Los Angeles at the time, to try "to get permission to build" on the site she had in mind (Barnsdall to FLW, 6 October 1918, FLWF). Since there is no evidence she was asking for his advice at this point, or that the site was unknown to her, it would seem that if Wright made certain suggestions about the choice of site, it had to be prior to then.

The first actual mention of the house in the correspondence is in a letter from Barnsdall to Wright of 30 May 1918. After noting that she "can't say anything more definate [*sic*] about the theatre . . . until the estate is settled," she says: "The house I can build in the fall, if its cost is not over $25,000" (FLWF). The earliest known record of payment specifically for drawings for the house is 27 September 1919. It is for $625, which is the "Balance of 2½% Commission of Preliminary sketches for Dwelling," meaning that at least one previous payment had taken place (Clarence Thomas to FLW, 27 September 1919, MS 1502.025, FLWF). This final installment followed directly on the signing of the contract for the house, the theater, a director's house, and a dwelling for actors, dated 15 September 1919 (MS 1502.025, FLWF). Bel Geddes later claimed that the house and theater were both preliminarily designed in 1916 (*Miracle*, 155, 161), but this would seem to have been impossible.

52. Barnsdall to FLW, undated note [1917?], Fiche B, FLWF. This note, which apparently has not been microfiched by the Getty, was filed in the Wright Archives between a letter of 2 December [1917?] and one of 4 January 1918. The information about the visit to the site by Barnsdall's father was kindly provided to me by Virginia Kazor. The visit took place in either December 1916 or January 1917. Barnsdall had referred to the need to get her father's consent in a letter to Wright of 27 July 1916 (see note 51 above). But, in a letter to Wright of early December possibly 1916 though probably 1917, Barnsdall speaks of the plans for the theater and asks: "Can you do anything without seeing the land?" (2 December [1917?], FLWF).

53. Barnsdall to FLW, 30 May 1918, FLWF. In this letter, written from Seattle, Barnsdall said: "I may have to begin here instead of L. A. Its [sic] makes no difference—'a thing of beauty is a joy anywhere.' Seattle is virgin soil not spoilt by 'art movements.'" In the undated note referred to above (note 52), Barnsdall hinted that cost might also have been a factor. She told Wright that the owners of the Olive Hill site were "holding it impossibly high, so I may have to look for another site when you come out."

54. Rudolph Schindler to Barnsdall, 6 April 1919, MS 1502.253, D. Blair Gift, FLWF. This letter, along with other letters and telegrams between Schindler and Barnsdall from 14 March to 9 June 1919, is in a group recently acquired by the Wright Archives. They document the discussions over the three-month period just prior to the purchase of Olive Hill and indicate that there was never, at least during this period of time, any question about the location of the site. I particularly want to thank Bruce Pfeiffer for making them available to me.

55. The highest point, just to the east of the circular pool, at the semi-circular band of lawn, is actually 488′6″ above sea level. The patio court is about 1′6″ lower. Griffith J. Griffith, who in 1896 gave the City of Los Angeles the three thousand-acre park on the slopes of the Hollywood Hills that bears his name, had intended to build a "large tourist hotel" on the Olive Hill site. See Edwin O. Palmer, *History of Hollywood* (1938; rev. and enl. ed., rpt. New York: Garland, 1978), 115.

56. Florence Lawrence, "Eminence to Be Made Rare Beauty Spot," *Los Angeles Examiner*, 6 July 1919, p. 5. See also Sutherland, "Strange Saga."

57. The chronology is worked out most carefully in Smith, *Wright, Hollyhock House and Olive Hill*, 48–117.

58. Bel Geddes, *Miracle*, 164, 162. Cf. Wendell Cole, "The Theatre Projects of Frank Lloyd Wright," *Educational Theatre Journal* 12 (May 1960): 86–93. For the evolution of Wright's theater design from 1915/16 through 1920, see Smith, *Wright, Hollyhock House and Olive Hill*, 204–10.

59. Wendell Cole has noted that "possibly Wright's Barnsdall Theatre shows the influence of the contemporary interest in California in so-called 'Greek' theatres." He points to the fact that by 1918 "at least five outdoor 'Greek' theatres had been built in California since the first had been constructed at Point Loma in 1901" ("Theatre Projects," 88–89). Friedman, "House Is Not a Home," 247–54, elaborates on the background of the open-air theater movement, citing John Galen Howard's Hearst Greek Theatre, Berkeley, Calif., built in 1903, and Sheldon Cheney's *The Open-Air Theatre* (New York: M. Kennerley, 1918) as significant occurrences.

60. As noted above (note 51), the first written evidence of Barnsdall's intention to build a house to accompany the theater occurred in late May 1918, at which point she already seemed to be deferring the construction of the theater in favor of her house. On 6 October 1918, she told Wright quite specifically what she wanted: "I wonder if you would find me a nice rug for my living room, while you are in Japan? I want all the living room and small alcove in light natural wood, much as your own house is—and much the same light & color—like sunshine on a late autumn afternoon. . . . I don't want pictures on my walls in ridiculous frames. . . . [I want] to have a house with some of the unity of the outdoors" (Barnsdall to FLW, FLWF).

61. On Schindler's role, see McCoy, *Vienna to Los Angeles*, passim. For these early years of Schindler's move to California, see also Kathryn Smith, *R. M. Schindler House, 1921–22* (West Hollywood: Friends of the Schindler House, 1987).

62. Barnsdall to FLW, 7 January 1920, FLWF.

63. FLW, "In the Cause of Architecture: The Third Dimension," 9 February 1923, MS III/2, J. L. Wright Collection, p. 12. This essay appeared in somewhat edited form in Wendingen 1925, 59.

64. Barnsdall to FLW, 30 May 1920, FLWF.

65. FLW, "Why I Love Wisconsin," in Gutheim, *FLW on Arch.*, 158.

66. *A* II, 226 (the phrase "in the changed circumstances" was added in the second edition); *A* I, 227; and *Sixty Years of Living Architecture*, [8].

67. *A* II, 226 (in the original edition, Wright said "sentimentality"); and *A* I, 240. Cf. Esther McCoy, *Five California Architects* (New York: Reinhold, 1960); and David Gebhard, "The Spanish Colonial Revival in Southern California (1895–1930)," *JSAH* 26 (May 1967): 131–47.

68. Reyner Banham remarked on the "geometrical banalities of its

conspicuously *beaux arts* plan" in "The Wilderness Years of Frank Lloyd Wright," *JRIBA* 75 (December 1969): 515. It should be noted that both the Imperial Hotel and Midway Gardens had stages terminating the central axis. In the Imperial Hotel, it was a one-thousand-seat theater with a revolving stage; in Midway Gardens, it was a semicircular orchestra shell, similar in shape to the stepped seats around the circular pool at the eastern end of Hollyhock House.

69. The reporter for the *Hollywood Citizen News* (2 September 1921) described entering the patio from the "courtyard entrance" under the "bedrooms . . . built across the east end of the house" ("New Home for Aline Barnsdall"). All the site plans of 1919–20 show this path quite clearly.

70. Although the color of the stucco is now beige, the original color of the exterior was almost surely a pale greenish-gray. In 1921 the reporter for the *Hollywood Citizen News* described the tint "as near an approach as possible to the silver green slopes" of the "foothills of the Sierras" ("New Home for Aline Barnsdall"). In an article in the *Los Angeles Examiner*, which appeared right after she purchased the site, Barnsdall was quoted as saying that "Mr. Wright and I have differed on only one point. He wants my house to be white, and I think a white house is too glaring for Southern California. So no matter what he says my house will not be white" (Lawrence, "Eminence to Be Made Rare Beauty Spot"). In the letter of 29 January 1920, Barnsdall told Wright that she did not "want [the house] to *look* green but to *feel* green as a background for the rich hollyhock and rose reds." That statement, however, came up in the context of a discussion of the interior decoration of the house and therefore may not be relevant to the exterior. Hoffmann, *Wright's Hollyhock House*, 37, says the exterior walls were stained "a light gray-green" in order to "suggest the subtle tint of olive leaves."

71. Lawrence, "Eminence to Be Made Rare Beauty Spot."

72. Kathryn Smith first suggested the connection between the court and its possible use as an outdoor theater in "Wright, Hollyhock House, and Olive Hill," 27–28. In her more recent book, *Wright, Hollyhock House and Olive Hill*, she emphasizes the formal similarities over the actual function, noting that while the space *could have* served as a theater, "Wright and Barnsdall left no documentary evidence that the court was designed as an outdoor theater" (pp. 79, 217n5). Friedman, "House Is Not a Home," 247–49, concludes that the court's role as a theater was probably more symbolic than real.

One should note, however, that in 1927 Francis William Vreeland referred to the "patio theatre" as "a gem of architectural, engineering and landscaping invention, ingenuity and charm," indicating that its use for dramatic productions had already been established by that time ("New Art Centre," 65). He went on to describe "its patio-embraced 'auditorium'" as "a sunken, grass-rugged garden," with a "circular lily pool" being "situated immediately beneath a massive, vine-draped proscenium." "The proscenium span and supporting piers," he added, "provide visible and concealed exits to and from the house for the actors and a complete equipment for hidden flood and spot lights for spectacular illumination of the stage area. Three rising steps in concrete form the rear boundary . . . and make an inverted or receding semicircular 'apron' for the elevated stage . . . the steps mounting to and establishing the stage level." Describing the uses to which the house would be put when it became the property of the California Art Club, he said: "In the patio theatre pageants, classical, interpretive and costume dances and out-of-doors dramatic performances will be given." It is also interesting to note that, in his description of Hollyhock House in his article entitled "Frank Lloyd Wright" that originally appeared in *Wendingen* in 1921 and was republished in 1925, Berlage spoke of "the architecture of a summer garden with an open-air theatre" (repr. in Wendingen 1925, 84). Since he knew the building only from plans and photographs, it is interesting to speculate on the origin of this information.

73. The reporter for the *Hollywood Citizen News* (2 September 1921) referred to the upper-level terrace as a "roof observatory" and the free-standing hollyhocks as "totem-pole looking concrete posts" ("New Home for Aline Barnsdall"). The roof was to have been entirely paved with tiles, but this was never done. Only the low area over the living room loggia is tiled.

The roof garden of Hollyhock House is one of the earliest examples of this modernist idea, which Le Corbusier codified in his "five points of modern architecture." It should also be remembered that Schindler and Neutra, who both worked with Wright before going out on their own, made such outdoor living, especially in their early designs for the Lovells, a conspicuous part of their approach to modern architecture. Wright remarked that "Hollyhock House became known as a work of fine art in the various ateliers of the continent where [Barnsdall] would go every summer. Europeans came and saw in it something of the higher harmony of the spirit of man" (*A* I, 233).

74. FLW, "In the Cause: Third Dimension," 12 (italics added).

75. Quoted in Ronnie, "Hollyhock," 20. Lloyd Wright, who helped supervise the building of Hollyhock House, always claimed that the Pueblo influence was paramount. According to him, Hollyhock House "was called modern and Mayan; but no one realized what father was giving them. He had submerged himself into the area in spirit and developed a true expression or architectural characteristic of the Southwest—his Romanza. What he had built was a mesa silhouette, terrace on terrace, characterized and developed by Pueblo Indians" (ibid.). In an interview with me in August 1976, he repeated the same thought. See also Smith, "Wright, Hollyhock House, and Olive Hill," 27n35; Gebhard and von Breton, *Lloyd Wright*, 30–32, 72n17; and Banham, "Wilderness Years," 515. It should be noted that in 1912–13, while Lloyd Wright was working in his office, Irving Gill designed one of the earliest and most interesting Pueblo Revival projects, the Casas Grandes housing scheme for Homer Laughlin.

76. For the impact of Maya architecture in particular on Wright, and the Precolumbian in general, see Dimitri Tselos, "Exotic Influences in the Architecture of Frank Lloyd Wright," *Magazine of Art* 47 (April 1953): 160–69, 184; Gabriel Weisberg, "Frank Lloyd Wright and Pre-Columbian Art—the Background for his Architecture," *Art Quarterly* 30 (Spring 1967): 40–51; Tselos, "Frank Lloyd Wright and World Architecture," *JSAH* 28 (March 1969): 58–72; and Scully, *Wright*, 24–25. More interesting than the citing of specific sources is the collocation of Mesoamerican and North American Indian references. The cultural continuity of these two major groups, one traditionally considered a "high" culture and the other a "low" one, was being firmly established in progressive anthropological thought at the time and would emerge on a more popular level by the later 1930s (see Chapter IX). For a general overview of the so-called Mayan Revival, see Marjorie I. Ingle, *The Mayan Revival Style: Art Deco Mayan Fantasy* (Salt Lake City: G. M. Smith, Peregrine Smith, 1984).

77. On the German Warehouse, see Randolph C. Henning, "The A. D. German Warehouse: A Rehabilitation and Adaptive Reuse Design," M. Arch. thesis, University of Wisconsin, Milwaukee, 1980 (Ann Arbor: University Microfilms, 1985); and Margaret Scott, *Frank Lloyd Wright's Warehouse in Richland Center, Wisconsin* (Richland Center: Richland County Publishers, 1984). On the Bogk House, see Harriet Riddle, "F. C. Bogk House, Milwaukee, Wisconsin," *FLWN* 2 (1979): 1–4. The starting date of the German Warehouse project is usually given as 1915. Margaret Scott points out that the Badger Hotel, on the site of which the warehouse would be built, was not demolished until late 1916, after being auctioned off on 18 November of that year. Approximately a month before, Albert Dell German, who owned the hotel, made public his plans for the site, saying that Wright was at work preparing a project (Scott, *Wright's Warehouse*, 99–112). The building was left unfinished in 1921.

Alofsin, *Lost Years*, 225, notes that Wright visited the Panama-California Exposition in San Diego in 1915 with Alfonso Ianelli, where he saw the exhibition of Precolumbian art and culture in the main California Building. The exhibition featured a large relief map of Central America indicating the distribution of the major archaeological sites; sculptural casts from Palenque and Quiriguá; frescoes by Carlos Vierrà of the sites of Copan, Tikal, Palenque, Quiriguá, Chichen Itzá, and Uxmal; and large-scale architectural models of the pyramid at Chichen (El Castillo) and the Governor's Palace at Uxmal. For an overview of the exhibition, see Edgar L. Hewett, "Ancient Art of the Panama-California Exposition," *Art and Archaeology* 2 (November 1915): 64–102.

78. D. H. Lawrence, "America, Listen to Your Own," orig. pub. *New Republic* (1920), repr. in *Phoenix: The Posthumous Papers of D. H. Lawrence, 1936*, ed. Edward D. McDonald (1936; Harmondsworth: Penguin, 1978), 90–91. Vincent Scully was the first to note the relation between Wright's search for "new roots to fix himself upon the continent" and Lawrence's contemporaneous writings in *Studies in Classic American Literature* (1923) about the "Spirit of Place" in America revealed to him through his contact with Indian culture when he visited Taos in the late teens (Scully, *Wright*, 24).

In his classic account of Maya sites, John L. Stephens wrote: "It is the spectacle of a people skilled in architecture, sculpture and drawing, . . . not derived from the Old World, but originating and growing up here, without models or masters, having a distinct, separate, independent existence; like the plants and fruits of the soil, indigenous" (*Incidents of Travel in Central America, Chiapas and Yucatan*, 2 vols. [1841; rpt. New York: Dover, 1969], 2: 442).

79. FLW, *A Testament* (New York: Horizon Press, 1957), 111; and Brownell and FLW, 33–34.

80. Ibid.; and *A* I, 239. Wright spoke of the "*stone-built*" character of Maya decoration in "In the Cause of Architecture, III: The Meaning of Materials—Stone," *ARec* 63 (April 1928): 352. Ironically, most classic Maya architecture is actually closer to Hollyhock House in structure than Wright thought, since the carved stone was generally simply a revetment of the rubble core.

81. FLW, *Testament*, 111–12.

82. In her early article on Hollyhock House, Kathryn Smith stated that the water was pumped first to the square pool in front of the living room, whence it flowed to the circular pool under the bridge. In conversation, she has assured me that it probably went the way I describe it, that is, from the circular to the square pool. This is the way Hoffmann, *Wright's Hollyhock House*, 65, also describes it. A pump house, variously called the spring house or fountain house on the plans, is located to the southeast of the house, slightly down the slope, at the far end of what was to have been a swimming pool. It would have fed the lower lake, planned for the Vermont Avenue facade of the theater, through a stream running down the hillside and under a bridge on the southern flank of the theater.

83. In the earlier Dana House, there is a pool of water diagonally opposite the fireplace in the entrance hall, along the wall leading to the garden; and in the nearly contemporaneous Bogk House, Wright again placed a pool inside the house near the fireplace, this time creating a kind of conservatory separating the dining room from the living room. But Hollyhock House is the first time he set the fireplace itself within a pool of water. Just after that, in one of the houses for the Doheny Ranch Development project of 1923 (House C), Wright set the two-sided fireplace within a pool giving onto the rear courtyard and allowed the stream of water coming down the hill to run under the front court and reappear below the prow in a waterfall (fig. 141). This idea obviously culminated in the combined images of water and fire in Fallingwater. Thereafter Wright sometimes returned to the trough idea of Hollyhock House with less symbolic purpose as, for example, in the Brown House in Kalamazoo, Mich. (1950).

84. The living room is approximately 24 feet long by 48 feet wide. The fireplace mass, from pier to pier, is a little over 12 feet wide. The decorative mantel is approximately 63 inches high by 124 inches long.

85. The fireplace of the Winslow House, by contrast, is on the long wall of the central entrance hall, directly opposite the door, and is therefore seen head-on upon entering the house. In the Dana House, the fireplace occupies a similar position in relation to the entrance, but it is on the short side of the galleried, two-story entrance space. In the Henderson House in Elmhurst, Ill. (1901), the fireplace is on the long side of the living room, but one enters the room from behind it. The same is true in the project for the Clarke House in Peoria, Ill. (1904), the project for the Shaw House in Montreal (1906), the project for a "Fireproof house for $5,000," published in the *Ladies' Home Journal* (1906), the project for three rental houses for Edward Waller for River Forest, Ill. (1909), Taliesin (fig. 72) and the Bagley House in Grand Beach, Mich. (1915). In the Glasner House (fig. 53) and the May House, Grand Rapids, Mich. (1908–1909), the fireplace is located in the long wall opposite the entrance to the room, though not in its visual center. The second scheme proposed for the Adams House in Oak Park (1913) comes closest to the eventual situation in Hollyhock House.

86. Although the painted mantels in the lounges off the main lobby and promenade of the Imperial Hotel were asymmetrical, they nonetheless remained purely decorative, like those in Midway Gardens. For the reading of the Hollyhock House mantel, I am particularly indebted to my wife, Gillian, and to Anne Higonnet.

87. It is interesting to note that Louise and Walter Arensberg, whose unique art collection included major works by Duchamp, Picabia, and Brancusi, moved to Los Angeles in the early 1920s and lived at Residence A on the

Barnsdall estate soon after it was finished (Smith, "Wright, Hollyhock House, and Olive Hill," 31). Wright would have had a chance to see the new European art in the Armory Show exhibition, which traveled to Chicago in 1913 and which Wright referred to obliquely in *A* I, 179–80, in the discussion of Midway Gardens.

88. This was described to me by Lloyd Wright in an interview in Los Angeles in August 1976 and is repeated in Smith, "Wright, Hollyhock House, and Olive Hill," 27n5. Bruce Pfeiffer has said that the fireplace relief was named "The Princess and the Desert" (*FLWPS*, vol. 10, 1).

89. Sometimes, in radial sandpaintings, the center of the composition marking the place of action is identified with a body of water, such as a pool or lake, by an actual bowl or cup of water sunk in the ground flush with the surface of the painting, and thus occupying the spot where the fire would normally be.

90. The furniture, which can be seen in early photographs, was reconstructed in 1990 based on survey drawings by Roderick Grant.

91. The "modern primitivism" of Brancusi's work, with its references both to contemporary streamlining and to organic nature, bears a powerful resemblance to Wright's work from this time on. In the five levels of the totem-like *King of Kings* (c. 1920), Brancusi intended to symbolize the realms of earth, water, fire, air, and ether.

92. The pool was apparently supposed to contain goldfish ("New Home for Aline Barnsdall"). The sunlight during the day must have been quite strong, and a shed roof over the skylight was added later. This surely explains the heavy curtain in early photographs, as well as the bleached-out appearance of the grid containing the glass. Edgar Tafel, who visited the house as a Taliesin apprentice in the 1930s, wrote that the skylight over the fireplace allowed one to "see the stars and the moon reflected in the water" and this was "the *romanza* element" (*Apprentice to Genius: Years with Frank Lloyd Wright* [New York: McGraw-Hill, 1979], 122).

93. Brownell and FLW, 19.

94. John Steven McGroarty, *Los Angeles from the Mountains to the Sea*, 3 vols. (Chicago and New York: American Historical Society, 1921), 1: 228; and Frank Fenton, *A Place in the Sun*, quoted in Carey McWilliams, *Southern California: An Island on the Land* (1946; rpt. Santa Barbara and Salt Lake City: Peregrine Smith, 1973), 269. Wright added the word "midwest" in the second edition of his *Autobiography*.

95. Palmer, *Hollywood*, 24. Cf. McWilliams, *Southern California*, 200–204. There were earthquakes in Los Angeles in 1920 (Inglewood) and 1933 (Long Beach–Compton), and one in Santa Barbara in 1925.

96. FLW, *Experimenting with Human Lives*, 1.

97. Bel Geddes, *Miracle*, 157.

98. Smith, *Wright, Hollyhock House and Olive Hill*, 43, uses this invention to support her contention that the site was merely an "imaginary" one in these early drawings. The low, saddle-backed Silver Lake hill does in fact rise up directly to the east of Olive Hill. Although it is nowhere near as monumental as Wright made it seem, it could have been his starting point.

99. FLW, "Hollyhock House, Hollywood," pp. 6–7, MS 4201.035 B, FLWF. Cf. the paragraph that comes shortly after this in the published version: "Now, with a radical client, like Aline Barnsdall, a site like Olive Hill, a climate like California, an architect himself head on for Freedom, something had to happen—even by 'proxy.' This 'Romance' of California had to '*come out.*' I couldn't *play* it, more's the pity perhaps. And yet, there would have been no Hollyhock House if I could. To 'play' it would have been the only alternative" (*A* I, 229; italics added).

100. Barnsdall commissioned the design in March 1923 for a twenty-four-acre hillside site on Summit Ridge Drive, north of Pickfair, the estate of Mary Pickford and Douglas Fairbanks. The house was designed to be built in concrete block, the system of construction Wright began experimenting with at that time (see Chapter VI). Nothing eventually came of this commission. See Smith, *Wright, Hollyhock House and Olive Hill*, 164–71.

101. For a most moving description of the inspirational quality of Hollyhock House in its state of disuse, see Harris, *Architecture as an Art*.

102. Quoted in John W. Cook and Heinrich Klotz, *Conversations with Architects* (New York and Washington: Praeger, 1973), 183. Kahn began this answer to the interviewer's question by saying: "No. Never build for need! . . . As an art a space is made a touch of eternity. I think a space evokes its use. It transcends need" (p. 183).

Chapter VI
From Los Angeles to Lake Tahoe and Death Valley

1. FLW, review of *Towards a New Architecture*, by Le Corbusier, *World Unity* 2 (September 1928): 393–95. The publisher of *World Unity*, Horace Holley, was a friend of Wright. The review itself was relatively favorable. Though pointing to the debt the younger Europeans owed to his and Sullivan's work, Wright was nowhere as acrimonious as he would become a few years later. For Wright's relations with Europe at this time, see Heidemarie Kief, *Der Einfluss Frank Lloyd Wrights auf die Mitteleuropäische Einzelhausarchitektur: Ein Beitrag zum Verhältnis von Architektur und Natur im 20. Jahrhundert*, diss. Darmstadt, 1978 (Stuttgart: Karl Krämer, 1978), esp. 100ff.

2. See, e.g., Hugh Ferriss, *The Metropolis of Tomorrow* (New York: Ives Washburn, 1929); and Giorgio Ciucci et al., *The American City: From the Civil War to the New Deal* (1973; trans. Barbara Luigia La Penta, Cambridge, Mass.: MIT Press, 1983), esp. 389–528 (Tafuri, "The Disenchanted Mountain: The Skyscraper and the City").

3. For an early assessment of the importance of this period for Wright's career as a whole, see Reyner Banham, "The Wilderness Years of Frank Lloyd Wright," *JRIBA* 76 (December 1969): 512–19. For a precise documentation of Wright's concrete-block designs of the decade, we now finally have Sweeney, *Wright in Hollywood*. I am grateful to the author for making his manuscript available to me while I was in the process of editing my text. The best contemporaneous publication of Wright's work of the first half of the twenties is H[einrich] de Fries, *Frank Lloyd Wright: Aus dem Lebenswerke eines Architekten* (Berlin: Ernst Pollak, 1926).

4. See Kathryn Smith, "Frank Lloyd Wright and the Imperial Hotel: A Postscript," *Art Bulletin* 67 (June 1985): 307–10; and Charles Lockwood, "Searching out Wright's Imprint in Los Angeles," *NYT*, 2 December 1984, sec. 10, pp. 9, 32.

5. Since 1915, in fact, Darwin Martin had been encouraging Wright to "circularize" his ideas in the West (Martin to FLW, 8 November 1915, Box 4-2, Wright-Martin Papers).

6. FLW, "In the Cause of Architecture: Second Paper," *ARec* 35 (May 1914): 407.

7. FLW to Martin, 20 August 1922, Box 4-13, Wright-Martin Papers.

8. Cf. H. Allen Brooks, *The Prairie School: Frank Lloyd Wright and His Midwest Contemporaries* (New York: W. W. Norton, 1972), 295ff.

9. H. P. Berlage, "Frank Lloyd Wright," orig. pub. *Wendingen* 4 (1921), repr. in Wendingen 1925, 79–85; and FLW to Berlage, 30 November 1922, FLWF. Wright repeated these same thoughts in "In the Cause of Architecture: The Third Dimension," in Wendingen 1925, 57–58. Berlage's reversal from his earlier, more positive position must also be seen in the light of the growing nationalism and anti-Americanism of European modernism in the twenties. Berlage concluded his article by questioning Wright's possible influence and wondered aloud: "Admiration for Wright . . . is comprehensible and . . . is more in evidence on this side of the Ocean than on the other. Even our own country (Holland) where at this moment a modern national architecture is growing, has here and there been unable to escape this 'foreign slur.' But should one regard such a leader with a jealous eye?" Berlage answered that there probably was not too much to fear, since such "outside influences" are usually "of a passing nature" (pp. 84–85). For more on this, see the Conclusion.

10. Cf. Dione Neutra, comp. and trans., *Richard Neutra: Promise and Fulfillment, 1919–1932, Selections from the Letters and Diaries of Richard and Dione Neutra* (Carbondale and Edwardsville: Southern Illinois University Press, 1986), esp. 89–168; Thomas S. Hines Jr., *Richard Neutra and the Search for Modern Architecture: A Biography and History* (New York: Oxford University Press, 1982), 45–67; and "Richard Neutra, Last Writings, Last

Works," *Architettura* 16 (November 1970): 422–72. See also Bruno Zevi, "From the Loos-Mendelsohn-Wright Triangle," *Architettura* 16 (November 1970): 425; and Zevi, *Erich Mendelsohn: opera completa—architetture ed immagini architettoniche* (Milan: ETAS/KOMPASS, 1970).

11. See especially Kenneth Silver, *"Esprit de Corps": The Art of the Parisian Avant-Garde and the First World War, 1914–1925* (Princeton: Princeton University Press, 1989). Henri Matisse, who was almost exactly Wright's age, left his suburban Paris home in 1917–18 for Nice, where he lived until the early 1930s, painting *odalisques* and other scenes of bourgeois luxury that have generally been interpreted as superficial, regressive, and escapist. Wright's atavistic return to ancient American sources, such as the Precolumbian, might well be compared in this connection to Matisse's and Picasso's return to Gallic and Mediterranean roots.

12. Cf. Kenneth Silver, "Purism: Straightening Up after the Great War," *Artforum* 15 (March 1977): 56–63.

13. As noted above (note 3), the definitive study of this structural system is Sweeney, *Wright in Hollywood*. As he points out, the system did not emerge fully developed, but only gradually found its typical form in the year 1923. According to Sweeney, Wright first employed the term "textile-block" in 1927. Sweeney points to a number of important precedents for Wright's use of concrete block, including Lloyd Wright's Bollman House in Los Angeles (1922), Walter Burley Griffin's "Knitlock" system (1916–17), and William E. Nelson's Nel-stone (1920–25). See esp. pp. 204–27. Earlier offerings on the subject are: A. N. Rebori, "Frank Lloyd Wright's Textile-Block Slab Construction," *ARec* 62 (December 1927): 449–56; Donald Leslie Johnson, "Notes on W. B. Griffin's 'Knitlock' and His Architectural Projects for Canberra," *JSAH* 29 (May 1970): 188–93; Charles Lockwood, "Frank Lloyd Wright in Los Angeles," *Portfolio* (February–March 1980): 74–79; Charles Calvo, "The Concrete Block Designs of Frank Lloyd Wright," *Forum voor Architectuur en daarmee verbonden kunsten* 30 (1985–86): 166–75; and Kenneth Frampton, "The Text-Tile Tectonic: The Origin and Evolution of Wright's Woven Architecture," in Robert McCarter, ed., *Frank Lloyd Wright: A Primer on Architectural Principles* (New York: Princeton Architectural Press, 1991), 124–49. In the early 1950s, Wright rebaptized the textile-block system "Usonian Automatic" and gave it a new lease on life.

14. As noted above, Wright began using the term "textile-block" only in 1927.

15. Comparing his invention to the great Renaissance architects' rediscovery of Rome, Wright wrote in the *Autobiography*: "Palladio! Bramante! Sansovino. Sculptors—all! Here was I the 'Weaver.' What might not now grow out of this little commonplace circumstance?" (I, 245). On Semper's theory of the role that textiles played in the origin of architectural form, see Gottfried Semper, *The Four Elements of Architecture & Other Writings*, trans. Harry Francis Mallgrave and Wolfgang Herrmann (Cambridge and New York: Cambridge University Press, 1989); and Herrmann, *Gottfried Semper: In Search of Architecture* (Cambridge, Mass., and London: MIT Press, 1984). Semper's 1869 lecture *Über Baustyle* was first translated in America by Daniel Burnham's partner, John Root, with the aid of Fritz Wagner, and published as the "Development of Architectural Style" in the Chicago-based journal *Inland Architect and News Record* 14 (December 1889): 76–78; (January 1890): 92–94; 15 (February 1890): 5–6; and (March 1890): 32–33. I should like to thank Robin Middleton for stressing to me this connection between Wright and Semper. It was picked up by Frampton in his "Text-Tile Tectonic."

16. Richard J. Neutra, *Wie Baut Amerika?* (Stuttgart: Julius Hoffmann, 1927), esp. 59–77. Neutra conflated Lloyd Wright's concrete-block buildings with his father's and pointedly illustrated them in comparison with the Pueblo examples (pp. 73–75).

17. Wright's description of the Pasadena house is in *A* I, 239–50. An earlier, shorter version was published as "A Building Adventure in Modernism: A Successful Adventure in Concrete," *Country Life* 56 (May 1929): 40–41. George Millard, who died in 1918, had been manager of the rare-books department of McClurg's in Chicago until the couple moved to Pasadena around 1913 and established a business out of their house. Sweeney, *Wright in Hollywood*, 27, maintains that Wright was so eager to build and test out his ideas for concrete block that he may have initiated the commission by "offering to design a new house without charging the standard architect's fee, while reserving an interest in the building in the form of a lien."

18. Cf. Henry-Russell Hitchcock, *Frank Lloyd Wright*, Collection "Les Maîtres de l'Architecture Contemporaine" (Paris: Editions "Cahiers d'Art," 1928), n.p.; and Alfred H. Barr, Henry-Russell Hitchcock, Philip Johnson, and Lewis Mumford, *Modern Architecture: International Exhibition*, 10 February–23 March 1932 (New York: Museum of Modern Art, 1932), 36–38 (Hitchcock, "Frank Lloyd Wright").

19. Wright commented on the "earthquake proof" nature of the textile-block system in *Sixty Years of Living Architecture: The Work of Frank Lloyd Wright* (New York: Solomon R. Guggenheim Museum, 1953), [9].

20. Sweeney, *Wright in Hollywood*, 17–19. The plot plan is #2104.009, FLWF. Doheny's wife, the former Carrie Estelle Betzold, a Midwesterner like her husband, was a major collector of rare books and is known to have been a client of Millard, but that relationship may only have begun in the late twenties or early thirties. See Ward Ritchie, *The Dohenys of Los Angeles*, Los Angeles Miscellany 3 (Los Angeles: Dawson's Book Shop, 1974), 32.

To add to the confusion, Wright identified Doheny as E. H., not E. L., on the drawings, and placed the site in the Sierra Madre or San Gabriel Mountains, rather than the Santa Monica foothills. He also dated the project to 1921.

The Dohenys used the land for ranching purposes and for a weekend home. If indeed Doheny had intended to develop it, the Senate investigation and criminal proceedings of the Teapot Dome scandal would probably have prevented him from doing so. He satisfied himself with having a house built for his son on the southeastern corner of the tract between 1925 and 1928. It was designed in Norman Baronial style by the Los Angeles architect George B. Kaufmann and called Greystone. The Doheny Ranch was subdivided as the Trousdale Estates after World War II.

21. Sweeney, *Wright in Hollywood*, 11, makes the point that the two overall perspectives illustrated here do not simply represent different points of view, but also different stages in the development of the design, fig. 139 being earlier (perhaps as early as late March 1923), fig. 140 being later (October ?) and involving the use of a true textile-block method of construction.

22. As mentioned above, four textile-block houses were built, plus the Little Dipper School and Community Playhouse. The one house that will not be discussed here is the Storer House, begun in late 1923 and based on the project of late 1922 for the Lowes House in Eagle Rock, Los Angeles. One should not forget, in this context, the Yamamura House in Ashiya, Japan, which makes use of a thirty/sixty-degree geometry in its plan. Although preliminary plans apparently date from 1918, the house was not built until 1924. See Massami Tanigawa, *Measured Drawing: Frank Lloyd Wright in Japan* (Tokyo: Gurafuiku [Graphic]-sha, 1980), 32–65. I should like to thank Jonathan Lipman for bringing this project to my attention, and William Coaldrake for supplying me with Tanigawa's publication.

23. Kathryn Smith, "Frank Lloyd Wright, Hollyhock House, and Olive Hill, 1919–1924," *JSAH* 38 (March 1979): 29–31; and now Smith, *Frank Lloyd Wright, Hollyhock House and Olive Hill: Buildings and Projects for Aline Barnsdall* (New York: Rizzoli International, 1992), 180–89. In view of the gift of the site to the city, Wright included on some of the drawings for the school and playhouse a contiguous pergola and terrace to the north as a memorial to Theodore N. Barnsdall, Aline Barnsdall's father.

24. The diagonal plan of the Little Dipper may well owe something to an earlier project by Norman Bel Geddes for a theater based on what he called "the diagonal axis principle." The stage was placed in one corner of a square space and the rest of the auditorium followed a diamond-shaped configuration. This plan was first published in 1915 in Bel Geddes's own little magazine, *In Which*, a copy of which Aline Barnsdall gave to Wright, according to Bel Geddes (*Miracle*, 162). Claude Bragdon republished the project in "Towards a New Theatre," *ARec* 52 (September 1922): 171–82, following a lecture by Bel Geddes on the subject at the Architectural League in New York. The basic form of the theater, as well as its application by Wright in the Little Dipper, has always made me think of the American baseball diamond, an appropriate reference at least for a children's playhouse.

25. Esther McCoy, *Vienna to Los Angeles: Two Journeys* (Santa Monica: Arts and Architecture Press, 1979), 65–66, 79. On the Freeman House, see the

excellent "Historic Structure Report: Samuel and Harriet Freeman House, Hollywood, California, Frank Lloyd Wright, 1924," prepared for the School of Architecture, University of Southern California, by Jeffrey Mark Chusid, 1989; and Chusid, "Concrete and Light: A Fabric for Living: The Freeman House of Frank Lloyd Wright," *Antiques and Fine Art* 7 (January 1990): 76–83. An interview with Samuel Freeman is published in Patrick J. Meehan, ed., *Frank Lloyd Wright Remembered* (Washington, D.C.: Preservation Press, National Trust for Historic Preservation, 1991), 61–64. The first set of working drawings for the house was produced in January 1924 and a revised set the following month. Construction began in April.

Leah and her husband Philip Lovell later commissioned Schindler to design their beach house in Newport Beach (1925–26) and Neutra to design their main residence in Los Angeles, known as the "Health House" (1928–29).

26. The canted corner window of decorative leaded glass in the nursery of Hollyhock House is a bit earlier, and the corner window in the dining room of the Ennis House may be coeval. There does not seem to be any earlier European example. The contemporaneous Schröder House by Rietveld has a corner window that is framed out to its edges.

27. FLW, "In the Cause of Architecture, VI: The Meaning of Materials—Glass," *ARec* 64 (July 1928): 13. On the previous page, opposite the view of the Freeman House, is a photograph of the corner of the Hollyhock House nursery (p. 12). According to Sweeney, Schindler's refurnishing dates from 1928 (*Wright in Hollywood*, 79).

28. For the "butterfly plan," see Jill Franklin, "Edwardian Butterfly Houses," *ARev* 157 (April 1975): 220–25. On the Cooper House and related issues, see H. Allen Brooks, "Frank Lloyd Wright—Towards a Maturity of Style (1887–1893)," *AA Files: Annals of the Architectural Association School of Architecture* 2 (July 1982): 44–49.

29. Wright surely picked up this idea of rotation from working with Sullivan, whose ornament was often generated by such a procedure. Cf. Louis Sullivan, *A System of Architectural Ornament According with a Philosophy of Man's Powers* (New York: American Institute of Architects, 1924).

30. Cf. Kasimir Malevich, *The Non-Objective World* (1927; trans. Howard Dearstyne, Chicago: Paul Theobald, 1959); Wassily Kandinsky, *Concerning the Spiritual in Art* (1912; trans. Michael Sadleir et al., Documents of Modern Art, New York: Wittenborn, Schultz, 1947); and Kandinsky, *Point and Line to Plane* (1926; trans. Dearstyne and Hilla Rebay, 1927; rpt. New York: Dover, 1979).

31. See E. A. Carmean Jr., *Mondrian: The Diamond Compositions* (Washington, D.C.: National Gallery of Art, 1979); Hans L. C. Jaffé, "The Diagonal Principle in the Works of Van Doesburg and Mondrian," *The Structurist* 9 (1969): 14–21; Donald McNamee, "Van Doesburg's Elementarism: New Translations of His Essays and Manifesto Originally Published in *De Stijl*," in ibid., 22–29; and Theo Van Doesburg, "Painting: From Composition to Counter-Composition" and "Painting and Sculpture: About Counter-Composition and Counter-Sculpture. Elementarism (Fragment of a Manifesto)," trans. in Jaffé, *De Stijl* (New York: Harry N. Abrams, 1967), 201–17.

32. It was, in fact, the argument with Van Doesburg over the explicit use of diagonality that finally caused Mondrian to leave the De Stijl group in 1925.

33. For a discussion of Wright's geometry especially as it relates to the Imperial Hotel, see Otto Antonia Graf, *Die Kunst des Quadrats: Zum Werk von Frank Lloyd Wright* (Vienna, Cologne, and Graz: Hermann Böhlaus Nachf., 1983), 2: 307ff.; and now also Alofsin, *Lost Years*, 261–86. Wright first experimented with diagonal motifs in a tentative way in the decorative concrete blocks of Midway Gardens (1913–14).

34. Wright wrote that, to make the structure "flexible" rather than "rigid," he imagined "a building made as the two hands thrust together palms inward, fingers interlocking and yielding to movement, but resilient to return to its original position when distortion ceased." The resulting form would express a "flexing and reflexing in any direction" (FLW, "Why the Japanese Earthquake Did Not Destroy the Hotel Imperial," *Liberty* 4 [3 December 1927]: 63).

35. London Lects., 3; and FLW, "Plasticity, Terminals, Third Dimension, Music and Architecture," lecture to the Taliesin Fellowship, 27 August 1952, FLWF. One of the first times he associated diagonality with "graceful reflexes" is in his discussion of Ocatilla and San Marcos-in-the-Desert in *A* I,

303. For an important and early discussion of the subject in relation to Michelangelo, see Vincent Scully, "Michelangelo's Fortification Drawings: A Study in the Reflex Diagonal," *Perspecta* 1 (1952): 38–45.

36. Wright dated the drawings to 1922 and 1923. Probably because it is earlier, the 1922 date has been the one usually given in the literature. In his description of the Millard House in the *Autobiography*, however, Wright noted that he was "called away to Tahoe" as construction on La Miniatura was about to begin (I, 249). A telegram from Wright to his son Lloyd about drawings for the project and about "NEGOTIATING WITH ARMSTRONGS" reveals that work was still underway in 1924 (FLW to Lloyd Wright, 6 May 1924, MS 1033.102, FLWF). A plot plan of the Armstrong property, dated September 1922, is also in FLWF.

37. For a summary of what is known of the Armstrong-Wright negotiations, as well as the possible financial involvement of Wright himself, see Sweeney, *Wright in Hollywood*, 103–7. See also Bruce Brooks Pfeiffer, *Treasures of Taliesin: Seventy-six Unbuilt Designs* (Fresno, Calif., and Carbondale and Edwardsville, Ill.: Press at California State University, Southern Illinois University Press, 1985), n.p. The property was sold for $250,000 in 1928 to Lora Josephine Knight. In the following year she commissioned the Swedish architect Lennart Palme, her nephew by marriage, to design a summer house for her near the southern tip of the lakeshore, in a Nordic style. See Helen Henry Smith, *Vikingsholm: Tahoe's Hidden Castle* (privately printed, 1973), 7–8. For a general history of the area, see Edward B. Scott, *The Saga of Lake Tahoe* (Crystal Bay, Lake Tahoe, Nev.: Sierra-Tahoe, 1957), esp. 121–35. I am grateful to Mina Marefat for information and insight on this and the Death Valley project provided during a seminar she took with me on Wright's works of the twenties.

38. Mark Twain [Samuel L. Clemens], *Roughing It* (1872; New York: Harper & Brothers, 1959), 156; and George Wharton James, *The Lake of the Sky: Lake Tahoe in the High Sierras of California and Nevada* (Pasadena: pri-vately printed, 1915).

39. James, *Lake of the Sky*, 222.

40. Two photomontages were published in De Fries, *Wright*, 46. They may well have been prepared especially for this publication by either Richard Neutra or Werner Moser, both of whom had been working in Wright's office. It was, in fact, in Germany that the technique of photomontage received its greatest development, following Lissitzky's introduction of it to the Bauhaus in 1922–23.

41. Wright commented on the appropriateness of Amerindian forms to wood construction in "In the Cause of Architecture, IV: The Meaning of Materials—Wood," *ARec* 63 (May 1928): 481, 487. He adapted the tepee forms of the Tahoe project for the Nakoma Country Club in Madison, Wisconsin (1923–24).

42. Cf. Banham, "Wilderness Years," 516–17; and Banham, *Scenes in America Deserta* (Salt Lake City: Peregrine-Smith, 1982), 31–35.

43. A very brief discussion of it is in Banham, "Wilderness Years," 516. This is based in large part on Wright's description in *A* I, 252–53. The only biographer of Wright to have gone into the subject in any detail is Finis Farr, *Frank Lloyd Wright: A Biography* (New York: Charles Scribner's Sons, 1961), 177–80. But see now Sweeney, *Wright in Hollywood*, 107–14. I am particularly grateful to Susan Buchel, former Museum Curator, Scotty's Castle, and her staff for making available to me much previously unpublished material as well as for commenting on an early version of this text.

44. For a history of Death Valley, and an extensive bibliography, see Richard E. Lingenfelter, *Death Valley & the Amargosa: A Land of Illusion* (Berkeley, Los Angeles, and London: University of California Press, 1986).

45. For this project, see FLW, "In the Cause of Architecture, VIII: Sheet Metal and a Modern Instance," *ARec* 64 (October 1928): 334–42; and *A* I, 253–57.

46. On Albert M. Johnson and Death Valley Scotty, see Hank Johnston, *Death Valley Scotty: The Fastest Con in the West* (Corona del Mar, Calif.: Trans-Anglo Books, 1974); Levering Cartwright, "A Sacrifice to Death Valley," *Best's Insurance News: Life Edition* 67 (August 1966): 24–26, 28–31, 34–38; (September 1966): 10–11, 14, 16, 19–20; (October 1966): 10–11, 14, 16–17, 20, 22, 24, 26, 28, 30–31; and 68 (August 1967): 21, 23–24, 26, 28. See also Lingenfelter, *Death Valley*, 242–74, 441–67; Orin S. Merrill, *Mysterious Scott: The Monte*

Cristo of Death Valley (Chicago: privately printed, 1906); Clarence P. Milligan, *Death Valley and Scotty* (Los Angeles: Ward Ritchie Press, 1942); and Johnston, *Death Valley Scotty: The Man and the Myth* (Yosemite, Calif.: Flying Spur Press, 1972). On Scotty's Castle, in particular, see Dorothy Shally and William Bolton, *Scotty's Castle* (Yosemite, Calif.: Flying Spur Press, 1973).

47. Quoted in Shally and Bolton, *Scotty's Castle*, 9. Johnson's famous explanation of the relationship was later published in the 1937 Sunday supplement of the King Features Syndicate: "I've been paying Scotty's bills for years—and I like it. He repays me in laughs" (quoted in C[arl] B. Glasscock, *Here's Death Valley* [Indianapolis and New York: Bobbs-Merrill, 1940], 220).

48. Among these are *Shadow Mountains* (1919) and *Lost Wagons* (1923) by Dane Coolidge; and *Tales of Lonely Trails* (1922) and *Wanderer of the Wasteland* (1923) by Zane Grey.

49. This spelling of Staininger follows Lingenfelter; it can also be spelled Steininger. The road was built by Jack Salsberry around 1907 to connect his Ubehebe Copper Mines and Smelter Company with the Las Vegas and Tonopah railroad line.

50. Shally and Bolton, *Scotty's Castle*, 9, claim this work took three years to complete, meaning that construction may still have been going on when Wright visited the site.

51. Although he may have known of Wright through his earlier business dealings in Chicago, Johnson more than likely was persuaded to commission Wright by Alfred MacArthur, a younger officer of the National Life Insurance Company. MacArthur, who later became a friend of Wright, was a fellow member of the Tavern Club. He was deeply impressed by Wright's architecture and tried to buy his Oak Park house in the teens, with the intention of helping Wright out financially and, it would seem, preserving the house. (He and his family lived in the Oak Park house during that period of time as renters.)

In 1924 MacArthur spoke of Wright to Darwin Martin as "the world's greatest architect" (MacArthur to Martin, 16 April 1924, Box 4-14, Wright-Martin Papers). MacArthur was apparently also responsible for introducing Gordon Strong to Wright; see Mark Reinberger, "The Sugarloaf Mountain Project and Frank Lloyd Wright's Vision of a New World," *JSAH* 43 (March 1984): 39. According to Reinberger, the first meeting between Wright and Strong took place at Taliesin in 1924, when MacArthur brought Strong there to see the drawings for the Johnson skyscraper project. MacArthur knew Death Valley well, having been sent there by Johnson in 1908 "to gain Scott's confidence" so that he might reveal the location of his mine (Johnston, *Death Valley Scotty: Man and Myth*, 33). MacArthur wandered around the valley with Scotty from January until April without seeing any trace of a mine.

Wright later maintained that Johnson was impressed with the way the Imperial Hotel had survived the 1923 earthquake and hoped to see the hotel's structural principles developed further in his company's skyscraper.

Dione Neutra, the architect's wife, wrote to her parents in July 1924: "Today the air in Taliesin . . . was charged with electricity. A big industrialist [A. M. Johnson] with wife, daughter, and son-in-law were houseguests, and it was to be decided whether Wright would be commissioned to build a skyscraper. All his hopes were based on this. For weeks all had been prepared for this visit" (D. Neutra, *Richard Neutra*, 126). On 19 July 1924, Johnson sent Wright a contract, saying "we would like to have you, as Architect, take up a preliminary study" (A. M. Johnson to FLW, FLWF). Wright always claimed that the original studies for an office building on which the National Life Insurance Company was based were begun as early as 1920. The drawings published in the October 1928 *ARec* are dated May 1923. These drawings, therefore, may be the ones "prepared" for Johnson to look at in July 1924 to provide the basis for a decision as to whether to commission Wright to go ahead with the project on his behalf. It might also explain why Johnson, according to Wright, insisted he wanted an original design, "a Virgin" (*A* I, 252). According to a chronology of Wright's activities between 1922 and 1932 that Robert Sweeney has prepared for the catalogue of the forthcoming exhibition *Frank Lloyd Wright: Shaping an American Landscape, 1920–1929*, Centre Canadien d'Architecture, Montreal, and Library of Congress, Washington, D.C., 1996, Schindler notified Neutra on 2 February 1924 that Wright, who was in Los Angeles until the end of the month, was currently involved in a skyscraper project for Chicago, though he did not specify for whom.

52. Sweeney, *Wright in Hollywood*, 108, suggests the December 1923 date for the visit based on the recollections of George C. Lyon, a student in the 1920s at the Deep Springs school, just north of Death Valley, which Johnson visited with Wright on their way to his ranch in Grapevine Canyon. (The school was founded and run by a friend of Johnson, L. L. Nunn of the Telluride Foundation, whom Johnson apparently helped find the land for his educational venture.) But according to Jan Vleck, a more recent graduate of Deep Springs who has been engaged in research on the period in question, Wright and Johnson visited Deep Springs "in early March 1924," at which time "Wright gave a lecture on the survival of his Imperial Hotel during the 1923 Tokyo earthquake, and apparently agreed to draw up a house plan for Martin Sachse during his stay in Death Valley" (Vleck, "A House to Live In . . . ," unpublished typescript).

Martin Sachse, a German immigrant, was a master mechanic who taught machine shop at Deep Springs. After becoming engaged to Kate Park, whom he met in Los Angeles, he returned to Deep Springs in November 1923 with the thought of building a house for the two of them. According to correspondence between Sachse and Park dating from late March and early April 1924 (a summary of which was kindly supplied to me by Vleck), Sachse asked Wright to design the house but never received any drawings from him. (Wright always mistakenly referred to the client as Arthur Sachse and dated the house to 1922.) The correspondence also reveals that the Wright-Johnson visit and Wright lecture occurred on 2 March 1924 and that Wright probably made at least one other return visit toward the very end of the month. In a letter to Park on 30 March 1924, Sachse wrote: "By the end of next week I shall have a chance to talk with . . . Mr. Wright (architect) who is at J[ohnson] place" (personal communication from Jan Vleck, 2 August 1994). Recollections by another student who was at Deep Springs at the same time as Lyon confirm the March date of the Wright-Johnson visit and lecture (James S. Mansfield, "A Visit from Frank Lloyd Wright") as well as the fact that "Wright visited Deep Springs several times though not regularly" (Mansfield to Vleck, 1 December 1989). I am grateful to Jan Vleck for providing me with this information. The early March date for the initial visit would appear to be corroborated by a letter Johnson sent Wright on 16 March 1924 supplying him with information of a specifically topographical nature (#2306.002, FLWF).

On Nunn and Deep Springs, see *Telluride Association and Deep Springs: An Account of Their Origin and Plan*, prepared by a Committee of Telluride Association (privately printed, 1928); and *Telluride Association and Deep Springs* (Ithaca, N.Y.: Telluride Association, 1938).

53. Dione Neutra's opinion was quite different. She thought Johnson was a "harmless, benevolent, little, dull-looking man" whom "one would never suspect . . . to be a millionaire" (*Richard Neutra*, 127).

54. The photograph is an Eastman Bromide Enlargement made by Charles W. Beam, 5070 Hollywood Boulevard, Los Angeles. This is the only case I am aware of in which Wright used a photograph as the basis for a sketch. It should probably be related to the use of photomontage in the Tahoe project. Richard Neutra worked on the drawings as a member of Wright's staff (D. Neutra, *Richard Neutra*, 130). That he or Werner Moser also worked on the preliminary design is evidenced by the German spelling of the word for "house" in the early sketch plan (fig. 163).

55. The word comes from the Malay *kampung* or *kampong*, meaning an enclosure containing a cluster of buildings, usually occupied by foreigners.

56. It was on top of this hill that Scotty was eventually buried.

57. A spire, decorated in a herringbone pattern, was added to the octagonal chapel in the final stages of the design. A domed, two-story octagonal living room appears in the preliminary plans for the Beverly Hills house Wright designed for Aline Barnsdall in 1923.

58. A similar profile appears in Wright's project for the Foster House in Buffalo (1923) and the contemporaneous remodeling of the Moore House in Oak Park. In the Johnson House project, two bridges cross under the vault of the living room to connect, at a mezzanine level, the terrace platform above the rear kitchen area with the one above the front third of the room.

59. In the early stages of the project, the bedroom wing was only one story high. In the final plan, there are two smaller bedrooms on the upper floor, plus a corbel-vaulted master bedroom.

60. Two other examples of such radical asymmetry are the coeval Little Dipper and Yamamura House.

61. Richard Neutra noted in a letter to his mother-in-law in November 1924 that "Wright desires that his building should look like a sprouting cactus" (quoted in D. Neutra, *Richard Neutra*, 130).

62. Johnston, *Death Valley Scotty: Fastest Con*, 104. Sweeney, *Wright in Hollywood*, 114,offers the opinion, based on a reading of a letter from Johnson to Hitchcock of 1941, that the reason for aborting the project was fundamentally financial. What Johnson told Hitchcock, however, is not quite that simple. He said: "His [Wright's] estimate . . . ran into several hundred thousand dollars and I did not feel like assuming that investment at the time although a little later [hardly more than a year!] I did put up a couple of buildings and the cost of these ultimately exceeded by many times Mr. Wright's estimate." He then noted that these buildings "followed the type of architecture known as 'provincial Spanish.'" (Albert M. Johnson to Henry-Russell Hitchcock, 18 June 1941, Scotty's Castle, Death Valley National Monument). I should like to thank Blair Davenport for making this letter available to me.

Levering Cartwright says that Johnson turned against the project "when Wright advised using local stone [*sic*] and blending the castle into the environment" ("Sacrifice" [September 1966], 19).

63. Although the Death Valley project was rejected out of hand, the project for the National Life headquarters apparently dragged on into 1928–29. One suspects that the problems between Wright and Johnson went beyond simply matters of design. In the fall of 1924, Wright met Olgivanna Lazovich Hinzenberg, a married woman with a child, and soon began living with her. In a letter to his friend William Norman Guthrie, regarding the St. Mark's-in-the-Bouwerie Tower project, Wright implied that the Johnsons' Christian morality may have had something to do with the ultimate rejection of the office building project and the earlier house design: "He [Johnson] is a fundamentalist—and, although convinced of the practical virtues of the ideas, a personal matter, given undue publicity, holds it where it is for the present" (FLW to Guthrie, 26 October 1927, quoted in *LClients*, 275). It would appear that Johnson rejected the Death Valley project after the second fire at Taliesin, which occurred in April 1925, and thus after Olgivanna had moved in with Wright. When Alexander Woolcott visited Wright soon after that event, the project was on Wright's drawing board, and he went away believing that Wright had built Scotty's Castle. See Samuel Hopkins Adams, *Alexander Woolcott: His Life and His World* (New York: Reynal and Hitchcock, 1945), 309–10; and George Palmer Putnam, *Death Valley and Its Country* (New York: Duell, Sloan and Pearce, 1946), 113–14.

64. Quoted in Bourke Lee, *Death Valley* (New York: Macmillan, 1930), 19.

65. Federal Writers' Project of the Works Progress Administration of Northern California, *Death Valley: A Guide*, American Guide Series (Boston: Houghton Mifflin, 1939), 48. It is now usually less fancifully translated as "Duhveetah's Carrying Basket."

66. In the section of the *Autobiography* dealing with Ocatilla and San Marcos-in-the-Desert (1928–29; see Chapter VII), Wright wrote that "out here [in the desert] obvious symmetry soon wearies the eyes, stultifies imagination, closes the episode before it begins. . . . Any sound constitution [in the desert] is pregnant with graceful reflexes" (I, 303). He also noted that the eroded "mountain ranges are all 60–30 triangles" and that "a cross-section of the talus at the base of the mountains is the hypotenuse of a 30–60 triangle" (*Sixty Years of Living Architecture*, [9]).

67. London Lects., 3; and FLW, "Plasticity, Terminals."

68. Wright often quoted Victor Hugo on the subject, attributing to him the phrase: "The desert is where God is and Man is not" (*A* I, 304).

69. Guy Debord, *Society of the Spectacle* (1967; rev. trans., Detroit: Black and Red, 1977).

70. The project was completely unknown until its publication in 1986 in *FLWPS*, vol. 10, 83–84, having never been mentioned by Wright or even listed among his works. I would especially like to thank Bruce Pfeiffer for making the project known to me before that publication and for sharing his thoughts about it with me, in particular, its possible relevance to the Death Valley project. The date Wright later inscribed on the drawing is 1921. This is clearly much too early, as is the case with the dates on the Johnson ranch drawings and the Sachse project. A common date of 1924–25 would be much more logical.

71. This area of the northern reaches of the desert seems most likely, based on the configuration of the land and its accessibility and availability.

Grapevine Springs was also part of the original Staininger holdings. When Johnson acquired it in the late teens, it was known as Lower Grapevine Ranch (as opposed to Upper Grapevine Ranch, where he planned to build his house). When visitors became too numerous in the late twenties following the tremendous publicity surrounding the building of the "Castle," Scotty felt the need for a hideaway. In 1929 Johnson built a small house for him on Lower Grapevine Ranch. Facing south-southwest on a ledge at the base of the Grapevine Mountains, the site (marked Scotty's Ranch in fig. 161) conforms quite closely with the one indicated in Wright's sketches.

72. The plan is very similar to those for some of the small shore cottages and houseboats in the Tahoe project.

73. Other early examples include the libraries of the McAfee House (fig. 26), the Baldwin House project, Oak Park (1895), and the communal lounge of the River Forest Golf Club (1901). One can postulate a source for this plan, especially as regards the Baldwin House, in H. H. Richardson's small suburban and rural libraries. For the medieval origins of the form, see especially André Grabar, *Martyrium: Recherches sur le culte des reliques et l'art chrétien antique*, 2 vols. plus album (Paris: Collège de France, 1943–1946); and Richard Krautheimer, "Introduction to an 'Iconography of Medieval Architecture,'" *Journal of the Warburg and Courtauld Institutes* 5 (1942): 1–33. The prototypes for the martyria and baptistry were the domed rotundas of the Church of the Nativity in Bethlehem (built over the grotto in which Christ was born) and the Church of the Holy Sepulchre (built over the tomb from which Christ was supposed to have risen). The octagonal shape reappeared in Wright's work of the twenties in the plan of the two-story living room of the Barnsdall Beverly Hills house (1923) and in a number of the cabins and houseboats for the Tahoe project (1923–24). After the Death Valley designs, it was used for the central meeting room of the Nakoma Country Club project (1923–24) and for the project for a silo and barn at Taliesin (c. 1925).

74. Cf. FLW, "In the Cause of Architecture, V: The Meaning of Materials—The Kiln," *ARec* 63 (June 1928): 555–61:

The natural material here is of the earth itself. But to produce this material known as Ceramics, another element, that of the artificer, has entered with Fire.

This product should therefore be nearer man's desire molded, as it is, by himself. His creation is seen in it. What he has sensed of the story of his creation, he has put into it. (P. 555)

The interest in the fired-clay product brought Wright back to Sullivan at just the point when he began to see Sullivan once again on a regular basis. "Modern terra-cotta," Wright noted, "has known but one creative master—only one—Louis H. Sullivan." "And it is the greatest opportunity for the creative artist of all the materials he may choose. It is, of course, burned clay in any color or glaze for entire buildings—pottery buildings! Earthenware on a great scale" (p. 556). Wright went on to ask: "Where is the pottery-building beautiful in form and texture and color—as *such*?" (p. 559). "In the terra-cotta or pottery of Earthenware building," he believed, "we may have, today, the sum and substance of all the kiln ever gave to architecture" (p. 558).

75. Commenting a few years later on this spatial model of architecture, Wright noted: "This interior conception took architecture entirely away from sculpture, away from painting and entirely away from architecture as it had been known in the antique. The building now became a creation of interior-space in light" (FLW, *Two Lectures on Architecture* [Chicago: Art Institute of Chicago, 1931], 25–26). And again, in 1939, referring to Lao-tse's metaphor of the water pitcher in Okakura's *Book of Tea* as proving "that the reality of the building consisted not in the four walls and the roof but inhered in the space within," Wright added: "That idea is entire reversal of all pagan—'Classic'—ideals of building whatsoever. If you accept that concept of building classical-architecture falls dead to the ground. An entirely new concept has entered the mind of the architect and the life of his people" (London Lects., 3).

76. Brownell and FLW, 24–25. Cf. Alfred Vincent Kidder, *Introduction to the Study of Southwestern Archaeology, with a Preliminary Account of the Excavations at Pecos* (New Haven: Yale University Press, 1924), esp. 78, 81, 119–23.

77. This is not to deny the important sources in the theoretical literature

of the nineteenth century for such "non-architectural," "nonclassical" archetypal models. Here, Viollet-le-Duc and Gottfried Semper come to mind, both of whose work Wright was acquainted with.

78. The theory of evolution from basket making to fired-clay pottery was summarized at just this time in Kidder, *Southwestern Archaeology*, 49, 118–35. Wright retraced, in effect, the sequence from weaving, to pottery making, to building in his description of the textile-block method in his *Autobiography*. "Concrete is a plastic material," he wrote, "susceptible to the impress of imagination. I saw a kind of weaving coming out of it. . . . Then I saw the 'shell.' Shells with steel inlaid in them. Or steel for warp and masonry units for 'woof' in the weaving" (I, 245). The final outcome would be "hollow wall-shells for living in! The 'shell,' as human habitation" (p. 235).

79. Brownell and FLW, 24–25. Bruce Pfeiffer pointed out to me that this section of the book was part of a larger history of architecture Wright began working on after finishing *An Autobiography*. A reflection of this unpublished manuscript can be seen in FLW and Iovanna Lloyd Wright, *Architecture: Man in Possession of His Earth*, ed. Patricia Coyle Nicholson (Garden City, N.Y.: Doubleday, 1962), 50ff.

It should be pointed out that Wright quite consciously wavered between the cave and the tree as early man's first abode, finally admitting that "it is perhaps better to say he first lived sometimes in trees and sometimes in stone caves" (Brownell and FLW, 23). This distinction is significant, for it represented in Wright's thought a difference between those who lived in the north, which "always demanded most from [man] in the way of building," and those in the south, where "the builder was satisfied with some grass and leaves raised on a platform of sticks, or with some kind of tent that he might fold up and take with him on his horse as he rode away" (ibid., 23–24). The cave dweller became the prototypical man of the north, and the tree dweller that of the south. Thus, when he later had to acknowledge that the traditional classical wood "hut" in fact preceded the "large clay cave or pot of the cliff-dwellers" ("but previously better forms of houses had come from the sticks that had been conferred upon him by his friendly companion, the tree") to produce "lighter, more scientific house-shapes" (ibid., 24), Wright was able to maintain the priority of the cliff dweller for the environment of the north with which he himself was concerned. In any event, he noted that the southerners' huts "were at first conical" (ibid.).

Wright's mythical history of architecture, reflecting conditions of the American subcontinent and thus going back to its prehistoric cultures for a model of origins, is repeated in his son John Lloyd Wright's short dissertation on the subject in *My Father Who Is on Earth* (New York: G. P. Putnam's Sons, 1946), 129–31.

80. FLW, "In the Cause of Architecture, IX: The Terms," *ARec* 64 (December 1928): 512. Both Vincent Scully and William Jordy have remarked on the significance of the container, or "vase," in the later work of Wright, but without giving it the representational meaning I have or taking it back to its sources in his work and thought of the teens and twenties. See, for example, Scully, *Wright*, 30; and William H. Jordy, *American Buildings and Their Architects*, vol. 4, *The Impact of European Modernism in the Mid-Twentieth Century* (Garden City, N.Y.: Doubleday, 1972), 353–59. Both Scully and Jordy refer Wright's concept of the spatial container to the aphorism of Lao-tse that Wright often quoted from the *Book of Tea* in the later years of his life. But, see note 81.

Wright's articulation of a spatial definition of architecture in the 1920s coincides with the development in Europe of what Le Corbusier called the "free plan" and may owe something to the contemporary discussion in Europe of architecture as space.

81. London Lects., 3. Bruce Pfeiffer has suggested that the date was 1922 (in conversation, August 1993). The short book by Kakuzo Okakura, entitled *The Book of Tea*, was published in the United States in 1906, two years after its author had emigrated to Boston and five years before he became curator of Chinese and Japanese art at the Boston Museum of Fine Arts, succeeding his mentor, Ernest Fenollosa. Although Okakura was an important member of the circle around Isabella S. Gardner and his work was well known among artists and intellectuals of the time, there is no indication that Wright actually read *The Book of Tea* until the 1920s. One of his first references to it was in 1938 in the January issue of *AF* devoted to his work (p. 35). In the London lectures of the following year, he wrote: "To go back now for a moment to the central

thought of organic architecture, it was Lao Tze, five hundred years before Jesus, who, so far as I know, first declared that the reality of the building consisted not in the four walls and the roof but inhered in the space within, the space to be lived in" (London Lects., 3). In recounting the circumstances of this discovery, Wright explained how the passage from Lao-tse's *Tao-tê-ching* was not a revelation of something new but rather a confirmation of something that he had been thinking about for quite some time:

My own recognition of this concept has been instinctive; I did not know of Lao Tze when I began to build with it in my mind; I discovered him much later. I came across Lao Tze quite by accident. One day I came in from the garden where I had been working and picked up a little book the Japanese Ambassador to America had sent me and in it I came upon the concept of building I have just mentioned to you. It expressed precisely what had been in my mind and what I had myself been trying to do with a building: "The reality of the building does not consist of walls and roof but in the space within to be lived in." There it was! At first I was inclined to dissemble a little; I had thought myself somewhat a prophet . . . only to find after all, that I was an "Also Ran." The message had been given to the world thousands of years ago. . . . So what? I could not hide the book nor could I conceal the fact. For some time I had felt as a punctured balloon looks. But then I began to see that, after all, I had not derived that idea from Lao Tze; it was a deeper, profound something that survived in the world, something probably eternal therefore universal, something that persisted and will persist forever. Then I began to feel that I ought to be proud to have perceived it as Lao Tze had perceived it and to have tried to build it! (Ibid., 3–4)

Wright repeated the story to John Peter in a tape recording made in 1957 and edited by Wright (MS 2401.386 A/B, FLWF). What is curious is (1) that Wright apparently took so long to come into contact with this celebrated work, given his earlier connection to the museum curators and collectors of Japanese prints; and (2) that he never quoted Lao-tse's words accurately but always preferred to phrase them in his own way. Perhaps this was because, in Okakura's translation of Lao-tse's "favorite metaphor" of the empty vessel, the positive concept of space was rendered as a negative image of "the Vacuum" (K. Okakura, *The Book of Tea*, ed. Everett F. Bleiler [New York: Dover, 1964], 24). According to Okakura, "he [Lao-tse] claimed that only in vacuum lay the truly essential. The reality of a room, for instance, was to be found in the vacant space enclosed by the roof and walls, not in the roof and walls themselves. The usefulness of a water pitcher dwelt in the emptiness where water might be put, not in the form of the pitcher or the material of which it was made. Vacuum is all-potent because all-containing" (ibid.).

In his recent study of *Frank Lloyd Wright and Japan: The Role of Traditional Japanese Art and Architecture in the Work of Frank Lloyd Wright* (New York: Van Nostrand Reinhold, 1993), Kevin Nute tries to make the case for an earlier acquaintance with both Okakura and Lao-tse. He says that Wright "would probably have taken an interest in the appearance of Okakura's influential *Book of Tea* in 1906, especially since [his friend] Gookin gave it an enthusiastic review soon after its publication" (p. 51). Based on Wright's spelling of Lao-tse's name, Nute argues that Wright may also have read Paul Carus's translation of *Lao-Tze's Tao-Teh-King*, which first appeared in the Chicago journal *The Open Court* in 1896 and was then published in book form two years later (pp. 123–24).

82. For a fuller discussion of the issue of the "spectacle" and the "view," see my "Questioning the View: Seaside's Critique of the Gaze of Modern Architecture," in *Seaside: Making a Town in America*, ed. David Mohney and Keller Easterling (New York: Princeton Architectural Press, 1991), 240–59.

83. Brownell and FLW, 17.

Chapter VII
Writing *An Autobiography*, Reading the Arizona Desert

1. Martin to FLW, 5 April 1926, Box 4-23, Wright-Martin Papers. Wright put his son John in charge of the Martin summer house when he became preoccupied with his own and his family's safety in late 1926. Much of the

construction was unsupervised, and the results tell. For correspondence regarding the Lloyd Jones House, see *LClients*, 40–66. On Ocatilla, see pp. 201–6 below.

Until recently, historians have tended to disregard the Arizona projects in favor of Wright's more "modernist" designs for the St. Mark's-in-the-Bouwerie project (1928–30) and the Elizabeth Noble Apartment House (1929–30). Wright owed the former commission to his old friend William Norman Guthrie, rector of the downtown New York church. It was mooted as early as the fall of 1926, but Wright refused to do any sketches without a firm offer of the job (*LClients*, 275–77). Discussions dragged on, and designing began only in 1929 on the heels of the more pressing Arizona work. The New York project was shelved in early 1930 following the stock market crash. The Elizabeth Noble Apartment House for Los Angeles came to Wright through the intermediation of Harold McCormick late in 1929 and was mainly designed in 1930. With their prismatic glass curtain-walls (St. Mark's Tower) and de Stijl–like cantilevered concrete balconies (Elizabeth Noble Apartments), these projects tended to overshadow Ocatilla and San Marcos-in-the-Desert in the eyes of most critics and historians for reasons of style and taste as well as for their greater accessibility in terms of program and content. Writing in November 1929, Wright said that, while "the New York work [St. Mark's] is exceedingly interesting . . . and will be profitable," his "heart [was] in the project out in the desert." "It means more to me than anything else and I have already put into it more of myself . . . than anything else I have ever put my mind to" (FLW to Alexander Chandler, 9 November 1929, FLWF).

2. Wright noted in *A* I, 279, that he began the writing at the "earnest solicitation" of his new lover, Olgivanna Lazovich, while hiding out with her in a rented cottage on Lake Minnetonka in September–October 1926.

3. The second edition of the *Autobiography*, published in 1943, divided Book One ("Family Fellowship") into two separate books and added a Book Five ("Form"). The posthumous 1977 edition added a Book Six ("Broadacre City"). I owe a number of important observations on this subject to the paper written by Michael Desmond, who took my seminar on Taliesin West and did a remarkably original study of the *Autobiography*, particularly the graphic design of its title pages.

4. It carried a subtitle, "From Generation to Generation," which was dropped in the later editions.

5. Wright always maintained that the term *Usonia* came from Samuel Butler, but scholars have failed to locate the specific source. It is generally considered that Usonia was Wright's "acronym for the United States of North America" and that it first appeared sometime between 1927 and 1930 (Anthony Alofsin, "Broadacre City: The Reception of a Modernist Vision," *Center: A Journal for Architecture in America*, vol. 5, *Modernist Visions and the Contemporary American City* (Austin: Center for the Study of American Architecture, School of Architecture, University of Texas, 1989), 13. For more on the utopian dimensions of the name, see Chapter VIII, note 23.

6. FLW to Martin, 7 September 1929, Box 5-25, Wright-Martin Papers.

7. The first edition of 1932 was reviewed in the *NYT Book Review, Saturday Review, New Republic, Chicagoan, Wisconsin Magazine of History*, and *Virginia Quarterly Review*, as well as *ARec, AF, Shelter*, and the *American Magazine of Art*.

8. Wright noted in *A* I, 200, that he invited her to meet him in his Chicago office, but "she preferred to come after office hours." Noel told her side of the story, confirming the suggestive timing of the first meeting, in a memoir she apparently wrote in 1928, two years before her death. It was serialized as "The Romance of Miriam Wright" in the Boys and Girls Section of the *Sunday Magazine* of the *Milwaukee Journal* in 1932, no doubt to coincide with the publication of Wright's *Autobiography* (8 May 1932, p. 1; 15 May 1932, p. 3; 22 May 1932, p. 6; 29 May 1932, p. 2; and 5 June 1932, p. 9). Noel claims she had a letter of introduction to Wright from Paris (perhaps from Wright's friends the Horace Holleys) that she mailed the day she arrived in New York. Upon reaching Chicago, where one of her daughters lived, there was already a response from Wright, which she was shown only after dinner. She made up her mind to visit him right away.

Noel placed their initial meeting in the fall, before Thanksgiving. However, the first letter from Noel to Wright that we have is from her Chicago address and is dated 12 December 1914. It begins, "Because I stand aghast at the immensity of your sorrow," and thus seems to be the initial one (FLWF). Wright responded on 14 December (FLWF). Noel wrote back on 17 December, offering "my friendship" if it "can serve you in any way" (FLWF). Apparently still not having met her, Wright responded on 19 December, inviting Noel to show him her work: "Your work would be safe with me and I want to see it. Could you bring something here where I work to show me its character and where I could show you something of mine or what do you suggest?" (FLWF). That preliminary letter of invitation seems to have caused some disturbance on the part of Noel. We do not have her response, but on 22 December, Wright wrote to her:

> *I know that you are not young! and probably not pretty, and how you are dressed matters little. . . .*
>
> *About you otherwise I know nothing except what you have yourself sent me, so we start abreast in leaving the facts about us for each to discover from the other.*
>
> *. . . I had intended to spend Christmas alone—Your quiet heart will be welcome. . . .*
>
> *My letter was susceptible of many interpretations—some unpleasant in superficial hands—but I felt no need to insure my meaning even though you do not know me—*
>
> *So—come, —you will be welcome here at my workroom at five on Thursday [Christmas Eve]—we can plan our evening as we will—.* (FLWF)

Noel spent the night at Wright's house, which she acknowledged having done in her memoir, speaking of her "deep love for the man to whom I had given myself" ("Romance of Miram Wright," 15 May 1932). But by leading the reader to believe that the courtship had been of at least a month or two's duration, she no doubt hoped to assuage obvious implications of immorality, not to speak of forwardness, on her part.

The most complete picture of Noel so far is in Secrest, *Wright*, 236ff., to which I owe the reference to her memoir.

9. "Love Truce at Wright Cote; Live in Fear," *CT*, 8 November 1915, p. 1; and *A* I, 201.

10. Noel to FLW, Friday–Christmas Day [25 December 1914], FLWF; and M. N. Wright, "Romance of Miriam Wright," 15 May 1932.

11. Noel to FLW, 17 December 1914; FLW to Noel, 19 December 1914; and Noel to FLW, [25 December 1914]. Noel was a Christian Scientist, and her letters to Wright were filled with religious rhetoric of an "exalted" sort.

12. Noel to FLW, Thursday [early 1915], FLWF; and Noel to FLW, [25 December 1914].

13. Noel to FLW, 12 December 1914. In his *Autobiography* (I, 201), Wright noted on first meeting Noel that "a trace of some illness seemed to cling to her in the continuous shaking of her head, slight but perceptible." She told him that "'her health . . . had been broken by the tragedy of the luckless love affair'" (ibid.). Secrest, *Wright*, 238–40, describes Noel as "dangerously self-delusory" and a "fantasist" but, most significantly, "a morphine addict."

14. "'Miriam' Letters to Wright Range from Joy to Despair," *CT*, 7 November 1915, p. 6; and "Love Truce at Wright Cote," p. 6.

15. Wright described her situation in an almost clinical way: "Strange disabilities began to appear in her. All would go happily for days. Then strange perversions of all that. No visible cause. An unnatural exaggeration of emotional nature grew more and more morbid. More violent the mystifying reactions until something like a terrible struggle between two natures in her would seem to be going on within and tearing her to pieces. Then peace again for a time" (*A* I, 203–4). Wright's unprofessional diagnosis seems to be borne out by the existing correspondence. Aside from the letters between Noel and Wright, published and unpublished, there is a particularly telling one from Wright's friend Ruby Darrow, the wife of Clarence Darrow, expressing disbelief and grave concern over recent actions of Noel (R. Darrow to FLW, 15 August 1916, FLWF). Secrest, *Wright*, 281–83, explains Noel's behavior in terms of her morphine addiction and Wright's diagnosis of it in psychological terms as a "useful" way of shifting the "dilemma . . . from a subject that could not be discussed to one that would explain everything" and that was based on contemporary belief that addiction was but "a symptom of a disordered libido."

16. Quoted in Finis Farr, *Frank Lloyd Wright: A Biography* (New York: Charles Scribner's Sons, 1961), 124.

17. *A* I, 203–4. For a firsthand account of the Wright-Noel relationship in Tokyo, see Antonin Raymond, *An Autobiography* (Rutland, Vt., and Tokyo: Charles E. Tuttle, 1973), p. 76.

18. *A* II, 260. The divorce was granted on 13 November 1922. The marriage took place on 19 November 1923. It should be noted that Wright's mother, who apparently did not get along with Noel, died on 2 February 1923.

19. For Wright's description of her, see *A* I, 274–75; and II, 508–14. See also William Marlin, "Olgivanna and Frank Lloyd Wright: Convictions and Continuity," *Arizona Living* 14 (May 1983): 11–15. Olgivanna's first husband's name is sometimes spelled Hinzenburg rather than Hinzenberg. She is often referred to in the literature as Olga Milanov or Milanoff, that being her mother's maiden name.

20. For the best account of these and the following events other than Wright's own, see Robert C. Twombly, "Frank Lloyd Wright in Spring Green, 1911–1932," *Wisconsin Magazine of History* 51 (Spring 1968): 211–13. Olgivanna Wright's article, "The Last Days of Katherine Mansfield," *The Bookman* 73 (March 1931): 6–13, recounts some of her experiences at the Institute in France. For a discussion of the impact of Olgivanna's background on Wright's later development, see the excellent study by Twombly, "Organic Living: Frank Lloyd Wright's Taliesin Fellowship and Georgi Gurdjieff's Institute for the Harmonious Development of Man," *Wisconsin Magazine of History* 58 (Winter 1974–75): 126–39.

21. The commission for the Nakoma Country Club was apparently in Wright's office by late 1923, and preliminary designs were done by the end of December; working drawings were completed by August 1924. See Paul E. Sprague, ed., *Frank Lloyd Wright and Madison: Eight Decades of Artistic and Social Interaction* (Madison: Elvehjem Museum of Art, University of Wisconsin, 1990), 77–82. The contract for the Gordon Strong project was signed on 22 September 1924. The design was worked on through the early part of 1925 and presented to the client in August. Strong rejected it on 15 October. See Mark Reinberger, "The Sugarloaf Mountain Project and Frank Lloyd Wright's Vision of a New World," *JSAH* 43 (March 1984).

22. It should be stressed that the architects who felt closest in spirit to Wright were the Expressionists and not those who would come to be linked to the International Style. Henry-Russell Hitchcock later differentiated the two groups as the "New Traditionalists" and the "New Pioneers" and squarely placed Wright ("the full New Traditionalist") in the former camp despite certain straddling tendencies (Hitchcock, "Modern Architecture, I: The Traditionalists and the New Tradition," *ARec* 63 [April 1928]: 337–49; and "Modern Architecture, II: The New Pioneers," *ARec* 63 [May 1928]: 453–60).

23. Wright's description of these events is in *A* I, 257–60 and 274–95. Aside from letters preserved in the Wright Archives, another extremely important resource is the Wright-Martin Papers, Boxes 4-5.

24. For more on this, see below pp. 197ff.

25. Baraboo and Dodgeville are towns near Spring Green.

26. Wright was particularly struck with the aptness of the name for his own situation and wrote to his son John in 1928: "Phoenix seems to be the name for me too" (FLW to J. L. Wright [early April 1928], MS XIII/7, #90, J. L. Wright Collection). The best recent study of Phoenix is Bradford Luckingham, *Phoenix: The History of a Southwestern Metropolis* (Tucson: University of Arizona Press, 1989). For an overview of the Hohokam and the early Native American settlement, see Emil W. Haury, *The Hohokam: Desert Farmers & Craftsmen. Excavations at Snaketown, 1964–1965* (Tucson: University of Arizona Press, 1976); Robert H. Lister and Florence C. Lister, *Those Who Came Before: Southwestern Archeology in the National Park System* (Globe and Tucson: Southwest Parks and Monuments Association, University of Arizona Press, 1983); and Randall H. McGuire and Michael B. Schiffer, eds., *Hohokam and Patayan: Prehistory of Southwestern Arizona* (New York and London: Academic Press, 1982).

27. Quoted in Luckingham, *Phoenix*, 85.

28. An additional tract of four hundred acres was set aside for the development of private houses. On the Arizona Biltmore and Wright's role in it, see "The Arizona-Biltmore Hotel, Phoenix, Arizona. Albert Chase McArthur, Architect," *ARec* 66 (July 1929): 19–55; Letters from Albert Chase McArthur and

FLW, "Behind the Record," *ARec* 89 (June 1941): 7; Margaret Dudley Thomas, "The Arizona Biltmore: The Queen of Internationally Honored Resort Hotels," *Arizona Highways* 50 (April 1974): 14–23; Olgivanna Lloyd Wright and Bruce Brooks Pfeiffer, *The Arizona Biltmore: History and Guide* (Scottsdale: Frank Lloyd Wright Foundation, 1974); Warren McArthur Jr., "The Arizona Biltmore, the McArthur Brothers, and Frank Lloyd Wright, *Triglyph: A Southwestern Journal of Architecture and Environmental Design* 6 (Summer 1988): 36–47; and now Sweeney, *Wright in Hollywood*, 120–40.

Within the first year of operation, the McArthur brothers were forced to borrow heavily from William Wrigley, who took over effective control of the hotel in June 1929 and became owner two years later.

29. Finis Farr reproduces a telegram from Wright to McArthur: "TEXTILE BLOCK IDEAL FOR YOUR PURPOSE. . . . SHOULD COME OUT TO HELP YOU START PERHAPS" (*Wright*, 168). Sweeney, *Wright in Hollywood*, 123, accepts this interpretation and notes that the date of McArthur's original request was 2 January 1928. He dates the preliminary McArthur scheme to the previous May.

30. "Memorandum of Agreement," McArthur Bros. Inc. Co., Albert Chase McArthur, and Frank Lloyd Wright, 25 January 1928, Box 5-1, Wright-Martin Papers. In February–March 1928, Wright lived at 129 North Country Club Drive. From 1 May to 15 June, he rented a small bungalow nearer the center of town, at 108 West Almeria Road.

31. In 1929, Wright wrote to Alexander Chandler: "I, —who stood behind the scenes [of the Arizona Biltmore], . . . I had a role to play and played it to the end as best I knew how" (1 August 1929, FLWF). The six perspectives that Wright drew, which are called "original sketches" in O. L. Wright and Pfeiffer, *History and Guide*, were no doubt the ones Wright produced in November–December 1928 at Taliesin, after construction of the hotel was begun. They were based on photographs McArthur sent him and were clearly done for financial reasons. What McArthur intended to do with them is unclear, although one would suspect he hoped to use them either for fund-raising or for publication. The arrangement between McArthur and Wright is spelled out in their correspondence of October–December 1928, FLWF. Sweeney, *Wright in Hollywood*, 128, however, takes them to be evidence of Wright's design input.

32. *A* I, 301; and FLW to J. L. Wright [early April 1928]. Wright later elaborated on what he meant by "undefiled" by rewriting the phrase in the 1943 edition of the *Autobiography* as "undefiled-by-irrigation" (II, 306).

33. FLW to Chandler, 28 December 1929, FLWF. It would appear that Chandler was constantly under pressure, at least from prospective West Coast backers, to continue in the Spanish Colonial style of the original San Marcos Hotel.

34. On Chandler, see Robert Conway Stevens, "A History of Chandler, Arizona," *University of Arizona Bulletin* 25 (October 1954): 5–106 (*Social Science Bulletin*, no. 25); and *History of Arizona: Biographical*, 4 vols. (Phoenix: Record Publishing Co., 1930), 3: 112–16.

35. Luckingham, *Phoenix*, 133. Wright was impressed with Chandler's interest in town planning and remarked to his son on "the development of Chandler itself along ideal lines" (FLW to J. L. Wright [early April 1928]).

36. Despite its founder's idealistic ambitions, little of note was realized from the point of view of town building. Only the northwest corner of the plaza, occupied by the hotel, was completed in any sort of monumental style. The rest was quite makeshift and remained so until very recently (1990), when the Sheraton chain bought the dilapidated San Marcos Hotel and initiated a process of restoration of the hotel and renovation of the town center.

37. George Wharton James, *Arizona: The Wonderland* (Boston: Page Company, 1917), 445. The chapter is entitled "The Realized Mirage—Chandler and the San Marcos." Benton built the main part of the hotel in 1912–13. Hunt apparently added the patio, the Spanish Dining Room, and the gallery in 1914. He also did several bungalows in 1925. Reginald Johnson built an earlier group of bungalows in 1916–17.

38. On 30 March 1928, Wright wrote to Chandler: "We all enjoyed our stay at San Marcos and thank you for a pleasant two days," adding, "I am eager to work with you" (FLWF).

39. FLW to Chandler, 30 March 1928. A year and a half later, Wright wrote that "if I can be of service in helping you present the project, making other drawings, helping sell the project to any prospect, just let me know and I will get alongside" (FLW to Chandler, 9 November 1929, FLWF). Within two

months of that offer, Wright wrote to his old friend Harold McCormick to tell him that "plans are ready to go" on "what might be the finest resort hotel of any description anywhere in the world" and to ask him: "Don't you want to go into partnership with me in the endeavor to get some real building going out there on the West Coast, and in Arizona? Preferably in Arizona for I believe it to be the 'coming' play string now. I believe such enterprise could be not only profitable to you, which it could not fail to be on a gratifying scale, but a lot of satisfaction besides. . . . Think this over and we'll talk about it when I come out—about the middle of January—to Los Angeles" (FLW to H. McCormick, 31 December 1929, FLWF).

The San Marcos-in-the-Desert Hotel, though the most important by far, was only one of a number of commissions that Wright received from Chandler over the succeeding months. The others included: San Marcos Water Gardens (1929); Auto Camp (1929); Citrus Camp Cabins for Chandler Land Improvement Company (1929); and Chandler Block House (1929). Of these, only the camp for a citrus tract owned by the Chandler Land Improvement Company was built. It was composed of wood-and-canvas tent-like structures that remained in existence for only a few years. The Chandler Block House was a revision of the Sachse House for Deep Springs, Calif., of 1924 (see Chapter VI, note 52). In the 1930s, when Wright was planning to build his own permanent winter headquarters in Arizona (Taliesin West), Chandler again asked him for a design for a facility in the desert. Wright produced the project for the Little San Marcos-in-the-Desert (1935–36), but it was never built.

Among the very few studies of Wright's work in Arizona during the second half of the twenties, prior to Sweeney, *Wright in Hollywood*, are: Reyner Banham, "The Wilderness Years of Frank Lloyd Wright," *JRIBA* 76 (December 1969): 512–19; and Edgar Kaufmann Jr., "Frank Lloyd Wright's Years of Modernism," *JSAH* 24 (March 1965): 31–33. See also Banham, *Scenes in America Deserta* (Salt Lake City: Peregrine-Smith, 1982), 69–77; and Kaufmann, "Frank Lloyd Wright: Plasticity, Continuity, and Ornament," *JSAH* 37 (March 1978): 34–39.

40. FLW to Chandler, 30 April 1928, FLWF. He noted in this letter that he was "anxiously awaiting the plat and aeroplane views." He said: "I have the 'stills' out and put together as they belong, making a good panorama. I will do this for you with your prints. The view is splendid and tempting." Fig. 188 shows one of these panoramic views. As mentioned earlier, Wright first started using photography as an aid to design in the Death Valley and Lake Tahoe projects.

41. Chandler to Frank Lloyd Wright, Architect, Incorporated, 25 September 1928, Box 5-10, Wright-Martin Papers. From the beginning, Wright intended to camp near the site of the future hotel in order to become more fully acquainted with it. In view of the lateness of the season, he wrote to Chandler at the end of April 1928: "It is only that to start any actual building experiment such as I contemplated when I thought of camping down near the building site, will have to be postponed. It would be unwise to undertake construction experiments unless I can be right there for some little time at the beginning" (30 April 1928).

42. See note 41 above; and Chandler to Wright, Inc., 25 September 1928.

43. FLW to Chandler, 12 December 1928, FLWF. Regarding accommodations, Wright wrote: "I would like to ask what arrangements I could make for my little family after say the middle of January at Chandler. I don't imagine we could stay at the hotel and if there was a little house somewhere of some kind that we might rent and do our light housekeeping, it might be the best thing for us." Curiously, nothing was written in the contract about living arrangements, despite the assumption that Wright would spend a good deal of time in Chandler. He was apparently to be fully responsible for the expenses incurred by his family and staff.

Chandler notified Wright in a letter of 31 December 1928 that "there are no houses in Chandler at present, for rent. Everything has been taken and hundreds of applicants have been turned away on account of lack of houses" (FLWF). Wright wrote in *A* I, 302, that, when the group arrived in Chandler, they found "that suitable quarters in which to live and work . . . would cost several thousand dollars," a sum well above what they could afford. Having "always wanted to camp in [the] region," he "took the idea to Dr. Chandler and said that if he would give me a site . . . we would build the camp ourselves." In a letter to Mrs. Darwin Martin of 1 February 1929, Olgivanna Wright said: "We looked for the place to live but all impossible [*sic*] expensive—so

decided to put up temporary camp. . . . Oh it was cold! But we simply had to come out—we could not afford to live in the hotel, and we could not afford to eat in the restaurants" (Box 5-17, Wright-Martin Papers).

Before going to Arizona, Wright had written to Albert McArthur to ask if he could use his office. McArthur replied in a telegram: "YOUR IDEA TO SHARE MY OFFICE WOULD NOT BE SUCCESSFUL ON ACCOUNT OF LACK OF PRIVACY . . . BUT PERHAPS SOMETHING COULD BE WORKED OUT AFTER YOU COME" (McArthur to FLW, 9 January 1929, FLWF). To this Wright responded: "Wire just received from Chandler suggesting we come there. We are fifteen, office and selves. May build sightly camp somewhere and live and work there" (FLW to McArthur, 11 January 1929, FLWF).

44. The nursemaid's name was Mrs. Daigle. The six draftsmen were Heinrich Klumb, Donald Walker, Vladimir Heifitz (or Karfick), Cy Tomblins (or Jahnke), George Kastner, and Frank Sullivan. Will Weston was the carpenter/handyman, and his wife the cook. Their two children came to join the two Wright children. See Margerie Green Archaeological Consulting Services, "A National Register Evaluation of Camp Ocatillo and Pima Ranch," for Genstar/Continental Homes, January 1983, p. 7; and Sweeney, *Wright in Hollywood*, 145–48. In the first edition of his *Autobiography*, Wright left Sullivan off the list (I, 306), but corrected this error in the second (II, 310). In early May, the engineer Paul Mueller came to consult on the steelwork for the hotel and lived in the camp's guest cabin. Alice Millard and Lloyd Wright also visited.

45. On Ocatilla, see: *A* I, 302–10; "Desert Camp for Frank Lloyd Wright, Arizona. Frank Lloyd Wright, Architect," *ARec* 68 (August 1930): 189–91; Siegfried Scharfe, "Frank Lloyd Wright," *Baugilde* 13 (25 July 1931): 1164–71; Margerie Green Archaeological Consulting Services, "A National Register Evaluation of Camp Ocatillo and Pima Ranch," for Genstar/Continental Homes, January 1983; and Bruce Brooks Pfeiffer and Yukio Futagawa, *Frank Lloyd Wright: Selected Houses*, vol. 3, *Taliesin West* (Tokyo: A.D.A. EDITA, 1989), 8–11, 24–29.

A note on spelling. The candlewood, or vine-cactus, is ordinarily spelled *ocotillo*, as is the nearby town in Arizona, although a reporter for the local newspaper did spell it "ocatilla" in an article on the San Marcos-in-the-Desert Hotel project (Addison N. Clark, "San Marcos-in-the-Desert Will Be Nation's Finest Host," *Chandler Arizonan*, 21 March 1929, p. 7). Whether it was to distinguish his camp from the town, or to give the spelling the asymmetry he felt was characteristic of the desert ("So, there should be no obvious symmetry in building in the desert, none in the camp,—we later named it 'Ocatilla' and partly for this reason" [*A* I, 303]), Wright chose to spell it, at first, with an initial *O* and two *a*'s. This was the spelling used on the original drawings and in publications up to the early 1940s. In the second edition of the *Autobiography*, Ocatilla was changed to Ocatillo, thus taking on a very definite symmetry. In his various publications, Bruce Pfeiffer has spelled it Ocotilla, returning to the camp a kind of asymmetry, though not the one Wright initially assigned to it. I have chosen to retain Wright's original spelling for historical as well as expressive reasons.

Sweeney, *Wright in Hollywood*, 147, says the name was suggested by Olgivanna Wright.

46. I use the past tense to describe not only the camp—which was partially destroyed by fire in June 1929 and then left to disintegrate or to be cannibalized—but also the site. It, too, no longer exists as such. Following the National Register Evaluation for Genstar/Continental Homes in 1983, a series of subdivisions was begun in the foothills of South Mountain Park, starting with Ahwatukee. The photographs of the site were taken in the spring of 1985, just prior to the commencement of construction (or destruction) in the area.

47. These "box-board wall" cabins, as Wright called them, were similar, except for the pitch of the roof, to the tents Johnson and Scotty had used in Grapevine Canyon before and while building the Death Valley Ranch, and were characteristic of the times.

48. FLW, "In the Cause of Architecture: Arizona," 29 June 1929, p. 2, MS 2401.063, FLWF. The temporary residence Wright built for himself in 1938 on the site of what was to be Taliesin West was called Sun Trap (see Chapter IX).

49. FLW to Martin, 24 July 1928, Box 5-7, Wright-Martin Papers. Wright was referring in particular to his design for the Whittier School in Hampton, Va. (1928). He later used the same roof section in the drafting room for the Taliesin Fellowship at the Hillside Home School in the additions of 1933. Le

Corbusier had previously used it in the house/studio for Amédée Ozenfant in Paris (1922–23).

50. "Frank Lloyd Wright," *AF* 68 (January 1938): 64; and *A* I, 305.

51. FLW, "In the Cause: Arizona," 1–2; and *A* I, 305. Wright similarly compared the wood-and-canvas cabins designed for the San Marcos Water Gardens to the concrete-block San Marcos-in-the-Desert Hotel: "I should like these small edifices to be to the royal dignity and solidity of San Marcos-in-the-Desert what a butterfly might be to the rock on which it might alight" (FLW to Chandler, 14 September 1929, FLWF).

52. FLW, "In the Cause: Arizona," 8.

53. Wright's framing of the discussion of Ocatilla in terms of the issue of impermanence versus permanence recalls Hugo's opposition of the "durability" of stone building to the "imperishability" of the printed word in his novel *Notre-Dame de Paris* (bk. V, chap. 2, "This Will Kill That"). Hugo noted that whereas architecture made thought "permanent in stone," printed matter made it "ubiquitous": "You can demolish a great building, but how do you root out ubiquity?" (*Notre-Dame of Paris* [1832; 8th ed., trans. John Sturrock, Harmondsworth: Penguin, 1978], 196). Wright recalled this in saying that he would not "grieve long" over the "*short life*" Ocatilla had, "because our machine [age] so easily gives it, as a design, to the mind's eye of all." Wright viewed the press as Ocatilla's medium of preservation: "'Ocatilla' was published in German magazines two months after it was finished. Thank the machine, at least, for this *ubiquity* of publicity" (*A* I, 306, italics added). In the second edition of the *Autobiography*, where he added that "the Indians carried it [the camp] all away," Wright entitled the section about Ocatilla "Ubiquity" (*A* II, 312). Wright would always remain acutely aware of the value of the press and publicity for the dissemination of his ideas.

54. In a draft of the Ocatilla section, Wright specified that the petroglyph boulders were seen "from our translucent draftingroom" (FLW, "Arizona," June 1929, p. 3, transcribed by Heinrich Klumb, Klumb Archive). This means that the "mounds" in question were the ones immediately to the northeast of the camp, where the San Marcos Desert Lodge was located. For reasons that he never explained, Wright excised the paragraph about the petroglyph boulders from the second edition of the *Autobiography*. This was published right after he completed the first campaign of building of Taliesin West, where he used a number of such boulders found at the site as an integral part of the design (see Chapter IX). For a survey of archeological evidence, see Ernest E. Snyder, "Petroglyphs of the South Mountains of Arizona," *American Antiquity* 31, no. 5 (1966): 705–9.

55. Although important work had been done by Jesse W. Fewkes at Casa Grande and published by 1912, it was not until Kidder's *Introduction to the Study of Southwestern Archaeology* (1924) that a "new archaeology" came into existence. In 1928 the Arizona Museum was founded in Phoenix with a staff of three archaeologists. In the same year, Harold Colton set up the Museum of Northern Arizona in Flagstaff, and Harold Gladwin built Gila Pueblo near the town of Globe as a center for research into the Hohokam culture of the Salt-Gila basin. It was Gladwin's group, including Emil Haury, that was to excavate Snaketown and publish the most important work about the Hohokam in the 1930s (see Chapter IX).

56. See especially D. H. Lawrence, "New Mexico," orig. pub. *Survey Graphic*, May 1931, repr. in *Phoenix: The Posthumous Papers of D. H. Lawrence, 1936*, ed. Edward D. MacDonald (1936; Harmondsworth: Penguin, 1978), 141–47; and Lawrence, *Studies in Classic American Literature*, (1923; rpt. Harmondsworth: Penguin, 1971), 7–14 ("The Spirit of Place"). Cf. pp. 140–41 above.

57. This remark was immediately followed by certain exceptions:

Egyptian and Mayan came nearest and did best.

The American Indian in default of masonry, did well. He 'belonged.' He was becoming enough with his tepee, beads, wampum, and feather-dress,—his pots and tanned animal skins.

His was a forth-right spirit in keeping with it all.

58. FLW, "In the Cause: Arizona," 4–5.

59. For Wright's descriptions of the hotel, see *A* I, 301–2 and 308–10; and *AF* 68 (January 1938): 64. For a local, boosterish newspaper report on the project, see Addison N. Clark, "San Marcos-in-the-Desert Will Be Nation's

Finest Host," *Chandler Arizonan*, 21 March 1929, pp. 6–7. Clark was the secretary of the Chandler Improvement Association. In his article in the *Chandler Arizonan*, he noted that he "turned and looked far off to the south and east where, almost a hundred miles away, could be seen the jagged peaks of the Catalina Mountains that beetle above Tucson" (p. 7). I am grateful to Bruce Pfeiffer for indicating to me where the site was and for helping me to appreciate its character before it was destroyed by housing developments.

Aside from the drawings done by the draftsmen Wright brought with him from Wisconsin, a number of the finished sketches and perspectives were produced by Lloyd Wright.

60. FLW to Chandler, Summary of Costs, 20 November 1929, p. 2, FLWF. Wright told Chandler he would make use of the "solid rock" for foundations because "I do not want to dig into the water-washed surface of the Desert" (24 July 1929, FLWF).

In the Specifications, sent to Chandler on 20 November 1929, Wright stated:

The 60–30 degree, or 1–2 triangle being characteristic of all mountain regions and the approximate cross-section of the talus at the mountain base, has been freely used as a "stock angle" in the various parts of the ground plan in order to associate them with a proper grip upon the nature-forms of the ground they surmount.

The elevations however, are all cut to level, the triangular forms disappearing to reappear only in minor parts as an occasional copper-crowning of the blocks. The building silhouettes when seen from below, only, will show this triangular influence as does the region itself.

The masses of the building thus remain quiet, the triangular movement of the plan qualifying it only as an influence felt, but not seen for its own sake at any point whatsoever. . . .

"Of the desert, not on it" is the slogan that fits the building scheme, and the Desert, as it is, has been measured carefully, the building arranged to fit it and make the most of its native beauty. (FLW, "San Marcos in the Desert, for Alexander Chandler, Chandler, Arizona. Frank Lloyd Wright, Architect," p. 1, MS 2401.520 B, FLWF)

61. Bruce Pfeiffer has pointed out that one of the revolutionary ideas in the hotel was that the rooms, or apartments, were to be rented on a "time-sharing" basis (*Treasures of Taliesin: Seventy-six Unbuilt Designs* [Fresno, Calif., and Carbondale and Edwardsville, Ill.: Press of California State University, Southern Illinois University Press, 1985], n.p.)

62. Realizing the problem with sound transfer in reinforced-concrete construction, Wright claimed that "the building process [goes] on from floor to floor without regard to finished floors which are all laid after construction is completed and the sound-proofing members are in place" (Specifications, 2). The corridor floors were to be covered with cork.

63. FLW, Specifications, 1–2. Wright stated that "the structure is, in a real sense, '*fabricated*,'" reinforcing the analogy with weaving. He noted that, "were all concrete removed," the interwoven reinforcing rods "would show the forms of the building as steel wicker work" (pp. 1–2).

64. Ibid., 3. The costs broke down as follows: construction of hotel building alone, $483,846.60; construction of service unit, $40,000.00; architect and engineering fees, $52,384.66; furnishings, $167,738.45. The total came to $743,969.71. Wright often later quoted the figure of $480,000 (*AF* [January 1938]: 64), leaving out the furnishings.

65. The horizontal movement along superimposed ledges can be related to the Doheny Ranch project and to Le Corbusier's planning strategies of the twenties. One should also note the similarity to the Villa Savoye in the combined use of spiral stairs (here encased in triangular housings) and ramps in the main volume of the hotel.

66. For a further elaboration of this idea, see my "Questioning the View: Seaside's Critique of the Gaze of Modern Architecture," in *Seaside: Making a Town in America*, ed. David Mohney and Keller Easterling (New York: Princeton Architectural Press, 1991).

67. Wright was particularly conscious of this change in his work and linked it directly to the effect of the desert. He wrote in 1929: "Arizona is Architecture in tremendous sense. It will make any rightminded architect sick of everything he has done ever in his life. . . . For the Desert . . . comes to the

Artist as an inner experience. . . . When it does come it comes . . . as a beneficent simplifying influence" ("In the Cause: Arizona," 1).

Wright's first mention of the International Style comes in the third book of the *Autobiography*, in the section entitled "The Box," which immediately precedes the section on "Arizona" (I, 300). Wright's critique of the "straight line" and "flat plane" of the International Style's "cardboard box for boxing up space" is clearly illustrated by his choice of the terms "dotted line" and "textured, broken plane" to describe an architecture for the desert (I, 304). The "straight line" and "flat plane," he states, are antithetical to the environment and result in a building "divorced from nature by nature" (I, 300). The "dotted line" and "textured, broken plane" allow the building to accept the sun, to "take the light and play with it and break it up and render it harmless or drink it in until, sunlight blends the building into place with the creation around it" (FLW, "To Arizona," 27 March 1940, pp. [4–5], MS 2401.150, FLWF). The St. Mark's Tower and Elizabeth Noble Apartment House projects of 1928–30 give evidence of Wright's adoption of more straightforward modernist formal devices for the urban environment.

68. A I, 309; and *AF* (January 1938): 64. In the Specifications, Wright referred to "the exterior wall [of the building as] being scoriated like the walls of the sahuaro, the horizontal joints only appearing slightly as a dotted line" (p. 2). See also note 67 above.

69. I use the term *non-objectivity* here as it was customarily used from the 1930s to the 1950s: to distinguish an art like Wright's or Picasso's, which simplifies, clarifies, reorganizes, and "abstracts" natural objects, from a "non-objective" art like Mondrian's, Le Corbusier's, or Mies's, which starts from "pure" geometric forms that are in and of themselves understood to be nonrepresentational. For more on this distinction, see the discussion of Hilla Rebay and the Guggenheim Museum in Chapter X.

70. *AF* (January 1938): 64; and *A* I, 302.

71. FLW, "In the Cause of Architecture, III: The Meaning of Materials—Stone," *ARec* 63 (April 1928): 350. There may have been more to this remark than meets the eye. Wright wrote to Darwin Martin on 5 April 1928 that "there is a Fred Harvey Hotel at the Grand Canyon to take the place of El Tovar, in regard to which I am in a pretty good position already" (Box 5-5 [should be 5-4], Wright-Martin Papers). Wright never got the job, however.

Wright returned to the theme of the Grand Canyon in his Princeton lectures of May 1930. In the fifth lecture ("The Tyranny of the Skyscraper"), he pitied Michelangelo for not having been able to experience the Grand Canyon, insinuating that the entire history of Western architecture might have been different had he had the opportunity:

Michelangelo built the first skyscraper, I suppose, when he hurled the Pantheon on top of the Parthenon.

. . . The new church dome that was the consequence was empty of meaning or of any significance whatever except as the Pope's mitre has it. . . . [T]he great dome was just the sort of thing authority had been looking for as a symbol. . . .

Yet, as a consequence of a great sculptor's sense of grandeur in an Art that was not quite his own, we may see a tyranny that might well make the tyrannical skyscraper of the present day sway in its socket sick with envy. . . . How tragic it all is! It is not only as though Buonarroti himself had never seen the Grand Canyon, which of course he never could have seen, but it is as though no one else had ever seen it either, and monumental buildings therefore kept right on being domeous, domicular or dome-istic—on stilts because they knew no better. (Princeton Lects., 84–85)

72. FLW, "Meaning of Materials—Stone," 356.

73. FLW, "In the Cause of Architecture, VII: The Meaning of Materials—Concrete," *ARec* 64 (August 1928): 99, 102–4.

74. FLW, "Arizona," June 1929, p. 3; FLW, "To Arizona" [1929], p. 2, transcribed by H. Klumb, Klumb Archive. In "Arizona" Wright also included references to the "patterns of the rattlesnake, the Gila-monster, [and] the chameleon."

75. *AF* (January 1938): 64; and *A* I, 309.

76. FLW, Specifications, 1.

77. Perfectly catching that quality of movement and life in the plan,

Wright wistfully described it to Chandler in 1930 as "our lizard out in the desert" (FLW to Chandler, 18 February 1930, FLWF).

78. In a preliminary version of this text, in which the order of the paragraphs differs, Wright immediately followed the description of subsidence and erosion with a reference to the sun, based on Mallarmé's poem "L'Azur": "In Mallarmé's poem L'Azur, the addict who, in his plight, would shun the sky 'the blue' if he could, —notwithstanding all his efforts to get away from it, found, 'the blue' forever there. There was no escape for him. So there seems no mortal escape even in death from this Earth principle of *growth*, or 'Vegetation,'— that creative-creature of the Sun" ("In the Cause: Arizona," 2–3). This represents one of Wright's rare references to modern European poetry and can certainly be taken as another indication of his interest in modernism as it was being defined at the time, especially in France.

79. In a graduate seminar on Taliesin West that I gave at Harvard University in the fall of 1988–89, Danny Abramson pointed out the significance of this idea for Wright in the late twenties and how it affected his design of Taliesin West in the following decade.

80. We have already seen the sexual metaphor at work in the early Romeo and Juliet Tower and, especially, in the "marriage" of house and hill in Taliesin. In the late twenties, that idea became explicit once again. Speaking of the impress of imagination on material (in this case concrete), Wright described the process as "coition at last" and the effect as "the third dimension triumphant" (FLW, "In the Cause of Architecture, IV: Fabrication and Imagination," *ARec* 62 [October 1927]: 321). Expanding the reference to the relation of building to landscape, Wright remarked that, when "our sense of depth becomes that sense of the thing, or the quality in it that makes it *integral*," then "the human spirit is free to blossom in structure as organic as plants and trees" and thus "buildings, too, are children of Earth and Sun" (FLW, "In the Cause of Architecture, V: The New World," *ARec* 62 [October 1927]: 322).

81. FLW, "Notes and Comments: Surface and Mass, —Again!" *ARec* 66 (July 1929): 92. This article, dated 5 April 1929, was written in response to articles by Douglas Haskell and Henry-Russell Hitchcock that described Wright's work as romantic, traditionalist, and even historicist by comparison with that of the younger Europeans.

82. FLW, "Fabrication and Imagination," 321. In the second edition of the *Autobiography*, he added the following regarding San Marcos-in-the-Desert: "Human habitation here comes decently in where God is [cf.: "The desert is where God is and Man is not"]. Man is come in as himself something of a God. And just that is what Architecture can do for him—not only show appreciation of Arizona's character but qualify him in a human habitation to become a godlike native part of Arizona for so long as any building ever endured" (II, 314).

83. The concept of fate, combined with the associated idea of serenity, finds its first expression in Wright's thought in his description of the 1925 fire at Taliesin (see *A* I, 258–60, 271–73).

84. FLW to Martin, 9 May 1929, Box 5-20, Wright-Martin Papers.

85. FLW to Chandler, 24 October 1929, FLWF.

86. After Fallingwater and Taliesin West were built, Wright wrote that, with the San Marcos and Ocatilla projects, "something had started that was not stopping thus, later you will see the consequences" (*A* II, 315).

Chapter VIII
The Temporal Dimension of Fallingwater

1. The Johnson story is told, among other places, in Johnson's own collected *Writings* (New York: Oxford University Press, 1979), 192, in the commentary by Robert A. M. Stern. Johnson has more than once denied the story. See most recently Edgar Tafel, *About Wright: An Album of Recollections by Those Who Knew Frank Lloyd Wright* (New York: John Wiley, 1993), 50 (interview with Johnson). The quotation from Wright comes from a letter to Fiske Kimball, of 30 April 1928, published in "American Architecture: Correspondence of Walter Pach, Paul Cret, Frank Lloyd Wright and Erich Mendelsohn with Fiske Kimball," *ARec* 65 (May 1929): 434. A further dimension to the Johnson story was added by Wright in 1955 when, upon meeting his younger

colleague at Yale, he is reported to have said: "Why, Philip, I thought you were dead!" (originally quoted in Selden Rodman, ed., *Conversations with Artists* [New York: Capricorn, 1961], 53; this version in Vincent Scully, "Frank Lloyd Wright and Philip Johnson at Yale," *Architectural Digest* 43 [March 1986]: 94). One might well assume from this that Wright had heard a version of the original story close to the one referred to in the text.

2. "Usonian Architect," *Time* 31 (17 January 1938): 29–32; *AF* 68 (January 1938): 1–102; John McAndrew, *A New House by Frank Lloyd Wright on Bear Run, Pennsylvania* (New York: Museum of Modern Art, January 1938). Wright designed the cover and frontispiece for the special edition of *AF* that was "devoted to the new and unpublished work" of his (p. 1). He was responsible for the choice of material as well as the layout. *AF* was published by Time, Inc., which was owned by Henry R. and Claire Booth Luce, soon to become good friends of the Wrights. The editor at the time was Howard Myers. Myers had originally written to Wright in the fall of 1936 to get the rights to publish the Johnson Wax Building. By the summer of 1936, discussion had shifted to doing an entire issue on Wright's recent work. See *LArchitects*, 153–60 et seq.

The two one-building exhibitions at the Museum of Modern Art prior to that of Fallingwater were: "A House by Richard C. Wood," and "Project for a House in North Carolina by William T. Priestly," both held in 1933. I would like to thank Matilda McQuaid for this information.

3. The older view of Wright's return to prominence in the late 1930s that I refer to here divided his career into two major and distinct periods: the Prairie Style up to 1909, and the Usonian after 1936. Looking from a modernist perspective, it viewed Wright's early work as a precursor of European developments and his later work as a response to and outgrowth of them. In 1942, Henry-Russell Hitchcock described the period of the thirties as a "revival" (Hitchcock, *Materials*, 89–90); later he characterized it as Wright's "renewal" and "'second' career" (Hitchcock, *Architecture: Nineteenth and Twentieth Centuries*, Pelican History of Art [Harmondsworth: Penguin, 1958], 528–30). Norris Kelly Smith spoke of it as a "resurgence" (Smith, *Wright*, 129ff.); and Robert Twombly described it as a "resuscitation" and a "renaissance" (Twombly, *Wright*, 236, 240). The religious connotation of these descriptions is both personal (Wright's "second coming") and ideological (Wright's "conversion" to modernism). Hitchcock wrote in 1942: "There are no projects leading up to the Kaufmann house unless it be the 'House on the Mesa' [of 1931]. It seems to have sprung as suddenly from the brow of Wright as did the River Forest Golf Club more than a generation earlier, with the difference that the world was now prepared to appreciate it, and to receive with loud acclaim a building that seemed to epitomize the aspirations not of Wright alone, but of all modern architects" (Hitchcock, *Materials*, 91).

Matisse's career has been interpreted in a similar way by those committed to a strict construction of modernism. His work from approximately 1917 to the mid-1930s is excluded from the canon for being *retardataire*, bourgeois, and essentially representational. (This is when Matisse spent most of his time away from the Parisian art scene at Nice in the south of France.) Such an interpretation limits the interest in his work to the periods up to 1905–1907 and after 1935, a chronology that corresponds closely with the typically modernist view of Wright. Cf. Yve-Alain Bois, *Painting as Model* (Cambridge, Mass., and London: MIT Press, *October* Book, 1990), 3–63.

For a recent study of Wright's architecture and thought of the 1930s, which appeared after this chapter was written, see Donald Leslie Johnson, *Frank Lloyd Wright versus America: The 1930s* (Cambridge, Mass., and London: MIT Press, 1990).

4. Princeton Lects.; FLW, *Two Lectures on Architecture* (Chicago: Art Institute of Chicago, 1931); and FLW, *The Disappearing City* (New York: William Farquhar Payson, 1932). For its final two stops, the exhibition traveled to Milwaukee and Eugene, Oregon.

Wright spoke of the "complete works" to Darwin Martin in a letter of 21 October 1929: "I worked several days at the Record . . . on the forthcoming book. They are putting fifty thousand dollars into a complete publication of my writing and building to date,—should appear sometime in the spring" (Box 5-26, Wright-Martin Papers). In an inventory prepared for Darwin Martin and the shareholders of Frank Lloyd Wright, Inc., in April 1930, Wright listed, among his present publications, a "book of my work published this coming fall by Architectural Record of New York underway" (Box 5-29, Wright-Martin

Papers). By 1931, Scribner's had apparently taken over the rights to the work, but nothing came of it. Texts and a mock-up for "Creative Matter in the Nature of Materials" are in MS 2401.531, FLWF.

5. See esp. Robert C. Twombly, "Organic Living: Frank Lloyd Wright's Taliesin Fellowship and Georgi Gurdjieff's Institute for the Harmonious Development of Man," *Wisconsin Magazine of History* 58 (Winter 1974–75): 126–39. For early discussions of the Fellowship, see: FLW, "The Taliesin Fellowship," *London Studio* 4 (December 1932): 348–49; "Taliesin Fellowship," *American Magazine of Art* 26 (December 1933): 552–53; FLW, "The Taliesin Fellowship," *Wisconsin Alumni Magazine* 35 (March 1934): 152–53, 176; John Gloag, "Frank Lloyd Wright and the Significance of the Taliesin Fellowship," *ARev* 77 (January 1935): 1–2; FLW, "Taliesin: Our Cause," *Professional Art Quarterly* 2 (March 1936): 6–7, 24, and (June 1936): 39–41; FLW, "Apprenticeship-Training for the Architect," *ARec* 80 (September 1936): 207–10; and *A* II, 381–94 ("An Extension of the Work in Architecture at Taliesin to Include Apprentices in Residence").

6. FLW, "The Hillside Home School of Allied Arts," 10 December 1928, pp. 6, 12–13; and Ferdinand Schevill, "Summarized Statement of the Project for a School of Allied Arts at Hillside, Wisconsin," p. 1, Box 5-14, Wright-Martin Papers. In the second of his Princeton lectures of 1930, Wright presented some early thoughts for an "Art School . . . in which the Fine Arts would be not only allied to the Industries they serve, but would stand there at the center of an industrial hive of characteristic industry as inspiration and influence in design-problems" (Princeton Lects., 41).

7. For Cranbrook, see *Design in America: The Cranbrook Vision, 1925–50* (New York: Harry N. Abrams, Detroit Institute of Arts, and Metropolitan Museum of Art, 1983), esp. 21–45. The earliest discussions between George G. Booth, the founder and benefactor of the Cranbrook schools, and Saarinen go back to 1924. Plans were made in 1924–25, and the first buildings were begun in 1926. The decision to establish an academy was made in 1927; in 1929, it was decided to integrate the school of arts and crafts into the academy. Its buildings were begun in 1929; the first students arrived in 1931; and the official opening took place in 1932. Among the numerous accounts of the Bauhaus, see Herbert Bayer, Walter Gropius, and Ise Gropius, eds., *Bauhaus, 1919–28* (New York: Museum of Modern Art, 1938); and Hans M. Wingler, *The Bauhaus: Weimar, Dessau, Berlin, Chicago* (1962; rev. and enl. ed., Cambridge, Mass., and London: MIT Press, 1969).

As noted above (Chapter IV, note 34), Wright had become acquainted with C. R. Ashbee's Guild of Handicraft in Chipping Camden when he visited it in the fall of 1910.

8. See Alfred H. Barr et al., *Modern Architecture: International Exhibition*, 10 February–23 March 1932 (New York: Museum of Modern Art, 1932), 15 (Barr, "Foreword"); and Henry-Russell Hitchcock and Philip Johnson, *The International Style* (1932; 2d ed., New York: W. W. Norton, 1966), esp. 11–39. See also now Terence Riley, *The International Style: Exhibition 15 and the Museum of Modern Art*, Columbia Books of Architecture, Catalogue 3 (New York: Rizzoli, Columbia Books of Architecture, 1992).

For Wright's reaction to recent European architecture and the MOMA exhibition, see FLW, review of *Towards a New Architecture* by Le Corbusier, *World Unity* 2 (September 1928): 393–95; "Surface and Mass,—Again!" *ARec* 66 (July 1929): 92–94; "The Logic of Contemporary Architecture as an Expression of This Age," *AF* 52 (May 1930): 637–38; Princeton Lects., 27–44, 65–80, 101–15; "Highlights," *AF* 55 (October 1931): 409–10; "For All May Raise the Flowers Now for All Have Got the Seed," *T-Square* 2 (February 1932): 6–8; "Letters to the Editor," *T-Square* 2 (February 1932): 32; and "Of Thee I Sing," *Shelter* 2 (April 1932): 10–12 (written on the occasion of the MOMA exhibition and intended for distribution at the museum while the exhibition was in progress). Wright continued the criticism throughout the remainder of his career, sometimes in jest, sometimes quite acerbically. For an example of the latter, see FLW, "Frank Lloyd Wright Speaks Up," *House Beautiful* 95 (July 1953): 86–88, 90. This was written in reaction to MOMA's 1952 exhibition of *Built in USA: Post-War Architecture*.

9. Some of the most important reviews of Wright's work, or significant references to it, are: Jean Badovici, "Frank Lloyd Wright," *Cahiers d'art* 1, no. 2 (February 1926): 30–33; Henry-Russell Hitchcock, *Frank Lloyd Wright*, Les Maîtres de l'Architecture Contemporaine, no. 1 (Paris: Cahiers d'art, 1928);

Hitchcock, "Modern Architecture, I: The Traditionalists and the New Tradition," *ARec* 63 (April 1928): 337–49, and "Modern Architecture, II: The New Pioneers," *ARec* 63 (May 1928): 453–60; Lewis Mumford, "American Architecture To-day," pt. 2, *Architecture* 57 (June 1928): 301–8; Douglas Haskell, "Organic Architecture: Frank Lloyd Wright," *Creative Art* 3 (November 1928): li–lvii; Mumford, "Frank Lloyd Wright and the New Pioneers," *ARec* 65 (April 1929): 414–16; Hitchcock, *Modern Architecture: Romanticism and Reintegration* (1929; rpt. New York: Hacker Art Books, 1970), 113–18 (English translation of essay in Les Maîtres de l'Architecture Contemporaine series); Sigfried Giedion, "Le Corbusier et l'architecture contemporaine," *Cahiers d'art* 5, no. 4 (1930): 205–13; Badovici, "Frank Lloyd Wright," *Architecture Vivante* 8 (Summer 1930): 49–76; Mumford, *The Brown Decades: A Study of the Arts of America, 1865–1895* (1931; rpt. New York: Dover, 1955), 165–81; Giedion, "Les Problèmes actuels de l'architecture à l'occasion d'un manifeste de Frank Lloyd Wright aux architectes et critiques d'Europe," *Cahiers d'art* 7, nos. 1–2 (1932): 69–73; and Catherine K. Bauer, "Exhibition of Modern Architecture, Museum of Modern Art," *Creative Art* 10 (March 1932): 201–6.

10. FLW, "Surface and Mass," 93; FLW, review of *Towards a New Architecture*, 395; and FLW, "Wright Speaks Up," 88.

11. FLW, "All May Raise the Flowers," 8; Princeton Lects., 3; and FLW, "Surface and Mass," 93. Cf. FLW, "Wright Speaks Up," 90.

12. FLW, "Highlights," 409.

13. Henry-Russell Hitchcock, in Alfred Barr et al., *Modern Architecture*, 37; FLW, "Of Thee I Sing," 10, 12. The words *hide* and *horns* were probably references to the journal *Hound & Horn: A Harvard Miscellany* with which Hitchcock had been associated and in which some of his earliest pronouncements about modern architecture appeared.

14. Quoted in Gutheim, *FLW on Arch.*, 136. In a similar vein, at the time of his European traveling exhibition, Wright wrote on 23 July 1931 an open letter "To My Critics in the Land of the Danube and the Rhine," sent to Wijdeveld, Mendelsohn, Klumb, and the *Frankfurter Allgemeine Zeitung*. It ended: "And realize that I am still at work with greater appreciation of life. What you have seen from my hand is yet unfinished" (MS 2401.097, FLWF).

In *Modern Architecture: Romanticism and Reintegration* (1929), Hitchcock described Wright as "unquestionably eclectic in style" and thus the consummate representative of the "New Tradition in the Twentieth century . . . in America." He qualified this only by saying that Wright's "eclecticism in opposition to the revival of European styles by his contemporaries in America has thrown him back consciously or unconsciously on the Far East, the Ancient East, and the Maya of Mexico" (pp. 104, 117). Fundamentally, Hitchcock had made the same points in his pathbreaking article of the previous year, "Modern Architecture, I: The New Tradition." The position elaborated by Hitchcock was restated by Douglas Haskell, who wrote in the fall of 1928: "Frank Lloyd Wright is more of his time than his disciples like to think. . . . He belongs still to that imperialistic period . . . which we generally associate with the Roman structures of McKim, Mead & White: the very lavishness of his ornament proclaims it. . . . And the imagination belongs, after all, to the eclectic period. McKim, Mead & White took 'Italian Renaissance' and modelled it; Frank Lloyd Wright ranged over the world's architecture and digested it. Not for nothing are some of his constructions related to Japanese, some to Maya, some to Egyptian art" (Haskell, "Organic Architecture," lvi–lvii).

15. FLW, "Surface and Mass," 93; FLW, "Logic of Contemporary Architecture," 638; and FLW, "Of Thee I Sing," 11.

16. See note 8 above. See also my "Abstraction and Representation in Modern Architecture: Frank Lloyd Wright and the International Style," *AA Files: Annals of the Architectural Association School of Architecture* 11 (Spring 1986): 3–21 and errata.

17. Wright's original proposal of 1928 for the Hillside Home School of the Allied Arts was accompanied by a somewhat different plan for the expansion of the former Hillside Home School. A courtyard, surrounded by the men's dormitory, connected the 1901–1903 buildings to a transverse, skylit shop wing on the north, paralleling the original buildings. Behind that were to be instructors' houses, and to the east, connected by the dining room, was to be a wing running perpendicular to the state highway, serving as the women's dormitory. For the plan and perspective, see *FLWM*, vol. 5, 54–55. This plan

served as the basis for those developed for Taliesin West and Florida Southern College (both begun 1938).

18. "Frank Lloyd Wright," *AF* (January 1938): 18. The other major space located in the renovated buildings was the playhouse. It used a thirty/sixty-degree geometry to create a "reflex arrangement of seating" that would fit into the rectangular shape of the old gymnasium (ibid., 23). The drafting room replaced the men's dormitory court of the 1928 plan.

19. *AF* (January 1938): 18. Wright described the condition of the existing structures and his intentions in reusing them in *A* I, 384–89.

The Midway Barn complex was built in the later 1930s to early 1940s, and a new entrance court and farm-workshop area were added to the upper (northwest) corner of the house. It was also at this time that the access drive of Taliesin was diverted from its circuitous route around the east and south slopes of the hill to merge with the former exit drive on the northwest as part of a new two-way road system. The new entrance was located under the original drafting room, to which one now mounted (from the northwest) by foot through the loggia between the house and the studio. This removed traffic from the inner court and hill garden, turning that space into a more private, domestic "backyard" for the Wrights and their guests. I should like to thank Danny Abramson for clarifying a number of these important changes in a paper he did in a graduate seminar on Taliesin at Harvard University in the fall of 1987–88.

20. Sweeney, *Wright in Hollywood*, 196, claims that the House on the Mesa had no real client, but was simply inspired by a trip to Denver in December 1930. Each of the architects in the International Style show at MOMA was asked to submit a model of an important new project or building, and Wright chose the House on the Mesa. In the catalogue of the exhibition, Henry-Russell Hitchcock praised the design as indicating that "the distance between him [Wright] and even Le Corbusier . . . grows ever less" as the "community of feeling" between their work increases (in Barr et al., *Modern Architecture*, 36). The plan for the Oregon newspaper plant served as the basis for the later Johnson Wax headquarters.

21. George Collins described Broadacre City as "a sort of WPA project" in his "Broadacre City: Wright's Utopia Reconsidered," in *Four Great Makers of Modern Architecture: Gropius, Le Corbusier, Mies van der Rohe, Wright, Verbatim Record of a Symposium Held at the School of Architecture, Columbia University, March–May 1961* (New York: Trustees of Columbia University, 1963), 67. Collins's article still remains one of the best on the subject. Among the other studies in this quite extensive bibliography are: Meyer Schapiro, "Architect's Utopia," *Partisan Review* 4 (March 1938): 42–47; Lionel March, "Imperial City of the Boundless West—Lionel March describes the impact of Chicago on the work of Frank Lloyd Wright," *Listener* 83 (30 April 1970): 581–84; Robert Fishman, *Urban Utopias in the 20th Century: Ebenezer Howard, Frank Lloyd Wright, Le Corbusier* (New York: Basic Books, 1977), 91–160; Giorgio Ciucci, "The City in Agrarian Ideology and Frank Lloyd Wright: Origins and Development of Broadacres," in Ciucci et al., *The American City: From the Civil War to the New Deal* (1973; trans. Barbara Luigia La Penta, Cambridge, Mass.: MIT Press, 1983, 293–387; March, "An Architect in Search of Democracy: Broadacre City," talks broadcast on BBC's Third Programme, 7 and 15 January 1970, in H. Allen Brooks, ed., *Writings on Wright: Selected Comment on Frank Lloyd Wright* (Cambridge, Mass., and London: MIT Press, 1981), 195–206; Herbert Muschamp, *Man About Town: Frank Lloyd Wright in New York City* (Cambridge, Mass.: MIT Press, 1983), esp. 45–87; and, most recently, Anthony Alofsin, "Broadacre City: The Reception of a Modernist Vision," *Center: A Journal for Architecture in America*, vol. 5, *Modernist Visions and the Contemporary American City* (Austin: Center for the Study of American Architecture, School of Architecture, University of Texas, 1989): 8–43.

Among Wright's numerous presentations of the project, the most important are: *The Disappearing City* (1932; rev. and enl. as *When Democracy Builds*, Chicago: University of Chicago Press, 1945; rev. and enl. as *The Living City*, New York: Horizon Press, 1958; and rev. and enl. as *The Industrial Revolution Runs Away*, New York: Horizon Press, 1969); "'Broadacre City': An Architect's Vision," *NYT Magazine*, 20 March 1932, pp. 8–9; "Broadacre City: A New Community Plan," *ARec* 77 (April 1935): 243–54; "Broadacre City: Frank Lloyd Wright, Architect," *American Architect* 146 (May 1935): 55–62; "An Autobiography, Book Six: Broadacre City" (1943), typescript prepared for *A* II but not included until the posthumous 1977 edition (*A* III, 593–616). Wright stressed the oppositional character of his concept for Broadacre City in the *NYT Magazine* article and in *Disappearing City*, 29, 33.

22. The integration of living and work in an agrarian environment where subsistence farming would be an essential element is the most basic parallel. The administrative center of the regional (county) government was located around a man-made lake just beneath the hill in the corner of the model. On the hypotenuse of the lake was a long building intended for crafts and the industrial arts and for the office of the county architect. The architect was thus made a central figure in the regional planning of the scheme.

23. Wright described Broadacre City as "nowhere unless everywhere" (*When Democracy Builds*, 58; and " 'Broadacre City': Architect's Vision," 8), thus alluding to the utopian origin of the project. The title of Thomas More's book *Utopia* (1516), invented to describe an ideal commonwealth, was a neologism meaning "nowhere" (from the Greek *ou* ["not"] + *topos* ["a place"]).

Interest in Broadacre City, especially on the part of European architects and critics, has grown considerably since the late 1960s, often overshadowing interest in buildings and designs Wright would seem to have put more time and effort into. Since it is one of his least resolved and most easily criticized projects—on social, political, economic, as well as formal grounds—its prominence in the literature has often served a rather negative purpose.

24. FLW, *The Natural House* (New York: Horizon Press, 1954). For an excellent discussion of the underlying principles of Wright's domestic work from this time on, see John Sergeant, *Frank Lloyd Wright's Usonian Houses: The Case for Organic Architecture* (New York: Whitney Library of Design, Watson-Guptill, 1976). See now also Alvin Rosenbaum, *Usonia: Frank Lloyd Wright's Design for America* (Washington, D.C.: Preservation Press, National Trust for Historic Preservation, 1993).

25. Wright received the commission for the Willey House in the spring or early summer of 1932, following the publication of his *Autobiography* (March 1932) and the publicity generated by the International Style exhibition at the Museum of Modern Art (opened 24 January 1932). The first project was presented to the clients in late August of that year. Cost became an issue by April 1933, and a two-stage construction procedure was debated. It was then decided to redesign the project completely, which Wright did by the end of the year. The second scheme was finished by the end of February 1934. It was put out for bids in April and finished enough so that the Willeys could move in before Thanksgiving of that year. See *LClients*, 67–81.

For early publications and discussions of the Willey House, see: "Portfolio of Houses: House of Prof. Malcolm Willey in Minneapolis, Frank Lloyd Wright, Architect," *ARec* 78 (November 1935): 313–15; *AF* (January 1938): 24–31; and Lewis Mumford, "The Sky Line—at Home, Indoors and Out," *New Yorker* 13 (12 February 1938): 31.

26. For a fuller analysis of this, see my "Frank Lloyd Wright's Diagonal Planning," in Helen Searing, ed., *In Search of Modern Architecture: A Tribute to Henry-Russell Hitchcock* (New York, Cambridge, Mass., and London: Architectural History Foundation, MIT Press, 1982), 262–65.

27. *AF* (January 1938): 45. The house-as-sequestered-garden can already be seen in the 1931 project for the House on the Mesa. The cost of the first Willey project was estimated at $16,500, as compared to $10,000 for the second. In describing the difference in expression between the two projects to his former apprentice Heinrich Klumb, Wright said: "I have re-designed the Willey's House and they will now get Poetry instead of Drama. Drama always comes high I guess" (FLW to Klumb, 23 December 1933, Klumb Archive).

28. Eugène-Emmanuel Viollet-le-Duc, *The Habitations of Man in All Ages* (1875; trans. Benjamin Bucknall, Boston: James R. Osgood, 1876), 8–26. Wright called the Willey House a "northern house" (*AF* [January 1938]: 24). Viollet referred to his lean-to shelter as a "House of the Arya" (p. 11). Wright specifically referred to having read this book during his first year or so working in Chicago: "From the library of 'All Souls' I got two books you would never expect could be found there. Owen Jones' 'Grammar of Ornament,' and Viollet-le-Duc's 'Habitations of Man in all Ages' " (*A* I, 74).

29. In one of his earliest descriptions of the Usonian House, Wright noted in relation to his design of the Jacobs House in Madison, Wisconsin (1936–37):

In our country the chief obstacle to any real solution of the moderate-cost house-problem is the fact that our people do not really know how to live, imagining their idiosyncrasies to be their "tastes," their prejudices to be their predilections and their ignorance to be virtue where any beauty of living is concerned.

To be more specific, a small house on the side street might have charm if it didn't ape the big house on the avenue. . . .

. . . That house must be a pattern for more simple and, at the same time, more gracious living: new, but suitable to living conditions as they might so well be in the country we live in today.

This needed house of moderate cost must sometime face reality. . . .

. . . Simplifications must take place. Mr. & Mrs. Jacobs must themselves see life in somewhat simplified terms. (AF [January 1938]: 78)

30. The Willey House would also be published by Wright in *When Democracy Builds* as a model Broadacre City plan-type for any "steeply sloping site" (fig. [8]). After serving as the basis for Fallingwater, it gave the name of "Little Fallingwater" to the various Usonian Houses like the Sturges and Affleck houses that were based on it.

The Bay Region Style was championed in the immediate postwar period by Lewis Mumford, who clearly saw the debt of that movement to Wright. Among the proponents of the Bay Region Style, perhaps the most important, as well as the one most influenced by Wright, was Harwell Hamilton Harris.

31. For a documentation of many of these issues, see now Susan J. Bandes, ed., *Affordable Dreams: The Goetsch-Winckler House and Frank Lloyd Wright* (*Kresge Art Museum Bulletin* 6 [1991]) (East Lansing: Michigan State University, 1991). On Malcolm Willey and his academic career, see James Gray, *Open Wide the Door: The Story of the University of Minnesota* (New York: G. P. Putnam's Sons, 1958), esp. 425ff.

32. Wright described it both as a "forest lodge" and as a "country lodge" in *AF* (January 1938): 36. Kaufmann often referred to it as a "mountain lodge." There are now two books on Fallingwater: Donald Hoffmann, *Frank Lloyd Wright's Fallingwater: The House and Its History*, 2d ed. rev. (New York: Dover, 1993); and Edgar Kaufmann Jr., *Fallingwater: A Frank Lloyd Wright Country House* (New York: Abbeville Press, 1986). There is also a photomonograph: Bruce Brooks Pfeiffer and Yukio Futagawa, eds., *Frank Lloyd Wright: Selected Houses*, vol. 4, *Fallingwater* (Tokyo: A.D.A. EDITA, 1990). Wright's primary description of the house was published in *AF* (January 1938): 36. It was reprinted in McAndrew, *House on Bear Run*, n.p.; and Werner M. Moser, *Frank Lloyd Wright: Sechzig Jahre lebendige Architektur; Sixty Years of Living Architecture* (Winterthur and Munich: Verlag Buchdruckerei Winterthur AG, Verlag Hermann Rinn, 1952), 83–84. Other publications include: Max Putzel, "A House That Straddles a Waterfall," *St. Louis Post-Dispatch Magazine*, 21 March 1937, pp. 1, 7; Jay Peterson, "Nature's Architect," *New Masses* 26 (8 February 1938): 29–30; Mumford, "Home, Indoors and Out"; Augusta Owen Patterson, "Three Modern Houses, No. 3: Owner, Edgar J. Kaufmann, Pittsburgh; Architect, Frank Lloyd Wright," *Town and Country* 93 (February 1938): 64–65, 104; Talbot F. Hamlin, "F.L.W.—An Analysis," *Pencil Points* 19 (March 1938): 137–44; Kaufmann, "Frank Lloyd Wright's Fallingwater 25 Years After," *Architettura* 8 (August 1962): 222–80; Bruno Zevi, "Il vaticinio del Riegl e la casa sulla cascata," *Architettura* 8 (August 1962): 218–21 (both of the above were repr. in Zevi and Kaufmann, *La casa sulla cascata di F. L. Wright; F. Lloyd Wright's Fallingwater* [Milan: ETAS/Kompass, 1963]); Martin Engel, "The Ambiguity of Frank Lloyd Wright: Fallingwater," *Charette* 44 (April 1964): 17–18; James D. Van Trump, "A House of Leaves: The Poetry of Fallingwater," *Charette* 44 (April 1964): 13–16; Futagawa and Paul Rudolph, *Global Architecture*, vol. 2, *Frank Lloyd Wright: Kaufmann House, "Fallingwater," Bear Run, Pennsylvania. 1936* (Tokyo: A.D.A. EDITA, 1970); Bernhard Hoesli, "Frank Lloyd Wright: Fallingwater," *A + U* 118 (July 1980): 155–66; and *LClients*, 82–109. Aside from the drawings and correspondence preserved in the Wright Archives (FLWF), there is a sizable amount of documentation in the Special Collections of the Avery Library at Columbia University. Given by Edgar Kaufmann Jr., the collection includes blueprints and correspondence, as well as miscellaneous published and unpublished material.

33. FLW to Edgar Kaufmann, 26 December 1934, in *LClients*, 82; and *AF* (January 1938): 36. Information about the family's use of "Bear Run" is from Kaufmann, "Fallingwater 25 Years After," 255.

Brendan Gill has written that the name Fallingwater "simply—and delightfully—reversed 'waterfall,'" although he admits, at the same time, that the family "wasn't even particularly struck by the fact" (*Many Masks*, 347). Franklin Toker, in a symposium on Fallingwater at the Temple Hoyne Buell Center at Columbia University in 1986, noted that the consonants of the name repeated Wright's own initials, i.e., FLLW. (This had been previously commented on in an early, popular review of the house, "Modern Home Built Over a Mountain Brook," *We the People: Pennsylvania in Review* 3 [1 February 1938]: 12–13.) It has always seemed to me that the name bears some relation to Native American nomenclature, which would only reinforce the active, animistic interpretation of its meaning.

34. Futagawa and Rudolph, *Wright: Kaufmann House*, n.p. This six-page text by Rudolph is one of the most sensitive and beautifully written essays on Fallingwater.

35. FLW to Kaufmann, 25 October 1937, Box ST 22, Special Collections; and FLW to Kaufmann, 27 September 1948, Wright-Kaufmann Correspondence, File 23600, Pt. 12, Folder 4, Avery Library.

36. It should be apparent that, in my view, Fallingwater does not engage in any meaningful way the issues of the individual, the family, and the community that scholars like Norris Kelly Smith have found so crucial to Wright's thinking about domestic architecture. That is not to say that Wright's later work avoids those issues. On the contrary, that is what the Usonian House is all about. It is only to say that Wright took the commission from Kaufmann for what it was—an invitation to create a significant work of art dealing with themes suggested by the program and situation.

37. The projects Wright designed for Kaufmann include: Kaufmann Office, Kaufmann's Department Store, Pittsburgh, built 1936–38; Usonian House, Pittsburgh, 1939; Gate Lodge (for caretaker), Mill Run, 1940; Farm Cottage, Mill Run, 1940; Pittsburgh Point Park Civic Center, Pittsburgh, 1947–48; Self-Service Garage, Pittsburgh, 1949–50; "Boulder House," Palm Springs, Calif., 1951; Point View Residences, Pittsburgh (two versions), 1951–53; Rhododendron Chapel, Mill Run, 1952. Edgar Kaufmann Jr. commissioned a second project for a Gate Lodge in 1957. Of these, as noted, only the Department Store Office was built. Among other things, Kaufmann helped pay for the construction of the Broadacre City model (1934–35) and arranged for its exhibition in Pittsburgh following the Industrial Arts Exposition at Rockefeller Center in New York.

On the Kaufmann Office, see now Christopher Wilk, *Frank Lloyd Wright: The Kaufmann Office* ([London]: Victoria & Albert Museum, 1993); on the Pittsburgh Point project, see now Richard Cleary, "Edgar J. Kaufmann, Frank Lloyd Wright and the 'Pittsburgh Point Park Coney Island in Automobile Scale,'" *JSAH* 52 (June 1993): 139–58.

38. On Kaufmann and Kaufmann's Department Store, see: "Seller's Market," *Fortune* 30 (November 1944): 123–30; Leon Harris, *Merchant Princes: An Intimate History of Jewish Families Who Built Great Department Stores* (New York: Harper & Row, 1979), 91–111; and Stefan Lorant, ed., *Pittsburgh: The Story of an American City* (Garden City, N.Y.: Doubleday, 1964), 321ff. The marriage between Edgar and Liliane Kaufmann was characterized by Leon Harris as "stormy": "His numberless infidelities drove her to leave him temporarily, to threaten divorce, and occasionally to take lovers of her own, or so the gossips said. The same gossips suggested that whether Edgar had married her for love was less certain than that the stock she would inherit as the only child of Isaac [Kaufmann, Edgar's uncle] would give Edgar effective control of the store" (*Merchant Princes*, 95). Edgar Kaufmann had a daughter by another woman, as well as one son, Edgar Jr., with Liliane. Edgar Jr., who never married, refused to follow in his father's footsteps as head of the department store. It was for this reason that the store was sold out of the family in 1946.

39. "Seller's Market," 126, 124; Kaufmann, "Fallingwater 25 Years After," 255; Lorant, *Pittsburgh*, 373–455; and Cleary, "Kaufmann, Wright and 'Pittsburgh Point.'" The Lorant book was in fact commissioned by Kaufmann in 1954 to "show how the city has grown and how it became what it is today."

Kaufmann intended it to be "a special kind of book—something no other city has, not even London or Paris or Rome—a 'de luxe book'" about the city "he was inordinately proud of . . . and very much in love with" (Lorant, *Pittsburgh*, 6).

40. Cf. Harris, *Merchant Princes*, 95–101.

41. For this statement and for my account of the early history of the site and the commission, I am mainly following Hoffmann, *Fallingwater*, 3–25. Cleary, "Kaufmann, Wright and 'Pittsburgh Point,'" 141, however, refers to an unpublished paper in which Franklin Toker suggests that the influence was of the father on the son.

42. It should be noted that there has been some disagreement over the date of the first visit; see note 45 below.

43. Hoffmann, *Fallingwater*, 6. The Indian word is "Ohiopehelle."

44. "Kaufmann's Summer Club" brochure, 1926, Box ST 22, Avery Library.

45. A mid- to late December date for this first visit to the site is supported by the letter Wright sent to Kaufmann on 26 December 1934 (quoted below) describing his reaction to the site (*LClients*, 82). On 10 January 1935, Wright wrote to Kaufmann again, asking: "When do we get the contours of 'Bear Run'?" (ibid., 89). Edgar Kaufmann Jr.'s memories, however, create some confusion. In his 1986 book on the house, he stated that he joined his father and Wright on this first visit: "Before the year's end Wright stopped off in Pittsburgh to discuss several projects with my father; one was a country house to replace a rudimentary cottage that had served for over a decade. Father and Wright drove to the mountain property to consider a site; I went along. This was Wright's first view of our forested land and its waterfall. Sun, rain, and hail accented the rugged terrain and the swollen stream" (*Fallingwater*, 36). In 1962 he described the visit somewhat differently: "at our request he [Wright] came to view the property. The mountains put on their best repertoire to him—sun, rain and hail alternated; the masses of native rhododendron were in bloom; the run was full and the falls, thundering" ("Fallingwater 25 Years After," 256). It is obvious that if the rhododendron were in bloom, as Kaufmann remembered in the earlier account, the season had to be spring rather than winter. This is corroborated by the "fullness" of the run in both descriptions. Based on this account, it would appear that Edgar Jr. may only have accompanied his father and Wright on a second visit that we know took place in either mid-May or early July 1935 (Wright visited Pittsburgh on 18 May 1935; 29 June–3 July 1935; 19 October 1935; 19 April 1936; and 5 June 1936 [Eugene Masselink to E. Clinton (secretary to Kaufmann), undated, Box ST 22, Avery Library]). Blaine Drake, an apprentice in the Taliesin Fellowship, told Donald Hoffmann that he remembered "driving Wright to Bear Run sometime in the summer of 1935," but being unaware "at the time, that Wright already had seen the site" (Hoffmann, *Fallingwater*, 16). Edgar Tafel similarly recalls that the first visit and the commission for the house occurred in the summer of 1935, sometime between 18 June and 29 June, when he was in Pittsburgh with Blaine Drake for the exhibition of the Broadacre City model (*Apprentice to Genius: Years with Frank Lloyd Wright* [New York: McGraw-Hill, 1979], 3). It is unclear why the apprentices, including Kaufmann's own son, were unaware of the first visit in December 1934.

46. Putzel, "House That Straddles a Waterfall," 1; and *LClients*, 82.

47. The map is dated 9 March 1935. There is a note of 20 February 1935 in the files of Morris Knowles, the engineering firm responsible for the survey, from E. F. Twomey to Wilfrid Jupenlay saying that "Mr. Kaufmann is particularly anxious to have the survey cleaned up this week as he is thinking of building a house at the camp in the spring" (Box ST 22, Avery Library).

Hoffmann, *Fallingwater*, 14, says that the Kaufmanns could not get reservations in or near Chandler, thus implying that this meeting did not take place. A letter from one of the apprentices who was there (Robert F. Bishop) recently published in Tafel, *About Wright*, 114, however, confirms that the Kaufmanns did stay at the San Marcos Hotel. Cf. Kaufmann, "Fallingwater 25 Years After," 255. In his account of 1962, Kaufmann places this visit before the one to the site, which would support my conclusion that he accompanied his father and Wright only on their second visit, the one in the early summer of 1935.

48. Kaufmann to FLW, 5 July 1935, Box ST 22, Avery Library. Although Kaufmann had not yet seen any sketches by that time, he made it clear that he

assumed Wright would be "proceeding with the preliminary sketches and floor plans for the Bear Run house." This second visit to the site coincided with Wright's trip to Pittsburgh on 29 June for the closing of the Broadacre City exhibition, held in the Kaufmann's Department Store (Hoffmann, *Falling-water*, 15–16; and see note 45 above).

49. Tafel, *Apprentice to Genius*, 3. Cf. Kaufmann, "Fallingwater 25 Years After," 256. Although the overall design never varied, a number of important changes were made in 1936. In the original project, there was no trellis over the drive between the rear wall of the house and the cliff. According to Wright, there was "originally no corner window system . . . no pool and stairs . . . no fireplace fittings, no outside coating . . . etc. etc. etc." (FLW to Kaufmann, 25 October 1937, Box ST 22, Avery Library). Significant changes were also made in the shape of the fireplace and the outside parapet of the hatch (see pp. 234–35).

The question of drawings prior to the September 1935 meeting still re-mains open. Hoffmann, *Fallingwater*, 15, refers to a letter from Wright to Kaufmann of 15 June 1935 saying: "We are starting on the home at 'Bear Run,' a specially difficult project, but on which we will charge you the usual ten per-cent fee only. . . . You will see some drawings from us soon." Hoffmann also refers to a note that Tafel sent to Edgar Jr., perhaps in late August 1935, saying that "the office and house were both to some extent 'on paper'" (p. 16). What-ever that might have meant is not spelled out.

50. The famous perspective that shows the house from below the falls (fig. 225) was done while Wright was in Arizona, which is to say, sometime between mid-January and mid-April 1936. Among the blueprints in the Avery Library, there is a set of revised plans dated 27 May 1936 and another dated 27 July 1936. Further revisions were made in August and November.

51. Kaufmann, *Fallingwater*, 45; and Harris, *Merchant Princes*, 95. Harris claims that the eighteen-room Fox Chapel house cost $250,000.

52. The term *trays*, which seems perfectly appropriate to the shallow, container-like shape of the terraces, was used by Edgar Kaufmann Jr. in "Fallingwater 25 Years After."

53. Preliminary designs for the guest house show the bridge connecting it to the main house to be either a double-height affair, coming off both the second and third floors, or a single level joining at the third floor. It was finally decided to have a single level connecting to the second floor, leaving the top level of the house isolated.

54. Kaufmann, *Fallingwater*, 36. In an interview with Donald Hoff-mann, Blaine Drake, who was present at Kaufmann's visit to Taliesin in Sep-tember 1935, reported: "I remember E. J. [Kaufmann] being quite surprised that the house would be above the falls. He told F. LL. W. he had always ex-pected the house to be on the opposite side of the Run, looking at the falls from below" (quoted in Hoffmann, *Fallingwater*, 16). This is corroborated by Edgar Kaufmann Jr., who wrote: "Amazingly to us, the house did not look toward the falls, it sat above them. It seemed impossible to imagine the result" ("Falling-water 25 Years After," 256).

55. Putzel, "House That Straddles a Waterfall," 1.

56. As pointed out in note 49 above, the first plans (September 1935) had no connecting trellis. It was added in 1936.

57. Hoffmann, *Fallingwater*, 19. One of the givens was the bridge cross-ing the stream at a right angle to the shelf to join the original logging road on the north bank. In an early perspective of the project, this bridge was redrawn at a thirty/sixty-degree angle to the house, making the sweep of the access drive more gentle. The idea was never pursued, however, and the bridge re-tained its orthogonal relation to the house.

58. *AF* (January 1938): 36.

59. Hoffmann, *Fallingwater*, 59, points out that it was Kaufmann's idea to leave the top of the hearth boulder in its natural state, Wright having ini-tially thought to trim it flush with the floor (cf. fig.207).

60. Tafel, *Apprentice to Genius*, 7. Tafel reports that, during the first visit to the site, "after much walking, according to Mr. Wright, he [Wright] asked, 'E. J., where do you like to sit?' And E. J. pointed to a massive rock whose crest commanded a view over a waterfall and down into a glen. That spot, Mr. Kaufmann's stone seat, was to become the heart and hearthstone of the . . . house" (p. 3). Cf. Hoffmann, *Fallingwater*, 34. Kaufmann Jr., on the

other hand, denied that the boulder that protrudes through the floor is the one on which his father liked to sit, maintaining that Tafel and Hoffmann confused it with the flat rock below the falls to which Wright was led by Kaufmann to view the falls (remarks made at Fallingwater symposium, Temple Hoyne Buell Center, Columbia University, fall 1986; and *Fallingwater*, 31, 124). He claimed that the upper, easternmost boulder "lay amid a daunting tangle of trees, shrubs, and vines" and was "practically inaccessible" (ibid., 124). "What is the likelihood that Wright chose a particular boulder top as the hearth in the living room . . . because he thought it was 'Kaufmann's favorite spot for lying in the sun and listening to the falls'?" he rhetorically asked (p. 31). Kaufmann Jr. may well be right concerning his father's habits, but that does not change what Wright either heard or wanted to have heard.

61. FLW to Robert K. Mosher, 21 August 1936, FLWF (in *LApprentices*, 134–35); and FLW to Kaufmann, 2 April 1937, Box ST 22, Avery Library. Mosher, a Taliesin apprentice who was supervising construction of Falling-water at the time, confirms that the hatch was originally supposed to be used for access to the stream for swimming. His description of Fallingwater ap-peared in "At Taliesin," *Capital Times* (Madison), 22 January 1937, repr. in Randolph C. Henning, ed., *"At Taliesin": Newspaper Columns by Frank Lloyd Wright and the Taliesin Fellowship, 1934–1937* (Carbondale and Edwardsville, Ill.: Southern Illinois University Press, 1992), 232–34.

62. The walkway joining the main house to the guest house was given an S-bend made up of two semicircles that decrease in size as they descend the hill slope. This sinuous pattern is reflected in the disjoined S of the fireplace and hatch and, with that, forms a continuous, rippling double-S pattern. Because the upper walkway begins at a tub-like, above-ground swimming pool that appears more like an overflowing reservoir than anything else, one reads the continuous, double-S bend as a cascading stream of water that narrows and deepens as it descends.

The connection between a circular geometry and the element of water will be further explored in Chapter X. It should be mentioned here, however, that Wright apparently wanted the image of the circle to become almost a "heraldic device" for the house (Kaufmann, *Fallingwater*, 102). He had originally de-signed the end support for the cantilevered roof of the east terrace (the one over the plunge pool) in the form of a square of painted concrete with a circle cut out of it, the whole thing set vertically and suspended on steel rods joining the parapet to the roof. This so-called "moon window" would have been the first thing seen upon turning toward the entrance after the bridge. If it was a kind of "heraldic device," as Kaufmann Jr. suggested, then it surely was meant to symbolize and announce the water in the name Fallingwater. In 1939 Wright designed three gates for Taliesin, one based on the motif of the square, another on that of the triangle, and a third on that of the circle. The one with the squares was to have been for the main gate, located on the state highway; the one based on the triangle was to have served as the entrance to the Hillside Home School buildings; the gate with the motif of the circle was to have been at the dam, next to the waterfall, where the road crosses the lake and stream before climbing up the hill slope (fig. 223).

63. The triangular fireplace and curved hatch appeared by 27 May 1936. The semicircular fireplace, with its accompanying spherical kettle and hemi-spherical recess, was worked out between 27 July 1936 and late August. Early discussions about the location of the plunge pool, and the continuing relevance of the hatch and its stairs, took place in July–August 1936. The "moon win-dow" referred to in note 62 above was sketched in January 1937 (Blueprints, Folders I–III, Avery Library).

64. The stairs from the ground floor run inside the rear wall to allow all the upstairs rooms to open to the view over the stream. The glassed-in areas are nestled within the ell of the chimney mass and rear wall. The elongated ter-races that extend in three directions from the rooms on the second floor pin-wheel out from the chimney over the broad floating plane of the lowest tray. Where the upper terrace does not extend far enough to provide shade or cover-age, as over the hatch and library area of the living room, or the window of the sitting area opposite it, the lower slab is cantilevered beyond as a trellis or thin canopy. Structurally, this forms a folded plane that serves to stiffen the slab. The third-floor terrace is completely contained within the structural stone ell, except for the lower slab, which again is folded to extend out as a canopy

beyond the end of the chimney in one direction and to the far end of the terrace pointing toward the bridge in the other.

65. Kaufmann to FLW, 7 August 1937, and FLW to Kaufmann, 19 March 1937, Box ST 22, Folder 7, Avery Library; Kaufmann, "Fallingwater 25 Years After," 257; and FLW, "Memorandum: The Kaufmann House," n.d. [prob. January 1937], Box ST 22, Folder 5, Avery Library.

66. The most important analysis of Wright's relation to the International Style remains Vincent Scully, "Wright vs. the International Style," *Art News* 53 (March 1954): 32–35, 64–66. Cf. responses from Edgar Kaufmann Jr., T. H. Robsjohn-Gibbings, and Elizabeth Gordon, plus rejoinder from Scully, *Art News* 53 (September 1954): 48–49. Cf. also Henry-Russell Hitchcock, "The International Style Twenty Years After," orig. pub. *ARec* 110 (August 1951), repr. in Hitchcock and Johnson, *International Style*, 237–55. Indeed, there was so much in Fallingwater that was unprecedented in his own work that Wright felt compelled to defend himself against the charge of European influence. In the text published in the January 1938 *AF* issue devoted to his work (p. 36), reprinted in the McAndrew MOMA catalogue, he explained: "The ideas involved here are in no wise changed from those of early work. The materials and methods of construction come through them here, as they may and will come through everywhere. That is all. The effects you see in this house are not superficial effects." As evidence of an earlier building of his based on a similar formal device (i.e., cantilevering), Wright often cited the Gale House in Oak Park (1909). In the catalogue of his exhibition at the Guggenheim Museum in 1953, he noted: "The Gale house at Oak Park built in wood and plaster was its [Fallingwater's] progenitor as to general type" (*Sixty Years of Living Architecture: The Work of Frank Lloyd Wright* [New York: Solomon R. Guggenheim Museum 1953], [14]).

67. In Le Corbusier's work, one immediately thinks of the Villa Stein-de Monzie at Garches and the Villa Savoye at Poissy. In Mies, one thinks of the Tugendhat House and the Berlin Exhibition House of 1931. Curiously, Wright seems to have considered the contrapuntal device almost a cliché of modernism. In his fourth Princeton lecture of 1930, he said: "Most new 'modernistic' houses manage to look as though cut from cardboard with scissors, the sheets of cardboard folded or bent in rectangles with an occasional curved cardboard surface added to get relief" (Princeton Lects., 66). The relation of the curved hatch to the International Style may explain the references to a "machine esthetic" it suggests.

68. This point has often been made by Vincent Scully; see, e.g., his "Wright vs. International Style."

69. Writing at the time he was designing Fallingwater, Wright offered the image of the tree as the model for modern architecture: "Our arboreal ancestors in their trees seem more likely precedent for us at the present time than savage animals who 'hole in' for protection" (FLW, "Recollections: United States, 1893–1920," pt. 2, *AJ* 84 [23 July 1936]: 111). In 1932 he wrote in his *Autobiography*: "Conceive now that an entire building might grow up out of conditions as a plant grows up out of soil, as free to be itself, to 'live its own life according to Nature' as is the tree. Dignified as a tree in the midst of nature. . . . I now propose that ideal for the architecture of the machine age, for the ideal 'American' building. Grow up in that image. The TREE" (p. 146). Toward the end of the *Autobiography*, he raised the tree to a cultural symbol of historic proportions:

The Egyptians, for cultural symbol—the lotus.
The Greeks, for cultural symbol—the honeysuckle.
The Romans, for cultural symbol—the acanthus.
To our hoped for growth of organic culture in these United States—for cultural symbol—the tree. (P. 362)

The structure of the St. Mark's-in-the-Bouwerie apartment tower (1928–30), which became the model for all Wright's later tall buildings, was based on that of a tree.

70. *AF* (January 1938): 36. Wright used the term *arbor*, among other places, on pp. 40, 45.

71. FLW to Mosher, 21 August 1936.

72. *AF* (January 1938): 36; and *A* I, 146. The spherical kettle in the fire-

place can surely be read as a metaphor for the overall conception of Fallingwater in terms of the spatial model of a vessel. It should be remarked that it was really only in the late 1920s and especially the early 1930s that Wright began to speak of "plasticity as physical continuity," where "walls, ceilings, floors become *seen* as component parts of each other, their surfaces flowing into each other" (*A* I, 147). What has caused many scholars to read these thoughts into the earlier Prairie Style buildings is partly the fact that in the second book of the *Autobiography*, Wright discussed the concept of "plasticity" in the context of the Prairie House (pp. 146–48). To avoid such anachronism, it must always be borne in mind that the *Autobiography* was written in the late 1920s and finished in the early 1930s. A follow-up discussion of plasticity comes in the final pages of Book Four, under the heading "Twentieth Century Architecture" (esp. pp. 354–56). This section is based on the articles written for *ARec* in 1927–28.

The literal transformation of Fallingwater's rectangular trays into circular pools of water occurs in the 1940s in the projects for the Pittsburgh Point Park Civic Center and the Huntington Hartford Hotel and Sports Club for Los Angeles.

73. FLW, *The Future of Architecture* (New York: Horizon Press, 1953), 15 ("A Conversation" with Hugh Downs, NBC television, 17 May 1953).

74. Perhaps the most obvious example of Fallingwater's influence on Taliesin is the extension of the dining room terrace of the latter into the dramatically cantilevered Birdwalk.

75. FLW, "In the Cause of Architecture, III: The Meaning of Materials—Stone," *ARec* 63 (April 1928): 350.

76. The oya (tufa) stone used in the Imperial Hotel, it will be recalled, was not originally specified but only discovered by Wright after he got to Japan. Furthermore, it was used as a revetment rather than as a structural material, meaning it was laid vertically in plaques rather than horizontally in layers. Among the very few cases where stone was to be used in a structural way is the Nakoma Country Club (1923–24), but it was originally designed for textile-block construction.

77. FLW, "Meaning of Materials—Stone," 350.

78. FLW, "In the Cause of Architecture, VIII: The Meaning of Materials—Concrete," *ARec* 64 (August 1928): 99, 102–4; and "Meaning of Materials—Stone," 350.

79. Brownell and FLW, 19; and FLW, "Meaning of Materials—Stone," 356.

80. *AF* (January 1938): 36.

81. It is the spot to which Kaufmann Jr. said he and his father brought Wright to get a view of the falls. The view represented in the perspective is from the base of the well-hidden path and stone steps on the far (south) bank of the stream. The famous Hedrich-Blessing photograph was taken from this spot in November 1937 in preparation for the MOMA exhibition.

82. Mumford, "Home, Indoors and Out," 31.

83. Holes for three trees were also left in the concrete slab of the west (bedroom) terrace, but those trees did not survive. Wright first used the idea in the passage connecting his studio to the Oak Park house.

84. FLW to Kaufmann, 19 March 1937.

85. The footbath and fountain were apparently added by Wright in response to a request from the client. See Hoffmann, *Fallingwater*, 40.

86. Tafel, *Apprentice to Genius*, 7.

87. Wright reused the idea of a curved resonating chamber in the project for the Morris House, for an oceanside site at the edge of San Francisco (1944–46) (see Chapter XI). There, a well leading down through the base of the house to an opening along the shore would have transmitted the sound of the waves to the upper living floors. The hatch was used for the purpose of ventilation in the Affleck House in Bloomfield Hills, Mich. (1941).

88. The tree-house image, which is extremely powerful, was noted by early visitors to the house. One described the "arboreal airiness" of Fallingwater as so impregnated "with the spirit of the woods, that it might be a house in a tree for one of the 'little people'" ("Wright Western Pennsylvania Landmark Completed," *The Bulletin Index: Pittsburgh Weekly Newsmagazine*, 27 January 1938, p. 10; and Patterson, "Three Modern Houses," 64). Wright's own obsession with the tree as the "cultural symbol" of modern architecture (see

note 69 above) and of the tree house as an archetypal abode of the free human being can best be appreciated in *The Disappearing City*, 5–7, and Brownell and FLW, 22–23.

89. Wright wrote about the idea of synesthesia at the time he was engaged in designing Fallingwater. In the book co-authored with Baker Brownell in 1937, he described architecture, at least until the Renaissance, as "man's greatest work wherein his five senses were all employed and enjoyed. By way of eye, ear, and finger, by tongue and even by nostril he was creating out of himself greater delights for a super-self" (Brownell and FLW, 47–48). But unlike the traditional *gesamtkunstwerk* to which Midway Gardens and the Imperial Hotel might be related, Fallingwater is neither a collaborative effort of painters, sculptors, musicians, and architects nor a multimedia event staged by the architect. Rather, architecture alone, through the means peculiar to it as a medium, is made to appeal to and involve the various senses. Its synesthetic quality is therefore fundamentally modern in structure and form.

In the television interview with Hugh Downs in 1953, Wright said: "I think you can hear the waterfall when you look at the design" (in FLW, *Future of Architecture*, 14).

90. Continuing the analogy with the Baroque *vol d'oiseau*, it would not be inappropriate to compare this final view of Fallingwater to the view from the garden one would have of a Baroque country house or palace after passing through the entrance court and interior space.

91. Curiously, Robert Venturi, to whom this distinction in terms is owed, did not himself stress the ambiguities and complexities of Fallingwater. He described it in *Complexity and Contradiction in Architecture* as fundamentally a modernist design (Museum of Modern Art Papers on Architecture, no. 1 [New York and Chicago: Museum of Modern Art, Graham Foundation for Advanced Studies in the Fine Arts, 1966], 58).

92. Charles Jencks offered the opinion that the house should be seen as "frozen water." "The name 'Fallingwater,'" he wrote, "is taken up by these frozen, concrete horizontals: 'Stillwater' they could be called, because they take the white sheets of foam, evident as white planes in Wright's drawings, and turn them into architectural equivalents, metaphors of still, frozen water" (Jencks, *Kings of Infinite Space: Frank Lloyd Wright and Michael Graves* [London and New York: Academy Editions, St. Martin's, 1983], 44). This reading seems to force the connection between the ideas of "natural architecture" and "frozen music."

93. Again, the guest house is essential to this reading. Although it was not actually designed until 1938 (and built in 1939), it was clearly always part of Wright's site planning. Cf. Kaufmann, *Fallingwater*, 41.

94. FLW to Kaufmann, 19 March 1937. For a different, though related, interpretation of the tree/leaf imagery, see Van Trump, "House of Leaves," 13–14.

95. FLW, "In the Cause of Architecture: The Meaning of Materials—Wood," p. 1, MS 2401.044 B, FLWF. This is a draft of the article published in *ARec* 63 (May 1928). The section on the cult of Zeus at Dodona, which was to have introduced the article, was eliminated in the final copy. It was later published, with some slight variations and, somewhat misleadingly, at the *end* of the excerpts from the draft for the article on "Wood," in Gutheim, *FLW on Arch.*, 119. In transforming the idea of "rustling" leaves to "falling" leaves, Wright may have had Lake Tahoe in mind. One of the houseboats for it was called Fallen Leaf, based on the name of the small lake and town just south of Tahoe. It is now believed that the lake was named for the Delaware chief Falling Leaf, who guided one of the first white men to see and explore the area. There is also, however, a Washoe legend that links the dropping of leaves to the appearance of water and personal salvation. The story goes that a brave, being pursued by the Evil One, was given a branch with leaves by the Good Spirit, who counseled him to drop the leaves along the way. They "contained magical powers" that would cause water to spring up wherever they landed. In this way, the brave was able to escape over the Sierra Nevada into the Sacramento Valley, leaving behind Lake Tahoe and Fallen Leaf Lake, as well as Lilly, Grass, and Heather Lakes (Edward B. Scott, *The Saga of Lake Tahoe* [Crystal Bay, Lake Tahoe, Nev.: Sierre-Tahoe, 1957], 143).

It is also interesting to speculate whether Wright may have remembered the following passage from Ruskin's *Stones of Venice*:

> *The rock [of Mont Cervin] is indeed hard beneath, but still disposed in thin courses of . . . cloven shales, so finely laid that they look in places more like a heap of crushed autumn leaves than a rock; and the first sensation is one of unmitigated surprise, as if the mountain were upheld by miracle; but surprise becomes more intelligent reverence for the great builder, when we find, in the middle of the mass of these dead leaves, a course of living rock, of quartz as white as the snow that encircles it, and harder than a bed of steel.* (Vol. 1, ch. 5, par. 4)

I am indebted to Amy Kurlander for pointing out this passage to me and suggesting its possible relevance to Fallingwater.

96. According to Donald Hoffmann, McAndrew had heard of the house through the brother of a former student of his at Vassar College, who was related to Edgar Kaufmann's brother Henry. McAndrew was told by Liliane Kaufmann "that he was the first person from the outside world to see the house" (*Fallingwater*, 69–70).

97. This distinction is borrowed from Colin Rowe and Robert Slutzky, "Transparency: Literal and Phenomenal," orig. pub. *Perspecta* 8 (1963), repr. in Rowe, *The Mathematics of the Ideal Villa and Other Essays* (Cambridge, Mass., and London: MIT Press, 1976), 159–83. For our purposes, Bergson's most important discussions of duration are: *Essai sur les données immédiates de la conscience* (1889); *L'Evolution créatrice* (1907; trans. as *Creative Evolution*, 1911); and *Durée et simultanéité, à propos de le théorie d'Einstein* (1922). It should be remembered how important, at this time, Bergson's philosophy of vitalism was considered to be for Cubist art in general.

98. Sigfried Giedion, *Space, Time and Architecture: The Growth of a New Tradition*, Charles Eliot Norton Lectures for 1938–39 (1941; 4th ed. enl., Cambridge, Mass.: Harvard University Press, 1962). By the mid-1940s it had become almost a cliché, especially of Harvard-trained architects, to speak of the "flux" and "flow" of modern space. Cf. Vincent Scully, "Doldrums in the Suburbs," *Perspecta* 9/10 (1965): 281–90. For a more profound and perceptive reading of Wright's "temporalizing" of space, see Sergio Bettini, "Venezia e Wright," *Metron* 9, nos. 49–50 (January–April 1954): 14–31.

99. In an unpublished review of Giedion's *Space, Time and Architecture*, Wright spoke of the numerous "erudite, Harvardite Franco-Germanic attempts . . . to purge the European scene of Frank Lloyd Wright" (p. 1, MS 2401.243 A, FLWF). "I do not know where this author dug up the coincidences he rationalizes so freely," Wright said at the end of the piece. "But of one thing I am sure: such rationalizing goes pretty far wide of the truth underlying space and time where American Architecture is concerned. . . . Such books as this one serve merely to confuse, not clarify, the culture currents of our time" (pp. 1–2).

100. Reference to Ledoux's project for the House of Surveyors of the Loue River was made as early as 1944 in John Fabian Kienitz, "The Romanticism of Frank Lloyd Wright," *Art in America* 32 (April 1944): 99.

101. A very loose connection might be drawn between Fallingwater and the cliff dwellings of the Southwest, but it is one that seems to occur mainly in hindsight. In the majority of works after Fallingwater, beginning with Taliesin West and including the Guggenheim Museum and the Marin County Civic Center, Wright would return to historical references, in one form or another, to substantiate the temporal aspects of the building in relation to the site.

Chapter IX
The Traces of Prehistory at Taliesin West

1. No scholarly study of Taliesin West exists, nor has its history been documented yet. The two most perceptive accounts of it are the short discussion in Scully, *Wright*, 28–29, and the exacting description in Philip Johnson, "100 Years, Frank Lloyd Wright and Us," orig. pub. *Pacific Architect and Builder* (March 1957), repr. in Johnson *Writings* (New York: Oxford University Press, 1979), 196–98. The most important early publications are: Raymond Carlson, ed., "Mr. Frank Lloyd Wright, the Taliesin Fellowship, and Taliesin West," *Arizona Highways* 16 (May 1940): 4–15; Robert Mosher, "In the Arizona

Desert: Taliesin West," *Taliesin* 1 (February 1941): 30–33; "'Taliesin West,' Arizona, by Frank Lloyd Wright," *AJ* 93 (13 March 1941): 177–78; Elizabeth Gordon, "One Man's House," *House Beautiful* 138 (December 1946): 186–96, 235; Elizabeth B. Mock, "Taliesin West," *House and Garden* 94 (August 1948): 52–55, 91; "Frank Lloyd Wright," *AF* 88 (January 1948): 87–88, 152–55; and Carlson, ed., "Frank Lloyd Wright and Taliesin West," *Arizona Highways* 25 (October 1949): 4–15. Wright's description of the building is in *A* II, 452–55 ("The Conquest of the Desert"). Olgivanna Lloyd Wright's description is in *The Shining Brow: Frank Lloyd Wright* (New York: Horizon Press, 1960), 43–60, 91–123.

Other publications include: "The Immobile Idea: Home Grown," *AJ* 94 (24 July 1941): 56–57; George Nelson, "Wright's Houses," *Fortune* 34 (August 1946): 116–25; "Taliesin West, arkitekten Frank Lloyd Wrights vinterbostad i Arizona," *Byggmästaren* (Stockholm) 1 (1948): 8–12; "Journey to Taliesin West," *Look* 16 (1 January 1952): 28–31; "Un peruano visita Taliesin in Arizona," *Arquitecto Peruano* 20 (January–February 1956): 31–36; "Frank Lloyd Wright's Own Home in the Desert," *House and Home* 15 (June 1959): 88–98; Bruce Brooks Pfeiffer, "Out of the Desert's Mystery," *American Institute of Architects Journal* 59 (May 1973): 54–55; Edgar Tafel, *Apprentice to Genius: Years with Frank Lloyd Wright* (New York: McGraw-Hill, 1979), 194–203; and Bernard M. Boyle, "Taliesin, Then and Now," *Architecture* (March 1984): 129–33. The most recent publication, with a short though very useful text and excellent photographs, is Pfeiffer and Yukio Futagawa, *Frank Lloyd Wright: Selected Houses*, vol. 3, *Taliesin West* (Tokyo: A.D.A. EDITA, 1989).

2. Johnson, *Writings*, 197.

3. One can already see this interest at work in the differences between the Lake Tahoe and Death Valley projects, coeval in date but very separate in geographic terms. Around 1938–39 Wright began to particularize the imagery of his houses in a very explicit manner. I am thinking here, for instance, of the Jester House, Palos Verdes, Calif. (1938–39); Pauson House, Phoenix (1938–41); Smith House project, Piedmont Pines, Calif. (1939); Spivey House project, Fort Lauderdale, Fla. (1939); Watkins Studio project, Barnegat City, N.J. (1940); and Burlingham House project, El Paso, Tex. (1940–42). This development in the direction of regional and individual expression took place at exactly the same time Wright was standardizing the Usonian House.

4. Philip Johnson, "The Frontiersman," orig. pub. *ARcv* 106 (August 1949), repr. in *Writings*, 189–91; Ayn Rand, *The Fountainhead* (1943; New York: Signet Book, New American Library, 1971); Scully, *Wright*, 28; and Mock, "Taliesin West," 52, 91.

5. Hitchcock, *Materials*, 97; Johnson, *Writings*, 196–98; and Gordon, "One Man's House."

6. FLW to Fowler McCormick, 31 March 1949, in *LApprentices*, 31. Fowler McCormick was the son of Harold McCormick and a neighbor of Wright's in Scottsdale. He was a major landowner, responsible for the development of the McCormick Ranch property.

7. Olgivanna Lloyd Wright and Bruce Brooks Pfeiffer, *The Arizona Biltmore: History and Guide* (Scottsdale: Frank Lloyd Wright Foundation, 1974), 8.

8. Eugene Masselink, "The Arizona Trek: 1935," p. 1, MS 2401.572 R, FLWF. In *An Autobiography*, Wright predated the event, saying that "the trek across the continent began November, 1933" (II, 452). A later recollection is given in a talk by Wright to the Taliesin Fellowship entitled "Beginning of Fellowship; choice of site for Taliesin West; desire for a 'big job,'" 8 March 1953, Reel 63, FLWF.

9. FLW to Chandler, 19 September 1934 and 7 December [1934], FLWF. In a letter to Alden Dow written on 11 September 1934, Wright said: "But this winter I am going to take it easier with a group of some fifteen I will take with me to the grand scale of Arizona. A complete change. We will probably go in with Dr. Chandler until we get our own camp built" (in *LApprentices*, 26).

10. J. Lee Loveless to FLW, 31 May 1935, FLWF. Correspondence between Keith and Wright begins on 11 April 1935 and goes through 14 November 1936 (FLWF).

11. FLW to Chandler, 6 December 1935, FLWF.

12. Quoted in Paul R. and Jean S. Hanna, *Frank Lloyd Wright's Hanna House: The Clients' Report* (New York, Cambridge, Mass., and London: Ar-

chitectural History Foundation, MIT Press, 1981), 20. See W[illiam] T. Evjue, "Good Afternoon Everybody," *Capital Times* (Madison), 24 April 1936.

13. FLW to Loveless, 15 May 1936; and FLW to Chandler, 23 May 1936, FLWF.

14. FLW to Dewey Keith, 8 May 1936; Keith to FLW, 1 August 1936; and FLW to Loveless, 3 September 1936, FLWF. The land was in the same area as the "cove." Wright also wrote to Keith on 3 September: "Your proposition is up for consideration now and I may take you up. Will let you know later" (FLWF).

15. Chandler to FLW, 23 February 1937; and FLW to Chandler, 8 February 1937, FLWF. In his letter of 23 February, Chandler explained his reasons for buying the land: "I had in mind if the proper conditions should come again we might organize some kind of syndicate that would get possession of all the land in the cove . . . so that no part of the desert could be destroyed. I am sure it could be developed to make the whole thing most attractive for building sites."

16. FLW to Chandler, 29 September 1937, FLWF. A letter from Chandler, dated 2 September 1937 (but probably 2 October 1937) reiterates: "As San Tan is now, I do not doubt that Mrs. Wright would not care to be pioneering out there, but should I be able to get financed, we could completely change that place and make it nationaly [*sic*] and internationally [*sic*] famous" (FLWF). In her biography of Wright, Olgivanna Lloyd Wright stated: "I always liked Phoenix and was able to convince my husband to buy property some twenty miles away from town" (*Frank Lloyd Wright: His Life, His Work, His Words* [New York: Horizon Press, 1966], 104). In the letter to Chandler cited above, Wright went on to insist: "I'll never see anything I like better than the Dewey [desert?] 640 acres at San Tan and I would be willing to go there myself. But we will look over the situation to see [undecipherable]." This remark, however, may not be as straightforward as it appears. Knowing that Chandler now owned the Keith property, Wright may have had some ulterior motive.

17. *LApprentices*, 8–9; and *FLWM*, vol. 6, 38, 44. The early spring 1937 date is also given in Randolph C. Henning, ed., *"At Taliesin": Newspaper Columns by Frank Lloyd Wright and the Taliesin Fellowship, 1934–1937* (Carbondale and Edwardsville, Ill.: Southern Illinois University Press, 1992), 228. Edgar Tafel's account implies that the land was found before the fall of 1937. (*Apprentice to Genius*, 194). In his own account in the *Autobiography*, Wright makes it seem as if a full year passed between buying the land and building on it: "The land could be bought from Stephen Pool at the Government Land Office. . . . We got about eight hundred acres together finally [see note 19 below], part purchase, part lease. Next year we began 'to do something with it.' We made the plans and were all ready" (II, 453). What puts the spring 1937 date in some doubt is Wright's letter to Chandler of 29 September 1937 quoted above, in which he says that the Fellowship would "prefer to go nearer to Phoenix *if there is a suitable place* available" (italics added).

Site preparation for the Hanna House began in early January 1937. Wright's visit coincided with the pouring of the concrete mat, which was planned to take place around 15 March. See Hanna and Hanna, *Hanna House*, 40–59.

18. FLW to Chandler, 29 September 1937; O. L. Wright to Mr. and Mrs. Mendel Glickman, 12 November 1937, in *LApprentices*, 9; and FLW to Chandler, 7 December 1937, FLWF. On the other hand, Eugene Masselink wrote on 15 October 1937 that the Fellowship had plans for "driving in caravan to Arizona where we plan to build a desert camp near Phoenix—leaving about the first of December" (quoted in Henning, *"At Taliesin"*, 228).

19. Stephen D. Pool to FLW, 31 December 1937, FLWF. Pfeiffer, however, speaks of "a trip to Arizona in November and December of 1937 [during which time] Mr. and Mrs. Wright finally decided upon the site of land they wished to purchase" (*LApprentices*, 30). Cf. *FLWM*, vol. 6, 44. Henning, *"At Taliesin,"* 230, says the Wrights left Wisconsin for Arizona on Christmas Eve 1937.

The actual amount of land Wright originally purchased and/or leased has never been accurately documented. Estimates usually put it at around 600 acres (William Wesley Peters, in conversation, April 1990). In early 1941, Robert Mosher wrote that the holdings amounted to 640 acres ("Arizona Desert: Taliesin West," 30). A letter to Wright from Pool, from whom Wright bought and leased the original parcels, dated 17 October 1941, indicates that

Wright had in his possession by then 640 acres and was in the process of leasing another quarter section (160 acres) from the government (FLWF). In October 1949, Wright wrote that he owned 800 acres ("Living in the Desert," in Carlson, "Wright and Taliesin West," 15). According to Cornelia Brierly, a senior Taliesin Fellow, Sterling Rockefeller, a neighbor in Scottsdale and a principal in the Todd Company in Philadelphia (which built the Sun Top Houses), was responsible for "giving" some of the land to Wright (in conversation, April 1990). By the time of Wright's death in 1959, the Foundation controlled approximately 1,120 acres, of which 640 were owned outright and 480 were leased. See Richard Carney, "Land Swap Secures Buffer Zone for Taliesin West," *Journal of the Taliesin Fellows* 7 (summer 1992): 10.

Wright makes it appear in the *Autobiography* that Pool simply acted as the government agent for the entire transaction (II, 453). Pool's own property was the northeast quarter of section 16 (Tp. 3N, R. 5E). The government parcel was the southeast quarter of the same section 16. According to correspondence, the initial cost to Wright was $2,000 (Pool to FLW, 26 January 1938 and 3 February 1938, FLWF).

20. *IApprentices*, 30; and Masselink to D. Graeme Keith, 31 December 1937, FLWF.

21. See Carlson, "Wright and Taliesin West" (May 1940): 6–7. Bruce Pfeiffer told me that he only remembers the hill being referred to as "our hill" (in conversation, May 1983). The name Maricopa Hill, however, will be used for identification purposes only.

22. Black Mountain has recently come to be referred to sometimes as Saddleback Mountain, due to its shape. The second hump, which is behind, is barely visible, if at all, from Taliesin West.

23. See Richard E. Lynch, *Winfield Scott: A Biography of Scottsdale's Founder* (Scottsdale: City of Scottsdale, 1978); and Patricia Myers McElfresh, *Scottsdale: Jewel in the Desert* (Woodland Hills, Calif.: Continental Heritage Press, 1984). As noted above, one of the leading developers in the area was Fowler McCormick. Wright's neighbor as a winter visitor (in the early years) was Sterling Rockefeller.

24. I should like to thank Cornelia Brierly, Kenneth Lockhart, and Wesley Peters for sharing their knowledge of the site's prehistoric remains with me. I should also like to thank David E. Doyel, William Breen Murray, Anthony F. Aveni, and Barbara Gronemann for their help in understanding the earlier history of the site. Murray was kind enough to visit Taliesin West and provide me with a report of his investigations. Gronemann gave me a copy of her "Taliesin West Rock Art Site Report," Rock Art Recorder Class, Arizona Archaeological Society, Phoenix Chapter, October 1992. A thorough study of the site still remains to be done, but the fact that Wright and the apprentices working with him found evidence of early Native American occupation, which led them to make certain assumptions about the site, is in some ways even more important than the actual historical/anthropological/archaeological facts.

25. Cf., e.g., Landon Douglas Smith, "Archaeological and Paleoenvironmental Investigations in the Cave Buttes Area North of Phoenix, Arizona," *Arizona Archaeologist*, no. 11 (1977); and *Anthropological Research Papers* (Tempe: Arizona State University): James B. Rodgers, "An Archaeological Investigation of Buckeye Hills East, Maricopa County, Arizona" (no. 10, 1976); Rodgers, "Archaeological Investigation of the Granite Reef Aqueduct, Cave Creek Archaeological District, Arizona" (no. 12, 1977); T. Kathleen Henderson and J. B. Rodgers, "Archaeological Investigations in the Cave Creek Area, Maricopa County, South Central Arizona" (no. 17, 1979); and David E. Doyel and Fred Plog, eds., *Current Issues in Hohokam Prehistory: Proceedings of a Symposium* (no. 23, 1980), esp. Donald E. Weaver Jr., "The Northern Frontier, Hohokam Regional Diversity as Seen from the Lower Salt River Valley," 121–33.

Cornelia Brierly recalled that underground hot springs were found at the base of the McDowell Mountains, which might indicate a winter use for the site (in conversation, April 1990).

26. Cornelia Brierly and Wesley Peters (in conversation, April 1990). See also Gronemann, "Taliesin West Report."

The petroglyph boulders have been studied also by LaVan Martineau. A videotape of his initial impressions is in the Wright Archives, but he has not published these findings yet. The analogies he draws with Amerindian sign

language are intriguing, especially in terms of his contextual reading of the glyphs. Cf. LaVan Martineau, *The Rocks Begin to Speak* (Las Vegas: KC Publications, 1973).

27. Edwin R. Embree, *Indians of the Americas* (1939; rpt. New York: Collier, 1970). Cf. John Collier, *Indians of the Americas: The Long Hope*, (1947; New York: Mentor Books, New American Library, 1948). As early as 1916, Edgar L. Hewett, organizer of the exhibition of Precolumbian art and architecture at the San Diego Panama-California Exposition, wrote: "There has been a singular tendency to think of the ancient masterworks of the race found in Mexico, Central America, and South America as other than Indian art. It is necessary to repeat again and again that all native American remains, whether of plains tribes, mound-builders, cliff-dwellers, Pueblo, Navaho, Toltec, Aztec, Maya, Inca are just the work of the Indian. . . . The most homogeneous of all racial art is that of the American Indian. Chronologically it is without serious gaps, and ethnologically it is unbroken" (Hewett, "America's Archaeological Heritage," *Art and Archaeology* 4 [December 1916]: 260).

28. Randall H. McGuire, "A History of Archaeological Research," and Michael B. Schiffer, "Hohokam Chronology: An Essay on History and Method," in McGuire and Schiffer, *Hohokam and Patayan*, 101–52, 299–330; and Harold S. Gladwin et al., *Excavations at Snaketown: Material Culture* (1938; rpt. Tucson: University of Arizona Press, 1965), esp. 36–49.

29. This information was provided to me by Wesley Peters and by Emil W. Haury, who was in charge of the excavation (in conversation, April 1990).

30. *FLWM*, vol. 6, 38–39, 44–45. The lack of a complete and accurate building history makes any certainty about dates difficult. Given here are "best-guess estimates" based on available information. Sometime after Wright and his wife moved out of Sun Trap, it was remodeled as a house for their daughter Iovanna and renamed Sun Cottage. Serving also as overflow accommodations for guests, it was rebuilt in 1960 in more permanent materials.

31. Ibid., 44.

32. I am grateful to Bruce Pfeiffer and Oscar Muñoz for making this and another early plan available to me. They were apparently recently rediscovered by John Howe, one of the apprentices who worked most closely with Wright on the planning of the camp.

33. The east-southeast orientation was preserved, probably mistakenly, in the site plan published in Carlson, "Wright and Taliesin West" (May 1940), 6. It might be noted here that the lateral axis of Sun Trap was approximately six degrees north-northwest of the final orientation of the camp. This is indicated on a later plan of the complex (#3803.134, FLWF).

34. Another plan recently returned by Howe to the Wright Archives may well be the first version of the final design. The drawing (#3803.186, FLWF), which corresponds in most respects to the perspective published in Tafel, *Apprentice to Genius*, 197, is composed of cut-and-pasted elements, indicating that the diagonal rotation was effected as an operational overlay on a previously orthogonal plan. Another interesting aspect of this plan is the hexagonal observatory on the roof of the cinema-theater Wright called the kiva.

Taliesin West was originally planned for about thirty people. The apprentice court contained room for only some of the older Fellows. New members were expected to live in tents on the hill slope behind the camp.

35. Plan #3803.186 (FLWF), for instance, does not show the apprentice court. The corresponding perspective has neither the apprentice court nor the workshop building. Cf. Tafel, *Apprentice to Genius*, 194.

36. The plan for the Stanley Marcus House in Dallas, Tex., on which Taliesin West is based, seems to have developed in a similar manner. The rotated study at one end of the house and the corresponding garage at the other were not drawn in until the later stages of the planning process.

37. To these should also be added the 1933 project for the renovation and enlargement of the Hillside Home School (fig. 197), as well as the project for Little San Marcos of 1935–36.

38. Perhaps the most graphic indication of this reference is a thumbnail sketch of the Willey House plan on the bottom margin of one of the preliminary plans for the Marcus House (fig. 247). The Marcus House was commissioned in late October or early November 1934, a little over a month before Kaufmann commissioned Fallingwater. The first plans for the Marcus House were presented to the client on 15 August 1935, again about a month before the same was

done for Fallingwater. Discussions between Wright and Marcus dragged on for another six months or so, during which time the client considered changing the site and Wright obliged with a revised plan, sent off from Arizona on 13 March 1936. Marcus finally chose a local architect when the estimates on Wright's design came in one-third above the original limit of $20,000–25,000. Interestingly, the figure of $30,000–35,000 was exactly what Kaufmann and Wright agreed upon as their limit in November 1935 (which proved to be an underestimation of the final cost by more than one-half). The best publication of the Marcus House remains *AF* (January 1938): 50–53.

39. Wright characterized the house as "a Texas house" for the "Texas rolling prairie" in *AF* (January 1938): 50. It was to be "wide open" to the expansive landscape, he told the client, and "long drawn out to the breeze wherein every room looks at the landscape not slantwise but directly" (FLW to Stanley Marcus, 13 March 1936, FLWF). He noted in the same letter that "the attenuation of the design . . . is ideal for Texas climate and modern ways of living."

Wright described the movable "roof over the house [as] a screened-in deck like that of a ship" (*AF* [January 1938]: 50). The drawings, and especially the photographs of the model, emphasize the engineered look, so much so as to remind one of Buckminster Fuller's Dymaxion House of just a few years earlier. In the Marcus House, the booms of the exoskeletal roof structure may also allude to a Texas imagery of oil rigs and derricks.

40. Wright appears to have been particularly annoyed by Marcus's rejection of the design. He made that clear in his comments in *AF* (January 1938), where he quoted from Walt Whitman: "Are we to have wealthy and immense cities—but still through and of them not a single poet, savior, knower—lover? Are the infidels of these states to laugh all faith away? If one man be found with faith in him are the rest free only to set upon him? Is this the price of money, business, imports, exports, custom, authority, precedents, pallor, dyspepsia, smut, ignorance, unbelief? Frighten faith and you destroy the power of breeding faith" (p. 50). Wright clearly felt that such a house for the "poet, savior, knower—lover" was too good for the "infidel" businessman and should be reserved for the architect himself. Laying the rationale for the design of Taliesin West at about the time he began planning it, Wright added: "I believe—making provision against violent winds—a lighter, more transient construction would serve well enough, something between Ocatilla, the architect's camp in the desert, and the San Marcos block building itself. The experiment would be worth making" (ibid.).

41. This interpretation is particularly interesting because it was just shortly after Taliesin West was begun that Wright began discussing his method of diagonal planning in some detail. See London Lects., 3, 9–11. In the London lectures, he noted: "To put it very simply, that natural reflex [diagonal] expresses very directly the feeling we now have at Taliesin about what constitutes the basis of our buildings" (p. 10). In this context, it might be mentioned that the sculptor Tony Smith, who was to become an important member of the New York School and to incorporate the diagonal both in the plans and in the sections of his large-scale sculptures, was an apprentice at Taliesin in 1939–40.

42. The first, and until recently the only, person to remark on the alignment of Taliesin West with the main features of the surrounding landscape was Vincent Scully. In his short book on Wright, published in 1960, he compared the relationships Wright set up to those obtaining in Phaistos and other "Cretan palace sites" that Wright "knew and admired" (Scully, *Wright*, 28–29). Recently, Bruce Pfeiffer has described how "the site [of Taliesin West] and its relation to the mountain range of the north dictated the orientation of the plan. The axis is derived from this extended view, from the west, looking east to a group of isolated mountains: Black Mountain and Granite Reef Mountain" (Pfeiffer and Futagawa, *Selected Houses, Taliesin West*, 11).

43. Wright drew the axes in red and marked them "A" and "B" in plan #3803.138 (FLWF). On another plan (#3803.005, FLWF), he drew the spiral symbol of the Fellowship at the crossing.

44. Tafel, *Apprentice to Genius*, 196. The particular reference here is to Wright's reuse of certain petroglyph boulders, which he removed from the hillside for placement in his camp, where they were carefully angled to follow their original orientation (see p. 273 below).

45. FLW, "To Arizona" and "In Arizona: The Taliesin Fellowship," in Carlson, "Wright and Taliesin West," 8, 15. The term "desert rubble stone"

was Wright's (*AF* [January 1948]: 88). Hitchcock used the term "mosaic" in Hitchcock, *Materials*, 97. One should connect Wright's procedure with collage and assemblage techniques in post-Surrealist painting and sculpture. Max Ernst's paintings done in Arizona in the early 1940s (when he lived at Sedona) immediately come to mind.

46. Cf. William Wesley Peters, quoted in William Marlin, "Olgivanna and Frank Lloyd Wright: Convictions and Continuity," *Arizona Living* 14 (May 1983): 13; and Pfeiffer and Futagawa, *Selected Houses, Taliesin West*, 13. Wright later acknowledged the importance of the pot in the design of the focal corner of the living room of his domestic quarters. Just opposite the Cove, he hollowed out a small well-like court and set within its glass enclosure, framed as if floating miraculously in space, two ancient Chinese cinerary urns. They look like prehistoric relics, unearthed and newly brought to light, and thus dramatize the underlying image of the vessel as a symbol of regeneration. The image of the vessel became particularly important in Wright's work of the late 1930s and 1940s as he began to use circular geometries that related to the element of water. See my "Frank Lloyd Wright's Own Houses and His Changing Concept of Architectural Representation," in *The Nature of Frank Lloyd Wright*, ed. Carol R. Bolon, Robert S. Nelson, and Linda Seidel (Chicago and London: University of Chicago Press, 1988), 52–56; and Chapter X, below.

47. Originally, lapped boards laid lengthwise across the center of the beams reduced the area covered by canvas. Steel was later substituted for most of the wood beams; a plastic material replaced the canvas by the late 1950s; and glass was increasingly added to enclose the interior spaces from the mid-1940s on.

48. The reference may actually be more to the Hopi and Pueblo architectures of the Southwest. In the article "To Arizona," included in the first publication of Taliesin West in *Arizona Highways* (1940), Wright observed: "Nor is the Indian Hopi-house a desert house in any true sense. Even were the Hopi imitation no base imitation for us, it is too loud. The projecting poles soften it with shadows a very little; the native Indian got that far with it" (in Carlson, "Wright and Taliesin West," 11).

49. Wright spoke of the desert as a "titanic, ancient battlefield" where everything "speak[s] of terrific violence" (*A* I, 307). "In the desert," he said, "the supreme mistress of creation gives all her 'works' to bristle in self-defense with extraordinary weapons. Stylish. And their designer also patterns the creature inhabitants of the desert for defense. And seduction, too, it seems. In style the creatures all resemble in one way or another—and by way of pattern—the braided, branded, triangular terrain itself. No less than cacti she provides her reptiles with deadly weapons" (ibid.).

The wood-and-canvas roof clearly goes back to Wright's first experiments at Ocatilla. In between came the "abstract forest" drafting room at the Hillside Home School, the Little San Marcos project, and the project for the Marcus House. Each had an imagery specific to its locale. In Taliesin West, the Amerindian and desert-defensive imagery shades over into the nomadic one of tents and covered wagons it shares with Ocatilla.

50. Wright's most extensive discussion of the "historical" interplay of the archetypes of cave and tent occurs in the chapter "Some Aspects of the Past and Present of Architecture" in Brownell and FLW, esp. 22–25, published the year before Taliesin West was begun.

51. Cf. *A* II, 455. To the group of fully enclosed spaces should be added the original dining room, which faced the prow but received light only through a clerestory and skylight.

52. It is surely not merely a coincidence that in Taliesin West Wright returned to the original Death Valley expression of the transformation of the basket and pot into the cave and the pithouse. In both cases, he was involved in making a permanent residence for himself in the desert of the Southwest. In the article "To Arizona" included in the first publication of Taliesin West, Wright noted how "the Indian learned from the desert when he made pots or mats or beadwork or clothed himself. He got something of the desert into all those things as we may see" (in Carlson, "Wright and Taliesin West," 10–11).

53. In conversation, April 1990. Not all the construction work was done by the apprentices, as is commonly thought. Hired workers continued the construction at least through the spring and summer of 1938. See correspondence between FLW, Robert Mosher, James Garrett, and J. W. (Bill) Hatfield, 23 April–12 September 1938, MS 1502.034, FLWF.

54. Note by FLW (unsigned) appended to Mosher, "In the Arizona Desert" (February 1941): 33. The photographs in Hitchcock, *Materials* (1942), unfortunately show only the south- and west-facing parts of the complex. It is impossible to see either the apprentice court or the workshop building. In his *Autobiography*, Wright made the building of Taliesin West into a protracted campaign of biblical proportions by saying that it took "about seven years" to complete (II, 454). But in such a project as Taliesin West, where changes were constantly being made and parts were always being extended or added, it is really not possible to say when the complex was finally finished.

55. Cf. Mosher, "In the Arizona Desert" (February 1941); and Masselink to Pool, 2 February 1941, FLWF.

56. These names appear in correspondence between 1938 and early 1941 and on drawings of that period. A notation on a section through the loggia and Garden Room (#3803.031, FLWF), for instance, says:

Taliesin   Wisconsin
Alladin   Arizona

<u>ALADIN</u>

ALI̸AD̸DIN

See also Tafel, *Apprentice to Genius*, 198, 200.

57. The reference to Aladin is in the section on Midway Gardens. See also FLW, "In the Cause of Architecture, IV: Fabrication and Imagination," *ARec* 62 (October 1927): 318. In 1940–41, Wright named the remodeling of the Ennis House he proposed for John Nesbitt "Sijistan," after the Safavid Caliph's palace in what was then Persia.

58. *Tales from the Thousand and One Nights*, trans. N. J. Dawood (Harmondsworth: Penguin, 1973), 179.

59. Wingspread is the house Wright built for Herbert Johnson in Wind Point, north of Racine, in 1937; Eaglefeather is the house designed for Arch Oboler in Malibu, Calif., in 1940.

60. One can trace Wright's use of fragments and remains of previous construction to his rebuilding of Taliesin after the second fire of 1925. In *An Autobiography*, he described how the fragments of the many works of art he had brought back from Japan and built into Taliesin lay mutilated in the debris of the ruin, as "sacrificial offerings to—whatever Gods may be." He noted that he "put the fragments aside to weave them into the masonry fabric of Taliesin III." He "had not protected them," and so he felt as responsible for the loss of their "souls" as he was for the human losses in the first fire. His life would thus be dedicated to their regeneration. "They should live on in me," Wright said, for "I would prove their life by mine in what I did" (*A* II, 262–63). Wright described the rebuilding of Taliesin with Olgivanna in 1925–26 as an act of archaeological reconstruction. By building "history" into the "fabric" of the new building, a much richer story would be evoked, one that could almost tell itself: "The limestone piers, walls and fireplaces of Taliesin II had turned red and crumbled in the fire, but I saved many stones not so destroyed, dyed by fire, and built them together with the fragments of great sculpture I had raked from the ashes into the new walls adding a storied richness to them unknown before. Whereas the previous buildings had all grown by addition, all could now be spontaneously born" (*A* II, 272).

In the London lectures, given at the time Taliesin West was being built, Wright said: "Instead of sculpture . . . we have used native rocks written on centuries ago by the American Indians and which we found on our own piece of ground. The camp has grown out of the ground, according to the spirit of environment and climate" (London Lects., 23).

61. Wesley Peters, in conversation, April 1990. Cf. Tafel, *Apprentice to Genius*, 196.

62. Johnson, *Writings*, 196. See also his "Whence and Whither: The Processional Element in Architecture," orig. pub. *Perspecta* 9/10 (1965), repr. in *Writings*, 151–55.

63. Wright began referring to the yearly "trek" to the desert as a "hegira" as early as 1934 (FLW to Dow, 11 September 1934). In the *Autobiography*, he called it the "Fellowship's annual hegira" (II, 452). It was also often spoken of as an "annual pilgrimage" (see, e.g., "The Uncovered Wagons," *AJ* 91 [11 April 1940]: 379). Bruce Pfeiffer has noted that the intertwined double spiral can be related to the "nautical handshake" (in conversation, May 1983),

which would reinforce the aspect of "fellowship." It was also one of the signs employed in Hohokam petroglyphs. Wright in fact used a small boulder with one such sign to mark the entrance to the complex (fig. 265).

64. Bradford Luckingham, *Phoenix: The History of a Southwestern Metropolis* (Tucson: University of Arizona Press, 1989), 195.

65. That sign, which has since been moved, was placed there in 1953 according to Pfeiffer and Futagawa, *Selected Houses, Taliesin West*, 51.

66. A photograph showing a saguaro being transplanted is reproduced in Carlson, "Wright and Taliesin West," 8.

67. On the relationship between Taliesin West and Bronze Age architecture, see Scully, *Wright*, 28–29.

68. Bruce Pfeiffer first made me aware of this by showing me a film that Wright's client Gerald Loeb made recording his arrival at Taliesin West in the spring of 1945. Few other Fellowship members recall the road's being used very much, and some do not remember it at all. Pfeiffer suggested that one of its purposes may have been to access Sun Trap. A photograph taken from Maricopa Hill around 1940 or 1941, reproduced in *Frank Lloyd Wright: Architect*, ed. Terence Riley, with Peter Reed (New York: Museum of Modern Art, 1994), 105, shows the same view as my fig. 261, but without the road.

69. Before the Cabaret Theater and Music Pavilion behind Wright's office were built in the 1950s, you could see almost nothing of the other buildings when you entered the court. Maricopa Hill filled the field of vision. You could just make out, at the edges of this field, the sloping roofs of the office and the drafting room, which might at first have been taken to be part of the talus of the hill.

70. Wesley Peters told me that Wright visited the Casa Grande ruins at the time and remarked on the existence of the same double-spiral symbol in the petroglyphs there (in conversation, April 1990). The double-square spiral was repeated in the rotated square in the plan of the apprentice court as published in *Arizona Highways* in May 1940 (Carlson, "Wright and Taliesin West," 7).

71. LaVan Martineau suggests that the imagery is one of warfare relating to a battle at the site. The stone points to the hill to which the women and children were taken (videotape, FLWF). I had always assumed that the boulder was originally a single one, albeit consolidated by cement. Based on a comparison with early photographs of the boulders taken *in situ*, Barbara Gronemann has concluded that the boulder is actually a composite, formed of two completely separate elements ("Taliesin West Site Report").

72. Bruce Pfeiffer claims that Wright had already drawn up a plan around 1956–57 to create an addition on the north side of the living quarters that would have effectively blocked the axis (in conversation, April 1990). A "sun bath" and "library" entered off the "lanai" were to have been sunk four feet below ground, but the parapet surrounding it would have projected six feet above ground. Plan #3803.134 (FLWF) records this scheme.

73. The slight shifts and jogs in the axes at Taliesin West in no way contradict the determination of alignments. The multiple conical buttes to the southeast of the camp allowed Wright to provide different sightings depending upon where the visitor was standing. The prow-shaped termination of the platform at the entrance could be seen as a reflection of the conical mountain in the distance, similar to the way Wright drew House C in the Doheny Ranch project based on Hokusai's prints of Fujiyama (figs. 141, 142). This same effect occurs in Wright's perspective sketch of Taliesin West (fig. 262) and, in magnified form, on the main terrace of Taliesin West, where the prow of the terrace seems to reflect Thompson Peak directly above it (fig. 278).

74. The sequence of changes can be dated only in a very general way until a complete documentary history of Taliesin West is available. I have based my chronology on plans, photographs, slides, and films, which are themselves more often than not undated.

75. This plan was published in *AF* (January 1948): 87–88.

76. I owe this information, like so much else regarding the development of Taliesin West, to Bruce Pfeiffer. According to him, Wright acquired the "Chinese theater" plaque along with eleven others in 1950. See Pfeiffer and Futagawa, *Selected Houses, Taliesin West*, 67.

77. Vincent Scully, *The Earth, the Temple, and the Gods: Greek Sacred Architecture* (New Haven: Yale University Press, 1962). The major research for this book was done in 1958, two years before the publication of Scully's book on Wright (1960). It is important to recall that Scully later dealt with many of

these same issues of the relationship between architecture, nature, and ceremonial in the context of the Native American cultures of the Southwest in *Pueblo: Mountain, Village, Dance* (New York: Viking, 1975).

There is in the collection of the Wright Archives a typed excerpt from the book *Traveling Impressions of Western Crete*, published in 1918 by Michael Dephner, that describes "How the Minoan Column Originated" and refers to the sculpture relief panel of the Lion Gate at Mycenae as a prime example (MSS 2401.513 A-B, FLWF). The text is annotated by Wright, and there is a tracing of the Lion Gate relief. The interest in Minoan forms is also to be seen in the downward-tapering columns of the Johnson Wax Company headquarters (fig. 295).

78. Cf. Dimitri Tselos, "Exotic Influences in the Architecture of Frank Lloyd Wright," *Magazine of Art* 46 (April 1953): 160–69, 184; and Tselos, "Frank Lloyd Wright and World Architecture," *JSAH* 28 (March 1969): 58–72.

79. One of the plans showing the alignment of standing stones (# 3803.138, FLWF) was drawn over a print of the plan published in *AF* (January 1948): 87–88. The project, however, appears to have reached its final form around the time of the design for the pediment of the bridge. The increased interest Wright showed in the mid-1950s in marking the axis with standing stones and other elements coincided with his placement of the large ceramic tub on the hill crown at Taliesin.

80. An early plan of the area in front of the cinema-theater and hexagonal pool shows a spiral drawn on the ground at the point where the east-west and north-south axes cross (#3803.005, FLWF). A loggia connecting the living to the working areas of the combined studio-home goes back to Taliesin. There is a large outdoor fireplace on the far wall of the loggia at Taliesin West, which could be used for barbecues. The loggia was partially enclosed in 1952 to accommodate the dining room that previously overlooked the terrace prow. Its glass wall was further extended in 1958.

81. David Doyel, who looked at the hilltop with me, felt that the stone's position may be more the result of nature's doing than man's. On the other hand, he suggested that it might have been a marker put in place by white miners or ranchers rather than prehistoric Indians. Parts of it are patinated from constant rubbing.

The propped boulder is not the only enigmatic stone on the hill. There is a petroglyph boulder halfway down the slope and a little to the north that offers an extraordinary and apparently unique image of what looks like a solar calendar, or at least some form of astronomical calculation. Pecked strokes, dots, and circles appear to define the orbit of the sun, while the cardinal points, represented by pinwheeling lines ending in open or solid squares, seem to function in a site-specific way, relating the directions to actual topographical features. Experts have tended to regard the petroglyph as modern, rather than prehistoric, though not without some hesitation. If modern, it can only be assumed that it was done by one of the Fellowship or, if not, by a very gifted artist.

82. T. S. Eliot, *Four Quartets* (1943), in *The Complete Poems and Plays* (New York: Harcourt, Brace, 1952), 119. This line is from "Burnt Norton," the first of the *Four Quartets*, published separately in 1941.

83. Mircea Eliade, *Cosmos and History: The Myth of the Eternal Return* (1949; trans. Willard R. Trask, New York: Harper and Row; Harper Torchbooks, Bollingen Library, 1959), esp. pp. 141–62.

84. Adolph Gottlieb and Mark Rothko (with Barnett Newman), "Letter to the Editor," *NYT*, 13 June 1943, sec. 2, p. 9; and Gottlieb and Rothko, "The Portrait of the Modern Artist," mimeographed script of broadcast, "Art in New York," WNYC, New York, 13 October 1943 (both quoted in Irving Sandler, *The Triumph of American Painting: A History of Abstract Expressionism* [New York and Washington, D.C.: Praeger, 1970], 63–64). The name Myth Makers was used by Rothko in his introduction to the catalogue of Clyfford Still's first exhibition at Peggy Guggenheim's Art of This Century Gallery in New York in February–March 1946. For a general discussion of the subject and useful bibliography, see Sandler, *American Painting*, esp. 62–71. See also *Chimera* 4 (Spring 1946); and William Rubin, ed., *"Primitivism" in 20th Century Art: Affinity of the Tribal and the Modern*, 2 vols. (New York: Museum of Modern Art, 1984). Again, it should be noted that the sculptor Tony Smith, who returned to New York in 1945 and became a good friend of Pollock and Newman, forms a direct link between the worlds of Taliesin West and the New York

School. Gottlieb, whose first Pictograph dates from 1941, spent 1937–38 living in the desert near Tucson.

85. Robert Goldwater, *Primitivism in Modern Art* (1938; rev. ed., New York: Random House, Vintage Books, 1967). The exhibitions at New York's Museum of Modern Art devoted in part or in whole to "primitive art" included: "American Sources of Modern Art," 1933; "African Negro Art," 1935; "Prehistoric Rock Pictures in Europe and Africa," 1937; "Twenty Centuries of Mexican Art," 1940; "Ancestral Sources of Modern Painting," 1941; and "Indian Art of the United States," 1944. The exhibition, "Indian Art of the United States," which took place shortly after Wright's retrospective at MOMA, included a large wall of pictographs made specially for the show by Basketmaker artists from Barrier Canyon, Utah.

86. FLW to McCormick, 31 March 1949. In the catalogue *Sixty Years of Living Architecture* (1953), Wright wrote of his winter headquarters: "Taliesin West came from the same source as the early American primitives and there are certain resemblances, but not influences" (p. [19]). Wright, however, made disparaging comments about the tendency toward "primitivism" in modern art in the symposium "The Western Round Table on Modern Art," held in San Francisco in April 1949. For excerpts of this, see Robert Motherwell and Ad Reinhardt, eds., *Modern Artists in America*, 1st ser. (New York: Wittenborn Schultz, 1951), 30–31. For more on this event and the "gadfly" role Wright was intended to play in it, see Chapter X, note 68.

87. No history of "primitivism" in modern architecture has yet been written. The difference in degree of literalness of the appropriation that is apparent in a comparison of, say, Gottlieb and Wright, may be explained by the difference in the respective mediums and their means of representation.

88. Leo Steinberg, "Reflections on the State of Criticism," orig. pub. *Artforum* 10 (March 1972), repr. in Steinberg, *Other Criteria: Confrontations with Twentieth-Century Art* (New York: Oxford University Press, 1972), esp. 82–91.

89. See, e.g., Robert Morris, "Aligned with Nazca," *Artforum* 14 (October 1975): 26–39; and Robert Smithson, *The Writings of Robert Smithson*, ed. Nancy Holt (New York: New York University Press, 1979). For an overview of the subject, see Lucy R. Lippard, *Overlay: Contemporary Art and the Art of Prehistory* (New York: Pantheon, 1983).

90. The so-called Nazca lines were coincidentally "discovered" in 1941 when geographer Paul Kosok first took aerial photographs of them. He and Maria Reiche published their "Ancient Drawings on the Desert of Peru" in *Archaeology* 2 (1949): 206–15.

91. The term was probably first used by Le Corbusier in his description of the Maison La Roche in *Le Corbusier et Pierre Jeanneret: Oeuvre complète de 1910–1929*, ed. W[illy] Boesiger and O[skar] Stonorov (1929; 8th ed., Zurich: Editions d'Architecture, 1965), 60.

92. The processional type of movement, combined with explicit references to ritual and myth, emerged in Le Corbusier's work in the late 1940s, after his trip to the United States in 1946. The projects I have in mind are the pilgrimage chapel at Sainte-Baume in Southern France (1948); the capitol complex of Chandigarh (begun 1950); and the Chapel of Notre-Dame du Haut at Ronchamp (1950–55). Le Corbusier had used the spiral for the design of his Museum of World Culture for the Mundaneum project of 1928–29 (see Chapter X).

93. Frank Waters, *Book of the Hopi* (New York: Viking, 1963), 23–24, 35, 115.

94. See Jean Chevalier and Alain Gheerbrant, eds., *Dictionnaire de symboles: mythes, rêves, coutumes, gestes, formes, figures, couleurs, nombres* (Paris: Robert Laffont, 1969), 723–25; J. E. Cirlot, *A Dictionary of Symbols*, trans. Jack Sage, 2d ed. (New York: Philosophical Library, 1971), 305–7; Aubrey Burl, *Rites of the Gods* (London, Melbourne, and Toronto: J. M. Dent & Sons, 1981), 83–87; and Jill Purce, *The Mystic Spiral: Journey of the Soul* (New York: Avon, 1974).

95. As a geometric form, the spiral clearly held a meaning for Wright that had something to do with this idea of progress *with* circumspection, that is to say, the ability to move ahead while always seeing where one has come from. He described the spiral in *The Japanese Print: An Interpretation* (1912; rpt. Horizon Press, 1967), 10, as symbolizing "organic progress." He admired how "the Japanese approach to any matter is a spiral. Their . . . attack . . . is oblique and volute" (*A I*, 217).

96. See note 63 above. In the early years, the Fellowship left Wisconsin right after Christmas and returned after Easter. By 1948, as Wright was getting older, they began to leave for Arizona in November, to return to Wisconsin in May. This lengthening of the winter season may even have increased in some later years.

97. Eliade, *Cosmos and History*, 34–35. Wright's numerous references to the infinite and the timeless in his description of Taliesin West for the 1943 edition of the *Autobiography* appear to contradict his questioning whether art can express the timeless in the discussion with Baker Brownell that ends their *Architecture and Modern Life* published six years before (pp. 282–85).

98. Eliade, *Cosmos and History*, esp. 147–54; Eliot, *Complete Poems*, 136, 120 ("The Dry Salvages" [1941], and "Burnt Norton" [1941]).

99. See Sigfried Giedion, "The Need for a New Monumentality," in *New Architecture and City Planning*, ed. Paul Zucker (New York: Philosophical Library, 1944), 549–68; and "In Search of a New Monumentality," a symposium by Gregor Paulsson, Henry-Russell Hitchcock, William Holford, Sigfried Giedion, Walter Gropius, Lucio Costa, and Alfred Roth, *ARev* 104 (September 1948): 117–28.

It is well known that Wright opposed America's entry into World War II and saw that conflict as a disaster. Following his pacifist leanings, a number of the Taliesin Fellows registered as conscientious objectors.

100. For a survey of the subject of ruins, see Reinhard Zimmermann, *Künstliche Ruinen: Studien zu ihrer Bedeutung und Form* (Wiesbaden: Reichert, 1989). I am grateful to Danny Abramson for numerous observations relating to the subject.

101. We know that Wright visited the Casa Grande site. It would be interesting to know how many others in the area he visited. The relationship between Wright's incorporation of Hohokam remains at Taliesin West and his reuse of elements that escaped destruction in the second fire at Taliesin has already been pointed out (note 60 above). The conflation of ruin and wartime destruction was remarked upon by Katherine and Herbert Jacobs in relation to the construction of their second Wright house, the Solar Hemicycle, in Middleton, Wis. (1943–48): "Uncovered at last from the snow, the tracery of stones which outlined the house looked like those pitiful foundations unearthed by archeologists, from which one is supposed to imagine great pillared temples with spacious porticoes. Under Johnny's [the mason's] masterful and creative approach, as the stone walls began rapidly rising, the scene swiftly changed to resemble a picture of war's destruction" (Jacobs and Jacobs, *Building with Frank Lloyd Wright: An Illustrated Memoir* [San Francisco: Chronicle Books, Prism Edition, 1978], 98).

102. Gordon, "One Man's House," 195. One is reminded of Hitchcock's reference to "the prehistoric grandeur" of the camp. That this was part of the in-house explanation may be inferred from Edgar Tafel's remark that "Taliesin West would make one of the most interesting ruins of all time" (Tafel, *Apprentice to Genius*, 196).

103. Richard Carney, CEO of the Frank Lloyd Wright Foundation, informed me that Olgivanna Wright's remark was "made in the early stages of construction before the redwood trusses and canvas were in place" (by letter, 29 December 1986), implying that it was never meant to describe the finished building. In *Wright: His Life, His Work, His Words*, however, she reiterated that "the buildings of our camp *look* as though they were excavated rather than built, and yet they are prodigiously modern" (p. 104, italics added).

104. In the third edition (1977), that phrase was changed to "as though it had stood there during creation" (*A* III, 480).

105. Eliade, *Cosmos and History*, 3–48.

106. Here I am thinking particularly of Louis Kahn and the discussion of ruins spawned by his work of the 1960s and early 1970s.

107. For the most popular and widely read example of V. Gordon Childe's thought, see his *Man Makes Himself* (1936; rev. ed., New York and Scarborough, Ont.: New American Library, Meridian Book, 1983). The first chapter is entitled "Human and Natural History." In it, Childe declares that "human history joins on to natural history. Through prehistory history is seen growing out of the 'natural sciences' of biology, paleontology, and geology" (p. 3) so that "not only does prehistory extend written history backwards, it carries on natural history forwards. In reality, if one root of prehistoric archaeology is ancient history, the other is geology. Prehistory constitutes a bridge between human history and the natural sciences of zoology, paleontology, and geology. Geology has traced the building up of the earth we inhabit; under the aspect of paleontology it follows the emergence of various forms of life through several vast periods of geological time. In the last era prehistory takes up the tale" (p. 7).

108. Brownell and FLW, 17, 42.

109. Ibid., 31, 44, 49, 43. The affinity with Kahn's description of ruins (Chapter V) surely suggests a historical relation between the two.

110. Eliot, *Complete Poems*, 144 ("Little Gidding").

Chapter X
The Guggenheim Museum's Logic of Inversion

1. Hilla Rebay to FLW, 1 June 1943, in Bruce Brooks Pfeiffer, ed., *Frank Lloyd Wright: The Guggenheim Correspondence* (Fresno, Calif., and Carbondale and Edwardsville, Ill.: Press at California State University, Southern Illinois University Press, 1986; hereafter *Guggenheim Corres.*), 4. Brendan Gill dated this letter to 30 May 1943 (Gill, *Many Masks*, 527n1). The "three books" referred to by Rebay were, very possibly, the recently published second edition of *An Autobiography* (1943), Hitchcock, *Materials* (1942), and Gutheim, *FLW on Arch.* (1941).

2. FLW to Rebay, 10 June 1943, in *Guggenheim Corres.*, 4, 6. Wright's birthday on 8 June was traditionally celebrated at Taliesin by a party and gift-giving.

3. Rebay to FLW, 14 June 1943, in *Guggenheim Corres.*, 6.

4. Selden Rodman, ed., *Conversations with Artists*, (New York: Capricorn, 1961), 72. The truth of this statement would be hard to prove. Certainly Wright's relationships with clients varied over the years. My impression, however, is that it is a fairly accurate representation of his *modus operandi*.

5. In one of the question-and-answer periods during the London lectures of 1939, Wright said: "They [clients] think they know what they want. Sometimes they do. If they come to you, wanting you, believing that you know, they do know that much. . . . Any architect builds a building to please his client, certainly. . . . But were you as an architect to go out seeking a job, go after a piece of work, try to persuade a man to let you build a building for him, then perhaps you would have to please your client against your will, do what he told you, and serve you right, too! But to put yourself there in his power is unethical, of course" (London Lects., 21).

Or again in 1939: "No man can build a building for another who does not believe in him, who does not believe in what he believes in, and who has not chosen him because of this faith, knowing what he can do. That is the nature of the architect and client as I see it. When a man wants to build a building, he seeks an interpreter, does he not? He seeks some man who has the technique to express that thing which he himself desires but cannot do. So should a man come to me for a building he would be ready for me. It would be what I could do that he wanted" (in Gutheim, *FLW on Arch.*, 249).

6. Comparisons could be drawn here with Le Corbusier and Mme. Savoye, Mies and Edith Farnsworth, and Peter Eisenman and the Falks. Aline Barnsdall, as we know, commissioned Wright to design a second house for herself (in Beverly Hills) at the very moment she was disposing of the Olive Hill property.

7. In the first draft of a letter of 27 December 1958 sent to Harry F. Guggenheim, who had taken over as president of the Board of Trustees of the Solomon R. Guggenheim Foundation, Wright stated: "The opus greatly matters to me because it is probably the supreme effort of a lifetime of supreme effort" (MS 2401.397 T, FLWF). In his review of the building, Henry-Russell Hitchcock called it "the swansong of America's greatest architect." "Like the late quartets of Beethoven, like the last works of such long-lived artists as Michelangelo and Titian," Hitchcock went on to say, "the Guggenheim Museum does not belong to the time of its production; but like them, paradoxically, it probably belongs more to the future than to the past. Long after many of the current paintings whose acquisition is the pride of the Guggenheim Museum trustees and the present director are retired from exhibition, . . . this building will survive as one of the triumphs of the twentieth century" (Hitchcock, "Notes of a

Traveller: Wright and Kahn," *Zodiac* 6 [1960]: 17, 20). For more on the building's reception, see pp. 347ff.

8. Cf. Elizabeth Mock, ed., *Built in USA, 1932–1944* (New York: Museum of Modern Art, 1944); and, more recently, James D. Kornwolf, ed., *Modernism in America, 1937–1941: A Catalog and Exhibition of Four Architectural Competitions* (Williamsburg, Va.: Joseph and Margaret Muscarelle Museum of Art, College of William and Mary, 1985). For a relevant discussion of the United Nations building in this context, see Lewis Mumford's critical articles "UN Model and Model UN" (1947), "Buildings as Symbols" (1947), "Magic with Mirrors" (1951), "A Disoriented Symbol" (1951), "United Nations Assembly" (1953), and "Workshop Invisible" (1953), collected in *From the Ground Up: Observations on Contemporary Architecture, Housing, Highway Building, and Civic Design* (New York: Harcourt, Brace and Company, Harvest Books, 1956), 20–70. For the broader postwar context, see Sigfried Giedion, *Architecture, You and Me: The Diary of a Development* (Cambridge, Mass.: Harvard University Press, 1958). This contains the important article of 1944, "The Need for a New Monumentality" (pp. 25–39), which provoked the symposium "In Search of a New Monumentality," published in *ARev* 104 (September 1948): 117–28.

9. A number of important studies on the subject appeared at just the time the Guggenheim Museum was being designed: André Grabar, *Martyrium: Recherches sur le culte des reliques et l'art chrétien antique*, 2 vols. plus album (Paris: Collège de France, 1943–46); Richard Krautheimer, "Introduction to an 'Iconography of Medieval Architecture,'" *Journal of the Warburg and Courtauld Institutes* 5 (1942): 1–33; Karl Lehmann, "The Dome of Heaven," *Art Bulletin* 27 (March 1945): 1–27; Rudolf Wittkower, *Architectural Principles in the Age of Humanism*, Studies of the Warburg Institute, 19 (London: Warburg Institute, University of London, 1949), esp. 1–28; E. Baldwin Smith, *The Dome: A Study in the History of Ideas*, Princeton Monographs in Art and Archaeology, 25 (Princeton: Princeton University Press, 1950); and Louis Hautecoeur, *Mystique et architecture: Symbolisme du cercle et de la coupole* (Paris: A. et J. Picard, 1954). Krautheimer remarked in the postscript to the reprint of his article in his *Studies in Early Christian, Medieval, and Renaissance Art* (New York and London: New York University Press, University of London Press, 1969), 149, that "the ideas . . . must have been 'in the air.'" Smith was on the faculty of Princeton University, and Wright may have met him when he lectured there.

10. Cf. James Johnson Sweeney, "Chambered Nautilus on Fifth Avenue," and Philip Johnson, "Letter to the Museum Director," *Museum News* 38 (January 1960): 15, 25.

11. FLW, *The Japanese Print: An Interpretation* (1912; rpt. New York: Horizon Press, 1967)16; and "Frank Lloyd Wright Comments," *The Meeting House: First Unitarian Society, Madison-Wisconsin* (Madison: Friends of the Meeting House, n.d.), 13. As noted earlier, Wright also described the form of the spiral in physiologico-racial terms: "The characteristic Japanese approach to any subject is, by instinct, spiral. The Oriental instinct for attack in any direction is oblique or volute and becomes wearisome to a direct occidental, whose instinct is frontal and whose approach is rectilinear" (Brownell and FLW, 132).

One should also recall, in this context, Wright's 1939 project for three gates for Taliesin, each one based on one of the three primary geometric forms (see Chapter VIII, note 62).

12. See Wassily Kandinsky, *Concerning the Spiritual in Art* (1912; trans. Michael Sadleir et al., New York: Wittenborn, Schultz, 1947), and *Point and Line to Plane* (1926; trans. Howard Dearstyne and Hilla Rebay, 1927; rpt. New York: Dover, 1979). See also Angelica Zander Rudenstine, *The Guggenheim Museum Collection: Paintings, 1880–1945*, 2 vols. (New York: Solomon R. Guggenheim Museum, 1976), 1: 136–73, 204–391. In her book *Hilla Rebay: In Search of the Spirit in Art* (New York: George Braziller, 1983), Joan Lukach quotes the following from Gleizes's response to Wright's design for the Guggenheim Museum: "The idea of the spiral greatly captivates me because 'the spiral' is the traditional expression of the universal form. In my paintings as in my books since *Peinture et ses lois, ce que devait sortir du Cubisme* of 1922, I have continued to use it and to proclaim that non-figurative works must be founded upon 'cosmic laws of which the spiral is the ultimate formal expression.' . . . The spiral is love. . . . It is the alpha and omega of all form . . . and the very essence of God" (p. 265).

13. The commission from Strong came in the summer of 1924. The de-

sign was pretty much finalized by April 1925 and was presented to the client in August. It was rejected in mid-October. It is connected to the Death Valley project in a very direct way, because Alfred MacArthur, who worked for A. M. Johnson, probably acted as the middleman between Strong and Wright (see Chapter VI). On the Gordon Strong project, see Mark Reinberger, "The Sugarloaf Mountain Project and Frank Lloyd Wright's Vision of a New World," *JSAH* 43 (March 1984): 38–52. I am grateful to him for sending me a copy of his Master's thesis, "Frank Lloyd Wright's Sugarloaf Mountain 'Automobile Objective' Project," Cornell University, 1982. Secrest, *Wright*, 289, suggests that Strong held a kind of competition of ideas, commissioning projects from four other architects at the same time.

To be absolutely accurate about Wright's first use of the circle in planning, one should probably go back to the Little Dipper project of mid-1923 (fig. 144). Although the bowl of seats was not enclosed, its circular shape functioned as a key element in the plan. It is important to note that the circle was related to a public, educational, and cultural use in this early occurrence.

14. FLW to Gordon Strong, 20 October 1925, Stronghold, Inc., Dickerson, Md. In his attempt to justify the design to Strong, who seems to have disliked it on almost every score, comparing it to "a standard astronomical observatory which might be located on the highly scenic Mt. Wilson" (Strong to FLW, 14 October 1925, Stronghold Inc.), Wright defended the "natural and organic" form of the spiral design in terms of "the law of gravitation," comparing it to a "screw," a "spiral spring," and a "snail." He also referred to "the leaning Tower of Pisa" (FLW to Strong, 20 October 1925). Strong, for his part, was particularly unimpressed with the biblical reference. "I must admit that the exterior ramps are archaeologically right," he said. "They prove overwhelmingly your close adherence to tradition. In devising the latest type of structure, you have gone straight back to the earliest." He then sarcastically added: "Perhaps the particular view which I have of the Tower of Babel may not be in your collection on this interesting and important structure. I therefore venture to enclose a copy herewith. You will note in the foreground a gentleman who, according to the Bible, lost his voice, and according to the picture also lost his shirt; in endeavoring to explain that the structure under way possessed one thing any how—organic integrity. But the more he repeated the phrase, the less his hearers understood him. Finally their understanding became so mixed that they did not understand each other. Which was the end of the first attempt at an externally ramped automobile observatory." Strong ended by calling Wright "the world's greatest archaeologist and philologist," signing off with: "Confusion of tongues! Loss of shirts! Good night!!" (Strong to FLW, 14 October 1925).

15. FLW to Strong, 20 October 1925.

16. Ibid.

17. In his description of the project, Le Corbusier stressed, as Wright did, the panoramic aspect of the circulation given by the spiral: "At each turn, a new horizon; at each spiral a more extensive view." He equally stressed, as did Wright, the monumental and cosmic references of the overall pyramidal form: "The four angles of the Musée Mondial mark precisely the four cardinal points." In fact, there was even to be a planetarium (Le Corbusier, "'Mundaneum,'" *Architecture Vivante* 7 [Spring–Summer 1929]: 29, 31, 32).

It is not known whether Le Corbusier was familiar with the Wright project. Richard Neutra worked on the project, as he did on the one for Death Valley. Reinberger suggests that Erich Mendelsohn may have proposed the circular form of the building, based on a letter written by Mendelsohn when he visited Wright at Taliesin in November 1924 (Reinberger, "Sugarloaf Mountain Project," 48). Neutra's comment at the time that Mendelsohn "has some good qualities although he is apparently not on the side of a true effective building art" and that "Wright was rather against him" could be taken in different ways (Richard Neutra to Frances Toplitz, November 1924, in Diane Neutra, comp. and trans., *Richard Neutra: Promise and Fulfillment, 1919–1932, Selections from the Letters and Diaries of Richard and Diane Neutra* [Carbondale and Edwardsville, Ill.: Southern Illinois University Press, 1986] 130).

Recently, Bruce Pfeiffer has suggested that "in 1929 Wright was considering the use of the spiral for an art musuem," implying that it was for a site in France. He based this on a letter from Wright to Strong in that year requesting the return of his drawings: "It seems something of the kind is contemplated on the other side, in France, only in that case, it is a *museum*. Some interest has arisen in this idea as I have worked it out for you and I have been asked many times to see it" (quoted in Bruce Brooks Pfeiffer, "A Temple of Spirit," in *The Solomon R. Guggenheim Museum* [New York: Guggenheim Museum, 1994], 6). Though not having all the information Pfeiffer has, I read the comment not as referring to a commission but rather to Le Corbusier's scheme (and perhaps as a way of making Strong regret missing out on a good idea).

18. Cf. FLW, *The Disappearing City* (New York: William Farquhar Payson, 1932), 74–75; and FLW, "Broadacre City: A New Community Plan," *ARec* 77 (April 1935): 248.

19. It should be recalled that Wright's initial discussions with Edgar Kaufmann in 1934–35 centered on a plan for Pittsburgh involving the construction of a planetarium based on the Gordon Strong project. As a founding member of the Allegheny Conference on Community Development (1944), which took as one of its primary responsibilities the redevelopment of the downtown area known as Point Park, Kaufmann commissioned Wright in 1947 to prepare a project for the site. The first Pittsburgh Point Park Civic Center scheme of 1947 had at its center an enormous, fifteen-level ziggurat with a continuous ramp for access and parking. Within it were art galleries, a planetarium, concert halls, cinemas, convention facilities, an opera house, and a glass-covered "astrodome" for sports. For this project, see now Richard Cleary, "Edgar J. Kaufmann, Frank Lloyd Wright and 'Pitsburgh Point Park Coney Island in Automobile Scale,'" *JSAH* 52 (June 1993): 139–58. The Baghdad project will be discussed in Chapter XI.

20. There is a direct connection between this aspect of Johnson Wax and the design development of Fallingwater. The commission for Johnson Wax came in late July 1936. The spherical kettle and the curved recess in the fireplace were designed at precisely this moment and may well have been the first explicit connection Wright made between water and the geometry of the circle. On the Racine headquarters, see esp. Jonathan Lipman, *Frank Lloyd Wright and the Johnson Wax Buildings* (New York: Rizzoli, 1986).

21. Cf. *A* II, 472–75; and Smith, *Wright*, 153–64. Wright used the terms *rift* and *dendriform* in "Frank Lloyd Wright," *AF* (January 1938): 88. When the building was opened to the public in 1939, a reporter for the Milwaukee *Journal* compared it to "a woman swimming naked in a stream" (quoted in "New Frank Lloyd Wright Office Building Shows Shape of Things to Come," *Life* 6 [8 May 1939]: 15). Wright thought this comparison apt enough to include it in his description of the building in *A* II, 470. Vincent Scully noted the aqueous, Egyptoid imagery of Johnson Wax in Scully, *Wright*, 29.

22. Lipman, *Johnson Wax*, 25–37.

23. The references in Johnson Wax may well extend beyond the classical world to that of the Middle East. Arthur Drexler insisted that the brickwork of the building owed much to the Assyrian and Achaemenian palaces at Ninevah, Khorsabad, and Persepolis (in conversation, May 1980). This reading may also help explain the similarity between the Research Tower, in its relationship to the office block to which it was added in 1943–50, and the brick spiral minaret of the Great Mosque at Samarra, Iraq, in its relationship to the lower and broader mass of the brick-walled court and prayer hall (cf. figs. 296, 379).

24. Wright's growing interest in the dome is reflected in his discussion of the history of architecture in Brownell and FLW (1937), where the evolution of the dome, which he calls "the perfect masonry roof" (p. 26), becomes the barometer of historical change (pp. 35–40).

25. The project for the Jester House dates from late July 1938. The client was a movie director. Wright reused the scheme in a design for the Pence House in Hilo, Hawaii, in the following year. It was posthumously built, with certain variations, for Arthur E. and Bruce Brooks Pfeiffer in 1971, just to the east of the main buildings of Taliesin West.

26. Mary Jane Hamilton, "The Olin Terraces and Monona Terrace Projects," in Paul E. Sprague, ed., *Frank Lloyd Wright and Madison: Eight Decades of Artistic and Social Interaction* (Madison: Elvehjem Museum of Art, University of Wisconsin, 1990), 195–206.

27. FLW, "The Monona Terrace Project," 6 August 1958, p. 1, MS 2401.395 A; and FLW, "Monona Terraces: Civic Gardens constructed above the Lake, Facts concerning the Monona Project," 28 May 1941, p. 4, MS 2401.248 A, FLWF. In the 1941 text, Wright said the project was "designed as a great landscape feature," the "inner rooms [of] which are not buildings but elements in the park scheme" (pp. 1, 2).

28. The most apt comparison might be with the multilevel Jardin de la Fontaine in Nîmes.

29. FLW, "Monona Terrace," 1.

30. Wright's design is "people-oriented," to use the terminology of the late fifties and sixties. In comparison, say, with the Boston City Hall, Wright's structure refuses to express the power of city government, pushing it instead to the periphery or underground.

31. For Wright's rejection of the idea of the Michelangelesque "dome on stilts" as "the symbol of authority," see *A* II, 333–35; and Chapter VII, note 71.

32. Mary Jane Hamilton, "Olin Terraces and Monona Terrace," 199–204; and "Frank Lloyd Wright: A Selection of Current Work," *ARec* 123 (May 1958): 170–71. A reference to seasonal changes was already contained in the legend on the perspective of the first scheme (fig. 300): "SEVEN MONTHS WATER-DOMES, FIVE MONTHS EVERGREENS." Certain elements in the design of the mid-fifties, such as the cylindrical units, remind one of Eero Saarinen's work, like the Kresge Chapel at MIT (1953–55).

Interest in the project was rekindled once again in the early 1990s (after having been revived in 1962 and 1974), and a positive referendum vote took place on 4 November 1992 to build Monona Terrace as a convention center.

33. The project was commissioned in April 1938. See *LClients*, 158–86. There is no study yet of this important design. It has largely been left out of histories of American architecture and only barely treated in works specifically devoted to campus planning. Cf. Paul Venable Turner, *Campus: An American Planning Tradition* (New York, Cambridge, Mass., and London: Architectural History Foundation, MIT Press, 1984), 252–57. Arthur Drexler considered it one of Wright's most important designs and one of the most significant group-plans of the twentieth century (in conversation, May 1976).

The most useful publications to consult are: "Frank Lloyd Wright," *AF* (January 1948): 127–35; "Frank Lloyd Wright," *AF* 94 (January 1951): 102–3; "Florida Southern College Revisited for Glimpses of the Administration Group in Wright's Organic Campus," *AF* 97 (September 1952): 120–27; "The Frank Lloyd Wright Campus," *Bulletin of Florida Southern College, Lakeland* 69 (April 1953); and Bruce Brooks Pfeiffer and Yukio Futagawa, *Global Architecture*, vol. 40, *Frank Lloyd Wright: Pfeiffer Chapel, Florida Southern College, Lakeland, Florida. 1938; Beth Sholom Synagogue, Elkins Park, Pennsylvania. 1954* (Tokyo: A.D.A. EDITA, 1976).

34. *AF* (January 1948): 127. The plan is clearly an outcome of Taliesin West. As in that case, the preliminary scheme for Florida Southern was completely orthogonal. The diagonal may have been suggested by the angled line of the lakeshore.

35. Scully, *Wright*, 29.

36. As the focal element of the design, the proposed water dome was to function like the hill crown at Taliesin. Like much of Wright's design for the campus, it was never built according to the original plans. A drawing of 1946 shows that the total diameter of the pool was to be 160 feet. The jets on the circumference were to be set in an eight-foot-high band.

The Roux Library plan was based on that of the Little Dipper, which, as noted earlier, could be considered Wright's first circular design. For reasons of economy, the buildings were mainly constructed according to the textile-block system, with students providing the primary labor force.

37. Sometime in the later 1940s, Wright redesigned the outdoor theater and pool to form a complete circle, the diameter of which paralleled the lakeshore and defined the stage. The structure was relocated to the east, between the two main axes leading down to the lake, and the semicircular pool was surrounded by a lagoon created by a dam. Sometime after 1955, the theater/pool was returned to its original location, redesigned, and reoriented to follow more closely the original scheme.

38. A case can be made for the evolution of Wright's circular house designs from the hinged and pivoted Usonian House plan that first emerged in the Willey House of 1934; see my "Frank Lloyd Wright's Diagonal Planning," in Helen Searing, ed., *In Search of Modern Architecture: A Tribute to Henry-Russell Hitchcock* (New York, Cambridge, Mass., and London: Architectural History Foundation, MIT Press, 1982), 265–72. The most striking example of this would be the second house Wright designed for the Jacobses, in Middleton, Wis., between December 1943 and February 1944, at exactly the same time he was beginning the design of the Guggenheim Museum. Some of the most important circular house designs of the mid- to late forties include: Loeb House, Redding, Conn., 1944–46; Haldorn House ("The Wave"), Carmel, Calif., 1945; Morris House, San Francisco, 1944–46; Huntington Hartford House, Los Ange-

les, 1946–48; Marting House, Northampton, Ohio, 1947; Palmer House, Phoenix, 1947; Friedman House, Pleasantville, N.Y., 1948; McCord House, North Arlington, N.J., 1948; Windfohr House ("Crownfield"), Fort Worth, Tex., 1948–50; Meyer House, Galesburg, Mich., 1948; and Laurent House, Rockford, Ill., 1949.

39. FLW to Ludd Spivey, 31 August 1942, in *LClients*, 183.

40. There is no book or major study on the Guggenheim Museum. The most important essay to date is the chapter "The Encompassing Environment of Free-Form Architecture: Frank Lloyd Wright's Guggenheim Museum," in William H. Jordy, *American Buildings and Their Architects*, vol. 4, *The Impact of European Modernism in the Mid-Twentieth Century* (Garden City, N.Y.: Doubleday, 1972), 279–359. William J. Hennessey, "Frank Lloyd Wright and the Guggenheim Museum: A New Perspective," *Arts* 52 (April 1978): 128–33, was the first to make use of archival material at the Guggenheim Foundation. John Coolidge, *Patrons and Architects: Designing Art Museums in the Twentieth Century*, Anne Burnett Tandy Lectures in American Civilization, 2 (Fort Worth, Tex: Amon Carter Museum, 1989), places the museum in the context of other twentieth-century examples. On the occasion of the opening of the Gwathmey-Siegel addition (1992), the museum published a mainly photographic booklet, *The Solomon R. Guggenheim Museum*, containing a historical essay by Bruce Brooks Pfeiffer ("A Temple of Spirit," pp. 3–39).

In the past several years, two important publications appeared that have already sparked interest in further scholarly study of the building. The first is Joan M. Lukach's extremely interesting and well-documented study of the museum's first curator and director, *Hilla Rebay: In Search of the Spirit in Art* (New York: George Braziller, 1983). This includes two chapters specifically devoted to Wright and the building (pp. 182–210). The second is Bruce Brooks Pfeiffer's publication of *Frank Lloyd Wright: The Guggenheim Correspondence* (1986), which covers the entire sixteen years from June 1943 to April 1959. Although it does not include all of Wright's letters and includes very few of Rebay's, it is indispensable for an understanding of how the design was conceived and how it developed over time.

There are two studies of the Guggenheim family, each of which has relevant information about the museum: Milton Lomask, *Seed Money: The Guggenheim Story* (New York: Farrar, Straus, 1964), esp. 164–217; and John H. Davis, *The Guggenheims: An American Epic* (New York: William Morrow, 1978), esp. 198–231, 437–56. Brochures published by the museum include: *The Solomon R. Guggenheim Museum. Architect: Frank Lloyd Wright* (New York: Solomon R. Guggenheim Foundation, Horizon Press, 1960), which contains a selection of statements by Wright; and *The Solomon R. Guggenheim Museum: Frank Lloyd Wright* (New York: Solomon R. Guggenheim Foundation, 1975). Bruce Pfeiffer wrote the introductory text for Yukio Futagawa, ed., *Global Architecture*, vol. 36, *Frank Lloyd Wright: Solomon R. Guggenheim Museum, New York City, N.Y., 1943–59; Marin County Civic Center, California, 1957–70* (Tokyo: A.D.A. EDITA, 1975).

The most important presentations by Wright of the building are: "The Modern Gallery," *AF* 84 (January 1946): 81–88; FLW, "The Modern Gallery for the Solomon R. Guggenheim Foundation: New York City," *Magazine of Art* 39 (January 1946): 24–26; *AF* (January 1948): 136–38; "Frank Lloyd Wright's Masterwork," *AF* 96 (April 1952): 141–44; and "Frank Lloyd Wright: A Selection of Current Work," *ARec* 123 (May 1958): 182–90.

Among the numerous articles and reviews written while the building was being planned or shortly after it was finished, the most interesting and useful are: "Optimistic Ziggurat," *Time* 46 (1 October 1945): 74; "Speaking of Pictures: . . . New Art Museum Will Be New York's Strangest Building," *Life* 19 (8 October 1945): 12–13, 15; "Un Musée en spirale: Le Musée Guggenheim à New-York," *Mouseion* 55–56 (1946): 99–106; Max Huggler and Georg Schmidt, "Das Guggenheim-Museum von Frank Lloyd Wright in New York: Zwei Museumsdirektoren äussern sich zu einer grundsätzlichen Idee," *Werk* 34 (June 1947): 188–92; Aline B. Saarinen, "Tour with Mr. Wright," *NYT Magazine* (22 September 1957): 22–23, 69–70; George N. Cohen, "Frank Lloyd Wright's Guggenheim Museum," *Concrete Construction* 3 (March 1958): 10–13; Edgar Kaufmann Jr., "The Form of Space for Art: Wright's Guggenheim Museum," *Art in America* 46 (Winter 1958–59): 74–77; Peter Blake, "The Guggenheim: Museum or Monument?" *AF* 111 (December 1959): 86–93, 180, 184; Lewis Mumford, "The Skyline: What Wright Hath Wrought," orig. pub. *New Yorker*

35 (5 December 1959), repr. in Mumford, *The Highway and the City* (New York: Harcourt, Brace and World, Harvest Book, 1963), 124–38; James Johnson Sweeney, "Chambered Nautilus on Fifth Avenue" (includes excerpts of reviews by Mumford, Blake, and Alfred Frankenstein, plus Philip Johnson, "Letter to the Museum Director"), *Museum News* 38 (January 1960): 14–25; Henry-Russell Hitchcock, "Notes of a Traveller: Wright and Kahn," *Zodiac* 6 (1960): 14–21; Bruno Zevi, "L'incessante polemica sul Museo Guggenheim," *Architettura* 5 (April 1960): 798–99; Christian Norberg-Schulz, "Wright or Wrong?" *Byggekunst*, 42, no. 3 (1960): 80–84; and Carola Giedion-Welcker, "Zum neuen Guggenheim-Museum in New York," *Werk* 47 (May 1960): 178–81.

Herbert Muschamp, *Man about Town: Frank Lloyd Wright in New York City* (Cambridge, Mass.: MIT Press, 1983), has an extensive discussion of Taliesin the Third and Wright in New York (pp. 98ff.).

41. Aside from Lomask, *Seed Money*, and Davis, *Guggenheims*, one should also consult Harvey O'Connor, *The Guggenheims: The Making of an American Dynasty* (New York: Covici, Friede, 1937); and Stephen Birmingham, *"Our Crowd": The Great Jewish Families of New York* (New York, Evanston, Ill., and London: Harper & Row, 1967).

42. In 1939–41, Wright built a fairly extensive plantation-type country house, called Auldbrass, for C. Leigh Stevens in Yemassee. Stevens intended to use it primarily for hunting and riding. I do not know whether the Stevenses and the Guggenheims moved in the same social circles.

43. Lukach, *Rebay*, esp. 42–86. Cf. Davis, *Guggenheims*, 198–222; and Lomask, *Seed Money*, 164–82.

44. Lukach, *Rebay*, 34–36, 61–81.

45. Ibid., 209.

46. Solomon R. Guggenheim to Trustees of Solomon R. Guggenheim Foundation, adjunct to will [April 1949?], in Davis, *Guggenheims*, 219. Lukach also quotes from this letter but dates it to 19 March 1949 (*Rebay*, 289–90). Wright later maintained that Solomon Guggenheim's interest in "advanced modern painting" preceded his meeting Rebay. It "began in Paris," he wrote, "by the purchase of two paintings by Bauer. Subsequently, within a year or two thereafter he met the Baroness Hilla Rebay, . . . and the Baroness went to work with him to make the collection into the kind of museum . . . Mr. Guggenheim wanted" (in FLW, "The Story of the Solomon R. Guggenheim Memorial-Museum" [1958], MS 2401.389 B, FLWF). This account is not supported by Lukach's history (cf. esp. pp. 53–58) and may have been slightly doctored to meet the needs of the moment, that is, when Rebay was persona non grata and Wright was using the memory of Guggenheim to make sure the building would be built as closely as possible to the way it was planned when Guggenheim was still alive.

47. Rebay to Rudolf Bauer, 5 August 1929, 15 August 1929, and 16 April 1930, in Lukach, *Rebay*, 56, 62.

48. Lukach states that Wallace Harrison's 1933 plan "for a cultural mall to link the Radio City office buildings . . . with The Museum of Modern Art . . . indicated a 'Guggenheim Museum'" (*Rebay*, 83). It was to have been situated between MOMA and the Metropolitan Opera House. Frederick Kiesler, the Austrian-born émigré who had been introduced to Rebay by Mondrian, was to design the building in collaboration with Bauer and Edmund Körner, who had recently completed the Folkwang Museum in Essen (1929) and the Ford factory in Cologne (ibid., 135–38).

49. The first exhibition was held in Charleston, S. C., in 1936; the second in Philadelphia (1937); the third in Charleston again (1938); and the fourth in Baltimore (1939). Each was accompanied by an illustrated catalogue prepared by Hilla Rebay: *Solomon R. Guggenheim Collection of Non-objective Paintings*, 1 March 1936–12 April 1936, Gibbes Memorial Art Gallery, Charleston (Charleston: Carolina Art Association, 1936) (hereafter *1st Cat.*); *Solomon R. Guggenheim Collection of Non-objective Paintings*, 2d cat., enl., 8 February 1937–28 February 1937, Philadelphia Art Alliance (New York: H. Rebay v. Ehrenwiesen, 1937) (hereafter *2d Cat.*); *Solomon R. Guggenheim Collection of Non-objective Paintings*, 3d cat., enl., 7 March 1938–17 April 1938, Gibbes Memorial Art Gallery, Charleston (New York: Solomon R. Guggenheim Foundation, 1938) (hereafter *3d Cat.*); and *Solomon R. Guggenheim Collection of Non-objective Paintings*, 4th cat., 6 January 1939–29 January 1939 (New York: Solomon R. Guggenheim Foundation, 1939) (hereafter *4th Cat.*). The exhibition in New York was accompanied by Rebay, *Art of Tomorrow: Solomon R. Gug-*

genheim Collection of Non-objective Paintings, 5th cat., opening 1 June 1939, 24 East 54th Street, New York (New York: Solomon R. Guggenheim Foundation, 1939) (hereafter *5th Cat.*).

50. Lukach, *Rebay*, 141 ("like precious stones," quoted from *Art Digest*, 1 July 1939).

51. Charter, 25 June 1937, in Lukach, *Rebay*, 98.

52. S. Guggenheim to Rebay, 27 March 1939, in ibid., 142–43. Wright fully understood Rebay's position. In early January 1944 he remarked to her: "I guess [the] Foundation means *you* Hilla" (3 January 1944, in ibid., 178). Or again: "This whole building has been built for you and around you, whether you know it or not" (FLW to Rebay, 9 August 1945 (in *Guggenheim Corres.*).

53. For complete references, see note 12 above.

54. "Non-objective paintings are the height of art," Rebay wrote. "These masterpieces are education's most consequential factor—they develop intuition and spiritual joy through vision" (*4th Cat.*, 1).

55. *1st Cat.*, 8.

56. Ibid., 9–10; and *3d Cat.*, 5–6.

57. *3d Cat.*, 4; *5th Cat.*, 7; and *1st Cat.*, 13. Wright, like most contemporary critics, felt uneasy with the term *non-objective*. He wished Rebay could find a more "positive" way of describing the expressive geometry of the art. "Why not speak of just Free Painting," he wrote. "Or say 'Creative Painting' and let the 'non' appear as internal evidence only when the painting is seen?" (FLW to Rebay, 20 September 1947, in *Guggenheim Corres.*, 107).

58. *2d Cat.*, 5, 12; *3d Cat.*, 11; and *1st Cat.*, 11.

59. *3d Cat.*, 11.

60. *3d Cat.*, 11, 9, 12; *1st Cat.*, 11; and *2d Cat.*, 12.

61. *4th Cat.*, 3; *5th Cat.*, 5, 10, 8; *2d Cat.*, 9, 13, 12; and *1st Cat.*, 12.

62. *1st Cat.*, 12; *3d Cat.*, 8, 4; *5th Cat.*, 5; and *2d Cat.*, 4.

63. *3d Cat.*, 7; *2d Cat.*, 10; and *4th Cat.*, 1.

64. *4th Cat.*, 1; *5th Cat.*, 10; *3d Cat.*, 14; and *1st Cat.*, 8, 9.

65. *1st Cat.*, 12–13. In 1937 she wrote: "Non-objectivity will be the religion of the future. Very soon the nations on earth will turn to it in thought and feeling and develop such intuitive powers which lead them to harmony" (*2d Cat.*, 13).

66. *5th Cat.*, 7, 9; and Rebay to FLW, 23 June 1943, in Lukach, *Rebay*, 186. Rebay believed implicitly in the concept of genius, reminding one, in this regard, of her contemporary Ayn Rand, whose "objectivist" philosophy might otherwise be seen as the polar opposite of Rebay's. "New epochs are brought about by geniuses," Rebay declared (*1st Cat.*, 8). "Genius is a special gift of God to the elite of a nation" (*5th Cat.*, 4). This "advance guard of elite" is "usually neither helped nor understood by the masses," who, in time and through education, are enabled to "benefit from culture" (*2d Cat.*, 11). The "spiritual gift" of the great collector is the "intuitive capacity" of "discovering a genius while he is alive" and then believing in that artist enough to subsidize and encourage "new creation" (*1st Cat.*, 13).

The connection between Rand and Rebay can be seen even more clearly in the latter's equation of her "Maecenas's" connoisseurship with Guggenheim's business acumen: "His career in the field of mining was distinctive for the intuition he exhibited as an explorer of the earth, opening up new channels and forging ahead often in spite of predictions of failure. With courageous decision and self-reliant foresight he always turned his ventures into unusual successes. . . . The same intuitive capacity to discover the riches of the earth urged him to explore the spiritual world. His collection was made to give diversion, rest, joy and elevation to a creative mind in organic accordance with his unusual disposition to explore and love creation" (*1st Cat.*, 13). Both the religious frame of reference of Rebay's thought and the belief in the concept of genius prepared the ground for a sympathetic relationship with Wright.

67. *3d Cat.*, 14.

68. See esp. FLW, "Organic Architecture Looks at Modern Architecture," *ARec* 111 (May 1952): 148–54; and FLW, "Frank Lloyd Wright Speaks Up," *House Beautiful* 95 (July 1953): 86–90. It is difficult to know the degree to which Wright's public denunciation of modern art should be laid to real dislike, to provincialism, to bluff, or to the "competitive spirit." He no doubt had a certain distaste for contemporary art. In a manuscript note written around 1958, Wright criticized the idea of hanging paintings against a background of pure white walls, remarking: "And what then would become of the

noble art of Rembrandt—the profanities of Picasso—the inanities of Mondrian, the sprightly abstractions of Kandinsky—the platitudes of Bauer—etc. etc." ("Hanging the Picture Hanger," MS 2401.389 A, FLWF). In the symposium "The Western Round Table on Modern Art," sponsored by the San Francisco Art Association and held at the San Francisco Museum of Art in April 1949, Wright appeared along with Marcel Duchamp, Mark Tobey, and Darius Milhaud to represent "the artist." The only member of the panel known for his negative attitudes to the subject, Wright was apparently invited in part to act "as designated gadfly" (Bonnie Clearwater, "Trying Very Hard to Think: Duchamp and the Western Round Table on Modern Art, 1949," in Clearwater, ed., *West Coast Duchamp* [Miami Beach and Santa Monica, Calif.: Grassfield Press, Shoshana Wayne Gallery, 1991], 50). He did not let the group down, referring on numerous occasions to the "degeneracy" of modern art and modern culture. When asked by the moderator George Boas how a work of art should be "defined," Wright replied: "What passes for a work of art today is hardly worth defining. The test, so far as each person is concerned, is the extent to which he can respond to it." What at first might have come off as a real put-down can be read as a much more complex, even elliptical statement. It certainly is more interesting than Duchamp's response ("It can't be adequately defined") or Tobey's ("If the thing isn't a work of art, I think it is digested very quickly; a painting which is a work of art is digested very slowly and must have been lived-with long"). See "Modern Art Argument," *Look* (8 November 1949): 81. The comments included in the *Look* article represent a small fraction of the approximately nine hours of conversation recorded at the symposium, the complete transcripts of which have not yet been published. For excerpts, see also Robert Motherwell and Ad Reinhardt, eds., *Modern Artists in America*, 1st ser. (New York: Wittenborn Schultz, 1951), 25–38.

Wright defended the Guggenheim collection and projected museum at the San Francisco symposium: "I believe this art which you call 'modern' is taking an upward trend by way of 'non-objective' art. I believe that line, form and color are a language in themselves. You can, by means of them, create amazing refreshment for the human soul and mind [note the Rebay phraseology]. The museum I have made is in the spirit of this very thing. 'Non-objective' art can't go into the static form of the old building and live. It must have a new background, a quality, an atmosphere, to go with it" ("Modern Art Argument," 82). For a similar argument, see Wright's comments to Aline Saarinen in "Tour with Wright," 23.

For a summary of the usual views about Wright's attitude toward modern art, see James Marston Fitch, "Frank Lloyd Wright's War on the Fine Arts," *Horizon* 3 (September 1960): 96–102, 127–28; and Edgar Kaufmann Jr., "Frank Lloyd Wright and the Fine Arts," *Perspecta* 8 (1963): 40–42.

69. Rebay to FLW, 12 August 1943, in Hennessey, "Wright and Guggenheim," 130. See also note 66 above.

70. Hennessey (ibid., 130, 132) quotes a letter from Rebay to Wright (18 July 1943) in which she notes that Guggenheim referred to the museum as "Hilla's Museum," after which she says that Guggenheim told her: "Well, now you have got your architect for your museum, it is up to you to make it a success." Cf. Davis, *Guggenheims*, 215; and Lukach, *Rebay*, 182–83.

71. Rebay to Laszlo Moholy-Nagy, 12 May 1943; Moholy-Nagy to Rebay, 21 May 1943; and Rebay to Moholy-Nagy, 28 May 1943, in Lukach, *Rebay*, 182–83.

72. Rebay to FLW, 1 June 1943, in *Guggenheim Corres.*, 4. Lukach quotes from this letter with some textual variations (*Rebay*, 183). Gill, as mentioned in note 1 above, dated the letter to 30 May 1943 (Gill, *Many Masks*, 527n1). According to Lukach, Rebay "had assumed the seventy-year-old architect [Wright] was dead" (*Rebay*, 183), a mistake she apparently later confessed to Olgivanna Lloyd Wright (ibid., 335n3). Wright corroborated the story of the search in the somewhat self-serving account of the commission he wrote in the late fifties, at the time that any mention of Rebay in a good light might prove deleterious to his getting his way in completing the structure: "First suggested to him [Solomon Guggenheim] as his architect by his wife Irene—a Rothchild [sic]—and subsequently by the Baroness Hilla von Rebay" ("Story of the Guggenheim Memorial-Museum," 1–2). Irene Guggenheim would no doubt have known of Wright through her Speyer connection with Pittsburgh, and she may well have known Edgar Kaufmann personally. Could she also have met Wright, or heard talk of him, in Yemassee, in connection with the work he was

doing for Leigh Stevens? (See note 42 above.) Rebay apparently met Wright's sister Maginel Wright Barney before June 1943, at which time, Rebay said to Wright: "She told me you would be interested in our work" (Rebay to FLW, 1 June 1943, in *Guggenheim Corres.*, 4). How much before the 1 June date, however, is unclear.

73. Rebay to FLW, 18 July 1943, quoted in Hennessey, "Wright and Guggenheim," 130. Lukach noted that Rebay later told Wright that "Guggenheim had had reservations and agreed to the choice only through confidence in her [Rebay's] judgement" (*Rebay*, 207). Wright later recalled the first meeting with Guggenheim, during which the latter supposedly said "that he did not want to give his beloved City of New York 'just another museum.' He said he wanted to give the city something more in the nature of the advanced painting which he loved: painting wherein line, color, and form are a language in themselves, to be used freely by the artist independently of objects" (FLW, "By the Architect, Frank Lloyd Wright," 26 April 1956, MS 2401.553 A, FLWF). Much the same is repeated in FLW, "Story of the Guggenheim Memorial-Museum."

74. Solomon R. Guggenheim Foundation to Frank Lloyd Wright Foundation, 29 June 1943, in *Guggenheim Corres.*, 8–9. The contract stipulated that "the entire establishment, exclusive of the site, is to cost not more than $750,000., and it is contemplated that the site will be acquired for about $250,000. If the site can be acquired for less, the difference may be added to the cost of construction."

75. In a letter to Guggenheim of 14 July 1943, Wright summarized the visit with Moses (in *Guggenheim Corres.*, 9–12). The site opposite the Museum of Modern Art, on 53d Street, turned out to be "out of the question." The one that was available for $350,000 was on 54th Street, next to the museum's garden. There were two sites next to one another on Park Avenue, the Blumenthal House and the Arthur Curtis James House, on the corners of 69th and 70th Streets. For an account (including letters) of his relations with Wright regarding the Guggenheim Museum, see Robert Moses, *Public Works: A Dangerous Trade* (New York: McGraw-Hill, 1970), 855–72.

76. FLW to Guggenheim, 14 July 1943, in *Guggenheim Corres.*, 10–12. Wright's initial enthusiasm for the exurban park site may lie behind later rumors that the building was originally designed for a park rather than a typical New York City block.

77. This site was mentioned by Wright to Rebay before the end of July 1943 (FLW to Rebay, 26 July 1943, in *Guggenheim Corres.*, 15–17).

78. FLW to Rebay, 13 March 1944, in *Guggenheim Corres.*, 44–45. The decision occurred sometime between 13 March and 20 March; cf. *Guggenheim Corres.*, 44–45. The Morgan site was purchased the same year by the Lutheran Church in America.

79. *Guggenheim Corres.*, 8.

80. Rebay to FLW, 1 June and 14 June 1943, in ibid., 4, 6.

81. Lukach, *Rebay*, 61ff. Lukach noted that Rebay was in touch with her friend Robert Delaunay in 1930 at the time he was actively involved in the creation of a Museum of Contemporary Art in Nesles-la-Vallée, outside Paris, for which Le Corbusier did the design. That project, which was the first of Le Corbusier's square-spiral museum designs for "unlimited growth," will be referred to on pp. 350–51.

82. Rebay to Bauer, 16 April 1930, in Lukach, *Rebay*, 62.

83. Rebay to Bauer, 22 October 1936, in ibid., 137.

84. Bauer to Rebay, 17 February 1939, in ibid., 139; and Bauer to Rebay, 1938, in Hennessey, "Wright and Guggenheim," 129–30. Hennessey specifically remarks on the "resemblance between Bauer's description and the Guggenheim Museum as built," although his summary description of Bauer's four-story, apparently square, central-court structure leaves the issue somewhat vague (p. 129). Bauer placed all administrative and support areas in a separate building, noting that "there are no offices in a church" (p. 130).

85. This was stated by Hennessey, with reference to a second letter from Bauer to Rebay, from which he did not quote ("Wright and Guggenheim," 130). Whether the ramps were merely to take the place of stairs or were actually to function as gallery spaces is unclear.

86. Rebay to FLW, 11 September 1946, in Hennessey, "Wright and Guggenheim," 132. Lukach does not mention this letter, nor is it reproduced in *Guggenheim Corres.* There is a curious echo of it in Davis's book, where he states that Harry Guggenheim wrote the following to the board of trustees of

the Foundation sometime in the early fifties: "To the plans of the museum Miss Rebay gave the first design, indicating a building with no entrance to be seen, with no staircases, but a slowly ascending ramp to show paintings without a break of thought or feeling due to staircases" (Davis, *Guggenheims*, 215). It may well be that Rebay never sent Wright the letter referred to by Hennessey, and that Harry Guggenheim later found it in the Foundation's files when he was preparing a report about Rebay's activities for the board.

87. This project is discussed more fully in Lukach, *Rebay*, 139–40.

88. Rebay to FLW, 23 June 1943, in ibid., 186.

89. FLW to S. Guggenheim, 14 July 1943 and 14 August 1946, in *Guggenheim Corres.*, 10, 85. Wright's respect for Guggenheim seems quite genuine. Wright later liked to remark how Guggenheim was "the only American millionaire of whom I knew or had heard of who died facing the Future. All others cuddled up to the Past. When death stared them in the face they became reactionary. Not so, S.R.G. His faiths were not so fragile" (FLW to Albert E. Thiele and Trustees of Solomon R. Guggenheim Foundation, 4 October 1951, in ibid., 151).

90. S. Guggenheim to Trustees of Guggenheim Foundation, April 1949, adjunct to will, in Davis, *Guggenheims*, 218. Lukach published what must be an earlier draft of the statement, with the date 19 March 1949, in *Rebay*, 289–90.

91. S. Guggenheim, quoted in Lomask, *Seed Money*, 166–67; and Guggenheim to Rebay, 19 December 1944, in Lukach, *Rebay*, 179.

92. FLW, "The Solomon R. Guggenheim Memorial: A Statement by Frank Lloyd Wright," *ARec* 123 (May 1958). 181, quoted in Saarinen, "Tour with Wright," 69; and FLW to Harry F. Guggenheim, 18 December 1958, in *Guggenheim Corres.*, 278.

93. FLW, "Story of the Guggenheim Memorial-Museum"; and Saarinen, "Tour with Wright," 69.

94. S. Guggenheim to Rebay, 19 December 1944; and S. Guggenheim to Trustees, 19 March 1949, adjunct to will, in Lukach, *Rebay*, 290.

95. FLW to S. Guggenheim, 31 December 1943, in *Guggenheim Corres.*, 25.

96. Rebay to Bauer, 18 February 1944, in Lukach, *Rebay*, 181; and *3d Cat.*, 13.

97. Robert Moses to FLW, 27 March 1947, in Moses, *Public Works*, 861; and FLW to S. Guggenheim, 14 July 1943.

98. Rebay to FLW, 12 August 1943; and Rebay to Bartels, 2 August 1945, in Lukach, *Rebay*, 187.

99. FLW to Rebay, 5 November 1943, in ibid., 188. Pfeiffer, "Temple of Spirit," 7–11, dates a number of the early schemes to the fall of 1943, noting that one sketch for the display of works of art (fig. 318) is dated September 1943.

100. FLW to H[erbert] F. Johnson, 8 October 1943, in *LClients*, 233. The Research Tower was commissioned on 4 October 1943, and the first project was pretty much done by early December of that year. Revised plans were completed by early November 1944. Owing to war shortages, construction was not begun until November 1947. The building was completed three years later. See Lipman, *Wright and Johnson Wax*, 121–73.

101. FLW to Rebay, 18 December and 30 December 1943, in *Guggenheim Corres.*, 22, 25.

102. FLW to S. Guggenheim, 31 December 1943, in ibid., 25; and S. Guggenheim to FLW, 5 January 1944, in Lukach, *Rebay*, 189.

103. FLW to Rebay, 4 January 1944, in Lukach, *Rebay*, 187. A few days before, he had told her he was thinking of a "perpendicular" building for an urban block—a "nice little" skyscraper (FLW to Rebay, 31 December 1943, in ibid.). See also FLW to Rebay, 20 January 1944, in *Guggenheim Corres.*, 40–41; and Lukach, *Rebay*, 188.

104. FLW to Rebay, 20 January 1944, in *Guggenheim Corres.*, 40–41.

105. Ibid. At this very early stage, Wright was thinking of the ramp ascending rather than descending. Wright ended a *nota bene* to the letter with the epigrammatic phrase: " 'A wheel chair from bottom to top'!" (FLW to Rebay, 20 January 1944, in Lukach, *Rebay*, 186).

106. FLW to Rebay, 20 January 1944, in *Guggenheim Corres.*, 40. In Lukach, *Rebay*, 187, the text reads "no steps anywhere."

107. FLW to Rebay, 20 January 1944, in *Guggenheim Corres.*, 40–41. Wright gave, as a sort of minimum lot size, "125 feet by 90 feet" (p. 41). The galleries along the sides were mentioned in the *nota bene* to the letter quoted

by Lukach (*Rebay*, 186), which is not included in the version in *Guggenheim Corres.*, 41.

108. FLW to Rebay, 26 January 1944, in *Guggenheim Corres.*, 42. The curious description would almost seem to indicate that Wright had decided it would be "top side down," since "down side top" amounts to the same thing.

109. Cf. FLW to Rebay, 5 July and 6 July 1944, in *Guggenheim Corres.*, 47–48. The recollections of the Jacobses help confirm that a set of fairly complete drawings existed by mid-February. When they asked Wright for plans for a new house in 1943, he first presented them with an orthogonal scheme (related to the Hein House) on 2 December. After the clients turned it down as "not for us," Wright wrote back on 30 December 1943, saying: "We are at work on a more simple scheme, as you propose. We hope it will be ready soon!" (Herbert Jacobs and Katherine Jacobs, *Building with Frank Lloyd Wright: An Illustrated Memoir* [San Francisco: Chronicle Books, Prism Edition, 1978], 78, 81). By 8 February 1944, the drawings for the "Solar Hemicycle" design were so nearly finished that Wright was able to invite the Jacobses to Taliesin to see them. When they arrived on 13 February 1944, they also saw "on the walls" of the room adjoining the drafting room "no less than eight colored sketches which we learned later were of the proposed Guggenheim museum" (ibid., 83).

Wright did not go to Arizona that winter until late March (for just three weeks). In the letter to Rebay of 20 January 1944, he said: "When I've satisfied myself with the preliminary exploration I'll bring it down to New York before going West." In the letter to her of 26 January 1944, he spoke about being in New York "in a week or so."

110. "News: New York Discovers an Architect," *AF* 80 (April 1944): 70. Along with the news of the purchase of a "now-vacant southeast corner" went the announcement that Wright was to design the new "museum to house the Guggenheim collection of non-objective paintings." An announcement also appeared in *Museum News* 22 (15 April 1944): 1.

111. FLW to Rebay, 20 March 1944, in *Guggenheim Corres.*, 45–46; and FLW to Rebay, c. 23 March 1944, in Lukach, *Rebay*, 189. The lot was approximately twenty-five feet shorter than the "imaginary" Morgan one.

112. Rebay to FLW, 5 April 1944, in Lukach, *Rebay*, 190; and FLW to Rebay, 21 March 1944, in *Guggenheim Corres.*, 46.

113. FLW to Rebay, 23 March 1944, in Lukach, *Rebay*, 191.

114. FLW to Rebay, 6 July 1944, in *Guggenheim Corres.*, 48. Cf. *Guggenheim Corres.*, 46–50; Lomask, *Seed Money*, 188; and Davis, *Guggenheims*, 217.

115. See Pfeiffer, "Temple of Spirit," 7, 11. It is doubtful that Wright ever intended to show Guggenheim more than one scheme. Bruce Pfeiffer has told me that Wright felt that Guggenheim had difficulty making decisions when too many options were left open for him.

116. S. Guggenheim to FLW, 27 July 1944, in *Guggenheim Corres.*, 49.

117. "Crystal court" is noted on the preliminary section for Scheme A (#4305.069, FLWF). It is unclear whether the four schemes were developed consecutively or concurrently. Pfeiffer, "Temple of Spirit," 7–11, argues for the consecutive, placing the hexagonal scheme C first, then the ziggurat scheme B, followed by the inverted ziggurat schemes D and A. The homogeneity of the drawings and the uniformity of the legends could support a conclusion of concurrency. I totally agree, however, with the conceptual evolution from C to B to D and A outlined in Pfeiffer's chronology and had already adopted it for my own analysis.

118. I am grateful to Bruce Pfeiffer for this information. Scheme D was taller than A by at least one story. The outside walls of the ramp did not slope but were perpendicular to the ground. The continuous skylight "rift" formed an overhanging lip rather than an inset band.

Using Wright's letter to Rebay as a guide, one could, as Pfeiffer has done ("Temple of Spirit"), date the hexagonal scheme C to 1943, the ziggurat scheme B to c. 20 January 1944, and the inverted ziggurat schemes D and A to c. 26 January 1944. Cf. *Guggenheim Corres.*, 25–26, 40–42.

119. "Taruggitz" appears to be written in the same hand and with the same lead as "Ziggurat." It was originally spelled with only one *g*. The *u* was made narrower to allow for the insertion of the second *g*. The German spelling of "ziggurat" in archaeological publications of the first half of the twentieth century is curiously inconsistent. Sometimes it is spelled with one *k* and two *r*'s, sometimes with two *k*'s and two *r*'s. Rarely does it appear with two *k*'s and one

r. The handwriting of "Zikkurat" on the drawing is slightly different from that of "Ziggurat" and is in brown colored pencil rather than plain graphite.

120. More will be said about the significance of this in the final section of this chapter.

121. Wright described the building, as it developed by late 1945, in the following way:

The interior is absolutely fireproof, dust-proof, and vermin-proof. A constant moisture content will be maintained throughout the changing seasons.

As people come into the museum through the entrance vestibule they pass across a perforated metal floor through which air-conditioning apparatus, operating like a vacuum cleaner, creates suction on feet and clothes, making it less likely for dust to come into the building. All entering air is washed, filtered, tempered, and discharged at slow speed into every portion of the building. ("Modern Gallery," *Magazine of Art*, 24)

122. FLW, "Guggenheim Memorial: Statement," 182; and FLW, "Experiment in Third-Dimension," quoted in *Solomon Guggenheim Museum* (1960), 19.

123. On the circulation, see note 105 above.

124. Rebay to FLW, 13 January 19[45], in Lukach, *Rebay*, 195. Cf. *Guggenheim Corres.*, 47–48 and 56ff.

125. Rebay to FLW, 13 January 1945, in Lukach, *Rebay*, 192.

126. FLW to Rebay, 1 March 1945, 2 August 1945, 27 August 1946, and 26 September 1947, in *Guggenheim Corres.*, 58, 66, 88, 106.

127. FLW to Rebay, 1 March 1945 and 2 August 1945, in ibid., 58–59, 65–66.

128. FLW to Rebay, 27 August 1946. Although it was not uncommon for Wright to compare architecture with music, the references to music in relation to the Guggenheim design are particularly numerous. As he was first developing the project, he wrote to Rebay that "this unique building is so symphonic in character that the least discord at any one point echoes throughout the entire structure" (12 May 1945, in *Guggenheim Corres.*, 60). In his statement for publication, Wright said: "For the first time, purely imaginative paintings, regardless of the representation of any natural object, will have appropriate, congenial environment suited to their character and purpose as harmonious works of art as music is for the ear" ("Modern Gallery," *Magazine of Art*, 24).

129. See "Museum Building to Rise as Spiral," *NYT*, 10 July 1945, p. 11; "Museum à la Wright," *Time* 46 (23 July 1946): 72; "Post-War Buildings," *Art News* 44 (August 1945): 6–7; Peyton Boswell, "Comments: Frank Lloyd Wright's Museum," *Art Digest* 44 (1 August 1945): 3; and "News," *AF* 83 (August 1945): 8.

130. See note 40 above and: "Guggenheim Art Museum Plans Spiral Building," *Museum News* 23 (1 September 1945): 1–2; "Model is Unveiled of New Museum Here," *NYT*, 21 September 1945, p. 38; "Architects on the Rampage," *Harper's Magazine* 191 (October 1945): 388, 390; "Monolithic Masterpiece," *AF* 83 (October 1945): 9; "Solomon R. Guggenheim Museum of Non-Objective Art, New York," *Museum News* 23 (1 October 1945): 1; "Frank Lloyd Wright's New Museum Plan," *Art News* 44 (15–30 October 1945): 29; and *Art Digest* 20 (15 October 1945): 14. The model was destroyed while being shipped back to Taliesin. A second, less elaborate one was built in 1947 and featured in the January 1948 *AF* and later publications.

131. The planning strategy followed that employed in the Jester House project of 1938. A thirty/sixty-degree geometry was settled on after a forty-five-degree one was tried. The increased fluidity in the manipulation of interlocking and intersecting arcs in the "Modern Gallery" plan, as compared with schemes A–D, may also reflect the work Wright was doing in early 1945 on the Haldorn House ("The Wave") and the Morris House, both of which were designed for sites overlooking the Pacific Ocean.

Unlike the "ocular" image of the first plans, this one for the "Modern Gallery" looks more like the planetary spheres, with their moons revolving around the sun—an image not too far removed from that of the celestial, spacey paintings of Bauer and Kandinsky.

132. The main, nine-story spiral reached a height of a little over one hundred feet. The ramp itself measured about three-quarters of a mile, rising at a grade of three and one-half inches for every twenty feet around the open central well that was about twenty-four feet wider at the top than at its base.

The size and proportions of the galleries remained more or less unchanged from the preliminary scheme. They ranged from ten to twelve feet in height and were about twenty feet in depth, except for the wider, final revolution just under the dome.

133. "Museum Building to Rise as Spiral," 11; and FLW, "Modern Gallery," *Magazine of Art*, 26. In June, he explained to Rebay that the building would be a "fibrous fabrication like a steel basket shot with gunnite (a high-pressure plastic concrete)" (FLW to Rebay, 2 June 1945, in *Guggenheim Corres.*, 62). The issue of "indestructibility" was important for Wright and came up often in his comments at the time. At the September press conference, he was reported to have said: "This building is built like a spring. . . . When the first atomic bomb lands on New York it will not be destroyed. It may be blown a few miles up into the air, but when it comes down it will *bounce!*" ("Modern Gallery," *AF*, 82).

134. *AF* (January 1948): 136. The struts were shown in one view of the model published in January 1946 in "Modern Gallery," *AF*, 88, but note was taken that Wright was working toward the "elimination of [these] interior columns" (p. 85). Jordy has a very good discussion of this and related structural issues in *American Buildings*, 311–29. There is also an interesting unpublished article by the engineer Jaroslav Joseph Polivka, who was brought in by Wright as a consultant in 1946 to help verify and refine the design and, especially, to see how to eliminate the struts (J. J. Polivka, "What It's Like to Work with Wright" [1957], Box 1-7, MS 48, Polivka-Wright Papers). The extensive correspondence between Polivka and Wright during the years 1946–1947 is in Box 1-1/4.

135. FLW to Rebay, 17 July 1945, in *Guggenheim Corres.*, 64.

136. FLW to Rebay, 6 February 1944, in ibid., p. 43; FLW to Rebay, 20 January 1944, in Lukach, *Rebay*, 185 (version in *Guggenheim Corres.* lacks reference to color); and Rebay to FLW, 19 June 1945, in Lukach, *Rebay*, 191.

137. *AF* (January 1948): 136.

138. The circular auditorium, which was connected to a film archive, had provision for front projection, rear projection, and ceiling projection. Aside from providing a choice between taking the elevator and walking up the ramp, Wright also intended that "motorized wheel chairs," based on ones used in Atlantic City, be available in the lobby for those who wanted "to go up . . . and come safely down again without undesired interruption." ("Modern Gallery," *AF*, 85; and "Modern Gallery," *Magazine of Art*, 24).

139. Oskar Fischinger to Rebay, 25 April 1944, in Lukach, *Rebay*, 214–15.

140. The tilt of the walls can be related to the Stevens "Auldbrass" plantation and to Taliesin West.

141. FLW to S. Guggenheim, 14 August 1946, in *Guggenheim Corres.*, 85.

142. FLW, "Modern Gallery," *Magazine of Art*, 24. Both built-in and movable seats and benches would permit the paintings to be viewed "comfortably," in the sedentary manner Rebay seems to have preferred.

143. In his description published in January 1946, he wrote that "the wall surfaces of the building itself automatically frame them [the paintings] in a setting suitable to each and every one" (FLW, "Modern Gallery," *Magazine of Art*, 24).

144. *AF* (January 1948): 136. Wright intended to dramatize the effect of overhead light by night as well as by day. Around the base of the dome was a "lighting trough" programmed so that "changeable prismatic illumination plays upward and outward from electrically controlled fountains of light, not only illuminating the great open space of the grand-ramp but going outward over terraces and gardens" (FLW, "Modern Gallery," *Magazine of Art*, 24). The trough was hidden by a ring of planters forming "hanging gardens" just under the base of the dome.

145. The sales desk on the main (second) floor was eliminated. It is difficult to know whether Wright was aware that Le Corbusier also intended the visitor to his Musée Mondial of 1928–29 to begin the visit of the interior at the top of the square-spiral ziggurat.

146. FLW, "Modern Gallery," *Magazine of Art*, 26.

147. Quoted in Saarinen, "Tour with Wright," 70; and FLW, "An Experiment in the Third-Dimension," 16 May 1958, in *Solomon Guggenheim Museum* (1960), 20. The effect of buoyancy described by Wright would have been made physically evident to the visitor by the special feeling induced by the plunger-type elevator as compared to that of the suspended-cage type.

148. FLW to S. Guggenheim, 14 August 1946, in *Guggenheim Corres.*, 85; and FLW, "Modern Gallery," *Magazine of Art*, 26.

149. FLW to J. J. Sweeney, 9 January 1959; and FLW to H. Guggenheim, 27 December 1958, in *Guggenheim Corres.*, 295, 283.

150. FLW to Rebay, 5 January 1944, in *Guggenheim Corres.*, 38; FLW to H. Guggenheim, 27 December 1958; and FLW, "Experiment in Third-Dimension," 21. Wright contended that the backward and upward tilt of the paintings would "make viewing much more natural to the viewer . . . thus making the picture itself more natural to the sweep of the building." The paintings would be "perpendicular . . . to the line of vision" rather than to an abstract horizon line (FLW to H. Guggenheim, 27 December 1958).

151. FLW, "Experiment in Third-Dimension," 19, 21; FLW to H. Guggenheim, 17 March 1958, in *Guggenheim Corres.*, 263; and FLW, "Story of Guggenheim Memorial-Museum," 6.

152. FLW, "Experiment in Third-Dimension," 19.

153. While the project remained in abeyance, both Guggenheim and Rebay continued to question Wright about matters of installation relative to the slope of the floor, the angle of the walls, and the direction of the lighting. Guggenheim warned Wright that "the paintings should be in no danger of being overwhelmed by the building" and "must not be subjugated to [it]" (S. Guggenheim to FLW, 20 August 1946, in *Guggenheim Corres.*, 86). Wright assured his client that there was absolutely nothing to fear in this regard. Quite the contrary: "Adaptability and wide range for the individual taste of the exhibitor, whoever he or she might be, is perfectly provided for and established by the architecture itself." "All this has been so carefully considered in this building," Wright maintained, "that the whole interior would add up to a reposeful place in which the paintings would be seen to better advantage than they have ever been seen" (FLW to S. Guggenheim, 14 August 1946, in ibid., 84–85). It is unclear whether Guggenheim's apprehensions about the building had any bearing on his unwillingness to move ahead faster.

154. Frank Lloyd Wright Foundation to Solomon R. Guggenheim Foundation, 1 November 1946, in *Guggenheim Corres.*, 93–94. Wright apparently began studying the option of a welded steel structure in November 1945. See Polivka, "Work with Wright"; and Polivka-Wright Papers. Note was made of this in the January 1946 *AF* article on "The Modern Gallery" (p. 85). Polivka worked on the Guggenheim project in a concerted way from May 1946 to January 1947. He was apparently on the payroll only for the first three months, however (Polivka-Wright Papers).

155. The plans published in January 1946 in "Modern Gallery," *AF*, already show an expansion in width of the site by approximately twenty-five feet. It is unclear, however, whether the additional parcel was actually purchased by them. The additional square footage and the annex are reflected in the model and plans published in *AF* (January 1948): 137–38. Wright's plans for the annex are dated 20 September 1947. The project was vetoed by Guggenheim in November (*Guggenheim Corres.*, 101–9).

156. FLW to S. Guggenheim, 19 April 1948, in *Guggenheim Corres.*, 116. Cf. ibid., 121–23. The cost of the reduced project was estimated by Wright at $1.5 million.

157. See FLW to Rebay, 23 June 1949; FLW to S. Guggenheim, 1 July 1949; and FLW to Arthur Holden, 9 November 1949, in *Guggenheim Corres.*, 123, 124–26, 128–29. For very sketchy details of Guggenheim's will, see Lomask, *Seed Money*, 188; Davis, *Guggenheims*, 218–19; and Lukach, *Rebay*, 205. In a letter drafted to Wright on 5 July 1949, though apparently never sent, Guggenheim said: "You will recall that before the recent wars both Germany and France were prosperous countries, but today their currencies are valueless. . . . My great fear is that unless we in this country are most careful, the politicians will bring the United States to the same pass. While I have provided liberally for both the museum building and its endowment it could be that, when the time comes for materialization of our plans, money in this country will have much less value than today" (quoted in Lomask, *Seed Money*, 188).

158. FLW to Albert E. Thiele, 9 February 1950, in *Guggenheim Corres.*, 132.

159. "Guggenheim Fund to Build New Museum," *NYT*, 17 April 1951, p. 31; and "Museum of Non-Objective Painting Buys Property," *Museum News* 29 (15 June 1951): 2.

160. Aline Louchheim, "Museum in Query," *NYT*, 22 April 1951, sec. 2, p. 8. (Louchheim married Eero Saarinen in 1953 and took his last name.)

Louchheim's criticism of Rebay and the Museum of Non-objective Painting should be understood in the light of postwar developments in modern art in the United States, and especially New York. By 1951, it had become clear that America was producing some of the most significant painting in the world, and this was to a certain extent highlighted by a growing sense of cultural nationalism. Rebay and her institution represented, to all intents and purposes, a European art that was considered to be, if not in decline, at least of the past.

161. S. R. Guggenheim Foundation to F. L. Wright Foundation, 5 February 1952, in *Guggenheim Corres.*, 164–65; Aline Louchheim, "Museum Will File Plans for New Building," *NYT*, 30 March 1952, sec. 1, p. 63; and "Guggenheim Museum Files Revised Building Plans," *Museum News* 30 (15 May 1952): 1.

162. See Jordy, *American Buildings*, 311ff.; and "Wright's Masterwork," *AF* (April 1952): 144.

163. Ibid.; and FLW, Statement, March 1952, in *Solomon Guggenheim Museum* (1960), 17, from which one quote in "Wright's Masterwork" was excerpted.

164. FLW, Statement, March 1952, in *Solomon Guggenheim Museum* (1960), 16, 18. The idea of a "temple in a park" was very much the result of the Foundation's having been able to acquire the entire frontage on Fifth Avenue between 88th and 89th streets.

165. *Guggenheim Corres.*, 147–78; and FLW, Statement, March 1952, in *Solomon Guggenheim Museum* (1960), 17.

166. FLW, "Experiment in Third-Dimension," 21; and FLW, "A Few Words of Explanation," p. 1, MS 2401.397 E, FLWF. Such "architectural" sculpture should be compared, in style and symbolic form, to other contemporary examples, like Harry Bertoia's piece for Saarinen's Kresge Chapel at MIT.

167. Among the other violations cited were the excessive overhang of the top story, inadequate mechanical appurtenances, and illegal use of materials such as plastic and cork. See"Wright's Masterwork," 141–44; *Guggenheim Corres.*, 168–222; "Wright Retreats on Museum Plans," *NYT*, 29 July 1953, p. 21; "Naughty Nautilus," *Time* 62 (10 August 1953): 70; John Haverstick, "To Be or Not to Be," *Saturday Review* 38 (21 May 1955): 13; "Approve Spiral-Ramp Museum," *ENR* 155 (29 December 1955): 24; "News: Skies Clearing for Wright's Ramp Museum, Synagogue," *AF* 104 (February 1956): 9; and "Guggenheim Museum to Rise: Victory for Wright in 12-Year Design Battle," *AF* 104 (June 1956): 13.

168. "Modern Gallery," *AF*, 85.

169. Jordy, *American Buildings*, 327–28, vaguely suggested that this was the first of *two* final schemes. A drawing relating to this solution is dated Revised 7 August 1953 (#4305.342, FLWF). But something resembling Jordy's description also appears in the very late section published by Wright in May 1958 in "Wright: Current Work," 184.

170. A preliminary drawing for this scheme, without the lunette cutouts but with a "glass stalactite" hanging down from the center, is dated Revised 1 October 1954 (#4305.336, FLWF). On 7 October 1954, Wright wrote to the new Director, James Johnson Sweeney: "There is now a good chance to use murals in connection with the sky-lighted top of the Museum. I have so changed it" (in *Guggenheim Corres.*, 209). The final drawings for this scheme are dated 1 August 1955–20 February 1956.

171. Jordy, *American Buildings*, 311, reported that Wright told his supervising architect, William H. Short, that the Guggenheim Museum was "My Pantheon." Wright visited Rome in August 1956, after a trip to Wales. He had previously been to Rome in 1951. The similarity between the hairpin-ribbed structure and the octagonal dome of the Vatican Museum staircase by Giuseppe Momo (1932), which has led a number of observers to compare its spiral form with the Guggenheim, may well have been a result of the 1956 trip also. Wright could have visited the Vatican Museum in 1951, but it is doubtful he knew of the staircase when he originally designed the Guggenheim. It is quite possible that the final form of the skylight owes something to Momo's example.

The drawings for the coffered solution are on sheets dated 1 August 1955–1 August 1956, but with revisions dated 7 September 1956. A note on the plan (fig. 332) says that the "inner dome" was revised on 1 October 1956. For a discussion of the structure, see "Spiral Museum Is Built Like a Work of Art," *ENR* 159 (5 December 1957): 42.

172. A final change in the project should be noted, especially as it affects so strongly the visual perception of the building's interior from the entrance. In his effort to extend the space of the central court beyond the closed circle of the spiral and at the same time to create a fitting climax for the final revolution of the descent, Wright cut a wide, double-height arch into the Grand Gallery where previously there was only a small door and a screen-wall of circular holes. Seen directly on axis from the entrance, at the elbow of the final swing of the ramp, this large, segmental opening provides a point of reference and orientation in relation to the elevator diagonally across from it. Its thickness and its shape have as much to do with Wright's late interest in classical detailing as does the coffered dome design to which it is related.

173. Louchheim, "Museum Will File Plans." For Wright's immediate reaction, see *Guggenheim Corres.*, 168–71. Sweeney officially took over as director on 15 October 1952.

174. As one of his conditions for accepting the directorship, it would appear that Sweeney demanded a free hand in redesigning the interior of the building. This might help explain a request from Thiele in early June 1952, asking Wright for an outline of provisions made for office space for staff and employees, for space for preparation of loan exhibitions, for conservation, etc. Wright responded to Thiele on 18 June 1952 (in *Guggenheim Corres.*, 172–73).

175. FLW to Sweeney, 5 October 1955, in ibid., 214; and FLW to William Wesley Peters, 16 March 1956, in *LApprentices*, 183. Wright wrote to Thiele that Sweeney was a person "whose very guts Uncle [Solomon Guggenheim] would hate, not to mention the fool he [Sweeney] would make, if he could, of Uncle Sol's ideas for which he has registered the greatest contempt" (18 September 1956, in *Guggenheim Corres.*, 232).

176. FLW to H. Guggenheim, 10 April 1954; and FLW to Sweeney, 7 October 1954, in *Guggenheim Corres.*, 201–2, 208.

177. FLW to Sweeney, 14 February 1958, in ibid., 260; and "Wright: Current Work" (Wright statement on "Guggenheim Memorial"), 182. In 1966–68 a three-and-one-half-story, five-thousand-square-foot office annex was built to take care of some of the "business" of the museum. Until then, what could not be crammed into the small Monitor was allowed to overflow onto the top two levels of the main ramp, which were consequently closed off to the public. This compromised the building's processional space, since "the upper floor," as Wright said, was "the great feature of the museum" whence "the easy downward drift" along "the grand-ramp" was to originate (FLW, Statement, 10 December 1958, and "Experiment in Third-Dimension," *Solomon Guggenheim Museum* [1960], 18–19). At the same time this office annex was planned by Wesley Peters, of Taliesin Architects Associated (1963), the Justin Thannhauser Collection of late nineteenth- and early twentieth-century art was acquired, and it soon occupied the library and work space of the curatorial staff located on the second-floor bridge, over the entrance, between the Monitor and the main gallery. The library eventually replaced the restaurant, which was later restored to the complex by filling in the entrance loggia. Almost all of this was changed by the Gwathmey-Siegel addition (1988–92), which not only provided much-needed office and storage space but also entirely reconfigured the exhibition space of the building. New galleries link up with the spiral through openings in its wall, while the upper floors of the Monitor have been transformed into exhibition space and the lower floor into commercial space.

178. It was perhaps as some form of compensation that Wright conceived the idea, in 1954, of renaming the building The Archeseum. While many have taken this as proof of Wright's egomania and of his negative attitude toward modern art, it seems that his interest was less in asserting the architectural implications of the prefix *arch-* than in distinguishing the building from its associations with the "museum as a business." Wright said he got the idea for the neologism from the Ramesseum in Thebes (FLW to Alicia Guggenheim, 27 June 1958, in *Guggenheim Corres.*, 269). He hoped it would "signify" to the visitor "not exactly 'museum,' but . . . a building in which to see the highest" (FLW, "By the Architect," April 1956, 1). When the Board of Trustees asked him to remove the term from his drawings and restore the word "Museum," Wright told Harry Guggenheim:

MU has already firmly taken the place of ARCH. AMEN.
At least the challenge will make a good many people think about the meaning of MUSEUM. I can't myself say whether we go from MU to SEUM or from SEUM to MU. (6 July 1956, in *Guggenheim Corres.*, 226)

179. FLW to H. Guggenheim, 17 March 1958, in *Guggenheim Corres.*, 263. Sweeney's reinstallation and rehanging of the collection in the museum's temporary quarters already revealed the bias he had toward "dead white walls, and . . . very intense illumination" (Hitchcock, "Notes of a Traveller," 17). It was done in consultation with José Luis Sert, who took over the chairmanship of Harvard's Architecture Department from Gropius in 1953.

180. Hilton Kramer, "Month in Review," *Arts* 34 (December 1959): 51. It should be pointed out, in all fairness to Kramer, that he was no more disturbed by Sweeney's work than by Wright's, considering the combined effect one that "brings the museum to the brink of complete nullity."

181. Pfeiffer, introductory notes, *Guggenheim Corres.*, 248; and FLW to H. Guggenheim, 22 April 1958, in ibid., 265. Wright apparently sent copies of the brochure to Bruno Zevi, Carlo Scarpa, and André Bloc. It should always be borne in mind that Rebay never intended sculpture to be exhibited in the museum. Sculpture was, in her view (as in the opinion of many other critics at the time, notably Clement Greenberg), an art that was too "material" ever to achieve pure abstraction or what she called non-objectivity. Cf. Rebay, *3d Cat.*, 9.

182. See *Guggenheim Corres.*, 271–83 (esp. FLW to H. Guggenheim, 18 December 1958, 280). Secrest, *Wright*, 559, states that "Wright refused to allow Short [his supervisor] to cooperate on Sweeney's plan or present his own in a competition."

183. Sanka Knox, "Museum Designed by FLW to Rise," *NYT*, 7 May 1956, p. 29; "Spiral Museum: Work Begins after 12-Year Delay on Wright's Design," *ENR* 156 (10 May 1956): 27; and H[ilton] K[ramer], "The New Guggenheim Museum," *Arts* 30 (June 1956): 11. According to Lomask, *Seed Money*, 192, the base contract bid of George Cohen, president and general manager of the Euclid Contracting Company, accepted in May 1956, was $2,609,742.00. The final total was $3,733,924.21, excluding the cost of the land, which amounted to $478,544.31. On the choice of contractor, see FLW to Moses, 6 October 1955, in Moses, *Public Works*, 864–65; and *Guggenheim Corres.*, 207, 212–14.

184. "Spiral Museum Built Like Work of Art," 42–45; George Cohen, "Wright's Guggenheim Museum," 10–13; "Guggenheim Memorial," *ARec* 123 (May 1958): 182–90; Herbert Mitang, "Sidewalk Views of That Museum," *NYT Magazine*, 12 October 1958, pp. 14, 73; "Guggenheim Museum Spirals toward Completion," *PA* 40 (July 1959): 75–77; and Sanka Knox, "New Art Museum Opens on Fifth Avenue," *NYT*, 21 October 1959, pp. 1, 38.

185. Printed in full in "Letters: The Guggenheim Museum," *Arts* 31 (January 1957): 4. See Sanka Knox, "21 Artists Assail Museum Interior," *NYT*, 12 December 1956, p. 46. The letter is repr. in *Guggenheim Corres.*, 242, but misdated to 1957. A very critical letter from the painter Carl Holty, claiming the building was "flippantly disregardful of the paintings it will house," was published in "Letters to the Times," *NYT*, 12 May 1956, p. 18.

186. FLW to Fellow Artists [December 1956], in *Guggenheim Corres.*, 243; and Saarinen, "Tour with Wright," 69. Cf. "Guggenheim Chides Critics of Museum," *NYT*, 22 December 1956, p. 2; and FLW, "Concerning the Solomon R. Guggenheim Museum: Frank Lloyd Wright," 14 December 1957 [should be 1956], in *Guggenheim Corres.*, 244–45. Clement Greenberg's essay "The Crisis of the Easel Picture" was published just a few years earlier in *Partisan Review* (April 1948).

187. Saarinen, "Tour with Wright," 69.

188. For a representative sampling of the critical reception, see: John Canaday, "Wright vs. Painting," *NYT*, 21 October 1959, pp. 1, 38; Canaday, "Two Torch Bearers: A New Museum and a Familiar Statue," *NYT*, 25 October 1959, sec. 2, p. 23; Robert M. Coates, "The Art Galleries: The Guggenheim and Zorach," *New Yorker* 35 (31 October 1959): 179–82; T[homas] B. H[ess], "First View of the Guggenheim," *Art News* 58 (November 1959): 46, 67–68; Russell Lynes, "After Hours: Mr. Wright's Museum," *Harper's Magazine* 219 (November 1959): 96, 98–100; "Last Monument," *Time* 74 (2 November 1959): 67; Katharine Kuh, "Architecturally Successful but the Paintings Died," *Saturday Review* 42 (7 November 1959): 36–37; Walter McQuade, "Architecture," *Nation* 189 (7 November 1959): 335–38; Kramer, "Month in Review," 48–51; Blake, "Guggenheim: Museum or Monument?" 86–93, 180, 183; Mumford, *Highway and City*, 124–38 ("What Wright Hath Wrought"); Hitchcock, "Notes of a Traveller," 15–21; Sweeney, "Chambered Nautilus," 14–25; William Barrett,

"Observations: Frank Lloyd Wright's Pictorama," *Commentary* 29 (March 1960): 249–52; Francis Steegmuller, "Battle of the Guggenheim," *Holiday* 28 (September 1960): 60–61, 105–6; Zevi, "L'incessante polemica," 798–99; and Fitch, "Wright's War on the Fine Arts," 96–102, 127–28.

189. Hitchcock, "Notes of a Traveller," 17; and Blake, "Guggenheim," 87.

190. Mumford, *Highway and City*, 130, 137, 131, 138; Johnson, "Letter to Museum Director," 25; Rodman, *Conversations with Artists*, 70; and "Last Monument," *Time*, 67.

191. Kramer, "Month in Review," 48; Hess, "First View," 68; Canaday, "Torch Bearers"; and Canaday, "Wright vs. Painting," 1.

192. Sweeney, "Chambered Nautilus," 15.

193. It is interesting that those critics, like Hitchcock and Blake, who were most positive about the building also suggested that any full appreciation of it would entail a general reassessment of modernism. It is not by chance that I. M. Pei's addition to the National Gallery, the East Wing Building of 1971–78, takes its "modern" cue from the Guggenheim (via Le Corbusier).

194. A brief bibliography of relevant publications on the subject should include: Lawrence Vail Coleman, *Museum Buildings* (Washington, D.C.: American Association of Museums, 1950); Roberto Aloi, *Musei: Architettura, tecnica* (Milan: Ulrico Hoepli, 1962); Michael Brawne, *The New Museum: Architecture and Display* (New York: Frederick A. Praeger, 1965); Ludwig Glaeser, *Architecture of Museums* (New York: Museum of Modern Art, 1968); Helen Searing, *New American Art Museums* (New York, Berkeley, Los Angeles, and London: Whitney Museum of American Art, University of California Press, 1982); and Coolidge, *Patrons and Architects*.

195. The term comes from André Malraux, who developed the idea in a somewhat different and much more complex way in *Les Voix du silence* (Paris: Galerie de La Pléiade, NRF, 1951). One could say that Mies's museum (fig. 335), with its collaged photographs of well-known works of art, reifies Malraux's conception.

196. "Museum: Mies van der Rohe, Architect, Chicago, Ill.," in "New Buildings for 194x," *AF* (May 1943): 84–85. The project was commissioned by the journal in 1941 as part of a plan to develop ideas for the postwar era.

197. *Le Corbusier et Pierre Jeanneret: Oeuvre complète de 1910–1929*, ed. W[illy] Boesiger and O[skar] Stonorov (1929; 8th ed., Zurich: Editions d'Architecture, 1965), 194. Cf. Le Corbusier, "'Mundaneum,'" 27–32. Although Le Corbusier's circulation predicted the descending pattern of the Guggenheim, the movement in the Musée Mondial was centrifugal rather than centripetal. The relation between Le Corbusier's museums and Wright's Guggenheim has often been commented upon. The general view has been that Le Corbusier's spiral Musée Mondial was the source for Wright's design, even though Wright's Gordon Strong project predated Le Corbusier's by four years. For more on this, see note 17 above.

198. *Le Corbusier et Pierre Jeanneret: Oeuvre complète de 1929–1934*, ed. W[illy] Boesiger (1935; 8th ed., Zurich: Editions d'Architecture, 1967), 74; and *Le Corbusier: Oeuvre complète, 1938–1946*, ed. Boesiger (1946; 6th ed., Zurich: Editions d'Architecture, 1971), 16.

199. Once having arrived at the "extendable" plan-type, Le Corbusier essentially concentrated on such functional considerations as lighting. Indeed, the lighting "gallery" of Philippeville and Tokyo became a determining factor of the interior space, affecting both the installation of works of art and their experience by the visitor.

200. Wright often made this point in his correspondence with Rebay and Guggenheim, as well as in his published comments about the building. Cf. FLW to Rebay, 2 August 1945 and 26 September 1947, in *Guggenheim Corres.*, 65–66, 105–7; and "Wright: Current Work," 182 (Wright statement on "Guggenheim Memorial").

201. Kandinsky often spoke of the pure shapes of geometry in vaguely animistic terms. They took on figurative and emotional characteristics for him. "The circle," he wrote, "is a link with the cosmic." It represents "the synthesis of the greatest oppositions. . . . Of the three primary forms, it points most clearly to the fourth dimension" (Kandinsky to Will Grohman, 12 October 1930, in Rudenstine, *Guggenheim Collection*, 310). "The contact of the acute angle of a triangle with a circle," he wrote in 1931, "is no less powerful in its effect than that of the finger of God with the finger of Adam in Michelangelo's

painting" (ibid.). The plan of the Guggenheim, especially in its final form, can almost be read as a spatial diagram of Kandinsky's thought. Cf. Jordy, *American Buildings*, 330ff.

202. Wright's "rising spiral" can be interpreted as literally enabling the perception of non-objective art to take place on its own terms and within its own spiritual aura as described by Rebay:

To unfold the human soul and lead it into receptivity of cosmic power and joy is the tremendous benefit derived from the non-objective masterpiece.... In loving Kandinsky's paintings, we assimilate ourselves with expressions of beauty with which he links us to a higher world. Kandinsky's message of non-objectivity is the message of Eternity. (Rebay, Introduction to Kandinsky, *Point and Line to Plane*, 12)

203. Rebay's discussions of non-objective painting were predicated on a teleological vision that construed this form of abstraction as an ultimate conclusion to a process of exfoliation that began in the late nineteenth century. The catalogues she wrote in the late 1930s repeatedly lead the reader through this evolutionary cycle, using its "progress" as a primary means of exposition.

204. The most famous ancient descriptions are in Genesis 11:1–9; and Herodotus, *The Histories* 1.181–84. For Renaissance and post-Renaissance representations, see Evelyn Klengel-Brandt, *Der Turm von Babylon: Legende und Geschichte eines Bauwerkes* (Vienna and Munich: Verlag Schroll, 1982).

In actuality, the Tower of Babel was most probably the New Babylonian Ziggurat of Marduk (Etemenanki) enlarged by Nebuchadnezzar. A source for representations and reconstructions of it in a circular form is the spiral minaret of the ninth-century Great Mosque of Samarra, north of Baghdad (fig. 379). There is every reason to believe Wright was familiar with this monument, since the placement of the Research Tower of the Johnson Wax Company headquarters in relation to the quadrangle of the existing structure appears to be directly related to the plan of that building. Brick was the material common to both, which could also explain Wright's original intention to make the Guggenheim "Ziggurat" red. Wright's continuing interest in the Samarra minaret is evidenced by the design for the Monument to Harun ar-Rashid in the Plan for Greater Baghdad of the 1950s (fig. 375; see Chapter XI).

205. For the history of the ziggurat, see Heinrich J. Lenzen, *Die Entwicklung der Zikurrat von ihren Anfängen bis zur Zeit der III. Dynastie von Ur*, vol. 4, *Ausgrabungen der Deutschen Forschungsgemeinschaft in Uruk-Warka* (Leipzig: Otto Harrassowitz, 1941), 1–62; André Parrot, *Ziggurats et tour de Babel* (Paris: Albin Michel, 1949); and Henri Frankfort, *Art and Architecture of the Ancient Orient*, Pelican History of Art (1954; 1st pb. ed., Harmondsworth: Penguin Books, 1970).

206. Victor Hugo, *Notre-Dame of Paris* (1832; 8th ed., trans. John Sturrock, Harmondsworth: Penguin, 1978), 201–2.

207. In "Optimistic Ziggurat," 74. Wright apparently said this in the September 1945 press conference on the occasion of the public presentation of the model of the museum.

208. The loop-like quality of the circulation pattern can be compared to the movement through Unity Temple, where again it is an experience of social togetherness that awaits the visitor at the end (see pp. 41–44 above). Wright wrote in *Genius and the Mobocracy* (New York: Duell, Sloan and Pearce, 1949): "Life itself is a splendid unfolding—a coherent plasticity: so there can be no real *beginning* in this or any mortal conjunction on this earth. Nor . . . end to be foreseen" (p. 28).

209. "Optimistic Ziggurat," 74. For Boullée's description of the "pessimistic" character of the pyramid, see his "Architecture: Essai sur l'art," in Helen Rosenau, *Boullée & Visionary Architecture, including Boullée's "Architecture, Essay on Art"* (London and New York: Academy Editions, Harmony Books, 1976), 105–6.

210. Wright always maintained that the museum had political implications as well: "Every building signifies a state of affairs, social, therefore political. This building signifies the sovereignty of the individual—Democratic, instead of the solidarity of the mass led by one—Fascist. Therefore this building is neither Communist nor Socialist but characteristic of the new aristocracy born of Freedom to maintain it. The Reactionary, though perhaps fascinated by it, will not really like it. It will scare him." This was written in March 1952

and published in "The Solomon R. Guggenheim Museum," *Museums Journal* 53 (December 1953): 230; repr. in *Solomon Guggenheim Museum* (1960), 18.

211. "Modern Gallery," *AF*, 82. One of the inherent paradoxes of utopianism is reflected in this statement: to achieve an environment of pure harmony and cooperation often necessitates an underlying order and authoritarian control that is not acknowledged, or deemed of concern, because of its purported beneficial disposition. Cf. Lewis Mumford, *The Story of Utopias* (1922; rpt. New York: Viking Press, Viking Compass Edition, 1962).

212. Lewis Mumford, *From the Ground Up*, 60 ("United Nations Assembly").

213. It is important to emphasize that Wright consistently referred to the building not as a space or a place but as an "atmosphere" or "environment," carrying with it the sense of something palpable and laden.

214. Lehmann, "Dome of Heaven"; Smith, *Dome*; and Hautecoeur, *Mystique et architecture*.

215. FLW, Statement, March 1952, in *Solomon Guggenheim Museum* (1960), 16; *AF* (January 1948): 137; and Saarinen, "Tour with Wright," 70. In an interview with Aline Saarinen (formerly Louchheim) four years before, Wright said: "The eye encounters no abrupt change [in the museum], but is gently led and treated as if at the edge of the shore watching an unbreaking wave, or is that too fancy a phrase?" (Louchheim, "Frank Lloyd Wright Talks of His Art," *NYT Magazine*, 4 October 1953, p. 47). Earlier that year, he said: "[The building] is a shell, containing great fluctuations of space . . . undulating like a wave" (in Louchheim, "Wright Analyzes Architect's Need," *NYT*, 26 May 1953, p. 23). And in the interview with Selden Rodman in 1956, he said: "Just look at this plan. . . . It is like the relaxation you get from the unbroken but constantly moving waves of the sea!" (*Conversations with Artists*, 73).

216. An earlier example of the subsumption of the act of looking into the imagery of a building is Ledoux's celebrated engraving of the Theater of Besançon, in which the auditorium is depicted through an open eye.

217. FLW to H. Guggenheim, 27 December 1958; and FLW to Sweeney, 9 January 1959, in *Guggenheim Corres.*, 281, 296.

218. Cf. FLW, "Experiment in Third-Dimension," 19–20.

219. Ibid., 21–22. It would be too obvious to point out how Wright's built-in security measure has become almost a standard add-on by way of stanchions and ropes in contemporary museum installations of major traveling exhibitions.

220. Ibid., 22. In large part, of course, the success of this system would depend on the degree to which the works of art exhibited were made *without* the traditional conception of the flat wall and circumscriptive frame in mind. Wright's approach was prospective rather than retrospective. He believed that the art Guggenheim and Rebay collected justified this position.

221. FLW to Rebay, 27 August 1946; and FLW to Sweeney, 5 October 1955, in *Guggenheim Corres.*, 88, 215 (italics added).

222. Wright contrasted the "naturalness" of the Guggenheim's "environment" to the hothouse "artificiality" of the traditional museum (FLW to Trustees of S. R. Guggenheim Memorial Museum, 28 November 1958, in *Guggenheim Corres.*, 276). Leo Steinberg's discussion of the "flatbed picture plane," which deals with similar issues, emerged out of the "non-anthropomorphic" art that developed in the mid-1950s, especially in the work of Robert Rauschenberg. See Leo Steinberg, *Other Criteria: Confrontations with Twentieth-Century Art* (New York: Oxford University Press, 1972), 82–91 ("Reflections on the State of Criticism").

223. The first site-specific Judd piece of record is the rectangular one for the Pulitzer estate in St. Louis (1970–71). It is unclear when Judd began thinking about the Guggenheim version. The building itself, like all of Wright's architecture, was of great interest to him. Frank Stella's interest in Kandinsky was made particularly vivid in his Norton Lectures at Harvard (Frank Stella, *Working Space*, Charles Eliot Norton Lectures, 1983–84 [Cambridge, Mass., and London: Harvard University Press, 1986], esp. 103–25).

224. Thomas More, *De Optimo Reipublicae Statu, deque Nova Insula Utopia* (Louvain, 1516); published in English as *Utopia*. The most relevant study of utopias for Wright would have been Mumford's *Story of Utopias* (1922). Wright always claimed that his name for the United States—Usonia—was derived from Samuel Butler's utopian novel *Erewhon* (1872) (but see note 227 below). Wright was, by all evidence, well read in utopian literature. The

title of the Afterword to *When Democracy Builds* (1945), for example, was taken from Edward Bellamy's novel *Looking Backward* (1888).

225. Hugo, *Notre-Dame*, 201.

226. FLW, *A Testament* (New York: Horizon Press, 1957), 17.

227. Although Wright maintained that the word Usonia came from Butler's utopian *Erewhon*, it does not occur in the book. This has posed a problem for scholars. George Collins suggested that "the expression very probably lodged in Wright's mind during his first European trip in 1910 at which time there was considerable talk about addressing the States as U-S-O-N-A in order to avoid confusion with the new Union of South Africa" (Collins, "Broadacre City: Wright's Utopia Reconsidered," in *Four Great Makers of Modern Architecture: Gropius, Le Corbusier, Mies van der Rohe, Wright* [New York: Trustees of Columbia University, 1963], 70–71). But that still does not explain why Wright said the term came from Butler. I would argue that the word Usonia functioned for Wright as a cryptogram for utopia, and this is the reason for his insistence on the reference to *Erewhon*. Wright made a point of remarking in the late 1950s that the title of Butler's novel was " 'nowhere' spelled backwards" (*Testament*, 160), as if to provide a clue to the relation with the ideal (read: utopian) Usonian community of Broadacre City—"the city nowhere unless everywhere" (FLW, *The Living City* [1958; rpt. New York, Toronto, and London: New American Library, Plume Book, 1970], 122). For the utopian implications of the original Gordon Strong project and its perpetuation in Broadacre City, see Reinberger, "Sugarloaf Mountain Project," 49ff.

228. The movement through the Guggenheim Museum again reminds us forcefully of T. S. Eliot's *Four Quartets* (1943), where the theme of suspension in space and time becomes the precondition for the artistic experience:

At the still point of the turning world. Neither flesh nor fleshless;
Neither from nor towards; at the still point, there the dance is. . . .
("Burnt Norton")

What we call the beginning is often the end
And to make an end is to make a beginning.
The end is where we start from.

. . . . .

We shall not cease from exploration
And the end of all our exploring
Will be to arrive where we started
And know the place for the first time.
("Little Gidding")

The Complete Poems and Plays (New York: Harcourt, Brace, 1952), 119 and 144–45.

229. FLW, *Living City*, 122, 240.

Chapter XI
Signs of Identity

1. It was published soon after it was finished in "The New Curiosity Shop," *AJ* 110 (10 November 1949): 512, 516; "China and Gift Shop by Frank Lloyd Wright for V. C. Morris, Maiden Lane, San Francisco, California," *AF* 92 (February 1950): 79–85; Edgar Kaufmann Jr., "Wright Setting for Decorative Art," *Art News* 48 (February 1950): 42–44; and Alfred Roth, "Geschenkartikel-Laden in San Francisco," *Werk* 38 (December 1951): 379–82. It was also included as one of the four buildings by Wright in the Museum of Modern Art's 1952 exhibition *Built in USA: Post-War Architecture*, ed. Henry-Russell Hitchcock and Arthur Drexler (New York: Museum of Modern Art, Simon and Schuster, 1952), 118–19.

2. Wright's critical reception in this period will be analyzed more fully in the Conclusion.

3. See Bruce Brooks Pfeiffer, ed., *Frank Lloyd Wright: The Crowning Decade, 1949–59* (Fresno: Press at California State University, 1989); and Twombly, *Wright*, 303ff. For a selection of Wright's private and public utterances on his art, see Pfeiffer, ed., *Frank Lloyd Wright: His Living Voice* (Fresno: Press at California State University, 1987); Patrick J. Meehan, *The*

Master Architect: Conversations with Frank Lloyd Wright (New York: Wiley-Interscience Publication, John Wiley, 1984); and Meehan, *Truth against the World: Frank Lloyd Wright Speaks for an Organic Architecture* (New York: Wiley-Interscience Publication, John Wiley, 1987). Among the awards Wright received during this period were the Gold Medal of the American Institute of Architects (1949); Gold Medal of the American Academy of Arts and Letters (1953); Gold Medal of the Swedish Academic Society of Architects (1953); and honorary degrees from the University of Venice (1951), Yale University (1954), University of Wisconsin (1955), and University of Wales (1956).

Among the most important publications of Wright's work during the period are *Metron* 41–42 (May–August 1951): 17–87 (double issue devoted to Wright and serving as the catalogue for an exhibition at the Strozzi Palace, Florence); "Frank Lloyd Wright: A Four-Color Portfolio of the Recent Work of the Dean of Contemporary Architects, with His Own Commentary on Each Building," *AF* 94 (January 1951): 73–108; Werner M. Moser, *Frank Lloyd Wright: Sechzig Jahre lebendige Architektur; Sixty Years of Living Architecture* (Winterthur and Munich: Verlag Buchdruckerei Winterthur AG, Hermann Rinn, 1952); Edgar Kaufmann Jr., ed., *Taliesin Drawings: Recent Architecture of Frank Lloyd Wright Selected from His Drawings*, Problems of Contemporary Art, 6 (New York: Wittenborn, Schultz, 1952); "Frank Lloyd Wright," *Architecture Française* 13, nos. 123–24 (1952): 3–72 (special issue devoted to Wright); FLW, *The Natural House* (New York: Horizon Press, 1954); "The Dramatic Story of Frank Lloyd Wright," *House Beautiful* 48 (November 1955): 233–90 and passim (special issue devoted to Wright); "Frank Lloyd Wright: A Selection of Current Work," *ARec* 123 (May 1958): 167–90; FLW, *Drawings for a Living Architecture* (New York: Bear Run Foundation and Edgar J. Kaufmann Charitable Foundation, Horizon Press, 1959); and "Your Heritage from Frank Lloyd Wright," *House Beautiful* 101 (October 1959): 207–58 and passim (special issue devoted to Wright).

4. Norman Mailer, "The Big Bite," *Esquire* 60 (August 1963): 24. This was the second of two articles devoted to the subject of modern architecture's "totalitarian" facelessness. The first was "The Big Bite," *Esquire* 59 (May 1963): 37, 40. They were condensed and reprinted in "Mailer vs. Scully," *AF* 120 (April 1964): 96–97. The terms *anonymity* and *packaging* were part of the lingua franca of the period.

5. A[rthur] D[rexler] and W[ilder] G[reen], *Architecture and Imagery: Four New Buildings* (*Museum of Modern Art Bulletin* 26, no. 2 [1959]): 1; Reyner Banham, *The New Brutalism: Ethic or Aesthetic?*, Documents of Modern Architecture (New York: Reinhold, 1966); Jürgen Joedicke, *Architecture since 1945: Sources and Directions*, trans. J. C. Palmes (New York: Praeger, 1969); and Vincent Scully, *American Architecture and Urbanism* (New York and Washington, D.C.: Praeger, 1969), esp. 190–212.

6. Up to now, the particularly vituperative nature of Wright's criticism of postwar, late International Style modernism has usually been attributed to old-age crankiness. I would suggest that his characterization of Mies's Seagram Building as the "whiskey building" and the firm of Skidmore, Owings and Merrill as the "three blind Mies" reflects a deeper concern over the prospects for modern architecture. There is no doubt that his own polemical stance for "organic architecture" and against "modern architecture" grew more and more pronounced during this period. Cf. FLW, "Organic Architecture Looks at Modern Architecture," *ARec* 111 (May 1952): 148–54.

7. "Frank Lloyd Wright," *AF* (January 1948): 68 (italics added).

8. FLW, Talk to Society of Engineers of Baghdad, transcript of tape recording [22 May 1957], p. 1, MS 2401.377-78 C; and Talk "Delivered to the Society of Architects and Engineers of Baghdad," June [should be 22 May] 1957, p. 2, MS 2401.377-78 B, FLWF. In the edited transcript, he clarified what he meant by saying " 'Modern' is becoming a bad word in Architecture" (p. 1).

9. FLW, "This Venice Affair," 24 March 1954, p. 2, MS 2401.561 A, FLWF; FLW, "A Journey to Baghdad," 16 June 1957, in Pfeiffer, *Living Voice*, 52; and FLW, Talk to Engineers, p. 1. Wright's new-found interest in preservation might be related to the debate over the future of the Robie House in 1956–58, in which Wright took a positive stand for preservation. It should be recalled that the Larkin Building was torn down only a few years before (1950).

10. See Chapter V. Wright stressed this consideration in his account of the hotel in *A I*, 195–225. In the 1950s, he added: "I have sometimes been asked why I did not make the opus more 'modern.' The answer is that there was a

tradition there worthy of respect and I felt it my duty as well as my privilege to make the building belong to them so far as I might" (*Sixty Years of Living Architecture: The Work of Frank Lloyd Wright* [New York: Solomon R. Guggenheim Museum, 1953], [7]).

11. Giovanni Michelucci, "Lettere: La casa sul Canal Grande," *Metron* 51 (May–June 1954): 2.

12. The relevant correspondence between Lillian Morris, who took the initiative on the house, and Wright begins in November 1944 and continues through 1951, when the first scheme was effectively abandoned for economic reasons. A second, less elaborate design was proposed by Wright in 1955. This one was abandoned due to the death of Vere Morris two years later. The topographical plan for the original project is dated 11 February 1945. Working drawings were done by April 1946, and the perspective in fig. 349 is dated November 1946. The Morrises, like many of Wright's clients, were Christian Scientists. Vere Chase Morris was a native of Cleveland and taught at the Parsons School of Design in New York before moving with his wife, the former Lillian Isaacs, to California. She was from Oakland, Calif.

13. In a letter to Wright of 27 March 1956, Lillian Morris recalled "the symphony that I intended to bring in from without (mechanically)—the medley of sea winds and sea waves, and foghorns and sirens, all this music amplified and blended" (FLWF).

14. The original two-story brick building, probably built sometime around 1910, was designed by J. E. Krafft & Sons, a local architectural and engineering firm. The lower floor was divided down the middle into two stores fronted by large plate glass windows. A side entrance led to a general loft space above for storage, lit by skylights as well as by two bands of relatively tall, continuous windows. The building was first remodeled in the 1930s by Albert R. Williams, of the local firm of Williams and Grimes. The ground floor was turned into a single space, and a central door, with plate glass "show windows" to either side, replaced the double storefront. The upper part of the facade was left fundamentally unchanged. The brick was plastered, and a terracotta facing added as a base beneath the "show windows." When the Morrises bought the building, it was a French restaurant. White prints of the original building and the 1930s remodeling are in FLWF (n.n.). For early publications of Wright's design, see note 1 above.

15. A local precedent, which may have justified to Wright the adaptation of the Guggenheim *parti*, is the well-known City of Paris Store by Clinton Day, built in 1900. Based on late nineteenth-century Parisian models, it has a central skylit court with shopping floors arranged in galleries. It is just a block away from the Morris Shop. One should also remember that circular planning devices and furniture arrangements were typically adopted in store design of the period for reasons of ease of circulation and attractiveness to the customer. Numerous examples can be seen in the books cited in note 16 below.

16. Cf. Morris Ketchum Jr., *Shops & Stores* (New York: Reinhold, Progressive Architecture Library, 1948), 147. See also Emrich Nicholson, *Contemporary Shops in the United States*, with a foreword by George Nelson (New York: Architectural Book Publishing, 1945); and *Store Modernization, 1948: Clinics and Forums*, 2d International Store Modernization Show (New York, July 1948). Although Wright's facade design differed radically from those published in terms of the issue of transparency versus opacity, it could be related to them in its billboard-like character.

17. See my "Questioning the View: Seaside's Critique of the Gaze of Modern Architecture," in *Seaside: Making a Town in America*, ed. David Mohney and Keller Easterling (New York: Princeton Architectural Press, 1991), 245–52; and Ketchum, *Shops*, 148–50.

18. Wright added: "Just like a mousetrap" (in *FLWM*, vol. 7, 228).

19. In the article devoted to the building in *AF* (February 1950), Elizabeth Mock wrote: "And if Frank Lloyd Wright is as prophetic here as he has been in the past, we may confidently expect a revival of that half-forgotten, half-remembered element of architecture—the Wall" (p. 78). In his critique of Wright originally written in 1921 and republished in Wendingen 1925 (p. 83), Berlage noted that "Wright refuses to recognize almost every curve," although "he occasionally makes use of the manifold recessed, half-circle arch for his entrance and for his ceilings (and this I regard as a weakness)".

20. The entrance arch can, however, be read as an external sign of the geometry of the interior space. A small sketch of the facade by Wright showing this relationship (#4824.001, FLWF) bears a curious, though undoubtedly unintended, resemblance to August Endell's Atelier Elvira (Munich, 1898).

21. An article in a local San Francisco newspaper noted: "Frank Lloyd Wright, 'Father of Modern Architecture,' is a man who has long disdained to use the classic arch in his structures, which is why local architects are double-taking the fancy job he's doing for merchant V. C. Morris in Maiden Lane. There's an arch there, all right—possibly the first Wright-designed arch in 40 years (check, Gardner Dailey?) but it's satisfactorily unusual: half brick and half glass" (Box 2-18, Wright-Polivka Papers).

My interpretation of the Morris Shop owes much to Robert Venturi, who described its urban character in the following way: "Wright's Morris Store is another of the Master's exceptions that reinforce a rule. Its vivid contradictions between the inside and the outside—between the particular private and the general public functions—make it a traditional urban building rare in modern architecture" (Venturi, *Complexity and Contradiction in Architecture*, Museum of Modern Art Papers on Architecture, no. 1 [New York and Chicago: Museum of Modern Art, Graham Foundation for Advanced Studies in the Fine Arts, 1966], 86). Two precedents for this in Wright's work are the Sarabhai Calico Mills Store, planned for Ahmedabad, India (1945–46), and the Rogers Lacy Hotel for Dallas, Tex. (1946–47). Although both make use of extensive areas of plate glass on the ground floor, they fill out their sites and conform to the existing street line.

22. Cf. opinions of Colin Rowe and Vincent Scully referred to in my "Robert Venturi and 'The Return of Historicism,'" in *The Architecture of Robert Venturi*, ed. Christopher Mead (Albuquerque: University of New Mexico Press, 1989), esp. 50–52.

23. Arches appear in one of the preliminary designs for Wright's house in Fiesole (1910) as well as in a few projects done between 1911 and 1914, including: Park Gate and Town Hall for Sherman Booth, Glencoe, Ill. (1911); first scheme for Christian Catholic Church, Zion, Ill. (1911?); Little House ("Northome"), Wayzata, Minn. (1912–14); and preliminary designs for Midway Gardens (1913–14). There are also arches in the Doheny Ranch project as part of the viaduct road system.

24. Cf. my "Venturi and 'Historicism,'" 51–55. One can trace the arched roof-vault system Le Corbusier favored in the forties and fifties back to his Maison Monol project of 1919 and the so-called Weekend House at la Celle-St. Cloud of 1935.

25. See *FLWPS*, vol. 11, 172. There can be little doubt that Wright was aligning himself, whether consciously or not, with the Richardson-Sullivan axis that had been proposed by Mumford, Hitchcock, and others since the early thirties as the source for a modern American architecture of which Wright himself was assumed to be the heir (see Chapter I, note 36). The relation to Richardson's Glessner House was noted and illustrated in one of the first mentions of the Morris Shop in the professional press: Astragal [pseud.], "Notes & Topics," *AJ* 110 (8 December 1949): 639. Hitchcock described the entrance as "a Sullivanian—or Richardsonian—arch" in *Architecture: Nineteenth and Twentieth Centuries*, Pelican History of Art (Harmondsworth: Penguin, 1958), 330. Scully specifically related it to the "engulfing arches of Richardson" in Scully, *Wright*, 30.

26. The "rediscovery" of Sullivan's banks (and late work in general) by Scully, Venturi, and others during these years should be seen as an important part of this development. Buildings by Kahn and Venturi that come immediately to mind are the project by the former for the American Embassy at Luanda, Angola (1959); and the project by the latter for the Town Hall of North Canton, Ohio (1965), and Guild House in Philadelphia (built 1960–63).

27. One thinks here of the proto-Brutalist Y.W.C.A. for Racine, Wis. (1949), as well as the Bramlett Motor Hotel project for Memphis, Tenn. (1956), not to speak of the Mile High Illinois for Chicago's lakefront (1956).

28. One of the best accounts of the interest in Wright in postwar Italy is in Fabrizio Brunetti, *L'Architettura in Italia negli anni della ricostruzione*, Saggi e Documenti di Storia dell'Architettura, 9 (Florence: Alinea, 1986), 125–42. This reference, as well as other interesting aspects of the relationship between Wright and Italy during the period, was pointed out to me by Benedict Zucchi in a seminar he took with me at Harvard in the fall of 1988–89.

29. Different accounts of the origin of the exhibition have been published. Bruce Brooks Pfeiffer, in *LApprentices*, 174–75, notes that the initial

force behind the exhibition was actually an American; and indeed, like so many postwar exhibitions of American art in Europe and around the world, the idea had a political dimension: to counter the growth of Communism, especially in intellectual circles, by demonstrating the vitality and creativity of American culture. According to this account, Arthur C. Kaufmann, a cousin of Edgar and the owner of Gimbel's Department Store in Philadelphia, offered in 1949 to back such an exhibition following discussions with Claire Booth Luce, America's Ambassador to Italy. They apparently talked only in general terms; it was the Italians who later requested that the artist shown be Wright. On the other hand, Secrest, *Wright*, 529, reports that it was the Italians who first had the idea and that Gimbel's (and presumably A. Kaufmann) became involved only when money was needed to help pay for transportation. In her account, it was Oskar Stonorov, the organizer of the exhibition, who sought the support of Gimbel's. A transcript of a taped talk by FLW, "Exploitation of Italian Exhibition" (7 January 1951, Reel #19, FLWF), supports the Secrest version, although it may well be that the Kaufmann-Luce discussions took place earlier, even without Wright's knowledge.

On the "Sixty Years of Living Architecture" exhibition, see *LArchitects*, 174–203; "Editoriali: La grande mostra di Wright a Firenze," *Metron* 40 (1951): 4; Edgar Kaufmann Jr., "Frank Lloyd Wright at the Strozzi," *Magazine of Art* 44 (May 1951): 190–92; Giulio Carlo Argan, "De tentoonstelling van F. L. Wright te Florenze," *Forum* (Amsterdam) 11 (November 1951): 298–304; Carlo Ludovico Ragghianti, "Letture di Wright," *Edilizia Moderna* 47 (December 1951): 17–28; "Frank Lloyd Wright in Italia," *Urbanistica* 21, no. 7 (1951): 57; and Giancarlo de Carlo, "Wright e l'Europa," *Sele Arte* 1 (September–October 1952): 17–24. The double issue of *Metron* 41–42 (May–August 1951) served as the catalogue for the Italian exhibition. Moser's *Wright: Sechzig Jahre lebendige Architektur* was published for the Zurich stop of the exhibition in early 1952.

For the Philadelphia preview, see "Business and Culture," *Newsweek* 37 (5 February 1951): 76; Talbot Hamlin, "Frank Lloyd Wright in Philadelphia," *Nation* 172 (10 February 1951): 140–41; and "Architect F. L. Wright," *Art Digest* 35 (15 February 1951): 16. Although Louis Kahn was a Resident of the American Academy in Rome during the time the exhibition was in Philadelphia (January–February 1951) and had returned to Philadelphia by the time the show reached Florence (May 1951), one can assume he heard about the show from his former partner Stonorov during the preceding two years.

30. The medal given to him at the Strozzi Palace was the Medici Medal. Although Pfeiffer mentions only the Star of Solidarity in *Crowning Decade* (p. 13), it was apparently the *honoris causa* degree ceremony at the University of Venice that brought him to the city in the first place. See Elio Zorzi, "Ingiustificato allarme a Venezia per la nuova casa sul Canal Grande progettata dal famoso architetto Wright," *Metron* 8, no. 48 (1953): 64; and *AF* 95 (August 1951): 68. According to Pfeiffer, in *LArchitects*, 177, the United States government stepped in after the Florence exhibition to sponsor the rest of the international tour. Wright apparently traveled to most of the openings.

31. Savina Masieri to FLW, 19 December 1952, FLWF. For a portrait of Angelo Masieri and a review of his short career, see "L'architetto Angelo Masieri," *Metron* 9, nos. 49–50 (January–April 1954): 31–65 (contains articles by Giuseppe Samonà, Ernesto Rogers, and Alfonso Gatto). For a conspectus of the work Masieri did with Scarpa, see Francesco Dal Co and Giuseppe Mazzariol, *Carlo Scarpa: The Complete Works*, trans. Richard Sadlier (New York: Electa/Rizzoli, 1985), esp. 106–12. Paolo Masieri, Angelo's father, was an engineer and building contractor.

32. Zorzi, "Casa sul Canal Grande," 64. Cf. Alfonso Gatto, "Destino di Angelo Masieri," *Metron* 9, nos. 49–50 (January–April 1954): 35. It is curious that the literature on Wright generally fails to note that the commission for the house may go back to the June 1951 visit to Venice and, more importantly, that Wright supposedly saw the site at that time. In her letter of mid-December 1952, Savina Masieri reminded Wright that "you may perhaps remember that last year in Italy—where we had the pleasure and honour of meeting you personally, first in Venice and again in Florence—my husband had already mentioned his wish to you [to design a house for us], through Mr. Stonorov" (19 December 1952). No mention, however, is made of a site visit. In a memorandum of a message delivered by telephone to Lester Markel, of the *NYT*, on 15 March 1954, Wright stated: "Young Angelo Masieri commissioned me to building [*sic*] the building when I was in Venice to receive the ad honorem at the Ducal Palace June 1951" (FLWF).

33. Gino Valle, who was studying at Harvard's Graduate School of Design at the time, accompanied the Masieris for part of their sightseeing tour. Wright was not at Taliesin when the Masieris arrived.

34. Zorzi, "Casa sul Canal Grande," 8.

35. Masieri to FLW, 19 December 1952; and FLW to Masieri, 30 December 1952, FLWF. Wright's aversion to designing "monuments" or "memorials" as such was well known, which perhaps explains the discreet way in which Masieri phrased the subject.

36. The plans supplied to Wright are dated 20 December 1952 (#5306.006, #5306.007, and n.n., FLWF). Wright sent a telegram to Savina Masieri on 26 January 1953, saying that the drawings were "ready" and asking her how they should be mailed to avoid "certain complications" (FLWF). They were sent off on 5 February 1953. Wright made a number of changes as he worked on the project. They are reflected in the perspectives done after the initial submission. A key change made before 20 January 1953, however, was the removal of the rooftop belvedere from the left to the right side of the structure.

37. Masieri to FLW, 2 March 1953, FLWF.

38. On the Masieri Memorial, see "Frank Lloyd Wright: La casa sul Canal Grande," *Metron* 9, nos. 49–50 (January–April 1954): 2–31 (includes statements by Wright, drawings and plans, and article by Sergio Bettini); Luisa Querci della Rovere, "Il Masieri Memorial di Frank Lloyd Wright," in Lionello Puppi and Giandomenico Romanelli, eds., *Le Venezie possibili: Da Palladio a Le Corbusier* (Milan: Electa, 1985), 272–75; and Paolo Ceccarelli, *Fondazione Angelo Masieri*, undated brochure published by the Foundation. I am indebted to Giancarlo Pirrone for bringing the Pupi-Romanelli publication to my attention, as well as for other information and thoughts on the subject. References to the controversy over the building of the memorial are in note 50 below.

39. That Wright may have been troubled by the disparateness of the facade could be the reason for some of the changes he made (cf. figs. 362, 365). The most relevant in this regard are the increased projection of the mid-level, asymmetrically placed balcony on the extreme right; and the projection of a prow-shaped terrace at ground level beneath it. Both these elements mark the diagonal line of the mezzanine balconies along the rear wall of the interior space. The ground-level prow also picks up the line of the Palazzo Balbi facade and mediates between it and the direction the Rio Nuovo takes at that point.

40. As Wright moved toward a more dynamic facade composition between late January 1953 and early 1954, which involved the projection of the asymmetrical balcony on the right and the ground-level terrace-prow noted above, he tightened and "classicized" the surface treatment by bringing out the intermediate lintels to the same depth as the vertical fins. This decreased the "Gothic" verticality and skeletal construction while emphasizing the mass and thickness of the facade.

41. FLW, "This Venice Affair," 2; and FLW to Masieri, 19 February 1953, FLWF.

42. Sergio Bettini, "Venice and Wright," *Metron* 9, nos. 49–50 (January–April 1954): 30.

43. Ibid.; and Michelucci, "Casa sul Canal Grande," 2.

44. In submitting the project, Wright told Masieri that, "loving Venice as I do I wanted, by way of modern techniques, to make the old Venice Tradition live anew" (19 February 1953). In recounting his Venice visit to the Taliesin Fellowship, he said: "Venice was a wonderful experience, and of course it is the greatest sight, picturesquely, in all Italy. . . . I think that's the place we would like to go back to for a vacation some day. Venice is really beautiful. . . . You see the old Ducal Palace, which is one of the loveliest buildings on earth, right out of the heart of old Italy, and then next to it Sansovino's marvelously contrived and exquisitely academic facade" (in Pfeiffer, *Living Voice*, 150).

45. For Wright's perception of the mix of Gothic and classical in Venice, see his comments on the Doge's Palace and Sansovino's Library in note 44 above. One could compare Wright's approach with similar work by Franco Albini and Samonà, among others, in Italy. Perhaps the most famous building of the type is the Torre Velasca in Milan (1950–58) by Ludovico Belgiojoso, Enrico Peressutti, and Ernesto Rogers. The quasi-traditional look of Wright's design led some critics to see it as a return to his work of the 1920s (see note 53 below).

46. FLW to Masieri, 19 February 1953 and 28 December 1953, FLWF;

and *Frank Lloyd Wright at the National Institute of Arts and Letters by the Recipient of the Gold Medal for Architecture, May 27, 1953*, 3. Wright went on to say that, once "modernity" was understood in this way, it could be "a coming-alive of what was best and noble in local tradition of the Great Tradition." This characteristically modernist presumption of a style to end all styles was further expressed in a letter to Masieri in which Wright said, among other things, that he "wanted to show [in the Masieri Memorial] that Organic Architecture is not a style but is style and not only that, but able to revivify genuine traditions in Architecture no matter what their nationality—preserving them alive" (11 March 1953, FLWF).

47. Quoted in "A New Debate in Old Venice," *NYT Magazine*, 21 March 1954, p. 8. Wright's remarks appear to be particularly directed at the criticism of Antonio Cederna (see notes 50–51 below).

48. Aline Louchheim, "Wright Analyzes Architect's Need," *NYT*, 26 May 1953, p. 23. The show was occasioned by Wright's receiving the Gold Medal of the American Academy of Arts and Letters.

49. Masieri to FLW, 19 December 1953, FLWF. One rumor was that Wright not only intended to replace the relatively insignificant structure the Masieris owned but that he also intended to destroy the Palazzo Balbi to make room for his project!

50. A definitive bibliography of the controversy should accompany a much-needed monograph on the project. The following is a list of some of the materials I consulted and found useful: "Un palazzo in Canal Grande progettato dall'architetto Wright," *Il Gazzettino*, 28 June 1953; Antonio Cederna, "Wright s'adatta a Venezia," *L'Europeo* 403 (5 July 1953): 35; Elio Zorzi, "Ingiustificato allarme a Venezia per la nuova casa sul Canal Grande progettata dal famoso architetto Wright," *Metron* 8, no. 48 (1953): 64; Roberto Pane, "La laguna 'organica,'" *Il Mondo* 6 (2 February 1954): 11 (an abridged translation is in MS 2401.340 B, FLWF); Astragal [pseud.], "Notes and Topics: Early Wright," *AJ* 119 (4 February 1954): 145, 156; Cederna, "L'Operazione Wright," *Il Mondo* 6 (9 February 1954): 11–12 (an abridged translation is in MS 2401.340 C, FLWF); Pane, "Disaccordo architettonico," *Il Mondo* 6 (2 March 1954): 12; "Design by Wright Has Venice Astir," *NYT*, 9 March 1954, p. 3; "A New Debate in Old Venice," *NYT Magazine*, 21 March 1954, pp. 8–9; Carlo L. Ragghianti, "Cronache: Italia moderna," *Critica d'Arte* 2 (March 1954): 197–99; "Wright or Wrong," *Time* 113 (22 March 1954): 92; Roberto Papini, "Perchè sarebbe una stonatura il palazzotto di Wright sul Canalazzo," *Corriere della Sera* (Milan), 25 March 1954, p. 3; "Frank Lloyd Wright: La casa sul Canal Grande," *Metron* 9, nos. 49–50 (January–April 1954): 2–65; "Venice Bars Wright Bid," *NYT*, 22 April 1954, p. 6; "News: Question: is Venice ready for an FLLW palazzo?" *AF* 100 (May 1954): 39; Bruno Zevi, "La palazzina di Wright 'in volta del canal,'" *Cronache*, 8 June 1954; Ernesto N. Rogers, "Polemica per una polemica," *Casabella* 201 (May–June 1954): 1–4; Ragghianti, "Cronache: Italia moderna, eja!" *Critica d'Arte* 4 (July 1954): 397–400 (repr. as "Notizie da Venezia," *Sele Arte* 2 [May–June 1954]: 77–80); F. Sacchi, "Il dialogo dei sordi dall'una all'altra riva del canale," *La Stampa*, 14 May 1954; Giovanni Michelucci, "Lettere: La casa sul Canal Grande," *Metron* 10, no. 51 (May–June 1954): 2; Henry Saylor, "The Editor's Asides," *Journal of the American Institute of Architects* 22 (July 1954): 24–25, 44; J. M. Richards, "'Venice Preserv'd,'" *Royal Architectural Institute of Canada* 31 (August 1954): 281–83 (repr. from *The Listener*); John Barrington Bayley, "Communications: Frank Lloyd Wright and the Grand Design," *Landscape: Magazine of Human Geography* 4 (Summer 1954): 30–33; Letter of Mario Deluigi and response of Rogers, *Casabella* 202 (August–September 1954): ii; Michelucci, "La ragioni di una polemica," *La Nuova Città* 14–15 (1954): 48–52; and "Wright Design Rejected by Venetian Commission," *NYT*, 16 November 1955, p. 15.

51. Cederna, "Operazione Wright," 11; and Bayley, "Wright and the Grand Design." The first part of Cederna's statement about Michelangelo and the Grand Canal was quoted (in a slightly different translation) in "Wright or Wrong," 92. It is important to note that Wright's contextualism and "classicism" did not appeal to traditionalists like Bayley.

52. See, e.g., Michelucci, "Casa sul Canal Grande" and "Ragioni di una polemica"; and Pane, "Laguna 'organica,'" 11.

53. Richards, "'Venice Preserv'd,'" 282–83 (italics added). In an earlier editorial in the *AJ*, the magazine of which Richards was house editor, the pseudonymous Astragal characterized the building as "a modest, disciplined, marble-faced little structure in the early 20th century manner of the Master"

("Early Wright," 145). The building they may have been referring to is the Merchandising Building project of 1922, for Los Angeles, published in Wendingen 1925, 92–94. Sweeney, *Wright in Hollywood*, 29, notes that Alice Millard's friend Olive Percival characterized Wright's design for La Miniatura as "the Venetian Palace plan." Sweeney, however, assumes the reference had less to do with the facade treatment than with the placing of the main floor on the *piano nobile*.

54. Berenson was quoted in "A New Debate in Old Venice," *NYT Magazine*, 21 March 1954, p. 8. This version of the Hemingway statement is quoted in Twombly, *Wright*, 363. The letter from Beale to the mayor is quoted in "Wright or Wrong," 92. Henry Saylor reported that "Ernest Hemingway suggests that if Wright must build a house in Venice the best thing would be to set it afire when completed" ("Editor's Asides," 44). According to Bruce Pfeiffer, Wright responded with the following when asked for his reaction to the Hemingway statement: "Reaction? Why none, whatsoever. After all, that was nothing more than a mere voice from the jungle" (in *Treasures of Taliesin: Seventy-six Unbuilt Designs* [Fresno, Calif., and Carbondale and Edwardsville, Ill.: Press at California State University, Southern Illinois University Press, 1985], 55). Pfeiffer claims that "Hemingway said that he would rather see Venice burn than erect a Frank Lloyd Wright building" (ibid.).

55. Querci della Rovere, "Masieri Memorial," 272–73; "Wright Design Rejected," 15. In late June 1955, the architect Bruno Morassutti wrote to Wright on behalf of Masieri to say that the situation had become more "complicated" due to "the persistent refusal of the neighbours to an agreement about the part of the new building wich [*sic*] exceeds local regulations and laws" and to ask "for a new project of a dormitory with a limited number of rooms to be built within the limits of the existing building" (24 June 1955, FLWF). Wright responded on 11 July: "I will modify the facade to remove the neighbor's objections if they will write to me and tell me just what is needed" (FLW to Morassutti, FLWF). It does not appear that anything came of this. Regarding the perimeter, the alley between the new building and the Palazzo Balbi actually created a space where there had been none.

56. *FLWR*, note to pl. 175.

57. There is no study yet of Wright's Baghdad project, nor, for that matter, of any of the other projects commissioned concurrently by the Iraqi government. Wright described his proposal in "Frank Lloyd Wright Designs for Baghdad," *AF* 108 (May 1958): 89–101. His design for the opera house was posthumously built in a much simplified form as the Grady Gammage Memorial Auditorium at Arizona State University, Tempe, in 1962–64. This was planned in 1959, just before Wright died. See Stephen D. Helmer, "Grady Gammage Auditorium and the Baghdad Opera Project: Two Late Designs by Frank Lloyd Wright," *FLWN* 3, no. 4 (1980): 10–17.

58. In 1927, Wright did designs for a group of prefabricated beach cottages for the seaside resort of Ras el Bar, outside Dumyât, on the Mediterranean coast of Egypt. In 1945–46, he designed the Calico Mills Store for the Sarabhai family in Ahmedabad. A major reason the Sarabhai store was never built was the problem of foreign exchange between the United States and India (Gira and Gautam Sarabhai, in conversation, April 1991).

59. After the armistice of 1918, Faysal was initially given the Syrian throne, as head of an Arab government in Damascus. When the French received the mandate over Syria in April 1920, conflict arose between them and Faysal, resulting in his expulsion. After going to London, he was offered the throne of Iraq by the British, with the understanding that a treaty of alliance (October 1922) would replace the mandate and thus ensure the new nation a certain degree of self-determination. The Iraqi constitution was instituted in 1924.

60. Lord Salter, *The Development of Iraq: A Plan of Action* (Baghdad: Iraq Development Board, 1955), 126. In the original plan of May 1950, 100 percent of the revenues was targeted for development. The 30-percent reduction was a response to the enormous increase in revenues resulting from the fifty-fifty deal in royalties negotiated in February 1952. The most relevant studies of this economic development are: Fahim I. Qubain, *The Reconstruction of Iraq*, Foreign Policy Research Institute Series, University of Pennsylvania, 6 (New York: Frederick A. Praeger, 1958); Kathleen M. Langley, *The Industrialization of Iraq*, Harvard Middle Eastern Monograph Series, 5 (Cambridge, Mass.: Center for Middle Eastern Studies, Harvard University Press, 1961); Ferhang Jalal, *The Role of Government in the Industrialization of Iraq, 1950–65* (Lon-

don: Frank Cass, 1972); and Edith and E. F. Penrose, *Iraq: International Relations and National Development* (London and Boulder, Colo.: Ernest Benn, Westview Press, 1978).

The best study of Iraq's post–World War II political and social history is Hanna Batatu, *The Old Social Classes and the Revolutionary Movements of Iraq: A Study of Iraq's Old Landed and Commericial Classes and of Its Communists, Baʿthists, and Free Officers* (Princeton: Princeton University Press, 1978).

61. Langley, *Industrialization of Iraq*, 103ff.; and Jalal, *Role of Government*, 33. The report produced by Salter in 1955 was commissioned by the government in response to political pressures. For a summary of progress through 1957, see Waldo G. Bowman, "Iraq's Operation Bootstrap," pt. 1, "A Modern Mesopotamia Is Molded"; pt. 2, "Big Dams Instead of Hanging Gardens," *ENR* 159 (12 December 1957): 32–40; (26 December 1957): 32–40.

62. Salter, *Development of Iraq*, 118.

63. Discussions related to the Iraq Museum (museum of antiquities) began as far back as 1932, when the German architect Werner March was asked for a design. In 1951 he was called in again. Construction began on his revised plan in March 1957 and was completed by 1963. I am grateful to Jülide Aker, a student in a seminar I gave on Baghdad at Harvard University in the spring of 1992, for this information. J. Brian Cooper was also hired prior to the decisions resulting from the Salter report.

64. Some of the most important of the Doxiadis projects were for worker housing for western Baghdad, Sarchinar, Mosul, and Basra. On his work in Iraq, see Doxiadis Associates, *Progress of the Housing Program*, Monthly Report 46 [cumulative and final], Prepared for Government of Iraq, May 1959; Doxiadis Associates, *Iraq Housing Program, D. A. Review* 5 (September 1959); John Gulick, "Baghdad: Portrait of a City in Physical and Cultural Change," *Journal of the American Institute of Planners* 33 (July 1967): 252–55; and Ihsan Fethi, "Urban Conservation in Iraq: The Case for Protecting the Cultural Heritage of Iraq with Special Reference to Baghdad Including a Comprehensive Inventory of Its Areas and Buildings of Historic or Architectural Interest," 3 vols. (Ph.D. diss., University of Sheffield, 1977), 1: 295–324.

Le Corbusier was originally contacted about the stadium in June 1955 and responded positively in mid-July of that year. Nothing seems to have happened until the following summer, when he received the program. He was officially appointed on 25 December 1956. I owe this information to David Joselit, who conducted research at the Fondation Le Corbusier in Paris for my Baghdad seminar in the spring of 1992. For general treatments of the commission, see Suzanne Taj-Eldin and Stanislaus von Moos, "Nach Plänen von . . . Eine Gymnastikhalle von Le Corbusier in Baghdad," *Archithèse* 3 (May–June 1983): 39–44; and Taj-Eldin, "Baghdad: Box of Miracles," *ARev* 181 (January 1987): 78–83. I should like to thank Mohammed al-Asad for bringing the Taj-Eldin articles to my attention. The Garland volume of Le Corbusier's drawings devoted to the Baghdad project mysteriously date the first designs to 1953. See H. Allen Brooks, gen. ed., *The Le Corbusier Archive*, vol. 27, *Le Corbusier: Projet pour un Stade Olympique, Baghdad, and Other Buildings and Projects, 1953* (New York, London, and Paris: Garland Publishing, Fondation Le Corbusier, 1984), 101–514.

Two other buildings of the period were the United States Embassy by José Luis Sert (1955-61) and the Baghdad Hilton Hotel by Welton Becket (construction begun 1957).

65. Economist Intelligence Unit, *Three-Monthly Economic Review: Iraq and Arabian Peninsula* 7 (November 1957): 6. A group of younger architects, including Rifat Chadirji, Ellen Jawdat, and Nizar Jawdat, were apparently, consulted after they had expressed dismay over some of the earlier choices of architects.

The Minoprio-Spencely-Macfarlane plan is dated March 1956 and was published in *The Master Plan for the City of Baghdad, 1956*, Report prepared by Minoprio & Spencely and P. W. Macfarlane, London, April 1956. I am indebted to Thomas Doxiadis, a student in my Baghdad seminar of spring 1992, for providing me with a copy of the report. Minoprio & Spencely and P. W. Macfarlane did a master plan for Kuwait in 1951 and one for Dhaka in 1957–59. Their work in Great Britain included plans for Slough (1950) and Cwmbran New Town (1951); prior to that, Anthony Minoprio did, on his own, plans for Chelmsford (1945) and Crawley New Town (1947–49). Other British firms that

prepared master plans for Iraqi cities in the mid-fifties were Max Lock (Basra) and Raglan Squire (Mosul). See Raglan Squire, ed., "Architecture in the Middle East," *Architectural Design* 27 (March 1957): 74–78. The Minoprio-Spencely-Macfarlane plan for Baghdad was replaced by one prepared by Doxiadis for the Qasim regime in 1958–59, which in turn was replaced by one prepared by the Polish firm of Polservice in the mid-1960s.

66. D[hia] Jāfar, Minister of Development, to FLW, 15 January 1957; FLW to Minister of Development, 24 January 1957; and Jāfar to FLW, 9 March 1957, MS 1502.258, FLWF. I am grateful to Indira Berndtson for making these letters available to me. In the letter of commission of 15 January, Jāfar wrote: "The Development Board of the Government of Iraq in their meeting . . . held on 29/12/1956 have on our recommendation agreed to appoint you Consultant for the Engineering services required for the preparation of designs and the supervision of constructing the Opera for the City of Baghdad." See also "Wright Going to Iraq to Design Opera House," *NYT*, 27 January 1957, p. 57; "Opera House for Baghdad," *NYT*, 28 January 1957, p. 22; and "Wright to Design Baghdad Opera: Opera and Poetry," *AF* 106 (March 1957): 97.

67. A note in Le Corbusier's sketchbooks, his first on the subject of Baghdad, reads: "January 9, 195[7] [mistakenly written 1956]//Goutail from Baghdad they have called on Wright Oscar Niemeyer Aalto//USA—Sert" (Françoise de Franclieu, ed., *Le Corbusier Sketchbooks*, vol. 3, *1954–1957* [New York, Cambridge, Mass., and London: Architectural History Foundation, MIT Press, 1982], K 45/812). The *Three-Monthly Economic Review of Iraq and Arabian Peninsula* 5 (May 1957): 6, reported that the Wright and Ponti commissions were announced in Baghdad during the Development Week of 23–29 March 1957. In an article published in 1960, Ponti stated that the Development Board "simultaneously" commissioned Aalto, Wright, Le Corbusier, and himself (Gio Ponti, "Progetto per l'edificio del 'Development Board' in Baghdad," *Domus* 370 [September 1960]: 1). The *Three-Monthly Economic Review of Iraq and Arabian Peninsula*, on the other hand, first noted the "addition of M. Le Corbusier" to Iraq's panel of architects of world fame" in its report of November 1957 (no. 7, p. 6).

Gropius, apparently, was awarded the commission for the university in the late summer or early fall of 1957, even though he may have informally discussed the subject as early as 1954, when he visited his former students Ellen and Nizar Jawdat in Baghdad that summer. In a letter to the Gropiuses following that visit, Ellen Jawdat wrote: "We are more than ever convinced that we must find some way for you to make your contribution to this country" (3 October 1954, Gropius Correspondence, b MS ger 208 [956], *81M-84, Houghton Library, Harvard University; hereafter Gropius Corres.) The following year she added: "The university scheme is temporarily halted until the English firm of Minoprio & Spencely have made their recommendations for the Baghdad City plan and have settled on the site for the university center. So it still simmers and we keep talking. Reginald Squire . . . are blatantly publicizing themselves for the job" (Jawdat to Gropius [prob. mid-1955], Gropius Corres.). I am grateful to Elizabeth Dean Hermann, a student in my 1992 Baghdad seminar, for bringing these letters and other information about the project to my attention. The *Three-Monthly Economic Review: Iraq and Arabian Peninsula* announced in its January 1958 issue that "Iraq has added to the great names of Frank Lloyd Wright (who has now produced preliminary drawings for the Opera House), Le Corbusier, and Gio Ponti that of Gropius, whose firm was invited during the autumn to discuss the planning of Baghdad University" (no. 8, p. 8). Cf. Reginald R. Isaacs, *Walter Gropius: Der Mensch und sein Werk*, 2 vols. (Berlin: Gebr. Mann Verlag, 1984), 2: 1040–47; and "Planning a University," *Christian Science Monitor*, 2 April 1958, sec. 2, p. 1.

When Wright returned from his May 1957 trip to Baghdad, he told the Taliesin Fellowship on 16 June that "Corbusier is there doing a race track, no, not a race track, a stadium. And they've got Hilton in there to build a hotel. He's got his favorite architect building it [Becket], so the hotel is already merchandized and standardized to start with. I hope Corbu does better with the stadium—interesting to see what he will do. Then they have Aalto in there. They have a German architect whose name I don't remember [March]. And a British concern [Minoprio & Spencely and Macfarlane] has laid out the town, done the master plan of the city" (in Pfeiffer, *Living Voice*, 51). Although he did not mention Ponti, one would assume Wright would have noted the name of Gropius if he was already part of the group. According to Elizabeth Hermann, the *Iraq Times* announced the Development Board's decision to hire Gropius on 9 September 1957. Rifat Chadirji and Ellen Jawdat both maintain that Gropius was on the original list of architects (lecture, Baghdad Development Projects seminar, Harvard University, spring 1992; in conversation, 3 July 1993), but there is no documentary evidence so far to support the claim.

Given the extraordinary cast of characters involved, it is amazing that nothing has been written about the subject of these commissions and that most of the events remain clouded in mystery. Among the rare press reports dealing with the group of commissions as a whole are: "Architects Build a Modern Baghdad," *Christian Science Monitor*, 2 April 1958, sec. 2, p. 1; and "New Lights for Aladdin," *Time* 71 (19 May 1958): 80. See now also Rifat Chadirji, *Al Ukhaider and the Crystal Palace* (London and Cyprus: Riad El-Rayyes, 1991), esp. 118–23 (in Arabic).

68. See note 67 above. Wright was in Baghdad from 21 May through 27 May 1957. I am grateful to Jülide Aker for this information. Le Corbusier's sketchbooks reveal that he visited Baghdad in the second week of November 1957 and that he received the final program for the stadium on 9 November (*Le Corbusier Sketchbooks, 1954–1957*, L50/1056–74). For their help in documenting and understanding the work of Ponti and Aalto, I should like to thank Jak Cheng and Ahmet Ersoy, both students in my 1992 Baghdad seminar.

69. But see note 72 below. Le Corbusier tried to change the site of his stadium on his November visit to Baghdad to one near the river (ibid., L40/1072). While unsuccessful at this, he was apparently able to expand the program to include a gymnasium (sports hall), an outdoor amphitheater, a restaurant, tennis courts, and a swimming pool. Aalto was able to supplement his art museum with the commission for the Postal Administration Headquarters. Some time later, Gropius noted in a letter to his wife that, following discussions with the ministry, he thought he might get the opera house job in addition to the university (Walter Gropius to Ise Gropius, 26 February 1960, in Isaacs, *Gropius*, 2: 1044).

70. Wright reported the following to the Taliesin Fellows on 16 June 1957: "I saw they had allocated the university on the ground opposite the island, and the island was a cleavage right between the city and the university. So I went after that island" ("Baghdad," transcript of tape recording, 16 June 1957, p. 5, Reel #188, FLWF). The Karradah peninsula was described in the report on *The Master Plan for the City of Baghdad, 1956* as an "ideal" spot for a regional park: "It is on the fringe of the built-up area, and therefore easily accessible; and yet it has about it a certain atmosphere of remoteness. Its wonderful display of greenery, its date palm groves and the presence of the river, which bounds it on three sides, make it a real oasis of beauty, offering opportunities for mental refreshment and quiet that it is so essential a great city should provide its inhabitants" (p. 17). As "a possible alternative site for the University," the peninsula, "with its date palm groves and long river frontages, provides a magnificent site for a group of University buildings," although it is "a little far from the centre of the city" (p. 16).

Ellen Jawdat told me that the island site was reserved for Aalto, who was to design a library for it. According to Jawdat, when Wright was informed of this by her on the way in from the airport, he replied: "Aalto and I are friends and he'll give me the island" (in conversation, 3 July 1993). This story, however, corresponds with nothing else I have read. Aalto's art gallery was planned for the downtown civic center.

71. FLW, "Preface" (to proposal submitted to King Faysal and Development Board), [p. 7], MS 2401.379 GG, FLWF; Pfeiffer, *Living Voice*, 51; and *FLWPS*, vol. 11, 218.

72. "Wright, 88, to Design Iraqi Cultural Center," *NYT*, 8 June 1957, p. 6; FLW, "To the Minister and his Development Board, City of Baghdad, Iraq" (draft), n.d. [June or July 1957], MS 2401.379 BB, FLWF; and Pfeiffer, *Living Voice*, 50–52. The commission for the post office was decided on 27 May 1957, the day Wright left, and reported in the *Iraq Times* two days later. Following Wright's visit, the *Three-Monthly Economic Review of Iraq and Arabian Peninsula* 6 (July 1957): 6, reported "the appointment of Mr. Frank Lloyd Wright to draw the plans for a central post office and a cultural center, which will include a university building." Even before going to Baghdad, Wright had written to Fowler McCormick: "My share I believe is the opera—(probably meaning civic-center and a world-resort in the Garden of Eden) at the southern tip of Iraq" (10 May 1957, FLWF). Wright also mentioned the Basra resort

to Ray Rubicam (7 May 1957, FLWF). Ellen Jawdat confirmed that there may well have been discussion of such a project (in conversation, 3 July 1993). Although nothing came of it, Wright may have been inspired to rename Pig Island the Garden of Eden as a result. See p. 397 below.

73. FLW, "Proposed—This Nine-Year Plan for the Cultural Center of Greater Baghdad," June–July 1957, MS 2401.379 M, FLWF; and "Wright's Plans for Baghdad Cultural Center Shown," *NYT*, 3 May 1958, p. 5. Numerous drafts of the general proposal have been preserved. It was excerpted in "Wright Designs for Baghdad," 89–101. The *Three-Monthly Economic Review: Iraq and Arabian Peninsula* reported in its January 1958 issue that Wright had "produced preliminary drawings for the Opera House" (no. 8, p. 8). A "List of Drawings Actually Sent to Iraqui [*sic*] Government in Baghdad," dated 18 November 1963, specifies nearly fifty, including three colored renderings of which no copies were retained. The total number of drawings listed for the project runs to eighty-one (MS 1502.258, FLWF).

74. "Architects Build Modern Baghdad." Probably sometime in May 1958, Ellen Jawdat wrote to Ise Gropius of Wright's "Opera House having been consigned forever, we hope, to a dusty shelf" (n.d., Gropius Corres.). Wright himself seems to have had doubts about the government's will or ability to carry through with the project from quite early on.

75. See Republic of Iraq, *The Five-Years Detailed Economic Plan (1961–62)–(1965–66)* (Baghdad: Ministry of Guidance, 1961), 463–512.

As will be discussed below, Wright's design was much more tied to the Hashimite dynasty in terms of expression than any of the other projects. Their adherence to a more strictly functionalist form of expression allowed them to appear more in tune with Qasim's socialist-revolutionary aims. In the book edited by Ali Ghalib Aziz, *The Iraqi Revolution: One Year of Progress and Achievement* (Baghdad: 14th July Celebrations Committee, 1959), put out on the occasion of the first anniversary of the revolution of 1958, it was made clear that "the new policy was [to be] directed to constructing new public buildings of *modern* design" (p. 75, italics added).

Twombly, *Wright*, 361, claimed that "at first the new government said it would honor the [Wright] contract, but early in 1959, deeming Wright's plans 'rather grandiose,' declared that the people needed food, clothing, and shelter more than floating gardens, gold fountains, and a mammoth zoo. The new leaders wanted a university, but decided to look elsewhere for an architect." Gropius, of course, had already been hired by the Hashimite government; and the Qasim regime, despite early rhetoric against "luxurious buildings," such as "a lavish royal palace, parliament and government offices and . . . an opera house" (Fawzi el-Kaissi, "The Economic Development Policies of the Republic of Iraq," March 1959, in *The Republic of Iraq: Establishment, Policies and Achievements* [Washington, D.C.: Embassy of the Republic of Iraq, 1959], 9), completed and made use of the Royal Palace and Parliament. By the end of 1959, Qasim had decided not only to develop the zoo at the scale of London's Kew Gardens but to do it on the island site Wright had proposed for his scheme (Abdul Karim Qasim, *Objectives of Iraq's Revolution*, press conference, 2 December 1959 [Baghdad: Ministry of Guidance, 1959], 77). Gropius informed his wife on 26 February 1960 that his reputation was "sky-high in Baghdad" and that it looked as if the Opera House was also to be given to him, adding: "F. L. Wright would turn over in his grave" (quoted in Isaacs, *Gropius*, 2: 1044). An international competition for an Opera House was in fact announced in November 1962 (to close in July 1963), but nothing came of it.

The initial plans for the university, done in 1958, were presented to Qasim in early 1959. Changes were requested and a final scheme was approved in 1960. Construction began in 1962, although Qasim had laid the foundation stone as early as July 1959. Ponti's Development Board Building was sent out for bids in August 1960 (as the Ministry of Planning and Economic Planning Board Building) and was under construction by the following summer. Le Corbusier's project was kept on the books during the Qasim regime and remained a possibility throughout Le Corbusier's life. The site was changed, and a new plan was drawn up in 1964. Well after Le Corbusier died, it was revived in a very reduced form during the second Ba'th regime under Saddam Husain. Georges Présenté, Le Corbusier's former associate, produced the final working drawings for yet another site, and oversaw construction of the Sports Hall, called Saddam Husain Gymnasium, in 1973–80.

76. FLW, Talk to Engineers [22 May 1957], 1–3. Edward Said has point-

edly emphasized the Orientalist's resort to this dichotomy in *Orientalism* (New York: Vintage Books, Random House, 1979). Wright, however, did not imply a distinction between the dynamism and progressivism of the "materialist" West and the inertness and static aspect of the "spiritualist" East that Said sees as endemic to the Orientalist's disregard for his or her own cultural bailiwick.

On his return to the United States, Wright told the Fellowship that he "talked to them [the Society] in a very unrestrained fashion. . . . And they were very appreciative and they printed it. Recorded it and printed it and distributed it all through Iraq," noting that as a result of the attitudes expressed in the talk "we'll probably bring a whole battery of ambitious criticism down on our heads" ("Baghdad," 16 June 1957, 2, 8).

The transcript of the Baghdad talk is edited by Wright. There are six further edited versions (MS 2401.377–78, A, B, D, E, F, G, FLWF). I presume the final version was either sent or intended to be sent with the project.

77. FLW, Talk to Engineers, 2, 6, 5, 8. Wright specifically distinguished himself, on all these issues, from the standardized, commerical modernism of the West.

78. Ibid., 6, 7, 1 (words in brackets added by Wright in edited version). In a number of the edited versions Wright ended on the following note: "Your culture needs the dignity and strength of the Kingdom of your great past, and in IRAQ monarchy has proved worthy" (MSS 2401.377–78 D, G).

79. "Wright Designs for Baghdad," 95. It would be interesting to look at Doxiadis's work further in this regard. Some of his housing makes a tentative effort in the direction of what Frampton later called "critical regionalism." See Kenneth Frampton, "Towards a Critical Regionalism: Six Points for an Architecture of Resistance," in Hal Foster, ed., *The Anti-Aesthetic: Essays on Postmodern Culture* (Port Townsend, Wash.: Bay Press, 1983), 16–30.

80. The Aalto museum was a translation of his design for the Art Gallery at Reval (Tallinn), Estonia (1936), which he reused, at the same time as the Baghdad commission, for the 1958 Aalborg Museum competition in Denmark (built 1969–73). See Elissa Aalto and Karl Fleig, *Alvar Aalto*, vol. 3, *Projects and Final Buildings* (Zurich: Verlag für Architektur Artemis, 1978), 150–53. Le Corbusier, *My Work*, trans. James Palmes (London: Architectural Press, 1960), 132, pointed out that the Baghdad Stadium project was a reprise of the Centre National de Réjouissances Populaires he had designed for the outskirts of Paris in 1936–37. That proposal itself was made with the intention that it could be implemented at any one of three different locations (Bois de Vincennes, Gentilly-Cité Universitaire, or Gennevilliers). For the Gropius-TAC University, see John C. Harkness, ed., *The Walter Gropius Archive*, vol. 4, *1945–1969: The Work of the Architects Colloborative* (New York and London: Garland Publishing, 1991), 189–238. For earlier publications, see "TAC: The Architects Colloborative," pt. 1, "The University of Baghdad," *ARec* 125 (April 1959): 147–54; "The Architects Collaborative International Limited: La città universitaria di Baghdad," *Casabella* 242 (August 1960): 1–31; "Planning the University of Baghdad," *ARec* 129 (February 1961): 107–22; and Walter Gropius et al., *The Architects Collaborative, 1945–1965* (New York: Architectural Book Publishing Company, 1966), 119–37.

81. The American embassies built in the 1950s under the guidelines of the State Department's Foreign Buildings Office made a particular point of deriving character and expression from local climatic conditions. See "USA Abroad," *AF* 107 (December 1957): 121; Jane C. Loeffler, "The Architecture of Diplomacy: Heyday of the United States Embassy-Building Program, 1954–1960," *JSAH* 49 (September 1990): 251–78; and Ron Robin, *Enclaves of America: The Rhetoric of American Political Architecture Abroad, 1900–1965* (Princeton: Princeton University Press, 1992). The *Forum* article noted how, in Sert's Baghdad Embassy, "sun control devices create rich, textured east and west walls" (p. 121), and how, in Paul Rudolph's embassy project for Amman, Jordan, "the curved precast ribs form a parasol shading the flat roof beneath the colonnade [which is] calculated also for vertical sun shade" (p. 122).

82. "TAC: University of Baghdad," *ARec*, 148; and "Planning a University," *Christian Science Monitor*, 1. The abstractness of Gropius's thinking is particularly apparent in the following remark: "The interrelationship of the individual buildings and the landscaped open spaces with their water fountains between them . . . will cause a significant rhythm. This rhythm tends to express the meaning of Universitas, which is 'wholeness,' offering the creative setting for a full, well-integrated life of the students" ("Planning a University,"

1). Aalto's response to "working in Baghdad, one of the world's hottest cities," is cited in Göran Schildt, *Alvar Aalto: The Mature Years* (New York: Rizzoli International, 1991), 206. Two aspects of the design directly related to this were the "heavy" masonry construction ("to minimize the use of air conditioning") and the roof consisting of "a double parasol of louvres." It should be noted that Aalto intended the walls to be "clad with ceramic tiles in the local tradition," stating that "the entire project calls for great tact, so as not to destroy the character of the city"(ibid.).

83. Ponti, " 'Development Board' in Baghdad," 1, 5. Ponti referred to the continuous portico as the special "invention" relating the building to local conditions (p. 1). For Ponti's justification of standardization as what he preferred to call "representativeness," see his "Primo e dopo la Pirelli," *Domus* 379 (June 1961): 29–32. On the Development Board Building, see also Lisa Licitra Ponti, *Gio Ponti: The Complete Works, 1923–1978* (Cambridge, Mass.: MIT Press, 1990), 202.

84. The one issue aside from historical tradition that Wright consistently referred to as a major determinant of his design was the "traffic problem" and the accommodation of the automobile. See "Wright Designs for Baghdad," 91, 98; FLW, "Proposed—Nine-Year Plan," passim; and Meehan, *Truth against the World*, 418–19. It is interesting to compare his use of the spiral ziggurat for parking with Louis Kahn's coeval designs for Philadelphia and, especially, to note that Wright, like Kahn, used the term "harboring" as a synonym for parking ("Wright Designs for Baghdad," 91).

85. The main literary sources for our knowledge of ancient Baghdad are the ninth-century accounts of Abu Ja'far Muhammed al Tabari and Ahmad al-Ya'kubi, and the eleventh-century one of Al-Khatib al-Baghdadi. For the early history of Baghdad, see K.A.C. Creswell, *Early Muslim Architecture*, 2 vols. (Oxford: Oxford University Press, 1932–1940), 2: 1–38; *Encyclopaedia of Islam*, new ed., s.v. "Baghdad" (Abdul-Aziz Duri); Mustapha Jewad et al., eds., *Baghdad: An Illustrated History* (Baghdad: Iraqi Engineers Association, 1969) (in Arabic); Jacob Lassner, "The Caliph's Personal Domain: The City Plan of Baghdad Re-Examined," in A. H. Hourani and S. M. Stern, eds., *The Islamic City: A Colloquium*, Papers on Islamic History, 1 (Oxford and Philadelphia: Bruno Cassirer, University of Pennsylvania Press, 1970), 103–18; and Lassner, *The Topography of Baghdad in the Early Middle Ages* (Detroit: Wayne State University Press, 1970).

86. The 1959 edition of the *Petit Larousse* French dictionary, for instance, reproduces a reconstruction of one of the gates of ancient Babylon as "the Assyrian gate of Baghdad" (p. 1185). Wright may also have been confused on the matter. In the talk he gave to the Society of Engineers of Baghdad, he said in his opening remarks: "And my first visit comes to what once was to me the center of the Orient, I find myself mistaken but that does not matter; the feeling is there just the same" (Talk to Engineers, 1). It is also possible that Wright was confused as to the original location of al-Mansur's Round City.

87. Wright may not only have confused Babylon with Baghdad, as so many of his generation still did, he also confused the reign of Harun ar-Rashid with that of al-Mansur, conflating the two into one. His definition of a ziggurat was based, no doubt, on popular Renaissance-Baroque images from Western sources, which in turn were related more to the circular spiral shape of the minaret of the Great Mosque of Samarra than to any extant or presupposed ancient example. His belief that the Garden of Eden was located about sixty miles southwest of Baghdad was based on a long literary tradition.

There is no record of what sites Wright visited in Baghdad or what other places he may have been taken to in Iraq, such as Samarra or Ctesiphon. We do know that on the return trip he stopped off in Egypt. See Tawfiq Ahmad 'abd al-Gawad, "Frank L. Wright Visits Cairo," *Majállat al-'Imara* 3 (1957): 37–41. I thank Rebecca Foote for bringing this article to my attention.

88. FLW, "To Minister and Development Board," [2]. Here again Wright confuses Harun ar-Rashid with al-Mansur.

89. "Wright Designs for Baghdad," 91; and FLW, "The Crescent Opera and Civic Auditorium," p. 5, MS 2401.379 II, FLWF (draft marked "sent"). Wright interpreted the ancient ziggurat as circular in form, rather than square. In the "Preface" to his exposition of the project, Wright added:

Such ceramic buildings as these here presented are devoted to the welfare entertainment and uplift of the Baghdad citizenry. All should be . . . so built as to give a revived sense of the arts and crafts value of his great heritage from his

Arabic Past. . . . Effort such as here suggested to the Baghdad body-politic if put to work would serve essentially to fortify this political social issue of character at a time when the tide of civilization seems drifting toward international conformity to universal mediocrity. (Pp. 8–9, MS 2401.379 GG, FLWF)

90. FLW, "The University of Baghdad," p. 1, MS 2401.379 HH, FLWF; and "Wright Designs for Baghdad," 91. The phrase about copying ancestors was included in the "Note" Wright affixed as a "Fore-Word" to the explanatory text sent to Faysal and the Development Board ("Proposed—Nine-Year Plan," 1).

91. One could argue that the University provided a program that gave Wright the scope to develop a plan that legitimates his entire project from a historico-contextual point of view.

92. The new boulevard would have passed directly by Le Corbusier's Stadium before arriving at the railroad station.

93. Aside from the Monona Terrace Civic Center, which Wright reworked in the early to mid-1950s, the Pittsburgh project, with its enormous ziggurat for parking and for housing multiple cultural facilities, as well as its bridges and roads connecting to the rest of the city, is the most important precedent for the work in Baghdad. It is therefore no surprise that the general plan of Pittsburgh should have been on Wright's mind when he did the design.

94. See note 87 above. The twelve circular landscape elements surrounding the central open space (fig. 376) may well reflect the cosmic implications of the original circular plan of al-Mansur. One might also relate Wright's circular plan to the history of utopian city plans that would include, as its foremost representative, Ebenezer Howard's diagram of a "Garden City" in *To-morrow: A Peaceful Path to Real Reform* (1898), republished in 1902 as *Garden Cities of To-morrow*.

95. "Wright Designs for Baghdad," 98. John Rattenbury, who was responsible for the rendering of the University, told me that Wright drew the mosque himself, but later whited it out (in conversation, 26 August 1993). Fig. 378 shows the design as it was published in 1958 and, presumably, as it was submitted to the client. Ellen Jawdat informed me that she accompanied Wright to the Khadimain Mosque and that he was impressed (in conversation, 3 July 1993).

96. The term *culture industry* comes from Max Horkheimer and Theodor W. Adorno, *Dialectic of Enlightenment* (1944; new ed., trans. John Cumming, New York: Continuum, 1988), 120–67.

97. There had been a gradual shift during the 1940s and 1950s from the pan-Arabism of Faysal I to a more "separatist" position emphasizing the unique heritage of Iraqi culture. This was particularly true among the more progressive artists and writers, something Wright may have become aware of during his short trip. Government propaganda, at the international level at least, stressed the dual heritage of Iraq's past, that is, its pre-Islamic ancient civilizations and its Islamic medieval and modern cultures. For instance, *An Introduction to the Past and Present of the Kingdom of Iraq*, published in English by a Committee of Officials in 1946, devoted about two-thirds of its section on pre-twentieth-century history to ancient Mesopotamia and the remaining third to the Islamic period. The purpose of the brochure *Iraq Today . . .*, put out by the Directorate-General of Propaganda in the year Faysal II acceded to the throne, was to provide an overview "of the various phases of development now taking place in this modern kingdom that stands on such ancient foundations" (Baghdad: Ministry of Interior, May 1953, 3). The later Ba'thist regime followed a similar pattern of relating medieval and modern Islamic traditions to Iraq's ancient, pre-Islamic past. For different views on this, see Amatzia Baram, *Culture, History and Ideology in the Formation of Ba'thist Iraq, 1968–89* (New York: St. Martin's, 1991); and Samir al-Khalil [Kanan Makiya], *The Monument: Art, Vulgarity and Responsibility in Iraq* (Berkeley, Los Angeles, London: University of California Press, 1991). I should like to thank my colleague Cemal Kafadar for this latter reference as well as other helpful insights.

98. Wright referred to this often in his descriptions of the project: "The Garden of Eden was located at an old city named Edena which was on the great canal taken from the Tigris to the Euphrates . . . south of Baghdad. So we are calling this little island . . . the Isle of Edena, and we are going to make a big feature of Adam and Eve when we do the building" ("Baghdad," 3–4). It should also be recalled that, at one point, Wright either had, or at least enter-

tained the thought that he had, a commission for a "world-class resort in the Garden of Eden" near Basra (see note 72 above).

99. Richard Ettinghausen and Oleg Grabar, *The Art and Architecture of Islam: 650–1250*, Pelican History of Art (Harmondsworth: Penguin, 1987), 86–88.

100. FLW, "Preface," 2–3. Gulick, "Baghdad," 254, discusses the importance of the riverfront *kazinu* in the social life of Baghdad. In a preliminary sketch of the island plan (#5733.037 B, FLWF), Wright placed a casino along the shore of the island, opposite the university. The geometric shapes of the kiosks, like so many other aspects of the Baghdad project, should be compared with Kahn's later work.

101. According to Rifat Chadirji, the key supporter of the Opera House project was Fadil aj-Jamali, who had been Minister of Foreign Affairs in the late 1940s, then Director General of Education in the early 1950s, and Prime Minister in 1954. Educated in the United States and married to a Canadian, he had one of the largest collections of classical European music in Baghdad (lecture, Baghdad seminar, Harvard University, spring 1992). On the intentions of the Qasim government, see *Three-Monthly Economic Review: Iraq* 26 (August 1962): 10; and 27 (November 1962): 10. See also note 75 above.

102. The stated capacity of the house differs considerably from one version of Wright's text to the next. Pfeiffer says that "the auditorium itself was created to seat 3000" *(FLWPS*, vol. II, 218). Wright gave the figure of 1,600 (auditorium proper) plus 3,700 in "Wright Designs for Baghdad," 95. The expanded civic auditorium idea may not have been Wright's alone, although it is difficult to assess how much discussion there was with the Development Board.

103. One is particularly reminded of the drawn-back curtains in doorways or arcades in Byzantine and Western Medieval mosaics and manuscripts.

104. In order to eliminate the need for a fly-loft, the revolving circular stage was designed to be lowered for scenery changes.

105. FLW, "Crescent Opera and Civic Auditorium," 1; and "Wright Designs for Baghdad," 95.

106. The Tallahassee project was published in G. E. Kidder Smith, "Beethoven and Basketball," *AF* 106 (March 1957): 114–17. This was the same issue in which the news of Wright's commission for the Baghdad Opera House appeared ("Wright to Design Baghdad Opera"). Gropius reused the Tallahassee design for the main auditorium building of Baghdad University, but without the arch.

107. "Wright Designs for Baghdad," 95; and FLW, "Crescent Opera and Civic Auditorium," 2.

108. From the Assessors' Report, in "Sydney Opera House Competition," *Architect and Building News* 211 (28 February 1957): 275. Cf. also D[rexler] and G[reen], *Architecture and Imagery*, 3.

109. The results of the Sydney competition, which was opened in 1955 and judged in late January 1957, were widely published in February–April 1957. An article appeared in *AF* in March and another in *ARec* in April. In addition, Utzon had visited Taliesin in the late 1940s and must therefore have been personally known to Wright. According to Sigfried Giedion, "in 1949 a scholarship took him first to the USA and then to Mexico. He spent a short time with Frank Lloyd Wright in Taliesin West and Taliesin East" (Giedion, "Jörn Utzon and the Third Generation," *Zodiac* 14 [1965]: 38). Utzon was apparently never formally a member of the Taliesin Fellowship.

110. FLW, "The Crescent Opera and Civic Auditorium," 1. The first reference to the tales, as noted earlier, was the mural in the Oak Park house playroom, done in 1895. In his talk to the Society of Engineers of Baghdad, Wright began with a reference to the tales: "I am still one of the 'subjects' of Harun Al-Rashid by way of the tales of the 'Arabian Nights' and I know nearly every tale of the Arabian Nights even now as I knew them when a boy" (p. 1).

The "framing" character of the arch not only relates to the "framing" narrative of Shahrazad and Shahrayar but also physically frames the procession through the spaces in a way that distantly recalls Bernini's colonnade at St. Peter's. This processional aspect becomes even more pronounced when one takes into account the fact that the crescent arch was to be built not perpendicular to the ground but tilted back, so as to embrace the visitor's movement in depth.

111. The crescent (*hilal*) in Islamic culture stands for the new or waxing moon. It is important in the Islamic calendar, which is lunar- rather than solar-based, because its appearance determines the date of pilgrimage to Mecca

(*hajj*) as well as the beginning and end of Ramadan. Used as a military and religious symbol by the Turks during the Ottoman Empire, it became in the nineteenth century a sign of Islam (in contradistinction to the Christian cross) and was adopted by many Arab countries in the twentieth century for their national flags.

Wright may also have had in mind the early Sassanid arch of the Palace at Ctesiphon (the capital of Mesopotamia just prior to al-Mansur's construction of the Round City), which remained an important symbol of Iraqi culture. In FLW and Iovanna Lloyd Wright, *Architecture: Man in Possession of His Earth*, ed. Patricia Coyle Nicholson (Garden City, N. Y.: Doubleday, 1962), the caption for the photograph of the Palace at Ctesiphon gives this arch primacy of place in the history of architecture: "The arch was first used in this land between the Tigris and the Euphrates because wide openings had to be spanned with units no larger than brick. The evolution from the Sumerian architecture of great ramps, terraces and roadways to the more delicately ornamented arched and domed architecture of the Persians has created a lasting wealth of architectural ideas" (p. 77).

112. "Wright Designs for Baghdad," 95. The tale of Aladdin was not part of the original *Thousand and One Nights* as the stories were recorded in the late thirteenth and fourteenth centuries. It first appeared in Antoine Galland's early eighteenth-century French translation, although it soon became one of the most famous of the tales, especially in the late nineteenth-century translation by Richard Burton. It was the Burton translation that Wright apparently owned and read.

113. In a preliminary sketch plan of the overall scheme (#5733.037 B, FLWF), the Opera House was placed at the center of the Garden of Eden and the two statues and water domes were to either side of it. Without specifically referring to the Baghdad project, Norris Kelly Smith pointed out in his last chapter the general significance of Edenic imagery in Wright's work (Smith, *Wright*, 175ff.).

114. Ulrich Conrads and Hans G. Sperlich, *The Architecture of Fantasy: Utopian Building and Planning in Modern Times* (1960; trans. and ed. Christiane Crasemann Collins and George R. Collins, New York: Frederick A. Praeger, 1962). The operative term in the German title was *phantastisch*, which is really closer to the concept I am referring to here than is "fantasy." The latter can be all too easily confused with personal delusion.

115. Samuel Taylor Coleridge, "Kubla Khan: or, A Vision in a Dream. A Fragment," 1798; and Said, *Orientalism*, passim.

116. It is fairly clear that the Development Board saw building as a form of technology (i.e., public works) rather than as an aspect of culture. Nor did they see tourism as an industry. Wright thus appears to have seriously misjudged their intentions in more ways than one. In the letter he wrote "To the Minister and his Development Board" accompanying his designs, he said that he realized that he "had come too late to save the Asian East from the invasions of the Professional Architects of the West" (p. 1), which is probably exactly what they did not want to hear.

Although Wright deliberately rejected certain "modernist" ideas in favor of a historicizing contextualism, he still followed a basically early twentieth-century approach to traffic planning, laying out broad streets and wide spaces that contrasted in their scale with the traditional medieval Islamic city. It was only in the late 1960s and 1970s that architects would begin to look with favor on such patterns based on a pedestrian scale.

117. Upon his return from Baghdad, Wright told the Fellowship on 16 June 1957: "We are not there to slap them in the face but to do honor to them according to our ability" (in Pfeiffer, *Living Voice*, 52).

118. Tzvetan Todorov, *The Fantastic: A Structural Approach to a Literary Genre* (1970; trans. Richard Howard, Ithaca: Cornell University Press, Cornell Paperbacks, 1975), 25. Todorov helps us to distinguish between fantasy—or, more properly speaking, the fantastic—as a category of artistic expression and fantasy as a psychological state of the artist. It is only the first that should interest us here. Todorov defines the fantastic (in literature) as a "particular case of the more general category of the 'ambiguous vision'" (p. 33). It issues from a "hesitation between a natural and a supernatural explanation of the events" on the part of the reader (p. 32):

In a world which is indeed our world, the one we know, . . . there occurs an event which cannot be explained by the laws of this same familiar world. The person who experiences the event must opt for one of two possible solutions: either he is the victim of an illusion of the senses, of a product of the imagination—and the laws of the world then remain what they are; or else the event has indeed taken place, it is an integral part of reality—but then this reality is controlled by laws unknown to us. . . .

. . . The fantastic is that hesitation experienced by a person who knows only the laws of nature, confronting an apparently supernatural event. (P. 25)

119. Wright liked to point out that Baghdad was almost midway between the biblical and the ancient sites to which he referred. It became, thereby, a palimpsest of Mesopotamia's cultural history: "The Garden of Eden is only sixty miles away, and the Tower of Babylon is only about forty miles away. So there is Mesopotamia, the very center of all that has happened since" (FLW, "On Production," 21 October 1957, in Meehan, *Truth against the World*, 155).

120. See notes 75 and 98 above.

121. A major argument for the quite tenuous legitimacy of the Hashimites was based on their supposed descent from Fatima, the Prophet Muhammad's daughter. The propagandistic *Introduction to the Past and Present of the Kingdom of Iraq* (1946) stressed that "by choosing a Hashimite as head of the State she [Iraq] also restored to the throne the very family from which the Abbasid Caliphs themselves had sprung" (p. 3).

122. I should like to thank my colleague Gülru Necipoglu for pointing out the close relationship between Wright's Opera House and literary descriptions of palaces and pavilions in the *Thousand and One Nights*. She also noted that Wright's device of backlighting a fountain to create a rainbow effect has its parallel in a number of Mughal palaces, where candles were placed in niches behind fountains.

123. FLW, Talk to Engineers, 8 (words in brackets in edited versions). The populism of Wright's design, which many have seen as kitschy and vulgar, predicts in certain ways the public art of the later Baʿth regime of Saddam Husain. As part of that regime's appeal to popular taste, sculptures of the *Thousand and One Nights*, for instance, have been placed at important sites in Baghdad. Cf. Baram, *Culture, History and Ideology*; and al-Khalil, *The Monument*.

124. There are now two books on the Marin County Civic Center: Evelyn Morris Radford, *The Bridge and the Building: The Art of Government and the Government of Art*, rev. ed. (New York: Carlton Press, Hearthstone Book, 1974); and Aaron G. Green and Donald P. DeNevi, *An Architecture for Democracy: Frank Lloyd Wright—The Marin County Civic Center* (San Francisco: Grendon, 1990). Two earlier publications include important visual and documentary information: *Marin County Civic Center* (San Rafael: Board of Supervisors, 1962); and Yukio Futagawa and Bruce Brooks Pfeiffer, *Global Architecture*, vol. 36, *Frank Lloyd Wright: Solomon R. Guggenheim Museum, New York City, N.Y., 1943–59; Marin County Civic Center, California, 1957–1970* (Tokyo: A.D.A. EDITA, 1975). The text of the talk Wright gave at the San Rafael High School on 31 July 1957 is reproduced in Meehan, *Truth against the World*, 381–411. Among the publications of the building in professional journals, some of the most comprehensive are: "'The Good Building Is One That Makes the Landscape More Beautiful Than It Was Before'—FLLW," *AF* 117 (November 1962): 122–29; "Centre Civique de Marin County, California, Etats-Unis," *Architecture d'Aujourd'hui* 34 (February–March 1963): 10–17; "Uffici amministrativi e biblioteca de Marin County, San Rafael, California, 1959–62," *Casabella* 274 (April 1963): 44–55; "L'Ultima opera di Wright costruita negli Stati Uniti," *Domus* 406 (September 1963): 1–6; and Giulio Veronesi and Bruno Alfieri, eds., "Civic Center, Marin County, San Rafael, California," *Lotus, Architectural Annual, 1964–1965*, 18–25. I should like to thank Bonnie Ruder for supplying me with a copy of her typescript "Frank Lloyd Wright and the Marin County Civic Center: An Architectural and Historical Study," 1990.

125. As was his wont, Wright, in the question-and-answer period following the talk at the San Rafael High School in July 1957, singled out the "realtor" for destroying any semblance of "nature" in his subdivision of the landscape (in Meehan, *Truth against the World*, 399, 402). The distinction between "nature" and "real estate" comes from Harris Rosenstein. In "the dominating business-technological complex" of our age, he wrote, "nature is real estate, and real estate is outside the window (if there is a window) or something on both sides of the highway you drive on, behind and less significant

than the signs and the billboards. . . . The urban in our consciousness has entirely swallowed up the rural; the pastoral is gone" (Rosenstein, "Climbing Mt. Oldenburg," *Art News* 64 [February 1966]: 58).

126. The Richmond–San Rafael Bridge opened in 1956, adding a second important link to Berkeley and Oakland. Radford's *Bridge and Building*, 13–83, contains an informative history of Marin County. See also Mel Scott, *The San Francisco Bay Area: A Metropolis in Perspective* (Berkeley and Los Angeles: University of California Press, 1959); William Chapin, Alvin D. Hyman, and Jonathan Carroll, *The Suburbs of San Francisco* (San Francisco: Chronicle Books, 1969), 123–81; and Jack Mason and Helen Van Cleave Park, *The Making of Marin (1850–1975)* (Inverness: North Shore Books, 1975).

127. Another important woman involved in the project was Mary Summers. She was planning director of the Marin County Planning Commission and sat on both the site committee and the architect selection committee (which she chaired). Radford was unable to ascertain who was actually responsible for thinking of Wright: "Whether Vera Schultz or Mary Summers, or Mary's husband engineer Harold Summers first conceived the idea of asking Frank Lloyd Wright to consider the job is lost in memory" (Radford, *Bridge and Building*, 92). Ruder, "Wright and Marin County," 9, implies that it was Vera Schultz's suggestion: "During the New Year's holiday of 1957, Vera Schultz and Mary Summers were conversing about the project. Mrs. Schultz had been reading an issue of *House Beautiful* devoted to the work of Frank Lloyd Wright, and by the end of the conversation they enthusiastically agreed to contact the world-renowned architect."

Radford, *Bridge and Building*, 92, dates the first meeting between Wright and the architect selection committee to 26 April 1957, saying it took place in San Francisco at the office of Aaron Green, a former Taliesin Fellow and associate of Wright. She also says they went to hear Wright's lecture at Berkeley that evening. Aaron Green, on the other hand, who helped arrange the meeting and was present at it, places the event over two months later. He says that "in early July 1957, Mr. Wright was scheduled for a series of lectures at the University of California, Berkeley, and I was able to arrange the initial meeting in conjunction with that trip" (Green, *Architecture for Democracy*, 21). According to a story in the *San Francisco Examiner* of 26 April 1957, Wright had arrived the day before and was "here to deliver the first of a series of lectures tonight at the University of California, honoring . . . Bernard Maybeck" ("F. Lloyd Wright 'Blows' into S.F.," sec. 1, p. 14). The story goes on to say: "Today he meets with Marin County officials for a preliminary interview on the design of a county civic center north of San Rafael."

128. Radford, *Bridge and Building*, 92, and Meehan, *Truth against the World*, 382, both state that the Marin County Board of Supervisors voted four to one on 20 June 1957 to retain Wright as architect (the one negative vote was cast by William D. Fusselman, who opposed Wright on every score). Ruder says the vote took place on 27 June ("Wright and Marin County," 12); whereas Green places it on 26 July (*Architecture for Democracy*, 22). That last date would have given Wright only three or four days to prepare for the visit to San Rafael and the lecture he gave at the high school. The transcript of "Frank Lloyd Wright's Address at San Rafael High School" is dated 31 July 1957 (MS 2401.612 A, FLWF). The cover letter sent by Mary Summers forwarding the transcript to Wright for him to edit confirms that date (M. Summers to FLW, 26 August 1957, FLWF). The contract was supposed to be signed at a formal meeting of the board the day after the lecture. The four pro-Wright members had been warned that there would be an effort by Fusselman and others to prevent that, so a copy of the contract was brought to the high school and was signed on the evening of the lecture. At the formal meeting of the board, Wright was accused by members of the American Legion of being a Communist sympathizer, and he walked out. Notwithstanding that, he visited the site later that morning, accompanied by the four supportive supervisors, the members of the architect selection committee, and Aaron Green (Ruder, "Wright and Marin County," 13).

Radford, *Bridge and Building*, 92–93, also notes that between 26 April and 27 June 1957 there was "a flurry of protests from local architects and a last-minute push from Richard Neutra." He "brought models of proposed government buildings to the Board of Supervisor's [*sic*] chambers and spent an afternoon explaining his theories of architecture to the Board and the Civic Center Committee." Neutra tried to undercut Wright by offering to work "with a local architect for a fee of 8%" rather than Wright's standard 10 percent fee.

Neutra gave a lecture in San Rafael on 10 June 1957 in which he urged the citizens of Marin County to "do a lot of thinking" about what they really wanted and "talked with local architects assuring them that he would be glad to work with whichever one of them the county would choose."

129. The model was requested by the Board of Supervisors in June 1958 and received in early September. (It is still on display on the ground floor of the building.) Green says that program development "required more than three months" and that "several weeks after [he] forwarded the space program" to Wright, he flew to Taliesin to see the initial results. That would probably have been sometime in November or December. He goes on to say that it then took "less than three months from the time I had seen the first sketch" to develop the preliminary presentation drawings and cost estimates (Green, *Architecture for Democracy*, 25, 63, 66). A number of the presentation drawings are dated 24 December 1957.

The board's final vote, which again was four to one (with Fusselman the negative), took place on 28 April 1958. To spread costs over a longer period of time, Wright had proposed not only to build the two wings of the Civic Center in different stages but also to construct the initial wing for the administrative offices in two or three stages. A first stage would have resulted in an initial two-story structure with an open, flat roof deck. In a second stage, that deck would have formed a second floor by being roofed with another flat terrace. Only in the third stage would the vaults have been built to enclose the top story. The Board of Supervisors, however, voted to build the entire wing at once and to include the domed rotunda and television antenna tower in the contract sent out for bid.

130. Contract drawings for the first phase (administration wing) were completed by 10 September 1959 and approved 10 November. The contract was let in January 1960, and groundbreaking ceremonies took place on 15 February. The tower was hoisted into place in December 1961, and the wing was dedicated on 13 October 1962. The U.S. Post Office, also designed by Wright, was the first building to be completed. The Veterans Memorial Auditorium, designed by Taliesin Associated Architects, was completed in 1971, though neither in the same location nor in exactly the same form as stipulated in the Wright master plan. In addition to articles cited in note 124 above, see: "Ground Is Broken for Wright's Marin County Civic Center," *PA* 41 (April 1960): 82; "First Building in Wright's Marin County to Be Completed this Month," *ARec* 131 (June 1962): sup. 4–5; "Wright's Post Office," *PA* 43 (September 1962): 76; "First Phase of Marin County Center Is Completed," *ARec* 132 (November 1962): 12; "Marin Centre: Frank Lloyd Wright's Last Work?" *ARev* 133 (February 1963): 83; "Wright, Marin County," *Architettura* 11 (June 1965): 108–9; "Gold in the Hills of California," *Fortune* 72 (August 1965): 162–64; "Wright's Last Stab at Immortality" and "Future Projects at Civic Center," *California Architecture* 2 (October 1966): 10–12, 13, 25; "Wright's Ship of State," *PA* 48 (February 1967): 30; Roger Montgomery, "Frank Lloyd Wright's Hall of Justice," *AF* 133 (December 1970): 54–59; and "Parasol for the Arts," *AF* 135 (July–August 1971): 5.

131. Quoted in Meehan, *Truth against the World*, 390, 393, 411, 389. In the transcript of the text edited by Wright, the phrase "good building" is in quotation marks and "characteristic" is underlined ("Wright's Address," 4).

132. Introduction by Henry Schubart Jr. to "Wright's Address," 2; and "Wright's Address," 9. The text reproduced in Meehan represents a much edited version (by Wright) that often goes well beyond the original transcript.

133. Radford, *Bridge and Building*, 92. It may well be that the idea of adapting the "campus plan" to such programs as corporate headquarters, industrial parks, and shopping centers goes back to Eliel and Eero Saarinen's seminal plan for the General Motors Technical Center in Warren, Mich. (designed 1945–48; built 1949–57). In any event, the idea became popular around then, and Eero Saarinen was certainly one of those who most consistently favored it.

134. Quoted in Meehan, *Truth against the World*, 398; and "Wright's Address," 12. Wright described the *parti* to his apprentices as a response to the need for flexibility: "It had to grow, had to be flexible and was almost impossible at first thought until we got this idea of making the one unit out of it, a growing unit, that could proceed from hill to hill" (30 March 1958, in Pfeiffer, *Living Voice*, 55).

135. According to Aaron Green, *Architecture for Democracy*, 21, Wright hit upon the basic idea soon after arriving at the site. Within less than a half-

hour there, he apparently said: "I'll bridge these hills with graceful arches." Bruce Pfeiffer reported that Wright was told by one of the board members accompanying him on that visit: "If the hills are a problem, we can easily flatten them out, and give you a more suitable building ground that way." To which Wright replied: "To the contrary, those hills will be the feature of the design, the building will be a bridge between them" (in *FLWM*, vol. 8, 320).

136. The oculi were a late change in the design. Early sketches and presentation drawings show an arcade on the top floor just under the roof. At this stage, by contrast, there were oculi in the ground-floor arcade of the larger Hall of Justice wing. (One should not be confused by the early drawings that show either just two stories with a flat roof, or three stories: they simply represent Wright's proposal for a staged construction process, which was rejected by the county [see note 129 above].) It is unclear whether the existing oculi were designed by Wright or added after his death.

137. Green, *Architecture for Democracy*, 94. Green says that Wright consciously employed such elaborate decorative designs in the roof for the very traditional and classical reasons of concealing poor workmanship in the building of the vaults: "Placing precast ornamental units on the roof over the barrel shell overcame any appearance of imprecise workmanship, which otherwise would have been evident. This meant that the roof shell did not have to be an exact labor-intensive effort. . . . Similarly, the decorative facias (roof edges), the spheres, made it possible for the long, extended, straight-line roof edges to be visually tolerable as they disguised variations in line" (ibid., 89–90). Green remarks that the fairly intense pinkish cast was chosen to counteract fading due to the strong California sunlight. He recalls Wright saying that "the structure will melt into the sunburnt hills" (in ibid., 66).

138. There is, in fact, a two-level difference between the wings. The fourth floor of the later Hall of Justice lines up with the second-floor garden-terrace level of the administration wing. Wright had originally placed the jail on the top floor of the northern wing so as to afford the prisoners the best view. A corridor ultimately had to be placed between the cells and the exterior walls for security reasons. Green, *Architecture for Democracy*, 63, says that Wright strove for flexibility in the office areas of the administration wing and essentially left the interior disposition up to him.

139. Green, *Architecture for Democracy*, 84, states that the "natural spring which continuously seeped into the lagoon" was only "uncovered" during the "excavation" of the site. At one of my site visits, however, I was told by the owner of the gas station on North Pedro Road, opposite the entrance, that he knew the site when it was still used for farming and grazing cattle and that there was a stream that more or less followed the line of the building and eventually emptied into the lake. An early aerial perspective suggests that Wright was aware of this and wanted to represent it in the aqueduct-like form of the building and the fountain, pool, and cascade leading to the lagoon.

140. The Marin County Fair was more oriented to cultural activities than to farm displays, having grown out of the Marin Art and Garden Fiesta and Center. See Radford, *Bridge and Building*, 31. The tradition of World's Fair pavilions, to which this design makes obvious reference, was pointed out by Pfeiffer, who specifically relates it to Wright's 1931 project for Chicago's Century of Progress Exhibition of 1933 (in *FLWR*, note to pls. 198–99).

141. See Green, *Architecture for Democracy*, 104–5. Wright's outdoor theater and pool was not a fantasy but was directly occasioned by one of the major cultural activities of Marin County, Gladys Hodgson's ballet aquacade group. Weather studies, however, proved that his amphitheater would not work.

142. I am indebted to David Van Zanten for this observation. The Civic Center thus combines in the same environment a day at the office and a day in the country.

143. Wright characteristically denied the explicitness and deliberateness of the reference. At a talk given in San Rafael on 27 March 1957, at the time the plans were presented to the community, he reportedly warded off any accusation of making a building that looked like a Roman aqueduct by telling his audience that the "pendant crescents" should be viewed as "scalloped arches dropping like curtain folds across the front of the structure to shield the largely glass facade from the sun" (in Editorial, *San Francisco Examiner*, 28 March 1958, quoted in Radford, *Bridge and Building*, 97). To the Fellowship, he later said: "The thing looked, to most people, I think, like a Roman aqueduct, but I had to tell them that they were not arches, they were pendant crescents, re-

sembling arches, and then we were in deep water!" (quoted in Pfeiffer, *Living Voice*, 54).

144. "A Skyscraper Bridge Proposed for Chicago," *ARec* 63 (April 1928): 383; and Arthur Tappan North, ed., *Raymond Hood*, Contemporary American Architects (New York and London: Whittlesey House, McGraw-Hill, 1931), 86–87. Although Reyner Banham, *Megastructure: Urban Futures of the Recent Past* (New York: Harper & Row, Icon Editions, 1972), 7–8, cites Le Corbusier's 1931–32 Projet Obus for Algiers as the "most general ancestor" of modern megastructures, he does not analyze its typological dependence on the viaduct or aqueduct.

It is highly unlikely that Wright did not know Morgan's project, since Wright's own article "In the Cause of Architecture, III: The Meaning of Materials—Stone" was published in the same issue of *ARec* (pp. 350–56). The Morgan design was also published in "Rainbow Bridge Suggested for Outer Drive," *Chicago Sunday Tribune*, 15 January 1928. For the terms of Wright's limited partnership with Morgan, see FLW to Charles Morgan, 12 December 1929, in *LArchitects*, 79–80. I am grateful to Mary Jane Hamilton for information provided about Charles Morgan.

145. FLW to Martin, 7 October 1931, Box 6-1, Wright-Martin Papers. Wright was in Rio in September–October 1931. The Carioca Aqueduct has a double range of arches, which predicts the split section of the Marin County Civic Center. It also has oculi-like roundels in the spandrels of the arcade.

146. Nikolaus Pevsner, "The Return of Historicism," orig. pub. *JRIBA*, 3d ser., 68 (1961), repr. in Pevsner, *Studies in Art, Architecture and Design*, vol. 2, *Victorian and After* (London: Thames and Hudson, 1968), 242–59. For further discussion of this point, see my "Venturi and 'Return of Historicism,'" 52–55.

147. The very conscious historicism of Wright's work of the fifties emerges first in the "Greek" designs for the lakeside pool and theater at Florida Southern College. The Annunciation Greek Orthodox Church in Wauwatosa, Wis., outside Milwaukee, is another important example. It was commissioned in the fall of 1955, designed in 1956 on Byzantine prototypes, and built in 1959–61. On the other hand, the 1954–55 redesign of the Monona Terrace Civic Center is very similar, especially in its use of arcades, to the more decorative and generalized detailing of Yamasaki, Stone, Johnson, and particularly Eero Saarinen. The more deliberate aspect of Wright's historicism in Marin County, however, should be compared with the work that Kahn and Venturi began to produce in about 1959–60. To those buildings mentioned in note 26 above could be added Kahn's design for the Meeting House of the Salk Institute for Biological Studies in La Jolla (begun 1959–61) and Venturi's Vanna Venturi House, Chestnut Hill, Pa. (1961–64).

148. Manfredo Tafuri described the Civic Center as "a gigantic fragment of a planetary city" that produces an "effect of alienation" rather than integration with the landscape, thus illustrating how "Wright's attitude toward nature likewise changed in his last works" (Tafuri and Francesco Dal Co, *Modern Architecture* [1976; History of World Architecture, trans. Robert Erich Wolf, New York: Harry N. Abrams, 1979], 357). Kenneth Frampton, *Modern Architecture: A Critical History* (New York and Toronto: Oxford University Press, 1980), 189, viewed it as the culmination of a decadence that set in at least two decades before: "From now on [1937], aside from his remarkably practical Usonian houses, Wright continued to develop a curious kind of science-fiction architecture which, judging from the exotic style of his late renderings, seemed intended for occupation by some extraterrestrial species. The selfconscious exoticism fell to the level of ultra-kitsch in his Marin County Courthouse." In Jürgen Joedicke's view, the problem could be taken back to the twenties, when Wright supposedly first contradicted the modern principles governing his Prairie Style: "The projects and buildings of his later years repeat the fairy-tale features of those of the twenties, and one is bound to wonder where, if anywhere, their significance lies or how, in Wright's view, the 'inner nature of the problem' produced such solutions. Wright the theorist [meaning Wright of 1893–1909], indeed, stands in conflict here with Wright the creative practising architect" (Joedicke, *Architecture since 1945*, 32).

149. The reference here is to the genres in painting that, in the hierarchy of classical theory, were often considered, along with their analogues in literature, as a model for architecture.

150. It should be reemphasized, however, that such "invention" was in no way at odds with an environment located between the wineries of the So-

noma and Napa Valleys and San Francisco, often described as the most European of American cities.

151. Wright's project for the Arizona State Capitol, produced between February and April 1957, called "Oasis—Pro Bono Publico," should be viewed in similar City Beautiful terms. It is a symmetrical scheme based on a conventional bicameral plan. The structure is placed in a formal park setting. The tent-like covering Wright meant to "resemble a dome" was intended, in his words, to be "suitable to the character and beauty of the State of Arizona and its unique landscape" (quoted in Pfeiffer, *Treasures of Taliesin*, n.p.) Both the Arizona and the Marin County projects exemplify, through their "regional" inflections, the later phase of the City Beautiful movement that can be seen in such schemes of the 1920s as the one by Arthur Brown for Pasadena.

Conclusion
Wright and His/story

1. Andrew Saint, *The Image of the Architect* (New Haven and London: Yale University Press, 1983), 1–18, sets Wright up as the scapegoat of the book by prejudicially defining his role, in terms of Ayn Rand's image of Howard Roark, as "The Architect as Hero and Genius." Forming the first chapter of the book, this textual gloss is decontextualized and dehistoricized even in relation to Saint's own chronological development of the subject in chapters 2–8. The historical construction of most of the other stereotypes will be discussed below in the context of Wright's critical reception.

2. Ludwig Mies van der Rohe, "A Tribute to Frank Lloyd Wright," orig. pub. *College Art Journal* 6 (August 1946), repr. in H. Allen Brooks, ed., *Writings on Wright: Selected Comment on Frank Lloyd Wright* (Cambridge, Mass., and London: MIT Press, 1981), 129–30. It should be noted that this was written much later than the period in question, but at precisely the moment Wright's work was beginning to have its greatest public impact, that is, the 1940s. The reference to "secessionism" is in G[eorge] H. Edgell, *The American Architecture of To-day* (New York: Charles Scribner's Sons, 1928), 79.

3. J.J.P. Oud, "Architectural Observations Concerning Wright and the Robie House," orig. pub. *De Stijl* 1 (1918), repr. in Brooks, *Writings on Wright*, 135–36; and "The Influence of Frank Lloyd Wright on the Architecture of Europe," in Wendingen 1925, 88–89. Oud allowed that "Wright's work smoothed to a great extent the way for cubism itself" but that "the irony of fate has willed . . . that the lyric charm of this architectonic piper of Hammeln at the same time impaired the purity of the sound which began to be heard in the architecture of Europe" ("Influence of Wright," 88). Berlage's 1921 critique of Wright was reprinted in the same publication as Oud's (see Chapter VI, note 9, above).

4. Henry-Russell Hitchcock and Philip Johnson, *The International Style* (1932; 2d ed., New York: W. W. Norton, 1966), 19, 18, 26; Alfred H. Barr et al., *Modern Architecture: International Exhibition*, 10 February–23 March 1932 (New York: Museum of Modern Art, 1932), 37, 15; and Johnson, "Style and the International Style" (talk given in 1955), in Johnson, *Writings* (New York: Oxford University Press, 1979), 74. In his article on Wright in Wendingen 1925, 89, Oud spoke of "a new—an unhistorical!—classicism." Hitchcock described the younger Europeans as "classicists" in contrast to Wright the "romantic" in Barr, *Modern Architecture*, 37.

5. In Barr, *Modern Architecture*, 37, 29, 31. The term "frontiersman" comes from Philip Johnson, "The Frontiersman," *ARev* 106 (August 1949), repr. in *Writings*, 189–91. Wright's putative ignorance of history became a trope of modern criticism. In 1941, Sigfried Giedion wrote: "What is the explanation of the fact that Wright is the only architect so far ahead of his own generation, a man who is ever today creating works that have a strong impact? The answer is rather simple: he had less debris to clear away than the Europeans" (Giedion, *Space, Time and Architecture: The Growth of a New Tradition*, Charles Eliot Norton Lectures for 1938–39 [1941; 4th ed. enl., Cambridge, Mass.: Harvard University Press, 1962], 395–96). For the subject of the Noble Savage, especially in its American context, see Hugh Honour, *The New Golden Land: European Images of America from the Discovery to the Present Time* (New York: Pantheon Books, Random House, 1975); Jean Franco, "The Noble Savage," in David Daiches and Anthony Thorlby, *Literature and Western Civ-*

ilization, vol. 4, *The Modern World I: Hopes* (London: Aldus Books, 1975), 565–93; Gaile McGregor, *The Noble Savage in the New World Garden: Notes Toward a Syntactics of Place* (Toronto and Bowling Green: University of Toronto Press, Bowling Green State University Popular Press, 1988); and, also, Henry Nash Smith, *Virgin Land: The American West as Symbol and Myth* (Cambridge, Mass.: Harvard University Press, 1950). I am grateful to Lucy MacClintock for sharing her knowledge of the subject with me.

6. Manfredo Tafuri and Francesco Dal Co, *Modern Architecture* (1976; History of World Architecture, trans. Robert Erich Wolf, New York: Harry N. Abrams, 1979), 357.

7. Sigfried Giedion, "Les Problèmes actuels de l'architecture: à l'occasion d'un manifeste de Frank Lloyd Wright aux architectes et critiques d'Europe," *Cahiers d'art* 7, nos. 1–2 (1932): 70, 72; and Giedion, "Theo van Doesburg," *Cahiers d'art* 6, no. 4 (1931): 228.

8. Giedion, *Space, Time and Architecture*, 412–21, 423. The reference to "the organic perception of the world" is in the section "The Urge toward the Organic" (p. 415). The fact that Giedion stopped with the Johnson Wax Building may well explain why that building is the last of Wright's to appear acceptable to so many Europeans and why it has had such an appeal for contemporary architects, like Stirling, trained in the European modernist tradition.

9. P. Morton Shand, "Scenario for a Human Drama," pt. 6, "La Machine-à-Habiter to the House of Character," *ARev* 77 (February 1935): 64 (italics added).

10. Nikolaus Pevsner, "Frank Lloyd Wright's Peaceful Penetration of Europe," *AJ* 89 (4 May 1939): 734, 732. Pevsner indicated, in a general way only, that the story came from Wijdeveld himself; but he admitted that "it seems unlikely that . . . Le Corbusier can have been in complete ignorance of Wright." Paul Turner published a letter from Le Corbusier to Wijdeveld (5 August 1925) that finally puts to rest this supposed ignorance. In it, Le Corbusier speaks of first seeing "reproductions" of Wright's work "around 1914 or 1915(?)" and of being "strongly impressed." He ends the note by saying that "we are all too much in the habit of forgetting quickly those who have been directly helpful to our orientation" (in Turner, "Frank Lloyd Wright and the Young Le Corbusier," *JSAH* 42 [December 1983]: 351, 359). For an American critique of Wright at this time that takes him seriously to task for the "reactionary character" of his Broadacre City project in political, social, and economic terms, see Meyer Schapiro, "Architect's Utopia," *Partisan Review* 4 (March 1938): 42–47.

11. Colin Rowe, in conversation, Spring 1980; Reyner Banham, *Theory and Design in the First Machine Age* (New York: Frederick A. Praeger, 1960), 221; and Banham, "The Wilderness Years of Frank Lloyd Wright," *JRIBA* 76 (December 1969): 514. But see, again, Turner, "Wright and Le Corbusier," 351. To be fair, Banham went on to do important research and writing on Wright, though he concentrated almost exclusively on the early work. Colin Rowe did an extremely intelligent analysis of Wright's skyscraper designs in "Chicago Frame," *ARev* 120 (November 1956), repr. in *The Mathematics of the Ideal Villa and Other Essays* (Cambridge, Mass., and London: MIT Press, 1976), 89–117.

As a final put-down in this sequence of Americophobic reactions to Wright on the part of second- and third-generation British modernists, see Andrew Saint's closing comments in *The Image of the Architect*. "A last word on Wright may be left with Raymond Hood's friend and sometime colleague, Ralph Walker," the classically trained, stereotypical corporate architect whom Saint then quotes: "'Wright does not have a social sense,' remarked Walker. 'His buildings are designed on the principle "Treat the client rough"'" (p. 17). This would be like giving Umdenstock the last word on Le Corbusier!

12. In *Modern Architecture: A Critical History* (New York and Toronto: Oxford University Press, 1980), Kenneth Frampton, for instance, dismisses almost everything of Wright's after 1936, with the notable exception of the Usonian Houses, on the basis of bad taste. Were it not for the client's sense of restraint, even Fallingwater would have been turned into a "kitsch gesture" by Wright's intended use of gold leaf as a surfacing material. Contemptuously referring to the "apricot"-colored paint finally chosen, Frampton makes it clear that there was no real way of controlling Wright's utter lack of refinement. "Kitsch" and even "ultra-kitsch" finally come to characterize his late work (pp. 188–91). Recently, Frampton revised his assessment forward to include the Guggenheim Museum as "first conceived in 1943 . . . as the last truly

potent work, prior to Wright's precipitious descent into the kitsch of his last years" (in *Frank Lloyd Wright: Architect*, ed. Terence Riley, with Peter Reed [New York: Museum of Modern Art, 1994], 75). Here again the lineage can be traced back to Henry-Russell Hitchcock, who wrote in the late 1920s of the architecture of the New Tradition—of which Wright's was for him a prime example—as "pandering to the bourgeois taste for representational prettiness" in contrast to the "aristocratic, even Olympian" New Pioneer, who is "capable of appreciating architecture for itself" (Hitchcock, "Modern Architecture, II: The New Pioneers," *ARec* 63 [May 1928]: 456). As noted earlier (Chapter V), Hitchcock lambasted the Imperial Hotel for its "redundant . . . unskillfully exotic ornament," which he said made the interiors appear "incomparably worse than those however Louis XVI of any coëval Ritz" (*Modern Architecture: Romanticism and Reintegration* [1929; rpt. New York: Hacker Art Books, 1970], 115).

13. See Chapter XI, pp. 374ff.

14. In "What Is Happening to Modern Architecture?: A Symposium at the Museum of Modern Art," *Museum of Modern Art Bulletin* 15 (Spring 1948): 10. Hitchcock's change of position relative to Wright's significance can be traced through the following articles by him: "The Architectural Future in America," *ARev* 82 (July 1937): 1–2; "Wright's Influence Abroad," *Parnassus* 12 (December 1940): 11–15; "Exhibitions and Collections: Frank Lloyd Wright at the Museum of Modern Art," *Art Bulletin* 23 (March 1941): 73–76; "The Architecture of Bureaucracy and the Architecture of Genius," *ARev* 101 (January 1947): 3–6; and "The International Style Twenty Years After," orig. pub. *ARec* 110 (August 1951), rpr. in Hitchcock and Johnson, *International Style*, 237–55.

15. In "What Is Happening to Modern Architecture?" 10. The comparison with Michelangelo goes back at least to 1941, when the reviewer for *Time* magazine spoke of Wright's retrospective at the Museum of Modern Art during the winter of 1940–41 as revealing "as exciting a body of architectural thinking as has come from the brain of anyone since Michelangelo" (quoted in *Current Biography: Who's Who and Why 1941*, ed. Marie Block [New York: H. W. Wilson, 1941], 938). From 1948 on, the comparison of Wright to Michelangelo became a commonplace of architectural criticism. Manfredo Tafuri naturally bridled at Bruno Zevi and Paolo Portoghesi's portrayal of Michelangelo in their 1964 exhibition in Rome of "Michelangelo the Architect" as "a raging iconoclast extending his hand across the centuries to Pollock and Frank Lloyd Wright" (*two* Americans, no less!) (Tafuri, *History of Italian Architecture, 1944–1985* [1986; trans. Jessica Levine, Cambridge, Mass., and London: MIT Press, 1989], 79).

16. Colin Rowe, "The Mathematics of the Ideal Villa," orig. pub. *ARev* 101 (March 1947), rpr. in Rowe, *Mathematics of the Ideal Villa*, 1–27; Philip Johnson, "Frontiersman," in *Writings*, 191; and Johnson, "Style and International Style," in ibid., 74–75. Considering his eulogy of Michelangelo in *Vers une architecture*, one wonders how Le Corbusier felt about the academic coupling with Palladio. For a belated Wright-Palladio pairing, see Daniel Treiber, "Frank Lloyd Wright," *CREE* 3 (August–September 1974): 113.

17. The establishment of a set of appropriate standards and models was one of the fundamental preoccupations of the academy in this period. Sigfried Giedion wrote in *Space, Time and Architecture*: "What is to be grasped, what can be observed of his [Wright's] direct influence, is often only superficial and leads to misunderstanding. Whoever as an architect has tried to imitate or even to follow him, whether in Europe or America, has misused his work and misinterpreted his spirit" (p. 423). Following the same line, Jürgen Joedicke said in *Architecture since 1945: Sources and Directions*, trans. J. C. Palmes (New York: Frederick A. Praeger, 1969): "Wright's buildings are too closely tailored to his personality to serve as schoolroom models. The impact of his personality obscured everything in its shadow" (p. 31).

18. Vincent Scully, "Heritage of Wright," *Zodiac* 8 (1961): 12.

19. In Patrick J. Meehan, ed., *Truth against the World: Frank Lloyd Wright Speaks for an Organic Architecture* (New York: Wiley-Interscience Publications, John Wiley, 1987), 389; FLW, "Civilization and Culture," 18 January 1953, in Bruce Brooks Pfeiffer, ed., *Frank Lloyd Wright: His Living Voice* (Fresno: Press at California State University, 1987), 105; and FLW, "Room for the Dead," in Gutheim, *FLW on Arch.*, 210.

20. Philip Johnson, "100 Years, Frank Lloyd Wright and Us," orig. pub. *Pacific Architect and Builder* (March 1957), rpr. in *Writings*, 193–94, 195–98.

21. Harold Bloom, *The Anxiety of Influence: A Theory of Poetry* (London and Oxford: Oxford University Press, 1973). Bloom generally restricts his use of the concept to the defensive reaction of one individual to another in a transhistorical battle between the "strong poet" and his precursor(s). Wright's case poses the problem on a more general historical and cultural plane, involving the collective repression of a specific artistic production. Two minor but interesting examples might be cited as illustrations. First, the 1967 *AIA Guide to New York City*, in which Norval White and Elliot Willensky list eight pages of "New York Milestones" that include, among buildings, the UN Headquarters, Lever House, Lincoln Center, Seagram Building, World Trade Center, and CBS Building. The Guggenheim Museum, somehow, did not make the list! Second, an article in the Sunday *NYT* Arts and Leisure section in 1990 in which Witold Rybczynski blithely credits Le Corbusier with inventing the idea of "set[ting] the window glass directly into a groove in the concrete wall, thus doing away with the window frame altogether, and producing the unexpectedly rustic impression of an opening cut directly into the wall," completely ignoring the fact that Wright made the device a trademark of his work almost fifteen years earlier ("Architecture View: It Seems That God Isn't in the Details, after All," 16 December 1990, sec. 2, p. 44).

22. James Stirling, who suspected as early as 1955 that "eventually somebody will have to consider the numerous similarities between Le Corbusier and Frank Lloyd Wright" ("Garches to Jaoul: Le Corbusier as Domestic Architect in 1927 and 1953," *ARev* 118 [September 1955]: 145–51), visited the Johnson Wax headquarters on his first trip to the United States in 1949. Le Corbusier spent a number of months in the United States in 1946 as part of his work on the UN Headquarters, and he acknowledged that it was during a visit to America that he got the idea for the shape of the roof of the chapel at Ronchamp: "The shell of a crab picked up on Long Island near New York in 1946 is lying on my drawing board. It will become the roof of the chapel" (Le Corbusier, *The Chapel at Ronchamp* [London: Architectural Press, 1957], 89). He did not, however, acknowledge any debt to Wright's church. Among the striking similarities between the Le Corbusier and Wright churches are: the way in which they both open out bell-like to the landscape; the use of a contemporary form of medieval stained glass (in Wright's published project); and the relationship of the floor to the sloping ground. Although one could point to the primitivizing masonry of the villas at Le Pradet and Mathes of the 1930s, the switch by Le Corbusier from a steel structure to the *béton brut* of the Unité d'Habitation at Marseille would seem to be much more related to the precedent of Taliesin West's use of raw concrete. Eero Saarinan's rubble and concrete walls at Yale's Morse and Stiles Colleges (1958–62) are unquestionably indebted to Wright's example. On the relation between Wright and Le Corbusier, see Thomas Doremus, *Frank Lloyd Wright and Le Corbusier: The Great Dialogue* (New York: Van Nostrand Reinhold, 1985). Wright, however, is virtually non-existent in Reyner Banham's account of *The New Brutalism: Ethic or Aesthetic?* (New York: Reinhold, 1966).

23. Vincent Scully, especially, has lectured and written about the influence of Wright's early work on Kahn and Rudolph. See, e.g., his "Frank Lloyd Wright and Twentieth-Century Style," in *Problems of the 19th & 20th Centuries: Studies in Western Art*, Acts of the Twentieth International Congress of the History of Art, 4 (Princeton: Princeton University Press, 1963), esp. 17–21. As to the question of acknowledging his debt, it is interesting to note that Kahn told Scully "that he was never consciously influenced by Wright" (Scully, *Louis I. Kahn*, Makers of Contemporary Architecture [New York: George Braziller, 1962]). Scully said: "I do believe him in this," but added that "Kahn seems to have fully experienced no building by Wright until 1959 when, sadly enough after the latter's death, he was taken to see the Johnson Wax Building and, to the depths of his soul, was overwhelmed" (pp. 30–31). Regardless of Kahn's actual experience of a Wright building, it is difficult to believe he did not closely follow the design and construction of Wright's Beth Sholom Synagogue in the North Philadelphia suburb of Elkins Park (1953–59). One should also remember that the major exhibition of Wright's architecture that opened in Philadelphia in 1951 before traveling to Florence was organized by Kahn's former partner Oskar Stonorov. Although Kahn was in Italy when the exhibition was in Philadelphia and back in Philadelphia by the time the show arrived in Florence, it is doubtful he was unaware of its contents.

The most obvious example of Wrightian circular planning by Johnson is the John Lucas House project for Nantucket (1953). This followed closely on the heels of the Museum of Modern Art's exhibition *Built in USA: Post-War Architecture*, which included Wright's second Jacobs House in Middleton, Wis. (1943–48), and his Friedman House in Pleasantville, N.Y. (1948–50). (Johnson contributed the preface to the exhibition catalogue.) One could also point to Johnson's Underground Painting Gallery in New Canaan, his addition to Dumbarton Oaks, and his project for the National Immigration Museum and Park, Ellis Island, New York.

Among the most obvious examples in Scarpa's work are: Torre de Mosto Parish Church project, Venice, 1948; Apartment Building project, Feltre, 1949; Il Cavallino Book Pavilion, Castello Gardens, Venice, 1950; Pavilion, 36th Venice Biennale, 1952; Veritti House, Udine, 1956–61; Taddei House project, Venice 1957; and Brion Tomb, San Vito d'Altivole, begun 1969. On Scarpa and Wright, see especially Maria Antonietta Crippa, *Carlo Scarpa: Il pensiero, il disegno, i progetti* (Milan: Jaca, 1984), 34–38, 52–59; and Scully, "Between Wright and Kahn," in Francesco Dal Co and Giuseppe Mazzariol, *Carlo Scarpa: The Complete Works*, trans. Richard Sadleir (New York: Electa/Rizzoli, 1985), 267–70.

24. The Wright redevelopment projects were extensively published in the late forties and fifties and included in the 1951 "Sixty Years of Living Architecture" exhibition that traveled around the world. The influential projects of Wright's from the late thirties through the Living City designs of the late fifties were all included in the major exhibition of Wright's drawings at the Museum of Modern Art in 1962, which was probably the occasion for a younger generation's first real chance to see and study the work. It is perhaps significant that Colin Rowe's only article about Wright dealt with the skyscraper-type often favored in those projects, that is, the tree-like mast with clipped-on or attached living capsules ("Chicago Frame"). The type appears in Isozaki's Space City project of 1962 and Peter Cook's Plug-in City of 1964, for instance. Although Buckminster Fuller and Raymond Hood had produced designs of this sort in the late 1920s, Wright made the idea almost a trademark of his tall-building designs, from the St. Mark's Tower of the late 1920s and the Research Tower at Johnson Wax of the 1940s, to the Mile-High Illinois for Chicago of 1956. One should also relate Bertram Goldberg's "organic" design for Marina City, in Chicago (1963–67), to Wright's conception.

25. Vincent Scully has often spoken and written of Venturi's debt to early Wright, especially the relation between the Vanna Venturi House and Wright's own Oak Park house. See Scully, *The Shingle Style and the Stick Style: Architectural Theory from Downing to the Origins of Wright* (1955; rev. ed., New Haven and London: Yale University Press, 1971), 164; and *The Shingle Style Today, or the Historian's Revenge* (New York: George Braziller, 1974), 29–32. In his biography of Aalto, Göran Schildt argues that Wright's influence beginning around 1940 involved Aalto's entire conception of himself as an architectural "personality" (*Alvar Aalto, The Mature Years* [1989; New York: Rizzoli International, 1991], 303–5).

26. Cf. *L'Architects*, 105, 109–12; and Philip Johnson, "House at New Canaan, Connecticut," orig. pub. *ARev* 108 (September 1950), repr. in *Writings*, 212–25. The only mention of Wright is a parenthetical disclaimer: "The Eighteenth Century preferred more regular sites than this and the Post-Romantic Revivalists preferred hilltops to the cliff edges or shelves of the Romantics (Frank Lloyd Wright, that great Romantic, prefers shelves or hillsides)" (p. 216). Given the importance Johnson attached to the "processional" approach to the Glass House, which he related to Le Corbusier and Choisy, one should recall his comments on the "hieratic" spatial sequencing of Taliesin West, where this concept seems to have made its first appearance in Johnson's thinking (see Chapter IX, pp. 256, 274 above).

27. A perfect case in point is the following sequence of remarks of Philip Johnson to Edgar Tafel. After claiming that Wright's "actual" buildings had only a "minimal" influence on him, Johnson went on to say: "Yet there isn't a day that doesn't go by without my thinking of Mr. Wright; there isn't a day that I don't feel—when I have a pencil in my hand anyhow—that the man isn't looking over my shoulder. *It's funny. I've never thought of that before*" (in Edgar Tafel, *About Wright: An Album of Recollections by Those Who Knew Frank Lloyd Wright* [New York: John Wiley & Sons, 1993], 47–48; italics added).

In light of the psychoanalytic possibilities of the above, it would be interesting to deconstruct Peter Eisenman's choice of the title of Wright's Princeton lecture criticizing Le Corbusier's houses ("The Cardboard House") to represent his own exploration and extension of modernist practices in what he called, at first, "Cardboard Architecture: House I," and "Cardboard Architecture: House II" (in *Five Architects: Eisenman, Graves, Gwathmey, Hejduk, Meier* [1972; rpt. New York: Oxford University Press, 1975], 15–17, 25–27) and then fragmented into *House of Cards*, the book about his work published by Oxford University Press in 1987. The name "Romeo and Juliet" that Eisenman gave to his Venice project (1975) probably also has multiple references, at least one of which extends from the historical scene of the play to Wright's landmark windmill at Taliesin.

28. To which Moore added the spiteful emotional twist: "or at least to waves of irrelevance, because it's a lousy street tree and won't survive automobile exhaust" (in "FLW: His Future Influence," *PA* 49 [September 1968]: 142–43. This is one of the most interesting collections of statements concerning Wright's impact on contemporary architecture. At the beginning of the piece, Arthur Drexler is quoted as saying that he "feels that current architectural leaders such as James Stirling and Louis I. Kahn 'derive more from Wright than any other source, and do indeed, follow principle and not precept'" (p. 140).

Moore's comparison of Wright to a tree (the tree of knowledge?) should be related to Mies's earlier description of Wright as "resembl[ing] a giant tree in a wide landscape, which, year after year, ever attains a more noble crown" ("Tribute to Wright," 130). The comparison of Wright to a natural object follows the Noble Savage paradigm.

29. In his review of the second edition of *An Autobiography*, Talbot Hamlin spoke of Wright's "creation for himself of a kind of life that is in its own way as extraordinary and unexpected a work of art as are the amazing series of buildings which he has designed. For that life, as evidenced in Taliesin and Taliesin West, is a kind of fairy-tale creation won apparently against the most impugnable odds" ("Book Notes," *Wisconsin Magazine of History* 27 [December 1943]: 228). In a letter to Mrs. Darwin Martin, Olgivanna Wright spoke of the prospective Taliesin Fellowship as a "fairy tale" (21 July 1932, Box 6-3, Wright-Martin Papers). Smith, *Wright*, esp. 134–44, compares Taliesin to Camelot and the Order of the Round Table.

The "Aladdin motif," as a sign of artistic creativity, made its first appearance in Romantic literature with Adam Oehlenschläger's play *Aladdin, oder: die Wunder-lampe* (Breslau: Verlage bei Josef Mar und Ramp, 1839).

30. Walter Benjamin, "The Storyteller: Reflections on the Works of Nikolai Leskov" (1936; trans. Harry Zohn, in *Illuminations*, ed. Hannah Arendt, New York: Schocken Books, 1968), 102, 108. Benjamin specifically distinguishes "the art of storytelling" from "the dissemination of information." The latter, in his view, "lays claim to prompt verifiability," even though "often it is no more exact than the intelligence of earlier centuries was" (p. 89).

The most useful general studies of fairy tales and folktales from the point of view of child development are: Bruno Bettelheim, *The Uses of Enchantment: The Meaning and Importance of Fairy Tales* (New York: Vintage Books, Random House, 1977); Jack Zipes, *Breaking the Magic Spell: Radical Theories of Folk and Fairy Tales* (New York: Methuen, 1979); Ruth B. Bottigheimer, ed., *Fairy Tales and Society: Illusion, Allusion, and Paradigm* (Philadelphia: University of Pennsylvania Press, 1986); and Zipes, *Fairy Tales and the Art of Subversion: The Classical Genre for Children and the Process of Civilization* (New York: Methuen, 1988). Wright's use of the fairy tale as a "transitional object," in D. W. Winnicott's terms, might make the subject of a fruitful study. Cf. Simon A. Grolnick, "Fairy Tales and Psychotherapy," in Bottigheimer, *Fairy Tales and Society*, 203–15.

31. I have used the terms *fairy tale* and *folk-tale* interchangeably since that is the way Wright and most of his contemporaries did. Scholars still do not agree completely on the distinction, as is evidenced in Zipes, *Breaking the Magic Spell*, 20–40. Cf. Linda Dégh, "Folk Narrative," in *Folklore and Folklife*, ed. Richard M. Dorson (Chicago: University of Chicago Press, 1972), 53–84. For another view of Wright's interest in kindergarten training, see David Van Zanten, "Frank Lloyd Wright's Kindergarten: Professional Practice and Sexual Roles," in *Architecture: A Place for Women*, ed. Ellen Perry Berkeley and Matilda McQuaid (Washington, D.C.: Smithsonian Institution Press, 1989), 55–61.

32. Bruce Brooks Pfeiffer, ed., *Frank Lloyd Wright: The Crowning Decade, 1949–1959* (Fresno: Press at California State Univeristy, 1989), 195–99; *FLWM*, vol. 8, xi; and FLW, "The Wonderful World of Architecture," MS 2401.511, FLWF. Viollet-le-Duc's late storybooks, which were almost immediately translated into English, included the pseudo-autobiography *Histoire d'un dessinateur: Comment on apprend à dessiner* (Paris: J. Hetzel, Bibliothèque d'Education et de Récréation, 1879).

33. Wright willingly acknowledged his debt to Viollet. In *A* I, 74, he wrote that when he first began working in Chicago he got "Viollet-le-Duc's 'Habitations of Man in all Ages'" from the library of All Souls Church, having "read his 'Dictionnaire,' the 'Raisonne' [*sic*] at home, got from the Madison city-library." "The 'Raisonne,'" he went on to say, "was the only really sensible book on architecture in the world. . . . I got copies of it later for my sons. That book was enough to keep one's faith in architecture in spite of architects." John Lloyd Wright *My Father Who Is on Earth* (New York: G. P. Putnam's Sons, 1946), 69, reports that, after giving him Viollet's *Discourses on Architecture*, his father said: "In these volumes you will find all the architectural schooling you will ever need. What you cannot learn from them, you can learn from me." Cf. Donald Hoffmann, "Frank Lloyd Wright and Viollet-le-Duc," *JSAH* 28 (October 1969): 173–83.

34. Le Corbusier, *The City of To-morrow and Its Planning* (1924; trans. Frederick Etchells, 1929, rpt. Cambridge, Mass.: MIT Press, 1971), 160. This is how Le Corbusier began his description of the "discovery" of the scheme for the 1922 Contemporary City for Three Million Inhabitants. The entire description reads as follows: "Proceeding in the manner of the investigator in his laboratory, I have avoided all special cases, and all that may be accidental. . . . My object was not to overcome the existing state of things, but *by constructing a theoretically water-tight formula to arrive at the fundamental principles of modern town planning . . .* [these] being as it were the *rules* according to which development will take place." Hannes Meyer likewise noted that the "artist's studio has become a scientific and technical laboratory" in his article "Die Neue Welt," published in *Das Werk* in 1926 (quoted in K. Michael Hays, *Modernism and the Posthumanist Subject: The Architecture of Hannes Meyer and Ludwig Hilberseimer* [Cambridge, Mass., and London: MIT Press, 1992], 102). Cf. Walter Gropius, *Scope of Total Architecture*, World Perspectives, 3 (New York: Harper & Brothers, 1955).

35. Le Corbusier, *Towards a New Architecture* (1923; trans. Frederick Etchells, 1927, rpt. New York: Holt, Rinehart and Winston, 1976), 102 (cf. 97, 105, 135, 138); *Le Corbusier: Oeuvre complète, 1938–1946*, ed. W[illy] Boesiger (1946; 6th ed. Zurich: Editions d'Architecture, 1971), 170; Le Corbusier, *The Modulor: A Harmonious Measure to the Human Scale Universally Applicable to Architecture and Mechanics* (1950; trans. Peter de Francia and Anna Bostock, Cambridge, Mass.: Harvard University Press, 1958), 5, 58; *Le Corbusier: Oeuvre complète, 1946–1952*, ed. Boesiger (Zurich: Girsberger, 1953), 182–83; and Le Corbusier, *Modulor 2: 1955 (Let the User Speak Next)* (1955; trans. de Francia and Bostock, Cambridge, Mass.: Harvard University Press, 1956), 84, 144, 289.

36. Wright specifically referred to the figure of Aladdin in these terms in *A* I, 178; "In the Cause of Architecture, IV: Fabrication and Imagination," *ARec* 62 (October 1927): 318; "In the Cause of Architecture, III: The Meaning of Materials—Stone," *ARec* 63 (April 1928): 356; and in a letter to Hibbard Johnson outlining his ideas for the Research Tower, 14 December 1943 (in *LClients*, 234–35).

37. Mircea Eliade, "Myths and Fairy Tales" (1956), repr. in *Myth and Reality*, trans. Willard R. Trask (New York: Harper Torchbooks, Harper & Row, 1975), 201. Louis Kahn also liked to define his "creativity" in terms of the fairy tale. In a lecture at the University of Pennsylvania in 1968, he said: "The wish of a fairy tale is our inheritance of first desires. When you have desire but you have no means, all you can do is wish, and it is still a fairy tale" (in Richard Saul Wurman, ed., *What Will Be Has Always Been: The Words of Louis I. Kahn* [New York: Access, Rizzoli, 1986], 33). In the same year, he expanded on the idea: "If I were asked what I would now choose to be, I would say 'to be the creator of the new fairy tales.' It is from the sense of the incredible that all man's desire to make and to establish comes. The simple structures of shelter seem like the markers of a dominating desire to establish a claim out of the vastness of the land, a place from which to dream of anticipated enterprise, full

of the promise of a kingdom where the house or the castle is not yet in the mind" (in Clovis Heimsath, *Pioneer Texas Buildings: A Geometry Lesson* [Austin and London: University of Texas Press, 1968], foreword [n.p.]). And in the following year, he told a student audience at Rice University: "If I could think what I would do other than architecture, it would be to write the new fairy tale, because from the fairy tale came the airplane, and the locomotive, and the wonderful instruments of our minds . . . it all came from wonder" (Kahn, *Talks with Students*, Architecture at Rice, no. 26, 1969, 2).

38. Albert Kahn wrote disparagingly of Wright in 1939 as "The Wizard of Taliesin," *Architect and Engineer* 139 (December 1939): 75. Vincent Scully spoke of Wright as a "shaman" in a lecture given at the Fallingwater Symposium at the Temple Hoyne Buell Center of American Architecture, Columbia University, 1986. Cf. also Gill, *Many Masks*, passim.

39. Louis Sullivan, "The Tall Office Building Artistically Considered," orig. pub. *Lippincott's* 57 (1896), repr. in Sullivan, *Kindergarten Chats and Other Writings* (New York: George Wittenborn, 1947), 208; and FLW, *Genius and the Mobocracy* (New York: Duell, Sloan and Pearce, 1949), 83.

40. Shand, "Scenario for a Drama," 64; and Oud, "Influence of Wright," 85–86.

41. Wright specifically used the phrase "once upon a time" in the draft of his description of the Romeo and Juliet Tower for *An Autobiography* (FLW, "Romeo and Juliet," p. 1, MS 2401.031 A, FLWF); and in the foreword to *The Living City* (1958; rpt. New York, Toronto, and London: New American Library, Plume book, 1970), xiii. One should remember his description of the Imperial Hotel as a place "wherein the Old was in the New and the New was in the Old" (*A* I, 225); and, even more pointedly, that of Taliesin: "For the story of Taliesin, after all, is old: old as the human spirit. These ancient figures [of Japanese and Chinese sculpture] were traces of that spirit, left behind in the human procession as Time went on, and they now came forward to find rest and feel at home. So it seemed as you looked at them. But they were only the story within the story: ancient comment on the New" (*A* I, 177).

42. The following discussion owes much to Jean-François Lyotard, *The Postmodern Condition: A Report on Knowledge* (1979; trans. Geoff Bennington and Brian Massumi, Theory and History of Literature, 10, Minneapolis: University of Minnesota Press, 1984).

43. This recalls the archetypal narrative situation in which a former narratee (here the Taliesin Fellow) becomes the new narrator (the guide), and the present narratee (the visitor) is primed to become a future narrator.

44. Cf. Lyotard, *Postmodern Condition*, esp. 18–37; and Benjamin, "Storyteller," esp. 87–98. One should probably relate Wright's adoption of the storyteller's mode of narrative to his preoccupation with Hugo's theory of the replacement of architecture by literature in the battle for significance among the arts. Where Hugo meant the novel, and eventually the newspaper, to be the winner, Wright clearly chose the preindustrial, oral form of the tale as his model because of its much greater similarity to the shared and embodied experience of architecture.

45. Cf. Charles Perrault, *Histoires ou contes du temps passé* (Paris: Barbin, 1697); and *Parallèle des anciens et des modernes en ce qui regarde les arts et les sciences* (Paris: Coignard, 1688–97).

46. In addition to the works by Benjamin, Eliade, and Bettelheim previously cited, see also Ernst Bloch, "The Fairy Tale Moves on Its Own in Time" (1930) and "Better Castles in the Sky at the Country Fair and Circus, in Fairy Tales and Colportage" (1959), repr. in *The Utopian Function of Art and Literature: Selected Essays*, trans. Jack Zipes and Frank Mecklenburg (Cambridge, Mass., and London: MIT Press, 1989), 163–85; Michel Butor, "On Fairy Tales," trans. Remy Hall, in *European Literary Theory and Practice: From Existential Phenomenology to Structuralism*, ed. Vernon W. Gras (New York: Delta, 1973), 350–62; and V[ladimir] Propp, *Morphology of the Folktale* (1928; trans. Laurance Scott, 2d ed. rev. and ed. Louis A. Wagner (Austin: University of Texas Press, 1968).

47. In a talk to the graduate seminar I gave on Taliesin at Harvard in the fall of 1987–88, Tom Beeby spoke very movingly about this aspect of Wright's work.

48. "Sun, space, and greenery" was Le Corbusier's (and CIAM's) well-known synonym for nature.

Bibliographical Note

This bibliography does not list all the published and unpublished material used in the research and writing of this book. The complete documentation of works and sources is recorded in the notes. The purpose of the following compendium is to provide a broad and concise overview of the Wright literature and archival collections that may be most useful for further research and study.

Monographs and General Art Historical Studies

The essential documentation of Wright's entire corpus of buildings and projects is:

Bruce Brooks Pfeiffer and Yukio Futagawa, eds., *Frank Lloyd Wright.* Tokyo: A.D.A. EDITA, 1984–88. Vols. 1–8, *Monograph*; vols. 9–11, *Preliminary Studies*; vol. 12, *In His Renderings.*

Until this twelve-volume series containing plans, drawings, and photographs, as well as descriptive texts, became available in the mid-1980s, the fundamental work covering Wright's output up to 1941 was:

Henry-Russell Hitchcock. *In the Nature of Materials: The Buildings of Frank Lloyd Wright, 1887–1941.* New York: Duell, Sloan and Pearce, 1942. Rpt., with a new foreword and bibliography by the author, New York: Da Capo Press, 1975.

The Hitchcock text remains an authoritative analysis of Wright's career and formal development. Other general studies that offer significant interpretive advances are:

Bruno Zevi. *Frank Lloyd Wright.* Milan: Il Balcone, 1947.
Vincent Scully Jr. *Frank Lloyd Wright.* Masters of World Architecture Series. New York: George Braziller, 1960.
Norris Kelly Smith. *Frank Lloyd Wright: A Study in Architectural Content.* Orig. pub. 1966. Rev. ed. Watkins Glen, N.Y.: American Life Foundation & Study Institute, 1979.

Studies of Individual Buildings or Groups of Buildings

Most important studies of Wright since the late 1970s have focused on a single period, an individual building, or a group of typologically related buildings. References to these writings will be found in the relevant notes. For convenience, the following is a list of notes containing bibliographies for buildings or projects discussed at some length in the text:

Oak Park House and Studio: Chapter I, note 19; Chapter II, note 5.
Winslow House: Chapter I, note 39.
Willits House: Chapter II, note 21.
Larkin Building: Chapter II, note 33.
Unity Temple: Chapter II, note 40.
Robie House: Chapter II, note 56.
Taliesin: Chapter IV, note 3.
Imperial Hotel: Chapter V, note 2.
Hollyhock House and Olive Hill Cultural Center: Chapter V, note 41.
Textile-block houses and designs: Chapter VI, notes 13, 17, 25.

Johnson Death Valley Compound: Chapter VI, notes 43, 46.
Ocatilla and San Marcos-in-the-Desert Hotel: Chapter VII, notes 45, 59.
Broadacre City: Chapter VII, note 21.
Fallingwater: Chapter VII, note 32.
Taliesin West: Chapter IX, note 1.
Johnson Wax Company: Chapter X, note 20.
Florida Southern College: Chapter X, note 33.
Guggenheim Museum: Chapter X, notes 40, 130, 167, 188.
Morris Shop: Chapter XI, note 1.
Masieri Memorial: Chapter XI, notes 38, 50.
Baghdad Opera House, Cultural Center, and University: Chapter XI, notes 57, 66, passim.
Marin County Civic Center: Chapter XI, notes 124, 130.

Biographies

The biographical component of the study of Wright's architecture has always been an important one. Three recent biographies stand out either for their critical approach to the subject or for the new information they provide:

Robert C. Twombly. *Frank Lloyd Wright: His Life and His Architecture.* New York: John Wiley & Sons, Wiley-Interscience Publication, 1979. Rev. and exp. version of *Frank Lloyd Wright: An Interpretive Biography.* New York: Harper & Row, 1973.
Brendan Gill. *Many Masks: A Life of Frank Lloyd Wright.* New York: G. P. Putnam's Sons, 1987.
Meryle Secrest. *Frank Lloyd Wright.* New York: Alfred A. Knopf, 1992.

For other biographies, see Introduction, note 19.

For published correspondence, talks, interviews, miscellaneous writings, and personal recollections of those who knew and/or worked with Wright, see Introduction, note 15, and Chapter XI, note 3.

Significant Publications of Wright's Work during His Lifetime

Among the most important primary sources for understanding Wright's architecture in its historical context are the publications of his work in his lifetime. Key among these are:

Robert C. Spencer Jr. "The Work of Frank Lloyd Wright." *Architectural Review* (Boston) 7 (June 1900): 61–72.
Frank Lloyd Wright. "In the Cause of Architecture." *Architectural Record* 23 (March 1908): 155–221. Repr. in Frederick Gutheim, ed., *In the Cause of Architecture, Frank Lloyd Wright: Essays by Frank Lloyd Wright for Architectural Record, 1908–1952.* New York: Architectural Record Books, 1975.
————. *Ausgeführte Bauten und Entwürfe von Frank Lloyd Wright.* Berlin: Ernst Wasmuth, 1910[–11]. Republished in Japanese (1916), German (1924, 1986), and English. The American editions have carried the following titles: *Buildings, Plans, and Designs.* New York: Horizon Press, 1963; *Studies and Executed Buildings by Frank Lloyd Wright; Ausgeführte Bauten und Entwürfe von Frank Lloyd Wright.* Palos Park, Ill.: Prairie School Press, 1975; *Drawings and Plans of Frank Lloyd Wright: The Early Period (1893–1909).* New York: Dover, 1983; and *Studies and Executed Buildings by Frank Lloyd Wright.* New York: Rizzoli, 1986.
————. *Frank Lloyd Wright: Ausgeführte Bauten.* Berlin: Ernst Wasmuth, 1911. Republished in English as *Frank Lloyd Wright: The Early Work.* New York: Horizon Press, 1968; and *The Early Work of Frank Lloyd Wright: The "Ausgeführte Bauten" of 1911.* New York: Dover, 1982.
H[endrikus] Th[eodorus] Wijdeveld, ed., *The Life-Work of the American Architect Frank Lloyd Wright.* Santpoort, Holland: C. A. Mees, 1925. Orig. pub. "Frank Lloyd Wright." *Wendingen* 7, nos. 3–9 (1925): 1–164. Repub-

lished as *The Work of Frank Lloyd Wright: The Wendingen Edition*. New York: Horizon Press, 1965; and *Frank Lloyd Wright: The Complete "Wendingen" Series*. New York: Dover, 1992.

H[einrich] de Fries, ed., *Frank Lloyd Wright: Aus dem Lebenswerke eines Architekten*. Berlin: Ernst Pollak, 1926.

Jean Badovici. "Frank Lloyd Wright." *Architecture Vivante* 8 (Summer 1930): 49–76.

"Frank Lloyd Wright." *Architectural Forum* 68 (January 1938): 1–102. Entire issue devoted to Wright.

"Frank Lloyd Wright." *Architectural Forum* 88 (January 1948): 65–156. Entire issue devoted to Wright.

Werner M. Moser. *Frank Lloyd Wright: Sechzig Jahre lebendige Architektur; Sixty Years of Living Architecture*. Winterthur and Munich: Verlag Buchdruckerei Winterthur AG, Hermann Rinn, 1952.

"Frank Lloyd Wright: A Selection of Current Work." *Architectural Record* 123 (May 1958): 167–90.

Wright's Own Writings

A number of collections of Wright's writings exist:

Frederick Gutheim, ed., *Frank Lloyd Wright on Architecture: Selected Writings, 1894–1940*. New York: Duell, Sloan and Pearce, 1941.

Edgar Kaufmann and Ben Raeburn, eds., *Frank Lloyd Wright: Writings and Buildings*. Cleveland and New York: Meridian Books, World Publishing, 1960.

Bruce Brooks Pfeiffer, ed., *Frank Lloyd Wright: Collected Writings*, 5 vols. New York: Rizzoli, Frank Lloyd Wright Foundation, 1992–95. Vol. 1, *1894–1930*; vol. 2, *1930–1932*; vol. 3, *1931–1939*; vol. 4, *1939–1949*; vol. 5, *1949–1959*.

Perhaps the single most important document of Wright's thoughts on architecture and life in general is:

Frank Lloyd Wright. *An Autobiography*. London, New York, and Toronto: Longmans, Green, 1932. New ed., rev. and enl. New York. Duell, Sloan and Pearce, 1943. New ed., rev. and enl. New York: Horizon Press, 1977. Repr. in Pfeiffer, vols. 2, 4.

Among the other texts that most fully represent the evolution of his thinking are:

Frank Lloyd Wright. "The Art and Craft of the Machine." Orig. pub. Catalogue of the *Fourteenth Annual Exhibition of the Chicago Architectural Club*, 1901, n.p. Repr. in Kaufmann and Raeburn; and Pfeiffer, vol. 1.

———. "In the Cause of Architecture." *Architectural Record* 23 (March 1908): 155–65. Repr. in Gutheim, *In the Cause of Architecture*; and Pfeiffer, vol. 1.

———. Introduction, *Ausgeführte Bauten und Entwürfe von Frank Lloyd Wright*. Berlin: Ernst Wasmuth, 1910[–11], n.p. Repr. in Pfeiffer, vol. 1.

———. *The Japanese Print: An Interpretation*. Orig. pub. 1912. Rpt. New York: Horizon Press, 1967. Repr. in Pfeiffer, vol. 1.

———. "In the Cause of Architecture." Parts 1–5. *Architectural Record* 62 (May, June, August, and October 1927): 394–96, 478–80, 163–66, 318–21, 322–24. Repr. in Gutheim, *In the Cause of Architecture*; and Pfeiffer, vol. 1.

———. "In the Cause of Architecture." Parts 1–9. *Architectural Record* 63 (January, February, April, May, and June 1928): 49–57, 145–51, 350–56, 481–88, 555–61; 64 (July, August, October, and December 1928): 10–16, 98–104, 334–42, 507–14. Repr. in Gutheim, *In the Cause of Architecture*; and Pfeiffer, vol. 1.

———. *Modern Architecture, Being the Kahn Lectures for 1930*. Princeton: Princeton University Press, 1931. Repr. in Frank Lloyd Wright. *The Future of Architecture*. New York: Horizon Press, 1953; and Pfeiffer, vol. 2. A reprint edition of the original text was published by Southern Illinois University Press (Carbondale and Edwardsville, Ill.) in 1987.

———. *The Disappearing City*. New York: William Farquhar Payson, 1932. New ed., rev. and enl. *When Democracy Builds*. Chicago: University of Chicago Press, 1945. New ed., rev. and enl. *The Living City*. New York: Horizon Press, 1958. Repr. in Pfeiffer, vol. 3.

Baker Brownell and Frank Lloyd Wright. *Architecture and Modern Life*. New York and London: Harper & Brothers, 1937. Chapters by Wright repr. in Pfeiffer, vol. 3.

Frank Lloyd Wright. *An Organic Architecture: The Architecture of Democracy*, Sir George Watson Lectures of the Sulgrave Manor Board for 1939. London: Lund Humphries, 1939. Repr. in Pfeiffer, vol. 3.

———. *Genius and the Mobocracy*. New York: Duell, Sloan and Pearce, 1949. Repr. in Pfeiffer, vol. 4.

———. *The Natural House*. New York: Horizon Press, 1954. Repr. in Pfeiffer, vol. 5.

———. *A Testament*. New York: Horizon Press, 1957. Repr. in Pfeiffer, vol. 5.

Research Tools and Archival Collections

The definitive bibliography of writings by and about Wright up to 1977 is:

Robert L. Sweeney. *Frank Lloyd Wright: An Annotated Bibliography*. Art and Architecture Bibliographies, no. 5. Los Angeles: Hennessey & Ingalls, 1978.

The most comprehensive guide to Wright's buildings is:

William Allin Storrer. *The Frank Lloyd Wright Companion*. Chicago and London: University of Chicago Press, 1993. This is a much expanded and revised version of *The Architecture of Frank Lloyd Wright: A Complete Catalog*. Orig. pub. 1974. 2d ed., rev. and enl. Cambridge, Mass., and London: MIT Press, 1978.

The voluminous Wright correspondence preserved in the Frank Lloyd Wright Archives at the Frank Lloyd Wright Foundation, Taliesin West, is indexed in:

Anthony Alofsin, ed., *Frank Lloyd Wright: An Index to the Taliesin Correspondence*. 5 vols. New York and London: Garland, 1988.

The many collections containing archival materials on Wright can be found in:

Patrick J. Meehan, ed., *Frank Lloyd Wright: A Research Guide to Archival Sources*. New York and London: Garland, 1983.

The most important collection of original drawings, correspondence, manuscripts, photographs, works of art, and other archival materials is:

Frank Lloyd Wright Archives, Frank Lloyd Wright Foundation, Taliesin West, Scottsdale, Ariz.

Other significant holdings can be found in:

Research Center, Frank Lloyd Wright Home and Studio Foundation, Chicago.

Manuscript Division, Library of Congress, Washington, D.C.: Frank Lloyd Wright Papers, 1894–1940.

University Archives, State University of New York, Buffalo: Frank Lloyd Wright-Darwin D. Martin Papers, MS 22.8; Jaroslav Joseph Polivka. Papers Concerning Frank Lloyd Wright, 1945–1959, MS 48.

Department of Special Collections, Stanford University Libraries, Stanford, Calif.: Frank Lloyd Wright-Darwin D. Martin Papers, MS 355.

Drawings and Archives, Avery Architectural and Fine Arts Library, Columbia University, New York: John Lloyd Wright Collection; Edgar Kaufmann-Fallingwater Collection.

Manuscripts Division, Special Collections, University of Utah Libraries, Salt Lake City: Taylor Woolley Archive, MS 452; Clifford Evans Scrapbooks, MS 466.

Archivo de Arquitectura y Construcción, Escuela de Arquitectura, Universidad de Puerto Rico, San Juan: Henry Klumb Archive.

List of Illustrations

N.B. All buildings are by Wright except where otherwise noted. All drawings in the archives of the Frank Lloyd Wright Foundation are © 1996 The Frank Lloyd Wright Foundation. Dates of buildings and projects are inclusive (from commission through completion). Dates in parentheses refer to the specific drawing or photograph (if taken prior to 1960). All maps and site plans are oriented north unless indicated otherwise.

Index